CHINA IN THE WORLD ECONOMY

China in the World Economy

THE DOMESTIC POLICY CHALLENGES

ORGANISATION FOR ECONOMIC CO-OPERATION AND DEVELOPMENT

ORGANISATION FOR ECONOMIC CO-OPERATION AND DEVELOPMENT

Pursuant to Article 1 of the Convention signed in Paris on 14th December 1960, and which came into force on 30th September 1961, the Organisation for Economic Co-operation and Development (OECD) shall promote policies designed:

– to achieve the highest sustainable economic growth and employment and a rising standard of living in Member countries, while maintaining financial stability, and thus to contribute to the development of the world economy;

– to contribute to sound economic expansion in Member as well as non-member countries in the process of economic development; and

– to contribute to the expansion of world trade on a multilateral, non-discriminatory basis in accordance with international obligations.

The original Member countries of the OECD are Austria, Belgium, Canada, Denmark, France, Germany, Greece, Iceland, Ireland, Italy, Luxembourg, the Netherlands, Norway, Portugal, Spain, Sweden, Switzerland, Turkey, the United Kingdom and the United States. The following countries became Members subsequently through accession at the dates indicated hereafter: Japan (28th April 1964), Finland (28th January 1969), Australia (7th June 1971), New Zealand (29th May 1973), Mexico (18th May 1994), the Czech Republic (21st December 1995), Hungary (7th May 1996), Poland (22nd November 1996), Korea (12th December 1996) and the Slovak Republic (14th December 2000). The Commission of the European Communities takes part in the work of the OECD (Article 13 of the OECD Convention).

OECD CENTRE FOR CO-OPERATION WITH NON-MEMBERS

The OECD Centre for Co-operation with Non-Members (CCNM) promotes and co-ordinates OECD's policy dialogue and co-operation with economies outside the OECD area. The OECD currently maintains policy co-operation with approximately 70 non-Member economies.

The essence of CCNM co-operative programmes with non-Members is to make the rich and varied assets of the OECD available beyond its current Membership to interested non-Members. For example, the OECD's unique co-operative working methods that have been developed over many years; a stock of best practices across all areas of public policy experiences among Members; on-going policy dialogue among senior representatives from capitals, reinforced by reciprocal peer pressure; and the capacity to address interdisciplinary issues. All of this is supported by a rich historical database and strong analytical capacity within the Secretariat. Likewise, Member countries benefit from the exchange of experience with experts and officials from non-Member economies.

The CCNM's programmes cover the major policy areas of OECD expertise that are of mutual interest to non-Members. These include: economic monitoring, structural adjustment through sectoral policies, trade policy, international investment, financial sector reform, international taxation, environment, agriculture, labour market, education and social policy, as well as innovation and technological policy development.

Publié en français sous le titre :

La Chine dans l'économie mondiale

LES ENJEUX DE POLITIQUE ÉCONOMIQUE INTÉRIEURE

FOREWORD

To reap the full benefits of further integration in the world economy, the Chinese economy must undergo fundamental adjustments. A substantial reallocation of resources among economic sectors and a major restructuring of the business sector will be needed to correct widespread inefficiencies. The government will face demands from society to ease the pressures created by this historic transition.

Many OECD Member countries which have undergone similar economic upheavals have found that international co-operation in the framework of the OECD can provide valuable support in designing institutions and policies that maximise the benefits of liberalisation while minimising its costs. This landmark study grew out of what the OECD perceived as a strong interest by the Chinese authorities in sharing the collective knowledge and experiences of economic development that OECD Member countries have accumulated through this process.

Since 1995, China and the OECD have engaged in a fruitful dialogue on many policy issues of common interest in the framework of a comprehensive programme of co-operation managed by the Centre for Co-operation with Non-Members.

This study takes stock of the results of these activities and develops the analysis of the policies that will have to be adjusted in order to meet the challenges of further trade and investment liberalisation. It is published under my responsibility.

I hope that this work can provide the Chinese authorities and people with tools and encouragement to continue their momentous undertaking.

Donald J. Johnston
Secretary-General
OECD

ABOUT THE STUDY

This study has been undertaken in the framework of the ongoing OECD-China programme of dialogue and co-operation, managed on the OECD side by the Centre for Co-operation with Non-Members. Although the study draws on the understanding gained from several years of dialogue with a number of Chinese Ministries and Agencies, this remains an independent study of the OECD Secretariat and is published under the Secretary-General's responsibility.

ACKNOWLEDGEMENTS

This study has been produced by a cross-Directorate team led by Charles Pigott (Senior Economist for China in the Economics Department) under the supervision of Silvana Malle (Head of the Non-Member Economies Division) and has been co-ordinated by Frédéric Langer (Head of the China and Asia Unit of the OECD Centre for Co-operation with Non-Members).

OECD Contributors: Jón Blöndal, Peter Börkey, Sang Mok Choi, Andrzej Kwiecinski, Christina Tebar-Less, George Holliday, Marie-France Houde, Bernard Hugonnier, Xiande Li, Marie-Ange Maurice, Krzysztof Michalak, Elena Miteva, Makoto Nakagawa, Young-Sook Nam, Stilpon Nestor, Charles Pigott, Anders Reutersward, Udo Pretschker, Sally Van Siclen, John Thompson, Peter Whiteford, Terry Winslow, Aki Yamaguchi, Gang Zhang.

Outside Contributors: Chunlai Chen, Hunter Colby, Sylvie Demurger, Gerry Dickinson, Jean-François Huchet, Scott Jacobs, Gilles Lelong, Shantong Li, Wayne Morrison, Albert Park, Scott Rozelle, Jian-Guang Shen, Qihong Sun, Cunzhi Wan, Wei Wang, Shiqiu Zhang, Zhujian Zhou.

Research support: Chuen-Mui Wu   Final copy editor: Kathleen Gray

The CCNM wishes to thank the experts from OECD Member countries and China who participated in the informal seminar under the auspices of the Economic and Development Review Committee on 10 December 2001 in Paris, contributing important comments on the draft study results. Experts from China, who took part in their personal capacity, were Mr. Wen Hai, Deputy Director, China Centre for economic research, Beijing University, Mr. Jun Han, Director General, Research Department on the rural economy, Development Research Center of the State Council (DRC), Mr. Kang Jia, Director, Institute of Fiscal Science, and Mrs. Shantong Li, Director General, Department of Development Strategy, DRC.

TABLE OF CONTENTS

SYNTHESIS OF THE MAIN FINDINGS OF THE STUDY

China's progress during the economic reform era that began in 1978 has been one of the great economic success stories of the post-war era. China has become the world's seventh largest economy and second largest recipient of foreign direct investment. Only Japan and Korea achieved a comparable record of sustained rapid growth during the latter half of the 20th century. China's performance is all the more remarkable in that its reforms have been gradual and its development has occurred despite extensive, though declining, state ownership and intervention in the economy.

The accession of China to the World Trade Organisation (WTO) marks an important milestone along the reform path China has been following for more than twenty years, rather than a new direction. China has been liberalising its international trade and investment policies since the mid-1980s and is now as open as some present WTO members. Although China stands to gain significantly from the opening of its export markets under the terms of its accession, the depth and breadth of its commitments to liberalise access to its domestic economy are acknowledged to be more extensive than those agreed to by previous adherents to the WTO. This willingness reflects the fact that opening to international markets promotes market discipline, access to technology, and other qualities that have been important goals of domestic economic reforms. In this respect, WTO entry is a complementary aspect of the next phase of China's reforms.

This report synthesises the main findings and recommendations of the OECD horizontal study of the domestic economic policy challenges posed by China's further trade and investment liberalisation (TIL). The study comprises 22 detailed reports prepared by nine OECD directorates covering the adjustments and policy challenges facing the key sectors of the real economy over the next decade, and their implications for the policies that will be critical to success in meeting these challenges. The study represents an OECD perspective drawn from the experiences of its Member countries with economic transformations, and from the work of the OECD with China and other emerging economies over the past decade. The basic question the study addresses is: how can China best reap the benefits of its opening and other economic reforms over the next decade in order to meet its basic development objectives? The reports analyse the current problems impeding China's economic development and identify key priorities and objectives, along with some suggested specific steps, in order to maximise the benefits of China's opening and other reform efforts. These analyses highlight the interdependence, and increasing need for co-ordination of policies in different areas.

Messages

The studies document the impressive progress China has made in transforming its economy during the reform era. At the same time, they indicate that the important engines that have driven China's growth in the past are losing their dynamism. The main reason is that China's economy has become badly fragmented and segmented, and this has led to increasing under and inefficient utilisation of resources. Trade and investment liberalisation, although it will require difficult adjustments by some segments of the economy, will stimulate other segments and bring positive net benefits to the economy as a whole over the longer-term. However by itself, trade and investment liberalisation is unlikely to solve the basic problems now impeding China's economic development.

As it has throughout the reform era, the realisation of China's economic potential, including the full benefits of trade and investment liberalisation, rests on its success in continuing and strengthening its domestic economic reforms. However China's economy has reached a stage that calls for some important changes in the way economic reforms are carried out. As the economy has become increasingly exposed to market forces and the scope for self-contained development of individual sectors has declined, economic problems have become more and more interdependent. Conditions in particular segments of the economy, such as rural labour markets, industry, the financial system, and regional development, now depend as much or more on developments in other areas of the economy than on developments or policies in that specific segment. Economic distinctions among various parts of the economy that have been accorded different treatment are breaking down. This interdependence has led to several "vicious circles" in which problems in a number of areas interact in a mutually reinforcing fashion to impede progress in the overall reform process. Particularly difficult is the vicious circle involving the weak performance of many of China's enterprises and the problems of the banking system.

In China's present situation, the outcomes of particular reforms depend increasingly on the interaction among measures taken by the economy's key actors – government, enterprises, workers, and the financial system – acting in markets whose functioning is shaped by key framework conditions such as competition, property rights, and corporate governance. Rather than emphasising particular sectors, reforms now need to focus more on *economy-wide* policies to promote more efficient allocation of resources and to bolster the effectiveness of markets. The study highlights three objectives as the key to the success of China's overall reforms over the next decade.

- The first and most immediate is to lay the foundation for improving the utilisation of China's resources, by removing present obstacles to business sector restructuring and by achieving better integration among various segments of the economy that have been developed separately under different sets of rules.

- The second is to improve competition law, property rights, enterprise governance and other frameworks that are essential to efficient market functioning so that resources are efficiently allocated in the future.

- And the third is to improve the capacity of the government to support economic development, by strengthening the effectiveness of macroeconomic policies while refocusing the role of regulatory policy on establishing and enforcing rules for market behaviour.

In achieving these objectives, reforms need to be both concurrent and carefully sequenced. Individual reforms to address particular problems need to be accompanied by complementary reforms in other areas in a comprehensive and co-ordinated fashion that is mutually reinforcing. Preferential development of individual sectors to "lead" the overall economy is likely to have much lower payoffs than in the past, and pose greater risks of negative outcomes. At the same time, reforms cannot be made all at once and care needs to be taken to establish the pre-conditions needed for follow-up measures.

Both principles will be particularly important to the achievement of three objectives which the study identifies as needed to break through the vicious circles now impeding reforms and establish the pre-conditions for sustained progress in the future. These are to:

- restore solvency to the financial system;
- bolster market based mechanisms as the dominant force for restructuring of the business sector;
- and establish public finances on a sound and sustainable basis.

Taking stock: the progress that has been made and the problems that need to be overcome

China's economy has undergone extensive transformations over the past twenty years (Table 1). The characteristic feature of the government's economic strategy has been to create separate channels for development outside the state sector, operating under different rules and conditions, in order to progressively increase the scope for market forces while phasing out central planning. This process, which has been termed "growing out of the plan",[1] has been highly successful but it has become increasingly apparent that its ability to push China's economic development further is coming to an

Table 1.   **The transformation in China's economy**

	1980	2000
GDP per capita[1]	168	727[2]
Percentage of population in urban areas	20	31
Share of GDP (per cent) in:		
Agriculture	30	16
Industry	49	51
Services	21	33
Share of employment in:		
Agriculture	69	50
Industry	18	23
Services	13	27
Trade/GDP (%)[3]	12	42

1. In constant 1995 US$.
2. Figure is for 1998.
3. Exports plus imports as share of GDP.
Sources: World Bank, *World Development Indicators*, 2000; *China Statistical Yearbook*, 2000; IMF, *International Financial Statistics*.
          Figures for shares in GDP and employment for 2000 are from Chapter 1, Table 1.1.

Figure 1.   **Real GDP growth**

3 year moving average

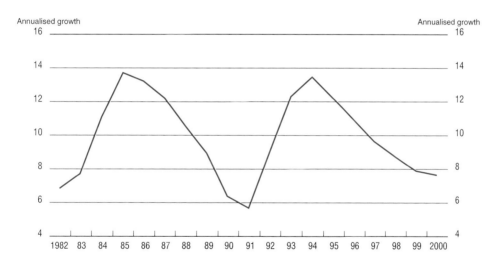

Source: China Statistical Yearbook, 2000.

end. Structural problems in the real economy have worsened progressively during the 1990s, leading to growing under-utilisation of labour and a protracted slowdown in real growth (Figure 1). These structural problems are substantially attributable to a lack of integration in factor markets, among business segments, and among regions.

Obstacles to resource utilisation in the rural economy[2]

China's agriculture employs about 50 per cent of the country's workforce and is characterised by relatively scarce land in relation to labour and small-scale production using little mechanisation. As in Japan and Korea, output per unit of land is high by international standards but output per worker is low. Land-intensive crops, notably wheat, corn, soybeans, and cotton are produced mainly in the northern

11

part of the country while most of China's rice and sugar crops are produced in the southern half. Cultivation of vegetables, which are labour-intensive, is concentrated in coastal provinces and in areas adjacent to cities. Meat production is more evenly dispersed and largely carried out in small "backyard" facilities. Agriculture supplies less than half of total rural income. Per-capita incomes of rural households are 40 per cent of those in urban areas and, due largely to greater access to off-farm jobs, are highest in coastal areas.

Policy toward the rural economy continues to be carried out under frameworks and institutions distinct from those governing other parts of the economy. The Ministry of Agriculture is responsible not only for agricultural activities but also for general oversight of township and village enterprises (TVEs). The property rights regime in rural areas, in which village collectives formally own agricultural land, is distinct from that applying in urban areas. China's population registry system (*hukou*) includes provisions that impede migration of rural-born workers by preventing them from becoming legal residents of cities. Education resources per-capita and the average level of schooling are significantly lower than in urban areas. Pensions and other social benefits provided in urban areas are largely unavailable to the rural population.

Limits on integration with the rest of the economy did not prevent the rural sector from providing two key sources of China's development during much of the reform area. The first came from a major transformation in the policy environment in agriculture in the early 1980s. The tightly-controlled commune system of pre-reform times was replaced by a household based system in which individual farmers lease their land from the collectives, are largely autonomous in their production decisions, and bear the profits or losses from their operations. Market forces have largely replaced government plans and targets. And with the important exception of grains,[3] government intervention in the production, pricing, and marketing of agricultural products is now limited.

These policies have been instrumental in raising agricultural productivity and living standards during the reform era. The increase in agricultural productivity provided the first major impulse to the take-off in China's growth during the first half of the 1980s. However, the physical constraints on China's land and environmental resources make it difficult to increase productivity further within the existing pattern of production. Fertiliser use is already exceptionally high and the scope for increasing the use of pesticides is limited by their adverse environmental impacts. Water shortages and other environmental problems pose increasing barriers to higher agricultural productivity.

Fundamental improvements in agricultural productivity depend on substantial reallocation of resources away from land-intensive products toward labour-intensive products. However, the scope for reallocation is limited by certain government agricultural policies, the most of important of which is the grain procurement system. The policy has also had adverse consequences for macroeconomic performance in recent years: grain surpluses and falling market prices have depressed agricultural incomes and contributed to a marked slowdown in rural consumption growth.

The changing role of agriculture within the rural economy has provided a second major source of China's growth and development. In 1980, agriculture employed virtually the entire rural workforce and supplied nearly all of its income. However, rising productivity within agriculture was accompanied by the large-scale exit of workers from agriculture to industry.

In order to employ the workers coming from agriculture, local governments were encouraged to foster the growth of rural non-agricultural enterprises (REs), commonly known as TVEs.[4] These REs have been the main vehicle for absorbing this exit of workers from agriculture. REs are small and medium-size enterprises (SMEs) in rural areas that specialise in labour-intensive products, and along with foreign funded enterprises produce most of China's exports. Exemption from central planning restrictions, backing from local governments, business relations with state-owned enterprises (SOEs), greater exposure to market discipline compared to SOEs, and access to cheap rural labour, led REs to flourish beginning in the mid-1980s. They were the largest contributor to growth in aggregate GDP and employment from the mid-1980s through the early 1990s, and by 1996 employed 131 million workers, or 28 per cent of the rural workforce. The development of REs in turn has transformed rural income generation, with more than 40 per cent of rural incomes now coming from non-agricultural activities

Table 2.   **Rural household incomes by source**

Net income *per capita*, per cent

	Year				
	1985	1990	1995	1998	1999
Total income (monetary and in-kind)	100	100	100	100	100
Of which: farming and related activities[2]	75	74	63	57	53
Memoranda:					
Total annual income in 1999 RMB[3]	1 311	1 370	1 718	2 132	2 210
Annual real growth rate, per cent[1]	..	0.9	4.6	7.5	3.7

1.   Average growth rates for the periods between indicated years.
2.   Including animal husbandry, forestry, fishing, hunting and gathering.
3.   RMB amount deflated by the consumer price index.
Source: Figures are taken from Chapter 16, Table 16.4, which gives additional details. Data come from *China Statistical Yearbook* 2000, Tables 10-14 and 10-15. The data are derived from official household budget surveys using partly different definitions in urban and rural areas. Wages are assumed to be paid entirely in money.

(Table 2). The overall effect has been to increase the interdependence between the rural and urban economies, even though the traditional administrative distinctions have largely remained.

The large-scale shift of workers from lower productivity occupations in agriculture to higher productivity jobs in industry has been an important engine of China's growth, as it has been for other rapidly developing countries in the past. However, in China the bulk of the shift has taken place within the rural economy rather than through migration from rural to urban areas, due to government regulations that have impeded migration from rural to urban areas. These impediments, which amount to disincentives to migration rather than outright barriers, derive primarily from two sources. The first is related to the *hukou*, and has effectively denied services, other benefits, and most formal sector jobs in urban areas to rural migrants. The second impediment arises from the rural land tenure system, under which farmers who are absent for prolonged periods of time from their rural residences risk losing the land-use rights that are their primary old-age insurance.

Moreover, the shift of agricultural workers into REs has also been quite uneven. These industries have developed mostly in coastal provinces and have much less of a presence in the interior provinces, particularly those in the west. Even during the most dynamic phase, the growth of REs has not been sufficient to fully absorb the exit of workers from agriculture. The result has been the development of a substantial surplus of under-employed rural workers. A large portion of these workers – as many as 100 million – have become "floating" migrants who have taken up unregistered informal sector employment in urban areas.

The impetus to aggregate growth from REs has also waned in recent years. Since 1996, RE performance has deteriorated sharply, and employment has fallen by nearly 2.5 million. The slowdown in China's export growth after the 1997 Asian crisis can explain only a small part of this deterioration, which is rooted in fundamental structural problems. China's REs are suffering from financial problems and operating inefficiencies nearly as severe as those afflicting the SOE sector. The exemption from central planning restrictions and sponsorship by local governments, which gave REs an advantage in the past, have become less important as constraints on SOEs have been relaxed. The disadvantages of REs, in terms of distance from infrastructure and other facilities that benefit businesses in urban areas and which limit the scale of operations REs can achieve, have become more prominent. The degree to which these disadvantages are offset by access to lower cost but also lower skilled labour is unclear.

China's further opening to international markets offers opportunities to revive the growth forces from the rural economy but does not ensure the opportunities will be exploited. China's undertakings in agriculture under the WTO include tariff reductions and higher import quotas, elimination of the privileged position of state-trading enterprises (STEs), and increased scope for private traders in the marketing of agricultural products. The opening to international markets implies a shift of resources away from land-intensive products, notably grains (except rice) and cotton, and an increase in resources in labour-intensive products such as vegetables and horticultural products. However, several policies not covered by China's WTO accession agreement, notably government control of grain procurement prices and distribution, will need to be changed if this reallocation is to occur to more than a limited degree.

Nor does opening appreciably alter the scale of the challenge of employing China's rural workers. Estimates suggest that, even with no further opening, nearly 70 million additional workers will exit agriculture between 2000 and 2010.[5] WTO itself is expected to add only 2 to 3 million further to this decline. The analysis in the chapter on rural industries indicates that, even under optimistic assumptions about how much their performance can be improved, REs are unlikely to be able to take up more than a fraction of the rural workers who will need to find jobs outside the agricultural sector. This further underscores the fact that the development of the rural economy is increasingly dependent on conditions and policies affecting the economy as a whole.

Structural impediments to further industry development[6]

Two related structural changes have provided much of the impetus to China's industrial development during the reform period. The first is the shift from a wholly state-owned industrial sector at the beginning of the reform period toward one increasingly dominated by "non-state" enterprises, starting with TVEs and other collectively owned businesses, followed by foreign-funded enterprises, and more recently by private domestic enterprises. Enterprises either wholly owned or controlled by government entities now account for less than 30 per cent of industrial output, although they still employ nearly half of the urban workforce in the formal sector.

This transformation of industry ownership contributed to growth in at least two ways. First, it fostered a shift of resources toward enterprises that have been more efficient and more effective in responding to changing market forces than most SOEs. The fact that non-state enterprises have faced harder budget constraints than many SOEs partly accounts for this superior performance.

Second, ownership transformation helped to spur growth by increasing competition. The entry of non-state enterprises engendered particularly fierce competition in export industries and industries supplying foreign goods, where the state has allowed relatively free access. Competition has been increased further by the curtailing of central planning mechanisms and freeing of prices: nearly 90 per cent of retail prices are now completely market determined, the main exceptions being energy and other utility prices. Increased competition has helped to raise the overall profit orientation of industry. The advance of competition has, however, been uneven. Protected industries reserved entirely or mainly for SOEs include major utilities such as electricity and petroleum/gas extraction, but also mineral extraction, steel and other metallurgical industries, automobile production, basic chemicals, and tobacco.

The second structural change is the progressive opening of the Chinese economy to foreign trade and investment. China's average tariff rate has fallen from above 40 per cent in the early 1990s to 15 per cent in 2001. Since 1979, China has received a cumulative total of US$ 350 billion in foreign direct investment (FDI) and in recent years, foreign investment has averaged 4-5 per cent of GDP (Table 3). The performance admittedly has been uneven: the bulk of foreign direct investment has come from Chinese Taipei, Hong Kong, China, and other Asian countries with large ethnic Chinese populations, while China has been less successful in attracting foreign direct investment from OECD countries.[7] Foreign direct investment has been largely concentrated in coastal provinces, mainly because most of the special economic zones (SEZ) granting preferences to foreign investment have been established in those regions.

The opening to international trade and investment has increased competition, spurred the growth of domestic labour-intensive industries, especially REs, and helped to develop China's exports. Foreign-invested enterprises (FIEs) in China have also been instrumental in developing China's export industries, particularly in recent years as foreign direct investment inflows have shifted toward capital-

Table 3.   **Ratio of foreign direct investment inflows to China's GDP and gross capital formation**

	Total foreign direct investment inflows (US$ billion)	China's GDP (US$ billion)	Ratio of total foreign direct investment inflows to China's GDP (%)	China's domestic GCF[1] (US$ billion)	Ratio of total foreign direct investment inflows to China's domestic GCF[1] (%)
1983	0.916	300.375	0.31	101.483	0.90
1985	1.661	305.254	0.54	115.300	1.44
1990	3.487	387.723	0.90	134.705	2.59
1995	37.521	700.278	5.36	285.928	13.12
1996	41.725	816.490	5.11	323.148	12.91
1997	45.257	898.244	5.04	343.285	13.18
1998	45.463	958.990	4.74	356.964	12.74
1999	40.319	989.621	4.07	368.446	10.94

1.   GCF refers to gross domestic capital formation.
Source: The Table is adapted from Chapter 10, Figure 10.2. Data come from various issues of the *China Statistical Yearbook*.

and technology-intensive export sectors. Foreign investment has also helped to raise industry productivity and to improve industry technology, know-how and the skills of workers.

As in agriculture, the dynamism to industry imparted by structural shifts seems to be weakening. Industry financial performance has deteriorated sharply since the early 1990s. Profits fell to nearly zero in 1998, with more than one-third of enterprises making losses, and despite noticeable improvement during 1999-2001, financial performance remains weak in many sectors. Growth in industry employment and capital spending has declined markedly. The deterioration has been pervasive and not simply confined to SOEs. The performance of collective enterprises has worsened nearly as much as that of SOEs; and the SME sector generally is in particularly dire straits.

The poor industry performance can be traced in part to the accumulation of policy burdens arising from the long-standing use of enterprises to accomplish social policy goals. These burdens, which amount to government resource extraction through regulation, include excess labour, high debt loads, and responsibilities for public pensions, housing, education, and other social benefits that in other countries are the responsibility of government or individuals. Policy burdens are heaviest on SOEs but they are also borne by REs. Authorities have made significant progress in recent years in reducing excess labour and excess capacity and in reducing debt burdens of larger SOEs. However less progress has been made in reducing other policy burdens, and there has been much less improvement for other SOEs or non-state enterprises.

The biggest problem impairing industry performance is widespread inefficiency in enterprise operations. Presently, much of industry operates with inadequate resources that are poorly managed by the firms that control them and which are misallocated across firms. In contrast to formerly centrally planned economies in Eastern Europe, China's industry is characterised by widespread sub-optimal scale in production facilities, fragmentation and duplication. There are 200 separate producers of automobiles, most of which complete only a few thousand units per year. Much of the plant and equipment is outmoded. Economies of scope are also poorly exploited, as illustrated by the nearly 8 000 independent cement firms in China compared to 110 in the United States, 51 in Russia, 58 in Brazil, and 106 in India.

Inadequate technology and limited capacity to innovate are particular weaknesses of much of Chinese industry. Technology standards for a large portion of domestic firms are below international standards. China devotes proportionately fewer resources, and produces less scientific outputs such as patents, than OECD countries, as well as other large developing countries such as India. Industry also plays a relatively smaller role in technology development and innovation. Moreover, the technology transferred by foreign enterprises to Chinese firms seems to have been limited in both amount and scope.

These inefficiencies are attributable to a range of factors at the firm level, in the external environment, and in the relation between government and business. The poorly skilled and insufficiently profit-motivated management that characterises much of domestic business has neglected technology. Weak financial discipline, which has effectively presented firms and their government backers with a zero cost of capital, has been a major impetus to the development of unproductive and redundant capacity. The pre-reform policy of encouraging regional self-sufficiency together with low capital mobility has left a legacy of limited regional specialisation in production. The resulting inefficiencies have persisted and accumulated because key corrective market mechanisms have been severely impaired. Exit via bankruptcy and liquidation has been relatively rare, although it is becoming more common; and regional protectionism and other administrative barriers have severely restricted the scope for value-enhancing mergers and acquisitions (M&A). These factors have become a mutually reinforcing vicious circle (Figure 2). Government interference leads to poor SOE management and inefficient operations, which foster low profits and high debt; this in turn makes it more difficult to restructure to improve efficiency and prompts government interventions that spread the problem by extracting resources from stronger enterprises to prop up those that are failing.

Industry problems have become acute at a time when the traditional distinctions among ownership forms are becoming less and less meaningful in functional terms. Smaller SOEs and REs are blending into the broader universe of SMEs. Non-state enterprises are moving closer to enterprises formally recognised as private. The blurring of distinctions among ownership classes has not, however, appreciably levelled the playing field among enterprises even though it has modified the boundaries. The different ownership classes are still subject to distinct legal and regulatory frameworks. Differences in treatment – among smaller *versus* larger enterprises, among enterprises in competitive versus sheltered sectors, and among enterprises that receive backing from central or local governments versus those that do not – remain and in some cases have increased.

Figure 2. **The vicious cycle of poor enterprise performance**

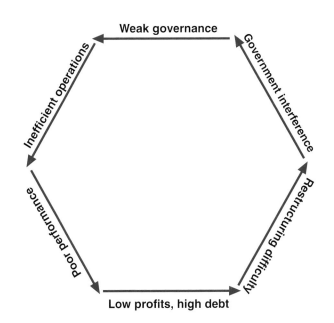

Source: OECD Secretariat.

The contrast in performance among industry segments has likewise become starker. Large SOEs remaining under government control receive preferential treatment from the government and are often sheltered from competition, but their performance is often lacklustre and their flexibility is constrained by government intervention in their management and by various policy burdens. A contrasting segment includes less favoured SOEs and collectives that have become highly competitive in national, and in some cases international, markets, in large part because they have been freer of government interference, more exposed to market discipline, and better managed as a result. Within this group are enterprises in consumer goods and other labour-intensive industries that have been tempered by fierce competition and have successfully integrated into international production chains. Between these groups lie a large portion of (mainly) SMEs in poor financial condition and in dire need of restructuring, but whose ability to restructure is circumscribed by limited access to financing and other impediments.

China's further opening to international markets will force substantial adjustments in industry.[8] Studies indicate that production of textiles, particularly lower value-added segments, could more than double once the Multi-Fibre Agreement (MFA) is phased out in 2005. Other labour-intensive industries are expected to gain, although not as dramatically. Domestic firms in a number of capital or technology intensive industries are expected to lose ground, at least initially, to foreign competition. These include automobiles along with segments of the chemical and metallurgical industries. Foreign direct investment is also expected to rise substantially, by as much as two-fold annually by 2005 compared to the level that would otherwise prevail. Higher foreign direct investment will create jobs but will put competitive pressure on current domestic enterprises, even in sectors where China has a comparative advantage.

Trade and investment liberalisation is unlikely by itself, however, to restore dynamism to China's industry. To take full advantage of trade and investment liberalisation, the real economy will require extensive restructuring of firms, improvement in their governance and management, and reallocation of resources. The benefits of trade and investment liberalisation to particular industries will depend not only on their theoretical comparative advantage but also upon their ability to restructure and upgrade operations to meet the challenges of world markets that in important respects have become more difficult over time. For example, higher end segments of the textile industry will need to improve technology and quality if they are to keep up with competitors in other emerging Asian economies. Firms producing labour intensive products will need to integrate into international production chains if they are to be successful in export markets. Trade and investment liberalisation should help to improve some of the mechanisms needed to accomplish the necessary restructuring, by increasing competition, expanding opportunities for alliances between foreign and domestic firms, and spurring government officials to take measures to improve the business environment. However, key obstacles that now exist to improvement in industry performance, such as continued government interference in enterprise management, poor financial discipline, and restrictions on exit and other modalities for re-deploying resources, need to be addressed if the potential benefits of trade and investment liberalisation are to be realised. Furthermore, a more comprehensive and effectively enforced competition law will be needed to prevent incumbent firms and governments from erecting new protectionist barriers to subvert trade and investment liberalisation and the adjustments it will necessitate.

Growing constraints from the financial system[9]

China's financial system has made important progress in recent years. The stock market has expanded impressively since its inception in the early 1990s, reaching a market capitalisation of more than 50 per cent of GDP by 2001 (Figure 3). The past decade has also seen the creation of new nation-wide banks, significant expansion of the insurance sector, development of a domestic money market, and the more recent emergence of consumer and housing finance. The financial supervisory and regulatory structure has also been thoroughly reorganised and rationalised along lines consistent with international best practices.

Figure 3. **Equity market capitalisation: ratio to GDP in selected countries, 2000**

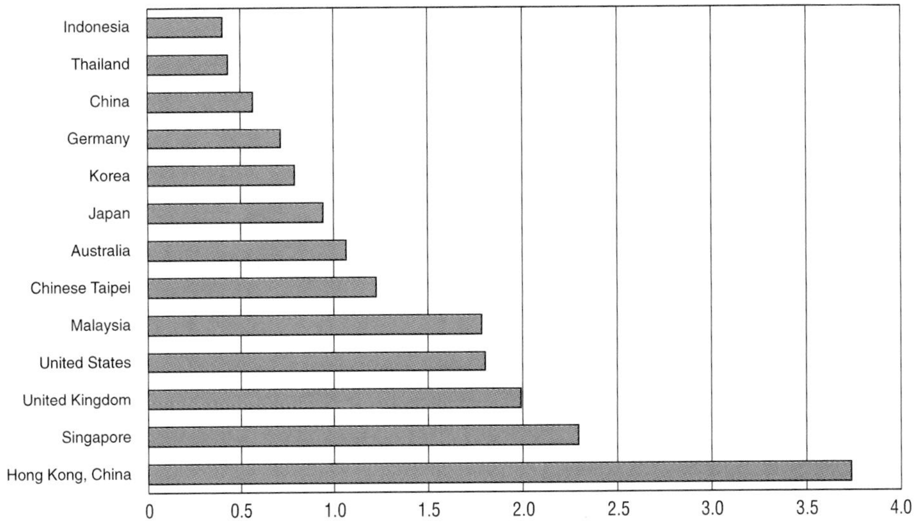

Note: Figure is from Chapter 15, Figure 15.1.
Source: International Federation of Stock Exchanges and OECD Secretariat Estimates.

Despite this progress, the financial system still performs inadequately in carrying out several of its basic functions in the economy. Although savings appear to be mobilised reasonably effectively,[10] credit is inefficiently allocated. SOEs receive the bulk of funds allocated by the formal financial system, while non-state enterprises receive a much lower share than warranted by their importance in the overall economy.[11] Non-commercial considerations, such as the need to sustain loss-making SOEs, continue to influence bank lending. These distortions, together with the limited ability to vary interest rates to reflect risk, mean that the effective cost of credit varies widely among borrowers of comparable credit worthiness. There is limited diversity in financial outlets and capabilities. The interbank market and other available facilities provide only limited scope for transferring funds among financial institutions or regions. Insurance companies and other institutional investors are underdeveloped even compared with other emerging market economies such as India and Brazil. The government and other bond markets are small, fragmented, and illiquid, and the stock market, despite its rapid growth, is subject to limitations on access and trading that impair its effectiveness. Financial instruments to deal with liquidity fluctuations, manage risk, and provide for other specialised needs are limited.

The external discipline provided by the financial system has also been a major weakness. Years of government-mandated lending together with weak contract enforcement and bankruptcy regimes created a distorted credit culture in which banks have had limited incentives – and even less ability – to maintain strict lending standards and enforce loan contracts. Government mandates and weak lending standards created "soft budget constraints" for many enterprises that were a major factor in the over-investment that occurred during 1992-94, and whose legacy of excess and inefficient capacity now afflicts the Chinese economy. The overall weakness in discipline has been aggravated by its unevenness across enterprises. Due in part to the limited development of capital markets, but also to government intervention in enterprise operations, the financial system lacks means to support enterprise restructuring, re-deploy resources, and provide a market for corporate control.

These weaknesses in the financial system are partly a reflection of the fact that China is still a developing country. However they also reflect the fact that evolution of the financial system has lagged that of the real economy. Despite the substantial growth of the non-state sector in the real economy, the financial system remains virtually entirely state-owned (Table 4), with only a single privately owned

Table 4. **State ownership of banks**

	State owned or controlled banks: share of banking system capital	
	1998	1994
China	99	100
Other emerging economies:		
Hong Kong, China	0	0
India	82	87
Indonesia	85	48
Malaysia	7	9
Philippines	n.a.	19
Singapore	0	0
Thailand	29	7
Russia	36	n.a.
Argentina	30	36
Brazil	47	48
Chile	12	14
Mexico	28	0
Peru	0	3
South Africa	2	2
OECD *countries:*		
Australia	0	22
Canada	0[1]	n.a.
France	0[2]	n.a.
Germany	47	50
Italy	17[1]	n.a.
Japan	15	0
United Kingdom	0[1]	n.a.
United States	0	0
Czech Republic	19	20
Hungary	9[1]	81[3]
Poland	46	76

1. 1999.
2. The government has a controlling interest in several financial institutions that provide services similar to those of commercial banks.
3. 1990.

Sources: Chan-Lee, James with Sanghoon Ahn (2000), *Measuring the quality of financial systems in 29 market economies: an indicators approach with an extension to East Asia*, Asian Development Bank Institute, July; Barth, James R., Gerard Caprio Jr., and Ross Levine (2001), *The regulation and supervision of banks around the world: a new database*, World Bank, February; national sources and secretariat estimates.

domestic bank. The four major state-owned commercial banks (SOCBs) established in the early reform period to finance SOEs, and which are still heavily oriented toward this enterprise segment, dominate the financial system, accounting for nearly three-quarters of domestic lending. Credit facilities are segmented between the cities and rural areas. Operations of most commercial banks, with the exception of the SOCBs and 13 newer joint-stock banks, are restricted to their home city.

These structural features reflect the heavy past involvement of the government in lending decisions to support central planning mandates in the real economy and to use bank lending as a substitute for government spending to promote various non-commercial objectives. The latter practice was spurred in part by the steady decline in government tax revenues from the early 1980s through the mid-1990s (see Chapters 18 and 22 on tax policy and macroeconomic issues respectively). The resulting substitution of government mandates for sound credit standards is substantially responsible for the massive accumulation of non-performing loans by banks and other financial institutions. Government involvement, and the perception that financial institutions will ultimately be backed by the government regardless of their performance, has also inhibited the development of a commercially oriented internal culture focused on the maintenance of sound lending standards and rigorous management of risks.

Beginning in the mid-1990s, the pace of financial reform has accelerated sharply in an effort to address the system's weaknesses. The banking law enacted in 1996 led to a significant tightening of bank lending standards by improving internal controls and strengthening accountability by holding bank loan officers and their management responsible for new problem loans. This step, together with the earlier establishment of three "policy banks", was intended to free commercial banks from government mandates. In 2000, authorities transferred RMB 1.3 trillion (about US$150 billion) of SOCB non-performing loans (NPLs), amounting to nearly 18 per cent of their total loans, to bank asset management companies (BAMCs). New joint-stock banks with nation-wide scope have been established since 1995 in order to create more diversity in the financial system. Authorities have also sought to reduce restrictions on the joint-stock banks to encourage their development and are planning to introduce governance reforms for SOCBs.

However, while important, these steps have not proved sufficient to remedy the weaknesses in financial system capabilities. Credit quality has improved but a large portion of SMEs now face a virtual credit crunch. While many of these enterprises are in poor financial condition, surveys suggest that lack of access to funding has become a key impediment to SME restructuring. Financial discipline has become if anything more uneven than before, as large SOEs with government backing continue to have good access to bank credit and have been the main beneficiaries of the additional financing provided by the stock market. Government intervention in lending decisions has been reduced but the continued provision of working capital loans to poorly performing SOEs suggests it has not disappeared. Furthermore, while the tightening of lending standards helps to contain new non-performing loans, it is unlikely to be sufficient to foster the managed risk-taking characteristic of commercially oriented financial institutions, and which will be increasingly needed in China to facilitate the adjustments to trade and investment liberalisation.

Financial weakness has made these problems all the more difficult to deal with. Despite the carve out of non-performing loans in 2000, the SOCBs along with many other financial institutions almost certainly would have negative capital if their loan portfolios were valued realistically. non-performing loans remaining with the SOCBs after the transfer of loans to BAMC were nearly 27 per cent of total loans in mid 2001 according to official figures, and would probably be higher if the international accounting and loan classification standards China is gradually introducing were fully applied. Joint stock banks also have high non-performing loans and rural credit co-operatives are widely acknowledged to be in especially bad shape. Moreover, financial institutions have little cushion to write down non-performing loans: capital adequacy ratios are barely at the BIS minimum in the best cases and Ministry of Finance restrictions have left loan provisions at levels that are quite low by international standards. Bank profits have fallen steadily through the 1990s to very low levels that would probably be close to zero, or even negative, for SOCBs if international accounting standards were applied.

In a proximate sense, the ongoing problems of financial institutions reflect the poor condition of their enterprise customers. A severe vicious circle has developed (Figure 4). Poor enterprise performance contributes to bank non-performing loans and lowers bank profits by eliminating much of their core market. By themselves, financial institutions themselves cannot hope to restore their financial solvency unless and until enterprise performance improves substantially. But high non-performing loans make it difficult for banks to provide the funds for the enterprise restructuring needed to improve their performance. While common to countries in financial distress, this vicious circle is aggravated in China by behaviours derived from the traditional relations among financial institutions, SOEs, and the government that reforms have not yet decisively transformed. Limited government revenues to facilitate SOE restructuring and its consequences continue to require bank lending to sustain loss-making SOEs. This in turn weakens efforts to improve the internal credit culture and commercial orientation of the banks, while blunting incentives of SOEs to improve their own governance and management. The combination of financial weakness and inadequate governance of financial institutions and enterprises also creates risks that inhibit the development of healthy capital markets as alternative financial outlets.

Figure 4. **The vicious circles of bank and enterprise problems**

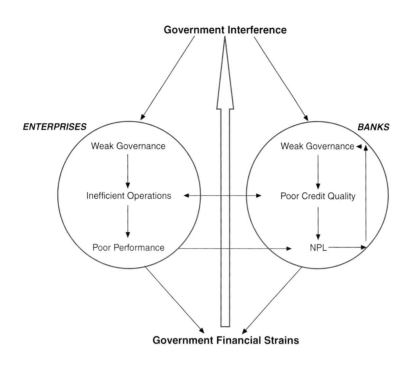

Source: OECD Secretariat.

As in other areas, trade and investment liberalisation offers opportunities but cannot itself guarantee that domestic problems will be appreciably reduced, and it presents some risks if these domestic reforms are not effective. Trade and investment liberalisation in principle allows much greater scope for foreign banks, insurance companies and securities firms to participate in the domestic market. Concerns within China that domestic banks will lose a substantial market share to foreign banks appear to be overstated, however. Foreign banks are likely to be very selective in their activities and to largely avoid lending to domestic enterprises until their performance improves substantially.[12] As argued in the chapter on the banking sector, the development of China's domestic banks depends on the success of reforms to improve their capabilities and governance *and* to facilitate restructuring of their enterprise customers. Given success in these areas, foreign entry into banking and other financial services should help to develop the financial system, and ultimately benefit Chinese firms that succeed in improving their capacities to operate effectively. Trade and investment liberalisation is also likely to increase foreign investment in China's capital markets. This is likely to help develop these markets over the long-term, but it may put near-term pressures on Chinese equity markets, where domestic shares appear overvalued compared to those on international markets. Opening of the capital markets to foreign participation on any sizeable scale implies liberalisation of the capital control regime – which will require substantial improvement in financial discipline and supervision if risks to financial stability are to be contained.

Emerging weaknesses in macroeconomic performance[13]

China's macroeconomic performance has been enviable in many respects. Impressive growth in real GDP has been accompanied by even more rapid growth in foreign trade and investment that have made China one of the more open of the world's largest economies.[14] The external balances have remained healthy. China has undergone several episodes of overheating and inflation during the reform period, but has avoided the prolonged bouts of very high inflation suffered by many other developing countries.

In recent years, however, several signs of a weakening in China's macroeconomic performance have emerged. The first is the slowdown in real growth noted earlier. Real GDP growth since 1996 has averaged slightly above 8 per cent, nearly 2 percentage points below the pace of the prior fifteen years. Fiscal stimulus, which contributed nearly 1 percentage point to growth during 1998-2000, prevented an even greater slowdown. Employment growth has fallen even more sharply (Figure 5), to below the rate needed to absorb new entrants into the labour force plus those laid off from SOEs and other activities. The result has been a marked rise in urban unemployment – which by some estimates is over 10 per cent – and a further increase in under-employed rural workers.

The slowdown is not fundamentally cyclical. China was hit only moderately by the 1997 Asian crisis and growth has remained low by past standards even as Asian countries recovered. Nor does the slowdown seem to reflect the natural decline in potential growth that occurs as countries run out of opportunities to transfer labour from low productivity to higher productivity occupations and to absorb readily available technology and know-how from abroad. The labour surpluses and widespread inefficiencies in industry suggest that these processes have been slowed by structural distortions but are not exhausted. Rather the growth slowdown is more plausibly viewed as the result of the drag on aggregate demand engendered by the problems of banks and enterprises, together with structural problems in the rural economy.

The slowdown in real growth also poses challenges to authorities as they seek to foster the adjustments needed to alleviate the structural problems. Adequate growth is needed to generate the demand, profits, and government revenues required to finance industry upgrading, facilitate reallocation of resources among sectors, and support workers displaced by the transition. Achieving full employment of the labour force is likely to require an extended period of growth above China's potential rate at some future point.

Efforts to support growth through macroeconomic stimulus have underscored the limits on monetary and fiscal policy instruments. As has happened in OECD countries during periods of banking stress, expansionary monetary policy has had only a limited impact because of the credit crunch resulting from banks' reluctance to risk incurring new problem loans. Although the central bank interest

Figure 5. **Aggregate employment growth**

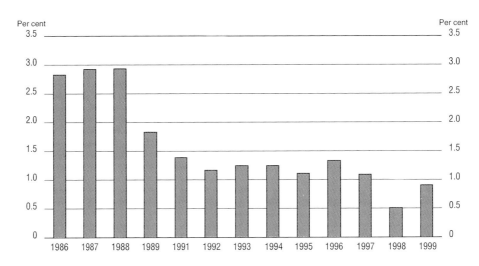

Source: China Statistical Yearbook, 2000.

Table 5.   **Government on-budget revenues as share of GDP**
Figures for 1999

	Percentage share
China	20.4
OECD average	37.8
United States	31.0
European Union	45.0
Japan	37.6
Other emerging market economies	
Brazil	31.7
India	18.8
Indonesia	17.3
Russia	29.8

Source: OECD Secretariat compilations and estimates based on national sources. Date include payments to social insurance funds.

rate has been lowered progressively, to below 1 per cent currently, bank-lending rates have been allowed to fall by less in order to avoid further aggravating the weak profitability of the banks.

As a result, fiscal policy had had to supply most of the macroeconomic stimulus. Official figures suggest that China's fiscal position is healthy and that there is ample scope for fiscal expansion. While the general government deficit rose to nearly 3 per cent of GDP in 2000, domestic and foreign government debt together still amount to only about 32 per cent of GDP.[15] However, this picture is misleading because it is widely acknowledged that the government will need to take on debt obligations not yet explicitly recognised. The main obligation, the funds needed to restore solvency to financial system, could more than double the government debt ratio initially.[16]

China's debt-carrying capacity is probably less than its GDP might suggest because government revenues are relatively low. Tax revenues fell steadily relative to GDP between 1980 and 1996 and, although they have recovered somewhat, are still less than 15 per cent of GDP. General government revenues, including "extra-budget" fees collected by local governments and contributions to social insurance funds, are about 21 per cent of GDP, a relatively low level compared to OECD countries as well as a number of emerging market economies (Table 5).

The relative scarcity of government revenues has had broader consequences. Government spending on education, research and development, and other social purposes have been low by international standards. The imposition of policy burdens on enterprises and the use of bank lending as a substitute for explicit government spending is due at least partially to the scarcity of government revenues. Limited revenues at the local government level, due in part to distortions in the present fiscal federalism arrangements, have encouraged the widespread imposition of unsanctioned *ad hoc* charges and other forms of resource extraction on enterprises and rural residents. These distortions account for a striking paradox in China's fiscal system. Government financial resources to facilitate economic reforms and meet other key social needs are limited; yet the burden of government resource extraction is heavy for most segments of the real economy – including those that appear to receive preferential treatment in the formal tax system.

The macroeconomic consequences of China's WTO entry are difficult to predict.[17] Much will depend on the success of the economy in making the necessary microeconomic adjustments and on the degree to which economic reforms allow the potentially large dynamic gains from trade and investment liberalisation to be realised over the long term. Adjustment to trade and investment liberalisation will stimulate some sectors but engender deflationary pressures from sectors that lose ground. Macroeconomic policy is likely to have to deal with a shifting balance between these positive and negative forces over time. Recent commentaries point to the possibility that the current exchange rate parity may need to be changed at some point as trade and investment liberalisation proceeds – but they differ as to the direction. These considerations suggest that greater flexibility will be needed in macroeconomic demand management instruments and in the exchange rate regime and capital control regimes.

Growing imbalances in regional development[18]

China's growth during the 1990s has been accompanied by growing inequality among its regions. Incomes and living standards have risen in nearly all areas, but growth has been most rapid in the coastal provinces, followed by provinces in the central region, and least rapid in the western regions (Table 6). Geographic disparities in income have been rising steadily since the late 1980s.

The divergences in growth rates and increasing gaps in living standards among China's regions, and between urban and rural areas, are fundamentally reflections of their poor integration. Transportation and communication infrastructure within China's interior provinces, and that linking the interior with the coast, is generally much less developed than in the coastal provinces. Segmentation has been accentuated by differences in market rules and conditions across regions, and in the way government policies are applied. The scope for non-state enterprises has been considerably less in interior provinces than on the coast, and the heritage of SOE dominance and past central planning is greater.

Table 6. **Per capita GDP and real GDP growth by province**

	Per capita GDP RMB/capita		Rank in the year		Change of rank	Growth rate of GDP	
	1980	1999	1980	1999	1980-99	1980-90	1990-00
Eastern							
Beijing	1 582	19 803	2	2	0	8.8	10.9
Tianjin	1 392	15 932	3	3	0	7.3	11.5
Hebei	427	6 913	12	11	−1	9.2	12.8
Liaoning	768	9 958	4	8	4	8.4	9.4
Shanghai	2 738	30 805	1	1	0	7.4	12.2
Zhejiang	468	11 981	9	4	−5	11.1	15.0
Jiangsu	544	10 699	6	7	1	11.6	14.0
Fujian	343	10 969	20	6	−14	11.4	15.4
Shandong	405	8 648	14	9	−5	10.1	19.6
Guangdong	473	11 739	8	5	−3	12.8	14.6
Guangxi	281	4 264	26	27	1	7.2	11.6
Hainan	278	6 227	27	15	−12	11.7	12.5
Central							
Shanxi	437	5 117	10	18	8	8.7	9.4
Inner Mongolia	345	5 400	19	16	−3	10.6	9.8
Jilin	384	6 302	17	14	−3	9.5	10.4
Heilongjiang	685	7 660	5	10	5	6.9	8.4
Anhui	285	4 710	25	21	−4	9.9	12.2
Jiangxi	342	4 673	21	23	2	8.8	11.7
Henan	317	4 899	23	19	−4	9.6	11.5
Hubei	428	6 511	11	13	2	9.2	11.9
Hunan	365	5 227	18	17	−1	7.8	10.5
Western							
Chongqing	−	4 852		20	−		
Sichuan	315	4 356	24	26	2	8.1	10.0
Guizhou	219	2 463	30	31	1	9.5	8.7
Yunnan	367	4 444	28	25	−3	11.8	9.3
Tibet	259	4 262	29	28	−1	6.4	9.2
Shaanxi	335	4 107	22	29	7	10.0	9.1
Gansu	388	3 595	16	30	14	8.8	9.4
Qinghai	475	4 707	7	22	15	7.1	8.2
Ningxia	409	4 477	13	24	11	9.7	8.5
Xinjiang	405	6 653	15	12	−3	11.1	9.7

Source: *China Statistical Yearbook, 2000.*

Capital mobility has been limited, due in part to the limited outlets for transferring savings among regions and to protectionist barriers to business establishment across regional jurisdictions. Largely as a result of the pre-reform policy of regional self-sufficiency together with limited capital mobility, there is relatively little regional differentiation in industrial production structures, suggesting that regional comparative advantages are not adequately exploited. There are several competition bodies and conditions governing business establishment often differ among provinces. Until recently, interior provinces were given much less freedom to offer preferential treatment to attract foreign direct investment compared to the coastal provinces, and in some cases have been further disadvantaged by the closure of their resource sectors to foreign participation. As discussed in Chapter 9, the relatively inefficient distribution system has increased costs of marketing products nationwide and has fostered regional segmentation in some product markets.

Government policy to favour the development of coastal provinces has increased their integration with the international economy to a degree that in some respects exceeds their integration with the rest of the domestic economy. While the policy is intended to catalyse the development of the economy as a whole, the spillover benefits are limited by the poor integration of the coast with the interior. The focus in the current five-year plan is to continue to rely on the coast to lead China's growth while improving infrastructure in the interior, mainly western, provinces and allowing their governments to offer financial and other preferences to attract foreign direct investment and domestic capital. These efforts are intended to provide a foundation for the much longer-term goal of reducing disparities in growth and, eventually, in living standards. Apart from these measures, explicit regional policy has largely been left to provincial authorities. Financial and other key reform policies at the national level have few explicit regional dimensions.

China's approach to regional policy presents a marked contrast to the experience of the European Union. From the beginning, EU policy emphasised the integration of its internal markets in parallel with liberalisation of its international trade and investment regimes. The example of the United States, which has enjoyed a high degree of internal integration for many years, has been a motivating factor behind this emphasis. Internal integration in the EU has been an explicitly broad based effort to allow free movement of goods, services, capital, persons, and businesses. In order to create comparable conditions for business operations across member countries, the European Commission is assigned responsibility under the Treaty of Rome for enforcing competition law, and has undertaken complementary initiatives toward greater harmonisation of tax and other policies affecting the business environment. The motivation for this move to a "single market" has been that internal integration can have benefits at least comparable to those from external integration, and indeed is necessary to fully realise the benefits of external trade and investment liberalisation.

Trade and investment liberalisation is widely expected to increase pressures for divergences among China's regions – despite the initiatives being taken under the western economic development programme. Although governments in interior provinces are making strong efforts to attract foreign investment, most foreign direct investment is expected to go to coastal provinces. The labour-intensive industries that will benefit most are also concentrated in coastal provinces. Their proximity to international markets and their infrastructure also favour coastal producers of vegetables and other labour-intensive agricultural products. Without further policy efforts, income inequalities among regions are expected to grow, and could even accelerate with trade and investment liberalisation.

Improving the utilisation of China's resources

China's economy is clearly operating below its productive potential. Human, capital, land, and other resources are under-employed, misallocated among economic sectors, and inefficiently used. Achieving better resource utilisation is the most basic challenge China faces in seeking to meet its development objectives. As discussed in this section, better integration among the various segments China's economy is likely to be essential if resource utilisation is to be improved. Many of the priorities and suggested steps outlined below, and summarised at the end in Box 2, will need to be supported by complementary policies to improve market framework conditions and to strengthen the capacity of the government to support economic development.

Raising labour utilisation[19]

The task of achieving full employment of China's workforce is daunting. Rough projections indicate that China's aggregate labour force will increase by more than 70 million over the next decade. To absorb these new entrants along with the millions of workers expected to leave agriculture, while making progress toward reducing the number of under-employed, will require substantially more rapid employment growth in industry and services than has been attained in recent years. Given the widespread structural distortions in the economy, macroeconomic policy, although it has an important complementary role to play, can do little in the medium-term if inflation is to be contained. Instead, achieving better labour utilisation is fundamentally a structural challenge. Labour market reforms are a necessary pre-condition to achieve this goal, but broader reforms discussed later will also be required.

The key priority for improving the capacity of labour markets is *"… to overcome an inherited pattern of labour market segmentation and establish a national labour market"*.[20] This is necessary because, whatever purposes they may have served in the past, impediments to rural-urban migration and other impediments to mobility have become major obstacles to absorption of excess labour and improvement in labour productivity. Removal of labour mobility constraints is necessary not only to allow workers to find jobs but also to reduce other distortions. In particular, access to a wider array of jobs should improve incentives for rural workers to increase their human capital. Increasing the supply of labour to urban areas should stimulate development of urban businesses. Integrated labour markets should foster business location to areas offering the greatest comparative advantages in terms of access to resources, suppliers, and markets.

An essential step toward creating a national labour market is to begin to progressively phase out the constraints on migration to urban areas and other barriers to the recruitment of non-local workers by urban enterprises. Reform of the *hukou* is necessary to reduce these impediments and has recently been endorsed in principle by the Chinese authorities. Several local experiments with its relaxation are underway. The step has broader implications that condition its timing: in particular, the phase-out might begin with medium-sized cities followed later by larger cities. Furthermore, to genuinely improve labour mobility and integration, *hukou* relaxation needs to be accompanied by reforms of the rural land tenure system if rural migrants are not to face a prohibitively large loss of their land assets. Reform of land tenure, whose terms vary widely, is also necessary to ensure that migration incentives are comparable across regions.

While a key step, elimination of *hukou*-related constraints on rural-urban migration and land tenure reform are only first steps. Other complementary measures need to be taken, beginning in the near-term and extending over a longer period, to improve labour market flexibility and to ensure that improved mobility results in greater and higher productivity employment in the economy as a whole. Local preferences and other measures within and between urban areas that inhibit migrants from seeking education or finding jobs in the formal sector also need to be eliminated in a timely fashion. Development of the unemployment insurance system to replace the transition arrangements being used to help laid-off SOE workers should help to improve incentives for efficient job-search. OECD experience suggests that unemployment insurance reforms can be reinforced through the establishment of a modern employment service that works with businesses to improve collection and dissemination of information – but which does not seek to interfere with hiring decisions.

Over a longer period, development of SMEs in or near cities in interior provinces needs to be fostered along with the expansion of existing cities and creation of new cities in areas where they are economically viable. This will be necessary to ensure that rural migrants from these provinces can find jobs without a mass exodus to coastal cities, and the attendant excessive congestion and negative externalities such an exodus would likely create.

Improved labour market performance also depends importantly on broader reforms to social programmes. Achieving higher educational standards in order to improve human capital is a key priority in this regard, particularly in rural areas where education expenditures and attainment lag those in urban areas considerably. A longer-term goal suggested by OECD experience would be to raise the average duration of formal education from the current 9-10 years to 12 years, and to increase the portion of students that complete the first level of higher education (*i.e.* 16 years) to 25 per cent (see Annex 3 for a discussion of tertiary education issues).

Better integration of the markets also depends on reforms to increase the coverage and portability of pensions and other social benefits. While achievement of these objectives is necessarily a longer-term goal, more attention needs to be paid in the medium-term to relieving distortions that arise from the unevenness in financing burdens for the government-run first tier of the pension system. These distortions are greatest between rural and urban enterprises, and between the informal and formal sectors within the urban sector, and are due to the currently limited and uneven coverage of pension benefits. These differences have worsened as required contribution rates for enterprises subject to the formal pension system have increased. A first step would be to reduce disparities that now exist among urban areas, possibly by pooling financing of the first tier of the pension system at the provincial government level, rather than at the municipal level as is now the case. Over the longer-term, coverage will need to be extended to rural workers and those now in the informal sector in cities, but with flexibility to allow some local variations in contribution and benefit rates.

Making better use of land and environmental resources[21]

The key to improving productivity in the agriculture sector is to "... foster cropping patterns and other agricultural decisions based on emerging market opportunities and regional comparative advantage, rather than on the traditional yardstick of increasing grain output in all areas at any cost".[22] As indicated in the last section, land and other resources now devoted to grain production need to be shifted toward more labour-intensive crops if China is to be able to exploit its comparative advantage under trade and investment liberalisation. To achieve this goal, the current system of government control over grain procurement prices and the related interventions should be phased out as import restrictions are eliminated. This is likely to be needed in any case to contain fiscal burdens on the government.

This step will have greater benefits if accompanied by other complementary policies. These include development of information systems concerning output and input prices and improved marketing channels. Improvement in product standards and quality that are consistent with international norms is particularly important if China is to fully benefit from the opening of foreign markets to agricultural products in which it has a comparative advantage. Infrastructure investment to better link farmers with their markets is also important, particularly in interior provinces. As the experience of European transition economies has underscored, restructuring in agriculture, and in the rural sector as a whole, requires adequate financing. Improvement in the functioning of the rural credit co-operative network and its better integration with the rest of the financial system is basic in this respect. Development of other micro-financing and informal credit channels, provided they can be structured and supervised to prevent abuse, could be particularly effective in the small-scale and low-income farming environment in China.

Reallocation of agricultural production will help to promote an important environmental goal, which is the severe shortage of water and degradation of water quality in Northern China. Water use has expanded sharply over the past twenty years due to increasing use of irrigated land and to growing demands from rural industries and urban centres. Reduction of land-intensive grain crops should release water resources to accommodate urbanisation or other uses. The recent adoption of a more market-oriented water pricing policy, based in part on actual supply costs, should also help to promote more efficient use of water resources.

China's other major environmental problems are extensive air and water pollution. Nearly one-third of the country suffers from acid rain, urban air pollution is quite severe in larger cities, and there are growing pressures on solid waste disposal facilities. These problems can be traced to a variety of factors, including low energy efficiency and the reliance on soft coal in energy generation, the increased use of fertilisers in agriculture, urbanisation, and the explosion in the automobile population in urban areas. The trend away from heavy toward lighter and generally less polluting industries has moderated these forces somewhat, but not enough to prevent a continuing deterioration in environmental quality.

China's government has been making strong efforts to alleviate pollution problems. Environmental standards have been tightened substantially and the authorities have been encouraging more efficient energy use and a shift away from coal toward oil and other less polluting sources. Local governments have been shutting down enterprises that are in violation of pollution standards. These and other steps have substantially established the legal and regulatory framework needed to achieve China's environmental goals. However, as in many other areas, the effectiveness of the framework is limited by implementation problems.

Trade and investment liberalisation will potentially contribute to alleviating China's environmental problems by spurring the shift toward more labour-intensive industries. However the extent to which the environmental benefits are realised depends on reducing three main barriers that are limiting the effectiveness of current policy. The first is better enforcement of environmental regulations, particularly of national standards that are often evaded or ignored at the local level. The power of courts to interpret environmental laws and to adjudicate disputes between legal and regulatory provisions needs to be strengthened. Second, subsidies, price distortions, and other adverse incentives that encourage pollution and inefficient energy use need to be phased out. And third, there needs to be better co-ordination among government agencies to develop a more comprehensive environmental strategy and to redress the significant gaps and "responsibility vacuums" in environmental policy formulation and enforcement at all levels.

Bolstering the capacity of the business sector to productively employ resources[23]

Labour market reforms can improve the conditions under which labour is supplied but improvement in the capacity of the business sector to productively employ both labour and capital is equally critical. An important longer-term goal is to foster the development of China's service sectors, particularly labour-intensive services, but the pace at which this occurs will depend on further increases in urbanisation. The more immediate priority is to restructure China's industrial enterprises through consolidation and reorganisation to achieve a more efficient structure of industry as a whole. Technology also needs to be upgraded and industry's capacity to innovate and to absorb new technology strengthened.

China's government has long been heavily and directly involved in industry restructuring. Since the 1980s, authorities have sought to develop large enterprises and enterprise groups as "national champions" to compete in international markets with multinationals from more advanced economies – although these efforts have met with little success. More recently, the government has intervened extensively and directly to reduce excess labour and other policy burdens of SOEs, to lower surplus capacity, and to manage SOE restructuring. While these efforts have had important benefits, they have also distorted the restructuring process, for example by requiring stronger enterprises to merge with weaker firms. Much of the government involvement reflects its continued intervention in SOE management. Government efforts have also been focused on large SOEs destined to remain under state control.

A key message of the study is that *market mechanisms need to be strengthened so that they play the dominant role in China's business restructuring*. Fundamental improvement in the performance of China's industries will involve extensive reallocation of resources, and changes in ownership and control extending across thousands of enterprises in both the state and non-state sectors. SMEs are critical to this effort and their importance will further increase as the economy shifts toward more labour-intensive activities. These changes will need to come about primarily from market driven processes in which individual enterprises reorganise to maximise the long-term value of their operations. While trade and investment liberalisation offers opportunities to large Chinese enterprises, success in international markets has come to depend less on the scale of a multinational's operations than on the sophistication of its management and the effectiveness of its governance – qualities over which government can have little direct control. Given these conditions, government policies to promote restructuring need to focus on establishing conditions that support market restructuring processes, such as improving competition and clarifying property rights, while limiting direct interventions to matters, such as the disposition of SOE assets, where market processes alone are insufficient to accomplish the task.

The most pressing need is to remove obstacles that now exist to market driven business restructuring. Two sets of policies are most essential to accomplish this objective. The first is financial system reform, as discussed further in the next sub-section. It will not be possible to shift resources toward enterprises that can use them most efficiently unless credit allocation is much more firmly based on strict commercial criteria than is now the case. For this to happen, banks and other financial institutions will need to have greater capacity and better incentives to lend to productive outlets. Financial markets need to be more flexible and open if they are to facilitate transfers of ownership and create a market for corporate control. OECD experience also offers lessons for improving access to external financing for creditworthy SMEs, as part of broader efforts to develop this key enterprise segment.

The second key step is to end government interventions that constrain enterprises' ability to reorganise, distort their incentives to do so, and which block their exit when needed. SOEs particularly need to be given autonomy to choose the partners and terms for mergers and acquisitions based on their long-term economic value, without being burdened by non-commercial requirements imposed by government authorities. SOEs also need to have clearer claims and control over their assets if they are to be able to restructure their operations in a productive manner. Regional barriers to capital mobility and to cross-provincial business location also need to be curtailed. Policies that have the effect of creating cartels or price floors (including rules that define pricing below industry average cost as "predatory") should be avoided wherever possible since these tend to limit incentives for restructuring and to slow exit. Equally important are reforms to facilitate and accelerate exit, since large numbers of China's present enterprises are not competitively viable and will need to leave the market if industry is to become more efficient.

While such measures are essential first steps, their ultimate payoff depends on reforms in other areas. These include measures to eliminate external conditions that would tend to distort restructuring decisions, such as unequal social benefit burdens and incentives that encourage regional protectionism. Equally important are reforms to corporate governance and other framework conditions discussed in the next section that are needed to ensure that enterprises have the capacity and incentives to exploit value-enhancing restructuring opportunities. In light of experience and the more demanding international market environment, authorities might also review the current policy of developing national champions and consider narrowing its focus to areas where China's current advantages give it a better chance of success than in the past.

The technology challenges facing Chinese industry further underscore the importance of strengthening market forces while improving the quality of government intervention. Meeting these challenges involves more than simply making more technology available to the market. Other key objectives are to foster the improvement of capacities at the firm level to innovate and to use and absorb technology; to improve technology diffusion; and to enhance the technological pay-off from foreign direct investment. Explicit technology policies cannot achieve these objectives by themselves without broader reforms. In particular, bolstering firm abilities and incentives to keep up with market technology standards requires improvements in management and governance, competition, and other framework conditions necessary to ensure that firms are adequately profit-oriented. Equally important are reforms to improve protection for intellectual property rights to encourage technology sharing and the development of venture capital facilities. Further opening of knowledge-based service sectors to foreign participation would also help to foster technology transfer from abroad.

The government has an important role to play in improving China's technological capabilities but there needs to be a change in emphasis. The government is likely to have to supply much of the resources to bring funding for basic science up to levels more comparable to international norms. OECD experience suggests that China's government can contribute to technology diffusion by providing support to regional

---

Box 1. **Improving technological capabilities –
Some potential lessons from OECD experience**

OECD experience offers some lessons for fostering the development, diffusion, and absorption of technology. It shows that successful new technology-based firms – which are responsible for an increasing share of innovations – require not only superior governance and management capabilities but also an enabling infrastructure of business services.

The experience of OECD countries indicates that effective implementation of technology diffusion programmes requires organisational improvements and strategic changes in firms, the building of interactive relations between different players, exploitation of existing resources and a local presence. To accelerate technology diffusion, OECD governments are focusing on addressing market and systemic failures through four types of operational strategies:

- *Supply-driven initiatives* that transfer technologies developed under government sponsorship to the private sector. An example is the Canadian Space Agency's Space Station Program, which involves competitive bidding of private firms for contracts to develop and commercialise dual-use space technologies.

- *Demand-driven programmes* seek to diagnose and enhance the technological absorptive capacity of firms. The Manufacturing Extension Partnership in the United States assists smaller manufacturers to implement appropriate technologies and improve their business practices.

- *Network-building initiatives* develop bridging institutions and inter-firm partnerships to facilitate information flows. Innovation Centres in the Netherlands strengthen both vertical and horizontal network links at the regional level.

- *Infrastructure-building programmes* upgrade the technology diffusion infrastructure at the national level. Korea adopted various schemes of spreading new technology and promoting network links as part of the country's developmental strategy.

Absorption of technology is a long-term process in which acquiring firms need to develop long-term partnerships and trust with technology providers. Case studies of the electronic and semiconductor industries in Korea and Chinese Taipei suggest that it is important for domestic firms to engage in progressively more advanced forms of technology transfer with foreign partners over time (for example, from subcontracting, to technology licensing to original equipment manufacturing, to original design manufacturing, to joint product R&D and strategic alliances).

---

university and other research centres, for example. There is also a need to embed government technology policies in a broader framework that exploits complementary relations with other industrial policies. This is likely to require greater co-ordination between the Ministry of Science and Technology, which has been largely responsible for technology policy, and other Ministries responsible for programmes concerning financing for SMEs and other industrial policies.

Despite its impressive performance, there is significant room to improve China's foreign direct investment performance in both quantitative and qualitative terms. The strengthening of intellectual property rights protection under China's accession agreement should help to attract more foreign direct investment from developed country businesses, which have sometimes been reluctant to invest in the domestic market out of concern that their advanced technologies and production techniques will be inadequately protected. Given the worldwide trend toward the use of M&A in cross-border investment, establishment of market based mechanisms for domestic M&A would also help to attract investment from more advanced economies. Adoption and effective enforcement of a comprehensive competition law, and reduction in administrative and other barriers beyond those required by the WTO, would encourage more foreign investment aimed at the domestic market. Further opening of protected industries, for example by allowing more foreign participation in extractive activities, would also help to attract foreign direct investment as well as increase efficiency.

Other measures could help to improve the pay-off to the domestic economy from foreign investment. Improved competition and better enforcement of contracts would encourage more local sourcing of inputs, such as packaging materials, used by resident foreign enterprises. Reduction of government interference in the operations of domestic enterprises could help to foster more fruitful partnerships with foreign firms possessing advanced technology.

Improving the effectiveness of the financial system[24]

Improvement of the capabilities of the financial system to promote efficient resource utilisation is fundamental to the restructuring of industry, achieving better integration among regions, bolstering macroeconomic performance, and allowing China to open its financial markets to the world without undue risk to financial stability. As noted earlier, despite the important steps taken over the past five years, the fundamental capabilities and incentives of the financial system to allocate credit efficiently remain impaired.

As discussed in the previous section, the problems of the financial system are closely linked to those of the real economy and to the shortage of resources effectively available to the government. As emphasised in the chapter on the banking sector, China's banks are unlikely to become fully healthy and effective until the performances of their enterprise customers improve substantially. Nevertheless, international experience strongly indicates that timely and decisive reforms of the financial system are essential to break through the vicious circle China now faces. Three key objectives need to be achieved if the financial system is to become an effective support, rather than obstacle, to the broader reform process.

The first and most pressing objective *is to restore capital adequacy to financial institutions within the near-term*, through direct government financial support as needed. International experience suggests there are a range of specific modalities that could be used to accomplish this objective, but that three important principles need to be observed if the benefits are to be realised.

- First, the rehabilitation needs to be thorough, comprising measures to deal with non-performing loans (through removal from banks' balance sheets of non-performing loans that cannot be dealt with out of provisions or through write-downs) and increases in capital, to at least the BIS minimum initially.

- Second, the clean up should complete the financial rehabilitation of SOCBs, and address the non-performing loans of other commercial banks and credit co-operatives that are also in distress.

- And third, the clean up and its aftermath should also involve strict conditions on the financial institutions, under which management is held accountable for, and given the requisite autonomy to improve, future performance. For example, authorisation for banks to enter new lines of business could be made conditional on their maintenance of adequate capital and adherence to prudential standards.

While a necessary precondition, balance sheet clean up cannot itself guarantee sustained improvement in the effectiveness of the financial system. Perhaps the most basic lesson from other countries' experiences with financial distress is that clean up needs to be accompanied by stringent measures to correct the conditions that led to the stress. In China's context, measures to establish and strengthen the governance of financial institutions as commercial entities and further improve their internal systems for credit assessment and management of risk are essential, along with the strengthening of the independence and capabilities of bank supervisors. These are particularly necessary given the inevitable difficulty of ensuring that government-owned financial institutions, particularly large ones, are truly commercially oriented.

Nevertheless, international experience strongly suggests that breaking the vicious circle China is now in requires early intervention to restore financial system solvency as other measures to improve conditions in the real economy that require more time are undertaken. Inadequately capitalised financial institutions tend to have weak incentives to maintain sound lending standards or manage risk.[25] Indeed, financial weakness can spur perverse incentives to hide loan problems or to take excessive risks ("gamble for redemption"). In China's case, stronger balance sheets are necessary to allow other reforms to improve the fundamental health of financial institutions to proceed. These include the ability of banks to restructure to meet increased foreign competition and to access external funds to bolster their capital. Moreover, given their low profitability, China's financial institutions are unlikely to be able to achieve capital adequacy out of their own resources within a reasonable time. In fact, balance sheet clean up is probably key to their longer-term ability to improve their profitability.

While the current rapid pace of loan growth might suggest that banks could "outgrow" their high non-performing loans rates given sufficient time and continued rapid growth in the real economy, such a strategy carries important risks. It would leave banks in even worse shape if loan or deposit growth were to slow. It could also pose a difficult dilemma between improvement in banking system conditions and fostering the growth of alternative financial outlets which might divert business from banks. As the experience of other countries, most recently Japan, has underscored, relying on real sector recovery to restore the health of financial institutions is more likely to impede real recovery, allow financial problems to get worse, and increase the ultimate cost of their resolution.

There has been concern that a government sponsored clean up will undermine financial institutions' incentives to sustain a strong credit culture. Against this must be set the fact that only SOCBs benefited from the first non-performing loans programme, and the widespread perception within and outside China that the government will always back the solvency of the SOCBs in order to prevent a financial crisis. Delay in restoring solvency is more likely to increase and prolong expectations of multiple and open-ended bailouts. A second concern is whether China's government can afford the cost of a thorough financial system clean up, given the limits on its fiscal resources. The cost is likely to be high, on the order of those facing other Asian countries that experienced severe banking problems in the aftermath of the 1997 crisis.[26] However, as argued in the last section of this summary, the cost should be affordable provided that government revenues continue to rise relative to GDP, social benefit programmes are established on a sustainable basis, and further non-performing loans are kept to minimal levels. China does not now face an intractable dilemma between cleaning up the financial system and maintaining the sustainability of its fiscal accounts. But further delay, since the ultimate costs are likely to rise, increases the risk that such a dilemma will develop in the future.

Restoration of solvency will also help to promote the second, if longer-term, objective, *to create a more diverse and balanced system in which financial outlets other than SOCBs have a much greater role*. The SOCB orientation toward SOEs is likely to continue, as they become "lead banks" for the large firms that will remain under state control. This, together with their size and potential ability to tap domestic and international financial markets, gives them a strong comparative advantage in serving multinational and other larger enterprises. The other commercial banks and credit co-operatives probably have stronger comparative advantages and incentives to lend to SMEs, but their ability to expand their market share is circumscribed by regulatory and other limits on their access to funding. Accordingly, relaxation of policies that restrict the ability of joint stock and other smaller institutions to expand, as part of broader efforts to create a more level playing field among commercial banks, are necessary first steps toward greater diversity in the financial system. A more active longer-term policy to restructure the SOCBs along regional or functional lines would also help to promote greater diversity and to increase competition.

Greater diversity would also help to improve the commercial orientation of the financial system as a whole. Although strong efforts are being made to develop a more commercially oriented credit culture in the SOCBs, the task is inevitably difficult given the traditional role of these banks in central planning, their continued strong ties to the government, and, not least, their "too big to fail" status. The joint-stock banks enjoy more autonomy from government mandates, are generally better managed and more commercially oriented. Increasing the importance of these banks would help to make the overall banking system more responsive to market forces.

The third key objective to improve financial system capabilities *is to foster the development of China's capital markets*. The government bond market needs to be able to absorb the large increase in public debt that is likely to occur in the next several years. Capital markets are also necessary to allow enterprises to achieve a better debt and capital structure and to provide the instruments for retirement savings that will be needed as the second and third tiers of the pension system develop. However, China's capital markets are not yet capable of adequately carrying out these functions. Most listed companies are SOEs and only about one-third of their shares are actively tradable. The market has been prone to manipulation and overvaluation. The bond, as well as money, markets are behind the stock market in their development and lack liquidity and breadth. As argued in Chapter 15, the markets as a whole will need further strengthening to accommodate new financial instruments, greater foreign participation and increased exposure to international financial markets at acceptable risk.

As in other areas, the priorities for improving the capital markets start with several near-term steps to remove obstacles to their effective functioning and development. These steps have been endorsed by the authorities (or at least raised by senior officials), but in some cases their implementation has been delayed.

- The first is to increase the share of SOE equity that can be traded within the three year time-period authorities have specified, following a pre-announced timetable.

- The second is to open stock market listing to all firms, including collectives and private firms, based on their ability to meet the supervisory requirements – thereby ending the preferential treatment large SOEs still receive in this area. This, together with the first step, is basic to improving the discipline offered by the stock market and to creating a market for corporate control.

- The third step is to integrate the equity markets by eliminating the distinction between ("A") shares that can be held by Chinese citizens and the ("B") shares that can be held by foreigners within the near term. This step does not depend upon achievement of capital account convertibility, but it will need to be carefully timed to avoid disruptions arising from the now considerable differences in share valuation across the segmented markets.

These near-term steps should open the way for, but also need to be reinforced by, other policies to promote the development of the capital markets over the medium and longer-term. These include policies to improve corporate governance and to allow foreign financial institutions to enter the capital markets, and implementation within the medium-term of official plans to improve the government bond market. Frameworks for mortgage bond and mortgage-backed bond markets will need to be established in order to facilitate the increased demand for real-estate credit as housing reforms proceed.

Achieving better integration among China's regions[27]

Better integration among China's regions is not simply important on equity grounds. Lack of integration is becoming an impediment to other development goals and is likely to become a greater obstacle over time if not addressed. Without greater integration, coastal and a few interior cities are likely to bear the brunt of the migration of workers who will need to find jobs in cities. The resulting pressures on urban land, the environment, and other resources could lead to sharply diminishing returns from agglomeration, and thereby degrade the advantages that have given these urban areas their vitality. Greater integration is needed to make full use of China's land and agricultural resources – which cannot be transferred to the coast. Continued segmentation among regions limits the productivity gains from regional specialisation and restricts the ability of enterprises to achieve adequate economies of scale and scope.

To achieve better integration, China needs a much broader and comprehensive regional development strategy focused on the creation of national markets for products and productive factors. This implies a shift in emphasis, away from the granting of selective exemptions from government regulations and tax preferences, in favour of measures to allow greater scope for national market forces and to improve the ability and incentives of local governments to respond to those forces. OECD experience underscores several pitfalls in regional development strategies that are potentially relevant to China, including:

- over-reliance on government interventions to develop specific areas or sectors ("growth poles") to catalyse regional development, a strategy which tends to be quite expensive and has proved to not be very successful;

Box 2.   **Key priorities for improving resource utilisation**

Problem	Priority objectives	Some suggested steps
Labour market segmentation is preventing full employment of human resources	Create a national labour market by removing impediments to labour mobility	*a*) Beginning in the near term, progressively phase out *hukou* related restrictions on migration and reform rural land tenure *b*) Continue to develop the unemployment insurance system and reduce disparities in social benefit burdens over time
Government policies impede a shift away from land-intensive toward labour-intensive crops	Foster cropping patterns in line with market forces and regional comparative advantage	In the near term, phase out controls on grain procurement, prices and distribution
Environmental problems impair efficient resource allocation	Improve enforcement and achieve better co-ordination of environmental policies among government agencies	Strengthen the powers of courts to interpret and enforce environmental laws and regulations; eliminate distortions that encourage pollution and inefficient energy use
Business sector restructuring is hampered by lack of market mechanisms	Foster market-based mechanisms as the primary vehicle for restructuring	*a*) In the near term, remove government imposed obstacles to enterprise restructuring *b*) Develop capital markets over the longer term *c*) Improve protection for intellectual property rights; increase government resources devoted to basic R&D
Technology is sub-standard and capabilities for innovation, diffusion, and absorption are weak	Develop a comprehensive framework to foster technology capabilities of enterprises	
Credit allocation is inefficient, financial discipline is weak, and financial facilities to support business sector restructuring are limited	*a*) Restore financial system solvency *b*) Improve diversity in financial institutions and develop money and capital markets	*a*) Restore capital adequacy to financial institutions in the near term subject to strict performance requirements. *b*) Remove regulatory barriers impeding the functioning and development of money and capital markets as soon as possible *c*) Over a longer period, foster a greater role for joint-stock and other smaller commercial banks; foster development of capital markets, in part by liberalising access of foreigners to the capital markets
Regional fragmentation is becoming an obstacle to broader development needs	Develop a comprehensive regional development strategy, focused on the creation of more uniform framework conditions and improving internal capital mobility	*a*) In the near term, eliminate administrative and other regional protectionist barriers *b*) Reform central-local government fiscal relations within the medium-term *c*) Promote development of national money and capital markets

- the launching of major infrastructure projects without taking realistic account of regional demand; and

- maintenance of direct assistance to declining sectors in order to protect local economic activities.

In addition to infrastructure development, a comprehensive regional development strategy for China involves three basic objectives. The first is to ensure that common framework conditions for competition, property rights, business establishment, and taxation apply to all regions and localities. As the experience of the EU suggests, this is likely to require a sustained and broad initiative from the central government. The principle that sub-national governments may not impose barriers to domestic trade, which is contained in current law but lacks enforcement provisions, needs to be strengthened. This might be accomplished (as in the European Union and Russia) partly through the application of national competition law provisions.

The second objective is to improve the mobility of capital among regions. Development of national capital markets and improvement in the commercial orientation of financial institutions are the ultimate keys to promoting a more efficient geographic allocation of capital over the longer-term. In the near-term, administrative burdens on local business need to be reduced and transparency in regulations increased if provincial governments in the interior are to be competitive in attracting foreign direct investment as well as domestic capital. Reduction in administrative barriers and local protectionism that impede cross-border business establishment and mergers and acquisitions is also important. In the medium term, further development and liberalisation of the money markets and expansion in the geographic scope for city bank operations in the interior would facilitate the ability to transfer savings among regions. Opening of protected resource sectors to foreign investment would also help to attract foreign direct investment to resource-rich central and western provinces.

Regional integration also depends on a third objective, reform of central-local government fiscal relations. The current system contributes to the unevenness in tax burdens among regions. As discussed in the last section of this synthesis, the allocation of government revenues and division of responsibilities for spending need to be realigned among government levels in accordance with need rather than the economically arbitrary administrative criteria. China needs not only to raise the total amount spent nationally on education but to give equal priority to increasing resources for education in rural areas, particularly those in the interior, where standards are now low but the potential payoff in terms of improved human capital is relatively high.

Realisation of the benefits of greater integration also depends on promoting greater balance in urbanisation by fostering market-driven creation and development of new cities in interior provinces. City building along with the exit of workers from agriculture will help to equalise strains on urban resources and provide an impetus to regional growth as agglomeration economies are exploited. Expansion of existing medium-sized cities by accretion of bordering rural townships that are already experiencing rapid growth of new enterprises should also help to invigorate growth. Creation of new cities, however, is a complex process in which the most productive role of government is to foster conditions conducive to their formation. These include access to financing and sufficient flexibility in labour markets to attract essential labour skills, along with sufficient autonomy for regional and city planning authorities to formulate and implement development strategies based on local resources and comparative advantage.

Strengthening the institutional frameworks for market functioning

The success of the steps to break down barriers to resource reallocation and to ensure that resources are efficiently used in the future depends critically upon governance, property rights, competition, and other frameworks essential to effective market functioning. Considerable effort has been made over the past several years to strengthen several of these frameworks, but their impact has been blunted by the more limited progress made in complementary areas. Fundamental ambiguities in the property rights framework have not been resolved; market discipline is still inadequate; and while organisational structures and many of the basic laws have been established, their effectiveness has been limited by inadequate enforcement. This section outlines the priorities for strengthening the frameworks; these are summarised in Box 3. at the end.

Strengthening enterprise governance[28]

Establishing governance structures so that enterprises behave as autonomous profit-seeking commercial entities has been a key goal of China's economic reforms since the early 1990s.[29] The difficulties facing China in accomplishing this task are hardly unique. OECD countries have experimented for several decades with various modalities for ensuring that publicly-owned companies perform adequately – but with only limited success. The difficulties in China are likely to be even greater, given the close ties between the government and SOEs.

Since 1999, corporate governance reform focused on SOEs has become a key priority in China. The strategy has sought to create governance structures patterned on best practices derived from OECD-country experience.[30] One component of the strategy is the conversion ("corporatisation") of SOEs into legally independent joint-stock companies and the establishment of boards of directors and supervisors together with laws defining their responsibilities and those of managers. With this, the authorities have sought to curtail direct government intervention in enterprise management by creating separate organs to manage state-owned assets. The second component, which has been given increasing emphasis, is to list corporatised SOEs and diversify their ownership in order to provide further discipline on the boards and managers. Nearly half of SOEs have so far been corporatised. Authorities plan to corporatise the SOCBs within the next several years.

The tangible results of the governance reforms have fallen short of expectations, however. Actual corporate governance practices deviate considerably from OECD standards, and surveys indicate that China is still seen as comparing unfavourably to its Asian competitors in this regard.[31] Weaknesses in the structures themselves are one reason for the limited success of the reforms. The boards of directors and supervisors mandated by corporatisation do not yet have sufficiently distinct identities within the enterprise and their independence is limited. Top managers continue to be appointed by local authorities or political officials. The boards tend to function more as an extension of management than as its monitor, and are effectively bypassed in exercising genuine oversight. The autonomy of managers is weakened by their dependence on government or political authorities for their position, their low salaries, and their lack of a direct stake in the firm's profit performance.

Two related steps needed to improve the functioning of the existing corporate governance framework are to *strengthen the independence and powers of boards of directors and to foster greater accountability and professionalism among managers*. Greater use of qualified independent directors, including outside directors, should be part of this effort. With this, the scope for political participation in enterprise governance should be limited to advice and consultation. These steps would help to lay the foundation for development of a market for managers, which is now lacking, and for the more widespread adoption of performance-based compensation.

The greater obstacles and necessary solutions to the present weaknesses in corporate governance lie outside the corporate governance structures themselves. Much of the difficulty in creating SOEs that are autonomous, profit-oriented, and accountable to their state owners can be traced to the ambiguities in the property rights framework discussed further below. Partly as a result, SOEs have gained only limited autonomy as the result of corporatisation, and have continued to be subject to government restrictions on their ability to lay off workers, dispose of assets, and engage in mergers and acquisitions.

As in other countries, stronger market discipline is critical in establishing a firm and lasting foundation for effective corporate governance. In China, competition is often limited in sectors in which the current listed SOEs are concentrated. Apart from the continued weakness in discipline from financial institutions, limited access to the market and the withholding of the majority of listed SOE shares from trading effectively prevent the stock market from carrying out the disciplining role it has been assigned in the overall corporate governance reform strategy. The impact of ownership diversification has so far been blunted by the fact that nearly all of the minority shareholders are other public entities, whose own profit-orientation is often weak.[32] Strengthening external disciplines is particularly important because once the basic legal structures are established, their functioning depends most critically on market incentives for enterprises to maintain effective governance.[33]

Finally, corporate governance issues in China do not simply involve SOEs. Collective enterprises have multiple owners and stakeholders and their internal control, allocation of residual claims, and ties to local governments are also ambiguous and of limited transparency. Many collectives seem to be evolving into forms equivalent to joint-stock companies but without being required to adopt the governance structures of the latter. The need to establish a good credit standing and business reputation should create incentives for larger collectives to adopt governance norms more in line with those required of corporate firms. The degree to which this will be true for other collectives is less clear.

Reforming property rights and insolvency mechanisms

Property rights and their embodiment in contracts have been one of the major gaps in China's frameworks for market functioning. An essential step toward remedying this gap was taken in 1999 with the enactment of a Unified Contract Law to replace the formerly scattered collection of laws, by-laws, and regulations based on numerous and not always consistent legislative provisions. The new law creates clearer and more even rules of the game for contractual transactions among businesses of all types and establishes a national framework to which local authorities are subject. The law also reduces the scope for regulatory restrictions on contract provisions that are not sanctioned by other legislation.

The key remaining objective is to develop a coherent framework clarifying property rights and ensuring their equal application to all economic segments. Property rights remain highly ambiguous due to the unresolved status of state assets and the relation between public and non-public ownership. Different sets of rules apply to private, collective, and state-owned property. SOEs cannot freely dispose of their land or of rights to its use.

Lack of clarity about the effective owners of SOEs is a major obstacle to their restructuring and improvement in their governance. SOEs are effectively owned by a collection of ministries and agencies at all government levels with unclear and often conflicting claims that are not adequately defined by existing law or regulations. This creates a situation that has been characterised as "agents without owners",[34] in which multiple owners have limited incentives to monitor the enterprises or to hold their managers and boards accountable. It also produces conflicts that slow and distort business restructuring and exit.[35]

Ambiguous property rights are also impeding restructuring in other parts of the real economy. Apart from the potential barrier to labour mobility posed by the rural property rights regime, the uncertain status of state assets poses obstacles to the development of private enterprises. Private enterprises are unlikely to realise their full potential until the rules for acquiring state assets are better defined.

There is thus a pressing need to develop a coherent framework and supporting laws clarifying rights to property and to ensure their equal application to all segments of the economy. Explicit protections for private property, and better definition of the rights of the enterprise as a legal entity *vis-à-vis* holding groups, regulatory agencies, and political bodies, are key elements of this framework.

Ambiguous property rights are also an impediment to China's insolvency mechanisms. Although bankruptcies and liquidations have increased markedly in recent years, they have occurred mainly among smaller firms and those in the private sector. Passage of the reformed comprehensive bankruptcy law that was first drafted in 1994 will be an important step toward establishing uniform rules applying to state and non-state enterprises and in defining the rights of debtors, creditors and shareholders. But further efforts are likely to be needed to improve the independence of bankruptcy courts and the professional skill of judges so that they can more effectively implement the legislation.

More also needs to be done to clarify the rules if insolvency mechanisms are to be able to accommodate the large-scale re-deployment of assets from nonviable enterprises that will be needed in coming years. Presently, exit is often blocked by legal and administrative barriers to disposal of claims of banks, bank asset management companies, social benefit funds, and agencies responsible for supporting displaced workers. The government agencies that are ultimately responsible for these bodies need to be held liable for these claims so that they do not prevent the liquidation of insolvent firms.

Improving the competition framework[36]

By some standard indicators, China's product markets appear to be reasonably competitive: market concentration at the national level is relatively low; and there has been substantial entry of new firms. Economic rivalry is fierce in many sectors. These measures are deceptive, however, because the limits to competition in China are manifest in other ways. Government restrictions are more prominent as barriers to competition. Limited transport facilities, local protectionism, and other barriers to geographic integration allow enterprises to exercise monopoly power in local markets to a degree that is not apparent in national concentration ratios. Moreover, as noted earlier, competition is uneven across sectors.

The main weaknesses in the competitive environment in China can be listed as follows.

- As has happened in other countries, established enterprises and local governments often seek to prevent entry by newcomers and thereby extract monopoly rents. Product market competition is limited in some cases by overt barriers, by distortions in the tax code and distribution system, and, probably most importantly, by locally imposed restrictions on outsider's ability to establish or acquire a local business.[37]

- The different legal and regulatory frameworks applying to state-owned, collective, private and foreign enterprises, along with complex and opaque requirements for business establishment and business scope, often limit competition. Examples include the high minimum capital required of private limited companies and their need to undergo an elaborate regulatory approval process to make even modest changes in their lines of business.[38]

- While prices are reasonably free to vary for most products and markets, they continue to be restricted in some, notably energy and tobacco. The temporary price floors imposed in industries with excess capacity also limit competition as well as impede exit.

- A substantial number of key sectors are wholly or mainly reserved to SOEs, including not only natural monopolies but, as noted earlier, automobile and steel production. Authorities plan to reduce the role of SOEs to "strategic sectors" but have not specified what those sectors will be.

The present competition law framework rests on the 1993 Unfair Competition Law and the 1999 Price Law, together with various specific regulations and decrees banning certain regional protectionist practices. These laws are enforced by the State Administration for Industry and Commerce (SAIC) and the State Development Planning Commission (SDPC). Together these laws outlaw some overt anti-competitive practices, such as price fixing, and prohibit unauthorised actions by local government agencies or officials that prevent competition. However these laws do not constitute a comprehensive legal framework for competition. In particular, existing Chinese law does not clearly prohibit other practices, such as monopoly abuses, cartels, or restrictive distribution arrangements, that effectively prevent entry and restrict competition. Current prohibitions on anti-competitive practices by government agencies lack sanctions and have had little if any practical effect.

Given this situation, the key objective is to establish a national competition framework to ensure that laws and regulations support rather than interfere with market competition. Adoption of such a framework is particularly important since incentives to engage in anti-competitive practices are likely to increase with trade and investment liberalisation. An essential first step is to enact and implement a comprehensive competition law along the lines of that now being drafted by the State Economic and Trade Commission (SETC) and SAIC. This law should include effective sanctions against the maintenance of "administrative monopolies" by government agencies. As in OECD countries, China's government could usefully apply competition principles to identify existing and proposed laws and regulations that interfere with competition, with a view to eliminating those that are otherwise unwarranted. Special scrutiny should be given to laws that restrict entry based on the legal form or ownership of an enterprise. Competition policy principles should also be incorporated in the design of natural monopoly regulation.

Beyond these measures, steps need to be taken to reduce the incentives for anti-competitive behaviour, particularly that fostered by government entities. In this respect, reforms to social security, the financial system, and other conditions that encourage government entities to extract resources through anti-competitive behaviour are ultimately important to ensure a competitive environment.

Developing financial regulatory and supervisory capabilities[39]

The financial regulatory and supervisory (FRS) framework is key to the success of the steps discussed earlier to improve the capabilities of the financial system and to allow its further development without creating unacceptable risks to financial stability. China's financial regulatory and supervisory authorities face especially great challenges given the adverse incentives inherent in extensive state ownership of financial institutions.

Important steps have been taken since the mid-1990s to provide a modern institutional base for financial regulation/supervision comparable to that of OECD countries. In 1999 the People's Bank of China (PBC) was reorganised into nine regional branches in order to reduce local government interference in its operations and to provide a platform for more effective bank supervision. The PBC now has responsibility for all depository financial institutions, including the rural credit co-operatives. The previously fragmented responsibility for regulation and supervision of the stock exchanges, bond markets, and securities and investment companies has been consolidated in the China Securities Regulatory Commission (CSRC), while responsibility for insurance companies has been lodged with the China Insurance Regulatory Commission (CIRC).

The key objective now is to strengthen the autonomy of financial supervisory authorities and to endow them with the necessary physical and human resources to accomplish their tasks. China's financial regulators face a particularly daunting task in maintaining prudential standards in state-owned financial institutions subject to other, sometimes conflicting, government mandates. As the essential starting point, supervisors need to have the authority and independence to exercise surveillance over supervised institutions solely in the interest of prudential soundness and in a way that is not constrained by other government objectives. Supervisors need to be able to require prompt corrective action by institutions subject to their jurisdiction when problems are found. While their authority has been strengthened in recent years, supervisory authorities still lack full control over some basic prudential standards, such as the power to impose realistic norms for bank provisioning and loan write-offs.[40] Financial supervisors will also have to continue to acquire the necessary physical and human capital to accomplish their tasks. Adaptation of internationally accepted supervisory norms and practices to Chinese circumstances is an important means to these ends – and one which will also provide a foundation for the ultimate opening of the financial system to international markets.

Supervisory structures and responsibilities also need to be further refined to keep up with the development of financial markets. The concentration of authority over capital markets in the CSRC and expansion of its institutional capacity have been essential steps toward ensuring effective oversight of the markets. However, the authority of the CSRC to investigate abuses and order remedies needs to be further strengthened, and accounting, disclosure, and audit standards should be aligned more closely with international practices. Newer financial vehicles, notably investment funds that take money from the public, need to be brought within a formal regulatory framework, preferably one based on models provided by major financial markets outside of China. The CSRC and supervisory authorities responsible for the insurance and pension fund sectors need to co-ordinate their efforts to ensure a level playing field for institutional investors.

Ultimately, the effectiveness of financial supervision in China, as elsewhere, rests on its success in ensuring that market participants have adequate internal incentives and capabilities to maintain prudential standards. Supervision needs to progressively increase the responsibility of market participants for in-house compliance with prudential standards, risk management, and adherence to industry standards. Effective corporate governance of all financial market actors is crucial to these goals. To this end, efforts to strengthen shareholder rights and to raise standards of corporate governance are an essential element of the supervisory process.

Improved transparency in the operations of all enterprises is essential for effective regulatory oversight and effective monitoring by investors and stakeholders. Several steps now underway should help greatly to improve transparency once they are completed. These include the implementation of new accounting standards for financial institutions that are more in line with international norms; and the extension to all non-financial enterprises of the modernised accounting standards that have been required of listed SOEs. Transparency needs to be accompanied by improved disclosure and measures to ensure the accuracy of the information reported. To this end, enterprises need to be further encouraged to bring in independent outside auditors to assist in preparing their annual reports. This should be facilitated by the increased scope foreign auditing firms are scheduled to receive with trade and investment liberalisation. Supervisory authorities, together with the relevant professional associations, need to make further efforts to increase the independence of auditing firms and their compliance with regulatory standards.

Improving the enforcement capacity of the judicial system

Weak enforcement of improved legal and regulatory frameworks has been a recurrent theme of China's economic reforms, ranging from enforcement of contracts, commercial codes, competition law, and environmental codes. The Chinese authorities are committed under their WTO agreements to

---

Box 3. **Key priorities for improving frameworks for effective market functioning**

Problem	Priority objectives	Some suggested steps
Corporate governance reforms have had limited success	Address remaining weaknesses in governance structures while clarifying property rights and strengthening market incentives	a) In the near-term, improve independence and accountability of managers and boards of directors a) Remove restrictions on trading of SOE shares as soon as possible and take other steps over the longer-term to improve financial market discipline
Ambiguous property rights hamper corporate governance and mechanisms for business sector restructuring	Develop a coherent framework and supporting laws ensuring that property rights are well defined and apply equally to all economic segments	In the near term, clarify and strengthen SOE rights to property and other assets; clarify rules governing use of and acquisition of state assets by non-state entities
Bankruptcy and other insolvency mechanisms are too weak to allow resources to be re-deployed from firms that are not competitively viable	Establish a more uniform framework for insolvency and strengthen the autonomy and enforcement powers of bankruptcy courts	In the near term, enact a comprehensive bankruptcy law with uniform rules and clear rights of debtors, creditors, and shareholders; clarify responsibility for debt of failing enterprises to banks and social benefit funds so that they do not block exit
Competition is uneven across sectors; anti-competitive practices and in some cases legal/regulatory frameworks impede entry or limit competition among incumbents	Develop a comprehensive framework for fostering competition nationwide with clear definition of the responsibilities of government agencies	a) In the near term, enact a comprehensive competition law; and establish a clear code of conduct sanctioning anti-competitive practices by government entities b) Except for natural monopolies, open sectors now reserved for SOEs to other enterprises
Weak financial discipline encourages misallocation of resources, weakens incentives of enterprises to operate efficiently, and poses risks to financial stability	Strengthen the independence and capabilities of financial regulators/supervisors; improve the ability and incentives of financial institutions and markets to provide discipline	a) In the near term, restore solvency to financial institutions while continuing to improve their accountability for maintaining sound prudential standards b) Move rapidly to strengthen enforcement powers of financial supervisors c) Improve transparency and remove restrictions on financial markets that inhibit discipline
Laws and regulations are poorly and unevenly enforced	Strengthen the independence of the judiciary and clarify its jurisdiction	a) In the near term, reduce the judiciary's financial dependence on government and political authorities and strengthen the jurisdiction of courts over government agencies

---

improve judicial enforcement of contracts and other business codes, including those governing intellectual property and counterfeiting.

However, there has been little fundamental change in the judicial mechanisms for enforcement. Neither the independence of the courts nor their jurisdiction is adequately established. Although the Chinese constitution states that judicial proceedings are to be free of interference from other government and political entities, judges, courts, and other judicial organs remain under their supervision and dependent on them for funding. The legal obligations of other government entities to enforce or obey court decisions are not adequately established, and court decisions are often ignored as a result. The relations among courts are also unclear, which makes it difficult to reconcile conflicting rulings in different jurisdictions or to build a body of case law. Enforcement is further hampered by the limited experience of China's courts (which traditionally have been devoted to criminal matters) with civil law proceedings, and the limited training of judges and other judicial personnel.

To improve enforcement the key objective is *to strengthen the independence and clarify the jurisdiction of courts, particularly with respect to government bodies*. The Supreme People's Court has developed a plan for independent funding of the judiciary to curtail its dependence on local governments. For this to be effective, however, the process of appointing judges will need to be made more professional and less subject to political influence.

Improving the government's capabilities to support economic development

The need to periodically redirect the role played by government as the economy develops is not unique to China. OECD countries have gone through a comparable process during the post-war period, in building, restoring, and maintaining sound public finances, in seeking to develop tax structures that impose as little distortion as possible on the real economy and in undertaking regulatory reforms to improve market functioning. As discussed further below and summarised in Box 4., improvement in the ability of China's government to foster a successful adjustment to trade and investment liberalisation and to promote its longer-term development rests on the achievement of three key goals. The most immediate is to bolster public finances to establish a sustainable fiscal position in which adequate revenues are raised to meet the development needs of the economy. Reform of central-local government fiscal relations is an important element of this effort. The second goal is to strengthen and increase the flexibility of the policy instruments needed to maintain macroeconomic stability in the face of the diverse shocks the economy is likely to experience in coming years. And the third goal is to establish a comprehensive framework for regulatory policy to promote effective market functioning.

Bolstering public finances[41]

The strains on China's public finances are manifest in the under-funding of research and development, education, and other areas important to the economy's development, the difficulty of finding adequate government revenues to facilitate restructuring of SOEs and to expand social benefits, as well as the proliferation of *ad hoc* fees and charges imposed by local governments. As noted earlier, demands on public finances will grow substantially even in the medium term. The scale of these demands has led at least one prominent scholar to warn that China's fiscal position may be heading for a crisis.[42] However a crisis should be avoidable provided that three conditions are met.

The first is an *increase in tax revenues in relation to GDP to levels needed to accommodate increases in spending for development needs*. Tax revenues have been rising relative to GDP in recent years (Table 7) and there is significant scope within the current tax structure for them to increase further. The potential yield from improved collection of the value-added tax (VAT),[43] which accounts for more than one-third of total tax revenue, is especially great. Taxes on services and personal income are likely to increase relative to GDP as services and urban household incomes continue to grow rapidly, and could be increased further if collection were improved. There is also scope for enterprise income taxes to rise relative to GDP provided that restructuring succeeds in raising their profitability. Rough calculations suggest that these

Table 7. **Annual growth in tax revenue, 1994-99**

	Growth (%)	Share of total 1999
Total	15.8	100
Value-added taxes	11.0	36.3
Business taxes	20.0	15.6
Consumption taxes	11.0	7.7
Tariff revenue	15.5	5.3
Corporate profits taxes- total	6.3	9.6
SOE	0.9	6.0
Collective enterprises	11.7	1.6
Foreign-funded enterprises	35.3	2.0
Personal income taxes	41.5	3.9

Note: Value-added taxes are levied primarily on industry while business taxes are levied on revenue of service and some other tertiary activities.
Source: *China Statistical Yearbook*, 2000.

factors, together with changes in tax provisions that authorities are now contemplating, could raise tax revenues by a further several percentage points of GDP over the next five to ten years.[44]

Improvements in the tax structure and administration and better mechanisms for budget planning, formulation, and monitoring would also help to increase tax revenues and to maximise their benefits. The potential gains from better collection and compliance underscore the pay off from devoting resources to improvement of the efficiency of the tax administration. Central government authorities are consolidating numerous extra-budget fees imposed by local governments into a more coherent and efficient system of taxes that are more even across jurisdictions. Authorities are also considering other changes in the tax system, including a phased convergence of the tax treatment of foreign and domestic enterprises, that have the potential to raise substantial revenues and which are ultimately needed to establish a more level playing field among enterprises.

Effective mechanisms for planning, formulating, and monitoring the government's budget are also essential to ensure that revenues are efficiently used. The budget is typically the single most important overall government-planning tool in OECD countries but is much less important in China. Government authorities endorse the need for budget reform and are planning to establish a Treasury Single Account to monitor outlays and resources of government organs. This will provide essential institutions for more advanced reforms. However, capabilities to formulate comprehensive budgets that, 1) include all government revenues and expenditures, 2) are based on realistic forecasts of revenues and expenditures, and 3) are embedded in a multi-year planning context, are still some way off.

The second key objective is to *establish a sustainable system of pension and other social benefits*. Even with no change in the present limited coverage, benefits will rise more rapidly than GDP as a result of population ageing. Extension of social benefits to the nearly 80 per cent of workers that are not now covered will not be feasible at current pension benefit rates, which are quite generous by international standards (Table 8). However, in contrast to the situation that has faced some OECD countries, the authorities are not yet locked into untenably high benefit rates.

Significant progress has been made in providing the institutional basis for sharing the financing of social benefits. A three-tier pension system has been established along lines recommended by the OECD and the World Bank. The government is directly responsible for the first tier, which is a defined benefit plan financed by a payroll tax and intended to cover one-third of targeted pension benefits.[45] The remaining two-thirds will be supplied by second and third (voluntary) tier defined contribution plans. The financing of health care benefits has been established on a similar basis.

Recent reforms have gone part of the way toward reducing future pension benefits and the new pension system provides the basis for further reductions over time to levels that are sustainable.[46] The challenge in the medium term is to manage the transition between the presently high benefits

Table 8. **China's pension system compared with selected regions in the world**
(China in 1999 compared with regional averages in the mid-1990s)

Region	Participation as share of labour force (%)	Contributions as ratio to wages (%)		Average income replacement ratio (%)	Average pension as per cent of GDP per capita	Pension spending as per cent of GDP
		Pensions	All social insurance			
China (1999)	18[1]	25[2]	30[3]	77[2]	99[2]	3
OECD	90	19	34	38	54	10
Range	79-98	6-35	14-57	25-49	23-98	5-15
Asia and the Pacific	26	14	17	na	na	1
Range	3-73	3-40	4-46	*na*	*na*	0-3
Central and Eastern Europe[4]	66	22	31	44	39	7
Range	32-97	20-45	24-61	24-69	13-92	2-14
North Africa and Middle East	41	13	23	55	71	3
Range	30-82	3-27	13-48	36-78	22-144	0-6
Sub-Saharan Africa	6	10	17	na	135	1
Range	1-18	3-24	6-33	na	40-207	0-3
Latin America and Caribbean	33	12	21	39	50	3
Range	11-82	3-29	8-46	13-64	26-64	0-13

1. The regular urban pension system and that for civil servants.
2. The regular urban pension system. N.B. employee contribution rates increased every year 1997-2001.
3. Approximate national average.
4. Including the former Soviet Union.
Source: The Table is adapted from Chapter 16, Table 16.8, which gives further details. Figures are based on calculations using World Bank data.

promised under the first tier to current middle-aged and older workers and the lower benefits that younger workers will receive. Currently, younger workers in the formal sector are effectively taxed to pay for the higher benefits to those nearing retirement, which creates incentives to work in the uncovered informal sector. These disincentives could be reduced by allowing lower contribution rates for younger or lower paid workers, while making up for the loss of payroll contributions out of other revenues. There is also a need to start preparations for organising social insurance for rural workers. This might be done by initially extending coverage with lower benefit and contribution rates to selected agricultural areas bordering the cities, with a view to gradually raising the rates over time.

The third objective is to *contain future non-performing loans and so avoid the need for another financial system cleanup after the one that needs to be undertaken now.* This is absolutely essential: the possibility that new non-performing loans will not be adequately contained is probably the single greatest risk to fiscal sustainability in China. Thus financial reforms to ensure that financial institutions have the incentives and capabilities to maintain rigorous lending standards and manage risk are critical to maintaining sound public finances.

Conditions for fiscal sustainability:

– *Raise tax revenues sufficiently to accommodate increased needs for spending on development.*

– *Establish sustainable benefit levels for social insurance programmes.*

– *Contain future non-performing loans by sustaining sound lending standards*

Reforming central-local government fiscal relations[47]

China's fiscal system is relatively decentralised, with local governments accounting for 71 per cent of government expenditure. Since the major reform of central-government fiscal relations in 1994, the VAT, business, personal and other on-budget taxes have been subject to explicit revenue-sharing formulae. Expenditure responsibilities are also explicitly divided, with the central government responsible for national defence while local governments have the main responsibility for education, agriculture, and most social welfare payments. Transfers between the central and local government are also relatively large, accounting for nearly 42 per cent of central government revenues and nearly 5 per cent of GDP.

Despite this decentralisation, many local governments are starved for revenues to meet local needs. While due partly to the low level of tax revenues for government as a whole, the scarcity at the local level is aggravated by the current fiscal federalism system. The system has also resulted in large disparities among richer and poorer regions. *Per-capita* government expenditure in Shanghai is six to eight times greater than in most central and western provinces; budget revenues relative to local GDP are two to three times higher on the coast than in most western provinces. The fiscal system therefore accentuates the imbalances and lack of integration among regions.

One of the underlying causes of these problems is the fact that expenditures are more decentralised than tax revenues. Sub-national governments – provincial governments and the local levels subject to their jurisdiction, receive about 55 per cent of total tax revenues, but these account for less than half of their spending, with the remainder coming from extra-budget funds and from transfers from the central government. The expenditures assigned to sub-national government are among the most rapidly growing components of overall government spending. They are also the areas where the need for further increases is greatest. Sub-national governments are mainly responsible for supporting SOE workers displaced by labour shedding and for making up shortfalls in contributions to pay for social welfare benefits. Sub-national governments have little (sanctioned) flexibility in setting the criteria for spending or in determining the rates even on those taxes assigned entirely to them. Indeed, under-funded mandates from the central government have added to the pressures on local finances in recent years. Local governments' flexibility, even to smooth out fluctuations in their revenue, is limited by the requirement that their budget be balanced each fiscal year. The squeeze on sub-national revenues is further heightened by inefficiencies in spending, such as the maintenance of an excessive number of government staff.

A second problem lies with the central-local government transfer mechanism. This mechanism is based in part on the earlier system in which transfers to a province were related to its success in raising revenues above a targeted base amount. Partly as a result, the transfer system does not appreciably offset discrepancies between the tax bases of rich and poor provinces. A third problem lies with the inefficient distribution of revenues between provincial governments and their local governments. This is attributable in part to the influence of political and other non-commercial considerations, and in part to the lack of formal national criteria governing the allocation.

Establishment of a better balance between local government resources and their spending is a key objective of broader fiscal reforms. Reform of central-local government fiscal relations is important to reduce the incentives for regional protectionism and other distorting resource extraction by local governments, and to improve regional integration. OECD experiences suggest that the appropriate division of responsibilities among various levels of governments to meet these objectives depends heavily on country circumstances, in particular the capabilities and incentives of the various levels of government, and may have to change over time.[48] However the overall objectives of the reforms should be, first, to bring tax revenues of sub-national governments in to line with their expenditure needs. This is likely to require both review of the current assignment of tax revenues and expenditure responsibilities and reform of the transfer mechanism. The second objective is to improve revenue and expenditure within provinces by setting clearer standards at the national level and by giving provinces more flexibility in administering their finances, including some ability to set rates on local taxes and to borrow to meet short-term liquidity needs.

Improving the flexibility of macroeconomic policy instruments[49]

The diverse forces that will impact China's economy from trade and investment liberalisation and the restructuring of the domestic real economy will place heavy demands on China's macroeconomic policy instruments. As the earlier discussion suggests, macroeconomic policy will need to be able to support higher real GDP growth in order to reduce the current slack in labour markets – once structural problems have been alleviated enough to allow higher growth without igniting inflation. The exchange rate necessary to maintain China's external balance may also change, but the amount and direction cannot be predicted in advance. The study points to three priority objectives for improving the effectiveness and flexibility of China's macroeconomic policy instruments to deal with these prospective changes.

The first is to *improve the effectiveness of monetary policy in managing aggregate demand* so that the burden does not fall disproportionately on fiscal policy, as is now the case. Important steps have been taken in recent years toward developing instruments for "indirect" monetary policy management of domestic credit. At least for the medium term, the next challenge is largely one of strengthening monetary policy transmission mechanisms. One important source of the weakness in the transmission mechanisms – the poor financial conditions of enterprises and of banks that together are responsible for the present credit crunch – is likely to take some time to fully remedy.

However, much progress could be made in the near term on two other important steps. The first is to deregulate interest rates on bank loans and on large deposits. Interest rates in the inter-bank market have already been freed and authorities have announced plans to liberalise bank loan (and some deposit) rates within three years.[50] Acceleration in this schedule would be desirable. The current restriction on bank loan rates limits the ability of central bank operating instruments to control the effective cost of credit to final borrowers. The second step is to improve the flexibility of the money markets. While development of the money markets is also a longer process, broadening access to the market and liberalising the positions permitted to participants would help to distribute the effects of monetary policy changes more broadly and evenly.

A second objective is to *accelerate the development of the government bond market* in order to accommodate the large increase in government debt that is likely to be needed over the next several years. The current government bond markets are limited by their segmentation into two tiers, the stock market and inter-bank market, low liquidity in both the primary and secondary markets, and by disincentives to active trading. Banks are the largest holders of government bonds but are only able to trade in the interbank market (since they have been banned from the stock exchanges), and tend to follow a buy and hold strategy encouraged by the positive gap between bond interest rates and bank loan rates. Integration of the two tiers would probably be the most effective step in the near-term to improve the liquidity and breadth of the market. As the stock of debt grows, it will be increasingly important to broaden access by domestic institutional investors, and, at a suitable point, to allow foreigners to purchase government bonds. Development of the money market and liberalisation of bank loan rates is also important to bond market development, for example to help securities dealers to fund inventories of government bonds.[51]

The third objective, and the most difficult challenge, is *to progressively increase the flexibility of the exchange rate and capital control regimes*. The Chinese authorities have been considering technical means in the near-term to make exchange rate management more flexible, notably by widening the band within which the rate is allowed to vary. However, greater flexibility is likely to be needed beyond the near term to allow the nominal exchange rate to vary in line with the requirements of external balance while avoiding the speculative disruptions that have often accompanied adjustable parity regimes in the past. Ultimately, a floating exchange rate regime may well be most suitable to China's conditions, in part because of the ability it will allow for more independent monetary policy once the capital account is liberalised. Capital account liberalisation, however, is essential to ensure that the foreign exchange market is sufficiently broad and efficient to determine a price for the domestic currency that is in line with its underlying competitiveness. Progressive liberalisation of the capital account will also be needed to allow domestic businesses sufficient access to international financial markets as trade and investment liberalisation progresses, and to help spur the development of domestic financial markets.

Identifying the concrete steps needed to balance these considerations is very difficult. Recent international experience has graphically illustrated the risk to macroeconomic stability posed by capital account liberalisation when domestic financial markets are insufficiently developed or subject to distortiums. The risks of premature liberalisation are now especially great in China because of the poor financial conditions of enterprises and financial institutions, weak corporate governance, and the incomplete development of the financial supervisory and regulatory system. However, delay in liberalising the capital account also involves a cost, since it limits the degree to which the exchange rate regime can be made more flexible as well as the potential benefits of liberalised capital flows to the domestic economy.

In the near term, the stability afforded by the present exchange rate regime is probably beneficial to China's economy but there is also a need to establish a foundation for greater flexibility in the future. To this end, it would be useful to partially relax existing capital controls over the next several years to give enterprises more flexible access to foreign exchange and to create a broader and more efficient foreign exchange market. Once supervisory mechanisms have been adequately strengthened, further relaxation of controls on portfolio capital flows, starting with equity and government bond markets, would be useful.

Creating the framework for a market-based regulatory system[52]

Regulatory reform is a major part of the policy effort to realise the full benefits of trade and investment liberalisation. Establishment of the conditions needed to integrate the internal economy and the frameworks for market functioning is a process involving new regulation in some areas, deregulation in many others, and revised regulation nearly everywhere. The overall objective is to focus regulation on establishing and enforcing the rules and processes for effective market functioning, rather than on resource extraction or government-directed resource allocation.

One of the most basic lessons OECD countries have learned from their experiences over the past fifty years is that regulation is not simply a collection of laws and regulations in individual areas but a process in its own right. To be fully effective, the regulatory process, and not simply its individual components, needs to be based on a comprehensive and coherent long-term framework with clearly defined priorities and strategies. There is a growing body of evidence that a coherent regulatory process can yield significant economic benefits in terms of lower costs to business, greater choices for consumers, improved innovative capacity, and other gains.

The potential benefits of a comprehensive regulatory framework are especially great for China for at least three reasons:

- First, it would help to level the playing field for domestic firms in competing with foreign enterprises that benefit from a coherent regulatory framework in their own countries.

- Second, a comprehensive framework is needed to harmonise regulatory policies that up to now have largely been developed sector by sector, or driven by outside commitments such as those under WTO. It would also help to improve co-ordination, consistency, and accountability in the regulatory efforts of the myriad government agencies and levels that too often operate in isolation, and sometimes at cross-purposes, in China.

- Third, an overall regulatory framework can contribute to China's effort to establish a market economy by providing a more rigorous basis for balancing purely economic objectives with other social values, such as equity and the need to provide support to those displaced by economic transformation.

OECD experience, and the work of OECD experts with non-member countries, underscore that there is no single blueprint for an effective regulatory framework that is applicable to all. The appropriate institutions and strategies depend heavily on the traditions and circumstances of each individual economy. However, OECD experiences suggest several guiding principles. The first is the need to develop the institutional structures within government for regulatory planning, co-ordination, and accountability across all its components and levels. Most OECD governments now have central regulatory co-ordination agencies with government-wide scope. In the United States, for example, the Office of Management and Budget provides this co-ordinating role. China presently does not have such a function, but several current organs reporting directly to the State Council have more limited co-ordination roles that could serve as the basis for development of a broader regulatory co-ordinating body. Development of such a capability could help greatly to overcome administrative blockages and delays in mandated reforms and to achieve a clearer definition of responsibilities for particular regulatory areas across government agencies. Over a longer period, a regulatory co-ordinating body could serve as a catalyst for more fundamental rationalisation of regulatory policies that are now carried out by numerous bodies.

A second principle is that regulatory authorities need to have tools to objectively evaluate the impact of proposed policies and the trade-offs they involve. Such tools are particularly important when, as in China, developing markets and institutions are subject to distortions that increase the risk that poorly designed regulations will have perverse effects. In China, policy evaluation is most often carried out through consultations with local government officials, the testing of certain policies at selected local

---

Box 4. **Priorities for strengthening the government's capabilities to foster economic development**

Problem	Priority objectives	Some suggested steps
Public finances are insufficient to adequately meet development needs while maintaining fiscal sustainability	Bolster the capacity of the fiscal system by raising revenues relative to GDP, completing the establishment of a financially viable system of social benefits, and contain further non-performing loans	*a*) In the medium term, continue to improve tax collection and compliance; reform tax provisions to reduce distortions; and strengthen public management of the budget *b*) Over a longer period, reduce pension benefit rates to viable levels as coverage is extended
Local government fiscal resources are insufficient to meet their responsibilities and very unevenly distributed	Establish a better balance between local government resources and expenditure responsibilities	*a*) In the near term, review current assignment of revenue and expenditure responsibilities *b*) Over a longer period, reform the transfer mechanism to better direct funds on the basis of need; and establish criteria for a more efficient allocation of fiscal resources within provinces
Macroeconomic policy instruments are insufficiently flexible	Bolster the effectiveness of monetary policy instruments; accelerate the development of the government bond market, and move toward greater flexibility in the exchange rate and capital control regimes over time	*a*) Liberalise bank loan rates in the near term and remove restrictions that inhibit the money and government bond markets *b*) Over the longer term, liberalise the capital account and exchange rate regimes in line with development of domestic financial markets and improvements in financial discipline and supervision
The regulatory framework needs to be better aligned with the needs of an integrated market economy	Develop a comprehensive government-wide regulatory framework in which the government is an arms-length formulator and arbiter of rules for the market	*a*) In the near term, develop bodies to co-ordinate regulatory policy for the government as a whole *b*) Continue efforts to improve transparency and develop explicit tools to evaluate regulatory impacts

levels before nationwide implementation,[53] and by commissioning government and academic think tanks to develop policy options and assessments of the impact of proposed actions. However, more formal tools that could be applied directly by government agencies are likely to be needed as regulatory policy develops. In OECD countries, competition policy is often used to evaluate not only the impact of particular regulations on competition but also their trade-offs in terms of efficiency, environmental standards, and other broader goals. The regulatory framework needs to explicitly require the use of such tools by regulatory agencies and to specify their applicability and priority in particular areas.

Transparency is the third requirement of an effective regulatory framework and is the area where China's regulatory system most lags behind that of OECD countries. Transparency is essential to all phases of the regulatory process, from formulation, to implementation, and to ongoing administration. Transparency rests first on the principle that those regulated, as well as the general public, need to be accurately and thoroughly informed about regulatory rules and their changes. Public knowledge of the rules is necessary not only for those regulated, but also to ensure that government agencies at all levels are fully aware of their obligations, to ensure accountability, and to prevent capture of regulatory organs by special interests. Disclosure of regulations also serves as a commitment by regulatory authorities to the public that can help to buttress their credibility. Efforts to inform the public need to go beyond purely formal but *ad hoc* means (such as announcement in the speech of a senior official) to include a pro-active effort to inform the public through channels that can be easily accessed.

Finally, an effective regulatory system requires strong enforcement mechanisms that are consistent with the rule of law. Regulatory enforcement in China is decentralised to lower government levels to a greater extent than in most OECD countries. Regulatory authorities at these levels are hampered by interference from local governments are prone to capture by special interests, and often lack effective sanctions for violators. Operating without clear mandates or guidelines from the central government, local regulation is often excessive and intrusive. OECD countries typically have enacted explicit laws to clarify the scope of regulators and sanction abuses. The study suggests that China could build on several existing administrative laws to develop a more effective legal framework to achieve the same goals.

Conclusions

Collectively, the chapters of this study highlight the impressive progress China has made in recent years to prepare for further integration into the world economy. In nearly all the areas examined, the authorities have been moving in the direction needed to deal with inherited problems and to foster conditions to allow the benefits of trade and investment liberalisation to be realised. The chapters highlight areas where, based on OECD experiences and perspectives, further changes are likely to be needed to reinforce policies now underway or planned, and to improve prospects for achieving China's economic development objectives.

Although China has already opened considerably to international markets, the potential gains from further trade and investment liberalisation are very great. However, as the individual chapters illustrate, realisation of these gains is neither inevitable nor automatic, and depends crucially on progress on domestic economic reforms. Trade and investment liberalisation does not radically alter the priorities for domestic economic reforms, but it does make some steps all the more urgent.

The overall conclusion that emerges from the study is that China's development has now reached a stage that calls for a somewhat different emphasis in reforms from that prevailing earlier. Past policies to develop individual segments of the economy were based in part on the limited development of markets and their supporting mechanisms in the early stages of the reform era. As the scope for market forces has progressively increased and development has advanced, the administrative distinctions among these segments have come to have less and less economic meaning. Thus the problems and challenges of SOE and non-state enterprises are becoming more and more similar; conditions in the rural economy now depend more on national economic developments than on developments specific to the agriculture sector or rural industries themselves. Problems in individual areas and the policies needed to deal with them have become increasingly interdependent. As a result, the benefits to separate development of preferred sectors have reached sharply diminishing returns, and the risk that they will impose distortions that will be counter-productive for the overall economy has increased. Rather than seeking to replicate past policies, future policies need to be based on their underlying lessons, the most important of which is that allowing greater scope for market forces is the key to successful development.

Future economic reforms need to continue and broaden the trend in recent years toward measures with economy wide scope, focused on two essential objectives. The first is to foster the integration of the domestic economy in order to realise the benefits of trade and investment liberalisation and to sustain China's development over the longer term. As underscored by the high degree of internal integration of the United States economy, and the strenuous efforts the European Community has been making to achieve it to a comparable degree, internal integration is essential to the development of an advanced continental economy. Domestic integration in China is essential to achieving better utilisation of labour and other resources as well as to ensure that resources are efficiently employed in the future. Integration of the domestic economy involves the elimination of internal barriers to mobility in factor and product markets, creation of a more level playing field among enterprises and other economic segments, and greater scope for market forces in certain areas. Integration among China's regions, and between rural and urban areas, needs to become a major priority, not simply to improve equity, but to sustain the development of the economy as a whole. Development of interior provinces is likely to have to depart somewhat from the model suggested by China's coastal development, with the emphasis on integration with the rest of the country and improvement in the local business environment, rather than on special zones or other government preferences, as the keys to success.

Success in integrating the domestic economy also depends on achievement of a second key objective, which is to strengthen the framework conditions necessary for efficient market functioning. This is an ongoing process that continues even in the most advanced economies. However, in developing countries such as China, limited institutional development and the distortions left by central planning make framework reforms a critical priority. The study has identified five priorities for these reforms. These are to clarify property rights and strengthen exit mechanisms so that state-owned as well as other assets can be allocated to their most efficient uses; to improve competition and, in the process, break down regional and other protectionist barriers; to bolster enterprise governance by making managers and their boards more independent and accountable while strengthening external discipline; to buttress the powers and capabilities of financial supervisory authorities; and to underpin reforms generally by improving the independence and enforcement capabilities of the judiciary. While likely to take some time to complete improvement in framework conditions needs to be given high priority in the near and medium term since the adjustments entailed by trade and investment liberalisation are likely to create incentives to interfere with competition and impose other distortions to market functioning in order to protect incumbent interests.

More than in the past, success in achieving these objectives will require co-ordinated policies on a broad range of fronts that takes account of the increasing interdependence among current problems. At the same time, policies need to be carefully sequenced in order to establish the pre-conditions for subsequent reforms. In this regard, measures to break through the vicious circles that are blocking progress on broader reforms take on a particularly high near-term priority. Timely restoration of financial system solvency is important *not* because it will be sufficient by itself but because international experience suggests it is necessary to allow broader financial and real sector reforms to proceed. Government imposed and other obstacles to enterprise restructuring need to be removed as soon as possible if the business sector is to keep up with the imperatives that will come with trade and investment liberalisation. And government financial resources need to be bolstered in order to provide the support needed to facilitate these and other reforms that will need to be undertaken in the medium term.

Finally, China's government will need to continue to play a key role in the economic reform process. The chapters identify measures to bolster public finances, reform central-local government finances, improve the effectiveness of macroeconomic policy instruments, and develop a more comprehensive regulatory policy framework in order to improve the capabilities of the government to support reforms. These changes point to a broader need to re-orient the role of the government in the economy that is not unique to China. Public ownership of enterprises, the use of tax, regulatory, and other policies to influence resource allocation, and reliance on credit rationing and other direct interventions in macroeconomic policy were much more common in OECD countries during the 1950s and 1960s than they are now. Public governance in OECD countries has since evolved toward a more effective framework based on the following principles. The task of public finances is to extract sufficient resources to achieve the government's objectives through means that minimise distortions to market forces. The task of macroeconomic policy is to sustain internal and external balance in the economy through market-based policy instruments. And the task of government regulation, including regulatory reform, is to formulate, enact, and enforce rules to sustain competition and other framework conditions needed for market functioning. With this evolution, has come a need to rationalise government structures and capabilities in order to ensure that policies are adequately co-ordinated, understood by those they affect, and are carried out in a mutually reinforcing and consistent manner over time. Public governance in China is already moving in this direction and will need to continue to do so as the domestic economy develops and integration with the outside world proceeds.

NOTES

1. Barry Naughton (1995), *Growing out of the plan: Chinese economic reform*, 1978-93, Cambridge University Press.

2. This section is based mainly on Chapters 1-3 on agriculture and the rural sector.

3. Grains account for nearly two-thirds of total cultivated land. As throughout the reform period, the government establishes procurement prices and delivery quotas for major grains, including wheat, corn, and rice, and controls grain marketing, while allowing farmers to sell their surplus above the quota in the open market. The Governors' Grain Bag Responsibility System (GGBRS) introduced in 1995 sought to increase production by raising prices to farmers. The result has been led to rising surpluses. Despite progressive reduction in support prices in recent years, the gap between procurement and market prices has continued to widen. The grain procurement system is not covered by China's WTO agreement but is likely to become increasingly expensive to maintain once the domestic market is opened to lower cost imports from abroad.

4. REs, as the term is used in this synthesis, include all rural non-agricultural enterprises, including single owner and other private firms. This term is equivalent to TVEs as they are defined in Chapters 1-3. TVEs are sometimes defined more narrowly as rural collective enterprises; these account for most rural industrial output.

5. See the simulations discussed in Chapter 4 on industry implications and in Annex 2.

6. This sub-section is based on Chapters 4-6 on industry issues and Chapter 10 on foreign direct investment.

7. China ranked only eighth among developing country recipients of foreign direct investment in 1999. Studies cited in Chapter 10 on foreign direct investment suggest that China does not outperform other developing countries on average once its size and other characteristics are taken into account.

8. Empirical evidence on the impact of trade and investment liberalisation on China's industries is reviewed in Annex 2.

9. This section is based on Chapter 7 on banking, Chapter 8 on insurance, Chapter 14 on priorities for the financial system and financial regulatory policy, and Chapter 15 on capital market development.

10. China's financial system is relatively large, as measured by the ratio of domestic credit to GDP, compared to countries of comparable development. (See Chapter 14 on financial system priorities, Figure 4).

11. As mentioned in Chapter 7 on the banking sector, a recent People's Bank of China survey indicates that a significantly higher portion of bank lending goes indirectly to non-state entities than is apparent from official figures on their direct lending. This pattern is indicative of the importance of informal credit channels in China. However the degree to which non-state non-financial businesses are recipients of these indirect funds is unclear. Much of the indirect financing probably goes through informal financial channels into the stock market or other investments that banks are not allowed to engage in directly.

12. Foreign banks' ability to lend foreign currency will be constrained by the underdeveloped domestic interbank market and foreign exchange and other regulatory constraints not covered by WTO accession. See Chapter 7.

13. See Chapter 22 on macroeconomic issues.

14. China's trade (merchandise exports plus imports) to GDP was 38 per cent of GDP in 1999, compared to 26 per cent for the Euro area, 19 per cent for the United States, and 17 per cent for Japan. China ranks third among the five largest developing countries by this measure, behind Russia and Indonesia but substantially above Brazil and India.

15. China's domestically held public debt is about 22 per cent of GDP.

16. See the estimates discussed in Chapter 14.

17. Studies reviewed in Annex 2 suggest that real GDP growth could be boosted by an amount ranging from virtually negligible to as much as 0.5 per cent annually through 2010. The estimated effects on employment are small.

18. See Chapter 21 on regional issues.

19. See Chapters 2-3 on the rural sector and Chapter 16 on labour market and social policies.

20. See Chapter 16, on labour market and social policies.

21. See Chapter 17 on environmental issues and Chapter 1 on the agricultural sector.

22. See Chapter 1, concluding section.

23. See Chapters 4-6 on industry implications.

24. See Chapters 7 and 8 on the banking and insurance sectors, respectively, Chapter 14 on financial system priorities, and Chapter 15 on capital markets.

25. Partial clean-ups that simply reduce the amount of negative capital tend to have little impact on internal incentives to maintain prudential standards or to monitor loan contracts. See Aghion, Philippe, Olivier Jean Blanchard, and Wendy Carlin (1994), "*The economics of enterprise restructuring in Central and Eastern Europe*", *Centre for Economic Policy Research Discussion Paper* No. 1058.

26. Chapter 14 on priorities for financial system development presents rough illustrative calculations suggesting that the cost to China's government of a thorough clean up in the near-term could range between 30 and 60 per cent of GDP, depending on the true extent of non-performing loans, the recovery rate, and other circumstances. This range is comparable to the costs incurred by other developing countries that have undergone severe banking crises. The cost to China's government could be lower if the clean up were less comprehensive, or authorities were to rely substantially on the banks to "grow out" of their problems, but as argued in the text and in the chapters on the financial system, this is a risky strategy that could easily lead to greater costs in the future.

27. See Chapter 21 on regional economic issues.

28. The issues summarised in this and the following sub-section are discussed in detail in Chapter 13 on enterprise governance issues.

29. A basic step was taken in 1993 with the enactment of the Company Law providing for the establishment of legally autonomous limited liability and joint-stock companies, and specifying the rights of shareholders, and powers of managers and their boards of directors and supervisors. The company law does not cover all types of enterprises. Collective enterprises are subject to an earlier law. Private enterprises were not officially sanctioned until 1998 and are still subject to ambiguities about their legitimate scope.

30. Chinese authorities, including the Chairman of the China Securities Regulatory Commission, have explicitly stated that they regard the OECD Principles on Corporate Governance as the international benchmark in this area.

31. See the *Economist* article cited in Chapter 13 on enterprise governance.

32. Discipline is further constrained by the limited rights of minority shareholders.

33. As noted in Chapter 4, enterprise governance has improved most in sectors that are competitive.

34. Cyril Lin, *Corporate governance in China* (2000).

35. The decentralisation of state administration has effectively increased the number of "owners". Creation of separate asset management companies has not resolved this problem because the companies tend to function very similarly to the line government agencies from which they are typically derived. The separation of SOEs from their controlling line agencies may have had the perverse effect of making it easier for other government entities to interfere in their operations.

36. This section is based on Chapter 12 on competition law and policy but also draws on Chapter 11, on regulatory reform.

37. Overt barriers to product market competition are focused on a few products, such as automobiles and beer, and have been declining as a result of central government crackdowns.

38. These amount to RMB 300 000, or US$36 000, in retail trade and RMB 500 000 (US$60 000) in wholesale trade and manufacturing. See Chapter 13 on corporate governance.

39. See Chapter 14, the section on regulatory/supervisory policies, for further discussion of these issues.

40. This power now lies with the Ministry of Finance.

41. The issues for this sub-section are discussed in detail in Chapters 16 (section on pensions), 17 (public budget management) and 18 (tax policies), as well as Chapter 22 on macroeconomic implications.

42. See Nicolas Lardy (2000), "Fiscal sustainability: between a rock and hard place", *China Economic Quarterly*.

43. A 1997 study by the World Bank estimated that only 70 per cent of the VAT due to authorities was actually collected and there seems to have been only limited improvement since that date. See, World Bank, *China 2020* (1997).

44. See Chapter 22 on macroeconomic policy issues and Chapter 18 on tax policies.

45. Under current policy the first tier benefit replaces 20 per cent of a worker's average wage, although changes now being considered could raise this to 30 per cent.

46. Calculations developed in Chapter 16 suggest that a 20 per cent replacement rate in the first tier could be financed by a payroll tax of 10 per cent, even with the expected rise in the dependency ratio.

47. Further discussion of these issues can be found in Chapter 20 on central-local government fiscal relations.

48. This conclusion is further supported by recent Secretariat economic surveys of Russia and Brazil. See the chapters on central-local government relations in the OECD *Economic Surveys* for Russia (2001) and Brazil (2001).

49. These issues are discussed in detail in Chapter 22.

50. As with other policies, the exact timetable implicit in official announcements is not entirely clear, but three years from the time this plan was first stated would be in 2003.

51. As discussed in Chapter 15 on capital markets, China could improve the liquidity and depth of the government bond market by adopting techniques already used in major markets, such as standardising terms on bond issues, consolidating issues into a limited number of categories, and establishing a pre-announced schedule of regular issues.

52. These issues are discussed in Chapter 11 on regulatory policy; see also the portion of Chapter 12 on competition policy.

53. An example is the housing reform now applying nation-wide but which was first tested for several years in Shanghai.

Part I
SECTOR STUDIES

Chapter 1

AGRICULTURAL PROSPECTS AND POLICIES

TABLE OF CONTENTS

AGRICULTURAL PROSPECTS AND POLICIES[*]

Introduction

Although the role of agriculture in the Chinese economy has declined, it continues to contribute 16 per cent of GDP and provides about 50 per cent of employment. Over the last 20 years, Chinese agriculture has been transformed from a tightly controlled, centralised system of commune-based farming into a household-based system increasingly driven by markets rather than government targets and plans. In response to this change, agricultural output has surged, rural incomes have increased, and market integration has considerably improved. Today, with the exception of grains, the production, distribution and marketing of crops and livestock products are free from significant government intervention. Grain production, pricing, marketing, and distribution, however, continue to be subject to a relatively large amount of government control through monopoly purchasing, minimum purchase pricing, and state trading.

China's accession to the WTO and the accompanying liberalisation of China's trade system will see China reduce many of its agricultural tariffs and implement a tariff-rate quota (TRQ) system for the key commodities of wheat, rice, corn, cotton, vegetable oil and wool. However, the impact of trade liberalisation alone on China's agricultural trade, domestic production levels and patterns is likely to be minimal. This impact is expected to be significantly stronger if trade liberalisation is combined with domestic agricultural policy reform.

China's WTO commitments do not explicitly require China to eliminate state trading or many of its distortionary domestic policies. Nonetheless, trade liberalisation, including the requirement of allocating minimum amounts of the import quotas to non-state trading enterprises, will reduce the power of state trading enterprises and stimulate the ongoing process of agricultural policy reform.

The impact of trade liberalisation on agricultural labour reallocation will be of particular importance. China has long maintained a strict policy to prevent labour migration from rural to urban areas through a household registration system. Although many millions of farmers have migrated during the 1990s, the policy has effectively inhibited the flow from rural to urban areas. As agriculture is expected to come under pressure from trade liberalisation, the impact on rural incomes will be closely tied to whether surplus farm labour is able to move to the urban areas where trade liberalisation is likely to increase demand for services and labour-intensive industrial production.

The impact of trade liberalisation will differ markedly between crops and between regions. Adjustment costs for farmers in various regions will themselves differ depending on their agricultural comparative advantage and on government policy. China will likely see increased imports of land-intensive crops such as grains and oilseeds after trade liberalisation. The impact of these imports will be weaker in China's central and western regions not only because of those regions' relative comparative advantage in land-intensive crops, but also because of poor transportation linkages and imperfect market integration across regions. Land intensive grain and oilseed crops in the coastal regions are expected to bear the brunt of adjustment costs as imports increase, though off-farm labour opportunities are also most likely to increase in this region. In addition, producers in the coastal regions will have increased opportunities to shift into labour-intensive crops such as fruits and vegetables. These products are increasingly demanded by wealthier urban consumers and also for export to nearby nations such as Japan.

Trade liberalisation will challenge China's policy-makers to find creative solutions to problems arising from the new trade arrangements. The current system of government intervention in grain pricing, marketing, and distribution, for instance, will be less effective once grain trade is liberalised. Alternative means of supporting grain farmers and meeting the government's goal of ensuring food security will need to be developed. Some relatively straightforward options are to separate commercial and state intervention functions on grain markets, to increase funding for agricultural research and

---

[*] This chapter was prepared by Andrzej Kwiecinski, Principal Analyst, Division for Agricultural Policies in Non-Member Economies, Directorate for Food, Agriculture and Fisheries, OECD, with the help of Xiande Li and Hunter Colby, consultants.

extension, and to develop better agricultural price information systems, product standards, and marketing channels.

While this chapter deals with agriculture and agricultural policy measures, it should be emphasised that adjustment processes in agriculture will depend to a large degree on developments in other sectors of the economy. In particular, an outflow of agricultural surplus labour will depend on non-agricultural job creation linked with the availability and mobility of capital. Moreover, agricultural policy measures alone will not be sufficient to ease adjustment processes in agriculture. The policy agenda has to include labour market reform to soften the labour migration restrictions; education reform to provide the rural population with sufficient skills to compete on labour markets; fiscal policy reform combined with local administration reform to diminish the government-imposed burdens on rural households ("peasant burden"); and social policy reform to diminish the gap in access to social benefits between the rural and urban populations. Various aspects of these reforms are discussed in detail in other chapters of this study.

Current state of the agricultural sector and related policies

The role of agriculture in China's economy

Agriculture has made important, but declining contributions to China's economic development in terms of gross value added, employment, capital accumulation, urban welfare, and foreign exchange earnings. The declining importance of agriculture is historically common to all developing economies. Population growth and limited land resources will further shift China's comparative advantage from land-intensive economic activities like agriculture to labour-intensive manufacturing and industrial activities (Anderson, 1990).

Although the importance of non-agricultural activities has grown rapidly over the last 20 years, agriculture continues to account for 16 per cent of GDP and provides about 50 per cent of employment. China's agriculture supplies food for about 1.3 billion Chinese citizens and contributes to the net exports of agro-food products at about US$4 billion (as of 2000). According to the latest population census 64 per cent of China's population continues to live in rural areas. The declining role of agriculture in China's international trade is particularly striking. The share of primary (mainly agricultural) products in total exports was 50 per cent in 1980, but it fell to just 10 per cent in 2000. Over the same period, the share of food export in total exports fell from 17 per cent to 5 per cent only and the share of food imports in total imports fell from 15 per cent to just 2 per cent (Table 1.1).

Table 1.1.   **Role of agriculture in China's economy, 1980-2000**

	1980	1990	2000
Share in GDP			
Agriculture	30	27	16
Industry	49	42	51
Services	21	31	33
Share in employment			
Agriculture	69	60	50
Industry	18	21	23
Services	13	19	27
Share in export			
Primary products	50	26	10
Foods	17	11	5
Share in import			
Primary products	35	19	21
Foods	15	6	2
Share of rural population in total population	81	72	64

Sources: National Bureau of Statistics of China (NBS), *China Statistical Yearbook*, various issues; *China Rural Statistical Yearbook*, various issues; China Statistical Abstract, 2001.

Table 1.2. **Composition of China's agriculture by sectors (%), 1980-2000**
(Per cent shares of gross value of agricultural output)

	1980	1985	1990	1995	2000
Crops	75.6	69.2	64.7	58.9	55.7
Livestock	18.4	22.1	25.7	29.7	29.7
Forestry	4.2	5.2	4.3	3.5	3.8
Fisheries	1.7	3.5	5.4	8.9	10.9
Total	100.0	100.0	100.0	100.0	100.0

Sources: National Bureau of Statistics, *China Statistical Yearbook,* various issues; China Statistical Abstract, 2001.

Cropping is the dominant sub-sector within agriculture. It contributed 76 per cent of the gross value of agricultural output in 1980, but by 2000 its contribution fell to 56 per cent. The shares of livestock and aquatic output increased particularly rapidly during the same period (Table 1.2).

Agricultural production structures

Agriculture in China is dominated by very small, family-run farming operations. This is partly due to a high population density, but also a direct result of the 1978 reform of the commune system of agriculture and the introduction of the Household Production Responsibility System (HPRS). The HPRS broke up commune production teams and made the farm household the basic unit of production in agriculture. Households lease land from the village collectives (Box 1.1). The HPRS boosted production incentives, encouraged farmers to reduce costs, take risks, and enter new lines of production. As a result, agricultural output rapidly increased during the 1980s (Lin, 1992; Colby *et al.*, 2000).

Currently, China has about 238 million farm households. Based on the new, revised estimate of total cultivated land, each household has an average of only 0.55 hectares of arable land available for farming.[1] On a per capita basis, China's arable land area is much larger than its East Asian neighbours, but compared with a land-rich country such as the United States, China is very land poor (Figure 1.1.). Limited arable land and a large rural labour force mean that China tends to have a comparative

Figure 1.1. **Population density per hectare of arable land, 1998**

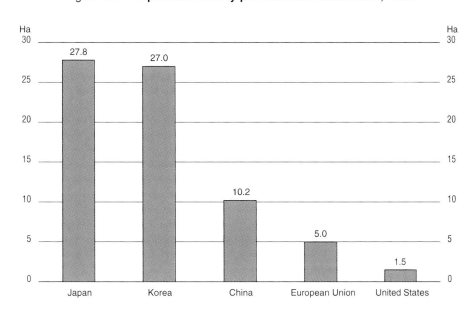

Source: FAO.

Box 1.1.   **Agricultural land tenure system in China**

The land tenure system in China is based on land lease contracts. Farmland is owned by village collectives, which extend land lease contracts to individual farm households. Households have most of the property rights: they can use, sub-lease and transfer land, but they cannot sell the land. The first round of lease contracts was granted in the framework of the household responsibility system in the late 1970s for periods of 20 years. A new round of leases, typically for 30 years, was completed over the last several years. Farmers pay for their leased land with a proportion of their production or with a cash equivalent. However, within this general framework there are many regional differences. In fact, surveys indicate that land-tenure rights differ from village to village, even within one county or township area, and that local government officials have an important influence in determining local land tenure regulations (Krusekopf, 2001).

There are two important aspects of the current land tenure system in China: land is considered a part of the social security system in rural areas and the majority of the rural population is still attached to the collective ownership of land. There is an underlying assumption that every member of the village should have access to a parcel of collectively owned land. Therefore, any change in the demographic situation in a village (birth, death, marriage, in- or out-migration) creates pressures for the administrative reallocation of land. In fact, reallocation of land (partial or involving all households) occurs on average every three to five years, which contrasts with the central government policy to extend the length of lease contracts between villages and households to 30 years. Reallocations are less frequent in more developed villages, less attached to egalitarian rules. Moreover, even if large numbers of rural wage earners no longer rely on land, they keep their use rights to land. This is partly due to regulations which require them to deliver *e.g.* grain quotas, but partly because land is their only subsistence guarantee if they lose their jobs (Vermeer, 2001).

Within this system there is rather limited room for land market transactions. If agricultural households leave their village to take non-farm jobs and allow their land to go fallow, then, depending on the local regulations, they may permanently forfeit their use rights. These problems faced by households wishing to migrate out of agriculture are handled by leaving a family member in the village or by sub-leasing land to another farmer, who takes on the obligation for payment of taxes and fees and grain quota supply to the procurement agency. However, as these payments are high, those who leave are often obliged to cover the costs involved from other income sources. These costs may amount to RMB 100-200 per mu (1/15 ha), meaning between RMB 750-1 500 per average farm per year. This could be an equivalent of 1.5-3 times average monthly wages rural migrants may earn in the cities.

The current system can lead to conflicting situations between village leaders and farmers, both in cases of administrative reallocations of land and when local regulations limit land-transfer rights. There are also cases when local leaders, assuming the role of landowners, decide to lease land to external investors without proper compensation to local farmers losing access to land. Such situations are possible within the current distribution of power at the local level. While the head of village (*cun zhang*) is elected through democratic procedures and at least partly accountable *vis-à-vis* the local population, his position is still much weaker than that of the nominated village Communist Party Secretary (*cun zhi shu*). In 2000, the National People's Congress proposed a new land contract law which is intended to establish a legal framework for various land relationships between farmers and collectives and, thus, to enforce farmers' rights to the land, but sales of land will not be allowed.

advantage in the production of labour-intensive crops such as fruits and vegetables and a disadvantage in the production of land-extensive crops such as grains and oilseeds.

Livestock production in China is highly fragmented. The majority of meat in China is produced by small, part-time "backyard" operations. Full-time household operations, so-called specialised households, and commercial operations have grown rapidly, but still account for less than 20 per cent of pork production (Fang, *et al.*, 2000).

China's crop and livestock production activities are scattered throughout the country, based to a large extent on agronomic conditions. Nevertheless, certain regions in China account for a disproportionate share of the output of many key crop and livestock products, partly due to distorting policies applied in the past.

North China[2] accounts for the largest or second-largest shares of seven out of ten major crops produced in China, including wheat, corn, soybean, peanut, cotton, fruits and vegetables. East and Central China are major producers of rice and rapeseed. In contrast, Southwest China is not a major producer of any crop. The only major crops not produced in North China are rice and sugar crops (sugar cane and sugar beets).

Production of meat products in China is somewhat more spread out than crop production, but North China is also a major producer of seven key livestock products and all four of the key meat products. Northwest China is a major producer of mutton, milk and sheep wool. Southwest China is an important producer of pork, almost half of which is produced in Sichuan province.

Agricultural policy environment

The overall thrust of China's agricultural policy strategy has remained relatively constant for more than 50 years, even during the period of dramatic reform and liberalisation after 1978. In its most basic guise, agriculture's role in national economic strategy is to produce food for the nation and to act as a source of funds to support the development of a modern industrial sector. Up until the end of the 1980s, agriculture was also seen as an important vehicle for earning foreign exchange through exports, though this role has faded as China's industrial exports have supplanted agriculture as the key engine of foreign exchange earnings. And finally, agriculture is the means of keeping China's vast rural population employed. This role has increased in recent years as competitive pressures have reduced the ability of China's state-owned industrial sector to absorb additional labour.

In more specific terms, the main goals of the current policy regime are to stabilise grain output, promote domestic food self-sufficiency, maintain large state grain reserves, boost farm incomes, provide inexpensive food to urban residents, and maintain social and political stability. Within these policy goals, the focus of government policy has changed over the years, giving more importance to raising farm incomes and improving the standard of living of rural residents. Nevertheless, the extraction of resources from agriculture continues. Previously, the central government relied on procuring farm products at below market prices to extract resources from agriculture. To some extent, that flow has reversed in recent years as the government instituted price floors that resulted in above-market prices paid to farmers. And where once the central government was the principal recipient of the flow of resources, local and provincial governments now increasingly rely on direct financial flows from rural residents, in the form of taxes and fees, to support schools, hospitals, and other government expenses (see Chapter 3).

Grain policy

The single most important agricultural policy in China is the "Grain-Bag Policy" or Governors' Grain-Bag Responsibility System (GGBRS). The GGBRS, introduced in 1995, shifted the responsibility for the development of agriculture and food production from the central government to provincial governments (Crook, 1998). The impetus for the new policy came from the four-year stagnation of grain production between 1990 and 1994 (Figure 1.2) and was further stimulated by growing concerns raised by domestic and international analysts that China would have difficulty meeting its future grain requirements. The main thrust of the GGBRS was to make China's provincial leaders responsible for managing grain supply and demand situations within their own provinces. The policy mandated that individual provinces:

- Maintain an overall balance of grain supply and demand within their province.
- Stabilise grain area, production, and stocks.
- Use provincial or local grain reserves to regulate markets and stabilise prices.

In combination with an earlier (in 1994) rise in the procurement price for mandatory grain sales to the government by approximately 40 per cent, these policies were successful in stabilising the grain area and prompting a series of record food grain harvests. This, in turn, allowed China to shift from a

Figure 1.2. **Total grain production, 1979-2000**

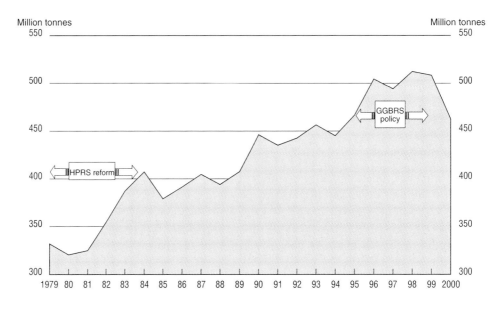

Source: China Statistical Yearbook.

major net importer of grain in the mid-1990s towards a net exporter of grain by the end of the decade. However, the policy focus on grain production and procurement caused a number of problems in China's grain storage and distribution system. Grain stocks kept rising to levels that became burdensome to maintain, while the low quality of grain stocks made it increasingly difficult to bring grain back into the consumption cycle. It also made it necessary to maintain an ever-increasing administrative apparatus, characterised by low efficiency, and alleged fraud and misuse of subsidies. It has also contributed to widespread overuse of selected inputs (Box 1.2), particularly nitrogen fertilisers, and aggravated existing environmental problems.

Although the GGBRS is still in place, the government started to implement new policy measures in 1999/2000 to address negative consequences of this policy package.[3] These new measures included: cutting the amounts of grain procured within the quota system, lowering the quota price and the so-called "protective" price (Box 1.3), introducing more stringent quality requirements for grains purchased within the quota system, and excluding low quality *indica* early rice, wheat and corn in southern China and spring wheat in the north-east regions from the set of products covered by the quota and the protective price system. For the varieties withdrawn, the state allowed certain categories of enterprises (engaged in grain processing; feed mills; animal raising and pharmaceutics production) to be involved in grain purchasing, provided these enterprises have received approvals from the State Administration for Industry and Commerce (SAIC) and from the Grain Administration. The agencies and companies of the former State Grain Reserve Bureau are being transformed into the China Grain Reserve Management Company (CGRM), which has been made responsible for the grain reserve, as well as edible oil.

The combined impact of the government's policy and the serious drought in the North China Plain in 2000 was a fall in grain production by 9 per cent or nearly 46 million tonnes from the previous year. The fall in production, together with subsidised exports of corn,[4] helped to reduce excessive grain stocks and to start the gradual replacement of low quality government stocks with high quality grains. New policies stimulated the reallocation of land from grains to other crops and helped improve the quality of grains produced and procured. For example, the area allocated to low quality early rice decreased while the area devoted to high-quality rice varieties increased substantially.

Box 1.2. **China's agricultural input subsidies**

Over the past 20 years, China's agricultural input policy has changed in parallel with the transformation of China's agricultural system. Prior to 1985, input policy focused on providing an inexpensive supply of fertilisers, agricultural chemicals, and other inputs. In the case of fertilisers, the largest component of input use, the policy directly subsidised production and distribution in order to reduce the prices paid by farmers. The government monopolised fertiliser marketing under the All-China Federation of Supply and Marketing Co-operatives (SMC).

In 1985, policy shifted from strict government control over input production, distribution, and pricing, to a mixed system of government control and private competition. Some degree of competition now exists in the markets for fertilisers, pesticides, insecticides, animal feed, agricultural machinery, and diesel fuel.

Under the post-1985 system, the government, through the State Development and Planning Commission (SDPC), continues to set and allocate import quotas and provide price guidance for imported fertilisers. Low-income farmers are provided with free seeds and other production materials. Central and provincial governments invest in scientific research and large rural infrastructure projects such as irrigation, water control and transportation. The central government exempts enterprises producing agricultural inputs and all imports of fertilisers from value-added taxes (VAT). And finally, the government subsidises water use by agricultural producers relative to other users.

Following the 1985 change in input policy, however, it has become difficult to identify direct or indirect government subsidies that reduce the ex-factory or purchase prices of fertilisers. In part this is due to the current two-tier price system for fertiliser producers where small enterprises sell all of their output at market prices but large and medium-size enterprises only sell a certain percentage of their output at market prices after fulfilling government plan targets. The central government also pressures provincial governments to impose price controls on fertilisers, most commonly in the form of mandatory ex-factory price ceilings and wholesale or retail marketing margin limits for SMC sales.

This mix of direct and indirect subsidies, combined with the new role of provincial governments in controlling fertiliser prices and the general lack of data, makes it difficult to determine China's current level of agricultural input subsidies. An assessment, based on the Policy Analysis Matrix for Chinese agriculture, indicated that policies were reducing input costs by between 13 and 30 per cent on average between 1996-1998 (Fang and Beghin, 2000). However, in recent years agricultural input prices have risen at a faster rate than overall price inflation, suggesting that subsidies may be declining (ERS, 2001a).

Farmers also tended to replace low quality early rice with cotton, oilseeds, vegetables and other more profitable crops.

In 2001 new pilot grain marketing reforms were initiated in Zhejiang province, later expanded to seven other provinces or municipalities (Shanghai, Fujian, Guangdong, Hainan, Jiangsu, Beijing and Tianjin). The reform included the cancellation of the grain quota delivery obligations for farmers, further liberalisation of grain prices and opening of grain market operations to a larger number of enterprises. While this initiative is in line with market-oriented reforms, its current geographical coverage is limited to the coastal, developed region, and the main challenges of including major grain producing areas of central China are still to be undertaken.

Cotton policy

Until 1999, the state monopoly on cotton purchasing and pricing, originally designed to ensure the development of China's textile industry in the context of a centrally planned economy, had failed to allow the sector to adapt to the fluctuating world market prices of competing crops and changing global economic conditions (ERS, 2001a). Chinese farmers continued to raise more cotton than planners wanted and government-held stocks strained physical storage capacity and financial resources as consumption weakened in the face of declining textile exports and soft domestic demand. Minor policy and price adjustments and administrative pressures on local officials to reduce the area failed to control the mounting problems and costly inefficiencies in the government-run cotton system.

Box 1.3. **The two-tier price system for grains**

The procurement price system for grains (in particular rice, wheat and corn) is the backbone of agricultural price policies. The system requires farmers to deliver a fixed quantity (quota) of the grain produced at an administrative price (procurement or quota price) to the government grain stations. For most of the last two decades, the quota prices were kept artificially low, placing a considerable tax on producers of grain. This made it possible to keep urban food prices low and helped meet the overall development objective of "supporting industrial development by assuring stable supplies of reasonably priced food". The effects of the system have changed markedly over the past six years. With renewed emphasis on grain production in line with the GGBRS programme launched in 1995, market prices started to fall below quota price levels. This meant that the implicit tax of the quota prices on agricultural products turned into a subsidy in more recent years. When prices for wheat and maize declined drastically in 1997, the government introduced another policy price for the remaining amount of grain farmers wanted to sell. This so-called "protective" price, though below the quota price level, should allow for cost coverage and include a small profit. It also sets a floor price for grain sold to the government. Both quota and protective prices have been cut every year since 1998. But the oversupply situation on grain markets contributed to even faster falls in market prices for all major varieties of grains. As a result, market prices have constantly been below quota prices and in 2000 they fell even below protective prices (Figure 1.3).

Figure 1.3. **Market and procurement prices for wheat, 1997-2000**

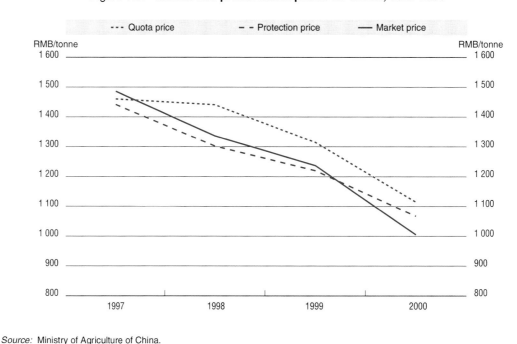

Source: Ministry of Agriculture of China.

Problems in the cotton sector worsened during the 1998/99-crop year, prompting government leaders to liberalise the market. The key provisions of the reforms were implemented in September 1999 and involved the cotton purchase, pricing, marketing and distribution systems (Box 1.4). As a result, China began the 1999/2000-crop year with no official government procurement price. Instead, market conditions were allowed to determine the price of cotton. The long-standing

---

Box 1.4. **Cotton market reform**

The four key provisions to liberalise the cotton market reform introduced in September 1999 are as follows:

1. The government no longer mandates cotton procurement or sales prices. Instead, it announces a non-binding guidance price based on its determination of market supply and demand, production costs, competing crop prices, and world cotton prices.

2. The China National Cotton Exchange was opened in Beijing in September 1999. The exchange provides a market for authorised domestic cotton firms, textile enterprises, and cotton import or export companies to buy and sell cotton. But the government may intervene in the market, through the Cotton and Jute Corporation (CJC), which buys and sells state-owned cotton reserves on the exchange in order to influence cotton supply, demand, and price.

3. The CJC monopoly over cotton procurement was ended and state subsidies were terminated. Cotton ginning enterprises under the Ministry of Agriculture, state farms, and a limited number of large, state-owned spinning mills or textile enterprises are now legally authorised to purchase cotton directly from farmers or co-operatives. Textile enterprises can now contract with government-certified cotton processors for ginning and baling.

4. As part of a push to improve cotton quality, the China Fiber Inspection Bureau is implementing new cotton grading standards. Once in place, the new grading standards will include four measures: grade, length, micronaire (measuring fibre fineness and maturity), and trash.

The legalisation of alternatives to the government's official cotton procurement system could introduce profound changes in the distribution of China's cotton. However, there are still several policy measures, which would suggest partial continuation of the previous administrative system. In particular, it is unclear how much competition will actually be allowed in the domestic market because individual cotton merchants and uncertified mills will continue to be officially prohibited from buying, processing, or operating cotton-related businesses. Certification of enterprises is the responsibility of provincial Industry and Commerce Administrations and local Bureaux of Technical Supervision.

The government will also continue to monopolise all cotton imports and exports. CHINATEX (China National Textile Import and Export Corporation), the Xinjiang CJC, and Xinjiang's Production and Construction Corps are the only authorised state trading companies for cotton. Government policy still focuses on encouraging domestic textile enterprises to consume domestic cotton in lieu of imports. Cotton imported to produce products destined for re-export will face close scrutiny in order to prevent leakage onto the domestic market. Moreover, other administrative measures – such as a moratorium on new cotton ginning enterprises – will be applied and the current policy forbidding the sale of used ginning equipment or spindles will continue.

Source: Colby and MacDonald, 2000.

---

state-monopolised purchase and sale system was ended. The most immediate impact of the reform has been a sharp decline in China's cotton prices, which have nearly fallen to world market levels (Figure 1.4). As China adjusts to the new marketing and pricing system, cotton farmers will see decreased incomes. However, lower cotton prices are expected to increase the competitiveness of China's textile exports. Lower prices may also increase domestic consumption, as lower costs mean cotton is better able to compete with synthetic fibre.

Oilseed policy

Compared to grains, there is relatively little government intervention in the domestic oilseed sector. Other than a small quantity of soybeans procured at fixed government prices by the Heilongjiang provincial government, all oilseeds are purchased at market prices. In addition, trade in

Figure 1.4. **World and Chinese cotton prices, August 1998-end 2000**

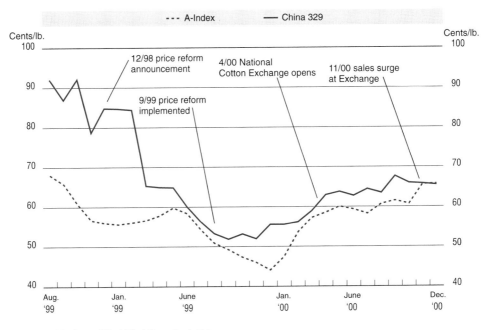

Source: Cotton Outlook A-Indiex and East West Consultants Ltd..

oilseeds has been more liberalised than grains. There are six entities authorised to import edible oils (as opposed to a single state company, CEROILS, for grain), and the government manages oil trade through import quotas and licenses. There are no restrictions on the enterprises that import oilseeds or oilseed meal.

Current government oilseed policy is focused on providing sufficient quantities of oilseeds for the country's growing crush capacity. In 1998 and 1999, the government initiated a series of actions that resulted in an increase in oilseed imports and a reduction in oilseed product (meal and oil) imports. First, the government reduced edible oil import quotas and tightened up the issuance of import licenses. Second, it initiated a strict crackdown on smuggling of edible oils, frequently conducted through under-invoicing of declared import quantities. And finally, it reversed its earlier policy of providing a rebate on the VAT for imported soymeal. The resulting surge in oilseed imports increased crushing facility capacity utilisation, reduced unit costs, and increased the competitiveness of the crushing sector (Schmidhuber, 2001).

Livestock policy

China's livestock sector is still primarily made up of small-scale household producers. China's livestock policy does not rely on direct intervention in the marketing or pricing of domestic livestock animals or meat. However, to a limited extent the government supports the livestock sector through indirect programmes aimed at increasing the role of specialised household and commercial livestock operations, ensuring adequate feed supplies to state-owned feed mills, and through the so called Mayors' Responsibility System.[5] In addition, the government supports development of the infrastructure necessary to have a vibrant animal product market, particularly increasing the availability of inspection and disease services, as well as increasing the supply of cold storage, transportation, and modern slaughter facilities (Tuan *et al.*, 1998).

Overall implications of trade liberalisation on the major segments of agriculture

Major shifts in output composition

China's accession to the WTO will bring about several important changes for its agricultural trade regime (see Annex I). Changes include tariff reductions and larger import quotas, as well as more transparent and contestable rules for the application of sanitary and phytosanitary trade measures. In addition, the role of State Trading Enterprises (STEs) – traditionally the key trading agents for cereals and cotton – will be curtailed and private traders will receive access to a portion of the tariff rate quotas (TRQs).

The impact of WTO on China's agricultural economy is likely to be mixed. While labour-intensive crops are likely to enjoy expanded access to international markets, some land-intensive sectors, notably wheat and corn, could contract after accession. An important factor making assessment difficult is uncertainty over the relative price levels on Chinese and world markets. Even if farmgate prices in China remain low and often below farmgate prices abroad, which would suggest price competitiveness at the farm level, they may not be low enough to allow effective competition for the final product at the border (Schmidhuber, 2001). This reflects a lack of infrastructure, an inefficient domestic handling system, high processing margins due to the inefficient processing industry, and significant quality gaps relative to internationally traded produce.

Assessing the impact of trade liberalisation on China's agricultural sector is further complicated by the fact that there are two types of changes that must be incorporated into the analysis: changes in barriers to trade, both tariff and non-tariff, and adjustments in domestic agricultural policies in response to trade liberalisation requirements and/or potential competitive pressures. The changes to China's trade barriers are, for the most part, detailed and explicit. Similarly, certain specific policy adjustments, such as opening up domestic distribution systems to non-state entities, are required by China's WTO commitments. Other possible agricultural policy changes, however, though not required, may be desirable and even necessary in order to minimise the burden on government finances or to limit the costs of social and economic adjustments arising from trade liberalisation. The two sections below examine the impacts on output composition under two sets of assumptions: reduction of trade barriers alone and reduction of trade barriers combined with adjustments in domestic agricultural policies.

Impacts of trade barrier reduction

A recent analysis by the OECD Secretariat estimated that the impact on China's agricultural trade of just the tariff reductions and the implementation of a TRQ system would not result in major changes in China's projected agricultural trade volumes. Therefore, the changes to China's domestic agricultural production levels and patterns resulting directly from the tariff and TRQ changes would also be rather small. The main reason is that under this scenario domestic agricultural policies would remain largely unchanged, meaning that both the administrative pressures of the "governors" grain responsibility system and the input subsidy system would remain in place, thus encouraging farmers to produce more, in particular grains and oilseeds, than under free market conditions (OECD, 2000; Schmidhuber, 2001). Another reason is that the fall in China's average tariffs on agricultural products would be limited, from 22 per cent in 2000 to 17.5 per cent in 2004, compared to tariff reductions from 24.6 per cent to 9.4 per cent, for the same years, for industrial products.

Under this scenario, grain imports would increase by just 2 million tonnes in 2005 *vis-à-vis* baseline results (non-WTO accession). There would be a somewhat greater impact on vegetable oil and oilseed imports, particularly soybeans. Oilseed meals are already relatively freely traded, so trade liberalisation is not expected to see a large change in meal imports. The analysis found that the relaxation of oil import quotas and the reduction in oilseed tariffs increased import volumes. Domestic supply of meals would increase, reducing import demand (Schmidhuber, 2001).

The study also found that a reduction in tariff rates would have a modest impact on meat trade, but the impacts on domestic consumption and production of meat would be significant. Higher real incomes and lower import prices, due to lower tariffs, should stimulate domestic demand for meat. At the same time, trade liberalisation would reduce costs of the major feed inputs (grains and oilseed meals), thus stimulating meat production and lowering upward pressure on import demand. However, these changes would not be equal across all livestock production systems. The largest increases in production were observed in the commercial and specialised household producers because of their relatively intensive use of compound feed. Backyard producers would experience less growth because of their greater reliance on non-grain feeds and low rates of oil meal use (Schmidhuber, 2001).

Impacts of trade barrier reduction accompanied by other domestic agricultural policy changes

The analysis becomes more complex when the question of domestic agricultural policy change is also addressed. China's WTO commitments do not explicitly require elimination of State Trading Enterprises (STE) or many other distortionary domestic agricultural policies. However, trade liberalisation, including the requirement to allocate minimum amounts of the import quotas to non-STEs, will exert strong pressure on STEs, reduce their power and stimulate the ongoing process of agricultural policy reform. It is likely that the combined effects of trade system changes and expected agricultural policy adjustments on trade flows would be much stronger than the impacts of trade system changes alone (Schmidhuber, 2001).

In addition to reducing the power of its STEs, China also committed itself to allow foreign companies (and by extension, joint ventures) to have full trading and distribution rights, including rights in retailing, wholesaling, warehouse, and transportation. This will clearly be incompatible with China's current agricultural marketing and distribution system – one based on government control over procurement, distribution, storage and allocation of priority agricultural commodities (primarily wheat, rice, and corn). The changes required in China's domestic marketing and distribution system, combined with the loss of control by STEs over a significant portion of the trade in grain, cotton, and edible oils, will either raise the costs of the current policy regime so as to be unsustainable or else reduce the efficacy of the policy to such an extent that it no longer fulfils its purpose (Colby, Diao, and Tuan, 2001).

While the actual extent of agricultural input subsidies is not clear (see Box 1.2), it is likely that, with trade liberalisation, input subsidies will be diminished and/or at least partly reallocated to less distortive policy measures. This would result in an increase of prices of some inputs such as fertilisers and could possibly have a negative impact on crop production. However, in a more liberal trade and investment environment, farmers could benefit from access to cheaper and much more efficient imported technologies. Currently, imports of some inputs such as pesticides and herbicides are restricted. Moreover, inadequate intellectual property rights, lack of regulations, and obsolete distribution systems limit foreign direct investment opportunities in the agricultural input sector (Huang *et al.*, 2000).

A change in China's agricultural policies, particularly a rollback of the GGBRS and related grain self-sufficiency and grain stock policies, or at least a weakening of the effectiveness of those policies due to the WTO accession commitments, will result in the reallocation of resources within agriculture and will bring an increase in imports of a wide range of agricultural products, but particularly grains, oilseeds, oilseed products, and cotton. The rise in imports should, however, be matched by an increase in exports of vegetables, fruits, and perhaps meats – all products for which China has a comparative advantage. China's low labour costs mean production of these products can be highly competitive on international markets if China can raise its processing and packaging quality to meet international standards (Box 1.5).

This production shift generally corresponds with China's international trade patterns over the last 20 years. Broadly speaking, the long-term trend in China's agricultural trade is following conventional trade theory. Trade liberalisation is likely to strengthen this tendency (Lu, 2001).

There are some concerns in China that agricultural production restructuring and, in particular, cuts in grain production may have gone too far. Moreover, farmers' incomes are still perceived in China to be

Box 1.5. **Likely agricultural trade and production adjustments
for main commodities**

Corn

China is currently a large corn exporter with exports supported by subsidies. Such subsidies will not be allowed now that China has joined the WTO. China's corn imports were on average less than half a million tonnes annually over the last three years. However, imports are expected to increase steadily because of the TRQ provision that creates effective market access opportunities for non-state trade companies in corn imports, because of the demand that already exists, particularly in South China, and finally, because government agricultural policy will provide less support to maintaining domestic output levels (see (Figure 1.5).

During the 1990s, transportation bottlenecks and high costs made the cost of moving domestic corn from North to South China more expensive than importing corn. However, for the most part the central government did not allow corn imports, forcing South China feed mills to procure more expensive corn from North China. With WTO membership, less government support will result in reduced domestic output in more marginal production areas, particularly in East and South China. Production in the North China corn-belt will continue, though perhaps with more of a focus on producing for nearby Asian export markets such as South Korea. And the liberalisation of trade under the TRQ system will allow South China to rely much more heavily fon imports.

Wheat

China has imported less than 2 million tonnes of wheat each year over the last three years, and stocks are relatively high. Nevertheless, imports are expected to increase under WTO membership because of demand for high-protein-content wheat in urban areas and a decrease in trade barriers for the previously banned US Pacific Northwest soft white wheat. While stock adjustments could delay rising imports, even relatively modest changes in production and consumption would quickly drive imports above previously expected levels (see Figure 1.5). Recent changes in government procurement policy are expected to reduce marginal areas planted to winter wheat in Northwest China and the region south of the Yangtze River, and spring wheat areas in Northeast China. South China is the likely destination for much of the additional imports needed to meet the demand for high-quality wheat (for noodles, cakes, biscuits and pastries). North China should continue to be supplied primarily by domestic production, though it too relies on imported wheat for blending purposes.

Figure 1.5. **Net import value in 2005 after the WTO accession**

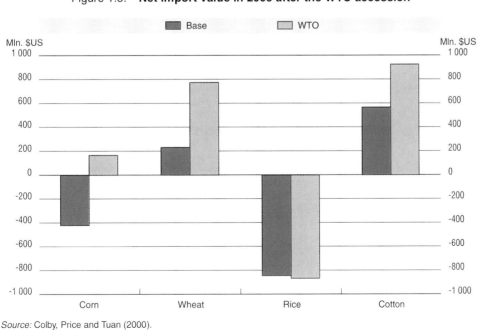

Source: Colby, Price and Tuan (2000).

Box 1.5.   **Likely agricultural trade and production adjustments**
for main commodities (*cont.*)

Rice

China is traditionally a large net exporter of rice and is likely to remain so (see Figure 1.5). However, because of the cap on domestic subsidies and likely reduction in government price support, China's internal prices could drop, reducing rice production as well as exports to third-country markets. China currently imports *indica* rice almost exclusively, mainly premium Thai jasmine for high-income urban consumers. This trade pattern is likely to continue. In terms of domestic production changes, production of high quality *japonica* rice is likely to continue to expand to meet growing domestic and export demand for high quality rice. On the other hand, production of the lowest quality rice, particularly early season *indica*, is likely to decline.

Cotton

The government's tight control over cotton purchase, marketing and distribution was loosened for the 1999/00 crop year. Although the new marketing system has only been in place for a short time, to date the transition to the new liberalised cotton system has been quite successful. The cotton sector will be able to adjust to trade and investment liberalisation much more readily than the grain sector. Nevertheless, cotton imports are expected to increase relatively sharply under the TRQ system (see Figure 1.5). In particular, the fact that two-thirds of the quota is reserved for non-state trade will provide an immediate boost to imports. Even with the new liberalised marketing system, China's domestic prices are roughly 10 cents/lb. higher than comparable world prices. This suggests that China's imports, particularly by joint-venture mills in East China, should increase. The impact on production, however, will be mixed. Domestic prices are expected to decline to be more in line with comparable world prices. This is likely to reduce production in higher cost producing areas, but not dramatically. For the most part, returns to cotton are higher than returns to other available competing crops. Therefore, the final impact on cotton area and production will be determined by the relative impacts of cotton and competing crops.

Oilseed complex

The impact of trade liberalisation on the edible oilseed complex will be almost entirely a function of the liberalisation of China's trading rules. The oilseed sector is already relatively open compared with grains. Therefore, it can be argued that the impact on oilseed complex trade is primarily a response to the implementation of the soy oil TRQ, and the elimination of government control over oilseed imports (and continuation of free trade in meal), and less a response to additional changes in domestic policy. In contrast, Schmidhuber (2001) suggests that a reduction in input subsidies would provide an additional and significant boost to oilseed complex imports. Loss of input subsidies, it is argued, would reduce domestic production, raise prices, and increase the competitiveness of imports, particularly of oilseeds and edible oil.

Horticultural products

China is a large net exporter of fruits, vegetables and their products. In the 1990s, the harvested area rose by nearly one-third for vegetables and nearly one-half for fruit. This trend is likely to be continued as policies stimulating grain production are expected to be relaxed, thus allowing more land to be allocated to more profitable fruit and vegetable production. However, China will also substantially reduce its import tariffs on a number of fruits, vegetables and their products, thus making imports more competitive on China's domestic market, in particular for processed products and high quality produce for hotel/ restaurant trade and large-scale city supermarkets (ERS, 2001*b*). While WTO membership gives China a way to appeal the unfavourable decisions of bilateral trade dispute settlements, thus helping China remove or reduce barriers erected by several foreign countries (such as Japan, Republic of Korea and the United States) on imports of several horticultural products, environmental concerns for rapidly growing chemical inputs in horticultural production will have to be addressed in the near future. The improvement of quality combined with a wider use of grade standards, basic marketing practices (such as modern packing and packaging techniques) and product promotion will be needed to bring Chinese horticultural products to international standards.

Box 1.5. **Likely agricultural trade and production adjustments
for main commodities** (*cont.*)

Livestock products

The importance of livestock output has been rapidly growing in China. While the vast majority of livestock output is destined for the domestic market, China is also a large net exporter. Livestock product marketing was liberalised more than a decade ago, but several policy and institutional constraints, such as lack of standardised national quarantine and phytosanitary inspection procedures and shipping documents applicable to all interprovincial commodity transport, still impede marketing efficiency. While there is relatively little doubt that in particular pork and poultry producers will profit from lower feed prices, the impact on beef, mutton and milk producers will depend to a large extent on the impact of trade liberalisation on domestic prices, which remains a controversial issue. An indirect positive impact on livestock production may come from investment liberalisation, which should contribute to the creation of more competitive domestic meat and milk processing industries in China. Such developments would not only contribute to the improvement of the quality of products, but would also force these industries to operate with smaller margins, thus lessening the downward pressures on farmgate prices.

---

strongly linked with grain prices. However, even if agriculture comes under pressure after China's WTO accession, there are several factors that will buffer adverse effects, both in the short and the long run. These factors include various policy safeguards, high transaction costs and isolated regional markets, and the specificity of small household responses (see Chapter 3). In fact, under the accession agreement, China's TRQ levels are set at levels modest enough and the above quota tariff rates, at rates high enough, to minimise any damage, either real or perceived. For example, after bringing in imports up to its TRQ level (*e.g.* 9.636 million tonnes for wheat), China could legally assess a tariff of 65 per cent on any additional imports of grains. At such high tariff levels, China's wheat producers would almost certainly be shielded from any other competition from international producers for many years.

Implied changes in labour utilisation due to trade liberalisation

Impacts on total agricultural employment

Total employment in China's agriculture increased until the beginning of the 1990s when it reached its highest level of above 340 million, before dropping to below 330 million in the mid-1990s.[6] In more recent years it increased again, mostly due to the overall cooling of the Chinese economy and a fall in employment in township and village enterprises (TVEs) – until the mid-1990s the major employer of redundant farm labour. As employment in other sectors of the Chinese economy increased at high rates, the share of agricultural labour in the total declined from 71 per cent at the end of the 1970s to 47 per cent at the end of the 1990s (Figure 1.6).

It is estimated that direct trade liberalisation impacts on agricultural employment in China will not be large. Estimates differ, but according to the most recent simulation based on a computable general equilibrium (CGE) model, agricultural employment would fall by around 78 million between 1997 and 2010 with China joining the WTO, compared to the baseline scenario (no WTO entry) estimating the fall at 75 million (Zhai and Li, 2000). Relatively more people would be employed in livestock, but fewer in grain production. Overall, the trade liberalisation impact on agricultural employment can be considered as minimal. Therefore, the question is not how to absorb the additional flow of labour from agriculture to other sectors of the economy stimulated by trade liberalisation, but rather how to profit from the positive trade liberalisation framework to bring into practice policies which would ease the overall flow, so vitally needed to improve farmers' incomes.

Figure 1.6. **Evolution of employment in Chinese agriculture**

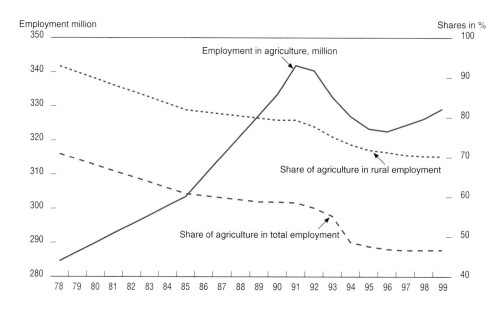

Source: China Statistical Yearbook.

Unofficial estimates suggest that between 30 and 40 per cent of the current agricultural workforce is not productively employed, even under China's currently low level of technology in agriculture (Carter, 2001; Du, 2001). The high level of excess labour has brought low labour productivity in agriculture, low agricultural incomes, and hidden unemployment in rural areas, and has become a driving force behind the ongoing rural workforce migration to urban areas. The income gap between rural and urban households is wide and growing (see Chapters 3 and 16). A more competitive economic environment following trade liberalisation is likely to bring a relative fall in farmgate prices in China and lower agricultural incomes. However, numerical simulations show that if trade liberalisation leads to labour market reforms, this will dramatically boost the gains to agricultural labour. It is estimated that if 35 per cent of China's agricultural labour force exits agriculture and takes up jobs in urban industries after China's WTO accession, the current almost 3:1 urban/rural income gap would close (Carter, 2001). Therefore, the greatest challenge for the Chinese authorities will be providing alternative employment opportunities for redundant farm labour. Experience from other nations suggests that this migration can be managed successfully. In South Korea, for instance, over 50 per cent of the workforce was engaged in agriculture in 1970, but by 1997 this had declined to only 11 per cent.

Impacts on agricultural employment by region

China's agricultural labour force is spread unevenly across regions (Figure 1.7). Over 45 per cent of agricultural labour is concentrated in just two regions of North and Southwest China, while the largest share of cultivated area (based on revised Agricultural Census estimates) is in North, Northwest, and Southwest China. The largest per farmer availability of arable land is in Northeast and Northwest China, at 1.1 and 0.8 hectares, respectively. In the other regions the availability is approximately 0.3 hectares per farmer.

The theory of comparative advantage suggests that regions producing land-intensive agricultural products will tend to incur a greater share of the adjustment costs of trade liberalisation, while regions with a domestic advantage in labour-intensive agricultural products will tend to accrue relatively more of the benefits of increased trade. Figure 1.8 shows estimates of average provincial concentration ratios

Figure 1.7. **Regional agricultural labour and cultivated area, 1999**

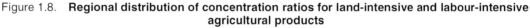

Agricultural labour ▢ Arable land

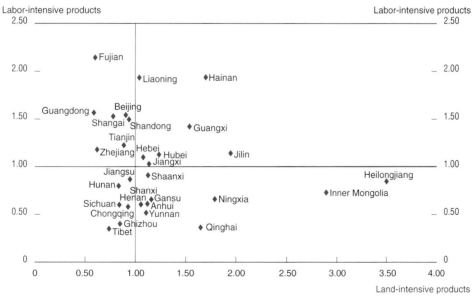

Note: See Note 2 for the list of provinces in each category.
Source: China Statistical Yearbook.

Figure 1.8. **Regional distribution of concentration ratios for land-intensive and labour-intensive agricultural products**

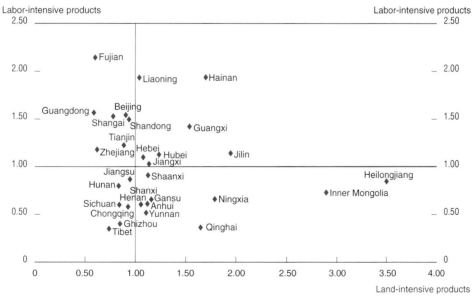

1. Weighted average index of concentration ratios for land-intensive products and simple average index of concentration ratios for labour-intensive product for each province. For crops these are ratios of rural per capita sown area for a given product in a given region to national average of rural per capita sown area of the same product. For meat and fishery products these are ratios of rural per capita output of a given product in a given province to national average of rural per capita output of the same product.
Source: Lu (2001).

on land-intensive and labour-intensive products in China for the period 1997-1999. Land-intensive products include grains, oilseeds, cotton, and sugar, while labour-intensive products include vegetables, fruit, meat, and aquatic products.

Not surprisingly, the estimates indicate that coastal provinces have relatively more production of labour-intensive agricultural products, indicated by a concentration ratio greater than one. In contrast, central and western provinces tend to have land-intensive concentration ratios greater than one. Based on the calculation of each province's relative concentration in land or labour intensive agricultural products, likely potential adjustment costs or benefits under trade liberalisation can be determined (Table 1.3). Provinces with a concentration ratio for land-intensive products above one and labour intensive products below one are likely to experience relatively large adjustment costs and receive relatively few benefits. Those with labour-intensive ratios above one and land-intensive ratios below one will incur relatively fewer adjustment costs but reap more of the benefits of trade liberalisation.

Table 1.3. **Agricultural adjustment costs and benefits from trade and investment liberalisation by province**

		Adjustment costs from potential import growth	
		Large	Small
Benefits from potential export growth	Large	Beijing, Fujian, Guangdong, Shandong, Shanghai, Tianjin, Zhejiang	Hainan, Guangxi, Hebei, Hubei, Jiangxi, Jilin, Liaoning
	Small	Chongqing, Guizhou, Hunan, Jiangsu, Sichuan, Tibet	Anhui, Gansu, Heilongjiang, Inner Mongolia, Ningxia, Qinghai, Shaanxi, Shanxi, Xinjiang, Yunnan

Source: Lu (2001).

Based on this analysis, grouping individual provinces into coastal and non-coastal (central and western) regions, the relative potential gains and benefits from trade liberalisation are clearly defined. With few exceptions, the concentration ratios would suggest relatively large benefits and small costs for provinces in the coastal region, and relatively small benefits and large costs for the central and western regions. However, the underlying assumption of such an approach is that farmers are equally linked with the domestic and international markets, which is not the case. Therefore, the initial impact of trade liberalisation and adjustments will differ depending on the degree farms are linked with markets.

For instance, the increased imports will tend to compete most directly with the land-intensive grain and oilseed production along China's coast. Competitive imports will reduce China's domestic prices by the margin they exceed world prices. To the extent that certain provinces possess a competitive advantage in a particular crop, for instance *japonica* rice production in Heilongjiang province (Zhong, 2001), then production will likely increase. However, the overall comparative advantage in the coastal region suggests that many farmers will continue to reduce areas planted to grains in order to increase areas planted to vegetables and fruit. To the extent that agricultural producers along the coast can either shift labour to newly available non-farm employment opportunities created by trade liberalisation, or can adjust production patterns to take advantage of the demand for higher value crops such as fruit and vegetables, these agricultural households may suffer only temporary income setbacks, if any, during the initial adjustment period. Producers in regions that concentrate on grains where China's comparative advantage is relatively low, however, such as corn production in Jilin province, are likely to face more substantial difficulties during the adjustment process.[7]

Central and western provinces will be insulated to a large extent from the competition with imports because of high marketing costs, partly due to poor transportation linkages. Moreover, China's small-scale farming, in particular in the central and western regions, is characterised by a large proportion of production used directly by households (60-70 per cent in the case of grains) and only partly destined for markets. This sector will to a large extent be immune to any external market signals or shocks. This has been the experience of many Mexican regions dominated by small-scale farming after Mexico joined NAFTA. In addition, production of grains and oilseeds in central and western regions takes advantage of relatively abundant land resources. Therefore, the likely negative impact of lower grain prices will be rather weak in these provinces.[8]

Conclusion: Policy priorities to facilitate adjustment

Trade and investment liberalisation is likely to accelerate the ongoing processes of agricultural policy reform and restructuring of Chinese agriculture.

China's Governors' Grain Bag Responsibility System, government management of grain storage, distribution, and marketing, and state control over major agricultural commodity imports through STEs are all parts of a system that implements government agricultural and food security goals. Trade liberalisation reduces the ability of the government to control agricultural imports. It will therefore reduce the effectiveness of the institutions the government uses to manage grain storage, distribution, and marketing as foreign and domestic competitors are allowed to enter. This situation provides an opportunity to put in place a new set of institutions and policies that will be better able to assist adjustments to a more open trading environment and to meet the goal of food security. Such policy measures should be based on the following principles:

- Clear separation of commercial and policy functions to parallel the separation of commercial and state grain reserves. The commercial companies should be responsible for farm procurement and interprovincial grain transfers, with financing independent of the state budget.

- Clear separation of central and local government responsibilities. Buffer stocks for price stabilisation and disaster relief stocks should be the responsibility of the central government. Local governments should be responsible for implementing income stabilisation policies (*e.g.* food stamp or welfare programmes) and should not attempt to intervene in markets.

- Clear separation of old and new grain debts. The current grain financing debt represents largely defaulted policy loans with the balance representing borrowing for commercial operations. Policy debts should be serviced by the fiscal system, and commercial debts should be restructured and their repayment decoupled from current operations.

Government policy should attempt to foster cropping patterns and other agricultural production decisions based on emerging market opportunities and regional comparative advantage rather than on the traditional yardstick of increasing grain output in all areas at any cost. In the new market-oriented system the development of better agricultural price information systems, grading standards, and marketing channels is needed to support diversification of farm production patterns away from traditional practices. A more effective agricultural research and extension system is also needed in China to provide farmers with the varieties and knowledge necessary to compete.

Restructuring of agricultural production should be supported by investment in rural infrastructure to better link farmers with the markets and to attract other investors to rural areas. An adequate network of finance and credit institutions is particularly needed to ease agricultural transformation. In this respect micro-credit systems, co-operative credit institutions, and various types of informal financing could be particularly well suited to the small-scale and low-income farming dominating in China. A further reform of the land use and land ownership system would provide farmers with the opportunity to use land as collateral. It has to be emphasised that all polices mentioned above, and budgetary expenditures linked with them, are considered to be "Green Box" items, and as such do not fall under the agricultural support ceilings that China will have to abide by under WTO rules.

To benefit from international markets more open to its agro-food exports, China needs to improve the quality of agricultural commodities produced and exported. Tackling this problem would help China gain access to OECD markets for products (*e.g.* processed vegetables) where lower factor costs, particularly labour, provide a comparative advantage that could be exploited. With lower tariff barriers, other trade obstacles regulated under the Sanitary and Phytosanitary (SPS) and Technical Barriers to

Trade (TBT) agreements will become increasingly important in importing countries, particularly for processed food. Of crucial importance for China is the establishment of a sound, scientific, consistent, and transparent approach to determining the pest and disease risks associated with the agro-food trade, both to be able to participate effectively in the possible disputes over the SPS measures applied by other countries, but, even more importantly, to apply the appropriate, least trade restrictive measures to manage that risk on animal and plant imports. In many cases, these measures should meet internationally agreed standards.

Whatever short-term changes are made in the current agricultural policy regime in response to trade liberalisation, the most effective and sustainable method of boosting the incomes of farm households is to provide off-farm opportunities to work. As discussed in the next chapter, this involves the development of non-agricultural employment opportunities in rural areas on the one hand, and easing the flow of rural labour to urban areas on the other.

Trade liberalisation will present China with numerous opportunities and challenges. The changes and adjustments that China will need to make in terms of altering domestic institutions or adjusting domestic policy will be difficult. Nevertheless, in the late 1970s, China was successful in transforming its struggling collectivised agricultural system into the vastly more productive mixed socialist-market system that it has today. This dramatic transformation was a success by almost any measure – and one that provides a considerable measure of optimism for this next transition.

NOTES

1. Up until 1995, the National Bureau of Statistics reported that China had 95 million hectares of cultivated land. However, the 1997 Census of Agriculture issued a revised national cultivated land total of 130 million hectares, an increase of 36.9 per cent. The issue of cultivated (or arable) land is one of many important data problems that complicate any analysis of China's agriculture sector.

2. In this paper, China's regions are classified as follows: Northeast: Heilongjiang, Liaoning, Jilin; North: Shandong, Hebei, Beijing, Tianjin, Henan, Shanxi; Northwest: Shaanxi, Gansu, Inner Mongolia, Ningxia, Xinjiang, Qinghai; East: Zhejiang, Jiangsu, Shanghai, Anhui; Centre: Hubei, Hunan, Jiangxi; South: Guangdong, Guangxi, Fujian, Hainan; Southwest: Chongqing, Sichuan, Guizhou, Yunnan, and Tibet.

3. China's government launched a first attempt to reform its grain economy in 1998. This policy reform was known as the "four separations and one perfection". However, in fact, it did not seriously address the fundamental problems of China's grain economy (overproduction, inefficiencies in the storage and distribution system) introduced by previous policy packages. As a result, this reform contributed to the additional debt accumulation by state grain traders and largely failed (OECD, 1999).

4. Corn exports reached 10.5 million tonnes in 2000, up 143 per cent compared to 1999. To support corn exports, China subsidised exports at a widely reported rate of RMB 368 per tonne (US$44). The subsidy was provided to state agents to compensate them for storage costs and debt accumulated on corn stocks purchased at high prices several years ago.

5. The Mayors Responsibility System, or what is sometimes referred to as the "vegetable basket programme", is an adjunct to the Governors Grain Bag Responsibility System. Initiated in 1988, the programme placed the responsibility on mayors to secure sufficient supplies of non-staple foods (meat, eggs, vegetables and fish) for large metropolitan areas. Under this programme, large cities promote development of large-scale greenhouse agriculture in the suburbs and nearby countryside in order to increase the available vegetable supply. They also support the development of commercial livestock operations in the suburbs and nearby countryside by providing subsidised animal feed and other inputs. Since its inception, the policy has significantly increased the quantity and quality of these foods around major cities.

6. This is an official estimate. For a discussion on agricultural labour statistics see Chapter 16.

7. Vast areas of Jilin are planted to corn, and if many producers attempt to shift to other crops, the adjustment process is likely to be more difficult and protracted given the current focus on a single grain crop.

8. There will also be some positive impacts, such as for cotton production in the far Northwestern province of Xinjiang, where agronomic conditions make cotton very profitable and competitive (notwithstanding the transportation issues that Xinjiang faces in moving products east to consumers or for export).

BIBLIOGRAPHY

Anderson, K. (1990),
Comparative Advantages in China: Effects on Food, Feed, and Fiber Markets, OECD, Paris.

Carter, C. (2001),
"China's Trade Integration and Impacts on Factor Markets," China's Agriculture in the International Trading System, OECD Proceedings, Paris.

China Agriculture Yearbook,
China Agriculture Publishing House, Beijing, China, various issues.

China Statistical Abstract (2001),
National Bureau of Statistics, Beijing, China.

China Statistical Yearbook, Compiled by the National Bureau of Statistics (formerly State Statistical Bureau), China Statistics Press, Beijing, China, various issues.

Colby, H., X. Diao and F. Tuan (2001),
"China's WTO Accession: Conflicts with Domestic Agricultural Policies and Institutions", China's Agriculture in the International Trading System, OECD Proceedings, Paris.

Colby, H., X. Diao and A. Somwaru (2000),
Cross-Commodity Analysis of China's Grain Sector: Sources of Growth and Supply Response, USDA, Economic Research Service, Washington, DC, Technical Bulletin No. 1884, May.

Colby, H. and S. MacDonald (2000),
"China's New and Improved Cotton Market", China International Agriculture and Trade Report, US Department of Agriculture, Economic Research Service, March.

Crook, F. (1998),
"Agricultural Policies in 1998: Stability and Change", China International Agriculture and Trade Report, US Department of Agriculture, Economic Research Service, July.

Du, Y. (2001),
"China's Agricultural Restructuring and System Reform Under Its Accession into WTO", China's Agriculture in the International Trading System, OECD Proceedings, Paris.

ERS (2001a),
"China Policy" China Briefing Room, US Department of Agriculture, Washington, DC, January, www.ers.usda.gov.

ERS (2001b),
"China's Fruit and Vegetable Sector: A Changing Market Environment", Agricultural Outlook, June-July.

Fang, C., and J.C. Beghin (2000),
Self-Sufficiency, Comparative Advantage, and Agricultural Trade: A Policy Analysis Matrix for Chinese Agriculture, mimeo.

Fang, C., F. Fuller, M. Lopez, and F. Tuan (2000),
"Livestock Production Slowly Evolving from Sideline to Principal Occupation", China International Agriculture and Trade Report, US Department of Agriculture, Economic Research Service, March.

Huang, J., S. Rozelle, L. Zhang (2000),
"WTO and agriculture: radical reforms or the continuation of gradual transition", China Economic Review, No. 11.

Krusekopf, C.C. (2001),
"Diversity in Land Tenure Arrangements under the Household Responsibility System in China", Has China Become a Market Economy?, International Conference on the Chinese Economy, Clermont Ferrand, 17-18 May.

Lin, J.Y. (1992),
"Rural Reforms and Agricultural Growth in China", American Economic Review, No. 82.

Lu, F. (2001),
"Regional Pattern of the Impact from China's WTO Accession on Its Agricultural Sector", China Enters WTO: Pursuing Symbiosis with the Global Economy, I. Yamazawa and K. Imai, (editors), Institute of Developing Economies, Japan External Trade Organisation.

OECD (2000),
    Agricultural Policies in Emerging and Transition Economies, Paris.

OECD (1999),
    Agricultural Policies in Emerging and Transition Economies, Paris.

Schmidhuber, J. (2001),
    "Changes in China's Agricultural Trade Policy Regime: Impacts on Agricultural Production, Consumption, Prices, and Trade", *China's Agriculture in the International Trading System*, OECD Proceedings, Paris.

Tuan, F., X. Zhang and E. Wailes (1998),
    "China's Pork Economy: Production, Marketing, Foreign Trade, and Consumption", *China International Agriculture and Trade Report*, US Department of Agriculture, Economic Research Service, July.

Tuan, F. and B. Ke (1999),
    "A Review of China's Agricultural Policy: Past and Present Developments", *Agriculture in China and OECD Countries: Past Policies and Future Challenges*, OECD Proceedings, Paris.

Vermeer, E.B. (2001),
    "Readjustment Issues in Rural China in the 21st Century", The International Symposium on the WTO and Chinese Rural Development in 21st Century, Maoming, China, 26-29 June.

Zhai, F. and S, Li (2000),
    "Quantitative analysis and evaluation of the impact of entry to WTO on China's economy", *China Development Review*, Development Research Centre of the State Council of the People's Republic of China.

Zhong, F. (2001)
    "Regional Comparative Advantage in China's Grain Production: Implications from Policy Reform", *China's Agriculture in the International Trading System*, OECD Proceedings, Paris.

Chapter 2

RURAL INDUSTRIES

TABLE OF CONTENTS

RURAL INDUSTRIES [*]

Introduction

Township and village enterprises (TVEs) have been a major driving force for the restructuring of the Chinese economy. They have emerged as an important sector, accounting for 30 per cent of China's GDP, almost one-fifth of total employment, and more than 40 per cent of total exports. This chapter attempts to assess the effects of trade liberalisation on rural industries with a special focus on their capacity to absorb the likely rapid shift of labour from agriculture to the non-agricultural sector.

Over the last two decades, TVEs have enabled millions of farmers to benefit from new employment opportunities in the non-agricultural sector. However, even during periods of strong expansion, market imperfections for output, capital, and labour have contributed to uneven patterns of TVE development with a strong concentration of TVEs in the coastal provinces. During the second half of the 1990s, TVE performance stagnated throughout rural China: their contribution to growth slowed, their number declined, and employment fell substantially. But a large part of collective TVEs have gone through an important ownership transformation process and labour productivity has improved. Nevertheless, there is great concern about whether TVEs can provide expected employment opportunities for Chinese farmers in the future.

As a large share of TVE industrial production is located in labour-intensive industries, which will potentially benefit from trade liberalisation, and a relatively small share is in capital-intensive and strongly protected industries that are likely to lose, the TVE sector as a whole should benefit from China's WTO accession. This should enable TVEs to absorb an important part of labour moving out from agriculture. It is realistic to expect that TVEs will be able to create about 2 million new jobs annually by the year 2010, which would mean employing about one-third of the simulated annual outflow of labour from agriculture. Such a scenario would require overcoming the fall in TVE employment of the second half of the 1990s, but would not entail a return to the TVE expansion period of 1984-1996.

There is a wide range of policies that should be put in practice to make such a scenario feasible. In particular, policies should address broad failures in the functioning of financial, labour and distribution markets as well as in fiscal and administration systems. In particular, banking and finance reform would be needed to improve the incentives for, and ability of, domestic banks and possibly other financial institutions to lend to rural enterprises. Further ownership restructuring of collective TVEs should contribute to their better management and governance practices. More transparent taxation as well as business and export licensing would be needed to create a level playing field for all types of enterprises. As competition intensifies and market demands shift from quantity to quality of goods and services TVEs will need to improve their outmoded equipment and low technology.

It is likely that in the future the relative importance of TVEs in the Chinese economy will decline compared to the period of 1984-1996, when they emerged as a response to imperfect state institutions and profited from a number of privileges provided by local authorities. However, after further restructuring they are likely to develop into a vital part of the dynamic sector of small and medium-sized enterprises in China.

The role of rural enterprises in China's structural transformation

TVEs, here defined to include all rural non-agricultural enterprises, including private firms, contribute nearly one-third of Chinese GDP, employ almost one-fifth of total labour and provide half of China's total industrial production (Table 2.1). About 95 per cent of TVEs are small-scale, usually household-based enterprises, employing less than eight workers. In contrast, the number of collective TVEs (narrow definition of TVEs) is rather small, but as they are on average much larger and more,

---

[*] This chapter was prepared by Andrzej Kwiecinski, Principal Analyst, Division for Agricultural Policies in Non-Member Economies, Directorate for Food, Agriculture and Fisheries, OECD, with the help of Xiande Li, consultant.

Table 2.1. **TVEs in China's economy, 1990-1999**

	Number (million)	Employment (million)	Share of national employment %	Share of national GDP %	Share of national exports[1] %
1990	18.5	93	14	14	16
1995	22.0	129	19	25	43
1996	23.4	135	20	26	48
1997	20.2	131	19	28	46
1998	20.0	125	18	28	45
1999	20.7	127	18	30	48
2000	20.8	128	18	31	42

1. Measured as TVE export delivery value related to the total value of exports. As "export deliveries" are likely to be higher than the actual value of exports, this indicator may overestimate the TVEs' share in total exports.
Source: *China Township and Village Enterprise Statistical Yearbook*, Ministry of Agriculture (MOA), various editions.

technologically advanced than private TVEs, their share in the total value of production and employment is relatively high. However, as the process of ownership restructuring advances,[1] the importance of collective TVEs has been progressively declining as indicated by the fall in their share in total TVE value added from 64 per cent in 1995 to 40 per cent in 1999. TVEs are strongly concentrated in the coastal provinces. In 1999, the share of coastal provinces varied between 44 per cent of the total number to 92 per cent of total TVE export value, while the share of western provinces was 19 per cent and just 1 per cent, respectively.

The majority of TVEs are industrial enterprises, accounting in 1999 for 57 per cent of total TVE employment and for 71 per cent of total output. But there is a large number of tertiary sector TVEs including (in order of number of employees) construction, commerce, transportation and services, accounting for 39 per cent of total TVE employment and 27 per cent of total TVE output (Figures 2.1 and 2.2). Non-industrial activities are relatively more important in interior areas where industrial TVEs have faced difficulties.

TVEs have gone through various stages of development (Box 2.1), but overall they have made an extraordinary contribution to China's rapid economic growth and have been a major engine for growth during the reform period. From 1985 to 1999, their output value increased more than thirteen-fold in real terms. TVE productivity growth has consistently outpaced that of state-owned enterprises (SOEs),

Figure 2.1. **TVE employment by sector, 1999**

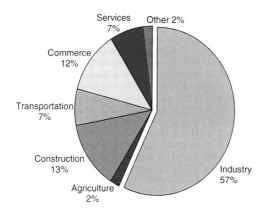

Figure 2.2. **TVE output value by sector, 1999**

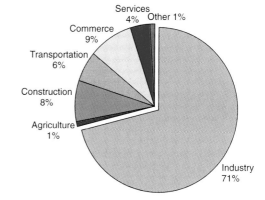

Source: China Township and Village Enterprise Statistical Yearbook, Ministry of Agriculture, 2000.

Box 2.1. **TVE development stages**

1949-1978: Embryonic stage

Rural industries originated from the rural sideline and handicrafts industry started in the late 1950s as "commune and brigade enterprises" (*she dui gongye*). By 1978 their number had reached 1.5 million and employed 28.3 million people.

1979-1983: Restricted development stage

The Third Plenum of the 11th Party Congress in December 1978 initiated major reforms in agriculture. Subsequently, in 1979, a new law placed commune and brigade enterprises within the framework of the collective economy. Several policy decisions provided an institutional guarantee for the development of these enterprises, but at the same time imposed various restrictions on them. In particular, to avoid competition with SOEs, the state imposed the principles of "3 Jiudi" (local community constraints): using local resources, processing locally, and marketing locally. Despite these constraints, the value of production rose rather quickly. However, employment grew moderately to reach 32.4 million in 1983.

1984-1988: High growth stage

In 1984, China's rural reforms were extended to urban sectors and the government encouraged the development of individual and jointly established enterprises. The commune and brigade enterprises were renamed as township and village enterprises (TVEs). Between 1985 and 1987, the government took measures to create a favourable environment for TVEs: long distance transportation became legal (encouraging commerce); farmers were allowed to enter the transportation sector; the household registration system (*hukou* system) was partly relaxed to allow farmers to enter and settle in small towns; and preferential credit and tax policies for TVEs were implemented. However, private enterprises were still discriminated against, encouraging many to register as collectively owned, a phenomenon commonly referred to as "putting on a red hat" (*dai hong maozi*). Employment rose three-fold during this period, reaching 95.5 million in 1988.

1989-1991: Policy retrenchment stage

In 1988, TVEs suffered from political controversies about their role in the economy and an austerity programme to combat overheating of the economy. Many TVEs were closed down and production fell by 8 per cent. Several million rural inhabitants returned to their villages and to farming.

1992-1996: Overall development stage

Following Deng Xiaoping's inspection tour of the southern coastal provinces in 1992, when he expressed his support for building "a socialist market economy with Chinese characteristics", the 14th Congress of the CCP in 1992 reaffirmed the importance of TVEs in the Chinese economy. Discrimination against private ownership was reduced. In 1994, TVE ownership reform started to be implemented. Many TVEs began taking off their "red hats". TVEs share of industry value-added reached 52 per cent in this period and employment grew to a historical high of 135.1 million at the end of 1996.

1997-2000: Structural adjustment and institutional innovation stage

The decision of the 15th Congress of the CCP in September 1997 to undertake large-scale privatisation of the state sector spurred an acceleration of the ongoing privatisation of collective TVEs. Due partly to the 1997 Asian crisis, growing financial problems and lagging competitiveness, TVE growth slowed sharply and employment fell.

and was sustained even through the mid-1990s when the rate of productivity growth in the state sector turned negative (Jefferson and Singh, 1999). In addition to its direct effects on growth, this rapid expansion of rural industry also contributed to China's overall economic performance by putting competitive pressure on SOEs (Naughton, 1995), financing the provision of local public goods, and enabling the transfer of part of agricultural surplus labour to non-agricultural activities with higher levels of productivity.

The role of TVEs in the rural economy

TVEs created 83 million new jobs from 1984 to 1996, *i.e.* 7 million per year, and were a major channel for shifting labour from the agricultural to the non-agricultural sector. TVEs contributed to a fall in the percentage of labour engaged primarily in agriculture from 71 per cent in 1978 to 47 per cent in 1999. In 1996, TVE employment peaked at 135 million. By 1998 it had fallen to 125 million, but increased moderately in the following two years to 128 million in 2000 when it represented 27 per cent of rural labour and 18 per cent of the national labour force. Due mainly to the development of TVEs, the share of rural household income from non-agricultural activities has increased from just 22 per cent in 1990 to 43 per cent in 1999.

Wages in TVEs are substantially higher than the average rural income, and the gap is constantly growing. This suggests that while TVEs are contributing to a rise in rural incomes, they have had a rather limited effect on incomes in other sectors of the rural economy, in particular in agriculture. The average wage in TVEs is also growing faster than the average wage in the state sector and while the former is still lower than the latter, the gap has been constantly narrowing, from almost one-half in 1980 to one-third in 1998 (Table 2.2, see also Chapter 16).

Table 2.2. **Wages in the state and TVE sectors and incomes in rural areas**

	Annual average wage in the state sector	Annual average wage in the TVE sector	Rural labour annual net income	TVE/state wages	TVE wages/rural incomes %	State wages/rural incomes %
	A RMB/person	B RMB/person	C RMB/person	B/A %	B/C %	A/C %
1980	762.0	398.0	433.0	52.2	91.9	176.0
1985	1 148.0	676.0	690.0	58.8	97.8	166.4
1990	2 140.0	1 219.0	1 128.0	57.0	108.1	189.7
1995	5 500.0	3 406.0	2 454.0	61.9	138.8	224.1
1997	6 470.0	4 465.0	3 259.0	69.0	137.0	198.5
1998	7 479.0	4 987.0	3 344.0	66.7	149.1	223.7

Source: National Bureau of Statistics, *China Statistical Yearbook* 1999; Ministry of Agriculture, *China TVE Statistical Yearbook*, various editions.

Deterioration in TVE performance

Several indicators of TVE performance deteriorated considerably in the second half of the 1990s. In particular, TVEs' capacity to absorb labour fell, and the marginal propensity of TVEs to create jobs fell significantly even as output continued to increase (WB, 1999). Also, the number of TVEs fell from 23.4 million in 1996 to 20.2 million in 1998 and only slightly increased to 20.8 million in 2000. The drying up of non-agricultural employment opportunities, along with falling agricultural commodity prices has led to much slower rural income growth in recent years (Park, 2001).

However, while employment fell, other indicators provide a more mixed picture. Value added, exports and profits continued to grow, but at significantly slower rates than in the first half of the 1990s. Labour productivity increased substantially. In fact, the available data suggest that the value added/employment ratio improved by 90 per cent between 1995 and 2000 (on the basis of Table 2.3). Ratios of before-tax profits to assets and to sales did not show any marked deterioration tendency and remained well above China's average (Table 2.3 and OECD, 2000). The debt to asset ratio (available for collective TVEs only) remained high at around 60 per cent and was only slightly lower than the national average for SOEs at 65 per cent in 1997 (OECD, 2000). The percentage of loss-making TVEs doubled in the

Table 2.3. **TVEs economic performance, 1995-2000**

	1995	1996	1997	1998	1999	2000
Before-tax profits (1990 billion RMB)[1]	191.0	219.0	246.0	269.0	323.0	339.0
Value added (1990 billion RMB)[1]	756.0	889.0	1 047.0	1 168.0	1 342.0	1 425.0
Exports (1990 billion RMB)[1]	279.0	302.0	351.0	361.0	418.0	455.0
Before-tax profits/assets (%)	14.1	14.6	15.7	12.9	13.2	n.a.
Before-tax profits /sales value (%)	5.5	5.6	6.5	5.1	5.9	6.0
Debt/assets (%)[2]	53.4	62.0	60.2	60.3	58.9	57.7
Loss-making TVEs (%)	5.0	8.4	6.8	6.7	10.2	3.5

1. Nominal values deflated by ex-factory price indices of industrial products.
2. Collective TVE.
Source: TVE Department, Ministry of Agriculture (2000); *Xinhua Monthly*, No. 6, 2000; *China TVE Yearbook 2000*; *China Township Enterprises Daily*, 26 July 2001.

second half of the 1990s to 10.2 per cent in 1999, but fell to just 3.5 per cent in 2000. This compares to a national average of 38 per cent for SOEs in 1997 (OECD, 2000).

Even if TVEs appear to perform significantly better on average that SOEs, a slow-down in TVE development is clearly visible. There are several explanations for this stagnation:

- TVEs' access to lending significantly deteriorated in the second half of the 1990s.

- The privatisation of collective TVEs resulted in temporary adjustment costs and led to a loss of some earlier privileges provided by local authorities.

- The 1994 tax reform increased the effective rate of taxation for TVEs, in particular in western and central provinces.

- A softening in external demand from the 1997 Asian crisis and in internal demand as real GDP growth slowed during the latter half of the 1990s led to a shift from buyers' to sellers' markets for TVE products. The result was intensified competition on the domestic market (Park, 2001) and fierce price-cutting. TVEs were also forced to incur additional costs to improve quality.

- The deepening of reforms of state owned enterprises (SOEs) reduced the organisational advantages that TVEs had enjoyed over SOEs in the area of enterprise autonomy (Ho, Bowles and Dong, 2000).

- More stringent environmental legislation led to the closing down of 170 000 polluting TVEs.

Some of the above-mentioned causes can be considered as temporary (*e.g.* consequences of the Asian crisis), or even one-time factors (*e.g.* closing-down enterprises for old bad loans or environmental reasons), but there are several structural processes and impediments that will have a longer-term impact on TVEs' performance in the future. Some of these factors, such as privatisation, output markets, labour markets, the tax system and, in particular, the difficult access to formal financing, are examined in greater detail below.

Property rights reform

In the past, collective TVEs were a type of enterprise owned by local government that emerged as an organisational response to imperfect state institutions. Under the then existing conditions this type of enterprise worked much better than either conventional private or state owned enterprises (Che and Qian, 1998). In fact, collective TVEs were quite often a complementary and brighter side of SOEs, but not entirely distinct from them.

In the mid-1990s, while the vast majority of TVEs were already private, small-scale enterprises, collective TVEs accounted for almost half of total TVE employment and 64 per cent of total TVE value added. To face the new challenges, ownership reform of collective TVEs was deemed necessary. The 15th CPC National Congress held in 1997 further accelerated this process. Property rights reform of collective TVEs can be considered as one of the most striking trends in recent years.

The overall statistical assessment of the scope of property rights reform is not easily available and sometimes confusing. According to official statistics, 193 000 collective TVEs had been transformed by 1999 with 87 per cent of them becoming so-called "joint-stock co-operatives", and 13 per cent shareholding enterprises. The capital ownership structure of the transformed TVEs is mixed. In 1999, local collectives and the state accounted for one-third of total capital (collectives 32 per cent and the state 2 per cent), individuals for 38 per cent, other legal identities for 23 per cent, and foreign capital for 6 per cent (TVE *Statistical Yearbook*, 2000). In fact, the majority of large and medium-size collective TVEs have been transformed into shareholding companies with the majority of shares owned by the managers and employees. Both in transformed and newly-established TVEs, local communities often own a minority of shares. This share is used to meet the formal requirement imposed on TVEs to serve agriculture and rural communities. Small TVEs, particularly those making small profits or those making losses, were usually sold or went bankrupt.

Another indication of the progress in property rights reform can be provided by the fall in importance of collective TVEs, whose share of the total number fell from 7.4 per cent in 1995 to 4.5 per cent in 1999. But as collective TVEs are usually much larger than the average TVE, their share in total TVE employment, while substantially falling, remains high at about 35 per cent. The structural reallocation of resources within TVEs can be demonstrated by the fact that while employment in collective TVEs fell by 17 million between 1995 and 1999, it increased by 15 million in private TVEs over the same period. But even for firms that have remained collective, managerial contracts have increasingly given managers greater profit retention and decentralised decision-making authority (Chen and Rozelle, 1999).

Foreign direct investment (FDI) plays an active role in the property rights reform of relatively large TVEs, mainly in the form of joint ventures with participation of investors originating in most cases from Hong Kong; China; Macao; and Chinese Taipei. At the end of 1999 there were 26.6 thousand TVEs with participation of foreign capital, about 0.1 per cent of the total number. Up to the end of 1999, foreigners invested about US$30 billion in TVEs, or about US$1.1 million per TVE with foreign capital (China TVE Statistical Yearbook, 2000). Between 1979 and 1999, total FDI inflow into China was US$306 billion, meaning that almost 10 per cent of the total was invested in TVEs. In 1999 alone, foreign investment in TVEs amounted to US$3.5 billion, accounting for 8.6 per cent of total FDI inflows (*China Statistical Yearbook*, 2000).

The market environment

Output markets

While there is no doubt that output markets have become more integrated, authors differ in their opinion on the extent to which market integration has been achieved. The importance of local contacts in procuring inputs and in marketing outputs, deficiencies in the communication and transportation systems, and administrative barriers to factor mobility (see below) may all still contribute to the development of rather dispersed, small-scale production oriented to local markets (Hare and West, 1999). In many places, government regulation discourages entry in business areas with a large SOE presence (IFC, 1999). However, Naughton (1999) has challenged this argument with data from provincial input-output tables, which suggest very high levels of inter-provincial trade (similar to US states).

Credit markets

Financing has emerged as a major constraint to TVE development (Park, 2001). TVEs are very sensitive to credit policies, as evidenced by a fall in TVE gross output in 1989 and low growth periods in 1988, 1990 and 1994, which coincides with a fall in lending or low credit expansion (WB, 1999). The financing problem reflects innate structural problems rooted in the continued channelling of financial resources to state enterprises as well as the growing financial fragility and management challenges facing Chinese banks.[2] The share of TVEs in total lending has fallen steadily in the second half of the 1990s and in 2000 was just 6.1 per cent, far below TVEs' importance in the Chinese economy measured by their share in total industrial production or in total exports. Also, the ratio of TVE loans to revenues fell from 8.2 per cent in 1994 to 6.1 per cent in 1999.

In addition to the traditional preference for channelling the bulk of state bank funds to the state-owned sector, in particular during periods of monetary retrenchment (Brandt and Zhu, 1999), there are several objective reasons that led to the fall in lending to TVEs, in particular to collective ones. Financial reforms have heightened the commercial incentives of bank managers (Park and Sehrt, 2000), reducing the incidence of "political" lending to local enterprises (Park and Shen, 2000). Surveys find that the amount of non-performing loans to TVEs increased substantially from 1994 to 1997 in Zhejiang (Brandt, Park, and Wang, 2000). Much of this has to do with the high debt/asset ratio for the collective TVEs. In combination with greater financial competition and higher real interest rates, poor collective TVE performance has led to a collapse in confidence in the ability of TVEs to remain solvent. While in the past bankers relied on township leaders to assume joint-liability for obligations of collective TVEs in their township (Park, 2001), privatisation weakened this relationship, thus making local governments more reluctant to provide such guarantees. On the other hand, privatisation has only partly released TVEs from various non-profit maximisation objectives imposed on them by local authorities. Together with weak property rights over firm assets, ambiguous bankruptcy rules and procedures, vague accounting procedures, and weak legal enforcement, these obligations undermine TVEs' economic viability and accountability, thus undermining their creditworthiness.

Lack of access to finance may prevent TVEs from seizing the new opportunities coming with greater trade integration. This difficulty troubles not just TVEs but also SME, SOE and the private sectors of urban areas, which are to an increasing extent an important source of potential employment growth.

Labour markets

China maintains administrative barriers on labour flows, such as the residence permit (*hukou*) system, restrictions on access to public education and health services, and job category restrictions for migrants (Solinger, 1999). An important evidence of significant rural-urban mobility restrictions is the growing gap between rural and urban incomes since the mid-1980s (see Chapters 3 and 16).

The privatisation process of both SOEs and TVEs may prove beneficial to the development of more integrated labour markets. The more commercial the orientation of enterprise managers, the less willing they will be to bear the costs of making employment decisions based on political considerations such as the desire to pass on rents to employees or maximise employment (Park, 2001). More integrated labour markets should result in smaller discrepancies in labour remuneration between urban and rural areas and across regions. This may, however, work to the disadvantage of some TVEs, which have profited so far from abundant and cheap labour because of the various administrative measures mentioned above that limit opportunities to migrate to urban areas.

TVEs and local governments

Although privatisation of TVEs is reducing the direct role of local governments in TVE management, the relationship between the two remains complex. While TVEs profit from some advantages, such as low or no rents for land, and proportionally lower formal taxes than in the case of SOEs, they remain a major source of revenue for local governments. TVEs are also required to provide contributions to self-raised funds for the provision of social and technical infrastructure, such as schools, health care and transport facilities. Moreover, TVEs have to pay various fees, penalties and contributions that go beyond regular taxes and contributions based on the TVE Law and other national regulations (see Box 2.2). There are several explanations for this situation:

- As discussed further in chapters 18 and 20, local government revenues tend to be insufficient to meet the expenditure responsibilities they are assigned under the central-local government fiscal arrangements.

- Heavy overstaffing of government administration, especially at county and township levels, making limited budgetary allocations far too low to cover the administrative costs.

Box 2.2. Charges and fees imposed on rural industry

The TVE Law, passed in 1996, defined TVEs as various types of enterprises that are funded mainly by rural collective economic organisations or farmers in townships and towns (and villages under their jurisdiction) designed to carry out the *obligations to support agriculture*. Both these obligations and regular taxes paid by the TVE are referred to below as *legal charges*. Apart from that, there are various fees and obligations imposed on TVEs that are referred to below as the TVE *burden*.

Legal charges

Taxes

The most important taxes include: value-added tax at 17 per cent; corporate income tax (*ying jiao suode shui*) at a flat rate of 33 per cent; and a so-called management fee of 0.5 per cent of sales value. The management fee is paid to local governments to cover the costs of local administrative units supervising TVEs and to contribute to local TVE Development Funds.

The fiscal reform of 1994 increased the effective rate of taxation of TVEs. Prior to the reform, China applied progressive corporate income tax rates ranging from 10 per cent to 55 per cent. As the vast majority of TVEs are small, in 1992 the average effective rate was 21 per cent compared to 29 per cent for state owned enterprises (SOEs). The reform brought an increase to a flat rate of 33 per cent. To partly compensate TVEs for their support to agriculture and rural infrastructure, the government decided to reduce the corporate tax to be paid by TVEs by 10 per cent, which brings the effective rate to slightly below 30 per cent.

Obligations to support agriculture

The TVE Law stipulates that TVEs should pay contributions from after-tax profits to support agriculture and take responsibility for the construction of physical and social infrastructure in rural communities. Both the amounts to be paid and the management of funds raised are to be determined by each province (Article 17 of the TVE Law).

According to the TVE Bureau of the Ministry of Agriculture, the total value of "support for agriculture" provided by TVEs amounted to about RMB 100 billion between 1996 and 2000. Half was contributed to various funds and half for rural infrastructure. Township- and village-owned TVEs contribute to their respective governments. Privatised TVEs pay bonuses reflecting the collectively owned share in total capital. Contributions by private enterprises depend on their individual and benevolent initiative.

TVE burden

The TVE burden can be defined as additional fees, penalties and contributions imposed on TVEs by authorities at various levels that go beyond regular taxes and contributions based on the TVE Law and other national regulations (Lu and Li, 1997). These various institutions impose more than 1 000 payments on TVEs that can be classified into four categories: apportionments, penalties, funds collection and fees. Some administrative units charge arbitrary fees for their services that are much higher than the amounts set by state regulations (*Outlook Weekly*, No. 38, 2000). Others force TVEs to make financial contributions under "donations" or "support". Some administrative services originally free of charge have become payable.

According to some estimates, in 1999 the "TVE burden" amounted to RMB 110 billion, accounting for about 20 per cent of TVE after-tax profit (*Farmers' Daily*, 5 June 2000). This burden commonly costs more than the regular taxes paid by TVEs.

- Traditionally strong position of local administration *vis-à-vis* local inhabitants and enterprises, making it possible to impose otherwise unjustifiable charges.

- Lack of clear distinction between the local government and the TVE management – which leaves a large margin for local government intervention in TVE affairs.

- Vague definition of "obligations to support agriculture" (see Box 2.2), which provides local authorities with the opportunity to justify additional fees and charges on TVEs.

This interference has become less evident in more recent years due to the privatisation process and it is clear that significant changes in the relationship between enterprises and local government have already occurred, in particular in terms of increased managerial autonomy in enterprise decision-making. However, local administrations remain deeply implanted in local economic structures and this is manifested in at least three important ways. Firstly, local governments have managed to secure large shares in the largest local enterprises undergoing privatisation. Secondly, the extensive regulatory environment which enterprises face with respect to investment project approval, safety standards, tax compliance, labour and environmental regulations etc., requires enterprise managers to maintain a good relationship with the local government. Thirdly, the funds accumulated through leasing and selling enterprise assets and managed by the Collective Assets Management Company (CACM) (*jiti zichan jingying gongshi*) provide local governments with important sources of economic influence (Ho, Bowles and Dong, 2000).

Anticipated effects of China's membership of WTO

TVE *employment*

Industry is the most important TVE activity, accounting for 71 per cent of total TVE output value and 58 per cent of total TVE employment in 1999 (Figures 2.1 and 2.2). Therefore, the trade liberalisation impacts on TVE employment will materialise mainly through the impacts on TVE industrial employment. The most important sectors (in order of numbers employed) are mineral and metal products, textiles and clothing, mining and quarrying, other manufacturing, and food, beverages and tobacco. In total, these industries account for almost 70 per cent of total TVE industrial employment.

TVEs are heavily involved in the export sector. In the first half of the 1990s, TVE exports grew in real terms by 45 per cent annually and their share in China's total exports increased from 16 per cent in 1990 to 48 per cent in 1996. In the second half of the 1990s, the rate slowed and in 2000 fell below the national average leading to a fall in the share to 42 per cent (Table 2.1). Three leading industries account for about half of TVE exports: light industry, textiles and clothing. In the 1990s there was quite an important structural change in TVE exports: while the share of the clothing sector remained high and rather stable, the share of textiles fell substantially and the importance of other light industry products strongly increased. Other important export categories include handicrafts as well as local products, foodstuffs and machinery. China continues to have a strong relative cost advantage in producing labour-intensive consumer goods compared to most Asian competitors, but competition is growing from South Asia and Vietnam, as well as from Southeast Asian countries where currency devaluation following the Asian crisis has made them more competitive.

Thus, while TVEs are engaged in a wide range of industrial and non-industrial activities, exports are heavily concentrated in light industrial consumer goods, clothing, and textiles. These include industries that stand to make the greatest gains from China's WTO entry (see Chapter 4). On the other hand, the biggest potential loser from WTO, the automobile industry, is almost non-existent in the TVE industrial structure. TVE firms, like all industrial firms, will face increased domestic competition. This will increase the importance of shifting production lines to those for which China has a comparative advantage.

However, to benefit from trade liberalisation TVEs will have to substantially improve the quality of products destined for export. Partly due to the relatively easy period of TVE development until the mid-1990s, the current product structure of TVEs is predominated by manufactured goods, which are in most cases characterised by low value-added, low and outdated technological standards, high energy and wasteful raw material consumption and, in certain cases, environmental pollution.

In order to assess the potential trade liberalisation impact on TVE employment in quantitative terms, the simulation results obtained from the dynamic computable general equilibrium (CGE) model applied for the Chinese economy will be used. Another part of this study provides very detailed analysis of these results for Chinese industry as a whole (Zhai and Li (2000)). The model compares WTO impacts on various variables, including employment, for 53 sectors, including 34 industrial sectors. The base year for the data and the model is 1997. The model simulates WTO impacts against baseline

93

scenario (no WTO entry) for subsequent years up to 2010. Trade liberalisation impacts on TVE employment are estimated below, on the assumption that the percentage changes by industrial sector in TVE industries are the same as for Chinese industries as a whole. As the overall TVE industrial structure is rather out-dated (1995), detailed and more up-dated (1999) information on the collective TVE industrial structure is used as a proxy for the overall TVE industrial structure.

Taking into account these highly approximate assumptions, the simulation suggests that the WTO impact on TVE industrial employment will be positive, with overall industrial TVE employment higher in 2010 by 2.0 per cent compared to the baseline scenario (no WTO entry). This compares to simulated 0.9 per cent growth in employment over the baseline scenario for the Chinese industry as a whole. This relatively positive result for TVEs reflects the fact that the share of labour-intensive manufacturing sectors, which tend to gain in total TVE industrial production, is relatively high, while the share of capital-intensive or highly protected sectors, which tend to lose, is relatively low.

The results also suggest that employment gains in TVE enterprises are expected to be strongly concentrated in the broadly defined textile sector, which includes textiles, garments and chemical fibres. The simulation suggests that 92 per cent of employment gains will be in this sector. In contrast, employment losses are expected to be more evenly distributed with machinery and other manufacturing losing the most in terms of total employment numbers, but the falls in percentage terms are expected to be negligible.

Under the above-mentioned assumptions, a rise in industrial TVE employment by 2.0 per cent would represent an increase of between 1.5-2.2 million industrial TVE workers over the baseline scenario results. Therefore, industrial TVEs would be likely to absorb a large part of the 3.1 million agricultural workers, shown by the simulation results as losing jobs in agriculture due to China's WTO accession.

However, it has to be underlined that the WTO impacts on employment will be negligible compared to the simulated overall employment changes that would happen even if China were to remain outside the WTO. The baseline (no WTO entry) simulations suggest that overall employment in non-agricultural activities (secondary and tertiary sectors) would increase from 282 million in 1997 to 454 million in 2010, i.e. by 61 per cent, and that agricultural employment would fall from 354 million to 280 million, i.e. by 21 per cent.

There is an important question as to what extent labour moving out from agriculture would be absorbed by non-agricultural activities in rural areas and what percentage would migrate to urban areas. Two hypothetical scenarios are briefly discussed below. One is based on the assumption that there is no relaxation of China's labour market regulations and that TVEs would have to absorb, in the extreme case, all of the labour moving out from agriculture. Another scenario is based on the assumption that labour market legislation would be partially relaxed and that TVEs would absorb one third of labour moving out from agriculture, with the remainder finding employment in urban industries. Table 2.4 summarises basic assumptions and results.

Table 2.4. **Hypothetical TVE employment scenarios between 1997 and 2010**

	Number of workers leaving agriculture (Million)	Labour market legislation	Number of agricultural workers absorbed by TVEs (Million)	Number of agricultural workers absorbed by other sectors of economy (Million)	Annual increase in TVE employment (Million)
Scenario I	74.9	Hukou system strictly applied	74.9	0.0	5.8
Scenario II	74.9	Partial relaxation of labour market regulations	24.7	50.2	1.9

Source: Secretariat calculations based on simulations from Zhai and Li (2000).

The first scenario would necessitate an annual job creation by TVEs of 5.8 million between 1997 and 2010, which seems to be highly unrealistic taking into account recent developments in TVE employment, discussed above. Actually, to make up for a fall in TVE employment between 1997 and 2000 (3 million; see Table 2.1) and to absorb a fall in agricultural employment at 74.9 million, TVEs would need to create about 7.8 million new jobs annually between 2001 and 2010. This would be even more than in the most prosperous period of 1984-1996, when TVEs profited from the backing of local governments and were making strong inroads on SOEs. Moreover, taking into account growing competitive pressures, TVEs will be forced to improve quality, partly through improvements in technology, which will lead to capital for labour substitution, thus diminishing the possibility for absorbing new labour.

The second scenario would require that TVEs create annually 1.9 million jobs between 1997 and 2010. However, to make up for the fall in TVE employment between 1997 and 2000 and still to absorb the 24.7 million workers leaving agriculture, TVEs would need to create 2.1 million jobs annually between 2001 and 2010. This scenario requires that TVEs accelerate job creation compared to the last two years (about 1.5 million a year), which is fairly realistic, in particular if rural industries in interior provinces are better linked to domestic and foreign markets (see section below). However, even more importantly, such a scenario requires that labour market legislation allows for a large outflow of labour from rural areas.

Under the second scenario, urban areas would need to absorb two-thirds of labour leaving agriculture, *i.e.* about 50 million by the year 2010. This is not an unrealistic assumption. The relatively low urbanisation rate of 36 per cent in 2000, lower than would be expected if China's GDP per capita is taken as a reference,[3] indicates that the urbanisation process in China has so far been impeded and that there exists significant room for a larger shift of labour from rural to urban areas. Moreover, despite various administrative measures imposed on labour flows, there is a large migration from rural areas to the cities. This flow grew rapidly in the 1990s as networks developed among migrants from the same town, county, or even province, providing information and local contacts to locate work opportunities, largely for construction work, in large urban cities. This flow of migrants reportedly slowed in the late 1990s due to the cooling of the economy, but some estimates place the number of these migrants during the peak period of economic growth in the 1990s as high as 100 million.

Regional patterns

Firms located in the eastern provinces of China have always been privileged, with relatively easy access both to export markets and to large domestic markets in the densely populated and rich coastal regions. Partly as a result, rural industries in China have been heavily concentrated on the coast, despite periodic efforts to encourage the establishment of more TVEs in interior provinces.

Table 2.5 summarises various regional indicators of TVE performance in 1999. While the coast (Eastern provinces) contains 40 per cent of the nation's rural labour force, it accounts for 52 per cent of TVE employment and 63 per cent of TVE output value. This compares to 25 per cent, 14 per cent and only 9 per cent, respectively, for the west.

The distribution of TVEs directly linked to the international economy is much more biased than the patterns of overall TVE production (Park, 2001). In 1999, 92 per cent of TVE exports were produced in the coastal provinces. Fifteen per cent of TVE workers worked in exporting firms on the coast, compared to only 1 per cent in the west. In coastal provinces, 5 per cent of TVE workers were in joint ventures, compared to just 0.2 per cent in the west. Guangdong Province, next to Hong Kong, alone accounted for 33 per cent of national employment in exporting TVEs, and 25 per cent of employment in TVE joint ventures (*China TVE Yearbook*, 2000). The employment shares for Zhejiang, Jiangsu, Fujian, and Shandong were also more than or near to 10 per cent for both TVE exporting firms and TVE joint ventures (*China TVE Yearbook*, 2000). Regional concentration of production for export is not just a TVE phenomenon. Three-quarters of all Chinese exports (not only of TVEs) came from six coastal provinces in 1994

Table 2.5. **Regional indicators of TVE performance in 1999**

Share of national total, %

	East	Centre	West	China
National shares:				
Rural employment	40.0	34.7	25.2	100
TVE enterprises	43.8	37.5	18.7	100
TVE employment	51.8	34.2	14.0	100
TVE output value	63.3	28.0	8.7	100
TVE value added	60.9	30.8	8.2	100
TVE profit	55.2	36.8	8.0	100
TVE export value	92.2	6.8	1.0	100
TVE joint venture employment	93.9	5.1	0.9	100
TVE share of rural employment	35.0	26.7	15.1	27.1
Share of TVE employment in exporting firms	14.5	2.4	1.0	8.5
TVE export value/TVE output value	10.4	1.7	0.8	7.1
Share of TVE employment in joint venture firms	5.1	0.4	0.2	2.8

Note: East region includes Beijing, Tianjin, Hebei, Shandong, Liaoning, Guangxi, Jiangsu, Zhejiang, Shanghai, Guangdong, Fujian, and Hainan (12 provinces). Centre region includes Inner Mongolia, Heilongjiang, Jilin, Shanxi, Anhui, Henan, Hubei, Hunan, Jiangxi (9 provinces). West includes Shaanxi, Gansu, Ningxia, Qinghai, Xinjiang, Chongqing, Sichuan, Guizhou, Yunnan, Tibet (10 provinces).

Source: *China Township and Village Enterprise Statistical Yearbook* 2000, Ministry of Agriculture (MOA).

(Perkins, 1999). Also, from 1978 to 1998, FDI in the eastern coastal region represented 88 per cent, while the central region attracted 9 per cent and the western region only 3 per cent (Park, 2001).

Hare and West (1999) find that the spatial pattern of TVE development does not demonstrate strong characteristics of a trend toward greater regional specialisation as predicted by the theory of comparative advantage. They suggest that policies may contribute to such outcomes. State interventions in pricing and resource allocation decisions led to resource misallocation at the nationwide level. Moreover, the 1994 tax reform put the interior provinces at a disadvantage *vis-à-vis* the coastal areas. Actually, the tax reform, although successful in other respects, increased the tax burden for the interior from 21 per cent to 33 per cent, well above the favourable tax rates of 15 per cent in the special economic zones and 24 per cent in the development zones, most of which are in the East (Jian, 1997). Furthermore, the west continues to suffer from severe market handicaps in developing industry, such as poor transportation infrastructure, as well as relatively limited supplies of skilled or highly educated labour.

There is considerable room for specialisation based on comparative advantage within the TVE sector, and for linkages to agriculture in some areas, provided that state policies refrain from interventions in resource allocations. In particular, Li (2001) argues that TVEs producing food, drinks, tobacco and feed and providing services for the agricultural marketing channels (*e.g.* storage, packaging and transportation), characterised by high labour-intensity, close location to agricultural production and not requiring highly qualified staff, could be relatively easily developed in the western provinces, even within the more competitive framework of China's WTO membership.

Because WTO membership will open markets for goods produced by firms located primarily on the coast, it will be a great policy challenge to nurture linkages to the economies (and labour) of interior regions (Park, 2001). This can happen if rural labour from interior regions has better access to a national labour market, and if firms in the interior have supportive institutions that facilitate adjustment to the realignments in comparative advantage that will occur with more open markets and even greater export orientation of firms on the coast. The state should cease price controls of raw materials and should refrain from interventions in resource allocation decisions as they work against residents of inland provinces by holding down prices of these materials supplied to other regions and by keeping labour prices in these provinces at artificially low levels. Stronger state support for physical infrastructure and education services in central and western provinces would further support alleviating the interregional inequalities (Hare and West, 1999).

Summary and policy priorities in light of trade liberalisation

The direct impact of trade liberalisation on TVEs will be rather positive. A relatively large part of the industrial TVE enterprises are in labour-intensive manufacturing sectors, which are likely to gain, and a relatively small part of these enterprises are in industrial sectors that are likely to lose from China's WTO accession. Many TVEs are already export oriented and are relatively well integrated into international markets. A large part of collective TVEs have gone through the ownership transformation process, which has made them better prepared to compete on domestic and international markets. However, the recent deterioration in TVE sector performance provides important warnings of the institutional challenges that TVEs face in trying to fulfil their market potential (Park, 2001).

The relative importance of TVEs in the Chinese economy is likely to decline in the medium term as TVEs lose some of their privileges, and urban enterprises, including privatised and restructured SOEs and private SMEs, profit from easier access to domestic and foreign markets, to qualified labour, to financial institutions, and to better infrastructure. Labour market reforms that ease the access of rural labour to urban labour markets will promote convergence of wages and so reduce TVEs current privileged position in this respect. Reforms in social benefits will eventually lead to more uniform costs for these benefits across different types of enterprises (see Chapter 16). Urban enterprises will be released from some of their social obligations *vis-à-vis* their employees (such as provision of housing), while TVEs will probably face higher charges to provide their employees with social benefits similar to those expected to be enjoyed by urban employees (such as pensions). The gap in labour costs will therefore further close over time.

However, TVEs will still have an important role to play in rural areas and, in particular, in absorbing a relatively large part of labour moving out from agriculture. It is realistic to expect that TVEs will be able to create about 2 million new jobs annually by the year 2010, which would mean employing about one-third of the likely annual outflow of labour from agriculture. This scenario would require overcoming the fall in TVE employment of the second half of the 1990s, but would not entail a return to the TVE boom period of 1984-1996 when TVEs created about 7 million new jobs annually. The scenario is likely to be the net result of two diverging tendencies: while technological improvements, further restructuring of collective TVEs, and deepening of reforms in private enterprises will continue to exert a downward pressure on employment, the more efficient TVEs that result from this process, along with newly established TVEs, will create new employment opportunities.

Ultimately, the economic distinction between TVEs and urban SMEs is likely to disappear. TVEs will become a rural part of the SME sector in China. There is a wide range of policies that should create an enabling framework for further development of rural non-agricultural enterprises in China. Reforms of the second half of the 1990s resulted in a qualitatively new situation. These enterprises will struggle if enabling market institutions do not emerge. In particular, policies should address broad failures in the functioning of financial, labour and distribution markets as well as in fiscal and administration systems:

- Financing has emerged as a major constraint to TVE development. As competition intensifies and market demands shift from quantity to quality of goods and services, capital market distortions may prevent TVEs from realising their development capacity. TVEs are under growing pressure to adopt a new growth strategy based on technological innovation, and to undertake further restructuring in order to improve the quality and technological levels of product structures. This necessitates access to capital markets on equal terms with other types of enterprises. Privatisation of SOEs and financial market reforms should limit the level of funds channelled on privileged terms to the state-owned sector, but further reforms of bank lending and institutional innovation in the provision of finance (including in rural areas) would be needed to address this major constraint.

- All economic indicators are more favourable for TVEs located in the eastern provinces than for those in central and western provinces. The latter are disadvantaged by smaller local markets owing to the lower population and purchasing power in these regions, more difficult access to foreign markets, undeveloped infrastructure, higher transportation costs, lower education level of employees, and limited access to capital, qualified personnel and modern technology. Removing internal bottlenecks provides the benefits similar to those associated with external trade liberalisation. If western and central provinces are able to shift resources to activities in which they have a comparative advantage (*e.g.* food processing), they could benefit from more integrated markets even as they lose market share in other products that are purchased from coastal provinces. If they retain their old production structures or are unable to finance new investments to take advantage of new opportunities, the effects of liberalisation may be one-sided. Coastal provinces may benefit from internal trade liberalisation in the same way that they benefit from international trade liberalisation – gaining access to cheaper inputs and to larger output markets (Park, 2001).

- Ownership and contract reforms should be further encouraged to strengthen the profit incentives and promote healthy corporate governance structures of enterprises and financial institutions. This process of institutional development will play a critical role in achieving successful structural adjustment. The government should police against internal trade barriers and other distortions (*e.g.* local government fee extractions) that limit competition and the integration of internal markets. Other possible measures to support private enterprises could include the following: ensure transparent licensing that does not restrict entry to a business; ensure that export licensing is open to the private sector and is used for statistical purposes rather than as an approval process; enforce more strictly the 1993 Law on Protection Against Unfair Competition; strengthen the rule of law, including commercial laws, bankruptcy laws, and contract enforcement.

- TVEs are exposed to various overhead burdens, in particular extractive fees being charged by local governments faced with poor fiscal resources. This situation calls for further reforms in the tax and central-local government fiscal systems to find a better balance between local tax revenues and the redistributive role of the central government budget, for cuts in the size of local bureaucracy, and for the redefinition of the role of TVEs in rural areas to release them from legal obligations to serve agriculture and to change their legal status to make them similar to other private SMEs.

NOTES

1. The process of ownership restructuring means the conversion of collective TVEs into enterprises that are majority owned by non-state entities. Later in this text this process is referred to as property rights reform.

2. However, as documented in Chapter 7 on banking, non-state enterprises, including TVEs, get probably funds indirectly from banks, by borrowing from SOEs or local governments.

3. Urbanisation in China is at about the same rate as in India, but GDP per capita in purchasing power parity is more than two-fold higher in China than in India.

BIBLIOGRAPHY

Brandt, L., A. Park, and S. Wang. (2000),
  Are Financial Reforms Leaving the Poor Behind?: Regional Differences in Bank Performance and Fund Allocation in Rural China, *preliminary results*.

Brandt, L. and X. Zhu (2000),
  "Redistribution in a Decentralized Economy: Growth and Inflation in Reform China", *Journal of Political Economy* 108(2): 422-39.

Che, J. and Y. Qian (1998),
  "Insecure Property Rights and Government Ownership of Firms", *Quarterly Journal of Economics* 113(2): 467-96.

Chen, H. and S. Rozelle (1999),
  "Leaders, Managers, and the Organisation of Township and Village Enterprises in China", *Journal of Development Economics* 60(2): 529-57.

China Statistical Yearbook, National Bureau for Statistics (NBS),
  Beijing, China Statistics Press. Various editions.

China TVE Yearbook, Ministry of Agriculture (MoA),
  Beijing, Agricultural Press. Various editions.

Farmers' Daily. 2000. 5 June.

Hare, D. and L.A. West (1999),
  "Spatial Patterns in China's Rural Industrial Growth and Prospects for the Alleviation of Regional Income Inequality", *Journal of Comparative Economics* 27: 475-497.

Ho, S.P.S., P. Bowles, X. Dong (2000),
  Letting Go of the Small : The Political Economy of Privatising Rural Enterprises in Jiangsu and Shandong, mimeo.

IFC (1999),
  China Private Enterprise Study: A Draft Report, International Finance Corporation.

Jefferson, G. and I. Singh (1999) "Overview", in G. Jefferson and I. Singh, eds. *Enterprise Reform in China: Ownership, Transition, and Performance*, New York: Oxford University Press, pp. 1-22.

Jian, T. (1997),
  "Regional Economic Development, TVEs, and Tax Reforms in China", Development Discussion Paper No. 572, Harvard Institute for International Development, Harvard University.

Knight, J. and L. Song (1999),
  "Increasing Wage Inequality in China: Efficiency versus Equity?" University of Oxford Applied Economics Discussion Paper Series No. 211.

Li, H. and S. Rozelle (2000),
  "Saving or stripping rural industry: an analysis of privatisation and efficiency in China", *Agricultural Economics* 23 (2000) 241-252.

Li, W. (2001),
  "TVEs and Economic Growth in Rural China after the WTO", The International Symposium on the WTO and Chinese Rural Development in 21st Century, Maoming, China, 26-29 June.

Lu, L. and G. Li. (1997),
  "Reflections on the TVE Burden", *China TVE Yearbook*, MoA, pp. 385-388.

Naughton, B. (1995),
  Growing Out of the Plan: Chinese Economic Reform, 1978-92, Cambridge; New York and Melbourne: Cambridge University Press.

Naughton, B. (1999),
  "How Much Can Regional Integration Do to Unify China's Markets?", paper for a conference on Policy Reform in China, Stanford University, 18-20 November.

Outlook Weekly,
   No. 38. 2000.

OECD (2000),
   Reforming China's Enterprises, Paris.

Park, A. (2001),
   "Trade integration and the prospects for rural enterprise development in China", *China's Agriculture in the International Trading System*, proceedings from the OECD workshop, Paris, 16-17 November 2000, OECD.

Park, A., H. Jin, S. Rozelle and J. Huang. (2000),
   Market Emergence and Transition: Transaction Costs, Arbitrage, and Autarky in China's Grain Markets, mimeo.

Park, A. and K. Sehrt. (2000),
   Tests of Financial Intermediation and Banking Reform in China, mimeo.

Park, A., and M. Shen. (2000),
   Joint Liability Lending and the Rise and Fall of China's Township and Village Enterprises, William Davidson Institute Working Paper, University of Michigan.

Perkins, F. (1999),
   "Export Performance and Enterprise Reform in China's Coastal Provinces", in G. Jefferson and I. Singh, eds., *Enterprise Reform in China: Ownership, Transition, and Performance* (New York: Oxford University Press, pp. 241-263).

Solinger, D. (1999),
   Contesting Citizenship in Urban China, Berkeley, Los Angeles, and London: University of California Press.

TVE Department, MoA (2000),
   Analysis of the TVEs Economic Operation in 1999.

World Bank (1999),
   Rural China: Transition and Development, Washington, DC.

World Bank (2000),
   China: Overcoming Rural Poverty, Washington, DC.

Zhai, F. and S, Li (2000),
   "Quantitative analysis and evaluation of the impact of entry to WTO on China's economy", *China Development Review*, Development Research Centre of the State Council of the People's Republic of China.

Chapter 3

IMPLICATIONS FOR THE RURAL ECONOMY

TABLE OF CONTENTS

IMPLICATIONS FOR THE RURAL ECONOMY[*]

Introduction

China's rural economy is experiencing the best of times and the worst of times. Rural incomes have grown steadily for the last two decades, and millions have moved out of poverty. However, rural incomes are in general lower than those in urban areas and millions more remain at or below the poverty line. A growing share of rural incomes originates from non-agricultural activities, some local, others in nearby rural factories, and others in faraway cities and suburbs. At the same time, some farmers in China's poor areas are subsistence, while others who interact with markets frequently face high transaction costs. Markets have emerged in many parts of rural China, providing farmers with access to a growing number of channels for purchasing inputs and consumer goods and for selling their output. However, the household registration system, dividing all households into two categories – rural and urban, artificially fragments China's economy, putting those who live in rural areas at a strong disadvantage in obtaining access to high-paying jobs and China's welfare system. In fact, it is estimated that about 90 per cent of the rural population has no access to any formal welfare system. In general, with rising market integration, various barriers may be declining, but large initial discrepancies in resource, human capital, and locational endowments may require generations to equalise wealth levels.

Trade and investment liberalisation will have both negative and positive effects on rural households, but that, in general, positive effects for the rural economy will prevail. The most important effects may be due to the indirect impacts that trade liberalisation policies will have on the efficiency of the rural economy. The negative effects on rural households will be partly attenuated by policy safeguards and the ability of households to respond through their production and investment decisions. Households in the poorest regions will remain relatively unaffected because of their isolation from the markets due to extreme remoteness and/or high degree of self-sufficiency. In the short-run, the hardest hit group of households will be those in the middle-income areas, in particular those that are located in the far suburbs and the not-so-far-away rural areas.

China should combine trade and investment liberalisation with a number of other transition and rural development policies in order to push for as rapid an evolution towards a modern economy as possible. To address the existing problems in rural areas the new environment should include farm restructuring, land reform, the creation of a new paradigm for migration, improved access to education for rural populations, the development of integrated and competitive domestic markets, and the establishment of predictable and transparent relations with trading partners. In this new framework property rights for agricultural land should become better defined. The rule of law should improve, allowing companies that deal in advanced agricultural technologies to operate profitably. Markets should improve as infrastructure investments begin to reduce transaction costs. The rise of private traders should increase the reliability of markets, while the retreat of the state should reduce the propensity for local officials to intervene.

This chapter consists of four sections. The first section discusses a number of macro-forces that may have important impacts on rural incomes in China. It then traces out the record of rural incomes during the reform period. The second section examines in more detail the performance of non-agricultural employment in the rural economy during the past two decades. The third section attempts to assess the net result of the positive and negative impacts that trade and investment liberalisation may have on rural incomes and employment. Finally, the last section concludes with a discussion of policies that may assist policy makers in minimising the costs and maximising the benefits of liberalisation.

---

[*] This chapter was prepared by Andrzej Kwiecinski, Principal Analyst, Division for Agricultural Policies in Non-Member Economies, Directorate for Food, Agriculture and Fisheries, OECD, with the help of Xiande Li, Consultant. It was written on the basis of a report submitted by Scott Rozelle (University of California, US).

Rural incomes

Domestic macroeconomic dimensions[1]

The rural and urban sectors are dualistic and poorly integrated. China's rural sector has continuously transferred resources to the urban-industrial sector, including capital, food, industrial inputs, and to a lesser extent, labour. Constrained labour flows have contributed to the large differential in rural and urban labour productivity and income. The rural sector has also served to buffer the impact of macroeconomic shocks on the urban economy. The spread of market forces and increased reliance on competitive prices have tended to increase the flow of labour and other resources and improve integration in recent years. However, unless labour movement constraints are lifted, the dualistic nature will remain.

As China has moved from a planned to a more market-oriented economy, balanced sectoral growth and integration have become more important. The urban-industrial sector provides the demand for the rural sector's marketed surplus, and as the agricultural economy becomes an increasingly smaller component of the national economy (see Chapter 1), changes in growth rates of the industrial and service sectors will have increasingly strong effects on the agricultural and rural economy.

Domestic terms of trade

In most countries, growth in the total productivity of all production factors (land, labour and capital) – total factor productivity (TFP) – and slowly growing demand for agricultural products have led to declining agricultural terms of trade – despite various price support and subsidy programmes. In China, however, rising domestic demand for food, periodic strong rises in procurement prices fixed by the government, the growing role of market prices for agricultural products, and price controls over input prices contributed to a substantial improvement in agricultural terms of trade between 1978-95, as reflected in the ratio of prices received by farmers to prices paid by farmers. In the second half of the 1990s the terms of trade deteriorated, but in 1999 they were still more advantageous for farmers by about 50 per cent than at the beginning of the reform process. As China's agricultural markets are becoming more open to both domestic and international competition it may be expected that price tendencies prevailing in market economies will be transmitted into China. This may mean that in the long-run agricultural terms of trade will tend to deteriorate. However, other national policies and events, not effectively captured in terms of trade calculations, contributed in the past (in particular until the mid-1990s) to both implicit and explicit transfers from rural to urban sectors. These effects are discussed in the section below.

Fiscal and financial flows

Over the reform period direct budgetary expenditures to agricultural activities have been greater than tax receipts from agriculture, but the net *fiscal flow* to the rural economy declined during the 1990s. Fiscal expenditures include allocations for investments in irrigation, land improvement, specialty crop production bases, etc. However, as taxes from rural-based industries (TVEs) have been considerably greater than the net flow to agriculture, a net outflow from the rural economy has occurred. The net annual rural-to-urban fiscal flow averaged about RMB114 billion (constant 1995) over the 1994-96 period (Table 3.1).

Large amounts of off-budget funds (not included in Table 3.1) are generated in the rural sector through various fees and unofficial taxes-levied particularly on TVEs but also on agriculture (see Chapter 2 and Box 3.1). To the extent that these resources are *not* spent in rural areas, additional outflow of rural resources may occur through unofficial channels that are not captured in the consolidated fiscal statements. In fact, farmers in China are taxed through various taxes, levies and fees, which can be grouped into four categories: state or federal taxes, township levies, village levies and miscellaneous fees, levies and fines (Box 3.1). The first three categories are well recorded in official statistics, both at central and provincial levels. But the fourth category (miscellaneous fees, levies and fines) comprises payments that are arbitrary and mostly illegal, and as such not captured by statistics. According to some field surveys, the share of these payments in the total could be as high as 50 per cent (Fu, 2001; Chai, *et al.*, 1999).

Table 3.1. **Resource flows from agricultural and rural sectors
to non-agricultural and urban sectors**

RMB billion, constant 1995 prices

	Fiscal system		Financial system		Grain	Total resource flow	
	Agri. to non-agr. (1)	Rural to urban (2)	Agri. to non-agr. (3)	Rural to urban (4)	Marketing (implicit tax) (5)	Agri. to non-agr. (6)	Rural to urban (7)
1980	−38.5	−30.0	13.2	3.7	46.0	20.8	19.7
1985	−18.4	11.8	23.5	7.4	15.6	20.7	34.8
1990	−31.1	16.1	68.9	47.8	43.0	80.8	106.9
1991	−35.6	20.0	59.4	28.3	27.9	51.6	76.2
1992	−35.8	38.5	56.9	17.3	20.8	41.8	76.5
1993	−28.5	103.8	49.1	8.6	24.9	45.5	137.4
1994	−26.4	105.2	53.4	38.3	59.5	86.4	203.1
1995	−21.3	122.5	51.1	27.8	50.2	80.0	200.6
1996	−22.1	113.2	44.0	27.6	32.9	54.7	173.7

1. Total equals sum of columns (1),(3) and (5).
Source: Derived from *China Finance Yearbook* and *China Statistical Yearbook*, various years.

Box 3.1. **Taxes and fees paid by farmers**

Until 2000, farmers faced four categories of taxes, levies and fees. They add up to a considerable overall burden on farm households. The four major categories include:

1. *Government taxes*. They include the so-called agricultural tax, special agricultural product tax, and animal slaughtering tax. This part of the overall tax burden is relatively small, at least relative to farm incomes.

2. *Township levies*. These levies are to be paid under the so-called "Five Unified Plans" (*Five Tongchou*): Education supplement tax, social expenses, family planning, public (collective) transportation, and militia exercises expenses.

3. *Village levies*. These levies are to be paid under the so-called "three contributions" (*Three Tiliu*): contributions to the public accumulation fund, the public welfare fund and other administration fees.

4. *Miscellaneous fees, levies and fines*. They are to be paid to other government institutions at different hierarchical levels.

Moreover, each farmer has to contribute about one month of obligatory work for the local community in the framework of *"labour accumulation work"* and " *rural compulsory work"*.

As the various taxes, fees, and levies have presented a considerable and growing burden for farmers (*"peasant burden"*) and led to social unrest or even violent demonstrations against local authorities, the government declared, already in 1991, that the combined levies of categories 2 and 3 ("*Five Tongchou*" & "*Three Tiliu*") should not exceed a level of 5 per cent of farmers' net income earned during the previous year. As the measure was limited to only two of the four categories, the effect on controlling the overall tax burden proved to be very limited in practice. To circumvent the 5 per cent limit, fees in category 4 were increased or items of the tax base in categories 2 and 3 were shifted to category 4. As a result, the effective burden on farmers increased while the proportion paid under the "*Five Tongchou*" and "*Three Tiliu*" fell.

A new a pilot tax experiment in 50 counties of seven provinces was launched in 1996. This experiment was extended to the whole province of Anhui in 2000. It was called the "tax-for-fees" reform and was designed to replace all "unreasonable" fees and charges levied upon farmers ("*Tiliu and Tongchou*") by an agricultural tax set at 7 per cent of the value of agricultural output and an agricultural tax supplement at 1.4 per cent. While there were differences in the evaluation of the results of this experiment, it was initially decided to extend it to all other provinces in 2001, but later it was suspended due to inadequate financial resources. The success of reform will depend to a large extent on the restructuring of local administrations, including an estimated reduction of about 20 per cent in the number of administrative workers. Equally important will be the reallocation of fiscal resources from the central to local government budgets, as the reform will lower local tax revenues, and better governance at the local level, including more transparency in the funds' use.

China's financial sector, like those in other Asian economies, lagged behind the development of the real sector, remains structurally weak, and potentially puts rural growth and development at risk. Analysis of data from the banking system indicates a net transfer of financial resources from agriculture to industry throughout the reform period, although such findings need to be interpreted with caution because of concerns about the coverage of the available statistics (Park, Brandt, and Giles, 2000). Consolidated data on rural savings and loans exclude transactions of Rural Credit Foundations (RCFs), the smallest of the rural credit institutions, and results in a modest understatement of the *financial flows*. Conversely, the inclusion of Agricultural Development Bank (ADB) data contributes to overstating financial flows, as its lending is almost exclusively for agricultural procurement by government marketing agencies. Many deposits in the Agricultural Bank of China (ABC) are by urban residents. After making allowances for these shortcomings, it is clear that, although township and village enterprises (TVEs) absorb a portion of these transfers of agriculture to industry, a significant rural-to-urban financial flow (RMB31 billion per year in 1995 real terms) continued during the 1994-96 period (Table 3.1). Whether the financial flows reflect the response of rational investors moving funds from low-return to high-return sectors or whether they result from distortions in the financial and fiscal system is undetermined, but the massive movement of funds out of agriculture and the rural economy highlights the importance of the sector and emphasises the importance of keeping it healthy.

Rural income trends

One of the great achievements of China's first two decades of reform is the strong and steady growth of real per capita rural incomes (Table 3.2). Real rural income rose by 249 per cent between 1980 and 1999 (column 1). The rise from RMB616 per capita in 1980 to 2 210 in 1999 produced an annual rate of increase of 7 per cent (column 4).

The rate of increase, however, has not been the same across time or among all of the sub-groups in China. After rising by 14 per cent annually in the early reform years (1980 to 1985), the growth of rural incomes slowed in the late 1980s to only 3 per cent annually. Since then income growth rates have accelerated, rising by 5 per cent annually between 1990 and 1995 and then by 6 per cent annually in the late 1990s (derived from Table 3.2).

The rates in China's poor areas, while still positive and quite rapid in some periods, have lagged behind those of the rest of the economy during most of the reform era until recently (Table 3.2). Large discrepancies separate those living in the richer coastal area and those in the poorer inland areas. The average rural resident in the east has an income (RMB2 929) that is almost double that of the average resident living in the west (RMB1 502). Similarly, average expenditure levels are also almost double in the east, while the amount of income that a household is required to spend on food is much lower. The Gini coefficient of rural incomes rose from 0.24 in the early 1980s to 0.35 in 1999 (Table 3.2), although, in part because of the robust performance of those in poor areas, the rate of increase of the Gini ratios slowed in the 1990s. Intra-rural inequality is socially sensitive since rural residents may be more aware

Table 3.2. **Real incomes in rural and urban households in China, 1980-1999**

	Real per capita income index			Real per capita net income in 1999 prices (RMB)		
	Rural (1)	Poorest (20%) (2)	Gini coefficient (3)	Rural (4)	Urban (5)	Urban/rural ratio (6)
1980	100	100	0.24	616	2062	3.35
1985	189	165	0.26	1 193	2 605	2.18
1990	218	177	0.31	1 380	3 217	2.33
1995	272	193	0.33	1 702	4 713	2.77
1999	349	252	0.35	2 210	5 854	2.65

1. Gini coefficient of income distribution. Higher value indicate greater income inequality.
Sources: National Bureau of Statistics, 1989-2000, and rural household income and expenditure surveys.

Table 3.3.   **Rural poverty in China, 1978-1999**

	Rural population (million)	Absolute poverty (million)	Incidence (%)
1980	790.47	218	27.58
1985	807.57	96	11.89
1990	841.42	85	10.10
1995	859.47	65	7.56
1996	864.39	58	6.71
1997	866.37	50	5.57
1998	868.68	42	4.83
1999	870.17	34	3.91

Source: Poverty data for 1978-1989 are from *"China: Strategies for Reducing Poverty in the 1990s"*, World Bank, Washington 1992; for 1990-1999, data are from *China Agricultural Development Report*, various issues, Ministry of Agriculture (MOA); Rural population data are from National Bureau of Statistics, *China Statistical Yearbook*, various issues.

of the differences in standard of living between themselves and other rural counterparts (Rozelle, 1996). Some of the gap may be due to factors restricting the flow of labour and other resources between rich and poor rural areas.

The steady rise of incomes in rural areas, especially those in poor areas, has led to historic rates of poverty alleviation during the reform era, although China's poor still remain at very low levels of income (Table 3.2). Using China's own poverty lines (about US$0.70 per day), the number of people in poverty fell from 260 million in 1978 to 34 million in 1999. Measured as a proportion of China's rural population, the incidence of poverty fell from 33 per cent in 1978 to 4 per cent in 1999. However, China's poverty line is lower than the line applied by the World Bank to measure poverty in other countries (US$1 per day, World Bank, 2000). If the World Bank's standard is applied, although the progress in eliminating poverty is still remarkable (174 million people rose above the US$1 per day poverty line between 1990 and 1998), there are still more than 100 million people living below that income level (World Bank, 2000).

Rural-urban income dichotomy

The fact that during the reform era China has experienced an exceptional increase in inequality, is cause for concern. Gini ratios for the whole country (combining rural and urban residents) have been above 0.40 since the early 1990s and have continued to rise. China's rural-urban income gap is large by international standards. In nominal terms, the rural/urban per capita income ratio declined from 0.54 in 1985 to 0.35 in 1994, then recovered by five percentage points between 1994 and 1997, but fell again to 0.36 in 2000. These ratios compare poorly with Vietnam where the 1997/98 rural per capita income level was 67 per cent of that of urban incomes (Bales, 1998). Even when adjusting official rural and urban income data for housing costs and other poorly measured or excluded components of income, rural/urban income ratios do not improve. Further, Yang and Zhou's (1996) analysis of rural-urban income ratios for 36 countries over the 1985-1995 decade demonstrated that urban incomes are rarely more than twice rural incomes. Only one country (out of the 22 for which 1995 data were available) exceeded China's urban/rural income ratio. Using consumption as an income proxy, China also compares unfavourably with India in terms of its rural/urban inequality. In 1993-94 China's per capita rural/urban consumption ratio was 0.28, while India's was 0.61.

The rural/urban ratio using constant 1985 prices reflects the differential increases in the cost of living between rural and urban areas, and illustrates a similar but slightly more modest decline in relative incomes. However, these data underestimate both rural and urban in-kind income. Price deflators adjust for differential price changes but not price levels. Adjusting for this differential (15 per cent), imputing rent to rural incomes and adjusting urban incomes to include in-kind income for housing, education, health care, pensions and other subsidised services provide more accurate income estimates. These adjustments lowered rural incomes to 31 per cent of urban incomes in 1990-substantially less than the 45 per cent suggested by official data (World Bank, 1997).

The large rural-urban income gap stems from a large differential in labour productivity and to constrained factor mobility, especially labour and capital; it also reflects the arbitrary nature in which wage levels are set. Although only examining data through 1992, Yang and Zhou (1996) determined that the marginal productivity of labour in agriculture, TVEs, and SOEs was RMB601, RMB1 211, and RMB9 346 respectively, in 1992. Such large productivity gaps indicate that, among other factors, barriers to labour mobility impede a narrowing of the differential – despite large numbers of sanctioned migration and larger numbers of "floating" population. The government attempts to control the pace of migration to ensure urban services are not overwhelmed, and in part to assure urban grain sufficiency. Other factors also constrain migration. For example, housing, medical, education and other social services are unavailable to those migrating from rural to urban areas. Moreover, there is a lack of job information. Government policies continue to support and subsidise urban standards of living, including soft budget constraints for state-owned enterprises (protecting urban jobs), and low-cost capital for urban enterprises, although housing and enterprise reforms and taxation are mitigating these benefits as urban workers now pay higher rents and contribute more to their pension and medical benefits.

It is important to note that rural-urban income disparities have worsened during the reform period despite rapid growth in rural industrial employment, output, and wages (TVE wages have grown at 18 per cent annually), and the substantial direct and indirect contribution to the rural economy (see Chapter 2). Unquestionably, rapid TVE expansion prevented the income ratio from being even more adverse, but it was unable to reverse the worsening trend.

As a large part of rural incomes comes from agriculture, it will be very difficult to improve the trends in rural/urban income ratios without improving labour efficiency and productivity through increased capital/labour and land/labour ratios in agriculture. While making capital more accessible can increase the former ratio, significant increases in the land/labour ratio can be achieved only by transferring labour out of agriculture. During the early and mid-1990s, increasing agricultural prices contributed to increasing rural incomes, preventing further deterioration in the rural/urban income ratio, but additional reliance on agricultural price policy may be limited in the framework of China's WTO commitments. Shifting production to higher value commodities and continued improvements in total factor productivity will permit modest income growth in agriculture, but without additional land and capital per agricultural labourer, future per capita income growth will be slow in agriculture.

Rural labour

The importance of rural labour markets

For China to modernise successfully, the nation must rely on labour markets to facilitate the shift from a largely rural population to an urban one. Barriers to migration appear to be primarily on the urban side, although scholars still debate whether or not rural institutions affect migration decisions. Some researchers believe that significant barriers still exist in China's rural areas and that the absence of well-functioning rural labour markets may be hindering growth. For example, Meng (1990; 1996) finds substantial evidence of non-market labour assignment and allocation behaviour in the rural industrial sector. Several scholars have focused on institutional features in rural and urban areas that may constrain the movement of labour, despite high wage gaps and positive expected gains from migration. Mallee (1996) and Yang and Zhou (1996) believe a number of barriers, such as land tenure arrangements and mandatory delivery quotas, continue to increase the cost of out-migration and dampen off-farm labour market participation. Johnson (1995) worries that several prominent urban institutions, such as the household registration system and the absence of social and educational services for rural residents in cities, restrict entrance into the urban market.

It is important, however, to point out that other more recent work illustrates the emergence of well-functioning rural labour markets and the breakdown of institutional barriers. For example, Cook (1999) demonstrates the equalisation of off-farm labour returns between wage earning and self-employed workers in her rural Shandong sample. Zhang et al. (2000) show the rising significance of education as a determinant of off-farm earnings, a result that implies individuals are being better rewarded for their human capital. A number of papers document the absence or attenuation of institutional barriers to off-farm labour participation. Lohmar's (1999) analysis of the effect of land tenure and quota policies finds that, although more restrictive policies have some impact on household labour response to the off-farm sector, the magnitude is small. Knight and Song (2001) demonstrate how some urban firms have become less discriminatory in their hiring practices of those without an urban *hukou*. Zhang, Zhao, and Chen (1995), Rozelle *et al.* (1999), and NBS (1990 to 2000) and others have documented the explosion of migration and off-farm participation, which supports the hypothesis that labour markets have improved over time.

The evolution of rural labour markets in China

The overall goal of this section is to provide an update of the trends in off-farm labour participation. It compares how rural labour has fared after five years of relatively slow economic growth (between 1995 and 2000) relative to its performance in the mid-1990s (after a period of rapid economic growth). Second, a decomposition of the growth in off-farm employment is provided, examining what segments of the rural labour force are growing. The main part of the analysis will be based on the unique set of rural household data collected in the fall of 2000 that contains 20-year employment histories for more than 2 000 individuals from across China (see Box 3.2).

Box 3.2. Household data and definitions

The main data for this study were collected in a randomly selected, nearly nationally representative sample of 60 villages in 6 provinces of rural China (Hebei, Liaoning, Shaanxi, Zhejiang, Hubei, and Sichuan). To accurately reflect varying income distributions within each province, one county was randomly selected from within each income quintile for the province, as measured by the gross value of industrial output. Two villages were randomly selected within each county, and twenty randomly selected households, both those with their residency permits (*hukou*) in the village and those without, were surveyed per village. A total of 1 199 households were surveyed. The survey, supported by a grant from the US National Science Foundation to the University of California, Davis (NSF2000 Household Survey), was led by Scott Rozelle (University of California), Loren Brandt (University of Toronto), Linxiu Zhang and Jikun Huang (both from the Centre for Chinese Agricultural Policy, Chinese Academy of Sciences).

The survey gathered detailed information on household demographic characteristics, wealth, agricultural production, non-farm activities, and investment. Several parts of the household survey were designed to learn about migration from the household and other labour market participation across time. For roughly half of the households surveyed (610 out of 1 199), a twenty-year employment history form was completed for each household member and each child of the household head, some of whom were no longer considered household members. The form tracks the level of participation in off-farm employment, the main type of off-farm work performed, the place of residence while working (within or outside the village), the location of employment, and whether or not each individual was self-employed. All households surveyed were also asked a comprehensive set of questions about their demographic characteristics, agricultural production, other non-farm activities, and both productive and consumptive investments made over the past 20 years.

Using the employment history data, several broad categories of off-farm workers could be identified. Migrants were identified as people with off-farm jobs who did not live in the household while working. Local wage labourers (henceforth, wage earners) were identified as people who had off-farm employment, were not self-employed, and lived at home while they worked. Finally, all people who reported being self-employed off the farm were categorised as such. In total, the survey divided off-farm jobs into four types: migrant wage earners (henceforth, migrants); self-employed migrants; wage earners; and local self-employed. These definitions held for both members of the household and children of the household head. Additional questions related to the extent of the participation of each member, in each year, in the household's on-farm activities.

Participation rates were created by normalising by the total labour force, a figure calculated by aggregating all individuals above the age of 16 who indicated that they were either working in or searching for employment in agricultural and/or industry in each year. If a person over 16 indicated they had retired or could not work for health, full-time enrolment in school, or other reasons, they were not included in the labour force total.

Consistent with previous findings of other national studies of rural off-farm employment, the survey data show that the off-farm labour force (including migrant wage earners, self-employed migrants, local wage earners and local self-employed) expanded steadily between 1981 and 1995. In 1995, 34 per cent of the rural labour force found some employment off-farm, compared to around 16 per cent in 1981. Moreover, despite the Asian Financial Crisis, China's own structural reforms, and a general slowing of economic growth in the late 1990s, the survey data demonstrate that rural off-farm employment growth continued expanding between 1995 and 2000 (Figure 3.1). By 2000, 47 per cent of rural individuals participated in off-farm work, a rise of 13 percentage points compared to 1995.

Trends by job type clearly indicate that the focus of workers over the past 20 years has shifted from rural to urban destinations (Figure 3.1). In 1981, most rural individuals (84 per cent) not only spent all of their time in farming, but those who worked off the farm were more than twice as likely to live at home and work in or close to the village than to work out of the village. By 2000, almost as many off-farm workers were living away from home as in the village. Migrants composed both the largest and fastest growing component of the rural off-farm labour force. Other main findings are presented in Box 3.3 and suggest that rural labour markets have been increasingly dominated by young workers. More and more workers are drafted from those sub-sectors of the population that earlier had been excluded from off-farm activities, for example, women. Rural workers also showed signs of specialisation especially when examined by age group and education. Young and better-educated workers work much less on the farm than older workers in 2000. Moreover, the on-farm participation of young workers in 2000 is much less than in 1990 and 1981. Finally, household surveys prove that workers are moving further from home and developing ties in other rural areas (rural-to-rural migration). These findings provide evidence that despite still existing administrative and institutional barriers, trends on labour markets are consistent with an economy that is in transition from agriculture to non-agriculture and a population that is shifting from rural to urban.

Figure 3.1. **Percentage of rural labour force in different types of off-farm work, 1981-2000**

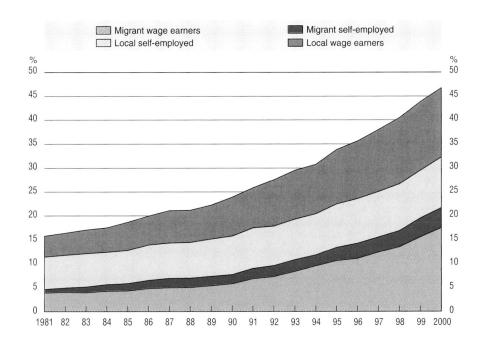

Source: S. Rozelle, L. Brandt, L. Zhang, J. Huang, NSF 2000 Household Survey.

Box 3.3. Off-farm employment patterns in rural China

Age. One of the most striking characteristics of China's changing employment patterns is the domination of younger workers in the shift towards off-farm employment. Workers in all age categories participated in off-farm work at similar rates in 1981 (ranging from 18 to 19 per cent) and 1990 (ranging from 20.5 to 33.6 per cent). By 2000, while there was an important rise in the off-farm participation rates in all age categories, there was a distinct acceleration in these rates among younger workers relative to older ones. In 2000, the youngest workers participated at rates more than twice (75.8 per cent for those in the 16-20-year old cohort) those of the older age category (37.6 per cent for those in the 41 to 50-year old cohort).

The rise in the off-farm participation rates of younger workers also shows their increasing specialisation in the off-farm sector. In 1990, for example, of those in the younger cohorts who had off-farm jobs, more than half spent time (either part time or during the busy season) working on the farm. By 2000, less than a quarter of the youngest cohort who worked off-farm spent any time in agriculture. In contrast, in 2000, of those in the 41 to 50 year old cohort who worked off the farm, over 80 per cent of them were still working in agriculture, either on a part-time or seasonal basis. These data illustrate the tendency for young workers to live away from home and not engage in any on-farm work.

Gender. The rise in labour markets has already begun to have a positive impact on increasing off-farm participation rates of women. Although women have participated at rates far below those of men throughout the entire 20-year sample period, since the early 1990s, participation rates have risen. In the 1980s, the participation rates of men (more than 25 per cent in 1981) far exceeded those of women (less than 5 per cent). Moreover, despite these low initial levels of involvement in the off-farm sector, the growth of participation rates of women remained below those of men in the 1980s. In the 1990s, however, the rate of growth of participation of women has risen faster relative to men.

The rising participation rates of women have been driven by the entry by women into all job categories, although the most striking absolute gains have come in migration. Throughout the entire 1980s decade, less than 1 per cent of women left their homes to work for a wage or become engaged in self-employed activities. Since 1990, however, the rate of growth has been higher than any category of job types for either men or women. By 2000, nearly 6 per cent of the female labour force was working as a wage earning migrant and nearly 3 per cent was working as a self-employed migrant.

Education. There is a significant shift to greater education among migrants. Although rural men generally have higher levels of education than rural women, the education of male and female migrants is roughly equivalent. Male migrants are slightly more likely than women to have either a high school or elementary education, which suggests that the range of opportunities for male migrants is wider. Multivariate analysis shows that in the 1980s, for each additional year of education, the probability of becoming a migrant rises by 10 per cent and the probability of working in a local wage-earning job rises by 6 per cent. By the 1990s, the probability of becoming a migrant rises by 18 per cent for each year of additional education and the probability of finding an off-farm job rises by 17 per cent. The participation in formal training and apprenticeship programmes also has a large and significant effect in increasing the participation in all forms of labour market activity.

Migration destinations. The destinations of migrants, both men and women, also changed and differ from region to region (Rozelle *et al.*, 1999). In coastal areas such as Zhejiang, more migrants stay within their home county than in other areas. Migrants from inland provinces move outside of their own provinces more frequently than others. Surprisingly, most migration destinations were short and medium distance, except in Sichuan and Hubei in 1995. However, the number of long distance migrants, especially women, has risen sharply. Nationwide, the proportion of migrant men moving to remote destinations rose from 28 to 42 per cent between 1988 and 1995; the proportion of women rose sharply from 7 to 41 per cent. Some areas had exceptionally high levels of outmigration. The proportion of men migrating to destinations outside the province increased from 61 to 74 per cent in Sichuan and from 14 to 46 per cent in Hubei.

Developing rural-to-rural linkages. Many of the new jobs in rural areas, created mostly by TVEs, go to workers from other villages. In 1988, only about 1 per cent of the rural labour force found employment in another rural village. By 1995, 5 per cent of rural workers were employed in a rural village outside of their home village. The increase in the size of the rural labour force, the rapid rise in the proportion of rural workers who leave their home village for work, and the increasing share of those workers heading to other rural villages have contributed to the expansion in rural-to-rural labour movement. Between 1988

On the basis of the earlier survey conducted in 1995 (Rozelle *et al.*, 1999), it is possible to differentiate several categories of villages specialised in different modes of production. When ranking the sample villages in terms of average income per capita and dividing them into four distinct groupings (Figure 3.2), it may be found that full-time farming is the dominant form of economic activity in the poorest of the poor villages (the poorest 10 per cent of the sample) and is far more common than in the better off villages – Panel I). In contrast, most of migration is occurring in villages in the lower-middle income categories (that is in villages that are in the 90th to 50th percentile in terms of their

Figure 3.2.   **Modes of production in various categories of villages grouped according to their average income, 1995**

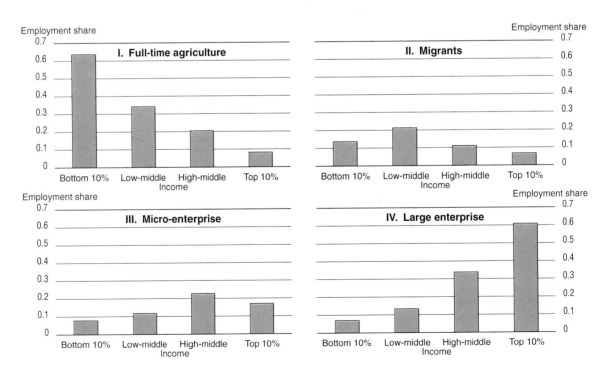

Source: Mohatrapa (2001).

Figure 3.3. **Modes of production in various categories of villages grouped according to their distance from the metropolitan core, 1995**

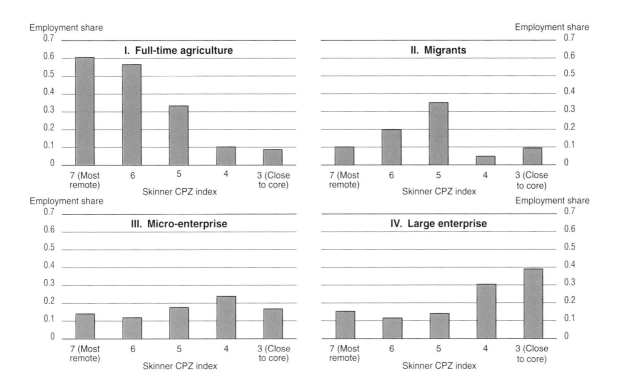

average income per capita – Panel II). Upper middle-income villages (those in the 50th to 10th percentile) have relatively specialised in micro-enterprise operation, and have participated in migration to a much lower extent. Finally, large-scale manufacturing dominates the economies of the richest 10 per cent of China's villages.

Nearly the same pattern of regional specialisation in employment and economic activity can be found when dividing villages into groups according to their "distance" from a major metropolitan region (Figure 3.3). For this illustration, measures of Core-Periphery Zones (CPZ), first used by Skinner (1994), are applied.[2] Those in the periphery (CPZ 6 and 7) are mostly engaged in full-time agriculture, especially when measured relative to other economic activities. In contrast, those in CPZ 5, rural residents that live in villages in areas that are fairly – but not extremely – remote, are those who have a propensity to migrate. As villages move closer to the core, the intensity of micro-enterprises and large manufacturing firms arise. A very large proportion (more than 67 per cent) of manufacturing firms occur in CPZ 3 or 4. These findings will be important in the rest of our analysis demonstrating the trade liberalisation impacts on various categories of rural households.

The impact of trade liberalisation on rural incomes and employment

This section reviews the various potential positive and negative impacts that trade liberalisation policies may have on the rural economy in China, on both those engaged in agriculture and those who rely on the rural industrial and service sectors. It then examines the different factors that will tend to minimise the impacts – in both the short and long runs. Finally, this section analyses how each factor may affect the different sectors of the rural economy.

Impacts

Direct negative effects

There is much discussion inside and outside of China about the negative impacts that trade liberalisation policies will have on the rural economy. However, one of the most important uncertainties regarding the question about how large an impact trade liberalisation will have on China's rural economy, especially its agricultural producers, is about the level of prices faced by China's agricultural producers *vis-à-vis* world market prices (see also Chapter 1). So far, there is almost no solid empirical basis for answering such a question. Most of the comparisons are done on the basis of comparing a single national price and a single world market price. Almost no adjustments are done to account for quality differences between imported and domestically traded products. Little thought has been put into accounting for regional differences among China's major producing regions. Also, many comparisons are done between China's farmgate and border prices, when it is known that transaction costs inside China are relatively high.

Despite these uncertainties most authors would agree that many of China's domestic producers of a number of major commodities, such as wheat, maize, cotton, and soybean, will suffer income declines from lower prices. Given the vast areas of China over which these crops are grown and the possibly large gaps in prices between domestic and international prices, it is likely that complete liberalisation would have a large impact on the producers of these crops inside China. Moreover, these pressures can be fairly sustained over time. Even if prices in the world rose temporarily if China were to dramatically increase imports, there is probably enough flexibility in world cropping systems for wheat, maize, cotton, and soybeans, that foreign producers would respond with greater production and in the medium-run there would be vast quantities of the products at relatively low prices ready to enter China's market.

To the extent that most of the industrial sectors that are most vulnerable to international competition are in the urban sector, a sector that is dominated by fairly high-paid urban workers, the largest negative, direct employment and income effects will likely fall upon urban workers, not those from rural areas. However, wage earners in some rural industries also will be affected negatively by the reduction in employment and wages. In Chapter 2, there is a discussion of the fact that a number of the TVE sub-sectors will become less competitive after trade liberalisation. In these sub-sectors, falling demand for labour and downward pressure on wages will hurt the interests of rural wage earners. And although direct competition between urban and rural workers is fairly limited, competition may intensify for rural workers in certain sectors from laid off urban workers who are searching for new work and/or self-employed business opportunities. In total, then, there should be limited negative impact of trade liberalisation policies on the employment and wages of a subset of rural workers.

Direct positive effects

The direct, positive effects will mainly occur as mirror images to the negative ones. The largest positive impact of trade liberalisation measures almost certainly will come from the rise in the demand for rural employment due to the increased demand for China's products overseas and the more relaxed investment environment inside China. If China's access to export markets increases, many of the sectors that most likely will be the largest beneficiaries will be those labour-intensive firms that hire large volumes of workers from rural areas, in particular in garment and textile industries.

As discussed in Chapter 1, trade liberalisation policies may have a positive effect on certain key subsectors of agriculture. For most of the past decade, China has exported more agricultural commodities in value terms than it has imported. As shown by Huang *et al.* (2000) and Lu (2001), most of the exports have been labour intensive horticulture, livestock and other processed products. Many of the products have been shipped to other Asian economies, though increasing quantities have been going to the United States. To the extent that trade liberalisation helps China's access to markets in other countries for products which it is able to export, agricultural producers of these commodities will benefit by higher prices and more export opportunities.

Trade liberalisation policies may also help China remove or reduce barriers to many of its agricultural imports that have been erected by foreign countries (such as Japan, Korea, and the United States) in recent years, if becoming part of the WTO gives China a way to appeal the unfavourable decisions of bilateral trade dispute settlements. In almost all cases, China is being accused of dumping, or selling commodities on international markets at a price that is less than its cost of production. In most cases, high countervailing tariffs have been placed on the commodities, effectively eliminating them from that market.[3] As long as China was not in the WTO, there was no appeal.

Less selectively, almost all agricultural producers will benefit from the falling tariffs and reduced trade barriers for key agricultural inputs, especially chemical fertilisers, pesticides, and seeds. Currently, state trading, licensing, and tariffs have protected domestic fertiliser and chemical pesticide markets. Falling non-tariff barriers could aid agricultural producers in getting access to better technology and higher quality agricultural inputs. For example, currently China requires that no more than 20 per cent of chemical pesticides can be imported. China's farmers have repeatedly expressed their high demand for foreign produced pesticides, which are frequently more effective and safer for both the user and the ultimate consumer. Quantitative restrictions and barriers to distribution have forced the price to rise in a number of markets and made the products completely unattainable in others. Similar restrictions keep parent stock of chicks for the broiler industry from being imported. Breeding stock can be imported, but only after extreme quarantine regulations are met, actions that limit their use.

Indirect effects

There are several ways that trade liberalisation policies could bring benefits to China's rural economy. For example, there are many foreign countries that might be induced into investing into the agricultural inputs sector or importing more once trade liberalisation policies are in place. Currently, there are many explicit and implicit barriers keeping foreign agricultural input firms from investing in China. Rozelle, Pray, and Huang (2000) delineate a number of the most restrictive measures. For example, manufacturers of pesticides are required to produce the active ingredients inside China. Since trade secrets are embodied in this process, a number of firms are hesitant about investing for fear that their product's manufacturing process could be stolen.[4] Farmers could also acquire large potential gains if restrictions on multinational seed companies were eliminated. For years, a number of international seed producers have been experimenting with their new varieties in China. According to their reports, their new varieties could produce important new gains in yields. Yet regulations require that the foreign partner cannot own more than 50 per cent of the firm. A number of restrictions on the import of seed stock and parent varieties also limit the flexibility of firms to get around other barriers in the industry.

Trade liberalisation policies are expected to stimulate investment and increase competition and efficiency in China's domestic markets. This will bring positive spillover effects on agricultural producers and rural industries. Currently, restrictions on wholesaling have kept a small number of large state-owned firms in control of the wholesale industry. Their buying and distribution practices often either purposely or inadvertently kept the products of foreign firms out of the market, and kept them from producers. Smaller rural industries were also forced to do their own marketing, limiting the expansion of their production capabilities. If trade liberalisation allows for the entry of foreign firms into the wholesaling industry, or at least encourages domestic firms to innovate and become more open, then all those in rural industry and agriculture stand to benefit. Similar positive effects could arise if trade liberalisation induces the development of better and more regular legal and accounting practices.

Opening agricultural markets to global competition may bring benefits to producers in sectors undergoing rapid technological change. Currently, when producers adopt new technologies there are two countervailing effects. Costs fall (or output rises with costs fixed) leading to positive efficiency gains. However, because China's economy is relatively closed to the world, as supply expands, the price of the commodity falls. Except for the case of the early adopters in the first year or two after the extension of the technology, in the longer run, some or all of the benefit from the fall in costs are negated by the fall in the price of the domestic good. If China's markets were open to the world, however, their demand curve would become more elastic and the negative effects on prices would be dampened.

Buffering effects

The effects of the impacts discussed above could be measured by the price differences between China's domestic price and the world price. If estimates of the supply and demand elasticities inside China were available and on world markets, then analysts could conceivably come up with a quantitative measure of the net overall gain (or loss). However, in this section, several arguments are raised about why even these calculations may not accurately measure the real benefits and costs that the economy will incur. In fact, in addition to policy safeguards discussed in Chapter I, high transaction costs, and household responses will also serve to buffer the effects of trade liberalisation policies on many who live in rural areas in China.

High transaction costs and isolated regional markets

To the extent that there are high transaction costs inside China and that certain domestic markets are isolated from others in the country – especially those inland areas that are isolated from port regions where imports arrive – it can be argued that both the positive and negative impacts of trade liberalisation will not be evenly distributed and that they will be greatly attenuated.

Although there has been a large improvement in agricultural markets integration, large parts of the country, especially poorer areas, are not completely integrated. Farmers in poor areas market only a small portion of their output (mostly maize) and sell it into local markets (for feed) that are not necessarily integrated into national markets. Moreover, even in the integrated regions, the transaction costs of moving commodities between producing and consuming regions are high; when measured on a cost per kilometre per ton, the cost of moving bulk commodities in China is nearly five times as great as in the United States (Rozelle *et al.*, 2000).

A study by Taylor (1998) shows that the impact of NAFTA on Mexican farmers varied dramatically between those in border regions and those in more remote regions that faced high transaction costs for marketing their output and buying inputs. In fact, Taylor finds that NAFTA has had little impact on those in the poorest areas mainly because they have been insulated from the changes by high transaction costs. Since most of their economic activities are in their own village or township, the prices that they are facing and selling for are determined locally and are not affected by what happens far away in the nation's border areas. Moreover, farm households in poorer areas are operating in economies that are characterised by poor, incomplete or absent markets for many factors, such as land and on-farm labour. Therefore, when they do interact with commodity or input markets, some of the impact of changes in prices is "absorbed" by changes in the shadow value of the un-marketed household resources, such as its land or labour (see Singh, Squire and Strauss, 1986, for a complete analytical description of this mechanism). For example, part of the fall in agricultural prices could affect the shadow value of land, which while "real" is unrealised since the household is not able to (or is not willing to) sell or rent the land in any case. Therefore, the complicated ways in which farmers in these economies respond to changes in prices and marketing opportunities usually mean that the effects are much smaller than they would be on households that live and work in completely commercialised economies.

Household responses

While in the previous section it is argued that there are many rural households in China that may be substantially isolated from the effects of trade liberalisation policies, there are many households that live in areas that are highly integrated into the rest of the economy and part of them will suffer the adverse consequences of trade and investment liberalisation. However, because of the ability of households to respond, even though there may be large negative effects in the initial period, the costs may diminish over time. For example, in the case of NAFTA's impact on Mexico, farmers in some of the border areas found their maize crop to be unprofitable in the first years after the onset of the free trade policies. Undoubtedly, their incomes fell substantially. These farmers, however, did not stand still and continue to produce at a loss. Instead, they responded and adopted new technologies and made investments that allowed them to take advantage of positive opportunities that arose in the wake of the free trade agreement. There are many cases in which farmers in Northern Mexico invested heavily – sometimes in partnership with US growers – in fruit and vegetable production since protection for US markets also fell. In many cases, profits after an initial investment period were higher for these Mexican farmers than previously, when they were producing for the protected domestic maize market. Not all farmers benefited, but because of the ability of farmers to respond, their losses in subsequent years can be substantially lower than in the initial year.

Hence, in China the magnitude and severity of the possible negative impact of trade liberalisation policies on agricultural production will depend in part on how well households are able to respond. The rapidity with which the rural economy has evolved in the past, when facing changes in the external environment, provides grounds for optimism. Trade liberalisation policies themselves may help the rural economy respond even faster if they promote more liberalised credit, more liberalised labour markets, better property rights, and the rise of wholesaling networks, and encourage foreign direct investment.

Trade liberalisation impacts on subsectors of the rural economy

So far, this chapter has discussed trade liberalisation policies' effects on the rural economy as a whole and how it is possible that different types of households in different regions of the country and subsectors of the economy might be affected differently. This section examines how the typical household in different regions of the country might be affected by trade liberalisation policies. If it can be shown that certain groups of households or certain regions of the country are particularly vulnerable, it may be possible to more accurately target aid to these regions to help producers during the post-trade liberalisation transition.

Relying on the categorisation that underlies Figures 3.2 and 3.3, and based on a number of assumptions (not the least of which is that the focus is primarily on examining the "typical" household in each region – recognising that all regions are fairly heterogeneous), it appears that certain regions will be affected more severely than others. If trade liberalisation policies stimulate manufacturing in light industry, the largest winners will be the richest of the rural areas. As seen in Panel IV of Figure 3.2 and 3.3, most of the labour force in the villages that are among the richest 10 per cent in the country (closest to the core metropolitan regions) will enjoy higher wages and more employment if manufacturing expands after the implementation of trade liberalisation policies. The richest rural areas will almost certainly enjoy higher investments by both domestic and foreign investors.

Higher demand for China's manufactured products may also be expected to help those outside of the richest areas, in particular those in the lower middle-income villages, through the higher demand for rural labour (Figure 3.2, Panel II). Previous analysis by a number of different research teams have found that most of rural migration is coming from villages that are below average but not those that are the poorest of the poor. In most of the households in these villages, the income from rural migration far exceeds income from other sources. Hence, even if there are some adverse consequences on agricultural incomes in these villages due to a fall in agricultural prices, the dominance of rural migration in these villages could make the typical household in these areas a net gainer from trade liberalisation policies.

While it might be thought that households in the poorest regions (who are mostly full-time farmers – Figure 3.2, Panel I) will be hurt the most by the changes to agriculture introduced by trade liberalisation policies, it may be that households in these villages enjoy the most buffering by a number of factors. They will remain relatively unaffected to the extent that they are self-sufficient, have lower levels of cash income, and sell their commodities into markets that are relatively isolated from the rest of the economy. The net effect will depend on a number of factors, but even if farmers sell a substantial amount of their output, if they primarily purchase agricultural inputs and other tradable stable commodities (such as wheat and soybean oil for which prices are expected to fall due to trade liberalisation), any fall in revenues will be attenuated. In short, it can be expected that the poorest of the poor in China will either not be affected at all because of their extreme remoteness and high degree of self-sufficiency, or because they will gain nearly as much as they lose.

Most probably, the largest negative effect of trade liberalisation policies will affect those in the middle-income categories. The typical household in these villages does not benefit universally either from the greater demand for labour from local investments by enterprises or from greater demand for local labour, since migration is not very common (Panel II of Figures 3.2 and 3.3). They are typically fairly well integrated into the rest of the economy and frequently highly commercialised. If agricultural prices fall, full-time farmers in these areas will be adversely affected. In fact, there is a higher propensity to be running a self-employed enterprise in these types of villages than in any other region (Panel III of Figures 3.2 and 3.3). If their businesses are connected with agriculture or with any other sector that is affected by trade liberalisation policies, they will be hurt in a second way. In short, those in these middle-income villages that are located in the far suburbs and the not so-far-away rural areas will be the ones most likely to be affected by trade liberalisation policies – at least in the short run. However, since these villages are in the regions that are fairly well-off it may be that these households are fairly flexible and may minimise the costs.

In summary, to the extent that the *mode* household in each area is examined, it may be argued that most regions have reasons to be fairly optimistic. The poorest regions will be unaffected due to their remoteness. The next to the poorest and richest should have substantial benefits if trade liberalisation policies increase the demand for China's rural industrial products or for rural labour in general. Those in the middle-income areas may be hurt. However, to the extent that they will respond, the first round negative effect may be reduced considerably. In short, there is reason to believe that most of the aggregate effects will not be too serious.

However, there are other households in rural China besides the "typical" ones. In rich areas there are commercial farmers who have invested in and are producing agricultural goods that may suffer large price falls when trade liberalisation policies are fully implemented. In a number of areas that are well-integrated into the rest of China's economy there are farmers who are on land that is best suited for wheat and maize production, two crops that will most likely see a large increase in imports (see Chapter 1). Many of these households have few feasible alternative crops that they can produce. In some areas, rural factory owners and their workers will suffer if they happen to be in an industry that loses its long-standing protection. In the long run, most of these households may adjust; in the short run, however, some may experience severe consequences.

Conclusions

The policy changes in the late 1970s and 1980s were successful in boosting per capita food production but incomplete in many other aspects. The implementation of the responsibility system in agriculture was revolutionary. But the lack of well-defined property rights has kept land consolidation and other farm structural changes from taking place. Markets have emerged and have become more integrated and competitive, but progress on market liberalisation has been slow: procurement channels and input supply lines for some commodities and farm inputs remain under state control. The government has maintained an active role in supporting investment in water, roads and research, but a lot more needs to be done in this respect. Although more than 100 million workers found employment off the farm in the past 20 years, there are still serious barriers to labour movement into the city. In several ways, state policies continue to discriminate against rural residents.

If the economy continues to be run as a partially reformed entity, many misguided policy choices may result. For example, if food production stagnated, and the government became concerned that China was becoming too reliant on world food markets, it is easy to imagine how the government would force domestic production back into grains and other staples. If WTO pushed down domestic prices, one could easily see how such policies would lead to more domestic policy intervention. With lower prices, the government would have to adopt strong-arm policies to ensure compliance. These policies would block the effect of markets and go against the spirit of the WTO. And with lower returns to agriculture, the rural-urban income gap would widen. In turn, an unhealthy rural economy would slow down aggregate economic growth.

There has clearly been enough progress in recent years, however, to support the view that reforms will continue and that China's leadership will find a way to move beyond today's policy regime with the support of the international community. In this scenario, the needs and welfare of the rural economy should become an integral part of the economic programme of the leadership.

New initiatives will be necessary to resolve the contradictions associated with China's land policies. Currently, farmers have poorly defined rights associated with the land they farm, while the village retains ownership rights. This has adverse impacts on investment. Weak land-use rights also undermine credit markets. As a result, farm households may have increased difficulty in accumulating wealth to finance retirement. Furthermore, weak land rights limit the possibilities for serious farm restructuring. Hence, the government should push through new policy initiatives, such as a proposal that is currently before a People's Congress working committee that would require banks to use 30-year land contracts as collateral for farm and non-farm business loans. Ultimately, either permanent-use contracts or even land privatisation seems necessary.

China has not taken as much advantage of specialisation or regional comparative advantage as it could. To do so, competitive internal grain trade is required, in which commercialised state and non-state enterprises operate under the same constraints, incentives, and commercial standards. This would facilitate more rapid responses to grain surpluses – including surplus stocks – and shortages, and stabilise both prices and availability more than the current regime. The tariff-rate-quotas (TRQs), if properly executed, could be the first crack in the armour of China's monopolistic state trading regime. Farmers would also have better access to quality inputs and technology than they presently enjoy.

With radical changes to land rights and the marketing environment (as well as equally radical changes in the individual ability to migrate, obtain credit, and enjoy other economic essentials), China's rural sector will undoubtedly be a very different place in three or four decades. Improved land rights, the elimination of migration restrictions and better education would give farmers an opportunity to choose between farm and city life. Hundreds of millions of rural workers may be expected to move to the cities over the next 50 years, some to the suburbs of large metropolitan areas, but many to small and medium-sized cities where their labour and capital become part of the largest urbanisation movement in the history of the world. With secure land rights, farmers could increase farm size through leasing. Larger farms could raise the returns to farming to at least the point where specialised households make a living on par with urban dwellers.

NOTES

1. This section draws on Nyberg and Rozelle (1999).

2. In Skinner (1994), the author argues that in analysing spatial data, provinces are not the appropriate unit of analysis. To rectify this problem, Skinner has assigned core-periphery zones indices (CPZ) to every county in China. A CPZ measure is assigned to each county using a macro-regional index of highly correlated variables, such as electricity use, meat output, and age structure. A measure of 1 to 3 means that the village is in a county that is in the immediate vicinity (suburb) of one of China's main 7 major metropolitan regions (*e.g.*, Beijing, Shanghai, Guangzhou, Wuhan, Chengdu, etc.). A measure of 7 means that it is in a periphery county that is most "remote" from the metropolitan core.

3. For example, in March 2001 Japan imposed prohibitive tariffs on imports of three commodities from China, including garlic and mushrooms. The US has taken trade actions in its Federal Trade Commission against a number of commodities, such as garlic, honey, apple juice concentrate, shrimp and crayfish, and tomato paste. In June 2000, Korea undertook similar actions on imports of garlic from China.

4. In the late 1990s, the experience of one large US manufacturer confirmed the worst fears of the industry. After less than six months of production in a new factory, a number of copy-cat factories began to produce the exact same chemical pesticides and were selling them at a price below the break-even point of the foreign direct investment factory.

BIBLIOGRAPHY

Bales, S. (1998),
"Analysis of Developments in Labour Markets in Vietnam over the Period 1992 to 1998", Working Paper, World Bank, Washington, DC.

Chai P., J. Zhou and J. Xie (1999),
"Empirical study on the rational farmers' burden", *Problems of Agricultural Economy*, No. 12.

Chai P., J. Zhou and J. Xie (1999),
"Empirical study on the rational farmers' burden", *Problems of Agricultural Economy*, No. 12.

Cook, S. (1999),
"Surplus Labour and Productivity in Chinese Agriculture: Evidence from Household Survey Data", *Journal of Development Studies*, Vol. 35, No. 3.

Fu, G. (2001),
"Survey report on the taxes and fees shouldered by farmers in seven counties of Hubei province", *Problems of Agricultural Economy*, No 4.

Huang, J., C. Chen, S. Rozelle, and F. Tuan (2000),
"Trade and Liberalisation in China's Agriculture". Working Paper, Department of Agricultural and Resource Economics, University of California, Davis.

Johnson, D.G. (1995),
"Is Agriculture a Threat to China's Growth?" Working Paper No. 95:04, Office of Agricultural Economics Research, University of Chicago.

Knight, J. and L. Song (2001),
"New Urban Labour Market Study", Paper Presented at CERDI Conference on Emergence of Markets in China, Clermont-Ferrand, France.

Lohmar, B. (1999),
"The Role of Institutions in Rural Labour Flow in China", Unpublished Ph.D. Dissertation, Department of Agricultural and Resource Economics, University of California, Davis.

Lohmar, B., C. Zhao, and S. Rozelle (2000),
"Rural to Rural Migration: New Channels of Off-Farm Employment in Rural China", Working Paper, Department of Agriculture and Resource Economics, University of California, Davis.

Lu, F. (2001),
"Regional Pattern of the Impact from China's WTO Accession on Its Agricultural Sector", *China Enters WTO: Pursuing Symbiosis with the Global Economy*, I. Yamazawa and K. Imai, (editors), Institute of Developing Economies, Japan External Trade Organisation.

Mallee, H. (1996),
"Agricultural Labour and Rural Population Mobility: Some Preliminary Observations", Paper Presented at the 1996 Conference on Rural-Urban Migration, Beijing, China, 25-27 June.

Meng, X. (1990),
"The Rural Labour Market." In William A. Byrd and Qingsong Lin, Eds., *China's Rural Industry: Structure, Development, and Reform*, Oxford University Press, New York.

Meng, X. (1996),
"Regional Wage Gap, Information Flow, and Rural-Urban Migration", Paper Presented at the Conference on Rural-Urban Labour Migration, Beijing, China, 25-27 June.

Mohatrapa, S. (2001),
"The Evolution of Modes of Production and China's Rural Economic Development", Working Paper, Department of Agricultural and Resource Economics, University of California, Davis.

National Bureau of Statistics (1990-2000),
China Statistical Yearbook, Beijing.

123

Nyberg, A. and S. Rozelle (1999),
    Accelerating China's Rural Economic Transformation, World Bank Monograph Series, Washington, DC.

Park, A., L. Brandt, and J. Giles (2000),
    "Rural Credit and Rural Economies", Working Paper, Department of Economics, University of Michigan.

Rozelle, S. (1996),
    "Stagnation Without Equity: Changing Patterns of Income and Inequality in China's Post-Reform Rural Economy", *The China Journal* No. 35.

Rozelle, S., G. Li, M. Shen, A. Hughart and J. Giles (1999),
    "Leaving China's Farms: Survey Results of New Paths and Remaining Hurdles to Rural Migration", *China Quarterly* No. 158.

Rozelle, S., A. Park, J. Huang, and H. Jin (2000),
    "Bureaucrat to Entrepreneur: The Changing Role of the State in China's Transitional Commodity Economy", *Economic Development and Cultural Change* Vol. 48, No. 2.

Rozelle, S., C. Pray, and J. Huang (2000),
    "Foreign Direct Investment and Agricultural Technology in China", Working Paper, Department of Agricultural and Resource Economics, University of California, Davis.

Rozelle, S., A. deBrauw, L. Zhang, J. Huang, and Y. Zhang (2001),
    "Rural Labour in China: Evolving, Growing, Transforming", Working Paper, Department of Agricultural and Resource Economics, University of California, Davis.

Singh, I., D. Squire and J. Strauss (1986),
    Agricultural Household Models in Rural Development, World Bank; Washington, DC.

Skinner, W. G. (1994),
    "Differential Development in Lingnan" in Thomas P. Lyons and Victor Nee (eds.).

Taylor, J.E. (1998),
    "Trade Liberalisation and the Impact on Small holders in Rural Mexico", Working Paper, Department of Agricultural and Resource Economics, University of California, Davis.

World Bank (1992),
    China: Strategies for Reducing Poverty in the 1990s, Washington, DC.

World Bank (1997),
    China Engaged: Integration with the Global Economy, Washington, DC.

World Bank (2000),
    China: Overcoming rural poverty, World Bank Report, Washington, DC.

Yang, D. and H. Zhou (1996),
    "Rural-Urban Disparity and Sectoral Labour Allocation in China", Research Papers in *Asian Pacific Studies*, Duke University, Durham, North Carolina.

Zhang, L., S. Rozelle, X. Dong, and Andrew Mason (2000),
    "Opportunities and Barriers in Rural China: Gender, Work, and Wages in Rural China", Working Paper No. WP-00-E25, Centre for Chinese Agricultural Policy, Chinese Academy of Sciences, Beijing, China.

Zhang, X., C. Zhao, and L. Chen (1995),
    "1994: A Real Description of Rural Labour's Cross-regional Flows", *Strategy and Management* No. 6, June.

Chapter 4

OVERVIEW OF INDUSTRY PROSPECTS

TABLE OF CONTENTS

OVERVIEW OF INDUSTRY PROSPECTS[*]

Introduction

China's industrial sector has undergone a rapid process of growth and transformation since the "reform and open door" policy started in 1978. Industry has been at the core of China's modernisation programme and the government has mobilised a very large amount of resources to develop the industrial sector. The result has been spectacular growth, with industry growing at an annual rate of 11.8 per cent between 1979 and 2000, compared to an average GDP growth rate of 9.6 per cent during the same period. China's industry has become a major production platform for multinational corporations and has been a large recipient of foreign direct investment (FDI). China has also managed to become internationally competitive in some technologically sophisticated products at a relatively early stage of economic development.

China's impressive industrial rise has been marked, however, by a number of striking contradictions. Despite the country's rapid integration into international markets, domestic markets remain highly segmented and fragmented. Industrial growth has been concentrated in pockets of regions, sectors and firms, while the rest have lagged. Although some highly efficient and internationally competitive Chinese firms have emerged, most Chinese firms remain relatively small, under-capitalised and poorly managed. Overcapacity and inefficiency characterise many industrial sectors that have been shielded from competition.

China's WTO entry is a potential watershed for industrial reform. WTO accession increases the need to remove protection from inefficient industries, promote market discipline, increase access to technology, and develop the legal and regulatory framework necessary for a well-functioning market economy, which have been important goals for the reform of the industrial sector.

This chapter addresses the question of how China's industrial sector can best realise the benefits of further trade and investment liberalisation and other broader economic reforms over the next decade. Joining the WTO should in principle create a better business environment that is conducive to more efficient allocation of resources across sectors, enabling China to regain momentum in restructuring its economy and increase the potential for higher growth in the longer term. However, the potential benefits from trade and investment liberalisation can be realised only when necessary domestic adjustments are undertaken in various sectors.

The impact of WTO entry and the extent to which the industrial sector realises its potential benefits will depend on the ability of China's industries to reallocate resources and restructure operations. Observers generally agree that China's industrial sector will benefit from its current comparative advantages in labour-intensive industries, while many inefficient industries and firms will lose initially. Successful industrial restructuring will induce resources to flow to the sectors with comparative advantage, while forcing less efficient sectors to restructure so as to be able to improve their efficiency and competitiveness.

Over the longer term, in order to sustain its industrial development China will have to move up the technological ladder, from lower to higher value-added industries. Success will depend on enterprise governance, financial discipline, competition, research and development (R&D), infrastructure, human capital development, and other framework conditions. The major policy challenge is thus to develop and sustain the business environment conducive to long-term industrial upgrading and development, while maximising the medium and shorter-term benefits created for labour-intensive industries, and minimising the disruptions to inefficient industries through a successful structural adjustment process.

---

[*] This chapter was prepared by Young-Sook Nam, Administrator, Non-Member Economies Division, Economics Department, OECD. The part on steel was prepared by Udo Pretschker, Administrator, Directorate for Science, Technology and Industry, OECD.

The next section provides an overview of the development and current situation of the industrial sector in China. This is followed by an analysis of the expected changes in the industrial sector in light of trade and investment liberalisation and broader economic reforms, and the adjustments that need to be made in order to benefit fully from those changes. These adjustments are discussed further in the context of selected industry sectors. This is followed by a discussion of the challenges of longer-term industrial development in China. The last section presents conclusions and policy implications.

Strength and weaknesses of China's industrial sector[1]

Compared with most other developing economies, China is endowed with comparatively favourable conditions for industrial growth and development. China's large domestic market, a seemingly unlimited supply of low-wage labour, and abundance of natural resources provide favourable potential for developing industrial capabilities. While the development of the industrial sector has benefited from these factors in the past, it is becoming clearer that the current structural and institutional features of the economy are blocking the full realisation of their potential benefits.

Growth and structure of the industrial sector

Economic growth in China has been largely driven on the supply side by increases in industrial output. Industrial output grew at an annual average rate of 11.8 per cent during the 1979-2000 period, while China's GDP increased by 9.6 per cent. The relative size of China's industrial sector – reaching around 50 per cent of GDP – is larger than any of the Asian newly industrialising economies (NIEs)[2] or ASEAN-4 countries, as shown in Table 4.1. When compared with a broader set of both developing and developed countries, the large size of industry relative to GDP in China stands out, as shown in Figure 4.1. In contrast, the relative size of China's service sector is among the lowest, and much lower than that of the ASEAN-4 countries (Figure 4.2).

Compared to its share of national output, China's industry employs a much smaller portion of the labour force. China's industrial sector accounted for 23 per cent of total employment in 1999, whereas agriculture employed around 50 per cent and the service sector employed 27 per cent. The current employment distribution across sectors, together with the output structure, indicates the relatively limited urbanisation and tertiarisation processes in the Chinese economy (see Box 4.1).

Both the large size and the rapid growth of the industrial sector in China reflect the overall development strategy taken by the government since the 1950s. During the pre-reform period between the 1950s and the late 1970s, China's industrial growth was based on the growth of chemical and heavy manufacturing industries. As with most planned economies, the Chinese government adopted a heavy

Table 4.1. **Structure of output in selected Asian economies**

	Agriculture value added as a % of GDP		Industry value added as a % of GDP		Manufacturing value added as a % of GDP		Services value added as a % of GDP	
	1980	1998	1980	1998	1980	1998	1980	1998
China	30	18	49	49	41	37	21	33
Chinese Taipei	8	3	46	35	36	27	47	63
Hong Kong, China	1	0[1]	32	15[1]	24	7[1]	67	85[1]
Korea	14	5	40	43	28	31	46	52
Singapore	1	0	38	35	29	23	61	65
Indonesia	24	20	42	45	13	25	34	35
Malaysia	22	13	38	44	21	29	40	43
Philippines	25	17	39	32	26	22	36	51
Thailand	23	11	29	41	22	32	48	48

1. Figures for 1997.
Source: OECD (1999); World Bank, *World Development Indicators*, 2000; *Taiwan Statistical Data Book*, 2001.

Figure 4.1. **Industry as a percentage of GDP, 1995-98, average**

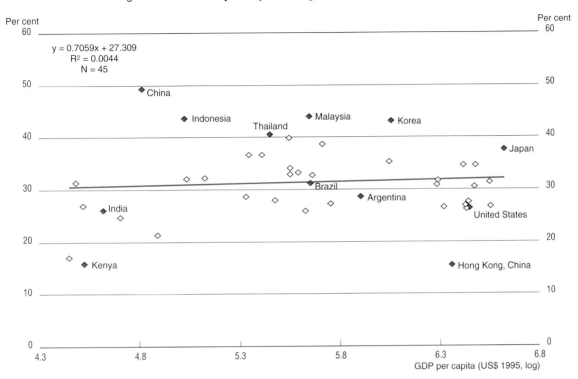

$y = 0.7059x + 27.309$
$R^2 = 0.0044$
$N = 45$

GDP per capita (US$ 1995, log)

Figure 4.2. **Services as a percentage of GDP, 1995-98, average**

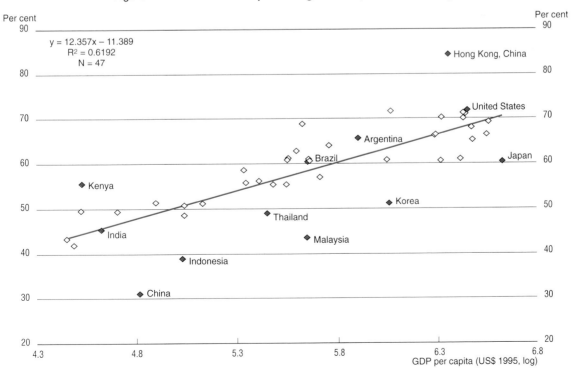

$y = 12.357x - 11.389$
$R^2 = 0.6192$
$N = 47$

GDP per capita (US$ 1995, log)

Source: World Bank, *World Development Indicators*, 2000.

129

Box 4.1. **Characteristics of the sectoral transformation in China**

Like most other countries, China's economic growth pattern has been characterised by the shift of factors of production, *i.e.* labour and capital, from the agriculture sector to the industry and services sectors. The changes in the sectoral shares of output and employment suggest that the Chinese economy has been undergoing the process of transition from a rural, agricultural society to an urban, industrial one. The share of the value added of agriculture declined from 28 per cent in 1978 to around 18 per cent in 1999, whereas the share of services increased from 24 per cent to 33 per cent during this period. The employment share of the agricultural sector also declined from around 70 per cent to 47 per cent during the same period, and was accompanied by a corresponding increase in the employment shares of industry and services.

While similar to the development pattern of many other countries, there are two major features that set China apart from other countries. First, the development of the services sector in China has been much slower compared to other countries at a similar level of development. In general, the share of the service sector tends to increase with the rise in GDP per capita. Compared with other countries, the share of services in China's GDP is much lower for its level of GDP per capita, whereas the share of industry is the highest among the countries shown in Figure 4.1. In many developing countries, the growth in the service sector has contributed greatly to absorbing surplus labour, as this sector tends to be more labour-intensive. The service sector provides a variety of crucial functions – the distributive infrastructure for extractive and manufactured goods, financing for enterprises, the administrative functions that enable a society to exist, the maintenance and recycling (renting/leasing) facilities for durable goods, and the activities (health, education, recreation) that enhance the quality of the labour force.* The growth of services has been a driving force underlying economic growth in most OECD countries. The underdevelopment of the service sector in China stems in large part from the low degree of urbanisation associated with the restrictions on labour mobility from rural to urban areas, and the high degree of regulation, including widespread market-entry restrictions and state monopoly in many service activities.

The second feature is the relatively low rate of labour absorption in non-agricultural sectors. Despite the rapid shift of labour out of agriculture during the last two decades, 70 per cent of the population currently resides in rural areas and 50 per cent of employment is in the agricultural sector. The agricultural sector has significant surplus labour. As discussed in Chapter 1, movement in labour from the agricultural sector to higher productivity occupations is inhibited by the land tenure system and impediments associated with the household registration system. This situation hinders realisation of the potential gains from more efficient allocation of labour.

The employment intensity of growth has markedly declined in the 1990s, compared to the 1980s. In particular, it declined markedly in the industrial sector since the second half of the 1990s, due in part to the acceleration of enterprise reform and industry restructuring. The prospect for an increased flow of labour from rural to urban areas highlights the need to foster growth of labour-intensive industries and services sectors to facilitate labour absorption in China.

---

* Riddle (1986).

---

industry-oriented development strategy in the 1950s, so that China could catch up with advanced countries. Thus, before the economic reforms started in the late 1970s, the Chinese economy had already been characterised by an unusually large share of industry in real GDP for its level of development. This was particularly striking given that the majority of the workforce remained in agriculture. Promoting the heavy industry-oriented development strategy in a capital-scarce, agrarian economy brought serious economic problems. One major problem was over-development of sectors heavily dependent on capital at the expense of labour-intensive sectors that were China's comparative advantage. Combined with lack of competition and poor incentives to improve efficiency, the priority given to the development of overly capital-intensive industries resulted in low economic efficiency and low growth (Lin, Cai and Li, 1996).

Since the late 1970s, China's reform and open-door policies have generated a very heterogeneous business landscape and transformed China's industrial structure to better align with its comparative advantage. Three strands of economic reform have contributed to this dynamic: product and factor market reforms; enterprise reforms; and reforms of trade and foreign investment policies. The combination of these interlocking sets of reforms has created a highly dynamic industrial landscape in China during the last two decades.

The economic reforms since the late 1970s initially shifted national resources towards agriculture, through a sharp rise in the procurement price paid for agricultural crops and what amounted to the privatisation of agriculture. However, during the 1980s, township and village enterprises (TVEs) in light industries producing labour-intensive products such as apparel and footwear began to grow rapidly, taking advantage of the abundant cheap labour in China. As a result, by the late 1980s, the share of industry in national output was again rising.

These reforms have transformed the industrial sector from an almost complete reliance on state-owned enterprises to one where non-state small and medium-sized enterprises (SMEs) play an increasingly important role. In many industries, various types of enterprises now coexist, including state-owned enterprises (SOEs), urban collectives (UCEs), rural enterprises or TVEs, share-holding enterprises, foreign-invested enterprises (FIEs), individual and private firms.[3]

The rise in non-state enterprises during the 1980s was spurred by the removal of entry barriers to industries that had been monopolised by government-protected SOEs. With increasing competition in the market for industrial products, the number of TVEs rapidly increased. The prior heavy industry-oriented development strategy had left a large market for consumer goods for TVEs to expand into light consumer goods such as garments, leather, beverages, furniture, and paper products (Otsuka, *et al.* 1998).

The period starting from the end of the 1980s has seen a rise in the number of FIEs in relatively high-tech manufacturing industries including consumer electronics and telecommunications equipment. Domestic demand for durable consumer goods such as household electronic appliances also started to accelerate. Combined with the growth in external demand for these products, this market provided for the growth of more technology-intensive manufacturing.

As shown in Figure 4.3, collective enterprises (UCEs and TVEs) grew much more rapidly than SOEs throughout the 1980s and the early 1990s, but their performance has faltered since the mid-1990s. On the other hand, starting from the mid-1990s, the share of "other" types of enterprises, *i.e.* FIEs, share-holding enterprises, and private enterprises, started to rise rapidly. By 1999, the industrial output of SOEs accounted for only around 28 per cent of total industrial output, while various types of non-state enterprises contributed the remaining 72 per cent.

As a result of this transformation, China has developed a highly diversified industrial structure, encompassing a wide range of industries from light labour-intensive industries such as textile, garments and food processing to capital-intensive industries such as steel, petroleum processing and automobiles, as shown in Table 4.2. After the chemical industry, the six largest sectors in terms of value added include: electric machinery, food products, textiles, iron and steel, transport equipment, and tobacco.

Industrial policy and sectoral divergence

As in many other developing countries, China has used industrial policy to promote particular sectors and industries in order to achieve structural change and economic growth. One of the main objectives of China's industrial policy has been to accelerate the pace of industrialisation by selecting and providing special support and protection to "strategic" or "pillar" industries, whose development is expected to have spillover effects on the rest of the economy.[4] Both China's trade and foreign investment policies have been formed as part of industrial policy with selective protection to specific industry sectors in accordance with overall development objectives. A large range of tariff and non-tariff barriers, including a broad array of quotas, licensing and tendering requirements, state trading, and other controls, apply to specific industrial sectors. Much of these restrictive measures are to be phased out gradually as part of China's WTO accession commitments (see Annex I).

Figure 4.3. **Industrial output, 1980-1999**

A. Shares of industrial output (cumulative percentage)

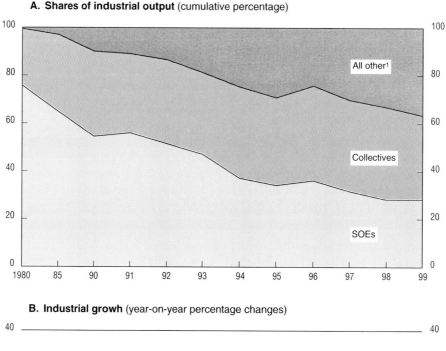

B. Industrial growh (year-on-year percentage changes)

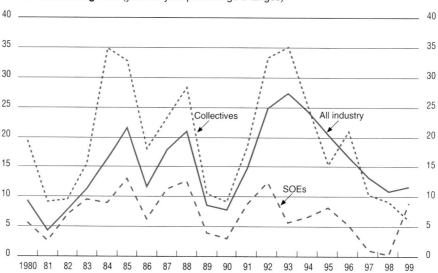

Note: Figures refer to gross industrial output of all industrial enterprises, with or without independent accounting system.
1. Other firms include private and foreign-funded industrial enterprises.
Source: China Statistical Yearbook, 2000.

The protected industrial sectors are dominated by the SOEs, and competition from non-state enterprises, especially FIEs, is largely limited. These sectors include mainly resource-based industries and heavy industries such as gas, electricity production, petroleum processing, ferrous metals, non-ferrous metals, transport, and basic chemicals. Within light industry, tobacco processing is monopolised by the state. Operating in these sectors are China's biggest industrial groups, which are regarded by the government as the flagships of Chinese industry (see Chapter 5). Large SOEs continue to receive preferential treatment from the government, including access to bank loans, trading rights, and monopoly positions in certain sectors.

Table 4.2. **Structure of China's manufacturing industry, 1981-1997**

% share of industry total

	Value added (at current prices)			Number of employees		
	1981	1991	1997	1981	1991	1997
Light industry	**36.0**	**32.4**	**32.9**	**28.8**	**33.5**	**33.8**
Food products	4.7	5.3	7.2	6.7	5.9	6.3
Beverages	2.1	3.0	3.5	1.7	2.1	2.3
Tobacco	4.9	6.3	5.2	0.7	0.6	0.5
Textiles	16.1	10.0	7.1	14.0	13.9	11.9
Wearing apparel and footwear	2.3	2.4	3.0	0.5	3.2	4.0
Leather products	1.1	1.1	1.9	0.7	1.5	2.2
Wood products, except furniture	0.9	0.6	1.1	0.8	1.4	1.5
Furniture, except metal	0.8	0.5	0.6	0.2	0.7	0.7
Paper and products	2.0	2.0	2.2	1.9	2.3	2.7
Printing and publishing	1.3	1.2	1.2	1.6	1.9	1.6
Chemical industry	**26.6**	**26.9**	**26.0**	**20.2**	**21.8**	**26.1**
Industrial chemicals	8.0	9.2	{ 11.5	7.5	7.0	{ 8.8
Other chemicals	3.5	3.7	{ ..	2.4	2.6	{ ..
Petroleum refinering	5.0	3.4	{ 3.8	0.7	1.0	{ 1.3
Misc. petroleum and coal products	0.2	0.2	{ ..	0.3	0.5	{ ..
Rubber products	2.2	1.7	1.3	1.2	1.4	1.5
Plastic products	1.5	2.0	2.3	0.5	1.9	2.5
Pottery, china, earthenware	0.5	0.6	0.7	0.7	0.7	1.3
Glass and products	0.9	0.8	0.6	1.2	1.0	1.0
Other non-metallic mineral products	4.9	5.3	5.7	5.7	5.6	9.7
Heavy industry	**37.4**	**40.7**	**41.1**	**51.0**	**44.8**	**40.0**
Iron and steel	6.9	7.5	6.5	7.8	5.6	5.5
Non-ferrous metals	2.0	2.1	2.0	1.8	1.6	1.9
Fabricated metal products	5.5	3.2	3.3	1.4	3.4	4.2
Machinery, except electrical	13.6	11.3	8.5	26.2	17.7	13.0
Machinery, electric	3.3	8.4	11.0	6.4	6.5	4.9
Transport equipment	3.1	4.9	6.4	4.8	4.2	6.7
Professional and scientific equipment	0.8	1.0	0.9	1.4	1.2	1.4
Other manufactured products	2.2	2.4	2.4	1.3	4.4	2.4

Source: United Nations Industrial Development Organisation (UNIDO), *Industrial Statistics Database*, 2000.

One major focus of China's industrial reform policy has been to develop large enterprises or enterprise groups that can compete successfully in the global market. Constructing large, globally powerful "national champions" is viewed as a key to China's future economic success. In pursuit of this objective, a few large enterprises or groups have been chosen in targeted industries, for example, AVIC in the aerospace industry; Shougang, Angang, and Baosteel in steel; Yiqi, Erqi, Shanghai Auto and Tianjin Auto in automobiles; and Sinopec and CNPC in oil and petrochemicals (Nolan, 2001). The chosen giant enterprises or enterprise groups have received government support through a range of measures, including preferred loans from state banks, protection from competition through various tariff and non-tariff barriers, and access to international stock markets. This policy has been strengthened since 1998 in anticipation of China's WTO entry.

In contrast, economic reforms have liberalised those sectors that are close to final consumption such as consumer electronics, textiles, clothing, and the food industry, which enjoy a high degree of price liberalisation and market competition. In these sectors, China's most successful medium-sized enterprises are present, as well as TVEs or other non-state SMEs. FIEs are mainly concentrated in the export-oriented sectors such as apparel, leather, cultural, educational and sports goods, and electronic and telecommunications equipment.

From the perspective of industrial organisation, the performance of an industry depends on the behaviour and performance of its enterprises, which in turn depends largely on their business environment. China's market-oriented economic reform policy has significantly changed the market structure within which different categories of Chinese industries and enterprises operate, and has hence affected the performance of China's industrial sector. In particular, different exposure to market competition has had a large impact on the performance of particular industrial sectors.

Data on enterprise profitability suggest that SOEs in many sectors tend to suffer from negative or low profit rates compared to non-SOEs. The financial performance of China's industrial enterprises, particularly of SOEs, deteriorated during the 1990s, although there has been some improvement in the last few years. SOEs showed negative or very low profit rates in many sectors in 1999.

Reasons underlying weak industrial performance

A number of factors account for the weak industrial performance during the 1990s, in particular, the poor performance of SOEs. One of the major factors can be traced to the imbalances created during the 1992-94 investment boom, which left many Chinese industries with very low capacity utilisation, high debt loads, and large overhangs of excess inventories. The over-investment behaviour was attributable to weaknesses in enterprise governance and in external financial discipline. The soft budget constraints most public Chinese enterprises face, combined with widespread availability of soft bank loans, resulted in strong incentives to maximise revenue by expanding capacity.

The investment boom has led to chronic oversupply in a wide range of Chinese industries. It is estimated that more than 80 per cent of industrial products are currently in oversupply. The chronic oversupply has contributed to the deflationary pressure in the Chinese economy, which began in 1997, by forcing firms to cut prices to maintain market share. This has further contributed to a worsening of profit performance in these industries. Nonetheless, there has been a lack of exit of loss-making enterprises due in part to local protectionism.

A remarkable degree of economic fragmentation characterises China's domestic markets. While China has a high degree of political centralisation, it has developed a decentralised economic structure under which each region tends to be operationally and financially autonomous. In contrast to the traditional Soviet model, the Chinese system has been and, to a large extent still is, based on regional planning whereby one government agency, *i.e.* the local government, governs most economic activities in one region across different economic sectors. Devolution of investment powers from the central government to the provinces gave local authorities an incentive to protect domestic enterprises, which they owned or from which they collected taxes.

The central government has largely removed inter-provincial barriers to trade in manufactured goods, although there are still local barriers to some specific commodities such as alcohol, tobacco and automobiles.[5] Barriers to capital market mobility are more important obstacles to the restructuring and consolidation of industries across provinces. The rise of local protectionism is partly attributable to the tax system. The control of marketing channels and investment by regional governments might also have added to the protectionist restrictions in imported goods from other provinces (Huang, 2001). Another factor is China's geography, which has added to the difficulty of inter-provincial trade because of underdeveloped transport and distribution networks between provinces.

One of the immediate impacts of market fragmentation has been the emergence of a repetitive and duplicative economic structure across provinces. Instead of specialising along the lines of their comparative advantage, China's regions and provinces strove to develop similar industries and product groups, resulting in a convergence of industrial production across different regions. This industrial dispersion violates the economic prediction that firms tend to cluster regionally in order to reap the benefits of agglomeration economies. This policy has also prevented Chinese industries from fully realising the benefit of the potentially large domestic market, particularly in sectors where scale economies are important. The fragmented market structure, combined with limited exit of inefficient producers, has become a major disadvantage of many Chinese industries, in particular, in capital- and technology-intensive industries.

Another major factor underlying the poor performance of industrial enterprises results from operating inefficiencies arising from inefficient and obsolete production capacity, backward technology, and low product quality. Widespread sub-optimal scale, a large number of small producers, and a high cost base characterise many Chinese industries, including the automobile industry, where larger scale is critical to achieving operational efficiency. This situation persists as local governments resist the pressure to close down inefficient or loss-making enterprises, due in part to the policy imperative to maintain employment levels.

The relatively poor performance of SOEs is further aggravated by policy-imposed burdens such as surplus labour that SOEs are not free to shed, expenses for social benefits such as medical care and pensions, and disproportionately high tax burdens. Policy burdens continue to hamper the performance of SOEs because of underdeveloped social benefit programmes and the scarcity of government revenue.

The poor performance of SOEs, however, stems more fundamentally from lack of good enterprise governance and management, which persists due in large part to weak financial discipline and lack of competition in some industries. Sustained improvement in enterprise performance will not be obtained without good managers who respond to market signals, even after SOEs are relieved from policy burdens.

The third major reason arises from lack of technological and innovative capabilities among Chinese enterprises. In particular, very few SMEs – including the vast majority of TVEs operating in low-tech, labour-intensive manufacturing industry – possess their own R&D and innovative capability. Another weakness of SMEs is their inferior technical endowment. The technical efficiency gap between China's small and large firms remains large although it has been narrowed in the last two decades. One of the major impediments that hinder SMEs' technological advancement is the lack of financial resources (Gregory and Tenev, 2001). Financing problems for SMEs have become even more difficult as bank loan officers have become more cautious about lending to SMEs, whose performances are often weak and which no longer enjoy as much backing from local governments, as was discussed in Chapter 2. In addition, small enterprises themselves do not have adequate personnel to develop technology or to exploit existing technologies. While TVEs are increasingly facing growing competition from other types of enterprises with relatively better technological and innovative capabilities, lack of technological base and managerial talent, scarcity of funds for innovation, and poor information access are the main obstacles that prevent the TVE sector from upgrading its industrial and product structures (see Chapter 6).

Recent measures to reform the industrial sector

Structural reforms to the SOE sector as well as to the financial system continue to be the top economic priority of the Chinese government in recent years. Reforms to SOEs have involved three major components: economic revitalisation, enterprise restructuring and corporate governance reforms (OECD, 2000a).

The first of these, economic revitalisation to improve financial performance and enhance competitiveness, has been a major focus of current efforts since it is the most immediate key to reviving growth in the medium-term. Efforts have been made to reduce the substantial amounts of excess capacity afflicting SOEs, particularly in the textile, energy, petrochemical, metals, and defence industries where the problems have been especially serious. A substantial number of excess workers in SOEs have been taken off enterprise payrolls. In addition, pension, health, and other social programmes that have been a major burden to SOEs are in the process of being restructured and socialised (see Chapter 16). Debt levels have also been significantly reduced for larger SOEs through debt-equity swaps.

Progress has also been made on enterprise restructuring to create more viable entities and diversify ownership. The majority of smaller SOEs in the coastal provinces, and a smaller but still substantial proportion in the interior regions, have been *de facto* privatised. Efforts to diversify ownership of larger SOEs are still at an early stage. However, the government is moving to sell state shares in listed companies, partly as a means to finance various liabilities, including pensions, as well as to promote development of the non-state sector. The government has also been encouraging the participation of foreign investors in the restructuring of SOEs.

As discussed in Chapter 13, establishment of effective corporate governance mechanisms has also become a key priority of reforms to ensure that SOEs function effectively in a market environment.

The overall industrial restructuring drive has been accompanied by an increase in merger and acquisition (M&A) activities. It is reported that there were 177 deals worth US$41.7 billion in 2000, up from 145 deals in 1999 worth US$10 billion. In one of the cases, China's largest shipbuilding company, China State Shipbuilding Corp., was established in April 2001 with the merger of Shanghai's Hudong and Zhonghua Shipyards. Bankruptcy of state and non-state enterprises has also become more widespread since the mid-1990s. The number of bankruptcies of all forms of enterprises reached 25 000 cases, with SOEs accounting for more than half of the number (World Bank, 2000).[6]

The government's various reform efforts appear to have resulted in some improvement of the performance of SOEs. According to the State Economic and Trade Commission (SETC), the three-year programme to turn around the performance of 6 600 loss-making SOEs achieved its goal. It is reported that over 70 per cent of these firms either became profit-making or were merged or reorganised by the end of 2000. Business surveys also show that there has been a general improvement in business conditions in recent years in China. As shown in Figure 4.4, the People's Bank of China survey suggests that general business conditions, profitability, cash flow, and industry capacity utilisation have all been improving since 1999. The inventory situation also seems to have improved in recent years.

While substantial efforts are being made, it is difficult to assess the degree to which reforms are leading to a fundamental improvement in industrial performance. Reform efforts have been hampered by a number of structural and institutional obstacles.

First, most improvement in SOE performance has been achieved by government measures to prop up the state-owned sector through massive fiscal spending since 1998. The major beneficiary of the government reform programme has been large SOEs, which have absorbed most of the large treasury bond issuance and other government support, including technological upgrading, debt reduction, and listing in the stock market. Some critics view this as propping up inefficient industries and enterprises, prolonging their life through subsidies. On the other hand, investment of non-state enterprises, which has been the key engine of growth, still lags significantly behind that of the state-owned entities. The recent improvement in industrial performance has also been highly uneven and concentrated in a relatively small number of large SOEs in certain sectors such as petroleum, power, telecommunications, and electronics.

Second, the impact of the reform efforts has tended to be blunted by continued government interference in business operations. These include restrictions on entry as well as on exit, and on M&A and other modalities for redeploying resources. For example, M&As tend to be heavily influenced by non-commercial objectives, such as the merger of financially stronger with weaker firms in order to limit the burden on government. The effectiveness of establishing good enterprise governance has also been limited because the government still interferes in the selection of senior management.

Furthermore, local protectionism continues to hamper industry consolidation. A good example is the automobile industry. The central government has tried to consolidate the industry through M&As but failed because of strong resistance from local governments. For the purposes of local tax revenues and employment, inefficient, small auto firms have been kept in operation by local authorities.

Figure 4.4. **Indicators of business condition of Chinese enterprises**[1]

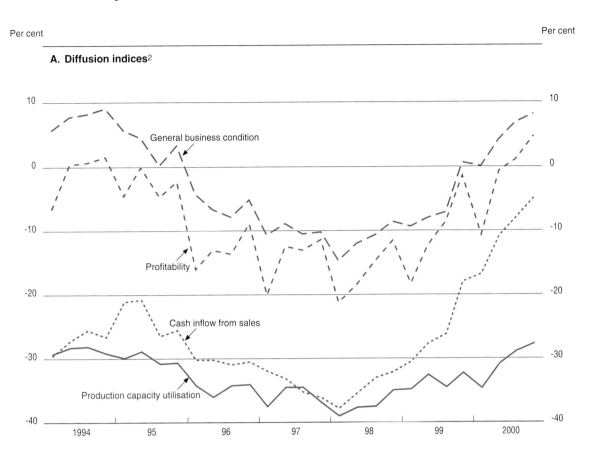

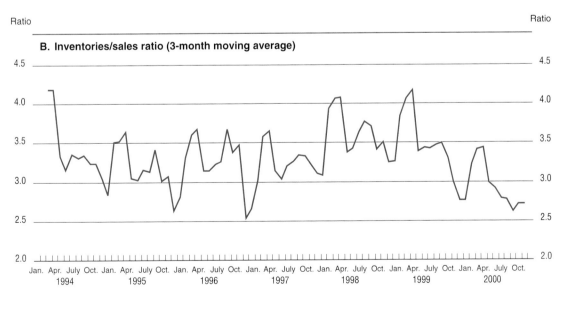

1. Indicators are based on the survey of 5 000 principal industrial enterprises.
2. Diffusion index is calculated as the percentage of positive responses *minus* the percentage of negative responses.
Source: The People's Bank of China Quarterly Statistical Bulletin, various issues.

International integration and China's comparative advantages

China's exports expanded rapidly during the last two decades, making China the world's ninth largest trading nation. China's selective trade liberalisation has led to an accelerated expansion of international processing activities, which have been the engine of the rapid diversification of its manufactured exports. China's rise in world trade has been underpinned by its integration of some of China's industries into global production chains. This process has a direct bearing on competitiveness and industrial upgrading in China, and should play an important role in shaping the prospects of some of China's industries in light of trade and investment liberalisation.

China's integration in the global production system

China's outstanding performance in trade in world markets since the mid-1980s is directly linked to its increased involvement in the international segmentation of production processes. This has been deliberately encouraged by the Chinese government through a selective trade policy granting preferential treatment to assembling and processing activities, through tariff exemptions on intermediate goods. Concessional import duties were also granted to equipment imported by foreign firms related to initial investment in affiliates in China (Lemoine and Ünal-Kesenci, 2001).

The growth of China's clothing and consumer electronics exports has been closely related to China's trade and foreign direct investment policy, which has allowed these industries to integrate into global production chains. This policy had a direct bearing on competitiveness and industrial upgrading in China. Clothing and consumer electronics, together with automobiles, are industries that are increasingly organised as integrated global production systems in which transnational corporations source from a variety of affiliates, supplier firms and locations (UNCTAD, 2000a). These industries are registering significant shares in world trade flows, and high rates of growth in both trade and investment.

Foreign affiliates, in particular those from the Asian region, have taken advantage of China's policy and have used China as a production base, relying on their international trade and production networks. In particular, the downstream, labour-intensive stages of production in Asian advanced economies have tended to migrate to China, taking advantage of the low level of labour costs. By 2000, FIEs accounted for 70 per cent of China's processed exports and three-fourths of imports for processing.

China's participation in the international division of production takes place in the final stages of production (assembling/processing) that are labour intensive, while the upstream, capital-intensive stages of production (semi-finished products and components) are imported. Its comparative advantage in the downstream stages of the production process thus relies on a comparative disadvantage in the upstream segments of production. This vertical division of production has allowed China to diversify its exports of consumption goods, and to exploit strengths in its exports of certain capital goods, especially in electrical machinery. Imports of parts and components embody a large share of high technology and could have been an important channel for the transfer and diffusion of high technology in Chinese manufacturing industry. However the actual situation, as discussed in Chapter 6, leaves much to be desired in this regard.

This selective trade strategy has led to a dichotomy between highly internationalised and competitive industries on the one hand, and a more traditional exporting sector based on domestic inputs, whose performance has remained sluggish, on the other. Tariff reductions accompanied by China's WTO accession represent a good opportunity for these Chinese domestic firms to have better access to foreign technology and equipment, which have been mostly imported by the internationalised sector, while at the same time they will face increased competition from cheaper imports of finished products.

Changing comparative advantages

Compared with more developed countries, China's productivity is relatively low.[7] However, given its low wage costs, China has been competitive in labour-intensive processing activities (Cable, 1996).

Figure 4.5. **Composition of China's exports**[1]

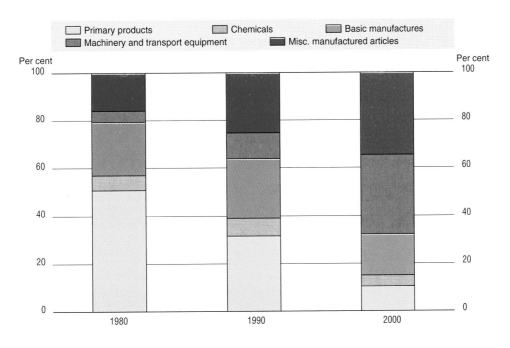

1. Excluding products not otherwise classified.
Source: China Statistical Yearbook, 2000; *China's Customs Statistics*, 12/2000.

During the last two decades, there was a large shift in China's export composition from primary products to manufactured goods as shown in Figure 4.5. During the 1980s there was a major increase in the share of traditional labour-intensive products, *i.e.* miscellaneous manufactured articles (SITC 8) such as apparel and footwear. During the 1990s, however, the share of relatively capital- and technology-intensive products – machinery and transport equipment (SITC 7) – started to increase rapidly. Within this category, China's exports were dominated by low-end labour-intensive products such as office machines and automatic data processing machines (SITC 75) and electrical machinery, apparatus and appliances (SITC 77). The shift in the overall export structure away from the traditional exports such as textiles and clothing, and in favour of electrical machinery and appliances, suggests the upgrading of China's comparative advantage.

The changing comparative advantage of China's exports can be examined by looking at the market share of various Chinese products in the world markets. In the G7 market, China's share in clothing doubled from around 10 per cent in 1989 to around 20 per cent in 1999, and its share in footwear increased more than five times, from around 7 per cent to around 38 per cent (see Figure 4.6). These were categories of exports for which the share of the Asian NIEs declined rapidly. Relying on its cost advantage in labour-intensive manufacturing, China was able to erode the market share of these countries, whose exports shifted toward more capital- and technology-intensive exports.

Figure 4.6 also shows that China, along with ASEAN countries, also gradually moved into more capital- and technology-intensive consumer durable products such as office machines and automatic data processing machines for which NIEs still hold a large market share. China also moved into telecommunications, sound recording, and reproducing apparatus and equipment (such as colour TV sets).

While China has upgraded its industrial structure during the last two decades, the development of its knowledge-based industries[8] is still significantly behind that of Asian NIEs or ASEAN countries such

Figure 4.6. **Developments in share of G7 market of selected products**

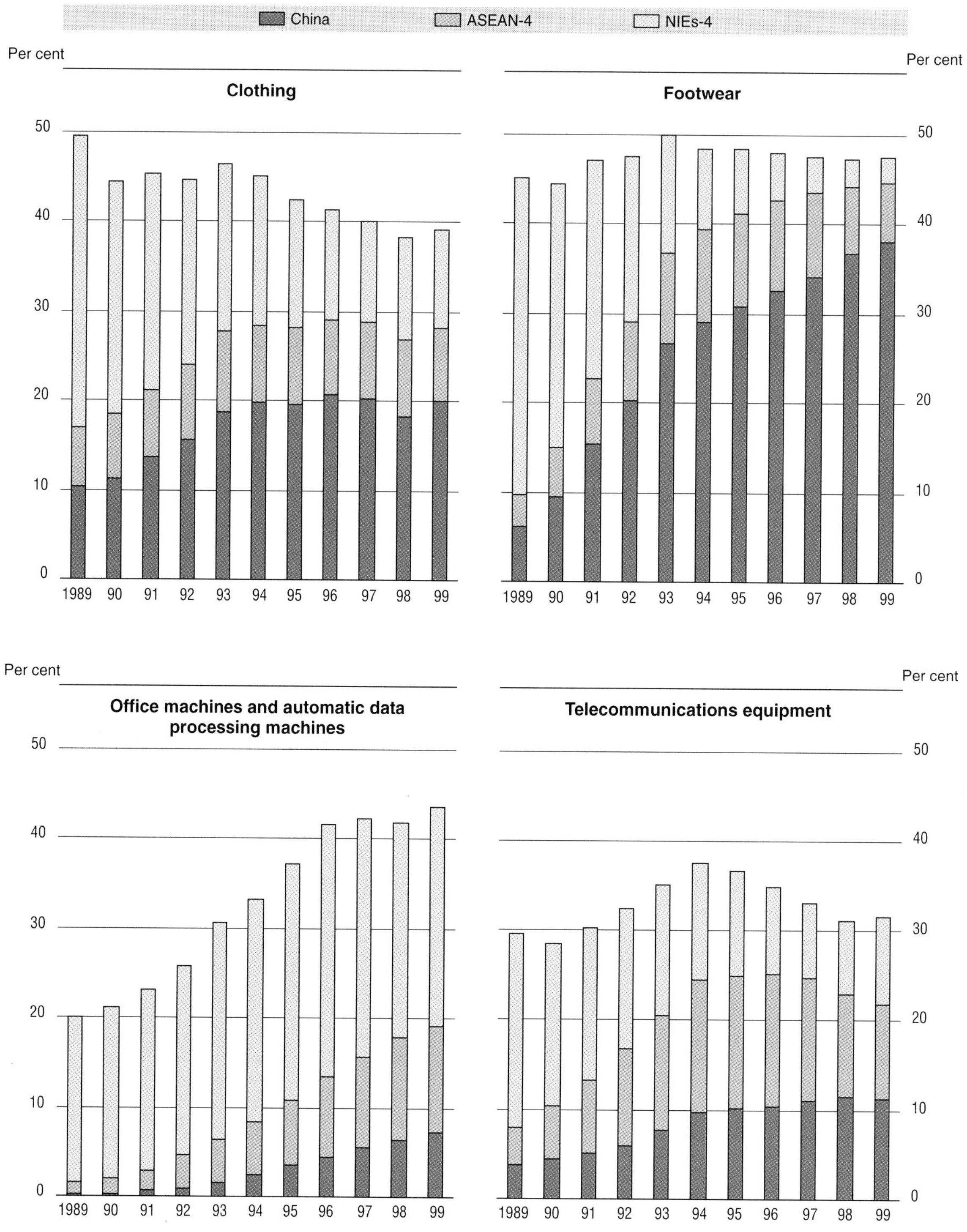

Legend: ☐ China ☐ ASEAN-4 ☐ NIEs-4

Per cent

Clothing

Footwear

Per cent

Office machines and automatic data processing machines

Telecommunications equipment

Note: Clothing: SITC 84; footwear: SITC 85; office machines and automatic data processing machines: SITC 75; telecommunications and sound recording and reproducing apparatus and equipment: SITC 76. ASEAN-4: Indonesia, Malaysia, Philippines, and Thailand. NIEs-4: Chinese Taipei; Hong Kong, China; Korea; and Singapore. G7: Canada, France, Germany, Italy, Japan, United Kingdom, and United States.

Source: OECD, Foreign Trade Statistics Database.

as Malaysia and Thailand. These industries in China suffer from low technological capabilities and limited absorption capacity for imported technology and know-how (OECD, 2000b). As discussed in Chapter 6, China records large trade deficits in technology, in particular in the areas of computer-integrated production, computers and telecommunications, aerospace, and microelectronics.

Industry prospects and the domestic adjustments needed in light of trade and investment liberalisation

The prospects for China's industrial sectors are likely to be shaped by three main forces. First, China's WTO accession and the implementation of its commitments are expected to create a new business environment that will have different effects across industry sectors. In addition, China's own economic growth path, along with the direction of government policies, should also have large implications for the prospects for different industry sectors. Another factor is the direction and size of foreign investment and participation in China's industrial sector, which in turn rely on the strategy of foreign firms. This section provides an overview of industry prospects in light of these forces. It also discusses the adjustments needed in order to reap the benefits arising from these forces, and to overcome the difficulties in a number of industrial segments.

Industry prospects in light of China's WTO accession

China has made very extensive commitments to liberalise access to its domestic market in its WTO accession agreements (see Annex I). Among the sectors, the most dramatic change in market access is promised for the services sector, in particular, banking, securities, insurance, distribution, and retailing. WTO accession will also bring potentially large changes to agriculture. For the industrial sector, as a whole, the change will not be as dramatic as in other sectors because many manufacturing industries have already been fairly open to international competition. Nonetheless, the potential impacts on some previously protected industrial sectors are likely to be significant.

China's accession to WTO impacts the industrial sector through several channels. The most immediate changes concern market access, i.e. the removal of tariff and non-tariff barriers, which directly affect industries and enterprises. China has committed to reduce its average tariff rate for industrial goods from the average of 14.8 per cent in 2001 to 8.9 per cent by 2005.[9] This includes eliminating tariffs on IT products by 2005. The WTO rules and China's commitments under its WTO accession also imply that China has to overhaul government policies, regulations, and administrative systems. These changes imply more equal treatment of enterprises regardless of ownership, and the phasing-out of many government rules and regulations concerning business activities. An array of domestic measures related to trade, investment and other rules and practices that are inconsistent with WTO membership will need to be removed, including direct and indirect support for SOEs. WTO entry also implies a significant change in the environment in which both domestic and foreign firms operate in China. Commitments to agreed rules and schedules of liberalisation change the corporate strategic environment in which firms plan and develop their activities.

Once these commitments are implemented, China will move towards a trade regime based on tariffs, phasing out quotas, licenses and other non-trade barriers. The protection of automobiles, electronics, petrochemicals, and textiles and clothing will decrease substantially. The actual reduction in protection of the automobile sector will be much greater than suggested by tariff reduction, since quotas are also to be phased out. As for China's exports, the main direct impact in terms of improved market access will come from the elimination of the Multi-Fibre Agreement (MFA) quotas on China's textile and apparel exports in 2005.

There have been a number of studies that simulate the impacts of China's WTO entry on trade, output, and employment across different industry sectors (see Annex II for a summary). Overall, the results of these studies suggest that labour-intensive manufacturing sectors are expected to gain in line with China's comparative advantage. In contrast, those previously protected sectors such as resource-oriented activities, chemicals, and automobiles are expected to lose, as a sharp increase in imports leads to a fall in output.

141

Figure 4.7 shows the top five industrial sectors whose output is expected to increase or decrease, suggested by one of the simulation studies (Zhai and Li, 2001). Overall, the "textile" sector (in its broad definition including textile, apparel, and chemical fibres) is expected to benefit the most in terms of output, and employment after WTO entry. This results from China's comparative advantage in labour-intensive manufacturing combined with the elimination of MFA quotas on textile and apparel exports. Some food sectors, such as processed food and grain mill and forage, should also increase their output and exports, which benefit from the reduction in costs of imported agricultural intermediate inputs. In contrast, capital-intensive industries like automobiles, petroleum, electronics, machinery and ferrous metals are expected to lose as protection for these sectors is gradually phased out.

This study also shows that the benefits of trade liberalisation will be spread unevenly across China's regions and provinces. As discussed further in Chapter 21, the coastal area will gain more from trade expansion and the increased export of labour-intensive goods, while the provinces in inland areas, especially the provinces that specialise in agriculture, are expected to experience losses. In particular, Guangdong, Fujian, and Shanghai are likely to be the major beneficiaries of China's WTO accession, as they are important producers of labour-intensive manufacturing products and the most export-oriented provinces.

These simulation studies mainly concern the impact of trade induced by the WTO accession. However, the actual prospects for industrial sectors need to be examined in light of two additional factors. First, the prospects for particular industries rely greatly on the potential for domestic demand growth for their products as well as domestic industrial policy, which could reinforce or offset any impact of WTO.

Figure 4.7. **Impact of WTO entry on the most affected sectors**

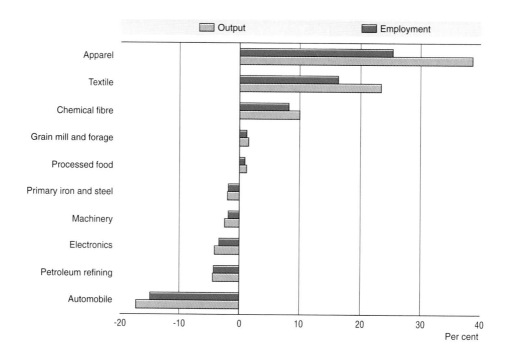

1. The figures refer to percentage changes in employment and output induced by WTO entry in 2010, compared to the benchmark case of no entry.
   Source: Zhai and Li (2001).

Given the stage of economic development and the pattern of consumption growth in China, most Chinese scholars or policy-makers believe that China is entering a new stage of domestic consumption. In particular, large consumption growth is expected in the automobile and housing markets. The rapid growth of housing construction and renovation, spurred by ongoing housing reform, combined with the western development strategy, is expected to boost construction materials industries like steel and cement. In addition, higher-end consumer electronics and information technology (IT) products like computers and mobile phones are believed to have high growth potential. The sectors with high growth potential during the Tenth Five-Year Plan (2001-2005) period include: electronics, medicine, automobiles, complete sets of machinery and equipment, household electronic appliances, leather and furs, furniture, soft drinks, and cultural/educational/sports products (Yang, 2000).

In addition, the government industrial policy is putting an increasing emphasis on the development of new and high-tech industries. The Tenth Five-Year Plan announced in March 2001 sets out two main objectives for the industrial sector:[10] enhancing the capacity of traditional industries with high, new and advanced technologies; and developing new and high-tech industries, using information technology. The government plans to invest US$500 billion in the IT sector by 2005, and envisages that China's electronic and information products manufacturing industry will become the "pillar" industry in the national economy.

A second factor shaping industry prospects is the inflow of foreign capital into China's industrial sector. WTO entry is also expected to bring more foreign direct investment inflows into China, although observers differ on the magnitude of the FDI increase. Not only does WTO entry open up previously closed sectors, but it is also expected to lead to more transparent, stable and predictable government policies, which should help build up foreign investors' confidence in the Chinese market. Furthermore, if the government relaxes the restrictions on cross-border M&As involving Chinese firms, China will also be able to attract more FDI inflows in the form of cross-border M&As which have become the largest component of FDI among OECD countries since the 1990s (OECD, 2001). According to one projection, FDI inflows might increase from the current level of around US$40 billion to an annual level of over US$60 billion in the medium-term, and could even reach US$100 billion if cross-border M&As should be permitted (UNCTAD, 2000b). While much of the additional inflow is expected to go to the services sectors, some industrial sectors are expected to attract more foreign investment after the WTO entry. These industries include labour-intensive processing industries, as foreign investors seek to gain from the increased export opportunities created for these industries, and resource-based industries such as the oil and natural gas exploration industry and mining (see Chapter 10).

As discussed in Chapter 6, foreign companies also show an increasing interest in investing in R&D-intensive industries and in forming R&D joint ventures in China. These investments tend to concentrate on such knowledge-intensive industries as software, telecommunications, biotechnology, and the chemical industry. This change partly reflects foreign companies' rising confidence in the long-term potential of the Chinese market, and a change in their investment strategies towards longer-term investment. It is also partly motivated by the cost advantage of Chinese R&D human resources.

However, many foreign investors still view China as a country where it is difficult to do business. An international survey of the quality or attractiveness of the business environment ranked China as 43rd out of 60 countries for the 2001-05 period.[11] Among the most unfavourable factors in China's business environment are: a high level of business taxes (54th); lack of skilled and qualified workers[12] (52nd); insufficient infrastructure (52nd); and ambivalent policy toward private enterprise and competition (50th). Among the 17 Asian-Pacific countries included in the survey, China ranked 11th in overall position.[13] In another international survey, China ranked 33rd on overall competitiveness among the 49 countries surveyed (IMD, 2001). In particular, China ranked low on business efficiency (40th) and infrastructure (39th). Within the category of infrastructure, China's ranked particularly low on technological infrastructure due in part to lack of technological co-operation between companies, unavailability of qualified IT employees, and low human capital development. These international comparisons highlight China's comparative disadvantages in education, human capital development, business efficiency, and in aspects of overall business environment.

Implications for domestic industry adjustments

The impact further opening up will have on the Chinese industrial sector will depend not only on the current comparative advantages and disadvantages of Chinese industries and firms, but also on their ability to reallocate resources and to restructure to enhance efficiency and competitiveness. Over the past few years, the Chinese government has made major efforts to prepare the industrial sector for the increased competitive pressure arising from anticipated WTO membership. The focus has been on industrial restructuring and enterprise reform along with financial sector reform. The extent to which the industrial sector realises its potential benefits from WTO entry will depend greatly on whether these ongoing efforts make real changes in the way Chinese industries and enterprises operate.

The foregoing discussion suggest that in the medium or shorter term, trade and investment liberalisation will put domestic industries and firms without comparative advantage under competitive pressure, forcing substantial adjustments. The expected higher inflows of foreign direct investment after WTO entry will also put competitive pressure on domestic firms. Domestic companies' profit margins could get squeezed and even eliminated if prices fall with tariff reduction and the removal of other trade barriers. Given the current problems of Chinese industries and enterprises, there have been concerns that China's WTO entry will allow foreign corporations to take over Chinese enterprises, surrendering the domestic markets to control by big foreign companies. While a genuine restructuring process is likely to result in bankruptcy and other forms of exit of domestic firms, there are some reasons to believe that the situation is much more complex.

The potential ability of China's industries to absorb the shocks should not be underestimated, as many of them are already exposed to fierce external competition. Compared to agriculture and services, much of the industrial sector has already been highly exposed to international competition, and the additional pressure is therefore expected to be relatively limited. The progress that has been made in recent years to prepare the industrial sector for WTO entry should also help cushion the shocks coming from further TIL.

Some industrial sectors have strong Chinese SOEs (*e.g.* petroleum) while other sectors have highly efficient, aggressive, medium-sized Chinese enterprises competing in sectors less controlled by the government (*e.g.* consumer electronics). The five-year transition period implied in the WTO agreements should give these Chinese firms a big head start as they already have strong legacy positions. In addition to entrenched market positions, domestic enterprises also have advantages in their understanding of the domestic market and customers.

In contrast, the competitive pressure generated by WTO entry will be particularly challenging for manufacturing SMEs, including TVEs, which suffer from structural problems like low profitability, under-capitalisation, small production scale, lack of technological capabilities, and heavy bureaucratic interference.

In order to realise the full benefits of further trade and investment liberalisation and other broader economic reforms, China's industries will need to make important adjustments. The major adjustments that need to be made in the post-WTO world include:

- Exit of inefficient, small-scale producers and improvements in economies of scale, in particular, in sectors like automobile and chemicals. This requires breaking down local protectionism and accelerating industrial restructuring and reorganisation

- Upgrade technology, improve operational efficiency, and reduce the number of redundant employees. These are of key importance for traditional industries such as textiles and steel. Reducing the policy burdens on SOEs is critical to improving their performance.

- Improve corporate governance of large Chinese SOEs by ending government interference in enterprise management and strengthening external discipline.

- Encourage foreign investment and co-operation to boost the efficiency and competitiveness of Chinese industries and to facilitate their restructuring.

Prospects for selected industrial sectors

This section discusses the implications for the prospects and adjustments in selected industries, *i.e.* textiles and clothing, steel, motor vehicles, consumer electronics, and information and communications technology (ICT) based sectors. As summarised in Table 4.3, these sectors have different growth prospects in terms of domestic demand, exports, imports, and FDI inflows.

Table 4.3. **Prospects for selected industries in light of China's WTO accession**

Industry sector	Domestic demand	China's exports	China's imports	FDI inflow
Textiles and clothing	→	↑	↑	→
Steel	↑	↑	→	↑
Motor vehicles	↑	→	↑	→
Consumer electronics	↑	↑	↓	↑
ICT-based sectors	↑	→	↑	↑

Note: ↑ increase; ↓ decrease; → no significant change.
Source: OECD Secretariat.

Textiles and clothing

China is one of the largest textile and clothing producers and exporters in the world. Relying on low labour costs, the Chinese textile industry is competitive in low value-added clothing, which accounts for 70 per cent of total textile exports. Much of China's clothing products are produced by foreign joint ventures or TVEs in the coastal area. While the textile and clothing industry in China remains one of the most competitive sectors in the international market, it faces a number of structural weaknesses (CASS, 1999):

- The textile industry in China is dominated by SOEs, many of which suffer from negative or low profitability due to excess capacity and operating inefficiencies.

- China has been facing increased competitive pressure from other developing countries, especially from some Asian countries like India, Thailand, Pakistan, and Vietnam where labour costs tend to be even lower than those in China.

- China's textile sector lacks high value-added, high quality products to compete with more advanced economies such as Korea and Chinese Taipei. China's chemical fibre industry, which provides the textile industry with important raw materials, is inferior to those in Japan, Korea, and Chinese Taipei in terms of technology, production scale, product quality and cost-efficiency.

- Many smaller enterprises in the textile sector are disadvantaged in their access to financing. They are also disadvantaged in their access to export outlets and necessary market information because of the monopoly of the state-owned import and export trading system in China.

- Chinese textiles suffer from a lack of technology, innovation and new product development, which seriously affects their potential to move up the value-added chain.

Entry into the WTO also obliges China to reduce its textile import tariffs from the present 25.4 per cent to 11.7 per cent by 2005. On the other hand, textile and clothing will benefit from the opening of the developed countries' markets once MFA quotas and other quantitative restrictions on China's textile and clothing exports are lifted in 2005. These sectors have been identified as the "winners" who will gain the most after China's WTO accession. The effects are likely to differ among the sub-groups of textile products:

- With the elimination of the current quota structure by 2005, the potential for clothing exports will be further exploited, in particular through increased flows of foreign and domestic capital into this sector.

145

- While tariff reduction is not expected to greatly affect the enterprises that produce lower-end textiles, the enterprises producing mainly high-grade materials and fabrics, especially chemical fibres, will face increased competition from the producers in more advanced countries such as Japan, Korea, and Chinese Taipei. Increased competition will accelerate the restructuring of the textile industry, especially SOEs in the value-added sectors like textile raw materials and high quality clothing.

In order to maximise the benefits from the increased opportunities in this sector, further industrial restructuring and enterprise reforms will be necessary so that Chinese enterprises remain competitive in the world market.

- Improve technological and innovative capabilities of textile and clothing enterprises.

- Stimulate the development of non-state enterprises, in particular, urban and rural collectives, shareholding enterprises, and private enterprises, which adjust more quickly to market signals. The measures might include: improving the financing for SMEs in this sector; expanding the trading rights for SMEs; and facilitating co-operation with foreign joint ventures or other larger firms including SOEs.

- Facilitate the process of shifting production to interior regions might also help firms take advantage of low wage costs.

- Accelerate the restructuring and reorganisation of SOEs through M&As and bankruptcies to dispose of non-performing assets and to improve operating efficiencies as well as technical upgrading. Migration of textile production from the coast to low-wage interior regions needs to be facilitated by reducing protectionist barriers.

Steel

The iron and steel industry is one of the most important industrial sectors of China, accounting for 6.5 per cent of value-added and 5.5 per cent of employment in manufacturing. In 1996, China became the world's largest crude steel producer. Since then, the growth in steel production has been maintained and in 2000 a crude steel output of 127.3 million tonnes was recorded – representing 15 per cent of total world steel production.

Chinese steel demand has also witnessed an equally important expansion. Demand for steel in China has more than quadrupled since 1980. China consumed more than 130 million tons of steel in 2000, surpassing the United States to become the largest market in the world. Chinese consumption is currently close to 16 per cent of world steel demand.

During the last two decades, China's steel industry has established a comprehensive structure covering mining, sintering, coke making, rolling, and the accessory departments including ferroalloys, refractory activities, carbon products, engineering and scientific research. However, its development has been hampered by the fragmented proliferation of small producers, which has resulted in losses or low profitability, high debts, low productivity and an excess of low-end products such as ordinary small sections (which include round bars and concrete reinforcing bars) and wire rods. At the same time, some high value-added products (particularly stainless steel, cold-rolled silicon sheets and galvanised sheets) have remained in substantial shortage.

As a result of the product mix, China relies heavily on imports of high value-added products. China is the world's second largest net importer of steel. In 2000, China recorded a negative trade balance of 10 million tonnes, which was largely due to voluminous imports of high value added products such as coated sheets and cold rolled products. On the other hand, the country's steel exports are mainly composed of semi-finished products and hot rolled flat products.[14]

Productivity, measured as crude steel output per worker, reached only 40 tonnes, less than one-fourteenth of the performance of developed steel-producing countries. With the exception of the Shanghai Baosteel Group (800 tonnes per worker) Chinese productivity even lags behind Eastern European countries such as Poland and Romania, for which this indicator was 200-300 tonnes per worker. After the strong cuts in the industrial working force in 1999 from more than 1 million in 1998 to 600 000 by the end of 2000, the Chinese authorities are planning to further reduce the number of employees engaged in steel production.

Given the steel industry's strategic importance, it has been one of the major targets of industry restructuring programmes during the 1990s. The central government programme has been aimed at restoring profitability to the main producers, which are still predominantly state owned, in addition to making the industry internationally competitive once again.

As a result of the restructuring effort, a more competitive structure of the domestic steel industry was achieved through mergers and acquisitions on the one hand, and the closing of non-viable small units on the other. By the end of 1999, 294 steelworks existed in China compared to more than 2 500 mills at the beginning of the 1990s. However, there is further room for industry concentration. The five largest producers, i.e. Shanghai Baoshan Iron and Steel (Baosteel) Group, Anshan Iron and Steel (Angang), Shougang Corporation, Wuhan Iron and Steel (Wugang) and Panzhihua Iron and Steel (Pangang) accounted for only 34.3 per cent of China's crude steel output in 1999. Seventy-one companies accounted for a total of 84 per cent of total steel production.

The modernisation of the steel mills, through technological upgrading and renovation, also accelerated in the second half of the 1990s. Production in open-hearth furnaces has sharply diminished, and will be totally phased out by 2002. The electric arc furnace and converter production means gained in importance. High priority was given to increase the production of continuously-cast steel, which accounted for 68.9 per cent of total steel output in 1999. However, this figure remains well below those of developed countries, where it is over 95 per cent. A number of joint ventures and strategic alliances with partners from abroad have been undertaken in recent years.

One of the challenges currently facing the Chinese steel industry is the reduction of redundant employees. While the large producers such as the Baosteel group managed to reduce their workforce drastically, smaller producers in underdeveloped regions remain burdened with redundant workers due to the lack of local funding for social benefits (see Chapter 5).

The Tenth Five-Year Plan (2001-2005) lists the objectives for the steel industry as enlarging product variety, implementing high technology, achieving higher quality, saving energy, increasing labour productivity and alleviating pollution. Efforts to increase capacities for the production of steel with a low self-sufficiency ratio are given a major focus. Major projects include the renovation and/or construction of continuous concasting mills at several sites, the renovation of cold-rolled silicon steel strip lines, the renovation of heavy and medium plate lines in Angang, Hangang, Baosteel and Jigang and the erection of stainless steel smelting and hot rolling mills by the Baosteel Group.

The small and medium-sized steel mills are encouraged to strive for "High-tech, specialisation, precision uniqueness and originality" as well as co-operation with the large companies. However, many SMEs will not survive these structural changes, and might be forced to close business either as a result of stronger competition on the domestic market or through administrative measures.

In light of the current crisis in the international steel trading system, which is characterised by overcapacity, historically low steel prices and millions of tonnes of excess steel, the integration of the Chinese steel industry into the global steel market through WTO membership comes at a very critical juncture. This will add to the pressure for reform generated by the Tenth Five-Year Plan, and give the Chinese steel industry a harder time during this period.

China has committed to lower tariffs on steel imports from the current level of 10.6 per cent to 8.1 per cent by 2004. Import quotas will be eliminated and import-licensing systems will be liberalised. Subsidy disciplines will be established. On the other hand, China's steel exports will benefit from permanent Most Favoured Nations (MFN) status with all WTO members. Tariff reductions and removal of non-tariff barriers will certainly lead to fiercer competition on the domestic steel market with an expected increase of steel imports. In particular, steel manufacturers in Japan, the Republic of Korea, and Russia have also shifted their focus to overseas markets due to sluggish domestic demand.

However, the direct impact of tariff reductions is expected to be relatively limited. China's domestic market has already been flooded with low-end foreign steel products, even when small domestic plants continue to overproduce these products. With regard to Chinese steel exports, the benefits from receiving MFN status should also not be overestimated.

Meanwhile, the most positive factor for China's steel industry is likely to come from the prospect of the surge in domestic demand, which is expected to more than double by 2010.[15] The expected increase in construction investment in China, particularly for infrastructure projects in the less developed western regions and urban private housing, combined with growing demand for durable goods such as automobiles, and electrical household appliances in the world's most populous country, point to an enormous potential for long-term growth of domestic steel demand.

It is estimated that annual demand is set to increase by 50 million tonnes, to more than 182 million tonnes, by 2005, but no more than 27 million tonnes of net planned expansion capacity can be identified in China (Woetzel, 2001). This implies a gap of up to 44 million tonnes in the supply of finished steel by 2005, a gap that can be filled only by imports or higher productivity. But steel is not a major investment area for the central government in the Tenth Five-Year Plan, because the central government is hoping that continued deregulation and consolidation will be catalyst enough for improvement. The government is forcing the large steel producers to go to the private sector for the funds they need for growth.

Foreign and local private investors, as well as regional governments, seem to have a great interest in the industry given the prospect of the booming demand, but many of them appear to be waiting for additional restructuring before they act (Woetzel, 2001). Thus, if the industry is willing to restructure, private and foreign capital is likely to flow into the sector. Significant growth of foreign direct investment in the Chinese steel industry and steel-consuming industries will boost efficiency. By bringing with it new technologies and processes such investment could be important for the restructuring of the steel sector.

Motor vehicles

China now ranks 10th in world production of all types of motor vehicles. The Chinese auto industry has a production capacity of 2.5 million motor vehicles but operates at about 70 per cent capacity. China also produces 3.2 million agricultural vehicles and 11.2 million motorcycles per year.[16]

The Chinese government has given high priority to developing an indigenous auto industry. High tariff rates and various non-tariff barriers have protected Chinese auto manufacturers from foreign competition. Although tariffs have been reduced from an average of 200 per cent in 1986 to the present 80-100 per cent, they have been high enough to guarantee a profit. Many provincial governments identified automobiles as their pillar industry and built their own auto plants. Protective provincial and municipal government policies, including high regional trade barriers, have supported weak local producers, (Wang, 2001).

As a result, there are currently more than 120 auto firms in China, exceeding the total of the United States, Japan and Europe combined. These auto firms are supplied by more than 3 000 companies delivering engines, components and spare parts (Posth, 2001). Production scales are small, resulting in extremely low productivity.[17] Other weaknesses include a technology level more than 20 years behind those in developed countries, and unclear property structures of auto companies owned by different government agencies.

Attracted by the huge market potential, almost all the leading 50 international auto companies are currently engaged in the Chinese market. Since production started in 1985, Shanghai Volkswagen has become the market leader in the sector. Together with a second joint venture of the VW-group (FAW-VW), the Volkswagen joint ventures have over 50 per cent of the market share. The potential of China's growing heavy-duty truck market has also attracted international automakers to seek co-operation with Chinese counterparts. In the auto parts sector, China's leading tire company, Shanghai

Tire and Rubber Co., signed agreements with the French firm Michelin to form a US$200 million joint venture in Shanghai.

In anticipation of China's WTO entry, the government has promoted rationalisation of the auto industry through the formation of three backbone auto groups including the First Automotive Works (FAW) in Changchuan, the Shanghai Automotive Industry Group (SAIG) and the Dongfeng Motors Group in Hubei. The Chinese automakers are also accelerating efforts aimed at recapitalisation and restructuring of their operation and product upgrading.[18]

China's WTO commitments include one of the steepest cut in tariffs for automobiles and auto parts among industrial products. China will lower auto tariffs from the current rate of 80 to 100 per cent to 25 per cent by 1 July 2006. Tariffs for auto parts will be cut to 10 per cent. China has also committed to scrap import quotas for autos by 2005. Due to the largest reduction rate in tariffs together with the comparative disadvantage in China's auto sector, simulation studies have identified China's auto industry as the "loser" after WTO entry, as previously discussed.

However, the actual situation is likely to be more complicated than the simulation studies might suggest. Although China's auto firms are not presently competitive, the domestic auto industry in China may not shrink even after China removes protection. Imports of luxury cars or those autos that are not produced in China will increase, but most of the economy cars are expected to be produced in China rather than imported (Hai, 2000). Once protection is removed, the small-scale auto production companies will disappear, but production of joint venture autos will expand. In other words, auto producers in developed countries are likely to prefer to produce economy cars in China rather than to produce the cars in their home countries and export them to China. Because of the growing market for small and medium-size economy cars, China is attracting foreign direct investment from the world's major auto producers. Therefore, while the trade impact of the WTO entry will reduce or shut down the small auto companies' production, the foreign direct investment impact will expand the production of Chinese-made foreign cars.

At the same time, the Chinese domestic market has a huge potential. According to one study, potential car demand in China is projected to reach 2 million by 2005 and 4 million by the year 2010 (Zhai, 2000). According to this projection, cars in use in China will reach 17 per thousand people by 2010, a level equal to that in Japan in the mid-1960s and that in Korea and Chinese Taipei in the mid-1980s. However, to turn such a huge potential demand into reality will require major adjustment of current policies. Removal of various restrictions on the purchase of automobiles and improvement of the environment for the use of automobiles will be of key importance to the development of China's automobile market and of its automobile industry.

The government has imposed a considerable number of restrictions on the consumption of automobiles, including large extra taxes and fees. The high production costs caused by the small production scale, together with extra taxes and fees, have resulted in high prices and slow sales of cars. The prices of Chinese cars are usually twice the international prices, too high for ordinary Chinese people. As a result, in 1998, the demand for cars reached only 0.5 million.

The removal of tariff and non-tariff barriers after WTO entry will put considerable pressure on small and less competitive auto firms to cut production costs, which in turn requires sharp increases in production scale. This pressure will force many of these firms to restructure or to seek co-operation and support from large enterprises in order to survive.

Observers, however, expect that the actual change in competitive positioning is likely to be less dramatic. Although many of the small, inefficient car producers will lose ground as imports flood in, new manufacturing entrants are less likely, since it will not be easy to outperform the relatively efficient, large-scale joint venture manufacturers such as SAIC-Volkswagen.

If China liberalises its policy concerning foreign participation in the automobile sector after WTO entry, China's automobile firms will benefit from more immediate and open access to foreign companies' global resources, technologies, and scale benefits. The competitiveness of the Chinese automobile industry should be enhanced through technological upgrading, product development, and improved management know-how as a result of the increased FDI inflows.

In particular, market liberalisation in the financial services and sales and distribution sectors will provide further opportunities for foreign investors to increase their presence in China. While it will put domestic manufacturers under additional pressure to improve their distribution and after-sales service networks, it has two other potentially important implications. Increased competition and improved performance in the sales, distribution, and after-sales service networks can provide a significant boost to consumer demand for autos in the domestic market. Even though domestic firms are likely to be disadvantaged initially, they may learn quickly and adapt to the new market situation by exploiting their location advantage. Along with other policy measures such as reduced vehicle taxation rates, elimination of *ad hoc* fees and increased financing availability, this scenario suggests that increased competition could create a win-win situation for domestic and foreign auto manufacturers.

Consumer electronics

China ranks third in the production of household electronic appliances, following the United States and Japan. In the last two decades, the Chinese consumer electronics industry has grown rapidly, with output increasing 20 to 50 per cent per year for most products. Through intensive internal competition, Chinese brands dominate the domestic market, accounting for 95 per cent of the market for refrigerators, 83 per cent for washing machines, 74 per cent for air-conditioners, 81 per cent for colour television sets and 71 per cent for microwave ovens.

This sector has been one of the largest recipients of foreign direct investment inflows in recent years, as foreign manufactures have moved production bases to China to lower production costs and raise competitiveness. For example, Japan's Toshiba Corporation moved its entire television production operation in Japan to China in April 2001. China also accounted for about 90 per cent of General Electric's overseas production in 2000, compared with only about 5 per cent in 1997.[19] Foreign production is highly concentrated on manufacturing for export and on traditional, low-value added products. Although foreign firms still have a very small market share, they rely on their technology advantage to compete in upper market niches for higher-technology products.

The consumer electronics industry has some of China's best companies – for example, Haier, KCL and Konka – that are highly efficient and internationally competitive. These firms grew in a highly competitive environment. For example, when China opened up its market for household appliances in the 1980s, it was soon dominated by foreign firms, particularly Japanese manufacturers. In 1983, colour television sets produced by local manufacturers accounted for only 15 per cent of the market. The opening of the market resulted in industry consolidation led by large domestic companies in the late 1980s and early 1990s through a series of M&As. As the industry consolidation deepened, domestic companies became more price-competitive, benefiting from economies of scale. Chinese enterprises started to aggressively regain their market share. By 1997, Chinese producers accounted for 81 per cent of total colour TVs sold in China and had started to expand into overseas markets (CICC, 1999).

Further opening of this sector through WTO membership will mean an intensification of competition in an already competitive sector. The home appliance sector has already been suffering from falling prices and extremely thin profit margins as a result of fierce domestic competition and oversupply. The situation has been aggravated by the presence of a large number of small-scale producers operating under the protection of local governments. The recent move by foreign electronic manufacturers to base production in China will also add to the problems for local producers. Given the already intense competition in the domestic market, domestic companies' profit margins might get squeezed if prices fall further once the tariffs are completely eliminated. This is likely to lead to another round of industry consolidation and enterprise restructuring in the home appliance sector. However, given the past experience in the sector, the leading domestic firms in this sector are likely to become more competitive after the adjustment process. The export competitiveness of these local firms should also improve as reduced tariffs further lower the price of many components they import.

ICT-*based sectors*

Growing by an annual average of 20 per cent since the early 1980s, China's ICT equipment industry is becoming one of the world's largest. In particular, telecommunications equipment is one of the most rapidly growing sectors in China and a major source of export expansion. The Chinese government envisages that the ICT manufacturing industry will become the "pillar" of the national economy and catch up to the production scale of the United States and Japan. To fulfil this objective, the Chinese government plans to invest US$500 billion in the information technology sector during the period between 2001 and 2005. China's Tenth Five-Year Plan (2001-05) predicts the output value of ICT products will reach US$303 billion by 2005 and foreign exchange earnings will reach US$100 billion.

China signed the WTO Information Technology Agreement (ITA) and is obliged to eliminate tariffs on 200 types of information technology products, including computers and computer components, telecommunications equipment and parts, semiconductors and components, software including disks, cassette and compact disks, and scientific research equipment. Elimination of tariffs will lead to an increase in the import of ICT products that, together with improved protection of intellectual property rights, will generate greater competitive pressures on Chinese manufacturers. China will reduce its current 10 per cent tariff on monitors to 3.8 per cent in 2002 and down to zero in 2003. For key monitor components, for which China relies heavily on imports, the tariff cuts may be even steeper. In the long run, the tariff cuts will be helpful in increasing the sales of liquid crystal display (LCD) monitors.

China is the world's most rapidly growing market for telecommunication services and products. For example, web users account for only 2 per cent of the population in China compared to 45 per cent in the United States and 21 per cent in Korea. The penetration of personal computers in China is very low – around 1 per cent currently – but expected to rise to 2.3 per cent by 2002. The penetration of mobile phones is relatively higher – close to 3 per cent in 1999 – and is expected to rise to almost 7 per cent by 2002 (Perkins and Shaw, 2000). China is also the fastest growing LCD monitor market in Asia, with 500 000 units sold in 2001, compared to only 11 000 units in 2000. It is expected that LCD monitor sales in China will grow by more than 80 per cent in 2002.[20]

Competition will further intensify in the ICT industry in China, in part between foreign and domestic producers. Foreign investment is already significant and is expected to grow further. Major international players in the ICT sector such as Motorola, Ericsson, Nokia and Siemens have heavily invested in China and plan to increase their investment. Construction is underway for Motorola (China) Electronics' US$1.9 billion semiconductor plant – one of the biggest in the world – in Tianjin, while Phillips also plans to build a US$1 billion semiconductor plant in Suzhou. Ericsson has business expansion plans that will create 29 000 new jobs in the next five years in China, and Motorola is to invest an additional US$6.6 billion in the coming five years. More multinationals – including Microsoft, Nokia, Intel, IBM and National – are also investing in research and development capabilities in China to strengthen their competitive positions. Sony Corporation has announced that it will manufacture and sell personal computers in China, becoming the first Japanese manufacture to do so, starting from 2003.[21] The computers will be sold in China, whose personal computer market is estimated at seven million units per year – about 50 per cent of Japan's own market.

The largest challenge facing the industry is to develop domestic technological capabilities and improve absorption capacity for imported technology and know-how. This objective will be best achieved by government reforms directed at improving the competitive environment, R&D infrastructure and other framework conditions, rather than insulating domestic firms from international competition through special support and protection.

Challenges for industrial development in China

China's further trade and investment liberalisation and broader economic reforms could bring great opportunities for industrial development in China. China's WTO entry should in principle help the necessary restructuring, by creating a better business environment through increased competition, a better functioning of market mechanisms, and an improved regulatory framework. Other ongoing

151

economic reforms aimed at enhancing the efficiency of the Chinese economy should also help improve the efficiency of industries.

Trade and investment liberalisation is, however, unlikely by itself to improve industry performance. The benefits of trade and investment liberalisation will depend critically on the ability of domestic sectors to restructure and upgrade operations to improve efficiency and competitiveness. The necessary domestic adjustments to boost international competitiveness have become all the more challenging as the rapid globalisation and technological change during the last decade have significantly altered the global business environment facing China's industries and enterprises. The changing domestic industrial landscape as well as the new global environment pose significant challenges to the industrial policy in China over this decade.

Market-based restructuring for industrial competitiveness

If trade and other reforms associated with WTO entry are successful, the comparative advantage of China's industry will be brought into full play so as to raise the overall international competitiveness of the industrial sector. As discussed in the previous sections, China's further integration in the international economy through WTO membership will provide an opportunity to further exploit its comparative advantage in labour-intensive industries such as textiles and garments. China should use this timely opportunity to let resources flow to these sectors and create jobs before it loses its current comparative advantage in these industries to other developing countries. The development of this sector will also be particularly important for the creation of additional employment, which will help relieve the social pressure coming from rising unemployment during structural adjustment.

However, at the same time, China will have to go through a process of longer-term industrial restructuring if these short-term benefits are to lead to sustained benefits. China's long-term growth will suffer if its competitive edge remains with low-wage, unskilled labour employed in the low value-added industries. China will have to continue to produce more goods for international markets as wages rise and lead to the phasing-out of labour-intensive exports. The experience of East Asian economies shows that the choice of appropriate industries and technologies consistent with the relative factor scarcities of the economy is a key to sustain economic development. These countries have developed in accordance with changing comparative advantages from labour-intensive to capital-intensive industries, and later to knowledge-intensive, high-technology industries.

Restructuring for industrial competitiveness means moving from static to dynamic sources of cost advantage in industry. This means moving up the technological ladder, from low to high value-added industries, in particular those that offer greater scope for technological advance and more spillover benefits to related activities. It also implies moving to more complex products and processes within a specific sector. Only such a structural shift allows a country to achieve long-term competitive industrial growth, instead of just remaining in a low-growth path. This sort of restructuring involves a complex learning process, calling for technological effort, skill building, networking and new organisational forms (UNCTAD, 2000a).

In order to sustain industrial growth, industrial restructuring will need to be accompanied by upgrading of technology and strengthening of industry's capacity to innovate and to absorb new technology. The technological and innovative capabilities of Chinese industries are generally weak, and the investment by the government and the enterprise sector in science and technology, R&D, and education and training has been quite low. These factors have led to a high reliance of Chinese industries on foreign technology, in particular among low value-added industries, as well as to limited technology diffusion.

The role of domestic policies is to create the conditions for successful industrial restructuring both in the shorter and longer terms. What is critical, however, is that restructuring decisions are based on strict commercial criteria and are not directed by the government's administrative and other non-commercial concerns. A successful market-driven restructuring process will enable China to overcome the medium-term adjustment challenges as well as to ensure longer-term industrial development.

Industrial policy in a changing global business environment

China's industrial development over this decade will be set against the background of rapid globalisation and technological change. During the 1990s, a distinctly different global economy emerged, characterised by rapid technological change, shorter product cycles, developments in information technology, widespread privatisation and deregulation, and rapid integration of global product and capital markets. Industries have to adopt new and often much larger-scale technologies, and have to operate at optimum efficiency. Otherwise, existing comparative advantages are rapidly overtaken by new competitors. This requires firms to develop the capacity to adapt continuously to technical change. Size alone is no longer sufficient.

While the protection of domestic industries might be justified on the grounds of the "infant industry" argument, this argument has also been frequently misused to prop up inefficient domestic firms, resulting in uncompetitive production (Bora, *et al.*, 2000). Protectionist measures usually create a moral hazard problem, which was common in many other Asian economies before the 1997 financial crisis, and can become a drag on longer-term growth and development. Attempts to induce industrial upgrading artificially by state intervention aimed at insulating some "key" sectors of the economy from productivity-enhancing international market competition can lower productivity growth rather than enhancing it, because they simply lift costs to other sectors in the economy and create rents, thereby wasting resources (Drysdale, 2000). Pursuing this type of industrial policy is likely to become even more problematic as China integrates further into the rapidly changing global economy.

The new global business environment has important implications for the objectives and instruments of industrial policy in developing countries. Firms in developing countries now face a far more competitive international environment. The experience of OECD countries suggests that the best way to respond to this situation is to liberalise business regulation and strengthen a competitive, market-based framework. Sustained improvement in operating efficiency depends on the ability of firms to effectively employ resources needed to upgrade the quality of their productive capacity and organisation.

In this context, much greater flexibility will be needed in the industrial policy framework to be more effective in the changing global environment after WTO entry. In particular, China's industrial policy framework will need to move from the current model based on state ownership and an interventionist mode of interaction with the business sector, to a market-based model of industrial development characterised by an efficient and flexible industrial sector in which enterprise decision-making is based on market principles. There are at least three current policy areas that need to be reviewed.

First, the current policy objective of developing large enterprises or enterprise groups should be carefully re-examined and re-addressed so that these enterprises or groups do not turn into inefficient, unprofitable entities that drag on other economic sectors. China's large enterprise groups tend to be characterised by weaknesses in their corporate governance mechanisms; weak financial discipline coming from implicit government backing; formation by government fiat with insufficient attention to their economic merits; and lack of clear exit mechanisms in place. Despite the government's continued efforts to establish globally competitive large enterprises or groups, China's leading large enterprises have not only failed to catch up with the global giants, but have also fallen much further behind the position they held when the industrial policy began almost two decades ago (Nolan, 2001). As seen in the case of the automobile industry, the central government's efforts to nurture a few globally competitive vehicle manufacturers through various protectionist measures have largely isolated China's auto manufacturers who, on their own, are unable to compete in the global market. Isolation from foreign as well as domestic competition has been especially disadvantageous to Chinese auto firms as the pace of change in global markets has continued to accelerate.

Large enterprise groups relying on continuous government support will have enormous difficulties in building competitive capabilities in the international markets. The liberalisation of trade and capital markets has created a "global level playing field" where global giant firms from advanced economies have dramatically increased business capabilities. These global giants benefit from massive expenditures on R&D as well as on marketing and brand building.

The second area needing re-examination is the continued commitment to retain substantial state ownership in the business sector, particularly in industries deemed to be "strategic". The experience of other countries strongly suggest that the contribution of SOEs to overall economic performance is likely to be greatest when they are confined to natural monopolies or other industries where extensive public ownership is clearly needed on economic or compelling social grounds. Although China is still a developing economy, defining the strategic industries where SOEs will dominate fairly narrowly is likely to be most conducive to economic growth and development. Ultimately, developing an efficient and flexible industrial sector that responds to market signals should require a significant reduction in state ownership in most industries.

Third, government interference in economic decisions has limited the effectiveness of reform measures in several areas, notably in M&As. The government should redefine and re-establish its role as a regulator of the industries, providing framework conditions conducive to market-based industrial restructuring and upgrading (see Chapter 11). Government agencies at various levels should also fully curtail their interference in the decision-making of SOEs and other public enterprises, in particular the selection of senior management.

Conclusions and policy implications

China's WTO entry, together with broader economic reforms, is a potential watershed for the reform and development of China's industrial sector. China's reform and opening-door policies since the late 1970s have transformed China's trade structure along with its comparative advantage, with broadly defined labour-intensive products comprising the bulk of China's exports. Further opening to international markets is expected to bring the production and export structures even more into line with China's comparative advantage.

Many manufacturing industries in China, however, are characterised by structural weaknesses such as over-capacity, lack of economies of scale, inefficient operations, and weak technological and innovative capabilities. Although the accelerated reform efforts over the past few years have led to significant improvement in some areas, widespread inefficiencies still exist in most sectors. China's WTO membership will put the inefficient and less competitive industries and firms under pressure, forcing them to restructure.

The major challenge to realising the potential benefits of trade and investment liberalisation is to improve conditions for long-term industrial upgrading and development, while maximising the medium and shorter-term benefits created for labour-intensive industries. In meeting these challenges, there is a potentially large role for government policy in improving competitiveness and facilitating industrial restructuring. However, the best outcomes are likely to be obtained if the government plays a role in optimising the business environment, instead of directly controlling or interfering with business activities.

In the near term, the most immediate objective is to accelerate market-based industrial restructuring and SOE reforms to improve efficiency and competitiveness. In particular, priority should be given to removing government imposed obstacles to industrial restructuring and providing a level playing field for enterprises regardless of ownership, size or location. At the same time, the government should redefine and re-establish its role as a regulator of the industries, providing framework conditions conducive to market-based industrial restructuring and upgrading.

- *Accelerate SOE reforms.* Of particular importance are tightening the budget constraints on SOEs and improving corporate governance. Government agencies should fully curtail interference in the decision-making of enterprises – in particular the selection of senior management. More drastic measures to reduce the state shares of SOEs will be needed so as to introduce a wider and deeper participation of foreign and private capital in the restructuring of the SOE sector.

- *Establish level-playing fields among enterprises.* More concrete efforts will be needed to establish a level-playing field for enterprises so that resources flow to the most efficient enterprises regardless of ownership, size or location. The special protection and preferences that are currently given to large SOEs should be curtailed. At the same time, restructuring of non-state enterprises, in particular non-state SMEs, should be fostered. This should include measures to facilitate financing, advance technological capacities, and improve the business environment for these firms. Increasing economic and technical co-operation between these firms and larger SOEs or foreign-invested firms could also help overcome the weaknesses in technical capacities of these firms.

- *Encourage and better utilise foreign direct investment inflows.* Efforts are needed to attract higher inflows of FDI in light of the global trend in cross-border M&As and to better utilise foreign direct investment to upgrade technological and other capabilities of domestic industries. In particular, more active measures to attract foreign direct investment to the central and western regions should help restructure inefficient industries and promote industrial development in those regions. Concrete measures to attract foreign investors to SMEs might also have a high payoff.

If reforms in these areas are to be successful, complementary reforms in other areas will be crucial. These include: financial sector reform aimed at commercialising state banks' lending decisions; reform of the social security system; and reforms to facilitate and accelerate bankruptcy and other insolvency mechanisms as discussed in other chapters. In addition, important complementary reforms include:

- *Remove regional barriers.* More active and systematic efforts by the central government to eliminate regional barriers to business establishments, M&As and competiton will be needed to improve the effectiveness of the industry restructuring process. As local protectionism has been one of the main reasons underlying the problems of over-capacity, lack of economies of scale, and inefficient operation, ending this situation is of key importance to improving industry performance.

- *Establish and enforce linkages between regions.* Particular attention should also be given to enhance the production, trade and technology linkages between the developed coastal regions and inland regions. These linkages have remained relatively weak, due partly to the unattractive business environment arising from local protectionism and inefficient infrastructure in western regions. China's current western development strategy should help this process by improving the infrastructure of inland regions, and the business environment.

Over the longer term, policy priority should be given to developing and ensuring the national business environment conducive to maximising the efficiency of competitiveness of industries and firms. This requires a multi-faceted approach involving enterprise governance; financial discipline; competition; R&D infrastructure, education and human capital development, and framework conditions essential to effective market functioning. In this context, maintaining and, where necessary, strengthening regulatory regimes to buttress competition and financial prudential policies is also of high priority.

- *Strengthen external discipline.* The effectiveness and sustainability of the reforms for the industrial sector will ultimately depend on the strengthening of external disciplines in the near term as well as in the longer term. Various areas of reform, such as financial and competition policies, should be designed and implemented to impose hard budget constraints upon firms.

- *Develop R&D infrastructure.* R&D and technology diffusion play a critical role in overall industry performance and are an important determinant of international competitiveness at the industry level. Given the low level of R&D infrastructure in China, there is a need to increase government resources devoted to basic R&D.

- *Foster human resources development*. China has a long-term need for skilled and qualified workers for sustained industrial development. As China moves up the technological ladder, the quality of the labour force will become a major contributor to business sector performance. More policy efforts to promote human resources development through education and training should help upgrade the skill levels of the workforce (see Annex III on education).

NOTES

1. In China, the category of "industry" includes manufacturing industries and mining/extraction industries. The analysis of this chapter follows this definition of industry, although the focus is on manufacturing industries.

2. The Asian NIEs refer to Chinese Taipei, Hong Kong-China, Korea, and Singapore, whereas ASEAN-4 countries are Indonesia, Malaysia, the Philippines, and Thailand.

3. An "individually owned firm" is defined as a privately owned firm with no more than 8 employees, whereas a "private firm" is defined as a privately owned firm with more than 8 employees.

4. Non-economic objectives such as national pride and prestige, the perceived need to promote "strategic" domestic industries, and the commitment to retain substantial state ownership in the economy have also influenced China's industrial policy.

5. Recently the central government has been acting to suppress local barriers to trade and investment in the automobiles sector.

6. According to the World Bank study, bankruptcies of all forms of enterprises rose from 277 per year in 1989-93 to 2 000 in 1994-95, and further to 5 640 per year in 1996-97.

7. For example, Chinese manufacturing GDP, converted into Germany's currency by PPPs, provides a labour productivity level lower than 7 per cent of the German level in 1995 (Ren and Bai, 2001).

8. Knowledge-based industries refer to those which are relatively intensive in their inputs of technology and human capital, including aerospace, chemicals/biotechnology, information and communication technologies (ICT) equipment and services, consumer electronics and the environment industry (OECD, 2000b).

9. The government already announced that the average tariff rate of industrial products would be lowered to 11.6 per cent in 2002 (Xinhua News Agency, 4 January 2002).

10. The government also continues to pursue a strategy of developing large enterprises and groups, considered to be critical to competitiveness in international markets. During the Tenth Five-Year Plan, the government plans to set up 30 to 50 large enterprises and enterprise groups through listing, M&As, co-operation and reorganisation.

11. The Economist Intelligence Unit Limited (EIU) *Country Reports*, 3 July 2001.

12. Foreign companies find that certain positions are difficult to fill locally, including financial controllers, internal auditors and planners; quality assurance managers; bankers; broad-based MBAs; biotechnology specialists; internet programmers, information technology specialists.

13. These countries include: Australia, China, Chinese Taipei, Hong Kong-China, India, Indonesia, Japan, Korea, Malaysia, New Zealand, Pakistan, the Philippines, Singapore, Sri Lanka, Thailand, and Vietnam.

14. Japan, followed by Chinese Taipei, Korea, Russia and Ukraine, are the most important steel exporting economies to China. On the other hand, Chinese Taipei and the Republic of Korea figure prominently among the destinations for Chinese steel exports.

15. Apparent steel consumption per capita of China reached 93.3 kg in 1999 after increasing from 46 kg in 1990. This indicator is still well below the world average of around 125 kg, and far below the OECD Member country average of 379.5 kg.

16. In contrast to the auto industry, which has made little real progress, China's motorcycle industry, despite little support from the state, has developed so rapidly that it has ranked first in the world in terms of output and sales.

17. Only five of the auto firms produced more than 100 000 vehicles a year. The top five auto manufacturers in terms of output are: First Auto Group, Shanghai Auto Industry Group, Dong Feng Auto Group, Tianjin Auto Industry Group, and ChangAn Auto. China's largest auto manufacturer, First Auto Group, produced 300 000 vehicles in 1998, compared with output of more than 7 million by General Motors (CICC, 1999).

18. For example, the participation of the Anhui Automotive Parts Co. in the Shanghai Automotive Industry Group (SAIG) by share transfer to establish the SAIG Chery Automotive Co. is described as the biggest

recapitalisation in the automotive industry in China. China First Automotive Group (FAG) has decided to withdraw from the FAW-Jinbei Automotive Co. as part of major restructuring efforts.

19. Emerson Electric Co. plans to invest about US$1 billion in China over the next few years. It includes US$30 million to build a washing machine component plant in Qingdao, where China's biggest electronic appliance maker Haier is based. Another part of the US$1 billion investment is to go toward the expansion of the production capacity of Copeland, Emerson's air-conditioning compressor subsidiary in Suzhou.

20. China Economic Information Service, 17 January 2002.

21. *Business Beijing*, 10 January 2002.

BIBLIOGRAPHY

Bora, B., P.J. Lloyd and M. Pangestu (2000),
"Industrial policy and the WTO", *The World Economy*, Vol. 23, No. 4, pp. 543-559.

Cable, V. (1996),
"The outlook for labour-intensive manufacturing in China", *China in the 21st Century: Long-Term Global Implications*, OECD, Paris.

China International Capital Corporation Limited (CICC) (1999),
Choose to Have No Choice: China's Accession to WTO, July 29.

Chinese Academy of Social Sciences (CASS) (1999),
The Research Report on China's Entry into WTO: The Analysis of the China's Industries, Social Sciences Documentation Publishing House (in Chinese).

Drysdale, P. (2000),
"The implications of China's membership of the WTO for industrial transformation", in Drysdale, P. and L. Song (eds.) *China's Entry to the WTO: Strategic issues and quantitative assessments*, London and New York: Routledge.

Gregory, N. and S. Tenev (2001),
"The financing of private enterprise in China", *Finance and Development*, Vol. 38, No. 1, March.

Hai, W. (2000),
"China's WTO membership: Significance and implications", *International Economic Review*, Vol. 2, Beijing.

Huang, Y. (2001),
Economic Fragmentation and FDI in China, Davidson Institute Working Paper Series No. 374, The William Davidson Institute at the University of Michigan Business School.

International Institute for Management Development (IMD) (2001),
The World Competitiveness Yearbook 2001, Lausanne, Switzerland.

Jefferson, G.H., I. Singh, X. Junling, and Z. Shouqing (1999),
"China's industrial performance: A review of recent findings", in Jefferson, G.H. and I. Singh (eds.) *Enterprise Reform in China: Ownership, Transition, and Performance*, Oxford: Oxford University Press.

Laurenceson, J. and J.C.H. Chai (2000),
"The Economic Performance of China's State-owned Industrial Enterprises", *Journal of Contemporary China*, Vol. 9, No. 23.

Lemoine, F. and D. Ünal-Kesenci (2001),
"China in the International Segmentation of Production Process", Paper presented at the workshop on *China's Economy*, organised by the CEPII in Paris on 12 December 2001.

Lin, J.Y., F. Cai, and Z. Li (1996),
The China Miracle: Development Strategy and Economic Reform, Hong Kong: Chinese University Press.

Nolan, P. (2001),
"China and the WTO: The Challenge for China's Large-scale Industry", Paper presented at the Fourth ECAN Annual Conference on "China's WTO accession: National and International Perspectives", Berlin, 1-2 February 2001.

OECD (1999),
Asia and the Global Crisis: The Industrial Dimension, OECD, Paris;

OECD (2001),
New Patterns of Industrial Globalisation: Cross-border Mergers and Acquisitions and Strategic Alliances, OECD, Paris.

OECD (2000a),
Reforming China's Enterprises, OECD, Paris.

OECD (2000b),
Knowledge-Based Industries in Asia, OECD, Paris.

Otsuka, K., D. Liu and N. Murakami (1998),
Industrial Reform in China: Past Performance and Future Prospects, Oxford: Clarendon Press.

Perkins, T. and S. Shaw (2000),
China in the WTO: What will Really Change?, McKinsey & Company.

Posth, M. (2001),
"China's automobile industry in the light of the WTO accession", Paper presented at the Fourth ECAN Annual Conference on "China's WTO accession: National and International Perspectives", Berlin, 1-2 February 2001.

Ren, R. and M. Bai (2001),
"A Benchmark Comparison in Manufacturing between China and Germany by ICOP Approach", Paper presented at the workshop on China's Economy, organised by the CEPII in Paris on 12 December 2001.

Riddle, D. (1986),
Service-Led Growth: The Role of the Service Sector in World Development. New York: Praeger.

UNCTAD (2000a),
The Competitiveness Challenge: Transnational Corporations and Industrial Restructuring in Developing Countries, United Nations: New York and Geneva.

UNCTAD (2000b),
World Investment Report 2000: Cross-border Mergers and Acquisitions and Development, United Nations: New York and Geneva.

Wang, H. (2001),
"Policy reforms and foreign direct investment: The case of the Chinese automobile industry", Paper presented at the Ninth GERPISA International Colloquium on "Reconfiguring the auto industry: merger and acquisition, alliances, and exit", Paris, France, 7-9 June 2001.

Woetzel, J.R. (2001),
"Remaking China's giant steel industry", The McKinsey Quarterly, Number 4, Emerging Markets.

The World Bank (2000),
Bankruptcy of State Enterprises in China – A Case and Agenda for Reforming the Insolvency System, Washington, DC.

Yang, J. (2000),
"Analysis of the Trend of Changes in the Industrial Structure and Choice of Leading Industries in China During the Tenth Five-Year Plan Period", China Development Review, Vol. 2, No. 2, Development Research Centre of the State Council, China.

Zhai, F. (2000),
"Forecasts of automobile demand", China Development Review, Vol. 2, No. 1, Development Research Centre of the State Council, China.

Zhai, F. and S. Li (2001),
"Quantitative analysis and evaluation of the impact of entry to WTO on China's economy", China Development Review, Vol. 3, No. 2, Development Research Centre of the State Council, China.

Chapter 5

INDUSTRY REORGANISATION AND RESTRUCTURING: PROSPECTS, PROBLEMS, AND POLICY PRIORITIES

TABLE OF CONTENTS

INDUSTRY REORGANISATION AND RESTRUCTURING: PROSPECTS, PROBLEMS, AND POLICY PRIORITIES[*]

Introduction

China's accession to the World Trade Organisation (WTO) constitutes a landmark decision for the Chinese economy reform comparable, to some extent, to the "open door policy" launched in December 1978. The agreements signed by the Chinese Government with its main trading partners for its accession to WTO will promote a broad trade and investment liberalisation which will bring positive effects for the Chinese economy in terms of foreign direct investment, increased competition in the domestic market, and a better legal framework for business operations, as well as helping the central government to break down some vested interests at different levels of the administration.

China should be able to cope with the challenges of a broad trade and investment liberalisation thanks to two decades of uninterrupted market transformation and the determination to move ahead with the market reforms required under WTO. There are reasons for optimism. First, the various agreements that China has signed with its different trading partners leave some room for a gradual adjustment. Second, most of the apparatus of a planned economy has been progressively dismantled (prices, procurements, quantitative plans). Chinese enterprises, even in the state sector, enjoy a relatively high degree of autonomy in their day-to-day management decisions. Finally, the level of competition on the domestic market has grown very rapidly since the beginning of the 1990s in most industrial sectors: township and village enterprises in rural areas (TVEs), private companies and foreign invested enterprises (FIEs) now represent more than half of industrial production.

Nevertheless, China's accession to the WTO will bring some substantial changes in terms of tariffs, industry regulation, competition through imports and FDI, rules governing public sector and opening up of services and domestic trade, which have been heavily protected up until now. Domestic firms and regions are indeed expected to respond to those changes in very different ways.

The industrial corporate landscape in the industry has dramatically changed during 20 years of reform. Some sectors, such as consumer electronics, textiles, garments, food processing, and steel, already enjoy a high degree of competition. Domestic leaders in these sectors that have established well-known brand-names (like Konka, Haier, Changhong) are already familiar with strong competition in their domestic market and have already incorporated a strong capacity for adaptation and reaction to the market into their management. Furthermore, they have invested massively over the past ten years in after-sales service networks, focusing on quality, which gives them a certain edge over potential competitors. Such companies should not suffer too much from trade and investment liberalisation. On the other hand, a majority of small and medium-sized enterprises (SMEs) in the state and urban collective sector suffer from structural problems like under-capitalisation, low profitability, lack of economies of scale and technological capabilities, poor management skills, and heavy control from the local bureaucracy in their decision-making process. These companies survive under the umbrella of local protectionism and with the help of the banking system, which funds their working capital. Their development in a more open environment will be a big challenge.

Trade and investment liberalisation may also affect regional economic growth and inequalities among regions that, in comparison with world standards, are already very high (see Chapter 21). The cost of transition from a planned to a market economy is very different from one region to another. Moreover, the benefits of 20 years of reforms and opening to foreign direct investment have been concentrated mainly in the coastal regions. In such a context, the impact of trade and investment liberalisation following China's accession to the WTO will have wide variations: Guangdong province, for example, expects to benefit from its comparative advantage on the international and the domestic

---

[*] This chapter was prepared by Jean-François Huchet from the University of Rennes and Ecole des Hautes Etudes en Sciences Sociales, France.

market for three main reasons: its share of the state sector in total industrial production is only 28 per cent: it has received 27 per cent of total foreign direct investment; and most private and collective companies are well integrated in the international division of labour. At the opposite end of the spectrum, provinces of the hinterland like Jilin, Inner Mongolia, Hebei, Shaanxi, Shanxi, Anhui, Jiangxi, Hunan, Sichuan, Chongqing, Guangxi, Guizhou, not to mention the remote western provinces like Ningxia, Gansu, Tibet, Xingjinang or Qinghai, are facing a very different situation. The share of the state sector in total industrial production is higher than 60 per cent; their private sector is undersized: and they have received little foreign direct investment. Furthermore, except in a few cases, companies originating from these provinces have neither been able to sustain competition on the domestic market nor to integrate efficiently into the international division of labour. These provinces have the highest concentration of SMEs in the state and urban collective sector that are suffering from structural problems. In this context, trade and investment liberalisation will require the implementation of urgent policies to help these provinces to cope with their restructuring needs.

More generally, in the matter of industrial restructuring, trade and investment liberalisation will confront the Chinese government with specific problems linked with the legacy of industrialisation during the pre-reform period and with the way reforms have been implemented between 1978 and the mid-1990s. The first problem lies in the fact that Chinese industry has witnessed a proliferation of inefficient enterprises. This dynamic birth rate of enterprises is without any doubt directly related to the impressive growth rate of the Chinese economy. Nevertheless, part of this phenomenon is also the result of an inefficient governance structure both at enterprise and government levels, as well as regional market segmentation.

In other words, despite its potential long-term benefits, trade and investment liberalisation will also bring some immediate challenges to Chinese industry, even though the WTO agreement allows a gradual implementation of the various aspects of the liberalisation process. Very different responses to the trade and investment liberalisation challenge are to be expected from regions, sectors and firms, depending on their current competitive strength. The reform agenda since 1999 has been on a fast track and there is little doubt that the Chinese government is using its accession to the WTO to give new impetus to the restructuring of its industry. But several current policies still manifest clear limitations and should be modified if China wants to take full advantage of further trade and investment liberalisation.

Challenges

The transformation of the industrial landscape

Compared to the situation prevailing in 1978, industrial firms now operate in a very different environment. Two decades of reforms and continuous restructuring have brought positive results to Chinese industry.

One of the most important changes lies in the rise of competition in Chinese industry, especially in sectors close to final consumption (electrical appliances, clothes, textiles, foodstuffs). This is the result of several converging factors:

- The dismantling of the planning mechanism, with the deregulation of prices, supply and distribution (Naughton, 1995). Over 90 per cent of retail prices in the industry and over 80 per cent of agricultural prices are set by the market. Plan obligations for procurement or subsidised inputs have also been abolished.

- The appearance of TVE, *i.e.* collective ownership in rural areas, where property rights status is unclear, and tolerance of private activities carried out by different categories of actors in the countryside and urban zones (Weitzman *et al.*, 1993). In 1999, the non-state sector was estimated to contribute nearly 77 per cent of total industrial production. The significance of this figure needs to be very strongly put in context as it hides important regional disparities, and does not cover important sections of the economy, such as services, transport, construction, and, above all, that it does not take into account the fact that an important number of companies in the non-state sector are actually under the control of public companies.

- The opening up of the internal market to direct foreign investment. Joint-venture companies with mixed capital today represent an important spur to competition in the domestic market. FIEs have become the dominant producers in four industrial sectors (instruments, electronic and telecommunications, sports goods, and leather, furs and related products), and have surpassed SOE production in thirteen other sectors competing directly with collective and private companies (Lemoine, 2000).

- Finally, from the mid-1990s, the duplication and poor planning of investments in most industrial sectors, together with a levelling-off in household demand have brought about a huge over-capacity in virtually the entire industrial sector. Companies thus found themselves in markets now dominated by supply, exacerbating even more the competitive pressures and elements of concentration around the most efficient ones (Huchet, 1999).

Since 1994, the monetary and budgetary tightening imposed by the government increased budget constraints on SOEs. Subsidies to SOEs, according to World Bank estimates, reportedly moved from 7.5 per cent of GDP in 1992 to 2.3 per cent in 1994, then to less than 1 per cent after 1995. Even if the major state enterprises continue to receive subsidies disguised as bank credits, heavily indebted SMEs are no longer able to obtain bank credits to finance new investments. Bank credits for this category of company is henceforth granted simply to finance the back pay of employees and pensioners, in order to limit the social cost of restructuring.

The opening up of the Chinese economy and its world-market niche have encouraged exports, especially from companies in the non-state sector. Increasing access to the foreign currency market has facilitated the acquisition of foreign technologies superior to those available on the internal market.[1] Finally, foreign investment has allowed receiving firms to acquire know-how, and enabled the development of durable high-quality consumer goods on the domestic market. The appearance of foreign competitors in certain branches of the domestic market has also increased the competitive pressure on state-owned enterprises operating in these markets, forcing them to press ahead with reforms (management, organisation, technology, finance) (Jefferson et al., 1994). China's membership of the WTO will increase these pressures to sectors that are still protected.

At the microeconomic level, reforms have brought about greater management autonomy and separation from public administration. Fifteen years after the "contract responsibility system" had been generalised to Chinese SOEs, managerial autonomy has increased significantly (Byrd, 1992; Lu et al., 1996; Warner, 1995). Although the bureaucracy still exercises its decision-making authority in some very important matters, Table 5.1 shows that management now enjoys a great deal of autonomy in decision

Table 5.1. **Degree of management autonomy in SOEs**

		% of enterprises declaring complete autonomy on decision making in the listed area
1	Selling	97
2	Production	96
3	Purchasing	94
4	Use of retained earnings	78
5	Right to decide on organisational structure	78
6	Pricing	73
7	Wages and bonuses	65
8	Right to hire workers	58
9	Right to manage personnel	55
10	Investment	47
11	Establishment of JV or mergers and acquisitions	40
12	Import and export	39
13	Right to dispose of assets	37
14	Right to refuse non-regulated government charges	21

Source: World Bank, *China – Reform of State-Owned Enterprises*, Report No. 14924-CHA, Washington DC, 1996.

making. By the mid-1980s, the centre had already relinquished nearly all its administrative power concerning small and medium-sized SOEs to the local level. Compared with the old centralised and planned system, the transfer of decision-making power has expanded the incentives for SOEs to invest in new production and respond to the needs of the market.

Unbalanced industrial structure

Despite these broad transformations, the legacy of the pre-reform industrialisation strategy and the way reforms have been implemented have created an unbalanced industrial structure for some time now. The concept of economic organisation was, as in other planned economies, an essentially functionalist concept. However, in contrast with the Russian policy, which favoured big production units, or that of East Germany, which set up its big Konzern during the 1970s, in China it was coupled with a preoccupation with local autonomy in terms of production. Thus, not only did each ministry have its own companies, but each province, sometimes each municipality, had to equip itself with as complete a production system as possible. The launching of reforms at the end of the 1970s did not bring about any real changes. Provincial and local officials were no longer judged on their political loyalty alone, but also on their ability to develop local industry. From this point of view, their control of the local banking syst em made it possible for them to embark on rapid industrialisation without considering the effects of the duplication of investment on the national scale.

China holds some unenviable world records when it comes to the fragmentation of its industrial structure. Thousands of undersized producers, manufacturing the same products, are spread all over the country. In the automobile industry for example, as mentioned in Chapter 4, there are still officially 123 independent automobile producers. Another example is the cement industry where there are still some 8000 independent operating companies, compared to a total of 1500 at world level (110 in the United states, 51 in Russia, 58 in Brazil and 106 in India). The leading Chinese company in the sector has only 0.6 per cent of the national market.[2] There was no consolidation between 1990 and 1996, despite a fierce price war between the various producers. The cement industry is a good illustration of the differences that exist between China and other countries where industrial organisation is concerned, differences based on the fact that each producer of cement in China is an independent company. As in many developing countries, low barriers to entry and sizeable constraints weighing on the transportation costs of cement can justify a large number of producers. But it is surprising that no group has managed to acquire enough companies to hold a dominant market share. Anhui Conch, the leading national company, has sought to consolidate its position on the market by recently acquiring another plant in its region, but it is still a long way from achieving the market share held by some of the leading companies in other countries which easily achieve 30 per cent of the national market, as in India, or 60 per cent in the case of Thailand.[3]

In general, Chinese industry faces a dual problem: low pace of consolidation in the different sectors and the slow exit from the market of inefficient producers. In 1994, the 500 leading Chinese groups accounted for only 16 per cent of GDP, considerably less than in the industrialised countries where the 500 leading companies generally account for at least 30 per cent of GDP. China's biggest company, Daqing Petroleum, had sales of US$3.6 billion in 1996, about half the figure of the company at the bottom of the Fortune 500 list of the world's biggest companies. The sales of Baogang, China's leading steelworks amounted to a mere 10 per cent of those of the Japanese giant Nippon Steel.[4] An analysis of the levels of concentration reveals different developments according to the industrial sector concerned. The available figures on consolidation are based on a survey of industrial companies carried out in 1995. As is shown in Table 5.2, in the 25 main industrial sectors, the market shares of the eight leading companies have increased only very slightly from 11.7 per cent to 12.2 per cent. However, these figures are highly aggregated by sector. A more detailed statistical nomenclature would be needed to analyse the evolution at a product level. Certain markets, such as consumer electronics, prepared food, or consumer chemical products have been undergoing a process of rapid consolidation. Nevertheless, inefficient producers are very slow to exit, as they are under the umbrella of local protectionism and are helped by subsidies (disguised in form of loans) from the banking system.

Table 5.2. **Evolution of concentration in Chinese industry between 1990 and 1996**

Sectors	Level of concentration (Market share of the 8 leading companies in the sector)		
	1990	1996	change
Chemical fibers	44.6	35.0	−9.6
Construction materials	2.6	2.7	0.0
Steel	31.0	29.7	−1.3
Non-ferrous metals	23.4	15.0	−8.4
Publishing and media	5.5	5.6	0.1
Chemicals	15.6	10.1	−5.6
Drinks	5.4	9.4	4.0
Paper	10.8	5.4	−5.4
Textiles	1.4	3.0	1.6
Basic machines	4.0	6.8	2.8
Woodworking	8.1	7.6	−0.5
Production of plastics	6.1	3.7	−2.4
Office equipment	10.5	11.8	1.3
Pharmaceuticals	9.7	11.8	2.1
Transport equipment	21.0	22.3	1.3
Metals	3.7	5.5	1.8
Rubber	12.7	18.5	5.8
Food	2.3	11.3	9.0
Furniture	5.4	6.1	0.7
Tobacco	26.0	37.1	11.1
Electric machines	9.3	10.0	0.7
Electronics and telecommunications	14.6	16.9	2.3
Cultural and sporting goods	8.8	11.7	2.9
Clothing	5.0	4.5	−0.5
Leather	4.2	4.1	−0.1
Average	**11.7**	**12.2**	**0.6**

Source: *Zhongguo gongye fazhan baogao*, 1997 (Report on industrial development in China).

Unbalanced industrial structures have several negatives consequences for Chinese industry. First, they are responsible for a tremendous waste of investment resources and a misallocation of the country's savings. Second, they have contributed to the rapid growth of non-performing loans (NPL) in the books of the main domestic state commercial banks (see Chapter 7). Third, they have contributed to huge over-capacity in nearly all industrial sectors. A survey conducted by the state Statistical Bureau revealed that production capacity utilisation, including for equipment, in close to half of 900-odd major industrial products has dropped to below 60 per cent.[5] This in turn is affecting the return on capital and profitability, especially in sectors where there is no brand-name awareness and where inefficient producers can produce and sell at a loss (steel, cement, construction materials, and other intermediary goods). Finally, in a more subtle way, though very important for the future of the industry, the low consolidation rate prevents the development of economies of scale. This not only represents an opportunity cost, but also hampers the development of technological competencies, which at China's stage of economic development, are mainly accumulated through economies of scale.[6]

Companies with different strength

Industrial organisation has become particularly heterogeneous, after two decades of reform. On top of the ownership differentiation among firms and a decentralisation of the Chinese administrative system, a second source of heterogeneity, related to the rise of competition in Chinese industry, has progressively emerged since the late 1980s. Each category operates in a different business environment and faces different constraints and challenges in terms of financing, technical capabilities, degree of control by the public administration, managers' behaviour, and the quality of their labour force. Most domestic industrial firms need to restructure but they face different problems.

Nine industrial sectors are still quite closed to competition, especially as far as FIEs are concerned: tobacco, petroleum and gas, electricity production, timber from logging, petroleum processing, ferrous metallurgy, non-ferrous metallurgy, transport, and basic chemicals. In these sectors the share of the state sector in total production is still above 50 per cent. They include China's biggest industrial groups. Out of the leading 100 Chinese groups in 1997, 94 are SOEs. Nearly all these companies are operating in non-competitive sectors: petrochemicals (34 firms), provincial public companies producing electricity (23 firms), metallurgy (18 firms), and, more tangentially, in the tobacco (15 firms) and automobile industries (four firms). Even if these enterprises have been corporatised and have set up new institutions to improve corporate governance, the power structure remains totally dominated by the central ministries, either directly or indirectly via the financial holding companies created since 1996 that operate like the former ministerial bureaux.

At the same time, these firms are living in a "culture" of soft budget constraints. Such enterprises have access to source of official financing, many approved by the authorities: subsidised loans, and stock market privileges. They are also the main beneficiaries of the debt-for-equity swap scheme put in place in 1999 to reduce their level of debt. Another factor working against any major change to the system of corporate governance in this category of enterprises lies in their role as an important link in the chain of financing and patronage. According to one of the few studies published in China, carried out by the Shanghai Stock Exchange and devoted to the decision-making processes of firms listed there, 99 per cent of the important investment decisions, or those related to the appointments of the top executive staff and their salary packages, are taken by the firm's CCP committee in conjunction with the CCP's local authorities.[7]

In this context, pressures to improve corporate governance need to come from competition policy, as well as from a vast reform of the banking sector. From this point of view, China's accession to the WTO could impose greater discipline in some still-protected sectors, such as the automobile and steel industries, machine tools, or even telecommunications, and speed up regroupings to withstand competition from foreign multinationals (Wang *et al.*, 2000). However, in China's WTO accession agreement, a lot of restrictions remain on the opening up of sectors that are still protected. In parallel, the WTO agreement has given renewed impetus to the debate on economic nationalism.[8] In spite of high levels of indebtedness, the Chinese government regards these groups as the flagships of Chinese industry. This should enable them to continue to have access to virtually free finance as "national champions".

In sectors such as electronics, household appliances, food industry, textiles and clothing, that have been marked by price liberalisation, a lowering of the entry barriers for producers, and the development of unbridled competition, the past ten years have witnessed the advent of a new type of corporate group in which the state has a majority control. These firms, leaders in their respective markets, like Haier, Huabao, Kelong (household appliances) Konka, TCL and Changhong (television sets), Legend (computers), have forged their reputations based on strategies that are in no way different from the major companies in capitalist economies. It is interesting to observe that they were far from figuring among the most well known domestic companies at the end of the 1980s.

These firms also won their management autonomy quite easily, in so far as the state did not regard them as priority companies. Their independence is also derived from their financing strategy. Not having benefited from the state's channels for funding in the 1980s, the first bank loans have been used in an efficient way, and profits were also reinvested efficiently, thereby avoiding over-dependence on loans from the state banks. All these firms have in common a relatively low debt-assets ratio, below 50 per cent in the majority of cases.[9]

Overall, strong competition, combined with management autonomy, have considerably improved corporate governance in these groups, even if their boards of directors and supervisory boards are less than effective. Trade and investment liberalisation should have an overall positive effect on these firms. While already exposed to strong competition in their domestic market, they have built a strong capacity for adaptation to market forces. Furthermore, massive investments over the past ten years in after-sales quality service networks give them a certain edge over foreign competitions. However, in the short to medium-term, such leading firms need external financing, not just to diversify and increase the quality of their products through R&D (see Chapter 6), but also to consolidate their position in their main market through large distribution networks, and the acquisition of firms in other provinces.

These firms should resist the temptation to continue relying on government support for R&D.[10] They will also have to institute effective instruments of corporate governance (outside experts on their boards of directors, recourse to the expertise of foreign investors). Considerable experience in co-operating with foreign companies (notably in terms of technology transfer and management methods), and their ability to combine an intelligent strategy of co-operation/conflict with foreign companies in China and abroad should foster improvement in this area.[11]

SMEs represent the bulk of state and collective enterprises in urban areas. For the industrial and state sector alone, they represented nearly 75 per cent of the some 110 000 SOEs in the peak year of 1996. Most of them are experiencing significant financial difficulties (OECD, 2000) and suffer from several structural problems: under-capitalisation, lack of competent management, obsolete technologies and low economies of scale. Furthermore, poor functioning of the internal control mechanisms (massive interference of the local bureaucracy in decision-making processes and inefficient management) is combined with inefficient external control mechanisms (local anti-competitive protectionism, huge subsidies dressed up as bank credits, an absence of bankruptcies until recently).

Trade and investment liberalisation will put strong pressure on such enterprises. Competition with foreign banks, as well as for the lowering of tariffs and a greater opening up to direct foreign investment in hitherto protected areas, should result in tighter budgetary constraints and fierce competition in the domestic market. Over the next few years a radical shake-up is to be expected. A minority of these firms will continue to exist. The others will be either bought up (best case scenario), merged, or will simply go into bankruptcy, although it cannot be excluded that conservative pressures from poor provinces will lead to some compromise and on-going local protection.

Another category brings together those private enterprises that have succeeded in reaching a critical mass in competitive sectors of industry. Private firms have indeed experienced rapid development since the end of the 1980s. Statistics vary depending on the source, the directory of private companies listing 1 280 000 officially registered firms, while a recent government study estimated a lower number (960 000 employing 13.5 million employees).[12] In the vast majority of cases, however, private companies are small in size and mainly based on households in the service sector, particularly in catering and small commercial activities in urban areas. Only a handful have managed to get beyond the frame of the small family business. New Hope (*Xinxiwang*), whose headquarters are in Sichuan province, is leader in the animal food industry, with a turnover of nearly 2 billion RMB (US$240 million) in 1998. Only three private companies (New Hope, Sichuan Tongwei, and Beijing Changning) had a turnover above one billion RMB in 1997.[13, 14] By way of comparison, the 1997 turnover of the top five Chinese groups (all state-owned enterprises) was 35 times greater than that of the five biggest private enterprises (Tung, 1997).

Political discrimination against the private sector is no longer authorised officially. The National People's Congress voted a constitutional amendment in 1999 recognising the place of the private sector alongside the state sector in the nation's economic development. These firms, like foreign companies, should benefit from progressive deregulation in still protected activities. Furthermore, the possibility for financing through foreign banks is eagerly awaited by such firms.

Finally, the last category, the TVEs in the rural collective sector make up a much more heterogeneous category of enterprises. Some literature emphasises their distinctive features, using the concept of "hybrid" property rights (Nee, 1992; Weitzman *et al.*, 1993; Jefferson, 1993; Jefferson *et al.*, 1994, Putterman, 1995; Oi, 1995; Rawski, 1995). Some firms that have become major groups since the early 1990s, such as Kelon, Chunlan, Dalian Bohai (which are now part of the country's top 100 groups) are in fact very close to the leading SOEs and private groups operating in the competitive sectors, and should adapt to trade and investment liberalisation without major problems. Another important part of collective rural enterprises is composed of smaller firms that are closer to the problematic urban state-owned and collective small and medium-sized companies run by local governments. For this type of TVEs, trade and investment liberalisation will represent a big challenge. The central government has already put pressure on local government to close thousands of inefficient TVEs operating in different sectors like mining, coal, textile, steel, cement, and construction materials.

In the coastal region TVEs are often well integrated in the subcontracting network working for the export market. They should normally benefit from China's membership of the WTO, especially in the sectors where China enjoys comparative advantages (textiles, garments, electronics, toys). Like private companies, they should also benefit from easier access to new sources of funding.

Regional discrepancies

Regional discrepancies in terms of economic development have greatly expanded during these two decades of reforms.[15] The cost and scope of transformation to a market economy vary greatly among provinces and will affect their capacity to adjust and cope with trade and investment liberalisation challenges. The cost of transformation is directly proportional to the importance of heavy industry and to the share of the state and urban collective sector in the local economy. One outstanding difference among provinces consists in the proportion of non-state companies – FIEs, TVEs or private companies – compared to SOEs. The share of the state sector in industrial production is below 50 per cent in all coastal provinces and is well over 60 per cent in northeast, western, and central provinces. Coastal provinces have received 88 per cent of all FDI, with 30 per cent for Guangdong province alone. Concurrently, Zhejiang, Jiangsu, Shandong have the greatest concentration of TVEs. The share of heavy industry in the total output is also a good indicator of the extent of restructuring that each province has to face. No province in the north-east, central and western regions has been able to eliminate the distortion in favour of heavy industry, a legacy of the planned economy.

At the same time, the regional industrial structure has a big influence on the volume of resources each province can use to smooth the restructuring process. Given the decline of fiscal revenues of the central government relative to GDP growth, provinces had to rely increasingly on their own resources to finance their development. Apart from Tibet, there is a high correlation between per capita budgetary revenue and budgetary expenditure in each province (Wang *et al.*, 1999; Wong, 2000). Each province relies to a great extent on extra budgetary funds that derive from taxes on the collective sectors, the private sector and other economic activities. Thus, overall, the coastal provinces that have received the majority of FDI and have been able to promote healthy rural collective and private sectors, have been able to generate much more fiscal revenues to finance their development than provinces of the hinterland. Furthermore, rich provinces, with a wide tax base, have been able to offer more tax concessions to attract new investors, reinforcing disparities between provinces. In the context of trade and investment liberalisation, the problem of fiscal transfer between provinces (see Chapter 20 on central-local fiscal relations) will therefore need to be addressed by the central government also to help comparatively worse-off provinces in their restructuring effort.

The coastal regions have also managed to set up a more efficient social security system than provinces in the hinterland, which has enabled them to progress more rapidly with the restructuring of their companies. Since the social security system in China is mainly organised at the municipal level, only the economically dynamic cities have been able to gradually finance unemployment, retirement or health insurance funds over the last few years. In contrast, regions of the north-east and of the interior that have to restructure the largest number of inefficient companies and provide for an effective social security system are encountering most difficulties in funding social security programmes.

To sum up, most of the northeast, central, and western regions risk being locked into a vicious circle of backwardness due to the dominant share in their economy of the state and urban collective sector and the inefficiency of their companies. Coastal regions have entered a virtuous circle based on a growing non-state sector, well integrated into the world economy. Without adequate policies the trade and investment liberalisation could accentuate locked-in regional discrepancies (see Chapter 21 for a further discussion of this issue).

Policies to accelerate industrial restructuring

Government policies to promote industrial restructuring in preparation for accession to WTO have moved in three directions: first, a programme of capacity reduction in several sectors, through mergers and initiation of bankruptcy proceedings. Second, debt-for-equity swaps for big SOEs, the launching of international public offerings on foreign stock exchanges, and the reform of credit policies in the banking system, have addressed the financial restructuring of industrial companies. Finally, the central government has decided to disengage from SMEs in the state and urban collective sectors. These policies have already produced encouraging results in solving some of the problems in industrial structure and in promoting a better business environment for domestic companies. Nevertheless, these policies are encountering problems in their implementation.

Reduction of capacity

Effectiveness of the new measures

Since the mid-1990s the central government has launched a series of restructuring plans in several industries in order to cut production capacities and push for further consolidation. Table 5.3 shows some examples, but nearly all central Ministries or bureaux have set up their own programme of industrial reorganisation. Capacity reduction relies on a series of measures:

- The formation of 156 big groups mainly in industry. This measure affects only the biggest SOEs with the objective of creating "national champions" in their respective industries. This policy involves mergers or take-overs by the biggest SOEs in each sector as well as other measures:

- The streamlining of unproductive assets, mainly the social welfare units of companies that are not directly related to the main activity of the SOEs or the urban collective enterprises.

- Weak enforcement of price controls in 12 sectors and price competition in some industries like consumer durables. This has further increased the degree of consolidation in several sectors and has pushed inefficient producers out of the market.[16]

- The promotion of mergers for SMEs in the state and collective sector by the local governments.

- Bankruptcies and closure of inefficient companies in the state and collective sector.

These measures have clearly brought some improvement in the structural problems affecting the domestic industry. As Table 5.4 indicates, the financial performance of state sectors has greatly improved. Industrial profits, losses, and inventories all show an improvement since 1999. Part of this positive trend is related to the evolution of the price of oil, lower interest rates which had a positive impact on SOEs' interest payments on debt, and also to the debt-for-equity swaps scheme for big SOEs (see below) that has enabled these companies to substantially reduce their debt. Accounting irregularities might also have an influence in artificially boosting SOEs financial results", given the alarming reports on accounting practices of SOEs published by the Audit Bureau of the State Council. Nevertheless, there are some clear indications that the reduction of capacities has also brought some positive results on finances of several industries.

First there has been a stabilisation of prices in most of the industries where some drastic plan of reduction of capacities has been implemented *i.e.*, in coal, steel, textiles, construction materials and sugar. In industries where prices have continued to fall – such as consumer electronics (refrigerators, air-conditioners, TV sets) – "price wars" have been orchestrated by big industrial groups at the national level and have contributed to pushing inefficient firms out of the market or to the take-over of under-performing firms by the market leaders. For example, in the refrigerator market, the number of domestic producers has shrunk from 40 in 1993 to eleven at the end of 1999.[17]

For the first time since 1978, there has been a drastic decline in the number of state and collective urban companies as well as in employee numbers (see Figure 5.1), despite a further increase in the number of private, shareholding companies and FIEs. After a peak in 1996, the number of SOEs has decreased from 126 000 to 61 300. Nevertheless, this reduction is not synonymous with closure in nearly

Table 5.3. **Progress on reduction of excess capacity in industry**

Industry	Overcapacity	Plan from the Government	Progress and Impact
Coal	Oversupplied at about 300 million tonnes (mt).	1999: to reduce production by 253 mt, but cut only 100 mt. 2000: to further cut production of 160 mt. To close 18 900 small coal mines.	Up to 2000: 34 000 coal mines have been closed, reducing 300 mt of production. Price increased slightly.
Oil	Inventory hit 8.8 metric tons(mt) by April 1998, but shortage now as demand rose.	1999: crude oil processing capacity controlled within 161 mt. No new refineries to be built nor capacity expanded in the near future. 120 small refineries closed, reduced 15 mt of capacity by year end.	Domestic oil price picked up following international price increases as well as from anti-smuggling moves in the area.
Electricity	Overcapacity due to unbalanced distribution among regions and between rural-urban areas.	1999: will not approve thermopower plant for next 3 years. Shut all thermopower generators with capacity below 1.8 m Kw.	Demand has been boosted by growth: development or transmission grids and promotion of national power transmission networks.
Steel	Overcapacity of normal steel production, but 7 mt high standard steel needs to be imported.	1999: cut capacity by 10%. No new plan approval within 3 years. Restrict control over imports. 2000: Cut production 16.3% to close 103 small steel plants.	1999: production up 7.5% not cut 10% as planned. 2000: export increased 150%.
Sugar	1997-98: 800 000 t surplus. 3 billion RMB loss due to low prices given over supply.	1999-2000 planting area reduced.	Production was controlled between January and May. Price rose to normal level around 3 000 RMB/t from 1 800 RMB/t.
Textile	25-35% of textile industry was loss making before 1998. 1.8 million workers in the sector.	1998: to cut by 5.1 m spindles. 3 billion government subsidy to reduce 10 000 spindles. 1999: to cut 4.5m spindles arrange 500 000- staff layoff and cut losses by 3 billion RMB. 2000: to cut further 4 m spindles.	1998: spindles cut 5 m and losses reduced by RMB 2.6 billion. 600 000 workers laid off. 1999: textile mills down from 2 226 to 2 829 in 1997.

Source: State Economic and Trade Commission, *China Quarterly Economic Review*, July 2000, p. 22.

Table 5.4. **Evolution of industrial efficiency in the State sector**

	1997	1998	1999	Janv.-Nov. 2000
Net industrial profits (billion RMB)	74.4	147.3	220.2	371.4
State sector	45.1	49.0	96.7	208.3
Total losses	134.1	155.6	130.0	100.0
State sector	74.4	102.3	85.1	84.6
Net industrial profits (% growth y-y)	16.8	−17	52.0	92.0
State sector	11.9	8.6	77.7	140.0
Memorandum:				
Industrial sales growth (%)	–	4.1	10.2	21.3

Source: National Bureau of Statistics, *China Statistical Yearbook*, and BNP-Paribas, cited in "BNP Paribas Peregrine" (2001), *Economic Outlook*, January, p. 14.

Figure 5.1. **Evolution of staff and workers by sectors and by ownership**
In millions

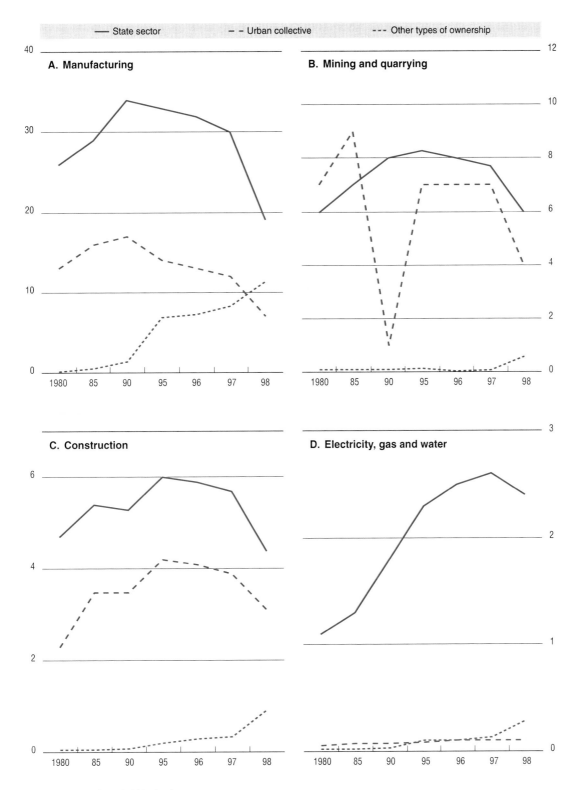

Source: *China Labour Statistical Yearbook*, 1999.

50 per cent of all SOEs. Part of this reduction comes from mergers, privatisation, especially for SMEs, and the transfer of some SOEs into the statistical category of shareholding entities.

In the most extensive study done on the bankruptcy situation in China, a recent World Bank report shows a clear acceleration of bankruptcy cases after 1995 (see Figure 5.2). Despite a respite in 1998 and 1999 during the Asian financial crisis, the level has grown again to reach a figure comparable to 1997. A special task force has been established by the central government to tackle the closure of inefficient enterprises in steel, sugar-making, coal, non-ferrous metal, defence, and textiles.[18] Moreover, the data in Figure 5.2 concern only bankruptcies under the Capital Structure Optimisation Programme funded by the People's Bank of China under instructions from the State Council.

Many bankruptcies are now declared outside this programme, and in 1997 alone 2 400 SOEs went into bankruptcy outside this quota system. Finally, a growing number of companies are effectively out of the market and have stopped producing. Bureaucratic battles and a lack of sufficient funding are preventing such companies from being officially declared bankrupt. In this respect, Beijing municipality has recently established a fund of 200 million RMB to help enterprises pay compensation for workers and creditors and begin bankruptcy proceedings.[19] Evidence on plant closures comes from different provinces. In Guangdong province – which has the biggest state sector of all provinces in absolute terms despite having FIEs representing 60 per cent of industrial sales – 80 cement plants, 12 refineries, and dozens of loss-making SOEs and urban collective companies have been closed over the last three years.[20]

The World Bank report shows that bankruptcy is slowly but surely emerging as an effective restructuring tool in the Chinese economy. More than 25 000 cases (state and non-state sectors) have been handled since the mid-1990s. This represents progress if compared to the situation between 1986 and 1994, when the few cases of bankruptcy had just a symbolic purpose. Since 1997, some large companies, like the Acheng Sugar plant in Heilongjiang province where creditors have agreed to write off 700 million RMB, or the GITIC case in Guangdong province where huge foreign liabilities were

Figure 5.2. **Evolution of bankruptcies and mergers under the Capital Structure Optimisation Program 1994-1999**

Number of cases implemented

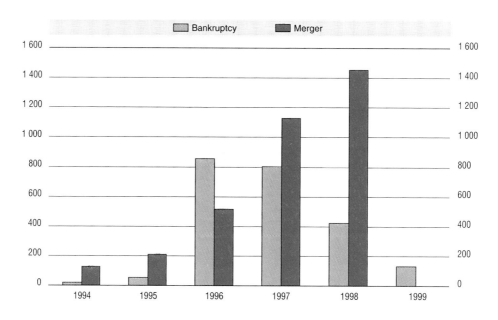

Source: World Bank, 2000.

involved, have gone bankrupt. The central government has set up the so-called "capital structure optimisation programme" in which the People's Bank of China is providing funds to write off the debt of companies filling for bankruptcy. In 1994-95 the quota provided by the People's Bank of China was only seven billion RMB per year, and applied to only 18 cities. But since 1997, the quota was expanded to 40 billion RMB a year covering 111 cities, allowing the handling of an increasing number of bankruptcies. Finally, considerable experience has been accumulated, not only within the courts but also at all level of administration, showing that "the notion and importance of bankruptcy are widely accepted among China's leadership and public" and can represent a much more efficient way to restructure companies than mergers.[21]

As was the case in former socialist countries, mergers in China have been the most privileged tools for restructuring companies for quite some time. They were used as an administrative way to avoid bankruptcy. Enterprises had little to say in the overall process of the merger and had to comply with bureaucratic decisions, which produced very inefficient results in terms of restructuring. Yet case studies carried out since the beginning of the last wave of mergers in 1996 (Huchet, J-F., 1999), show that in competitive sectors, leading companies that still had to comply with government's mergers could act with much more autonomy, and were therefore able to resist pressure to acquire loss-making state companies. It would thus seem that mergers do lead to more efficient results than in the past. In industries with fierce competition and a lot of take-over candidates, leading companies were able to bargain for good deals to expand their operations in different parts of China (reducing debt, acquiring companies with good technology).

More generally, two factors have been decisive in the evolution of restructuring. On the one hand, there are the sectors which are close to the end-user where consumer choice and competition (see Box 5.1) have led to a selection of companies and to a process of rapid concentration. In these sectors,

---

Box 5.1.   More flexibility and autonomy in mergers in competitive sectors*

The managers of Changhong (a leading company making TV sets) were frequently approached by officials from other provinces requesting them to acquire a problematic TV manufacturing company at an advantageous price. When they refused, the officials threatened to close the provincial distribution circuits to Changhong TVs or to favour their competitors. In certain cases, the Changhong managers avoided subcontracting agreements with these loss-making companies. Changhong also managed to avoid demands from the Ministry of Industry and Information (formerly the Electronics Ministry) and from the provincial authorities, to take over the Hongguan Company in Chengdu. This company makes cathode ray tubes for TVs, and its managers have recently been condemned for irregularities in the approval procedure of their company's market listing and in the use of funds raised on the market, setting off one of the most serious financial scandals on the Shanghai Stock Exchange. Changhong has nevertheless taken over two loss-making state companies which manufacture TVs, one in Nantong in the province of Jiangsu, and the other in Changchun in the Northeast of the country (Jilin).

The Haier group, the leader in domestic appliances in China, had already taken over close to 15 loss-making state companies in various provinces. Not only the central administration but also various local administrations regularly pressured the group to take over moribund companies in the sector. Nevertheless, the Haier group was able to select companies that produced good products, had good technology, and had a market, in spite of bad management. In this way the group was in a strong position to negotiate take-overs on favourable terms concerning the debts and the workforce of the acquired companies. Raising funds on the domestic and foreign exchanges was of much help in these operations. For example Kelon, another leading company in the domestic appliance sector was taken over by Huabao in 1998, a state company and a direct competitor established in the province of Guangdong. Here again, it seems that the strategic interests of both companies were considered by the tutelary administrations.

_____
*   See Huchet (1999).

---

domestic industry has entered into a new phase: after a fall in the number of enterprises in the 1980s, there has been a rapid process of consolidation, after which only a few domestic players will compete on the domestic market along with the global players. For example, there used to be more than 200 home electronics brands, but by 2000 the figure had dropped to about 20, and a recent survey by the Association of Light Industry predicts that after Chinese accession to the WTO only two or three domestic name-brand manufacturers will remain active in the market.[22] The other decisive variable has been the geographic concentration of industries and number of bureaucratic entities involved in this sector. The more an industry is concentrated in a relatively small area and the less bureaucratic entities are involved in the restructuring process, the easier it has been to reform it and to achieve economies of scale by promoting a concerted concentration not only by the market alone, but also by the administrative authorities (see Box 5.2).

Box 5.2.   **The case of the tobacco industry**

The tobacco industry in China is concentrated in the province of Yunnan. It is the industry where reform and restructuring projects decided at national level have been most successful. In 1995, there were almost 170 state companies operating in the tobacco industry in China. In 1995, the administration of the state Tobacco Monopoly, which supervises the industry, decided to implement a drastic restructuring plan by merging or closing down almost 50 companies over a five-year period, beginning with small companies whose annual production did not exceed 5 billion cigarettes. Between 1995 and 1997, ten companies had already been closed down. Even though this sector as a whole is still loss-making (about 40 to 50 per cent of the companies are still losing money), the geographic concentration of the industry has allowed for effective co-ordination between the centre and the provincial authorities. The rise in the concentration index in this industry has been the greatest in Chinese industry.

Limits and bottlenecks

Despite some progress in the way mergers have been used, this restructuring tool remains controversial. The authorities have preferred mergers under cover of a policy of promoting groups, in order to avoid bankruptcy procedures, which still remain very difficult to pursue, given the conflicts of interest between creditors and the inefficiencies of the social security system. Mergers are more of a way of concealing problems than a solution to the phenomenon of excess industrial capacities. Even for the leading companies in consumers' products that have managed to negotiate company take-overs in favourable terms, it is difficult to know whether they would have decided on a merger, had the authorities not pressured them. Many examples show that the state continues to intervene in an authoritarian manner in promoting groups (see Box 5.3). The smaller the size of the company, and the lower the level of the tutelary administration, the more mergers are carried out in an authoritarian fashion by the local authorities, who are not overly preoccupied with the strategy of companies, or the possibility of creating synergies in production, technology, financing, or the merging of distribution networks.[23] Furthermore, in the restructuring process, political patronage remains key, with fierce interdepartmental rivalry at the local level over allocation of state assets. Fortunately, following the Asian Crisis in 2000, the central authorities shifted their policy from mergers to bankruptcy and further deregulation to promote industrial restructuring through competition (see Box 5.4 for the automobile industry).

Efforts to streamline non-core assets in the SOE and urban collective sector (in-house social services, upward or downward activities non-directly related to core activities like transportation, electricity production) have been curbed by the slowness and the inefficiencies of social security system reforms. In the coastal area, where the funding of social security has not been too problematic, big companies have been able to sell or transfer their social in-house assets to their respective city

---

Box 5.3. Mergers difficult to refuse

Under the restructuring programme for petrochemicals, which aimed at diving the industry between two giants, Sinopec and CNPC, Sinopec was forced at the end of 1997 to take over two big state petrochemical companies in the province of Shandong. The two companies, Zibo Chemical Fiber and Zibo Petrochemical, with 50 000 employees, had accumulated three billion RMB in debts, with assets of only 2 billion RMB, and had registered losses since the beginning of the 1980s. In Sinopec's estimates, the two companies needed at least 1 billion RMB in new investment in order to modernise their obsolete production facilities.[1] Part of the recent IPO of Sinopec has been used to this purpose.

In the steel industry, a huge restructuring plan approved in 1997 called for a merging of the loss-making and undersized companies with larger companies and to form, by the year 2000, four big groups which would account for 40 per cent of national production. According to the official statistics, in 1998 there were 1 570 independent steel companies, of which only four had an annual production capacity exceeding five million tons (Baogang in Shanghai, Shougang in Beijing, Angang in Anshan and Wugang in Wuhan). The other 27 manufacture over a million tons per year.[2] The leading company in the Chinese steel industry, the Shanghai group Baogang, after having been at the cutting edge of the reforms since the end of the 1980s to the point of becoming a model for the whole industry, was forced to take over the Shanghai Metallurgical Holding, a group with ten times as many employees (120 000 employees, of whom only 30 000 engaged in steel production and the rest employed in various subsidiaries and social services) and which was staggering under the weight of its debt.[3] The model company of the city of Handan (Hebei), the Handan Steel Corp, for its part, had to take over the Wuyang Steel Corp, which was also heavily in debt (to the tune of nearly US$180 million),[4] while admitting to the press that this operation was in line with the new policy decided on at the 15th Party Congress in 1997. Both companies seem to have sought to anticipate the wishes of the government to prevent the closing down of steel mills of Wuyang and the Shanghai Metallurgical Holding.[5]

---

1. *Asian Wall Street Journal*, 12 November 1997.
2. "*Gangtie gongye: zengjia pinzhong tiaozheng jiegou*" (The steel industry: diversification and adjustment structures) (1997), in Zhongguo touzi yu jianshe (Investment and construction in China), No. 11, pp. 16-17, and *South China Morning Post*, 28 October 1998, p. 3, Business pages.
3. *Asian Wall Street Journal*, 5 May 1998, pp. 1 and 5.
4. *Ibid.*
5. Interview ING Barings, Shanghai, 19 September 1998, and *Asian Wall Street Journal*, 5 May 1998, pp. 1 and 5.

---

governments and to sell or lease their non-core activities. SMEs in the coastal area were also able to dismantle these activities more easily as city governments provided better medical care systems for employees and retraining for laid-off workers.

Cities in the northeast, central and western region, however, who have been struggling to fund their social security system, have been unable to take over the social assets of big companies that still have to provide most of the traditional social care services of the socialist firm. The steel industry provides a good example. If we take the production per employee as an indicator of the degree of the downsizing of non-core assets, Baogang steel company in Shanghai (before the wave of mergers in 1998), provides a striking example of success. After various agreements with the city government of Shanghai, Baogang, leader in the steel industry, had managed to cut its workforce to only 32 095 employees in 1998, each of them producing 307 tons of steel per year. In contrast, other major steel producers in the north-east or the hinterland provinces like Shougang in Beijing, Angang and Bengang in Liaoning province or Wugang in Hubei, or Taigang in Shaanxi, are all still struggling with over-employment in their non-core activity.[24]

Despite progress on this front, bankruptcy procedures encounter severe limits in their implementation and have a long way to go to become a normal tool for restructuring. In the entire state sector (industry, construction, transport and telecommunication, and commercial service sectors), only

---

Box 5.4.   **Still too many players in the automobile industry**

At the end of 1997, the central administration approved a plan for the restructuring of the automobile industry. The 13 biggest manufacturers were supposed to take over the smallest producers and transform them into subcontractors. According to the government plan, this would make it possible to develop economies of scale. The objective was to set up four big automobile groups in the country, each with a minimum production capacity of 400 000 cars. The plan also provided for greater control by the central administration in the approval of new joint venture projects in the industry with foreign companies. Mergers were to be carried out, not administratively as in the past, but on the basis of the market and of the strategic interests of the take-over. Case studies (Wang, *et al.*, 2001) indicate that since the middle of the 1980s, the central administration has met with multiple obstacles connected with local protectionism (see Table 5.5 and Table 5.6). Local governments have preferred, until recently, to subsidise companies which produce only a few thousand vehicles annually, rather than to open their market to outside producers. Local authorities have gone so far as to challenge the major projects to develop a nation-wide automobile industry. At the beginning of the 1990s, these projects envisaged limiting the number of Chinese and foreign joint ventures to three major centres: Shanghai (Volkswagen), Wuhan (Citröen) and Changchun (Audi-Volkswagen). Since then, Shanghai has welcomed Ford and General Motors; Tianjin has increased its co-operation with Daihatsu and Toyota; Honda has replaced Peugeot in Canton and Renault is said to be on the point of negotiating a joint production project, by itself or through Nissan.

Table 5.5.   **Indicators of the Chinese automobile industry (end of 1998)**

	Total	Automobiles	Motors	Parts
Number of firms	2 426.0	115.0	56.0	1 628.0
Output value (bn RMB)	278.7	139.2	9.8	55.7
Export (bn RMB)	5.2	1.3	0.24	2.3
Fixed assets (bn RMB)	141.8	67.0	5.7	39.7
Pre-tax profit (bn RMB)	19.7	9.7	0.53	6.5

Source: China Automotive Industry Yearbook (1999).

Table 5.6.   **Concentration in the Chinese automobile industry (Jan.-Sept. 1999)**

	Output (number of vehicles)	% of national total
Top 3 firms	431 947	23.75
Top 8 firms	867 415	56.77
Top 15 firms	1 155 937	87.64

Source: Wang et al. (2001).

16 360 companies have been put into bankruptcy which corresponds to only 0.6 per cent of the total number of enterprises created in the state sector between 1988 and 1996.[25] This reflects the extremely low mortality rate of companies in the state sector despite their continuing poor financial results (see Box 5.4 for the automobile industry).

The World Bank report insists that there is a strong anti-creditor bias, especially against banks, despite provisions in the bankruptcy law that give creditors a priority on the remaining assets. The low value of assets, the lack of legal protection in assets before and sometimes during the bankruptcy procedure allowing for irregularities, means that the remaining assets can sometimes only cover employees rehabilitation fees. In this context, the rate of recovery on initial loans by domestic banks is extremely low, between 3 and 10 per cent.

Given the lack of transparency and the complexity of property rights in the state sector, managers are trying to dump into state companies (which serve as the core company of a complex holding with different types of property rights) as much debt as possible and file for bankruptcy for the SOEs, which are striving to keep afloat the non-state companies that they control (Ding, 1999). In most bankruptcy cases, land use rights are the only remaining asset and the only source of finance for the social cost of bankruptcy – in a context of insufficient funding for the pension system, unemployment benefits, and retraining, particularly in the northeast, central and western regions, which are the most severely hit by restructuring. The World Bank report notes that the anti-creditor bias is even stronger against creditors from other provinces, sometimes other municipalities. All these facts explain the low rate of market exit for SOEs.

Financial restructuring

Debt for equity swaps

In 1998, the central government launched a programme of recapitalisation of the four biggest state commercial banks that has helped the biggest SOEs to reduce their debt. This programme allows banks to write-off from the balance sheet certain non-performing loans (NPLs) made to SOEs. The corresponding loans to the SOEs have been taken over by four liquidating companies created for the purpose (China Cinda, China Huarong, China Great Wall Asset and China Oriental) based on the American model of the late 1980s at the time of the Savings and Loan crisis. After taking over the assets, these asset management companies (AMCs) become responsible for selling them off. State bonds should finance the difference between the initial value of the asset and the amount recovered through recovery or the asset sale.

For example, the Shougang steelworks in Beijing signed an agreement in April 2000 with three of the four AMCs, enabling it to get rid of 3.5 billion RMB (US$430 million) worth of debts (or non-profitable assets).[26] The programme foresees the cancellation of nearly 1 500 billion RMB in debts coming exclusively from the major industrial groups in the state sector. In February 2001, the four AMCs had already bought back nearly 1 400 billion RMB worth of debts. The AMCs will try to collect on or sell these assets at the best price to recover part of the original net value of the assets. One of the AMCs, China Huarong has already started to put some of these assets on the market and has just signed a contract with Ernst and Young to help market nearly 20 billion RMB (US$3 billion) worth of assets to foreign investors (which represents just a fraction of the 407 billion RMB of NPLs taken over by Huarong).

Since the beginning of 2000, this programme has contributed to a substantial reduction of the huge debt of the largest SOEs, and has boosted the profitability of the public sector. It represents also a first step towards resolving the structural problem that links SOE investment performance and the evolution of state commercial bank lending practices. AMCs are normally not supposed to take over new NPLs (as declared after 1996) and to concentrate on old loans that are difficult to recover. This should help the state commercial banks to concentrate their efforts on reforming their credit lending practices on the new loans made since the mid-1990s as well to clean their portfolio.

Along these lines, the governor of the People's Bank of China declared in his annual speech in January 2000 that the cancellation of debts anticipated by this programme would constitute the last "free meal" to which the major state-owned enterprises would be entitled. Furthermore, AMCs have a clear mandate focusing on debt resolution and are expected to play a more active role than the banking system in forcing SOEs' restructuring. They are entitled to swap assets among themselves in order to become larger creditors and concentrate their effort on a more limited number of enterprises.

However, from the point of view of corporate governance, the programme does not get to the root of the problem. AMCs entering the boards of major state-owned enterprises are unable to play their role as "active" stakeholders, namely to control the actions of managers and to censure them, for a variety of reasons:

- An asymmetry in information: given the lack of transparency in the accountancy system and the poor functioning of the board of directors, managers of the SOEs still control access to strategic information on the firm.

- Their lack of human resources and skills to play a strategic role in the SOE's governance.

- The high number of companies affected by the programme, nearly 1 000 big SOEs which multiplies problems of competence. For Huarong alone, its 407 billion RMB of assets, involves about 71 000 debtor companies.[27]

- Finally, by their statutes, such companies lack an effective shareholder power, being subject to negotiation with the central and the local bureaucracies in charge of big SOEs. In several cases, AMCs have been unable to drastically restructure companies in a hopeless situation despite having become the main shareholder of these companies, or to combat the manipulation of bankruptcy procedures by local authorities (see Box 5.5).

Credit policy in the banking system

Some important reforms in lending practices have also been implemented in the state commercial banks, which dominate the credit market for industrial enterprises (for a full analysis of changes in the banking system, see Chapter 7). After the first step of the reform at the beginning of the 1980s, most lending was channelled through the state commercial banks, which received money from the People's Bank of China (PBOC). Banks were under the control of the local bureaucracy and lent money to SOEs without questioning the profitability of investments. This phenomenon has widely contributed to the proliferation of undersized investments in all sectors, and the lack of concentration in industry.

Box 5.5. China Huarong AMC against Monkey King Group[1]

Monkey King Group (MKG), an industrial conglomerate from Yichang city in Hubei province, is one of the country's 512 key SOEs and one of the big SOEs to benefit from the debt-for-equity swap scheme put in place by the central government. In August 2000, China Huarong Asset Management Company bought 622 million RMB in MKG debt from The Industrial and Commercial Bank of China (ICBC). Since then, Huarong, the main creditor of the group, has been unable to press MKG into a drastic restructuring plan. On the contrary, with the approval of Yichang city officials, in December 2000, MKG started a huge asset-stripping manoeuvre that has shrunk group assets from 2.42 billion RMB to 371 million RMB, according to Huarong. MKG then petitioned for bankruptcy to escape a restructuring plan coming from its main creditor Huarong, without informing the board of directors of its listed company. Last March, Huarong publicly questioned the fairness of the liquidation committee appointed by Yichang court, as it was composed only of representatives of local government agencies.

Similar difficulties have been reported in several cases involving AMCs, such as the controversial restructuring of the retailer Zhengzhou Baiwen in Henan province against China Cinda AMC's original plan to force this company into bankruptcy in March 2000.[2] They point to the difficulties encountered by the AMCs to play an active role in the restructuring of the biggest SOEs and reforming corporate governance in the state sector. It should be noted that MKG was far from being a good candidate for a debt/equity swap as it systematically infringed stock market regulations, and was engaged in different dubious financial practices. In 1999, MKG had already 162 pending lawsuits, had lost 513 million RMB in fraudulent investments on the stock market, and the group's total liabilities were reported at 2.77 billion RMB for 3.41 billions of assets.

---

1. All information is based on Matthew Miller, "Real Monkey Business", in *South China Morning Post*, 29 March 2001, Business post, p. 14.
2. World Bank (2000), p. 31.

After 1993, the government realised that NPLs were growing at an alarming rate and that this policy was not sustainable. The People's Bank of China reacted by significantly reducing both its subsidies to SOEs and its loans to commercial banks. As mentioned above, subsidies to SOEs were reduced from 7.5 per cent of GDP in 1992 to 2.3 per cent in 1994, then to less than 1 per cent after 1995. From 1994 to 1998, loans from the PBOC to state commercial banks grew at an average annual rate of 6 per cent as opposed to 20 per cent before 1994. It has been calculated that between 1996 and 1998 the stock of People's Bank of China loans to the banks actually declined from 142 billion RMB to 121 billion RMB.[28] A subsequent decision to turn the big four state banks into commercial banks, and to clean their balance sheets, made banks more conservative, knowing that bad loans were now less likely to be financed by new loans from the PBOC.

These steps were followed by a series of reforms to the banking system. The four state commercial banks have been required to increase their profits and to "clean up their balance sheets" by restricting bad debt. In this context, they are increasingly unwilling to lend money to companies that are already heavily in debt. Companies, for their part, are required, since 1996, to maintain accounts with only one bank (the principal bank system, called *zhuban yinghang*) and to close their accounts in other banks.[29] They are also subject to an evaluation of their financial situation by auditing firms or to ranking agencies. During the course of 1997, after the implementation of this measure, some 2000 large and medium-sized Shanghai state companies were audited and ranked according to their financial situation. Moreover, they were issued with a "loan certificate" summarising their credit track record, a document that they will have to present to their bank for any new credit request.

These reforms have contributed to speeding up the pace of restructuring. They constitute an important break with the practice of the 1980s. Thousands of inefficient SMEs in the state and collective sectors were progressively starved of funds. In tandem with a market dominated by demand, it is now more difficult for the local authorities not just to embark on industrial projects where demand is already saturated or dominated by efficient producers in other provinces, but also to sustain local companies. State commercial banks certainly continue to provide loans to unprofitable companies, on the orders of the central authorities. But there is no longer a policy, as in the 1980s, of granting loans to loss-making companies for purchases of production equipment or other costly investment projects. Bank loans are now handed out sparingly in order to reduce the social costs of transition, while waiting for these companies to be privatised, merged, or put into bankruptcy. These reforms, however imperfect they may be, are pushing the local authority to restructure SMEs in the state and collective sector.

Nevertheless, improvement is less obvious for the biggest SOEs. The expansionary fiscal policy carried out by the central government after the Asian crisis of 1997 contributed to channelling funds to big SOEs. This also partly explains the spectacular reversal in their financial indicators.[30, 31]

Privatisation of SMEs

The disengagement of the state in SMEs in the state and collective sector has occurred in various ways. On the principle of "grasping the big and releasing the small", local governments were empowered to choose how to reform state and collective SMEs. For example, in the province of Guangxi, between 1993 and 1998, 1 205 state SMEs (about 15 per cent of the total number of SMEs in Guangxi) were reformed in various ways: 93 were transformed into joint stock companies in which the state remained the major stakeholder; 222 companies were transformed into joint stock companies and sold to their workforce in the framework of the so-called co-operative shareholding system (*gufen hezuo zhi*); 29 were sold to a Chinese investor (without it being specified whether it was the director of the company, a local investor, or one from another province); 44 were merged with another company in the region; 469 were leased; 30 went into liquidation; and 318 were reformed using other, unspecified means (Wu, 1999). Another example, this time in a developed coastal city, the municipality of Shunde in Guangdong province has implemented an ambitious programme since 1992 to reform its 1 001 state companies. Only 94 remain under the direct ownership of the municipality in infrastructure, certain high technology industries, or those considered to be strategic at the national level. The government maintains a minority interest in another 70 companies.[32] All the other companies have been sold or leased.

Privatisation has been an important means of restructuring. Among the various methods of privatisation, the central authorities have chosen the sale of state shares rather than the free distribution of shares, in contrast with Russia or the former Czechoslovakia. The sale of capital to employees (in the form of shares) has in fact been the most widely used method to reform state and collective urban SMEs in difficulties. This method may have been applied, in the hinterland particularly, in almost a third of state and collective urban SMEs affected by the reforms (which amounts to much less if one takes into account the total number of state and collective companies).[33] The first experiment on a large scale, and which had comprehensive media coverage, took place in Zhucheng in 1994, a small city in the province of Shandong, where 210 state and collective companies were privatised.

This kind of shareholding was extended to all the cities in China in the wake of the 15th Congress of the CCP in the autumn of 1997. Although less frequently used than co-operative shareholding, another method has consisted of totally privatising the capital of companies by auctioning it off in the centres for the sale and exchange of state assets (guoyou zichan jiaoyi zhongxin), which were set up in all the larger municipalities. Total privatisation, accompanied by sale of the capital to outsiders, has mostly involved heavily indebted companies. Finally, another method used by local government has been partial privatisation with the maintenance of majority or minority ownership by the state. This method has been widely favoured by local authorities in companies in good financial condition, as it has made it possible to win the consensus of local officials and company managers who have acquired part of the capital of these companies.

Local statistics would suggest that a widespread move to privatisation has taken place in China. But lack of statistics at a national level makes it extremely difficult to evaluate the extent of privatisation of state and collective SMEs. Selling state assets should not be confused with the privatisation of companies. Not only have local authorities kept 100 per cent ownership of a relatively large number of urban state and collective SMEs, but they have also resorted to leasing that does not alter the property structure. In cases of partial privatisation, local authorities have maintained control through state asset management companies that have been set up in all China's large municipalities. Case studies found that these companies tend to behave in the same way as the old municipal industrial offices (Huchet et al., 2000).

Moreover, even when all or part of the capital has been sold, this does not necessarily mean that it has been acquired by the private investor, whether Chinese or foreign. On the contrary, some of the transactions in the assets of state and collective SMEs have taken place within the state and collective sector. Similarly, mergers have in most cases been organised by the local administrative authorities that have simply transferred all or part of the capital of a company to another state company organised as a group or holding company.

In some cases, foreign private investors have bought at knockdown prices production equipment belonging to state and collective SMEs that have gone out of business.[34] But in general, considering the large number of companies put on the market, very few foreign investors have ventured to take over these companies, because of both high transaction costs and unattractive assets. In contrast there have been quite a few take-overs by Chinese private investors. Case studies (Huchet, 2000) show many examples of aggressive taking over of state SMEs by outsiders from other provinces. The Xin Xiwang (New Hope) group in Sichuan, for example, has taken over 13 state SMEs in various provinces since 1993.[35]

The China Statistical Yearbook 2000 shows a sizeable decrease in the number of state companies in industry; these have fallen from 127 000 in 1996 to 61 300 in 1999. However, these figures include all state companies regardless of size, and do not indicate whether this drastic reduction is due to the closing of state companies, to the merging of public sector companies, or to the transfer to the heading of "joint stock companies" (gufenzhi jingji) of some of the state companies which have in fact been transformed into joint stock companies. By approximation, an estimate of between 23 000 and 30 000 state companies have been privatised in the industrial sector, or between 18 per cent and 23 per cent of public sector companies in the peak of the year 1996. This is a sizeable figure, which, if confirmed by precise statistics, would signal profound changes in the Chinese economy.

With regard to the effectiveness of restructuring, the most positive outcomes have been obtained by companies which were acquired by outside investors, whether Chinese or foreign. These companies have not only been freed from the stranglehold of the local bureaucracy, but they have also benefited from new, more dynamic management, a known brand name, and access to new markets. Their debt load with the banks has also been reduced, and the new owner has negotiated with the local authorities. The case studies on the private group Xin Xiwang (New Hope) have shown that two key players, the company director and the financial manager, were immediately replaced by senior managers from Xin Xiwang, with a view to rapidly introducing financial discipline and new methods of management. In fact this process of "subsidiarisation" through an active investor able to bring know-how and with the power to reform the company has already proved its effectiveness in capitalist economies, as well as in the restructuring of companies in the former socialist countries of Eastern Europe.

As for those companies whose capital has been sold to the workforce, the results seem so far rather negative. Once again it is difficult to get a precise assessment as no serious impact study has been published (or perhaps even carried out) by the central authorities. From case studies (Wu, 1999; Chenhong, 1999; Huchet, 2000; Dong, 1999; Zong, 2000), two major kinds of problem emerge, already documented for other countries in transition (Blasi, 1997). On the one hand, the injection of capital from the acquisition of shares by employees is insufficient to repay debts and upgrade production capacity. On the other hand, the management structure and the incentive system resulting from this kind of privatisation are often unable to generate any real reforming impulse (see Box 5.6).

There are some company directors with undeniable managerial know-how who take advantage of their new autonomy *vis-à-vis* the administration, and initiate profound reforms, as highlighted in the

---

Box 5.6.   **The co-operative shareholding system: the Zhucheng experiment***

The first experiment in the privatisation of SMEs in the state and collective sector was carried out in 1994 in Zhucheng, a town in the province of Shandong. This gradually extended to the whole of China, after the 15th Congress of the CCP in 1997. In July 1994, of the 288 state SMEs in the city of Zhucheng, 210 companies were entirely privatised for a total of 250 million yuan in shares. Almost 90 per cent of the employees bought shares, at 1 000 RMB a share. The employees bought between two and five shares each, while the company managers bought twice as many. The employees were unable to resell their shares outside the company. Because of this, the only shareholders outside the company are the handful of employees who left the company, but were unable to sell their shares to new or existing employees. All these companies have no prospect of being floated on the stock market and the shares circulate only inside the companies, according to the various regulations specific to each company. In the years immediately following the initial sale of shares, managers, with the help of loans from local banks, sought to buy back the shares of employees, and quickly became the majority shareholders. The workers sold their shares at a small profit, trying to recover their savings invested in shares that were non-negotiable outside the company. In 1997, the local authorities decided to raise company equity by 750 million RMB, or three times the previous issue. The contribution of employees (which was the majority holding in 1994) amounted then to only 180 million RMB (or 24 per cent of the total), the rest of the financing having been provided by the banks and outside investors who came into the capital of companies. The intervention of the local state banks was widely seen as a rescue mission and a partial renationalisation of the city's companies. The banks also lent heavily to company managers during the initial sale of shares, and again when the managers bought back the workers' shares in order to gain majority control of the companies. The various case studies carried out in Zhucheng show that the biggest shareholders are now the management teams, who control an overwhelming majority of the capital of companies. The case of Zhucheng is a good illustration of the ineffectiveness of the privatisation carried out in the form of co-operative shareholding.

---

*   This information comes mainly from Dong (1999), and from Zong (2000).

Chinese economic press. However, the impact on control is generally limited, for two main reasons. First, managers are still appointed by local political leaders and are still considered as local government officials. Party membership is also still crucial for their careers. Political allegiance is sometimes contrary to the interests of the company, but above all encourages rent-seeking, since company managers consider themselves to be both underpaid and not responsible for the destiny of the company (even if they are majority shareholders). Second, in spite of privatisation, no alternative decision-making power emerges within the company, even where the employees are the majority shareholders.

The lack of independent unions, the growth of unemployment, and the end of job security deprive employees of any means of bringing organised and official pressure to bear on their future or on that of the company (Leung, 1998). In a context similar to some other transition countries, none of the new institutions – such as boards of directors or supervisory committees – are able to exercise internal control over the behaviour and decisions of company bosses who, in most cases, also hold the position of chairman of the board of directors and supervision, chairman of the company, and Party Secretary.

Lastly, the workers' incentive system was supposed to have been improved by their new status as owners of the company. Where this influence existed, it was exercised only briefly, long enough for the workers to resell their shares, having realised that they had not gained any decision-making power. In reality, the threat of unemployment and the end of job security have proved to be much more powerful incentives to improve performance than shareholding (Zhao *et al.*, 1996; Lee, 1999).

Whatever the methods used, the effectiveness of restructuring has nonetheless varied very widely from one region to another. There is a fairly clear-cut difference between the coastal regions and those of the northeast and the interior. In the autonomous region of Guangxi, after five years of reforms, almost 70 per cent of companies had not recorded any improvement in their profits, while 25 per cent had registered a decline in profitability (Wu, 1999). Coastal cities such as Dalian, Shanghai and Canton, and provinces such as Shandong, Jiangsu, Zhejiang and Fujian, are apparently doing much better. The profitability and debt ratios of state companies in 1999 by province show that, with some exceptions (Yunnan where high profits come from the tobacco industry which is entirely state-owned, Tibet whose values are too low to be significant, and Heilongjiang which has surprising profitability given the size of its state sector), the coastal provinces are much better off than those of the north-east and of the interior, where state ownership remains above the national average.

This difference lies in the fact that restructuring in the coastal provinces has benefited from a more competitive environment, a more dynamic and transparent market for take-overs of these companies, and more competent managers. Also, higher land prices in coastal cities and opportunities to use their land-use rights have helped companies to restructure their activities (World Bank, 2000). In Xiamen, for example, 35 state companies in the old centre of the city have used this option in order to restructure, selling a total of 330 000 square metres of land for 1.24 billion RMB. These companies moved outside of the city and were thus able to recapitalise and acquire new technology (Chenhong, 1999). Furthermore, the viability of the social security system in coastal cities, especially the pension system, has allowed local government to proceed more rapidly in their restructuring process.

To sum up, privatisation in itself is not a sufficient condition for restructuring. In fact, improvement in performance depends above all on effective external control (depoliticisation of the banks that would make it possible to increase the budgetary constraints on companies, deregulation or abolition of local protectionism in order to expose these companies to competition) and the establishment of a social security system capable of reducing the social costs of restructuring.

Conclusions and policy recommendations

Despite some positive results following the implementation of a large program of enterprise restructuring since the mid-1990's, the analysis in this chapter has documented limits and bottlenecks in this reform process. China's accession to the WTO will bring some substantial changes in the business environment of domestic firms, and will more than ever confront the Chinese government with some specific problems that are linked with the legacy of the industrialisation process during the pre-reform period and with the way reforms were implemented after 1978.

Policy makers should tackle these limits and bottlenecks in a rather short period of time if they want to limit the social and financial costs of China's accession to the WTO. If the Chinese government does not address these problems, the gains from China's accession to the WTO could be seriously eroded.

- First a real risk exists that domestic enterprises are not sufficiently prepared to cope with the new competition. This risk is especially great for SMEs in the state and the collective sector.

- Second, international experience shows that industrial and financial restructuring should be swift and decisive in order to limit its costs. In this respect, and if the data are accurate and reliable, Chinese policy makers have a window of opportunity to accelerate industrial restructuring given the current level of their financial resources. Delaying reforms to achieve restructuring is likely to mean higher costs, both for public finances and for the economy as a whole.

In the short term, the government needs to implement reforms in three main areas. The first involves measures to *reinforce and accelerate corporate governance reform*, notably by limiting price controls in order to improve competition, and by reinforcing firm decision-making autonomy, particularly in mergers and acquisitions.

- **Limit price control policies.** Price controls have been introduced by the government and different associations of producers in different industries in order to deal with what is presented as destructive competition based on a "price war". Nevertheless, efforts to control and limit these strategies could be counterproductive in the context of a low degree of concentration and the rapid development of competition in the industry. Winners in a price war will be companies that invest aggressively in cost reduction, product development, and distribution networks. The best way to minimise the impact of the price war is to become the cost leader in the industry and to move to higher value added production. The most competitive industrial groups that are now emerging in China are all following this strategy regardless of whether they are state in non-state enterprises. Government should not intervene at this stage or it will prolong the consolidation process, reduce the number of exits from the market by inefficient producers, and lower the reaction capabilities of domestic producers in a context of increasing foreign competition following trade and investment liberalisation.

- *Reinforce company decision-making autonomy and enhance corporate governance mechanisms*. Even for SOEs, the government should refrain from intervening too directly in mergers and acquisitions, and should respect the strategic interests of the firms. Size still matters in terms of competition, but grandiose plans to create "national champions" only for the sake of economic national pride will probably serve neither the restructuring process nor the economic interest of China, as several experiences in the Republic of Korea, France and Italy have shown in the past.

For the large SOEs where the state will remain the principal stakeholder, the more it is able to implement and make them respect a system of objectives (exports, profitability, technological innovation) and sanctions (end of financing and assistance packages, disciplinary action for managers, privatisations, bankruptcies) that are clearly defined, the better they will restructure their activities under a more efficient corporate governance system, as has been observed in other developing countries (Amsden, 1989; Fields, 1995; Wade, 1990; Evans, 1995; Maxfield *et al.*, 1997).

Given the low effectiveness of the existing structure of corporate governance and pending radical reform in this area (see Chapter 13), competition in the goods and services market should be pursued as the most effective mechanism for regulating the behaviour of executives and guiding them to restructure and develop their activities (see Chapter 12 on Competition Law and Policy). China's membership of the WTO should have a positive impact in this field. Nevertheless, competition alone is not sufficient to lead to efficient corporate governance. The government therefore needs to work on several fronts at once. It needs to improve the functioning of other disciplinary mechanisms that will come to reinforce the effects of competition. This concerns the pursuit of reforms in the banking and financial sector (much more fundamentally than hitherto), the fight against regional protectionist measures, an improvement in the labour market, particularly regarding company managers, and the further development of the rule of law. Such reforms go well beyond the mere economic sphere, making them at once more complex and difficult to implement.

The second key area involves two sets of reforms to remove obstacles to implementation of bankruptcy and other mechanisms needed to accelerate the exit or restructuring of inefficient firms.

- **Reform of the social security funding system.** At this stage of the reform, one of the main problems in fostering restructuring lies in the inefficiencies of the current social protection system. The current funding system that consists of pooling resources at the municipal level represents a clear disadvantage for the regions that have the biggest needs and the greatest structural problems in terms of restructuring. Existing compensation funds between cities of the same province are clearly insufficient to counterbalance the lack of resources in municipalities of the northeast, the hinterland, and the western region. This lack of resources (for pensions, unemployment, medical expenses and retraining) is blocking the market exit of numerous inefficient companies. Since employees are privileged creditors, the state commercial banks make little effort to clean their balance sheets, as they would not recover much of their loans. In this context, the central government, in co-operation with the local authorities, should design a new funding system along the lines suggested in Chapter 16 on the labour market and social benefits.

- **Management of land use rights.** Land is an important asset in the restructuring process. As the recent World Bank report on bankruptcy stated, its management by the public administration should be enhanced in order to facilitate restructuring.[36] Enterprises that have to be restructured are often left with only one valuable asset: land. This explains why their restructuring opportunities are often linked with their location, which sets the price of land. This discrimination should be attenuated in order to help enterprises in bad locations to have access to some fund to restructure their activities. Enterprises do not own land but have land-use rights granted or allocated by the state for periods of time that differ from one industry to another. Local authorities could consider using the land-use rights granted to the local enterprises in a more efficient manner. The World Bank has suggested setting up a fund at an administrative level varying according to the local situation (city, province) "that pools the proceeds from selling land-use rights that have been taken back from all bankrupted enterprises of the region" and make them available to enterprises filing bankruptcies that do not have the opportunities from being in a good location to pays for their social costs and other rehabilitation fees.[37] Land-use rights should also be used in a more transparent environment (valuation, exchange or sale) in order to maximise value and smooth the restructuring process.

Finally, there is a need to *promote a more effective and mutually reinforcing division of responsibilities for* SOE *restructuring between central and local government authorities.* Restructuring has been being carried out by various institutions both at the central and local levels of the public administration. The distribution of responsibilities (in terms of privatisation, exchange and sales of assets, mergers, and bankruptcy) has followed the evolution of property rights in the state sector: the central government and its agencies for the biggest enterprises,[38] the municipal governments for the other state and urban-collective companies. This distribution of competence has some clear advantages in terms of agency costs as the central government lacks the capabilities to restructure the entire SOE sector by itself. It also enables local authorities to adapt their restructuring strategy to the characteristics of the local economy. Nevertheless, this institutional setting also has led to distortions that have constrained restructuring efforts. For example, in privatisation, local political leaders control the whole process of asset disposal, including allocation procedures all the way through to fixing the prices of the assets. Local leaders also have major influence over bankruptcy proceedings, as illustrated by the difficulties encountered by the bank AMCs in trying to impose thorough restructuring plans against the will of the local authorities. This distribution of responsibilities between various levels of government is also creating a regional compartmentalisation in the redistribution of assets, as local authorities tend to favour local investors, and encourages rent-seeking by public officials or managers. Thus an appropriate reform of the institutional framework governing the restructuring process, to achieve greater co-ordination, coherence, consistency and clearer rules, could help greatly to ensure that SOE restructuring and privatisation will promote the overall goal of improving the competitiveness of the industrial sector as a whole.

NOTES

1. The Chinese government nonetheless restricts access to foreign currency, to the extent that firms wishing to obtain foreign currency have to request authorisation from the exchange office. Moreover, not all firms have the right to participate in international trade, and only a part of the foreign currency earned by exports may be retained by such firms.

2. See China Research Team (1998).

3. *Ibid.*

4. Dongfang qiye yanjiuhui (1997), "Woguo xuyao yipi shejieji da gongsi" (China needs world size companies) in *Qiye wenhua*, No. 5, pp. 25-27.

5. *China Daily*, 27 January 1999.

6. See Teitel (1984), Lall (1990), and Dalhman *et al.* (1987).

7. Quoted by the *Financial Times*, 5 November 2000.

8. See the recent strident criticisms via the Chinese press against Philips or Toshiba in the *Financial Times* 21 August 2000.

9. Interview, April 1998.

10. The state has just granted 19 firms in this category US$2.7 million each in subsidies for R&D that may be extended over seven years. *Asian Wall Street Journal*, 11 September 2000.

11. Kelon and Konka are developing a foothold in Silicon Valley. Konka has made an alliance with Matsushita to sell its products on the Japanese market, and is seeking agreements with major distributors in the United states to commercialise its products; from the *Asian Wall Street Journal*, 8 May 2000.

12. Siren Qiye Nianqian (Directory of private Chinese companies), 1997.

13. Quoted by the *Asian Wall Street Journal*, 1 February 1999.

14. Zhongguo shehuikexueyuan gongyejingji yanjiusuo, Zhongguo gongye fazhan baogao (Report on industrial development in China) (1997), Beijing, *Jingii guanli chubanshe*.

15. A recent study in regional development stated "that despite its relatively low GDP per head (...) regional differences among China's thirty provinces are so large that they resemble the gap between the advanced industrial countries and the poorest countries in the world" (Wang *et al.*, 1999).

16. Glass, tractors, steel, sugar, passenger cars, fibre glass, colour TVs, caustic soda, urea, cement, aviation, see Warburg Dillon Read (1998), "China: price war and price control", December, Hong Kong, China, p. 15.

17. *China Light Industry Yearbook*, 2000.

18. *Asian Wall Street Journal*, 26 April 2001.

19. *Jingii Cankao*, 11 July 2000.

20. *South China Morning Post*, 20 February 2001.

21. *World Bank*, 2000, p.i.

22. *China Online*, 24 August 2000.

23. The Chinese economic press is full of examples of this phenomenon since the launching of the reform decided on at the 15th Party Congress. Case studies on the local and state asset-management companies of the big municipalities (Lu, 1999; Huchet, 1999; Lei *et al.*, 1999; Ma, 1999; Xu, 1999; Wu, 1999), which are directly in charge of carrying out these mergers on behalf of municipal governments, show that except for a few cases in Shanghai and coastal cities (Cheng, 1999; Wang, 2000; *Shanghaishi* guoyou zichan guanli moshi yanjiu kejizu, 1999), the formation of these groups was aimed at avoiding bankruptcies and concealing company losses.

24. *China Steel Industry Yearbook* (1999).

25. In the state Sector, between 1988 and 1996, 46 549 new enterprises were created in the industry, 213 657 in the wholesale, retail and catering trade, and 5 852 in the construction sector. Various issues of *China Statistical Yearbook*.

26. *Reuter*, 4 April 2000.

27. *South China Morning Post*, 19 February 2001.

28. *Asian Wall Street Journal*, 7 April 2000.

29. *Zhongguo jinrong xuehui* (Chinese Society for Financial Studies) (1997), *Zhongguo jinrong nianjian* (Chinese Financial Annual), Peking, *Zhongguo jinrong nianjian bianji bu*, p. 339.

30. Brandt, L. and X. Zhu, in *Asian Wall Street Journal*, 7 April 2000.

31. BNP Parisbas Peregrine (2001), "Inside China", March; Credit Lyonnais Securities (2001), "Emerging Markets"; SG Economic Research (2000), "Quarterly economic review, fundamental Asia", July.

32. *China Daily* (1998), "Business Weekly", 18-24 January.

33. See Lei *et al.* (1999) and Ma (1999).

34. See Cao *et al.* (1998).

35. Interview, *New Hope*, Chengdu, 20 April 1998.

36. World Bank (2000), *op. cit.*, p. 41.

37. World Bank (2000), *op. cit.*, p. 27.

38. In 1997, there were 2 097 large State-owned enterprises directly run by the central government.

BIBLIOGRAPHY

Amsden, A. (1989),
> *Asia's Next Giant: Republic of Korea and Late Industrialization*, Oxford University Press, Oxford.

Blasi, J. (1997),
> "Corporate ownership and corporate governance in the Russian Federation", in Lieberman, I.W., S. Stilpon, N. and R. M. Desai, *Between State and Market. Mass Privatization in Transition Economies*, The World Bank and OECD, Washington D. C., pp. 162-170.

Byrd, W. A. (1992),
> *Chinese Industrial Firms under Reform*, Oxford University Press, Oxford.

Cao, Y., Y. Qian and B.R. Weingast (1998),
> "The sale goes on. Transforming small enterprises in China", in *Transition*, February, pp. 5-7.

Chenhong, X. (1999),
> "Guanyu Xiamenshi guoqi gaige de jiaocha", (Research into the reform of state companies in the city of Xiamen), *Guoyou Zichan Guanli*, No. 4, pp. 52-54.

Cheng, E. (1999),
> "Shanghai guoyou zichan yunxing fenxi" (Analysis of the workings of state assets in Shanghai), *Guoyou Zichan Guanli*, No. 3, pp. 44-49.

China Research Team (1998),
> "China: price war and price control", in *Warburg Dillon Read*, December.

Dalhman, C.J., B. Ross–Larson and L.E. Westphal (1987),
> "Managing technological development: Lessons from the newly industrializing countries", in *World Development*, Vol. 15, No. 6, pp. 759-777.

Ding, X.L. (2000),
> "The illicit asset stripping of Chinese state firms", in *The China Journal*, No. 43, pp. 1-28.

Dong, Y. (1999),
> "Shandong Zhucheng gufen hezuozhi qiye yanshi fenxi" (Analysis of the co-operative share holding system of the city of Zhucheng in the province of Shandong), *Gongye Jingji Yanjiu*, No. 11, pp. 5-11.

Evans, P. (1995),
> *Embedded Autonomy. States and Industrial Transformation*, Princeton University Press, Princeton.

Fields, K.J. (1995),
> *Enterprise and the State in Republic of Korea and Taiwan*, Cornell University Press, Cornell.

Huchet, J-F. (1999),
> "Concentration and Emergence of Corporate Groups in Chinese Industry", in *China Perspectives*, No.23.

Huchet, J-F. (2000),
> "The hidden aspect of public sector reforms in China, state and collective SMEs in urban areas", in *China Perspectives*, No. 31, pp. 37-48.

Huchet, J-F. and X. Richet (2000),
> "Between bureaucracy and market: Chinese industrial groups in search of new forms of corporate governance", *Working Paper*, Centre d'Études Français sur la Chine Contemporaine.

Jefferson, G.H. (1993),
> "Are China's rural enterprises outperforming state-owned enterprises?", *Symposium on Economic Transition in China*, Haikou, China.

Jefferson, G.H., T.G. Rawski and Y. Zheng (1994),
> "Institutional change and industrial innovation in transitional economies", *Research Paper Series*, World Bank, Washington D. C.

Lall, S. (1990),
> *Promouvoir la Compétitivité Industrielle dans les Pays en Développement*, OCDE, Paris.

Lardy, N.R. (2000*a*),
"The challenge of bank restructuring in China", in *China Research*, CLSA *Emerging Market*.

Lardy, N.R. (2000*b*),
"Fiscal sustainability: between a rock and a hard place", in *China Economic Quarterly*, No. 26-41.

Lee, C-K. (1999),
"From organized dependence to disorganized despotism: changing labour regimes in Chinese factories", in *The China Quarterly*, No. 157, pp. 44-71.

Lei, Y., X. Huang, Y. Hu and Z. Ren (1999),
"Dui Sichuansheng qiye guoyou zichan linke guanli youguan qingkuangde yanjiubaogao" (Research report on the situation of the management and ownership of state assets in the companies in the province of Sichuan), *Guoyou Zichan Guanli*, No. 4, pp. 50-51.

Lemoine, F. (2000),
"FDI and the opening up of China's economy", CEPII *Working Paper*, Paris.

Leung, T.W.Y. (1998),
"S'organiser pour défendre ses droits ; Contestations ouvrières en Chine dans les années 1990", in *Perspectives Chinoises*, No. 48, pp. 6-23.

Lu, Z. (1999),
"Ruhe fangzhi guoyou zichan yingyun jigou biancheng fanpai gongsi, Shenzhen de shixian ji qishi" (How to prevent institutions in charge of state assets from becoming bureaucratised companies), *Zhongguo Gongye Jingji*, No. 7, Shanghai, Wuhan, pp. 18-20.

Lu, Y. and J. Child (1996),
"Decentralization of decision making in China's state enterprises" in Brown, D.H. and R. Porter (eds.), *Management Issues in China*, Domestic Enterprises, Vol. I, London: Routledge.

Ma, R. (1999),
"Guozi guanli tizhi gaige de youyi tansuo. Nanning shi zujianguozi jingying gongsi qingkuang de diaocha" (Exploration of the advantages of the reform of the state assets management system. Enquiry on the situation of state asset management companies established by the city of Nanning), *Guoyou Zichan Guanli*, No. 3, pp. 63-64, Xu Qing, *op. cit.*

Maxfield, S. and B.R. Schneider (eds.) (1997),
Business and the State in Developing Countries, Cornell University Press, Ithaca.

Naughton, B. (1995),
Growing Out of the Plan: Chinese Economic Reform 1978-1993, Cambridge University Press, Cambridge.

Nee, V. (1992),
"Organisational dynamics of market transition: hybrid forms, property rights and mixed economy in China", in *Administrative Science Quarterly*, No. 37, pp. 1-27.

OECD, (2000),
Reforming China's Enterprises, OECD, Paris.

Oi, J.C. (1995),
"The role of the local state in China's transitional economy", in *The China Quarterly*, No. 144, China's Transitional Economy, pp. 1132-49.

Putterman, L. (1995),
"The role of ownership and property rights in China's economic transition", in *The China Quarterly*, No. 144, China's Transitional Economy, pp. 1047-64.

Rawski, T.G. (1995),
"Implications of China's reform experience", in *The China Quarterly*, No. 144, China's Transitional Economy, pp. 1150-73.

Shanghaishi Guoyouzichan Guanli Moshi Yanjiu Kejizu (1999),
"Shanghai shi guoyou zichanguanli moshi zhong de lingkong xitong", in *Zhongguo Gongye Jingji*, No. 3, pp. 19-24.

Shen, Z. (1999),
New Developments of Enterprise Groups in China, Paper prepared for the International Conference on The Emergence and the Structuring of Corporate Groups in the P.R. China, University of Hong Kong.

Stark, D. (1997),
"Recombinant property in East European capitalism", in Grabher, G. and D. Stark (eds.), *Restructuring Networks in Post-Socialism*, Oxford University Press, Oxford, pp. 36-69.

Teitel, S. (1984),
"Technology creation in semi-industrial economies", in *Journal of Development Economics*, No. 16, pp. 39-61.

Wade, R. (1990),
Governing the Market. Economic Theory and the Role of Government in East Asian Industrialisation, Princeton University Press, Princeton.

Wang,. S. and A. Hu (1999),
The Political Economy of Uneven Development. The Case of China, Armonk, M.E. Sharp.

Wang, H. (2000),
Shunde Qiye Chanquan Gaige de Jiaocha (Enquiry into the reform of the property of companies in Shunde), No. 1, pp. 43-46, Gaige.

Wang, H., X. Richet and W. Wang (2001),
"Foreign direct investment in the Chinese automotive industry: country of origin effects", roneo unpublished, Paris.

Warner, M. (1995),
The Management of Human Resources in Chinese Industry, Macmillan, London.

Weitzman, M.L. and C. Xu (1993),
"Chinese township village enterprises as vaguely defined co-operatives", Development Economics Research Programme, London School of Economics, London.

Wong, C.P.W. (ed.) (1997),
Financing Local Government in the People's Republic of China, New York, Oxford University Press.

Wong, C.P.W. (2000),
"La nouvelle donne entre gouvernement central et les collectivités locales. La gestion des finances publiques et la réforme fiscale de 1994", in Perspectives Chinoises, pp. 56-67.

Wu, P. (1999),
"Dui shenhua guoyou zhongxiaoxing qiye gaige de sikao" (Reflections on the deepening of the reform of state SMEs),
Guoyou zichan Guanli, No. 4, pp. 35-37.

Xu, Q. (1999),
"Dangqian zhiyue Ningxia guoyou zhongxiao qiye gaizhi nandian wenti youxi" (Analysis of the problems in the reform of the state SME system in the province du Ningxia), Ningxia Shihuikexue, No. 3, 1999, pp. 47-52.

Zhao, M. and T. Nichols (1996),
"Management control of labour in state-owned enterprises: cases from the textile industry", The China Journal, No. 36, pp. 1-24.

Zong, H. (2000),
"Gufen hezuozhi de fazhan ji qi jiaojian" (Development of co-operative share holding), Zhongguo Gongye Jingji, No. 2, pp. 9-12.

Chapter 6

TECHNOLOGY CHALLENGES FOR CHINA'S INDUSTRIES

TABLE OF CONTENTS

Tables

Figures

Boxes

TECHNOLOGY CHALLENGES FOR CHINA'S INDUSTRIES[*]

Introduction

China's open-door policy, adopted since the late 1970s, has been rewarded with increased access to advanced technologies. As a result, China's high-tech industries have become an important sector accounting for 9 per cent of value added by industry, and 14 per cent of manufactured export goods (MOST 2000a and 2000b). China's electronic and information technology industry was the world's third largest in terms of turnover in 2000 (CND, 10 June 2001). In spite of this impressive achievement, the development of China's technological capability has lagged behind its economic development. China's already very low ratio of science and technology research and development (R&D) expenditure to GDP actually experienced a decline in the 1990s. Furthermore, Chinese enterprises are far from being the leaders in innovation. China still relies on foreign supply of advanced industrial technologies, and the lack of domestic progress in this area has further increased reliance on foreign technology. Poor domestic technological capability could lead to serious structural weaknesses in the Chinese economy.

Building technological capability is one of the areas in which China will face great challenges in the short- to medium-term. This concerns not only how China will be able to increase R&D but also, and more importantly, how effectively the institutional and structural weaknesses of its current innovation system will be addressed.

This Chapter outlines the technological and innovative performance of China's industry, analyses the factors that hampered, and continue to hinder, progress in innovation and proposes policy recommendations based on OECD experience to help meet the challenges of the development of a market-based advanced technological structure in China.

Science and technology

Science and technology expenditure

The level of China's science and technology (S&T) expenditures[1] as a share of GNP is still low. This share declined from 1.80 per cent in 1991 to 1.37 per cent in 1996 and since then has recovered to just 1.57 per cent by the end of the 1990s (see Table 6.1).

In the transition from a planned to a market economy, the Chinese Government has reduced its share of investment but still remains the main source of S&T funding. Government budgetary appropriation for S&T expenditures was RMB 54.5 billion in 1999, up from RMB 30.2 billion in 1995,

Table 6.1.   **S&T and R&D expenditure,1991-1998 (100 million RMB)**

	1991	1992	1993	1994	1995	1996	1997	1998	1999
S&T expenditure	388.5	490.4	622.5	738.9	845.2	930.7	1 060.1	1 128.5	1 284.9
Change from previous year in real terms, %	6.3	17.0	10.8	−1.0	1.1	4.0	12.8	5.9[1]	13.9[1]
R&D expenditure	150.8	209.8	256.2	309.2	348.7	404.5	509.2	551.1	678.9
Increase in real term over previous year	–	2 9,0	6,6	0,6	−0,6	9,5	24.9	10.9	26.0
Expenditure as share of GDP (%)									
S&T	1.8	1.84	1.80	1.58	1.45	1.37	1.42	1.42	1.57
R&D	0.70	0.79	0.74	0.66	0.60	0.60	0.64	0.69	0.83

1. in nominal terms
Source: Ministry of Science and Technology (MOST) 1999, p.41, 44; National Bureau of Statistics and MOST 1999. p. 7, and MOST, 2000a, p.2.

---

[*] This chapter has been prepared by Gang Zhang, Administrator, Non-Member Economies, Directorate for Science, Technology and Industry, OECD.

accounting for 42.4 per cent of the total S&T expenditure in that year. The S&T budgetary expenditure accounted for 4.1 per cent of total budget expenditure in 1999, down from the 4.4 per cent level reached in the mid-1990s. The Tenth Five-Year Plan (2001-2005) envisages spending RMB 15 billion (US$1.8 billion) in the civil programmes of the state high-tech R&D, three times more than the amount spent in the past 15 years.

Government research institutions (GRIs) and the enterprise sector combined accounted for over 88 per cent of China's total S&T expenditure in 1999. The enterprise sector, under pressure to improve competitiveness, has increased investment in innovation. The enterprise sector's share of S&T expenditure increased from 46.3 to 49.6 per cent between 1997 and 1999, while the share of GRIs dropped from 44.4 to 38.5 per cent. The contribution to innovation from higher education institutions, which accounted for less than 10 per cent of total S&T expenditure, is still relatively weak. However, the increase in the enterprise sector's share in China's S&T expenditure in recent years is partly a result of the transformation of a large number of GRIs into business entities.

R&D *expenditures*

China's R&D expenditure reached RMB 67.9 billion in 1999 (MOST, 2000a). On average, R&D expenditure increased by about 10 per cent per year in real terms between 1991 and 1997 (MOST 1999, p. 44). Despite the impressive rate of increase, China's R&D expenditure as a share of GDP remained low, averaging only 0.7 per cent for the 1990s (see Table 6.1). This level is not only far below that of OECD countries, which averaged 2.3 per cent between 1981 and 1996,[2] but also lower for instance than the level of India at 0.9 per cent of GDP in 1999.

There are also structural weaknesses in the allocation of R&D resources between basic research, applied research, and experimental development as shown in Figure 6.1.

The structure of China's R&D expenditure, compared with developed countries, is characterised by a relatively low share in basic research, and too large a share in experimental development.

As shown in Figure 6.2, the enterprise sector in 1999 accounted for nearly 50 per cent of R&D expenditure, up from 43 per cent in 1997, and the share of GRIs was 38.5 per cent, down from 43 per cent two years earlier. The share of R&D expenditure by universities decreased by 2.8 percentage points between 1997 and 1999, down to 9.3 per cent. GRIs, the enterprise sector, and higher education institutions tend to focus on different types of research. In 1997 GRIs were responsible for 54.8 per cent of R&D expenditure on basic research, and 53.1 per cent on applied research. While Chinese enterprises accounted for over 50 per cent of R&D expenditure on experimental development, they

Figure 6.1. **Structure of China's R&D expenditure, 1995-1998 average**

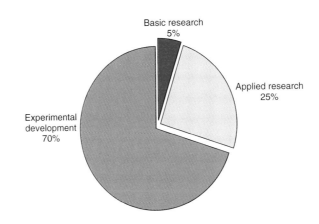

Source: National Bureau of Statistics and Ministry of Science and Technology, 1999, p. 7.

Figure 6.2. **Distribution of R&D expenditure by executing institutions, 1999**

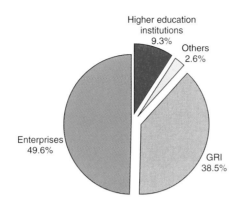

Source: Ministry of Science and Technology, 2000.

accounted for just 7.5 per cent of expenditure on basic research in 1997. Chinese higher educational institutions focus on basic research and applied research, accounting for 35.4 and 24.4 per cent of the R&D expenditures respectively in 1997.

S&T *human resource input*

Total S&T personnel[3]

As of 1999, there were 2.91 million people engaged in S&T in China, of whom scientists and engineers accounted for 54.9 per cent, and support staff accounted for 45.1 per cent. On average, there were only 0.6 R&D personnel per 1 000 of the population in 1998.

Over the past decade, there have been major shifts in the distribution of S&T personnel. Between 1991 and 1997, the share of GRIs in the total number of S&T personnel dropped from 36.5 per cent to 22 per cent, equal to an outflow of 200 000 people. Correspondingly, there was an increase of S&T personnel in the enterprise sector, which accounted for 62 per cent of the total in 1997. The proportion of scientists and engineers in total S&T personnel is 60.2 per cent in research institutions compared to 52.5 per cent in the enterprise sector. Thus, while the total number of S&T personnel has been increasing in the enterprise sector, the relatively low proportion of scientists and engineers points to possible low skills of S&T personnel in that sector.

R&D personnel[4]

China's total R&D manpower input, measured in full-time equivalents, was 8.22 million man-years in 1999. However, the proportion of scientists and engineers in the total R&D personnel input dropped from 70.3 per cent at the beginning of 1990s to 64.6 per cent in 1999. This could point to a decline of Chinese R&D skills input, even though the raw numbers increased for most of the 1990s. Compared to the high percentage of scientists and engineers in total R&D manpower input in higher education institutions, at 95.7 per cent, and in the R&D institutions at 71.2 per cent, the enterprise sector with only 49 per cent reveals its weakness in R&D.

The *higher education system*

The higher education system is of fundamental importance for the supply of R&D human resources. China's higher educational capacity increased markedly over time, especially in the 1990s. In 1995, the number of graduates increased to 805 000, and stabilised at a level of more than 800 thousand per year thereafter. China's higher education system is relatively strong in natural sciences and engineering, accounting for 62.3 per cent of the total number of registered students in Chinese higher education in 1997. As a result, although China does not have the world's largest student population in higher education, it had the third largest number of graduates in natural science and engineering (excluding medical science) in 1996, after Russia and the United States. However, the Chinese education system puts comparatively more emphasis on theory than in developing practical skills and innovative thinking, with implications for the innovative capability of Chinese scientists and engineers.

S&T outputs

Publication of scientific and technological papers in China[5]

The number of scientific papers published in China has increased 71 per cent, from 94 435 to 161 692 per year between 1991 and 1999. Industrial technology is by far the largest subject, accounting for around 44 per cent of S&T publications in China. In particular, subjects related to knowledge-intensive industries, such as chemistry, computer technology and biology, surpassed machinery and instruments and agricultural sciences on the top-six list of S&T publications in 1997. China is also relatively strong in international S&T publications fields such as chemistry; electronics, communications and automatic control, material sciences, power and electricity, and chemical engineering.

Patents

Applications for patents

Patents have an economically and statistically significant impact on firm-level productivity and market value (Bloom and Reenen, 2001). China's patent law, adopted in 1985, grants three types of patents, namely: patents for invention, patents for new utility design and patents for new appearance design. The statistics on patent applications between 1985 and 1999 are shown in Table 6.2. During the second half of the 1990s, the number of patent applications increased rapidly, at an average rate of 14.5 per cent per year, between 1994 and 1999.

It may also be noted from Table 6.2 that the number of patent applications filed by foreigners tended to grow faster than those made by Chinese applicants in the latter part of 1990s. As a result, the share of foreign applications in the total number of patent applications increased from 12 per cent in 1994 to 21 per cent in 1998. There could be different reasons for the increasing number of patent applications by foreigners in China. It may be attributable in part to the increasing degree of internationalisation of the Chinese economy and the effort by foreign firms to actively seek legal

Table 6.2. **Numbers of patent applications and of granted patents, 1985-1999**

	Applications for patents							
	1985-97	1985-93	1994	1995	1996	1997	1998	1999
Total	739 517	361 794	77 735	83 045	102 735	114 208	121 989	134 239
Granted	362 988	17 855	43 297	45 064	43 780	50 992	67 889	100 156
Portion of applications by (%)								
Chinese nationals	84.7	87.1	88.1	83.7	80.8	78.9	78.9	81.9
Foreigners	15.3	13.9	11.9	16.3	19.2	21.1	21.1	18.1
Portion granted to (%)								
Chinese nationals	91.5	90.4	93.2	92.9	92.1	91.0	90.4	92.0
Foreigners	8.5	9.6	6.8	7.1	7.9	9.0	9.6	8.0

Source: Compiled from the Ministry of Science and Technology (MOST) 1999, pp. 104-105, and MOST, 2000a, p. 26.

protection of their intellectual property rights when doing business in China. It may be related to the increase in transfers of foreign technology to China.

Application for innovation patents accounted for over 86 per cent of the total number of patent applications by foreigners in China between 1997 and 1999. This was in sharp contrast to the type of applications by the Chinese, of which innovation patents accounted for only 14.1 per cent, new utility designs 55.4 per cent, and appearance designs 30.5 per cent. Also noteworthy is that the share of applications for innovation patents by foreigners increased, while those by the Chinese fell in recent years. (MOST 1999, p. 105).

Patents granted

Between 1985 and 1997, China granted a total of 363 000 patents, less than half the number of applications (see Table 6.2). The number of approved patents increased between 1994 and 1997 by 5.6 per cent per year, less than half the rate of the increase in applications. Approximately 92 per cent of the patents were granted to Chinese applicants, and 8 per cent to foreigners.

Figures 6.3 and 6.4 show the breakdown by type of patents granted to the Chinese and to foreigners. The patents granted to Chinese applicants were predominantly in utility designs (56.6 per

Figure 6.3. **Types of patents granted to Chinese, 1997**

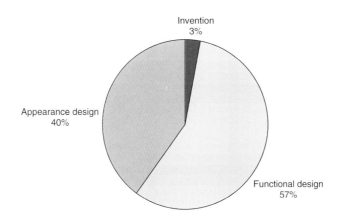

Figure 6.4. **Types of patents granted to foreigners, 1997**

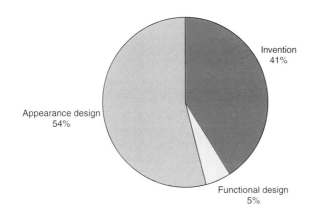

Source: Ministry of Science and Technology, 1999, p. 106.

cent) and new appearance designs (40 per cent), while patents for inventions accounted for merely 3.4 per cent. Inventions accounted for a total of 41 per cent of patents granted to foreigners, whereas utility designs accounted for only 6 per cent.

Not only was the share of inventions low for Chinese patents, but also the number of applications for invention patents dropped in the 1990s. Meanwhile, applications for invention patents by foreigners rapidly increased, and since 1995, have exceeded those by the Chinese. In 1997 and 1998, foreigners accounted for 62 per cent, and Chinese 38 per cent, of the applications for innovation patents. Since China's patent law was stipulated in 1985, the number of innovation patents granted to foreigners each year has by far exceeded those made by the Chinese, except for 1985-1988 (see Box 6.1).

Box 6.1.   **Chinese innovation patents granted to foreigners**

Between 1985 and 1997, China granted 21 252 patents for innovation to foreigners. Since the end of the 1980s, Japan has ranked number one, accounting for 31 per cent of granted patents, the US second with 28 per cent, with Germany occupying third place. Meanwhile, seven European countries, including France, the Netherlands, Switzerland, and the United Kingdom, together accounted for a combined 31 per cent. Republic of Korea's performance is interesting to note in this regard. It entered the league of top-ten countries in 1993 and since then has made a fast-growing number of applications for innovative patents in China. The number of Korean applications for innovative patents increased on average by a hefty 67.6 per cent per year between 1993 and 1997. As a result, since 1994, Republic of Korea has ranked fourth in relation to the number of applications for innovation patents in China.

Source: Most 1999, p. 108.

Foreign patents granted to Chinese innovators

Since China adopted its first patent law in 1985, there have been only limited numbers of applications for foreign patents filed by the Chinese. In 1995 and 1997, for example, the number of applications was 200 and 299 respectively, which was less than the number of applications filed by a major foreign company in China. Due to the limited number of applications, the cumulative total of foreign patents granted to Chinese nationals was very small, only some 508 patents until the late 1990s (MOST 1999, p. 113). Lack of financial resources may have acted as a constraint. It was reported that Chinese R&D institutes had to withdraw 60 patent applications from abroad in 1999 because of a lack of funds (STDRWP, 2000, p. 142).

Innovation in the Chinese enterprise sector

Generally speaking, China's enterprise sector is a weak part of the country's innovation system. As already discussed earlier, there is a systemic imbalance in the distribution of R&D resources between research institutions, the enterprise sector, and universities. Contrary to the situation in other OECD countries, where enterprises assume a leading role in national innovation systems, Chinese enterprises lag behind research institutions in carrying out innovative activities. This situation is partly reflected in the distribution of R&D resources among the three major parts of the innovation system. In terms of human resource inputs, R&D personnel in China's enterprise sector accounted for merely 42.7 per cent of the total R&D personnel in 1999, while this share is often above 50 per cent in the industrialised countries.

With regard to financial R&D input, several existing problems prevent the Chinese enterprise sector from playing a leading role in the national innovation system. First, R&D expenditure by Chinese enterprises is still extremely low. In absolute terms, the Chinese enterprise sector's R&D expenditure was estimated to be US$1.1 billion in 1995 (SCSR and PU 1999, p. 99). This level of R&D spending corresponds to only 1.1 per cent of that by US firms, 1.3 per cent of that by the Japanese, and 3.6 per cent of that by the Germans, in 1993. Measured by the ratio of R&D expenditure to the industrial value-added in 1995, the R&D intensity of Chinese industry is alarmingly low at only 0.33 per cent, even lower than the R&D expenditure-to-GDP ratio for China as a whole, at 0.6 per cent. A further problem concerns the enterprise sector's low share of R&D: nearly 50 per cent in 1999, of the total national R&D expenditures compared to over 60 per cent for industrialised countries.[6]

Moreover, Chinese enterprises are weak in technological inventions as can be seen in Figure 6.5 and Figure 6.6. These figures show the number of applications made for the Chinese invention patent, and subsequently granted by the Central Patents Office, for the period between 1996 and 1999.[7]

In terms of the number of applications for invention patents, the enterprise sector accounted for more than 50 per cent of the total, making it the largest contributor among universities, R&D

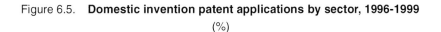

Figure 6.5. **Domestic invention patent applications by sector, 1996-1999**

(%)

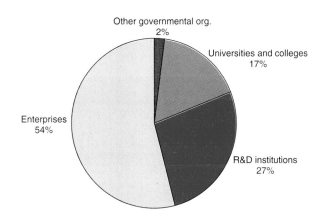

Figure 6.6. **Domestic invention patents granted by sector, 1996-1999**

(%)

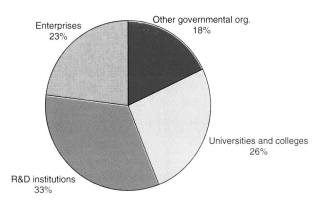

Source: China Science and Technology Statistics, 2000.

institutions, and other governmental organisations. Judging from the share of invention patents granted, however, Chinese enterprises are less important as a source of technological invention, (only 23 per cent during the period 1996-1999). Consequently, Chinese enterprises are also relatively weak in introducing innovative products, as discussed below.

R&D *in large and medium-sized enterprises*

Since the late 1980s, there have been some positive developments in the enterprise sector's R&D, although performance has been mixed. First, the number of R&D staff increased over time. Between 1987 and 1988, the total number of R&D personnel in the enterprise sector doubled, and their share in the national total of S&T personnel increased.[8] Judging from the ratio of R&D personnel to total employees in large and medium-sized enterprises (LMEs), which increased from 2.6 per cent in 1987 to 3.9 per cent in 1998, Chinese LMEs seem to have improved their R&D capacity over the past 10 years.

Box 6.2.   **Large and medium-sized enterprises in Chinese industry**

As of end 2000, there were 21 724 LMEs in China's manufacturing industries, accounting for 13.3 per cent of all state-owned industrial enterprises and non-state owned industrial enterprises with an annual sales revenue of over 5 million RMB. In 2000, LMEs were responsible for 57 per cent of industrial output value, 62 per cent of industrial value-added, and 72 per cent of the total profits of the industry enterprises in China.

Source: Complied from *China Statistics Yearbook* 2001.

Furthermore, there have been some improvements in the skills of R&D personnel employed by LMEs. The share of scientists and engineers in the total of R&D personnel improved steadily, from 28.2 per cent in 1987 to 54.4 per cent in 1998 (MOST, 1999).

With regard to financial R&D input, the amount of R&D funds has increased over the past 10 years from RMB 9.4 billion in 1987 to RMB 49.9 billion in 1997, averaging an annual increase of 8 per cent (MOST, 1999). However, this growth rate still fell below the rate of GDP growth (9.7 per cent on average), suggesting a weakening of the link between R&D support and GDP growth during this period. The main sources of R&D funding for the LMEs include government funding, enterprises' own funding, and bank loans, with enterprises' own funding accounting for an increasing share of the total R&D funds for the LMEs, as is shown in Figure 6.7.

The sources of R&D funds have changed over time. Between 1987 and 1998, the total share of enterprises' own funding increased from 45 per cent to 70 per cent, while government funding fell from 11 per cent to 7 per cent, and bank loans from 40 per cent to 18 per cent, respectively.

The number of R&D institutes affiliated with enterprises increased between the late 1980s and mid-1990s, reaching its peak in 1995, and thereafter declining. LMEs with their own R&D departments experienced similar changes. Their share in total LMEs increased from 48 per cent in 1987 to 54 per cent in 1990, and then fell to 32 per cent in 1997. Moreover, funding levels of R&D activities and equipment of R&D institutes also deteriorated in recent years. Within the enterprise sector, where 70 per cent of R&D institutes performed regular R&D tasks, half of them kept their level of R&D funding, and 56 per cent attained an acceptable level of testing and experimental conditions in 1997.

Figure 6.7. **Changing sources of R&D funding in Chinese enterprises, 1987 and 1998**

(%)

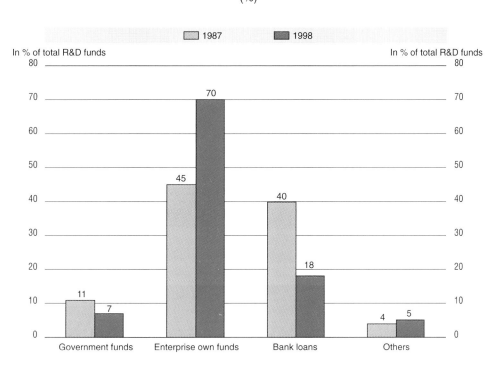

Source: Ministry of Science and Technology, 1999, p. 64-64.

R&D intensity, measured by R&D expenditure-to-revenue ratio, of Chinese LMEs remained at a low level of 0.5 per cent during the 1990s (MOST, 1999). Using a different measure of R&D intensity, *i.e.* the ratio of R&D to value added, it is estimated that the R&D intensity of a group of twelve OECD countries was 7.84 per cent, about seven times that of the Chinese manufacturing industry as a whole, at 1.15 per cent in 1995 (Sheehan, 2000).

Within ownership categories of LMEs, state-owned enterprises (SOEs) have the highest R&D intensity.[9] Sino-foreign joint-venture enterprises have an average R&D intensity; collectively owned enterprises had a below average R&D intensity; and foreign-owned enterprises had the lowest R&D intensity of all LMEs. It is also interesting to note that among different types of foreign-owned enterprises, joint ventures tend to engage in a comparatively higher level of R&D activities than the wholly foreign-owned entities, suggesting that the former may have played a relatively more positive role in enhancing the technological capability of Chinese industry.

Regarding output of R&D activities in the Chinese LME sector, new products accounted for 10.5 per cent of total output value, 10.1 per cent of total sales revenues, and 11.5 per cent of the pre-tax profits in 1996. While these figures suggest on-going improvements, a 1996 sample survey on technological innovation conducted by the government revealed problems in the technological level of product innovation. According to this survey, only 5.8 per cent of new products (under Chinese definitions) are such by international standards. New products accounted for only 3.3 per cent of export sales compared to 10.1 per cent share of new products in the total sales revenues (MOST 1999, p. 69). The survey also shows that the performance of state-owned enterprises lagged behind other types of enterprise in terms of introducing new products, share of new products in sales revenue, and percentage of new products sold to export markets.

203|

In sum, the level of innovative activities in Chinese LMEs is still low, both in terms of R&D inputs and level of technological product innovation. Although Chinese LMEs, including SOEs, are now paying more attention to innovation than they did previously, past influences still linger. Some enterprises still expect government funds for innovation, and struggle to have their innovation projects listed on the state plans in order to be entitled to state funding and other privileges. In addition, Chinese enterprise managers are faced with a major challenge in improving their knowledge and skills in innovation management.

Other types of enterprises

Township and village enterprises (TVEs)

TVEs, have emerged as an important sector in the Chinese economy, accounting for 30 per cent of China's GDP in value-added terms, 49 per cent of industrial value added and 40 per cent of total exports (see Chapters 2 on Agriculture and 4 on Industry). Despite its impressive performance in the past, the TVE sector suffers from a number of structural weaknesses. The vast majority of TVEs are small enterprises in low-tech, labour-intensive manufacturing industries, and few possess their own R&D and innovative capability. Consequently, primary manufactured goods dominate the product structure of TVEs. TVEs are faced with growing competition from other types of enterprises with relatively better technological and innovative capabilities. Lack of technological base and managerial talent, scarcity of funds for innovation, and poor information access are the main obstacles that prevent the TVE sector from upgrading its industrial and product structures.

TVEs have tried to improve their technology by hiring external consultants, co-operating with large and medium-sized enterprises, forming joint ventures with foreign companies, and engaging in joint research projects with universities and research institutions (Wu and Zou, 2001). TVEs have also become increasingly active in acquiring technology from the market. Their share in the total contract value of this market increased from 8.4 per cent to 17.4 per cent during the 1990s (NBS and MOST, 1999). However, as demand for quality goods and services increases in China, TVEs are under growing pressure to expand on technological innovation and to undertake fundamental restructuring. Given their importance in the Chinese economy, improving the innovative capability of TVEs will be crucial. So far, however, the Government has not promoted any effective policy solution.

Enterprises with foreign ownership or management control

One of the benefits of foreign direct investment is to facilitate the transfer of foreign technologies. Being a leading recipient of foreign direct investment (see Chapter 10 on foreign direct investment), China's foreign owned/invested enterprises grew from 0.2 per cent in terms of total industrial asset value and 0.3 per cent of total industrial output to 16.2 and 13.1 per cent respectively, during the decade to 1995. While foreign direct investment has undoubtedly played an important role in China's economic growth and modernisation, foreign-invested enterprises in China appear to have engaged in R&D to a limited extent. According to the 1995 industry census, the ratio of R&D expenditure to sales revenue, and the share of new products sales in the total sales revenue – two important indicators for R&D intensity – were only 0.4 per cent and 5.2 per cent respectively, among foreign-invested enterprises. These were far below the 1.1 per cent and 10.1 per cent respective indicators for the large and medium-sized Chinese enterprises as a whole (SCSR and PU 1999).

Only 1 per cent of the foreign-invested companies had R&D departments, of which nearly 40 per cent lacked the basic conditions for experimentation and testing equipment. Furthermore, when foreign companies acquired the management control of the joint-venture companies, they often closed down the R&D facilities in the Chinese partners' companies. This is especially common among joint ventures in light manufacturing industries, which attract most of the foreign direct investment. Foreign companies tend to treat their joint ventures in China primarily as a production base in their global business strategies. This could have resulted in increased technological dependence by Chinese industries on foreign technology supply.

There is, however, an increased interest by foreign companies to invest in R&D intensive industries and in forming R&D joint ventures in China (IIE, 1999, GEI, 1999). According to a study funded by the Ministry of Science and Technology in 2000, some 32 foreign companies possessed R&D facilities in China, up from two in 1994 (STDRWP, 2000). These investments tend to concentrate on a few knowledge-intensive industries, including software, telecommunications, biotechnology, and the chemical industry. The main forms of R&D investment include: R&D subsidiaries of foreign multinationals, product development departments within foreign-invested firms in China, and joint R&D facilities with Chinese research institutes and universities. Two factors seem to explain such a change: 1) foreign companies are now becoming convinced of the long-term potential of the Chinese market, and have changed their investment strategies towards longer-term investment, and 2) the cost advantage of hiring Chinese R&D personnel. In addition, the need to adapt products to the Chinese local markets have made joint R&D and product development necessary for certain industries such as, for example, the software industry. Since this type of R&D investment is limited to certain high-tech sectors, and concerns only a few major cities (IIE, 1999), its impact on the technological and innovative capability of Chinese industries as a whole is still limited.

S&T enterprises

The so-called S&T enterprises are often spin-offs of government R&D institutions, and to a lesser extent start-ups by R&D personnel. These enterprises are engaged, as a rule, in commercialisation of R&D results, technology transfers, and technological consultation and services. S&T enterprises started to emerge in the late 1970s with the transformation to a market-based economy. By the end of 1998 there were more than 70 000 such enterprises. The main ownership breakdown is as follows: 12 per cent are state-owned, 29 per cent collectively owned, 21 per cent privately owned, 6 per cent foreign owned, and 30 per cent belong to various forms of joint stock companies. They have all established strong market mechanisms in their operations. S&T enterprises had total business revenue of RMB 767 billion in 1998, with foreign exchange earned through export accounting for 4.5 per cent of the total revenue (Research Group 1999, p. 202).

S&T enterprises often enjoy advantages over other Chinese enterprises, including technological strength and freedom to adopt market principles in their management. With regard to technological strength, being either spin-offs from R&D institutions or set up by R&D personnel themselves, they enjoy strong network contacts with R&D institutions, and often have marketable research results on hand from the outset. They focus on the final stage of innovation, *i.e.* new product development. As regards management advantages, S&T enterprises enjoy a comparatively higher degree of autonomy in decision-making following experiments in reforming the S&T system in China. Today, they are an important asset in the national innovation system. Since these enterprises are not formally state owned, however, they are not always entitled to the policy incentives granted to other enterprises (IIE, 2000, p. 75).

Two types of these S&T enterprises, *i.e.* those associated with R&D institutes, and those with universities, are worth particular mention. Both types expanded their business and profit revenues in the 1990s. There were some 4 334 S&T enterprises associated with the R&D institutions in 1997, up from 3 314 units in 1992. These enterprises had a business revenue of RMB 17.5 billion, which was a 2.4-fold increase from the level in 1992. Their profit increased from RMB 639 million to RMB 1 702.3 million between 1992 and 1997, and their export value was US$202.3 million in 1997, reflecting a reduction by 17 per cent from the level in 1992. There were 2 564 S&T enterprises associated with Chinese universities, whose business revenue reached RMB 18.5 billion and with a profit of RMB 1.8 billion in 1997. These enterprises also provided internships for 519 thousand university students, and contributed to the postgraduate programmes of 617 doctoral students, and 2 111 Master's students.

Reportedly, the Chinese government plans to convert 4 000 scientific institutes into companies in an effort to increase the commercialisation of technology and knowledge (CND, 20 April 2000). Higher educational institutions with technical capabilities are encouraged to establish enterprises within universities with the aim of fostering entrepreneurial skills among students. The plan also requires large enterprises to set up their own R&D departments and encourages universities to engage in joint research with private businesses.

To facilitate further development of technology start-ups, the China Securities Regulatory Commission (CSRC) envisages opening a second-board market for high-tech enterprises that should help to raise capital in the stock market. This market should have lower entry requirements, but tougher disclosure rules as compared to the main boards (CND, 20 April 2000).

Private enterprises

China has a growing private enterprise sector. According to a survey published by the State Administration for Industry and Commerce in 2001 (CCPIT, 15 Jan. 2001), Chinese private enterprises had an average number of 55 employees by the end of 1999, of whom less than 10 per cent were technicians. While under-performing as to technical-intensive growth, private enterprises have strengthened the development of new products, technology and projects. An average of 2.3 persons in each enterprise is engaged in product development, an increase of 0.7 persons compared to levels reached in 1997. About 40 per cent of private enterprises co-operate with scientific research departments and researchers. The main forms of co-operation include hiring external technical personnel on a part-time basis, purchasing new technologies, and contracting professionals to conduct R&D for new products and processes. Some private enterprises accept technology as equity investment in their firms, but this practice is still very limited.

Transfer of foreign technology

There are various channels of transfer through which a country can obtain technology from other countries. These include, mainly, imports of industrial machinery and equipment, technology licensing, purchase of patents, the formation of joint business ventures, and joint R&D activities with foreign entities. In addition, diffusion within the country of the imported technology is important. This section discusses the main channels of transfer and the extent of China's reliance on foreign technology, as well as the diffusion of imported technology in China.

China's import of foreign technology

Since the opening of its markets in the late 1970s, the Chinese economy has become increasingly integrated with the world economy, including in the area of technology transfer. Between 1990 and 1997, China's international technology trade increased on average by 38 per cent per year, with export and import increasing by 28 and 44 per cent a year, respectively. In 1997 the total cumulative volume of technology trade reached US$86 billion, of which exports accounted for US$20.3 billion and imports for US$65.8 billion, pointing to an average annual deficit in international technology trade of more than US$10 billion.

Import and export of machinery and equipment (including core equipment), which accounted for more than 80 per cent in the total technology trade (Table 6.3) is the single most important item in China's technology trade. Nonetheless, the share of imports of complete equipment systems showed a declining trend in the 1990s. Meanwhile, the share of core equipment imports increased, reflecting a change in China's policy focus. Technology licensing ranked far below technology imports into China, accounting on average for about 9 per cent of total technology imports between 1993 and 1997. Other forms of technology transfers, such as technology services, consulting, and so on, had very limited importance.

China's reliance on foreign technology transfer

The ratio between the value of technology imports and the R&D expenditure of Chinese industry could be used to indicate China's reliance on foreign technology. For all years between 1991 and 1997, the expenditure on technology imports was well above R&D expenditure by Chinese industry, as well as for China as a whole. Statistics at the industrial level show an inverse relationship between the R&D

Table 6.3. **Structure of China's technology imports by type, 1993-1997**

% of the total

	1993	1994	1995	1996	1997	Average 1993-97
Equipment	88.0	88.3	86.3	81.5	85.9	86.0
– Complete systems	83.7	85.7	69.7	43.4	49.2	66.3
– Core equipment	4.3	2.6	16.6	38.1	36.7	19.7
Technology licenses	7.3	9.5	11.3	11.0	6.5	9.1
Technology services	1.3	1.6	1.5	3.3	0.9	1.7
Technology consulting	0.3	0.5	0.9	0.3	1.5	0.7
Others	3.1	0.1	0	3.9	5.2	2.5
Total	100	100	100	100	100	100

Source: Compiled based on the Ministry of Science and Technology (MOST), 1999, p.116.

expenditure by different Chinese industries and the cost of their technology imports, suggesting a substitution effect between technology imports and domestic R&D. Interestingly, it is the low R&D intensive Chinese industries, such as textiles, beverages, garments, and food processing, that tend to have a higher ratio of expenditure on technology imports to their R&D spending. This suggests that greater reliance on technology imports, in particular among some of the low technology Chinese industries, is also the result of low domestic R&D input.

During the 1990s, the gap between expenditure on technology imports and R&D expenditure further widened. Between 1995 and 1997 expenditure on equipment imports and other forms of technology transfer increased on average by 57 and 66 per cent per year, respectively, whereas China's R&D expenditure increased by 17 per cent per year pointing to an increasing dependence on technology imports during the 1990s.[10]

Foreign-invested units have served as an important vehicle in transferring high technology to China, primarily through imports of high-tech intermediate inputs and equipment, as discussed earlier. Foreign-invested units accounted for 60 per cent of the total imports of high-tech products in 1996, and the state-owned firms for 37 per cent, with the residual 3 per cent being shared by the rest of Chinese industries (MOST 1999, p. 125). Correspondingly, foreign-invested units accounted for nearly 59 per cent of China's high-tech exports; state-owned firms for only 39 per cent, with the rest being shared by all other categories of firms.

Although firms with foreign investments serve as a main channel of technology imports to China, in most of these cases the core technology involved is still controlled by the foreign partners of the joint venture, or by their headquarters. In China, foreign invested firms perform some parts of the manufacturing process with little technological innovation or product design. This channel of technology diffusion is thus rather limited. The lack of effort on the Chinese side to promote diffusion of imported technology, which is discussed below, has certainly further weakened the impact of foreign technology transfer on domestic technological capability.

There are four major areas of China's dependence on foreign technology. Statistics on technology imports from the late 1990s show that China's technology imports mainly concentrated on computer-integrated production technology, computer and telecommunication technology, aerospace technology, and microelectronics technology. These four areas taken together accounted for more than 90 per cent of China's technology imports in the late 1990s, and this pattern was relatively stable over the years.

This picture conceals some progress that deserves attention. Despite heavy dependence on foreign technology in some areas, China enjoys a net trade surplus in weaponry, nuclear technology, biotechnology, and opto-electrical technology.

207

The diffusion of imported technology

Problems in the diffusion of imported technology within China may have to do with SME strategy. Large and medium-sized Chinese enterprises spent RMB 32.2 billion on technology imports in 1996, but just 1.4 billion on technology absorption and diffusion (SCSR and PU 1999, p. 110). This compares badly with the ratio between expenditures on technology imports and technology diffusion in advanced industrialised countries, which is on average one third. Low absorption has reduced the opportunity for improving the technological capabilities of Chinese industry through reverse engineering. This may lead to increased dependence on foreign technology in the future. As imported technologies become outdated over time, China will need to rely on new imports. The limited efforts made in technology diffusion have also resulted in a limited "spillover effect", preventing more enterprises from benefiting from the imported technology.

Key factors affecting the impact of trade and investment liberalisation on the technological capability of Chinese industry

A number of factors will have a direct impact on China's access to international technology, and China's technology capability more generally. These factors primarily include relevant WTO regulations concerning technology transfer and other conditions related to foreign direct investment, R&D subsidies, the protection of intellectual property rights, as well as the business strategy of foreign firms regarding technology transfer to China.

Issues related to Intellectual Property Rights (IPR) protection

The level of protection of IPR affects the willingness of foreign partners to transfer technology to China, and infringement of IPR has been a major concern to foreign investors in China (QBPC, 2000). Now that China has become a WTO member, the protection of IPR will have to be brought into line with China's obligations according to the Trade Related Intellectual Property Rights (TRIPs) Agreement of the WTO (see Annex I). This obligation will entail costs and benefits. The cost for Chinese enterprises to obtain access to foreign technologies will increase, since they will not be able to copy or imitate the patented technologies and processes of foreign companies. This will also increase the cost of certain products and, therefore, reduce the market competitiveness of Chinese manufacturers in certain industries. On the other hand, this may force Chinese industries to increase their investment in R&D and industrial innovation, leading to faster growth of domestic technological capabilities.

However, for some industries, such as pharmaceuticals, the costs of R&D for developing new products and processes are excessively high. Given the existing low R&D capability of Chinese industries, it will prove very difficult for them to obtain needed technologies through their own R&D, meaning an increased reliance on foreign technology. Meanwhile, foreign technology holders are likely to reassess their decisions on technology transfers, depending on the nature of the technology and the intensity of market competition for the products concerned. It has been argued that enhancing IPR protection will entail making it more expensive and/or difficult for the Chinese industries to obtain advanced foreign technologies (STDRWP, 2000, p. 9-10). The way in which IPR-related issues are handled under the present TRIPS Agreement has been an issue of concern to many emerging market economies who are members of the WTO and who are concerned about the effects on economic development.

WTO regulations concerning R&D subsidies

The WTO Agreement on Subsidies and Countervailing Measures limits public subsidies for *basic industrial* R&D to 75 per cent, and for *pre-competitive development activities* to 50 per cent, whereas in *other types of* R&D these are limited to 62.5 per cent of project costs. This will effectively restrict the Chinese government's support to a large number of national R&D plans, including the State Key New Product Plan, and the State Key Industrial Experiment Plan, affecting the allocation of a substantial portion of government science and technology R&D funding. Some argue that given the low level of China's S&T

expenditure, it is unlikely that foreign competitors will seriously object to public support to R&D by the Chinese government (STDRWP, 2000). Irrespective of whether this will be the case, it is inevitable that China will have to adjust R&D policies and ways of financing R&D activities. This requires a reduction of the government's direct involvement (in the form of R&D plans and financing) in commercial R&D activities, while enhancing the enterprise sector's role in undertaking this type of R&D.

This can lead to several positive changes. First, it can free up financial resources needed for fundamental R&D, which is currently under-funded in China. Second, it may lead the government to shift from directly supporting commercial R&D in the enterprise sector to supporting research activities carried out jointly by enterprises, R&D institutions, and universities, which are not prohibited by the WTO regulation on subsidies. Third, it may also make it possible for the government to reallocate some of the resources freed up from direct R&D subsidy to supporting the purchase of patents, technologies, and know-how from abroad. Fourth, as the government will be restricted from directly subsidising commercial R&D, it could speed up the development of a market-based system for financing R&D, including venture capital. Fifth, it could also provide a much needed opportunity for developing other market institutions, such as the R&D-related service sector, and mechanisms, such as bidding for publicly-funded R&D contracts, for the development of a market-based national innovation system in China.

WTO *regulations concerning technology transfer and other conditions attached to foreign direct investment*

China has so far adopted a "market for technology" strategy when it comes to technological aspects of foreign direct investment. Following this principle, it normally imposes conditions, such as transfer of advanced technology, local content and trade balance requirements, for approving foreign direct investment projects. The Agreement on Trade-Related Investment Measures (TRIMs Agreement) prohibits trade-related investment measures, such as those mentioned above, that are inconsistent with the basic provisions of GATT. This will not only restrict China's ability to use conditionality as leverage for getting access to foreign technology, but also have other implications for the technological progress of Chinese industries. Once China can no longer impose transfer of technology conditions for foreign direct investment project appraisal, it increases the freedom for foreign investors to decide whether, and what types of technology that they may eventually transfer to their operations in China. It may lead to reduced interest by foreign investors in transferring more advanced technologies to China, and consequently have a negative impact on China's access to foreign technology.

These changes will also reduce China's influence on foreign companies' decisions to set up R&D facilities in China, which is treated by the Government as an effective way to improve China's own R&D capability. From the available information, it seems that the main motivations for foreign companies to set up R&D facilities in China are: first, to exploit the quality and the cost advantage of Chinese R&D human resources, and second, to serve their global business strategy by carrying out activities in countries that offer the cost advantages of the key inputs to the activities concerned. Some companies have clearly stated that their R&D in China is not undertaken in order to serve the Chinese market, but for their global business needs. In such cases, the interests of foreign companies in engaging in R&D activities in China might not be affected by the fact that the Chinese government would not be able to attach it as a condition for foreign investments in China.

The effects of abolishing conditions touching on foreign exchange balance and local contents implies that foreign companies will be able to decide freely the extent to which they need to import machinery and equipment, and intermediate inputs, for their operations in China. This can lead to reduced demand for Chinese inputs, limiting the "spillover" effect through up- and down-stream linkages between foreign-invested industries and Chinese suppliers. Supplying foreign companies in China serves as one means of technology transfer, from foreign contractors to Chinese suppliers, as well as an opportunity for learning by doing vis-à-vis processes, technical standards and designs.

The adjustments to foreign companies' strategies for technology transfer

Opinions regarding ways in which foreign companies in China will adjust their strategies for technology transfer in response to China's WTO accession were divided between the following two scenarios:

- As the Chinese market becomes more open to free trade in goods and services, foreign firms will be able to choose more freely between exporting goods to China and producing them in China. This can have a negative impact on the transfer of technology to China, if the number of foreign firms, which for various reasons prefer to export to China rather than producing there, were to increase. Foreign companies, especially those that are presently engaged only in production in China, are competing with each other in setting up subsidiaries for trading, and they see this as necessary for securing their future competitive positions in the China market.[11]

- As the Chinese market becomes more competitive, foreign companies may be forced to compete more vigorously in it, leading to increased R&D and use of more advanced technology in their operations in China. This scenario would mean a positive effect on the chances of China importing and getting access to more advanced technology from abroad. The fact that more foreign companies have started R&D activities in China, as mentioned above, could support this scenario. However, for foreign companies in China, their decisions on technology transfer would be based on the type of technology required for them to compete effectively in the Chinese market. Firms normally need to employ more advanced technology when they operate in more competitive markets. Thus, a competitive environment should help increase the possibility of technology transfer by foreign companies to China.

Key factors affecting the progress of Chinese enterprise's technological capability

The influence of the planning system remains profound. Under a planned economy, enterprises lacked the incentive to invest in R&D or to respond to market changes. This legacy continues to influence Chinese enterprises, especially the large and state-owned ones, despite the enterprise reforms of the past decade or so. This explains to a large extent the lack of R&D and innovation in state-owned enterprises. It has also had serious implications on R&D resources available to different types of Chinese enterprise. As SOEs are connected to state development plans, they are in a favourable position to receive state allocations of various funds for innovation and technological upgrading.[12] Moreover, because of their state ownership, they enjoy better access to the capital market for financing. China's limited R&D resources have therefore been channelled to SOEs, which lack the incentive to undertake R&D, while the smaller and non-state enterprises, which are more motivated to innovate, cannot get the resources they need. The legacy of the planning system is also reflected in the allocation of human resources in Chinese enterprises. Since fulfilling production targets was the most important objective for enterprises under the planning system, enterprise managers assigned the most qualified personnel, including skilled workers and engineers, to the production lines, leaving less qualified personnel to work on technological innovation, which is a relatively low priority.

Market competition is very important for promoting R&D and innovation by enterprises. In China, many market imperfections distort competition. On the one hand, administrative intervention interferes with the functioning of market mechanism; on the other, improper and illegal competitive behaviour and local protectionism hamper competition. Market institutions are still underdeveloped and effectively inadequate to regulate market behaviour in China (see Chapters 11 to 13). Consequently, technological advantage does not necessarily determine which of the enterprises will win competition, as other factors tend to play a more important role. This market environment has discouraged Chinese enterprises from undertaking R&D and other efforts to improve their product qualities and technical standing. Therefore, even though an increasing number of Chinese key enterprises have set up R&D facilities following the government's requirement, it did not reflect an initiative on the part of enterprise due to the effect of market competition.[13] For the same reason, R&D activities in Chinese enterprise are often weakly related to market demands (IIE, 1999).

Meanwhile, local protectionism is also a serious disincentive to firms' interest in investing in R&D. Under these conditions, enterprise managers tend to face a disincentive to allocate resources, including human and capital resources, and manager's time, to R&D and technology upgrading, and an incentive to put resources elsewhere, including lobbying for local protection and government intervention in market prices, bribery, and rent-seeking activities. To a large extent, local protectionism in China is related to local governments' striving to build a complete industrial structure in their localities as discussed in Chapters 4 and 5.

The Chinese market lacks an exit mechanism, which results in significant damage to competition. The lack of exit of non-viable firms results in serious over-capacity in Chinese industries, which further intensifies price competition in the product markets. As the majority of Chinese firms lack the technological and innovative capacities to compete on the basis of product and process innovation, product differentiation and quality improvements, their only recourse is price competition. As a result, excessive price competition drives down profit levels of even viable firms, consequently weakening the financial ability of these firms to invest in R&D and innovation.

Enterprise reform should aim at further transforming Chinese enterprises into market entities, which are profit-driven, innovative and very responsive to market demands. China's enterprise reform has not yet transformed SOEs into real market entities, since bankruptcy is far from a real threat to many of them, and their survival is not entirely determined by economic performance. The governance reform of Chinese enterprises is far from being fully carried out, and there is a lack of good governance for investment decisions in Chinese firms. In many SOEs, managers are still appointed by their superior administrative agencies and careers are not determined, or significantly influenced, by the performance of the enterprises that they manage. Since many of these managers' posts are of a political nature, and they are likely to be reassigned to a new post in a few years time, managers tend to be more interested in working on short-term issues with low risks. However, since investment in R&D often carries high risk and may take a long time to deliver economic returns, R&D tends to be treated as a low priority by SOE managers. The present stage of enterprise reform gives rise to distortions in the incentives to enterprise managers, who then react accordingly in their decision-making for resource allocation.

Lack of managerial competence is pervasive in Chinese enterprises, in particular in managing technology and innovation. Technological innovation and management, in particular R&D, has traditionally been a low priority and is, consequently, weak in Chinese enterprises. This legacy influences objectives set by enterprise managers, and explains the poor competence in managing R&D and technological matters in Chinese enterprises. Today, even though more and more Chinese enterprises are beginning to understand the importance of R&D and to pay attention to it, their managers often have very little knowledge about or experience of managing R&D and technological upgrading. This lack of managerial competence is not only one of the most important factors responsible for the poor performance of Chinese enterprises in innovation and technological upgrading, but it has also rendered ineffective policies for promoting enterprise innovativeness.[14] Managerial competence is thus one of the areas, even more than technical competence, where human resources are severely lacking in China.

Lack of enterprise investment in **R&D:** In the past, the planned economic regime created a shortage economy in China where enterprises could sell everything they managed to produce; therefore, they had little need to be concerned about product quality, not to mention innovation of new products. R&D was not given any priority and technological upgrading was far from being a major concern to Chinese enterprises. Today, although shortages of goods no longer characterise Chinese markets, their influence on enterprise R&D behaviour remains. There is a lack of incentive for Chinese enterprises to devote their resources to R&D since returns on investment in other activities tend to be higher and more immediate, because of the above-mentioned market imperfections.

Intellectual property rights protection is important as it provides incentives for enterprises and individuals to invest in innovation and research. Chinese enterprises are adversely affected by the poor protection of IPR in two ways. First, as many enterprises rely on copying and imitating others' production technology and product designs, they find little need to invest in their own R&D and innovation. In enterprises that do put resources into R&D, their investment interest is hampered by the fact that their R&D results cannot be effectively protected in the market. Furthermore, concerns with IPR protection have effectively reduced many inventors' interest in commercialising their R&D results. China needs to deal adequately with issues regarding the treatment of intellectual property rights for public research institutions and company researchers. The former is important for facilitating the transfer of research results from public research institutions to enterprises, and the latter is important for inducing efforts among R&D personnel in the enterprise sector as well as those in research institutions. While China has improved its legal framework for the protection of intellectual property rights since the mid-1980s, there remain serious problems in the enforcement of the laws.

Skill shortages and the labour market: China ranked the lowest with regard to the availability of qualified engineers in a comparison of 47 countries (IMD, 2000). This shows that although China has the third largest number of S&T personnel in the world, the quality of the Chinese R&D personnel is generally low and unsatisfactory. The problem appears to start from the Chinese education system, which as mentioned above, emphasises theoretical and exam-oriented learning at the expense of practical and problem-solving skills. In industries, since Chinese enterprises traditionally carried out very limited R&D and innovation, technical personnel's main duties were to ensure the functioning of equipment and production processes at the enterprises. This meant that Chinese technical personnel have had neither the opportunity to acquire sufficient knowledge of R&D and innovation from their formal education, nor experience from working in industry. This is further worsened by the lack of investment in personnel training in the enterprise sector, which limits the knowledge upgrading of technical personnel.

China has experienced a major brain drain in the last two decades which has affected Chinese industry's innovative and technology capability. First, this is because a large number (approximately 400 000 to 500 000) of educated Chinese went to study abroad, and the majority have not yet returned to China.[15] Second, there has been a serious human resource flow from the domestic sector to foreign firms in China. Today, the severe lack of human capital, including both technological and managerial personnel, is often recognised as one of the more serious constraints to upgrading enterprises' technological capability in China (STDRWP, 2000, p. 129).

However, things have started to look different in recent years. Increasingly, overseas scholars are becoming interested in opportunities on their return to China, and the number of returning scholars seems to be slowly increasing. In the domestic labour market, there are reportedly cases of Chinese personnel leaving jobs in foreign companies to start their own businesses and/or to take up senior positions in domestic companies, carrying with them the knowledge and know-how they gained through working for foreign employers. Although it will take a long time before massive overseas Chinese talent returns to China, and the flow of human capital from domestic to foreign firms will probably continue for some time before it reverses the current direction of movement, it is still important to improve conditions for more overseas Chinese talent to return from abroad, and to find ways to encourage the exchange of knowledge between domestic and foreign firms, in order to speed up knowledge diffusion. More generally, a functioning labour market is a prerequisite for knowledge-diffusion (Eliasson, 2000) between universities and industries on the one hand, and between firms, on the other hand. This is because the diffusion of tacit knowledge and know-how can be only carried out through the movement of people with such knowledge.

Financial instruments for R&D and innovation are poorly developed in China. The planning system and the corporate finance system are not designed to meet the needs of R&D funding and innovation. The State Development Planning Commission system is charged with the responsibility of allocating funds for the construction of new industrial facilities, while the State Economic and Trade Commission is responsible for channelling resources for renovation and technological upgrading (mainly through machinery and equipment upgrading) of existing SOEs. However, these channels provide scant resources for R&D and innovation in enterprises. China's corporate finance system stipulates that a certain percentage of revenues should be allocated to financing innovation (through an innovation fund). This resource is, however, both inadequate and often misused by enterprise managers. The banking system is not well suited to financing risky ventures such as innovation and R&D activities because it is difficult to judge the level of risk of, and the returns from, such activities (see Chapter 7 on Banking).

Moreover, Chinese banks' concerns regarding the risk of lending to R&D are well founded, judging from the poor record of financial disciplines of many Chinese enterprises. Thus, it is no surprise that the share of bank loans in total financing for technological upgrading of Chinese enterprises fell from 32 per cent in 1995 to 18 per cent in 1998 (IIE, 2000). The inability of banks to efficiently channel China's huge savings (US$800 billion, IHT, 4 June 2001) to enterprises represents an important resource loss. Stock markets in China have served as a channel for listed enterprises to raise capital, but they have functioned poorly in monitoring and controlling enterprise investment decisions (see Chapter 15 on Capital Markets). Due to the lack of incentives to invest in R&D, and because of the lack of competence in managing innovation in Chinese enterprises, capital raised through stock markets is not efficiently used in R&D and innovation. Venture capital, as a source of R&D funding, is not widely available to many Chinese enterprises, as it is still new and underdeveloped, and often run by the government in China.[16] While venture capital can provide effective solutions to financing certain types of innovative activities, it functions as a *supplement* to, but not a *substitute* for, resources for ordinary R&D, which should be financed from the revenue of the enterprises. However, as argued above, few enterprises would have an incentive to treat R&D as a priority.

Technology diffusion is fundamentally important for technological upgrading. As already noted above, Chinese industries devoted very limited efforts and resources to technological diffusion in the past. This is related to some institutional factors. The departmentalisation of the government agencies in charge of different industries proved to be an obstacle to technological diffusion across different industries. Between regions in China, there has been a tendency to compete with each other for technology imports, which has led to repeated imports of the same technologies from abroad to different industries as well as in different Chinese regions. The import of 130 colour TV production lines is one example. Furthermore, enterprises all wish to benefit from importing original technology and equipment from abroad, but are not interested in being involved in the technology diffusion process. This is because the diffused technologies tend to be technically inferior (at least in the initial stage) to the original ones, and hence cause technical troubles and failures for the enterprises.

However, since many enterprises with the privilege of accessing imported technologies are still state-owned and receive government funding for technology upgrading, they have very little incentive to economise on investment costs. So all enterprises prefer the import of technology, which is more expensive, to technology-diffusion, and this leads to different government agencies, and regions as well as enterprises, competing for government funds for importing technology. Furthermore, enterprises have vested interests in importing technology from abroad, because of opportunities such as visiting foreign countries and personnel training abroad, which are often attached as conditions when purchasing foreign technologies.

Technological-diffusion is also hampered by the lack of a financing channel within China's current investment system – as with financing innovation and R&D, there are few channels by which enterprises can obtain funds for technology diffusion in China. More broadly, technology markets and channels for commercialisation of scientific results are still underdeveloped in China. Statistics show that every year China produces some 25 000 ministry-level scientific research results, although only 10-15 per cent of them are commercially developed, (CND, 24 Sept 2001). The absence of technology transfer channels to diffuse research results from public-funded research institutes to industry is a major bottleneck of the Chinese innovation system. This needs to be urgently addressed.

Research collaboration with universities and R&D institutions is an important way of enhancing industrial R&D capability. Promoting research collaboration has become an important policy in OECD countries and China ranks very low in world comparisons in these terms (IMD, 2000). Again, there is an institutional barrier to research collaboration in China. As industries, universities, and R&D institutions belong to different administrative systems in China, it prevents the free flow of resources and knowledge between them. Furthermore, research collaboration is hampered by enterprises' low valuation of R&D results. As enterprises have difficulties in assessing the commercial value of R&D results, R&D institutions tend to be underpaid by the enterprises for the transfer of their R&D results. Chinese R&D institutions are subsequently more interested in direct commercialisation of R&D results than in research collaboration with enterprises. Insufficient technical assimilation capability on the part of enterprises, and the lack of transfer channels are considered as other factors seriously hampering technology transfer from the research institutions to enterprises in China (APEC-STPRC, 2001, p. 79).

Technological co-operation between companies in China is also weak, ranking 35 out of 47 countries in the world (IMD, 2000). One of the reasons cited is the weakness of the Chinese legal system in enforcing contract laws. The departmentalisation between both government agencies in charge of different industries and across Chinese regions has been another key obstacle for different firms to co-operate in R&D.

FDI *policies* can affect the transfer of technology. China has adopted certain policies that restrict foreign direct investment from entering into certain industries, that encourage foreign direct investment in priority industries, and that impose limits on the share of foreign ownership in joint ventures and the choice of investment forms in some other cases (see Chapter 10). These types of policies have had restrictive effects on the transfer of foreign technology to China. While protecting certain industries from foreign direct investment eliminates the possibility for technology transfer to these industries, policies aimed at leading foreign direct investment to certain priority industries, and away from the discouraged sectors can have the effect of reducing the total amount of technology transfer, as foregoing technology transfers to discouraged industries represents a lost opportunity. Moreover, these policies tend to contribute to enlarging the technological disparity between different industries, leading to further structural imbalances.

Restrictions imposed on the share and forms of foreign ownership have a direct impact on foreign investors' interest in transferring technologies to their operations in China. It is well understood that unless foreign investors can have majority control of enterprises, their interest in transferring core technology is limited. China is in the process of reviewing its foreign direct investment policies and the above-mentioned restrictive policies on foreign direct investment are being revised. As trade and investment liberalisation continues, it will enlarge the potential for technology transfer to China. To the extent that these policies will be kept for the purpose of achieving other policy objectives – often related to protecting national industries – the damaging effect of these policies on technology transfer should be carefully weighed against the gain. One should also prevent a tendency to use non-tariff barriers, such as technical standards, while policies restricting foreign direct investment are being phased out.

Foreign direct investment is not only a carrier of codified knowledge such as technology, but also important for the transfer of tacit knowledge. China has benefited from the presence of foreign knowledge-workers in foreign companies in China. However, some policies tend to limit the number of foreign employees in foreign companies in order to push for a speedy localisation of foreign firms in China and to create more (well-paid) jobs in foreign companies for the Chinese labour force. It reflects a shortsighted view that undervalues the importance of foreign knowledge and know-how. Such a policy is not conducive to the transfer of foreign knowledge and know-how to China.

China in recent years has seen increasing foreign direct investment in the area of R&D, as mentioned above. However, policies for encouraging R&D are not yet well developed, and foreign direct investment in R&D is affected by some concerns. While the protection of intellectual property rights for R&D is still low, the unfavourable infrastructure, the legal framework and labour market conditions in China constitute some of the main concerns for foreign investors (GEI, 1999) and China is concerned about the risk from the brain drain. There is also a misperception that R&D activities generate fewer jobs and smaller tax revenues for China, as compared with manufacturing activities by foreign companies. This view tends to influence policies favouring foreign direct investment in manufacturing above other types of activities. The evaluation of the R&D contribution to the Chinese economy should look far beyond direct economic revenues, taking into account the benefits of improving China's long-term R&D and innovative capabilities, on training R&D personnel, and on transferring R&D management expertise and know-how. To reverse the effect of the brain drain, the government should improve the economic environment in general and the functioning of the labour market in particular in order to facilitate the exchange of human resources between the domestic economy and foreign-invested firms. With increased international labour mobility in a global economy, it is increasingly important that all countries tap into the global knowledge network on a give-and-take basis.

Some international experiences: improving technological capability and technological diffusion

Improving corporate innovative capability: OECD experiences[17]

Lack of corporate innovative capabilities – the issues

There is increasing evidence that innovative capabilities of most firms, especially small and medium-sized enterprises (SMEs), are limited even in OECD economies. Due mainly to market and systemic failures, firms often find themselves suffering from the following weaknesses:

- The "low capability trap". Until a firm has learnt something, it cannot properly specify what it needs to learn. Moreover, many firms lack competencies to manage innovation, especially when it involves developing and mastering external linkages in the innovation process.

- Organisational inadequacies, inadequate availability of information, and/or deficiencies in managerial skills. These prevent sound self-diagnosis of needs and reduce the perceived value of organisational changes and external (e.g. consulting) market services.

For innovative firms, their levels of innovative capability vary. One can broadly distinguish four levels of innovativeness, irrespective of firm size and activity.

- Level 0 – the *static firms* innovate seldom or not at all, but may have a stable market position under existing conditions.

- Level 1 – the *innovating firms*, which have the capability to manage a continuous innovation process in a stable competitive and technological environment.

- Level 2 – the *learning firms* that have, in addition, the capability to adapt to a changing environment.

- Level 3 – the *self-regenerating* firms are able to use core technological capability to reposition themselves on different markets and/or create new ones.

The new technology-based firms (NTBFs) play an increasingly important role in innovation systems. However, all NTBF start-ups do not succeed, and many fail due either to defective business plans, or absence of a corporate governance structure able to adjust to changing conditions. This illustrates well the existence of "competence thresholds' and the implications for government policy. The OECD experience shows that a successful NTBF requires superior governance and management capabilities, including comprehensive understanding of product technology, manufacturing technology, market research, financial planning, accounting, and legal aspects, contracts and networking, as well as a supportive environment of relevant business services (OECD 1998).

Implications for Government Policy

A key policy challenge is to help non-innovative firms acquire basic capabilities and more competent firms to increase their level of innovativeness. Governments can indirectly help spur management and innovation capabilities by supplementing or catalysing private initiatives in three major ways:

- Development of infrastructure to correct information imperfection in the business service market.

- Public provision of innovation management tools or benchmarking services.

- Promotion of the development, diffusion and adoption of management know-how.

It has become increasingly clear that firms need to collaborate in R&D in order for them to be innovative. This need stems from, on the one hand, increasing specialisation of firms, and, on the other, growing competition and globalisation and the rapid advancement of technologies, which require that new technologies and innovative concepts have a wide variety of sources, most of them outside the direct control of firms. Thus, creating appropriate conditions for such collaboration poses a new policy challenge to all governments.

Evaluation of existing policies to promote innovation management capabilities demonstrates that there is much scope for improving policy responses in this area. This requires, however, better understanding of the main capacities that underlie firms' innovative behaviours. On the basis of a review of more recent thinking on innovation research and best business practices, six major capacities are identified as underlying innovation in all types of firms and sectors. These are the capacities in 1) managing the competence base, 2) vision and strategy, 3) creativity and idea management, 4) intelligence, 5) organisation and process, 6) culture and climate.[18]

The OECD experience also suggests that government policies should avoid the following common policy bias and mistakes:

- Project-oriented, which neglects to relate firms attributes to more generic abilities to manage technological changes.

- Focused on industry, which neglects the increasing importance of innovation in the services sector.

- Dominated by high-tech sectors, which neglects the innovation in low-tech sectors.

- Modelled on the experiences of large firms, which fails to take into account the specific needs of SMEs.

Technology diffusion: OECD experiences[19]

Technology diffusion, which is essentially the widespread adoption of technology by users other than the original innovator, is widely recognised as necessary for the ability of OECD economies to generate higher economic growth and incomes. Several studies on the effect of technology on productivity indicate that the productivity of firms and whole industries often depends more on technology developed elsewhere than on their own innovation. Recent firm-level studies point to a positive association between some form of innovative activity (formal R&D, technology adoption, and so on) and the ability of firms to grow and create jobs.

OECD governments maintain a variety of technology-diffusion initiatives to aid firms in identifying, absorbing, and implementing technology and know-how. Programmes to diffuse technology are intended largely to address *market and systemic failures*. Firms may lack information about technologies or face disadvantages due to scale requirements or high learning costs, resulting in under-investment in new technology. At the system level, failures may arise from weaknesses in linkages and interactions among different actors in the national innovation system. In addition, part of the rationale for public support to technology diffusion lies in maximising returns from public investment in R&D and technology development programmes. Other economic goals such as competitiveness, regional economic development, and job creation are also reasons for government initiatives to disseminate technology.

Government initiatives and programmes to promote technology diffusion have evolved considerably over recent decades from the transfer of public research results to enhancing the technological absorptive capacity of firms. During the 1980s, against a background of slow productivity growth, many OECD countries established national networks of manufacturing extension centres to promote the adoption of specific technologies (*e.g.* machine tools, robotics). However, it was realised that many of the obstacles to successful adoption and use of technology stemmed from deficiencies in labour, management, and organisational change at the firm level. In the early 1990s, OECD countries began launching business advisory/consultancy services and networking initiatives, using information technologies, to help firms adopt new management practices, implement organisational changes and enhance workforce skills in the interest of improving overall innovative capacity and use of technology.

Given the broad range of objectives, government programmes and initiatives may be categorised in a variety of ways. The OECD has proposed a three-tiered typology wherein the general goals of technology diffusion programmes can be identified. On the *first level* are programmes to improve the adoption and adaptation of specific technologies. On the *second level* are programmes to improve the general technology receptor capacity of firms, such as technical assistance projects and information networks. On the *third level* are programmes to build the overall innovation capacity of firms, including the use of tools such as sector roadmaps, diagnostics and benchmarking. Table 6.4 provides a summary of the different types of the programmes.

Table 6.4. **Typology of technology diffusion programmes**

Goal	Programme types	Objectives
Level 1: Improve the adoption and adaptation of specific technologies	Technology-specific	To diffuse a specific technology to a wide number of firms and sectors
	Institution-specific	To promote technology transfer from specific institutions
	Sector-specific	To diffuse technology to a particular industrial sector
	Demonstration	To demonstrate the practical implementation of technologies
Level 2: Improve the general technology receptor capacity of firms	Technical assistance	To assist firms in diagnosing technology needs and in problem solving
	Information networks	Access to information on technology sources, etc.
	Assistance for small-scale R&D projects	Build capacity for autonomous technology development
Level 3: Build the innovation capacity of firms	Sector-wide technology road maps	Systematic planning for future strategic technology investments
	Diagnostic tools	Assist firms to develop innovation-oriented management (includes organisational change)
	Benchmarking	Transmit best practice from elsewhere
	University-industry collaboration	Upgrade the knowledge base of the firm

Source: OECD, 1997.

Furthermore, based on operational focus, technology diffusion programmes in OECD countries may fall into the following four basic types:

- *Supply-driven initiatives* are essentially programmes to transfer and commercialise technology from government research programmes to private enterprise. They are targeted to lower-technology industries as well as high-technology sectors.

- *Demand-driven programmes* generally start with the firm and aim to identify technology gaps, needs and opportunities facing enterprises, especially smaller businesses; increasingly they attempt to diagnose and enhance the technological absorptive capacity of firms.

- *Network-building initiatives*, many of which operate at the regional level, aim to develop and enhance the role of bridging institutions and inter-firm partnerships in promoting information flows and the diffusion of technology.

- *Infrastructure building programmes* are those that work from a system-wide perspective to upgrade the technology diffusion infrastructure at the national level.

Supply-driven initiatives seek to transfer and commercialise technology, including basic or mission-oriented research and technology programmes out to the private sector. In most cases, the research or technology is sponsored by public funds through a university, technology centre or government agency. An example is the Canadian Space Agency's Space Station Program (CSPP) that supports the transfer of dual-use technology to Canadian firms, including small and medium-sized enterprises. In contrast to traditional transfer initiatives, the CSPP has made the commercialisation of dual-use space technologies (*e.g.* robotics) an explicit objective of the two main R&D programmes within its portfolio. This involves competitive bidding for research and commercialisation contracts by private firms as a way to leverage resources and obtain industry leadership. Technology management, commercialisation rights, and intellectual property protection are integral parts of the contractual and implementation processes. Contracting firms may obtain licences without royalties but are required to develop and adhere to a commercialisation plan. The CSPP, through its industry contracts, has helped firms develop and commercialise the application of dual-use technologies in areas as diverse as agriculture, automation, and toxic waste management. Such supply-side initiatives are not necessarily targeted to high-technology sectors. In Spain, there have been successful efforts to transfer technology from public research to private enterprises in traditional areas such as in the cutting of leather for shoe-making.

Demand-driven programmes represent a second general approach to encouraging technology diffusion. Here, the primary aim is to identify and assess technological gaps, needs, and opportunities facing enterprises, especially SMEs. In contrast to supply-driven approaches that tend to focus on commercialising publicly-developed advanced technologies, the technologies involved in demand-side initiatives are frequently pragmatic, well tested, and available through off-the-shelf private sources and consultants, as well as through public technology assistance centres. Public demand-side approaches generally seek to complement existing (and probably more important) private technology diffusion mechanisms. While demand-driven programmes vary in specific characteristics, they all share core strategies of building trust with business customers, identifying customer needs and then applying appropriate expertise and resources.

In many instances, demand-driven programmes assist firms with associated managerial, marketing, training, and financial problems in an attempt to ensure a comprehensive developmental strategy. A case in point is the Manufacturing Extension Partnership (MEP) in the United States, a national network of state-level manufacturing extension centres. This initiative aims to help smaller American manufacturers (many of whom lag behind in their use of modern technologies and methods) to not only implement appropriate technologies but also to improve their business practices. At the level of the extension centre, field agents assess the company's needs in terms of business systems and management, product market development, quality certification, and use of technology. In addition to providing access to technology and related services, the MEP disseminates information on best practices in manufacturing, management and workforce approaches related to technology implementation. As a way of building on existing local, state, and national resources, the MEP provides links and referrals to other public institutions such as federal laboratories (for technology), the Environmental Protection Agency (for environmental technology) or the Small Business Administration (for financing and business planning).

Other examples of demand-driven initiatives include Norway's BUNT (Business Development Using New Technologies) programme and Austria's MINT (Managing the Integration of New Technologies) programme. Norway's BUNT programme focuses on developing the problem-solving capacities of firms and their organisational ability to incorporate technology. Firms receive training in conducting strategic analyses of technology needs, including evaluations of technological possibilities. BUNT also provides funding for consultants to help firms in general evaluation, followed by the development of a strategic plan for technology use and company development. Austria's MINT programme – established by the European Union and carried out by the Austrian Institute for the Promotion of the Economy (WIFI) – provides comprehensive management consultancy services for some 200 SMEs, mainly in the wood, metal, and plastic processing sectors. Through a network of trained consultants, the programme has helped firms make innovation an integral part of their business plans. Services include overall company analysis, evaluation of strengths and weaknesses, and identification of organisational changes as a complement to introducing technology.

The network-based approach emphasises the development of bridging institutions and partnerships to promote information flows and new technology diffusion and commercialisation. An example of a network-based programme is the case of Germany, which aimed to capitalise on the existence of many technological institutions and a variety of private and public users of technology in a geographical region. It is an approach with several aspects, including the enhancement of interaction in "bio-regions" of technology developers and users, the development of projects to involve regional actors in the development and dissemination of specific new technologies, and incentives to foster co-ordination and networking within regional technology infrastructures. Similarly, in the Netherlands, a regional system of Innovation Centres (ICNs) acts as intermediaries between firms and private and public sources of knowledge. Despite the expansion of private information sources, particularly through information technologies, firms still lack awareness of available technology or of their own innovative capacity or they may need information on financing or industry trends. ICN counsellors advise firms and refer them to public research institutions, commercial suppliers of knowledge, and private consultants. In this way, the Innovation Centres develop both vertical and horizontal network links, which strengthen diffusion at the regional level.

A fourth type of technology diffusion strategy is one of system-wide **upgrading of technology-diffusion infrastructure**. In this context, policy attention is targeted not to specific lagging firms, sectors, or regions or to particular new technology opportunities, but to the national technology infrastructure as a whole. Efforts to promote system-wide upgrading are often conscious of technology diffusion infrastructures and models in other countries, which are then adapted or at least used to motivate new policies in the host country as part of broader developmental strategies. This was evident in the review of technology diffusion programmes in the Republic of Korea, which described (and provided a preliminary assessment of) a series of Korean initiatives to strengthen technological institutions and the spread of new technologies to industry. In light of rising labour costs, the Republic of Korea maintains a mix of supply-driven programmes to help firms adopt advanced manufacturing technologies, particularly their automated processes. Some initiatives such as the Regional Research Centres (RRCs) aim to improve linkages between universities and regional industries, particularly with SMEs, while other programmes promote the diffusion of software and information technologies. There is also current interest in Japan to improve and change fundamental elements of its technology-diffusion system, including promoting greater industry interaction by universities and other public researchers, increasing the mobility and flexibility of researchers and reducing regulatory and intra-governmental restrictions.

Different OECD countries pursue a varying mix of technology-diffusion programmes that reflect not only their national systems of innovation but also specific regional and broader economic dynamics.

Rationale for technology-diffusion programmes

One of the most fundamental questions is why are or should governments be involved in technology diffusion? The classical economic justification has been to rationalise government intervention on the basis of market failures that may arise when firms lack information about new or established technologies or are disadvantaged because of the size or scale of production requirements, and due to weak organisational, human resource development, and/or managerial capacities. The other important rationale for policy intervention concerns "systemic" failures, arising from weaknesses in linkages and interactions among different actors in national innovation systems. Public research institutes, for example, may lack the links and incentives to co-operate with smaller firms in the commercialisation and licensing of technology. Such market and systemic failures can limit the development of the absorptive capacity of firms, or their general ability to identify, access and use technology.

A further rationale for supporting technology diffusion stems from the need to maximise economic, as well as social, returns from public investments in R&D. Efforts to demonstrate broader returns from public R&D spending also reflect programme needs to maintain ongoing support in the budgetary process. Industrial and technological competitiveness, regional economic development, job creation, and business stabilisation are also reasons for intervention, particularly in the case of demand-driven types of technology-diffusion programmes.

Problems in technology diffusion

The fact that technology-diffusion programmes not only embody multiple rationalisations and objectives but also include varied *stakeholders* and partners gave rise to discussion about the complications involved in implementation. Technology diffusion generally has to be delivered locally (since this is where the firms are) and programmes, if they are to be comprehensive, often involve alliances and cross-sectoral networks as well as institutional investments and business incentives. Conflicts can arise between local and national levels of government over management practices and programme goals (with competitiveness stressed at the national level, while jobs are important locally).

It can be arduous to get firms to collaborate with one another, especially in developing and diffusing product-related technologies. Effective technology diffusion takes time and money and can be difficult to measure and evaluate; technology diffusion also requires flexibility in operation to meet diverse and emerging company needs. Available experiences from using market-driven non-governmental organisations to provide services suggest that it is not possible for these service providers to be entirely funded through customer revenues, meaning that a base of public investment is necessary.

Further problems concern what should be the *targets* of technology diffusion initiatives. Firms that already had advanced capabilities were often targeted in supply-driven technology commercialisation initiatives and in regional projects to develop and diffuse specific high-end new technologies, while most of the other programmes tended to focus on mature small and medium-sized firms. In addition, diffusion strategies developed in, or targeted to, particular regions might preclude involvement by firms and institutions from other regions within the same country.

Best practices in technology diffusion

There are a number of trends in OECD technology diffusion programmes, which also reflect on emerging agreement on **best practices at a general level:**

- **Ensuring quality control** – Technology-diffusion programmes should take steps to ensure the quality of service providers, the appropriate training of consultants and the effectiveness of local delivery systems.

- **Focusing on customers** – Technology-diffusion programmes should start with a focus on customers and users and aim at meeting the changing technical needs of companies.

- **Upgrading the innovative capacity of firms** – Technology-diffusion programmes should promote a general awareness of the value of innovation among management and stimulate demand for technical and organisational change within firms.

- **Integrating with national innovation systems** – Technology-diffusion programmes should build on existing inter-relationships with national innovation systems and have greater coherence between programme design (*e.g.* targets, objectives, modes of support) and service delivery.

- **Building in evaluation and assessment** – Technology-diffusion programmes should have mechanisms for assessment, to guide and improve their operation and management on a continuing basis.

In addition to the above, the following OECD experiences may be of particular relevance to China:

- **Geographical proximity.** The importance of a local presence and a local delivery system to ensure close and easy interaction with firms.

- **Building on existing resources**, rather than duplicating new ones, and integrating different types of institutions and service providers to comprehensively address technology-diffusion needs and opportunities. The development of integrated partnerships makes it easier to provide complementary services essential to support technology diffusion, such as training, marketing or finance.

- **Promoting organisational development and strategic change** as well as technology deployment. The experiences of many OECD countries indicate that efforts to diffuse specific technologies have usually been accompanied by organisational improvements and strategic changes in firms. This is evident at the macro level, for instance in Japan, where organisational barriers in both the private and public sectors are seen as substantial obstacles to more effective technology diffusion. In some OECD countries, technological-diffusion programmes explicitly introduced consultants to promote organisational change and strategic rethinking within firms.

- **Developing trust and close links between different players** Effective technology diffusion requires trust and long-term relationships to be formed between companies and technology-diffusion service providers. To improve polices and programmes, it is important that technology centres maintain close relations between industry groups and associations, so that feedback on current programmes and information on technological demands can be obtained.

The experience of some Asian countries in improving their technological capability is also worth considering (see Box 6.3).

Policy recommendations

The policy recommendations below are made primarily from the point of view that these policies affect R&D and innovation of *firms*. These policy recommendations are aimed at achieving five mid-term objectives: 1) enhancing the framework conditions for a competitive economic and business environment, 2) providing conditions for and assisting the capacity building of firms' technological capability, 3) improving technology diffusion, and 4) enhancing the role of foreign direct investment in improving the technological capability of China's industries. Finally, 5) a comprehensive policy approach is called for because of the comprehensive nature of the technology challenge to be addressed. The first set of policies may include those for improving framework conditions, competition, IPR, while the second set may consist of policies for improving technology and the absorptive capability of firms as well as human resources, training, and financial and venture capital markets as important supporting conditions. The third, fourth, and fifth categories of policies are explicitly stated below.

221

Box 6.3. Improving technological capability: Experiences of Chinese Taipei and the Republic of Korea

Both Chinese Taipei and the Republic of Korea have developed, albeit through different strategies, their high-technology industries, such as electronics and semiconductors, through successfully adopting foreign technologies from more advanced countries. Over time, they have also managed to rapidly upgrade their technological capabilities, while utilising and absorbing foreign technologies.

The experience of Chinese Taipei and the Republic of Korea indicate that for firms to benefit from partnership with foreign companies they have to reach a threshold level of technological absorptive capability to ensure the efficiency of technology transfer and learning.* Furthermore, acquiring technological capability is a long-term process, and it requires consistent efforts in building long-term business partnership relations with foreign technology providers, often the leading companies in certain areas of technology. Lasting, long-term relationships are not only important for continuous and progressive learning, but also for developing trust, which is a crucial factor affecting the transfer of technology. Case studies of electronic and semiconductor industries in the Republic of Korea and Chinese Taipei suggest that it is important for firms in partnership with foreign companies to engage through time in progressively more advanced forms of technology transfer, from, *e.g.* subcontracting, to technology licensing to OEM (Original Equipment Manufacturing), to ODM (Original Design Manufacturing), to joint product R&D and strategic alliance. It seems of particular importance for leading domestic companies to acquire advanced core technologies in the long run.

The Korean and Chinese Taipei experiences suggest that governments can play an important and positive role in assisting domestic industry to acquire technological capability. However, the governments of Chinese Taipei and the Republic of Korea have adopted different approaches in supporting their industries. The Korean government's approach may be manifested by more direct support and involvement in the development of targeted industries, such as electronics and semiconductors, but meanwhile, it had a clear objective for building the R&D capabilities of Korean industries. The approach taken by the Chinese Taipei government may be characterised as relatively indirect measures, such as the programme for technology transfer from public research institutes to industries, and public purchasing, while leaving the industries to manage the development of their R&D capability. In this regard, the success of Chinese Taipei's public research institutes, most noticeably the Industrial Technology Research Institute (ITRI), in transferring technology to industries is worthy of note.

The results of these two approaches have also been different. In terms of long-term effects on technological capability, the Korean government's conscious objective of building domestic industry's technological capability and its more direct interventionist approach appeared to have helped the major Korean companies to better develop their technological capabilities, which are today considered to be above those of their Chinese Taipei counterparts (APEC-STPRC, 2001). That Korea's industrial structure is dominated by big *chaebols*, whereas that of Chinese Taipei is dominated by small and medium-sized enterprises (SMEs), which generally lack the financial resources for R&D as compared to large firms, can also partly explain why the Republic of Korea has outperformed Chinese Taipei in obtaining technological capability. However, there are some side effects from the Korean approach, which should also be borne in mind. The lack of technological co-operation in the Republic of Korea both between industries and universities and, more seriously, among companies, appears to be related to the relatively strong position of individual Korean firms, and hence the lack of interest in co-operation. In contrast, Chinese Taipei scored significantly higher than the Republic of Korea in technological co-operation of both kinds (IMD, 2000), which appears to be the result of firms seeking co-operation to upgrade their technological capabilities. Other problems stemming from direct government support include, notably, corporate governance in Korean firms, and the structural weaknesses due to the dominance of the *chaebols* in the Korean industry structure (OECD, 1999*a*), as well as the difficulty in withdrawing government support later on, and in solving these problems more generally in the Republic of Korea.

---

* This is also confirmed by the experience of other countries, *e.g.* Czech manufacturing industries (see Kinoshita, 2000).

Securing framework conditions that are conducive to innovation

Science, technology and innovation policies need to operate in a stable macroeconomic environment and complement broad reforms in other fields. These include competition policies to increase innovation-driving competition but also facilitate collaborative research; education and training policies to develop human capital; regulatory reform policies to lessen the administrative burden and institutional rigidities; financial and fiscal policies to ease the flow of capital, especially to small firms; labour market policies to increase the mobility of personnel and strengthen tacit knowledge flow; communication policies to maximise the dissemination of information and enable the growth of electronic networks; foreign investment and trade policies to strengthen technology transfer; and regional policies to improve complementarity between different levels of government initiative (OECD, 1999b).

All factors that discourage investment in general, such as macroeconomic instability, high inflation and interest rates, will have a negative influence on innovation and technology diffusion. Specifically, the following factors reduce the attractiveness and feasibility of innovation: lack of financing channels, a weak financial sector unable to assess innovative projects, weak protection of intellectual property rights with the effect of reducing the rewards to creativity, and uncertainties in economic environment and government regulations, which increase risks and costs of commercialisation of innovative products and processes (OECD, 1999b). Some of the policy areas mentioned here are further discussed in the rest of this section, to reflect their importance for improving the innovation capability of Chinese industries.

Improving market competition

Through various economic reforms carried out since 1978, the Chinese market has become increasingly competitive. However, there are still market distortions and government interventions that create disincentives for firms to innovate. To improve market competition, the following reforms need to be considered (see also Chapters 11, 12 and 13 on institutional framework). First, governments at all levels should further withdraw from interfering with the functioning of the market. In this regard, reducing local protectionist interventions should be a priority. It is important for local governments to recognise that government protection will result in low productivity growth and weaken a firm's interest in innovation. Second, it is important to create market exit channels for non-viable firms to quit the market. As many firms are being protected, in one way or another, by the government, their existence is not only a waste of resources but also has a damaging effect by distorting market competition, which dampens incentives for healthier firms to innovate. The exit of non-viable firms thus would not only free up resources for other economic activities, but would also reduce market distortion, and force existing firms to innovate. Third, there is also a need for the government to examine policies that affect business start-ups. Market entry of new firms is not only necessary for keeping the pressure of market competition, it has become an increasingly important way of commercialising new technology and innovation. Governments should therefore remove regulatory barriers to market entry by new firms, such as excessive requirements and complicated procedures for new business registration, and provide convenient information and advisory services for business start-ups in order to spur the development of new firms. Fourth, government should design new policies that can help shift the focus of competition from resource- and investment-based to innovation-based.

Improving IPR legislation and implementation

As an economy in transition from a planned to a market system, China is faced with the great challenge of developing market institutions, including legislation for the protection of intellectual property rights. Strong and stable IPRs are needed for providing a legal basis for research-industry collaboration and for the commercialisation of research results. Also, intellectual property rights protection needs to be improved in order for China's venture capital to develop. Trade and investment liberalisation requires China to revise its IPR legislation according to international standards, especially in accordance with the TRIPs. While various laws are being improved upon, it is a common view that the enforcement of existing legislation presents a more urgent problem than the legislation itself. The central government has been making some progress in improving the enforcement of IPR laws, in particular in fighting against the counterfeiting of intellectual products. However, the uncertain and unreliable enforcement of IPR in China is often related to local protectionism, which makes the investigation of cases very difficult, and influences the result and enforcement of court rulings in favour of the local defendants. Thus, China still needs to continue its effort in improving the enforcement of IPR laws, especially at the local levels. Apart from enhancing IPR enforcement, China will also need to review its IPR legislation on issues such as the employer-employee relations with regard to property rights, the property rights of research results of publicly-funded research institutions, and the transfer of know-how.

Improving firms' innovative and absorptive capabilities

The majority of Chinese firms lack R&D and innovation capability due to a number of reasons, with some of the key ones being analysed in this study. Given the significance of reaching an initial level of innovation capability for firms to become innovative, it should be a policy priority for the government to help firms acquire the basic skills, knowledge, and experience in innovation. Above all, the government should put in place the required framework environment to generate pressures on firms to become innovative, and provide the infrastructure and conditions that facilitate the process for firms to do so. Apart from the framework conditions, all firms, large or small, face some common needs, which form important elements for a firm's innovation capability. These include commitments from the leader (or business owner); an integrated view of innovation strategy and business strategy; a clear idea of the firm's distinct competencies; openness to constructive ideas and contributions from all staff; and, a structured way of watching and responding to changes and opportunities in the business environment (OECD, 1999b). The previous section provides some experiences of OECD countries useful for designing government policies to help improving firms' innovation capability. When designing government policies and programmes to help firms to improve innovativeness, it is important to note that small firms differ from large firms in the skills and professional training of their managers, and in the profile of their innovation capacities. Furthermore, smaller firms tend to have more limited financial and human resources, and have less ready access to information, and shorter time horizons. This thus justifies a government policy of focusing on SMEs to help them acquire the needed elements for greater innovation capability (OECD, 1999b).

Investing in human skills and learning and improving labour mobility

Investing in skills and personnel training is necessary for updating the competence of the labour force, not least because technology today is rapidly advancing. China is faced with huge needs to retrain its workforce, as many of them lack the skill and knowledge required for working in modern industries. The government should provide incentives for firms to invest resources in personnel training, such as tax exemption on revenues used in personnel training.

Personnel training should be combined with policies for enhancing labour mobility, in order to facilitate technology and knowledge diffusion. A functioning labour market is necessary to ensure the mobility of skilled labour, which is in turn crucial for achieving higher efficiency of human resource allocation in the economy and for providing individuals with incentives to acquire knowledge and skills. A well-functioning labour market will also be necessary for people to take off-the-job training and education, as it can provide them with good opportunities to gain new employment afterwards. The retraining of the labour force should be made part of the active labour-market policy, as implemented in some OECD countries such as in Sweden, where unemployed people are paid through unemployment benefit for taking part in retraining and adult education.

Furthermore, as a foundation, education policy must emphasise multidisciplinary and lifelong learning. Education should also aim to equip the labour force not only with knowledge of modern science and technology, but also with skills such as working in teams, adapting to changes, effective interpersonal communications and networking (see Annex III).

Improving innovation financing, and venture capital markets

Financing innovation presents a host of special problems in economies plagued with weak legal and financial institutions. Indeed, the lack of financing has been the main bottleneck that contributed to the lack of innovative activities in Chinese enterprises. To improve this, the government should first consider taking measures to reduce the financial burden on firms so that resources can be made available for investing in R&D and innovation. Second, the government should assist the development of a venture capital market and the second tier stock market for start-up firms by providing the legal framework and regulations, but should withdraw from being directly involved in running these businesses. Third, experiences of other transition economies show that the lack of institutional investors, such as insurance companies and pension funds, severely limits the domestic venture capital supply. China has just opened its stock market to institutional investors, and the same needs to be done for the venture capital market. Fourth, China should improve the legal environment to attract foreign venture capital funds so that foreign venture capital and, more importantly, foreign expertise can be tapped in to speed up China's venture capital development. Fifth, the government should mitigate the deficiency of the existing investment channels in financing firms' R&D and innovation. Sixth, in the development of financial institutions, further emphasis should be placed on building expertise on accessing risks related to innovation. Seventh, small and medium-sized industries have particular problems in financing innovation in financial markets, so there is a special need for the government to correct the market failures. There is currently a lack of government programmes that focus on improving the innovative capability of SMEs.

Enhancing technology diffusion, emphasising commercialisation of R&D

Technology diffusion is particularly weak in China's innovation system. China has a relatively sound science and technology R&D capacity, which, due to the influence of the pre-reform science and technology management system, was to a large extent separated from industry. Thus, strengthening technology diffusion should be a priority in the strategy for improving the innovation capability of firms. The present reform of the scientific research system, which aims to transform the majority, if not all, of the government research institutions into self-sustaining, and profit-making economic entities, has resulted in research institutions engaging in direct commercialisation of their research results. This can lead to the weakening of China's basic and general research capability on the one hand, and low efficiency in the commercial activities that research institutions are engaged in doing, on the other, simply because research institutes lack knowledge in commercial activities. China's research capability should be strengthened, and efficiency in resource use could be improved through division of labour between R&D and technology diffusion. An alternative approach could be to strengthen technology diffusion by developing the R&D service sector that specialises in technology diffusion and the commercialisation of research results. This will help to avoid weakening China's research capability, and improve the efficiency of resource use. The same should apply to the universities, where researchers tend to engage in commercial activities at the cost of lowered input and quality in performing their teaching and research functions.

Details of OECD experience as outlined above on technology diffusion could help design policies and programmes for strengthening technology diffusion. It should also be noted that governments at different levels need to look carefully at the balance between support to the high-technology part of the manufacturing sector and support aimed at fostering innovation and technology diffusion throughout the economy. They should direct their diffusion efforts across a wider range of firms, including not only technologically-advanced ones and firms in emerging sectors, but also those with lesser capabilities and firms in traditional sectors, and not only firms in manufacturing industries, but also those in services industries (OECD, 1999*b*).

Improve conditions for foreign direct investment, especially for joint R&D, for tapping global knowledge

China has been very successful in attracting foreign direct investment in past decades, and the inflow of foreign direct investment will continue to be strong, benefiting from China's further trade and investment liberalisation. While the inflow of foreign direct investment has contributed to upgrading technological standards in Chinese industry, as discussed above, it has had a limited impact on improving the innovation capability of Chinese firms. China's government needs to improve foreign direct investment policies in order to realise better the benefits of foreign direct investment on the technological and innovative capability of Chinese firms. First, the focus of foreign direct investment policy should be shifted from emphasising the importance of foreign capital and technology (mostly embodied in machinery and equipment) to emphasising the importance of both capital and technology as well as the transfer of foreign knowledge and know-how. To achieve this, the government should pay more attention to providing favourable conditions for attracting foreign direct investment in the high value-added services sectors, including not only financial services, but also others such as business services, consulting services, and R&D. When carrying out trade and investment liberalisation, the government should not hesitate to open up the service sector to foreign direct investment, it should emphasise the importance of foreign direct investment in services in order to speed up the transfer of tacit knowledge and know-how. In all the service sectors, China lags behind advanced foreign countries, and the potential gain from opening these sectors to foreign direct investment in terms of knowledge transfer is therefore particularly huge.

Second, the OECD guidelines for multinational enterprises (OECD, 2001*b*) promotes the diffusion by multinational enterprises of the fruits of research and development activities among the countries where they operate, thereby contributing to the innovative capabilities of host countries. Joint R&D with multinational enterprises is an effective way of advancing the technological and innovative capability of developing countries. Taking advantage of trade and investment liberalisation to realise the potential and benefits from tapping into the global knowledge network should be one of the objectives of China's new foreign direct investment policy. China should develop specific policies and improve specific conditions, such as the protection of IPR, to encourage joint R&D.

Third, it will remain important for China to make further efforts to tap the global knowledge network through attracting foreign workers with technological know-how to come to work in China. The Chinese government needs to provide further incentives and improve relevant policies such as those restricting the number of foreign employees in the foreign-invested companies. Apart from specific policies, to absorb foreign knowledge and know-how will also require the domestic economy to be more open and ready to adopt foreign management techniques and firms to undertake the necessary organisational changes.

Fourth, China has traditionally had a policy to attract foreign direct investment to high-tech industries as a way to speed up the development of modern high-tech industries. However, China is also faced with a huge need to transform traditional manufacturing industries. From the point of view that foreign direct investment to traditional industries can also help improve technology and transfer knowledge, foreign direct investment sectoral policy should be reviewed in order to provide incentives for foreign direct investment to traditional industries as well.

Call for a better co-ordinated approach to government policy

Departmentalisation of government ministries can hamper policy co-ordination and policy implementation. Developing firms' technological and innovation capabilities is a complex issue, which depends on a number of economic and institutional factors, including science and technology policies, education policy, competition policies, labour market policies, tax policies, IPR protection, financial market and venture capital, enterprise reform policies, as well as foreign direct investment policies. Dealing with this complex issue requires high-level co-ordination of policies among government ministries. There seems to be a tendency within the Chinese government to treat the issue of innovation as mainly the responsibility of the Ministry of Science and Technology. However, unless other relevant policies and conditions are provided for, the policies for improving firms' innovation capability cannot be fully effective. Furthermore, there are important issues, such as technology diffusion between industries, and across regions, that can only be effectively handled when barriers of departmentalisation and regionalism are removed.

Therefore, there is a need to strengthen co-ordination between government ministries, as well as between regional governments, in order to improve the effectiveness of government polices. Co-ordination should not only be effected for the purpose of formulating policy, but also be maintained throughout the process of policy implementation, evaluation, and readjustment of policies. At the same time, the number of issues that require complex co-ordination can be reduced if and when government withdraws from intervening in various economic activities. These activities should be handled according to market principles. However, this approach would not work if only one of the government agencies involved decided to stop intervening, as other ministries would take the opportunity to exert greater influence on the issue. Thus, government co-ordination will also be needed in reviewing and agreeing on the areas from which the government should withdraw its intervention.

NOTES

1. Science and technology funding refers to all economic input into R&D activities that include the application of R&D results and the related S&T services, carried out by governmental R&D institutions, higher education institutions, and enterprises sector (MOST 1999, p. 40).

2. OECD (2000b), OECD here refers to OECD high-income group, which include 23 countries with 1998 GNP per capita of US$9361 or more.

3. S&T personnel include both S&T professionals and support staff in S&T activities. The statistics cover technological staff engaged in R&D within the enterprise sector, governmental research institutions, and S&T personnel at the higher educational institutions (excluding teaching staff).

4. R&D personnel refer to people who are engaged directly in R&D activities and support staff.

5. Scientific and technological papers published in China refer to those published in the selected 1 200 Chinese academic and scientific and technological journals, and, in addition, these papers must meet certain criteria set for being included in this statistic (MOST 1999, p. 94).

6. The very rapid increase of enterprises' share during the late 1990s may be in part attributable to reforms of China's S&T system, which had transformed many R&D institutions into enterprising businesses.

7. These figures exclude patents applied and held by individual inventors.

8. These statistics vary between different official sources. For example, in the report by SCSR and PU (1999), the share of LMEs R&D personnel in the national total of S&T personnel was 41.6 per cent in 1996, i.e. 9 per cent lower than the figure that was compiled from the official S&T statistical yearbook.

9. This may have to do with the fact that SOEs tend to benefit from state R&D funding or subsidies (see below).

10. Regarding whether China should develop its own innovation capacity, Fang Gang, a well-known Chinese economist, holds the following view. For a long period, China should mainly rely on imports of technology. This is because the innovation cost is higher than that of imports. He holds that import will allow China to realise the late-comer's advantage, as long as importing is a cheaper alternative to own innovation. (DRCnet news, 3 March 2000.)

11. Interview with representatives of foreign companies in China, April 2001.

12. For example, RMB 13 billion of subsidised loans were provided to 648 SOEs for technical upgrading during 1998, which represented 22 per cent of the total investment by these enterprises (OECD, 2000a).

13. The State Economic and Trade Commission instructed 520 key national enterprises to set up R&D facilities by the end of 2000, and 294 out of the 520 key enterprise met the technical requirements set for R&D facilities by mid-2001. In addition, some 1000 medium-sized enterprises administrated by provincial governments have acquired R&D facilities.

14. Interview with a senior official from the State Economic and Trade Committee, 24 April, 2001.

15. It was estimated that around one third of Chinese scholars returned to China (OECD, 2001a).

16. China's venture capital was estimated to account for 1 per cent of the total funding needed for commercialising R&D results in China, and funds from the government and banks consisted of 70 per cent of China's venture capital in 1999 (CEI, 22 Sept. 99).

17. This section draws primarily on OECD (1999).

18. For more details, see Little (1998).

19. This section draws primarily on OECD (1997).

BIBLIOGRAPHY

APEC-STPRC (Asian Pacific Economic co-operation and Science and Technology Policy Research Centre) (2001),
The role of innovation systems within the APEC, Chinese Taipei: STPRC.

Bloom Nichlose and Reenen John Van (2001),
"Real Options, Patents, Productivity and Market Value: Evidence from a Panel of British Firms", Institute for Fiscal Studies, Working Paper No. W00/21, February 2001.

CCPIT (China Council for the Promotion of International Trade),
Trade Information (various issues).

CEI (China Economic Information),
various issues, at *www.cei.gov.cn*.

CND (China News Digest),
various issues, at *www.cnd.org*.

Drcnet (Development Research Center Economic Information Net),
at *www.drcnet.com.cn/*.

Eliasson Gunnar (2000),
"Industrial policy, competence blocs and the role of science in economic development", in *Journal of Evolutionary Economics*, (2000) 10: pp. 217-241.

GEI (Great-wall Enterprise Institute) (1999),
Research Report on Multinational Enterprises R&D Investments in Beijing. Topical Research Report No. 5. March 1999.

IIE (Institute for Industrial Economics, Chinese Academy of Social Sciences) (1999),
China's Industrial Development Report (1999), Beijing: Economic Management Publishing House.

IIE (Institute for Industrial Economics, Chinese Academy of Social Sciences) (2000),
China's Industrial Development Report (2000), Beijing: Economic Management Publishing House.

IMD (Institute for Management Development) (2000),
World Competitiveness Yearbook 2000.

IHT (International Herald and Tribune),
A New Chinese Vanguard: Private Firms, 4 June, 2001.

Kinoshita Yuko (2000),
R&D and Technological Spillovers via FDI: *Innovation and Absorptive Capability*, William Davidson Institute Working Paper No. 349, Nov. 2000.

Little Arthur D. (1998),
The Innovative Company, Report prepared for the National Innovation System Focus Group on the Innovation Firm, Cambridge.

Liu Xielin and Steven White (2000),
China's National Innovation System in Transition: An activity based analysis. Draft study prepared for the project on "Constructing China's Market-based Innovation System" funded by Ministry of Science and Technology.

MOST (Ministry of Science and Technology) (1999),
China Science and Technology Indicators, 1998. Beijing: S&T Literature Press.

MOST (Ministry of Science and Technology) (2000a),
China Science and Technology Statistics 2000, Department of Development Planning, MOST.

MOST (2000b),
Statistics on China's High Technology Industry. Department of Development Planning.

NBS and MOST (National Bureau of Statistics and Ministry of Science and Technology) (1999),
China Statistical Yearbook on Science and Technology 1999, Beijing: China Statistical Press.

OECD (1997),
Diffusing Technology to Industry: Government Policies and Programs. Paris: OECD.

OECD (1998),
> Technology, Productivity, and Job Creation: Best Policy Practices. Paris: OECD.

OECD (1999a),
> Asia and the Global Crisis: The Industrial Dimension, Paris: OECD.

OECD (1999b),
> Managing National Innovation Systems, Paris: OECD.

OECD (2000a),
> Reforming China's Enterprises, Paris: OECD.

OECD (2000b),
> Knowledge-based Industries in Asia at www.oecd.org/dsti/sti/industry/indcomp/prod/ind-asia.htm

OECD (2001a),
> International Mobility of China's Resources in Science and Technology and its Impact, Paper presented at the Seminar on International Mobility of Highly Skilled Workers: From Statistical Analysis to the Formation of Policies, 11-12 June, Paris.

OECD (2001b),
> "Policy brief: The OECD guidelines for multinational enterprises". OECD Observer, June 2001.

QBPC (Quality Brands Protection Committee of the China Association of Enterprises with Foreign Investment) (2000),
> Report on Counterfeiting in the People's Republic of China, March 2000.

Research Group for China's S&T Development Research Report (1999),
> China's Science and Technology Development 1999. Beijing: Economic Management Press.

SCSR (State Commission for Systemic Reform) and PU (People's University) (1999),
> International Competitiveness Report 1999: Science and Technology Competitiveness. Beijing: People's University Press.

Sheehan Peter (2000),
> China's Innovation System in a Global Context, paper presented at the International High-Level Seminar on Technological Innovation, Beijing, 5-7 September 2000.

Shi Qingqi and Zhao Jingche, Eds. (1999),
> China Industrial Development Report 1999, Beijing: China Zhi-Gong Publishing House.

Smith Craig S. (2001),
> "China's high tech industry approaches critical mass" International Herald Tribune, May 29, 2001.

STDRWP (S&T Development Report Working Group) (2000),
> Research Report on China's Science and Technology Development (2000) – Globalisation of Science and Technology, and the Challenge facing China. Beijing: Social Sciences Literature Publishing House.

WTO (2001a),
> Agreement on Subsidies and Countervailing Measures ("SCM Agreement"). At www.wto.org/english/tratop_e/scm_e/scm.htm, accessed May 2001.

WTO (2001b),
> Basic Introduction to the WTO's Intellectual Property (TRIPS) Agreement. At www.wto.org/english/tratop_e/trips_e/trips_e.htm#Top, accessed May 2001.

WTO (2001c),
> Summary of Agreement on Trade Related Aspects of Investment Measures (TRIM). At www.wto.org/english/docs_e/legal_e/ursum_e.htm#eAgreement, accessed May 2001.

Wu Tianzu and Zou Gang (2001),
> "Research on technology transfer to small enterprises in China", Tech Monitor, Jul-Aug. 2001.

Zhu Lilan (2000),
> Welcome Speech at the Opening Ceremony of the International High-Level Seminar on Technological Innovation, Beijing, 5-7 September 2000.

Chapter 7

CHALLENGES TO CHINA'S BANKING INDUSTRY

TABLE OF CONTENTS

CHALLENGES TO CHINA'S BANKING INDUSTRY[*]

This chapter assesses the development prospects of the Chinese banking system in light of the increased competition from foreign banks that will come with China's trade and investment liberalisation. Fears that foreign banks will take substantial amounts of business and critical skilled staff from domestic banks have been among the most serious concerns within China concerning the effects of WTO entry. On the other hand, experiences in other countries suggest that foreign bank entry could help to improve the efficiency and quality of the domestic banking system.

The analysis focuses on three basic questions:

- What are the likely consequences of increased foreign participation on the competitive position and financial conditions of China's banks?

- What are the prospects in light of increased foreign bank participation for improvement in the abilities of the Chinese banking system to allocate capital efficiently, provide market discipline over enterprise behaviour, and support financial stability?

- Which policies will ensure that the potential benefits from foreign competition are secured, and promote the development of a more effective banking system than now exists?

Three sets of factors will shape the evolution of the Chinese banking system and the role of foreign banks within it. The first are the intrinsic comparative advantages and disadvantages of Chinese versus foreign banks. The second are the regulatory and other conditions in the Chinese banking environment and the economy at large that determine the extent to which various banks are able to exploit their comparative advantages. And the third are global considerations, such as regulatory policies in major financial centres and competitive pressures among multinational banks that determine the particular focus of the activities of foreign banks in emerging markets. Experiences of other developing countries with foreign bank entry, which are reviewed later in the chapter, provide useful insights for how these factors are likely to be manifest in China.

Overall, the analysis suggests that foreign banks are likely to play an important but limited role in China once the market is liberalised, on the order of that played by foreign banks in other Asian emerging economies and less than that found in several Eastern European and Latin American countries. This is despite the fact that foreign banks are more efficient and technically sophisticated than Chinese banks, and therefore capable in principle of gaining a substantial share of the market. In practice, however, given the high risks and costs involved in domestic lending, regulatory constraints not directly affected by the terms of China's WTO entry, and their own global strategies, foreign banks are likely to concentrate, at least at first, on a limited range of high profit activities. The primary risks to the development of the domestic Chinese banks are their own weakened financial conditions and the poor conditions of a large portion of their domestic customer base. These conditions also seriously weaken their ability to meet the needs of the real sector. Entry of foreign banks could seriously aggravate the problems of Chinese banks if conditions in these two other areas do not improve substantially, and the banking market remains relatively underdeveloped and unprofitable. On the other hand, success in reforms to restore domestic banks to financial soundness and improve the performances of enterprises is likely to result in greater profitability for both domestic and foreign banks – even if it leads to a larger foreign bank presence. The net benefits of foreign bank entry under these circumstances are potentially substantial. In this sense, improvement in the performance of domestic banks and expanded scope for foreign banks are complementary rather than competing.

---

[*] This Chapter was prepared by Charles Pigott, Senior Economist, and Young-Sook Nam, Economist, Non-Member, Economics Division, Economics Department, OECD. Jian-Guang Shen, Consultant, contributed the material for Box 7.4.

The current situation of the Chinese banking system

China's banking system has undergone significant changes in the last two decades in the course of its transformation from a mono-bank system typical of centrally-planned economies, to an increasingly diversified multi-layered system comprising a central bank together with a growing number of domestic and foreign commercial banks. China's banking system is now among the world's largest, particularly in relation to GDP.[1] As with other sectors of the economy, parts of the banking system are comparable in sophistication and market orientation to those found in other emerging economies and are rapidly modernising further, while other parts are still heavily influenced by the legacy of the past central planning system. At present, China's banks face several major immediate problems that seriously threaten their ability to deal effectively with increased foreign competition as well as their overall development. These problems are rooted in long-standing structural features of China's banking system that complicate the task of improving the competitiveness of the domestic banks and impair the effectiveness of the overall banking system.

The analysis here focuses on the formal commercial banking sector comprising the domestic commercial banks plus foreign banks, whose role is discussed further in the next section. The domestic banks fall into three distinct segments: the four major state-owned commercial banks (SOCBs); the 12 joint stock banks (JSBs) and the city commercial banks (CCBs). Further information about the characteristics of these segments is given in Box 7.1. Closely related to the commercial banks are the three "policy banks" created in 1994 to take over non-commercial lending previously carried out by the commercial banks. The policy banks are most similar to development banks in other countries, although they have been diversifying into some more traditional commercial banking activities. In addition, China also has a postal savings bank, which takes deposits but does not make commercial loans, along with a large network of urban and rural credit co-operatives that provide services similar to those of the commercial banks, although they are not formally commercial banks under the current regulatory framework. The urban co-operatives are due to be converted into commercial banks in the future.

The immediate problems impairing the competitiveness of domestic Chinese banks

China's domestic commercial banks possess important competitive advantages in terms of their extensive branch networks for raising deposits and servicing customers, and their close relations with and knowledge of their Chinese clients. Their close ties to the government, in particular their priority role in financing SOEs and government infrastructure projects, also confer some important advantages, although they also impose significant burdens. While certainly less sophisticated in many areas than foreign multinational banks, Chinese banks' capabilities have increased significantly as a result of the gradual but extensive opening of the economy to international markets over the past fifteen years, and the entry of foreign-invested enterprises into the domestic economy.

Despite these advantages, China's domestic banks now face the following three major problems that, unless resolved, jeopardise their ability to deal with increased foreign competition:

- low profitability;

- poor asset quality (high non-performing loans) together with inadequate (or barely adequate) capital;

- and impaired ability to control loan quality.

As with China's enterprises more generally, these problems are partly due to an accumulated stock of burdens arising from past distortions and partly to ongoing weaknesses in their governance and operating capabilities. Especially in recent years, the problems of the banks have been greatly aggravated by the poor conditions of their enterprise customers in the real sector. All three sets of problems will need to be addressed if there is to be a lasting improvement in banks' performance. In addition to their harmful effects on the banks' competitiveness, these problems also undermine the effectiveness with which banks are able to allocate credit and to exercise financial discipline over enterprises, and could pose serious risks to financial stability if they persist. While essential, the efforts

---

Box 7.1. The main domestic bank segments

The SOCBs, which were created from the mono bank early in the reform era, remain the backbone and dominant segment of the commercial banking system. The banks had combined assets equivalent to US$1.3 trillion at end-1999, some 150 000 branches, and a workforce of nearly 1.7 million. Operations of these banks are nationwide, extending to all provinces, cities, and, in the case of the Agricultural Bank of China until recently, to rural townships and villages. These banks have overseas offices in a number of OECD countries, and the Bank of China and the Industrial and Commercial Bank of China have banking and other financial subsidiaries in Hong Kong, China, and other major financial centres. The SOCBs have been the main suppliers of funds to state-owned enterprises and virtually monopolise lending and other financial services to the largest SOEs that are envisaged to remain indefinitely under state ownership. Traditionally their lending activities have been quite distinct: the Agricultural Bank of China lent mainly to agriculture and rural business; the China Construction Bank focused on real estate and infrastructure projects; the Industrial and Commercial Bank of China provided credit to SOEs for working capital or longer-term investment; while the Bank of China dominated foreign exchange financing. These distinctions have been breaking down in recent years, and competition among the banks has been increasing.

Joint-stock commercial banks (JSBs) together with the city commercial banks make up the remaining two segments of the domestic commercial banking sector. Joint stock banks have diverse ownership, with local governments and SOEs typically holding most of their equity. The one exception is the China Minshen Banking Corporation, whose dominant shareholders are non-state entities, and which is the only private Chinese bank. Although the regional banks were originally geographically restricted, all the joint stock banks are now allowed to conduct business throughout China. All of the nationwide banks and several of the regional banks have branches in major cities in China's interior, although their business is concentrated in the coastal provinces (in the case of the regional banks in their home province). Compared to the four largest SOCBs, the joint stock banks have much more limited branch networks and their enterprise lending is more concentrated on "second tier" larger SOEs outside the core of very large SOEs served by the four major banks, small and medium-sized SOEs, and non-state enterprises. The two oldest and largest of these banks, the Bank of Communications and the Everbright Bank of China are somewhat of an exception in that they serve several of the largest SOEs in China, such as Baosteel in the case of the former, but these are typically based in the banks' home territory. The city commercial banks have emerged out of the consolidation and transformation of urban credit co-operatives beginning in the mid-1990s. These banks, now 92 in number, are joint stock entities whose shares are primarily held by local governments and urban enterprises. Business is restricted to the municipal region in which they are incorporated, and their main customers are urban SMEs and collectives, and local residents. With the exception of a few banks in the largest cities, the city commercial banks are relatively small.

Closely related to the commercial banks are the three state-owned policy banks that were created since 1994 to take over non-commercial ("policy") lending tasks then being carried out by the SOCBs. The policy banks have only limited deposit networks and raise the bulk of their funds from government deposits and through the issuance of government guaranteed bonds that are largely held by the commercial banks. As with their counterparts in other countries, the policy banks engage mainly in state infrastructure financing and are major vehicles for the government's strategy of developing China's western provinces. However, the creation of the policy banks has not completely freed the SOCBs from lending to support loss-making SOEs or for other purposes deemed socially necessary but which do not meet strict commercial lending standards. Part of the reason is that explicit government subsidies and backing for the policy banks are limited. This may also help explain recent moves by some of the banks to develop commercial banking activities related to their core business.*

---

* See "China Development Bank: Benefits and Constraints of a Development Bank", JP Morgan Emerging Markets Research, 21 February 2001.

---

of the banks themselves are unlikely to be sufficient to fully deal with these problems. As discussed in the next sub-section, the problems are rooted in long-standing structural features of China's banking system and the real economy, whose reform depends critically on government policies.

The *profitability* of Chinese banks has declined steadily over the last ten years to levels that are in most cases quite low. By 1999, reported profits before tax of the four largest SOCBs ranged between slightly negative as a ratio to total assets for the Agricultural Bank of China, to 0.33 per cent for the China Construction Bank (Table 7.1). Even allowing for some recovery since 1999,[2] the profitability of these banks is quite low by international standards. The smaller joint stock banks generally have had better performances and account for the bulk of banking system profits.

Moreover, the situation is almost certainly worse than official figures suggest because bank profits tend to be overstated by several practices. One is the accrual of interest on loans classified as performing under China's standards, but which would not be regarded as performing by international standards. Profit figures are also overstated by relatively low charges for loan provisions. Banks are allowed to set aside only 1 per cent of total loans as provisions, a relatively low figure by international standards, and especially unrealistic given the financial condition of China's banks. Even more importantly, Chinese banks have been allowed to take only very limited write-offs of bad loans. Under practices more in line with international standards, profits of the SOCBs would probably be negative, while the financial performances of the joint stock banks would appear less favourable.

The low-level of profits, although not their secular decline, is partly attributable to inefficiencies that lead to excessively high costs in bank operations. The extent of such inefficiencies is difficult to gauge from aggregate data (Box 7.2). Nevertheless, there is evidence at the individual bank level of substantial inefficiencies and accompanying excessive costs in operations.[3] In particular, the extensive branch networks of the four largest commercial banks include large numbers of offices that are too small and/or poorly located to be economically viable. The SOCBs, and to a lesser extent other commercial banks, also have substantial amounts of excess staff. Bank costs are further inflated by the relatively high turnover tax rate imposed on bank loans (8 per cent until 2001, when it was lowered to 7 per cent).

Table 7.1. **Banks' profitability in China and Hong Kong, China, 1999**

	Assets	Capital asset ratio	Pre-tax profit	Return on capital	Return on assets[1]
	US$ million	%	US$ million	%	%
China					
Industrial and Commercial Bank of China	427 546	5.13	498	2.3	0.12
Bank of China	350 736	4.35	798	5.3	0.23
Agricultural Bank of China	274 876	5.91	−43	−0.3	−0.02
China Construction Bank	265 845	4.96	890	7.0	0.33
Bank of Communications	72 233	4.19	324	11.1	0.45
Everbright Bank of China	20 278	5.10	82	9.8	0.40
China Merchants Bank	19 866	7.57	184	14.8	0.92
CITIC Industrial Bank	19 003	4.62	138	16.5	0.72
Shanghai Pudong Development Bank	12 466	7.53	142	21.2	1.14
Hua-Xia Bank	7 383	5.20	62	16.4	0.84
Fujian Industrial Bank	5 940	6.59	53	13.7	0.89
Xiamen International Bank	1 097	13.79	2	1	0.15
Hong Kong, China					
Hong Kong and Shanghai Banking Corp.	210 770	4.45	3 178	32.6	1.51
Bank of East Asia	18 703	9.39	208	12.2	1.11
Doa Heng Bank	17 003	834.00	180	13.0	1.06
Nanyang Commercial Bank	11 047	11.62	86	6.9	−1.78
Wing Lung Bank	7 687	8.17	131	22.2	1.71
Shanghai Commercial Bank	7 433	11.68	134	16.3	1.8
Wing Hang Bank	6 491	8.85	103	18.9	1.59
Po Sang Bank	6 350	17.58	133	12.5	2.09
CITIC Ka Wah Bank	6 278	10.97	14	2.1	0.23
National Commercial Bank	6 210	11.92	31	4.3	0.50
China State Bank	6 176	10.82	31	4.7	0.50
Dah Sing Financial Holdings	5 713	7.75	85	20.0	1.49

1. After-tax return.
Source: *The Banker*, October 2000.

Box 7.2. **Aggregate data on the efficiency of China's banking operations**

Although analyses of individual banks and the actions of their management indicate substantial overstaffing and other inefficiencies, aggregate data are less clear. For example, the ratio of bank employees to the total population in China is lower than in nearly all OECD countries and does not seem out of line with its *per-capita* income (Table 7.2). China's major banks average about US$727 million in assets per 1 000 employees, well below the level of virtually all OECD countries (except Poland). This figure suggests that average labour productivity, measured in terms of loan or other transactions per worker is significantly lower in China than in most OECD countries. However, given China's low labour costs, banking services are likely to be produced with more labour intensive, and hence lower labour-productivity techniques. Operating expenses, the bulk of which are staff costs, do not appear to be obviously out of line in relation to total assets compared to other countries. Neither do Chinese banks' operating expenses – estimated from their income statements – appear high in relation to those reported by banks in other countries. Admittedly, such comparisons need to be regarded with caution because of differences between Chinese and OECD accounting and other reporting standards.

Table 7.2. **Comparison of Chinese and OECD Banks**

	Bank employees per 1 000 of population	Assets/bank employee: million US$/1 000 staff	Net non-interest/net interest income (%)
China	**2.7**	**727**	**0.13**
OECD countries			
Australia			0.86
Austria	3.7	7 397	0.90
Belgium	7.5	10 768	0.62
Canada			1.10
Czech Republic		1 483	5.32
Denmark			
Finland	3.0	5 525	0.99
France	3.4	10 645	2.03
Germany	2.7	8 651	0.74
Greece		2009	0.79
Hungary	2.8	1 106	0.13
Ireland (all banks)	14.1	4 973	0.59
Italy (all banks)	5.4	5 372	0.60
Japan	2.6	16 682	0.14
Korea	1.6	5 083	−0.08
Mexico	1.2	1 253	0.61
Netherlands (all banks)			0.74
New Zealand (all banks)			0.60
Norway	3.4		0.43
Poland	3.9	588	0.64
Portugal	5.7	4 530	0.44
Spain	3.3	4 627	0.57
Sweden	4.3	7 112	1.25
Switzerland (all banks)	16.2	12 776	1.66
Turkey	2.6	984	0.19
United Kingdom	6.9	5 126	0.67
United States	6.1	3 451	0.76

Note: Figures for China refer to the total number of employees in banking and insurance taken from the *China Statistical Yearbook* 2000 and are therefore an upper bound. Figures for total employees in banking only are not available but the Secretariat estimates suggest a figure of 1.5 to 2.0 per thousand of population.

Source: OECD figures are from OECD, *Bank Profitability*, 2000.

237

Finally, although normal for developing countries, the use of low or outmoded technology, particularly in branches, further contributes to relatively low productivity in bank operations. Except for excess branches, these problems are shared by virtually all of China's banks, but they are probably most severe for the four SOCBs.[4]

The main proximate reason for the decline in profitability of the SOCBs is a marked drop in their net interest income in relation to total assets. This decline has occurred despite the fact that the loan spread over deposit rates has fallen as interest rates have come down since 1996.[5] Rising non-performing loans, which have reduced the accrued interest banks can count as income, appear to be primarily responsible for the fall in net interest income.[6] An additional contributing factor has been a rise in the proportion of government bonds in bank portfolios, whose interest rates are below those of most bank loans. The increase in bonds held by the banks is partly the result of quotas imposed on their purchase of infrastructure bonds issued by the government in 1998-99. However, banks' preference for government bonds has also risen as the perceived risks of lending to enterprises have grown. These factors suggest that banks' low profitability is partly a reflection of the financially troubled state of their enterprise customers and the extremely cautious lending approach they are taking in response to the consequent risks. The negative impact on total profits of declining profits from lending has been aggravated by the limited diversity in bank products and consequent low amount of non-interest income (see next sub-section).

Non-performing loans, although there has been much controversy about their magnitude, appear to have grown quite sharply since the mid-1990s, as SOE profitability deteriorated, and as uneconomic loans originally made during the 1993-95 investment boom became due and were not repaid. Estimates by outside experts suggest that NPLs peaked in the late 1990s at 50 per cent or more of the total loans of the SOCBs.[7] Official estimates of NPLs have been substantially lower until recently, due in part to the difficulty of accurately evaluating loan performance given the numerous branches, limited central oversight of their operations, and significant differences in accounting procedures often employed from one location to another. However, despite the transfer of nearly 20 per cent of SOCB problem loans to four bank asset management companies (BAMC) in 2000, it is clear that the banks retain substantial NPLs. Recent estimates reported by the People's Bank of China (PBC) indicate that NPLs on the books of the SOCBs were (on average) about 27 per cent of their total loans in mid-2001. Moreover, the PBC figure is based on China's traditional loan classification system and would probably be somewhat higher if international standards were applied.[8]

Other estimates indicate that JSBs, which did not participate in the loan carve-out programme, also have serious balance sheet problems, with NPLs in most cases ranging between 10 and slightly above 20 per cent in 1999 (Wong, 2000).[9] This suggests that JSBs have had a significantly lower incidence of NPLs than SOCBs prior to 2000, which is consistent with their greater autonomy and less exclusive focus on SOEs. Although hard estimates are lacking, many of the city commercial banks are also thought to have high NPL ratios.

China's banks also have low levels of capital as a cushion against NPLs. Official capital injections made in 1998, together with the effective reduction in required capital from the subsequent swap of NPLs for government guaranteed bonds of the BAMC, have brought officially-measured SOCB capital ratios to around 7-8 per cent on average, near to the BIS minimum of 8 per cent. (The capital ratio is thought to be substantially lower for the Agricultural Bank of China.) Precise information on the capital ratios of JSBs, other than those that have been listed, is not available. The inadequate capitalisation of Chinese banks is further underscored by the fact that the BIS minimum is increasingly regarded as insufficient for emerging market economies, many of which have raised their capital ratios to 10 per cent or more.[10]

The nexus of low capital, high NPLs, and low profitability is a potentially large obstacle to the ability of Chinese banks to respond to increased foreign competition. Even after the transfer to the BAMC in 2000, NPLs in the banking system remain near or above the peaks reached in the Republic of Korea and Malaysia during their 1997 crises; and Chinese banks also have substantially fewer provisions than banks had in the Asian crisis countries. The financial weaknesses directly limit the capacity of the institutions to invest in improvements in their capabilities, to raise funds in domestic or foreign financial markets, and to form alliances with foreign banks. The same conditions also tend to weaken internal incentives to assess and monitor credit risks.

The prospects that the banks in China, particularly the SOCBs, will be able to "outgrow" their NPL problem on their own are not good, unless their profitability improves substantially. Although objectively in better shape than the SOCBs, these problems may pose the greater risk to the development of the joint-stock banks. The risk that poor financial performance will lead to a runoff of deposits or curtail access to financial markets is limited for SOCBs by the implicit government guarantee conferred by their "too big to fail" status and their close ties to the central government and leading SOEs. Lacking such status, and in the absence of a formal deposit insurance system, JSBs and other smaller banks are likely to be more vulnerable to such problems.

Improvement in the ability to control loan quality is ultimately the key to any lasting solution of the NPL problem, as well as to improved credit allocation and financial discipline in the economy. Banks' chronic inability to limit NPLs stems from a combination of problems of information, incentives, and control stemming from both internal and external factors, as summarised in Figure 7.1. External factors, mainly the reliance by the government on policy lending rather than direct fiscal outlays to support projects unable to earn a commercial rate of return but deemed socially necessary, has been the most important factor in the build up of NPLs, at least for the SOCBs.

Since the inception of the new banking law in 1996, the authorities have taken several important steps to improve bank-lending standards. Direct quotas on bank lending were abolished and replaced with required ratios of assets to liabilities ("asset liability system") to regulate aggregate credit. Banks were required to establish a strict separation between loan origination and loan approval. Accountability has been further strengthened by making higher-level bank offices responsible for compliance with lending standards by their lower branches, and by making lending officers and their senior management accountable for new bad loans. These measures reinforced the earlier (1994) creation of the three "policy banks" to take on government directed or other preferential lending previously carried out by the commercial banks. These reforms have substantially reduced, although not entirely eliminated, overt government direction of credit, and have significantly improved lending standards and credit quality.[11]

However, a number of developments suggest that non-commercial considerations continue to influence lending decisions, if to a lesser degree and through more indirect channels than before. In particular, SOCBs were allocated minimum quotas for matching lending to infrastructure projects

Figure 7.1. **Factors impairing bank's ability to control loan quality**

Internal to the bank	External to the bank
Information	
Defects in internal credit assessment and classification	Limited amount and poor transparency of information available from credit applicants
Incentives	
Weak governance and internal accountability	Weak market discipline and limited enforcement means
Control	
	Use of banks for policy lending
	Poor credit standing of a large portion of bank customers

Source: OECD Secretariat.

financed by the government's special bond issues in 1998, although they were free in principle to choose the specific projects. The continued operation of numerous loss-making SOEs unable to service their loans strongly suggests that banks continue to provide at last working capital to firms that would not meet basic standards of creditworthiness. The authorities have also periodically "suggested" that banks increase lending to non-state enterprises and for particular purposes. Such measures can send mixed messages to bank management and loan officers and thereby interfere with efforts to establish a strong "credit culture". The situation now prevailing in China in some respects resembles that of other Asian countries, such as the Republic of Korea, in the years before the 1997 crisis, where, despite the absence of overt government-directed credit, close ties among banks, major industrial customers, and the government made it difficult to contain imprudent lending.

Internally, bank efforts to maintain sound lending standards and monitor loan performance continue to be hampered by a number of problems. High NPLs limit incentives to maintain sound lending standards and to monitor and enforce loan contracts, because the banks have little or no capital at risk, and responsibility for bank performance is difficult to assign when financial problems are severe. Banks' incentives are further impaired by weaknesses in the judicial system and other factors that make it difficult to enforce loan contracts. The problems are further aggravated by banks' inadequate ability to charge interest rates commensurate with loan risk.[12] Efforts to control loan quality are also hampered by weaknesses in accounting and other internal systems for assessing creditworthiness, by the limited and often inaccurate information available about enterprise conditions, and by the poor financial position of much of the enterprise sector. These conditions have induced banks to severely curtail or avoid lending to a large segment of enterprises. This policy, while it limits the risk of accumulating new NPLs, contributes to low profitability.[13]

Structural features of the banking system underlying the current problems

Underlying the above problems are several long-standing and distinctive features of China's banking system. These features are partly symptomatic of distortions arising from the legacy of central planning and the limited state of development of the financial system as a whole, although they have been perpetuated to some degree by more recent regulatory policies. While these features are being eroded as the banking system evolves, in many cases they remain a serious impediment to efforts to address Chinese banks' problems.

The most distinctive feature of China's banking system is the virtually complete public ownership and control of the domestic banks. In contrast, although more important in the 1950s and 1960s, public ownership of banks has largely disappeared in most OECD countries, as authorities have sought to improve the efficiency of the banking sector and reduce burdens on public finances and financial distortions that have not infrequently resulted from state ownership. There has also been a general trend away from public ownership in emerging market economies. Moreover, direct government involvement in fundamental policies and business operations of the state-owned banks is relatively high in China. Admittedly, there are important differences in the form of government control. The SOCBs are directly subject to the central government and function in many respects as government agencies. Without a fundamental change in their relation to the government, it will be very difficult to fully transform the SOCBs into genuine commercial institutions. JSBs, with multiple public owners below the central government level, tend to have greater management autonomy, are less subject to government pressure in their lending decisions, and have greater flexibility in their personnel policies than the SOCBs.[14] Nevertheless, JSBs (and CBs) are not yet fully commercialised banking institutions, particularly as their main controlling shareholder is typically a local government facing policy dilemmas similar to those that have led the central government to use the SOCBs as fiscal vehicles.

A second and related feature is that despite the entry of new banks over the past fifteen years, the SOCBs remain overwhelmingly dominant. As shown in Table 7.3, the big four accounted for 83 per cent of total deposits of the banking system and nearly 72 per cent of total loans.[15] This concentration in the banking system is very high compared to most other countries including developing and transition economies. Although size itself need not be a competitive disadvantage for an individual bank, the

Table 7.3. **The distribution of assets, loans and deposits in China's banking system, 1999**

	Assets		Loans		Deposits	
	Billion RMB	Share of banking system total (%)	Billion RMB	Share of banking system total (%)	Billion RMB	Share of banking system total (%)
Big 4 commercial banks	10 403	73.2	6 249	71.7	7 618	83.0
City commercial banks	554	3.9	271	3.1	441	4.8
Foreign banks	263	1.9	180	2.1	43	0.5
Joint-equity commercial banks	1 456	10.2	704	8.1	1 038	11.3
Policy banks	1 540	10.8	1 312	15.1	37	0.4
Total	14 218	100.0	8 718	100.0	9 179	100.0

1. Assets, deposits and loans refer to consolidated figures including domestic and foreign currency.
Source: *The Banking Industry in China*, 2000.

dominance of the big four raises potential problems for the competitiveness and development of the Chinese banking system as a whole. Given their traditional role and their size, SOCBs are most suited to lending to large enterprises, particularly to SOEs destined to remain under state control. Indeed this role is implicit in the government's plans to foster a "main bank" type system for large SOEs. SOCBs are generally less suited to smaller-scale lending to non-state enterprises or SMEs, on the basis of objective commercial criteria rather than administrative regulations. JSBs and other smaller banks should have greater advantages in such lending (and also in lending to enterprises in interior provinces) but are constrained in their expansion possibilities by their more limited access to deposits or other funding. Moreover, continued dominance by the SOCBs, given their character and the inherent difficulties of strengthening their governance, could slow improvement in commercial standards of the overall banking system. In addition, the central position of the four major banks in the payments system creates an inevitable tension between the objective of increasing competition in the banking system and the need to safeguard financial stability – one that is greatly increased by the very weak financial conditions of the major banks.

A third feature is the disproportionate concentration of bank lending in the SOE sector and relatively low portion of lending to non-state enterprises. The figures for rural collectives (TVEs) are indicative: these enterprises received about 6.5 per cent of total outstanding financial institution loans in 1999, less than half their share of total industrial output. Private enterprises received a minuscule fraction of total credits, again well below their contribution to aggregate GDP.[16] The portion of SOCB loans going to these sectors is particularly low, reflecting their heavy orientation toward SOEs. The JSBs have been more active in lending to non-state enterprises, as a reflection of their greater concentration on SMEs.[17]

A somewhat different picture of financial flows going to non-state enterprises is conveyed when credits received indirectly by non-state enterprises are taken into account. According to a recent survey by the PBC, non-state enterprises were recipients through such indirect as well as direct channels of 47.7 per cent of loans from all non-financial institutions in 2000 (Table 7.4).[18] This is more than four times their direct share of bank loans. Non-state enterprises received a higher portion in coastal provinces, where they dominate economic activity, and a lower share in Western provinces where SOEs still dominate.

The substantial amount of funds flowing indirectly to non-state enterprises is an indication of the importance of informal credit channels in China. However, the degree to which the funds are received by non-financial enterprises in the non-state sector, thus helping to make up for their disproportionately low share of direct loans, is unclear. Some of the indirect lending, quite possibly a substantial amount, probably goes through formal and informal investment funds into the stock market – which banks are

Table 7.4. **Share of loans going to the non-state sector**

a. Share of short-term loans going to selected components of the non-state sector

	Financial institutions			State banks	
	1997	1998	1999	1997	1998
	(%)	(%)	(%)	(%)	(%)
TVE	6.7	6.4	6.6	2.6	2.6
Private enterprises and individuals	0.5	0.5	0.6	0.3	0.3
Foreign joint ventures	2.5	2.9	3.2	2.9	3.3

b. Share of outstanding loans going directly and indirectly to the non-state sector

	1996	1998	2000
Total	38.9	41.8	47.7

c. Share of new loans going directly or indirectly to the non-state sector, by selected provinces, 2000

	Province	Share
Coast	Jiangsu	65.0
	Shandong	49.8
	Zhejiang	74.2
Northeast	Helongjiang	37.8
Central	Hubei	37.6
West	Sichuan	47.0
	Shanxi	42.1
	Xinjiang	22.8

Sources: *Almanac of China's Finance and Banking* 1999; *The People's Bank of China Quarterly Statistical Bulletin*.
Figures refer to credits extended directly to the categories. The table does not include the entire non-state sector as credits to urban credit co-operatives and some other types of enterprises are included in official statistics with credits to SOE in loans to industry or other segments.
Source for parts b and c: People's Bank of China. Figures are based on a survey taken by the People's Bank of China.

not allowed to invest in directly, or into real estate. In any case, credit to non-state firms from indirect sources is apt to be vulnerable to changes in the financial condition of the SOEs or other providers. Furthermore, maintenance of sound lending standards and loan monitoring is also likely to be more difficult for credits provided indirectly.

Direct lending by domestic banks, including SOCBs, to non-state enterprises has grown rapidly in recent years, but from a very small base, and is likely to continue to increase as the share of SOEs in the economy continues to shrink. However in the near term, as discussed further in Chapter 14, banks' preoccupation with avoiding new NPLs, and the large-scale divestiture of smaller SOEs, has led to a severe worsening of external credit access for SMEs generally. The problems of SMEs and their importance to China's future development accentuate the need to foster the development of JSBs and other smaller commercial banks to increase the diversity and flexibility of the financial system as a whole.

A fourth feature that has important implications for the future development of the banking system is the virtually exclusive dependence of bank funding on deposits and central bank money. The money market is still quite small in size and its use is confined to short-term liquidity adjustments. Banks are prohibited from taking extended net positions.[19] Other vehicles for gathering wholesale deposits and transferring funds among banks, notably certificates of deposits, are severely limited by lack of negotiability and consequent low liquidity. Although not unique, the limited development of such facilities in China is an impediment to competition in the banking system and to its ability to allocate funds efficiently. In particular, the limited short-term financial markets represent a serious obstacle to the development of joint-stock and city banks. The disadvantages of the JSBs are compounded by a disproportionately small share of PBC loans to the banking system (they received less than 1 per cent of the total between 1994 and 1998) and regulatory limits on the number of new branches they are allowed to establish in a given year. The underdeveloped state of these markets also has potential implications for the financing of regional development, since the SOCBs, together with the central government, are now the main conduits for inter-regional financial flows.

Finally, a characteristic of many developing countries, but which is more pronounced in China, is the limited array of bank products and services. Basic lending to enterprises is the overwhelmingly dominant activity of nearly all the banks, while most other business lines are quite limited. These include not only "high technology" products such as derivatives but also more traditional products, such as bankers acceptances and letters of credit that are prominent bank activities in other comparably developed economies. The limited diversity of products is reflected in a very low ratio of income generated from financial activities other than core lending. Limited product diversity can be viewed as a contributing factor to banks' currently low profitability and makes their income and cash flow more sensitive to swings in interest rates and loan demand than otherwise would be the case.

Regulatory policy is substantially responsible for the limited array of bank products and activities. Until fairly recently, foreign exchange business was largely reserved to the People's Bank of China and foreign banks. PBC regulations limit the maturity and other characteristics of bank loans and other products. Banks typically have to obtain specific approval to offer new products or even to modify existing products, a process which often takes considerable time. Prudential considerations have further limited banks' scope for expanding the range of their activities, as illustrated by the order given to banks in 1999 to divest their trust and investment subsidiaries, which was prompted by widespread financial abuses.

Strategies being followed to improve the competitiveness of China's banks

Recognising the importance of the banking system to the overall economic reform effort and the need to prepare for increased foreign competition, supervisory officials and the banks themselves have been making strong efforts over the past several years to correct the weaknesses noted above.

The SOCBs have been closing smaller outlying branches and transferring their business to larger city branches or headquarters. Nearly 21 000 offices were closed between 1997 and 2000.[20] Major efforts are also being made to cut surplus staff. By the end of 2000, the banks had cut staff by a reported 110 000, or about 6.5 per cent of the total number. Banks at all levels are also investing extensively in equipment and other facilities to modernise and improve the efficiency of their operations. These efforts are expected to continue over the next several years and are probably the areas where the banks themselves have the most control and should be able to make the most progress.

Apart from cost cutting, the business strategies of China's banks are focused on two objectives: improving credit quality, and diversifying and strengthening their products in areas of their greatest comparative advantage. With strong encouragement from supervisory authorities, banks have tightened internal controls on lending through the steps mentioned earlier, and are upgrading their internal accounting and other information systems. A new loan classification standard based on international principles, and which should significantly improve banks' ability to monitor their credit risk exposure, is being gradually introduced. The often rapid changes China's enterprises will undergo in response to trade and investment liberalisation only increases the critical importance of effective and forward-looking credit assessment capabilities for China's banks. However, continued government influence over lending in some areas and the performance problems of enterprises continue to be significant impediments to progress.

Efforts by domestic banks to strengthen their competitiveness are based on exploiting their key advantages of close ties with and knowledge about domestic enterprises and households. On the corporate side, the objective is to strengthen ties with domestic enterprises with good credit standing, particularly in industries with high growth potential; and to develop consumer lending. Many of the specific efforts in these areas involve formation of alliances among domestic banks or with foreign banks to exploit their complementary advantages. The target customers differ according to the characteristics of the particular bank, with the largest SOCBs (the Agricultural Bank being something of an exception) focusing on very large SOEs, while joint-stock banks give more emphasis to SOEs in their home region. Banks are also seeking to develop more business with creditworthy non-state enterprises, including private firms. Cash management, foreign exchange, and other services aimed at corporate customers are being developed in order to improve profitability and enhance the banks' ability to retain their most profitable enterprise clients, including foreign joint ventures that they now serve. Consumer lending, which is now relatively small, is seen as a particularly attractive growth area for domestic banks. During the past several years, banks have been rapidly expanding lending for housing, which is expected to receive a major boost from reforms to encourage home ownership, and more recently for automobile purchases and other consumer durables. All the larger banks and several of the smaller joint-stock plans have announced plans to introduce credit cards and to develop lending for purchases of other consumer durables.

The thrust of recent *government efforts* has been to improve bank balance sheets and to introduce corporate governance reforms into the SOCBs as a means of improving their functioning as commercial institutions. Authorities have stated that they do not intend to undertake a further carve out of non-performing loans along the lines of that undertaken for the four SOCBs in 1999-2000. They are, however, facilitating the listing of banks as a means of injecting capital and allowing current NPLs to be written off. Three JSBs have already been listed and several others expected to follow over the next two to three years. Listing of SOCBs, although probably somewhat later, is also planned. The authorities also recently set a target for the reduction of SOCBs' NPLs of 3 percentage points of their loans per year over the next three years.[21] To help improve profitability, the turnover tax will be further reduced to 5 per cent by 2003. While no change in government control of SOCBs is envisaged, the authorities intend to establish supervisory boards and other governance mechanisms along the lines of reforms of non-bank SOEs, and to diversify their ownership in order to further strengthen governance.

Several important questions surround these efforts. First, official targets, taken at face value, indicate that SOCBs will continue to have high NPLs and low capital for some years. Cleaning up the balance sheets of JSBs is also likely, on current plans, to take at least several more years to be completed and no timetable has been given for resolving the financial problems of CCBs (nor have there been any clear official indications of the magnitude of these problems). This amounts to a relatively extended timetable for restoring financial soundness. In contrast, most OECD countries experiencing major banking system distress have acted more rapidly and comprehensively to restore bank capital once problems became acute (Box 7.3). The most notable exceptions, the United States during its savings and loan crisis in the 1980s and Japan during the 1990s, underscore the dangers of an unduly protracted process of financial restoration. Delay in both cases – and in similar cases in non-OECD countries – substantially raised the ultimate cost of the cleanup and, in Japan, imposed a significant drag on real growth for a number of years. In China, there is the further risk that continued financial weakness will interfere with efforts to improve bank efficiency and maintain sound lending standards.

Second, the degree to which banks will be capable of raising capital and dealing with remaining NPLs without substantial additional government support is also uncertain. Significant improvements in balance sheets is a precondition for successful listing of the banks and, for the reasons noted earlier, it is doubtful whether they will be able to generate the required resources on their own. In practice, the authorities have had to provide funds to clean up the balance sheets of JSBs sufficiently to allow them to be listed on the stock market. While no further official commitments to the SOCBs have yet been made, more funds will almost certainly be needed if they are to be able to write off their remaining NPLs on schedule while maintaining adequate capital.

A third question is the degree to which the governance reforms planned for the banks will improve their functioning. Experiences with governance reforms of large non-financial SOEs suggests that the establishment of boards of directors and other modern corporate structures by itself has only limited impact, since continued state ownership tends to perpetuate the influence of government agencies that

Box 7.3. **OECD experiences with banking system distress**

Since the 1980s, 13 OECD countries, including the three transition countries that are the newest members, have grappled with major episodes of banking system distress.* While generally milder than the problems China is now facing, the problems involved substantial government outlays to restore financial soundness and significant macroeconomic costs in terms of slower real growth. The following summaries illustrate several themes: the tendency for financial weakness to encourage excessive risk taking; the need to improve bank supervision and contain incentives for excessive risk taking during financial deregulation; the risks of undue delay and excessive "forbearance" in dealing with banking problems; and the need to improve prudential standards and restructure the banking system as an accompaniment to efforts to restore financial soundness.

S*pain* began to experience pervasive problems in its banking sector beginning in the late 1970s that lasted into the mid-1980s. The problems were precipitated by excessive speculation, particularly in real estate, and driven in many of the cases by "connected lending" and related abuses arising from the close ties between problem banks and financially troubled industrial groups. Excessive fragmentation of the banking system arising from the prior financial liberalisation also played a role, as suggested by the fact that most of the problem banks were of small or medium size. Official efforts to cope with the problems were hampered for several years by serious weaknesses in banking regulation and oversight. Effective supervisory mechanisms to prevent financial irregularities were lacking, and prevailing accounting standards often gave a misleading view of banks' true financial condition. Bank of Spain examiners were inadequate in number, largely confined to checking compliance with official regulations, and poorly equipped to deal with serious problems when they were discovered. In response, the authorities moved to correct the supervisory weaknesses and in 1980 established a formal deposit insurance scheme that became the key mechanism for dealing with problem banks. Under the supervision of the fund and after financial injections, most of the troubled banks were sold to stronger institutions and their management changed. Although substantial public funds were required, the condition of the banking sector improved considerably in the latter part of the 1980s.

The U*nited States* suffered its most serious banking problems since the 1930s with the onset of the savings and loan (S&L) crisis in the early 1980s. The problems of the S&L were precipitated by regulatory changes that increased competition for deposits from commercial banks and other financial institutions and from rising interest rates, which sharply lowered the value of their mortgage portfolios. For some years after the problems emerged, the regulatory authorities exercised "forbearance" in allowing S&L with sub-standard financial positions to continue to operate in the hope that their conditions would improve with time. To help, S&L were given increased latitude to invest in assets other than the home mortgages that were their traditional specialisation. These efforts backfired, however, as institutions with impaired capital took excessive risks ("gambled for redemption") in the knowledge that their owners were largely insulated from any further losses. As a result, the situation continued to worsen until the late 1980s, when the Resolution Trust Corporation was established to take decisive action. By that time, the net cost of resolving the problems had risen to nearly 3 per cent of GDP. Another set of banking sector problems, arising from commercial bank lending to the commercial real estate sector emerged in the early 1990s. In response, the authorities instituted a system of graduated penalties and incentives ("prompt corrective action") for banks to act decisively to restore their capital to adequate levels. Although the problems contributed to a protracted period of credit stringency during 1991-92, they improved fairly rapidly as the economy began to recover in 1993, and public outlays were much smaller than for the S&L crisis and entirely covered by existing funds in the deposit insurance fund.

Three N*ordic* countries, Finland, Norway, and Sweden, experienced major banking crises during the early 1990s. The crises were the direct result of excessive and imprudent bank lending into speculative real estate booms whose collapse, together with severe recessions, led to a sharp rise in non-performing loans and virtual insolvency of a significant portion of their banking sectors. The prior environment of heavy regulation and poorly implemented deregulation during the 1980s also played an important role. Banks' inexperience with a more liberal and competitive environment led them to take excessive risks and speculators were further encouraged by the buoyant economic expansions and continued tax-deductibility of interest on borrowing for real estate investment. Bank supervisors were also inexperienced in monitoring risks and initially slow to recognise that problems were accumulating. However, authorities in all three countries acted fairly quickly and comprehensively once the problems became acute. Resolving the problems involved substantial cost to the governments, particularly in Finland where it is estimated to have reached 9-10 per cent of GDP. However, by 1993, several years after the onset of the crisis, financial conditions had begun to recover, due substantially to the revival in economic activity but also thanks in part to the relatively comprehensive government measures taken earlier.

Box 7.3. **OECD experiences with banking system distress** (*cont.*)

In *Mexico*, large foreign exchange losses of the corporate sector in the wake of the 1994 depreciation led to a massive rise in non-performing loans and banking crisis in 1995. In response, the government moved to tighten prudential requirements while providing direct public funds to bolster financial institutions and to provide corporate debtors with support and time to restructure their obligations to the banks. The authorities took over 11 institutions pending their restructuring and re-capitalisation and subsequent re-privatisation. To ensure that stockholders bore a substantial portion of the ultimate cost, financial assistance to surviving banks was provided via subordinated debt or purchases of problem loans under a swap arrangement requiring the banks to share in the burden of any losses. The total cost of the financial assistance, including that provided to debtors, is estimated at 14.4 per cent of (1998) GDP. The authorities also initiated an extensive programme of mergers and acquisitions to bolster the strength of the banking system. With the active encouragement of the government, foreign participation in the banking system increased markedly and, besides providing capital has helped to improve competition and the technical skills of the banking system. Since the crisis, the condition of Mexican banks has improved significantly. By the end of 1999, non-performing loans were down to 8 per cent of total loans, provisions and profits were up considerably from several years before, and a capital adequacy ratio of more than 16 per cent had been achieved.

The *Republic of Korea's* banks were already suffering from low profits when the 1997 currency crisis led to a dramatic further deterioration. Increased non-performing loans virtually eliminated the capital of two major banks and pushed capital adequacy ratios of 12 others to below the BIS (and the Republic of Korea) required minimum. In response, the authorities acted rapidly to provide funds to carve out bank problem loans and boost capital, while tightening prudential standards and initiating steps to restructure the banking system around a core of healthy institutions. Major emphasis was put on improving the accuracy and transparency of reporting by financial institutions as part of a broader effort to raise supervisory standards to international norms. Banks were required to submit detailed plans for restoring capital adequacy within two years, and several were forced to merge with healthier partners after their plans were rejected as inadequate by the authorities. Public outlays committed to the financial rescue reached 25 per cent of GDP by mid-2000, although the final cost will depend upon the amount of problem loans that are recovered. Capital adequacy has been restored to most banks, although profits remain low in many cases, due in part to increased loan provisioning.

Japan's banking problems first emerged in the early 1990s with the collapse of the stock market and real estate prices. To an extent that was underestimated by both the authorities and outside experts, banks had become heavily exposed to the real estate sector indirectly through lending to real estate companies. Despite the seriousness of the problems, official policy maintained a policy of forbearance for most of the following five years and the full extent of bank non-performing loans did not begin to become clear until quite recently. This policy seems to have been motivated by the potentially high cost of an official bail out, concerns that official intervention would weaken bank incentives to improve their lending practices, and hopes that asset prices would revive. The problems of the banking system continued to fester, however, and have been an important factor in the weak macroeconomic performance of the economy since the early 1990s. The authorities have had to apply continual macroeconomic stimulus to make up for weak domestic demand. But with monetary policy impaired by the problems of the banking sector, the burden has largely been borne by fiscal deficits that have brought government debt from a very moderate level in the early 1990s to above 100 per cent at present. As a result, public support to restore the banking system poses a much greater potential problem for public finances than it would have earlier. While the direct costs of Japan's banking crisis have yet to be tallied, it is clear that the indirect costs in terms of the economy's overall performance have been severe.

Finally, the *Czech Republic, Hungary, and Poland* have grappled with large non-performing loans of state-owned banks arising from circumstances similar in some respects to those in China. Problem loans in Hungary began to rise soon after the creation of the 3 major state owned banks in 1987, due in part to the collapse of Hungary's traditional Eastern European markets. The problems were not decisively addressed for some years in the hope that banks would grow out of the problems. Instead, the true level of non-performing loans was seriously underestimated; banks continued to roll over loans that were not being serviced; and banks were not required to set aside adequate provisions. By 1993, problem loans had risen to nearly 28 per cent of total bank loans. In response to the worsening situation, the authorities began a series of direct interventions of increasing intensity. Although these steps substantially improved the situation, it was not until the latter 1990s, following extensive privatisation and the development of a major foreign bank presence, that banking system health was firmly established.

Box 7.3. **OECD experiences with banking system distress** (*cont.*)

Governments in the Czech Republic and Poland intervened somewhat earlier in the development of problem bank loans. In late 1992, about two years after the creation of the post-transition banking system, the Czech authorities began a series of efforts to purchase problem loans, inject new capital, and require banks to increase provisions. Partly because of the ongoing financial weaknesses of enterprises, these efforts proved insufficient and problem loans reached nearly two-thirds of all bank loans by the end of 1997. Poland took a distinctive approach to the problem loans built up just before and during the early years of its transition. Although the government supplied substantial funds to raise bank capital, the banks were left to work out their problem loans within a government-imposed framework that encouraged enterprise debtors and creditors to arrive at loan restructuring agreements. The framework provided conciliation procedures under which debtors were required to submit detailed plans for repaying their loans in return for a bank agreement to defer payments, engage in debt-equity swaps, or other provisions to reduce the burden of debt service. Banks proved within this context to be good restructuring vehicles and a substantial portion of problem loans were dealt with by these means within a considerably shorter time than that required in Hungary.

---

*   In addition to the OECD surveys of these countries, useful analyses of particular country experiences can be found in OECD (1997), and OECD (1993). See also the overview by Hawkins and Turner (1999).

---

is the main source of weak SOE governance.[22] Improving the governance of the SOCBs is likely to be especially difficult given their central role in a range of government policies. Ownership diversification, seen as a key means of improving governance for JSBs (and at some point SOCBs), is also no panacea for the state banks' governance problems. This is particularly the case given that minority shareholders in China, even when they have fairly large stakes, tend to have little influence over the choice or discipline of banks' management, or strategic decisions taken by the enterprise.[23]

A broader question concerns the priority to be accorded to strengthening the SOCBs versus promoting the development of joint stock and other domestic commercial banks. Official statements and recent policies do not clearly define the ranking of these policies, nor do they indicate how they are to be reconciled. As with other reforms, government resources have been concentrated on the larger banks but this is not necessarily inconsistent with a longer-term strategy of reducing their dominance. The policy of requiring SOEs to maintain deposit accounts at one ("main") bank, while intended to prevent financial abuses, favours SOCBs (although the SOEs remain free to borrow from other banks). The authorities have indicated that they intend to continue to relax quantitative restrictions on branch expansion by JSBs and other smaller commercial banks. They also indicated that they may allow the entry of additional nationwide, possibly even private, banks at some future point – but no specific plans or timetable have been announced.[24, 25] The direction of policy with respect to the development of domestic bank alternatives to the SOCBs is likely to be quite important to the longer-term success of China's banking system reforms. Although both bank segments need to be bolstered in the medium-term, ultimately the relative size of the four majors will almost certainly have to decline if the new smaller banks are to come to play the role likely to be required for a more efficient financial system.

The current situation of foreign banks in China

Foreign banks have been expanding their presence in China since the authorities permitted their entry after reforms started in 1978. Foreign banks were first allowed to establish representative offices in 1979 and later were allowed to establish commercial branches in 1986. The foreign banks in China have faced strict geographical and customer limitations, which have been designed to protect the state commercial banks from "excessive" competition. The share of foreign banks in China's banking sector is thus currently very low. In 1999, foreign banks accounted for only about 2 per cent of the total bank assets in China. The currently unfavourable environment for foreign bank operation in China is, however, expected to change significantly following China's WTO entry. China's WTO commitments require the phasing out of several key restrictions on foreign bank operations over the next five years (see Annex I on China's WTO agreement). Partly as a preparation for WTO membership and also in the context of overall financial reform in China, the authorities have recently been gradually relaxing some of the regulations.

Regulatory treatment

Prior to WTO entry, the establishment and operation of foreign bank branches has been subject to the *Regulations on the Management of Foreign Financial Institutions* promulgated by the State Council in 1994. According to the *Regulations*, a foreign financial institution must first establish a non-operational representative office in order to enter the Chinese market. An application to establish a foreign bank branch can be made two years after opening the representative office. Among the various requirements, the foreign bank must have minimum global assets of US$20 billion; minimum registered capital of RMB 300 million; paid-up capital of at least 50 per cent of registered capital; and the operational capital of at least RMB 100 million in convertible foreign currencies. Prior to 1999 foreign bank branches were allowed in only 13 cities, but this geographical restriction has been removed since January 1999.

Apart from representative offices, foreign banks are allowed to operate through three organisational forms: branches, wholly owned subsidiaries, and Sino-foreign joint-venture banks. At the end of 1999, there were 248 representative offices, 157 foreign bank branches and 13 locally incorporated banks. The 157 foreign bank branches were established by 69 foreign international banks from 16 countries. Of the 13 locally incorporated foreign commercial banks, six were wholly owned and seven were joint venture banks. Among the largest foreign banks in China are the Bank of East Asia, the Hong Kong and Shanghai Banking Corporation (HSBC–mainly through its Hong Kong-based subsidiary Hang Seng Bank) and Standard Chartered Bank, all of which have long been present in China.

The business scope of foreign banks is severely limited due to the restrictions placed on the customer base and the lines of businesses that are permitted to them. Foreign banks, their branches, and foreign joint-venture banks are only allowed to provide services to foreign residents and foreign and joint-venture enterprises. Their business with Chinese corporations and individuals is generally limited to approved foreign currency lending, and import and export settlement services for Chinese enterprises. Even with their limited customers, foreign banks' activity is largely restricted to foreign currency business because their local currency (renminbi) operations are heavily constrained.[26] Prior to 1996, foreign banks were not allowed to accept renminbi deposits or to make renminbi loans.[27] In 1996, the PBC started permitting selected foreign banks to engage in limited renminbi services in the Pudong district of Shanghai. By 2000, the PBC had allowed a total of 32 foreign banks in Shanghai and Shenzhen to engage in renminbi services, including deposit-taking and lending, to foreign-invested enterprises and foreign residents.[28, 29] However, foreign banks with renminbi licenses are currently only allowed to receive renminbi deposits from foreign-funded enterprises and foreign residents. They are only allowed to extend renminbi loans and provide guarantee services to foreign-funded enterprises or to Chinese enterprises specifically authorised to receive such services.

Foreign banks also enjoy legal preferences *vis-à-vis* domestic banks, notably in tax treatment, similar to those accorded foreign investments in other areas. Foreign banks pay less than half the profit tax rate levied on domestic banks (15 per cent versus 33 per cent), are exempt from profit tax in the first year of operation, and enjoy further exemption on a declining basis through their fourth year of operation.

The current focus of foreign bank activities

The restrictions that the PBC has imposed have created a number of disadvantages for foreign banks *vis-à-vis* Chinese commercial banks, in particular in terms of customer base, branch networks, and deposits. On the other hand, foreign banks have comparative advantages in a number of other areas, *i.e.* good asset quality, superior skills and technology, international expertise, overseas networks and access to global markets, flexible management structures, and good risk control. These comparative advantages and disadvantages of foreign banks have shaped the current operation of foreign banks in China, which can be characterised by the following three main features.

First, due in large part to the restrictions placed on their customer base and geographical locations, foreign bank branches are mainly concentrated in the centres of foreign investment, *i.e.* large cities in the coastal area including Beijing, Shanghai, Shenzhen, Guangzhou, Tianjin, Dalian and Xiamen. The number of foreign bank branches in the five leading cities (Shanghai, Shenzen, Beijing, Guangzhou, and Tianjin) accounted for 75 per cent of the total number of foreign bank branches in China in 1999. But this geographical concentration is also related to the fact that their major customers are multinational corporations operating in these coastal cities.

The second set of features conditioning the current operations of foreign banks is their lack of stable and long-term renmimbi resources and the regulatory restrictions on their customer base. As a result, credit from a foreign bank office's offshore parent is the main source for its foreign currency loans. The amount of deposits held at foreign bank offices in China accounted for less than 1 per cent of total banking system deposits in 1999 and less than 0.1 per cent of renminbi deposits. Although foreign banks are allowed to borrow renminbi funds from Chinese banks on the interbank market, regulatory limits and the immature nature of the market have made it a costly and insufficient funding source. Borrowing from the market is limited to one and a half times an office's capital. The interest rates in China's interbank market tend to be relatively high, above the PBC lending rate as well as commercial bank deposit rates. The liquidity of the interbank market is low. Moreover, until 1999 foreign banks were only allowed to borrow short term, *i.e.* with the maturity limited to four months or less. This restriction was removed by the PBC in August 1999, and since then there has been a surge in foreign banks' renminbi fund raising. The weak deposit base, combined with small branch networks and the constraints on their customer base, have significantly restricted foreign banks' lending, with their loans accounting for 2 per cent of the domestic total in 1999. Foreign banks' renminbi lending has been further restricted by regulations specifying that renminbi loans may not exceed eight times (or in some cases four times) the branch capital, or be greater than 50 per cent of its foreign currency liabilities.

Although precise data on the operations of foreign banks in China are difficult to obtain, it is known that the Chinese operations of most foreign banks generate low profits, with a lower return on their equity than they typically earn elsewhere.[30] Even those foreign banks that have obtained renminbi licenses hardly make significant profits due to the heavy restrictions on their operations. Disappointing results have prompted some banks to withdraw from the market.[31]

The third feature is that most foreign banks in China have focused mainly on wholesale banking and have made significant inroads in areas including trade financing, foreign exchange transactions, and the underwriting of Chinese overseas listed equity and bonds. This largely reflects the various restrictions placed on their activities, but it also shows the comparative advantages foreign banks enjoy *vis-à-vis* Chinese domestic banks in these areas. Foreign banks have been the primary source of foreign currency loans for multinational corporations and trading companies, and by 2000 accounted for 23 per cent of all foreign currency denominated loans in China. Foreign banks also offer a range of other services to multinational corporations, which, combined with hard currency financing, are considered important to fostering and maintaining relationships with their customers worldwide. While foreign banks are not permitted to underwrite domestic securities, they are allowed to underwrite the overseas issuance of equity and bonds by Chinese enterprises. Although the overseas issuance of securities applies only to selected large SOEs with overseas operations, the number of these companies has recently been increasing rapidly. Foreign investment banks have dominated the underwriting business of Chinese overseas listed equity and bonds, taking up over 90 per cent of market share in this area.

Foreign banks also offer a range of products that are not usually offered by Chinese banks. Some foreign banks have been active in arranging loan syndication for working capital, property development, and project finance such as power and infrastructure projects.[32] Some foreign banks also offer hedging of loan and foreign-exchange risks through currency and interest-rate swaps, and supply other derivatives designed to reduce risk and increase flexibility in managing funds.

China has pledged to open up the banking sector to foreign competition within five years after its accession to the WTO (see Annex I). This opening is ultimately expected to redefine the activities of foreign banks and accord them in principle something approaching "national treatment". Foreign banks will be allowed to conduct local currency business to domestic individuals five years after China's accession to the WTO. In retail banking, the highly profitable segments of the market such as mortgage financing or fee-based businesses like credit cards will be most attractive to foreign banks. However, given the relatively low income level of Chinese households as well as the absence of tradition in consumer loans, it will take a while before foreign bank operation in this area justify the cost of establishing an extensive network. Although Internet technology might provide an advantage to foreign banks in this regard, the computer ownership of Chinese households is still low and telecom infrastructure is yet to be developed. Meanwhile, domestic banks are likely to try to acquire advanced technology and skills quickly, so that they are able to offer products competitive with those available from foreign banks to their established customers. Chinese banks have already started paying more attention to consumer loans and credit card business, as discussed in the last section.

However, WTO provisions do not directly affect several major current constraints on the ability of foreign banks to conduct local currency business. In particular, several regulatory provisions, including required ratios of foreign currency borrowing to domestic lending, and the ratio of domestic currency lending to an office's capital, are not ruled out by WTO provided they are not applied in a discriminatory manor. So long as these are maintained, the ability of foreign banks to fund domestic lending by swapping foreign currency or borrowing from the money market will remain quite limited. The restrictions will become less binding if foreign banks are able to attract substantial funds from Chinese enterprises, but the extent to which they will be able to do so is at least uncertain.

The advantages and strategies of multinational banks in other emerging markets

As noted in the introduction, the activities of foreign banks in host markets reflect the interaction among their intrinsic advantages versus host country banks, regulatory and market conditions within the host country, and global consideration shaping the activities of multinational banks more generally. In assessing how these factors are likely to work out in China, it is useful to review the specific factors that have shaped the activities of foreign banks in other countries, particularly in developing countries.

The increased international trade in goods and financial services has been accompanied by the expansion of the activities of multinational banks. Banks expand internationally by establishing foreign subsidiaries and branches or by taking over established foreign banks. The internationalisation of the banking sector has been facilitated by the liberalisation of financial markets worldwide. Both developed and developing countries now increasingly allow foreign ownership of domestic banks or the entry of foreign bank branches.

The extent of foreign ownership in the banking system differs greatly across the OECD countries. As seen in Table 7.5, the share of foreign banks (defined in most cases as banks with more than 50 per cent of foreign capital and branches of foreign banks) ranges from 52.6 per cent of total banking sector assets in the United Kingdom and 18.6 per cent in the United States, to less than 5 per cent in continental European countries such as Germany, Italy, Austria and Portugal.[33] The presence of foreign banks in emerging markets has increased considerably since the second half of the 1990s, although there have been divergent trends across different regions. The most rapid and extensive expansion of foreign ownership has been observed in some Eastern European countries, in particular Hungary, Poland and the Czech Republic (Box 7.4). Foreign participation in the banking system has also become substantial in recent years in Latin American countries, particularly in Argentina, Brazil and Mexico. In contrast, foreign participation in most Asian countries remains relatively low. In recent years, however, many Asian countries have also been in the process of deregulating their financial systems, and allowing more access of foreign investors and financial service providers to their domestic markets.

Why do banks enter and operate in other markets abroad? Theoretical and empirical literature on multinational banking has hypothesised a range of factors that drive foreign bank entry as well as the

Table 7.5.   **Foreign bank participation in selected OECD countries, 1998-1999**

	Share of foreign bank assets (%)		Share of foreign bank assets (%)
United States	18.6	Korea	6.3
Japan	5.3	Luxembourg	13.6
Germany	4.2	Mexico	18.6
Italy	4.0	Norway	5.8
United Kingdom	52.6	Portugal	4.0
Canada	6.6	Spain	4.5
		Sweden	5.8
Australia	9.8	Switzerland	6.5
Austria	3.8	Turkey	1.7
Belgium	7.4		
Denmark		Czech Republic	27.3
Finland	7.3	Hungary	56.6
Greece	13.4	Poland	47.2

Source: OECD, *Bank Profitability* 2000.

Box 7.4.   **Where foreign banks have a major share of the domestic market**

Foreign banks have acquired a major share of the domestic banking market in a number of Eastern European and Latin American countries, but the circumstances are somewhat special. Foreign controlled banks account for nearly 75 per cent of banking system capital in Hungary and roughly 44 per cent in Poland. The importance of these banks is a direct result of government policies to encourage foreign entry as a means of restoring and privatising the domestic banking sector in the wake of the problems suffered in the early 1990s (see Box 7.3). It also reflects the relatively small size and openness of the two economies and their close economic ties with the European Union – most of the foreign banks in the two countries come from other European countries. Foreign banks in Hungary and Poland tend to specialise in lending to long-standing multinational clients with operations in the countries, corporate services, investment banking, and other relatively sophisticated and profitable activities, while they have been selective and cautious in entering retail banking.

Foreign banks have long been present in the banking sectors of major Latin American countries but their participation increased sharply in the 1990s through a wave of acquisitions encouraged in some cases by a more receptive regulatory environment. Foreign banks now control nearly 50 per cent of bank assets in Argentina and Chile and smaller but substantial shares in a number of other countries. Foreign banks not only have a large aggregate market but also control some of the leading banking institutions in most major Latin American countries, except for Brazil. Cultural ties have provided a key impetus to the development of the foreign bank presence. The two largest Spanish Banks, Banco Santander Central Hispano (BSCH) and Banco Bilbao Vizcaya (BBV), have acquired controlling shares of nearly 30 major banks in ten Latin American countries, control nearly 40 per cent of the region's pension fund business, and have more employees in Latin America than in their home markets. In contrast, with the exception of Citibank and Bank of Boston, the role of banks from the United States is relatively limited. As in Eastern Europe, foreign banks in Latin America have traditionally focused heavily on business with large corporate customers. However, there are signs that this pattern is changing, as foreign banks in Argentina have recently been increasing their presence in traditional lending to SMEs and to individuals.

factors that determine the pattern of foreign banks' expansion abroad. One of the frequently raised issues concerns the sources of the comparative advantages that banks exploit in operating outside their home country and which enable them to profit from extending their operations into other national markets. Banks will establish facilities in foreign countries where they have some type of comparative advantage (Dunning, 1980; Yannopoulos, 1983). These comparative advantages derive from three basic sources.

First, a bank might find it desirable to establish operations overseas if it possesses ownership-specific advantages. These can include specialised banking services, creditworthiness, a reputation for efficiency, managerial skills, technological edges, economies of scale, and easy access to hard currencies. Large banks from developed countries are likely to be able to exploit these advantages in developing countries and thereby earn relatively high returns from entering those markets. For example, foreign banks with high asset quality might be valued by the domestic borrowers that seek a banking relationship as a means of "certifying" their business operations to the financial markets.

Second, a bank may be able to use its ownership-specific advantages to derive further internal advantages ("internalisation advantages") that it can exploit. Obtaining and preserving client information is one of the major sources of internalisation advantages for banks. If banks are to maintain accurate, up-to-date information on their overseas borrowers, having a direct overseas presence may be crucial to overcoming asymmetric information problems. Also, following their clients to overseas markets can serve to enhance the information capital that has been built up. Thus, multinational banks can exploit the advantages they acquire as they build up informational capital through their operations linking different national markets. Informational advantages and access to the deposit bases in different national markets can give multinational banks superior capabilities in maturity transformation. Banks with a large and geographically diverse customer base will be able to reduce transaction costs by bringing together customers with offsetting needs. A network of foreign assets can also contribute to lower variability in earnings for a multinational bank as compared with a domestic bank.

Third, country specific endowments can confer location-specific advantages in the host country. In general, banks are likely to be at a disadvantage in information production when operating overseas due to lack of familiarity with the local market, but the presence of customer groups with which they are already familiar (*e.g.* multinational corporations) will help to overcome this disadvantage. Following multinationals into a particular country represents a location-specific advantage. Given the existence of a prior relationship, these banks have informational advantages over other banks. In addition, growth opportunities arise for these banks from the expansion of multinational corporations in the foreign markets. The "follow-the-client" hypothesis predicts that foreign banks provide services in countries with high levels of FDI from the home country. A number of empirical studies have identified the expansion of direct trade and investment ties to a country by multinational corporations as one of the most important motivations behind the entry of foreign banks (Parkhe and Miller 1998, Nigh *et al.* 1986). Opportunities to service trade-related business are an important inducement for the range of American banks with branches abroad (Goldberg and Johnson, 1990). One study found that the growth of foreign banks in China during the period between 1980 and 1994 was largely determined by the growth in trade and FDI (Leung, 1997). That is, most foreign banks entering the Chinese market followed their multinational clients in trade and investment.

In addition to the advantages based on the relationship with multinationals, country-specific regulations and entry restrictions can also confer other location-specific advantages to certain banks. The host country's laws and regulations can strongly influence the advantages enjoyed by foreign banks, and have been an important factor in determining the degree and type of foreign bank activity. For example, the activity of US banks abroad is to a large extent determined by the host country's regulatory action (Goldberg and Johnson, 1990). The economic and financial conditions of the host country may also affect the advantages enjoyed by foreign banks. Foreign banks might be interested in entering a country with large growth potential. They are also likely to be drawn to foreign locations where local banking conditions are relatively favourable. For example, exploiting the window of opportunity created by the poor conditions of many domestic US banks in the 1980s, many foreign banks entered the US corporate banking market and increased their market share by extending both domestic and international credit. However, as the US banking industry started to restructure and consolidate and became increasingly competitive, foreign banks had to find niche strategies offering high returns in order to survive (Walton, 1994). The potential opportunities in the domestic market, and not simply the prospect of profits from servicing multinationals, were an important factor encouraging foreign banks to enter the markets of Japan and the Republic of Korea (Ursacki and Vertinsky, 1992).

Once foreign banks establish operations within a country, however, the degree and type of their activities can differ considerably. For example, some banks may choose to focus on off-balance-sheet business, such as foreign exchange trading, rather than making loans. The strategic orientation of the parent bank can strongly affect the degree and type of activities of foreign bank operations outside the home market. In particular, marketing and product strategies influence the decisions as to which products from the home office can be transferred profitability to other markets, as well as the specific market niche a bank targets. The geographical interests of the parent bank may also influence the rate at which its growth objectives are implemented in different countries.

The wholesale market has been an important factor in FDI in banking since the 1960s, as have the markets for trade finance and services to corporate clients for a much longer period. The main operations performed by multinational banks include: corporate financing; foreign exchange trading; trade finance; project financing; securities dealing; certain non-finance activities; and leasing. In the case of US banks, branches were initially set up to serve the multinational clients of the head office. Retail banking, especially deposit taking, has not been a major focus for foreign branch activity, largely because of the restrictions that host countries impose, as well as the disadvantages in competing with the networks of local banks. The bulk of profits for foreign banks have come from wholesale banking, which has justified the cost of maintaining a branch. Typical borrowers have been multinational corporations of industrialised countries, banks, and governments of developing countries. As such, foreign branches in the major financial centres have been increasingly engaged in loan syndication, loan management, leasing, project financing, and other activities geared to the large, complex, and often risky lending required for major industrial projects or general economic development. Corporate money management, a service introduced in the 1970s for multinational corporations, has increased in importance and is bringing a steady-fee income for international banks. Banks also provide fee-based advice and assistance on setting up acquisitions and mergers or on investing in US companies, and sell advisory services on foreign stock investments to trust departments of client financial institutions.

While retail activities have tended to be considered as least important, partly because of heavy regulatory restrictions as well as high set-up costs, some banks, notably Citibank, have been more aggressive in entering into retail banking in overseas markets. Since the 1960s, Citibank has pursued an explicit strategy of international retail banking, establishing such operations wherever regulations permit. But other banks who have established retail operation abroad (for example, Barclays Bank, Chase Manhattan, Bank of America, and the Hong Kong, China and Shanghai Bank) seem to have done so as a result of historic accident or passive acceptance of such opportunities, rather than as a result of following a deliberate strategy (Tschoegl, 1987). In many other cases, retail banking developed out of trade finance or to follow established customers, activities that permitted the bank to learn the local environment and enabled it to acquire local retail operations when an opportunity arose. This "opportunistic" strategy can be contrasted with a more deliberate strategy whereby the parent bank establishes and maintains such retail operations in the expectation that it has advantages in terms of managerial and technical skills sufficient to overcome the problems of operating in an unfamiliar environment against local competitors with initially superior networks and information.

Since the early 1990s, there has been a large shift in multinational bank strategies, and subsequently the nature of the activity of multinational banks has undergone significant changes. Partly because of the international lending market, which has become extremely competitive and whose profit margins have gone down to nearly nil, but also in response to the increasing complexity of the international market and capital adequacy requirements, many branches have been cutting costs and diversifying their business away from a reliance on traditional lending and deposit-taking. As banks continue to search for higher returns and strive to define, measure, and manage risks effectively, they have been performing fewer traditional functions and instead have been increasing their off-balance-sheet activities, which require less capital coverage and are fee based. Banks have been evolving into "financial service companies" that face lower risks than those entailed by traditional lending, and entering markets traditionally occupied by insurance companies. One good example of the successful turnaround of this kind is Chase Manhattan: In order to survive, Chase Manhattan bundled together three businesses – regional retail banking, national financial services, and global investment banking. It

253

has given up retail banking overseas, and the bank's earnings from global wholesale banking now account for a growing proportion of earnings. It expects to earn more from fee income and less from the holding of loans. The foreign exchange, derivatives, and debt-trading markets are already a considerable proportion and a fast growing proportion of total of revenues. The bank states that its future strategy is to become an intermediary in capital flows, adding value in processing transactions, hedging, translating currencies, and providing advice (Khambata, 1996).

The move toward developing fee-based services and securitisation is expected to dominate the global strategy of multinational banks as they continue to move out of the shrinking core of traditional banking. These banks will continue to emphasise off-balance-sheet, liquid and other high quality transactions that do not tie up capital and which involve limited exposure to risk. Activities with these characteristics include foreign exchange trading, leasing services, currency futures and options, and fee services. Other alternatives include long-term swaps, cash management services, capital raising advice, customised financial packages, and acting as agents in putting parties or deals together or as lead manager in syndications. A new area of fee income relates to trade financing; banks put together transactions such as counter trade and bartering deals and receive a fee by participants. As investors prefer the capital market for raising money, banks also collect lucrative fees for handling issues. Banks will be increasingly looking for lending opportunities that involve more than just lending, such as expertise, management, and advisory services for which they can charge fees. Project financing has become attractive because it entails putting together a financing plan and package for which the bank can levy a charge.

Multinational bank strategies in other Asian emerging economies

The way banks have sought to apply these strategies in Asian emerging markets is of particular interest for assessing their likely strategies in China once their access is liberalised. Banking in Asia has been characterised by a high degree of government control and various discriminatory measures have been imposed on foreign bank operation by the respective governments and regulatory bodies. The participation of foreign banks in the domestic banking business in Asian countries is still low, although there are cross-country differences (Lang and So, 2001). Hong Kong, China and Singapore provide the most liberal environment, with least discrimination against the operations of foreign banks. In a number of other Asian countries, major restrictions limit the business activities of foreign banks, as well as the number of their branches and the amount of credit they can extend. Recently, however, particularly in the wake of the 1997 Asian financial crisis, many Asian countries have been in the process of deregulating their financial systems, and opening up their domestic markets to foreign banks and investors.

Due largely to the restrictions imposed on branching, lending, and funding, foreign banks have had to develop their own market niches. Most foreign banks in Asian countries have focused on wholesale and investment banking, making use of their comparative advantages in technology, international banking experience and networks (see Table 7.6). In most countries, foreign banks are particularly focused on the financing and provision of foreign exchange services. Highly open economies such as Malaysia represent huge market opportunities to foreign banks in these areas because of the importance of international trade to the economy. In Thailand, foreign banks have focused on wholesale banking, with trade financing and foreign exchange becoming their major business. Foreign banks in Indonesia also concentrate on corporate lending, trade finance and foreign exchange, although they are permitted to accept deposits and make local currency loans.[34] Foreign banks in India are required to allocate a minimum percentage of their loan portfolio to export and other designated priority sectors. Because of these restrictions, foreign banks tend to focus on trade finance, corporate lending to large business groups, wholesale banking, and investment services such as financial consulting. Even in a relatively free market such as that of Japan, foreign banks find it difficult to acquire business from domestic enterprises and tend to focus on business with clients from their home countries and to emphasise high value-added activities in preference to more conventional credit products.

Table 7.6. **Niche Business Activities of Foreign Banks in East Asian Economies**
Panel A: Niche Banking Activities

East Asian Economies	Project financing	Trade financing	Foreign exchange	Wholesale banking	Investment/off-shore banking	Retail banking	Corporate lending
Cambodia		✔*	✔				✔
China		✔	✔*	✔			✔
Hong Kong, China			✔	✔*	✔		✔
India		✔*		✔	✔	✔	✔
Indonesia		✔*	✔				✔
Japan		✔	✔*	✔			✔
Laos		✔	✔*				✔
Malaysia		✔	✔	✔		✔*	
Myanmar	✔*						
Philippines		✔	✔	✔	✔		
Singapore		✔	✔	✔*	✔	✔	✔
South Korea				✔	✔	✔	
Taiwan				✔		✔	✔
Thailand		✔	✔	✔*	✔		
Vietnam		✔*	✔	✔			

* Primary activity.
Source: Lang and So (2001).

Overall, foreign banks tend to have very limited retail business in Asia. Retail banking has been ignored to a large extent due to lack of branch networks, along with regulatory restrictions on their local currency deposit-taking in many cases. Foreign bank retail branches are very often used mainly to serve their home-country clients and their employees. An apparent exception is Malaysia, where foreign banks have taken a substantial share of the retail business, despite major restrictions imposed on foreign bank operation. However, this has been possible because some foreign banks (such as HSBC, Overseas Chinese Banking Corporation, Standard Chartered, and Citibank) which built extensive retail networking during the period of British rule have been allowed to retain those networks despite a subsequent regulation restricting operations of others to a single branch. These banks have been successful in competing in the local retail market because of their financial strength, efficient services, and international reputations. Other foreign banks in Malaysia, however, engage heavily in wholesale and international banking. Even in the absence of restrictions, foreign banks have also often stayed away from retail banking in markets where, as in Hong Kong, China, local banks are very strong competitors.

When foreign banks do engage in retail banking, they tend to target a specific segment, usually high value-added, of the retail market. For example, in India, the retail banking business of foreign banks usually targets high-value activities such as ATM services and mobile banking, and Internet banking to non-residents and the more affluent local people. In the Republic of Korea, where some lending and branching restrictions remain, foreign banks such as Citibank have reacted by concentrating their retail business in the capital city, and do not operate extensive branching networks throughout the country. Even so, investment and wholesale banking remain major sources of business for foreign banks in the Republic of Korea. In Chinese Taipei, the recent lifting of a number of regulatory restrictions has encouraged foreign banks to look to retail banking services, such as consumer loans and credit cards, as new profitable niches where they can exploit their advantages.

Prospects for China's banking system in light of expanded participation by foreign banks

This section attempts to assess the implications of the three sets of factors for the development of foreign and Chinese banks in the aftermath of liberalisation. The time horizon is the medium term (say five years) after foreign banks are allowed to engage in domestic currency lending with businesses (*i.e.* two to three years after accession under current terms of China's WTO agreement). As argued below, foreign banks are likely to assume an important but limited place in the Chinese market, one

Table 7.7. **Summary of comparative advantages and disadvantages of Chinese and foreign banks**

	Chinese banks		Foreign banks
	SOCB	JSB *and other*	
Advantages	Knowledge of market and customers Close ties to domestic customers Priority role with government		Skills, technology and products Access to global markets Financial strength Ties to foreign enterprises
	Access to funding Dominant market position Government preferences		
Disadvantages	Weak financial positions Weak credit assessment and control capabilities Limited skills and technology Limited product lines		Limited ties to local market Limited access to local currency
	Extensive government intervention	Limited branch networks and other access to funding	

Source: OECD Secretatiat.

comparable to that now prevailing in other Asian emerging economies. However, the possibility that foreign banks, even with a limited share of the market, will have serious adverse impacts on the financial performances of Chinese banks cannot be ruled out. Whether or not this occurs will depend critically on how the overall banking system develops, and in particular on the evolution of the third, "external" set of factors.

Three preliminary observations can be made on the basis of the previous discussions of the present situation of domestic and foreign banks in China, together with the review of the approaches foreign banks have taken in other emerging markets. First, foreign banks have intrinsic comparative advantages in China (ownership specific and localisation) qualitatively similar to those they enjoy in other countries, but with some differences in degree. In particular, foreign banks enjoy superior technical skills and products over Chinese banks in a wide range of areas (see Table 7.7). They have the added advantages of extensive access to international financial markets as well as to their home markets, and close ties to foreign enterprises that have, or will have, operations in China. Moreover, banks owned and largely managed by ethnic Chinese in Hong Kong, China and several other economies have advantages of cultural familiarity and ties to Chinese customers similar to those that have fostered the success of Spanish banks in Latin America. Foreign banks' advantages are further magnified, more than in many other emerging economies, by the low profitability, poor balance sheet quality, and weak ability to control credit quality of Chinese banks. Their advantages are also enhanced by the growing importance of foreign trade and investment to China's economy, although probably not to the same degree as in more open economies such as Malaysia, Thailand, and the Philippines. Against these advantages, Chinese banks have major strengths in terms of their knowledge of the market, access to deposit and other funding sources, and their priority role in the implementation of government policies, such as infrastructure spending.

If these advantages alone were determining, there would be little to prevent foreign banks from gaining a major share of the market in China, even one comparable to that they have achieved in several Eastern European and Latin American countries. However, three conditions in the banking market in China are likely to play a key limiting role, even more in some respects than in other emerging markets. These are regulatory policies mentioned earlier that limit foreign banks' ability to exchange foreign currency for renminbi and to make renminbi loans; the limited development of domestic money markets; and the poor financial conditions and limited transparency of Chinese enterprises. Improvement in the first two conditions is critical to the ability of foreign banks to expand in areas requiring local currency funding where they have advantages. Poor financial conditions and limited transparency are likely to keep foreign banks from lending to most domestic enterprises until conditions improve considerably. These constraints are likely to be most important in the medium term and diminish over a longer period as financial liberalisation and the development of domestic financial markets proceeds, and enterprise financial performances improve. However, changes in these areas depend on broader considerations, such as policies toward capital account liberalisation and progress on enterprise reforms.

Global considerations are likely to act as a further restraining force on the expansion of foreign banks in China. Foreign bank activities in host countries are conditioned by the need to conserve capital, earn a return commensurate with that available in alternative uses (as well as that required to raise additional capital in home or international markets), and limit their risk exposures. To date, foreign banks in China have been willing to endure low profitability in large part because of their limited commitment of capital and the potential opportunities from liberalised participation in a large and growing market. However, the profit threshold may well rise after liberalisation as foreign banks have to commit additional capital to expand their activities. This is likely to accentuate foreign banks' tendency to be selective in expanding their activities, since high profit opportunities in traditional banking are presently comparatively limited in China. Regulatory policies in foreign banks' home markets are likely to act as a further restraint. Lending by foreign bank branches to Chinese enterprises with weak financial positions or limited transparency – even if the enterprises were prepared to take the risk – would be unlikely to meet prudential requirements applied by regulators in many OECD countries.

Where foreign banks are likely to make greatest (and least) inroads

The three sets of factors discussed in the last section, together with consideration of the key "inputs" required to produce various bank products, provide a rough framework for assessing the relative competitive strengths of foreign and Chinese banks in various banking activities. For example, lending to domestic enterprises requires ample and reasonably priced access to local currency funding and reasonably good knowledge of the operations and conditions of the borrower – both clear advantages of Chinese banks. However, the ability to provide cash and risk management services and access to foreign markets – in which foreign banks have the main advantage – is also important in attracting large multinational enterprise customers. Accordingly, Chinese banks' comparative advantage in lending to these enterprises is probably less than in lending to medium-sized enterprises. Foreign banks have a more clear-cut advantage in risk management tools and other sophisticated products where high-technology innovation skills and experience are critical.

Table 7.8 summarises the implications for the relative strengths of the foreign banks in terms of their intrinsic comparative advantages, global strategies, and the external environment. This provides an indication of where foreign banks are most likely to make significant inroads. For example, foreign banks are clearly disadvantaged in lending to domestic enterprises, although somewhat less so in lending to the largest. However, given their global strategies and the poor risk/return profile resulting from the weak financial conditions and limited transparency of domestic enterprises, foreign banks are likely to largely avoid lending to Chinese businesses, at least initially. Moreover, while foreign banks may make some inroads in lending to Chinese businesses once the external environment improves, Chinese banks, given their intrinsic advantages, are likely to retain a dominant share. Apart from the important area of credit card services, foreign banks are also unlikely to become major players in consumer lending, at least not for a considerable time after full liberalisation.

In contrast, foreign banks have the potential to make large inroads in domestic currency lending to foreign joint ventures, which, as noted in the last section, is one of the greatest incentives for them to expand operations in China. They are potentially limited in this area, however, by their access to local currency funding. They are also likely to continue to dominate foreign currency lending to foreign joint ventures. Foreign banks are also likely to become major players in foreign exchange services, management consulting, cash and risk management, and in at least some securities related activities. Compared to local currency lending, these activities are much less hampered by limited access to local currency funds and expose much less bank capital. The prospects of further privatisation and economic

Table 7.8. **Summary of factors shaping foreign bank prospects in China**
Factors affecting foreign bank strategies in China

Business line	Comparative advantage	Global priority	External constraints	Size of market	Growth potential	Main domestic competitor
Core lending						
Leading SOE	Medium	Low	H:R,P,F	Large	Average	SOCB
Other SOE	Low	Low	H:P,F,R	Large	Low-average	SOCB
Non state enterprises	Low	Low	H:P,R	Moderate	High	JSB
Foreign JVs	High	High	L	Moderate	High	All
Consumer lending	Medium	Low	M:F	Small	High	All
Infrastructure finance	Low	Low	M:R,F	Large	Average	SOCB
Foreign exchange services	High	High	L	Moderate	High	SOCB
Securities and investment banking	High	High	M:R	Small	High	SOCB
Risk and cash management services	High	High	L	Small	High	All
Intermediary services	Medium-high	Moderate	L	Moderate	High	All

Notes: H, M, L: high, medium, or low limiting factor overall; R: regulatory; P: poor financial conditions; F: access to local currency; All: all domestic Chinese banks.
Source: OECD Secretatiat.

restructuring in China present a good opportunity for investment banking. The initial public offerings (IPOs) of large Chinese SOEs have been active recently and are expected to accelerate further as the Chinese government continues to pursue the privatisation process of Chinese SOEs. As discussed earlier, foreign investment banks have already captured the bulk of the underwriting business of Chinese overseas listed equity and bonds. Based on their comparative advantage in this area, they are likely to continue to capture a significant share of the domestic market in this highly profitable business area.

While indicative, this depiction is admittedly oversimplified. There is considerable diversity in the specific activities under each of the major headings in Table 7.8. Foreign banks, SOCBs, and JSB/CCB are each likely to find specific "niches" in most of the major areas in which they have a substantial share. All three segments have potentially important advantages in particular securities-related activities: for example, SOCBs are likely to be leading actors in arranging domestic mergers and acquisitions, while foreign banks provide risk management, advisory, and other ancillary products to facilitate deals.

Even more important, the three sets of factors are also subject to change over time. As has happened in other countries, domestic Chinese banks are likely to absorb skills, innovations, and technology brought in by their foreign competitors. This absorption process will increase their competitiveness versus the foreign banks over time. It is changes in the external environment, however, that will largely shape the development and performance of foreign and domestic banks. This environment is likely to change markedly over the next decade, in ways that will be shaped not only by China's trade and investment liberalisation but also by the content of economic reforms. In particular, foreign banks' participation in domestic lending is likely to expand if and when Chinese enterprises, particularly those that are listed, improve their corporate governance and meet the prudential standards imposed by the foreign banks' business strategies.

A key point suggested by Table 7.8 is that foreign banks have a comparative advantage in most of the activities that, given the direction of current policies, have the most favourable market growth prospects. This is partly because foreign-invested enterprises are likely to be one of the most rapidly growing segments of the business sector. In addition, demand for the sophisticated foreign exchange, cash, and risk management products foreign banks can offer, while quite limited now, is likely to grow rapidly as China's enterprises increase their international activities and improve their financial management systems. These activities also tend to be among the most profitable. The main potentially "high growth" activities where Chinese banks have an advantage are consumer lending and lending to non-state enterprises. The future profitability of consumer lending may well be limited by competition among the banks, however, which is likely to be particularly intense in this area. The profitability of lending to non-state enterprises is currently limited by the difficulty of assessing their credit worthiness, their often poor financial conditions, and to some extent by the smaller scale of their average borrowing.

In contrast, lending to SOEs, currently the largest market in which Chinese banks have a clear comparative advantage, also has the weakest longer-term growth prospects and currently quite low profitability. The weak longer-term growth in the SOE market reflects the prospective further decline in their share of the economy as reforms to "let go" all but the largest enterprises proceed. The medium-term prospects for this segment are potentially better, given that the *effective* size of the SOE loan market, that is the enterprises that are capable of borrowing on commercial terms, is now sharply restricted by the fact that a large segment of enterprises are not creditworthy. Success in SOE reforms, along with improvement in banks' capabilities to service non-state enterprises, make the potential for growth in loan markets where domestic banks have a comparative advantage much more favourable.

These patterns suggest two related observations concerning the development of China's banks. First, current efforts to expand non-core lending activities, while important to diversify the banks' activities, are unlikely to be panaceas for their currently low profitability, since they are likely to face stiff competition from foreign banks in most of these areas. Second, improvement in the profitability and exploitation of the opportunities for lending to enterprises, particularly in the most rapidly growing areas, are the key to more profitable performance of the domestic banks. Improvement in this area will also be conditioned by how SOE financial conditions develop. These points are illustrated by the scenarios for the development of China's banking system outlined below.

Scenarios: share of market or share of profits?

Two scenarios illustrate how the factors discussed above may interact to shape the development of China's banking system and its main segments over the next five to ten years. These scenarios are driven by different assumptions about developments in external environment of the banks, including regulatory policies and economic reforms. In each scenario, the banks are assumed to continue to cut costs, upgrade efficiency, expand the range of their products, and to improve their internal systems for assessing and managing credit risk. However their efforts are conditioned by their profitability and by external conditions, both of which differ among the scenarios. The scenarios are not intended as a prediction. Rather they are intended to suggest the range of possible outcomes and circumstances likely to be associated with them. However, they serve to underscore the critical role policies toward the banking system together with broader economic reforms are likely to play in determining how China's banks will fare in response to foreign competition.

In the first scenario, enterprise and banking sector economic reforms continue at a gradual pace, consistent with the targets in present policies but with no major new initiatives. As has been the case, resources for SOE reform remain heavily concentrated on the largest enterprises, with much less for small and medium-sized SOEs or non-state enterprises. Enterprise restructuring efforts, the development of SMEs and the formation of new enterprises continue, but are still seriously hampered by government intervention and regional protectionism. Partly as a result, the financial performance of the SOE sector improves only slowly, with a large segment of enterprises still making losses or only marginal profits after liberalisation. Performance in some sectors, such as automobiles, may worsen in the medium term, as the impact of foreign competition is manifest. While continuing to grow relative to SOEs, non-state enterprises continue to suffer serious financial problems, as well as regulatory and other obstacles to their restructuring and development. The government provides only a limited amount of additional financial injections to the SOCBs, although JSB balance sheets have improved sufficiently to allow the listing of most by the time the full liberalisation of foreign bank participation is implemented. The authorities seek to limit inroads on the SOCBs and to that end PBC funding to the JSBs/CBs continues to be disproportionately low and their activities continue to be significantly limited. The money market expands slowly, in part because authorities liberalise lending rates gradually and only partially in order to avoid a squeeze on loan margins that would adversely affect the SOCBs. JSBs – whose number is increased further by the formation of several private or quasi-private banks – become increasingly commercially oriented in their operations. Modern governance structures are established for the SOCBs and their ownership is diversified somewhat. However, the impact of these reforms is limited by continued government intervention in their lending and other decisions.

The outcome for the banking system in this scenario is likely to be one of slow and restricted development, in which there is only limited change in the problematic features described earlier. While avoiding lending to domestic enterprises virtually completely, and confining their activities to coastal provinces, foreign banks gain a major share of the loan market for foreign-invested enterprises, and establish major and growing positions in foreign exchange and "off-balance-sheet" activities requiring wide access to international markets and sophisticated skills. As in other emerging economies, foreign banks are generally more profitable than local banks. The situation for JSBs is likely to be more problematic. Healthier balance sheets and better management should raise their competitive advantages, but their ability to exploit those advantages is likely to be limited by their restricted access to funding and by continued difficulties in finding sufficient creditworthy non-state enterprises to lend to. The JSBs are likely to be further squeezed as foreign banks take a significant amount of JSBs' loan business with foreign invested enterprises and limit their expansion in profitable fee and other off-balance-sheet activities. They may be further squeezed to the extent that the government attempts to limit their activities to protect the SOCBs. The SOCBs remain dominant in the financial system but very weak financially. Despite some success in diversifying away from core lending, profitability remains quite low. With very limited ability to write down bad loans, NPLs remain a serious problem and vulnerable to further increase if financial performances in automobiles and other sectors are sufficiently badly hit by foreign competition. In terms of effective governance and management, the SOCBs remain partly government agencies, and only partly commercial institutions. This mixed orientation impairs the effectiveness of efforts to improve credit quality and to expand lending to non-state enterprises.

From one superficial perspective, this scenario appears favourable: foreign banks do not take a major share of the overall market and Chinese banks retain a dominant position. However, the outcome is much less favourable in fundamental terms. Although foreign banks' share of the banking market is, by conventional measures, limited, their share of the total profits of the banking system is likely to be substantially larger. Given that growth in total banking system profits is likely to be constrained by the problems of the banks' customers, there is a real possibility that the profitability of Chinese banks could actually fall further. More broadly, despite the breathing space they may seem to gain from limited foreign bank expansion, Chinese banks' fundamental ability to compete does not greatly improve, and the opportunities for banks as a whole remain constricted. In addition, there is little improvement in the major weaknesses of the banking system in carrying out its economic functions. Credit allocation is still inefficient, with an oversupply to SOEs and coastal provinces, and insufficient supply to non-state enterprises and interior provinces. Financial discipline remains weak in key areas. And the financial weaknesses of the banks pose a potential risk to financial stability.

A second and much more favourable scenario is based on greater improvement in enterprise performances and more rapid and broader financial reforms than in the first. Enterprise profits recover rapidly over the five years following liberalisation, due in part to moves to decisively end government interference in enterprise management, to allow market forces greater play in enterprise restructuring, and to implement targeted programmes to improve access to financing. The non-state sector also grows faster than in the first scenario, and its growth in interior provinces is particularly rapid. Government authorities provide further injections of funds in the near-term with a view to reducing SOCB NPLs to below 10 per cent within several years, and in the same timeframe take decisive steps to end policy lending and place SOCB operations on a purely commercial footing. These measures, together with the nationwide adoption of the new loan classification system, the upgrading of internal accounting and reporting standards at banks and enterprises, lead to a substantial improvement in banks' ability to assess credit quality and to identify good credit risks. The authorities also promote the rapid expansion of the money market by liberalising loan interest rates and relaxing restrictions on access and maximum positions allowed. They also accord JSBs/CBs equal treatment relative to SOCBs in lending by the PBC, and in the permitted scope of their activities.

In this second scenario, the business of all three major segments, foreign banks, SOCBs, and JSBs/ CBs is likely to grow significantly more rapidly than in the first. Better access to funding and improved prospects for non-state enterprises and SME SOEs should allow JSBs (and to a lesser extent city commercial banks) to significantly increase their market share. Foreign banks are also likely to gain more market share than in the first scenario and may start to expand, if selectively, into lending to domestic enterprises. While gains by the other two segments will gradually erode SOCB dominance, the improved condition of SOEs should provide a near-term expansion in the effective market for lending to these enterprises. While foreign banks are likely to have a somewhat larger overall share of the market than in the first case, it is likely to remain close to that in other Asian countries, and domestic banks as a whole should continue to have the leading role.

Equally important, total profits of the banking sector are likely to be substantially greater in this second scenario, and the profitability of both groups of domestic banks should be higher. Thus, despite their greater share of the market, foreign banks are likely to have a smaller share of overall banking profits. For the domestic banks, a somewhat smaller share of a bigger and better market generates more profits than the larger share of the less favourable market associated with the first scenario. Access by non-state enterprises, SME SOEs, and enterprises in interior provinces is also better than in the first scenario, and credit standards are more uniform and more effective in sustaining financial discipline over enterprises. Lower NPLs, higher capital, and improved profitability of domestic banks reduces the risks to financial stability in the overall economy.

The difference between the scenarios cannot be ascribed entirely to government policies and depends importantly on developments in the overall economy, such as the growth in world markets and success of the business strategies of Chinese enterprises in dealing with increased foreign competition, neither of which are easy to control or predict. However, these scenarios underscore two basic points. The first is that the development of Chinese banks in the face of increased foreign competition depends less on the intrinsic advantages they now possess than on their future ability to exploit those advantages. In order to do so, the banks need to be restored to financial soundness, and the government interference that now impairs their ability to control credit quality and diversify their activities needs to be ended. Second, the development of both Chinese and foreign banks depends upon improvement in the quality of the markets that the banks serve. In this respect, the fate of China's banks and the development of the banking system depend importantly on the success of broader reforms to improve business performance and remove distortions in the real economy.

Conclusions and recommendations

The analysis in this paper suggests two basic conclusions concerning the impact of liberalised foreign bank participation in the Chinese market. The first is that while foreign banks will almost certainly expand their access in China and come to play an important role in the banking system, they are very unlikely to dominate major domestic business segments, with the exception of lending to foreign-invested enterprises. The intrinsic advantages of Chinese banks with domestic customers, constraints imposed by their global strategies on lines they are likely to enter, and limited access to local funding, are likely to result in a foreign bank share in line with that in other Asian countries. Moreover, foreign banks are likely at some point to lose some of their initial market share gains as domestic banks become more sophisticated over time, and providing their financial soundness is restored and maintained.

The second conclusion is that foreign bank entry itself poses less of a risk to the future performance of Chinese banks than two other "home grown" conditions. These are the weak financial positions of the domestic banks and their impaired capacity to control credit quality; and the distortions in the external environment that limit the quality of the market for the services of all banks, but especially blunt the intrinsic comparative advantages of the domestic banks. Without significant improvement in these conditions – especially the first – within the next several years, there is a risk that foreign bank entry could add to the weakness of domestic banks. The benefits foreign banks can bring to the domestic banking system are also likely to be restricted in this case, in part because foreign banks will most probably limit their alliances with domestic banks and other activities where such transfers of expertise are most likely to occur. These risks should recede if reforms to improve the two conditions are reasonably successful. In that case, domestic banks would probably become more profitable and the role of JSBs and CBs would be likely to expand even as the market share of foreign banks also increases. The overall banking system would then be more competitive and efficient, and the allocation of credit and financial disciplined would improve.

The analysis in this chapter has suggested several priority steps for banking reforms that will help to improve the prospect for such a "win-win" outcome from foreign bank entry. The success of these steps will be further enhanced by progress on reforms affecting the banks' customers that are discussed in other chapters. In rough order of importance and urgency, the priorities for banking reforms are as follows.

- Accelerate the restoration of financial soundness to the domestic banks, using further injections of government funds as necessary. A reasonable goal would be to reduce NPLs of SOCBs, JSBs and CCBs to no greater than 10 per cent by the time restrictions on foreign bank local currency lending to domestic enterprises are lifted, and to concurrently raise their capital levels to at least 8 per cent initially.[35] As far as possible, government support should be structured to provide incentives (*e.g.* by making permission to expand into new activities conditional on reforms) for banks to strengthen their governance structures and to develop and sustain improvements in lending standards, loan monitoring, and risk management. To this end, banks should be required to set aside adequate provisions, to write-off problem loans according to prudential standards (rather than subject to approval by the Ministry of Finance) and, over time, to raise capital adequacy ratios toward the levels prevailing in other emerging market economies.

  As discussed further in Chapter 14 on the financial system, and in Chapter 22 on macroeconomic implications, such a programme will involve a substantial increase in government debt but, provided other feasible steps are taken to bolster public finances, should not pose a risk to fiscal soundness. Delay in comprehensive financial restructuring of the banks is likely to increase the ultimate cost, undermine current reforms to improve the incentives and performance of domestic banks, and impair their ability to deal with increased foreign competition.

- Pursue a more active strategy to encourage the development of JSBs, CBs, and possibly new banks and increase their scope and overall share of the market. In particular, regulatory constraints that disadvantage JSBs and CBs should be phased out. City banks, starting perhaps with the larger banks in interior provinces, could be authorised to expand their business beyond their current jurisdictions. While likely to remain the largest players for the foreseeable future, the decline in market share of the SOCBs should be regarded as a natural and desirable development and a more explicit strategy to manage this downsizing could help in improving their performance. At the least, expansion of SOCBs into new lines of business should be made conditional on targets for improvement in their financial performance. Dividing SOCBs into one or more independent subsidiary units could benefit their overall performance as well as improve competition, and should be given consideration.[36]

  The difficulty of reforming the SOCBs makes expansion of the scope for JSBs and other banks all the more important to improving the commercial functioning of the banking system and ensuring that all enterprise segments have adequate access to bank lending. The key priority is to increase the share of new funds going to and loans from JSBs and other smaller banks.

- Continue and strengthen efforts to remove non-commercial considerations from bank lending and to tighten bank-lending standards. One possibility is to expand the role of policy banks in lending to exceptionally risky or financially troubled SOEs that need to be maintained, or to create separate agencies to guarantee loans for such purposes.[37] To improve professionalism, boards of directors (which should be established as soon as possible) should take over the responsibility of appointing senior bank management, subject to the PBC approval in accordance with strict "fit and proper" criteria. Several additional steps by supervisory authorities could also help. These include prompt nationwide implementation (in the next year or two) of the new loan classification system; and reinforcement of the mandate of the PBC to strictly apply rigorous prudential standards in its bank examinations. A requirement that all banks undergo a regular outside audit by an accredited public accounting firm, with the results to be publicly disclosed, would also reinforce incentives to observe prudential and commercial norms. Banks also need to have more effective means to enforce loan contracts by taking possession of collateral and stronger bankruptcy procedures.

Although important steps have been taken, credit quality has improved in part because banks have withdrawn from lending in key areas and it is not clear that a rigorous credit culture has become firmly and pervasively embedded. To sustain sound lending standards and effective loan monitoring, ties between the banks and political or government authorities need to be weakened and accountability to supervisory authorities strengthened.

- Accelerate the development of the domestic money and other channels needed to facilitate transfers of funds among financial institutions and regions. The interbank and other money markets need to become both larger and more flexible over the next five years if the JSBs and other bank alternatives to the SOCBs are to expand to the extent needed. A similar case can be made for improving the liquidity and negotiability of certificates of deposit and similar financial vehicles to allow banks to borrow and lend wholesale funds more easily. Improvement in the interregional flow of funds, which is likely to be important to the development of China's interior provinces, also depends on expansion of these facilities. Money markets are likely to expand rapidly once limits on market access, constraints on the positions particular banks are allowed to take, and bank interest rates are liberalised.

NOTES

1. Although sometimes viewed as symptomatic of "over banking" or excessive investment in unproductive assets, the unusually high ratio of bank assets to GDP is probably mainly a reflection of China's high savings rate and the relative lack of alternatives to banks as an outlet for those savings.

2. The increase appears in any case to have been fairly modest. For example, the Bank of China reported an increase of 3.5 per cent in profits from its consolidated operations in 2000, leaving its return on assets the same as in 1999. See Bank of China, *Annual Report*, 2000 (English version), p. 2.

3. See the study by the Chinese Academy of Social Sciences, 2000; and Wong, 2000.

4. As reported by Wong, 2000, the four largest SOCBs had 95 per cent of employees in the state banking industry, versus only about 85 per cent of deposits.

5. This is, of course, contrary to the usual pattern during falling interest rates, although it is not unusual in periods of bank distress. Bank loan spreads also rose in Japan during the latter 1990s as interest rates fell.

6. The share of bonds and other instruments with generally lower interest rates has thus risen. Profit figures in 1999 may also have been artificially depressed by the attribution of interest earned on bonds acquired during that year to 2000; this would also partly explain the reported rise in bank profits in 2000.

7. See in particular, Lardy, 1999 and 2000.

8. The Bank of China recently reported an NPL figure of 28 per cent of loans based on the new classification system now being introduced and which is more in line with international standards (Bank of China, 2000). The NPL ratio of the BOC is probably neither the lowest or highest of the SOCB. This suggests that the true average is probably on the order of 30 per cent.

9. The independent estimates are probably subject to less downward bias than the official figures, and to that extent exaggerate the NPL problems of joint-stock banks relative to those of the four major SOCBs.

10. Core capital reached 11.4 per cent of risk-adjusted assets in Thailand at the end of 2000, and was above 12 per cent in Malaysia in early 2001. Capital ratios in Hong Kong, China and the Philippines are also well above 12 per cent.

11. This conclusion is based in part on discussions with experts at the PBC and other government agencies.

12. Since 1996, banks have been permitted to vary interest rates for working capital loans (but not other loans) by 10 per cent of a central rate set by regulatory authorities. At the present level of interest rates, this limits the interest rate charged to the most risky borrowers to about 60 basis points above the central rate. This is a relatively narrow risk spread by international standards. By comparison issuers of single A-rated US corporate bonds, who are regarded as relatively safe credit risks, pay nearly as great a premium over top-rated (triple A) corporate issuers.

13. Perverse incentives detrimental to overall financial discipline have also arisen in this environment. Some SOEs that are not objectively creditworthy are able to obtain loans because of the implicit guarantee conferred by their backing from central or local government agencies. Other less favoured SOEs and non-state enterprises face much stricter lending conditions imposed by their banks.

14. In contrast to the JSBs, SOCBs are still subject to civil service salary, promotion, and other personnel policies. The JSBs have also been innovation leaders and have been especially active in tapping foreign expertise and in improving their accounting and other information systems to increase transparency.

15. The loan share is down significantly from the early 1990s, but much of the drop is due to the assumption of loans of the SOCBs by the policy banks, rather than the growth of the other commercial banks.

16. Admittedly, the identifiable loans made directly to non-state enterprises – less than 10 per cent of the total – reported in official figures is an understatement since loans to urban collectives along with some loans to non-state enterprises are included with SOE in lending to specific sectors, such as industry or commerce, and cannot be separated out. In particular, direct loans to private enterprises are probably significantly greater than official figures suggest, although the official figures for TVEs should be closer to the true ones.

17. For example, roughly 70 per cent of new lending by the Everbright Bank of China reportedly now goes to non-state enterprises.

18. The figures refer to all financial institutions, and presumably take account of loans going directly to non-state firms but classified elsewhere in official figures, as well as loans going via SOEs or other non-financial institution channels. However, the dominance of commercial banks and the large gap between Panel a and Panel b of Table 7.4 suggests that the non-state total share of bank loans must be substantially above their direct share.

19. The relatively high level set for the money market interest rate relative to loan rates further limits incentives to take extended short positions, even if banks were allowed to do so.

20. Country briefing by the Economist Intelligence Unit, "China finance: China to cut number of trust and investment firms", as reported by *ChinaOnline*, 18 January 2001.

21. *South China Morning Post*, 7 February 2001, *op. cit.*

22. For further discussion of the problems of these reforms, see OECD (2000*a*), Chapter 5, and the references cited there.

23. OECD (2000*a*), Chapter 5.

24. Moreover, they appear to have been unwilling, so far, to approve requests to grant major city commercial banks nationwide status. (This latter observation is based on interviews with officials in one of China's western provinces).

25. The competitive implications of the government's effort to develop a "main bank" system are also not clear at this point. Under this system, enterprises are supposed to designate one bank as primary repository for their deposit accounts. However enterprises are free in principle to choose among banks in borrowing.

26. According to the *Regulations*, foreign banks, foreign bank branches and joint venture banks in China may engage in some or all of the following foreign currency businesses: foreign currency deposit-taking; foreign currency lending; foreign currency bill-discounting; approved foreign exchange investments; foreign exchange remittance; foreign exchange guarantee; import and export settlement; foreign currency dealing and brokerage; exchange of foreign currencies and foreign exchange bills as an agent; foreign currency credit card payment; custodial service; and credit verification and consulting.

27. Before 1996, foreign banks were allowed to handle renminbi only in the course of carrying out swap transactions in the foreign exchange market.

28. Foreign banks located in Shanghai and Shenzhen must meet the following requirements before they can apply for RMB business, banks must have had: three years of operation, two consecutive years of profit making, a minimum average month-end foreign currency lending balance of US$150 million for foreign bank branches (US$100 million for wholly-owned or joint-venture banks), and a foreign currency lending balance exceeding 50 per cent of their total foreign currency assets.

29. The banks currently engaged in the renminbi business have been allowed to expand their services into the neighbouring provinces, namely, Jiangsu and Zhejiang provinces for the Shanghai based banks and Guangdong, Guangxi and Hunan provinces for those based in Shenzhen.

30. *The Banker Supplement*, May 2000.

31. For example, the Royal Bank of Canada turned in its renminbi license in 1998. See Australia Foreign Affairs Ministry, p. 304.

32. Syndications are often organised by a group of banks working closely with senior government officials.

33. At least in some cases, the figures in the Table may understate the true extent of foreign control, since effective control can often be secured with a less than 50 per cent share of total equity.

34. In Indonesia, full bank licenses have been denied to foreign banks since 1972. The existing ten foreign banks operating in Indonesia entered the country before 1972.

35. Following the example of a number of other Asian countries, bank capital ratios also should be raised significantly above the BIS minimum, albeit on a longer time frame, to deal with the greater risks banks tend to face in emerging economies.

36. For example, it has been suggested that SOCBs be eventually split up into regional units. Another possibility would be to devolve a substantial portion of operations along functional lines into separate subsidiaries in which the main bank would retain the controlling share.

37. Alternatively, consideration might be given to creation of a special agency within the government, or in a subsidiary or internal unit of the SOCB, to provide explicit guarantees (backed by and approved by the government) for loans not meeting strict commercial standards but which are deemed socially worthwhile.

BIBLIOGRAPHY

Almanac of Finance and Banking (1999),
  China Financial Publishing House.

Australia Department of Foreign Affairs and Trade, East Asia Analytic Unit (1997),
  China Embraces the Market: Achievements, Constraints and Opportunities, Canberra.

Bank of China (1999),
  Annual Report 1999.

Bank of Communication (1999),
  Annual Report 1999.

Bank for International Settlements (1999),
  Strengthening the Banking System in China: Issues and Experience.

Burdisso *et al.* (1998),
  "A note on the profitability of the foreign-owned banks in Argentina", The Central Bank of Argentina Research Papers.

Cantrell, W. (1994),
  "Getting a global grip on custody", US *Banker*, November.

Chinese Academy of Social Sciences (2000),
  Research Report on China's Entry into WTO.

China Financial Development Report 2000,
  Shanghai University of Economics and Finance Publishing House.

Classens, S. and T. Glaessner (1998),
  "The internationalisation of financial services in Asia", *Policy Research Working Paper*, The World Bank, April.

Economist Intelligence Unit (2000),
  Country Finance 2000: China.

Dermirgüç-Kunt, A. and H. Huizinga (1999),
  "Determinants of commercial bank interest margins and profitability: some international evidence", *The World Bank Economic Review*, Vol. 13, No. 2.

Dunning, J.H. (1980),
  "Towards an eclectic theory of international production", *Journal of International Business Studies*, 11:1, pp. 9-31.

Goldman Sachs (1999),
  Investment Research, 23 November 1999.

Goldberg, L.G. and D. Johnson (1990),
  "The determinants of US banking activity abroad", *Journal of International Money and Finance*, 9, pp. 123-137.

Hawkins, J. and P. Turner (1999),
  "Bank restructuring in practice: an overview", in BIS (editor) *Bank Restructuring in Practice*, BIS Policy Papers No. 6, August, pp. 6-105.

He, L. (2001),
  "WTO accession: likely impacts to China's banking and securities industry", Paper presented to Fourth EU-China Academic Network Annual Conference, "China's WTO Accession: National and International Perspectives", Berlin, February.

Huang, Y. (2000),
  "It takes more than recapitalisation to fix China's banks", article published in *China Online*, September.

International Monetary Fund (2000),
  International Capital Markets.

Jiao, J (2000),
  WTO and the Future of China's Financial Industry, China Finance Publishing House.

JP Morgan (2001),
  "China development bank: benefits and constraints of a development bank", JP Morgan Emerging Markets Research, February.

Khambata, D. (1996),
  The Practice of Multinational Banking: Macro-Policy Issues and Key International Concepts, Quorum Books.

Konopielko, L. (1999),
  "Foreign banks' entry into central and east European markets: motives and activities", Post-Communist Economies, Vol. 11, No. 4.

Lang, L.H.P., and Raymond W.S. (2001),
  Banking in East Asia, background paper for this study.

Lardy, Nicolas R. (2000),
  "When will China's financial system meet China's needs?" Paper presented to the Conference on Policy Reform in China, Stanford University, 18-20 November 1999 and revised February 2000.

Lardy, Nicolas R. (1998),
  China's Unfinished Economic Revolution, Brookings Institution Press.

Leung, M-K. (1997),
  "Foreign banks in the People's Republic of China", Journal of Contemporary China, 6(15), pp. 365-376.

Liu, T. (2000),
  The Banking Industry in China 2000, China Financial Publishing House

Marashdeh, Omar,
  "Foreign Banks Activities and Factors Affecting Their Presence in Malaysia", Asia Pacific Journal of Management Vol. 11, No. 1, pp. 113-123.

OECD (2000a),
  Reforming China's Enterprises, Paris.

OECD (2000b),
  Bank Profitability 2000, Paris.

OECD (1997),
  The Banking Landscape in Central and Eastern Europe: Country Experience and Policies for The Future, proceedings of a joint conference sponsored by the OECD and the Vienna Institute for Comparative Economic Studies, held in December, 1996 in Vienna.

OECD (1993),
  Transformation of the Banking System, Paris.

Parkhe, A. and Steward R.M. (1998),
  "Foreign operations of US banks: Impact of environmental differences and ownership advantages on organisational form preferences", Journal of International Management 4:1, pp. 59-83.

The People's Bank of China,
  "Fiscal and Finance Issues", Monthly Journal of the PBOC, various issues 1998-2000.

The People's Bank of China (2000),
  China Financial Outlook 2000.

Pogson, K. (2001),
  "China's banking sector: an uneven playing field", FinanceAsia.com sector report, 14 February.

Standard and Poor's (2000),
  Bank Industry Risk Analysis: China, 20 September.

Tschoegl, A.E. (1987),
  "International retail banking as a strategy: an assessment", in Journal of international business.

Thompson's Bankwatch (1999),
  Banking Company Profile, Bank of China (January); Agricultural Bank of China (January); Everbright Bank of China (September).

Ursacki, T. and I. Vertinsky (1992),
  "Choice of entry timing and scale by foreign banks in Japan and Republic of Korea ", Journal of Banking and Finance, 16, pp. 402-421.

Walton, A.J. (1994),
  "What next for foreign banks?", The Bankers Magazine, January/February.

Watanabe, M. (ed.) (2000),
China's Non-Performing Loan Problem, Japan Institute for Developing Economies, March.

Wengel, J.T. (1995),
"International trade in banking services", Journal of International Money and Finance, Vol. 14, No. 1, pp. 47-64.

Wong, R. (2000),
Competition in China's Domestic Banking Industry, Parts I and II, Hong Kong Centre for Economic Research, October.

Wu, J. (1996),
Research on the Behaviour of China's State-Owned Banks, China Finance Publishing House.

Chapter 8

THE DEVELOPMENT OF CHINA'S INSURANCE INDUSTRY

TABLE OF CONTENTS

THE DEVELOPMENT OF CHINA'S INSURANCE INDUSTRY[*]

Introduction

This chapter analyses the development of the Chinese insurance sector and identifies the regulatory and market challenges that will have to be met if the sector is to fulfil its potential within the wider economic and financial system. The first section of this chapter outlines the role insurance plays within a modern economy in order to benchmark the progress of the Chinese insurance sector. The second provides an analysis of the development and structure of the Chinese insurance sector, especially from the early 1990s to the present time. The system of regulation and supervision is then discussed, focusing on the 1995 Insurance Act and its subsequent amendments and the policy measures taken by the China Insurance Regulatory Commission (CIRC) since its establishment in November 1998. The final section discusses the key challenges still facing the insurance industry, including the need for greater market liberalisation, and a set of policy priorities that should be considered by the CIRC and the insurance industry to ensure that the Chinese insurance market continues to develop.

Role of insurance in the economic system

Introduction

In a modern economic and financial system the insurance sector plays three main roles (see Box 8.1). First, it provides individuals, corporations and other organisations with a mechanism for transferring some of the non-entrepreneurial risks that they face. Second, it provides a means for mobilising long-term savings and investing them profitably in the capital market, thus indirectly stimulating the growth of the capital market itself. Third, it complements state social insurance programmes, especially in the areas of pensions, disability and health care financing.

Insurance companies provide an effective risk-transfer mechanism. They can bring together a large portfolio of insurable risks where the incidences of these losses are reasonably independent of each other, and thus reduce the overall risk through portfolio diversification *i.e.* the law of large numbers. In order to underwrite these risks insurance companies must be able to price them. This means collecting credible information to allow them to estimate the frequency and severity of future losses. In addition, the risk absorption capacity of individual insurance companies is increased dramatically through reinsurance. Reinsurance is a well-established network of risk sharing between insurance companies allowing large risk exposures to be spread not just within a national market but globally. Hence the collective capital and risk assessment resources of the world insurance market can be drawn on to finance catastrophic losses.

Insurance companies play a major role in mobilising small-scale savings from across the economy, which can collectively appreciate substantially if well invested in the capital market (Box 8.2).Insurance companies generate private sector saving in a variety of ways. First, all insurance contracts, whether life or non-life (property and casualty) insurance, give rise to some form of private saving. This arises primarily from insurance premiums being paid in advance by customers, while claims and policy settlements paid back to consumers at a later date, after covering operating and marketing costs. This time lag between the receipt of premiums and return payments to consumers varies between different classes of insurance. Clearly, the time lag is longer for life insurance contracts than for non-life insurance contracts, hence the accumulation of investable funds is higher. In addition, the plough back of investment returns earned on the accumulation of these invested funds by insurance companies also contributes to the total level of saving. Second, life insurance contracts, especially endowment and

---

[*] This chapter was prepared by Gerry Dickinson, consultant for the Directorate for Financial, Fiscal and Enterprise Affairs, OECD.

Box 8.1. Role of the insurance sector as a mechanism for risk transfer

Insurance companies provide an effective risk transfer mechanism since they can exploit risk diversification benefits by pooling together a large portfolio of reasonably independent risks. In a competitive insurance market the effective pricing of risk is also essential. The failure of an insurance company to price insurable risks adequately will tend to lead to financial problems. If the pricing of the risk is too low, then the insurance company will, over time, become unprofitable, since its claims payments will exceed those assumed in its pricing and this can lead to insolvency. Moreover, if an insurance company consistently underprices its insurance contracts, it can weaken the solvency of other companies in the market since they may be tempted to follow suit in order to maintain their market shares. On the other hand, if an insurance company sets its prices too high, these prices cannot be sustained in a competitive market since other insurance companies will charge more appropriate prices and hence the insurance company will not attract business. In a competitive insurance market, fair or risk-discriminating pricing is a necessary condition for ensuring an efficient and sustainable supply of private insurance.

If a market is not properly supervised, competitive pressures can drive insurance prices below the level at which companies are adequately compensated for risk, hence leading to insurer insolvency. It is for this reason that in some insurance markets, especially in less developed markets, national regulation requires the approved structure of prices in operation. These systems of approved or minimum insurance prices are called "tariff pricing" systems. Regulatory systems that have approved prices also have approved insurance products and contracts, since approved prices must relate clearly to the defined contractual conditions that give rise to an insurance claim. However, as insurance markets become more developed and the supervisory authorities become more sophisticated, there is a move away from price and product regulation towards the financial solvency assessment of individual insurance companies, not least to allow for more price and product competition to take place.

An important aspect of the insurance risk transfer mechanism is that not only do insurance companies have access through reinsurance to a network of other insurers but also that large potential losses can be spread across domestic and international markets. Essentially, the mechanism of reinsurance is one of accessing the capital of other insurance companies. When an insurance company buys reinsurance, the premium paid is effectively a payment for the use of the capital of the reinsurer. Due to reinsurance, therefore, the capital of a national insurance market is extended internationally since it allows domestic insurance companies access to the combined capital base of the global reinsurance market.

Economic benefits of an efficient risk transfer mechanism

Transferring insurable risks onto efficient insurance markets has potential benefits in the following ways. When operating in competitive markets, industrial, commercial and trading enterprises have to take business risks in order to make profits. By being able to transfer some of the risks associated with these commercial and investment decisions, the decision-taking process is made less risky. Hence, decision-makers faced with less uncertainty will be more prepared to undertake more adventurous and potentially more profitable activities. Insurance markets also provide protection against some of the risks associated with international trade, *e.g.* damage or loss of goods in transit and credit risks associated with non-payment by foreign customers. Cargo marine insurance and international credit insurance thus helps to lubricate the flow of international trade.

The risk transfer facility provided by insurance companies can be viewed in terms of the efficient use of capital. Industrial, commercial and trading enterprises would have to hold more precautionary capital to run their enterprises if there were no insurance markets. In effect, insurance companies supply contingent equity capital to industrial and commercial enterprises. This means that across the economy as a whole less equity capital is needed to support commercial and trading activities. Insurance companies also provide some risk support for banks in their role as financial intermediaries. One area of support is the risk transfer facilities provided by credit insurance. Credit insurance is input into the supply of banking lending products. In addition, when commercial and mortgage banks have sought to increase the liquidity within their asset portfolios through the securitisation of their loans, the bonds issued from this process have often been purchased by life insurance companies, because their long-term liabilities require them to hold long-term asset positions. Long-term liabilities, and strong cash flow positions, mean that life insurance companies are "natural" investors in the capital market. This transfer of long-term interest rate risk through loan securitisations into life insurance companies indirectly stimulates the development of the capital market.

Box 8.2. Role of the insurance sector in savings accumulation and investment

Life insurance has historically been an important method through which individuals with relatively low incomes have been able to save and invest effectively for the longer term. By designing relatively simple life insurance and savings contracts, which can be purchased in small amounts on a regular basis, insurance companies have been able to accumulate large amounts of money from across a large proportion of the population. By pooling these savings from many small investors into large accumulations of funds, insurance companies are able to invest these in a wider range of financial assets than individuals would be able to do so themselves, as well as in larger scale and more uncertain investment opportunities. This pooling benefit to individuals is not unique to life insurance; it is provided by other saving instruments, especially collective investments (CIS). In addition, because in life insurance there is a regular or contractual payment by consumers, the level and stability of personal saving may be increased, compared to what would be the case if the saving arrangement were more discretionary in nature. Life insurance companies often have active marketing strategies that encourage myopic individuals to save rather than consume. However, aggressive marketing strategies are sometimes used and this can lead to consumers purchasing inappropriate saving products. This is a negative aspect of active marketing, but these adverse effects can be minimised by a combination of statutory regulation, market self-regulation and sound corporate governance systems for insurance companies and other institutional investors. Evidence exists that an active life insurance sector increases the level of long-term saving in emerging economies, not least because it provides an alternative to bank deposits for smaller investors, but also because the CIS sector does not develop until the capital market itself is relatively well developed (see Chapter 15 on Capital Markets).

Economic benefits of the saving and investment role

What are the wider economic benefits derived from the stimulation of private sector saving and its subsequent investment in the capital market? Firstly, these savings can be made available, either in the form of equity or debt capital, to manufacturing, agricultural, energy, trading or service enterprises. New companies can be set up and finance is available for existing companies to increase their level of capital expenditure in new plant, equipment etc. Moreover, particularly for life insurance, since the time horizons for investment are long-term, these savings can be tied up for a long period of time and hence can be made available for capital expenditure decisions that will only produce profits in the future. Since banks can frequently only provide short-term finance to manufacturing and other enterprises, this investment activity of life insurance complements the lending practices of the banking system because of the short-term nature of their deposits.

The long-term savings generated by life insurance companies can also be made available to help fund large-scale projects to strengthen economic infrastructure. Such infrastructure investment is especially important in emerging economies not only to underpin the growth of domestic enterprises but also to encourage foreign companies to enter the market and invest further. Other possible financial assets for insurance companies are government bonds and mortgage or mortgage-backed securities. The latter stimulate the development of the housing market.

linked-life policies and those concerned with pension provision, have a more significant saving element. This arises not just from the fact that premiums are paid by customers in advance but also because insurance contracts entail a deliberate financial commitment by the consumer to save for the future. Here saving is of a different kind: it represents a voluntary saving as opposed to an involuntary saving from the pricing practice of paying insurance premiums in advance. Again, the plough back of investment income earned on the accumulation of these invested funds over time also contributes to the saving process.

It is through the investment of premiums paid by policyholders (and also the investment of shareholder funds) that the transmission of saving is fed into the wider economy through the capital market. The range of financial assets in which an insurance company can invest its funds will depend on the degree of development of the domestic capital market. Savings mobilised and invested in a capital market by insurance companies clearly act as an important stimulus to the growth of the capital market itself. However the relationship between the level of saving generated through life insurance and private pension contracts and the development of a capital market is a two-way process. This is because life insurance and private pension contracts usually involve a voluntary decision to save on the part of consumers. Consumers will not wish to save through these contracts if the investment opportunities available to insurance companies in the capital market are not attractive. Hence there is a dynamic interaction process at work, with the development of saving through life insurance and the development of the capital market both evolving together, with one assisting the other.

In many OECD and emerging market economies (EMEs), governments are seeking to reform their social security or social insurance systems to reduce the current and future burden of these systems on government finances. Pressures for reform arise from a combination of factors: demographic changes, rising standards of living, and increasing public expectations. Retirement provision, health care and disability support feature as a major component of social security budgets. Through these reforms, the insurance sector and other parts of the financial services industry are increasingly being seen as potential government partners. Pension and annuity schemes, private heath insurance and accident and disability insurances are core businesses of insurance companies. At the heart of this synergy, social insurance programmes and the insurance sector are both concerned with providing income maintenance to individuals and to families, in the face of adverse circumstances. Experience shows that partnerships between the state and the insurance sector work most effectively if two conditions hold. First, the government ensures that the scope of the partnership, and the conditions under which it operates, do not change much over time, or do so only in a reasonably predictable way; they are not subject to short-term political exigencies. Second, the government recognises that insurance companies, and other financial services enterprises, can only operate if they are allowed to earn an adequate rate of return on their shareholder funds.

Development and structure of the Chinese insurance sector

The Chinese insurance market prior to 1979

The insurance industry in China took root in the middle of the nineteenth century. Foreign-owned companies, initially European and then American and Japanese, set up domestic operations, mainly in Shanghai and Hong Kong, China. This expansion into China was part of a wider international expansion in trade and investment until the First World War, and more sporadically until the 1930s. Initially, foreign insurance companies operated through local agencies and branches, but when the scale of local operations justified it, these agencies and branches were converted into local subsidiary companies, and occasionally joint ventures with indigenous partners. As the market expanded, Chinese-owned insurance companies were formed. Until 1949, foreign insurance companies had by far the largest share of the Chinese life and non-life insurance markets, a pattern found in many emerging economies around the world during this colonial period.

In 1949, soon after the establishment of the People's Republic of China, the People's Insurance Company of China (PICC) was set up as a state monopoly and by the early 1950s all other insurance companies, both domestic and foreign, had been required to leave the market. The PICC retained this market monopoly until the mid-1980s, supplying both life and non-life insurances. However, its activity was severely curtailed from 1959 to 1979, as the role of insurance within the economic system was downplayed, with the effect that state-owned enterprises stopped purchasing insurance and thus commercial and personal insurances were largely curtailed. There were some exceptions: some types of compulsory accident insurances, foreign trade-related insurances, and civil aviation on international routes. Moreover, a number of life insurance companies were allowed to continue to transact business in Shanghai, mainly insurances for expatriates. The PICC continued to operate but its activities were largely restricted to meeting the needs of Chinese commercial interests outside of China, mainly in the Southeast Asian region.

Emergence of a more market-orientated approach after 1979

Under wider structural reforms after the Cultural Revolution, the role of insurance was reassessed and was subsequently considered to play a useful economic and social role. This reappraisal was also influenced by a number of large losses during the 1970s from earthquakes in Xingtai, Haicheng and Tangshan and later the flood losses in Sichan and Shanxi provinces, which were uninsured, where costs fell on central and provincial state budgets. On 1 January 1980, the PICC was allowed to recommence a more active supply of life and non-life insurances within China, and in anticipation of new insurance companies being granted licences, it was also given new powers to write reinsurance. An ordinance of the State Council in 1985 permitted the establishment of domestically owned insurance companies. The first of these were Ping An Insurance Company, which was set up in 1988 and granted a license to operate in Shenzhen, and China Pacific Insurance Company, established in 1991 with a licence to operate in Shanghai, both of which were state-owned enterprises. During the 1990s other domestically owned insurance companies, all owned by SOEs, were granted licences often with a restricted geographical scope of operation. By 1996, there were eleven domestically owned companies. A few of these companies were granted the authority to supply life and non-life insurances, but the majority were granted a licence to write either life or non-life insurance. These new companies were all granted licences to provide some competition to the PICC's dominant market position and to ensure a wider development of insurance across the country.

In addition, regulation allowed new types of insurance products to be offered. This change in economic policy consequently meant that state-owned enterprises (SOEs) themselves were now required to assume greater responsibility for their own profits and losses, creating a clear incentive to SOEs to purchase external insurance to protect their assets and to stabilise their profit flows over time. The period also saw the government recognise the benefit of having a more active life and health insurance sector in order to reduce the dependence of families on the social security system and on state finances from the rising costs of pensions, premature death or incapacity of individuals. The State Council also increasingly recognised that life insurance could be an effective means of mobilising long-term saving and could act as a stimulus to the growth of the capital market.

Gradual entry of foreign insurance companies

In 1992, with the promulgation of the "Foreign Insurance Institutions Temporary Management Provisions", the Chinese market was re-opened to foreign insurance companies. The American International Group received the first licences to offer life and non-life insurances in Shanghai, followed by the Tokyo Marine and Fire in 1994 with a more limited licence to supply only non-life insurance business in Shanghai. Other licences were granted later, so that by mid-2001 17 foreign insurance companies had received licences. These licences to foreign insurance companies were awarded with a more restricted geographical and product scope than for domestically owned insurers. The main restrictions were: *a*) licences were limited to operations in specially designated economic areas in Shanghai and Guangzhou; *b*) licences were limited to conduct either life insurance or non-life insurance – no joint licences were awarded to write life and non-life insurances; *c*) after 1996, foreign insurance companies wishing to supply life insurance were required to do so through a joint venture, with the local partner, approved by the insurance supervisory authority, and having a maximum 50 per cent foreign ownership stake. These joint ventures were permitted to sell only individual life and accident insurance contracts, but not group contracts to employers or others; *d*) foreign non-life insurance companies were granted more ownership rights in that they could operate through a local wholly-owned branch, but with an even more limited target market, mainly insurances for businesses which were financed, partly or in whole, by foreign capital.

A key reason for the gradual opening of the market to foreign competition was to allow time for the PICC and the new domestically owned insurance companies to establish themselves so that they could compete. These foreign insurers wishing to enter the Chinese market were among the world's leading insurance companies, with much greater financial, technical and management resources than their Chinese counterparts. Another reason was that there were at the time no detailed regulations governing the supervision of foreign insurers. In addition, there was a further factor governing the licence approval process, which accelerated in the late 1990s. The Chinese government had an eye on joining the WTO and wished to open its market selectively by choosing the leading insurance companies from a wide range of countries: a wide dispersal of licences was viewed as providing an international signal of this intention.

The pattern in granting licences to foreign insurance companies wishing to offer life insurance products changed in 1996 when joint ventures became the preferred policy. This policy change was initiated with the joint venture company, Zhong Hong Life, which was set up between Manufacturers Life (Canada) and Sinochem, the large SOE. Subsequently, all licences awarded to foreign life insurers have been through joint ventures, with the Chinese supervisory authority having to approve the Chinese joint venture partner. This switch in emphasis to joint ventures has been to permit a greater transfer of technical know-how and to ensure that the Chinese partner has the resources and management commitment to provide a balanced partner in this fast growing area of insurance. In non-life insurance, the policy of allowing foreign insurers to have a 100 per cent owned branch office has been retained, not least because of the need for sizeable capital strength to absorb large risk exposures and the fact that insurance contracts are of shorter duration.

Further market restructuring

In October 1996, the People's Insurance Company of China (PICC) was broken up into three separately managed entities: PICC Life Insurance, PICC Property Insurance and PICC Reinsurance Company, under a new group holding company structure. This separation of life and non-life insurance business of the PICC was a consequence of the 1995 Insurance Law which stipulated that new insurance companies could not supply life and non-life insurance within one insurance company, a policy which was subsequently extended to all existing insurance companies in 1999.

In 1999 there was a further restructuring of the PICC group, with a break-up of the PICC holding company, whereby the constituent companies were spun off into totally separate joint stock companies, but still being 100 per cent directly state-owned. PICC Life Insurance became the Life Insurance Company of China (China Life), PICC Reinsurance became China Reinsurance Company and PICC Property Insurance transformed into PICC. In addition, the international operations of the PICC were separated out in the 1999 restructuring into a new company, China Insurance Company, with its headquarters in Hong Kong, China. This restructuring had the effect of revitalising these companies as they now had more autonomy, new management and greater incentives to operate on a commercial basis. In addition, the creation of these companies as new joint stock companies was seen as permitting a possible future flotation on the stock market, in order to attract new capital to finance future growth, even though the government would wish to retain the majority of shares. As separate companies this would also increase the potential level of competition in the market. For example, the PICC, which currently only supplies non-life insurance, could well decide to apply to the CIRC to extend its licence in future to allow it to supply life and accident insurance, which it could do under a new holding company structure, ensuring the necessary operational separation. This would allow PICC to offer a full range of insurances, in the same way as Ping An and China Pacific can, and it would also be in line with the international pattern for large insurance companies.

In the mid-1990s, there were a few Chinese-owned insurance companies that had used assets derived from their non-life operations to cover increasing liabilities on their life insurance business due to over-ambitious interest rate guarantees on life contacts sold when interest rates were high. The interest rate problems facing these companies intensified in the second half of the 1990s, as interest rates fell further. Soon after its formation, the CIRC adopted a much tighter enforcement of this asset-liability separation to avoid cross-subsidisation and to reduce the risk of contagion from one group of policyholders to another. However, an insurance group in China can offer both life and non-life insurance contracts, if licensed to do so, through separate companies under a holding company structure. This is an acceptable solution and it is common practice in most OECD countries.

Table 8.1. **Growth in number of life insurance companies 1985 to mid-2001**

	State-owned enterprises	Domestic-owned insurance cos.	Joint-venture cos. with a foreign insurer or foreign branch
1985	1	0	0
1986	2	0	0
1987	2	0	0
1988	2	1	0
1989	2	1	0
1990	2	1	0
1991	2	2	0
1992	2	2	1
1993	2	2	1
1994	2	2	1
1995	2	2	1
1996	2	4	2
1997	2	4	4
1998	2	4	6
1999	2	4	6
2000	2	8	10
2001 (mid)	2	8	10

Source: Compiled from data in *Almanach of Chinese Insurance* (annual).

Table 8.2. **Growth in number of non-life insurance companies 1985 to mid-2001**

	State-owned enterprises	Domestic-owned insurance cos.	Foreign-owned branch operations
1985	1	0	0
1986	2	0	0
1987	2	0	0
1988	2	1	0
1989	2	1	0
1990	2	1	0
1991	2	2	0
1992	2	2	1
1993	2	2	1
1994	2	3	2
1995	2	4	2
1996	2	7	3
1997	2	8	3
1998	2	8	4
1999	2	8	4
2000	2	8	7
2001 (mid)	2	8	7

Source: Compiled from data in *Almanach of Chinese Insurance* (annual).

The growth in the number of new insurance companies can be seen in Tables 8.1 and 8.2. In particular there was a rapid increase in 2000, with licences being granted to four domestic companies and to four foreign companies. By mid-2001, there were thirty-seven companies licensed to supply insurance on the Chinese market, twenty allowed to supply life insurances and seventeen non-life insurances (see Table 8.3). Of these, seventeen were foreign insurers operating either through joint ventures or branch operations.

The size and growth of the Chinese insurance market

Figure 8.1 shows the size and growth of the insurance premiums received by Chinese insurance companies from 1982 to 2000. These are given in total and divided into the two main classes: non-life insurance (property and casualty insurances) and life insurance. As can be seen, the insurance market has grown sharply, from negligible levels in the early 1980s, with a compound growth rate of over 30 per

Table 8.3. **Life insurance companies licensed on Chinese market at June 2001
and non-life insurance companies licensed on Chinese market at June 2001**

Life insurance companies licensed on Chinese market at June 2001	
State-owned enterprises	2
SOE-owned enterprises	8
Joint-venture companies owned by foreign insurers and local partners (SOEs)	9
Foreign-owned branches	1
Total	20
Non-life insurance companies licensed on Chinese market at June 2001	
State-owned enterprises	2
SOE-owned enterprises	8
Foreign-owned branches	7
Total	17

Source: Compiled from data in *Almanach of Chinese Insurance* (annual).

Figure 8.1. **Size and growth of China's insurance market, 1982-2000**
(Gross premium income in RMB billions)

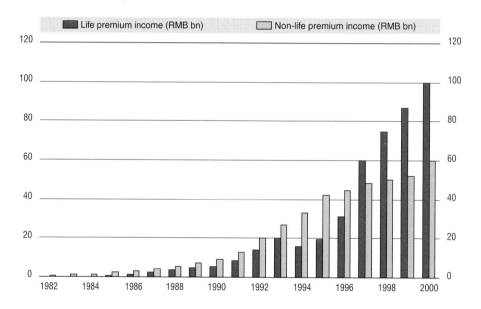

Source: Based on data from the Information Centre, China Insurance Regulatory Commission.

cent per annum from 1982 to 2000, albeit from a very low base in the early 1980s. A different pattern of growth is evident between life insurance and non-life insurance. In the years up to 1996, spending on non-life insurance was higher than for life insurance but this pattern changed after 1996 when life insurance grew more quickly. The changes in the state pensions system in 1997, which allowed life insurance companies to offer supplementary pensions to the state system, was a significant factor in this growth. This is evidenced by an increasing proportion of the new premium income earned by life insurance companies from this source of business. An active promotion campaign that was mounted by the government in the media provided an important boost to the marketing efforts of insurance companies.

Figures 8.2 and 8.3 relate to the level of spending on insurance as a percentage of per capita income and as a percentage of GDP, respectively. As can be seen, insurance spending increased relative to both. However, it is still very low by international standards. Total insurance spending, life and non-life, was just over 1.6 per cent of GDP in 1999. Figure 8.4 sets this ratio for China against a cross

Figure 8.2. **Insurance premiums per capita (insurance density) in China, 1982-2000**

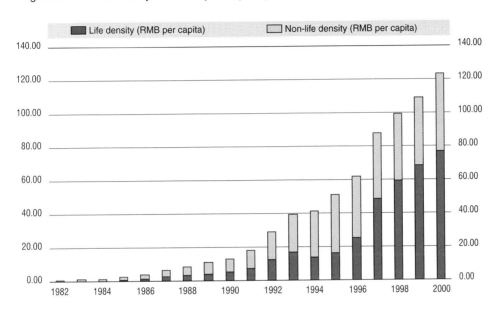

Figure 8.3. **Insurance premiums % of GDP (insurance penetration) in China, 1982-2000**

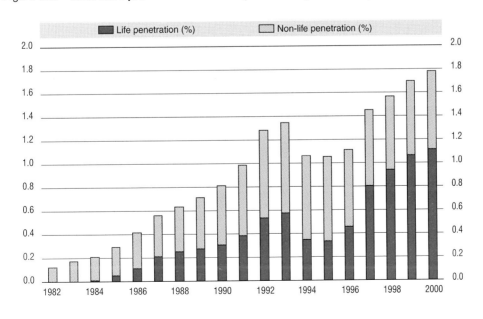

Source: Based on data from the Information Centre, China Insurance Regulatory Commission.

Figure 8.4. **Comparing China's insurance market penetration**
(*i.e.* total insurance premiums (life and non-life) as % of GDP in 1999

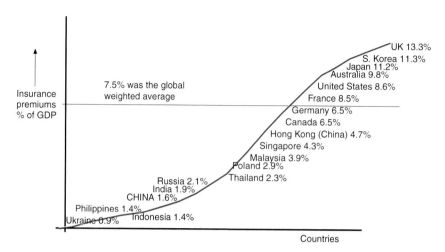

Source: Based on data from *Sigma*, No. 9, 2000, Swiss Re.

section of countries, both developed and emerging. China's ratio is lower than a number of other large emerging markets, such as India and Russia. The global weighted average of total premiums to GDP in 1999 was 7.5 per cent, which is dominated by the large, developed insurance markets of the OECD countries. But there is much scope for further market growth. Empirical evidence shows that the growth of insurance markets tends to follow an S-shaped curve, starting slowly, then accelerating and finally levelling off. It is likely that the Chinese insurance market will grow faster than its GDP for the foreseeable future.

High level of market concentration

The degree of market concentration, as measured in premiums received by insurance companies, is very high by international standards. PICC still holds a dominant market position in non-life insurance, with a market share of 77.6 per cent in 2000, while China Life, the former PICC life subsidiary, had a 64.5 per cent share of the life insurance market in 2000. The three largest companies had a 97.1 per cent share of the non-life market and a 95.5 per cent share of the life insurance market (see Tables 8.4 and 8.5). Hence the combined market shares held by the other Chinese-owned and the foreign-owned insurance companies and joint ventures are small. A key reason for the high level of concentration has arisen from the geographical restrictions that have been imposed on the newer market entrants. Only the PICC, China Life, CIC, Ping An and China Pacific have been granted licences to operate on a nationwide basis, and those granted to Ping An, China Pacific and CIC have only been awarded recently. Other domestically owned insurance companies have been restricted to one or a few

Table 8.4. **The largest three non-life insurers' market share in 2000**

Company	Gross premium income (US$ bn)	Market share %
PICC	5.61	77.63
China Pacific	0.83	11.44
Ping An	0.58	8.07
Others	0.21	2.86

Source: Various news releases of insurance companies on www.china-insurance.com and the Information Centre, Chinese Insurance Regulatory Commission.

Table 8.5. **The largest three life insurers' market share in 2000**

Company	Gross premium income (US$ bn)	Market share %
China Life	7.77	64.5
Ping An	2.71	22.5
China Pacific	1.02	8.5
Others	0.55	4.5

Source: Various news releases of insurance companies on *www.china-insurance.com* and the Information Centre, Chinese Insurance Regulatory Commission.

provinces, because the insurance supervisory authority has not considered them to possess the resources or proven management competence to operate more widely. Foreign insurers have had greater geographical limitations placed on them, in addition to the restrictions on the insurance products that they can offer and the consumers that they can serve.

Pattern of product growth

A notable characteristic of the development of an insurance market is that the diversity of insurance products also increases over time. In Figures 8.5 and 8.6, a pattern of product diversification found in many insurance markets is shown. An analysis of the Chinese insurance market indicates that it can be characterised to a significant degree by this pattern of development and thus it offers some guide to future product evolution. In non-life insurance, the pattern of product development is to protect physical assets (various types of property insurances), to develop first, and for insurance products that protect income or financial assets (*e.g.* business interruption, credit insurance) and against the protection of being sued for negligence (liability insurances) to grow later in relative importance. The demand for accident, disability and health insurances also increase as the insurance market matures. At the same time, corporate insurances emerge faster than personal insurances, since corporate buyers usually recognise earlier than individuals the benefits of insurance, but gradually the market becomes more equally balanced between the two groups of consumers.

Figure 8.5. **Market development and the growth of non-life (P&C) insurance product diversity**

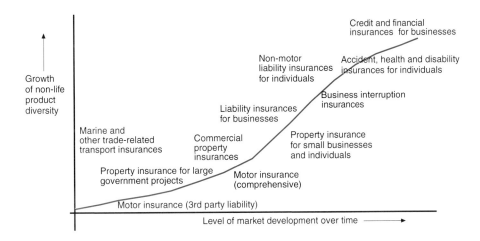

Source: G. Dickinson.

Figure 8.6. **Market development and the growth of life insurance product diversity**

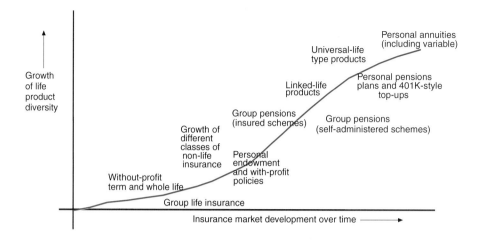

Source: G. Dickinson.

In a life insurance market, product development reveals a gradual shift from life protection to saving products, with saving products being increasingly concerned with retirement provision. There is a gradual move away from standardised life and saving products that are organised on a group basis toward more tailor-made products sold to individuals, reflecting rising standards of living and a greater consumer awareness.

Encouraging stock market listing of local insurance companies

During the late 1990s the government sought to strengthen the competitive ability of local insurance companies by encouraging them to seek listings on the stock market and thus to raise new capital resources, while accepting the increased obligations of a public listing. This has been part of a wider commercial policy across all state-owned enterprises. The insurance supervisory authority has given initial approval to twelve companies to gain a listing on either the Shanghai or Shenzhen stock markets, but no insurance company has yet come onto the market.

Pensions reform and its impact on the life insurance sector

In China, the pension problem has been made more acute by the one child family policy introduced in the late 1970s. There will be rapid changes in the age distribution over the next fifty years. It is estimated that 7 per cent of the population was 65 years or over in 2000 and this will rise to 20 per cent by 2050. For a country with such a large population and with a state pension system that is largely unfunded, this poses a major challenge. A large proportion of the population is still employed in the agricultural sector, and the rising number of individuals who are self-employed or employed in small-scale enterprises, especially with the restructuring of SOEs, poses additional problems. Even though the social insurance system in China dates back to the early 1950s with the adoption of the "Regulations of Labour Insurance" in 1951, the State Council has recognised the growing scale of the problem. The current pensions reform process can be considered to have begun in 1991, when the State Council introduced a new multilevel pension insurance system. These reforms introduced the concept of a combination of social pooling or social solidarity, with a high degree of cross-subsidisation, and of individual accounts, where future pension benefits would reflect the contributions that had been paid in. These early reforms also recognised the concept that pension contributions needed to be shared between the government, employers and individuals. The administrative responsibility for running the system was devolved away from the SOEs to the provincial governments and to autonomous regions and municipalities, not least to widen the potential scope of the pension provision with changing employment patterns. Some degree of funding in relation to the individual accounts was intended, but in reality there has been limited funding since the enhanced contributions were mainly used to pay for the basic state pension. There was no role for life insurance companies or other financial institutions within this system; it was entirely a state scheme.

The problem of funding, the lack of universal coverage and the limited portability of these individual pension accounts when workers changed their employment required further reforms. A more effective and more unified pensions system was sought. As a result the State Council introduced a new system in 1997, which drew on the experience of various overseas countries. This saw the introduction of a three-pillar system (see also Chapter 16 on Labour and Social Benefits). The first pillar is an unfunded basic pension. Above this minimum, there is a second pillar consisting of individual employee accounts organised on a group basis through an employer, and based on contributions from employers and employees. It was envisaged that these individual employee accounts would move from an unfunded to a fully-funded basis over a specified period of time, but this has not taken place as quickly as planned. One major innovation in the new system is the introduction of a third pillar in the form of supplementary pension plans. The third pillar is voluntary, whereas the first two pillars are compulsory. The third-pillar pensions allows for individuals, personally or with financial assistance from their employers, to top-up their second-pillar pension accounts. The social insurance bureaux, which are also responsible for managing the first two pillars, can offer these supplementary pensions but there is also the option for financial institutions, including life insurance companies, to offer these top-up pensions, as well as to employers that had the requisite in-house expertise. Even though these are individual pension plans, they have so far been mainly organised on a group basis *i.e.* through the employer. These third pillar pensions are on a defined contribution basis and are required to be fully funded. The rapid growth of the life insurance market from 1997 onwards has been due in no small measure to this change in the state pension system. But only selected, wholly-owned Chinese life insurance companies, and other approved financial services companies, have been able to offer these supplementary third pillar pensions on a group basis; foreign companies, even through their local joint ventures, have so far not been allowed to do so.

The 1997 pension reform did not extend to rural workers. A new pension system for those employed in the rural areas was subject to a separate pension reform, promulgated by the Ministry of Civil Affairs. The benefits this scheme provides are more limited, reflecting the different wage levels and social setting in these areas compared to urban areas. It was estimated at the end of 2000 that about 135 million employees were covered under the basic state pension system, and 82 million under the rural pension arrangements. This is only about 20 per cent of the overall working age population, although coverage in the urban population is much higher; it is estimated that coverage in the urban sector, including civil servants, is around 65 per cent. Although growing, the number of individuals contributing to these supplementary voluntary pensions, and the contributions paid in, remain relatively small and the levels are insufficient to provide an adequate retirement income.

There are several challenges facing the Chinese pension system. First, coverage has to be increased to cover a higher percentage of the population, especially outside the main cities and for those not employed in the large state-owned enterprises. Second, the authorities have announced the objective of gradually moving towards a more funded basis. However, it also likely that the pension benefits levels may have to be scaled down and/or there may have to be an increase in the age at which pensions become payable. Third, a greater and more effective role can be played by the life insurance industry and the fund (asset) management industry more generally. There is a case for arguing that the role of the life insurance companies and other approved financial services companies should initially be confined to developing supplementary pensions. In the longer term there is a potential role in the second pillar on a partnership basis with the social insurance bureaux at the provincial, city and prefecture levels, under the overall supervision of Ministry of Labour and Social Security. The Ministry of Labour and Social Security is already having to co-ordinate policy supervision with the CIRC, because of the involvement of life insurance companies, and this co-ordination will increase over time.

283

Experience in other countries, such as in Poland and Chile, shows that the life insurance sector and other parts of the financial services industry can play an active role in the provision of second pillar pensions. However, it should be noted that a second pillar based on individual employee accounts would, in essence, consist of personal pensions organised on a group basis, if they were fully funded. Such personal pension schemes are a core product of life insurance companies and other financial services companies and hence there is a potential future role for the financial sector. But such a partnership role will emerge more easily in time when the life insurance sector is more developed, has wider geographical coverage across the country and when the necessary internal reforms have been made to the operation and structure of the second pillar system.

For larger SOEs there is also the scope in the longer term to develop their own self-administered or occupational pension schemes, but corporate governance concerns must ensure that they are set up on an arm's-length basis, with the invested funds being kept separate from the finances of the enterprise. The system of appointing independent trustees to ensure that the funds are secure and well managed has fulfilled this role effectively in most OECD countries. If SOEs do not have proven in-house investment expertise, they can outsource the investment of funds to professional fund (asset) management companies, which will tend to be the asset management subsidiaries of larger banks, investment houses and insurance groups.

The system of regulation and supervision

The 1995 Insurance Law and the creation of the CIRC

After five years of investigation and planning, including fact-finding visits to a number of overseas countries, a new Insurance Law was introduced in June 1995, and its further extensions in "Provisional Rules for Insurance Regulation" in July 1996. This law sought to impose more discipline on the market and strengthen regulatory powers. The Law covers a variety of areas including the types of insurance that can be supplied; aspects of insurance contracts detailing the respective responsibilities of insurers and consumers; operational rules governing the conduct of business, including higher minimum capital requirements; approval of senior management; maintenance of contingency reserves; reinsurance requirements and restrictions on the investment of funds; aspects of supervision and control, including the approval of prices (rates) and policy conditions; accounting and actuarial monitoring; the regulation of insurance agents and other sales intermediaries; fines for non-compliance; and wind-up procedures.

The 1995 Law, and its subsequent amendments, have been well drafted and have brought the regulatory regime broadly into line with recognised standards, given the level of development of the insurance market. However, the challenge has been one of implementation, with the growing complexity of business, the entry of foreign insurers into the market and the geographical size of the country. Since 1949, the supervision of insurance rested with the People's Bank of China, which was also responsible for the supervision of the banking and securities industries. Hence it was considered necessary to have a better-resourced and more technically competent supervisory body for the insurance industry. The CIRC was set up in November 1998 and began its operations on 1 January 1999. Staff to run the CIRC were drawn from the People's Insurance Company of China (PICC), the People's Bank of China and the Ministry of Finance.

One policy priority of the CIRC has been to increase its own operations across the country in order to be able to have in place effective on-the-spot supervision. By 2001, the CIRC had set up 31 offices nationwide.

Strengthening solvency standards

The central concern of any supervisory body is to ensure the solvency of the insurance companies that it licenses. One aspect of solvency in insurance is capital adequacy. Under the 1995 Act, the system adopted for capital adequacy was based on the solvency margin system in use in the EU, and the wider European Economic Area, and not the newer risk-based capital systems that operate in a few countries, such as the United States, Japan and Australia. A solvency margin system was considered easier to administer. This was a sound decision. Until there are more transparent accounting and actuarial valuation systems, and better internal risk management systems are more widespread, the maintenance of a solvency margin system is appropriate. The minimum solvency margins levels are higher in China, for both life and non-life business, than they are in Western Europe, which is encouraging. Moreover, the CIRC has pursued a recent policy of requiring new insurance companies that have been set up to have a much higher initial paid-up capital level. In 2000, the minimum capital requirement for an insurance company with a licence to operate nationwide was raised to RMB 500 million, which is high by international standards.

It is also being increasingly recognised that the solvency of insurance companies does not depend only on their capital adequacy. It depends on the adequacy of premiums, reliable reinsurance arrangements, sound actuarial reserving methods and the appropriate risk matching of assets and liabilities. One aspect of technical supervision that is currently being strengthened is the requirement that insurance companies should have internal actuarial planning and controls systems in place. There is at present a shortage of actuaries in China, but this deficiency is being solved by encouraging the development of a national actuarial profession and by bringing in expertise from international actuarial consultancy firms.

One serious solvency problem has arisen in a few Chinese life insurance companies in recent years. In the early and mid-1990s a few life insurance companies issued life insurance contracts containing long-term interest rate guarantees which were set when interest rates were high. During the second half of the 1990s interest rates began to fall such that the investments would be unlikely to earn rates of returns that would be sufficient to meet these interest rate guarantees. In one or two cases it is estimated that their existing capital is unlikely to cover this asset shortfall. Hence it may be that these life insurance companies could be technically insolvent, under a not unreasonable interest rate scenario. This interest rate risk is the main source of insolvency for a life insurance company. The situation is not unique to China: similar problems have arisen during the 1990s in Japan, Korea and in some European countries. There are several lessons that the CIRC is drawing from this experience. One lesson is that it has to check that the interest rate guarantees offered by life insurance companies are not unreasonable in the light of long-term interest rate expectations. Another lesson is that life insurance should be encouraged to adapt modern asset-liability modelling techniques to measure and control their interest rate risks. On a wider front, if the Chinese government were to issue more longer-dated bonds, then life insurance companies would be able to lock in interest rates that are more appropriate to the duration of their liabilities.

In addition, a complete insurance regulatory system should also have a backstop in the event of failure of an insurance company. There is a growing trend worldwide to have in place a guarantee scheme or a protection fund that will ensure that consumers do not lose out financially in the event of the insolvency of an insurance company. These schemes usually take the form of levy on the rest of the insurance market. Setting up a comprehensive guarantee scheme in China has been considered by the CIRC, and this is a policy direction that should be encouraged.

A system of approved product and prices in non-life insurance

An integral part of the regulation of non-life insurance in China has been a system of approved insurance products and prices. The main classes of approved products in non-life insurance are: motor insurance; property insurance for enterprises; employers' liability; credit insurance; and fidelity guarantee. This regulatory practice of prior approval of insurance contracts and approved prices (tariff prices) is a common feature in many emerging markets. These approved prices have been put in place to avoid undue price competition that can undermine the solvency of insurance companies.

Experience in most countries shows that approved insurance contracts and pricing tends to be phased out by governments over time, since they run counter to wider competition policy. In the European Union, such regulatory practices were common prior to the mid-1990s but they have now been removed, except for compulsory insurances in a few countries. Another disadvantage of the system of approved insurance contracts and prices is that it slows down new product innovation.

Recently, there has been some relaxation in the system of prior approval for new insurance products. The CIRC has allowed a "file and use" system to evolve, whereby an insurance company can introduce a new product and set its own pricing for a trial period. The insurance company then reports back to the CIRC who checks the insurance contracts, pricing, and claims experience. If this new product and its associated pricing seem sound, the company is allowed to continue and expand its marketing and production. This flexibility in the regulatory system is to be commended.

Regulating prices for insurance is a complex issue for an emerging insurance market, since unbridled competition can force down prices to such low levels that they endanger insurance company solvency. The current policy overall is to retain regulated prices in the short term, but then to gradually phase them out, with prudential supervision placing more emphasis on capital adequacy and other aspects of financial solvency assessment.

The regulation of the investment policies of insurers

Since the opening up the market in the late 1980s, a few insurance companies have suffered financial losses from investing in risky corporate loans and poor quality equity and real estate investments. This was due in part to the lack of an adequate regulatory framework. One of the features of the 1995 Law was to tighten up these regulations. Under the Act, the investment of life and non-life insurance funds was restricted to bank deposits and government bonds. Other investments required official approval. These restrictions were also put in place because the supervisory authorities did not consider that insurance companies had the adequate in-house investment expertise to assess risk in these areas. A limited and thinly traded stock market was a further conditioning factor. With falling interest rates, and some deepening of the stock market in the second half of the 1990s, investment regulations were partly liberalised. With the permission of the supervisory authority, insurance companies could invest 5 per cent of their total assets in separately managed, closed-end CIS (collective investment schemes), but they were not allowed to invest directly in the stock market. The 5 per cent ceiling was raised to 10 per cent and to 15 per cent for selected companies in late 2000. Foreign non-life insurance companies operating through wholly-owned non-life branch operations, and restricted to providing local insurances to foreign-owned enterprises in foreign currencies, were granted limited flexibility to invest directly in the stock market and in large-scale infrastructure projects. In addition, to help develop the corporate debt market, insurance companies were allowed to invest in corporate bonds that were guaranteed by the central or provincial governments, provided that they had at least an AA+ rating.

This loosening of investment policies has been a sensible decision as it allows insurance companies, especially life insurance companies offering third pillar supplementary pensions and linked life contracts, to earn more competitive rates of return, thus encouraging more long-term saving. It is essential that investment regulations are not applied too rigidly. Some additional flexibility is being granted to the more financially sound insurance companies, in particular: a) companies holding capital and reserves that are significantly higher than the statutory minimum; b) life insurance companies that have not been financially weakened by offering high interest rate guarantees; c) companies possessing proven internal investment capability, including risk assessment skills. There is a case for allowing direct investment in the stock market on a limited scale, providing that the insurance company can show that it has internal investment competence. There is a growing recognition by the CIRC that adequate risk management systems should be in place within insurance companies, and that investment decisions should be set within an appropriate asset-liability framework.

The liberalisation of investment rules is conducive to the long-term development of the capital market. In many countries, the life insurance industry has emerged as the most important institutional investor. Encouraging the gradual liberalisation of investments by the life insurance sector requires having in place responsible, yet flexibly applied, investment regulations. However, a too rapid liberalisation of investment policy when capital markets are fragile can cause a destabilisation, not least because volatile stock and bond markets can adversely affect public confidence in an embryonic life insurance and private pensions industry. A balanced step-by-step process has been shown in other insurance markets to be the best approach. In addition, there is case for gradually reducing the restrictions on foreign investment. Greater flexibility to invest overseas allows more effective currency matching of the assets and liabilities for non-life insurance companies, for direct and reinsurance business, and for life insurance companies it increases the risk/return profile for long-term savers.

Large insurance groups in OECD countries, which have built up significant investment expertise over time, have tended to set up separate fund or asset management companies within their groups allowing them to offer mutual funds and investment services to individuals and to smaller institutional investors. In January 2001 there was a regulatory change that allowed the larger insurance groups to follow the trend, when fund management was recognised as a defined area of business by the Chinese Securities Regulatory Commission (CSRC). Large insurance companies, including foreign-owned or joint ventures, will be able to set up a separate fund management company under a holding company structure to supply these services, which will be supervised directly by the CSRC. Consequently, there will be a need for supervisory co-ordination between the CSRC and the CIRC to ensure that there are no adverse effects at the group or holding company level.

Reinsurance and risk spreading

One aim of the government has been to build up a viable reinsurance sector within China. This has been both to conserve foreign exchange and to have an adequate domestic risk retention capability. Current regulations require that 20 per cent of gross premiums received by all non-life insurance companies are paid to the government-owned reinsurance company, China Reinsurance Company. A policy of compulsory reinsurance cessions to a government reinsurance monopoly has been pursued in many emerging markets in the past. But usually over time they are discontinued, because of the lack of sustained capacity and inadequate technical pricing and risk management expertise. This 20 per cent compulsory cession to the state reinsurance company was lowered from 30 per cent in 1995, reflecting a recognition that risks should be spread more widely. The major floods in China in 1998 gave a further warning of the danger of over reliance on internal risk retention. The commercial imperative to spread large risk exposures internationally is well recognised, even in the large OECD countries. The reinsurance market in Hong Kong, China offers some reinsurance support, but this is mainly a conduit to the wider international reinsurance market.

Ensuring responsible marketing and distribution

One primary concern of the CIRC has been to curtail aggressive marketing practices and to increase the professionalism of insurance intermediaries, e.g. agents, brokers, etc. This problem arises from the fact that insurance, because of its intangible and contingent nature, has to be actively marketed to consumers. Most insurance products in China are sold though agents, including part-time agents who sell insurance as an ancillary source of income to their main employment. Although there is a requirement that agents and brokers must be approved by the CIRC and to gain this approval they must pass an examination in order to operate, these are only minimum requirements. Insurance companies have been encouraged to put more resources into training these part-time agents and their own sales staff, not just to improve their technical competence but to instil in them ethical practices.

One problem in the Chinese market, in common with other insurance markets, is that agents or other insurance intermediaries have strong bargaining power with insurance companies, since customer allegiance often rests with them. This bargaining power reflects itself in a tendency for commission rates paid to intermediaries to rise, with the attendant problem that insurances tend to be switched from one company to another. These are costs that have to be borne by consumers over time in the form of higher prices or in a lower quality service. This has been a feature of the Chinese insurance market, especially as new companies have been entering the market. Some attempt to contain this was an agreement between the supervisory body and the insurance companies in October 1997 to place a 10 per cent ceiling on commission rates, with an attendant agreement to prevent rebating of some of the premiums back to consumers. Failure to adhere to this commission ceiling and rebating to consumers still remain problems, and these issues are currently being given a high priority by the CIRC.

The CIRC is also encouraging more professionalism within the intermediary system. Since 2000 insurance brokers have been allowed to operate in the market. Several insurance brokerage firms have been licensed so far. Although none of these are foreign-owned brokers, granting licenses to the large, foreign insurance brokers would strengthen the market. As a complement to formal regulation and standard setting, CIRC has been seeking to increase self-regulation among the agents and brokers through the establishment of trade organisations and professional bodies. This is a sensible initiative, since these organisations can impose standards of ethical practice on their members and they also have their own penalties for malpractice. In life insurance, more attention is being placed on improving advertising standards, especially when presenting investment performance. Exaggerated advertising and aggressive selling techniques may have a short-term pay-off, but they can damage the future growth of the insurance industry, as disappointed consumers turn to alternative long-term saving products or do not save at all. There is now greater self-regulation by agents and brokers through the establishment of their own trade organisations and by the creation of professional bodies, which set standards of good practice with their own internal penalties for malpractice. Self-regulation complements statutory regulation; it does not have the same degree of deterrence as formal regulation but because it is market-based, potential problems can be identified more quickly.

A further market development has been the increased role of banks in the marketing of insurances, especially life insurances. Since the late 1990s, the CIRC has been encouraging the large banks to become more active in helping stimulate the demand for insurance though their networks of offices. At the same time, banks must be able to justify that they have adequately trained their staff to sell insurance products. Elsewhere in the world, banks have played a growing role as a distribution channel for insurances to individuals and small businesses. Over time, the trend has been for banks to own insurance companies and not just be marketing outlets. Since 2000, the CIRC has allowed banks to own insurance companies, providing they are separate companies under a holding company structure. The licensing of a new insurance company, Minsheng Insurance Company, which is a subsidiary of the Minsheng Banking Corporation, created a precedent. The Bank of China has also indicated its intention of setting up an insurance company within its group. These diversification strategies can be expected to expand the insurance market. There has been a secondary reason for allowing the large Chinese banking groups to extend their activities into insurance. This is to allow them to gain the overall economies of scale and scope in order to allow them to compete more effectively with the larger foreign financial services groups in the future, as the financial services sector liberalises.

Monitoring claims-paying efficiency

One current concern in non-life insurance is the fairness and speed of claim payments to policyholders when they have a loss. Consumers can only test the efficacy of an insurance contract when a claim is made. The CIRC is encouraging the introduction of professional loss adjusting and surveying services into the market, and it has recently developed an index to measure and assess the claim-paying effectiveness of insurance companies. If insurance companies fall below an acceptable level on the index, they will be penalised, including the possibility of being publicly denoted as a "specially supervised company" or to have their licences suspended. It is worth observing that leading international rating agencies, Standard and Poor's, Bests and Moody's, have developed sophisticated models to assess the claims-paying ability and performance of insurance companies as an extension of their core rating activities. Closer liaison with these rating firms might be explored to see if new approaches can be learnt from this wider experience.

In addition, there are inevitable disputes that arise between insurance companies and consumers over claim payments. There is currently only a limited legal system to handle such disputes, which includes an appeal procedure within the CIRC itself. One solution is to establish an Ombudsman scheme, which is an independent body to arbitrate between insurance companies and consumers. Ombudsman schemes operate successfully in a number of European countries.

A further challenge in improving claims settlement efficiency is that consumers first turn to their agent when a loss occurs, and a problem arises when the insurance agent changes company or moves to another region. Hence an attempt is being made to ensure greater co-ordination between the CIRC and agent trade associations to handle this problem.

Increasing corporate governance standards and internal market discipline

In most regulatory systems throughout the world, there are growing attempts by governments to share some of the responsibility for supervision with the companies themselves by promoting improved corporate governance. This is also occurring in other branches of financial services. As noted in Chapter 14 on the financial system and financial regulatory policies, this is also increasingly the practice in other areas of financial services, such as banking and securities. There are powers under the Insurance Law for the CIRC to approve senior management positions within insurance companies. These powers can also be exercised on an on-going basis as part of the annual licence approval process. In addition, insurance companies, in common with other Chinese companies, have supervisory committees or boards to which their executive management are accountable and must report. The strengthening of the responsibilities of supervisory committees would be a positive step forward, with a requirement that there should be an audit sub-committee, which includes a risk auditing function.

Trade associations can play an effective role in self-regulation across the insurance market as a whole, as has been shown in many OECD countries. The Insurance Association of China was set up in November 2000, with a membership across all insurance companies and with a regional structure. Trade associations can assist in the following areas: introducing more transparent accounting systems; pooling claims experience, especially on large risks, to assist individual insurance companies to have more soundly based pricing policies as regulated or approved pricing is gradually phased out; working with the CIRC, to effect better public education on the value of insurance, including what it offers and what it does not; and setting codes of best practice for investment policies and claims management.

Market liberalisation

Recognition of need for more foreign investment

Developing the Chinese insurance market will require much more investment, not just of capital but a strengthening of the technical capabilities within the market and its ability to introduce new products. One challenge is that insurance development has been most evident in the major cities and the coastal regions, with the rural areas and smaller towns, especially in remoter western regions, inadequately provided for. In a service industry such as insurance, effective production and distribution require a local presence. The Chinese government is increasingly recognising that foreign insurers should play a key role in this. The policy has been to phase in the introduction of foreign insurers into the market. There have been two aspects of this policy. The government wishes to ensure that there was a balance between domestic and foreign ownership, given the size and experience of the foreign insurers that wish to expand in the market. At the same time, the government needs to ensure that too strong competition from foreign insurers does not threaten the solvency of the less efficient domestic insurers and hence undermine consumer confidence in the market.

Widening the market scope for foreign insurers

A major restriction on foreign non-life insurers has been that they can only supply insurance products for foreign businesses, a restriction that is reinforced by their geographical limitations. These restrictions will be gradually widened to allow insurance to be supplied to these foreign businesses across China without geographical restriction, thus allowing them to supply a more effective service to their customers with operations in more than one region. Moreover, direct participation in the underwriting of large infrastructure projects will be allowed in the short term. But it is envisaged that the restrictions on supplying non-life insurances to Chinese individuals and businesses, such as motor, property, liability, marine and credit insurances, will only be relaxed gradually. The restrictions on motor insurance are significant since it represents some 60 per cent of the total non-life insurance market at the present time. Even so foreign insurers with a local presence are helped to some degree by the restriction that foreign businesses must insure their risks within China.

Currently, life insurance supplied by foreign joint venture companies can supply insurance to both Chinese and foreign nationals, but they are subject to severe geographical restrictions. Also there are limitations on product restrictions not faced by domestically owned life insurance companies, in particular they cannot supply group life or group pension products. This is a binding restriction, since a significant proportion of life insurance is carried out through group schemes, especially the third-pillar pensions that are mainly offered on a packaged basis through employers. Similarly, foreign life insurers have not been allowed to offer health and disability insurance. There will be no major liberalisation immediately after China's accession to the WTO, but there is a minimum timetable within which the liberalisation process will take place. It has been agreed that foreign joint ventures will be able to sell health insurance within the next four years and group life and pension products within five years.

Strategic foreign investment in existing insurance companies

One aspect of the policy of the CIRC in strengthening domestically owned insurance companies has been to allow the major international insurance companies to take strategic stakes in them, but there are limits on this. Foreign insurance companies can collectively have a maximum shareholding of 25 per cent, with a single foreign insurer having a maximum of 10 per cent. These limits have been raised recently. The 25 per cent limit was raised from 20 per cent in 1999 and the 10 per cent limit from 5 per cent in 2000. The encouragement of these strategic investments has also had another purpose: to increase public confidence, especially as a number of the larger domestic companies are planning to list on the stock market.

Key challenges in developing the insurance market

Earlier the three key roles that insurance plays in a modern economic system were discussed. These roles were: *a*) to provide an efficient mechanism for the transfer of risk; *b*) to mobilise long-term saving from a wide section of the population and to invest these savings on capital markets; and *c*) to act as partner with the state in the provision of pension, disability and health care financing benefits. In this section, policy areas are identified that would strengthen the Chinese insurance sector in fulfilling these economic roles.

Increasing the capacity to absorb large risks

One challenge facing the Chinese non-life insurance market is to have sufficient capacity to underwrite very large risk exposures. These risk exposures arise from large-scale projects such as the Three Gorges Dam development and nuclear power stations, but also protection against natural catastrophes to which parts of China is prone, *viz.* earthquakes, floods and windstorms. These large risk exposures require major capital resources and the on-the-spot risk assessment expertise. Hence international expertise and financial resources need to be brought in to strengthen the local market capability. Major risk concentrations, even within a large economy such as China, will always need to be well diversified internationally. By October 2001, the only large specialist reinsurance company allowed to operate on the Chinese insurance market was the state-owned China Reinsurance Company. But it does not have a monopoly, since domestic insurers and the branches of foreign insurers can supply reinsurance above the 20 per cent compulsory limit. However, none of the large international reinsurance companies have so far been granted licences to operate. This restriction on their activities has been to allow the China Reinsurance Company and some of the large domestic insurance companies to grow and build up their local capability. International reinsurance is allowed if a case can be made that there is insufficient local capacity. This external reinsurance is usually arranged in foreign currency and placed with international reinsurers based in Hong Kong, China or directly into the wider international reinsurance market. Some evidence exists to suggest that the level of risk retention within China is higher than the real absorption capacity of the local market. Only if a very large loss occurs will this risk retention capability be fully tested, and then it will be too late. One option that has been advanced by the Chinese Government is to set up a Reinsurance Exchange to which local and foreign insurers and reinsurers could subscribe as members. Experience in establishing reinsurance exchanges have not been promising, for example in New York, Miami and Bermuda. One reason for the failure is that, over time, the large reinsurers and insurers find a conflict arising between their corporate strategies and those of the exchange itself. Lloyd's or the International Underwriting Association in London are particular types of exchange, but their success depends on the active role of insurance brokers. However, over time advances in IT networking systems for risk placement may make reinsurance exchanges work. A second option is to allow the large specialist reinsurers to enter the market by allowing them to have their own wholly owned branches or subsidiaries. Experience elsewhere shows that large reinsurers will invest more if they can have wholly-owned local operations which can be more easily integrated into their global corporate policies, including their own risk transfer ("retrocession") mechanisms. But these two options are not necessarily mutually exclusive.

One factor that has slowed down the granting of licences to large foreign reinsurance companies is the lack of specific regulation covering reinsurance operations. This problem of having specific regulation for reinsurance operations is not confined to China. The European Commission is currently working on a new directive to help to standardise the regulation of the reinsurance sector across the European Economic Area. Indeed, the CIRC is close to completing new regulations for reinsurance and when these are finalised, this will allow the large foreign reinsurers to be granted licences more easily.

Allowing foreign reinsurance companies to operate on the national market also strengthens the ability of domestically owned insurance companies to compete more effectively against large foreign insurers. This is because reinsurance companies stand behind a local direct insurer by providing it with capital indirectly, through the reinsurance arrangement, and by providing it with technical know-how and IT and training support.

Building up the capacity of the domestic reinsurance industry will tend to reduce an undue dependence on the international reinsurance market in the long term, but there will always be a need to spread large risk exposures internationally. International reinsurance contracts will tend to be denominated in foreign currencies, but there should be some encouragement that these foreign currencies are strong currencies. Indeed there is an advantage in this for China itself, since if there were a large natural catastrophe and this caused a depreciation of renminbi, the cost of imported replacement goods and services would increase. By having reinsurance protection denominated in strong foreign currencies thus affords an implicit currency hedge.

In addition, because of the very large potential loss exposures, there is a case for considering the development of pools to which insurance companies can participate and spread the risk, with external reinsurance support, possibly with some government involvement. Two risk-sharing pools currently exist in China: one for satellites and one for nuclear power stations. In addition, there is a case for the development of risk securitisation and Alternative Risk Transfer mechanisms that allow some of these large risk exposures to be transferred directly onto global capital markets. There are a number of existing mechanisms that can be studied to see how they might be adapted to fit the particular Chinese situation. These are the Californian Earthquake Authority and the new proposed risk pool for Turkey.

Encouraging a greater role for the life insurance sector

One further challenge for China is to encourage a greater role for the life insurance sector. As discussed earlier, life insurance companies provide an effective way of mobilising small savings across the whole economy and hence generate long-term funds for investment in the domestic capital market. However, for life insurance companies to fulfil their potential they must be able to offer appropriate savings products and their associated sales and marketing practices must be professional. Over-aggressive sales and marketing practices that force inappropriate products on consumers and which raise unrealistic expectations on future investment performance, or high commission payments that reduce the rate of return on savings products, have the effect of harming the development of the life insurance industry.

There are also clear lessons to be learned from the marketing practices in the mid-1990s when Chinese life insurers offered guaranteed interest rates higher than the life insurance companies could deliver. The introduction of linked life insurance contracts since early 2000, which pass on the investment risk to consumers but which also provide higher long-term returns, should be encouraged further. Linked life insurance contracts are the fastest growing area of life insurance around the world.

One further problem is that the growth of the life insurance market is uneven; it is concentrated too much in the larger cities and insufficiently in the rural areas. This concentration within the more affluent cities and regions is a normal pattern of development, but it is now time for a more active policy to extend life insurance across the country. There may well be a need to change the product range and distribution channels for these less affluent areas. A greater emphasis on group schemes, organised through employers, trade and farmers associations and other affinity groups suggests itself. In addition, the commercial banks should be encouraged to be more active in the marketing of life insurance products, and this would enable them to use their nationwide branch office networks. Given the scale of the country, this is beyond the financial and technical and management resources of the domestically owned life insurance companies, especially as some of these have their capital tied up in the interest guarantee business sold during the 1990s. This requires not just permitting more foreign insurers to set up joint ventures, but more importantly allowing foreign insurers that are already operating in the market to set up branch offices across the country. Foreign life insurers operate in other emerging markets and so they can deploy this international experience. Domestically owned insurance companies should be encouraged to gain stock market listing to allow them to raise the additional capital to finance this market expansion.

Given the ageing structure of the Chinese population, the government recognises the need for a more effective implementation of its pension reforms. There is a key role in this for the life insurance industry, as has been the case in most countries of the world in recent years. Allowing foreign life insurers to play a more active role through their joint ventures will be important in developing the potential of the non-state pensions market. The current restrictions on foreign life insurers, even through joint ventures, from offering group pensions, and other group schemes, such as disability and accident, clearly hinders the planned reform of the social insurance system. These restrictions are also exacerbated by the geographical restrictions of these insurers. The fact that all pensions-related activities of life insurance companies will be carried out on a funded basis will also help to ensure that the pension system as a whole is put on a more sustainable footing. The gradual liberalisation of the investment restrictions on insurance companies that can show that they have the management competence to invest their funds would facilitate this process.

Widening product choice

The development of the market also requires new products to be developed. In non-life insurance, earthquake insurances that were withdrawn in the 1990s are now being introduced on a limited quota basis for the stronger domestic insurance companies. There is a need to expand the scope of earthquake, flood and windstorm protection so they are more generally available within personal and commercial property insurance policies. Allowing a greater role for foreign insurers in supplying the requisite capital and risk assessment and pricing expertise would allow this widening of protection. In addition, increasing the international reinsurance support against these natural catastrophes is also necessary to allow an adequate supply across the country and to ensure that very large losses do not bankrupt domestic insurers. During 2001, international excess of loss reinsurance arrangements began to be put in place to allow the supply of earthquake, flood and windstorm insurance protections in property insurance contracts. This policy needs to be extended further to allow an even greater supply.

At the same time, there is scope for commercial and personal non-life insurances to grow. Home contents and personal property insurances are underdeveloped, as are personal accident and disability insurances. Health and medical insurances are also underdeveloped. One characteristic of the Chinese market is that private health insurance is considered to be a part of life insurance, whereas in other countries it can be written by non-life insurance or life and non-life insurance companies. There is a case for amending the insurance legislation so that non-life insurance can offer health insurance as well as life insurance companies. This would allow the insurance sector to be more active not just by increasing the potential supply but by being able to offer a wider range of health insurance and disability products. For the commercial non-life sector, there is also the scope to develop the business interruption insurances and the new types of insurance covering operational and enterprise risks.

Credit insurance is another area where there is scope for greater product development and availability. In 2001, the China Credit Insurance Company was set up from a merger between the China Import and Export Bank and the credit insurance activities of the state-owned property insurer, PICC. This merger was to strengthen the capability of the credit insurance market and to allow a better co-ordination between the credit insurance for Chinese enterprises for their domestic and their international commercial and trading activities. It is proposed that the product experience of leading international credit insurance companies should also be called on. Their experience is especially useful, as they have developed their businesses during the last decade in part following decisions by national governments to outsource or to privatise their short-term export credit insurance activities.

One area of potential product development is in the field of liability insurances: professional liability, employer liability, product liability and general liability insurances. The current insurance legislation in China allows these liability insurances to be supplied, but the main constraint on supply has been the concern of CIRC with the ability of the local insurance companies to underwrite these more complex insurances. The experience of foreign companies in these areas of insurance would permit the market to develop further.

In general, the diversity of insurance products and the supply capability in the Chinese market are closely linked to the issue of market liberalisation. As more foreign insurers are allowed to enter the market, their capital resources and their technical and management expertise will allow the insurance market to meet the large untapped demand potential. Domestically owned insurance companies can also develop their business in these new product areas, since they can learn from these foreign insurers, because there are no patent laws in insurance and because the general skill level within the market will tend to increase.

Conclusions and recommendations

The size of the Chinese insurance industry relative to the wider economy, as measured by the ratio of insurance premium spending to GDP, was 1.6 per cent in 1999 and 1.8 per cent in 2000. Although this ratio is low by international standards, it is not greatly out of line with that of other large emerging economies, such as India, Russia and Brazil. This ratio can be expected to be within the 2 per cent to 3 per cent range by 2005, but it could be at the upper end of this range if there is sufficient new investment into the insurance sector and consumer confidence is not undermined by insurance company insolvencies. To ensure an adequate level of investment will require a continuation of the current policy of greater market liberalisation by allowing financially strong and well-managed foreign insurance companies to enter and expand in the market. It also requires that domestically owned insurance companies should gain listings on the stock market in order to attract new capital to finance this potential growth.

It is clear that there needs to be a wider geographical coverage of insurance company operations. In a service industry, such as insurance, the effective supply of insurance depends on an adequate local presence to assess risks, to underwrite and price these risks, and to ensure that there is a sound system for claims assessment and payment. Insurance supply is still over-concentrated in the major cities and in the coastal areas. There are an insufficient number of branch offices of insurance companies in the rural areas and in the western regions. Gaining a wider geographical coverage should be seen as an integral part of the process of market development. But it is more than this. By having a broader market, insurance companies can exploit the risk-spreading benefits inherent in the law of large numbers, thus increasing the capacity of the market and reducing the potential cost of insurance. In life insurance, a wider geographical coverage also helps to ensure that insurance companies can be more effective in providing third pillar supplementary pensions and other insurances, such as disability, accident and medical insurances, which complement the wider social insurance benefit structure. A social insurance system must have national coverage, and so it is essential that insurance companies, and other relevant financial service providers, have a similar geographical spread, if they are to be useful partners in the reform process.

If the CIRC is to strengthen its supervisory role it must have the necessary resources to attract and retain well-qualified staff. Its current staff of 400 should be increased, especially as the CIRC is developing a network of offices across the country to allow more effective local monitoring. It should be kept in mind that the responsibilities of the CIRC are not confined to supervision: they also embrace the development of the insurance market itself. A key problem is to ensure that staff salaries do not get out of line with those that are paid outside, especially within the insurance industry. Experience in many emerging insurance markets shows that if the salary structure of middle and senior staff within a supervisory agency is low relative to that within the insurance sector, key staff are often tempted away to work for insurance companies, especially foreign companies. It is not just a question of maintaining staff quality but ensuring continuity; a supervisory authority must deliver a consistent monitoring policy, which it cannot do with a high staff turnover.

The CIRC should seek to follow more closely the Core Principles that have been recently formulated by the International Association of Insurance Supervisors (IAIS), which is the system of best practice laid down by insurance supervisors from both OECD and emerging countries. The fact that the CIRC has recently gained membership in the IAIS should assist in this, since it can exploit the associated technical and training support that the IAIS offers to its members. The standards on insurance accounting and actuarial valuation practices that are being developed by the IAIS should be adopted as soon as practicable.

It has been recognised by the CIRC that effective supervision also depends on self-regulation within the insurance industry and on sound corporate governance. Further efforts should be made to ensure that the CIRC works more closely with the insurance trade associations that have recently been set up. Corporate governance standards can be increased by requiring that published accounts be more transparent and by placing a greater responsibility on the supervisory committees or boards of insurance companies.

The size of the losses within the Chinese life insurance sector arising from the interest rate guarantees offered in the mid and late 1990s requires attention, and greater efforts should be made to quantify these losses. Due to a lack of accounting and actuarial transparency, the scale of the problem is not known with any degree of accuracy nor are the identities of the insurance companies that are most affected. However, any assessment of the actuarial deficit will depend on a variety of financial assumptions, not least the future pattern of interest rates (or the long-term rates of return on investments) and the future profits expected to be earned on new business. The best solution to the problem is to encourage financially strong companies, including foreign insurers, to acquire strategic stakes in those insurance companies that are most affected. This would inject capital quickly into these companies and also create the necessary stock market confidence that will allow them to gain an early listing to raise more capital.

The domestic reinsurance market within China is underdeveloped and its internal risk-absorption capacity is inadequate. To allow large foreign reinsurance companies to enter the market to provide this capacity is a priority, and this is clearly complementary to the current plans to phase out the 20 per cent compulsory reinsurance cessions to the China Reinsurance Company. But while building up the domestic reinsurance market, it should not be forgotten that very large risk exposures still require to be spread further through international reinsurance, which will require payment in foreign currencies. In addition, there should be a continuing monitoring by the CIRC of potential risk accumulations within the non-life insurance sector. International risk spreading and the monitoring of risk accumulations across the market are necessary to ensure that no significant systemic risk is building up. Moreover, effective reinsurance transfer arrangements, both domestically and internationally, depend on the active role of professional reinsurance brokers, risk management consultants, and loss adjusters. Granting licences to leading foreign broking firms and loss adjusters should therefore be seen as a part of the process of building up this domestic reinsurance capability.

The current policy of widening the range of distribution channels for insurance and requiring that insurance intermediaries are well qualified should be continued. Experience shows that growing insurance markets possess a broad range of distribution channels and have effective sales and marketing policies in operation. There is a causal link between the two. This is because consumers are not naturally aware of the benefits of insurance, because of its contingent nature, and when making long-term saving provision, especially for retirement purposes, they are often myopic. Banks should be further encouraged to act as distribution outlets for insurance and direct marketing through telesales and through the Internet. Widening distribution channels places an additional burden on a supervisory authority, but this is a responsibility that has to be accepted.

BIBLIOGRAPHY

Arkell, Julian (1997),
"The Service Liberalisation Agenda of the World Trade Organisation: What are the Issues?" *The Geneva Papers on Risk and Insurance*, No. 84, July.

AXCO (2000),
Insurance Market Report on China, London.

Brostoff. S. (1999),
"Insurers Praise Pact for China to Entry to WTO" *National Underwriter: Life and Health/Financial Services*, 22 November.

Carter, Robert L. and Dickinson, Gerry (1992),
Obstacles to the Liberalisation of Trade in Insurance, for the Trade Policy Research Centre. London: Harvester Wheatsheaf

Chinese Academy of Social Sciences (2000),
Research Report on China's Entry into WTO.

China Financial Development Report 2000, Shanghai University of Economics and Finance Publishing House.

China Insurance Regulatory Commission (various publications).

CIRC-OECD (2000),
"Experts Meeting on Insurance Regulation and Supervision" *Meeting Materials Volumes* A *and* B, Beijing, January 20-21.

CIRC-OECD (2001),
"2nd Experts Meeting on Insurance Regulation and Supervision" *Meeting Materials Volumes* A *and* B, Tianjin, July 9-10.

Classens, S. and T. Glaessner (1998),
"The Internationalisation of Financial Services in Asia", *Policy Research Working Paper*, The World Bank, April.

Daykin, Chris (1999),
"The Role of the Actuary in the Supervision of Insurance" in *Insurance Regulation and Supervision in Asia*. OECD, Paris.

Dickinson, Gerry (1998),
"The Economic Role of the Insurance Sector in the Risk-Transfer-Capital Market Nexus" *The Geneva Papers on Risk and Insurance*, No. 89, October.

Dickinson, Gerry (1999),
"The Changing Focus in the Supervision of Insurance Company Investment" in *Insurance Regulation and Supervision in Asia*. OECD, Paris.

Dickinson, Gerry (2001),
"Overview of Chinese Insurance Market and its Challenges" *Volume A of Proceedings*, 2nd CIRC-OECD Expert Meeting on Insurance Regulation and Supervision in China, Tianjin, June.

Fung, K.C. and Lawrence, J.L. (1999),
New Estimates of the United States-China Bilateral Trade Balance, Institute for International Studies, Stanford University, April.

Gautier, J-P and Peng (2000),
Insurance in China: an Historic Approach to Understanding the Chinese Insurance Market, London: Informa Publishing.

Giarini, Orio (1987),
editor, *The Emerging Service Economy*, Oxford: Pergamon Press.

Group of Ten (1997),
Financial Stability in Emerging Market Economies, Report of the Working Party on Financial Stability in Emerging Market Economies.

Han, Dawei, Li Fang and Wu Jiaheng (2000),
Pension Reform around the World-Lessons for China. Beijing: Publications of Science ad Economy.

Insurance Institute of China (2000),
   Almanac of China's Insurance. Beijing.

Jiao, J (2000),
   WTO and the Future of China's Financial Industry, China Finance Publishing House.

KPMG (2000),
   "China Issues Insurance Firm Regulations" in Insurance Insider, January.

Lim.P. and Bai, E. (1998),
   China Insurance Industry , Market Reports, National Trade Data Bank, August.

National People's Congress of China (1995),
   Insurance Law of the People's Republic of China, Beijing.

OECD (1996),
   Policy Issues in Insurance: Investment, Taxation and Insolvency, Paris.

OECD (1999),
   Insurance Regulation and Supervision in Asia. Paris.

OECD (2000),
   Reforming China's Enterprises. Paris.

Rosen, D.H. (1999),
   China in the WTO, a Great Leap Forward, "Institute for International Economics", June.

Santermero, A.M. (1997),
   "Insurers in a Changing and Competitive Financial Structure" Journal of Risk and Insurance, No. 4.

Shen, Yiming (2000),
   "China's Insurance Market: Opportunity, Competition and Market Trends", The Geneva Papers on Risk and Insurance, Vol. 25, No. 3, July.

Skipper, H.D. Jr. (998),
   International Risk and Insurance: An Environment-Managerial Approach , Irwin McGraw-Hill.

Skipper, H.D. Jr. and Klein, R.W. (2000),
   "Insurance Regulation in the Public Interest: the Path towards Solvent, Competitive Markets", The Geneva Papers on Risk and Insurance, Vol. 25 No. 4.

Souter, Gavin (2000),
   "Changes seen in China's Regulatory Crackdown anticipates WTO Membership' Business Insurance, May 3.

Wang Caiyu (1999),
   Development of Commercially Managed Pension Funds in China, MSc degree dissertation, City University Business School, London.

Wasow, B. and Hill, R.D (editors) (1986),
   Insurance Industry in Economic Development, New York University Press.

Wei Hualin and Li Kaibin (2000),
   "Joining the WTO and the Construction and Development of China Insurance Organisation Structure", Journal of Insurance Markets, April.

Woodrow, R. Brian (1997),
   "The World Trade Organisation and Liberalisation of Trade in Insurance Services: Impact and Implications of the 1995 Protocol on Financial Services" The Geneva Papers on Risk and Insurance, No. 84, July.

Yu, Michael (2000),
   "WTO and its Implications: a Case of the Chinese Insurance Market" Unpublished paper. London: China Insurance Company.

www.china-insurance.com

www.chinaonline.com/

www.circ.org

www.chinavista.com

www.circ.org

www.insure.com

ww.insurenet.com

Chapter 9

THE DEVELOPMENT OF CHINA'S DISTRIBUTION SECTOR

TABLE OF CONTENTS

THE DEVELOPMENT OF CHINA'S DISTRIBUTION SECTOR[*] [1]

Introduction

As the basic link between producer and consumer, the distribution sector is vital to the functioning of a market economy. Not only can an efficient and competitive distribution sector help promote the interests of the consumer, but it can also improve the efficiency of the economy as a whole.

Changes in the delivery of goods and services are a microcosm of China's wider, national economic transformation. In two brief decades China has gone from a central monopoly on buying, selling and trading to a condition where almost all materials for production and consumption move according to market supply and demand. To achieve this change, an administrative transformation was launched and sustained, dissolving collective distribution by turning centrally controlled wholesalers into local operators.

The market share of non-state-owned distributors rose from nothing in 1979 to four-fifths by the end of the century. During that period more than half of the incremental growth of jobs in distribution came from outside the realm of public ownership.

As distributive activity is being opened to global competition, we can look to international experience outside China to anticipate effects inside China. Expansion of the scale and scope of products and services available to the Chinese people is inevitable. This will stimulate increases in efficiency as well as the creation of jobs and provide a boost to trade, internally and internationally. As a result, the formation of a modern, competitive and efficient distribution system will provide net gains to the overall economy.

The development gap between distribution in China and in OECD countries is profound. The distribution sector is in its infancy in China. No better example illustrates this than the following: if a company has two warehouses in two locations and goods are moved from one to another, then the local tax bureau must treat the transfer as a sale and tax it accordingly.

In the immediate stage after WTO accession, China's distribution sector will feel the effects as foreign distributors enter the market. Traditional distributors, especially large wholesalers, will lose ground as foreign companies make inroads into the territory they used to dominate. Small distributors will continue to be disadvantaged in rules covering exports, for instance, unless remedies to administrative obstacles are identified and implemented.

What is true in broad-brush economic terms for China as a whole applies with equal validity within the distribution sector, where the chief handicap to the realisation of gains from liberalisation is a direct result of having so many different levels of government. There is a great need for the Chinese government to disentangle the welter of contradictory regulations, among which it is not obvious which set of rules holds primacy. Clarity from the centre is a necessity to overcome grave constraints in distribution, such as unfair rules on market access and arbitrary limits on where and how a distributor can operate. The deepening of reforms to solve these problems must take place in the very near term if the potential gains in distribution from trade and investment liberalisation are to be realised.

The chapter begins with a brief overview of the reform and opening process as it has affected China's distribution sector over the past 20 years. This is followed by a discussion of the structure of the sector and its significance in the overall economy. The next two sections consider, respectively, the challenges and problems currently faced by the distribution sector, and the implications of liberalising the sector in light of Chinese and international experience. The chapter concludes with a summary of policy changes that are necessary if the potential contributions of the distribution sector to the economy are to be realised.

---

[*] This chapter was prepared by Ms Wei Wang, Research associate, Development Research Centre of the State Council, China, and consultant for the Economics Department, OECD.

Overview of the evolution of the distribution system

As one of the most important components of the planned economy, the traditional distribution sector before 1978 was a closed system with a state monopoly over the purchase and selling of almost all products. At that time, all distribution activities were undertaken by the state-owned, collective distribution companies in accordance with planning mandates and at prices fixed by the government. Neither producers nor individuals enjoyed the freedom to sell products or purchase materials for production. In line with the requirements of a planned economy, the distribution network was shaped as a three-tier wholesale system consisting of: the administrative planning level; a retail system with vast numbers of small shops selling limited varieties of products; and a few department stores supplying almost the entire gamut of consumer goods.

Distribution reform and the domestic opening

In the evolution of the economic system since the 1979 reform that aimed to break the traditional system of central planning and establish a market economy, changes to the distribution system were from the outset treated as a breakthrough and an opportunity to reinforce broader reforms. The following aspects of policy reform stand out: First, *mandatory planning provisions governing product purchasing and selling have been gradually abolished over the past 20 years.* As a result, the proportion of products exchanged through the market has constantly increased. By the end of the Eighth Five-year Plan period, most industrial products and consumer goods were allocated according to market supply and demand; only a certain portion of key products such as grain, cotton, coal, heavy oil, and automobiles still fell within the ambit of the state's mandatory plan.

Second, price-setting power reverted to the market as opposed to state-controlled price mechanisms. Under the system of central planning, prices were merely accounting devices set by the government. In the process of price reform since 1979, the government's price-setting power has been narrowed significantly. At the time of writing, prices for 95 per cent of all consumer goods and production materials were determined by market forces of supply and demand; at the same time, however, ten kinds of state-controlled prices or price guidelines on goods and services remain in force, such as the pricing of rail transportation and aviation, and products of strategic value like crude and refined oil.

Third, the planning distribution network was dismantled. At one level, the vertical, three-tier wholesale network and its linkage to retailers was disassembled and control of all wholesale enterprises and outlets was transferred to each relevant locality, turning centrally controlled wholesalers into local operators. At another level, all wholesalers, retailers and manufacturers were granted the freedom to choose purchasing and selling channels for most commodity products. Besides the power to accord operational autonomy to companies, every distributor could operate independently and separately, experiencing progressively less administrative intervention from the various levels of government. The rupture of traditional distribution linkages under central planning provided opportunities to develop new kinds of linkages, as well as market-driven distribution networks.

Fourth, the distribution sector was opened to the entire domestic market and, with the exception of several important product areas, all domestic enterprises and individuals were encouraged to participate in this sector.[2] This broke the monopoly of state-owned, collective distribution. Competition and then distributive efficiency improved significantly. By the end of 1999, the market share of the non-state-owned distributors had reached 81.8 per cent, from almost zero in 1979.

Thanks to the combined effects of distribution reform and the policy of comprehensive economic reform, China's distribution sector experienced great changes and profound development after 1979. From 1979 to 1999, the output of the Chinese distribution sector increased each year at an average rate of 9.4 per cent, close to the average growth of economy-wide GDP (9.6 per cent) in the same period. Employment in distribution also grew substantially: at an average of 6.4 per cent during the period 1980-99.

Opening the distribution sector to the outside

For a long time, China's government showed a cautious attitude to the opening up of distribution to the outside world, applying progressive liberalisation on a pilot basis after 1992. Compared with the industrial sector and some tertiary sub-sectors, it could be said that distribution had been opened comparatively late.

It was in 1992 that China started its trial opening of distribution to the outside world. Chinese foreign retailing joint-ventures were allowed to establish and operate in specific areas including six cities: Beijing, Shanghai, Tianjin, Guangzhou, Qingdao and Dalian; and five special economic zones: Shenzhen, Zhuhai, Shantou, Xiamen, and Hainan. Only one or two retailing joint ventures were approved by the central government. However, retailing joint ventures were not allowed to engage in wholesale trade and the ratio of import and export volume could not exceed 30 per cent of annual sales. All approved retailing joint ventures had to be controlled by a Chinese partner with a shareholding ratio of more than 51 per cent of total shares.

In 1997, in the *Catalogue for the Guidance of Foreign Invested Industries* (first version) issued by the State Development Planning Commission (SDPC) of China, the distribution sector was listed among those in which foreign investment activities were restricted. It highlighted that the Chinese partner would be the majority-holding party or play a dominant role, and that only central government has the authority to approve the establishment of commercial companies with foreign investment. Prior to 1999, the central government had approved 30 commercial Chinese-foreign joint ventures in distribution.[3]

In 1999, the State Economic and Trade Commission (SETC) and Ministry of Foreign Trade and Economic Co-operation (MOFTEC) jointly issued the pilot provision on commercial foreign-invested enterprises, which could be viewed as the first transparent policy to open the distribution sector to the outside. The provision contains a set of restrictions on foreign participants entering the Chinese distribution sector, including limits on location and operations along with qualification and application procedures.

Besides opening the distribution sector to the outside world, domestic distribution enterprises also provide access to international markets. While domestic and international distribution were originally separate, beginning in the early 1990s China's government permitted some qualified domestic enterprises to apply for trading rights. A recent notice issued by the MOFTEC and SETC clarified applicant qualifications as follows: 1) firms under central administration, and enterprises in raw materials and equipment distribution in coastal areas with annual sales of RMB 200 million (in the west and central regions the threshold will drop to annual sales of RMB 50 million); 2) retailers, including franchises, with annual sales of RMB 50 million. Although more recently adopted standards provide equal opportunities for all kinds of applicants, together with a lowering of the annual sales threshold, special requirements do remain for distribution companies. For example, applicant procedures for commercial and materials distribution companies require an application report, a general survey of applicants, opinions of the competent government department, plus documentation of a two-year track record. So it is rather difficult for distributors to obtain trading rights, especially for emergent private and mixed-ownership distribution companies.

By the end of year 1999, there were 293 commercial enterprises with a total investment of US$2 billion from outside the mainland of China. In retail trade there were 193 foreign invested commercial companies with annual sales above RMB 5 million. The share represented by foreign invested retail companies accounted for only 1.8 per cent of national sales of consumer goods. As indicated in Table 9.1, among designated wholesale enterprises, foreign invested wholesale enterprises have less than a 1 per cent share of outlets, employment or annual sales. The above analysis indicates that the degree of access by the distribution sector to the outside world is still quite low.

Table 9.1. **A picture of wholesale and retail enterprises in China**
Per cent share of total

	Number of enterprises	Number of outlets	Employment
1. Wholesale trade	**100**	**100**	**100**
Domestic-funded enterprises	**99.4**	**99.2**	**99.5**
State-owned enterprises	63.3	65.9	66.8
Collectively-owned enterprises	17.9	16.7	17.7
Limited liability and share-holding corporations	12.0	12.0	12.6
Private enterprises	2.4	1.6	0.6
All others	3.7	3.0	1.9
Enterprises with investment from Hong Kong, China, Macao, China and Chinese Taipei	**0.3**	**0.3**	**0.1**
Foreign-invested enterprises	**0.3**	**0.5**	**0.3**
2. Retail trade	**100**	**100**	**100**
Domestic-funded enterprises	**98.2**	**95.8**	**96.1**
State-owned enterprises	48.4	44.6	45.1
Collectively-owned enterprises	26.7	22.9	16.6
Limited liability and share-holding corporations	13.8	21.2	27.9
Private enterprises	3.7	2.4	2.2
All others	5.4	4.6	4.3
Enterprises with investment from Hong Kong, China Macao, China and Chinese Taipei	**1.0**	**1.0**	**1.7**
Foreign-invested Enterprises	**0.8**	**3.2**	**2.2**

Notes: Figures refer to wholesale trade enterprises with annual sales of more than RMB 20 million and more than 20 employees; and to retail trade
enterprises with annual sales of more than RMB 5 million and more than 60 employees.
Source: *Chinese Market Statistics* 1996, published by the National Bureau of Statistics of China.

Significance and structure of the distribution sector

As a major component of the economy, China's distribution sector has been one of the important contributors to the overall economy, especially to its tertiary activities. Its contribution to GDP rose to 8.4 per cent in 1999 from 5.5 per cent in 1979. Table 9.2 shows that distribution's contribution to total GDP reached its high point during the period from 1985 to 1992. Changes in that ratio track the stages of reform as follows: the initial stage from 1979 to 1984; the comprehensive development stage from 1985 to 1992; and the stage of stabilisation and restructuring from 1993 to the present. These features of distribution development match the three stages of China's market evolution since the 1979 reform.[4]

An important contribution by the distribution sector is that it has provided a growing number of jobs. As Table 9.3 indicates, the number of those employed in distribution[5] increased from 13.6 million in 1980 to 47.5 million in 1999, while distribution's share of total employment grew from 3.2 per cent to 6.7 per cent. In the past 20 years, the sector provided about 16.9 million new employment positions, of which about 10 million, or 60 per cent, are attributable to private commercial enterprises and self-employed individuals.

Table 9.2. **The weight of the distribution sector in GDP**
Per cent share

Year	Distribution sector[1]
1980	4.7
1985	9.8
1990	7.7
1995	8.4
1999	8.4

1.   Including wholesale, retail and catering trade services.
Source: *Zhongguo Tongji Nianjian* (2000), *China Statistical Yearbook*, 2000.

Table 9.3. **Employment in the distribution sector**

Unit: 10 000

	Distribution sector (total)	Self-employed in distribution	Share of distribution in total employment (%)	Share of self-employed in total distribution sector employment (%)	Share of tertiary employment in distribution (%)
1980	1 363	57.1	3.2	4.2	24.6
1985	2 306	325.0	4.6	14.1	27.6
1990	2 839	431.2	4.4	15.2	24.0
1995	4 292	1 265.8	6.3	29.5	25.5
1999	4 751	2 024.7	6.7	42.6	25.0

Source: *Zhongguo Tongji Nianjian* (2000), *China Statistical Yearbook*, 2000.

Among tertiary activities, distribution has been the biggest contributor in terms of value-added and employment for the past two decades. The ratio of value-added in distribution to the total for tertiary industry since 1990 has been around 27 per cent, while the employment share of distribution within the tertiary sector has been a steady 25 per cent (Table 9.3). Compared with the overall growth of tertiary value-added as a whole, growth of distribution after 1991 was measurably lower.

In OECD countries, the contribution of the distribution sector to GDP ranges from 8 per cent in Germany and Ireland to over 15 per cent in United States, Italy, Australia, Belgium, Mexico and New Zealand (Table 9.4). And its contribution to economy-wide employment is usually even greater

Table 9.4. **The distribution sector in OECD countries**

OECD countries	Share of, 1993:		Average annual growth, 1979-94		
	Total GDP	Total employment	Output	Employment	Productivity
United States	15.7	15.5	3.84	1.76	2.04
Japan	12.5	18.4	4.74	0.58	4.14
Germany	7.8	11.3	2.22	0.96	1.24
France	12.2	13.8	1.84	0.18	1.65
Italy	15.3	19.3	2.47	1.46	1.00
United Kingdom	12.8	17.1	2.53	0.72	1.80
Canada	10.0	16.4	2.86	1.51	1.33
Australia	17.9	20.8	1.94	1.97	−0.02
Austria	12.8	14.4	3.13	1.31	1.80
Belgium	15.4	15.9	0.82	−0.11	0.93
Czech Republic	10.7	16.4	n.a	3.13	n.a
Denmark	10.7	10.8	2.20	−0.96	3.19
Finland	8.4	12.5	0.89	−1.10	2.02
Greece	9.6	15.5	1.61	3.15	−1.50
Hungary	10.8	12.4	n.a	n.a	n.a
Iceland	8.9	11.9	n.a	1.51	n.a
Ireland	7.9	14.3	n.a	1.70	2.80
Korea	11.7	22.0	7.42	4.50	2.02
Luxembourg	13.5	15.9	3.46	1.40	−0.16
Mexico	22.6	14.9	1.12	1.28	1.79
Netherlands	12.7	16.2	3.42	1.61	n.a
New Zealand	15.2	12.4	n.a	n.a	n.a
Norway	9.7	13.9	n.a	0.40	n.a
Poland	8.9	16.4	n.a	n.a	1.13
Portugal	14.1	13.2	1.55	0.42	0.56
Spain	14.2	16.7	1.93	1.36	3.45
Sweden	8.3	11.9	2.79	−0.64	n.a
Switzerland	14.7	13.9	n.a	n.a	n.a
Turkey	16.0	12.5	n.a	n.a	

n.a. not available.

Source: Pilat (1997).

than that of GDP, typically equalling around 15 per cent of total employment. This reflects the labour-intensive nature of activity in this sector.

Obviously, the contribution of distribution to China's economy as a whole has remained lower than that in OECD countries. This indicates that there exists a vast opportunity for China to improve the development of distribution.

Intensified competition in distribution

Over the past 20 years, one of the purposes of distribution reform has been to dismantle the monopoly by state-owned and collective commercial distribution enterprises and to introduce competition to the sector. As a result, competition in distribution has improved significantly and in the latter 1990s has intensified further.

As Table 9.5 indicates, the market share of state-owned and collective commercial enterprises dropped from 54.6 per cent and 43.3 per cent respectively in 1978 to 18.2 per cent and 15.6 per cent respectively in 1999. Conversely, the market share held by other commercial distribution enterprises and self-employed individuals, which took advantage of lower costs, more convenient service and more flexible methods, rose from almost zero in 1979 to 66.2 per cent in 1999 – a significant rise. Retail price trends since 1979 could furnish another important way to illustrate intensified competition in distribution in recent years. Retail prices before 1996 increased due to price reforms and supply deficiencies. However, retail prices dropped in the latter 1990s, reflecting a transformation of supply-and-demand relationships. This also indicates that competition in distribution has been fiercer than ever before. In the past few years, most retailers have adopted the principle of discounting sales as the primary means of competing.

Table 9.5. **Market share of distribution by type of enterprise**

Per cent

	1978	1995	1999
SOE	54.6	29.9	18.2
CE	43.3	19.3	15.6
Private	0	2.5	⎧
Mom-and-pop	0.1	30.3	⎨ 43.2
Others *	2.0	18.0	23

*   Others include share-holding enterprises, joint ventures, and foreign-invested enterprises, including those from Hong Kong, China Investment, from foreign and Hong Kong. CE- collectively-owned enterprises.
Source: Market Statistics Yearbook of China, 1999.

It should be noted that the degree of competition in distribution varies in different sub-sectors and regions. The competition in the retail market in big cities is now fiercer than ever before. In Shanghai, for example, there were 84 Chinese-foreign retail joint ventures with total annual sales of RMB 10 billion, and which accounted for about 8 per cent of total sales of consumer goods in Shanghai. Fierce competition existed not only between the domestic and Chinese-foreign joint ventures, but also among the foreign partners. In some senses, the Chinese market is transforming itself into the frontier of competition between international commercial giants.

Traditional participants in distribution

Within the distribution sector, a distinction is usually made between wholesale and retail trade. The retail sector sells directly to the consumer, whereas wholesalers normally take an intermediary role between manufacturers and retailers. However, this distinction is becoming increasingly more difficult to make as the distribution system is becoming more integrated (Pilat, 1997).

In China, the participants in the retail sector vary from big department stores to mom-&-pop shops, from e-commerce through the Internet to free market bazaars and even peddlers. Among the variety of retail formats, department stores, bazaars and mom-and-pop shops are the most popular and together have the dominant market share in retail trade.

The department store is a well-established and popular format in China, introduced during the era of central planning to serve as the main point of distribution for manufactured consumer goods. There are now about 7 000 such stores with annual sales of more than RMB 230 billion, accounting for approximately 35 per cent of sales of durable goods and clothing. Chinese consumers, especially those living in the big cities, still rely on department stores for a large portion of their important shopping and they visit them frequently. As Table 9.6 indicates, about 41 per cent of large and medium-sized Chinese retailing enterprises have adopted the department store as the default format for their operations. This figure implies that department stores constitute the leading commercial format for large and medium-sized retailers in China.

In 1999, there were about 88 000 bazaars (free markets) spread throughout urban and rural areas and engaging in the consumer goods trade. Total sales in 1999 for such bazaars amounted to RMB 2 170.8 billion, equivalent to almost two-thirds of the national annual retail sales of consumer goods. The distribution of bazaars is quite different in urban compared to rural areas. The number of bazaars in rural areas accounts more than three-quarters of the total sales, indicating that bazaars remain the main retail channel for rural residents to obtain manufactured consumer goods and to sell their agricultural products.

There are about 15.4 million mom-and-pop shops throughout the country. In one sense, mom-and-pop shops could be regarded as the principal retail format in the Chinese retail sector, since they account for almost 88 per cent of all retailing outlets and represent more than 30 per cent of retail market share, as well as providing 75 per cent of working opportunities in retail trade in China.

New retail formats like chain stores, supermarkets, hypermarkets, discount stores and even electronic commerce (e-stores) have been introduced into the Chinese retailing market. Take development of the chain store as an example. It was introduced into China in 1992 and since then has experienced double-digit growth. By the end of 1999, there were about 1 800 chain stores with more than 26 000 outlets in operation. Annual sales in 1999 totalled about RMB 150 billion and accounted for 7 per cent of national retail sales of consumer goods.

According to the "retailing development cycle" theory, the development of retailing was driven by innovation in the retail format. Retail development can be divided into different stages, characterised by distinct dominant retailing formats. China's retail sector is still in its initial development stage since department stores and traditional retail formats like mom-and-pop shops and bazaars dominate. In many OECD countries distribution is moving to a higher stage of development, as traditional small shops selling basic products are disappearing and are increasingly being replaced by modern retail formats such as larger supermarket or hypermarket chains and shopping centres.

Even though the frontiers of wholesaling have fluctuated with the changes in the distribution sector, China's traditional wholesalers still remain much in evidence. The chief participants are usually classified in the customary way as wholesale trade companies, sales branches and subsidiaries of the main manufacturers and various types of agencies. In the latter 1990s, the biggest market share (70 per

Table 9.6.   **Large and medium sized retail enterprises by form**

Total retail enterprises	Depart. stores		Supermarket		Specialty store		Other	
	Number	Ratio %	Amount	Ratio %	Amount	Ratio %	Amount	Ratio %
11 627	4 822	41.4	451	3.9	3 386	29.1	2 968	25.6

Note: Large-medium retailing enterprises refer to firms with annual sales of more than 5 million RMB and more than 60 employees.

Source: *Market Statistics Yearbook of China*, 1999.

cent of sales revenue of wholesale trade) belonged to manufacturers' sales branches and subsidiaries. This highlights the domination by manufacturers over traditional wholesaling activities.

For domestic manufacturers, there are three ways to distribute products to retailers: 1) regional sales outlets of their own, such as those maintained by big electronic appliance manufacturers like Haier, and Changhong; 2) direct sales to retailers, as is the case with small manufacturers, especially of fresh food and clothing; and 3) sales through local agents or wholesalers.

For manufacturers with investment from overseas, distribution channels may be divided into two categories. One is the direct channel between the well-capitalised foreign producer and the most modern Chinese retailer. An example is the consumer goods channel between Wal-Mart, a global discount store, and brand-name global producers such as Proctor and Gamble or Unilever. The other channel comprises various domestic distributors such as the wholesaler, the agent or even the retailer. Automobile distribution furnishes the best example. Under the relevant Chinese regulations applying before WTO accession, no foreign investment-backed auto producers were allowed to have distribution rights within the domestic market; they were required to take their Chinese partner as the exclusive selling agent, as in the case of Shanghai General Motors Company and the Shanghai company for auto sales.

It should be noted that the role of the wholesale trading companies, especially the state-owned wholesaling companies, declined with the gradual disappearance of central planning. Some private individuals have ventured into wholesaling, but mostly on a small scale. As for state-owned and collective-owned wholesalers, they have lost most of their market share and in the aggregate are making losses. However, a few state-owned wholesalers have stayed in good shape since they still enjoy special approvals or licenses to distribute certain key products, such as refined oil, tobacco, publications and various agricultural production materials.

Low level of consolidation and integration in the distribution sector

Large distribution firms have been very successful in many parts of the market. As a result, the distribution sector has become more consolidated. Such consolidation also happens to be one of the most significant trends in distribution in the more developed countries. This is manifested both in terms of the emergence of a number of large operators, and in terms of closer links between manufacturer, wholesaler and retailer, particularly through the creation of networks (WTO, 1998).

The degree of concentration in China's distribution sector is quite low since it is still dominated by a multiplicity of small-scale distribution establishments, while large operators are in need of further improvement. According to Chinese statistics, retail enterprises with annual sales over RMB 5 million and more than 60 employees are identified as large or medium-scale (meaning that the enterprise has grown above the original designated size), while large and medium-sized wholesale firms are defined as those with annual sales over RMB 20 million and more than 20 employees.

In the Chinese retail trade sector in 1999 there were 11627 large and medium-sized enterprises. Their annual sales totalled RMB 364.1 billion and accounted for 11.7 per cent of national retail sales. The big operators in retailing include the department stores. The ten largest department stores controlled 9.8 per cent of the market in that sub-sector, or 6.0 per cent of the retailing market as a whole. This highlights the low degree of concentration in department stores, most of which operate regionally. For example, China's top 200 retailers operate across the 100 largest cities. The second largest retail operators are the chain stores. Although chain stores in China have been in existence for less than ten years, they demonstrate great potential for consolidation. By 1999, the top three and ten chain store companies controlled about 22.2 and 34.6 per cent of the food and beverage market respectively.

In most OECD countries, concentration in distribution is more advanced. Taking food retailing in Europe for instance, the highest concentration is to be found in northern Europe, where the top three companies control more than 80 per cent of food retailing. Concentration is somewhat lower in other European countries, where the market share of the top three retailers ranges from 25 to 50 per cent.

Another important indicator of the degree of concentration in Chinese distribution is the number of shops owned by self-employed individuals (single shops or sole proprietorships). By the end of 1996, there were 12.79 million individually owned or small distribution establishments, and these accounted for 93.6 per cent of the total number of distribution establishments.

According to OECD experiences, distribution is a function of the structural characteristics of a country, such as population density, degree of urbanisation, public policy (for example, zoning laws and restrictions on large stores). However, the reasons behind the fragmented Chinese distribution market are quite complicated. Apart from the above factors, the economic structure of production can and does make a special and fundamental contribution to the fragmentation of the distribution market. In China's industrial and agricultural sector, most firms and operational units lack economies of scale: for example, family-based agricultural producers and millions of small or individual workshops predominate. This fragmented distribution structure, based mostly on small shops and even bazaars, is consistent with the requirements derived from the structure of production.

Integration and co-operation have been at their infancy in China's distribution sector. As in the OECD countries, the main purpose of integration and co-operation in operations within a distribution channel is to make it easier to compete in an increasingly dynamic and concentrated market. Since market concentration and comprehensive competition are less advanced in China, integration and co-operation along the distribution chain have not become a popular business development strategy. The chain store, for example, represents one kind of integration within retailing, but only 9.5 per cent of the retailing outlets are linked as chain stores.

In theory, market forces drive integration and co-operation. In China, however, integration has sometimes been organised by the government. For example, during one industrial restructuring, refined oil distribution channels were integrated and two regional oil distribution networks, China Petroleum and China Petrochemicals, were established. These were authorised to control all manufacturing, wholesaling and most retailing establishments in the southern and northern parts of the Chinese market respectively.

Main challenges and problems in light of liberalisation in the distribution sector

Although the government has long highlighted the domestic opening policy in distribution and has in recent years introduced foreign participants on a trial basis, there remain barriers and problems affecting the liberalisation of the domestic market.

Barriers to market entry

On paper, enterprises have autonomy of operations under China's company law. In practice, however, some regulations and policies impose limits on their operational autonomy, especially on their ability to enter particular markets.

The business administration registration system can be considered a reflection of the variety of regulations on market entry. According to China's business administration registration regulation, any commercial entity should be registered with the local business administration bureau and obtain an operating license to engage in approved business activities locally. Limits to market entry in distribution are manifest in provisions relating to the geographic scope of operations, the nature of the activities themselves (*e.g.* wholesale or foreign trade), the category of commodity distributed, and other factors. If enterprises wish to enter into a special business area like foreign trade, or refined oil distribution, they must meet all qualifications and conditions in the relevant regulations.

This registration system effectively limits a company's ability to choose the "playing field" on which it will operate. Even though the business administration bureaux have relaxed some controls on approved business areas and usually identify several business activities in an operating license, Chinese enterprises still suffer from high costs of market entry and other constraints.

Limits on trading of commodities

Three kinds of limits on commodity trading are manifest within the domestic market in China. They arise from national policy, local administrative protection and various sector-specific constraints.

At the state level, commodity trade has been distorted by inappropriate design of various policies. Most complaints on the distribution side identify the tax system and collection measures, especially for value added tax (VAT). VAT was introduced as the main tax revenue both for central and local government in the fiscal reform of 1994. However, unsettled issues remain concerning VAT calculation and collection on the value-added progression from manufacturers to retailers (see Chapter 18 on tax policies).

One of the examples is the treatment of certain activities as sales even when no actual sale occurs. Many normal distribution activities are treated for tax purposes as if they were sales, and the rules allow for the imposition of VAT irrespective of the final outcome: For example, physical movement of products between different regional locations – even among different facilities within a single company – can be treated and taxed as sales. Since there is no law on VAT collection (only a provisional regulation), tax collectors at various government levels have flexibility in the way they apply the VAT to commodities as they circulate. Such distortions in the application of taxes raise costs, and adversely affect efficiency in the distribution sector. Similar instances may be observed for other taxes in China.

At the local government level, there are many limits on commodity circulation across different regions. The basic reason stems from institutional arrangements within the Chinese economic system. For most national economic laws and regulations affecting the economy, each level of local government has some latitude to implement measures according to local circumstances. In the absence of supervision from the central government regarding relevant local laws and regulations, firms can face quite different business environments in distribution and production. Many local governments have applied administrative measures or have taken actions to protect their own stakes in local products and enterprises. A recent reported example was that of a county-level government office in Anhui province that was found to have been promoting local products since 1996.[6]

Limits on commodity circulation have also arisen from sector regulations and various policies of different government institutions. This is especially the case for sectors in which state-owned enterprises (SOEs) still enjoy a dominant or monopoly position, as in the case of refined oil, chemical fertilisers and agricultural drugs.

Concerns about the competitive strength of domestic distribution enterprises

China's distribution sector is described as featuring "low concentration" since small firms and traditional mom-and-pop shops still take the lion's share of the market. While more than 30000 large and medium-sized enterprises are engaged in distribution, their current condition, especially that of most domestic distributors, offers cause for concern because their competitive strength is quite weak.

Almost 99 per cent of large and medium-sized distribution companies are domestic entities, which indicates that the degree of opening in distribution remains rather low. Among domestic distributors, state-owned firms in retail and wholesale trade account for 48.4 per cent and 63.3 per cent respectively of the total large and medium-sized enterprises, while collective retail and wholesale enterprises account for 26.7 per cent and 17.9 per cent respectively. In other words, large and medium-sized distribution companies are still dominated by state-owned and collective enterprises.

Table 9.7 shows selected financial indicators for large and medium-sized distribution companies and helps to illustrate their comparative strengths. First, most of these domestic distribution enterprises bear a heavy burden of liabilities. Analysis of the ratios of liabilities to assets indicates that domestic distribution firms, excluding stock-holding companies, have liability burdens above 70 per cent. This is a relatively heavy debt load and implies that, according to international standards, such enterprises are at risk of bankruptcy.

Table 9.7. **Selected financial indicators of distribution enterprises by ownership**

	Assets (RMB 10 000)	Liability ratio (%)	Turnover ratio (%)	Profit ratio (%)	Exports (RMB 10 000)
State-owned	570.5	81	14.0	1.1	19.3
Collective	7.9	80.4	3.9	0.5	0.2
Private	0.9	73.2	0.4	1.3	0
Joint venture	334.5	71.7	12.1	1.5	4.3
Share-holding corporations	2293	64.6	39.2	2.9	66.6
Investment from Hong Kong, China, Macao and Chinese Taipei	615	69.4	11.1	0.8	5.7
Foreign-invested enterprises	684.6	70	14.9	2.5	3.6
Others	14.7	73.3	4.5	2.0	0.2

Source: *Chinese Market Statistics* 1996, published by the National Bureau of Statistics of China.

Secondly, the marketing abilities of most domestic distribution firms are quite low. Analysis of each category of large and medium-sized distribution enterprises shows that more than 65 per cent of their turnover was contributed by stock-holding and foreign-invested enterprises, which account for less than 10 per cent of the total number of the enterprises. A similar pattern is found in distributors' export ratios.

Thirdly, differences in profitability of different kinds of distribution enterprises suggest substantial disparities in their competitive capabilities. The most profitable entities remain the stock-holding companies with a profit ratio of 2.9 per cent, 1.8 points higher than for state-owned distribution enterprises.

From the above analysis, stock-holding distribution enterprises could be seen as the strongest competitors in the Chinese distribution market, having experienced the transition from state-owned to publicly-quoted company at a time when funds were available from the capital market and various other types of outside investors. But for most domestic distribution enterprises, their financial condition and competitiveness are more questionable. If this condition does not improve soon, it will interfere with the development of an efficient distribution system and make it difficult for domestic distributors to deal with the increased foreign participation that will come with TIL.

Problems of the state-owned distribution enterprises

As is the case for SOEs in the economy as a whole, the competitiveness of state-owned distributors has tended to decline, despite government policies to favour them. Three kinds of problem confront SOEs in distribution:

One problem is their debt burden stemming both from the traditional planning system and from transitional reform policies. State-owned distributors used to assume a plethora of responsibilities, including maintenance of price controls and procurement and storage functions for the government. Collateral responsibilities like these have left SOEs in the distribution sector burdened by debt; this is, especially true for state-owned wholesale companies. Such problems, however, have been neglected since SOEs in the industrial sector have been given the priority in government policy reform. The high ratio of liabilities to assets constitutes the chief constraint preventing state-owned distribution companies from improving their competitive strength.

The second problem is that the operational and management mechanisms of the state-owned distribution companies have failed to keep up with changes in the market. As the standard of living in China improves, the trend in the Chinese consumer market tends to be more dynamic and diversified. Hampered by their complicated decision-making process and lack of qualified professional management, the state-owned distribution companies have suffered serious losses in market share.

The last problem is related to the management regime of state-owned distribution enterprises. At present, most state-owned distribution companies are under the control of local governments and only a few of them are owned and managed by the central government. This kind of arrangement has confined state-owned companies to development within their regions, with the result that they became the leading companies in their local domestic market. Restructuring in the distribution sector has in many cases been confined to the local market. For example, most of the M&As in the distribution sector have taken place within the same region.

Implications of trade and investment liberalisation for China's distribution sector

The distribution sector is central to the economy, not only in terms of its direct contribution to output and employment, but also in terms of its crucial role in domestic and international trade. Under the terms of its WTO accession agreement, China will wholly open the distribution sector within three to five years (see Annex I on WTO commitments). Once foreign direct investment in distribution has been fully realised, a series of changes, not simply in distribution but throughout the economy, will be manifest.

Opening policies in line with trade and investment liberalisation in the distribution sector

According to the protocol commitments for WTO entry agreed between China and the United States, the distribution sector will be almost wholly opened to the outside world in the next five years. The following picture emerges from these commitments (see Annex I).

- In the field of retailing, commission-earning and wholesaling, Chinese-foreign joint ventures will be allowed to establish and engage in the importing, retailing and wholesaling of all domestic manufactured products excluding newspapers and magazines, pharmaceuticals, drugs for agriculture, chemical fertilisers, and refined and crude oil. The prohibition on these products will be phased out gradually over the next five years.

- In franchising, foreign companies will be allowed to operate in the Chinese market by way of franchises and all existing limitations will be abolished before 2003.

- In direct selling, China will negotiate with WTO member countries and will draft regulations on direct selling.

- In distribution services, all foreign-invested manufacturing enterprises will be allowed to distribute products manufactured within China and to provide auxiliary services.

- Foreign companies and individuals will remain prohibited from engaging in the wholesaling of tobacco and salt as well as tobacco retailing.

International experience in distribution liberalisation

It has long been argued that Chinese distribution would suffer after China's WTO accession. In this regard, the worldwide evolution of foreign investment in distribution could provide a lens through which China might evaluate the implications of trade and investment liberalisation on this sector.

Based on foreign direct investment (mainly joint ventures plus M&As), internationalisation within the distribution sector has been one of the major trends in the developed countries. According to OECD research, internationalisation is limited to a number of countries, typically those with a highly developed retail sector whose firms seek opportunities abroad to expand their markets. In terms of direct investment in distribution-related activities relative to GDP, the most internationalised market is the European mainland, particularly the Netherlands.

Other evidence indicates that domestic wholesale and retail services generally account for the bulk of sales within developed countries. According to the statistical office of the EU, total turnover for wholesale and retail trade in nine reporting countries was ECU 2 089 billion, of which ECU 369 billion (17.6 per cent) represented the activity of the foreign-owned enterprises.[7] The leading retailers in most countries most often have domestic origins, a characteristic that applies even to the most internationally oriented retailers.

Foreign direct investment in distribution has been undertaken by large, leading global enterprises. Among the world's top 20 retailers (measured by sales), all of which are multinational, seven are of

United States origin, eleven are of European origin and two are of Japanese origin. For most internationally-oriented distribution enterprises, their home markets still accounted for two-thirds or more of their total turnover. In developing countries international retailers may face more constraints and restrictions than they do in developed countries.

Of US direct investment abroad in wholesale trade in 1997, only 25 per cent went outside the OECD to developing countries. In the Asia and Pacific region, United States direct investment was focused on Hong Kong, China and Singapore. The ratio of US direct investment in Chinese wholesaling to its total foreign direct investment outflow in this sector was less than 0.5 per cent, which can be taken as a reflection of the fact that wholesale trade in China is largely closed to foreigners.

Difficulties in the internationalisation of distribution have been attributed to differences in market tastes and national regulation. Successful retailing formats and strategies originating in a particular OECD country may not always be allowed under legislation in another OECD country. Differences in tastes and demand patterns also help to constrain the local and domestic character of retailing in many countries.

Given their labour-intensive character, the implications for employment of introducing international retail giants has become a matter of concern for developing countries. Restrictions on large retail outlets have typically been designed to protect employment in small stores. However, OECD analysis suggests that removing restrictions on larger retail outlets has few negative effects on overall retail employment. This is because larger retailers require a significant amount of threshold labour (to keep their stores open at all times), and because liberalisation often leads to traditional stores being replaced by new retail formats and more specialised stores. Employment in the distribution sector has continued to grow over the past decades in almost every OECD country, notwithstanding substantial productivity gains (Pilat, 1997).

General implications for distribution after trade and investment liberalisation

In general, liberalisation in trade and investment will offer a clear net gain to distribution in China from the medium term to the long run, through a range of predictable impacts. Once distribution is opened up to the outside world, foreign investment in Chinese distribution will doubtless increase significantly, but is unlikely to make major inroads in terms of market share and commercial presence.

The first benefit is the most obvious: the expansion of distribution services. By lowering trade barriers and changing regulations in line with international standards, industrial and some agricultural production as well as imports and exports will experience significant increases. This will no doubt result in considerable expansion in the amount and variety of products circulating in the economy.

Second, liberalisation will provide the distribution sector with both incentives and models to restructure and upgrade its capabilities in order to raise its competitiveness. Competition and innovation in distribution have improved since China's opening to the outside world. There will be a considerable increase in foreign direct investment flowing into distribution. It will attract new competitors, new types of commercial formats, and advanced managerial and operating techniques. This provides the chance for Chinese distributors to compete with their international rivals by learning modern managerial skills and marketing techniques. It also provides domestic distributors with opportunities to develop their comparative advantages and to increase specialisation by concentrating on core businesses (business activities with comparatively high efficiency). So, as time goes on, a more efficient and diversified distribution sector should emerge.

Third, benefits will accrue from China's access to distribution channels abroad, which in turn will stimulate commodity exports. Domestic distributors, which have been barred from international distribution for so long, will be able to use their trading rights together with the distribution network of foreign partners to move into the international markets and to export Chinese commodities.

Finally, liberalisation in the distribution sector will help to enhance consumer welfare as competition and efficiency improve. Foreign retailers have contributed greatly to price competition in some of the big cities. Average prices of foreign-invested retailers, like Makro and Metro, have been

5-10 per cent lower than those among local rivals because of their high turnover and their networked global purchasing power. In China price competition will become more intense as more foreign participants enter the big consumer market. Price competition will doubtless squeeze distributors' margins and contribute to lower prices.

It is undeniable that there will be a considerable impact on the distribution sector, with some domestic distributors losing ground to foreign companies. The extent of the change will be quite different across different sub-sectors of China's distributive activities, depending on their openness to competition as well as their degree of development. The near-term negative consequences for some segments will be offset over a longer period by increasing gains originating from the forthcoming expansion, deepening and upgrading of the entire distribution sector. The gains resulting from trade and investment liberalisation will be manifest in substantial growth in distribution-related GDP and its contribution to the whole economy. According to a study on China's WTO accession by the Development Research Centre (DRC) of the State Council, the distribution sector will benefit in terms of increased output and employment (DRC, 2000). The study projects that by 2010 employment in distribution will be 1.1 million higher as a result of WTO entry, or 1.2 per cent, compared to the projected outcome in the absence of WTO.

Impacts on retailing

For foreign investors there are some obvious fields to enter in the Chinese retail market. A priority is to establish a commercial presence in those cities with high residential densities and quite high standards of living. Targets for foreign investors will include all big Chinese cities, especially those in coastal regions, plus some provincial capital cities and regional economic centres in the central and western regions. Most cities thus defined have been included in the official agenda for opening up to the outside world.

A second field of interest will be in the retailing of food and clothing through the media of chain stores and franchising. For most large international retailers, establishing outlets in other countries (mainly through joint ventures and M&As) can be seen as typical ways to expand internationally. For manufacturers with international brand names, the best choice will be to establish retailing franchises in China (like the Kodak film-developing shops in China).

The third type of outlet attracting foreign investors will be new emerging retail formats and related services, like shopping centres and electronic commerce. As urbanisation increases in China, establishing and operating shopping centres will become worthwhile for foreign investors.

In terms of market share held by foreign participants, the effects of trade and investment liberalisation on retailing will, in the long run, be limited. With a gargantuan market driven by growing demand among almost 1.2 billion consumers, there is no possibility for any single type of retailer to take over the entire Chinese retail trade. Another consideration is that the degree of openness in the domestic retailing sector is already quite high since government rules no longer protect such business from competition. Competition in retailing tends to be intense, especially in cities with higher population density and income, which will likely be the destination for foreign retailers. Even if foreign direct investment in Chinese retailing were to surge, their market operations and, in turn, their market share, would increase initially but would be limited to selected regions and the more profitable market segments.

Nevertheless, the potential benefits of foreign participation in developing China's retail sector are potentially large. Because foreign retailers enjoy considerable competitive advantage over their Chinese rivals in terms of economies of scale, advanced management and operating techniques, and worldwide supply chains, their participation will challenge domestic retail enterprises with fierce competition. Such competitive pressure from foreign participants will provoke some profound changes in the Chinese retailing market. First of all, Chinese retailers will modernise by learning from and imitating foreign participants. The changing face of Chinese retailing will include not only the application of new commercial formats but of improved operating and managerial techniques as well. Second, there will be a structural shift in the retail market in terms of concentration. Coming up against the world's leading international retailers will lead to a strengthening in the competitiveness of Chinese domestic retail enterprises. As a direct result, some will grow to be leading participants in the domestic or even in the international retail market. WTO accession and trade and investment liberalisation favour an improvement in the retailing environment because the Chinese government has expressed a strong desire to provide a level playing field in line with international standards. This will make it possible for China's retail market to modernise and thus to catch up with changes and developments in international retailing.

Impacts on wholesaling

In the short run there will be more negative impacts than benefits on domestic wholesale enterprises because a new and efficient wholesale system requires time for improvement. Nevertheless, Chinese wholesalers will benefit from the opening of their markets in a number of ways over time. Benefits will be generated by improving economic efficiency and competitiveness, by the removal of regulatory barriers in domestic trade and import monopolies, by increased access to export markets and by the acquisition of modern managerial skills and marketing techniques.

The immediate impact of trade and investment liberalisation on wholesaling is that the market share of domestic wholesalers is likely to shrink. International experience shows that foreign investment entry into China's wholesale market will be driven mainly by foreign direct investment in manufacturing and retailing, especially for mass production and distribution products. There being no sound wholesale distribution network now for multinationals, the rational choice for them will be to establish their own sales forces and to aim to control the whole distribution chain instead of using existing domestic wholesalers. Another choice for multinational distributors is to bypass the wholesalers and go directly to the larger retailers. The likely result, given the current state of Chinese wholesaling, is that domestic wholesalers, especially the traditional wholesale trading companies, will lose market share.

The next impact concerns the growing body of large retailers. As the big international retailers move in and the leading domestic retailers mature, links between retailers and manufacturers will become closer and will soon play a vital role in distribution. Bigger retailers will emerge to become purchasing centres and will establish networks that buy directly from manufacturers. This will further shrink the market for domestic wholesalers.

Finally, impacts will arise from the conditions of domestic wholesalers themselves. The high ratios of liabilities to assets and the widespread shortage of capital have damaged the functional basis for domestic wholesalers. Most domestic wholesalers enjoy only the most limited ability to provide services in purchasing and selling, or to offer financial support and information for manufacturers and retailers. In this regard, the competitive strength of most domestic wholesalers is cause for concern.

TIL will also provide the overall Chinese wholesale sector opportunities to develop. In order to increase distributive efficiency and concentrate on core business, a large number of manufacturers and retailers will take more control of the sales transaction itself and will outsource various related activities, such as logistics, to outside suppliers. This will further promote the division of labour and specialisation in distribution and will create new specialities in business services. Specialisation in wholesaling, in terms of functions like sales agencies, logistics services and so on, will create conditions for domestic wholesalers to develop. In this sense, liberalisation in wholesaling implies reallocation of wholesale resources among the whole gamut of distribution participants, and the creation of a new wholesale system to meet market requirements.

Implications for industry

Liberalisation in distribution will provide companies with full freedom to compete in crucial areas like after-sales support and channel management, each of which can become a source of competitive advantage (Perkins and Shaw, 2000).

The opening up in specific areas of product distribution will have considerable effect on entire industries such as automobiles and petrochemicals. Take the auto industry as an example. In the international automobile market, competition is between different integrated networks of manufacturers and distributors. The product concept is not confined merely to physical utilisation itself but includes before- and after-sales services as well. The efficiency of its distribution networks has been a major source of competitive advantage for the auto industry.

In China, automobile distribution has improved in terms of the increase in variety of wholesalers, agencies and maintenance service companies, but such changes have been limited to domestic enterprises. Foreign companies and even Chinese-foreign joint ventures have been unable to engage in automobile distribution and after-sales servicing. Car manufacturers' sales outlets and their sales agency systems have been playing an increasing role in the distribution of vehicles. Nonetheless, the automobile distribution market remains too fragmented to contribute to the competitive advantage of China's own auto industry.

The opening of the auto distribution and service market will make it possible to introduce international models and to draw on foreign experiences with auto distribution through the participation of foreign auto manufacturers – and distributors – in the domestic market. Based on experiences in other countries, foreign auto producers, once they obtain distribution and auxiliary service rights, are likely to seek to reorganise existing distributors in the Chinese market. This will provide access to the Chinese market for their auto products manufactured both domestically and abroad. Since most Chinese carmakers have established joint ventures with international automobile manufacturers, liberalisation in trade and investment will provide a new internal market place within which the international auto giants may compete with one another.

Thus, the distribution sector is set for tremendous challenges and innovations as manufacturers, distributors and retailers strive over time to achieve supply chain efficiencies and marketing effectiveness.

Effects on exports and imports

Liberalisation in trade and investment in China will break the trade monopoly by state-owned trading enterprises and provide more choice in international distribution channels for both Chinese companies and for foreign companies. This will increase the volume and quality of China's international trade.

As a developing country, one of the benefits for China from the opening up of distribution relates to increased access to export markets. Foreign partners involved in Chinese distribution will facilitate market access for domestic goods through their international channels. The best example in China is that of the United States-based retailer, Wal-Mart. While successfully operating its discount stores in several cities in coastal regions, Wal-Mart purchases considerable amounts of consumer goods from the Chinese market for export via its distribution system to its retailing outlets worldwide.

Once foreign direct investment in the distribution sector is allowed, there will likely be an import surge – since the requirement that foreign firms use Chinese distributors has hitherto been a major constraint on imports in some areas. The decline in tariffs will discourage smuggling, which will choke off an important source of low-cost supply for local mom-and-pop stores. This will make it easier for other retailers to earn adequate profit margins.

Policy changes to stimulate further reform in the distribution sector

Liberalisation in distribution will indeed produce net benefits for the Chinese economy overall as well as for the sector itself. But in the near term the Chinese government will need to undertake some structural reforms if it is to remove the constraints to the development of the distribution sector. For a healthy outcome for the economy as a whole and for distribution in particular, it is crucial to establish a regulatory framework that is consistent with international experience. Deep reform of the macro-economic and regulatory roles of government is not merely necessary, it is a *sine qua non* to sustain healthy development in the distributive sector. The one follows the other. Further changes in distribution reform policy should include the following:

- To revise corporate law in line with international standards and to grant autonomy to enterprises.
- To reform business registration and to liberalise regulatory requirements requiring government approval for market entry.
- To undertake tax reforms, especially of the VAT, so as to stimulate trade by applying international experience (for example, drawing on the reform of the VAT as part of the programmes to create a single market in Europe).[8]
- To consider the withdrawal of SOEs from distribution.
- To adjust institutional arrangements and undertake regulatory reforms to unify the domestic market by removing local and sector barriers to trade and market entry.

NOTES

1. The concept of distribution in this chapter relies on the definition of the United Nations provisional Central Product Classification (CPC), which includes four major services: commission agents' services, wholesale trade services, retail trade services and franchising. This chapter is mainly focused on wholesale and retail trade services due to China's very limited database.

2. Limitations still exist on distribution rights for some key products. One is for gold (as a raw material), the distribution right being controlled by the People's Bank of China (PBC); other limitations are on agricultural products, crude and refined oil, chemical fertilisers and published material. Distribution rights for these products were granted to specific state-owned trading enterprises. Finally there is a specific monopoly for the distribution of tobacco.

3. There were strong incentives within various levels of local government as a result of which more than 300 foreign invested commercial companies are now operating in the main cities of China.

4. DRC (1995).

5. According to *China Statistical Yearbook* (2000), p. 114 , the coverage of statistics in employment included all urban and rural economic entities.

6. Refer to *www.news.xihuanet.com/20010619/649261.htm*.

7. Statistical Office of the European Communities (EUROSTAT) (1997).

8. Background information based upon OECD research. See Pilat (1997) and OECD (2000).

BIBLIOGRAPHY

References in English

Boylaud, O. (2000),
"Regulatory reform in road freight and retail distribution", OECD *Economics Department Working Papers*, No. 266, Paris.

Statistical Office of the European Communities (EUROSTAT) (1997),
Basic Statistics of the Community, Luxembourg.

McKinsey&Company (1997),
"China's retailing markets are evolving more quickly than companies anticipate", *The McKinsey Quarterly*, No. 2.

OECD (2000),
"The OECD service economy", *Business and Industry Policy Forum Series*, Directorate of Science and technology Industry, OECD, Paris.

OECD (2001),
Structural Statistics for Industry and Service, Statistics Directorate, OECD, Vol. 1, Paris.

Perkins, T. and S. Shaw (2000),
"China in the WTO: What will really change?", McKinsey and Company research report, at *www.McKinsey.com*.

Pilat, D. (1997),
"Regulation and Performance in the Distribution Sector", OECD *Economics Department Working Papers*, No. 180, Paris.

WTO (1998),
Distribution Service – Background Notes by the Secretariat, Council for trade in Service, World Trade Organisation, June, (S/C/W/37), Geneva.

World Bank (1999),
Foreign Direct Investment in Services and the Domestic Market for Experience, Washington.

References in Chinese

CASS (2000),
The Research Report on China's Entry into WTO–Analysis of China's Industries, Social Scientific Documentation Publishing House, June, Beijing.

Development Research Centre of the State Council (DRC) (1995),
Chinese Market Development Yearbook, China Development Press, (English version).

DRC (1996; 1998; 1999; 2000),
Chinese Market Development Yearbook, China Development Press.

DRC (2000),
"Implication of China's WTO accession on distribution sector and countermeasures", DRC report, January.

Huang, H. (2000),
"Reform and openness in Chinese distribution sector", Seminar on China 2000: Target, Policy and Prospect, January, Beijing.

Ren, X. (2001),
"Implication of opening distribution and policy suggestion", DRC report, January.

Wang, W. (1998),
"Structure and its trend: distribution sector in China", Series Report of DRC on Chinese Economic Structure.

Wang, W. (1999),
"Characteristics and problems: Current situation of market development in China", DRC report.

Chapter 10

FOREIGN DIRECT INVESTMENT: PROSPECTS AND POLICIES

TABLE OF CONTENTS

Tables

Figures

Box

FOREIGN DIRECT INVESTMENT: PROSPECTS AND POLICIES[*]

Introduction

This study examines the effects foreign direct investment has had on China's economy and, based on that experience and other evidence, evaluates the effect WTO accession is likely to have on future foreign direct investment inflows. The evidence developed predicts that, after China's accession to the WTO, foreign direct investment inflows into China will increase moderately in the short term and then increase rapidly in the medium- and long-term. By the year 2010 annual foreign direct investment inflows into China could reach US$100 billion if China were to fully implement the WTO agreements and complementary domestic economic reforms. These reforms include further reductions in trade and investment barriers and liberalisation of domestic markets, reform of state-owned enterprises, and strengthened protection of intellectual property rights.

The study argues that while remaining a very important host for investments from developing countries and economies, particularly Hong Kong, China, Chinese Taipei, and the other East and Southeast Asian economies, China will become an increasingly important destination for investments from the developed countries as it strengthens intellectual property rights protection, opens more economic sectors – especially the services sector – to foreign direct investment, and encourages cross-border mergers and acquisitions (M&As).

In terms of regional distribution of foreign direct investment inflows after China's accession to the WTO, the study reveals that, in the short run, the uneven regional economic development, and hence, the uneven regional distribution of foreign direct investment between the east region and the central and the west regions in China, will probably be reinforced. However, in the medium and long run, with the implementation of the Western Economic Development Strategy, and economic development in the central regions, it is reasonable to predict that more foreign direct investment would gradually flow into interior provinces.

The study also reveals that the sectoral distribution of foreign direct investment in China will undergo major changes. Opening the service sector has been one of the most important issues in the bilateral negotiations of China's accession to the WTO. China has made some important and concrete commitments to the WTO in opening its service sector to foreign investors. Therefore, it is expected that there will be a big surge of foreign direct investment inflows into China's service sector, especially into finance, insurance, telecommunications, domestic commerce and auxiliary service industries. As a result, the share of foreign direct investment inflows into the manufacturing sector is likely to gradually decline, while the share of foreign direct investment inflows into the services sector should increase significantly.

This chapter is structured as follows. The next section provides an overview of the growth and economic impact of foreign direct investment in China. This is followed by a summary and evaluation of China's current foreign direct investment policy regime. The subsequent sections discuss the implications of China's WTO accession for foreign direct investment inflows into China, the composition of foreign direct investment sources, and the likely future regional and sectoral distribution of foreign direct investment inflows. Finally, the concluding section summarises the main findings and recommendations.

The growth and economic impact of foreign direct investment in China

During the past two decades, China has attracted a large amount of foreign direct investment inflows. As shown in Figure 10.1, the growth of foreign direct investment inflows into China from 1979 to 1999 can be broadly divided into two phases: 1979-91 and 1992-99. At the initial stage of the first

---

[*] This chapter was prepared by Chunlai Chen, Professor, School of Economics, Australian National University, under the supervision of Marie-France Houde, Manager of OECD Foreign Direct Investment Policy reviews, OECD Directorate for Financial and Fiscal Affairs.

Figure 10.1. **FDI inflows into China**

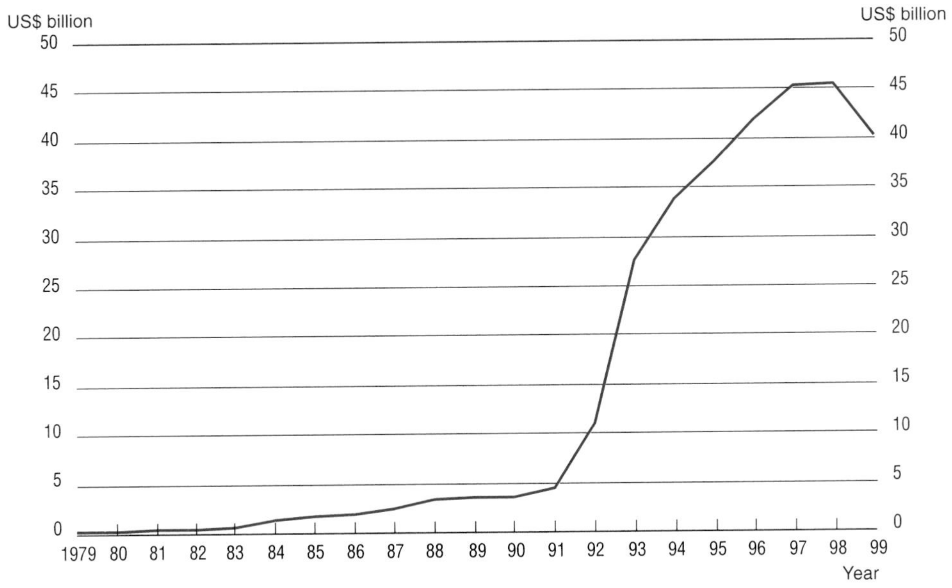

Source: Various issues of the State Statistical Bureau, *Zhongguo Tongji Nianjian (China Statistical Yearbook])* *Zhongguo Tongji Chubanshe,* Beijing.

phase, following the establishment of the four Special Economic Zones (SEZs) in Guangdong and Fujian provinces,[1] foreign direct investment inflows into China were highly concentrated in the four SEZs, and the total amount of foreign direct investment inflows were very limited. In 1984 Hainan Island and fourteen coastal cities across ten provinces were opened to foreign direct investment. Following this trend, in the second half of the 1980s more and more regions and areas were opened up, including the Yangzi River delta, the Pearl River delta, the Min Nan region, the Shanghai Pudong New Development Area and the entire coastal areas. At the same time, a series of laws and regulations were stipulated and implemented to encourage foreign direct investment inflows. Consequently, foreign direct investment inflows into China increased rapidly with an annual growth rate of nearly 20 per cent from 1984 to 1991.

The second phase was initiated by Deng Xiaoping's tour to China's southern coastal economically opened areas and SEZs in the spring of 1992. Deng Xiaoping's visit, which turned out to be a landmark, set the scene for China's move away from the uneven regional priority toward nationwide implementation of open policies for FDI. The Chinese government then further liberalised its foreign direct investment regime and implemented a series of new policies to encourage foreign direct investment inflows into China. The results were astounding. The inflows of foreign direct investment to China surged from US$11.01 billion in 1992 to US$45.46 billion in 1998. Although foreign direct investment inflows into China declined in 1999 for the first time in two decades, it still attracted US$40.32 billion, far exceeding the amount of foreign direct investment into any other developing country.

There are several factors contributing to the large amount of foreign direct investment inflows into China. First, with the implementation of economic reform and open door policies in late 1978, and especially since the early 1990s, China has gradually liberalised its foreign direct investment regime. China's foreign direct investment regime is still relatively restricted – especially in some economic sectors, particularly services – and in the terms permitted, such as the maximum foreign ownership share in a domestic business and participation in cross-border merges and acquisitions (M&As). China has substantially reduced investment barriers and improved its investment environment by opening more and more regions and economic sectors to foreign investors and by formulating and implementing a series of laws and regulations governing foreign direct investment. In addition, China also initiated many preferential policies to encourage foreign direct investment into its targeted regions and industries especially those that are export-oriented or technologically advanced.

Second, with the largest population in the world, China has potentially huge markets. Although China's per capita GDP is still low, its rapid economic growth and rising purchasing power along with cheaper labour and land costs than other developing countries, have provided tremendous business opportunities to overseas investors, and made China's markets more attractive to foreign direct investment.

Third, since the early 1990s, the world has witnessed a rapid development in international economic integration and globalisation of production, which has been driven by falling trade and investment barriers due to economic and trade liberalisation worldwide. As a result, world foreign direct investment flows have increased rapidly since 1993, particularly inflows into developing countries. This rising trend of world foreign direct investment flows contributed to the rapid growth and high level of foreign direct investment into China during the 1990s.

Fourth, since the 1980s, the Asian newly industrialising economies (NIEs) have joined other developed countries to become important capital suppliers. Owing to the rising costs of labour and the upgrading of industrial structure at home, many firms from these countries have increased their investment abroad, especially to ASEAN countries and China, where relatively cheaper labour is available and dynamic economic changes have occurred.

Finally, China's extensive connection with overseas Chinese business networks has greatly helped in attracting investments from overseas Chinese investors. In fact, more than half of China's foreign direct investment has come from overseas Chinese investors.

Capital formation

One general indicator measuring the importance of foreign direct investment in a host country's national economy is the share of foreign direct investment inflows to the host country's GDP. This indicator is also used to measure a country's openness or dependence towards inward foreign direct investment. Foreign direct investment inflows into China have attained increasing importance in China's national economy during the last two decades. The share of foreign direct investment inflows to China's GDP was only 0.3 per cent in 1983, increasing to over 1 per cent in 1991 and reaching its peak of 6.2 per cent in 1994. Since 1995, the share of foreign direct investment inflows to China's GDP has declined slightly, following the unprecedented growth during the early 1990s, but has remained above 4 per cent.

As Figure 10.2. illustrates, foreign direct investment has provided an important source of external finance for China's economic development. In terms of domestic gross capital formation, foreign direct investment inflows only accounted for 0.9 per cent of China's domestic gross capital formation in 1983. However, since then the share of foreign direct investment inflows in China's domestic gross capital formation has increased steadily, reaching the highest level of 15.11 per cent in 1994, staying around 13 per cent from 1995 to 1998 and falling to around 11 per cent in 1999.

The above figure, however, may overestimate the real contribution of foreign direct investment to China's domestic capital formation. In fact, total foreign direct investment inflows into China have not all been used for long-term fixed capital investment. There is evidence that fixed capital investment made by foreign invested enterprises accounted for only a portion of the total foreign direct investment inflows into China each year. Foreign invested enterprises' gross fixed capital investment accounted for nearly 80 per cent of the total foreign direct investment inflows into China in the late 1990s, and the figure for earlier years was much lower. The remainder (around 20 per cent) of foreign direct investment inflows may have been used by the foreign invested enterprises as working capital and for inventory investment. If so, foreign direct investment inflows actually accounted for around 11 per cent of China's domestic gross fixed capital formation in the late 1990s.

325

Figure 10.2. **FDI inflows to GDP, GCF and GFCF ratios in China**

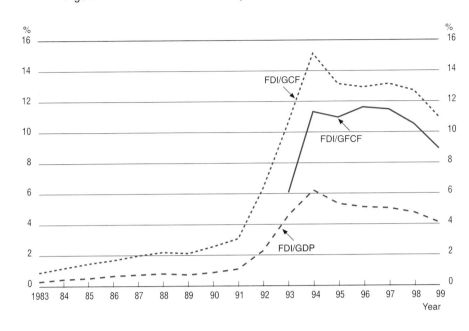

Source: Various issues of the State Statistical Bureau, *Zhongguo Tongji Nianjian (China Statistical Yearbook)*, *Zhongguo Tongji Chubanshe*, Beijing.

Employment opportunities

In the developing countries, where capital is relatively scarce but labour is abundant, one of the most prominent contributions of foreign direct investment to the local economy is the creation of employment opportunities. In general, foreign direct investment involves direct and indirect employment effects in a host country's economy.

Direct employment impacts refer to the total number of people employed within the foreign invested enterprises. Indirect employment effects refer to employment opportunities indirectly generated by foreign direct investment activities in the host country's domestic economy. Indirect employment effects have three aspects. The first relates to the macroeconomic consequences. These include the employment indirectly generated throughout the local economy as a result of spending by the foreign invested enterprises' workers or shareholders. The second regards the horizontal consequences. These include the employment indirectly generated among other local enterprises as a result of competition with the foreign invested enterprises. The third aspect concerns the vertical consequences. These include the employment indirectly generated by the foreign invested enterprises among their local suppliers and customers. The indirect employment effects of foreign invested enterprises on host countries' employment are very difficult to measure. However, the results of a series of country case studies conducted by the International Labour Organisation (ILO) show clearly that the indirect employment effects associated with inward direct investment may sometimes be as, if not more, important than the direct effects (Dunning, 1993).

Because of the difficulties in measuring the indirect employment effects of foreign direct investment, the following analysis will be confined to direct employment effects of foreign direct investment in China. However, the importance of the indirect employment effects resulting from foreign direct investment activities in China's economy should not be underestimated.

Table 10.1. **FIEs' urban employment in China by regions**
1999

Province	Share of FIEs' urban employment (%)
East region	7.2
Central region	1.1
West region	0.8
China Total	2.9

Source: National Bureau of Statistics (2000), *Zhongguo Tongji Nianjian 2000 [China Statistical Yearbook 2000]*, Zhongguo Tongji Chubanshe, Beijing.

Foreign invested enterprises' urban employment increased significantly during the 1990s.[2] While they employed 1.6 million workers or about 1 per cent of China's urban employment in 1991, the figures have almost quadrupled in 1999 to 6.1 million workers or 2.9 per cent of China's urban employment (Table 10.1).

Foreign invested enterprises' urban employment in China is overwhelmingly concentrated in the east region provinces, which account for 86 per cent of foreign invested enterprises total urban employment in China. Within the east region, foreign invested enterprises' employment is relatively concentrated in several coastal provinces, for example Guangdong, Fujian, Jiangsu, Shandong, Liaoning and Zhejiang, and the three municipalities – Shanghai, Beijing and Tianjin. Together the above provinces and municipalities account for 82.52 per cent of foreign invested enterprises' total urban employment in China. In contrast, foreign invested enterprises urban employment in the central region and the west region is very small, accounting for only 10.10 per cent and 3.81 per cent of foreign invested enterprises' total urban employment in China respectively.

As a result, the contribution of foreign invested enterprises in China's urban employment among the three regions is very uneven. While foreign invested enterprises contributed 7.23 per cent of the urban employment in the east region, they only contributed 1.12 per cent and 0.83 per cent of the urban employment in the central region and the west region respectively. The revealed regional difference in the employment effects of foreign invested enterprises in China is not surprising given the uneven regional distribution of foreign direct investment inflows into China in the last two decades. However, the concern is that the uneven regional employment effects created by foreign invested enterprises may further exacerbate the existing situation of uneven regional economic development and widen the income gap between the east and the west regions in China.

Export promotion

There is considerable evidence that foreign direct investment contributes to the growth of host countries' international trade. The most direct way to measure the impact of foreign direct investment on China's trade growth is to examine the trade performance of foreign invested enterprises. Table 10.2

Table 10.2. **Trade performance of Foreign Invested Enterprises (FIEs) in China**
1980-1999

	Value of FIEs trade (million US$)			FIEs as % of China's total			Trade balance of FIEs (million US$)
	Total trade	Exports	Imports	Total trade	Exports	Imports	
1985	2 361	297	2064	3.4	1.1	4.9	−1 767
1990	20 120	7 814	12 306	17.4	12.6	23.1	−4 492
1995	109 818	46 876	62 942	39.1	31.5	47.7	−16 066
1996	137 110	61 506	75 604	47.3	40.7	54.4	−14 098
1997	152 620	74 900	77 720	47.0	41.0	54.6	−2 820
1998	157 679	80 962	76 717	48.7	44.1	54.7	4 245
1999	174 511	88 628	85 883	48.4	45.5	51.8	2 745

Source: Data for 1980-93 are from the National Bureau of Statistics (1995), *Zhongguo Duiwai Jingji Tongji Nianjian 1994 [China Foreign Economic Statistical Yearbook 1994]*, Zhongguo Tongji Chubanshe, Beijing. Data for 1994-99 are from various issues of the National Bureau of Statistics, *Zhongguo Tongji Nianjian [China Statistical Yearbook]*, Zhongguo Tongji Chubanshe, Beijing.

presents the trade performance of foreign invested enterprises in China from 1980 to 1999. As the table indicates, in terms of the total trade value, foreign invested enterprises' trade increased very fast from US$43 million in 1980 to US$174.5 billion in 1999, an annual growth rate of nearly 55 per cent.

China's policy in relation to foreign direct investment has been deliberately biased toward export-oriented foreign direct investment. As a result, foreign invested enterprises have rapidly become major exporters. In 1980 the value of exports from foreign invested enterprises were US$8 million, accounting for only 0.05 per cent of China's total exports. Two decades later in 1999, exports from foreign invested enterprises reached US$88.6 billion, accounting for about 45 per cent of China's total exports. In some years, notably 1983, 1993, 1996, and 1998, China's export growth was entirely driven by foreign invested enterprises, while exports by domestic firms declined.

However, despite fast export growth, foreign invested enterprises have incurred net deficits in their international trade in most years. The deficits were especially large in the mid-1990s, although the balances have improved considerably since then and have recorded surpluses in 1998-1999. Large trade deficits have at times presented problems for foreign invested enterprises in China given their need to balance their foreign exchange expenditure and receipts under China's foreign exchange control regulations.

This impediment was eased in December 1996, when the *Renminbi* (RMB) became convertible on current account. This includes all payments for international goods and services trade, repayments of loans and profit remittance. This policy change in foreign exchange management has not only assisted China's international traders but also greatly facilitated the business operations of foreign investors in China.

Despite the trade deficits run by foreign invested enterprises, their overall impact on the balance of payments has probably been favourable. The huge foreign direct investment inflows into China each year have not only compensated for the trade deficits of foreign invested enterprises, but have also greatly improved China's balance of payments and contributed to the large increase of China's foreign exchange reserves.

Technology transfer and productivity improvement

According to the industrial organisation theory of foreign direct investment, for a firm to invest overseas it must possess some ownership advantages. A firm's ownership advantage could be a product or a production process to which other firms do not have access, such as a patent or blueprint. It could also be some specific intangible assets or capabilities such as technology and information, managerial, marketing and entrepreneurial skills, organisational systems or access to intermediate or final goods markets. Whatever its form, the ownership advantage confers some valuable market power or cost advantage on the firm sufficient to outweigh the disadvantages of doing business abroad.

When foreign firms conduct foreign direct investment and start production, the ownership advantages they possess will be brought into the host country in which they operate. It is very difficult to directly measure the extent to which ownership advantages, such as technology and managerial skills, have been transferred by foreign direct investment firms. However, there are several alternative ways to measure them indirectly.

These ways include examining basic indicators of company characteristics, including the size, physical capital intensity, labour productivity and capital productivity of both foreign invested firms (FIEs) and China's domestic firms (DOEs).

On these various counts, foreign invested enterprises appear as having had a positive contribution to the Chinese economy. Their average size is 43 per cent larger than domestic enterprises (more so in labour and technology-intensive industries). Their capital to labour ratio is higher. Despite using more capital than domestic firms, they have a higher productivity. Labour productivity is also higher by 88 per cent than the productivity of domestic firms for the industry as a whole.

The role of foreign direct investment in technology transfer into China can also be seen in the changes in the industrial structure of foreign invested enterprises. Over the past several years, the

Table 10.3. **Industrial composition of FIEs in China's manufacturing (%)**

Manufacturing industries	Total assets			Value-added		
	Year 1995	Year 1999	Changes	Year 1995	Year 1999	Changes
Labour intensive industries	50.42	41.44	−8.98	46.80	40.75	−6.05
Capital intensive industries	22.73	25.35	2.62	21.02	21.94	0.92
Technology intensive industries	26.86	33.21	6.35	32.19	37.31	5.12

Source: Data for 1995 are calculated from the Office of the Third National Industrial Census (1997), *Zhonghua Renmin Gonghe Guo 1995 Nian Disanci Quanguo Gongye Pucha Ziliao* [Data of the 1995 Third National Industrial Census of the PRC], Zhongguo Tongji Chubanshe, Beijing. Data for 1999 are calculated from National Bureau of Statistics (2000), *Zhongguo Tongji Nianjian 2000* [*China Statistical Yearbook* 2000], Zhongguo Tongji Chubanshe, Beijing.

composition of foreign direct investment inflows into China's manufacturing sector has changed from heavy concentration in labour intensive industries towards more investment in capital intensive and technology intensive industries. This has led to significant changes in the industrial structure of foreign invested enterprises' in China's manufacturing sector. As Table 10.3 indicates, both in terms of total assets and in terms of value-added, the share of labour-intensive industries declined between 1995 and 1999, while the share of capital-intensive industries and especially that of technology-intensive industries increased. The changing industrial structure of foreign invested enterprises towards more investments in capital intensive and technology intensive industries is an indication that technology transfer into China's manufacturing sector by foreign invested enterprises may be increasing.

Overall, there is evidence to argue that foreign invested enterprises have brought advanced technologies and modern corporate management skills into China's economy. Over the past two decades, a lot of advanced equipment and technical projects have been introduced by foreign invested enterprises, which has not only filled some technological gaps between China and the outside world, but has also helped to develop many new products in China.

Competition

Foreign invested enterprises have helped to improve competition in China's economy. By the end of 1999, foreign invested enterprises accounted for 23 per cent of the total assets and nearly 27 per cent of the total value-added of China's manufacturing sector. In some manufacturing industries, foreign invested enterprises have gained the dominant or at least significant positions. In 1999, in terms of value-added, FIEs' shares of value-added reached 68 per cent in electronics and telecommunication equipment, 60 per cent in cultural, education and sports goods, 54 per cent in leather and fur products, 50 per cent in instruments and meters, 49 per cent in clothing and other fibre products, 43 per cent in plastic products, 41 per cent in furniture manufacturing, 40 per cent in chemical fibres, 37 per cent in food manufacturing, 32 per cent in rubber products, 31 per cent in metal products, and 30 per cent in transport equipment, electrical equipment and machinery. Undoubtedly, the increasing importance of foreign invested enterprises in China's economy, together with their superior technology and better performance, has put intense pressure on China's domestic firms and increased competition in China's markets.

With the implementation of trade and investment liberalisation after China's accession to the WTO, the market shares of foreign invested enterprises are expected to rise further as more and more large multinational enterprises (MNEs) enter China's markets. It is expected that the new MNE entrants will mainly target China's huge domestic markets. The presence of foreign invested enterprises has forced, and will continue to force, China's domestic firms to improve their performance in order to prevent their market shares from shrinking even further. These impacts of foreign direct investment on China's domestic economy are much more profound and important than those likely to be produced by comparable levels of other types of foreign capital inflows.

329|

China's current foreign direct investment policies

Foreign direct investment in China was highly restrictive prior to 1978. Since then, the foreign direct investment regime has been liberalised gradually, aiming at attracting a high level of foreign direct investment inflows and accelerating the transfer of technology and modern management skills. However, China's foreign direct investment policy regime still needs further liberalisation. On the one hand, China's current foreign direct investment policy is still relatively restricted in terms of foreign direct investment entry forms, foreign ownership shares, access to certain activities, and performance requirements. Moreover, China still extensively uses fiscal and other incentive policies to encourage some specific types of foreign direct investment, for example, the export-oriented and technologically advanced foreign direct investment, and to induce foreign direct investment flows into some targeted regions and industries. The remainder of this section will discuss China's major foreign direct investment policies and regulations.

Policies affecting the forms of foreign direct investment

According to China's laws and regulations, foreign investors can choose between three different forms to invest in China, namely contractual joint ventures, equity joint ventures, and wholly foreign-owned enterprises.

The Equity Joint Venture Law issued in 1979 was China's first law permitting the establishment and operation of foreign economic entities in its territory. For ideological reasons as well as the primary interest in acquiring advanced technologies through FDI, China restricted foreign investment to joint ventures in the initial stage of attracting FDI. Wholly foreign-owned enterprises were only permitted within the SEZs. It was not until 1986, after the passing of the Wholly Foreign Owned Enterprise Law, that wholly foreign-owned enterprises were allowed to establish in China nationwide.

As some studies (Powell, 1987; Stein, 1987; Behrman, 1988; *et al.*) have revealed, there are many reasons for foreign investors to prefer to create wholly owned ventures to joint ventures. However, two are most important. One is to maintain maximum operating independence from Chinese participation. Another is to access fully all corporate resources and technology from the parent company and to more effectively protect their technologies. This latter consideration is especially important when the foreign enterprises are in technology-intensive industries. The role of private property rights is a critical determinant of the entry mode of foreign companies. Due to the nature of their firm's specific asset they will seek to prevent its dissipation in foreign markets by choosing the form of entry that will deliver the most protection. That form is usually a wholly foreign-owned entity.

Despite China's continued priority for attracting foreign direct investment with advanced technologies, there remain restrictions on the organisational forms of foreign direct investment entry. There are 31 industries that are not allowed the establishment of wholly foreign-owned enterprises, and 32 industries in which the Chinese partners must have majority share holdings or are in a dominant position (Table 10.4). It is worth noting that nearly half of these industries are high technology industries. It is very likely that these policy restrictions would not only discourage foreign direct investment inflows from developed countries but also undercut China's effort to attract high technology foreign direct investment.

Cross-border mergers and acquisitions

China has not yet permitted all forms of cross-border mergers and acquisitions (M&As) prevailing in the world. However, over the past several years, foreign investment in China has taken a number of traditional M&A forms, including purchase of registered capital in a foreign invested enterprises, asset purchase, share purchase, and merger.

Table 10.4. **Industries in which the Chinese partners must have majority share**

1. Construction and management of key water projects for comprehensive utilisation of hydraulic resources.

2. Design, construction and management of transportation facilities, including city subways, trunk railways, airports, aviation, and water transportation.

3. Coal mining and dressing by water.

4. Construction and management of unclear power stations.

5. Ethylene with an annual output of or exceeding 600 000 tons.

6. Polyvinyl chloride resin.

7. Construction and management of oil and gas delivery pipelines, as well as oil depots and oil wharves.

8. Manufacture of turbine compressor and combined powder machine for the complete set of equipment for an annual output of or exceeding 300 000 tons of synthetic ammonia, 480 000 or more tons of urea, and 300 000 or more tons of ethylene.

9. Design and manufacture of civil aeroplanes; engines; satellites, their payloads and carrier rockets.

10. Manufacture of motor vehicles, their engines, and radial tires.

11. Development and production of grain, cotton and oil seeds.

12. Addictive narcotic drugs and psychiatric drugs.

13. Manufacturing of high-tech vaccines (AIDS, Type III hepatitis, contraceptive, etc.).

14. Repairing, designing and manufacturing of special, high-performance ships and ships at or above 35 000 tons.

15. Designing and manufacturing of diesel engines, auxiliary engines, radio communications and piloting equipment, as well as parts and components thereof.

16. Domestic commerce.

17. Foreign trade.

18. Medical institutions.

19. Printing and publishing business.

20. Producing, publishing, distributing of audio and visual products.

Source: Foreign Investment Administration, China's Ministry of Foreign Trade and Economic Co-operation (MOFTEC) (1998), *Tax Exemption Policies on Importation of Equipment by Enterprises with Foreign Investment*, Foreign Investment Administration of MOFTEC, Beijing.

Purchase of registered capital in an FIE

The registered capital in a foreign invested enterprises can be sold, either to one of the other equity holders in the joint-venture (if the investment is through joint venture) or to a third party. The transactions are subject to the Regulations Concerning Changes in Equity Interest of Investors in Foreign Investment Enterprises issued by the Ministry of Foreign Trade and Economic Co-operation (MOFTEC) and the State Administration of Industry and Commerce (SAIC) of May 1997. The change in the equity interest will be in accordance with the provisions of Chinese laws and regulations concerning the fields of industry prohibited or restricted to foreigners. For example, the Equity Change Regulations stipulate that MOFTEC must not approve the equity sale from the Chinese party to a foreign party in a joint venture if, as a consequence of the foreign party's purchase, the joint venture would be converted into a wholly foreign-owned enterprise in an industry in which the establishment of a wholly foreign-owned enterprise is restricted.

The Equity Change Regulations also clearly prohibit the total equity share held by foreign investors from falling below 25 per cent of the registered capital through such a sale, unless all of the foreign party's interest is to be acquired by the Chinese party. The Equity Change Regulations do not apply to joint stock limited companies.

Asset purchase

China's law does not permit the acquisition of a domestic company's productive assets by a foreign entity unless the foreign acquirer has established or concurrently establishes a registered presence in China. This presence must take the form of either an equity or contractual joint venture, a wholly foreign-owned enterprise or, more recently, a joint stock limited company. In addition to the respective regulations applying to joint ventures and wholly foreign-owned enterprises, these entities are theoretically subject to the relevant provisions of the Company Law, which also govern the establishment and operation of joint stock limited companies.

Therefore, asset acquisitions of Chinese targets must be made through a China-registered foreign invested enterprise in which the foreign investor owns at least a 25 per cent interest. All acquisition transactions are subject to government approval. Whether an acquisition of the assets of a Chinese target is permissible will depend in large part on state policies concerning industrial development and priorities for the direction of foreign direct investment.

Share purchase

Under MOFTEC's 1995 Provisional Regulations on Several Issues Concerning the Establishment of Joint Stock Limited Companies with Foreign Investment, China's law allows foreign investors to acquire shares in a Chinese company (other than as a passive B shareholder). In a share purchase transaction, the target company may be a listed or an unlisted joint stock limited company. A foreign investor may either acquire the shares from existing shareholders, typically a holding company set up to hold state-owned shares, or from a Chinese legal person holding legal person shares. It may also acquire newly issued shares directly from the joint stock limited company.

There are fewer potential targets for a share purchase because of the relatively small number of existing joint stock limited companies in China. However, foreign investors may start to choose this strategy more often as an increasing number of state-owned enterprises convert to joint stock limited companies, and new companies of that type are established due to the efficiency of asset transfer with joint stock limited companies.

Mergers

Mergers in China are governed by specific provisions of the Company Law. Two forms of merger are permitted. The first is merger by absorption, in which one company absorbs one or more other companies and the absorbed companies are dissolved. The second is merger by establishment, in which two or more companies are merged into a newly created company and the parties to the merger are dissolved. Mergers directly involving foreign companies and China's domestic companies are still not possible in China. But as foreign investors seek to restructure their existing Chinese holdings, there have been a growing number of mergers among foreign invested enterprises.

Current global foreign direct investment flows have been dominated by M&As, particularly in the service sector. M&As in China have been very limited due to the tight restrictions imposed by the Chinese government. However, China has made substantial commitments under its WTO agreement to open up the service sector to foreign direct investment (see Annex I) and it is expected that more foreign direct investment will flow into services in coming years. Elimination of restrictions on M&A activities is likely to be needed if China is to realise its potential for attracting such inflows. In the Tenth Five-Year Plan on foreign direct investment, the Chinese government has given priority to reforming its relevant laws and regulations in order to encourage foreign investors to participate in state-owned enterprise reform through cross-border mergers and acquisitions.

Industrial policies concerning foreign direct investment

China has comprehensive industrial polices aimed at guiding foreign direct investment into targeted industries in accordance with China's economic and industrial development strategy. The "Provisional Regulations on Guiding Foreign Investment" and the "Industrial Catalogue on the Guidance of Foreign Investment" were issued in June 1995 and later amended in December 1997. The regulations classify foreign direct investment into "encouraged", "permitted", "prohibited" categories along with two forms of "restricted" categories (see Table 10.5). Under the regulations, China seeks to encourage both a greater geographic dispersion of foreign direct investment inflows domestically and to increase foreign direct investment inflows into the targeted economic sectors, such as agriculture, resource exploitation, infrastructure, export-oriented and high technology industries.

Foreign investments in the industries listed under the encouraged and restricted-B categories are entitled to a set of fiscal incentives. First, foreign investments in these categories are eligible for tariff and value added tax exemption treatment for imported equipment and technology. Second, foreign investments in encouraged categories are offered a set of income tax incentives, as discussed in more detail below.

Table 10.5. **China's industrial guidance on foreign direct investment**

Encouraged

1) agricultural new technologies, comprehensive development of agriculture, and the building of energy sources, communications and important materials industries;
2) new or advanced technologies which can improve the quality of products, conserve energy and raw materials, raise technological and economic efficiency of enterprises, or can manufacture products to alleviate the shortage of such products in the domestic markets;
3) projects that meet the needs of the international market, raise the grade and quality of products, open up new markets, or expand and increase exports;
4) investments related to comprehensive use of renewable resources and new technologies and equipment for environmental protection;
5) investments that can give full play to the advantages of labour and natural resources in the central and western regions.

Permitted

foreign direct investments that are not under the categories of encouraged, restricted and prohibited are permitted.

Restricted

1) projects which have been developed domestically, projects the technology of which has been imported and projects the production capacity of which can meet domestic demand;
2) trades in which the state is still experimenting with utilising foreign investment in sectors where a state monopoly still exists;
3) projects involving the prospecting and exploitation of rare and valuable mineral resources;
4) trades that must be put under the overall plan of the state;
5) other projects restricted by state laws and administrative regulations.

Prohibited

1) projects that endanger state security or harm social and public interest;
2) projects that pollute and damage environment, destroy natural resources or harm people's health;
3) projects that use up large tracts of farmland, that are not beneficial to the protection and development of land resources, or that endanger the security and the effective use of military facilities;
4) projects that manufacture products by applying China's special industrial arts or technology;
5) other projects that are prohibited by state laws and administrative regulations.

Source: Foreign Investment Administration, China's Ministry of Foreign Trade and Economic Co-operation (MOFTEC) (1998), *Tax Exemption Policies on Importation of Equipment by Enterprises with Foreign Investment*, Foreign Investment Administration of MOFTEC, Beijing.

Tax policies toward foreign direct investment

Since introducing tax incentives for foreign invested enterprises in the SEZs and open coastal cities in the early 1980s, China has extensively but selectively used them as "economic levers" to guide foreign direct investment into designated regions, economic sectors, and industries.

At the beginning of 1994 China adopted a new taxation system that applies to both domestic enterprises and foreign invested enterprises. Foreign invested enterprises will ultimately be subject to the same business income tax rate of 33 per cent and value added tax rate of 17 per cent that applies to domestic firms. This is to be accomplished by gradually phasing out the preferential treatment for foreign invested enterprises in order to establish a level-playing field with domestic firms. With the implementation of the policy, the preferential policies including tax incentives given to foreign invested enterprises will be gradually reduced and abolished. However, as shown in Tables 10.6 and 10.7, at present foreign invested enterprises still enjoy substantial tax incentives.

China's tax incentive policy for foreign invested enterprises have two key features. First, tax incentives offered in the SEZs and Economic and Technological Development Zones (ETDZs) located in

Table 10.6. **National business income tax exemption and reduction for FDI firms**

FDI firms	Income tax exemption and reduction
1. Productive FDI firms scheduled to operate for 10 years or more.	Commencing from the first profit-making year, 2 years exemption plus 3 years 50% reduction.
2. Joint-venture FDI firms engaged in ports construction scheduled to operate for 15 years or more.	Commencing from the first profit-making year, 5 years exemption plus 5 years 50% reduction.
3. FDI firms located in Hainan Special Economic Zone engaged in infrastructure construction of airport, port, railway, highway, power station, coal mine, water conservancy, and in agricultural development and production scheduled to operate for 15 years or more.	Commencing from the first profit-making year, 5 years exemption plus 5 years 50% reduction.
4. FDI firms located in Shanghai Pudong New Economic and Technological Development Zone engaged in the construction of airport, port, railway, and power station scheduled to operate for 15 years or more.	Commencing from the first profit-making year, 5 years exemption plus 5 years 50% reduction.
5. FDI firms located in SEZs engaged in service industries with investment over US$5 million scheduled to operate for 10 years or more.	Commencing from the first profit-making year, 1 year exemption plus 2 years 50% reduction.
6. Wholly foreign owned banks and joint-venture banks located in SEZs and government permitted areas with investment over US$10 million scheduled to operate for 10 years or more.	Commencing from the first profit-making year, 1 year exemption plus 2 years 50% reduction.
7. High and new technology joint-venture FDI firms located in government designated national high and new technology development zones scheduled to operate for 10 years or more.	Commencing from the first profit-making year, 2 years exemption.
8. Export-oriented FDI firms if they export 70% or more of their annual products after the expiration of the initial period allowed for exemption and reduction.	Further 50% reduction after the expiration of the initial period allowed for exemption and reduction.
9. Technologically advanced FDI firms if they still are classified as technologically advanced enterprises after the expiration of the initial period allowed for exemption and reduction.	Further 3 years 50% reduction after the expiration of the initial period allowed for exemption and reduction.
10. FDI firms engaged in agriculture, forestry, and animal husbandry, or located in economically less developed and remote areas.	Further 10 years 15%-30% reduction after the expiration of the initial period allowed for exemption and reduction.

Source: Wang Luolin *et al.* (eds) (1997), *Zhongguo Waishang Touzi Baogao: Waishang Touzi de Hangye Fenbu* [*Report on Foreign Direct Investment in China: Industrial Distribution of Foreign Direct Investment*], Jingji Guanli Chubanshe, Beijing, pp. 360-361.

Table 10.7. **Other tax incentives for FDI firms**

FDI firms	Tax Incentives
1. Firms engaged in industries and projects classified as encouraged and restricted.	Tariff free and value added tax exemption for imported equipment and technology.
2. Firms engaged in industries and projects classified as encouraged.	Local business income tax exemption and reduction possible.
3. Technologically advanced and export-oriented FDI firms, and FDI firms located in Hainan Special Economic Zone engaged in the projects of infrastructure construction or agricultural development.	100% refund for income tax paid on the reinvested portion if reinvestment allows an operational period of no less than 5 years.
4. All FDI firms.	40% refund for income tax paid on earnings reinvested over an operational period of not less than five years.
5. All FDI firms and foreign investors.	No restriction on profits remittance and capital repatriation. Foreign investors are granted tax exemption on repatriated profits.

Source: Wang Luolin *et al.* (eds) (1997), *Zhongguo Waishang Touzi Baogao: Waishang Touzi de Hangye Fenbu* [Report on Foreign Direct Investment in China: Industrial Distribution of Foreign Direct Investment], Jingji Guanli Chubanshe, Beijing, pp. 361-362.
Foreign Investment Administration of the Ministry of Foreign Trade and Economic Co-operation (1998), *Tax Exemption Policies on Importation of Equipment by Enterprises with Foreign Investment*, Foreign Investment Administration of MOFTEC, Beijing.

the open cities are much more favourable than in other open regions. Second, tax incentives are more favourable for technologically advanced and export-oriented foreign invested enterprises.

Admittedly, these tax incentives have had a positive impact on attracting foreign direct investment inflows into China. However, some tax incentives are more effective than others, some have more impact on one group of investors than on another, and some are ineffective.

First, the tax incentives granted to technologically advanced and exported-oriented enterprises, and the tax concessions offered to foreign invested enterprises engaged in low-profit operations or located in remote and poor areas, are consistent with China's needs to introduce advanced technology, to expand international exports, and to encourage the inflows of capital and technology into the targeted regions and sectors. Second, the tax refund on reinvestment has a large influence on decisions by foreign investors to reinvest their profits, particularly when such profits are distributed in RMB terms.

Third, the tax incentive package granting two years' exemption from income tax plus a 50 per cent reduction for three further years to joint ventures operating for at least ten years, has a stronger impact on cheap labour-seeking, export-oriented foreign direct investment than on market-seeking or strategic-position-seeking foreign direct investment. Cheap labour-seeking foreign direct investment, because its primary goal is to lower production costs and to make profits as soon as possible, has a strong short-term profit motive that can be significantly enhanced by tax exemptions or reductions. As a result, the tax incentive package has greater impact on the initial investment decisions of the cheap labour-seeking, export-oriented foreign direct investment. In contrast, market-seeking foreign direct investment and strategic-position-seeking foreign direct investment in general are motivated by longer-term profit expectations that can be little influenced by short-term tax holidays. Their initial investment decisions are mainly determined by the host country's overall investment climate and their own global expansion strategy. Therefore, the tax incentive package has little impact on the initial investment decisions, and no influence on the length of operations of such enterprises once they have made their investments in China.

Fourth, a tax incentive package offered in the form of tax holidays has greater impact on investors from Hong Kong, China, Macao, Chinese Taipei, and other East and Southeast Asian countries (mainly the overseas Chinese investors) than on investors from developed countries. Overseas Chinese investors are usually modestly capitalised and possess middle-level technology mainly for labour-intensive activities.

335

These are more easily motivated by low labour cost and short-term profits. Therefore, the favourable tax concessions plus low labour costs and the advantages of cultural and geographical proximity with China have a greater impact on the incentives of the overseas Chinese investors to start or shift operations into China. Unlike overseas Chinese investors, most investors from developed countries are large multinational enterprises (MNEs). These generally have advanced technology, superior technical capabilities, larger scale, and greater geographical diversification. Their initial investment decisions are usually determined by the overall investment environment of host countries, long-term profit expectations and their own strategic global business expansion. Thus, in general, foreign direct investment from developed countries tends to be inelastic with respect to short-term tax concessions.

Fifth, to be cost-effective, exemptions and reductions on local income taxes need to affect where foreign investors choose to locate in China. However, since almost all provinces compete with each other to attract foreign direct investment by offering local income tax exemptions and reductions, the net effect is to eliminate their role in foreigners' decision as to which region to set up operations. In fact, the competition among provinces in offering tax incentives to foreign investors creates a well-known situation of a "prisoner's dilemma". "In the market for foreign investment, a prisoner's dilemma arises among countries when one country's increase in incentives is matched by increased incentives from a competitor. A point will be reached when the incentive levels stabilise and no country will be better off: unchanged relative incentives will produce the same market share as before. Indeed, both countries may be worse off because income is transferred to firms with no gain in market share" (Guisinger, 1985).

Finally, let us examine the effectiveness of these tax incentives on foreign direct investment in China from the aspect of different taxation systems adopted by source countries. There are two taxation systems prevailing in the world. One is the "territorial taxation system" and the other is the "global taxation system". Under the territorial system, a citizen or subsidiary earning income abroad needs to pay tax only to the host country governments, in other words, the home country government does not tax the income of its citizens or subsidiaries abroad. Whereas, under the global system, the home country government does tax the income of its citizens or subsidiaries, but grants a tax credit for taxes paid to host country governments. The tax credit system can complicate the effect of tax incentives on foreign direct investment.

According to the global taxation system, subsidiaries of foreign firms pay income taxes to the host country government based on the host's tax laws. However, when the subsidiaries repatriate income to their parent companies, they are liable to taxation at the home countries' rate, with a credit for any taxes paid to the host country governments. In the normal practice of the credit system, only taxes actually paid to the host country governments can be credited by the home country government. Under this system, a tax concession established by a host country simply reduces the amount the subsidiary can deduct from its liability to the home government. In effect, the foreign subsidiary is effectively prevented from benefiting from the tax concessions, whose value accrues to the home country tax authority The result is that not only are the tax concessions ineffective in influencing the investment decisions of foreign investors from the countries with a tax credit system, but host country governments lose tax revenues which they otherwise would have received had they not offered the tax concessions.

China has offered substantial tax exemptions and tax reductions to foreign direct investment firms, and some of its major foreign investors, including those from the United States, Japan, and the United Kingdom, are subject to global taxation under the tax credit system. In order to avoid the potentially adverse consequences of this combination, China has successfully negotiated a "tax-sparing" provision in tax treaties with its foreign direct investment source countries that allows a credit for taxes foregone by China's tax concessions, to be applied against the home country's tax on the income of its businesses in China.[3] However, the United States has consistently refused to include such a "tax-sparing" provision in its tax treaties with any country. The traditional justification is the principle of capital export neutrality, since a tax-sparing credit may favour certain foreign investment over domestic investment. Under this tax policy, overseas subsidiaries of United States' companies are liable for United States Tax on a portion of the tax forgone by their host countries. This has put the United States' subsidiaries in a disadvantageous position and effectively reduced their competitiveness compared to foreign invested enterprises from countries that recognise the tax-sparing credit. In addition, this tax policy creates an incentive to defer profit repatriation and, in the case of China, to take the advantage of the tax refund on reinvestment funds to reinvest their profits in China. The overall result is that the tax incentives offered by the Chinese government in the form of tax exemptions and tax reductions have virtually no effect on the investment decisions of the United States' investors.[4]

Foreign exchange policies

Foreign exchange policies directly affect the financial operation and international transaction of foreign invested firms. So foreign exchange policy in host countries is important for foreign investors. Undoubtedly, a stable foreign exchange rate, a more liberalised foreign exchange regime and a fully convertible local currency will greatly help the operation of foreign invested enterprises.

In 1994, China adopted the foreign exchange management system of sale-and-purchase through banks and the managed floating exchange rate system. In December 1996, RMB became convertible on the current account. In China, foreign invested enterprises are required to keep a balance between their foreign exchange receipts and expenditures. However, foreign invested enterprises can participate in the foreign exchange swap markets to balance their foreign exchange accounts. Therefore, foreign exchange balancing is a less important issue for foreign invested enterprises in China.

Admittedly, China has achieved substantial progress in its foreign direct investment policy reform within a relatively short period. However, comparing China's current foreign direct investment policy to the principles of the TRIMs agreement, there is still room for China to further liberalise its foreign direct investment policy regime in order to attract foreign investors and benefit from foreign direct investment in the long run.

National treatment is the cornerstone of any set of principles underpinning foreign investment policy. The implementation of national treatment to foreign invested enterprises has two aspects in China. First, since the Chinese government granted tax incentives to foreign invested enterprises, usually the foreign investors have been treated more favourably than domestic investors. As a result, domestic firms have been put in a disadvantageous position to compete with foreign invested enterprises. Therefore, with the application of national treatment the tax incentives granted to foreign invested enterprises will be gradually reduced and abolished in order to create a fair competition environment for both foreign and domestic firms. Second, the application of national treatment to foreign invested enterprises also involves the removal of various restrictions and performance requirements imposed on FIEs. China has made commitments in its WTO accession to reduce the restrictions on foreign direct investment and to eliminate the performance requirements to foreign invested enterprises.

As regards the principle of transparency, WTO member countries have an obligation to notify the WTO-inconsistent TRIMs and eliminate the notified TRIMs in a specified period. Until China has formally entered the WTO, there is no notification and publication of WTO-inconsistent TRIMs. Currently, China maintains a very complex application process for foreign direct investment, which needs to be simplified and made more transparent through further policy reform. China has extensive laws, regulations, and guidelines to foreign direct investment, which foreign investors view as among the most complex in the world. China therefore needs to increase the transparency of its foreign direct investment policy regime.

Implications of WTO accession for foreign direct investment inflows into China

China has made substantial commitments to liberalise the terms and conditions for foreign investment and the activities of foreign-owned or invested enterprises in the domestic economy. As summarised in Annex I, these include the reduction of existing restrictions on foreign enterprises and expansion of the sectors into which foreign investment may enter. In addition, accession to WTO obligates China to adhere to several longer-standing WTO agreements that will have important effects on the investment climate for foreign direct investment (see Box 1). The Agreement on Trade Related Investment Measures (TRIMS) and the Agreement on Trade Related Intellectual Property are

Box 10.1. Other WTO agreements bearing on FDI in China

With accession, China is now bound by several earlier agreements among WTO members that are intended to limit distortions to international trade and investment arising from domestic economic policies. The Agreement on Trade-Related Investment Measures (TRIMs) was achieved in the Uruguay Round multilateral negotiations of GATT. The Agreement recognises that certain investment measures can have trade-restrictive and distorting effects, and provides that no Member shall apply a measure that is prohibited by the provisions of GATT Article III (national treatment) or Article XI (quantitative restrictions).

Because of the difficulties associated with bringing disciplines on investment into the international trading framework, the TRIMs agreement has emerged as the shortest and most limited of the WTO agreements, with only nine Articles plus the Illustrative List set out in an Annex. The TRIMs agreement applies to investment measures related to trade in goods only. TRIMs themselves are not defined. Instead, the Illustrative List of measures which are deemed to be WTO-inconsistent refers to measures that are mandatory or enforceable under domestic law or administrative ruling, or compliance with which is necessary to obtain an advantage. A TRIM may fall into at least one of the following five categories:

- it requires a firm to source a specified minimum proportion of its purchases from local sources (local content requirement);
- it requires a firm to achieve a specified import/export ratio in relation to local product embedded in the exports (trade balancing requirement);
- it restricts a firm's level of imports in relation to its export or local production (trade balancing restriction);
- it restricts a firm's access to foreign exchange (foreign exchange balancing restrictions);
- it restricts a firm's level of exports (export restrictions).

The TRIMs agreement contains transitional arrangements allowing members to maintain notified TRIMs for a limited time following the entry into force of the WTO (two years in the case of developed country members, five years for developing country members, and seven years for least-developed country members). The Agreement also provides for an establishment of a TRIMs Committee which has responsibility for overseeing the operation of the agreement, including facilitating consultations, and for reporting annually to the WTO's Council for Trade in Goods.

Although the TRIMs agreement is the most relevant part of WTO agreements for FDI, it is not the only WTO instrument that has a bearing on investment measures. Other relevant WTO agreements include, for example, the General Agreement on Trade in Service (GATS) and the Agreement on Trade-Related Aspects of Intellectual Property Rights (TRIPs).

The GATS sets out the rights and obligations for non-discriminatory service trade. While it does not explicitly refer to investment or investment measures, it does implicitly include provisions on investment through references to commercial presence. Commercial presence is one of the four modes of supply identified in GATS (the other three are cross-border trade, movement of supplier, and movement of natural persons). Commercial presence is defined as any type of business or professional establishment, including through 1) the constitution, acquisition or maintenance of a juridical person, or 2) the creation or maintenance of a branch or a representative office, within the territory of a member for the purpose of supplying a service. Member countries are required to schedule their commitments to liberalisation in particular sectors (that is, to provide market access and national treatment) in terms of the four modes of supply. In addition, countries are required to apply the principle of MFN in all sectors. This means that even where countries do not specify greater liberalisation in particular sectors, the MFN obligation will still apply. Given the direct link between investment and establishing commercial presence, it is clear that further liberalisations will directly influence investment flows.

The TRIPs agreement does not refer directly or even indirectly to investment. However, to the extent that foreign investment is related either to investment in products or processes with an intellectual property content (that is, the value of the product is in part determined by the legal protection accorded to the intellectual property) or to licensing arrangements for technology transfer, decisions to invest may be affected by the level of intellectual property protection offered by the host government. The TRIPs agreement, which provides for minimal standards of protection and enforcement of intellectual property, may have some influence on the direction of investment flows.

particularly important in this regard. The effectiveness with which these WTO commitments are implemented will be a key factor in determining the course of future foreign direct investment into China and its impact on the overall economy.

From 1979 to 1999, China attracted a total of over US$300 billion foreign direct investment inflows, making it the largest foreign direct investment recipient among the developing countries and the second largest foreign direct investment recipient in the world. However this does not mean necessarily that China has performed better in attracting foreign direct investment inflows than other developing countries, and actually received more foreign direct investment inflows from the world than it should have, based on its economic and geographical characteristics. Chen Chunlai (2000*a*), using a multi-regression empirical model,[5] found that during the period 1987 to 1998, China attracted 8.22 per cent (cumulatively around US$22 billion) more foreign direct investment inflows than its potential based on economic and geographical characteristics. This ranks China number fifteen in terms of its performance in attracting foreign direct investment inflows among the thirty-two developing host countries in the study. Undoubtedly, China's performance in attracting foreign direct investment inflow is better than most developing countries. However, it is far from the best among the thirty-two developing countries in the study.

China is the largest foreign direct investment recipient among the developing countries and attracted around 30 per cent of the total foreign direct investment inflows into developing countries and nearly 50 per cent of total foreign direct investment inflows into the East and Southeast Asian economies from 1987 to 1998. Compared with the eight East and Southeast Asian economies, China's performance in attracting foreign direct investment inflows ranked number five, which is just in the middle, much better than that of the Philippines, Thailand, Chinese Taipei and the Republic of Korea, similar to that of Hong Kong, China, but much lower than that of Singapore, Malaysia and Indonesia. After discounting for its huge market size, fast economic growth, low labour costs, relatively well-educated human resources, and other economic and geographical characteristics, China's relative performance in attracting foreign direct investment inflows is only at a level moderately above average both among the developing countries and among the East and Southeast Asian economies.

From a dynamic point of view, the study also examined the annual performance of China in attracting foreign direct investment inflows from 1987 to 1998. As shown in Figure 10.3., China attracted more foreign direct investment inflows than its potential in 1987 and 1988. However, from 1989 to 1991 China received less foreign direct investment inflows than it might have received. China's poor performance in attracting foreign direct investment inflows during the period 1989 to 1991 was largely due to foreign countries' reaction to the Tiananmen Square event. Starting from 1992, foreign direct investment inflows into China surged at an unprecedented pace. As a result, China received much more foreign direct investment inflows than its potential from 1992 to 1996. However, in 1997 and 1998 China received less foreign direct investment than its potential, which might be attributed largely to the negative impact of Asian financial crisis on China's economy.

The slowdown of foreign direct investment inflows into China since 1997 could be explained by various factors. First, it is likely that the high foreign direct investment inflows into China during the early 1990s were exceptional and above the rate likely to be sustained in the long run. Second, there has been a slowdown from the surge in transfers of labour intensive activities from neighbouring Asian countries and economies, which has been particularly apparent after the Asian financial crisis. The Asian financial crisis occurred in 1997 and has substantially weakened outward investment from the East and Southeast Asian economies. In fact, except for Singapore, foreign direct investment flows into China from all other East and Southeast Asian economies have declined substantially since 1997. Third, market rates of return on investment in China have not been as high as foreign investors expected. In many cases foreign investors' high hopes for China's market have been slow to materialise. Informal relationships and corruption still hinder many business transactions by foreigners. In addition, inefficient state-owned enterprises still dominate many key sectors of the economy. Finally, there are still restrictions on foreign direct investment, such as on ownership shares, types of foreign direct investment, and regional and sectoral restrictions.

Figure 10.3. **Annual relative performance of China in attracting FDI inflows**

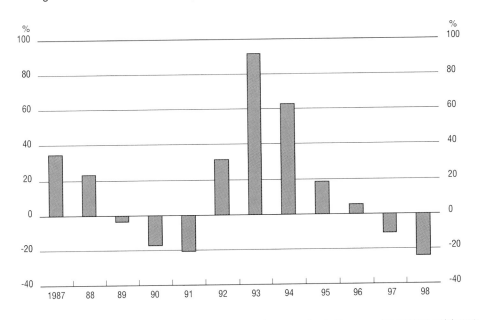

Note: Figures are the percentage difference between China's potential FDI inflows as estimated by regression analysis and the actual FDI inflows received.
Source: Chen Chunlai (2000*a*).

Therefore, China's accession to the WTO comes at a very critical time. China is facing difficulties in sustaining a high but normal level of foreign direct investment inflows. Could China's accession to the WTO revive a high level of foreign direct investment inflows? Since China applied to join the GATT then the WTO, there have been many studies on the impact that China's WTO accession would have on China's economy. However, most studies have focused on analyses of the impact of trade liberalisation on China's economy by examining the reduction of China's tariffs and the phase-out of textile and clothing quotas. There are only a very small number of studies that incorporate investment or financial liberalisation in their analyses and estimate foreign direct investment inflows after China's WTO accession.

McKibben and Wilcoxen (1998) explored the impact of China's WTO accession using a dynamic inter-temporal general equilibrium model (DIGEM). According to the authors, a key feature of the model is that it has well-defined financial markets that are based on valuation of the returns to real economic activities, with arbitrage between different activities within and across countries.[6] The authors attempt to use the model to separately measure the impact of trade liberalisation and financial liberalisation on China's economy.

The baseline model is estimated using data for the world economy from 1991 to 2020 and assumes no additional change in China's 1997 tariffs for the duration of the baseline. Two simulations are run: 1) China's 1997 statutory tariff rates are gradually reduced, beginning in 1998, to zero by 2010, and 2) China implements financial reforms that increase the returns from investing in China by 1 per cent in 1998, 2 per cent in 1999, and 3 per cent from 2000 onwards.

Under the first simulation, China's trade liberalisation causes the economy to slow somewhat in 1998 compared to the baseline, as trade liberalisation puts competitive pressures on China's domestic firms. After 1998, the economy grows more quickly, and by 2010, GDP growth is 0.85 per cent higher than in the absence of liberalisation. Real exports initially fall, and then rise in the long run; real imports increase sharply, to 3 per cent above the baseline in 2010. China's tariff cuts improve economic efficiency and raise the overall return to capital, which in turn increases foreign investment.

Under the financial liberalisation scenario, financial flows into China increase very quickly. Real exports decrease while imports increase as the inflow of foreign investment causes Chinese currency to appreciate; the current account and trade balance initially deteriorate by nearly 4 per cent of GDP, but then improve over time. The increased capital inflows permanently raise GDP above the baseline.[7]

Walmsley and Hertel (2000) estimated the economic effects of China's WTO accession by using a Dynamic GTAP model, which incorporates international capital mobility and ownership data. This model is used to examine the effects on China's economy from a delay in the effective implementation of MFA quota elimination, due to the use of safeguards that are permitted under the agreement (see Annex I). A baseline is developed for 1995 to 2020. The baseline includes the implementation and effects of prior WTO agreements made during the Uruguay Round, including projected effects of measures that are still being phased in. Tariff liberalisation China undertook before 2000 has also been factored into the baseline projection. Two alternative policy scenarios for China's WTO accession are then examined: 1) China enters as a developed country, reduces tariffs gradually from 2000 to 2005 based on its August 1998 WTO offer, and enjoys the elimination of MFA quotas by 2005; and 2) China enters the WTO and makes the tariff cuts, but the full elimination of the MFA quotas is not achieved until 2010, due to the use of safeguard provisions by China's trade partners.

In the first simulation, China's accession raises the rate of return for capital, therefore increasing foreign investment, particularly in the first five years following China's accession, leading to a rise in the capital stock (up by 7.8 per cent). Capital moves into China from competitor economies, where the rate of return has fallen as a consequence of China's WTO accession. Overall foreign ownership of China's capital increases relative to the baseline as a result of China's accession. The increased capital formation resulting from foreign investment leads to higher GDP growth, which increases over time to a cumulative difference reaching 8.6 per cent compared with the baseline in 2020. Economic welfare increases by US$27.1 billion.[8] In addition, real wages for skilled and unskilled workers are higher by 2.4 per cent and 3.1 per cent respectively. Exports and imports increase by 35.2 per cent and 39.4 per cent respectively. Employment in the textile and clothing sector grows sharply until 2005, and then levels off.

Under the second simulation in which MFA quotas are not eliminated until 2010, GDP growth is slightly lower than in the first scenario but real GDP is still above the baseline, by 8.3 per cent, in 2020. Economic welfare, exports and imports, and real wages are relatively unaffected. Employment in the textile and clothing sector grows less rapidly compared with the first simulation through 2005, but by 2020, it rises to the same level as under the first simulation. Foreign ownership increases as a result of China's accession to the WTO, but this increase occurs more gradually when the MFA is delayed. In the long run foreign ownership is greater than if the MFA had not been delayed (the first scenario).

The United Nations Conference on Trade and Development (UNCTAD, 2000) estimated that in the short term, WTO accession would have only a small effect on foreign direct investment flows into China, as investors take a wait-and-see attitude while reforms are being implemented. However, in the medium-term, UNCTAD predicts foreign direct investment flows into China could increase from current levels of about US$40 billion to US$60 billion and possibly to US$100 billion annually if cross-border mergers and acquisitions are allowed.

Goldman Sachs (1999) examined China's reported April 1999 offer to the United States and projected that China's WTO accession would significantly boost China's economic growth, foreign investment, and trade. According to the study, trade liberalisation and greater openness would boost productivity, increasing GDP growth by an additional 0.5 per cent per year by 2005. China's total trade (exports plus imports) and foreign direct investment flows would nearly double by 2005.

In summary, although the studies use different models, data sets, assumptions and time frames, there are some common results. First, China's WTO accession is expected to have a positive impact on its GDP growth mainly through efficiency gains resulting from trade and investment liberalisation. Second, China's WTO accession will boost both China's exports and imports. Third, China's WTO accession will accelerate foreign direct investment inflows into China and increase the foreign ownership share of China's assets.

341

The remainder of this section presents rough estimates of the quantity of foreign direct investment inflows into China after accession to the WTO by using an empirical model. First of all, it should be noted that the empirical model was initially designed to test the location determinants affecting foreign direct investment inflows into developing countries rather than to predict future foreign direct investment inflows. Second, when predicting future foreign direct investment inflows into a developing country, the empirical model assumes that the location variables of the other developing countries are unchanged, and the model can only predict the future foreign direct investment inflows into those developing countries that are in the regression data set. Third, the model used in the estimation is a simplified empirical model that only captures a group of key location determinant variables. Fourth, the implementation of the WTO agreements are not directly incorporated into the model, however, they are assumed to be captured by the other variables in the model, such as the economic growth rate, efficiency wages and economic distance, which are affected by the implementation of the WTO agreements. Therefore, because of the many deficiencies mentioned above, the estimation results presented below are only indicative, and the interpretation of these results requires extreme caution.

The simplified empirical model is a multi-regression model with pooled data. The data set contains 32 developing countries (including China) for a period of 12 years from 1987 to 1998. The dependent variable is foreign direct investment inflows into developing countries, and the independent variables include market size (GDP), GDP growth rate, efficiency wage, defined as the real wage rate adjusted by labour productivity, labour quality approximated by illiteracy rate of population, and economic distance defined as the weighted average distance of a developing country to the rest of the world, where the weights are the shares of the countries' GDP in the world total GDP. In the regression the independent variables are lagged by one year. All the independent variables are statistically significant at the 0.01 significance level, and the Buse-R^2 is 0.55, which indicates the relatively high explanatory power of the estimated equation.

To estimate future foreign direct investment inflows, the following assumptions are made for two scenarios. The baseline scenario assumed that China did not join the WTO. In this scenario, the annual GDP growth rate from 2001 to 2010 is assumed to be 7.66 per cent;[9] the efficiency wage increases by 1.5 per cent annually; the economic distance index increases by 0.25 per cent annually due to the relatively higher GDP growth in the rest of the world resulting from the efficiency gains of WTO; and the labour quality variable is kept constant.

The second scenario assumed that China joined the WTO in 2001. This scenario assumes that WTO accession will affect China's economy at a gradual but progressively accelerating pace. Thus, for the early period of WTO entry, the GDP growth rate rises from the 7.66 per cent in the baseline in even steps to reach 8.16 per cent in 2005, or 0.5 percentage points above the baseline. GDP growth accelerates further after 2005, reaching 9.16 per cent in 2010.[10] The efficiency wage decreases by 0.5 per cent annually during the projection period, under the assumption that productivity growth is higher than real wage growth due to the large efficiency gains from WTO accession; the economic distance index decreases by 0.25 per cent annually due to the relatively higher GDP growth in China than in the rest of the world; and the labour quality variable is kept constant at the level of the baseline scenario.

Based on the empirical model and the assumptions made above, future foreign direct investment inflows into China are estimated for the two scenarios. The estimation results are presented in Figure 10.4..

According to the estimation, foreign direct investment inflows into China are projected to increase from US\$40 billion in 2000 to US\$63 billion in 2005 and further increase to over US\$100 billion in 2010,[11] an annual growth rate of nearly 10 per cent. Compared with the baseline, after China enters the WTO and implements trade and investment liberalisation, foreign direct investment inflows into China would be more than 23 per cent higher in 2005 and more than 58 per cent higher in 2010, and the annual growth rate of foreign direct investment inflows would be double that of the baseline.

It should be noted that the above estimate of the quantity of foreign direct investment inflows into China is only the theoretical potential based on a group of key location determinants affecting foreign

Figure 10.4. **Estimation of future FDI inflows into China**

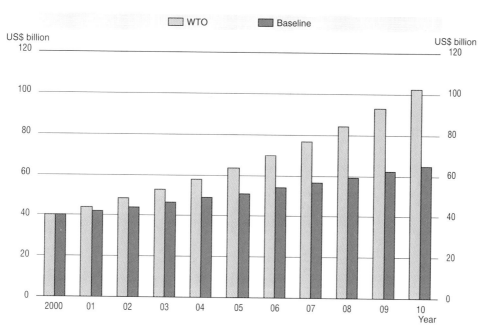

Source: Estimated based on the empirical analyses summarised in the text.

direct investment inflows. However, whether China can realise this potential in attracting foreign direct investment inflows will largely depend on how China implements its WTO commitments, further reduces and eliminates trade and investment barriers and opens up domestic markets, manages internal economic reforms, particularly the reform of state-owned enterprises, and enforces the protection of intellectual property rights.

Implications for the composition of foreign direct investment sources

Since China started to attract foreign direct investment, more than 100 countries in the world have invested in the country. However, foreign direct investment in China has been overwhelmingly dominated by the developing economies, particularly the Asian newly industrialising economies (NIEs). The four largest foreign direct investment suppliers to China are Hong Kong, China, Chinese Taipei, the United States and Japan.

Figure 10.5. shows the annual foreign direct investment flows into China from source countries and economies. The table reveals several important characteristics.

First, since 1983 Hong Kong, China has been the single largest and the most important investor in China among all sources. Chinese Taipei started to invest in mainland China relatively late compared with other major investors, but its annual foreign direct investment outflows increased very rapidly. The United States and Japan have been by far the largest investors among the developed countries investing in China.

Second, in the early 1990s the annual foreign direct investment flows into China from all source countries and economic groupings increased remarkably. However, comparing the two groups, foreign direct investment flows into China from developing source countries increased more rapidly than those from developed source countries. As a result, the gap in the annual foreign direct investment outflows to China between the developing and developed source countries has enlarged since the early 1990s.

343

Figure 10.5. **The main investors in China (1983-1999)**

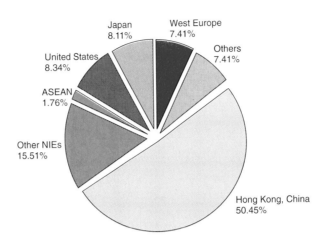

Japan
8.11%

West Europe
7.41%

United States
8.34%

Others
7.41%

ASEAN
1.76%

Other NIEs
15.51%

Hong Kong, China
50.45%

Source: Various issues of the State Statistical Bureau, *Zhongguo Duiwai Jingji Tongji Nianjian (China Foreign Economic Statistical Yearbook)* and *Zhongguo Tongji Nianjian (China Statistical Yearbook), Zhongguo Tongji Chubanshe,* Beijing.

Third, since 1997 the growth rate of investments in China from the developing source countries has slowed down, and investments by some major suppliers have actually declined in absolute terms. The main reason for the decline of foreign direct investment flows into China from developing source economies is the negative impact of the Asian financial crisis. The Asian financial crisis has substantially weakened the ability of most of the East and Southeast Asian economies to supply funds for outward investment. In contrast, since 1997, foreign direct investment flows into China from other developed source countries (except Japan, which has also been affected by the Asian financial crisis) have increased considerably, indicating an increasing interest in investing in China on the part of the developed source countries, particularly the United States and the Western European countries.

One way to assess a country' relative importance for its source countries' investments is to calculate the investment intensity indexes of source countries. The investment intensity index reveals the relative importance of a country as a host for a source country's investment as compared to its importance as a source for the rest of the world. This index is usually used as an indicator of investment relations between countries.[12]

The investment intensity index between China and its major investors are presented in Table 10.8. As the table shows, the investment intensity index for the major investors varies enormously. For the period from 1990 to 1998, the investment intensity indexes for Hong Kong, China, Chinese Taipei, Singapore, Republic of Korea, Thailand, Malaysia, Indonesia, and the Philippines are over 100 per cent, indicating that these countries have a higher share of total foreign direct investment in China than they do of total foreign direct investment to the rest of the world. In other words, China is more important as a host for these countries' investments as compared to the rest of the world. In contrast, the investment intensity indexes are all below 100 per cent for the developed countries, particularly for the Western European countries. However, among the developed countries, the investment intensity indexes of Japan, the United States, Australia and New Zealand are relatively high compared with those of the Western European countries, which may reflect the regional biases of these countries' investments in the Asia-Pacific region.

Why has China been successful in attracting foreign direct investment inflows from developing economies, especially from Hong Kong, China and Chinese Taipei, but has not been impressive in attracting foreign direct investment inflows from developed countries, especially from the West European countries, even though they are the major investors for world foreign direct investment?

Table 10.8. **Investment intensity index of major investors in China (%)**

Source countries and economies	Investment intensity index (1990-98)	Source countries and economies	Investment intensity index (1990-98)
Hong Kong, China	991	United Kingdom	19
Chinese Taipei	773	Germany	11
Singapore	417	France	10
Korea	340	Italy	20
Thailand	501	Netherlands	9
Malaysia	108	Switzerland	10
Indonesia	254	Norway	4
Philippines	1924	Denmark	10
Japan	87	Austria	11
United States	33	Sweden	4
Canada	19	Spain	3
Australia	58	Belgium	3
New Zealand	31	Finland	2

Notes: The equation of investment intensity index is as follows:

$$III_{ij} = \left(\frac{\frac{I_{ij}}{I_{*j}}}{\frac{I_{i*}}{I_{**}}} \right) \times 100$$

where:
IIIij = investment intensity index of i's investment in j
Iij = investment by i (source country) in j (host country)
I*j = investment from the world in j

Source: Calculated from various issues of:
National Bureau of Statistics, *Zhongguo Tongji Nianjian [China Statistical Yearbook]* and *Zhongguo Duiwai Jingji Tongji Nianjian [China Foreign Economic Statistical Yearbook]*, Zhongguo Tongji Chubanshe, Beijing.
United Nations, *World Investment Report*, United Nations Publication, United Nations, New York and Geneva.

It is generally agreed that the economic and technological development levels of the NIEs are above that of China but lower than that of the developed countries. In the past two decades the NIEs have been developing their economies relatively faster than other developing countries. This has led to both a rapid accumulation of human and physical capital and a rapid rise in real wages in the NIEs' economies. The changes in resource endowments of production factors have led to a process of economic restructuring and technological upgrading. Consequently, many labour-intensive industries have lost competitiveness, and investment abroad is seen as a means of utilising accumulated managerial and technical expertise and the established export markets by these industries. The labour-intensive production technology and the well established international export markets of the NIEs are well suited to exploit China's comparative advantages in labour intensive industries and to promote its exports. China is therefore a good location for the NIE investors to exploit overseas investment opportunities. In addition, Hong Kong, China, Chinese Taipei, and to a lesser extent Singapore and Republic of Korea, are geographically close to China. The common Chinese culture, language and close geographical distance greatly reduces the costs of doing business in China for these investors. As a result, it is not surprising that China has attracted a large amount of foreign direct investment inflows from NIEs.

There are many reasons for the low level of foreign direct investment flows into China from the developed countries. Apart from the relatively large economic and technological development gaps and long distance between most developed countries and China, several other factors may be very important in hindering foreign direct investment flows into China from the developed countries. First, the firms of developed countries usually possess more advanced technology and production techniques. Since the legal network for protecting intellectual property rights in China is poor, firms from the developed countries possessing advanced technology and production techniques are reluctant to invest in China. Second, the services sector in developed countries is very advanced and has recorded the highest growth rates in global foreign direct investment over the last decade. Most of China's services industries are closed to foreign investments. Third, the large multinational enterprises (MNEs) are the main carriers of foreign direct investment from developed countries and cross-border mergers and acquisitions (M&As) are the increasingly important means by which they carry out their FDI. However, M&A transactions by foreign investors in China have only been allowed in an experimental fashion with very strict restrictions. All of these factors have strong negative impacts on the investment decisions of developed countries' investors who are considering investing in China. Not surprisingly, the result is that the magnitude and the intensity of investment from developed countries in China are very low compared with their total investments worldwide.

The current composition of foreign direct investment sources in China needs to be diversified if China wants to benefit more from foreign direct investment. The diversification of foreign direct investment sources is not only necessary for China to attract a higher quantity of foreign direct investment inflows, but also to attract foreign direct investment inflows of a higher quality. China's accession to the WTO provides a great opportunity for China to improve and diversify its foreign direct investment sources and will therefore have significant implications for the composition of foreign direct investment sources in China.

Implications for regional distribution of foreign direct investment in China

Since China started to attract foreign direct investment into its economy, the regional distribution of foreign direct investment within China has been very uneven. (see Figures 10.6 and 10.7).[13]

Foreign direct investment inflows into China in the 1980s were overwhelmingly concentrated in the four SEZs and the two municipalities of Beijing and Shanghai. This is indicated by the huge foreign direct investment inflows into Guangdong, Fujian, Beijing, and Shanghai, whose combined share of annual foreign direct investment inflows was more than 66 per cent of the national total from 1983 to 1990.

Figure 10.6. **FDI inflows into China by regions**

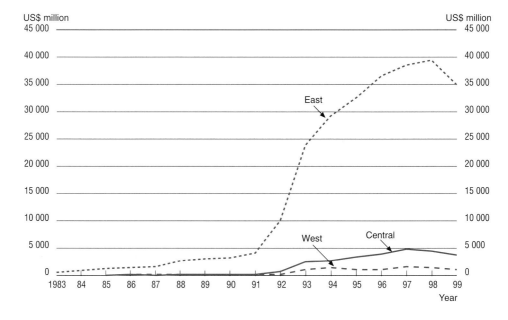

Source: Data for 1983-1991 are calculated from the State Statistical Bureau (1992), *Zhongguo Duiwai Jingji Tongji Daquan 1979-1991 (China Foreign Economic Statistics 1979-1991)*, China Statistical Information and Consultancy Service Center, Beijin. Data for 1992-1999 are calculated from various issues of the State Statistical Bureau, *Zhongguo Tongji Nianjian (China Statistical Yearbook)*, *Zhongguo Tongji Chubanshe*, Beijing.

Figure 10.7. **Regional distribution of accumulated FDI stocks in China, 1983-1999**

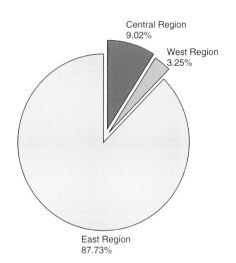

Central Region
9.02%

West Region
3.25%

East Region
87.73%

Source: Data for 1983-1991 are calculated from the State Statistical Bureau (1992), *Zhongguo Duiwai Jingji Tongji Daquan 1979-1991 (China Foreign Economic Statistics 1979-1991)*, China Statistical Information and Consultancy Service Centre, *Beijing.* Data for 1992-1999 are calculated from various issues of the State Statistical Bureau, *Zhongguo Tongji Nianjian (China Statistical Yearbook)*, *Zhongguo Tongji Chubanshe*, Beijing.

With the development of overall economic reform and the nationwide implementation of open policies for foreign direct investment in the 1990s, foreign direct investment inflows into China gradually spread from the initial concentrated areas to other provinces. Increasingly, the most important areas for hosting foreign direct investment are the Yangzi River Delta including Jiangsu, Shanghai, and Zhejiang, and the Bohai Gulf including Shandong, Hebei, Tianjin, and Liaoning. Several provinces, such as Jilin, Heilongjiang, Anhui, Jiangxi, Henan, Hubei and Hunan in the central region, and Sichuan and Shaanxi in the west region, also witnessed relatively large increases in foreign direct investment inflows from 1991 to 1999. Foreign direct investment inflows in the 1990s have therefore diffused from the initially concentrated southern coastal areas towards the southeastern and eastern coastal areas as well as towards inland areas.

The east, central, and western regions have experienced contrasting patterns in foreign direct investment inflows. Foreign direct investment inflows into the eastern provinces have been increasing steadily with a remarkably high growth rate, particularly during 1992 to 1998. For the other two regions, the inflows of foreign direct investment have been much lower, especially in the western region. Consequently, the gap between the east and the central and west regions in terms of the absolute magnitude of annual foreign direct investment inflows has actually increased since 1992. As a result, the east region provinces have overwhelmingly dominated the other two province groups in attracting foreign direct investment. As Figure 10.7 indicates, for the period from 1983 to 1999, the percentage shares in the cumulative national stock of foreign direct investment stock were 88 per cent for the eastern provinces, 9 per cent for the central region provinces, and only 3 per cent for the western region provinces. Per capita foreign direct investment in the east region is US$517, compared to US$61 in the central region and US$34 in the west. This uneven regional distribution of foreign direct investment has actually helped to enlarge the gap in economic development and income levels between the east on the one hand, and the central and western regions on the other.

Among the east region provinces, Guangdong's performance in attracting foreign direct investment has been very impressive. Its share of accumulated foreign direct investment from 1983 to 1999 was 29 per cent of the national total, far exceeding all other provinces including Jiangsu and Fujian, each of which possessed around 10 per cent of the national total, and ranked second and third among China's thirty provinces. However, if we analyse this pattern further, we find that the shares of each province have gradually changed. The share of Guangdong has declined from 46 per cent in the 1980s to 28 per cent in the 1990s. In contrast, the shares of other coastal provinces, such as Jiangsu, Fujian, Zhejiang, Shandong, Tianjin and Hebei, have increased steadily.

The share of the central provinces in the national total accumulated foreign direct investment stocks has increased gradually from 5 per cent during the 1980s to 9 per cent during the 1990s. The main contributors are Henan, Hubei, and Hunan provinces, and their shares of accumulated foreign direct investment in the national total doubled between the 1980s and the 1990s.

The less-developed western provinces have received a very small amount of foreign direct investment inflows. Their share in the national accumulated foreign direct investment stocks has been declining from around 5 per cent in the 1980s to around just over 3 per cent in the 1990s. However, Sichuan and Shaanxi attracted relatively more foreign direct investment inflows than the other provinces in this group.

In general, the above description of the provincial distribution of foreign direct investment has clearly revealed the uneven foreign direct investment distribution among China's provinces. This raises the question of identifying the location factors affecting foreign direct investment distribution across provinces in China. Chen Chunlai (2000b), using an empirical multi-regression model,[14] tested the location determinants affecting foreign direct investment inflows into China's provinces. The study found that the provincial differences in foreign direct investment inflows could be explained by the differences in provincial location factors. The provincial market size, the level of economic development, the level of previously-accumulated foreign direct investment, the intensity of transport infrastructure and the level of telecommunications are positive and statistically significant location factors affecting foreign direct investment in a given province. The provincial efficiency wage, the rates of illiteracy and semi-illiteracy, the proxy for labour quality, are negative and statistically significant location factors in affecting foreign direct investment inflows. In addition, the timing of the opening to foreign direct investment among provinces has had a strong impact on the provincial distribution of foreign direct investment inflows into China. Apart from the economic factors, the huge foreign direct investment inflows into the east region provinces were enhanced by policies that opened those provinces to foreign direct investment during the 1980s, before opening was allowed in the interior. The gradual but noticeable diffusion of foreign direct investment inflows into the inland provinces after 1992 is also partially due to the nationwide implementation of opening policies for foreign direct investment since the early 1990s. These, together with a series of foreign direct investment promotion policies in the early 1990s, had strong positive effects on attracting the foreign direct investment inflows throughout China.

One important implication for improving the uneven provincial distribution of foreign direct investment in China could be drawn from the study. It is essential for the central and the west region provinces to improve their location factors in order to attract more foreign direct investment inflows. Compared to the east region, the central and the western regions lag behind in almost all economic and social indicators (see Chapter 21 on regional developments and prospects), including those that are important location determinants in attracting foreign direct investment inflows. Although it is not easy for the economically backward provinces in the central and the west regions to improve these economic and social factors in the short run, such improvement is fundamental to their ability to attract more foreign direct investment to accelerate economic development in the long run.

This would indicate that the trade and investment liberalisation under China's WTO accession would bring more benefits to the east region than to the rest of the country, especially the western region. Therefore, economic growth in the east region is likely to continue to be higher than that in the west region and the east is likely to continue to receive proportionately more foreign direct investment than other regions.

The attractiveness of the east region to foreign direct investment derives from its relatively more liberalised and developed economy, closer connections with the outside world, better infrastructure, higher level of scientific research and technical innovation, and higher quality of its labour force.

Foreign direct investment inflows into the labour intensive export-oriented parts of the manufacturing sector in the east are likely to continue to play a positive role in export promotion, economic growth and employment creation. However, market-oriented foreign direct investment, especially foreign direct investment in the services sector, is likely to increase in importance in the east, as well as in the country as a whole, as a result of the further opening up of China's domestic markets.

To boost economic growth and thereby help to reduce the gap in economic development between the east and the central and western regions, the Chinese government launched the "Western Economic Development Strategy" in 1998 (see Chapter 21 for further discussion). This strategy emphasises infrastructure development, environment protection, industrial restructuring, development of science and education, and economic reform and openness. China's government has already begun to invest heavily in infrastructure development in the west in order to improve the climate for investment by enterprises and to boost economic growth in the region. As part of this strategy, enterprises, especially foreign invested enterprises, in the east region are encouraged to invest and to do business in the central and the west regions. The Chinese government has also issued a series of preferential policies to attract more foreign direct investment inflows into the central and the west regions.

In summary, it is most likely that China's accession to the WTO will initially tend to accentuate the unevenness in regional economic development and in the distribution of foreign direct investment between the eastern provinces and those in the interior. However, in the medium and long run, more foreign direct investment is likely to flow to central and western regions with the implementation of the Western Economic Development Strategy and further economic development in the interior.

Implications for the sectoral distribution of foreign direct investment in China

The sectoral distribution of foreign direct investment in China is characterised by the concentration of foreign direct investment in manufacturing, both in terms of accumulated foreign direct investment stocks and in terms of annual foreign direct investment flows (Figure 10.8). Between 1983 and 1999, the primary sector attracted 22 per cent of cumulative foreign direct investment into China, the manufacturing sector attracted 60 per cent, and the services sector attracted 38 per cent. Within the services sector, most foreign direct investment has gone to the real estate segment, which accounted for 24 per cent of the total cumulative foreign direct investment inflows into China. Other services industries received only 14 per cent of the total foreign direct investment.

Figure 10.8. **Sectoral distribution of accumulated FDI stocks in China, 1983-1999**

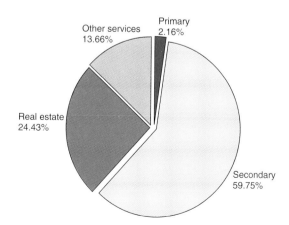

Source: Various issues of the State Statistical Bureau, *Zhongguo Duiwai Jingji Nianjian (China Foreign Economic Statistical Yearbook)* and *Zhongguo Tongji Nianjian (China Statistical Yearbook), Zhongguo Tongji Chubanshe,* Beijing.

In terms of the annual foreign direct investment inflows, the manufacturing sector has also been the largest recipient of annual foreign direct investment inflows into China, but its share has fluctuated. In the early stage of foreign direct investment into China, the manufacturing sector took the dominant share. In 1983, it attracted 67 per cent of total foreign direct investment inflows into China. However, during 1984 to 1986, the share of the manufacturing sector in the total annual foreign direct investment inflows declined to around 30 per cent, but subsequently increased very rapidly, reaching 80 per cent for three successive years from 1989 to 1991. After that its share fell back to just over 60 per cent from 1992 to 1999.

Although the manufacturing sector has dominated foreign direct investment inflows into China, the real estate sector has been a strong second. The interesting thing is that the changes in sectoral distribution of foreign direct investment inflows into China have been dominated by the share changes between the manufacturing and the real estate sectors. From 1984 to 1987, accompanying the overheating of economic growth in China, foreign direct investment inflows into the real estate sector increased substantially. It attracted more than one third of the total annual foreign direct investment inflows into China during this period, reaching a peak of 49 per cent in 1986. During the same period, the share of annual foreign direct investment inflow into the manufacturing sector declined correspondingly and reached its low of 22 per cent in 1984. In 1988, fighting against high inflation, the Chinese government introduced tighter macroeconomic control policies. As a result, the real estate sector contracted very sharply. From 1988 to 1991, the share of annual foreign direct investment inflow into the real estate sector was less than 10 per cent. Starting from 1992, with another economic boom in China, the real estate sector regained its momentum in attracting foreign direct investment, and its share of foreign direct investment inflows increased from 12 per cent in 1991 to 39 per cent in 1993, before declining from 1994 to 1999. The share of the primary sector in total foreign direct investment inflows in the national total has generally been lower than for manufacturing or services, but it has increased somewhat since the mid-1990s.

Thus, the distribution of foreign direct investment in China continues to be skewed towards the manufacturing sector. Although foreign direct investment inflows into the primary sector and the services sector has been on an increasing trend since the mid-1990s, the amount of foreign direct investment inflows into these sectors is still very low as compared to foreign direct investment inflows into the manufacturing sector.

China's WTO accession is likely to result in some changes in the distribution of foreign direct investment inflows among sectors. The portion of foreign direct investment in the manufacturing sector is likely to decline while the portion going to service sectors, particularly finance, insurance, commerce, telecommunications and auxiliary services, should increase. However, the extent of the changes in the distribution of foreign direct investment will depend primarily on success in implementing China's WTO commitments and on the degree of market opening to foreign investors. The remainder of this section will discuss the implications of China's WTO accession for foreign direct investment in different economic sectors, particularly services.

Primary sector

By the end of 1999, foreign direct investment in China's primary sector was around US$6.61 billion, of which US$4 billion was in agriculture and US$2.61 billion was in ocean oil and natural gas exploration, mining and other primary industries. It should be noted that most foreign investments in ocean oil and natural gas exploration are recorded as other foreign investments and are not included in the statistics of foreign direct investment in China.

Agriculture was one of the earliest sectors opened to foreign direct investment. However, the performance of agriculture in attracting foreign direct investment has not been impressive compared with the overall large amount of foreign direct investment inflows into China during the last two decades. There are many reasons for the poor performance of agriculture in attracting foreign direct investment but two are probably the most important. First, China's agricultural land tenure system, and the traditional small scale family based agricultural production methods that go with it, have greatly limited the inflows of agricultural foreign direct investment that require large-scale production and advanced technology. Second, government controls over production, pricing, purchase, storage, transportation, domestic sales, and international exports of grains and other major agricultural products (see Chapter I on agriculture) have had large negative effects on foreign investors to invest in China's agricultural sector.

In general, China has no comparative advantage in land-intensive grain production but does have a comparative advantage in labour-intensive horticultural and animal husbandry production. As discussed in Chapter I on agriculture, China's WTO accession provides opportunities to expand the production and exports of horticultural products and animal products. However, China's potential to expand exports of these products is limited by its deficiencies in technologies, capital, and marketing networks. This provides a great opportunity for foreign businesses to invest in areas such as quality upgrading, processing, fresh preservation, packaging, storage, and transportation. In addition, the development of animal husbandry will make the feed processing industry a very attractive sector for foreign direct investment.

The oil and natural gas exploration industry and the mining industry also have great potential to attract foreign investments if China removes the restrictions on foreign ownership shares, types of investment and scope of operations in these industries. It is expected that, after China's accession to the WTO, the oil and natural gas exploration and mining industries will attract more foreign direct investment inflows as China gradually reduces and eventually eliminates the restrictions on foreign direct investment in these industries. In addition, China's western region is well endowed with natural resources, particularly oil, natural gas, and mines. With the implementation of the Western Economic Development strategy and the improvement of the overall investment environment, it is expected that the western region should be able to attract more foreign direct investment inflows into its resource-based primary industries.

Manufacturing sector

China's labour-intensive industries accounted for 41 per cent of total foreign direct investment in manufacturing between 1983 and 1999, while capital-intensive and technology-intensive industries received 25 and 33 per cent respectively of the total. Studies predict that after accession to the WTO, China's labour-intensive manufacturing industries, especially textiles and clothing industries, will grow rapidly, led by the large expansion of exports. However, to realise this potential, China needs to introduce foreign capital, technology and advanced equipment to help upgrade its relatively backward labour-intensive industries in order to compete in the global markets (see the discussion in Chapter 4 on industry). Therefore, there are great opportunities for foreign investors to invest in China's labour-intensive and export-oriented manufacturing industries that could lead to an increase in foreign direct investment in these areas. As with foreign direct investment generally, the coastal region is likely to be the main receipt of the labour intensive and export-oriented foreign direct investment initially. However, as the central and the western regions become more attractive to foreign investors, they should receive increasing foreign direct investment flows into labour-intensive industries in the medium and long run. The result will be a gradual shift of labour-intensive foreign direct investment from the coastal region to the interior regions to take advantage of the comparative advantage conferred by lower wages in the interior.

In general, China's domestic capital-intensive and technology-intensive manufacturing industries have no comparative advantage in international markets, so these industries will face severe competition from foreign companies. Enhanced competition will put pressure on China's domestic enterprises to improve their management and technology and consequently increase their efficiency, but domestic enterprises that cannot make these adjustments face the possibility of being forced out of business. Loss-making state-owned enterprises in the traditional capital-intensive industries are particularly vulnerable in this regard.

State-owned enterprise reform is one of the essential issues to ensure the smoothness of China's accession to the WTO and is also very important for the successful implementation of China's WTO commitments. Currently, China's capital-intensive and technology-intensive manufacturing industries are still overwhelmingly dominated by state-owned enterprises. The successful reform of China's state sector will depend greatly on the means undertaken and the tools made available to foreign investors. Although the Chinese government has allowed private capital participation in the restructuring and modernisation of state-owned enterprises, controls over foreign ownership and the forms of foreign investment, such as cross-border M&As, continue to present major obstacles to that participation.

China's accession to the WTO will not only accelerate trade and investment liberalisation and improve the investment environment in China, but will also provide great opportunities for foreign investors to invest in China's capital-intensive and technology-intensive manufacturing industries. Foreign companies in capital-intensive and technology-intensive industries have more superior ownership advantages than China's domestic enterprises, and therefore have more advantages in competing in these industries. China should be able to attract more foreign direct investment, especially from large MNEs, into these sectors provided the government further relaxes the controls over foreign ownership; allows the direct transactions of cross-border M&As between foreign and domestic enterprises, especially state-owned enterprises; and effectively protects intellectual property rights. The most promising industries to attract foreign direct investment are new and high technology industries, for example, electronics, telecommunications equipment, synthetic materials, advanced building materials, pharmaceuticals, and automobiles.

The automobile industry is the only manufacturing industry where China has made specific commitments to liberalise conditions for foreign investment liberalisation in its WTO agreements. The auto industry was one of the industries opened earliest to foreign investors in China. In 1984, two joint ventures were set up: Beijing Jeep Corporation Ltd. (Beijing/US) and Shanghai Volkswagen Automobile Corporation (Shanghai/Germany). By the end of 1998, more than 400 Sino-foreign joint ventures in the auto industry had been approved, of which more than 50 are productive enterprises manufacturing all kinds of automobiles.

Currently, foreign direct investment in China's auto industry faces some policy restrictions. For example, there are restrictions on the share of foreign ownership, and, in particular, wholly foreign-owned enterprises are not allowed. Second, there are restrictions on production range and local content requirement. Third, foreign investors are not allowed to invest and operate in motor vehicle distribution and maintenance. However, China is committed to substantially relax these restrictions under its WTO agreement, in particular to allow non-bank foreign financial institutions to provide auto financing and to relax constraints on production, imports, distribution and sales networks, and the provision of maintenance and other services, along with liberalisation of approval and other administrative procedures (see Annex I for more details).

China's commitments in investment liberalisation in the auto industry provide great investment opportunities for foreign investors, and it is expected that they will increase their investments in China's auto industry after China's accession to the WTO (see also Chapter 4).

Services

The service sector was the last major sector of the economy to be opened to foreign investment and is still one of the most restricted. The Chinese government has opened some service industries to foreign direct investment, mainly in the eastern region in an experimental fashion, such as finance, insurance and commerce. By the end of 1999, the service sector had received a cumulative total of US$117 billion foreign direct investment, of which US$75 billion were actually in the real estate industry and only US$42 billion were in the other services industries. The limited share of these other service industries reflects the tight restrictions over foreign direct investment that have been maintained in these industries until now.

China's service sector has been under-developed in the national economy. For the past half century, from the 1950s to 2000, the share of services in China's GDP has been around 30 per cent with some decline during the 1970s to the mid-1980s. In an international comparison, the development level of China's services is also relatively low. The share of services in China's GDP is nearly 20 percentage points below the 50 per cent average for other countries at a comparable level of per-capital GDP. Although the Chinese government issued the "Decisions on Accelerating the Development of Services Sector' in the early 1990s, the targets set for the development of services have not been achieved. The under-development of services risks becoming a "bottle-neck" to the overall development of China's national economy in the future.

There are many reasons for the slow development of China's services. Most important, however, are their relative closure to foreign participation and the monopoly of state enterprises in many areas. During the last two decades of economic reform and opening up to the outside world of the Chinese economy, China's services have actually been relatively closed to foreign direct participation. Although the Chinese government has gradually opened some service industries to foreign investors in a very limited and experimental fashion, many services are still closed to foreign investors. This has effectively protected the state monopoly in the services sector. At present, China's many service industries are monopolised by state-owned enterprises, especially in the industries of finance, telecommunications and international trade.

Opening the service sector was one of the most important issues in the bilateral negotiations leading up to China's accession to the WTO. China has made important and concrete commitments to open its service sectors that are summarised in Annex I. The opening is expected to lead to a surge in foreign direct investment in services. The increase in foreign direct investment and its effects on the overall economy, are likely to be especially great in the following areas.

- In *banking*, while there are a substantial number of foreign bank offices, operations in most cases are restricted to foreign currency business and circumscribed in their geographic scope (see Chapter 7 on the banking sector). Foreign invested banks (32) in Shanghai and Shenzhen are permitted to engage in RMB business but are subject to regulatory constraints that severely limit their extent. China is committed to remove most regulations discriminating against foreign banks within the next five years.[15] Foreign direct investment into this sector is likely to increase to take advantage of these opportunities, although, as argued in Chapter 7, foreign banks are likely to focus on high-profit niche activities and to avoid most lending to domestic enterprises, at least at first.

- Foreign *insurance* companies were first permitted in 1992 and have been limited to joint ventures operating in a few major cities. By 2000 there were 26 foreign-invested insurance companies along with 196 representative offices. As discussed in Chapter 8, China's WTO commitments significantly increase the scope for foreign insurance companies. The permitted scope of operations will be expanded significantly, geographic restrictions will be lifted within three years after accession, and foreign non-life insurance companies will be permitted to establish wholly-owned subsidiaries within two years. Together with the rapid growth in demand for insurance services in China, the opening is expected to lead to a substantial expansion in foreign participation in China's insurance sector, and a consequent increase in foreign direct investment.

- Foreign *securities companies* also gain substantial expansion in their permitted scope under the WTO agreement. Together with the rapid growth of the domestic stock and bond markets and their related services (see Chapter 15 on the development of the capital markets), the opportunities afforded by the agreement to participate (through joint-ventures) in domestic fund management business and in some underwriting and trading activities is likely to encourage more foreign firms to enter the market as well as the expansion of existing foreign operations.

- *Telecommunications* has been largely closed to foreign participation but is due to open significantly after accession. Foreign firms will be allowed to establish joint ventures to supply value-added services and to sell those services nationwide by the end of 2003 (two years after accession). The potential for foreign direct investment is high, given the technological and other advantages of foreign firms as well as the rapid growth in domestic demand for telecommunications services.

- In *distribution*, foreign firms now account for less than 1 per cent of domestic wholesale or retail sales (see Chapter 9 for further discussion of China's distribution sector). Under WTO, product restrictions on foreign-invested distributors will be phased out (with some exceptions), geographic restrictions relaxed for retail firms and abolished for wholesalers, and foreigners will be allowed to acquire majority stakes in distribution firms. Foreign-invested automobile firms will also be able to establish their own distribution networks. As discussed further in Chapter 9, these changes are likely to lead to a significant increase in foreign participation in China's distribution sector.

In addition, WTO accession provides for significant openings in various other business and consumer services (see Annex I for details). In particular, the agreement permits (or liberalises existing entry terms for) foreign accounting, legal, along with computer, engineering, and other consulting companies to establish offices and/or joint ventures in China (over varying periods). Although business scope restrictions (*e.g.* those allowing law firms to conduct lawsuits in domestic courts on behalf of foreign clients only) will remain in some cases, these areas are likely to attract additional foreign direct investment given the rapid growth in demand for the sophisticated services they are able to offer. In some cases, such as accounting, the government intends to encourage the entry of foreign business service providers in order to help bring domestic standards into better alignment with those prevailing internationally. The WTO agreement also somewhat liberalises the scope for foreign invested health service providers (of which there are now 30 in China). Restrictions on foreign investment in tourism are also being relaxed to allow wholly-owned foreign subsidiaries in hotels and travel agencies within four to six years.

Conclusion

With its fast growth and large amount of inflows, foreign direct investment has greatly contributed to the Chinese economy in terms of capital formation, employment creation, labour training, export promotion, technology transfer, productivity improvement and competition. As a result, foreign direct investment has been playing an increasingly important role in the Chinese economy.

China has achieved substantial progress in its foreign direct investment policy reform within a relatively short period. However, China's current foreign direct investment policy needs to be further improved in all aspects. The provisions of the TRIMs agreement target two key specific government actions: performance requirements and restrictions. China uses both to guide and to restrict foreign direct investment into targeted areas and sectors. China's current foreign direct investment policy is still relatively restricted in terms of foreign direct investment entry forms, foreign ownership shares, and industry scope. Moreover, China still extensively uses fiscal and other incentive policies to encourage some specific types of foreign direct investment and to induce foreign direct investment flows into some targeted regions and industries. China's foreign direct investment policy regime needs to be further liberalised, particularly on competition policies, industrial policies and intellectual property rights' protection and enforcement.

China's entry to the WTO is a very important step toward integrating its economy into the world economy. In terms of investment liberalisation, China's commitments are mainly in the auto industry and some key segments of the service sector. However the WTO accession agreements do not directly affect other aspects of China's foreign direct investment policy regime. The limitations are mainly due to the fact that WTO rules affecting investment policies are still relatively limited. Further investment liberalisation in China, beyond what has already been undertaken or committed to under WTO, would be beneficial to the economy but will depend largely on its own policies to reduce and eliminate remaining barriers.

By using an empirical model, this study estimates that after China's accession to the WTO, foreign direct investment inflows into China will increase moderately in the first two years, reaching a level of around US$45 billion. Subsequently, foreign direct investment inflows into China are expected to increase rapidly and considerably, rising as high as US$100 billion by 2010.

However, as the analysis in this chapter has repeatedly underscored, China's success in attracting foreign direct investment and realising its potential benefits for the overall economy depends critically on the policies it undertakes after its WTO accession. Effective and thorough implementation of China's WTO commitments will be critical to its success in achieving its potential in attracting foreign direct investment, but it is not the only key to that success. Equally important will be China's success in carrying out complementary reforms, to further reduce trade and investment impediments and to open up domestic markets, to improve the performance of state owned enterprises, to better protect intellectual property rights, and to strengthen competition, judicial enforcement, and other framework conditions essential to the effective functioning of China's markets.

NOTES

1. Shenzhen, Zhuhai, and Shantou in Guangdong Province, and Xiamen in Fujian Province.

2. Data for FIEs' total and rural employment are not available in China's official publications.

3. The Chinese government has signed agreements on the avoidance of double taxation and prevention of evasion of tax with the following countries: Japan, the United States, France, the United Kingdom, Belgium, former Federal Republic of Germany, Malaysia, Norway, Denmark, Singapore, Finland, Canada, Sweden, New Zealand, Thailand, Italy, the Netherlands, Czechoslovakia, Poland, Australia, Yugoslavia, Bulgaria, Pakistan, Kuwait, Switzerland, former Soviet Union, Cyprus, Spain, Romania, Austria, Brazil, Mongolia, Hungary, Turkey, Malta, South Korea, and Indonesia.

4. However, if the United States' subsidiaries do not repatriate their profits to their parent companies located in the United States and, instead, reinvest the profits in China or send the profits to another subsidiary located in a third country, the tax incentives in the form of exemptions and reductions are still effective to their investment decisions.

5. The empirical model is a multi-regression model with pooled data. The data set contains 32 developing countries for a period of 12 years from 1987 to 1998. The dependent variable is foreign direct investment inflows into developing countries, and the independent variables include market size (GDP), per capita GDP, GDP growth rate, efficiency wage which is defined as the real wage rate adjusted by labour productivity, labour quality approximated by illiteracy rate of population, accumulated foreign direct investment stock, economic distance which is defined as the weighted average distance of a developing country to the rest of the world and the weights are the shares of the countries' GDP in the world total GDP, and a dummy variable for the countries who adopted the Export Promotion Development Strategy to capture the effects of trade and investment regime on foreign direct investment inflows.

6. The authors note that studies that use traditional CGE models to quantify the impacts of trade liberalisation in China focus only on the real sector, capital is exogenously fixed, and the role of financial assets and international financial markets is absent.

7. The authors present most of their findings in graphic form, but don't give actual data. GDP increases appear to average about 1.5 per cent annually over the baseline.

8. However, China's terms of trade decreases by 34.3 per cent.

9. This annual GDP growth rate of China is predicted by the World Bank, and most studies use it as the projected annual GDP growth rate for China in the baseline scenario.

10. In most studies on the impacts of China's WTO accession on the Chinese economy, the estimation for China's GDP growth rate is around 0.5 per cent to 1.5 per cent higher in the trade and investment liberalisation scenario than in the baseline scenario.

11. The value of the estimated foreign direct investment is at current US dollar prices, assuming that the deflator of US dollar increases by 2.5 percentage points annually from 2001 to 2010.

12. The equation of investment intensity index is as follows:

$$III_{ij} = \left(\frac{\frac{I_{ij}}{I_{*j}}}{\frac{I_{i*}}{I_{**}}} \right) \times 100$$

where:

III_{ij} = investment intensity index of i's investment in j

I_{ij} = investment by i (source country) in j (host country)

I_{*j} = investment from the world in j

I_{i*} = investment from i in the world

I_{**} = total investment in the world.

The index measures the relative importance of country j as a host for country i's investment as compared to the rest of the world. It can be interpreted as a measure of the relative resistances to foreign direct investment flows between countries reflected by the variations in the investment intensity index. If the index is above 100 per cent, it indicates that country i's investment in country j is more than the amount of its share of investment in the world. This implies that the relative resistance to foreign direct investment flows between country i and country j is lower than those between country i and the rest of the world.

13. The east region includes Beijing, Tianjin, Hebei, Liaoning, Shanghai, Jiangsu, Zhejiang, Fujian, Shandong, Guangdong, Guangxi, and Hainan. The central region includes Shanxi, Inner Mongolia, Jilin, Heilongjiang, Anhui, Jiangxi, Henan, Hubei, and Hunan. The west region includes Sichuan, Guizhou, Yunnan, Tibet, Shaanxi, Gansu, Qinghai, Ningxia, and Xinjiang.

14. The empirical model is a multi-regression model with pooled data. The data set contains 29 provinces for a period of 12 years from 1987 to 1998. The dependent variable is foreign direct investment inflows into provinces, and the independent variables include provincial market size (provincial GDP), provincial per capita GDP, provincial efficiency wage which is defined as the real wage rate adjusted by labour productivity, provincial labour quality approximated by illiteracy rate of the population, provincial accumulated foreign direct investment stock, provincial transport intensity index, provincial level of telecommunications, regional dummy variable for the coastal provinces, and the policy dummy variable for the increasingly more liberalised foreign direct investment regime in the 1990s. According to the model, the magnitude of foreign direct investment inflows into China's provinces is a function of a province's market size, per capita income, efficiency wages, illiteracy rates, level of existing foreign direct investment stock, levels of transportation and telecommunication infrastructure development, geographical location, and the implementation of economic reform and open policy.

15. As noted in Chapter 7, the extent to which foreign financial institutions are able to exploit their new opportunities also depends on regulatory policies that are not directly affected by China's WTO commitments.

BIBLIOGRAPHY

Behrman, J. (1988),
"Orientation and Organisation of Transnational Corporations", in Wenzao Teng and N. Wang (eds), *Transnational Corporations and China's Open Door Policy*, Lexington Books, Lexington, Massachusetts.

Chen Chunlai (2000*a*),
The Location Determinants of Foreign Direct Investment in Developing Countries: with special reference to comparing China's performance in attracting foreign direct investment with other developing countries, Research Paper to the MOFTEC/OECD co-operation programme on FDI.

Chen Chunlai (2000*b*),
Provincial Distribution of Foreign Direct Investment in China, Research Paper to the MOFTEC/OECD co-operation programme on FDI.

Dunning, J. (1993),
Multinational Enterprises and the Global Economy, Addison- Wesley, Wokingham, England.

Foreign Investment Administration, the Ministry of Foreign Trade and Economic co-operation (1998),
Tax Exemption Policies on Importation of Equipment by Enterprises with Foreign Investment, Foreign Investment Administration of MOFTEC, Beijing.

Goldman Sachs (1999),
Global Economics, by Fred Hu, Paper No. 14, April 26.

Guisinger, S. and Associates (1985),
Investment Incentives and Performance Requirements: Patterns of International Trade, Production, and Investment, Praeger, New York.

McKibben, W. and P. Wilcoxen (1998),
The Global Impacts of Trade and Financial Reform in China, Asia Pacific School of Economics and Management, Working Paper 98-3.

Office of the Leading Group for West Development of the State Council (2000),
Guojia Zhichi Xibu Dakaifa de Youguan Zhengce Cuoshi [State's Relevant Policies and Measures on Supporting the Development of West Areas].

Office of the Third National Industrial Census (1997),
Zhonghua Renmin Gonghe Guo 1995 Nian Disanci Quanguo Gongye Pucha Ziliao Huibian [Data of the 1995 Third National Industrial Census of the People's Republic of China], Zhongguo Tongji Chubanshe, Beijing.

Powell, B. (1987),
"The Wholly Foreign-Owned Enterprises in China: An Alternative to the Equity Joint Ventures", *Hasting International and Comparative Law Review*, Vol. 11.

State Statistical Bureau (various issues),
Zhongguo Tongji Nianjian (China Statistical Yearbook), Zhongguo Tongji Chubanshe, Beijing.

State Statistical Bureau (various issues),
Zhongguo Duiwai Jingji Tongji Nianjian [China Foreign Economic Statistical Yearbook], Zhongguo Tongji Chubanshe, Beijing.

Stein, L. (1987),
"Wholly Foreign Owned Ventures in China: A Comparison of 3M China, Ltd., Grace China, Ltd., and the New Foreign Enterprise Law", *China Law Reporter*, Vol. 4, No. 1.

United Nations Conference on Trade and Development (UNCTAD) (various issues),
World Investment Report, United Nations publication, New York and Geneva: United Nations.

Walmsley, T. and T. Hertel (2000),
China's Accession to the WTO: Timing is Everything, Centre for Global Trade Analysis, Purdue University.

Wang Luolin *et al.* (eds.) (1997),
Zhongguo Waishang Touzi Baogao: Waishang Touzi de Hangye Fenbu [Report on Foreign Direct Investment in China: Industrial Distribution of Foreign Direct Investment], Jingji Guanli Chubanshe, Beijing.

Part II
ECONOMY-WIDE ISSUES

Chapter 11

AN OECD PERSPECTIVE ON REGULATORY REFORM IN CHINA

TABLE OF CONTENTS

AN OECD PERSPECTIVE ON REGULATORY REFORM IN CHINA[*]

Introduction and major conclusions

An efficient and market-oriented regulatory environment is needed to create the incentives in which trade and investment liberalisation will support longer-term economic growth in China.

- In a narrow sense, regulatory reform can help China meet the legal obligations of the international trading system by removing barriers to trade and investment; improving transparency, neutrality, and due process; and building new institutions and practices expected by international norms, such as autonomous regulators in utility sectors. Effective regulatory reform can be a useful benchmark for credible commitment to the international trading system, and, as trade and investment develop, can help avoid costly conflicts between trading partners.

- In a wider sense, regulatory reform should be seen as a pro-active strategy that complements trade and investment liberalisation in boosting potential growth in China. As part of a mix of macroeconomic and structural policies, regulatory reforms, properly designed and implemented, can increase private investment (domestic and foreign), business start-ups, and incentives for efficiency among private and state-owned enterprises in China. These effects should improve over-all productivity performance and potential long-term growth, and they are a valuable tool in the national strategy for poverty reduction. As subsidies and monopolies for state-owned enterprises are eliminated, regulatory reform is also necessary as a defence against pressures on regulators to increase protection for incumbent firms.

Chinese authorities at national and regional levels have taken many positive steps since the late 1970s to construct the framework of credible rules, legal systems, and institutions needed for a market economy and to comply with WTO obligations. The high rate of economic growth in recent years is partly due to the success of these legal reforms. In the 1999 revision of the Constitution, the scope for market reform greatly expanded when the government and the Communist Party committed to protecting private ownership within a socialist market economy. Many other important laws in areas such as energy, communications, and competition policy will be issued in the coming years.

China's economic performance is, however, undermined by severe regulatory problems. First, regulatory risks are high, reducing investment and competition by increasing the cost of capital. Second, transactions costs are high due to an overly-complex, multi-layered, often arbitrary and interventionist regulatory environment that is vulnerable to corruption. Third, in many sectors, China suffers from substantial internal and external regulatory barriers to entry and competition. In other areas, regulation distorts incentives and misallocates resources. Fourth, there is substantial under-regulation. China suffers in many sectors from too little regulation, poor enforcement, and under-institutionalisation. Insufficient regulatory safeguards reduce confidence in markets by consumers and investors. Fifth, checks and balances, such as an effective judiciary to ensure application of the rule of law and efficient dispute resolution procedures between the state and market entities, are weak, reducing the capacity of outsiders to challenge market insiders. Sixth, infrastructure bottlenecks, partly due to the lack of market-oriented regulatory regimes, raise production costs throughout the economy. These problems will not be overcome quickly, and legal and regulatory inefficiencies and risks will be higher in China than in OECD countries for the foreseeable future.

Deregulation and creation of market-based regulatory regimes and administrative capacities are late compared to other market reforms, and this lag increases the risks of costly market failures. Even where high-quality national laws have been adopted, creation of new institutions and implementation capacities has lagged behind, and hence the effects of many legal reforms have not yet been felt in the marketplace.

---

[*] This Chapter was prepared by Scott Jacobs, Managing Partner, Jacobs and Associates, under the supervision of the Centre for co-operation with Non-Members (Asia and China Unit), OECD.

Transformation of the role of the state is occurring simultaneously with fast economic growth and rapid social change. Many problems arising in China's regulatory system are purely transitional issues normal during such rapid change, but other problems are structural and will be resolved only with continued, more co-ordinated, and more comprehensive reforms. The government must further develop its capacities to regulate behaviour in a competitive market. Ultimately, the success of regulatory reform will depend on the consolidation of the rule of law throughout China's complex governing structures, including regional, provincial, and municipal administrations. Better law enforcement is an urgent matter. In the global trading system, if China's domestic legal system cannot uphold legal obligations, disputes will move to international fora such as the WTO, where they will be multilateral, costly and damaging, and will raise the cost of foreign capital for the whole economy.

In addition, regulatory reform involves more than efficiency considerations, particularly in a country where social stability and regional inequities are continuing concerns and where there is no general safety net for the unemployed. Business failures and unemployment may increase as structural reform and the reform of SOEs accelerate, and may create major political problems. Many regulatory issues in China cannot be resolved only by regulatory reform, because they stem from larger issues of governance, accountability, and policy trade-offs such as how to manage change while preserving stability.

There is no universal model for the right regulatory system, since appropriate solutions must be designed to fit within the specific circumstances of a country's values and institutions, and stage of economic development. However, since China is competing in a global economy for capital and markets, international expectations and experiences for high-quality regulatory regimes can provide a source of valuable information. The rich pool of OECD-country experiences can be useful in setting goals and designing reforms. A consensus is growing among industrialised economies – with both common law and civil law systems – about good regulatory practices based on competition, market openness, and public management principles. This emerging consensus, based on a decade of work at the OECD, is increasingly used as the benchmark for international trade agreements. The key elements of this consensus are contained in the 1995 OECD Recommendation on Improving the Quality of Government Regulation and the 1997 OECD Report on Regulatory Reform.

Progress on regulatory reform in China

Regulatory reform in a transition country is not essentially a deregulatory task, but a mix of new regulation, deregulation, and re-regulation, backed up by legal and institutional reforms, to support increasingly competitive markets. Pro-market regimes are composed of economy-wide policies (such as commercial law, competition law, consumer protection, and corporate governance) and sector-specific policies (such as banking and telecommunications regulatory regimes), operating within the rule of law. As seen in Russia, and to a lesser extent in Eastern Europe and China, changes in ownership are not enough. Poor and inadequate regulatory structures permit abuses and corruption to flourish in emerging markets, undermine investor and consumer confidence, and destroy rather than create economic value.

China's long-term development plans (2010-2020) are to transform its planned economic system into a market-based economic system, which requires the reorganisation of state-owned enterprises so that they can compete better in an increasingly liberalised, open, and integrated economy. The Chinese government has stated that it aims to maintain a balance among reform, development and stability. Reform, as the motive force of development, should promote social and economic development to raise people's living standards. However, continuing ambiguity about the role of the government in the market economy will complicate the many difficult decisions facing the Chinese government with respect to the scope, intensity and speed of reform.

The Chinese government has recognised weaknesses in its legal and regulatory systems and has set a target to establish an appropriate framework for a market economy. Its current efforts follow more than two decades of reform.

- The first wave in 1978-1992 began with China's decision to open up to international co-operation and to welcome foreign direct investment. During the 1980s, a legal framework developed that helped China to become an attractive foreign direct investment destination among the emerging economies. The first comprehensive civil legislation – General Principles of Civil Law – was promulgated in 1986.

- The second wave of law reform began in the early 1990s, with the decision to establish financial markets that would be increasingly open to foreigners, and continued through end-2000. This was a period of intensive law making: more than 3 000 national laws were adopted, followed by 800 regulations by the State Council. The Provincial Peoples' Congresses adopted more than 7 000 regulations. Administrative regulations approved by central and local governments exceeded 30 000. China also signed many international agreements. This massive body of law covered nine aspects of legal reform: 1) regulations formalising market players, such as corporate law, joint ownership law, and joint ventures; 2) contract law and fair competition; 3) management of the budget and central bank; 4) social security issues such as labour law; 5) establishment of a framework for infrastructure and pillar industries such as railways, electricity, and civil aviation; 6) foreign trade law and customs law; 7) intellectual property rights (IPR) protection such as patent law; 8) conservation of natural resources and the environment, grasslands and forestry law; and 9) monitoring of market practices, such as administrative penalties. Progress was made in improving transparency and accountability throughout the regulatory system. In 1997, for the first time, the 15th National Congress of the Communist Party of China explicitly cited the rule of law as a guiding principle in its official document, and proposed to create a comprehensive legal framework with Chinese characteristics by the year 2010.[1]

- The current WTO-inspired wave of reform, which will probably continue for five to ten more years, has resulted in intense efforts to revise laws and regulations on trade, technology transfer, investments, banking, insurance, securities, taxation, customs, intellectual property, telecommunications, health, professional services and other subjects to bring them into compliance with the WTO regime and to make the adjustments required by market access commitments.[2] In this phase, the Chinese government will place more attention on improving the quality, efficiency, and implementation of law making and administration, including enforcement. SOE reforms will proceed in parallel.

Why is further regulatory reform needed in China?

A fundamental objective of regulatory reform is to improve the efficiency of national economies and their ability to adapt to change and remain competitive. OECD countries offer a persuasive body of evidence of the positive effects of regulatory reform (see Box 11.1). Regulatory reform has positive effects on the demand side, by increasing consumer income, and on the supply side, by increasing efficiency and innovation. Reform that reduces business burdens and increases the transparency of regulatory regimes supports entrepreneurship and market entry. Regulatory reform can have upstream and downstream effects by easing constraints on growth.

Like almost all OECD countries, China suffers high costs from many poor regulatory practices – monopolisation, over-regulation, under-regulation, inefficient and outdated regulation, and overt barriers to competition – that significantly hamper its economic performance:

- Regulatory risks are high, reducing investment and competition by increasing the cost of capital. High regulatory risks slow economic adjustment and act as a protective barrier to incumbent firms and insiders *vis-à-vis* new domestic and foreign market entrants. Regulatory risks are inherently higher in a transition period such as that in China, but much regulatory risk in China is systemic, not contextual, arising from economic management practices that can be improved by co-ordination, consultation, and better policy design and implementation. A recent white paper by the American Chamber of Commerce on China concluded "The business climate in China is characterised by a high degree of regulatory risk; that is, the risk of loss arising from sudden

---

Box 11.1. **The major benefits of regulatory reform in OECD countries**

The progress, strategies, and results of regulatory reform have been documented by the OECD in a multi-year programme of comparative research (see *www.oecd.org/subject/regreform/*). These assessments demonstrate how, against a backdrop of basic market rules, a comprehensive approach to regulatory reform across related policy areas creates positive synergies. Liberalising trade, empowering market competition, and reforming government institutions are mutually supportive elements of the first generation of reform. Stable macroeconomic policy, flexible labour markets, appropriate regulation of capital markets, and complementary structural reforms provide a supportive environment, and often a context of strong growth, that facilitate adjustments that follow from regulatory reform. A multi-sectoral approach also boosts gains, since the benefits of sectoral reforms are amplified when competition is vigorous in upstream and downstream sectors. The major benefits of regulatory reforms have been:

- *Boosting consumer benefits* by reducing prices for services and products such as electricity, transport, and health care, and by increasing choice and service quality. Price reductions are due mainly to *increased productivity*. After reform, gains are seen in all types of productivity: labour, capital and TFP. Service quality has generally improved after reform. Concerns that reform would reduce safety are not borne out, probably because regulatory protections were not reduced in reformed sectors.

- *Reducing the cost structure of exporting and upstream sectors to improve competitiveness* in regional and global markets. Improving productive efficiency by reducing costs for critical inputs such as communications, land, and transport services boosted the growth of Mexico's export sector. Reform also enhances investment. Inward investment in Japan grew fastest in deregulated sectors such as distribution, financial services, and telecommunications.

- A supportive effect of regulatory reform is to expand the scope for trade. In Japan, regulatory reform reduced trade tensions due to possible regulatory barriers, and improved the trading environment.

- *Reducing vulnerability to external shocks by addressing a lack of flexibility and innovation in the supply-side of the economy*, which will be an increasing constraint to growth. Dynamic effects of market opening are usually more important than anticipated through innovation and faster introduction of new technologies, services, and business practices that multiplied benefits for consumers and produced new high-growth industries. Direct and indirect effects of sectoral reform help increase flexibility in the labour market and elsewhere. These effects allow economies to adapt more quickly to changes in technology and to external shocks, and improve the trade-offs between inflation, growth, and unemployment.

- *Helping to increase employment rates by creating new job opportunities*, and by doing so reducing fiscal demands on social security. Programmes to increase competition create jobs, though costs may be borne by workers who face job losses. In many countries, positive employment effects of market liberalisation will be limited without further reforms to social security systems, labour market reforms, and active measures to upskill the workforce.

- *Maintaining and increasing high levels of regulatory protections* in areas such as health and safety, the environment, and consumer interests by introducing more flexible and efficient regulatory and non-regulatory instruments, such as market approaches. Many countries are adopting international standards that, while delivering high levels of protection, are also trade-friendly.

changes in law, policy, or individuals in office… the government is forced to respond rapidly to changing situations. It often does so pragmatically, to deal with short-term needs, and without good co-ordination among different agencies and levels of government".[3] In general, the more uncertain and risky the legal/administrative environment in which economic activity occurs, the more likely it is that aggressive rent-seeking and short-term profit-taking will replace longer-term investment in a competitive climate. That is, regulatory risk reduces the value of investment.

- Transaction costs are high due to an overly complex, multi-layered, often arbitrary and interventionist regulatory environment that is vulnerable to corruption. Inefficient and opaque government formalities are a major problem for market actors. Legal rights are often not clear, and public officials have too much discretion in interpreting and applying rules. Bureaucratic difficulties remain a top challenge for 67 per cent of responding companies, according to an American Chamber of Commerce survey. In the banking sector, for example, formal and informal procedures are inflexible and tailored, partly for historical reasons, to the "typical" state-owned enterprise. According to a 1999 survey, applying for a loan is a bureaucratic and costly process, and about 70 per cent of firms said that paperwork was a moderate or major obstacle to their application for a loan.[4] These kinds of problems raise the cost of production, reduce entrepreneurship, market entry, and business expansion, and hence hurt consumers and weaken competitive forces throughout the economy.

- Broad and systematic deregulation is a major task. In sector after sector, China suffers from substantial regulatory barriers to entry and competition. In other areas, regulation distorts incentives and misallocates resources.[5] Anti-competitive regulations are sometimes used to protect SOEs.[6] Discriminatory behaviour, such as preferential buying practices by state-owned firms, is common. Anti-market barriers to competition, such as provincial protectionism, reduce incentives for innovation and efficiency. Many regulations that prohibit market entry, such as current prohibitions on companies from distributing imported products and providing related distribution services of repair and maintenance, should be eliminated by WTO accession. In that sense, WTO accession is a strong deregulation policy. The Ministry of Foreign Trade and Economic Co-operation, MOFTEC, reports that WTO-related reviews of its 1 400 laws and other regulations abolished 500, amended 120, and created 26 new regulations.

- China suffers in many sectors from too little market regulation, poor enforcement, and under-institutionalisation. This has been noted in policy areas such as competition policy, consumer and environmental protection, taxation, procurement, intellectual property rights, and prudential regulation in the financial sector. The State Council has called attention to many "startling problems" in the market that are caused largely by ineffective regulatory regimes:

"Great attention must be paid to economic disorder in the market. For complicated economic, social, and ideological reasons, the economic situation in the markets of some sectors is still in chaos, mainly as follows: the markets are flooded with counterfeit and shoddy goods, activities like tax evasion, tax fraud, foreign exchange fraud and smuggling have not ceased despite repeated prohibitions, commercial cheating and debt evasion are becoming more and more serious, financial infidelities and violations of financial discipline are ubiquitous; fraud and deceptions in tender offering and bidding are quite severe in the field of engineering construction and the qualities of projects are inferior, the disorder in cultural market has caused intense complaints from the masses, and grave and super accidents occur frequently in production and management.[7]"

Insufficient regulatory safeguards reduce confidence in markets by both consumers and investors, and the costs will increase over time. Stiglitz has observed that China's high growth rate masked many institutional problems, but "as returns come down, investors will look more carefully at the long-run security of their investments. This will necessitate the development of a better institutional infrastructure".[8] Companies that comply suffer competitive disadvantages compared to companies that ignore the laws. In utility sectors where investment and higher productivity are desired, pro-competition regulatory regimes and independent regulators are needed to curb abuses by state-owned and dominant firms, and to encourage new market entry.

- Checks and balances, such as an effective judiciary to ensure proper application of the rule of law, rights of administrative procedure, and efficient dispute resolution procedures between the state and market entities, are weak, reducing the capacity of outsiders to challenge market insiders. This weakness is particularly debilitating when state-owned firms are competing with private firms, when policies are changing faster than administrative capacities, and when corruption is high. The result is an uneven playing field, confusion about property rights, and less investment.

Many of the regulatory challenges facing China will be resolved, not by adopting more laws, but by reducing intervention and, where intervention is needed, improving the capacities of its many layers of

Box 11.2. Regulatory institutions and the rule of law

Regulatory powers lie at the centre of the system of law. The foundation of a rule of law is built from respect by both government and citizens for the legitimacy of regulation, from high-quality regulations, from openness and clarity in the regulatory system, and from processes by which regulators can be held accountable for the contents of rules. In achieving respect, communication and consultation with the public is essential.

But what is the rule of law? While there is no model of the ideal "rule of law", characteristics of the rule of law are as important to economic activity as they are to principles of fairness and justice because, by preserving fair and orderly decision-making, they build confidence among investors and consumers:

- legality, that is, authorisation of all regulations and administrative actions by higher-level regulations;

- commitment at all stages of decision-making and implementation to protecting the rights of individuals (such as property rights) even while seeking social goods;

- fairness and redress (such as due process and appeals procedures in adverse actions, and the right not to face undue delays in administrative processes);

- equality before the law (treating like cases alike);

- transparency and openness in decisions and the reasons for them;

- clarity of legal requirements and easy accessibility to rules by those affected;

- accountability for administrative decisions and actions (through clear demarcation of responsibilities and control processes to detect abuses);

- broad access to decision-making (through consultation);

- orderliness and predictability in rule-making processes;

- definitions of rationality through concepts such as "proportionality" and "reasonableness".

These characteristics of rule making, and others important to fairness and economic decision-making, are longer-term values that do not emerge automatically. Rather, they must be built systematically into governing systems, institutions, and cultures. That is, they are products of institutional design and practice, of checks and balances within the administrative system and external to the administrative system (such as courts), and of administrative quality-control capacities. Particularly if these sorts of principles are not "natural" to the governing process, or are not accepted by officials as norms of behaviour, they must be carefully and explicitly built into the administrative system. This is particularly the case in transition societies, where powerful habits are opposed to the rule of law.

The degree to which governments adhere to specific principles becomes part of general expectations, influencing investors and entrepreneurs who make economic decisions. In fact, constraints imposed by the rule of law on policy-making and implementation can have a more significant impact on economic activity than do the policies themselves. In general, the weaker the rule of law, the more uncertain and risky is the legal/administrative environment in which economic activity occurs, and the more likely it is that aggressive rent-seeking and short-term profit-taking will replace longer-term investment in a competitive climate. Entrepreneurs, for example, threatened by inconsistent application of regulations will expend capital on bribes for inspectors rather than on productive improvements or even on compliance. That "reputations" for fair and orderly regulatory processes are powerful competitive factors should not go unnoticed.

Source: Adapted from Jacobs, Scott (1995) "Building Regulatory Institutions in Central and Eastern Europe", Proceedings of the OECD/World Bank Conference on Competition and Regulation in Network Infrastructure Industries, Budapest, 28 June-1 July 1994, pp. 301-317.

public administration – their skills, structures, accountability for performance, relation with and understanding of markets and consumer interests, and styles of operation. Administrative practices and cultures in the public sector at national and sub-national levels often do not support market competition. Nontransparent and unaccountable administration raises investment risks and risks of capture and corruption by established interests inside and outside the public sector.

Even with the highest-quality laws, regulatory reform will be unsuccessful without the consolidation of the rule of law throughout Chinese governing structures. Reform laws are often excellent in content, but slow in taking effect due to weak legal and implementing institutions. As the Chinese government has repeatedly stated, reforms in China should place priority on creating a strong legal system and credible, effective institutions that protect market competition against abuses, establish a level playing field for new market entrants, and promote appropriate incentives for efficiency. The principles of such a legal regime are legality, neutrality, transparency, efficiency, and accountability. Protecting these principles requires positive state action, as discussed below. Box 11.2 explains in more detail the characteristics of the rule of law as expressed in regulatory regimes.

Regulatory transparency in China

Transparency is essential for regulatory quality. The OECD recommends improvements to transparency in regulatory decisions and application because it helps cure many of the reasons for regulatory failures – capture and bias toward concentrated benefits, inadequate information in the public sector, rigidity, market uncertainty and inability to understand policy risk, and lack of accountability. Transparency has powerful upstream and downstream effects in the policy process. It encourages the development of better policy options, and helps reduce the incidence and impact of arbitrary decisions in regulatory implementation. Transparency will be particularly helpful to the Chinese government in speeding up reforms by weakening the resistance of insider groups, reconciling various interests, and reducing conflict. Moreover, transparency helps create a virtuous circle in the market – consumers and investors trust competition more because special interests have less power to manipulate government and markets. Transparency is also rightfully considered to be the sharpest sword in the war against corruption. Regulators must work to establish a climate of confidence in which suspicions of abuses are avoided.

Progress on regulatory transparency in China

Improving regulatory transparency is a high priority in China, since this is where China lags furthest behind OECD standards. China is not alone in facing transparency problems. In fact, regulatory transparency in OECD countries also falls short of good practices. Most regulatory transparency problems in China resemble those in OECD countries.

Already, China has moved steadily in the direction of increasing the frequency of consultation and the quantity of information available to market actors. In WTO negotiations, China has committed to further improving transparency in its legal system. It has agreed to publish and make readily available all relevant laws, regulations and administrative rulings of general applicability, including internal "normative documents", prior to their enforcement. Regulations and other measures will be published in a variety of ways before they are enforced, including publication in journals, newspapers, and Internet sites. Interested parties will have an opportunity to comment before implementation. In certain emergencies, opportunity for advance comment need not be provided, but a norm will never be enforceable prior to official publication. These practices are meant to be followed by all levels of government.

The Chinese government has not yet developed an operational strategy to implement these transparency commitments, and the WTO negotiations did not set a schedule. Cohen reasonably states that, "Implementing this enormously important change will take a few years to achieve",[9] but a general strategy with concrete steps for the short-term will help meet WTO obligations and speed up change. It is useful that the Chinese government has already carried out considerable education on the WTO disciplines at various levels of government. Businesses, too, are becoming aware of the WTO requirements. A much broader initiative should be launched, based on new transparency policies and legal concepts, human resources, and tools. Here, OECD experiences and standards for transparency may be useful in providing a menu of options.

Complaints from trade and investment partners about inadequate regulatory transparency in China have created friction within the international trading system that, without systemic reforms, will only worsen as the Chinese economy becomes more integrated.

Yet the most important reasons for improving regulatory transparency in China are not international agreements, but growing domestic expectations for more government transparency. Transparency strategies must be judged primarily on whether they meet the needs of Chinese citizens themselves. Increasingly, the Chinese people want to participate in decisions on public policies that affect their lives. There are recent cases where public debate and consultation were important in establishing policy. During development of China's Tenth Five-year Development Plan, the government asked for comments and ideas from the public. Changes to China's marriage laws followed an enormous campaign of consultation. The Chinese government is disclosing more information that was until recently deemed to be a state secret. For example, an air quality index for over 40 cities is now published daily on TV, partly due to requests from the public. A new law being drafted on disclosures of the results of environmental auditing will greatly increase the information available to citizens about environmental risks they face.

Another dynamic pushing for more government openness is the rise of Chinese NGOs, of which there are today about 70 000.[10] The term "NGO" is a misnomer, because, while some of these bodies are private, particularly those concerned with environmental protection, health care, education for poor children, women's issues, and rural development, most are privatised state-owned NGOs, such as trade unions, the Chambers of Commerce, and the All-China Women's Federation. To avoid creating a dual-level system of transparency in which international businesses have more access than domestic consumers, a transparency policy must clearly be designed with the capacities and expectations of these kinds of domestic audience in mind, rather than only those of the international community.

What is regulatory transparency?

In an operational sense, transparency is *the capacity of regulated entities to express views on, identify, and understand their obligations under the rule of law.* Transparency is an essential part of all phases of the regulatory process – from the initial formulation of regulatory proposals to the development of draft regulations, through to implementation, enforcement and review and reform, as well as the overall management of the regulatory system. Transparency practices take many different forms in OECD countries, but OECD countries have identified several practices that they deem essential to reach an acceptable level of regulatory transparency:

- Notification in advance of intent to regulate in order to increase confidence.
- Public consultation with all major interested parties on draft regulations before decisions are made.
- Publication of decisions in easily accessible form (increasingly, this means electronic dissemination of regulatory material).
- Registers of regulations and formalities with positive security.
- Legislative codification to ensure a coherent legal structure.
- Plain language drafting to improve readability, certainty, and clarity.
- Clarification and simplification of regulatory responsibilities within the public administration, including across levels of government, so that responsibilities are clear.
- Public explanations of the rationale for regulatory decisions.
- Controls on undue regulatory discretion by standardised procedures for making, implementing, and changing all regulations and decisions with regulatory effects such as licenses and permissions.

- Elimination of informal regulatory instruments, such as unpublished guidance and instructions, that have coercive effect.

In recent years, OECD governments have invested considerably in making more information available to the public, listening to a wider range of interests, and being more responsive to what is heard. Consultations are becoming standardised and the amount of information is increasing, particularly as regulatory impact analysis is made accessible. A greater variety and number of interest groups are becoming involved. Older and inefficient forms of consultation that were vulnerable to capture and bias, such as restricted advisory bodies and special relationships with interest groups, are being replaced with more open and flexible consultations open to all major interests. New information capacities are permitting the establishment of centralised databases with search engines, electronic filing, and institutional re-engineering through one-stop shops.

Domestic trends toward more transparency in OECD countries have been reinforced by a widening set of international trade-related disciplines on regulatory transparency, such as the GATS requirements. Regulatory transparency is also improved by the growing use of international standards, which reduce search costs and increase certainty for consumers and market players.

Two reform priorities in China: public consultation and accessibility

In the short-term, two high-priority transparency issues in China are i) improving public consultation in the regulatory development phase, and ii) accessibility to regulations after they are adopted. Consultation is the active seeking of the opinions of interested and affected groups. It is a two-way flow of information, which may occur at any stage of regulatory development, from problem identification to evaluation of existing regulation. It may be a one-stage process or a continuing dialogue.

Concepts of open access to government legal drafts are not widely accepted in the Chinese administration. Often, in fact, draft laws are secret, and consultation is a crime. Access is limited to those special interests with good contacts inside the administration. The usual approach to public consultation has been for the National Peoples' Congress to adopt a general law first. The government will then wait for six months to a year before issuing implementing regulations. If there are serious complaints in the interim, the implementing regulations may try to take the concerns into account. This approach is highly inefficient and unsuitable for a market environment. As consultation occurs too late in the policy process to assess market impacts, alternative approaches, and the need for regulation, it increases market uncertainties and the costs of mistakes. This approach also limits access to those interests that are most organised and most ready to confront the government, which may not be the interests that are most important. Market risks increase because clarifications are based on implementing regulations that can be withdrawn at any time, while the original law is unchanged. Hence, this approach is simultaneously unlikely to identify major errors or to be responsive to public views, is vulnerable to capture when it does respond, and is unsatisfactory to investors in any case due to the high cost of confrontation.

China's legal framework for new forms of public consultation is slowly developing. Since 1999, the Chinese government has had a policy on the use of hearings, under regulations issued by the State Development Planning Commission (SDPC), but this mechanism has not been much used and has not worked well when it was used. Similarly, hearings are recommended for national price determinations under the Price Law. After developing a price reform plan, the department should determine if a hearing should be held, and invite selected participants representing consumers, producers, and experts. Producers must give reasons for price increases and answer questions. On the basis of the comments, the department writes a report. But this procedure was not followed in the case of the deeply-unpopular increases in train ticket prices just before the 2001 spring holidays. The price increase was approved by the State Council based on a plan provided by the SDPC. No hearing was held, and the government was soundly criticised for the failing.

In an *ad hoc* fashion, other legal obligations for consultation are being created. National guidelines for water tariffs now require public consultation if tariffs are increased. Participatory mechanisms are being developed for rural poverty-reduction strategies: the land administration law amended in 1998, which addresses relocation after expropriation, requires public consultation on the relocation plan, requires the plan to be made public, and establishes a redress system that ultimately leads to the judiciary. In the telecommunications sector, regulatory changes to prices must be preceded by hearings that are open to the public. MOFTEC has also been experimenting with public hearings in cases that involve trade issues.

A key development in improving legal transparency was China's long-awaited, but flawed, Law on Legislation that came into force on July 1, 2000. Under the law, legislation must support "economic construction" while upholding socialism. The Law applies to the enactment, amendment and repeal of regulations issued by national and lower levels of government (military regulations have different requirements). The Law affirms the hierarchy of regulatory instruments and establishes general obligations for public consultation and publication. Regulations must be created, amended, and repealed in accord with statutory limits of authority and procedures. During the process of designing regulations, relevant government organisations and the relevant public should be consulted through workshops, meetings, or other fora. The instruments covered by the Law are:

- Laws (fa lu) adopted by the National People's Congress, in which case consultation is to be carried out by the relevant special committee of the National People's Congress, by the Legal Committee of the National People's Congress, and by an administrative body of the Standing Committee of the National Peoples' Congress.

- Regulations of the State Council (chin jun fa gui).

- Administrative regulations (gui jang) issued by committees of the State Council, national ministries, provinces, counties, and municipalities, and by other bodies such as the People's Bank of China regions, by counties, municipalities.

- Independent and autonomous regulations issued by special economic regions and minority groups with rule-making rights.

The Law-making Law has not, however, improved the quality or frequency of public consultation. It does not set minimum standards for the design of public consultation or the involvement of major affected interests, for the time period of consultation, or for the treatment of comments from the public. It does not set sanctions or remedies for failure to consult, only suggesting that regulations should be repealed or revised if procedures are not followed, nor does it establish any oversight of compliance. The WTO agreement on transparency also seems flawed, because it requires that interested parties have an opportunity to comment on regulations only before they are implemented. This kind of consultation is consistent with the usual Chinese process, but, as noted above, is far too late in the regulatory process to support any genuine discussion of the need for regulation or alternative approaches. It is unlikely to produce the benefits expected in terms of regulatory efficiency, reduced regulatory risk, or wider access.

China should move toward more standardised consultation procedures that are more open and systematic. The design of public consultation procedures must recognise the specific cultural, institutional and historical context of China, as these factors are crucial in determining the effectiveness and appropriateness of particular approaches. An approach that works well in one country might worsen transparency in other countries. Hence, it is not possible to take a prescriptive view of what consultative tools should be used or of how and when they should be applied. For example, in China, due to the need to move forward with legal reforms without substantial delay, efficiency is vital. Regulators will need a system that collects as much relevant information as possible, as quickly as possible. To reduce the risk of capture, wide access to major interests is important, though targeted consultation procedures might be suitable where the affected interests are small in number, for example, notice and comment could be used in a limited number of cases to assess specific trade impacts.

Flexibility in approach is needed because regulatory issues differ greatly in impact and importance, scope and number of affected groups, information needs, timing of government action, and resources available for consultation. Yet the OECD has recommended to its Members that a framework of minimum standards is needed across the whole of the government to provide consistency and confidence. Consistency in consultation approaches enhances the quality of the process in three ways. First, minimum standards provide clear benchmarks to all parties as to whether consultation has been properly undertaken, and so protects all interests. It provides clear guidance for regulatory policy-makers. This enhances confidence in the consultation process, and reduces the risk of capture by well-organised groups. Second, consistent procedures enhance participation by a wider variety of stakeholders. Because the procedures are more widely understood, opportunities for input are less likely to be missed. There will be a faster learning process for both regulators and interest groups. Third, adopting a consistent process permits better co-ordination for regulatory initiatives across policy areas. Allowing ministries significant discretion could endanger this, either because of a lack of understanding of the requirements of a good consultation process or because of capture of the ministry by specific interests. A consistent process is a key quality control mechanism. Where potentially important stakeholders are known to be harder to reach or less able to participate, specific efforts may be required to actively seek and ensure their input.

The second priority in improving transparency in China is ensuring accessibility by regulated entities to regulations. This is the aspect of regulatory transparency most closely related to the rule of law. Yet it is this aspect of transparency that receives the most criticism in OECD countries. Regulatory transparency requires that governments effectively communicate the existence and content of all regulations to the public. The 1995 OECD Recommendation asks if regulations are accessible to users and recommends that: "the strategy for disseminating the regulation to affected user groups should be considered." Concerns about growing regulatory complexity, fragmentation, inconsistency, unreadability, and problems with identifying relevant regulations are heard throughout the OECD area.

China, which faces similar concerns, has made considerable progress in improving accessibility to national laws and regulations after adoption. Publication of laws and other regulations in newspapers has improved, particularly for regulations affecting foreign trade, and the WTO obligations will place even tighter disciplines on publication. The two major sources for regulations are publications by the National Peoples' Congress and publications by the State Council of all important decisions by itself and by ministries. Its list of regulations is on its website. MOFTEC publishes trade-related regulations on the Internet (*www.moftec.gov.cn*). Ministries also produce their own publications. Foreign Investment Service Centres compile many laws for foreign investors. There are also private searchable databases. Each year the government translates key laws into English, but a continuing concern is that the Chinese and English versions are not always identical.

Accessibility worsens at lower levels of government, where regulations are sometimes not published at all, although some provinces such as Shanghai do well in making their regulations known.

As in China, the traditional OECD responses have been to simply publish new laws and regulations in official gazettes and to require regulating ministries and parliaments to keep copies of all current regulations available for inspection by the public. These mechanisms, while important, have come to be seen as inadequate. Regulatory inflation and rapid regulatory change mean that there is an increasing need for new efforts to permit the public to identify quickly the complete set of regulatory requirements. OECD countries use six tools to make regulations easier to find and understand:

- *Legislative codification*. Rationalisation and clarification of complex legal regimes that have accumulated haphazardly over the years often require comprehensive legal codification. Codification can improve juridical and substantive quality, and by doing so can improve accessibility and clarity.

- *Centralised regulatory registers*. The 1997 OECD Report to Ministers recommends that governments: "Create and update on a continuing basis public registries of regulations and business formalities, or use other means of ensuring that domestic and foreign businesses can easily identify all requirements applicable to them." Efforts to count and register regulations are also useful internal management tools. Registering the number of regulations assists co-ordination among regulatory authorities by ensuring a better and more systematic flow of information within the public administration. This reduces the risk of overlapping and inconsistent regulation. In

373

most countries that have established central regulatory registers, the rule of "positive security" has been adopted. This means that only rules that are included on the register can be enforced. Positive security has two advantages. For the user, positive security provides certainty that, if all rules on the register have been met, full compliance with the law is achieved. The regulator cannot demand compliance with rules not contained on the register, and the register is the authoritative source where any dispute arises as to different variants of a rule. Positive security also provides strong incentives for regulating bodies to ensure that all rules are registered and thereby ensures the integrity of the register. In China, it may be possible to create such a centralised registry of provincial, country, and municipal regulations. The Law on Law-making already requires that all regulations be registered. If a municipality makes a new regulation, it must register it with the county. Counties must register their regulations with provincial governments. Provincial governments register with the State Council. The Standing Committee of the People's Congress has a registry of all State Council regulations, all autonomous regulations, and all provincial regulations. These existing registration procedures could be tied to publication procedures, and compiled into public databases with positive legal security.

- Plain-language drafting of regulations. The need for plain-language drafting of regulation has long been recognised. Governments need to ensure that regulatory goals, strategies, and requirements are articulated clearly to the public. This requires that legal texts be comprehensible by non-experts. A number of OECD countries have had plain language drafting policies for many years, and most of these provide guidance on how to implement these policies. The 1995 OECD Recommendation recognised the importance of plain language drafting when it asked "Is the regulation clear, consistent, comprehensible, and accessible to users?" and recommends that "Regulators should assess whether rules will be understood by likely users, and to that end should take steps to ensure that the text and structure of rules are as clear as possible".

- Publication of future plans to regulate. Publication of lists of proposed future regulations is another strategy for improving transparency. Around 20 OECD countries currently have publicly accessible registers of forthcoming regulations. Publication promotes openness in the regulation-making process. Participation of interested parties in consultation is improved. Lists of plans to regulate also provide a means to review and co-ordinate regulatory policymaking.

- Electronic dissemination of regulatory documents. Advances in information technology, in particular improved data storage and the rapid development of the Internet, provide opportunities to improve the dissemination of regulatory material. As has China, most OECD countries have adopted some form of computerised dissemination of regulation, and this practice is quickly expanding. A wide variety of official publications, legal texts, administrative information, administrative forms and public procurement tenders is now available on the Internet. Access to the information is in almost all cases unrestricted and free of charge. One problem is that relevant information may be spread over different databases due to inadequate co-ordination between levels of government. In some cases, "information overload" may limit transparency gains if key data is not made readily accessible by adequate search capacities. Limited access to the Internet is also a factor, at least in the short term: while rapid growth is continuing, even the countries with the greatest Internet penetration boast no more than about one quarter of the population with Internet access.

- One-stop shops and regulatory streamlining. The "one-stop shop" creates an easily accessible source of information for businesses on regulatory requirements, and should be accompanied by a determined effort to eliminate unneeded and costly approvals, licenses, and permissions, of which there are many in China. Some progress is apparent. The city of Beijing, through a determined programme, cut its administrative approvals by 40 per cent in 2000. Search costs for business could be greatly reduced by a complete list of regulatory requirements from a single source. The one-stop shop usually focuses on licences, approvals, and permits, and produces a list of such requirements applicable to businesses. It can also provide application forms and contact details. In some cases, inter-governmental co-operation has allowed licence and permit requirements for all levels of government to be issued from a single point. Lists of applicable laws and lower-level rules are also now available in some countries, while delivery mechanisms have broadened to include CD-ROM copies of the database for purchase, access in public spaces such as libraries through "information kiosks" and use of the Internet. China has no one-stop shop at the national level, but Hong Kong, China has completed a government-wide stocktaking exercise of business-related regulatory activities and has established a computerised central database.

Capacities to choose efficient regulatory solutions

One of the most important capacities of a quality regulator is the ability to assess the market impacts of a regulation before it is adopted. The 1995 Recommendation of the Council of the OECD on Improving the Quality of Government Regulation emphasised the role of regulatory impact analysis (RIA) in systematically ensuring that the most efficient and effective policy options were chosen. RIA is a decision tool, a method of i) systematically and consistently examining selected potential impacts arising from government action and of ii) communicating the information to decision-makers.[11] The 1997 OECD Report on Regulatory Reform recommended that governments *integrate regulatory impact analysis into the development, review, and reform of regulations*.

The capacity to assess market impacts is particularly important in China. In the current transition phase, when market needs are changing quickly, the risk of making bad regulatory decisions is high.

The Chinese government has the capacity through several mechanisms to assess potential regulatory impacts:

- The National Peoples' Congress evaluates the quality of proposed laws, mostly through the debates of its relevant committees.

- Independent economists and analysts often write papers and reports for the State Council on new proposals for regulations. The State Council may organise, for example, investigating teams to assess reforms, as was done for the banking system.

- The practice of allowing local governments to draft and test regulations at local levels, and to report their results to the central government, is a form of market testing that can reduce the risks of failure later. For example, the reform of China's company law began with pilot projects at local levels. Based on their successes, local regulations were published and revised at the ministry level, and extended to national law.

These practices provide a basis for a more systematic approach to regulatory impact analysis. Yet there is room for considerable improvement in assessing market impacts and the scientific basis for regulations, and to incorporate those assessments into public consultation procedures. Investors in China cite many cases where important laws have been adopted without a clear understanding of market impacts, and had unintended negative impacts on investment and market development.[12]

In each of these cases, a simple RIA would have identified the major market impacts, and avoided confusion, embarrassment, and cost to China's credibility. There is nearly universal agreement among OECD countries that RIA, when it is done well, improves the cost-effectiveness of regulatory decisions and reduces the number of low-quality and unnecessary regulations. RIA also improves the transparency of decisions, and enhances consultation and participation of affected groups. The Chinese government may wish to investigate implementing a more systematic approach to RIA.

Regulatory planning, co-ordination and accountability

As indicated in this study, WTO accession by China will be more beneficial if accompanied by co-ordinated institutional reforms and sustained commitment. The OECD has arrived at the conclusion that structural reforms should be based on a longer-term, holistic approach to problems, rather than focusing on incremental changes to individual sectors and policy decisions. While this seems sensible, it vastly complicates reform, and is hard for governments to do. This is directly relevant to many of the issues arising in China, where the transition to market-led growth is so rapid that it is straining the capacities of regulatory institutions to perform important functions such as repairing market failures and maintaining policy effectiveness.

The central question here is: What new or strengthened regulatory institutions in China will increase the social welfare potential of market-led growth? Two institutional reforms that would contribute to the effectiveness of policy reforms are *i*) strengthening of a central capacity to co-ordinate a government-wide programme of regulatory reform, develop strategic planning, evaluate results, and keep reforms on track against resistance, and *ii*) rationalisation of fragmented regulatory institutions across the government.

A central capacity to co-ordinate reforms

The 1997 OECD report recommended that governments "*create effective and credible mechanisms inside the government for managing and co-ordinating regulation and its reform*". Country experiences show that a well-organised and monitored process, driven by "engines of reform" with clear accountability for results, is important for the success of the regulatory reform policy. Most OECD governments have established central regulatory co-ordination and management capacities with government-wide responsibilities. These central regulatory reform offices include the US Office of Management and Budget, the Office of Regulatory Review in the UK Cabinet Office, Korea's Regulatory Reform Commission, and the Regulatory Review Office in the Productivity Commission in Australia.[13] There is no corresponding function in the national Chinese government. In several countries, national legislatures have established committees for continuing oversight of regulatory reform activities.

There are three reasons why the Chinese government may want to consider strengthening oversight and responsibility for regulatory reform at the centre of the national government, such as in the State Council, and in the National People's Congress.

First, mechanisms at the centre for managing and tracking reform inside the public sector are needed to keep reform on schedule against delay and resistance. Certainly, the primary responsibility for reform must be at the level of the ministry, department, or regulator, where the expertise lies and where policies are formulated. Yet it is difficult for ministries to reform themselves, given pressures from vested interests. Promoting reform across years, across levels of government, and across multiple institutions requires the allocation of specific responsibilities and powers to agencies at the centre of government to monitor and promote progress as a whole. This will be necessary to ensure compliance with government-wide policies, such as new transparency disciplines, for example.

Second, it would be desirable if China took a more systematic approach to establishing the institutional and legal infrastructure to promote competition as discussed in Chapter 12 of the present study.

Third, accountability for results is poor. Ministries must report to the National Peoples' Congress on progress in implementing the five-year economic plan, but in practice there is little evaluation of the concrete effects of laws and other regulations once they are adopted. Evaluation tends to be crisis-driven, stimulated by major disasters and media attention. Each ministry may internally monitor the impacts of its policies, but these results are usually not reported to the State Council or made public. A system of periodic reporting to a central body such as the State Council and the National Peoples' Congress, perhaps supported by independent assessments by expert organisations, would help detect regulatory failures faster and permit timely mid-course corrections.

Managing a broad, coherent regulatory reform programme over several years is one of the most difficult tasks of governments, yet those countries that have succeeded, such as Hungary and Mexico, have shown the greatest gains in economic development. Economies in transition can particularly benefit from a strategic view of the reforms needed for the evolving market environment. A broad reform policy can help establish priorities across a wide range of reforms, keep reform moving to produce results more quickly, identify reform gaps, identify emerging risks of market failures during the transition due to regulatory inadequacies, and suggest synergies, linkages, and sequencing across reforms. Strategies are needed to help ensure that short-run regulatory decisions are consistent with broader longer-term policy objectives, so that regulatory change does not occur in an *ad hoc* manner. Conversely, reforms that are fragmented, episodic, or compartmentalised are likely to be incomplete, inconsistent, and vulnerable to capture by vested interests. This increases the risks of disappointment and costly policy failures. The risks of incoherent reforms increase in rapidly changing markets.

A lack of strategic planning in China reduces the benefits of the many reforms underway. Almost all reforms now underway in China are sectoral in nature. The major reforms are driven by external pressures – primarily financial risks and WTO negotiations – rather than by strategic planning to establish the foundations for growth over the next five to ten years. If regulatory reforms are *ad hoc* collections of sectoral market-opening measures designed to satisfy foreign critics, market liberalisation will be slow, unsatisfactory, and prone to failure. Strategic planning would reduce the risks of market failures in the transition period.

Over the longer-term, the evolution of the national regulatory system can be speeded up by the right management structure. Dynamic change can be driven by central units with longer-term, crosscutting views. The central regulatory reform units should be responsible for continuing adaptation and improvement of regulatory systems as external conditions change, information comes available, and new problems arise.

The design of a central regulatory reform unit is highly contextual, and depends on the legal and power relationships between various parts of the governing structure. The rapid pace of change in China has tended to reduce the capacity of the national government for longer-term planning. For example, the former State Commission on Economic Reform, which once prepared economic reform plans in the State Council, has become the Administration Office of Economic Reform, and its new functions are more concerned with short-term planning and crisis management. However, China has several bodies that might, working together, serve as the basis for more concentrated oversight of regulatory reform, such as the Office of Legal Affairs in the State Council, the State Economic and Trade Commission in the State, the WTO Leading Group at the level of the State Council and the National People's Congress Standing Committee.

In several OECD countries, central bodies are supported by other reform-minded bodies, such as ministries of finance, and competition and trade authorities that develop advocacy capacities. Competition authorities in about half of OECD countries have roles in reviewing regulatory proposals for their potential impacts on market entry and competition. When a competition body is created in China, it should have strong advocacy powers and capacities. Private sector bodies, such as advisory bodies or private initiatives, can also be helpful and should be encouraged.

Rationalisation of regulatory institutions

Another reform that would contribute to the effectiveness of policy reforms is rationalisation of fragmented regulatory institutions across the government. It is often difficult to identify not only the regulations in China, but also the regulators. The Chinese government has explicitly recognised this problem, and the State Council has ordered: "The division of responsibilities among various governmental departments shall be clear-cut, avoiding the overlapping of functions which may cause repetition or slips in management and thus harm the market economy."[14]

It is hard to escape the impression that, in many sectors, regulatory reform will be difficult or impossible without radical reform of the government institutions that regulate. Many of China's administrative bodies have regulatory powers derived or delegated from multiple and not always consistent laws. Institutional confusion often mirrors confusions in the underlying legal frameworks. Regulations are fragmented, both vertically and horizontally, across multiple agencies at national and sub-national levels, each with unclear and overlapping powers. Many regulatory powers are allocated based on historical and archaic duties, such as price controls and SOE oversight, perhaps working under different laws, rather than on the design of a coherent, transparent, and efficient regulatory regime. In the distribution sector, for example, regulators at the national level include the State Commission for Economy and Trade, the Internal Trade and Market Bureau, the State Development and Planning

Commission, the Price Bureau, and a quality and standards bureau under the State Council. Provincial governments have similar institutions. There is usually little co-operation and communication between regulators working on the same sectors, and no one has the authority to resolve conflicts. Some regulators also have commercial interests in the regulations that they promulgate.

As reform progresses in China, it will be important to rationalise these government structures. New regulatory institutions should be designed around the principles of simplicity, accountability, transparency, efficiency, and neutrality, with particular attention given to avoiding conflicts of interest and rapidly identifying and resolving any inconsistencies between regulators. These kinds of institutional changes are not easy, since they usually face deep resistance by the institutions being reformed and by their clients. OECD countries have found that the central regulatory reform body and a comprehensive strategy are useful in overcoming sectional interests and jurisdictional battles in developing new regulatory bodies.

Enforcement of regulations within the rule of law

China is rich in rules, but, as in most OECD countries, adopting a rule is easier than implementing it. The quality of the Chinese law enforcement system is improving as the national government takes steps to ensure fair and equitable enforcement, most notably in those policy areas where investors have the greatest interest. Accountability is getting better, partly due to more scrutiny by the media and complaints from foreign firms. The National Peoples' Congress has begun to carry out high-profile missions to monitor enforcement at local levels, as it did for the securities law in 2001. Ministries are using their current downsizing as an opportunity to upgrade the quality of their staff, and consistency of enforcement seems to be improving in areas such as customs, where all staff are employed by the national administration rather than local governments. In a few key areas such as banking, the national government has re-centralised regulatory authorities to ensure a consistent and neutral regime nationwide.

Judicial review is still a weak link in China in the overall structure of interlocking institutions that should establish the incentives and pressures for high-quality administrative action. The current situation should, however, be understood in light of the significant progress achieved over several years in reforming the judiciary. The court system handles well over five million cases a year. The legal profession includes about 120 000 practitioners, plus large numbers of government legal specialists and in-house counsel to PRC companies. The China International Economic and Trade Arbitration Commission (CIETAC) has become the busiest international commercial arbitration organisation in the world, and virtually every Chinese city of any size has its own domestic arbitration commission eligible to handle foreign-related as well as domestic disputes. Civil, administrative and criminal procedure codes and an arbitration law have been enacted, and laws governing the conduct of judges, prosecutors and lawyers have also been adopted. The quality of economic judgements from Chinese courts is improving, such as decisions settling disputes over contested Internet domain names. The Supreme People's Court has sought to educate the courts about the new tasks that will arise from China's entry into the WTO. In the WTO process, China has committed to improving judicial review of administrative actions relating to trade matters, and this reform could assist in broader reform of the administrative review system.

Yet there is room for considerable progress throughout the entire enforcement structure. Application and enforcement of China's laws and other regulations have lagged behind the establishment of national policy reforms, imposing unnecessary costs and uncertainties on the market, and allowing scope for unethical behaviour. Essential co-ordination between the public administration, the judiciary, and the police in enforcing laws does not always work well. Some commentators have indicated that a double standard exists in the enforcement of some regulations, differentiating SOEs from foreign firms and new market entrants.[15] Complaints about over-enforcement, inconsistent enforcement, and under-enforcement are common. Poor enforcement, and hence low regulatory compliance, threatens the effectiveness of policy reforms and undermines confidence in the rule of law.

Improving regulatory enforcement is a multi-faceted, political, and longer-term task that goes beyond regulatory reforms into consolidation of the rule of law, but useful progress could be made by certain legal and institutional reforms. In addition to larger governance issues such as accountability and relations with interest groups, which this chapter does not address in detail, there are many transitional and structural reasons for unpredictable enforcement in China:

Multiple layers of administration. China's regulatory enforcement system is highly decentralised and poses formidable co-ordination and consistency issues. The degree of decentralisation in regulatory enforcement in China is, in fact, greater than that in any federal country in the OECD, and even greater than that for European Union laws enforced by its member states. China's national government is quite small by OECD standards. Almost all of the staff who inspect and enforce regulations are employed at provincial, county and urban levels, with little accountability to the national ministries for their actions. Local governments have regulatory and enforcement powers in most policy areas, including investment project approval, safety standards, tax compliance, labour and environmental regulations. The State Administration of Industry and Commerce has local branches in all provinces and cities, which are responsible for approving businesses and issuing business licenses. Many local inspectorates must also be funded locally, further diminishing control from the centre. Even customs posts are financed by local governments or self-financed from fees. The flow of information between levels of government is insufficient, and national ministries usually do not know how vigorously the laws are being enforced, and have little authority to monitor or take corrective action. Local governments that do not implement laws face few penalties.

Local protectionism and capture of the enforcement process. The following section in this paper discusses the problem of opening China's internal market by reducing regulatory barriers to intra-China trade. Powerful, sometimes corrupt, interests at local levels often have strong influence on regulatory enforcement decisions affecting competitors.

Inadequate checks and balances on enforcement actions. A major problem is excessive discretion at national and sub-national levels of administration. Provincial, county, and municipal levels of administration exercise liberal powers of interpretation of regulatory requirements, a discretion not controlled by the Law on Law-making. China's administrative procedure laws do not define the rights of citizens affected by regulatory decisions with respect to disclosing compliance interpretations in advance, explaining decisions publicly, and limiting delays.

Despite reforms, judicial review of administrative actions is still very limited in China compared to OECD countries.[16] As a result, China's enforcement personnel are remarkably free from external judicial accountability under principles of administrative law. This is partly due to the fact that Chinese courts are not independent (despite the Constitution's guarantee of independence), but are in practice part of the local government and party. Judges have no tenure, and are usually appointed, promoted, compensated and removed by local party and government officials. They have strong incentives to give more weight to local interests and protections than to legal requirements.

The lack of effective judicial review in China, combined with expanding market needs for clearer rules, encourages a range of alternatives:

- Arbitration procedures in CIETAC (the China International Economic and Trade Arbitration Commission) are increasingly built into private contracts. While such arbitration has clear advantages over the current court system, the fact that larger and foreign firms are increasingly using arbitration mechanisms to avoid long judiciary procedures may discriminate against smaller and domestic entities, which rely more on the courts for redress.

- An administrative review system is being reformed to expand and speed up review of administrative decisions. In 2000, almost 70,000 individual cases were accepted for review.

- Businesses use their private contacts inside the relevant administration to resolve problems. Fear of disrupting these essential relationships with local officials, and perhaps of retribution by angry officials, discourages businesses from formally challenging decisions in court.

- The National People's Congress may provide quasi-judicial reviews. The 2000 Law on Law-making specified procedures by which the Congress' Standing Committee can be asked to review and invalidate administrative actions that violate Chinese law, and makes it possible to seek a determination by the Standing Committee that government actions violate the Constitution (China does not have an independent constitutional court).

379

- The State Economic and Trade Commission operates as a kind of ombudsman in trying to mediate complaints of businesses about problems at the provincial and regional levels.

- As part of the larger oversight strategy for regulatory compliance, the State Council is trying to strengthen what it calls "the social supervision system" consisting of "trade self-discipline, media supervision and mass participation". The State Council has resolved to "make full use of the functions of structures like chambers of commerce and trade associations, etc., to educate, supervise and constrain enterprises to consciously abide by the laws and rules.

The courts will only gradually assume the oversight role needed to improve certainty and due process for the public. In the coming years, it is particularly important that the Chinese government and courts provide an effective and practical judicial infrastructure for dispute settlement, since the government's role as mediator and arbitrator among interests will gradually diminish as its economic intervention is reduced.

Sanctions and penalties may not deter violations. A further problem is the enforcement of judgements and the collection of penalties. Court decisions are often not enforced promptly or at all. Sanctions are sometimes disproportionately low compared to the profits of violating the law.

Intrusive and excessive regulation. Inspectors in most policy areas have a wide range of opportunities to intervene in business decisions. Business licences, for example, are often given for very short periods, perhaps six months to a year. The frequent use of permissions and approvals rather than general regulations expands the enforcement problems, because these regulatory instruments inherently increase discretion, particularly when the criteria for these decisions are not clear and independent checks are not available. The build-up of regulations in the 1990s (30 000 new administrative regulations) has also made the problem worse. Contrary to what might be expected, reliance on more detailed regulations does not avoid delegation of broad discretionary powers to regulators because rules tend to concentrate on procedural details (obligations) rather than on setting down substantive criteria for decisions (policy results). In OECD countries, an accumulation of procedures actually increases the arbitrary nature of administration, because it be comes impossible to know or comply with all requirements, leaving administrators to decide which rules to enforce, and how. Paradoxically, the Chinese legal system seems to be characterised by both too much detail and too much discretion.

The regulatory reforms discussed in this paper will support the trend toward better enforcement in China. Certainly, a determined programme to eliminate the many unneeded and costly approvals, licenses, and permissions would go a long way to resolving the problem. However, full resolution of the interlocked institutional and structural weaknesses that undermine legal enforcement will require reforms that are well beyond the scope of this chapter, such as the development of a truly independent judiciary, essentially a political reform.

Based on the experiences of OECD countries, another tool that the Chinese government may wish to consider in controlling excessive administrative discretion is the elaboration of administrative procedure laws. China has already constructed a framework of administrative law, including an Administrative Litigation Law (1990), the State Compensation Law (1994, to respond to grievances of unlawful official conduct), the Law on Administrative Punishments (1996), and the Law on Law-making (2000, as discussed above). Similarly, many OECD countries are adopting or amending administrative procedure laws to improve the orderliness of administrative decision-making, to define the rights of citizens more clearly, and to detail standard procedures for making, implementing, enforcing and revising regulation. By adopting these practices in legislative form, they are effectively transformed into rights that the public can assert. By strengthening citizens' rights and controlling arbitrary regulatory actions, these acts are fundamentally changing the relationships between the public administration and the citizen. The importance of these kinds of reforms for improving certainty and reducing regulatory risk in the market, while enhancing accountability, can hardly be overestimated.

Administrative procedure acts are flexible tools. They can have wide scope, including requirements for:

- Making regulation: Consultation requirements at different stages of regulatory development, preparation of regulatory impact assessments; consideration of alternative instruments; publication requirements; dates of entry into effect; duration (including automatic "sunsetting") and disallowance.

- Implementation and enforcement: Accessibility of regulations; rules on incorporated material; general rules on extent and exercise of administrative discretions, including publication of objective criteria for judging applications, time-limits for decision-making, publication requirements for administrative decisions, requirements to give reasons for rejecting applications.

- Revision and amendment: Application of general procedural rules to amendments of existing regulation, rules on updating of incorporated material such as international standards.

- Appeals and due process. Hearing procedures before disciplinary actions for violation Rights of regulated entities in appealing rules and administrative actions such as enforcement and sanctions.

Box 11.3. Reform of the judiciary and appeals mechanisms in Hungary

Reforms in Hungary have concentrated on establishing a more independent and efficient judiciary. A clear separation between the executive and judicial branches was established. In particular, the courts became independent from the Ministry of Justice, and a specific management body for the judiciary, the National Judicial Council, was set up to execute a larger mandate to modernise the courts, organise training programmes, and oversee judges and take disciplinary actions. To improve efficiency and rapidity throughout the system, the government added a new level to the three-layer system involving local, county and supreme courts. The new level of courts inserted between regional courts and the supreme court will hear appeals in cases against decisions of the local or regional courts.

These reforms respond to the numerous criticisms of the past few years concerning the slowness and cost of the system. Usually, a plaintiff needs two or three years for a first decision; and this can extend to five years in complex cases. Consequently, an important backlog of cases accumulated in the courts, particularly at the local and supreme level. More independent management should also tackle the other two major weaknesses of the system. The first concerns the material conditions of the courts, which often lack support-staff and technical facilities. Second, the new National Judicial Council should be able to focus on the long-term challenge of improving judgements through better selection, training and skills of judges with skills to work in a market economy.

Hungary has a rich array of check and balance mechanisms in which constitutional bodies protect citizens against administrative abuses, and in particular regulatory excesses. As a complement as well as a substitute to its administrative and judicial system, a plaintiff in Hungary can use three other venues and institutions to complain against a regulation or a regulatory decision.

The *Public Prosecutor's Office* is entitled to examine the legality of an agency's decisions and may initiate a formal motion to review the decision. If the agency does not agree with its findings, the Public Prosecutor may turn to court or submit motions to the Constitutional Court for rulings on constitutional issues. An important point is that the Prosecutor's role goes beyond a pure supervision of legality, as he or she can act as a public attorney in the course of judicial proceedings. An advantage compared to the judiciary review is that it can intervene at an early stage, to investigate a potential unlawful action or practice and recommend redress. Another interesting feature is that the Public Prosecutor has local branches in addition to its headquarters in Budapest.

The *Ombudsmen* perform activities quite similar to those of the Prosecutor but are mainly concerned with violations of constitutional rights. They are appointed by the Parliament and report exclusively to it. Special ombudsmen have been set up to protect certain constitutional rights, such as the rights of ethnic minorities and data protection. The Ombudsmen can also act independently in their designated field. Based on past complaints, the Ombudsmen have suggested changes to laws and regulations in their annual report to the parliament.

The *Constitutional Court* has played an outstanding role since the change of regime. As in most countries, a specific procedure permits individuals to directly appeal to the Constitutional Court against alleged violations of their rights by a law or regulation. Additionally, if a court rules that a certain procedure violates the Constitution, it has the right to suspend such procedure through an injunction and turn the case to the Constitutional Court.

Opening the internal market in China

Opening the internal market in China could well boost China's overall growth as much or more than opening to external trade. China's domestic market is highly fragmented. Regulatory barriers to the movement of goods and services across regional, provincial, county, and even urban jurisdictions, create enormous hidden costs by weakening competition, increasing production costs, and reducing the quality of products and services. Such barriers affect markets for many products and services including construction, automobiles, chemicals, retailing, and procurement. The American Chamber of Commerce recently concluded, "There are very few truly national markets but rather an assortment of local markets regarding each other suspiciously".[17] Some foreign investors believe that local protectionism is now increasing, as subsidies decline and competition intensifies.

Fragmentation of the internal market in China arises from several sources. It is a result of the enforcement issues discussed above, in which the legal system has been captured by local interests; of the self-sufficiency doctrines of the previous period; and of under-financing of local governments who use approvals, fees, and fines to raise revenues. Not all of the local protections are illegitimate, however. Pressure is high on local officials to find jobs for the unemployed, and the easiest method is to protect local producers. A fully competitive internal market in China might exacerbate regional economic inequities by accelerating structural change in the least efficient and poorest regions. China's overall market structure is characterised by low national concentration and regions containing duplicate enterprises operating at less than minimum efficient scale. Chinese policy places a high priority on assisting the accelerated development of the central and western regions. A fragmented internal market in China is, therefore, part of the policy of stability and regional development, and reforms must be carefully designed.

Standardisation and centralisation of regulatory powers is not the right answer to local protectionism in most policy areas. This is partly a question of practicality in a country of China's size. The question may be raised as to whether it would be practical or even wise to attempt to enforce uniform administration of rules in different parts of a country possessed of such diverse regional conditions.

The State Council is maintaining decentralised decision-making in economic matters, with corrective oversight by the State Council where reforms are not progressing well. It has resolved that it will:

"Institute the system of full responsibility by the governor of a province (chairman of an autonomous region or mayor of a municipality). Governments of provinces (autonomous regions, municipalities) shall organise and lead the work of rectifying and regulating the economic order of their markets. Governments at all levels shall define the key points for the work of rectification, make specific arrangements and strengthen the supervision and inspection. For regions that have not done the work of rectification well, and for regions where the economic order of the markets is confused and cannot be rectified effectively for a long time, responsibilities of key responsible persons and related responsible persons of the local governments shall be investigated and affixed according to the law and the discipline."[18]

Just as important, China's decentralised governing structures can be beneficial for development. China's provincial, county, and urban system has advantages in speeding up regulatory reform, because it introduces flexibility and establishes positive incentives to compete on the basis of good economic management. Not all reform is top-down in China – many beneficial reforms are bottom-up. The two provinces that were the top recipients of foreign investment by end-1999 – Shanghai (a special economic zone since 1980) and Guangdong (among the very first of the provinces to open to foreign investment in 1979) – are precisely those with reputations for being better managed. The system of special economic and autonomous regions further increases flexibility and stimulates innovation, experimentation, and demonstration projects with substantial benefits for reform. The opening of coastal cities and special economic zones has been extraordinarily successful.

Consumer sophistication will erode protected local markets as consumers demand more choice and quality, but China will not simply grow out of this problem. Expansion of foreign trade after China's WTO accession is not likely in itself induce a large increase of interregional trade as documented in other parts of this study. Many of the issues are institutional and structural, and concrete steps are needed.

- The regulatory reforms discussed in this chapter – improved transparency and consultation, impact analysis, strategic planning and oversight, clearer rights and more precise requirements in administrative procedures, and market-based regimes for utility sectors – will help reduce internal barriers by disclosing conflicts, improving co-ordination, and identifying costs earlier. These good regulatory practices are needed in regions, provinces, counties, and municipalities to avoid undermining the benefits of regulatory reform at the national level. Assessments of the capacities of sub-national governments to implement good regulatory practices would be useful.

- To the extent that internal barriers arise from weaknesses in the legal system, consolidation of the rule of law will also gradually eliminate many barriers.

- National laws will not change practices quickly, but continued construction of a market-based legal system hostile to local protectionism is necessary, and is in fact proceeding. A tendering law adopted in 1999 for public construction projects mandates open and competitive bidding for all contracts over a low threshold (implementing regulations have not yet been issued), and a law under development will open all other government procurement to competitive bidding. New State Council regulations "Prohibiting the Implementation of Regional Barriers in the Course of Market Economy Activities" came into force in April 2001. These rules basically assert the rule of law by prohibiting "units and individuals … from obstructing, or interfering with, entry into the local market of non-local products or construction services' in any manner in violation of laws, administrative regulations or State Council regulations… thereby restricting fair competition". The regulations allocate responsibility among government departments for correcting types of protectionist conduct, and contain penalties for officials engaging in protectionist conduct. Remedies for injured parties are meagre: units and individuals have the right to reject regional barrier conduct, and the right to report such conduct to the appropriate authorities. In September 2000, amendments to the Product Quality Law came into force. Among other requirements, they prohibit the practice of excluding products produced outside the local area (or administrative system) if the goods meet quality standards, and introduce a system of review for parties dissatisfied with the results of spot checks.

- Reform has been fastest where clean lines of national control are established. In those few key cases where regulatory regimes have become too decentralised in China to operate efficiently in national markets, more centralisation should be considered, as was done for the banking sector, customs, and price controls. The vertical restructuring of banking supervision under the People's Bank of China has effectively stopped cases where local governments ordered banks to make loans to support local projects, blocked capital flows out of the area, and interfered with insolvency proceedings. (Although local governments still distort capital flows by guaranteeing bank loans to enterprises with state ownership, which reduces their costs relative to private firms).[19]

- Where regulatory powers and problems are shared between levels of government or between governments at any one level, more co-ordination and information sharing are essential to successful reform. The State Council is, in fact, encouraging more co-ordination in enforcement: "Co-operative action and co-ordination shall be made between all regions and departments in investigating transregional law-violating activities."[20] The centralised regulatory registry recommended in this chapter would be a substantial step toward more transparency in China's sub-national rules. Italy's experiences with its State-Regions Conference, a permanent body composed of the Prime Minister and the Presidents of the regions, might be interesting for China. Italy's Conference has been increasingly engaged in preparing and negotiating, promoting and monitoring agreements on co-ordination and activities between the centre and the regions. Italy's central government and its regions have co-operated through a series of administrative and regulatory relationships, such as obligatory sharing of information, joint proposals, requests for advice, conventions, consultations, and even sharing of offices.[21]

Like China, OECD countries – notably federal countries and regional groupings such as the European Union – have struggled with the tensions of decentralised regulations within national and global markets. They have also tried to balance local diversity and innovation with the need for national standardisation. Although China's domestic situation is unique for historical, geographic, and cultural reasons, OECD experiences with the many strategies needed to create efficient unified markets across multiple legal jurisdictions might offer concrete solutions to China in easing internal regulatory barriers. European single-market institutions such as the European court for internal trade issues might be adaptable. Concepts of commercial passports and mutual recognition might be used to avoid the situation where businesses must obtain individual licenses and approvals in every jurisdiction where they operate.

Building regulators in China for the utility sectors

Reform in China is beginning to address the utility sectors, which are "among the last remnants of the planned economy".[22] Substantial improvements in efficiency and service quality are possible in these sectors (see Chapter 12 for a sectoral discussion of these issues). To avoid dangerous market failures, however, it is imperative that liberalisation of China's utility sectors proceed on the basis of a thorough consolidation and rationalisation of regulatory institutions. The results of reforms in the utility sectors will be largely determined by the quality of the regulatory institutions set up to guide the multi-year reform process within the general policy framework. Transforming the structure of a network-based industry, such as electricity and communications, from monopoly to competitive markets requires a sophisticated and evolving regulatory structure. Timing and sequencing of policy changes can be crucial, as can flexibility in meeting changing technologies and competition.

In reform of these sectors, much attention is paid to the issue of the independent regulator (called "autonomous regulator" in this chapter). In China, a step toward more autonomous regulators was made in 1988, when regulatory powers were moved out of the line ministries, which were responsible for production, into the SETC in the State Council. The regulators in the SETC are not autonomous regulators by OECD standards, though, because they are still incorporated directly into the policy apparatus. Another step was taken in 1998, when more autonomous regulators were established for banking, securities, and insurance, although still under the State Council.

The reasons for setting up autonomous regulators – to shield market interventions from political and commercial interference and to improve transparency, expertise, stability, and commitment to optimal long-run policy – are well known.[23] In China's legal system, these are particularly attractive objectives. There is little doubt that, compared to regulatory functions embedded in line ministries without clear mandates for consumer welfare, autonomous regulators are a sound improvement. In OECD countries, the impacts of market opening have been greatest in precisely those sectors – financial services and telecommunications – where autonomous regulators are most prevalent (though the causality is not clear).

Yet things are not that simple. There is no single area of regulatory reform where more bad advice is given than in the design of autonomous regulators. As many countries have discovered too late, there is no single right institutional model for these institutions. Institutional designs must be contextual, and based on flexibility and responsiveness. In part, this is because the surrounding institutional and historical context is unique for each country. The "independent commission" model as it is used in the US system cannot be easily transplanted to other countries due to different constitutional structures between the executive and the legislative, differing roles for parliamentary and judicial oversight, differences between systems of governance, and different traditions of policy-making and public debate. In designing autonomous regulators, reformers have many options to consider.

Moreover, an over-emphasis on the autonomous regulator is a mistake. Autonomous regulators are not a panacea, and governments tend to rely too much on under-equipped and unsupported autonomous regulators to carry out tasks that are beyond their capacities. What is needed is a larger system approach to institutional redesign, since a regulatory regime is an interdependent system. The task of establishing a market-oriented regulatory regime should include all institutions with significant influence on policy design and implementation. This will help avoid unhealthy focus on single components of the system, to the exclusion of others.

Reformers in China should adopt the concept that autonomy is the result of a well-designed mix of incentives, authorities, and procedures, involving a range of actors. No single aspect of autonomy is the litmus test for success. Rather, the key question is *whether the checks and balances built into the overall system are sufficient to prevent capture and bias in decision-making contrary to the core mission of long-run consumer welfare.* This question of the right checks and balances can be answered only if we take into account the larger system in which the autonomous regulator operates. Institutional design, accountability, and transparency should be designed to work in an integrated fashion in the Chinese context. This will help put more emphasis on overall credibility and market results.

To establish the right checks and balances, for each utility sector at least two institutions should be designed, and a series of procedures should be established. The institutions to be designed are:

- A regulatory policy body within the relevant ministry or State Council body that is responsible for the broad policy framework for market liberalisation, network investment, restructuring, stranded costs, and financing of universal service obligations.

- An autonomous regulator that is functionally separate from the ministry, the State Council, and producers in terms of staffing, budgets, and major regulatory decisions, including licensing, pricing and cost modelling, access, and consumer protection.

Procedures should be created that ensure:

- Efficient and rapid dispute resolution
- Full consultation with market actors before a decision is taken
- Public disclosure of the rationale for decisions
- Ethical conduct of regulators
- Accountability for decisions against the criterion of maximising consumer welfare through efficient markets

Credibility among market actors (investors, producers and consumers) is the single most important characteristic of an effective regulator, in particular as new market actors such as foreign investors and consumers enter the market. The degree of credibility materially changes the risks of market entry and the behaviour of market actors. High credibility boosts market outcomes, while low credibility undermines or blocks the benefits of markets. Credibility comes both from design and performance. The behaviour of the regulator is not known in advance, but the regulatory institution and procedures can be designed explicitly to establish and maintain credibility, and reduce the risks of behaviour that reduce credibility.

China is moving to break up monopolies, separate public administration from commercial interests, and permit more market entry and competition in these sectors, but is still relying largely on marginal changes to regulatory institutions and regimes created for state-provided services. The policy interests of the state are not separated clearly enough from the interests of commercial entities. As a result, there is an increasing gap between institutional styles, capacities and regulatory frameworks, and the actual needs of competitive markets.

As discussed above, oversight of sectors is usually divided among several bodies at the national level: price controls are set by the SDPC, investments approved by the SDPC or other bodies, and other regulatory decisions by the relevant committee of the State Council and the responsible ministry. In some sectors, bodies with commercial interests still hold regulatory powers. Sub-national levels of administration also wield regulatory powers. In some sectors such as electricity, the national market is divided into several regional markets governed by different bodies. There is little capacity to co-ordinate and resolve conflicts and inconsistencies between these various regulatory and policy bodies.

A good example of the need for more attention to institutional reform is the energy sector. China has committed to modernise its energy sector, which is relatively inefficient and unable to prevent periodic power shortages. Reforms are in progress. The power sector, dominated by six regional integrated firms, has been corporatised, and decisions are increasingly taken on a commercial basis. Private ownership of power assets was legalised in the 1995 Electricity Law. Significant foreign investment has flowed into China's electricity sector: by 2000, foreign funds accounted for 10 per cent of China's total power investments through a variety of contractual arrangements such as BOT, TOT, and joint ventures. The State Power Corporation of China (SPCC), established in 1997, holds the ownership rights of the provincial power companies, through a holding company.[24] Investments above a threshold are approved by the central government, but are financed out of equity and debt. Prices are moving closer to costs, particularly in the richer coastal areas. SPCC is still a single buyer, but reforms plan to permit larger consumers to choose their suppliers (which would liberalise prices for those consumers), to integrate the regional markets, and to unbundle generation, transmission, and distribution.

Yet there are no corresponding decisions on the design of institutions to oversee the sector during this complex transition. Currently, the SDPC regulates prices for end-users and approves contracts with provincial-level units of the SPCC and all investment projects. The State Economic and Trade Commission has established a small new body on electricity power that regulates on the basis of the industrial reform plan. The Ministry of Finance oversees SOE operation and hence their profits. The SPCC (which is owned by the State Council) is responsible for grid maintenance and regulates access to the grid, becoming both regulator and owner. Another serious problem is regional protectionism. Provincial corporations are the most important market entities and routinely deny access to transmission to protect local generation. An unfortunate but predictable result is that IPPs (independent power producers) face increasing, not decreasing, discrimination in gaining access to the grid. Each of these regulatory bodies operates under a separate legal source and with different objectives, because there is no unified law for regulation of the sector. Expertise in identifying the correct market solutions is low throughout the regulatory system. Furthermore, there is no competition authority in China to support the regulator in enforcing competition principles against abuses of dominance. A weak judiciary will find it difficult to enforce decisions against incumbent firms.

A fundamental redesign of the regulatory institutions in the utility sectors should be based on international expectations. Standards of good regulatory practices are increasingly the benchmarks for judging investment risk, and hence the level and quality of investment. OECD countries have not reached any consensus on good designs for autonomous regulators, but their experiences, particularly where reforms have had several years to mature, will reduce the risks that China could put into place the wrong regulatory system, which would slow structural adjustment and impose costs for many years.

Conclusions

The opening section of this chapter summarised its main conclusions. Establishing the institutions and market environment needed for successful adjustment to trade and investment liberalisation requires a strategic and integrated regulatory reform policy. Experiences in OECD countries offer no model for China, but many of the wide range of tools accepted as good regulatory practices by OECD countries could be adapted to meet the development needs of China.

NOTES

1. Wang, Zhemin (2000) "The Developing Rule of Law in China", *Harvard Asia Quarterly http://fas.harvard.edu/~asiactr/ haq/200004/0004a007.htm.*

2. Opening Statement before the First Public Hearing of the US-China Security Review Commission by Jerome A. Cohen, Professor of Chinese Law, New York University, Adjunct Senior Fellow, Council on Foreign Relations, of Counsel, Paul Weiss, Rifkind, Wharton & Garrison, Washington DC. June 14, 2001.

3. American Chamber of Commerce in the People's Republic of China (2001). *White Paper on American Business in China*, January 22, 2001, Beijing.

4. Neil Gregory and Stoyan Tenev (2001) "The Financing of Private Enterprise in China", in *Financing and Development*, a quarterly magazine of the IMF, March 2001, Volume 38, Number 1.

5. For example, China's banking system shows "distortions arising from the legacy of central planning and the limited state of development of the financial system as a whole, although they have been perpetuated to some degree by more recent regulatory policies... Regulatory policy is substantially responsible for the limited array of bank products and activities... non-state enterprises continue to suffer serious financial problems, as well as regulatory and other obstacles to their restructuring and development". See Chapter 7.

6. "In many places, government regulation discourages entry in business areas with a large SOE presence. 30 per cent of managers report encountering market barriers of some sort (IFC, 1999)" as reported in Chapter 3.

7. State Council, "Resolution of the State Council on Rectifying and Standardising market economy order".

8. Stiglitz, Joseph (1998) "Second-Generation Strategies for Reform for China", Address given at Beijing University, Beijing, China, July 20.

9. See, among many others, the summary of Jerome A. Cohen, Opening Statement Before the First Public Hearing of the US – China Security Review Commission, Washington, DC, June 14, 2001. Cohen is Professor of Chinese Law, New York University and Adjunct Senior Fellow, Council on Foreign Relations.

10. A law on pension trusts adopted in April 2001 has a chapter on private charitable trusts that provides a legal framework for these kinds of NGO organisation.

11. Good RIA practices and case studies are available in OECD (1997) *Regulatory Impact Analysis: Best Practices in OECD Countries*, Paris.

12. A regulation on encryption first came to the industry's attention when a notification was published in the newspaper. No assessment of commercial issues or effects on IT development in China had been done, and the rule (requiring that Chinese encryption be placed on all software and hardware) would have greatly disrupted trade in computers and software. After an angry reaction from foreign firms, the government decided to clarify the rules.

13. In proposing reform approaches, it might be useful to examine experiences, not only in OECD countries, but also in the most developed parts of China. Since 1996, for example, Hong Kong, China has been carrying out a "Helping Business" Programme whose goal is to make Hong Kong, China attractive to domestic and overseas businesses. The Programme cut red tape, deregulated and transferred services out of the public sector to the private sector where appropriate market conditions prevailed. The aim of the Programme is to eliminate and simplify regulations that hinder Hong Kong, China's ability to innovate and grow, and provide a more open and fair environment to achieve growth and improve competitiveness, while maintaining the necessary standards and disciplines. The "Helping Business" Programme is being run with advice from a Business Advisory Group, which comprises a mix of prominent local businessmen and senior government officials. In April 1997, Hong Kong, China established The Business and Services Promotion Unit (BSPU), an organisation dedicated to assume responsibility for the "Helping Business" Programme.

14. State Council, People's Republic of China, "Resolution of the State Council on Rectifying and Standardising market economy order", Beijing.

15. It is claimed, for example, that "safety inspections' of electronic products are often more rigorous and expensive for imports than for domestic products. Testimony of Dave McCurdy, President, Electronic Industries

Alliance, before the United States-China Security Review Commission regarding Bilateral Trade Policies and Issues between the US and China, August 2, 2001.

16. By contrast, ministries in OECD countries are subject to various kinds of independent administrative courts and other forms of external judicial review. In France, for example, there are many control mechanisms, such as a network of Administrative Tribunals headed by the Council of State and the Mediator's Office, which are judicial bodies with the task of judging alleged administrative abuses against citizens.

17. American Chamber of Commerce, White Paper.

18. State Council, "Resolution of the State Council on Rectifying and Standardising market economy order".

19. Gregory, Neil and Stoyan Tenev (2001) "China's Home-grown Entrepreneurs", *China Business Review*, January-February 2001.

20. State Council, "Resolution of the State Council on Rectifying and Standardising market economy order".

21. OECD (2001) *Regulatory Reform in Italy*, Paris.

22. Wang, Junhao and Ping Chen (2001) "China modernises public utilities", *China Business Review*, July-August, pp. 46-50.

23. See Jacobs, Scott (1999) "The Second Generation of Regulatory Reforms", Paper presented at IMF Conference on Second Generation Reforms, 8-9 November 1999, Washington DC The paper can be found at *www.imf.org/external/pubs/ft/seminar/1999/reforms/jacobs.htm*

24. See State Development Planning Commission, China (2000) Report of the "Workshop: New Waves of Power Sector Reforms in China" with the assistance of the World Bank and The Energy Foundation, 9-10 October 2000, Beijing, pp. 9 and 11.

Chapter 12

THE ROLE OF COMPETITION LAW AND POLICY

TABLE OF CONTENTS

THE ROLE OF COMPETITION LAW AND POLICY[*]

Introduction

This chapter focuses on the role of competition law and policy in helping to ensure that China realises the anticipated benefits of its trade and investment liberalisation (TIL). By reducing barriers to entry by foreign enterprises' products, services, and capital, those reforms are crucial to enhancing competitiveness by stimulating domestic enterprises to respond more efficiently to market forces.

However, to fully realise the benefits from the opening of its borders to international competition, China will need to take further steps to remove, and prevent, anti-competitive restrictions within its borders. This will require two separate kinds of action.

First, China should prevent incumbent enterprises and local governments from limiting the benefits of trade and investment liberalisation by creating new barriers to entry. Worldwide experience shows that as policies directed at reducing international or domestic barriers to entry are adopted, vested interests seek to maintain the old *status quo*. This very risk led to the proposals, partially adopted in Doha, for negotiating WTO rules requiring that members enact and enforce competition laws. China is very vulnerable to this threat from vested interests.

- Incumbent enterprises seek to protect themselves from competition by abusing dominant positions, adopting restrictive distributions systems, or engaging in exclusionary boycotts. China's current competition-related laws have major gaps that make them unable to halt or deter such exclusionary conduct.

- Unauthorised and anti-competitive actions by local governments and their officials perpetuate sectoral monopolies, impose barriers to intra-regional competition, and otherwise favour incumbents. Legal bans including the Unfair Competition Law have not been fully effective. A comprehensive competition (anti-monopoly) law with real sanctions against regional protectionism should be adopted and enforced, and competition policy should be used to address such conduct when it is not subject to competition law.

Second, China will need to press ahead in its domestic reforms in order to maximise the benefits of the trade and investment liberalisation-induced entry. In addition to enacting a comprehensive competition law, China should focus on 1) repealing laws and rules that impose anti-competitive barriers to entry and other impediments to the creation and efficient operation of new and reorganised enterprises, and 2) reforming infrastructure industries that have natural monopoly characteristics.

Taken together, competition law and competition policy provide the tools needed for both kinds of actions. Competition law (also called anti-trust or anti-monopoly law) focuses primarily on halting anti-competitive activity by enterprises but can also be used against "administrative monopoly", including regional protectionism and other unauthorised local government restraints. One factor that may have delayed the enactment of a competition law is that there is a tendency in China to underestimate the extent of monopoly power possessed by enterprises (due to reliance on national concentration statistics that are not reliable indicators). Another factor in what may be a costly delay is apparently a concern that a competition law would interfere with China's ability to promote "national champions". That concern is misplaced; competition law does not interfere with promoting national champions (see Chapter 5 for a discussion of other issues relating to national champions).

Competition policy complements competition law by providing a means of addressing the economic costs of entry and other restrictions that are contained in laws and regulations. As noted in the previous chapter and discussed further below, it is important for China to continue eliminating

---

[*] This chapter has been written by Terry Winslow and Sally Van Siclen, respectively Principal Administrator and Administrator in the Competition division of the Directorate for Financial, Fiscal and Enterprise Affairs Department, OECD.

unwarranted government-imposed restrictions if it is to fully realise the benefits of trade and investment liberalisation.

This chapter begins by describing the nature and role of competition law and policy as it has developed in OECD and other countries. Thereafter, the chapter discusses competition law and policy in China and describes the current situation in Chinese markets. Finally, the chapter addresses in more detail the two separate kinds of actions that are central to the realisation of the benefits of trade and investment liberalisation – preventing vested interests from creating new barriers and removing the undue restrictions that remain in China's laws and regulations.

Competition law and policy in general and in OECD and other countries

Promoting economic efficiency is the principal goal of competition law and policy. In this context, "economic efficiency" does not only refer to efficient use of enterprises' resources – what microeconomics calls "productive efficiency". It also includes the best use of society's overall resources – *i.e.* "allocative efficiency" – and the development of new processes and products – "dynamic efficiency".[1] Thus, competition law and policy provide institutional support to maximise the overall welfare of society.[2]

To this end, competition law bans "anti-competitive" conduct by enterprises – that is, conduct that is likely to lead to a restriction of output and to monopoly pricing. The overpricing and waste caused by such conduct is very substantial.[3]

Complementing trade and investment liberalisation policies, competition policy is the tool OECD countries have increasingly used over the last 25 years to reduce inefficiency and waste without sacrificing other policy goals. The OECD Regulatory Reform Report issued and endorsed by Ministers in 1997 calls upon OECD countries to empower competition authorities to play a role in all regulatory analysis.[4]

There has been significant co-operation between China's government institutions and the OECD relating to competition law and policy in recent years. This co-operation has focused primarily on activities with China's State Economic and Trade Commission (SETC) and State Administration for Industry and Commerce (SAIC), which are responsible for drafting China's competition law. It has also included discussions with the Ministry for Foreign Trade and Economic co-operation (MOFTEC) and the Development Research Centre (DRC), and there has been increasingly close co-operation with the State Development Planning Commission (SDPC).[5]

In the wake of accession to WTO and ensuing policy challenges, it may be useful to summarise how efficiency and growth are stimulated by competitive markets, stifled by monopoly and unduly restrictive regulation, and protected by competition law and policy (Box 12.1). The remainder of this section expands on these concepts and seeks to provide a coherent framework for policy action.

The role of competition law

To stem inefficiency, waste, shortages, and high prices from anti-competitive behaviour, OECD Members and about fifty other economies have enacted competition laws. These laws typically ban *a*) anti-competitive agreements – both between competitors ("horizontal") and between sellers and buyers ("vertical"), *b*) unilateral enterprise conduct that abuses a monopoly position, and *c*) mergers and acquisitions that are likely to increase the risk of such agreements or abuses. The laws generally apply to state-owned enterprises (SOEs) as well as private ones, and to the activities of regulated, natural monopoly enterprises, with the exception of activities that are directed or specifically authorised by a regulatory agency. In some cases, competition law prohibits what is sometimes called "administrative monopoly" – unauthorised anti-competitive action by executive bodies of government and/or their officials.

Competition laws generally do not contain flat bans of specified conduct, but rather ban conduct that "substantially limits competition" or "creates or maintains a dominant position". Thus, the legality of conduct generally depends on its actual or likely effects on the market as a whole, which in turn

Box 12.1. **Benefits of and threats to competitive markets**

A competitive market may be described as one without significant impediments to entry or exit, or restrictions on price or output. Competition may be seen as the process in which enterprises seek to discover and satisfy consumer demand as efficiently as possible. A competitive market, then, is one in which enterprises have incentives to develop and produce goods and services at quantity, quality, cost, and price levels that make the best use of society's resources. Enterprises failing to meet these standards are vulnerable to take-over, reorganisation, or liquidation if competitive capital markets exist. Efficiency in innovation, production, and resource use leads to economic growth and increased aggregate welfare.

In addition to efficiency and growth, competitive markets provide economic opportunity, resilience, and innovation. In non-competitive economies, economic power is often concentrated in the hands of the few. Halting cartels and eliminating special treatment of protected businesses not only produces innovation and efficiency, but also gives more individuals a chance to contribute to, and benefit from, the resulting economic growth. In addition, competitive markets sustain macroeconomic stabilisation. Competition provides firms with incentives to adjust to internal and external shocks, thereby reducing the macroeconomic cost of adjustment to shocks.

There are two main threats to competitive markets: monopoly power possessed by enterprises, and government regulation that imposes undue restraints on enterprises' ability to respond efficiently to consumer demand. Monopolists and cartels obtain their monopoly prices by "restricting output", *i.e.*, by *deliberately creating artificial shortages*. This means not only supplying restricted quantities of goods or services, but also failing to discover and supply what buyers want. Monopolies and cartels tend to be *less innovative* and less likely to provide the varieties that consumers want. Regulatory barriers to competition operate in much the same way.

depend on whether the conduct is engaged in by an enterprise or enterprises with a dominant position or "market" or "monopoly" power (hereinafter monopoly power).

Two points merit emphasis. First, competition law does not ban the mere possession of monopoly power or its attainment by superior efficiency; it is only abuses of that power that are illegal.[6] Second, monopoly power is the power to increase profits by restricting output and raising price above the competitive level. It is not a function of overall firm size, but can exist only with respect to a particular product or group of products ("relevant product market") and a geographic area ("geographic market"). In this context product and geographic market concentration ratios (the percentage of production, sales, or some other measure accounted by the leading enterprises) provide some measures of competitiveness. Even with reliable data, however, concentration is not a meaningful measure of monopoly unless it is presented on the context of a "relevant market" so that it measures the choices that are actually open to buyers (see Box 12.2).

While focusing, as a rule, on the effects of conduct, many competition laws accord special treatment to "hard core cartels". This category is defined to include "an anti-competitive agreement, anti-competitive concerted practice, or anti-competitive arrangement by competitors to fix prices, make rigged bids (collusive tenders), establish output restrictions or quotas, or share or divide markets by allocating customers, suppliers, territories, or lines of commerce".[7] Because such cartels almost by definition have no efficiency justifications and are "the most egregious violations of competition law", many countries make them illegal without regard to their actual effects (sometimes called "illegal *per se*"). Still others require some evidence of anti-competitive effects but not the rigorous evidence required in other cases.

Until the last twenty-five years, there has not been much consensus on the goals or importance of competition law. Indeed, for much of the beginning of the last century, some OECD countries encouraged cartels, others considered them unavoidable evils and sought only to prevent their worst

---

Box 12.2. **Product and geographic markets**

Production or sales statistics presented on a national basis seldom reflect buyers' choices and are therefore misleading as an indicator of competitiveness. For example, an enterprise may be only one of many Chinese producers of a product but have monopoly power, whereas the sole producer of a product in China does not necessarily have monopoly power.

The contours of a geographic market are determined by economic reality – the area within which a buyer may obtain a product or service. The key factor is often transportation cost in relation to the price of the product or service, a consideration that is often very important in China. Administrative or political boundaries are relevant only if they reflect an economically significant barrier, such as a mountain range, or differing legal provisions, including licensing requirements. Thus, regional markets may consist of several provinces or only part of one province, and may be calculated as the area within a certain number of kilometres from one or more locations where buyers live or do business. A local geographic market may be an area surrounding a city or small town, but the official city or town limits are seldom relevant.

Similarly, it is clear that the categories in which production data are reported do not generally describe economically relevant product markets because they seldom reflect the demand side of the market. Information is usually collected on the basis of production methods or raw materials, meaning that a category might include, for example, all aluminium pots for cooking. Such a category is likely to be both too broad (including some pots appropriate for individuals, some only for restaurants) and under-inclusive (including no steel, copper, or ceramic pots).

Given China's size, its inadequate transportation infrastructure, and other shortcoming of the distribution system, many products and most services only compete in regional or local markets. Shipping between Chinese cities can often be more problematic than importing from abroad. Regional protectionism is another impediment to creating more unified, national markets. Since China's market structure is a legacy of traditional local self-sufficiency, it is clear that national concentration ratios tend to underestimate monopoly power in China.

---

abuses, and only a few prohibited them outright. Similarly, many OECD countries permitted and operated monopolies, and not merely in infrastructure industries where some monopoly may be "natural". It must be recalled, however, that during much of the period before World War II many countries also imposed high tariff and non-tariff barriers. It was not so much competition law that was controversial, but rather the entire notion of the value of competitive markets.

During the post-war period, as trade and investment barriers have fallen and the resulting competition has produced economic efficiency, innovation, and growth, consensus has grown among OECD countries concerning competition law's goals and importance. Because of the way competition law can help break down inefficient barriers to creating a unified market, the Treaty of Rome made it the *only* substantive law that is enforced directly by the European Commission. Economic efficiency became the predominant goal in most circumstances, and with this convergence on goals has come a convergence on the legal standards that competition laws should apply. Currently, all OECD countries have competition laws and many are giving them much higher priority than before. Moreover, almost all of the transition countries in Central and Eastern Europe and the former Soviet Union have enacted competition laws, and both formal studies and expert opinion consider that effective implementation of those laws contributed to the expansion of more efficient private firms.[8]

Most countries' competition laws apply essentially the same basic legal standard – the likelihood of substantially lessening competition or maintaining or creating a dominant position. This same standard can be used in countries with different economic conditions because most (sometimes all) prohibitions are based on the conduct's effect *in the particular relevant product and geographic market.*[9] However, differing economic conditions do call for differing law enforcement priorities. Competitive economies tend to focus on anti-cartel enforcement and on preventing anti-competitive mergers; many CIS countries focus on demonopolisation; for China, the focus should be on preventing exclusionary practices. In addition, differing economic conditions require different "rules of thumb" in predicting whether a given practice will have anti-competitive effects. Finally, competition laws do and indeed must contain differences reflecting different legal systems of which they are a part, and other differences reflecting values other than economic efficiency (aggregate welfare).

The role of competition policy

The basic principle of competition policy is that governments should permit markets to function to the maximum extent consistent with other social goals. Because of the central importance of "free" entry and exit to the existence of competitive markets, competition policy principles have long been used to analyse the effects of explicit barriers to entry such as tariffs and quotas. In addition, these principles were sometimes used when governments considered monopoly issues.

In the post-war period, as consensus grew among OECD countries concerning the benefits of trade and investment liberalisation and competition law enforcement, they began giving increasing and more systematic attention to competition issues in assessing government regulation. For example, during the 1930s it was common to regulate entry, prices, and profits in such industries as road haulage and airlines, based on the theory that the alternative would be "destructive" competition leading to price wars, bankruptcy, and unemployment. In the 1970s, when low productivity in industries subject to such "structural regulation" prompted OECD governments to reconsider this approach, they began adopting regulatory systems that restrict enterprises' conduct only to the extent necessary to achieve other social goals.[10]

Natural monopoly regulation, both through designated regulatory agencies and through government ownership, also came under increased scrutiny due to poor economic performance in infrastructure sectors. Breaking away from the traditional approach of applying entry, price, and service regulation (or government ownership) to an entire sector that had some elements of natural monopoly, OECD governments moved to reforming these sectors. They realised, on the basis of competition principles, that it is often possible and beneficial to reform the structure of such industries by separating out the natural monopoly element. Once that is done, market forces can be permitted to operate in the related markets; only the natural monopoly element must be controlled, as well as access to the monopoly element by competitors in the related markets.

As the authorities started to apply competition analysis more systematically to regulatory provisions, there was increasing recognition that entry barriers need not be explicit or absolute in order to harm competition and economic efficiency. Restrictions, which are not on the face of it total bans, may have that effect if, for example, they prevent realisation of economies of scale or scope. Also, barriers can be anti-competitive not merely by preventing "entry" in the sense of opening a particular kind of business, but also by restricting enterprises' ability to expand/enter into new product lines, start new plants or manufacturing systems, change distribution systems, and so on. Competition and efficiency can also be harmed by rules that prevent effective operation/entry by banning non-deceptive advertising, limiting operating hours, or otherwise interfering with firms' ability to respond efficiently to market forces. Thus, the concept of entry barriers expanded, and new emphasis was also placed on exit barriers, which, as discussed below, serve both to impede entry and to prevent efficient use of society's resources.

Thus, over the last 25 years, many competition law enforcers have become "competition advocates" within their governments, and competition policy has come to refer to a general approach to regulation under which a government seeks to foster market behaviour to the maximum extent consistent with other social goals. OECD Members apply a competition policy approach in many areas as a matter of discretion, and some have formalised it to a greater or lesser extent. Australia, for example, has an explicit National Competition Policy, overseen by a National Competition Council, which provides that regulations should not restrict competition unless it can be demonstrated that: *a*) the benefits of the restriction to the community as a whole outweigh the costs; and *b*) the regulatory objectives can only be achieved by restricting competition. And several years ago, the Korea Fair Trade

Commission was given special responsibility for competition policy analysis of other ministries' proposed regulatory schemes.

Competition policy's role in regulatory analysis is reflected in the OECD's 1997 Regulatory Reform Report. Box 12.3 contains information from the report on the benefits of pro-competitive reform, the

---

Box 12.3. Pro-competitive regulatory reform (1997 data)

Benefits of competition policy-based reform

- Permitting entry and rate competition reduced **airline** fares by 25 per cent in the United Kingdom, 33 per cent in the United States, and 50 per cent in Spain.
- Permitting entry and rate competition reduced **road freight service** by about 20 per cent while improving flexibility and productivity.
- Opening **financial service** markets led to financing innovations that increased home ownership.
- Eliminating a regulatory monopoly improved prices received by **milk producers**.

Types of competition advocacy activities

- The Australian Competition and Consumer Commission makes formal reports and submissions to other commissions and departments, makes appearances before Parliamentary committees, and maintains informal contacts and discussions with other parts of the government.
- The Canadian Competition Bureau offers policy and legislative advice within its own department, gives advice to other departments on request, participates formally in regulatory proceedings, and makes submissions to committees and tribunals.
- The German *Bundeskartellamt* has prepared formal statements on legislation at the ministry's request, and in particularly important situations, such as energy sector reform and telecommunications, Bundeskartellamt staff have testified to *Bundestag* committees and hearings.
- In Mexico, the Federal Competition Commission is a member of the inter-ministerial privatisation commission. In addition, it submits official statements to other bodies and uses informal means to advance competition and consumer interests.
- In Norway, the Competition Authority presents reports on regulatory issues at formal hearings and submits other presentations through its Ministry. The agency intervenes in regulatory proceedings on its own initiative, typically in response to complaints about regulatory barriers to entry.
- The Polish Anti-monopoly Office comments on all draft normative acts. Its president participates in meetings of the cabinet and the Government Economic Committee. It provides formal advice and opinion to Parliament and informally discusses anti-competitive regulations ministries.

Levels of competition advocacy activity

- In Finland, the Office of Free Competition has made competition policy-based regulatory reform a priority since 1988. The result has been over 900 actions in dozens of sectors, with the greatest number in agriculture, telecommunications, retail, financial services, health care, and transport.
- The Office of Economic Competition in Hungary estimates its annual output on regulatory and policy issues to be 20 comments within the government, ten in Parliament or the Cabinet, 30 in other formal settings, and 30 informally.
- In Italy, the Anti-trust Authority has, since 1990, submitted 65 written reports to public authorities, participated in three public hearings, and prepared twelve general fact-finding reports. About half of these actions involved telecommunications, professional services, maritime transport, or electric power.
- The United States Anti-trust Division and Federal Trade Commission have made about 2000 comments or other appearances about regulatory issues since 1975 (not including thousands of opinions on bank mergers and acquisitions).

types of competition advocacy OECD Members' competition authorities have engaged in, and the amount of such advocacy. The topics of the "best practice roundtables" held by the CLP Committee's Working Party on Competition Policy and Regulation are another measure of competition policy's relevance to regulation in other fields.[11]

Even in OECD countries, where there is very wide consensus on the importance of this regulatory approach, there is sometimes concern that competition policy gives more importance to competition than it does to other values, such as protecting consumers, the poor, or the environment. It is important to stress that this concern is not warranted. Competition policy acknowledges other values, merely providing that when considering rules to protect those values, governments should consider, among other things, whether the rules contain any unnecessary or unnecessarily broad restrictions on enterprises' ability to respond efficiently to consumer demand. Such restrictions by definition impose costs on society that are higher than needed to achieve the rules' goals. Thus, competition policy is a tool that can assist governments to reach other social goals at less cost, thereby freeing resources for other needs. Several examples from the OECD Regulatory Reform Report may help make this point.

- In Canada the Competition Commission pointed out, in support of electrical industry restructuring, that market-oriented reform could be done in a way that was not only consistent with environmental objectives, but could actually help to achieve them.

- Although competition policy recognises that licensing requirements and government standards can be useful protections for buyers when health or safety considerations are involved, it also recognises that even purported health or safety regulations can harm consumers. For example, in the United States, bans on the provision of optometry services in commercial settings such as shopping centres were found to raise costs without providing offsetting benefits.

- Competition policy can help a country strengthen its "safety net" for the disadvantaged, including those who have difficulties relating to the transition process. For example, inefficient monopolies in infrastructure markets were formed because the monopolies were considered necessary to ensure universal access. Competition policy has shown ways to ensure universal service at less cost without the monopolies, thus leaving countries with more resources for the safety net.

Competition law and policy in China

The nature of China's economic reforms of the past two decades and numerous declarations by the government make it clear that China, like OECD countries, generally regards competitive markets as a desirable goal in order to promote economic efficiency and growth. China's pursuit of a socialist market economy may imply a comparatively larger role for public ownership. But it is clear that competition law and policy have a substantial role to play in China's economic reform. A competition law's bans on exclusionary practices would make it illegal for enterprises and local governments to subvert trade and investment liberalisation by creating new barriers, while competition policy can do away with continuing legal barriers that would otherwise prevent the realisation of the benefits of trade and investment liberalisation. Both are flexible enough to accomplish these goals in a manner that takes into account China's economic conditions and societal values.[12]

The remainder of this chapter focuses on four key issues relating to the role of competition law and policy in realising the benefits of trade and investment liberalisation in China:

1. China's vulnerability to having trade and investment liberalisation subverted by new entry barriers created by enterprises. *Notably, monopoly power in China is currently more extensive than is often thought, and China's existing competition-related laws do not ban exclusionary conduct.*

2. China's vulnerability to having trade and investment liberalisation subverted by new entry barriers created by local governments. *Administrative monopoly and regional protectionism remain a substantial threat and the Unfair Competition Law's ban on such conduct has no sanctions.*

3. The persistence of unwarranted restrictions on entry and effective competition that are likely to prevent full realisation of the benefits of trade and investment liberalisation. *Despite substantial*

reform, many anti-competitive laws and policies impose direct and indirect barriers to entry, exit, and efficient resolution of the excess capacity problem created by earlier non-market policies.

4. The challenge of effectively regulating China's infrastructure industries. *Competition principles can assist in meeting this important challenge.*

The current situation in China's markets

Market prices and price controls

Pricing in China is governed by the Price Law, which came into effect on 1 May 1998. The law establishes two kinds of price controls – government-set prices and government-guided prices (prescribing a price range). The law provides that price controls are authorised for: 1) "an extremely small number of commodities vital for the development of the national economy and peoples' lives"; 2) "a small number of commodities the resources of which are rare or short"; 3) "commodities under natural monopoly management"; 4) "essential public utilities"; and 5) "essential non-profit services".[13] The law also provides for public participation in hearings to determine prices or price ranges for the last three of these categories.

Except for products or services whose prices are set or guided by the government, the Price Law provides that prices will be determined by the market. For those products and services, the law contains the same kinds of bans on anti-competitive pricing practices (price fixing, and so on) that are found in OECD competition laws.

It is not entirely clear exactly what sectors are currently subject to price controls. At a 1999 China/OECD seminar, the areas subject to price controls were described as including exported gas and petroleum, imported grain, cotton, salt, pharmaceuticals, electricity, gas, water, rare minerals (mainly gold and silver), the post, telecommunications and airlines. Other reports describe a wider range of products, including "sedan cars", civil aircraft, certain types of steel used by railways, salt sold at retail, tobacco, raw materials for certain synthetic fibres, rubber, pig-iron, additional types of steel, tractors, turbines, cement, copper, tires, and "car engines made by designated enterprises".[14]

Market-determined prices apply to over 95 per cent of products and services sold in China according to one estimate.[15] In light of the number and type of products described above as being subject to price controls, the accuracy or meaningfulness of these estimates are uncertain. Moreover, the fact that prices are not explicitly set or guided by the government does not mean that they are actually set by the market because monopolies and cartels do operate in China (sometimes apparently with extra-legal support from some government entities). Nevertheless, while estimates of market-set prices may well be exaggerated, and there appear to be sectors in which further price liberalisation is called for, it is clear that China's reform has succeeded in permitting most enterprises in China to compete on price.

Conditions of entry and exit

China's trade and investment liberalisation and other reforms have eliminated or reduced a vast number of entry barriers and there is every indication that this trend will continue. This is fortunate because there continue to be many significant barriers to entry and exit. An extensive and very useful analysis of these barriers is contained in a 1999 study by the Institute for International Economics (IIE).[16] Based on interviews with expatriates who work in enterprises operating in China, the IIE study analyses the difficulties involved in *a*) establishing an enterprise, *b*) hiring and managing human resources, *c*) running a productive plant, and *d*) marketing, distributing, and servicing a product. Some of the identified barriers apply only to foreign firms, but others apply equally (and some more severely) to domestic enterprises. The IIE study finds that for foreign enterprises, top in the list are market information problems, and that the lack of transparent, uniformly interpreted rules is also a major problem. In addition, the study calls particular attention to limits on plant location, steering foreign firms to specific partners, partnership and labour matters, and limits on scope of operations. Based on the IIE study and other sources including other chapters of this book, this section seeks to highlight and illustrate the nature of the problem and suggest priorities for future reform.

Barriers facing foreign-invested enterprises. Recent trade and investment liberalisation has not eliminated all of the important restrictions on foreign firms or joint ventures. In particular, WTO negotiations have addressed only part of the traditional restrictions on the ability of "foreign-invested enterprises" (FIEs) to market, distribute, and service their products. As just one example, it is reported that even after China's entry into the WTO, most foreign insurers will still need a separate license for each new city and will need to operate as joint ventures with domestic partners.[17]

Barriers facing domestic and foreign-invested enterprises. The intense scrutiny and change occasioned by the process of joining the WTO is an indication that China may be at a point where the greatest benefits would come from a review of its laws and policies in this area. For example, a variety of licensing, registration, and other regulatory/administrative requirements serve as barriers to entry by both FIEs and domestic enterprises.[18] The process of registering a new business is complex and was singled out by the World Bank in 1994 as an area warranting reform. In addition, government agencies must approve labour contracts, a process that can be very time-consuming since enterprises may be pressured to overstaff, and find themselves subject to numerous other formal and informal requirements. Another human resources problem faced at least by foreign enterprises is whether and how they can assure themselves of managerial control of personnel issues. With respect to running a plant, the central problem noted by IIE was the difficulty of enterprises with multiple operations or plants to manage money flows among their ventures. Restrictions on the scope of operations, which have been a focus of WTO negotiations, were also emphasised.

Discrimination among different kinds of enterprise. Rules such as those placing foreign firms or joint ventures on an uneven playing field clearly merit continued attention, but they are only part of a wider problem in which the rights and obligations of enterprises are determined by their ownership or other formal attribute. For example, "TVEs" (township-village enterprises) are at least in theory limited in the lines of business they can enter (see Chapter 2), and China has very different insolvency regimes for different types of enterprise (see Chapter 5). Eliminating barriers to entry based on enterprise form or ownership would appear to be an important goal to foster market competition. A new bankruptcy law has been prepared that will apply to all kinds of enterprises. China should follow that up with laws eliminating unwarranted discrimination in the ability of different kinds of firms to compete.

Discrimination in financing. China's policies on financing enterprises deter efficient entry and exit. Briefly, bank financing is crucial and has traditionally been directed by the state, based on non-market considerations. This distorts the meaning of competitiveness indicators for SOEs that are crucial in attracting outside investors' interest. It also means that financing policies deter entry from sectors in which entry is warranted by market conditions (and is most likely to stimulate efficiency and growth). Moreover, despite some reforms, there continue to be reports of banks giving "soft credit" or "policy loans" based on central or local government plans or preferences (see Chapter 7 on Banking).[19] This practice, together with subsidies and other policies by local governments, deters the exit of firms from markets with chronic excess capacity and the diversion of such firms' assets into more productive uses. It is also noteworthy that each of China's four state-owned banks has an area of specialisation and basically does not compete with the others.[20]

Distribution problems. Some distribution problems are attributable to the pre-reform emphasis on local self-sufficiency, which contributed to a neglect of transportation infrastructure. Moreover, before the reform process began, China controlled the distribution process through vertically integrated "state trading companies" that had statutory monopolies. The statutory monopolies have been eliminated, but a competitive distribution system has not yet emerged. There are real risks that in the absence of enactment and enforcement of a comprehensive competition law, private agreements among enterprises will impede China's movement towards a competitive distribution system and thus slow its realisation of the benefits of trade and investment liberalisation.

Barriers to exit. Banks and local governments apparently prevent enterprises from seeking or obtaining bankruptcy protection, permitting the accumulation of non-performing loans (NPLs) and having local governments make up for losses. In addition, local governments prevent enterprises from merging with companies located in other regions and/or closing down plants that are inefficient. By preventing exit from a loss-making business, the governments may avoid localised unemployment. But by not exiting declining markets, such enterprises prolong excess capacity in the unprofitable market. For the economy as a whole, this results in a net loss since assets are not put to their most productive use.[21]

Administrative monopoly. China has had significant problems dealing with "administrative monopoly", a term usually used to describe two ways in which local (including provincial) governments and officials abuse their power. One abuse is forcing enterprises to buy goods only from enterprises designated by them. The other is regional protectionism, which has been such a serious problem that it is discussed separately below. China's Unfair Competition Law already bans administrative monopoly, but the absence of sanctions has impeded enforcement, and there are proposals to include more effective provisions in the competition law China is planning to enact.

Regional protectionism

Regional protectionism has been a significant problem in China for many years. During the 1980s, state-owned distribution enterprises lost their statutory monopoly, while town and village enterprises (TVEs) were created at a rapid pace. One result of this rapid expansion was excess capacity in many markets. Moreover, the plants of some of these firms were below minimum efficient scale, and many others could only operate at profitable levels if they could sell their products in other regions. As these new firms sought to expand, often with some support from their own local governments, they found themselves in rivalry with firms supported by other local governments. In order to protect their local enterprises, which provided employment even if they were not efficient enough to survive in competition with firms in other regions, many local governments set up regional trade barriers consisting of everything from local customs posts to selective predatory pricing, from adopting discriminatory laws to slashing tires.[22] Many sectors were affected, from appliances to automobiles, and from chemical fibres to coal. And at least until recently, these "regional blockades" have been significant entry barriers with clear anti-competitive effects.

Regional protectionism has been a barrier to investment and restructuring through mergers, as well as to inter-provincial commerce in goods and services, and this may currently be the more serious restriction on competition.[23] The problem is that governments have prevented new entry that threatened local producers, forbidden mergers that would eliminate the separate identity of such producers, or used their power to allocate and manage market share. They have also prevented exit from unproductive businesses, both exit through bankruptcy and exit/reorganisation through merger.

The view that regional protectionism is wasteful is emerging among local government officials. However, such fees and other discriminatory policies, sometimes referred to as "vassal separatism" in reference to precursors of the practice throughout Chinese history, remain a problem.[24] Among other things, local governments' interference with mergers involving firms in their areas is a significant impediment to meeting the central government's laudable goals of reducing excess capacity and realising economies of scale. It is unfortunate that competition legislation in China is sometimes opposed on the mistaken belief that it would prevent mergers that would advance these goals. In fact, as some Chinese officials recognise, a competition law would not ban mergers to achieve minimum efficient scale,[25] and it could be used to ban the regional protectionism that actually is a barrier to efficient mergers.

Market information problems

In general, although many in China appreciate the efficiency of markets, there appears to be much less appreciation of the role information plays or the ways in which competitive markets generate much of the necessary information. The participants in any market need information. In a competitive market, buyers and sellers are in a dynamic and constantly evolving relationship, with producers' innovations shifting consumer demand, while changing consumer tastes suggest new directions for producers to explore. By the same token, lack of market information deters entry and otherwise prevents enterprises from discovering and responding appropriately to market changes.

The market itself can produce much of the information that market participants need. If the price of one commodity goes up, consumers are signalled to consider alternative goods, and existing or potential producers are signalled that they may have a business opportunity. If consumer tastes shift away from a product, increasing inventories and falling prices warn producers to reduce production or improve the product in some dramatic way.

One difficulty that arises in China, as in other transition economies, is that both buyers and sellers may lack experience in obtaining and using market information. A related difficulty is that a relatively large number of enterprises lack the incentive and the skill to adopt long-term strategies and may not "invest" in a key information-related asset – their reputation. These difficulties are an inevitable part of the economic transition process.

However, there are also a number of laws and policies that interfere with the market's ability to generate useful information. For example, in a competitive market, bank loans and other investment in a new enterprise reflect a conclusion that entry into a market is warranted by demand and supply conditions (and is therefore likely to generate efficiency and growth). Government-directed or encouraged loans to enterprises based on other considerations obscure this message, and the distortion is particularly severe if the loans purport to be commercial. Similarly, of course, direct subsidies to enterprises distort the meaning of price and profit information.

China's restrictions on foreign investment enterprises' engaging in distribution have also been a barrier to the efficient spreading of market information. These restrictions are being liberalised, but competitive problems in the distribution sector remain and contribute to information problems in the economy as a whole. Whether a producer sells its output directly or through independent intermediaries, distribution is not merely the means of getting existing products into the hands of buyers. It is a link that provides important information in both directions about such matters as market trends and the efficiency of alternative distributors and distribution methods.

There are also other problems that China should address in order to permit creation of the information markets need to be competitive. Statistical information about markets is subject to intentional and unintentional bias. Non-governmental reporting on financial matters has been discouraged. Moreover, China's law regulating market research in China requires research projects to be approved by the government in advance, and their findings reported to the government. The law may not have hampered market research as much as was originally feared, but it does deter research and would have a far greater effect if it were strictly enforced.[26]

Ambiguity and lack of transparency of Chinese laws

Poor market information is aggravated by persisting opacity regarding legal requirements, which also deters entry. China's traditional legal system was far less transparent than it is today, with the content of laws sometimes being deliberately withheld from the public – a system that gave enormous discretion to the government. From this perspective, China has made great strides. By 1997, it had developed a system of law in urban areas with publicly accessible laws and greater attention to private rights and to procedures. However, even in urban areas, it may be difficult to learn, for example, where and how to obtain a building permit. Moreover, even where the content of a law is known, officials may have considerable discretion in interpreting it. Interpretations may vary, and getting a written interpretation is reportedly impossible in many circumstances.

The ambiguity of China's legal system is in part a result of the relationship between the central government and the provinces. China is not a federal system; rather, sovereignty and legislative authority are vested in China's central government, which delegates legislative power in some areas to the provinces. Delegation has been increasing, which has sometimes led to multiple and partially conflicting laws being applicable to the same conduct. In addition, the central government sometimes tolerates provincial legislation that may or may not be strictly authorised and whose legal effect is unclear – a practice that has to some extent encouraged local protectionism,[27] but has also permitted some beneficial local experimentation.[28] On 15 March 2000, China's National Peoples' Congress enacted a Legislation Law that contains some guidance on dealing with conflicts between laws, but does not resolve other basic issues concerning the authority of provincial legislatures or what body has final responsibility for interpreting national law.[29]

Despite reforms, the legal requirements for doing business in China continue to be non-transparent in many situations. This non-transparency deters entry by raising transaction costs, making room for discriminatory policy. Enterprises with the right connections have access to public information that is as a practical matter denied to their competitors. Combined with the level of discretion officials possess, differential access to information can result in extra-legal privileges – such as increased production quotas or market share allocation, or changes in duty rates – being accorded to enterprises.

These attributes also create a situation in which corruption is reportedly rife. Reported practices vary from bribery that is clearly illegal under Chinese law to other measures that, although legal in China, would be illegal elsewhere. The IIE study discusses numerous means by which sanitised bribes are paid to affect sales or approvals.[30] For example, in order to get his firm's product on the list of approved hospital purchases, one executive was pressured to buy help from advisors to the provincial Minister of Health. Another reported that the way to have the import duty on an input lowered to the correct amount was to hire friends of the custom authorities to draft a report on whether the lower duty was appropriate. Another, who had needed to purchase "fire-testing equipment" from friends of the fire inspectors, stated, "every watchdog agency has its own consulting firm". Much of the corruption is apparently a form of "bid rigging" and could be directly attacked through competition law enforcement.

Enforcement of legal rights – China's court system

As discussed in the following chapter, China has enacted a number of very important framework laws to clarify property rights and provide for the enforceability of contracts. China has also been reforming its court system, but despite considerable progress, concern over individuals' and enterprises' ability to protect their rights remains a deterrent to entry into China or moving into other regions within China.[31]

China's court system has no real civil law tradition; the courts have traditionally dealt with criminal matters, while civil matters were handled by mediation. Moreover, the courts reportedly have little power and are vulnerable to pressures by local interests (including governments) and by government departments.[32] This vulnerability, together with courts' inability in practice to enforce judgements, contributes to the persistent problem of regional protectionism. In addition to informal pressures, there are reports of official interference with courts' jurisdiction by, for example, an administrative quota system that limits the number of enterprises that may be declared bankrupt in a year.[33]

China's court system is not independent. Formally, it is subject to supervision by people's congresses in order to ensure that courts carry out their function efficiently, but in the past it has consisted largely of "rubberstamping" reports prepared by the courts.[34] Recently, however, the Shenyang People's Congress signalled a new approach by rejecting the report submitted by its municipal Intermediate People's Court, which has been held responsible for corruption in the city. More generally, many reforms have been proposed, including a plan by the Supreme People's Court to reduce the local protectionism problem by making the judiciary economically independent of local governments.[35] Reform has occurred, but courts are still not considered objective. Moreover, few judges and lawyers are reported to be well trained.[36]

China's desire to accommodate the expectations of foreign investors has to some extent created a dual-track system in which FIEs have the faster and more reliable track. This reform has presumably benefited not only the FIEs but also elements of the Chinese economy. However, as the number of FIEs increases, such a system will become increasingly impractical. It is vital for the development of China's competitive markets that the two tracks be merged so that domestic producers have equal opportunity to enforce their rights.

Preventing the creation of new barriers to replace those removed by the trade and investment liberalisation

This section examines China's vulnerability to actions by vested interests to prevent the entry that trade and investment liberalisation is expected to bring. One example is exclusionary conduct by the enterprises that are losing from trade and investment liberalisation. Competition law bans such conduct, which is a reason for the proposal, partially adopted in Doha, to negotiate WTO rules *requiring* that members enact and enforce competition laws.

Local governments and their officials are another frequent source of resistance to further liberalisation. In developed market economies that have had competition laws for a long time, instruments other than competition law usually govern such activities. However, the Treaty of Rome and the experience of Russia and other transition countries show that competition law can be an important tool for breaking down such barriers to a unified market.

The vulnerability of China's economy to exclusionary conduct by enterprises

China's vulnerability to exclusionary conduct by enterprises is a function of both the susceptibility of China's economy to monopolistic abuses and other anti-competitive conduct, and the inadequacy of China's existing laws to halt and deter such conduct.

In truly competitive markets, individual enterprises do not have the necessary power to exclude competitors, and it can be difficult to hold together anti-competitive cartels. A common view in China is that its markets are competitive and therefore not susceptible to monopolistic abuses. However, the basis for this view appears to be that nationwide monopolies are rare and that there is intense rivalry in some markets. These propositions are correct, but they do not support the view that China's markets are not monopolistic or oligopolistic. Low concentration ratios in China as a whole are not an indicator of competitive markets because many product and most service markets are local, rather than national. And the intense rivalry that is seen, for example, in consumer electronics, is the result of market distortions – soft budget constraints, regional protectionism, and exit barriers – rather than an indicator of competitiveness.

Market concentration in China

As the World Bank noted in a comprehensive report in 1994, average enterprise size in China is not large, and many enterprises appear to operate at less than minimum efficient scale.[37] Many provinces have very similar industrial patterns, with a large number of industries represented in almost all provinces. Thus, it has often been noted that market concentration (the percentage of production, sales, or some other measure accounted by the leading enterprises) is relatively low in China as a whole, even compared to similar industries in developed countries. For example, the World Bank noted that the top five machine tool producers had 42 per cent of national production in Japan and 69 per cent in the United States, but only 20 per cent in China.

China's overall market structure, with low national concentration and a large number of regional enterprises operating at less than minimum efficient scale in the same field, does have important implications for policy in China. For example, the World Bank stated that since the "problem of monopoly is not pervasive"[38] and concentration of economic power "is not a major issue, at present", the emphasis in competition law enforcement should be on market conduct, rather than market structure.[39] The Bank noted that the Unfair Competition Law in fact contains some conduct-related provisions, but that "its coverage needs to be strengthened".[40] In that regard, the Bank pointed out the lack of a ban on cartel conduct other than bid rigging, and it noted the need for provisions against the abuse of "market power".[41]

While the World Bank report emphasised the structural difference between China and other transition economies and stressed what that difference meant in terms of competition law enforcement priorities, nothing in the report suggests that there are not significant monopoly problems in China. Three fundamental points merit emphasis.

First, as noted above, even when the underlying data is reliable, "market" concentration is not a meaningful indicator of competitiveness unless it reflects a market – the real-world choices that are open to buyers and sellers.[42] This requires defining relevant product markets and relevant geographic markets, a task that requires investigation into actual market operation. Available reports of concentration in China, however, are generally based on statistical product categories and political boundaries; such reports are not reliable and are often very misleading.

Second, although national concentration ratios can in principle overstate or understate actual market concentration, the way in which China's economy continues to reflect local self-sufficiency principles means that in the case of China, the national ratios clearly understate actual market concentration, as discussed above in Box 12.2.

Third, China's markets in fact manifest a variety of structural problems. Nine industrial sectors – including petroleum processing, ferrous metallurgy, non-ferrous metallurgy, transport, and basic chemicals – are still relatively closed to competition (see chapter on industry). Moreover, like the firms in the former Soviet Union, China's state-owned firms have engaged in excessive vertical integration, which has been continuing despite market reforms. This is due to the frequency of breaches of contract and the high transaction costs (or impossibility) of enforcing contacts.[43] Such excessive vertical integration creates barriers to entry as well as causing efficiency losses.

Another factor contributing to unwarranted optimism about the competitiveness of markets in China is the view that China does not have an "economic monopoly" problem, but only a problem of monopolies resulting from government restrictions on entry.[44] The distinction underlying this view is not valid. Worldwide, most "economic monopolies" derive power from government entry restrictions. And all monopolies protected by such entry restrictions are "economic monopolies" and may well retain their monopoly even after protection is removed.

Moreover, the substantial rivalry that is manifest in some Chinese markets does not warrant broad conclusions about the competitiveness of China's markets. The price wars and other forms of intense competition that have made headlines in fact reflect non-competitive features of China's economy – uneconomic investment, resulting in overcapacity, which is not diverted to more productive uses because of soft-budget constraints, regional protectionism, and exit barriers. Anecdotal evidence about even these markets suggests that monopoly elements sometimes exist, and there is certainly anecdotal evidence consistent with China's markets being susceptible to monopoly abuses and cartelisation.[45]

The most visible cartel conduct occurs in industries in which a combination of subsidies and exit barriers have created and maintained overcapacity. Price competition in those fields (especially consumer electronics) can be fierce and may – because of soft budget constraints and exit barriers – constitute "destructive competition" in that all producers may be pricing below marginal cost.[46] In this situation, it is obvious that enterprises have an incentive to cartelise but that incentives to cheat are also very large. Thus, there are some well-publicised cartel agreements, most of which do not last long.[47]

The failure of such cartels to endure leads some to believe that China's markets are too competitive to be subject to cartelisation. However, this appears to be an unduly optimistic view. In the first place, China is working to make budget constraints "hard" and to facilitate exit. As these reforms increasingly take effect, plants and other assets of the higher cost producers will be diverted to other uses. With higher concentration (for example, the top four tube manufacturers having 80 per cent of the market) and no excess capacity, collusion will be easier. In the second place, China has shortages (recently including LCD computer monitors) as well as overcapacity. Where excess capacity is not a factor and concentration higher (due to some combination of regional protectionism and transportation costs) collusion is not likely to be public, and is likely to be more enduring.

The adequacy of China's laws to protect against exclusionary and other anti-competitive conduct

Although China has no comprehensive competition law, two competition-related laws contain provisions against anti-competitive conduct. These provisions can address some of the kinds of

404

exclusionary conduct by enterprises that would subvert trade and investment liberalisation, but they have major gaps with respect to both exclusionary and other anti-competitive conduct. These gaps will need to be addressed by the new competition law (see below).[48]

The Unfair Competition Law

Although preceded by a number of regulations by the State Council dealing with, among other things, regional protectionism, the first important competition-related law enacted in China was the Unfair Competition Law, which came into effect on 1 December 1993. The law, which is enforced by the State Administration for Industry and Commerce (SAIC) at the central government level and by local AIC offices, bans various practices it defines as unfair competition. Most of the practices are the sort of fraudulent behaviour or misappropriation of property rights that are often referred to as unfair trade practices: commercial bribery, misleading advertising, deception (by "passing off" and other means), defamation of competitors, and misuse of trade secrets.[49] Like unfair trade bans in OECD countries, these provisions focus primarily on protecting enterprises from such dishonest practices by their competitors. In OECD countries, unfair trade laws often protect individual private rights, enforceable only by the injured competitor, though government-enforced consumer protection laws, as a rule, ban the same or similar practices when they harm consumers.

Unfair trade practices can be very harmful to competitors and, in the aggregate, to competition. In emerging market economies where the rules of the game are not well established, and where access to courts by injured enterprises or consumers is limited, government enforcement against unfair trade practices can be very important to the creation of competitive markets. At the same time, it is important to understand that bans of unfair trade practices or unfair competition are not generally referred to as being a part of "competition law". In general, the distinction is that an act violates competition law only if it is likely to injure market competition in the sense of leading to reduced output and monopoly prices, whereas acts covered by unfair competition laws are illegal without regard to market impact.

The Unfair Competition Law does prohibit four anti-competitive practices that would be covered by a competition law – predatory pricing, tie-in sales, a particular type of abuse by statutory monopolists and bid rigging. Bans on predatory pricing are often misused in ways that impede competitive pricing, and it is therefore noteworthy that the Chinese law identifies some situations in which below cost sales are not illegal. (It does not define just what "cost" a price must exceed, however.) It is unclear whether and to what extent the ban on tie-in sales has an efficiency defence. Another provision bans a practice akin to tie-ins – requiring buyers to obtain related products from specified sources. Interestingly, this provision applies to all (and only) statutory monopolies, which is unduly broad (since some statutory monopolies are not economic monopolies), and unduly narrow (for not covering economic monopolies that are not statutory). The law's ban on bid rigging is unexceptional in itself, but it is noteworthy that the law bans only bid rigging even though it is just one form of price fixing (which in turn is only one form of hard core cartel conduct). Illustrating the unclear relationship between central and provincial laws, Guangdong Province reportedly adopted China's first ban on price fixing as an implementing regulation under the Unfair Competition Law.[50]

The SAIC has been quite active in enforcing this law, and discussions with SAIC officials suggest that the enforcement has been useful.[51] It is important to emphasise, however, that these four provisions do not ban anywhere near all the forms of exclusionary conduct that could be so damaging to China. The predatory pricing and tie-in provisions could be used against some such conduct, but the Unfair Competition Law has no general ban on abuse of monopoly power, no ban on restrictive distributions systems, and no ban on exclusionary boycotts.

The Price Law

The Price Law contains a substantial number of bans on anti-competitive pricing practices by enterprises – price fixing, predatory pricing, price discrimination, and a variety of other "unfair price acts". While extending the Unfair Competition Law's ban on bid rigging to all price fixing is beneficial,

405

the Price Law only applies to conduct relating directly to price. Moreover, only its predatory pricing and price discrimination provisions could be used against exclusionary conduct; like the Unfair Competition Law, it has no general ban on abuse of monopoly power, no ban on restrictive distributions systems, and no ban on exclusionary boycotts. Finally, the SDPC is still developing the regulations necessary to implement the law's competition-related provisions.

Other Chinese laws

China has a number of other laws that have some applicability to competition law and policy, including a Bidding Law, a Product Quality Law and a Consumer Protection Law. While important, none of them bans exclusionary conduct. It should also be noted that no Chinese law prohibits mergers or acquisitions that would harm China's consumers and its overall economy.

China's draft competition law

It is not uncommon for countries to enact laws such as the Unfair Competition Law before enacting a competition law. However, anti-competitive activities such as cartels have been reported and criticised by the media since about 1988, and by 1993 Chinese officials had prepared drafts of a competition law. Some reformers were in fact seeking enactment of a complete (or more complete) competition law in 1993, and when that effort failed, it was expected that a separate competition law would be enacted fairly quickly.

One of the original reasons for delaying action on the competition law was a misguided concern that it might hinder mergers designed to create enterprises that could operate at above minimum efficient scale. Another factor has been the apparently unwarranted view that China's markets are competitive enough not to be subject to monopolisation. And recently, some policy-makers in China expressed concern that enacting a competition law would somehow prevent China from building up some of its enterprises as "national champions". This concern, too, reflects a fundamental misunderstanding of competition law. Although the trend in OECD countries is to give up national champions on policy grounds, some OECD countries maintain them, and their doing so does not raise any competition law problem. Some influential Chinese leaders understand that all of these concerns are unwarranted.

In preparing a competition law that incorporates market principles and is tailored to China's own situation, several general observations are noteworthy:

- The officials responsible for preparing the competition law have consistently emphasised that the law would contain a full set of provisions for halting and deterring exclusionary conduct by enterprises. Thus, the law would fill the major gaps in China's current competition-related laws.

- Like the European Union, the Russian Federation, and many other transition economies, China should include in its competition law provisions that can contribute to breaking down unauthorised local governmental protectionism within its borders and other forms of administrative monopoly.

- The substantive competition law provisions that China is contemplating are generally quite mainstream, which can be beneficial to China for a variety of reasons, including the encouragement of foreign investment. However, given China's intent to maintain a relatively high degree of public ownership, it should consider adopting special rules on predatory pricing for publicly owned firms. Moreover, if China considers adopting a system under which "recession" or "restructuring" cartels may be authorised, it should ensure that this option is available only in limited circumstances and for a limited period of time.

- Drafts of the competition law include important provisions to ban anti-competitive mergers and acquisitions. Those provisions would not deter the kind of beneficial mergers that are needed, for example, to achieve scale economies, and it may be that merger cases would be a very small part of competition law enforcement in China for some time. Nevertheless, it is important to have a ban on anti-competitive mergers. Otherwise, when cartel agreements or anti-competitive restrictive distribution agreements are found unlawful, the parties will be able to achieve their anti-competitive goals by merging. To ensure that Chinese officials are not required to waste resources by reviewing mergers that are not substantial threats to Chinese consumers, the competition authority should have discretion to challenge only the mergers it considers most harmful. For the same reason, the competition authority should be authorised, but not required, to establish a pre-merger notification system.

- The competition law will need an effective enforcement agency. This goal will require careful analysis of issues that have not so far received much attention. In particular, the competition law will overlap some provisions in China's existing competition-related laws, which are enforced by different agencies. OECD experience suggests that there would be significant benefits to having the core competition provisions of these laws enforced by a single agency. Institutional factors such as independence, transparency, and appropriate decision-making are critical for effective law enforcement and competition advocacy.

The relationship between competition-related laws and sectoral regulation

Competition laws generally apply to all or almost all sectors of the economy, and the same is true for competition-related laws such as the Unfair Competition Law. When countries establish special regulatory systems for particular sectors, such as infrastructure industries, the question arises as to how those regulatory systems should interact with competition-related laws. This issue has arisen in China with respect to, for example, the Unfair Competition Law and the Telecommunications Law. It will become even more important when China adopts its competition law.

Two related propositions are involved. First, the fact that an industry or a firm is subject to price and output regulation does not mean that it should be exempt from legislative bans on unfair or anti-competitive conduct. To the extent that a regulatory agency sets firms' prices and output, their price and output should not be subject to competition law, but there is no reason to exempt the firms or any practices by the firms that are not compelled or actively overseen by the sectoral regulator. In fact, in the transition countries of Central and Eastern Europe and the former Soviet Union, most of the competition law cases have been abuse-of-monopoly cases against regulated natural monopolists.

Second, even if the sectoral regulator is given general authority to prevent unfair or anti-competitive conduct for the firms it regulates, it is a good idea to leave the firms subject also to the general competition law. Different OECD countries have differing means of trying to deal with this situation, but there is a widespread belief that sectoral regulators should not have exclusive competition-enforcement authority because they lack competition expertise and may be subject to "regulatory capture". Co-operation between agencies can minimise conflicting policies, and the sectoral regulator may have the ability to confer immunity by adopting specific rules governing suspect conduct, but legislation exempting firms or industries can cause real problems. In China, the Telecommunications Law exempts regulated firms from the Unfair Competition Law, and the SAIC is therefore unable to prevent such conduct as requiring users to buy hardware from designated firms and requiring them to pay a "repair fee" without providing repairs.

The vulnerability of China's economy to exclusionary actions by local governments

Exclusionary actions by local governments and their officials are generally referred to in China as administrative monopoly, which for the purposes of this chapter may be defined by reference to Article 7 of the Unfair Competition Law. That article provides that local (including provincial) governments and their subordinate departments are prohibited from:

- abusing their administrative power by forcing others to buy the goods of operators designated by them so as to restrict the lawful business activities of other operators; and

- abusing their administrative power by restricting the entry of goods from other parts of the country into the local market or the flow of local goods to markets in other parts of the country.

The law is interpreted to apply to both actions by local governments themselves, such as the adoption of ordinances that discriminate against enterprises from other provinces or areas, and *ad hoc* actions by officials to favour a local firm directly or by creating barriers for its non-local competitors. Some forms of administrative monopoly are anticompetitive but not necessarily exclusionary. For example, the SAIC has been confronted by numerous instances in which insurance providers collude with government officials so that car owners and even kindergarten children must buy life insurance, or people who want a kind of insurance can buy it from only one firm. Thus, regional protectionism is, as a theoretical matter, a sub-category of administrative monopoly, but it is such a large and important sub-category that this chapter generally uses the terms as synonyms.

As discussed above, such local protectionism has been a significant problem in China. There, as in other countries or markets in which trade and investment liberalisation or other liberalisation reduces barriers to entry, local governments have often responded with protectionist activities ranging from flat bans, to discrimination (in taxes, standards, inspections, and so on), to physical intimidation. If the governments themselves do not engage in such activities, their officials may do so without authorisation in order to protect local interests or in exchange for extra-legal payments. The harmfulness of these activities is both described in the literature and reflected in the Unfair Competition Law's ban.

Article 7 was intended primarily to deal with practices such as refusing to permit a product such as tea to be transported out of the province except by a specified (and normally government-owned) distributor. Another example of such administrative monopoly was the practice of denying enterprises a license to do business unless they agreed to purchase all of their supplies from a specified enterprise.[52] The State Administration for Industry and Commerce has been able to achieve some notable successes through use of this provision, but the law's lack of sanctions and various other features prevent it from being truly effective. Local AIC enforcers are employees of the government that is engaging in the abuse, and there is no sanction for a violation. If the AIC finds a violation, its only power is to inform a higher level of the offending body. In this circumstance, enterprises have little incentive to make a complaint and the law enforcer has little incentive to act on complaints it does receive.

Activities such as these are not usually governed by competition law in developed market economies that have had competition laws for a long time. However, the Treaty of Rome included competition law as the *only* substantive law to be enforced by the European Commission in recognition of its usefulness in eliminating barriers to the creation of a single market. In addition, OECD and other countries that have enacted competition laws in the past ten years have frequently made at least some of their provisions applicable to governments and government officials. The Russian Federation, whose situation is the most analogous to China's in terms of overall size, variations in development, and actual examples of regional protectionism, has made good use of its competition law to combat both official protectionist policies and corruption.[53]

Continuing the reform process

In addition to combating attempts to frustrate China's trade and investment liberalisation, it is important for China to engage in further liberalisation of China's markets. This will require three kinds of activities: eliminating explicit entry barriers that lack justification; adopting and implementing a national competition policy; and using competition policy principles regulating natural monopolies.

Eliminating explicit entry barriers that lack justifications

In discussing the current situation in China's markets, this chapter referred to the existence of explicit legal barriers to entry (and exit) that are based on enterprises formal classification (TVE, FIE, etc.) or ownership. It is unclear how strictly these barriers are enforced in practice or how much actual harm they cause, but they serve no apparent purpose and create uncertainty that is itself a barrier. Reviewing such barriers is an important task, as is continuing to reduce the burden imposed by registration and other administrative requirements for opening and reorganising a business.

Adopting and implementing a national competition policy

More broadly, China should apply competition policy principles in assessing existing and proposed regulatory limitations on competitive activity. Examples of such limitations, which were noted in discussing the current situation in China, include restrictions that prevent the realisation of economies of scope and those whose overbreadth sweeps in legitimate activities as well as (for example) unsafe ones. Competition policy principles support the regulatory reform process discussed in the preceding chapter. And China is increasingly taking competition considerations into account in its regulatory policies. For example, the government's new "market-oriented" policy towards pricing water, in which water prices must take into account the cost of water, is a clear example of competition policy.[54] And the government appears to have moved away from policies adopted in 1998 that actually encouraged cartels by, among other things, suggesting that it was predatory pricing for a firm to charge a price below average cost for the industry as a whole. Given the consistency of this approach with China's goals, the government should consider adopting a formal national competition policy.

China should also apply competition policy to the analysis of issues relating to market restructuring. For example, news reports indicate that China recently merged all of the alumina production facilities in China into one enterprise that will produce 70 per cent of the alumina used in China; the other 30 per cent comes from imports. The firm will also produce 23 per cent of China's aluminium, and the government reportedly expects that the new firm will restrict output of alumina and thereby help prevent the creation of small and inefficient aluminium production facilities.[55] This implies that the government expects the enterprise to have monopoly power in the alumina market, *i.e.* that alumina imports will not rise enough to offset the enterprise's production cuts. In considering restructuring issues in such a situation, competition policy analysis would be used, for example, to assess how much economic waste will result from the monopoly and whether there are alternative, more efficient means of dealing with the underlying problem of over-investment in inefficient production facilities. Such over-investment is caused by market distortions, and competition policy would seek to find means to reduce the distortions rather than try to deal with their symptoms.

Using competition policy principles regulating natural monopolies

Infrastructure provides essential services to citizens and key inputs into all parts of an economy. Thus, ensuring an efficient infrastructure is important both for citizens' quality of life and for promoting economic growth. Efficient infrastructure is also important for attracting foreign and domestic investment and to enable China to benefit as an exporter from trade liberalisation.

China can benefit substantially from reforming its infrastructure sectors. This process is already underway, and China has considered the infrastructure reform experiences in OECD Member countries. A detailed review of Chinese infrastructure reforms is beyond the scope of this chapter. However, this chapter outlines some essential steps that must be taken to reform infrastructure sectors, focusing on the electricity, gas, rail, and telecommunications sectors.

The application of competition policy principles to the regulation of natural monopolies in the past twenty years has promoted efficiency, growth, innovation, and universal access. As noted above, the principle that governments should permit markets to function to the maximum extent consistent with other social goals led to the realisation that is often possible and beneficial to separate the natural monopoly element of an industry from those elements that could be competitive. Preceding or at least accompanying these structural changes, regulations and regulatory institutions are part of the reform bringing competition policy to natural monopolies.

Building a business environment for efficient infrastructure is part of a broad set of reforms whose components are discussed in various other chapters. Reforms in this area can be divided into two sets of steps.

First steps

The first set concerns the separation of regulation from business activity (see Box 12.4). This separation is vital for reform. In a country with state-owned incumbent enterprises, the government has potential conflicting interests and separation can help resolve those conflicts in socially desirable ways. Where the government has simultaneously played the roles of welfare provider, regulator and owner in some OECD countries, there have been a variety of undesirable results in different countries or sectors: prices that did not cover the costs of providing the infrastructure and its services; excessive costs due to a very high number of employees per unit of output (compared with other enterprises in the same business in other countries) and to poor procurement practices; under-investment in infrastructure and complaints from foreign investors of unfair treatment under the regulatory regime. These results are symptoms of inefficiency and, in the long-term, discourage private investment.

In addition, revenues to commercial enterprises, including those providing essential services such as electricity, should be fair and commensurate to quantity and quality. Metering and payment are both essential. If individual usage is not metered, then consumers cannot monitor their usage and receive no benefit from conservation. Non-paying customers are subsidised by other customers and taxpayers; any sustainable reform would need to take these cross-subsidies into account, or end them.

Second steps

The second set of steps uses competition policy principles to define the structure and the regulations to be applied to infrastructure sectors. These steps must take into account the economic features that distinguish infrastructure sectors from most other sectors. These features are:

- The services they provide, such as electricity and telecommunications, are important to citizens. Ensuring that citizens have access to them ("universal service") usually implies that a sustainable system of subsidies and definition of what will be provided on subsidised terms must be put into place.

Box 12.4.   **Reform steps: Separating regulation from business activity**

a) Define the boundaries between commerce and the state, and the respective roles of commercial enterprises to operate and the state to regulate. Competition is hampered where the division between state and commerce is unclear, because potential competitors to state-owned enterprise fear a "tilted playing field" and will hesitate to enter. Further, the separation means that government policy decisions must be made explicit in order for the commercial operator to carry them out. This is a first step towards, for example, developing sustainable universal service policies.

b) Establish state regulatory institutions that have the powers and the resources to regulate the commercial infrastructure enterprises so as to ensure that they achieve efficiency and other regulatory goals. These institutions will use regulations to create incentives for commercial entities. Such regulatory institutions can reduce regulatory barriers, promote entry and investment, and accelerate the development of competition. They can ensure fair and efficient access to essential facilities, such as electricity transmission or a gas pipeline, to which competing firms need access. They can also ensure predictable regulation: unpredictable regulation discourages private investment, and changing regulation renders sunk investment less efficient. Thus, a market environment requires regulatory institutions that make decisions that are neutral, transparent, and not subject to day-to-day political pressures or capture.

c) Put into place corporate governance systems to ensure adequate control and incentives for the commercial infrastructure enterprises.

- The sectors have elements that are natural monopolies; that is, the combination of production technology and market demand means that a single enterprise can serve the market at lower cost than two or more enterprises. Usually, the better solution to a natural monopoly is not to seek to introduce competition but rather to make the natural monopoly's price and output decisions subject to regulation in order to protect the public. But it is important to recognise that not every part of these sectors is a natural monopoly.

- Many of the costs in the sectors are "sunk", that is, once the costs are incurred the assets cannot be used to supply a different market. Thus, potential investors who have a choice of investment projects need to be convinced that the regulatory regime will allow them a stream of revenues and profits after the investments are made.

The design of a number of elements of reform – the structure of the sector, pricing of the natural monopoly, market design, institutional design and provision for universal service – must be coherent because the design of each element affects the feasible and desirable designs of the others.[56] It is critical to decide on the structural reforms and market design at an early stage, since the establishment of property rights makes subsequent change difficult. Reform design should be separated from implementation. Involving market participants in the design phase can help ensure technical coherence. However, implementation of the reform should be left to state agencies without a commercial interest in the sector. This arrangement best ensures that broader public objectives will be served, and it reduces the risk that consensus would be sought on each point, a process which can result in technical incoherence. Experience in OECD countries suggests that, while it is important to have a reform plan, it is equally vital to have a reform process that allows unexpected problems to be addressed while nevertheless progressing toward the reform's goals.

The second set of steps also uses competition policy principles to specify the structures of the sectors and the regulations applied to sectors so that they are efficient and meet universal service objectives. These reforms must take into account the main economic characteristics of each sector. In the infrastructure sectors these are: a political decision to provide universal service, elements of natural monopolies and "sunk" or irrecoverable costs.

Universal service

The structure and regulations of infrastructure sectors are usually designed so that efficiency and universal service are jointly achieved. The universal service objective follows directly from the observation that these sectors usually provide an essential service to citizens and key inputs into the rest of the economy. OECD countries have designed policies and structures to reduce the cost of universal service by introducing elements of competition.

Universal service implies that a sustainable system of subsidies must be put into place, along with a careful definition of what will be provided on subsidised terms. Universal service has different definitions in different sectors, at different places and times, since it is defined to achieve social goals within economic constraints. Universal service may mean ensuring that the infrastructure passes near each village, or that each citizen has access to a limited service at "affordable prices" or that prices for public services are geographically uniform. Since the amount of subsidies is necessarily limited, especially in emerging market economies (EMEs), careful trade-offs between health, safety, development and other objectives must be made to define what, exactly, are the current goals for universal service. In many countries, the economic constraints mean that subsidised access to services such as electricity is limited to consumers with low incomes or each consumer gets a limited quantity of subsidised services. Universal service of a low marginal-cost, difficult-to-exclude service such as rail transport usually specifies a frequency and a price available to any consumer.

Reform will fail unless the subsidies and cross-subsidies in the existing system, whether due to universal service or other policies like subsidies to energy-intensive customers or rural customers, are identified and either ended or funded from sustainable sources. If the incumbent must internally cross-subsidise, then free entry and competition will allow new entrants to undercut the prices offered by the incumbent to those customers currently providing cross-subsidies to undercharged customers. This makes the incumbent's position unsustainable.

Potentially sustainable sources of funds are other customers and the general tax and expenditure system. Under-investment is not sustainable and can harm other parts of the economy if it reduces the reliability with which the service is provided. Failure to introduce adequate funding for subsidies may well result in under-investment by the incumbent. The most sustainable source of funds for subsidies is a "non-bypassable" (unavoidable) transparent surcharge to which all consumers contribute. It should be non-bypassable so that subsidising consumers cannot leave the system. It should be transparent to ensure broad support for the universal service.

Competition can be used to identify the least-cost provider and technology of universal service. For example, where the obligation for universal service in specified areas has been sold by competitive auction, it was discovered that new entrants sometimes have lower costs than the incumbent.

A sustainable universal service regime specifies what is to be provided at subsidised prices, to whom it is provided, how the provider(s) is identified, and how the revenue shortfall is recovered. A reform plan that does not explicitly address funding those existing cross-subsidies that will be continued, and any additional subsidies that are adopted, is not sustainable.

Natural monopoly and the sunk cost characteristics

Many infrastructure sectors have elements that are natural monopolies and many of their costs are "sunk" or irrecoverable in the purpose of policy action. For the purpose of policy analysis, where a single enterprise can serve the market at lower cost than two or more enterprises, this market is defined as a "natural monopoly". Examples of natural monopolies are electricity transmission, gas transmission, and rail infrastructure.[57]

A natural monopoly has large fixed costs compared with variable costs. This does not allow for marginal cost pricing. A two-part tariff, where one part is usage-invariant and the other part varies with quantity used, is one method of recovering enough revenue to pay for total costs. Another method is to charge higher prices to consumers who have a lower elasticity of demand (those who have fewer options for cutting back their consumption so respond less to price changes). Since demand varies in a predictable pattern for many of these services, prices can also vary in order to generate revenues during high-demand periods to cover fixed costs. In OECD countries, all of these methods are used, and some natural monopolies, such as rail infrastructure, often receive subsidies.

Competition can be seriously impeded when a complement (a good that is used with other goods) is a natural monopoly. Where the same enterprise both owns the natural monopoly and is a competitor to supply a complement (such as owning the electricity transmission grid and one of several electricity generators), then that firm has incentives to deny access to the natural monopoly part, provide degraded service, and otherwise discriminate in the access it provides to its competitors. Competition in, say, electricity generation or gas supply, is distorted, costs are higher, and new investment by "outsiders" is discouraged. OECD Member countries have tried a variety of responses, each of them combining mandatory access regimes with some sort of unbundling or separation of the natural monopoly from the potentially competitive part. In light of the increasing recognition of the importance of full structural separation (separating the ownership of the natural monopoly from the potentially competitive parts), a recent OECD Recommendation encourages members to carefully balance the benefits and costs of separation versus integration in the course of regulatory decisions, especially in the course of privatisation and liberalisation. It also gives some guidance as to what benefits and costs to take into account when conducting this balancing.

One of the insights of the past two decades of economic reform in much of the OECD area is that sometimes only one part of a sector may be a natural monopoly, while other parts are potentially competitive. For example, the "wires" element of the electricity sector (the high-voltage transmission and low-voltage distribution systems) are natural monopolies over any given region, but competition is possible between electricity generators if they each have access to the electricity transmission system to transport their electricity to consumers. Similarly, competition is possible in telecommunications networks if new operators are ensured access to the network of the incumbent operator to originate and terminate calls.

Introducing competition into the competitive parts of these industries can benefit society through enhanced efficiency and greater innovation, but realising these benefits is difficult when the owner of the monopoly (or "bottleneck") participates in the competitive parts of the industry. The monopoly owner has a strong incentive and myriad ways to keep out other firms by delaying or denying them access to the monopoly element or raising the price for access. For example, an integrated railway company might restrict competition by such means as charging high prices for access to the track, denying rights to operate trains at certain times, or scheduling its own trains in front of rivals. Regulators have never been truly effective in preventing such behaviour (though they often can limit it) even when they require a regulated firm to separate its monopoly and competitive activities into different accounts or different enterprises under a single holding company.

OECD countries have therefore come to place increasing emphasis on preventing the owner of the monopoly facility from competing in the competitive parts of the industry. With this "ownership separation", the owner of the bottleneck no longer has an incentive to discriminate between the downstream firms or to prevent the growth of competition. To determine whether such separation is likely to be beneficial in any particular situation, the advantages from competition must be weighed against possible efficiency losses from the separation. This will depend, for example, on the feasibility of entry and on whether the corporate governance of the "competitors" is such that they have *incentives* to compete and seek efficiency gains. Also, the demand side of the market must also be developed to ensure that consumers and consuming businesses face prices that are higher during periods of shortage or higher costs, that they can respond to the changing prices by changing consumption, and that they can shop among competing suppliers. And the framework conditions in which these firms operate must be sufficient. For example, if contract disputes are costly to resolve, or the outcome of legal disputes too uncertain, the efficiency losses from separating potentially competitive bits from the natural monopoly bits may be too large.

Although separating the ownership of firms in monopoly and potentially competitive markets is not always the right approach, the increasing recognition of the importance of such separation recently led the OECD's Council to adopt a Recommendation on this topic. The Recommendation encourages Members to give serious consideration to full structural separation in the course of regulatory decisions, especially in the course of privatisation and liberalisation. It also gives some guidance as to what benefits and costs to take into account when conducting this balancing.

Many OECD countries changed the structure of their infrastructure sectors in anticipation of privatisation. These include Italy, the United Kingdom, and Hungary. In only a very few jurisdictions has partial or complete privatisation not followed soon after structural change. The incentives of owners and managers of an enterprise differ according to whether the enterprise is private or state-owned. In particular, competition between state-owned enterprises may not induce economically efficient behaviour: they may engage in destructive competition if they cannot be forced to exit by bankruptcy and can count on state subsidies. The electricity generators in New South Wales, Australia, engaged for a while in such conduct. Where partial or full privatisation is not envisaged in the medium term, the designers should take careful note of other countries' positive and negative experiences in providing efficiency-enhancing incentives under state ownership.

In addition to the natural monopoly characteristic, many of the costs of infrastructure sectors are "sunk". That is, once the costs are incurred then the assets cannot be used to supply a different market. The sunk characteristic is due to three factors: 1) the geographic location of the physical assets matters, 2) production is very capital intensive, and 3) the capital assets are long-lived.

Sunk costs make timing and beliefs about the future critical. Where there are sunk costs, investments are made at the outset, but revenues to pay for those investments only arrive later, over a period of years. Potential investors who have a choice of investment projects need to be convinced that they will be allowed the revenues that arrive years after the investments are made. For regulated industries, voluntary private investment requires credible, predictable regulation. Creating this credibility is one of the basic tasks of a new regulator. One reason for state ownership in many countries may have been the difficulty governments had in convincing private investors that they were committed to a regulatory regime permitting cost recovery. External guarantees that insure against regulatory risk may help overcome this barrier.

Structure and regulation of electricity, telecommunications, railways and gas in China

- Electricity

Demand for electricity is growing rapidly in China, particularly in the fast-growing eastern provinces. Generating plants are predominantly fired by coal. Reform is under way in the electricity sector. The dominant electricity enterprise, the State Power Corporation of China (SPCC) was separated from the ministry in 1998. In 1999, the State Council approved a plan to separate power generation from transmission and distribution. There is some foreign direct investment in the sector. Further reform should build upon the experiences in other countries to ensure that the difficult design does in fact promote efficiency and competition.

The Chinese electricity sector is growing rapidly and is expected to continue growing as per capita electricity usage "catches up" and some unserved rural areas gain access.[58] Most electricity is generated by coal, even as older and dirtier coal plants are being closed. Hydropower, in the centre and west of the country, is being developed. Four nuclear power stations are under construction and expected to begin generating electricity in 2005 or earlier.[59] Electric power flows predominantly west-to-east, and a major west-to-east transmission project is underway. There has been significant foreign investment in China's electricity sector. By 1999 24 GW of electricity was generated by plants with foreign investment, and in 2000, foreign funds accounted for 10 per cent of China's total power investments.[60]

Reform has already begun in this sector. The sector is principally governed by China's first electric power law which became effective in 1996. In 1998, China separated the enterprise functions into the State Power Corporation of China (SPCC), eliminated the Electric Industry Ministry, and placed the central government functions for the sector in the SETC. A comparable division of functions at the provincial level was to be completed in 2001, and the corresponding reorganisation at township and municipal level has already begun.

SPCC dominates the electric power sector in China. There are some power plants that are joint ventures between industrial companies and electric companies, but there are very few power plants that are solely owned by auto-generators.

Prices are regulated by the SDPC. Both the price at which electricity is sold by generators to the network and the price at which electricity is sold by the network to users are regulated. However, provincial and local governments can add surcharges. In 2000, electricity prices in rural areas were 45 per cent higher than in cities.[61] While the cost of supply in rural areas is higher than in urban areas, the government aims to equalise prices in the two types of areas.

Further structural change is planned. The State Council approved a plan to separate power generation from transmission and distribution in 1999. The longer-term plan is to introduce a "pool" system like the England and Wales system, where generators and consumers (at least large consumers) are able to sell and buy electricity.

Reforms are intended in regulation, too. Electricity has been regulated by administrative regulations. During the course of the Tenth Five Year Plan (2001-2005), a move toward greater use of economic regulation and market rules is planned.

Experience in OECD countries suggests that the plan to separate the competitive parts of the sector (generation, notably) from the natural monopoly parts (transmission and generation) is a major step toward successful reform. In making the separation, it will be important to ensure that there are indeed enough independent generating companies to provide effective competition, and to ensure that the buying side of the market has incentives to "push" the generators to compete. Hence, it is important that at least large consumers of electricity be free to switch among generators when seeking lower cost electricity. Since the transmission network is needed for all generators and users, access to it at fair and non-discriminatory terms is necessary for competition among generators. There are a number of design decisions that require technical coherence, such as the precise rules of the "pool" and the way in which "balancing" is performed. The structure and timing of reform and private investment are important to avoid the creation of excessive "stranded costs", such as long-term contracts that post-reform are rendered uneconomic and for which investors may need to be compensated. Finally, it is important for all of this to be overseen by a government body that is completely independent from the electricity companies.

Box 12.5. **Policy implications for reforms in electricity**

- In making the separation between generation on the one hand, and transmission and generation on the other, ensure that there are indeed enough independent generating companies to provide effective competition.
- Allow at least large consumers of electricity to be free to switch among generators when seeking lower cost electricity, so they can "push" the generators to compete.
- Ensure that access to the transmission network is at fair and non-discriminatory terms, so as to allow competition among generators.
- Ensure technical coherence of design decisions, such as the precise rules of the "pool" and the way in which "balancing" is performed.
- Structure and time reform and private investment so as not to create excessive "stranded costs", such as long-term contracts that are rendered uneconomic post-reform and for which investors may need to be compensated.
- Ensure that reform is overseen by a government body that is completely independent from the electricity companies.

- Telecommunications

Telecommunications in China are growing fast, with large investments and increases in the number of subscribers. The Ministry of Information Industry was established in 1998 as part of the separation of regulation from operation. China has committed to all the responsibilities contained in the WTO Reference Paper on pro-competitive regulatory principles.

China Telecom is the primary provider but China United Telecommunications Corporation ("Unicom") is the second telecommunications company. In addition, a few thousand carriers have been licensed to provide telecommunications services, of which over a hundred can provide inter-provincial services.

Competition in telecommunications in OECD countries has greatly reduced the cost of telecommunications services and accelerated the development and rollout of new technologies. Thus, developing effective competition should be the major objective of reform in this sector. In most countries, the issues for pro-competitive reform in telecommunications centre on re-balancing those tariffs that remain regulated, allowing new enterprises to enter into competition with the incumbent monopolist, providing access by competitors to certain facilities owned by the incumbent, and reducing customers' costs of switching between providers. Regulatory control over the sector has to be modified to control potential anti-competitive behaviour. Sometimes this takes the form of asymmetric regulation according to which the conduct by the incumbent is more tightly constrained than that of the entrants until the market power of the incumbent is sufficiently dissipated.

Tariff re-balancing is an issue only when regulation has been used to cross-subsidise a service and competition will be introduced in the services that had funded the cross-subsidy. In most OECD countries, local telecommunication service had been subsidised by long-distance and international services, and politically difficult tariff re-balancing had to begin before entry could reduce the price of long-distance and international services. Some countries have introduced a transparent surcharge to fund universal service in this sector.

Countries differed in how they introduced new entrants into the telecommunications sector. Some put in place a licensing regime where anyone who applies and meets the technical and legal standards is automatically given a license. Others have limited entry to only one or a designated number of entrants for each service. Experience in OECD countries is that a duopoly industrial structure in, for example, long-distance or mobile services, does not create effective competition. Thus, the trend is to grant licenses automatically and rapidly upon presentation of proof of meeting minimum standards. Of course, the exception is mobile operators where access to spectrum is necessary. Spectrum and mobile licenses are often but not always allocated according to competitive auction, a competition which is usually structured so as to allow additional entrants into the market. Some countries have allocated mobile licenses and spectrum by "beauty contests" where a number of attributes such as extent and coverage of promised investments, influence the allocation.

Entrants into telecommunications markets always need access to some of the facilities of the incumbent. Access that is delayed, degraded, or high-priced can be fatal to new entrants. Interconnection between networks can suffer the same shortcomings. Since the incumbent has an incentive to try to keep out entrants, it is important that, as a minimum, disputes about access and interconnection are rapidly and fairly resolved. Almost all countries regulate access and interconnection, and international practice has tended toward regulating access according to forward-looking long-run average incremental costs. This can be difficult to calculate, but the important features are that access prices are cost-based and do not protect the incumbent from its cost inefficiencies.

Regulation can reduce customers' costs of switching between providers. Allowing customers to keep their same telephone numbers when they switch providers ("number portability") means that small businesses, for example, do not have to bear the cost of informing their customers of their new number. Allowing customers to designate their "usual" provider and to change their designation ("carrier pre-selection") makes it easier to use other providers than the incumbent. Regulators must be alert to other means – for example, slow changes in the billing arrangements, "losing" requests to change providers – incumbents can use to hinder customers' switching. By making it harder for consumers to switch providers, the incumbent is able to discourage entry and the development of competition. It is for these reasons that incumbents are often subjected to tighter regulation than entrants, at least until the incumbents have lost some of their market dominance.

The broad experience in OECD Member countries in developing competition in telecommunications can be useful to China. In particular, establishing a licensing regime where licences are automatically granted when minimum standards set out in law or regulation are met, mandating access to certain facilities at regulated terms and conditions along with a rapid access dispute-settlement system, and ensuring that customers can in practice easily change telecommunications providers, will help in the development of competition in telecommunications.

Box 12.6.   **Policy implications for reforms in telecommunications**

- Establish a licensing regime where licences are automatically granted upon meeting minimum standards set out in law or regulation.
- Mandate access to certain facilities at regulated terms and conditions along with a rapid access dispute settlement system.
- Ensure that customers can in practice easily change telecommunications providers.

• Railways

Economic growth in China means that the already large rail system requires substantial further investment to relieve bottlenecks. A large fraction of freight and passengers in China is transported by rail. Revenues from user charges are insufficient for the required investment. The State Council sets charges, and rail services are provided directly by the Ministry of Railroads. Thus, in some respects reform of the rail sector lags reform in other sectors.

The major rail infrastructure projects in China are designed to relieve transport bottlenecks to allow greater economic development. It is estimated that the railways meet only 60 per cent of demand (at current prices).[62] The coastal region's boom has been constrained by limitations on coal supply, attributed to limited transport capacity and increased north-south transport of goods and raw materials. Thus, many projects aim to improve coal transport from northwest and southwest China to elsewhere in China. In addition, development of the rail system is seen as key to the economic development of the western and central areas.

Rail accounts for large fractions of total freight and passenger transport in China. Almost 40 per cent of freight and about 44 per cent of passengers were transported by rail.[63] Coal accounted for about 31 per cent of freight, other mining products 15 per cent, and oil four per cent.

Control over the Chinese rail system is highly centralised. The State Council sets the level of railway charges, including surcharges, and also approves rail construction plans as part of China's five-year development plan. Unlike the corresponding ministries for the electricity and telecommunications sectors, the Ministry of Railroads provides the railway infrastructure and services.

Foreign investment is limited in the Chinese rail system. The national rail system is not open to foreign direct investment but there is an emerging possibility that foreign investors may be allowed to own a stake in local railways. In any case, the absence of market-based pricing deters foreign investment at present.

The structure of the rail sector in other countries usually follows one of two basic models. The model followed in geographically larger OECD Member countries has vertically integrated rail companies, competing to provide services along alternative routes to the same centre. The rail companies own and operate the tracks, signalling, and associated infrastructure as well as owning and operating the trains. In regions where there are not competing rail companies or where competition is not provided by other transport modes, then the transport charges must be regulated. Rail companies may also negotiate to operate trains on the others' tracks, but this can result in monopoly pricing if not subject to state regulation or the threat of state regulation.

The second model is followed by most of the OECD Member countries that are also members of the European Union. These tend also to be geographically smaller countries, where road or water transport are often alternatives. In this model, trains are operated by a wholly owned subsidiary of the company that owns and operates the tracks and associated infrastructure, and the legal monopoly for operating trains is removed. In principle, this allows competition in train operation over the entire infrastructure, but in practice such competition has not yet developed. When the infrastructure and train operating companies have distinct economic incentives, it is more complicated simultaneously to provide economic incentives for efficient use of the existing network and for its efficient expansion and development.

The choice between models depends on the location of the rail tracks and the cost of resolving disputes between rail companies. Where alternative routes serve the same centres, then competition between vertically integrated rail companies can be feasible. Where the regulatory and legal structure is sufficiently mature for the cost of resolving disputes between the infrastructure and train-operating companies to be relatively low, then the vertically separated model can allow competition across much of the infrastructure. Consideration is being given to separating infrastructure from service and allowing competition in services in China. However, structural change of this type is probably several years away.

Whether trucks effectively compete against rail in freight transport is a major determinant of whether rail tariffs must be subject to state regulation. Demand for freight transport services is often differentiated on the basis of time-to-transport, variation in time-to-transport, and the ratio of weight or bulk to value. Thus, coal delivered to a power station has a high weight-to-value ratio, and the speed at which it is transported is less important than the variation in the transport time. (High variation means

417|

more and costlier inventory must be held at the power station.) In practice, in OECD countries it is sometimes necessary to regulate the tariffs for the transport of freight with high weight-to-value ratios, for which trucks cannot compete, but not to regulate tariffs for the transport of other freight, for which trucks provide effective competition.

Access to rail terminals that connect to sea transport or truck transport often requires regulation. Where the rail company is allowed to vertically integrate into sea or truck transport, it has incentives and the ability to discriminate against its sea or truck rivals. Sometimes sharing a terminal is feasible, but more often sharing is not feasible due to space and scheduling constraints. The constricted space and tight scheduling requirements make subtle discrimination possible. However, competing terminals owned by competing companies may be feasible only for large cities and ports.

A recurring issue in many countries is how to provide incentives to the rail company to make an efficient choice between self-provision of services and procurement, and to procure services effectively. While a "hard budget constraint" (so that the amount of transfer from the general budget does not vary with the rail company's deficit) is part of the answer, it is not the whole answer since the rail company can simply degrade its service. One country has entered into legally enforceable agreements with the state-owned rail company with performance standards and reporting requirements, and has specified those services that must be procured externally. It has regulations governing the procurement process to ensure it is competitive. More generally, rail companies are more efficient where there is competition between rail companies. This is partly because competition can force improvements in procurement practices.

Where there is a need to regulate, it is important to get the incentives right. That is, it is important that the rail company be provided with the economic incentives and regulations to achieve what is desired. For example, in the United Kingdom, the regulator rewarded the timeliness of train arrival. But by concentrating on this one measure, other important features of the rail system received relatively less attention so the network was allowed to run down. The economic incentives provided in one sector can have important effects in other sectors. For example, if the railway charges a price lower than the cost of transporting coal, then these subsidies distort trade in coal; it might be cheaper in China to import coal to east coast ports. Among the costs to consider are additional maintenance costs and the opportunity cost of passenger and other, higher-value, freight transport.

The development of the rail sector is important in the overall economic development of China. The shortfall between revenues and government transfers, on the one hand, and the cost of the rail system including building new infrastructure, on the other hand, can be addressed by re-examining the charges and the costs of the system. Putting into place incentives for efficiency may well reveal wide scope for improvement. Separation of commerce from regulation would be an early step. One part of this separation could be a contract between the government and the railway in which services and financial transfers would be specified. Finally, whether competition would be a means to increase efficiency, which model of competition would be best, and whether the same model would be appropriate for the entire rail network, depend on developments in the economic and legal environment in China, and the infrastructure.

Box 12.7.   **Policy implications for reforms of railways**

- The development of the rail sector is important in the overall economic development of China. Re-examine the charges and the costs of the system to address the shortfall between revenues and government transfers, on the one hand, and the cost of the rail system including building new infrastructure, on the other hand.
- Put into place incentives for efficiency. Separation of commerce from regulation would be an early step in this direction.
- Evaluate the advantages and disadvantages of the two models – competing vertically integrated rail companies or unified infrastructure and competing train operating companies – for the various regions of China.

• Gas

Most natural gas in China is used to produce fertiliser and petrochemicals rather than being burned directly to generate electricity. Plans to increase the proportion of gas-fired generation and to build the infrastructure to deliver the gas would introduce natural monopoly characteristics into the sector and raise competition issues centred on access to pipelines and other natural monopolies.

Natural gas has not, traditionally, been a major energy source in China. Natural gas accounts for only about 2 per cent of energy used, and about 3 per cent of electricity generation. About 60 per cent of natural gas is used to make fertiliser and petrochemicals. However, China plans to increase significantly the share of natural gas in energy supply, so that the share of natural gas will increase to 6 per cent by 2010 and to 10 per cent by 2020. Among the goals for the gas sector in the Tenth Five Year Plan are to create markets for gas, to improve gas transport infrastructure, and to formulate gas-pricing policies that are attractive to investors and gas consumers.

The International Energy Agency notes that obstacles to the development of gas include small and distant proven reserves, lack of infrastructure, high cost relative to alternative fuels, and lack of coherent government policy towards the natural gas industry.

Limited gas transport infrastructure means that there is no national gas market and gas prices vary significantly from city to city. Two major gas transport projects are almost under way, a west-to-east gas pipeline and a LNG (liquefied natural gas) import facility in Guangdong. Foreign investment is allowed up to 100 per cent of any joint venture related to gas pipeline construction or city gas networks. Experience in OECD countries shows that new gas transport facilities can reduce market fragmentation and substantially reduce variations in prices between regions.

Access to gas transport infrastructure is the main competition concern in natural gas markets in OECD Member countries. Competition can develop in the exploitation of gas fields, the retail supply of gas to businesses and consumers, and gas storage facilities. However, gas pipelines – both high-pressure transmission and low-pressure distribution – and re-gasification plants for liquefied natural gas are usually natural monopolies to which gas producers and gas retail suppliers require access. Increasingly in OECD Member countries, however, coalitions of shippers contract in advance to use a specified capacity of a gas pipeline before it is built; in essence, they share the natural monopoly. On the other hand, the economic feasibility of a pipeline may sometimes rest upon the owner's having exclusive rights to the pipeline or the right to charge an unregulated access tariff. Decisions about whether the State should mandate access under an "essential facilities doctrine" are normally taken on a case-by-case basis, bearing in mind the possible chilling effects on future investments of mandating access.

Natural gas is subject to a number of different pricing policies in China. Some gas is sold under the "centralised allocation and sale" system, under which the SDPC allocates a production quota to each producer and a consumption quota to each major consumer and sets a very low price. Another system, introduced in 1987, allows above-quota gas to be sold at prices within 10 per cent of a specified level. A third system, introduced in 1997, allows producers and consumers to fix prices through negotiations. (The 1997 "new-line new price" system was introduced to encourage new gas field development and new pipeline construction.) Today, the central government controls wellhead, mid-stream, and downstream prices, while municipal authorities set final end-user prices.

It is not unprecedented for gas extracted from the same field and passing through the same pipeline to be subject to different regulatory regimes. However, this type of price regulation causes inefficiency and waste. Prices in a competitive market for gas at a single location will not necessarily be identical, but regulation that imposes different prices for comparable transactions means that some gas that could be directed to a higher value use is being directed instead to a lower value use. This type of price regulation should be reformed so that identical transactions are treated identically.

The regulatory regime applied to the gas sector influences both investment in infrastructure and the subsequent development of competition and markets in the gas sector. After a regulatory institution is established, it should ensure that when it mandates access to pipelines, re-gasification plants, and other gas infrastructure, due account is taken of the possible discouragement of subsequent investments as well as effects on competition. Difficulties in regulating access to the infrastructure could be reduced by sharing agreements, though the legal infrastructure must be able to support such complex agreements. The existing multiplicity of regulations applied to the price of gas can impede efficient use of gas and, over the longer term, efficient investments in the sector and downstream sectors such as electricity generation. Thus, a coherent policy toward gas pricing should be developed.

Box 12.8. **Policy implications for reforms in gas**

- Establish a regulatory institution.
- When access to pipelines, re-gasification plants, and other gas infrastructure is mandated, ensure that due account is taken of the possible discouragement of subsequent investments as well as effects on competition.
- Develop a coherent policy toward gas pricing, treating similar transactions similarly.

Policy options

The basic policy framework applied in China to many of these sectors is moving away from government directly administering and providing the services. This is a positive development. In countries throughout the world, much of the infrastructure sectors are subjected to a policy framework that combines market competition and economic regulation.

The relationship between competition and economic regulation in these sectors is central to gaining efficiency. Many OECD countries, as well as developing countries, allow or create competition in the potentially competitive part of infrastructure industries, allowing free entry as well as freeing the prices of the competitively offered service. The idea is that competition will create pressure for efficiency and for satisfying consumers' wishes in terms of service quality and variety. Usually, access to the essential facility or natural monopoly (such as the electricity transmission grid or gas transmission lines) is regulated by the government.

In most OECD Member countries, most regulated industries are subject to the general competition law, enforced by the general competition authority. This ensures that competition is protected wherever it is feasible in an economy, and that the competition principles remain harmonised and predictable across industries. It is important that the economic regulatory authority and the competition authority work together. In this way, the competition authority can advise the regulator on which regulations help or harm competition. And the regulatory authority can achieve regulatory goals at lower overall cost to society.

Conclusions, recommendations, and policy options

This chapter's conclusions on the importance of competition law and policy in China and related recommendations are largely based on the OECD's institutional expertise from work with Members and non-Member countries. They also benefit from four years of competition law and policy co-operation with China. The policy implications are as follows.

1. In order to combat exclusionary conduct by enterprises and local governments to create new barriers replacing those removed by the central government's trade and investment liberalisation programme, China should:
   - Enact and implement a competition law, along the lines of the one being developed by the State Economic and Trade Commission and State Administration for Industry and Commerce,

that bans abuses of dominance, anti-competitive agreements, anti-competitive mergers, and "administrative monopoly". *The need for such a law is not fully realised in China, due in part to a tendency to underestimate the extent of Chinese enterprises' monopoly power. Moreover, the concern of some that the law would interfere with promoting national champions is misplaced. The most urgent need is to provide a legal basis for halting exclusionary conduct that will create new barriers to international and domestic trade and investment. The most urgent provisions, therefore, are a general ban on abuse of dominance, a general ban on hard-core cartels, and a ban with real sanctions to stop administrative monopoly.*

- Until a competition law is enacted, devote increased attention and resources to enforcing existing competition-related laws. *Enforcement of the Unfair Competition Law and the Price Law should increase, and preparation of implementing regulations for the Price Law should be expedited. If there is delay in enacting the competition law, China should consider amending the Unfair Competition Law to add a general ban on abuse of dominance and real sanctions to stop administrative monopoly, and amending the Price Law to add a general ban on hard-core cartels.*

- Apply competition law and other relevant laws to strike down regional protectionism that restricts the movement of goods, services, and capital within China. *Due in part to enforcement by the SAIC, "regional blockades" may have fallen off in recent years, but regional protectionism requires continuing and substantial attention. In this regard, regional restrictions on investment can be as damaging to competition as direct restrictions on the shipment of products.*

2. In order to remove legal barriers that impede realisation of the benefits of trade and investment liberalisation, China should:

- Continue economic reform aimed at reducing remaining barriers to entry and exit, together with other restrictions that maintain uneven playing fields. *Initial attention should focus on explicit barriers based on the form or ownership of an enterprise, together with unnecessarily burdensome requirements to opening a new business or reorganising an existing one.*

- Adopt a national competition policy that calls upon all parts and levels of government to review regulations that impose entry barriers and eliminate those found to be unwarranted. *The policy would not place competition above other regulatory or social goals, but rather provide a tool to help ensure that the pursuit of such goals is not more costly than necessary. The central government should take the lead both by its actions and by preparing guidelines for local governments.*

- Address its current problem of overcapacity by reforms aimed at the subsidies, soft loans, exit barriers, and other non-market policies that created it and that permit enterprises owned or favoured by government entities to continue operations in markets where they are not among the most efficient producers. *To the extent that such enterprises are being operated to prevent hardship from unemployment, China should focus on alternative policies, including direct subsidies to the unemployed, that would not create so much economic waste and impede realisation of the benefits of trade and investment liberalisation.*

- Use competition policy principles in designing and implementing reform of infrastructure industries that have natural monopoly characteristics.

NOTES

1. The tendency of planned economies to focus on productive (or "technical") and allocative inefficiency is discussed in Lin, Justin Yifu, F. Cai, and Z. Li, (1998), "Competition, policy burdens, and state-owned enterprise reform," *The American Economic Review*, May 1998.

2. This chapter does not address distinctions between "consumer welfare" and "total welfare". To greater or lesser degrees, most competition law systems also have other goals, such as ensuring the existence of a large number of competitors or protecting small business. In general, however, it is increasingly recognised that such goals sometimes conflict with the "aggregate welfare' goal, and that competition principles (and the authorities that implement them) are not well suited to resolving such conflicts. Similarly, some systems include a "public interest' standard that can raise similar issues. Thus, there is a tendency in OECD countries to focus on economic efficiency (aggregate welfare) as the main criteria in competition laws and to deal with other social goals in separate laws.

3. OECD (2000), *Hard Core Cartels*, Paris.

4. OECD (1997), *Report on Regulatory Reform Summary*, Paris.

5. Two China/OECD conferences have focused on China's draft competition law. The first was held in Beijing in November 1998, the second in Shanghai in December 1999. China's State Economic and Trade Commission, with some assistance from the OECD, arranged for the publication by the Publishing House of the Peoples' Court of a collection of papers delivered at or relating to those conferences. Most papers are only in Chinese.

6. In the United States and some other countries, it is not considered an illegal abuse for a monopolist to exercise its power by restricting output and charging monopoly high prices. This reflects the fact that in a competitive economy with few barriers to entry, charging monopoly prices generally encourages entry that can eliminate the monopoly power. In such economies, banning "monopoly high pricing' would mean creating a complex regulatory system that would tend to preserve the industry's monopolistic structure. In the European Union and some of its Member States and other countries, the law bans monopoly high pricing but the ban is rarely applied because doing so would prolong the monopoly. In transition and developing countries, however, capital market problems and other barriers mean that competition authorities cannot rely to the same extent on new entry to defeat monopoly pricing. In such situations, competition authorities are generally advised to seek to eliminate the entry barriers, but if that cannot be done they sometimes find themselves obliged to engage in a form of price regulation for which they are not well equipped.

7. OECD (1998), *Council Recommendation on Effective Action against Hard Core Cartels*. The Recommendation also provides that "the hard core cartel category does not include agreements, concerted practices, or arrangements that *i)* are reasonably related to the lawful realisation of cost-reducing or output-enhancing efficiencies, *ii)* are excluded directly or indirectly from the coverage of a Member country's own laws, or *iii)* are authorised in accordance with those laws." In addition to hard-core cartels, resale price maintenance is quite often subject to stricter standards or treated as automatically illegal.

8. Dutz, Mark A., and M. Vagliasindi, (1999), "Competition Policy implementation in transition countries: an empirical assessment", *European Economic Review*, Vol. 44, Nos. 4-6.

9. Moreover, even when conduct is banned without regard to its market effects – so economic differences are not automatically taken into account – there are relatively few variations because most countries that provide for automatic (or *per se*) illegality confine it to a few practices that are always or nearly always anti-competitive.

10. OECD (1992) *Regulatory Reform, Privatisation and Competition Policy*, Paris, at 13. *See also* OECD (1993), *Competition Policy and a Changing Broadcast Industry*, Paris; OECD (1990), *Competition Policy and the Deregulation of Road Transport*, Paris; OECD (1985), *Competition Policy and the Professions*, Paris; OECD (1979), *Competition Policy in Regulated Sectors with Special Reference to Energy, Transport and Banking*, Paris.

11. Among the roundtable reports of greatest potential interest to China are: *Relations between Regulators and Competition Authorities, Promoting Competition in the Natural Gas Industry, Railways: Structure, Regulation and Competition Policy, Application of Competition Policy to the Electricity Sector, Competition in Telecommunications, Developments in Telecommunications: An Update, Competition and Regulation in Broadcasting in the Light of Convergence, Competition and Related Regulation Issues in the Insurance Industry, Enhancing the Role of Competition in the Regulation of Banks, Promoting*

Competition in Postal Services, and *Competition in Local Services: Solid Waste Management*. Other relevant reports are: *Competition in Professional Services, Airline Mergers and Alliances, Competition Policy and Procurement Markets, Competition Policy and Intellectual Property Rights, Competition Policy and International Airport Services*, and *Competition Policy and Environment*.

12. As China's socialist market economy makes its transition and becomes more developed, it may be useful for both Chinese policy-makers and foreign observers to bear in mind two basic rationales for the adoption by governments of differing rules and policies, which may be called *market differences* and *value differences*. Like other transition and developing countries, China has many market differences from the most competitive OECD economies. Real market differences sometimes warrant different law enforcement or regulatory policies, but experience has also shown that proponents of the *status quo* often seek to justify their positions by pointing to irrelevant market differences. Competition policy can be used directly to assess when market differences justify policy differences from an efficiency perspective. Competition policy's role is useful but less directly so when deciding whether value differences (such as those reflected in China's conception of a socialist market economy) justify policy differences. Thus, competition policy may assist in calculating the cost of adopting a restriction on enterprise conduct in order to promote a social value (*e.g.* Sunday closing laws in Christian countries); it neither contributes to nor interferes with the value judgement that must in the end be made.

13. Beyond this, pricing in all markets is subject to the government's "macro" control, under which Article 27 of the Law says that the "government may establish an essential commodities reserve system and establish a price regulatory fund to regulate prices and stabilise the market." Moreover, in temporary emergencies, the State Council may take emergency measures to control prices and interest rates.

    The "vital commodities" category is very unclear but apparently includes the prices of natural gas and crude oil, and the purchase price of grain and cotton. "Rare resources" may not extend much beyond the purchase price of gold and silver. The "natural monopolies" and "utilities" categories are unclear in that they would appear to overlap. "Essential non-profit services" apparently refers to public services such as schools, hospitals, and parks. *New Pricing Law Follows Market Rules, Global News Network, Financial Times Information*, 30 April 1998.

14. "Government-Set Prices", *The China Business Review, Asia Intelligence Wire*, September 1998.

15. *Price Setting: New Prices for Old, China Economic Review, Global News Wire, Financial Times Information*, 23 November 1998.

16. Daniel H. Rosen, *Behind the Open Door: Foreign Enterprises in the Chinese Marketplace*, Institute for International Economics (Washington, DC, 1999).

17. The lack of a level playing field is reflected in the fact that one foreign insurer, AIA, is already allowed to operate without forming joint ventures and may sell more products, in more cities, than other foreign enterprises. "Insurer celebrates its foothold in mainland China", *Financial Times*, 20 February 2001.

18. "Non-State firms should play bigger role", *China Daily*, 20 February 2001, at 4.

19. An editorial in a monthly magazine published by China's Ministry of Foreign Trade and Economic co-operation recently condemned this situation as "an accident waiting to happen". *China International Business*, February 2001, at 3. It has been suggested that an unreformed investment mechanism is the main factor tilting China towards patterns typical of planned rather than market economies. Rawski, Thomas G., *China's move to market: How far? What next?*, 25 October 1999.

20. Lang, Larry H.P., and R. W. So, A *Survey of Banking in East Asia*, 31 January 2001. There have been calls for breaking up these four banks to permit competition. *e.g.* Reformist *Calls for Break-up of Big Four*, 8 February 1998.

21. An article that clearly identifies the role of exit barriers in China's overcapacity problems and also outlines other competition-related aspects of China's economic restructuring is Liu Shijin, "Proposed Measures for Strategic Economic Restructuring in China," *China Development Review*, Development Research Centre, July 2000.

22. The classic treatment of these trade wars in the 1980s is Wedeman (1995), *Bamboo Walls and Brick Ramparts*. See also Bing Song, "Competition policy in a transitional economy: the case of China," 31 Stanford L. J. 387, 405-11 (1995) (*e.g.* security bureau opened two firecracker shops while withdrawing the licenses of other shop owners; tax bureau opened restaurant and doubled tax of all competitors; province forbade local firms from buying 19 kinds of products from other provinces; local government required retailers show that at least 30 per cent of sales were locally made).

    An often-used example of such "regional blockades' is a 1999 Shanghai regulation imposing a much higher license plate fee on anyone buying any car other than one manufactured by the local Shanghai/German joint venture. A neighbouring province adopted a discriminatory fee of its own, and the "battle of the cars' attracted significant public attention. These regulations apparently violated the Unfair Competition Law and various other provisions but were not challenged under them. That particular matter was eventually resolved, as have other similar ones; in 2000, Chongqing, the largest industrial city in the west, repealed the additional fees it imposed on cars made in other provinces. *The legislative autonomy of the localities in China, China Perspectives*, No. 32, November-December 2000, at P16.

423

23. "Catch up by raising efficiency", *China Daily*, 17 January 2000; "Mergers make it better", *China Daily*, 22 March 2000.

24. "Local barriers stunt national trade", *China Daily*, 3 July 2000.

25. At a 1999 China/OECD conference in Shanghai, Mr. Wang Jaifu, a Member of the Standing Committee of the National Peoples' Congress, stated that a competition law would not ban mergers to achieve minimum efficient scale.

26. "Market Research Sector Survives Tough Legislation", *Reuters Business Briefing*, Economist Intelligence Unit, 3 August 2000.

27. *The Legislative Autonomy of the Localities in China*, China Perspectives, No. 32, November-December 2000, at 16.

28. Legislative ambiguity has sometimes played a positive role in bringing about pro-competitive reform of China's markets. At the central government level, deliberate ambiguity has sometimes permitted reformers to achieve *de facto* liberalisation where explicit *de jure* liberalisation may have been impossible.

29. Id. See also "The New PRC Legislation Law – The Emperor's New Clothes?", *Reuters Business Briefing*, 16 June 2000, Peter Cone, Consultant, Simmons and Simmons, Shanghai.

30. IIE P219.

31. See generally Holden, John L., "China's modernisation: The role of competition", Harvard University Asia Centre, 26 March 1999. On the importance of inter-regional competition and the problem that inter-regional disputes are handled by regional courts, see Li, Shaomin, Shuhe Li, and Weiying Zhang, "The road to capitalism: competition and institutional change in China", 28 J. of Comp. Econ. 269 (2000).

32. Sarah Biddulph, "Enhancing China's rule of law: supposedly yes but how", Asian Law Centre, University of Melbourne.

33. Id.

34. "A duty delegated by people", *China Daily*, 23 February 2001.

35. "Move to deter protectionism", China Daily, December 2, 1999.

36. IIE P208.

37. World Bank Country Study, *China: Internal Market Development and Regulation* (1994) (hereinafter WB). *See also* Bing Song, "Competition Policy in a Transitional Economy: the Case of China", 31 Stanford L. J. 387, 394-400 (1995).

38. WB P xviii.

39. Id. at 145. See also p. 138, where the report says that a competition law with merger-review provisions focusing on preventing undue market power would not be called for until after some of the more serious constraints on mergers had been removed.

40. WB P146.

41. WB P159.

42. The point can be illustrated by two simple examples. First, an enterprise may be one of many Chinese producers of a product but nonetheless have monopoly power. It may have such power either a) because it is the only seller in a geographic market that is less than national, or b) because its product is in a separate product market due to some feature that makes it uniquely valuable to certain buyers. By the same token, the only producer in China of a product does not necessarily have monopoly power. It will not have such power if Chinese buyers can a) buy the same product made by a foreign producer (*i.e.* the geographic market is international), or b) substitute other products (*i.e.* other goods are in the same product market).

43. Gary H. Jefferson and Thomas G. Rawski, "How Industrial Reform Worked in China: the Role of Innovation, Competition, and Property Rights", at n.8.

44. See, *e.g.*, "Anti-monopoly Law Crucial for Economy", *China Daily*, Financial Times Information Global News Wire, March 18, 1999 (distinguishing between "strong administrative monopolies, inherited from a planned economy", and "economic monopolies, [which] are not particularly prevalent in China at present") (and ignoring the fact that monopolies protected by administrative power can and do have real economic monopoly power when their statutory monopoly approximates or includes a relevant market). Another news report uses the term administrative monopoly to refer not to all statutory monopolies, but only to the monopolies in those infrastructure sectors that have natural monopoly characteristics. Reuters Business Briefing, 27 June 2000. See also "Antitrust Through the Eyes of a legal Scholar", Reuters News Service, 14 September 1998:

"Two kinds of monopoly exist in China: A) Administrative monopoly, wherein 1) the government monopolises some industries, interferes with state-owned enterprises, and even establishes companies itself; 2) the government places barriers upon industry admittance; and 3) local governments protect local enterprises from competing against outside enterprises; and B) economic monopoly whereby 1) excessive advantage of dominant market positions are taken; 2) over-centralisation of economic powers occurs during mergers, take-overs and/or regrouping; and 3) monopolistic agreements between oligarchies are formed (*e.g.* China Unicom and China Telecom)."

45. Some of the anecdotal evidence about markets in China is structural and conclusory. For example, it is reported that the People's Insurance Company of China has an 85 per cent share of insurance sold in Sichuan. "PICC Opens Hotline for Customers", *Reuters Business Briefing*, 7 February 2000. (It is typical of news reporting in China that this story contains both this astronomical "market share" data and a quotation referring to "white hot" competition in the insurance field.) Also, smugglers are said to have a "quasi-monopoly" for rubber and for diesel fuel in one area, a claim that is given some credibility from the fact that anti-smuggling campaigns apparently affected market prices even outside smuggling centres. Hans Hendrischke, "Smuggling and Border Trade on the South China Sea Coast", *China Perspectives*, No. 32, November-December 2000, at 26. Other anecdotal evidence stems from innumerable reports of monopoly abuses and cartel conduct. See, *e.g.*, "Measures to be Taken to Curb Price Cartel", *Global News Wire, Financial Times Information*, 9 August 1999 ("Wu Hanlong, an economics professor with the Beijing-based Renmin University of China, said he believed that the government stepped in [against cartels] because cartels, backed by industrial associations, have already failed to [solve] pricing problems. ... Until last week, ... nearly all industrial sectors that face a glutted market have resorted to price cartels.")

46. The Civil Aviation Administration of China has attempted to prevent what has been claimed to be destructive competition by forcing the airlines to reduce service, raise prices and stop offering price discounts, but its attempts at price fixing apparently failed when some airlines refused to go along with its plan. As discussed above, the price competition in the airline industry was once common in OECD countries on the theory that this was necessary to prevent destructive competition. That approach has been abandoned, however, and recent economic thinking has pointed out that the key to addressing destructive competition is to eliminate the exit barriers or other market distortions that permit it.

47. For example, one of China's television manufacturers at one point secured exclusive control over most television tubes manufactured in China. "Information Ministry Undecided Over Television Tube Monopoly", *Global News Wire*, Financial Times Information, 4 December 1998. That control apparently did not endure, and later eight tube manufacturers with 80-90 per cent of the market agreed to halt production for a month in order to raise prices; there are conflicting reports on the success of that cartel. "Output Halt Not A Wise Choice", *China Daily*, 3 June 1999. Price fixing agreements among the television manufacturers have not lasted long, which is perhaps to be expected in a sector with large overcapacity when no manufacturer has left the market in the past two years. "TV industry's price war has no winner", *Business Weekly*, 14 August 2001. See "SDPC Has No Plans to Curb Price-Fixing by TV Manufacturers", *Global News Wire*, Financial Times Information, 12 June 2000. An official from the Ministry of Information Industry initially supported this agreement to set minimum prices, "China TV Firms' Price-Fixing Agreement Does Not Break Price Law", *Global News Service*, Financial Times Information, 12 June 2000, but the Ministry later said that it violated the Price Law. "China MII Rules Price Fixing by 9 TV Makers Illegal", *Global News Wire*, Financial Times Information, 8 August 2000. (It is unclear why the Ministry of Information Industry, rather than the SDPC made this decision.)

A day after the SDPC liberalised gold jewellery prices (August 2001), several firms reduced prices and there was talk of charging by the piece (rather than by weight), thus creating a real jewellery market (rather than having simply a gold market). But an official of the Shanghai Gold Jewellery Association immediately announced its intent to "bring some discipline to the field", and an official of the World Gold Council offered the view that "The liberalisation of the gold jewellery price does not mean that the retailer can decide to price according to his own wish". "No more precious metal", *Hong Kong Edition*, 10 August 2001.

48. Li Jianzhong, *The Constantly Perfecting Legal System of Competition in China'* October 2000. See also Wang Lei, *Perfecting Competition Legal System in China*, October 1999.

49. See Snell, Steven L. (1999), "The development of competition policy in the People's Republic of China," 28 N.Y.U. J.Int'l L. & Pol. 575.

50. "Government-Set Prices", *The China Business Review, Asia Intelligence Wire*, September 1998.

51. See also "Curbing Unethical Competition", *China Daily*, Financial Times Information, 25 November 1998. "China Collects $100 million Fines for Unfair Trade Practices", *China Business Information Network*, Financial Times Information Global News Wire, 26 November 1998.

52. *See* Wang Yuankuo and M. J. Davison, "The law combating unfair competition in China: an approach to competition in a transitional eEconomy", 5 *Trade Practices L.J.* 88 (1997).

53. See, *e.g.* Sarah Reynolds, "Addressing Russia's economic crisis: open markets, public trust, and competition policy," OECD *Journal of Competition Law and Policy*, Vol. 1, No. 2 (1999).

54. "Officials: Water prices to increase", *China Daily*, 21 February 2001.

55. "China creates alumina monolith", *China Daily*, 24 February 2001.

56. Where several regulatory institutions are active in the same sector, *e.g.* national and regional levels of government, then responsibilities should be clearly delineated and a mechanism for developing common policies should be developed.

57. The term "natural monopoly" can be misused. For example, where rail and trucks compete to provide transport services to the same customers for the same loads, then clearly the rail company is not a natural monopoly in those markets. In the market for the transport of coal, however, the rail company very likely is a natural monopoly.

58. In 1998-99, however, there was oversupply of electric power in parts of the country due in part to slower Chinese economic growth and in part to demand reductions from closures of inefficient state-owned industrial units. (US Department of Energy, Energy Information Administration, 2001.)

59. *People's Daily*, January 11, 2001.

60. *People's Daily*, June 7, 2000.

61. *China Daily*, August 8, 2000

62. Pan and Pan, p. 66; Zhang p. 256 for Beijing-Guangzhuo line southern section.

63. Zhang p. 247 citing "Zhongguo Jichu Jianshe" Chinese Infrastructure Construction, Peregrine, Hong Kong, May 1994.

BIBLIOGRAPHY

APEC (1998),
"Reports on Recent Regulatory and Policy Developments: The People's Republic of China", Miyazaki, Japan, 10-13 March 1999 Telecommunications and Information Working Group (TEL), at *www.apecsec.org.sg/* on 9 August 2001.

China Daily (2000),
"Rural Consumers Need More Power, Water, TV Antennas", August 8.

People's Daily (2000),
"China strengthens international energy co-operation", June 7.

People's Daily (2000),
"Restructure in power sector urged", October 10.

People's Daily (2001),
"Four Nuclear Power Stations to Generate Electricity in Next Five Years", January 11.

Pan, Zhihong and Pan, Chi (1999),
Investing in China: Questions and Answers. Beijing: Foreign Language Press.

Rosen, Daniel H. (1999),
Behind the Open Door: Foreign Enterprises in the Chinese Marketplace, Institute for International Economics (Washington, DC).

Song, Bing (1995),
"Competition policy in a transitional economy: the case of China", 31 *Stanford* L. J. 387.

Zhang, Gang (1996),
"Rail Aid to China" in Marie Söderberg, eds, *The Business of Japanese Foreign Aid: Five Case Studies from Asia,* pp. 245-276. London: Routledge.

US Department of Energy, Energy Information Administration (2001),
"China Country Analysis Brief", *www.eia.doe.gov/emeu/cabs/china.html* on 24 July.

Chapter 13

ESTABLISHING EFFECTIVE GOVERNANCE FOR CHINA'S ENTERPRISES

TABLE OF CONTENTS

ESTABLISHING EFFECTIVE GOVERNANCE FOR CHINA'S ENTERPRISES[*]

Introduction

Trade and investment liberalisation (TIL) is expected to yield substantial welfare gains in the corporate sector, while at the same time it may stimulate adjustments on a large scale. Most importantly, trade and investment liberalisation is expected to impact on incentives for the corporate sector and bring about sustainable changes in the state and non-state sectors at the national and provincial levels. Efficiency of resource allocation (through increased specialisation according to China's comparative advantage) can be enhanced if the corporate sector is ready to adapt to a liberalised environment and the state institutions in charge of reforming it are in a position to speed up the process.

This chapter takes stock of certain framework conditions for the functioning of the corporate sector and attempts to analyse the impact of trade and investment liberalisation on their development in the future. More specifically, it examines some key aspects of the current legal and institutional framework of the Chinese corporate sector along with current developments in the corporate governance environment, and attempts to identify future policy options and concrete recommendations.

The legal and regulatory conditions of the Chinese corporate sector determine, to a great extent, its capacity to reap the benefits of its competitive advantages. The Chinese authorities have been proactive in amending the legal framework conditions of the corporate sector. Important legal reforms have led to clearer "rules of the game" for transactions and contractual relationships, greater business autonomy through corporatisation and better definition of the company as a legal entity, as well as a more comprehensive framework governing market exit.

In spite of marked progress in all these areas, China's accession to the rule-based WTO world requires further commitment to the reform of the legal and institutional framework, and a substantial effort at better implementation of existing rules. Important distortions need to be addressed in order to achieve coherence among commercial legal acts and their interpretation and enforcement at the central and local level, in order to establish a cohesive framework for the definition and recognition of property rights, in order to ensure the orderly exit of enterprises that have failed the market test.

Sound governance of Chinese enterprises is essential for its successful adjustment to a more competitive environment by improving access to low-cost financing through capital markets as well as long-term profitability and vitality. As a consequence of the positive trend towards greater commercial initiative in China, corporate governance has been significantly enhanced during the last few years. Of critical importance in the near future, however, is to address the intrinsic flaws in corporate governance of state-owned entities, stemming from their complex, multi-layer ownership and control structures, involving conflicting objectives, blurring the role of the state as a shareholder and regulator, and restricting its monitoring capacity. Accelerating the process of ownership diversification is important, as the potential gains for China are much larger than in other countries, given the large size of state holdings and the correspondingly high costs of monitoring by the state. Moreover, the state directly or indirectly controls almost 70 per cent of every single Chinese listed company.

More broadly, enhancing the credibility of the capital market as a corporate finance tool by a more open attitude towards foreign investors, by allowing and properly regulating the operation of private asset managers and other intermediaries; and by increasing the free float through further state sales, constitute an important incentive for companies to improve governance.

---

[*] This Chapter has been prepared by Stilpon Nestor, Head of Division, and Elena Miteva, Administrator of the Corporate Affairs Division of the Directorate for Financial, Fiscal and Enterprise Affairs, OECD.

The overall legal and institutional framework of the corporate sector in China

A coherent modern legal framework and well functioning implementing institutions are important elements in the sound development of the corporate sector in China. During the Cultural Revolution, the country's sophisticated legal traditions were abandoned, the lawyers and judges changed professions, and the courts were closed. From 1978, therefore, China had to make important efforts in legal reform. In the 1980s and 1990s, milestones with respect to the enterprise sector included new statutes for property, companies, commercial transactions (contracts), and bankruptcy.

The framework for contract law

The framework for contract law is a cornerstone for the legal framework of the corporate sector. Contractual relationships, if based on market principles, contribute to the efficient allocation of goods and hence, supply and demand should be the driving forces in determining contractual conditions. The legal framework of contracts should therefore be based upon the arm's length principle and should safeguard the enforceability of the rights and duties arising out of contractual relations. A comprehensive and stable contractual framework is important not only for the exchange of goods, services, and capital. Well-defined contractual relations are essential for the very existence of the company, for dealings in its shares, for decision-making, and as such, they serve as a facilitator of good corporate governance. The impact of the contractual relationship system on stakeholders might be even greater, as an effective contract law is a precondition for the protection of their rights.

Important steps have already been taken by the Chinese legislature in order to provide for a Contract Law that is broadly in line with these basic requirements.[1] The new Unified Contract Law (UCL)[2] that came into force on 1 October 1999 abolished the former system of contract laws characterised by too stringent regulation and a scattered, often conflicting, set of legislative rules.[3] Key improvements include:

- Uniformity is enhanced in several respects by the UCL. It creates a uniform legal framework at the national level by suppressing the possibility for local governments to modify those rules, and also eliminates previous artificial distinctions between the status of the contractual parties (*i.e.* private versus state-owned) and different categories of subject matter. However, it should be noted that the law still provides that if other regulations govern specific provisions in a contract, such provisions should prevail.

- The new law is the PRC's first comprehensive step to promote contractual freedom. It sets forth the principles of equal standing of the parties and the right of the parties to enter into contracts voluntarily "without any illegal intervention of work unit of individuals". However, there is no definition of what constitutes such illegal interference.

- The principle of freedom of contract is underlined by a number of specific provisions. For instance, the UCL contains mostly elective provisions that provide a fallback for when parties do not explicitly state their preferences. This gives the contractual parties the flexibility to stipulate their agreements according to their needs. The UCL also sets forth that contracts are generally based on offer and acceptance, as opposed to the formal procedures required under the earlier legislation. The UCL also introduces the concept of voidable contracts, thus giving the parties the freedom to continue the contracts despite their defects.

- The UCL provides for various market-based means to protect the interests of creditors, which have, in particular, been granted the right to unilateral termination or rescission of the contract in the event of a breach of contract. Additionally, the rules concerning consequential damages (*i.e.* those damages or those losses which do not arise immediately from the breach of the contract, but in consequence of such an act,) have been adapted to market economy standards.

The Contract Law is now broadly in line with the UNIDROIT Principles of International Commercial Contracts and consequently, the basic legal preconditions for trade and investment liberalisation seem to be set.[4] However, the new Chinese contract law still has important shortcomings, which could hamper the functioning of the corporate sector. For example, Article 38 of the UCL might erode market economy principles to a large extent, because it allows for parties to be forced into a contract. The provision reads: "Where the state has, in light of its requirements, issued a mandatory plan or state purchase order, the relevant legal persons and other organisations shall enter into a contract based on the rights and obligations of the parties prescribed by the relevant laws and administrative regulations." This does not entirely clarify the legal consequences of governmental organisations acting as contracting parties, given that the meaning of "state order purchase" is unclear. It might, if read broadly, even imply that, in spite of Article 2, the principles of the UCL are not applicable at all for Government contracts.[5]

The company as a legal entity and the notion of corporate ownership

In light of the greater competition stemming from trade and investment liberalisation, the Chinese authorities have carried out a series of measures aiming to enhance the autonomy of the corporate sector. A large part of these efforts was based on changes in the way companies are defined as legal entities. The Company Law, which was adopted only in 1993,[6] provides the national legal basis for the organisation and establishment of "limited liability companies" and "limited liability stock companies" (also translated as joint-stock companies). It requires SOEs that are converting into companies to inventory assets, to define property rights and to prepare themselves to be independent and self-sufficient entities. According to the law, companies are to conduct management independently and to carry sole responsibility for gains and losses. It also provides for mergers of enterprises. It enshrines fundamental legal concepts including the rights of shareholders, the powers of managers and the boards of directors and, thus, sets forth the basis of the Chinese corporate governance system (see Box 13.1).

Enterprises that exist as separate legal entities with their own commercial objectives as well as rights and obligations under the law, are likely to be more focused on achieving such objectives and to be held accountable for their performance than enterprises that exist as an integrated part of government departments. The current Company Law constitutes the legal basis for the drive to establish SOEs as separate legal entities through corporatisation. For China, corporatisation was a continuation of past gradual reforms and a new means to increase SOE autonomy while maintaining oversight by the state. The assumption is that corporatised SOEs would behave like privately owned corporates in an advanced market economy, even though they continue to be owned by the state.

One of the central corporate sector reform goals has been to commercialise the SOE sector and create a "modern enterprise system" by transforming SOEs into corporate entities. By the end of 1999, more than half of the industrial state-owned firms have transformed themselves into joint stock companies. In the light of the trade and investment liberalisation, this effort will need to be pursued in the remaining state entities. The formation of OECD-type corporate forms dates back to October 1993, following the Decision of the Fourteenth Congress of the Communist Party of China to launch the process of corporatisation (*gongsihua*). The transformation of SOEs into limited liability and joint stock companies became the core element of the "modern enterprise system", to be established in China, along with the fully-fledged establishment of a "socialist" market economy with "Chinese characteristics", *i.e.* a competitive market characterised by the predominance of state ownership.[7]

In practice, the conversion of SOEs into joint-stock companies effectively consolidated the role of central and local government departments in their role as *de jure* owners since they became legally the majority if not the sole shareholders. However, it is questionable whether the directors of joint-stock companies enjoy greater or full operational autonomy.[8]

According to the Company Law the "... ownership of state-owned assets in the company belongs to the state" (Chapter 1, Article 4). Together with other legal acts, it also defines the various categories of enterprises (see Box 13.2) existing in the state and private sector. Apart from the legal framework, the processes of decentralisation of state administration (*tiao tiao kuai kuai*) had an important impact on the property and control rights over the corporate sector. The representation of the state as owner through a multitude of ministries and administrations at many levels of government makes the exercise of ownership rights more ambiguous and difficult.[9] In this context, for example, the Company Law does not indicate how the "ownership" claims of multiple supervisory government units will be handled.

Box 13.1. The corporate governance system of China

The corporate governance system prescribed by the Company law is based on an organisational structure consisting of the shareholders' general meeting, the board of (executive) directors and the board of supervisors. This structure of corporate governance is modelled on the German system, which prescribes a two-tier structure of a board of directors and of an oversight supervisory board, with mandatory employees' representation on the supervisory board.

The general shareholder meeting is the highest authority within the company. Its rights and responsibilities are as follows:

- Determination of company strategy and operational business and investment plans.
- Appointment and dismissal of representatives of shareholders as members of the supervisory board, and determination of matters relating to their remuneration.
- Examination and approval of the company annual reports of the board of directors and supervisory board, as well as of the operating budget for the following year.
- Examination and approval of the company's profit distribution and dividend policy and of plans for meeting any losses.
- Approval of decisions on the increase or decrease in the company's registered capital, on the issuance of company bonds and on matters relating to mergers, de-mergers, dissolution and liquidation.
- A special shareholder meeting may be called when i) the number of board members attending the annual meeting is less than required; ii) the company has a loss exceeding one third of its owners' equity; iii) requested by owners with more than 10 per cent of the company's outstanding shares; iv) requested by the board of directors; and v) requested by the supervisory board.
- Shareholders present at the meetings are entitled to one vote for each share held. Resolutions of shareholders shall be approved with a simple majority of voting rights held by shareholders present. A two-third majority is required for the approval of resolutions on the merger, de-merger and dissolution of the company, as well as on the amendments to its charter.

The board of directors is the decision-making body of China's joint-stock companies. The size of the board ranges from 5 to 20 members, elected at shareholders meetings. The board is accountable to the general meeting of shareholders and directors' appointments should not exceed three years. The board is responsible for:

- Calling and hosting the annual or special shareholder meeting and reporting to shareholders.
- Executing resolutions passed by shareholders.
- Preparing the company's operating and investment plans, dividend policies and debt and equity financing plans.
- Drafting any plans for mergers, de-mergers or dissolution of the company.
- Appointing, dismissing and deciding on the remuneration of the company's general manager.

The board chairman is the legal representative of the company, and is elected by a simple majority of board directors. A board resolution can only be approved if more than half of the directors vote in its favour. Board directors and senior managers are to abide by the company charter and perform their duties diligently, to protect the interests of shareholders and may not use their position, roles and powers for personal gain. The general manager (*zhongjingli*) is in charge of the company's operation.*

The supervisory board of a joint-stock company comprise a minimum of three members, with a chairman of the board elected among and by its members. The board comprises representatives of shareholders and "proportionate" representation of the company's employees, to be decided by the company and stipulated in the company charter. The tenure of a supervisory board member is three years, which is renewable upon re-election and re-appointment by the shareholders' meeting. Members of the board of directors, managers, and the chief financial officer are not allowed to serve as members of the supervisory board. The responsibilities of the supervisory board members are to:

- Review and examine the company's finances.
- Supervise and oversee directors and managers to ensure non-violation of law, regulations and the company charter in the course of execution of their duties.
- Require any director manager to correct any act that is harmful to the company.
- Propose the convening of an extraordinary shareholders' meeting, when necessary.

---

* SOEs tend to adopt a form of governance known as the "key man model". As a rule, the key man is at the same time the chairman, chief executive, and a high-ranking party member who has almost total discretion over management, investment decisions and even internal auditing.

Box 13.2. **Categories of enterprises**

Enterprise reforms in general and the corporatisation process in particular have resulted in a highly diversified and complicated corporate landscape in China. Different types of enterprises exist reflecting the *de facto* and *de jure* ownership. **By ownership**, there are four categories of enterprises in China: SOEs, collectively-owned enterprises (COEs), individually-owned (or private) enterprises, and foreign enterprises. SOEs are the most numerous entity. They did not have proper legal basis until 1988. Several regulations determined the principles and procedures of their operation, while the Bankruptcy law of 1986 regulated insolvency of SOEs. Before the promulgation of the Company law in 1993, several regulations defined SOEs as legal persons, their liabilities, the main principles of their management, autonomy and monitoring by controlling authorities. COEs (*jiti qiye*) are subject to the Law on Collectively-Owned Enterprises of 1991. They are defined as a legal person with assets jointly owned by workers and other economic entities. The main subcategories of COEs are the rural (commonly referred to as township and village enterprises, xiangcun qiye or TVEs) and urban collectives.

Although *de facto* private enterprises were allowed after 1978, their legal status was approved only in 1988. Regulations classify those funded and run by one person as individual enterprises (*getihu*), and those with eight or more employees as private enterprises (*siren qiye*). Private enterprises under a contractual agreement were further defined as partnerships.[1] Enterprises in which the liability of investors is limited to their respective contribution and the company's liabilities to the extent of its assets were defined as limited liability companies.[2] Foreign enterprises, including joint ventures and wholly owned foreign enterprises, are subject to the respective laws that fix *ad hoc* provisions for each of them, or to the Company Law if they are established as limited or joint stock companies.

---

1. A Law on partnerships was promulgated in 1997.
2. Limited liability companies now fall under Company Law.

Moreover, for companies with mixed ownership, the law does not state how a conflict between private shareholders and state shareholders would be handled. Precedent in settling disputes between competing government agencies/claimants is also missing. Consequently, difficulties in identifying the real owner might significantly increase the potential for insider expropriation and abuses and hinder the efficient functioning of enterprises.

The balance among the different forms of ownership rights and their protection has also elicited a lot of debate. The state sector has not been the engine of economic development; the non-state and private enterprises have been the engine of growth. The leadership recognised that it is impossible to achieve sustained rapid economic development by solely relying on the state sector, and established the principle of the common development of economic sectors with different ownership.[10] An amendment to the Constitution of March 1999 put private ownership and private enterprise on equal footing with the state sector[11] (see Box 13.3). Furthermore, this is currently being put into practice through a wide-ranging ownership diversification effort encompassing not only small and medium-sized enterprises as was the case until recently, but spreading to the large ones, which are being divested mainly through the capital market.

For example, registered capital requirements for a private limited company in China are among the highest in the world. As reported in a recent World Bank study,[12] the minimum amounts for a limited liability joint stock company have to reach RMB 300 000 (US$36 000) in retail trade, and RMB 500 000 (US$60 000) in wholesale trade or manufacturing. Registration should be paid up before a business license is issued. High fees go also hand in hand with time-consuming and detailed *ad hoc* procedures and additional costs. Another constraint stems from the fact that entrepreneurs must define precisely their "scope of business" and go through a substantive review and approval process, every time it is modified. This is compounded by the new UCL that seems to mandate the adherence to a rigid interpretation of the "purpose" of the company. The "scope of business" doctrine has been abandoned

435

Box 13.3.   **Recent policies on relinquishing state control over the corporate sector**

A new policy approach to state control was approved in 1999. The first most important change in 1999 concerns a new layout of the state economy. Specifically, the state concentrates its control over four main types of enterprises, while gradually withdrawing from other areas. *i)* national security, *ii)* natural monopolies, *iii)* industries providing important goods and services and *iv)* certain sectors and enterprises in high and new technology industries. The second change launched in 1999 concerns the diversification of ownership structure for those enterprises over which the state still wants to maintain control. Except for a few enterprises in which the state intends to retain 100 per cent ownership, all other enterprises will become joint-stock companies with private domestic or foreign shareholders along with state and other state-controlled bodies. The third change concerns the development of corporate governance, considered for the first time in a Party document in 1999.

---

over the last century in most OECD countries. Entrepreneurs may avoid such barriers if they register under the Law for Wholly Individually-Owned Enterprises or the Partnership Law, but at the risk of unlimited liability for business debts and limited access to capital. The above disincentives are clearly hampering institutional development. They stand in the way of a modern system of standardised, tradable property rights, which is the hallmark of developed market economies.

The changing environment of bankruptcy

Enterprises facing enhanced competition and a rapidly changing economic environment need clear guidelines not only on establishment, growth, and enforceable commercial arrangements, but also on reorganising or closing down a business. Enterprise reform can succeed only if companies that fail to meet the market test engage in a process of shifting their assets and liabilities to other productive uses. Fears of social upheaval have resulted in a bottleneck in the reallocation of productive assets in China. However, factors such as the Asian financial crisis, the efforts towards trade and investment liberalisation and the consequent need to enhance performance of the enterprise sector, have underlined the urgency of reforming the bankruptcy framework.[13]

Notwithstanding some effort in this direction, enterprise exit through bankruptcy remains one of the weakest points of Chinese reforms. Although in this direction bankruptcy cases are occurring with increasing frequency, the overwhelming number of them deal with small and medium-sized industrial enterprises. Overall, the number of bankruptcies of state and non-state enterprises since the beginning of the 1990s remained modest. A little more than 40 000 cases have been heard by Chinese courts, until the end of 2000.

Reorganisation and liquidation decisions are often made through a closed negotiated process rather than transparent transactions. For example, a Capital Structure Optimisation Programme (CSOP) was developed for a pilot group of industrial SOEs in 1994. This Programme addressed social constraints by earmarking land use rights of the liquidated debtor to pay for the "rehabilitation" of its workers.[14] The selection of SOEs was based on administrative rather than market criteria and the proceedings were carried out by government officials rather than insolvency professionals or judges. Creditor banks related to the CSOP enterprises have allocated to these cases a substantial portion of their annual write-offs, which were capped by a special "debt write-off quota" determined under the CSOP.[15]

Bankruptcy cases started rising in the mid-1990s, not only under the CSOP. Thus, two years after the initiation of the CSOP programme, the total number of bankruptcy cases reached 6 000, which represents an approximately six-fold increase compared to 1994. In 1996-1997, more than half the cases were SOEs. In these two years together, as many as 1.5 per cent of all SOEs entered bankruptcy proceedings. Between 1998 and 2000, the number of bankruptcies stabilised at between 5 000 to

7 000 per year, partly due to the control of the central government in order to maintain social stability and avoid financial distress.[16] As a result, a great number of enterprises that are completely insolvent are still on the books, their assets remain idle, and their debts unpaid. Under such circumstances, a growing flow of bad debts through the already troubled banking sector and arrears might be expected in the future (see Chapter 7 on Banking).

Different insolvency regimes are currently applicable to different types of enterprises. These include, SOEs, non-state corporations and enterprises located in special economic zones. The current bankruptcy law, which is applicable only to SOEs, was adopted in 1986, but its implementation started only at the beginning of the 1990s. Bankruptcy proceedings under this law are plagued by procedural and institutional shortcomings. Moreover, there are various regulations issued by the central government that are applied to SOE bankruptcies *de facto* in priority over the law. On the other hand, non-SOE bankruptcies involving mainly firms with collective, private, and mixed ownership fall under various provisions in the Civil Procedure Code, the Company Law, and Opinions of the Supreme Court. The deficiencies of this sketchy framework have emerged in many bankruptcy cases involving large listed debtors or foreign creditors (see Box 13.4).

Legal shortcomings have been delaying bankruptcy not only in the state, but also in the non-state sector. A new comprehensive bankruptcy law, which has been drafted since 1994, is now ready for submission to the National People's Congress. It would apply to state, but also to non-state enterprises and personal firms. It envisages an administrator (trustee) who will run the estate, strengthens the role of the creditors' meeting, and provides a fairly sophisticated mechanism of court-supervised reorganisation that can be initiated by debtors, creditors or shareholders.

A recent comprehensive study of the World Bank[17] suggests that creditors of SOEs have little influence on the process and suffer violation of their secured claims for the sake of settling affected workers. On certain occasions, assets are distributed to local creditors while claims from other jurisdictions are disregarded. Sometimes major creditors such as commercial banks have a strong voice in the proceedings, while trade creditors are virtually ignored and are not even notified of the bankruptcy in writing. Creditors often note that proceedings lack transparency in some important matters such as the information on assets and claims, pre-bankruptcy transactions, liquidation fees and expenses, asset valuation, and disposal.[18]

Building judicial and court expertise in dealing with bankruptcy proceedings is another issue to be addressed. The judges of the so-called economic trial courts (recently renamed "second civil courts") of the people's courts at different levels are in charge of bankruptcy cases. Approximately 30 000 judges are practising in economic trial courts and dealing with a total of 1.5 million economic cases per year,

---

Box 13.4. **The case of the Guangdong International Trust and Investment Company**

In October 1998, a landmark case put the existing bankruptcy legislation to its most severe test yet. The so-called International Trust and Investment Companies (ITICs), the only Chinese enterprises allowed to borrow in foreign currency, are investment arms of local governments. When the ITIC of China's richest province, Guandong, defaulted along with several others, the central government made it clear that it had no intention of underwriting their debts. Two years of complex bankruptcy negotiations illustrated the flaws of the existing legal framework, especially the lack of concrete provisions in many areas starting from the formation of creditor committees to foreclosure. The banks eventually settled out of court, and for huge losses. The Guangdong ITIC's case clarified certain issues and set important precedents on procedure. For instance, it signalled that the claims of foreign creditors did not rank ahead of Chinese creditors, as the foreign banks had hoped – a decision that supported the principle of equality before the law.

most of which are disputes regarding commercial contracts.[19] The only specialised bankruptcy court was established by the Shenzhen Intermediate People's Court in December 1993. Until the end of 2000 it heard 486 cases and closed 373, which makes it the most active in the field of bankruptcy among all courts nationwide. Up to now it has formulated a series of professional instructions, such as the Operating Rules of Bankruptcy Court, the Instructions on Time Limit in Bankruptcy Cases and the Operating Rules of Liquidation Teams.[20] It has kept a list of bankruptcy practitioners, which is mainly composed of experienced lawyers, for appointment on liquidation teams.

The multiplicity of regimes applied to bankruptcy of different types of enterprises constitutes a serious challenge for the judges. Coping with the gaps and flaws of the current legislation is hard work. Another issue is the lack of entire independence of the courts from the government authorities, which has led to inconsistent treatment of creditors and abuses of their rights, mainly under pressures stemming from social concerns. It seems common practice that where assets of an insolvent SOE do not suffice to cover the entire rehabilitation expenses, and the government does not work out a satisfactory arrangement, the court would refuse to accept the bankruptcy case. Like other state authorities, courts are considered politically responsible for social stability.

The role of the judicial system

Legal reforms in China have made little progress with respect to the judicial system. The current system is based on a model combining Western civil law and the judicial tradition of centrally planned economies.[21] The independence of the courts is an important precondition for a sound legal system. However, the status of the people's courts is as yet unclear. Judicial organs have long been put under the supervision and control of the Party and various government organisations, despite a specific provision in the Constitution that clearly states that courts shall legally try cases without any intervention of administrative organs, social groups, or individuals. Thus, courts depend on such organisations for manpower, material, and financial resources, which leads to significant influence and potential for interference and capture of courts by the government and politicians.[22] Moreover, there have been allegations of corruption and influence trafficking that have not, as of now, been properly addressed. Finally, a judge in one court rarely studies judgements of other courts. This results in an incoherent, often conflicting and unpredictable interpretation of an already weak legal framework.

Key corporate governance issues in China[23]

Corporate governance has been recognised as a priority of enterprise reform in China since 1999. The challenge of improving corporate governance is gaining importance in the light of the trade and investment liberalisation in China. Effective corporate institutions are increasingly seen as important tools in generating growth and an efficient allocation of resources.

The corporate governance landscape

The Chinese equity markets have grown rapidly since their establishment ten years ago.[24] The ratio of total market capitalisation to GDP has reached almost 60 per cent in China, which is getting close to the European Union average of 87 per cent for 1998. It is higher than Republic of Korea (38 per cent) and much higher than countries like Poland (14 per cent) and Turkey (17 per cent). The average company market capitalisation, estimated at RMB 2 billion (US$240 million) is fairly large. There have been a growing number of purely private IPOs. Private companies currently represent close to 5 per cent of total market capitalisation. Authorities seem to be encouraging this trend and the CSRC (China Securities Regulatory Commission) seems bent on authorising more private flotations. Given the size, age, and profile of private companies, it might be important to create a second market for these companies to raise money.

However, the market mostly consists of state-controlled companies diversifying their ownership. Close to 70 per cent of the equity of the listed companies currently is still controlled by the state,[25] which reduces the free float to 30-35 per cent. The current population and profile of listed companies has been largely determined through geographical rationing of IPOs, adopted in the early/mid-nineties, including companies from all provinces in China in a roughly proportionate way. Many local authorities saw listing as an issue of political prestige rather than access to capital. While there is a listing requirement of three years of profitability before the IPO, this is easily evaded by carving out the most profitable parts of an SOE in the run up to listing – and leaving all the loss making parts in the holding structure. Consequently, a large part of the external capital generated from the listing is channelled to the SOE holding to cover losses and/or maintain the considerable social services/assets it provides to its workers and the local community. The rationing policy was abandoned in 2000 and the listing process is now based on more substantive criteria.

An important recent development has been the gradual integration between the A- and B-share markets (see Box 13.5 for a description of the types of shares in Chinese companies). Less than 10 per cent of listed companies now have outstanding B-shares in the two exchanges (Shanghai and Szenzhen). Until late 2000, B-shares were trading at a 70 per cent discount, reflecting the irrelevance of this excessively narrow market. This year the discount has lowered to 40 per cent, as Chinese investors were allowed to invest in B-shares. The market rose tenfold in terms of value. However, this is still an experimental market and it is not until the full integration of A and B share markets that Chinese companies will benefit from foreign portfolio investment in a substantial and sustainable way.

Non-state shareholders are often described as overwhelmingly retail. Indeed, there are over 60 million private equity accounts in China. The average daily turnover is very high, at more than 400 per cent the free float. This suggests a market based on small-time speculation with little institutional presence. Liquidity is quite spread out, *i.e.*, not limited to very few large issuers, as is often the case in many smaller markets.

However, retail might not be as important as it looks. Non-licensed funds, referred to as "grey" funds, are thought to manage more than ten times the amount of assets managed by the official state-owned/controlled fund industry (see Box 13.6). It is presumed that many of the 60 million retail accounts are in fact dummies for the operation of these illegal funds. The existence of the "grey" funds represents both a threat and an opportunity for the market. Their current unregulated non-transparent status creates great risks for stability given the lack of risk-weighted approach to investment. Given the amount of capital managed by "grey" funds, their collapse could take systemic proportions and have a lasting effect on market confidence, as has been the case in some other transition economies. Conversely, their legalisation and proper regulation could provide the market with the much-needed institutional presence and move it away from the current excessive retail-driven risk-taking mentality.

The official institutional investor sector holds only around 2.3 per cent of the market capitalisation. The existing 14 asset managers are owned either directly by the state or are joint ventures between the state and private domestic companies. While their shareholding has remained relatively small, their influence has been growing in the market as their research teams have become bigger and more competent. All of the trading/broking business is also state-owned.

The fact that these funds are still state-owned presents several disadvantages. The risk of interference in asset management policies is always present. In addition, access to capital and know-how is limited by their inability to ally themselves to the global fund management industry. However, the fund industry will be one of the first to benefit from trade and investment liberalisation. Within the next three years, foreign asset managers and securities firms will be allowed entry. This will exacerbate the downside of the state ownership for the incumbents. Chinese policy-makers should anticipate this development and take active steps in the state divestment of the asset managers.

In addition to the important corporate governance problems discussed below, narrow markets (because of a low free float) result in high volatility and increased opportunities for market manipulation. Hence, continuing state divestment is an important goal to pursue. Chinese authorities sometimes express the fear of flooding the market with new issues. As the recent history of stock market development in Europe shows, this should not be a concern in principle. State divestment has helped to increase market capitalisation in Europe at levels not seen since the early 20th century, in spite of

439

Box 13.5. Types of shares in Chinese companies

A variety of shares have emerged in the framework of enterprise corporatisation. Shares in China are classified by i) shareholder's identity, and ii) their listing location. In terms of type of owner, the shares are state-owned, legal person, and public shares. *Legal person shares* include domestic shares owned by the enterprise itself, or shares acquired by other enterprises and institutions.[1] Domestic institutions include stock companies, non-bank financial institutions and SOEs that have at least one non-state owner. Banks are legally prohibited from owning shares in companies. A sub-category is called *state-owned legal person* shares, referring to shares held by institutions in which the state is the majority owner but has less than 100 per cent shareholding. Legal person shares are not publicly tradable except by special approval of the state-authorised investing institution or department. *State-owned shares refer* to shareholdings of the central and local governments or by institutions and departments (including SOEs), designed by the State Council or by local governments. It was recently clarified that the ultimate owner of these shares is the State Council. State shares are subject to the same restrictions as legal person shares.

Public shares refer to shares offered to and freely traded by the general public. They are mainly held by individual public investors, staff, and employees of companies who are not promoters and institutional investors. Public shares are further classified according to their listing location. In *terms* of place of listing, the shares are domestically listed, *i.e.* called A- and B-shares or listed abroad, *i.e.* H-shares, listed in Hong Kong and N-shares, listed in New York. The transfer of A- and B-shares takes place at the Shanghai and Shenzhen stock exchanges, established respectively in 1990 and 1991. *A-shares* are traded in domestic currency and are reserved for domestic enterprises and individuals. There is a legal requirement that A-shares should account for not less then 25 per cent of total shares issued when a company goes for listing. *Employee* shares are offered to workers and managers of a listed company, usually at a substantial discount. They are registered under the title of the labour union of the company, representing employees in the exercise of their shareholder rights. After a holding period of six to twelve months, the company may require CSRC approval to sell the shares on the market.

By contrast, B-*shares* are traded in foreign currency and are available only to foreign individual and institutional investors. Despite their different names and places of listing, B-, H- and N-shares are held by foreigners and are commonly referred to as foreign shares. Foreign investors were given access to the Chinese stock market in 1992 with the introduction of the B-shares on both national exchanges.[2] On the Shanghai stock exchange they are traded in US$, and in Shenzhen in Hong Kong dollars. Initially, the A-share market was not supposed to open to foreign investors. However, in July 1994, following a year long decline of A-share prices, the Chinese authorities announced a series of measures, one of which was to allow foreign funds onto the A-share market by establishing joint-ventures. In addition, Chinese investors were also given access to the B-share market by allowing Chinese citizens residing abroad and other investors approved by CSRC to invest in B-shares. An important step towards building a unified mainland stock market represent the lifting of restrictions on local investors buying B-shares in February 2001.[3]

H-, N-, L- *and* S-*shares* refer to shares of Chinese companies listed, subscribed and traded in Hong Kong, New York, London and Singapore. In the early 1990s, some enterprises purchased controlling stakes in publicly quoted Hong Kong companies thereby obtaining "backdoor" listings on the Hong Kong stock exchange. This practice allowed Chinese enterprises to bypass both Chinese restrictions on sales of equity abroad and Hong Kong's regulations on new listings. These listings permitted Chinese companies to raise foreign funds by capital increases and sales of new shares on the Hong Kong stock exchange. The shares of such companies are referred to as "red chips". Co-operation between the Hong Kong stock exchange and the Chinese authorities continued on the establishment of a regulatory framework for such listings. Chinese enterprises have also listed shares on other stock exchanges. For example, the listing requirements of the NYSE have been modified for Chinese enterprises. Contrary to its regular requirements of a three-year financial track record, Chinese enterprises are listed on the basis of one-year audited accounts and unaudited financial results for the previous two years.[4]

In theory, all the shares entitle shareholders to the same dividends and voting rights. In practice, it is not uncommon for a company to pay its state owner cash dividends, but offer individual and legal person shareholders stock dividends and rights offerings, and legal person owners do likewise.

Box 13.5.   **Types of shares in Chinese companies** (*cont.*)

This is because new shares acquired by the state cannot be traded in the open market. For liquidity reasons, the state prefers cash dividends to stock dividends or rights offerings, and so do legal person owners. Regarding voting rights, tradable A-shareholders are in a disadvantageous position due to the lack of proxy voting procedures.[5]

---

1. The legal person shares should be distinguished from state-owned legal person shares traded on two automated quotation systems in Beijing, STAQ (Stock Trading Automated System) and NETS (National Exchange and Trading System). See Xu Xiaonian and Wang Yan, "Ownership Structure, Corporate Governance and Corporate Performance. The Case of Chinese Stock Companies", Policy Research Working Paper No. 1795, The World Bank, June 1997
2. S-Y Ma, "Foreign participation in Chinese privatisation", *Communist Economies and Economic Transformation*, Vol. 8, No 4, 1996.
3. If the move is successful, it might encourage the authorities to take further steps towards unifying the mainland market and making it completely open to foreign investors. The merger of the A- and B-shares was *inter alia* intended to take the heat off the A-share market, which has become dramatically over-priced. Richard McGregor and Joe Leahy, "China takes a 'giant step' towards unified stock market", *Financial Times*, 19 February, 2001.
4. Ma, *op. cit.*
5. Xu, *op. cit.*

---

similar flooding fears expressed earlier in the process. Provided that appropriate corporate governance reforms do take place, increasing the free float through more state disposals will be a highly beneficial stabilising factor for the markets.

Shareholder rights and treatment

The key issue in the shareholder area is the role of the state as a shareholder. While the Ministry of Finance represents the state as the owner of enterprises, control is exercised mostly at local level in a highly politicised and non-transparent fashion. Some local authorities have a relatively good reputation, but many have a negative record. There is a clear need for transparent processes for making state ownership more effective. In such a setting, it can be expected that most corporate governance improvements will come from empowering more outside shareholders and by letting the market take up a lot of control functions. This cannot be achieved unless a critical number of companies see direct or indirect state control fall under 50 per cent.

According to current rules, listed companies must have at least 1 000 outside shareholders and a 25 per cent free float. B- and H-shares usually represent a small fraction of a company's outstanding equity, and foreign shareholders play a very minor role in governance. While in theory they do have the right to vote, foreign investors seldom participate in the governance of companies.

There is a proxy mechanism provided for in Chinese company law, and the year 2000 saw a number of highly publicised proxy fights centred on director appointments. However, proxy regulation as well as the process of soliciting shareholder proposals and nominations in the context of the annual general meeting (AGM) are still in their infancy. In one of the two control contests, the issue did not even reach the AGM, as the company refused to put it on the agenda.

The company law does have provisions on pre-emptive rights and until now, share dilution has not been identified as an important threat to outsiders. In contrast, related party transactions constitute the most important problem as regards expropriation of outside shareholders. The current legal framework does have provisions stipulating that these transactions have to be disclosed in the press. When the transactions are large, they have to be discussed and approved by the shareholders in the AGM or at an extraordinary meeting, as well as audited by independent auditors. However, given the ownership structure, the AGMs are not necessarily a reliable mechanism for protecting the rights of outsiders. In a recent case, a liquor company bought a substantial amount of assets from its parent at rather inflated prices. In spite of AGM approval of the transaction, the CSRC questioned it, following minority shareholder complaints.

Box 13.6. **Investment Funds in China**

The mutual fund industry was established in 1991.[1] It is almost entirely state-owned. This step was taken in order increase market liquidity by encouraging the transfer of more than RMB 6 trillion (US$732 billion) from bank savings accounts[2] into stock market investments and also to reduce the volatility of the A-share-market. After a period of rapid growth, the development of the Chinese Fund Industry slowed down in 1993 when the People's Bank of China prohibited the establishment of any new investment fund without prior approval.[3] In November 1997[4] the State Council approved the "Administration of Securities Investment Fund Tentative Procedures", which improved and facilitated the establishment of new funds. Even though the first investment funds launched under the new legislation seem to have been a success, a further clean-up of the industry took place in 1998.

The regulatory framework, which is still in-force, presents serious shortcomings: the 1997 Funds Procedures apply only to 14 investment funds, whereas the remaining funds are outside their scope.[5] This is due to their diversified investment policy, which often includes industrial ventures. Yet the Funds Procedures only apply to funds exhaustively investing in listed securities. Hence, in 1999, the Finance and Economic Committee of the National People's Congress was asked to prepare a Law on Investment Funds,[6] the promulgation of which is planned only for the end of 2002.

In addition to the present legislative shortcomings, market monitoring is perceived as too lax. As a CSRC chief adviser comments: "There has been too much attention spent on approving funds and not enough on supervising them".[7]

A survey of the opinions of 3 600 private investment consultants[8] revealed a vast underground funds management market: whereas the official institutional investor sector holds only RMB 85 billion (US$10.2 billion) or around 2.3 per cent of the market capitalisation, "grey funds" are estimated to be worth around RMB 900 billion (US$108 billion). Hence, many of the 60 million retail accounts might in fact be dummies for the operation of these underground funds.

This illustrates that so far China's official fund industry failed to meet the goal of reducing volatility and improving corporate governance in the markets. Therefore, adopting a comprehensive legal framework and enhancing market supervision should become a priority in order to provide the fund industry with the means to achieve these goals (see Chapters 14 and 15 for further discussion of capital markets and the financial system).

---

1. China's first investment fund was the "Wuhan Securities Investment Fund" with a capital of RMB 10 million (US$1.2 million). See Chang, T. K., "Investment Funds: China's newest equity instrument", *China Law and Practice*, March 1998, p. 23.

2. By the end of February 2000, according to Zhang, D., "Savings up, loans too, says central bank", *China Daily*, 17.3.2000, p. 1.

3. See Chang T.K., *op. cit.*

4. The Administration of Securities Investment Funds Tentative Procedures, promulgated by the State Council Securities Commission on, and effective as of, November 14, 1997. For an English translation of the text see *China Law and Practice*, March 1998, p. 27.

5. According to interviews with the CSRC and Ding, M., "Legislation to safeguard infant investment funds", in: *China Daily Business Weekly*, November 15, 1998.

6. The different versions of the Draft Law can be found under *www.gtz-commercial-laws.org.cn*.

7. As cited in Bruce Gilley, "China's Dodgy Funds", *Far Eastern Economic Review*, December 14, 2000, p. 74. See also Anthony Neoh, "An Overview of the Chinese Domestic Capital Market at the Dawn of the New Millenium", in: *China 200 – Emerging Investment, Funding and Advisory Opportunities for a New China, www.asialaw.com/bookstore/china2000/*. As a consequence, illegal practices seem to be quite common among China's funds, as two recent reports suggest. Zhao Yugang, a researcher in the supervision department of the Shanghai Stock exchange, looked at 22 listed funds (see the report published by *Caijing Monthly*, in B. Gilley). Using detailed trading data, he found a lot of circumstantial evidence of wrongdoings like insider trading and misleading information policies. Hence, it is not surprising that most of the funds vastly under-performed. In the first 10 months of 2000, 19 of 31 listed funds under-performed on both the Shanghai and Shezhen stock markets.

8. See Richard McGregor, "New figures for China's unofficial funds sector", FT.*com site*, July 2, 2001, "Estimates grow for unofficial China funds", *Financial Times*, July 3, 2001 and "Spotlight falls on China's private funds "grey market", *Financial Times*, July 9, 2001.

Asset and cash-flow stripping of listed companies often occurs at a low, "everyday" level and thus cannot be directly addressed by existing regulations. Technically insolvent affiliates continue to benefit from large loan guarantees from the listed companies in the group. This explains large amounts of self-perpetuating receivables in listed company balance sheets. The listing process becomes a means of tunnelling external capital towards large loss-making, non-listed SOEs – previously bank-financed loss-making operations, which have led to mounting non-performing loans and the curtailment of corporate bank lending (see Chapter 7 on Banking).

Stakeholders

In China, the stakeholder issue takes a very different form than in OECD countries. Improving corporate governance is mostly about extricating companies from a very opaque set of stakeholder capture patterns and making the accountability lines clearer and more transparent to shareholders, as well as to other, existing and potential stakeholders.

Related party transactions are, as noted, the key threat to shareholder value. They are exacerbated by the need to maintain a vast array of social assets and services at the parent level. Often the relationship between a holding and a listed company is very close and problematic. This can be seen from the example of Sinopec, one of the largest Chinese listed companies, which underwent in-depth restructuring and corporate governance reforms, before listing (see Box 13.7). The CEO of Sinopec

---

Box 13.7.   **Restructuring and governance of the Chinese oil and gas sector: the example of Sinopec**

The decision to list the largest oil refinery in Asia, Sinopec, was taken in the spring of 2000. Prior to the listing, the refineries and chemical plants were separated from the Yanshan's power station schools, hospitals and other social concerns, which were to supply services to Sinopec on commercial terms before being definitively severed. They were transferred to the parent company, which also retains 76 per cent of the shares in Sinopec. The listing took place in the fall of 2000 – not only on the domestic market but also on the New York (ADR) and London (GDR) stock exchanges – and raised approximately US$3.5 billion. For the company, the listing was also seen as an opportunity to get exposure to market discipline under minority shareholder oversight in some of the toughest markets in the world. Investors were attracted by the possibility of obtaining a stake in one of the largest oil franchises in the world, notwithstanding the uncertainties related to the Chinese reform process and to the relations between Sinopec and its parent company.

Serious training programmes were organised for Sinopec's managers to prepare them for the cultural change brought about by the share offering, and to enable them to understand the main criteria against which the market will gauge the company. To ensure the success of the listing, the government relied on recommendations by international consultants. In the process of preparation, one issue proved particularly difficult to resolve, given its broad implications for the economy as a whole, namely the liberalisation of the retail price of Sinopec's main product, petrol, which was still regulated by the government.

According to the consultants, however, reforming corporate governance was a real revolution. Sinopec had to become a completely separate company from its parent, and carry out related transactions at arm's length. To reassure minority shareholders that their voice will be heard, Sinopec agreed that all "major" decisions (e.g. a new share issue) would have to be submitted to two separate votes, one at a general meeting, and one at a meeting for overseas shareholders only. The consultants also pressed for a board with independent directors. Three independent directors (two academics and one Hong Kong businessman) were appointed to the ten-member board. However, experience until now has shown that their independence is still to be proven in practice. According to reports, Sinopec is currently looking for a fourth independent director, possibly a foreigner from one of the oil majors that bought stakes in the company.

Source: The Economist, *op. cit.* and Baker, J., Lewis, S., *op. cit.*

heads both the SOE holding and the listed company. The listed company has 23 000 employees, while the holding has more than 1 million. As a Chinese official commented, most of his energy has to go to making sure that the social services that the parent company provides for all these employees are delivered. This impacts clearly on his capacity to focus on his role as CEO of the listed company.

The role of the Communist Party and its local representatives is at the heart of the stakeholder debate. In the past, the local/enterprise Party cells made most of the important decisions on the future of the enterprise. Evidence suggests that the Party is currently taking control of boards; the pattern is often that the local Party Secretary becomes the chair of the Board while the manager of the factory takes the CEO job in the new, listed company.

Another key issue is the very low pay of listed company management. This is mostly due to the fact that managers are still regarded as civil servants and have corresponding ranks. Also, the fact that many of the listed companies are located in far away provinces where overall salaries are very low makes it difficult to pay executives better than the local authority officials from a "fairness" perspective. Thus, people who manage substantial assets have annual salaries that are often less than RMB50 000 (US$6 000). Performance-based executive remuneration is still in its very infancy. While a few red-chips have "synthetic" options,[26] most listed companies do not have any incentives in place for executives. Stock options are not yet legal as such – although there is no agreement on their "illegality". CSRC is currently considering regulation that would facilitate their adoption by companies.

When listing in foreign markets, especially through depository receipts, Chinese companies might find it increasingly helpful to address up-front some key stakeholder issues such as their environmental record and labour practices. Recent experience with some large flotations (e.g. Petro China) in foreign markets has been quite painful in this respect. Stakeholder groups have managed to harm the Chinese companies' drive to raise capital, due to their poor performance in these areas. Increasingly important socially responsible investors might in the future create even more problems for Chinese corporations unless they take initiatives towards social responsibility on issues such as the environment.

Transparency and disclosure

Overall, most commentators agree that the quality of the Chinese accounting and auditing framework is quite good compared to other emerging/transition countries. However, transparency and disclosure practices are not up to international standards. Insiders often perceive transparency and disclosure of companies' operations and performance as unnecessary, as outsiders and other stakeholders are viewed as speculators. Financial management and reporting are plagued with fraud and pervasive irregularities. Particularly strong examples of the scale of this problem are the recent cases of financial mismanagement of the international trust and investment companies (see Box 13.7). However, it should be pointed out that the CSRC and the external auditors have played an important role in raising awareness of fraudulent accounting and financial practices. In some of the big international flotations, outside consultants have provided for a clearer perspective based on international shareholders, but implementation becomes the key issue.

Accounting standards in China are set by the Ministry of Finance. Its Advisory Committee, including representatives of the accounting profession, academics, the CSRC and the State Audit Committee, has the mandate to review draft legislation, but does not have a role in preparing it. Such an approach contrasts with the way accounting standards are set in most OECD economies, although it is better than the monolithic state-controlled method of some other transition countries. This approach might be responsible to a degree for the weakness of the accounting profession and the consequent weak implementation of the standards.

The Ministry of Finance claims that current 1999 standards are quite close to international accounting standards. Since 1985, the accounting system has been moving away from the old system devised for central planning. The accounting standards adopted in 1999 are applicable only to listed companies. The rest of the enterprise sector still applies older standards set in 1993. However, this situation is currently changing. A key difference between the old and the new system is that accounting disclosure and policy in the new system is effectively set by enterprises, not the government.[27]

However, there are some important gaps. Consolidation and business combination accounting is still in its infancy – a regulation is being prepared that would improve the situation and would throw a little more light on the control structures. Non-financial disclosure also needs serious improvement. Most importantly, ownership/control disclosures are almost completely lacking. Governance-related disclosures are also quite poor. The concept of continuous disclosure of items that materially affect the business is alien, but this is also quite new in some OECD economies.

In contrast to accounting standards, audit standards are set by the professional organisation, the Chinese Institute of Certified Public Accountants (CICPA). They are also said to be close to the International Standards of Audit (ISA), the global standard. However, this organisation has little independence and is headed by a deputy Finance minister. Moreover, it has reportedly been quite weak in creating the requisite guidance and adopting training programmes that would help lift the standard of implementation.

There are large domestic accounting firms in China but access by international accounting firms is quite limited. The big five have audited the banking sector and the handful of firms that have gone through offerings in international capital markets, but they have not been allowed a real presence in the domestic corporate sector. It can be expected that more foreign presence might lift the standards of implementation and increase the confidence of international investors.

The role of boards

The focal point of reforms right now seems to be on the constitution and operation of boards: the draft CSRC corporate governance code, now under consideration, will put them at the centre of corporate governance improvement. At present, boards do not have a separate identity in the company; they are rather viewed as a continuation of management. As in many Asian countries, including Japan, board power is very limited. However, shaping an effective board is the issue that Chinese authorities should address early on in order to gain a head start. Although in theory boards are supposed to appoint the management of a Chinese company, the latter is usually appointed directly either by the local authorities or by the SOE holding that controls the listed company. Few boards have independent directors and in the ones that do, non-executives have precious few responsibilities. The draft CSRC Code suggests having at least 30 per cent independent directors, and creating nomination committees that are majority-independent.

A key issue with respect to boards is how independent directors are nominated and appointed. It should be noted that the law does not allow civil servants to be directors of listed companies. This is a positive condition, which can be used to broaden independence in boards, although it does not guarantee true independence form the controlling shareholders. In China, parties (or the state holdings that usually control the listed companies) have enormous power and are quite monolithic under the conditions of little countervailing ownership power. In practice, local authorities and the Party, who are also in control of the holding companies, currently nominate most directors. The CSRC Code under preparation is presumably going to allow shareholders of at least 5 per cent of common stock to nominate directors.

The company law does not contain a duty of loyalty (neither a duty of care) for directors or other corporate officers. This facilitates capture by related parties or by management, even of independent directors. If such a duty were operational the situation at Sinopec described above would be more difficult to legitimise.

China has a board system similar to Japan's *kansayaku*, *i.e.* a second board of internal auditors. In Japan, the system is not working, as internal auditors are appointed by, and are dependent on managers. The draft Code envisages the possibility of a US-style unitary board with an Audit Committee. This could prove to be a good approach for China, as the system is not so much entrenched as it is in Japan. It should be noted that, in its new draft commercial code, Japan is also allowing enterprises to choose between the unitary system and an upgraded *kansayaku*.

The lack of available expertise is a stumbling block in the effective functioning of independent boards. Right now independent board members are mostly academics with very little training and knowledge of business. A possible solution for this might be to use management from other listed companies as board members, which is a common practice in most countries. Such an option is not being considered, as Chinese managers are perceived as being "too busy" running not only the business but also the social assets of enterprises. However, it seems more likely that the reluctance to serve on boards is due to the fact that these services are largely *pro bono*. In contrast to the financial/asset management sector, Chinese companies do not tap foreign managerial or board expertise. Only some of the red chips have allowed directors from outside the People's Republic of China.

Implementation and institutional issues

Chinese law does provide the possibility of sanctioning behaviour that is against the law of the articles of association of a company.

However, private investors have few *ex post* remedies when shareholder violations occur. Shareholder suits – especially a derivative suit – are not available under Chinese company law. Collective shareholder suits are also hard to launch. There have been instances where such remedial action has taken place in circumstances that resembled a class action suit.

Implementation is perceived as the key issue in strengthening corporate governance. In the last few years, the CSRC has become more powerful and more respected by market players. It has a broad authority to control listing and de-listing: CSRC takes the listing decision while the Exchanges take a de-listing one, subject to CSRC approval. It also seems to have broad powers in controlling self- and insider dealing, as well as market manipulation.

However, this is still a relatively inexperienced organisation with limited human and financial resources to use its powers effectively. Market monitoring is performed more by the stock exchanges. Instead of acting as increasingly commercial mechanisms as in many OECD jurisdictions, they often act as regulatory extensions of the CSRC. The CSRC has recently been more active in de-listing companies after three years of consecutive losses, as required by current rules. The third year of listing is critical for restructuring. The CSRC has also imposed some heavy fines on companies for various abuses. For example, the managers of a technology company were recently fined RMB1 million (US$120 000) for market manipulation. Overall, the CSRC imposed fines of RMB1.49 billion last year on more than 100 offenders.

A big advantage China has over other emerging market economies is the possibility (and its increasing willingness) to tap available expertise in Hong Kong. CSRC staff is often recruited from among bright young Chinese graduates of foreign universities. This is rather exceptional in the Chinese administration, which has a senior work record approach to promotion. Many asset management companies also hire Hong Kong and foreign experts among their research teams and senior management.

Conclusions and recommendations

The Chinese authorities have been promoting a more effective legal framework for the corporate sector. Important legal reforms have led to clearer "rules of the game" for transactions and contractual relationships, greater business autonomy through corporatisation and better definition of the company as a legal entity, as well as a more comprehensive framework governing market exit. These issues are paramount for the success of enterprise reforms in China, and would enable the corporate sector to adapt to and take advantage of the benefits stemming from a greater integration into the world economy (see Box 13.8).

In addition to the invisible hand of influence, other problems identified in this chapter are related to the uniform implementation of law in China. The Chinese legal system is somewhat "fragmented", as law can give both local and central authorities broad discretion in making certain decisions. Legislative and institutional coherence, and better definition of discretionary powers at different levels of

Box 13.8. The OECD Principles on Corporate Governance

Governance systems vary widely around the globe and, indeed, among the Member countries of the OECD. In April 1998, the OECD Ministers gave the OECD a mandate to develop a set of principles in the area of corporate governance, identifying common elements underlying good corporate governance across different systems. An *Ad hoc* Corporate Governance Task Force of representatives of 29 OECD governments, the EU Commission, World Bank, IMF, BIS, IOSCO, EBRD, business, labour and the investment community produced the OECD *Principles of Corporate Governance*, which were endorsed by the 1999 OECD Ministerial meeting.

The OECD Principles are expected to play an important role in helping countries to forge common standards for corporate governance. They are organised under five headings:

Rights of Shareholders. The first principle concerns the protection of shareholders' rights and the ability of shareholders to influence the behaviour of the corporation.

Equitable Treatment of Shareholders. The second principle emphasises that all shareholders, including foreign shareholders, should be treated fairly by controlling shareholders, boards and management. The Principles call for transparency with respect to the distribution of voting rights and the ways voting rights are exercised.

Role of Stakeholders. By far the most controversial issue, the stakeholder principle recognises that the competitiveness of a company is the result of teamwork, and that companies benefit from the contributions of a range of different resource providers, including employees, suppliers, creditors, and the communities in which companies operate.

Disclosure and Transparency. This chapter of the principles recommends that all material matters regarding the governance and performance of the corporation be disclosed. The importance of applying high quality standards of accounting, disclosure, and audit are underscored, and the Principles support the development of high quality internationally recognised accounting standards.

Responsibilities of the Board. The final principle states that the corporate governance framework should ensure the strategic guidance of the company, the effective monitoring of management by the board and the board's accountability to the company and the shareholders. It also states that independent directors can contribute significantly to the decision-making of the board. It is expected that they can play an important role with respect to the protection of minority investors' interests. (The full text of the Principles is available on the OECD's Website at *www.oecd.org/daf/governance/principles.htm.*)

The Principles, are the first inter-governmental attempts to develop international standards for corporate governance. As such, they are non-binding and are not meant to provide detailed prescriptions for legislation or regulation. Detailed codes and best practices should be established at national and regional levels reflecting the governance systems in use.

The Chinese authorities have recognised that intensified product market competition and the financial liberalisation that WTO implies might have a devastating effect on SOEs if the latter do not develop the means of attracting finance and of improving their performance and productivity through radically different incentive structures. To illustrate this, the September 1999 CCP Central Committee meeting, which set the stage for the most important current SOE reforms, endorsed the OECD *Principles of Corporate Governance*. They were referred to as the benchmark towards which Chinese enterprises should evolve. In the same vein, the Securities Regulatory Commission is currently developing a Code of Corporate Governance in which it is referring to the Principles.

government or the judicial system, is thus an urgent issue. These issues require special attention, as they are deeply entrenched and difficult to change. Constraining vested institutional interests in passing or enforcing regulations might need a coherent and decisive effort at all levels of government.

Evidence from the Chinese experience has shown that changing SOEs into new corporate entities with independent rights over their assets (corporatisation) did not allow them to achieve genuine autonomy. Corporatisation did help to make profits and losses more transparent, to establish book values of assets and to clarify, to a certain extent, the relationships among different investors. However, it did not manage to successfully separate enterprise management from state interference. Thus, the process of corporatisation needs to continue, in parallel with efforts aiming at effective separation between businesses and state administrations.

Despite a gradual improvement in the legal definition and recognition of property rights, a cohesive framework that would clarify, standardise, enforce and protect property rights in all sectors of the economy – without regard to the profile of the owner or its nationality – is still missing.

External disciplining measures to improve enterprise performance and foster enterprise restructuring are important in an increasingly competitive environment. The adoption and implementation of the new comprehensive bankruptcy framework that is now under discussion appears to be of essence. A change of perception also needs to take place in this respect. Reorganisation, liquidation, and bankruptcy proceedings need to be seen as a mechanism for facilitating the reassignment of assets to more productive uses. Better protection of creditors and enhancing the readiness of judges and courts to implement the new legislation, will also need to be addressed.

Intrinsic flaws of corporate governance in state-owned entities arise from the ambiguity of ownership rights. Under state ownership, the state acts as a principal on behalf of the public and delegates the decision-making over day-to-day operation of enterprises to managers (agents). The controlling authorities in China form a multi-layer governance system, which involves conflicting objectives, blurring the role of the state as a shareholder and regulator and restricting its monitoring and supervising capacity as owner. Under state ownership, the residual profits of enterprises are socialised, while losses are covered either explicitly through subsidies or implicitly through easier access to credit. Another critical impediment of corporate governance stemming from state ownership is the lack of market-based managerial incentives. All of this suggests that there are few incentives for the controlling authorities and the managers to ensure the efficient and profitable operation of SOEs.

State divestment of ownership is important for the establishment of an effective incentive structure for Chinese enterprises. The market rules of the game can replace many state-based, defective, and costly monitoring arrangements to ensure good enterprise performance and governance. In the case of China, the potential gains from diversified ownership and market incentives are much larger than in other countries, given the large size of state holdings and the correspondingly high cost of monitoring by the state alone. Thus, the current trend towards ownership diversification, greater commercial initiative and decentralisation of management needs to be accelerated, and investors should be allowed to become active owners. This is crucial for the success of the corporate governance reforms. An external environment of vigorous competition and financial discipline is also a key element of the success of corporate governance reforms.

It is also important to take steps in order to increase the free float in the market. This can be done through more state disposals, which could be highly beneficial for the markets especially in increasing liquidity and stability. Continuing ownership transformation in the form of IPOs, but also secondary offerings by state and SOEs, should be vigorously pursued in the medium term provided that market conditions do not become too unfavourable. However, they should be closely and carefully combined and sequenced with corporate governance improvements. This will also allow for state governance mechanisms to improve, as the control tasks of the government/shareholder will focus on a smaller number of companies.

Attracting better-governed companies to the capital market and enhancing its credibility as a corporate finance tool is important for capital market development in China. Thus, creating a second market addressed at purely private companies with more stringent corporate governance requirements and a more open attitude towards foreign investment might be a positive step. A second market tier could result in the relative de-coupling of investment in the new private sector from governance problems pestering the SOE listed sector. Experience in other emerging countries, such as Brazil, could be very useful.

Another way of attracting foreign portfolio investment in a substantial and sustainable way is the full integration of the Chinese A- and B-share markets. Recent developments have shown that the steps taken in this direction are rather encouraging. Chinese authorities should continue the process of integration of A and B markets in the near future. Promoting the development of large institutional investors is a measure that could also have an important positive spillover effect in increasing the quality of the Chinese market environment (see Chapter 15 on Capital Markets). As the experience in Europe shows, the presence of foreign institutions early on, through participation in European privatisation, has educated local institutions and helped them mature as equity market players. While carefully regulating the operation, Chinese authorities should therefore allow private asset managers and other intermediaries into the market, even ahead of relevant WTO deadlines in 2004.

The CSRC has an important role to play in improving corporate governance. It has quite large powers and is respected by market players. However, it is a still relatively young institution and its capacity to effectively fulfil its role will depend on the availability of human and financial resources in the future.

Capital market development will require a consistent effort to enhance existing shareholder rights and protection. Therefore, improvements of the technical regulations on shareholder proposals, nominations, and proxy solicitation by the CSRC, are important for the protection of outside shareholders, as the latter increase in number and importance.

Related party transactions are the key threat to shareholder value in China. They need to be addressed effectively by the regulator lest they undermine confidence in the nascent equity markets and close the door to this avenue of corporate finance. In this context, there is also a pressing need to shift the management of social assets away from the listed enterprises and increase the transparency of transfers towards the improvement of social infrastructure.

Related party transactions are also a threat for stakeholders. An important issue is the decision-making structure at the enterprise level, which often politicises resource allocation and hinders restructuring. The current government drive for modernisation in the corporate sector should allow for the de-politicisation of decision-making, while increasing its transparency.

Performance-based executive remuneration is still in its very infancy. The adoption of managerial incentives schemes and stock options might be a good measure in ensuring that the best people are attracted as managers of companies. Complete separation between civil administration remuneration and executives' remuneration is another priority in this respect. At this stage, stakeholder issues need also to be addressed by the rapid development of a social safety net and improvement of the overall regulatory framework for consumer and environmental protection. For example, when listing in foreign markets, Chinese companies might find it increasingly helpful to address up-front their environmental record and labour practices.

Transparency and disclosure constitute a key tool for encouraging better corporate governance as they ultimately ensure a lower cost of capital for companies. Investors are more willing to commit their capital if they feel they are appropriately informed regarding a company's prospects and risks. Therefore, the Chinese government should effectively expand the scope of the newly adopted accounting standard to the whole enterprise sector and not only to the handful of listed companies. In addition, a greater involvement of accountants in the elaboration of standards is also important, in order to enhance the role and quality of the accounting profession and the process of implementation of the new standards.

Non-financial disclosure also needs serious improvement, especially with respect to ownership/control structures and governance. Most importantly, the principle of auditor independence seems to be in need of proper implementation and a stronger compliance drive is needed by the relevant professional organisation.

Enhancing the role and independence of boards of directors is a central objective of the current Chinese corporate governance reform process. While board independence is a key building block in improving governance, it should not be perceived as a panacea. Strengthening board structures should be pursued, together with measures aiming to increase market efficiency through continuing supply of high quality shares in the context of ownership diversification.

449

Few boards have independent directors. In those that do, non-executives have precious few responsibilities. The corporate governance code under preparation by the CSRC will reportedly suggest at least 30 per cent independent directors and will create nomination committees that are majority independent. This would be an important step forward. A key issue with respect to boards is how independent directors are nominated and appointed.

Under Chinese control conditions of pervasive linkages between SOE holdings and listed companies, board independence becomes even more important. The CSRC draft code envisages allowing shareholders of at least 5 per cent of common stock to nominate directors. In addition, cumulative voting might be a good way to enhance the monitoring role of boards. It would empower outside shareholders and infuse boards with real independence. A related issue is the potential for capture even of independent directors by management or related parties. This is why the Company Law should be amended to include a duty of loyalty.

Another issue to be addressed is the competence of board members. A possible solution might be using management from other listed companies as board members, which is a common practice in most countries. Another option is to attract foreign expertise.

NOTES

1. As to the drafting process, see Charles Paglee, "Contract Law in China: Drafting a Uniform Contract Law", *www.qis.net/chinalaw/prccontract.htm* and Gianmaria Ajani, "Needs Analysis on the Law of Contracts", *gtz-commercial-laws.org.cn*.

2. Contract Law of the PRC, adopted and promulgated by the Second Session of the Ninth National People's Congress, March 15, 1999, *www.cclaw.net*

3. These included the Economic Contract Law of the PRC, the Law of the PRC on Economic Contract Involving Foreign Interests and the Law of the PRC on Technology Contracts, as well as more than a dozen by-laws (regulations, rules and measures).

4. Zhang Yuqing/Huang Danhan, "The New Contract Law in the People's Republic of China and the UNIDROIT Principles of International Commercial Contracts: A Brief Comparison", *www.unidroit.org/english/publications/review/articles/2000-3.htm*.

5. Compare again John Mo, "Uncertainties in the Mainland's New Code of Contract Law"; *Hong Kong Lawyer* June 1999, p. 32 and Ge Jun, "The PRC Contract Law: Where Lie the Uncertainties?", John Mo, "The PRC Contract Law: The Uncertainties Lie in Law; *Hong Kong Lawyer* January 2000, p. 82 and 87.

6. Company Law of the People's Republic of China (*Zhonhua renmin gongheguo gongsi fa*), adopted at the Fifth Session of the Standing Committee of the Eighth National People's Congress, December 29, 1993, *http://chinalawinfo.com*

7. For the full text of the Decision see *China Daily, Supplement*, November 17, 1993.

8. Thus, corporatised enterprises continued to be subjected to extensive state intervention. For example, enterprises remained subject to often rigorous state controls over labour, investment and production structure, cash flow allocations, disposal of assets and changes in capital structure. There was insufficient attenttion paid to formulating, and implementing governance was not positive, and on a number of occasions was negative because increased autonomy allowed managers, often in collusion with their controlling authorities, to form an insider group expropriating the state as owner. Cyril Lin, "Corporate Governance in China", paper presented at the OECD/ADB meeting on Corporate Governance of SOEs in China, Beijing, January 2000.

9. On Tam Kit. *The Development of Corporate Governance in China*. Edward Elgar. Cheltenham /Massachusetts: 1999.

10. As per 4th Plenum of the 15th CPC Central Committee, Decision on Major Issues concerning the reform and development of SOEs, September 22, 1999.

11. This was done by changing the original clause "the private economy is a supplement to public ownership" to "the non-public sector, including individual and private businesses, is an important component of the socialist market economy". *China Daily*, March 16, 1999.

12. World Bank, *China's Emerging Private Enterprises*, Washington DC, 2000.

13. Huaren Sheng (Chairman of the SETC), "The SOEs process of reforms shows an organic combination between state ownership and market economy", SETC *Communiqué* No. 27, October 2000, *www.setc.gov.cn*. Thus, the authorities fixed a three-year target to curtail loss-makers among large SOEs. Recent cases include some large SOEs, listed companies, joint ventures, financial institutions, and debtors with large foreign liabilities are an example to this effect.

14. The entitlement of labour affected by SOE bankruptcy can be quite substantial and reach up to 3-years of wages, which has deferred many bankruptcies for lack of funds.

15. Tight limits on the debt write-off by banks have also delayed many cases.

16. Wang Weiguo. "Strengthening Judicial Expertise in Bankruptcy Proceedings in China". Paper presented at the OECD meeting on Insolvency Reform in Asia, Denpasar, Indonesia, 7-8 February 2001, *op. cit.*

17. World Bank, "Bankruptcy of State Enterprises in China – A Case and Agenda for Reforming the Insolvency System", Washington DC, Draft September 20, 2000.

18. Wang Weiguo, *op. cit.*

19. Wang Weiguo, *op. cit.*

20. Furthermore, the judges of this court collectively wrote a book *The Trial Procedure for Bankruptcy Cases*, which was published by the People's Court Press in June 1997.

21. Weifang He (Vice-director, SETC). "Achievements and Disadvantages of China's Twenty Years in the Construction of its Legal System". *www.china.org.cn/*

22. This applies not only to China but also to other Asian countries, which have a unitary political tradition that does not separate the law-making and law-enforcing branches of government.

23. Unless stated otherwise, the information in this part of the paper is based on the results of fact-finding trips to China and on the proceedings of the OECD meeting on "Corporate Governance of State-Owned Enterprises", held in Beijing in January 2000 in co-operation with the Development Research Centre of the State Council.

24. See Chapter 15 on Capital Markets for details.

25. Approximately 30 per cent are directly under state ownership, while the rest are controlled by SOE holding company structures (the so-called legal person shares, see Box 13.6).

26. Systems that emulate development in share prices relative to a benchmark without the actual granting of options.

27. The 1999 amendments clarified the respective roles and responsibilities of the state, enterprise managers, and accountants. They make the corporate leadership legally responsible for the truthfulness of accounting information. The law sharpens the status of accountants, who are now responsible for themselves, rather than acting on behalf of the state. It also introduces a range of financial penalties for infringement. F. Narayan, and B. Reid, *Financial Management and Governance Issues in the People's Republic of China*, ADB, 2000.

BIBLIOGRAPHY

Ajani, Gianmaria,
 Needs Analysis on the Law of Contracts, http://gtz-commercial-laws.org.cn.

Chang, T. K. (1998),
 Investment Funds: China's newest equity instrument, China Law and Practice, March 1998, p. 23.

Cohen, Jerome,
 "Chinese Courts and Chinese Modernisation". *www.china.org.cn*

Comberg, Phillip (2000),
 "Grössere Sicherheit", *Asia Pacific News,* No. 5/June 2000, p. 11.

Ding, M. (1998),
 "Legislation to safeguard infant investment funds", in: *China Daily Business Weekly,* November 15, 1998.

Doods, Robert (1996),
 "State Enterprise Reform in China: Managing the Transition to a Market Economy", *Law and Policy in International Business,* Vol. 27, 1996.

The Economist (2001),
 "In Praise of Rules. A Survey of Asian Business", 7 April 2001.

Gilley, Bruce (2000),
 "China's Dodgy Funds", *Far Eastern Economic Review,* December 14, 2000.

McGregor, Richard/Leahy, Joe (2001),
 "China takes a giant step' towards unified stock market", *Financial Times,* 19 February, 2001.

McGregor, Richard (2001),
 "New figures for China's unofficial funds sector", FT.com site, July 2, 2001, "Estimates grow for unofficial China funds", *Financial Times,* July 3, 2001 and "Spotlight falls on China's private funds grey market'", *Financial Times,* July 9, 2001.

He Wiefang,
 Achievements and Disadvantages of China's Twenty Years in the Construction of its Legal System. www.china.org.cn/

Judges of the People's Court (1997),
 The Trial Procedure for Bankruptcy Case, published by the People's Court Press, June 1997.

Jun, Ge (2000),
 "The PRC Contract Law: Where Lie the Uncertainties?"; *Hong Kong Lawyer* 2000, p. 82.

Jiang, Ping (1996),
 "Drafting the Uniform Contract Law in China", *Columbia Journal of Asian Law,* 1996, p. 245-258.

Jiang Qiangui (2000),
 "Strengthening Law Enforcement (fazsi yisi) in Enterprise Management". Speech to managers working in priority SOEs *(guojia zhongdian quye). www.setc.gov.cn/.* December 28, 2000.

Lin, Cyril (2000),
 "Corporate Governance in China", paper presented at the OECD /ADB meeting on Corporate Governance of SOEs in China, Beijing, January 2000.

Lu, H. (1999),
 "Wall Economy and Unit Socialism", conference paper, Rice University, 1999, in: Baker, J., Nee, V., "Organisational Dynamic of Market Transition: Hybrid Forms, Property Rights and Mixed Economy in China", *Administrative Science Quarterly,* Vol. 37, 1992.

Ma, S.-Y. (1996),
 "Foreign participation in Chinese privatisation", *Communist Economies and Economic Transformation,* Vol. 8, No. 4, 1996.

453

Megginson, William/Boutc Hong Kongova, Maria,

"The Impact of Privatisation on Capital Market Development and Individual Share Ownership" unpublished research paper for the OECD and FIBV: *www.oecd.org/daf/corporate-affairs/privatisation/capital-markets/megginson. pdf*

Mo, John (1999),

"Uncertainties in the Mainland's New Code of Contract Law"; *Hong Kong Lawyer* June 1999, p. 32.

Mo, John (2000),

"The PRC Contract Law: The Uncertainties Lie in Law"; *Hong Kong Lawyer* January 2000, p. 87.

Narayan, F./Reid, B. (2000),

Financial Management and Governance Issues in the People's Republic of China, Asian Development Bank.

Neoh, Anthony (2000),

An Overview of the Chinese Domestic Capital Market at the Dawn of the New Millenium, in: *China 200 – Emerging Investment, Funding and Advisory Opportunities for a New China, www.asialaw.com/bookstore/china2000/.*

On Kit Tam (1999),

The Development of Corporate Governance in China. Edward Elgar. Cheltenham /Massachussets: 1999.

Paglee, Charles, *Contract Law in China: Drafting a Uniform Contract Law, www.qis.net/chinalaw/prccontract.htm*

Sheng Huaren (2000),

The SOEs process of reforms shows an organic combination between state ownership and market economy, SETC Communiqué No. 27, October 2000, *www.setc.gov.cn*

Wang Weiguo (2001),

"Strengthening Judicial Expertise in Bankruptcy Proceedings in China", Paper presented at the OECD meeting on Insolvency Reform in Asia, Denpasar, Indonesia, 7-8 February 2001.

World Bank (2000),

"Bankruptcy of State Enterprises in China – A Case and Agenda for Reforming the Insolvency System", Washington DC, Draft September 20, 2000.

World Bank (2000),

China's Emerging Private Enterprises, World Bank, Washington DC, 2000.

Yuqing, Zhang/Danhan, Huang (2000),

The New Contract Law in the People's Republic of China and the UNIDROIT Principles of International Commercial Contracts: A Brief Comparison, www.unidroit.org/english/publications/review/articles/2000-3.htm.

Xiaonian Xu, Yan Wang (1997),

"Ownership Structure, Corporate Governance and Corporate Performance. The Case of Chinese Stock Companies", Policy Research Working Paper 1795, The World Bank, June 1997.

Zhang, D. (2000),

"Savings up, loans too, says central bank", *China Daily,* 17.3.2000, p. 1.

Chapter 14

DEVELOPING THE FINANCIAL SYSTEM
AND FINANCIAL REGULATORY POLICIES

TABLE OF CONTENTS

DEVELOPING THE FINANCIAL SYSTEM
AND FINANCIAL REGULATORY POLICIES[*]

Financial system development is central to the economic development and transformation of all economies. Since the work of Gurley and Shaw (1956), theories of economic development, as they have evolved in response to experience, have given progressively greater weight to the financial system. Evidence continues to accumulate that efficient financial systems can increase economic growth potential by mobilising savings and by facilitating their allocation to the most productive uses. Conversely, historical experience amply illustrates that weak or distorted financial systems can lead to financial crises that damage economic performance.

Financial system development is particularly important to China's successful adjustment to trade and investment liberalisation, for several reasons. First, serious strains have developed, underscored by the mismatch in credit allocation among business segments and pervasive financial problems of financial institutions. These need to be addressed soon if the financial system is to support the adjustments in the real economy necessary to reap the benefits of trade and investment liberalisation. Second, financial system development is part of the broader process of developing the "framework" conditions such as competition policy, corporate governance, and other processes and institutions central to a market economy. And third, to fully exploit the opportunities offered by the international integration of China's real economy, the financial system will also have to become more open to international markets. However, as the 1997 Asian crisis illustrates, such an opening may pose risks to macroeconomic stability unless the present distortions in the financial system are corrected.

Previous chapters in the first part of this study have examined the development of key segments of the financial system. This chapter focuses on strategic issues concerning the overall architecture of the system that bear on its effectiveness in performing its main functions in the economy. The first section discusses the main weaknesses in the Chinese financial system's capabilities in fostering the efficient use of the economy's resources and examines the priorities for remedying those weaknesses. The second section considers the priorities for financial supervisory and regulatory policies to improve the functioning of the financial system and to preserve macroeconomic and financial stability in the overall economy

Improving the financial system's ability to promote efficient resource allocation

The effectiveness of the financial system in promoting efficient resource utilisation largely depends on how well it performs three basic tasks. The first is to mobilise savings. Developing country financial systems have not infrequently had difficulty in mobilising savings due to regulation of interest rates below market levels or other distortions that have discouraged savers from placing their funds in the formal financial sector ("financial repression").

The second task is to allocate credit to the most efficient uses. The ability of financial systems to gather and process information and lower transactions costs of moving funds from savers to investors is thought to be one of the key channels through which the financial system contributes to economic growth (Leahy et al., 2000; Tsuro, 2000). Particularly important in this regard is the success of financial systems in allocating funds to activities with high capacity for innovation and productivity enhancement. Financial systems also contribute to effective resource allocation over time while providing means to pool risks and smooth out fluctuations in liquidity (Tsuro, 2000).

The third task is to encourage efficient resource utilisation in productive sectors of the economy. Strict lending standards, the requirement that loans be repaid, and the monitoring of borrowers'

* This chapter was written by John Thompson, Counsellor, from the Directorate for Financial, Fiscal and Enterprise Affairs (DAF) Department and Charles Pigott, Economics Department, OECD. Dr. Cunzhi Wan, Deputy Director of the Statistics Department of the People's Bank of China contributed Box 14.3.

behaviour by financial markets provide incentives ("discipline") for economically efficient behaviour. Financial systems further contribute by providing means to reorganise enterprises, re-deploy resources, and transfer ownership and control. The effectiveness of these mechanisms depends not only on the characteristics of the financial system itself but also on the clarity of property rights, enforceability of contracts, and related aspects of the legal and regulatory framework for the economy as a whole.

Weaknesses in China's financial system capabilities

Judging from the amount of funds allocated (Figure 14.1), China's financial system appears to do a reasonable job of mobilising the economy's savings. Partly because inflation has been fairly well controlled (with the exception of a few fairly brief episodes – see Oppers 1997), financial repression has not been a serious problem. However the financial system performs much less well in carrying out the other two tasks.

In particular, there are several important and well-known distortions in credit allocation:

a) *Financial resources are inefficiently allocated among enterprise segments.* As documented in the chapters on banking and capital markets, SOEs receive a disproportionately high share of credits from financial institutions and markets, while the share directly received by non-state enterprises is low compared to their contribution to the overall economy. Within the SOE sector, larger enterprises, particularly those participating in central or local government industrial development efforts, tend to have more favourable access to credit than smaller SOEs, or those not so well connected. The low profitability of SOEs and their comparatively low growth rate further reinforces the impression of serious credit misallocation. Admittedly, the limited access of non-state firms to formal credit channels is partly offset by indirect borrowing through affiliated SOEs or other non-financial entities as well as through informal channels. However, the reliance on such indirect channels simply underscores the failings of the formal financial system

Figure 14.1. **Domestic credit, 1999**

As a percentage of GDP

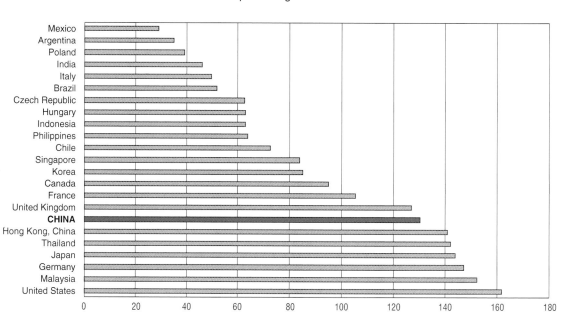

Note: 1998 for Hungary and India.
Source: IMF, *International Financial Statistics.*

in allocating credit. Moreover, such indirect channels are unlikely to be efficient and they increase the risks of financial abuses.[1] Recent developments have in certain respects increased divergences in credit access among enterprises. Banks' efforts to avoid incurring new non-performing loans have sharply reduced the access of SMEs, state owned and non-state, to bank credit, while larger SOEs backed by central or local governments are able to get loans largely because of the implicit guarantee that backing confers. This together with the divestiture of smaller SOEs from government control – and backing – has led to a virtual credit crunch for SMEs generally, one which could get worse as medium-sized SOEs are divested. In contrast, larger SOEs destined to remain under state control have been the main beneficiaries of the development of the stock market and SOEs continue to have nearly exclusive access to commercial paper and the corporate bond issuance.

b) *Non-economic considerations and various rigidities distort the pricing of credit.* Although bank-lending standards have been tightened for many enterprises, mandates to direct credit to priority sectors or projects (such as government infrastructure spending) together with continued lending to loss-making SOEs suggest that considerations beyond strict commercial criteria still play a role in a significant amount of lending. The four large, wholly state-owned commercial banks (SOCBs) in particular continue to be used in part as government agents in these efforts. Implicit government guarantees, which are unevenly distributed, play a major, indeed probably increasing, role in determining which enterprises receive loans. Access to stock market listing has been rationed on the basis of a mix of commercial criteria along with other criteria such as equity among regions and the desire to reduce state support for SOEs. Regulated interest rates do not allow adequate scope to charge appropriate risk premiums. The "credit culture" is weak since borrowers, especially large SOEs, face only limited sanctions if they fail to repay. The net result is that borrowers do not pay a cost for funds that is commensurate with their social opportunity cost or the associated risks.

c) *Facilities for channelling savings among financial institutions and markets are very limited.* The four large SOCBs have a major advantage, by virtue of their networks, in gathering savings but less of a comparative advantage in allocating savings to their most productive uses relative to smaller commercial banks and other financial institutions. Interbank, and other short-term markets that in other countries are important conduits for transferring funds among institutions, are growing rapidly in China but are still relatively limited. Bank certificates of deposits generally are not negotiable or transferable. Flows of funds among regions, although they have become more flexible in recent years, are limited by the same factors, as explained in Box 14.3.[2] The limited breadth of secondary markets for corporate and government bonds and commercial paper further constrains the ability of both savers and users of financial resources to deal with unforeseen contingencies.

d) Financial instruments – even basic ones to deal with liquidity fluctuations, manage risk, and deal with other specialised needs – are quite limited. For example, financial futures and options contracts are still not permitted. The fixed income markets are still quite limited, and even the government bond market lacks depth and liquidity (see Table 14.1). Consequently, institutions such as pension funds and insurance companies have a narrow range of investment options.

Due partly to these weaknesses, the financial system is seriously limited in its ability to promote efficient resource allocation more broadly.

a) *Financial discipline mechanisms are weak and uneven* due to government use of banks for non-commercial purposes, the unwillingness of authorities to allow larger SOEs to fail, the limited transparency of economic operations, plus weak property, contract, and bankruptcy laws and enforcement mechanisms. The tightening of lending standards that began in 1996 and efforts to make SOEs more autonomous and accountable have probably improved financial discipline to a significant degree for a large segment of enterprises. However, it is much less clear that larger

Table 14.1. **Funds raised by domestic non-financial sectors, 1999**
(100 million RMB)

	Total	Non-financial corporations	Households	General government
Total funds raised	19 201	13 543	840	4 818
Loans	10 988	10 148	840	
Securities	5 795	877		4 918
Bonds		42		4 918
Shares		835		
Foreign direct investment	3 622	3 622		
All other and errors and omissions	−1 204	−1 104		−100

Source: People's Bank of China, *Financial Outlook*, 2000.

SOEs face greater discipline. Competing government claims on enterprises, such as the effective seniority given to social security fund obligations (Lardy, 2000), impede loan contract enforcement and disclosure. These problems, together with their own financially weakened state, limit banks' incentives to effectively monitor their borrowers. The discipline provided by the stock market likewise is weakened by the relatively small share of equity that is listed, the limited powers of minority investors and the implicit government backing enjoyed by many of the listed firms. Existing evidence suggests that listing has had only limited impact on enterprise governance or performance.

b) Financial mechanisms to facilitate enterprise reorganisation, re-deploy resources, and provide a market for corporate control are developing but are severely impaired by government regulation and involvement in enterprise management as well as the weak property rights regime. Mergers and acquisitions are generally arranged by government agencies and their structuring is still influenced by non-economic considerations, such as employment maintenance, rather than based on maximisation of the value of the new entity (OECD, 2000*a*). The exclusion of a large portion of listed SOE shares from trading and other regulations largely rule out the possibility of hostile take-overs or even voluntary acquisitions apart from those actively sponsored by government authorities. Acquisitions or mergers that cross regional boundaries are hindered by government red tape and not infrequently by local protectionism. Together with factors that restrict the scope for bankruptcy or liquidation, these problems make it hard to reallocate resources or transfer control from inefficient to efficient enterprises.

These weaknesses stem in part from conditions common to developing and transition economies. Financial instruments are typically limited and bond markets play a small and narrow role in most developing countries. Unclear and conflicting property rights, weak commercial law enforcement, and limited bankruptcy regimes have been common issues in transition economies. As in European transition economies, financial institutions in China have massive non-performing loans and inadequate capital that need to be addressed if reforms to improve commercial functioning and tighten loan standards are to succeed. However two more distinctive features of China's financial system pose special challenges. First, although the degree of government direct control does vary, the almost complete public ownership of financial institutions poses major challenges to efforts to ensure that they operate according to strict commercial principles, exercise effective financial discipline, and observe prudential norms. Second, the concentration of financial activities on the four SOCBs and the relatively limited array of other bank and of non-bank financial institutions makes for particular difficulty in providing adequate financing to a large segment of enterprises critical to the economy's development, but which do not have the preferred status accorded to larger SOEs.

Implications of Trade and Investment Liberalisation for financial system development priorities

Remedying these weaknesses, the primary challenge to China's financial system, will involve extensive reforms in a range of areas. However, the priorities depend on the changes in the real economy likely to occur over the next five to ten years. Particularly important are the reallocation of resources and changes in enterprise organisation described in the first part of this study, together with the development of social benefit programmes and growth in government debt discussed later in this part.

The chapters on industry and agriculture indicate that the overall importance and numbers of enterprises that now have relatively limited access to formal financial outlets are going to increase greatly as trade and investment liberalisation proceeds. The shift of resources toward labour-intensive industries will increase the share of SME in industry output and employment. The importance of non-state, particularly private, enterprises is projected to rise rapidly and considerably as the downsizing ("letting go") of the SOE sector proceeds. Industry restructuring together with development of the service and high-technology sectors will provide a major impetus to formation of new enterprises.

All of these segments now face significant constraints in their access to external funding. The extensive survey conducted for the International Finance Corporation in 1999 (IFC, 2000) found that private enterprises relied almost exclusively on own funds for their development. Nearly 80 per cent of the firms surveyed cited lack of access to finance to be a serious constraint. Although commercial banks were important funding sources for the largest private firms, only 29 per cent of all private firms surveyed had received a bank loan within the past five years. While reliance on internal funds is typical for SMEs in all countries, Chinese SMEs appear to be even more dependent than firms in other advanced transition economies. Access by SMEs to external credit has deteriorated further in recent years, due in substantial part to the extensive financial problems in this sector but because of changes in the situation and policies of credit suppliers. As noted Chapter 7, banks have become very cautious in lending to all but the most obviously solid credit risks or to enterprises that are not firmly backed by central or local governments. The increased emphasis banks are placing on collateral backing for loans also disadvantages SMEs, particularly newer firms since they tend to have limited fixed assets (see OECD, 2000b). Officially encouraged efforts to improve commercial bank financing facilities for SMEs and private firms appear to have had at best limited success.[3] If this situation continues, the real sector adjustments that need to occur for China's economy to fully benefit from trade and investment liberalisation, including extensive restructuring and development of SMEs, are likely to be impeded.

As discussed further in Chapter 15 on capital markets, trade and investment liberalisation, along with other economic reforms, will also increase the overall importance of the capital market development. The priority now being placed on public listing as a means of improving firm capital structures and governance implies substantial expansion of the size of the stock markets as well as a more active role for the capital market in monitoring corporate performance. The expected growth of the insurance sector, together with the development of social benefit programmes, increase the need for both longer-term fixed income assets, as well as equity, to allow insurance and pension funds to manage their inherently longer term liabilities and the associated risks. Meanwhile, the likely substantial increase in the supply of government debt (see Chapter 22 on macroeconomic implications) will further increase the need for broader and more flexible bond markets. At the same time, better developed money- as well as capital markets are needed to allow joint-stock banks (JSBs) and smaller financial institutions to develop, and to provide facilities for the transfers of funds among regions needed to support China's regional development objectives.

The increased international activities of domestic businesses, and greater participation by foreign firms in the domestic Chinese market, implies a need for more flexible access to international financial markets than afforded by the present capital control regime. For example, Chinese multinationals, if they are to integrate their domestic and foreign activities efficiently and contain the risks arising from transactions in different currencies, will need greater flexibility to manage their foreign exchange positions. Capital account liberalisation, though, requires a certain level of development of domestic financial markets, particularly in those segments where controls are relaxed the most: liberalisation when there are serious distortions in domestic financial markets can greatly increase the risks of

461

destabilising capital flows and balance of payments crises (see Chapter 22). At the same time, liberalised capital flows can help to increase the depth and breadth of domestic financial markets while raising the level of sophistication of domestic issuers and intermediaries.

Strategic challenges and options for financial system development

Remedying the current weaknesses of the financial system and developing the capabilities to meet the demands that will arise over the next decade involve key strategic choices for financial reforms in a number of areas. The main challenges bearing on the financial system's ability to promote resource allocation are listed in Figure 14.2. The latter two – priorities for capital market development and the

Figure 14.2. **Principal challenges and options for financial reform**

Challenge	Central issue	Options
Restore Financial Stability	How fast; how much direct government intervention?	a. Comprehensive and near-term public injection of funds subject to conditionality
		b. Longer approach relying more on "growing out" of financial problems
Improve commercial orientation of financial institutions	How much to privatise? How to sustain commercial orientation of public financial institutions?	a. Privatisation
		b. Further measures to improve governance of public FI
Improve financing for SME and start-up enterprises		a. Develop facilities of JSBs and other smaller banks
		b. Foster "self-financed" credit guarantee funds and related facilities
		c. Provide government subsidies and direct guarantees
Ensure adequate diversity in financial outlets	What role for non-bank financial institutions?	a. Encourage development of JSBs and other smaller banks
		b. Encourage development of specialised non-bank financial institutions
Liberalise interest rates	How fast; which should come first?	a. Proceed slowly in line with market developments
		b. Proceed fairly rapidly in liberalising rates on lending and on large deposits and other market financial instruments
Prioritise development of money and capital markets	*What priorities should be given to stock, bond, and money markets?*	a. Continue to emphasise stock market development with a more gradual approach to bond markets
		b. Increase priority on money and bond markets while continuing to develop stock markets
Open up the capital account	*When and what segments to open? What are the domestic pre-conditions?*	a. Broad liberalisation in the medium-term
		b. More gradual and selective liberalisation retaining restrictions on short-term and other volatile types of capital flows

sequencing of capital account liberalisation – are discussed in other chapters. The remainder of this section discusses the main issues concerning the other challenges.

Restoring financial soundness

Despite the large transfer of non-performing bank loans to the bank asset management companies (BAMC) in 2000, China's banking system is still far short of being financially sound. As documented in the chapter on the banking sector, remaining non-performing loans of the four SOCBs are at least 25 per cent of their loan portfolio, between 10 and 20 per cent for the JSBs, and probably even higher than either figure for a substantial number of city commercial banks.[4] Despite their positive nominal capital ratios, all the SOCBs and many other Chinese banks would be effectively insolvent if evaluated by international accounting standards. A large segment of rural credit co-operatives are also reported to be virtually insolvent.

This situation of effectively negative capital is a major impediment to financial reform efforts. A central reform goal should be to establish financial institutions as profit-oriented commercial entities whose business is to place the capital of owners at risk with rewards or sanctions to shareholders and mangers reflecting the performance of their institutions. Under this paradigm, institutions must have positive incentives to seek out attractive opportunities while maintaining sound lending standards and effective means for credit monitoring and risk management. Institutions that cannot be closed but have negative capital are insulated from such market discipline. The threat of closure can provide incentives for smaller financial institutions – but it also creates incentives to take excessive risks and creates an uneven competitive playing field. High NPL and negative capitalisation further undercut internal incentives to maintain strict credit standards and effective loan monitoring by blurring responsibility for overall performance. While strict administrative penalties for bank officials may stem the growth of new NPL, they also foster overly risk-averse lending practices and limit incentives to take the prudent risks essential for a well-functioning financial system. Moreover, if allowed to persist, financial weakness will handicap domestic financial institutions in dealing with increased foreign competition and could limit authorities' flexibility to undertake capital control liberalisations.

The key choices for Chinese authorities in restoring financial soundness are the same as governments in other countries have faced during financial crisis: namely how rapidly to restore capital adequacy; and how much to rely on direct government injections of funds. Some countries have undertaken rapid and comprehensive government action to carve out NPL and restore capital adequacy, with the government assuming the bulk of the cost, at least initially. This was the approach taken by Finland, Sweden, and Norway during their banking crises in the early 1990s (Edey and Hviding, 1995) and has essentially been that followed by the Republic of Korea in the aftermath of the 1997 crisis.[5] A second approach is to undertake a "phased" approach in which substantial government funds are used *partially* to restore capital adequacy at the beginning, but with the remainder of the task left to the institutions to accomplish over a longer period. Except for the Republic of Korea and Indonesia, Asian countries that experienced crises in 1997 have taken this approach (OECD, *Economic Outlook*, 66) as did some European transition economies, notably Poland, earlier.

Whether rapid or more gradual, the key to the success of these efforts to clean up balance sheets has been accompanying measures to correct the adverse incentives and other distortions ("flow problems") that led to the accumulation of the NPL. Experience has shown repeatedly that these steps are critical to contain new NPL and prevent a recurrence of the crisis (Lindgren *et al.*, 1996; Goldstein and Turner, 1996). In most cases, government support has been conditional on efforts by recipient institutions to restructure their operations and make internal reforms to improve performance. It should be emphasised that recognising the costs of rehabilitation at an early stage can lessen the final costs of bank restructuring. If action is take to limit the emergence of new NPL and to maximise recovery from existing NPL, the total cost of the bank restructuring will be reduced. Similarly, if restructuring results in the creation of banks that are attractive to investors, some or all of the cost can be re-couped. Thus, in some of the Nordic countries mentioned in this paragraph, the government eventually recovered all

463

expenditure on bank restructuring even though at some points in the rehabilation process, the cost may have represented a large share of national income.

The advantage of the first, rapid, approach is that it promptly restores financial soundness, thereby containing the risks of a greater and more costly crisis subsequently and providing a fresh basis for reforms to improve financial institution behaviour. Of course, this approach will only work if management faces a new set of incentives. Once the bank is formally established on this path, the tasks of the management become 1) to prevent the development of new NPL and 2) to achieve earnings through cost cutting and focusing on the most profitable activities. A potential drawback is the creation of "moral hazard" incentives from the expectation that authorities will shield financial institutions from the consequences of future imprudent behaviour. A phased approach, though, may improve incentives for prudent behaviour over the longer term by imposing much of the burden on the financial institutions themselves. It may also involve lower costs to the government if external contributors to the financial crisis, such as economic recession, can be expected to improve within a reasonable time. However a phased approach that becomes too gradual can involve major risks, especially if authorities fail to enforce rigorous prudential standards in order to allow institutions to continue to operate. This lesson is underscored by the experiences of Japan during the 1990s and of the United States with its savings and loan institutions in the 1980s. Both countries allowed NPL to persist for years without ensuring adequate alternative means for the banks to restore their capital adequacy and engaged in "regulatory forbearance" that weakened market discipline over their activities. As a result the problems continued to worsen and the ultimate costs of the clean up were much higher than probably would have been the case if earlier and more comprehensive action had been taken. The most serious case of moral hazard arises where the remedies are insufficient to produce a bank with a strong balance sheet and where the management does not have a clear mandate to improve earnings and prevent new NPL. In these cases, management is likely to expect a second round of external support.

The current policy in China has been closest to the phased approach. Authorities have already provided substantial funds to carve out NPL from the SOCBs and increase their capital and have provided assistance to a number of JSBs in order to facilitate their listing on the stock market. They are also consolidating, as well as closing, many rural co-operatives and trust and investment companies. At the same time, authorities have repeatedly stated that there will be no further major loan carve outs or capital injections of the sort undertaken in 1999. By implication, banks are expected to use their profits and injections of outside equity from the stock market or other sources to "grow out" of their NPL and inadequate capital.

The considerations cited earlier, however, argue for a more rapid programme to restore financial soundness that is likely to require substantial further government funds. Given their low profitability and even with substantial funds from listing, Chinese financial institutions themselves are likely to be able to grow out of their problems on their own only (at best) quite slowly.[6] JSBs may be able to substantially improve their position through listing but this is likely to require substantial prior clean up of their balance sheets. A second but decisive round of support to the SOCBs is unlikely to add greatly to the moral hazard incentives already created by the banks' "too big to fail" status and consequent widespread market expectation that authorities will ultimately do what is necessary to maintain their viability. Indeed further delay could add to moral hazards by fostering the impression of an open-ended official commitment to prop up the banks, and by postponing the time when financial institutions' can be held fully accountable for their own performances.

A final and important consideration is whether the costs of a government financed "one-time" but comprehensive financial restructuring are affordable. This amounts to asking whether the additional government debt and associated servicing costs, together with other demands China's government will have to meet in coming years, are consistent with the maintenance of a sustainable fiscal position. The analysis in Box 14.1 and in the Chapter on macroeconomic issues suggests that such a clean up is affordable in this sense. The costs to the government, including those already incurred, of restoring capital adequacy to the (entire) banking system are estimated to be on the order of 23 to over 40 per cent of nominal GDP in 2000, depending on the actual amount of NPL, recovery rates, and other factors.

Box 14.1.   **Potential costs of restoring financial soundness**

This box presents a rough illustrative estimate of the order of magnitude of the costs of lowering NPL to manageable levels and restoring capital adequacy for the major segments of the financial system. The estimates include the costs of completing the clean up of SOCB balance sheets as well as costs of restoring financial soundness to other banks and to the rural credit co-operatives. The estimates should be viewed as only indicative given the considerable uncertainties about the present conditions of China's financial institutions.

Estimated cost of the clean up

Cleaning up balance sheets to restore capital adequacy involves two potential expenses for the government. The first is the cost of acquiring enough problem loans from the banks to reduce NPL to a level the banks can deal with out of their own resources. In China, low bank profits and loan provisions, and the difficulty of predicting the amount of problem loans that will arise from lending occurring now, suggests that bank NPL should be reduced to no more than 10 per cent of total loans. A lower target, of say 7.5 or 5 per cent would provide greater reassurance that the problems will not recur. The ultimate cost of assuming the loans is likely to be lower than the initial, gross, cost by an amount depending on the portion that banks and bank asset management companies (BAMC) are ultimately able to recover through collection, sale, or other means. Experiences in other emerging economies suggest that recovery rates vary from quite low, on the order of 20 per cent or less in the worst cases, to around 70-80 per cent in the best circumstances. The severe problems of enterprise borrowers, the slow pace of recovery, and very low recovery rates achieved so far suggest that China's recovery rate is likely to be in the lower end of this range. The illustrative calculations presented in the Table below assume a recovery rate of 15 per cent on a present discounted value basis.

The second potential expense involves raising core capital to adequate levels. All the major banking segments are, on average, still below the BIS minimum of 8 per cent of risk-adjusted assets. The calculations given below assume that capital ratios are initially raised to 8 per cent, and that the increase comes from government funds since the institutions presently have very low profits. In practice, this additional cost is likely to be fairly small since an exchange of NPL for government guaranteed bonds – the means used in 2000 – reduces required capital (because the bonds receive a zero risk weight under BIS rules while loans normally have at least a 100 per cent risk rate). Assuming further NPL are dealt with in a similar manner, and that authorities seek to achieve only the minimum capital ratio, implies that little or no new capital injections will be needed for SOCBs once the NPL are removed. As discussed further in the text, however, banks will probably need to raise their capital ratios further over time.

Very rough illustrative estimate of the cost of restoring financial soundness is summarised in the first table below, based on official estimates of NPL where available. While broadly consistent with estimates of banking sector clean up developed by other analysts, these figures are subject to numerous uncertainties, since precise information on the key parameters that determine the outcome is generally not available. NPL levels are particularly difficult to assess as in the past they have been fairly consistently under-estimated. If actual NPL are higher, the total cost could be substantially greater. On the other hand, the figures in the Table may overstate the ultimate costs if recovery rates turn out to be higher than assumed or bank profitability improves more rapidly (since it would allow banks to take on a greater share of the cost).

The table suggests three basic conclusions that seem reasonably robust to alternative assumptions. First, the ultimate cost of restoring financial soundness is likely to be large. Based on the official figures for SOCB NPLs, the estimated gross cost of restoring the commercial banks to financial soundness is 29 per cent of GDP, but significantly less, at 23 per cent of GDP, once the projected recovery of NPL is taken into account. While large, this cost is far from unprecedented as a number of other emerging economies have incurred even greater costs in the aftermath of financial crisis. About half of the total cost has already been incurred as a result of the carve out of SOCB NPL in 2000. Second, SOCBs account for nearly all of the bank clean-up cost. Extending support to JSBs and city commercial banks involves only modest additional cost and, as argued in the text, could reap a high payoff. Third, including the credit co-operatives is likely to raise the total cost significantly, to about 29 per cent of GDP on a net basis. While large, this cost would probably be worth incurring sooner rather than later since the problems of the co-operatives are likely to have to be dealt with at some point and could easily increase if not addressed now.

Box 14.1. **Potential costs of restoring financial soundness** (*cont.*)

Illustrative summary of costs of financial system clean up
(based on data for end-2000)

Amount (bn RMB unless otherwise indicated)	Total	All banks	SOCB	JS and City	Co-operatives
Assets	13 745	11 672	10 144	2 110	2073
Loans to non-financial entities[1]	10 038	8 452	7 606	1 171	1 586
Estimated NPL	4 164	3 371	3 202	234	793
Per cent of all loans (%)[2]	41	40	42	20	50
NPL to be assumed by government	3 160	2 526	2 441	114	634
Capital injections	65	33		33	32
Total gross cost/GDP (%)	36	29	27	3	7
Total cost net of recovery/GDP (%)	29	23	22	1	6

1. Excluding loans to the government and to other financial institutions.
2. Figures for SOCBs include the 1.3 trillion RMB transferred to asset management companies in 2000 and ssume an NPL rate on loans remaining with SOCBs of 25 per cent.

The figures assume that authorities reduce NPL to 10 per cent of total loans (excluding those to government and financial entities) and raise capital to at least 8 per cent of total risk-adjusted assets. Initial capital ratios are taken to be 7 per cent for SOCBs, 6 per cent for JSBs and city banks, and 4 per cent for co-operatives. The estimated net cost is the gross cost less the present discounted value of loans recovered, which is assumed to equal 15 per cent on a present value basis of the original NPL.

Although the final costs could turn out to be less under a more optimistic scenario (for example a higher recovery rate) they probably should be regarded as somewhat conservative. In particular, some outside experts believe remaining NPL with the banks are considerably above the official estimate of 25 per cent assumed for the Table (see in particular Lardy, 2000). Recent recovery rates on loans transferred to the asset management companies have been significantly lower than assumed for the Table. As indicated in the second Table below, the total cost could rise above 50 per cent of GDP under more pessimistic but possible outcomes. Lowering the bank NPL ratio further to a safer level of 7.5 per cent would add about 2 percentage points of real GDP further to the net cost. The estimates also do not include the possible cost of removing NPL and raising capital for policy banks, something that could cost a further 5 per cent of GDP. Overall, these considerations suggest that the cost of a comprehensive clean up are likely to range between 30 per cent of GDP in the most optimistic case and nearly 60 per cent of GDP in a pessimistic but not unrealistic outcome.

Range of possible costs of financial system clean up
(Per cent of GDP)

Net cost under baseline (see prior table)	30
With higher NPL[1]	44
Higher NPL plus lower recovery rate[2]	51
Memo:	
Additional cost of support for policy banks	~+5
Additional cost of lowering NPL ratio to 7.5 per cent	~+2
Range of possible costs	30 to 58

1. NPL for SOCBs of 40 per cent and co-operatives of 66 per cent.
2. Recovery rate of 5 per cent versus 15 per cent in baseline.

Although clearly high, the costs should not be prohibitive. Over time, the initial debt-GDP burden will fall as some of the NPL are recovered and as GDP increases. Under plausible assumptions about aggregate growth and the interest rate paid on government debt (see the Chapter on macroeconomic issues), the debt initially incurred should drop significantly in relation to GDP by 2010. Moreover, given its importance to financial institutions future performance, a rapid and decisive effort to restore financial soundness in the near term is likely to be less costly than allowing the problems to persist much further.

Most of this involves the clean up of the SOCBs. The costs of a more comprehensive clean up including credit co-operatives, would amount to somewhat more, on the order of 30 to just under 60 per cent of GDP. While large, this cost can be spread over a long period of time and is incurred largely through an increase in government debt that should be manageable, provided the share of government revenue to GDP continues to rise and the interest rate paid on government debt continues to be below the (nominal) growth of GDP. While the cost of the clean up is quite high, it is not out of line with that incurred by other emerging market economies that have experienced comparably severe financial difficulties. Moreover, the cost of waiting substantially longer to restore financial soundness could be considerably greater and more problematic.

The implication is that further initiatives in the near-term to complete the process of restoring financial soundness are both feasible and important to ensure that the financial system can accommodate the adjustments needed in the real economy. Such initiatives should involve smaller banks and non-bank financial institutions as well as the SOCBs. They are likely to be most effective if accompanied by clear and realistic targets and timetables and involve explicit conditions on the financial institutions to reform their internal operations. However implementation of such conditions also depends on reducing government involvement in the management of financial institutions, as discussed further below.

Ensuring that financial institutions operate as profit-oriented commercial entities

The almost complete government ownership of China's financial system presents a particularly acute challenge to ensuring that financial institutions operate as profit oriented institutions responsive to market forces. Government-owned financial institutions in OECD countries have declined in importance over the past several decades and now have a quite limited role. The main exceptions are transition economies, which are now privatising the financial institutions inherited from the central planning era: Germany, where banks owned by provincial (Länder) governments account for a substantial share of total assets, and other countries, notably Japan, where postal savings institutions are still major financial intermediaries.[7] Public ownership of financial institutions is more prominent in some emerging economies, such as India, but also has generally fallen over the past two decades (Table 14.2). Moreover, public ownership of financial institutions in China, while its form varies across different segments, involves a degree of direct government involvement in basic business decisions and in the choice of management that is unusual even in those other countries where government ownership is still significant.

The general decline in government ownership of financial institutions outside of China reflects a trend away from the use of banks as special institutions to promote "special objectives" (*e.g.* support of industrial policy, maintenance of employment, development of local communities and containment of the cost of servicing government debt) toward allocation of financial resources by market forces. Under this internationally accepted paradigm, banks are expected to develop modern corporate governance systems focused on 1) earning a competitive rate of return; and 2) maintaining prudential soundness. As experience in both OECD and non-OECD (especially Asian) countries shows, high government ownership and control – even when corporate governance structures have been established – interfere with the operation of banks as commercial entities. Banks that are expected to support industrial policy and other non-commercial objectives seldom can be held genuinely accountable for containing costs, earning adequate profits or observing prudential norms. The distortion in incentives is aggravated in many countries by regulatory restrictions that limit banks' ability to offer innovative products or control costs, and, particularly in Asia, by conflicts of interest arising from complex ownership and control arrangements of banks with industrial groups. The subordination of prudential policy to other objectives further compounds the problem by preventing bank supervisors from exercising effective oversight.[8]

While relevant to China, these considerations are conditioned by social objectives and other circumstances particular to that country. The need to replace administrative- with market-based credit allocation is a firmly accepted goal of official policy, but full privatisation of the financial system is not,

Table 14.2. **State ownership of banks**

	State owned or controlled banks: share of banking system capital	
	1998	1994
China	99	100
Other emerging economies:		
Hong Kong, China	0	0
India	82	87
Indonesia	85	48
Malaysia	7	9
Philippines	n.a.	19
Singapore	0	0
Thailand	29	7
Russia	36	n.a.
Argentina	30	36
Brazil	47	48
Chile	12	14
Mexico	28	0
Peru	0	3
South Africa	2	2
OECD countries:		
Australia	0	22
Canada	0[1]	n.a.
France	0[2]	n.a.
Germany	47	50
Italy	17[1]	n.a.
Japan	15	0
United Kingdom	0[1]	n.a.
United States	0	0
Czech Republic	19	20
Hungary	9[1]	81[3]
Poland	46	76

1. 1999.
2. The government has a controlling interest in several financial institutions that provide services similar to those of commercial banks.
3. 1990.
Source: OECD Secretariat.

at least at present. This raises two strategic questions. The first is how large a role will be allowed for private financial institutions. The second is how to improve, and sustain, commercially oriented behaviour consistent with prudential norms for financial institutions that remain government-owned. This second choice is critical for the period during which adjustments to trade and investment liberalisation will take place: even if privatisation were accepted to a much greater degree than is now the case, it would still take significant time to accomplish.

The current strategy to improve the commercial orientation of public financial institutions, notably the banks, is similar to that being followed for non-financial SOEs. The strategy relies heavily on the creation of modern corporate governance structures – boards of supervisors and directors consistent with international practice – and ownership diversification through stock market listing and other means. This process has been substantially accomplished for the JSBs (although further diversification through listing will occur over the next several years) but is only beginning for the SOCBs. Apart from tightening supervision, the means to improve commercial orientation of city commercial banks and non-bank financial institutions is less clear. The effectiveness of governance structures and ownership diversification is subject to the same limitations as for SOEs generally. The reforms have not ended the practice of government appointment of senior bank management, nor can they guarantee that imposition of non-commercial considerations on lending decisions will end. Ownership diversification may help eventually improve banks' governance and responsiveness to market forces, but its impact is likely to be very limited for some time to come by the continued role of financial institutions in implementing government policies and the limited mechanisms for securing the rights of minority shareholders in China. These limits are most severe for the SOCB but in principle they affect any institution whose majority owner is also a major customer and regulator, and which is responsible for, or has a major interest in, other major customers. This is true of virtually all the JSB and other smaller banks and non-financial institutions.

In addition to these explicit efforts, two other policies have potentially important bearing on the commercial orientation of financial institutions. The first comprises efforts to increase competition by encouraging the development of smaller banks and other financial institutions. While competition can be a powerful impetus to improved governance, the pace and degree to which authorities are prepared to countenance inroads into the markets of the SOCB is still unclear. Foreign financial institutions can also help to improve competition, although their overall impact may be limited by their likely tendency to avoid most lending to domestic enterprises, at least for some time. In addition to competition, regulatory policies to weed out poorly managed institutions and tighten prudential standards also help to improve governance. The effects are likely to be greatest on smaller institutions and are less clear for larger ones, however. Moreover, the co-existence of government and privately owned (or mixed ownership) financial institutions itself creates potential competitive distortions. Public institutions can enjoy significant funding advantages over less favoured competitors by virtue of their government backing and can operate with lower levels of capitalisation. Public institutions may be less sensitive to rating downgrades or other market signals when their creditworthiness is declining, but may gain at the expense of other domestic banks in times of financial turbulence, since the relative advantage conferred by their implicit state guarantee increases.[9]

These limitations suggest that it will be difficult to ensure that government-owned financial institutions function completely as commercial institutions, or that there is a level playing field in the financial system as a whole. However other countries' experiences also suggest further steps that might improve performance. In particular, as noted in the banking chapter, an important step would be to establish a much stricter "arms length" relation between financial institutions' management and government agencies along the lines taken in a number of other countries. Specific steps include establishment of professional standards requiring that top financial institution management have prior experience outside of line government agencies, further measures to improve accountability of local branches to head offices, and of head offices to the supervisory authorities, stricter and broader requirements for public disclosure of information on performance plus requirements for regular audits by independent outside public accounting firms. Establishment of explicit deposit insurance applying to all banks could help to reduce the advantage of SOCBs. Governance of the SOCBs might also be improved by dividing operations into a number of subsidiaries, which while majority owned by the parent holding company would have diversified ownership and considerable autonomy.

Ensuring adequate access to credit for SME and new enterprises

Financing for SMEs and new enterprises has been a difficult challenge in all countries. A focus of policy in OECD countries has been on improving financing for new firms and in particular, new technology-based, SMEs undergoing substantial expansion or modernisation of their capacities.[10] It should also be mentioned that as banks have become more adept at credit analysis in the 1990s and as banks have gained greater freedom to price credits, SME lending has emerged as a field of endeavour that is targeted by many major banks. Thus, with appropriate incentives banks can become active in this sector without large-scale government subsidies. In China, the priorities are broader and the task complicated by the shift away from administrative credit allocation by financial institutions, the priority of bank lenders to avoid new NPL, and the changing ties between SOEs and their traditional government backers. A key challenge is to ensure that non-state enterprises, together with SOEs whose official backing by governments has been severed, can obtain financing on equal terms with those that are still officially favoured.

Explicit government efforts in China to improve SME access to outside credit are fairly recent and at an early stage. The efforts are focused on strengthening commercial banks' facilities for lending to SMEs and on developing regionally based credit guarantee programmes financed by contributions from participating enterprises and local governments. Beginning in 1999, commercial banks were given an explicit if general mandate to establish special units for lending to SMEs, including private enterprises. The effectiveness of this effort is difficult to evaluate. Lending to private entities has been rising rapidly, but much is due to increased consumer and housing credit. While banks seem receptive to lending to SMEs that can demonstrate they are clearly creditworthy, few borrowers are able to meet the conservative criteria imposed. The inability to vary interest rates enough to fully reflect credit risks further limits the incentives to lend to SMEs. Interviews with government and bank officials together with anecdotal evidence suggest that there has been little if any improvement in credit access for SMEs as a whole. The degree to which the credit guarantee programme, which is still in an experimental stage and confined to a limited number of cities, has made a difference is unclear at this point.

OECD Member countries have developed a broad array of instruments over the past several decades to facilitate SME access to external credit. OECD programmes typically involve a mix of components whose emphasis varies across countries and which involve varying degrees of government intervention. The first, and arguably most *laissez-faire*, approach is to improve the availability of information bearing on the creditworthiness of target firms and to adapt regulatory codes and procedures that impose disproportionately heavy burdens on SMEs or newer enterprises. Governments in some countries, notably Canada, foster "partnership" associations between newer SMEs and larger or more established firms in order to improve access to technology, markets, and know-how in addition to finance. Many countries provide direct support for SMEs financing to some degree through selective interest rate subsidies and tax incentives, but predominately through credit guarantee facilities. SME programmes also sometimes include specialised institutions or facilities to either lend directly to SMEs and/or start-ups on non-preferential terms, or to encourage private financial institutions to do so by providing technical services or various types of incentives.

Although venture capital is most advanced in the United States, a major expansion of this sector occurred in the 1990s. This very rapid expansion peaked in 2000 with the sharp cutbacks on high technology investment and the sharp declines in "growth" exchanges. Most OECD countries have sought to foster the development of "venture capital" companies to finance start-ups. In many OECD countries such as the United States, several European countries, Japan and the Republic of Korea, special "growth" stock markets have been established to provide equity financing for high technology companies that are nearing the end of their initial venture capital stage and are ready to seek public listing. In most countries, venture capital firms are private but in many countries, special government programmes or institutions associated with other public financial institutions have played an important role in the raising of venture capital. Indeed, government venture capital support schemes have typically started when there was a need to compensate the lack of private supply in general. But with growing private supply they are now more targeted at areas where there is a perceived special market failure.

Several aspects of OECD country experiences are worth emphasising because of their potential relevance to China's efforts to improve SME finance. A basic principle ("best practice") of OECD countries efforts is to leave specific credit allocation decisions to private market forces. In particular, the programmes do not impose specific quotas for SME lending on private banks or other financial institutions. The targeting of specific sectors or enterprises is normally based on economic rather than social or other criteria. A second principle is that SME financing needs to be integrated into the broader framework of efforts to foster SME development. In many countries, government sponsored facilities to facilitate SME financing are subject to, or associated with, the overall umbrella agencies responsible for SME policy. Integrating financing with efforts to address other key SME needs – access to markets, technology, and managerial skills – helps to ensure that programmes are mutually reinforcing and

Box 14.2. Ensuring adequate diversity in financial outlets

China has a comparatively limited array of financial institutions apart from commercial banks and securities dealers. Until the establishment of the policy banks in 1994, there were no specialised development banks of the sort that have been prominent in many other developing economies. There are still no specialised savings and loan, or trust banks. Apart from the trust and investment companies and rural and urban co-operatives, specialised non-bank financial institutions (NBFI) such as finance companies have only a very small share of overall financial activity.[1] While such facilities together with mutual funds and securities companies are expected to develop more rapidly in coming years, the future of NBFI to serve smaller borrowers or specialised sectors that now have less access to bank credit is much less clear.

The limited array of financial institutions is not necessarily a sign of weakness. Functions performed by NBFI in other countries, such as lending to agriculture or smaller businesses are carried out in China by the credit co-operatives or smaller commercial banks. The commercial banks provide the savings outlets often performed in part by more specialised institutions in other countries. The array of NBFI in other countries at least partly reflects regulatory policies that prohibit or make it difficult for banks to carry out activities performed by the NBFI but which, in principle, they could perform if permitted to do so. However, a less favourable consequence of the present bank dominated system is that it concentrates risk on the financial segment closest to the payments system and hence most critical to overall financial stability.

Moreover, non-bank financial institutions have some potential advantages in financing comparatively risky projects or sectors that typically find it difficult to obtain bank credit. By specialising in credit assessment and risk management for a particular segment of borrowers, NBFI may enjoy economies in organisation and management that would be difficult to replicate in a commercial bank, whose "culture" and senior management expertise are not necessarily as conducive to those activities. Since NBFI do not take deposits, their failure does not pose the same direct risk to the payments system as a bank failure. As a result, NBFI may be able to engage in more risky activities without posing the systemic risks that could be entailed if they were carried out by commercial banks. Experience in other emerging economies suggests that the need for NBFI as well as specialised banks depends on the structure of relations between larger corporations and smaller enterprises that serve as their suppliers. In Japan, such smaller enterprises tend to be organised in networks centred on larger firms and, by virtue of that relation, enjoy access to bank financing. Where such networks do not exist NBFI play a more important financing role. On the other hand, a number of Asian countries have experienced significant problems in the NBFI sector. In some cases (*e.g.* Republic of Korea and Thailand) NBFI contributed to financial problems during the 1997 crisis.

China's experience with NBFI has been mixed. The major experiment with such institutions was the development of trust and investment companies (TIC) beginning in the late 1980s (Kumar *et al.*, 1997). These institutions were created by banks and local governments to raise funds in domestic and international financial markets to finance infrastructure and other projects as an alternative to bank lending. After rapid growth in the first half of the 1990s, the TIC became major participants in the investment bubble that burst in the mid-1990s after credit was tightened. The resulting problems became manifest after the 1997 Asian crisis with the failure of several major international TIC. These experiences underscored widespread financial weaknesses among TIC generally, resulting in substantial part from their use as vehicles to evade prudential regulations. Authorities are now in the process of reducing the number of TIC (from around 250 at their peak to 50-60 ultimately) as part of a broader programme to combat financial abuses.[2,3]

The experience with TIC underscores the tension between diversity in the financial system and the need to maintain strong prudential standards. This tension is present in all countries but has been particularly acute in China because of the influence on lending decisions exerted by central government agencies and local governments, the often loose control by head offices of branch activities, and limited resources available to examiners and other supervisory authorities. However, some further expansion of NBFI in China may be necessary, as, for example, the development of credit guarantee facilities is likely to involve the creation of specialised institutions responsible for administering the guarantees. There may be a need to develop further specialised institutions to facilitate adjustments in the real sector if the present obstacles to banks' ability to serve important segments persist. Indeed, the continued importance of indirect channels and informal unsanctioned

```
Box 14.2.  Ensuring adequate diversity in financial outlets (cont.)
```

channels in mediating credit flows – despite periodic official efforts to rein them in – may be symptomatic of the need for greater diversity and flexibility in formal financial outlets.[4] For these reasons, development of a coherent framework for the structure, supervision and regulation of NBFI is an important priority for China's financial regulatory authorities.

1. For more detailed discussion of the development of institutional investors and other capital market based financial institutions, see the chapters on the insurance sector and on the development of capital markets.
2. To curb their use to avoid prudential requirements, TIC owned by banks are to be divested.
3. The conversion of urban credit co-operatives into commercial banks and the reforms being undertaken for rural credit co-operatives are partly to impose bank prudential standards in place of the generally weaker standards applying to co-operatives.
4. "Spotlight falls on China's private funds "grey market", *Financial Times*, 8 July 2001, which is based on a recent study by the People's Bank of China, provides an indication of the importance of such unsanctioned facilities. In 1999, officials moved to terminate unsanctioned equity trading in a number of regional centres. While the move was aimed at curtailing abuses, potentially beneficial trading to restructure smaller enterprises and reallocate resources to more efficient uses were almost certainly curtailed as well.

thereby make efficient use of the public resources involved. There is also substantial co-ordination between SME policies at the central, regional and local government levels. The integration of SME programmes is less far along in China, partly because the overall framework is still developing. However, such integration is likely to become increasingly important, given the relatively scarce public funds available and the comparatively large needs to be served.

The need to "leverage" scarce government resources and preserve incentives for beneficiary companies to operate efficiently has been an important influence on the structure of OECD SME programmes and is equally relevant for China. OECD countries typically have used partial guarantees and subsidies together with co-financing as a means of spreading public funds as widely as possible, sharing the risks with the private sector, and sustaining incentives for beneficiary firms to remain in good credit-standing.[11] Partnership programmes involving other enterprises in SME development also help to leverage and maintain standards. In some countries, SME and venture capital finance firms have developed new financial instruments better tailored to SME needs and which help to improve their access to private funding.[12] OECD experience, including problems that have arisen in the past, is that the financial entities responsible for extending guarantees or subsidies need to be subject to rigorous supervision by relevant regulatory bodies if abuses are to be prevented and funds used in a productive manner. These experiences also suggest that public entities involved in SME financing function better if required to meet commercial objectives, at least in part. To this end, for example, the Business Development Bank of Canada has been required since 1995 to earn a positive rate of return and pay dividends to its government owner.

Interest rate liberalisation

Interest rate liberalisation is key to improvement of the capabilities of China's financial system in several ways. First, preventing interest rates from adjusting to market forces inevitably involves rationing of financial flows, which tends to perpetuate the influence of administrative mechanisms that are at the root of many present distortions. Second, as noted earlier, interest rates are not sufficiently flexible to fully account for credit or other risks faced by lenders; as a result, higher risk projects that would be a worthwhile use of resources for society as a whole receive less than socially optimal levels of financing. Third, restrictions on nominal interest rates can magnify fluctuations in real interest rates by preventing nominal rates from adjusting to changes in inflation (see Figure 14.3). Fourth, limited interest rate flexibility is an obstacle to the development of money and capital markets, which need to

Figure 14.3. **Interest rates**

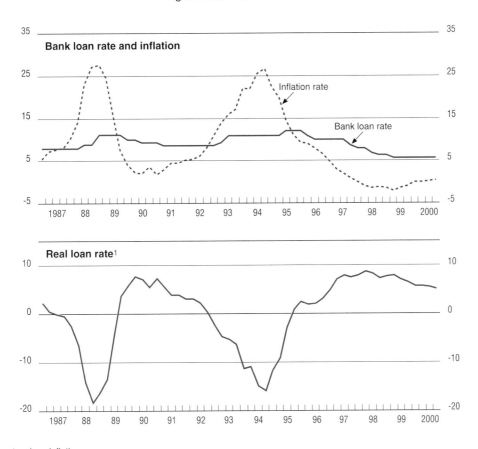

1. Bank loan rate minus inflation
Source: IMF, *International Financial Statistics.*

allow free play of market forces to function effectively but which are subject to distortions if interest rates in other components of the financial system are not allowed to vary also. In particular, greater interest rate flexibility is necessary for a more efficient foreign exchange market and to reduce the risks that capital account liberalisation will lead to destabilising capital flows.

China is arguably relatively advanced toward interest rate liberalisation for countries at a comparable stage of development. Money market interest rates have been substantially liberalised and banks are allowed some, if limited, flexibility in setting loan rates. This flexibility is comparable to that prevailing in Japan during the late 1960s and in Republic of Korea in the early 1980s. Liberalisation of rates on domestic currency loans and deposits has been viewed as more problematic, in part because of concerns that it would drive down loan spreads and reduce the already quite low level of bank profits. Recently, however, Chinese authorities have announced plans to free key domestic interest rates over the next three years, beginning with remaining restrictions on money market instruments and followed by the freeing of rates on loans and large fixed term deposits.

This plan, if it proceeds on schedule, should help significantly to improve the effectiveness and flexibility of the financial system to meet the changing financial demands that will be coming from the real economy. The scope and schedule of the interest rate liberalisation should also allow authorities adequate flexibility to manage any changes in capital control policy that become appropriate. Liberalisation of interest rates on smaller deposits, while desirable as an ultimate goal, is likely to have to wait until there has been a substantial and sustained improvement in bank profitability. Experiences

473

Box 14.3. **Mechanisms for funds transfer among regions in China***

The imbalance in regional economic development remains a key problem in China. The coastal provinces and cities have witnessed robust development while the economic performance of inland provinces and cities has been hampered by problems such as the loss of share in traditional markets and limited ability to attract inflows of funds from more prosperous areas.

Initially, these problems led to regional protectionism. The less-developed regions refused to accept goods from other regions and requested or pressured officials of local bank branches to prevent locally collected funds from flowing to other regions. One result was the emergence of serious duplication in industrial capacity. In addition, developed regions could not easily get raw materials from other regions and were reluctant to allow their own banks to lend to less-developed regions out of fear that the risks were too great. Furthermore, macroeconomic policy tended to respond to the conditions of the developed regions and the needs of less-developed regions were seldom completely met. This aggravated regional protectionism, a condition barely perceived by regional protectionists themselves.

The mechanism for transfers of funds among regions in China has changed substantially since the inception of reform and the opening to the outside world.

Since the mid-1990s, the People's Bank of China, as a central bank, has paid much attention to the development of China's financial markets so as to promote the appropriate allocation of funds among both industries and regions, and to maintain stability of both prices and economic performance in different regions. The focus is on redirecting monetary policy from plan-oriented direct operation to market-oriented indirect operation.

The first step is to establish a system of money supply statistics and to monitor the performance of monetary aggregates as a medium-term target of monetary policy instead of using the credit ceiling, which had been the traditional macro-adjustment tool and had led to shortages of funds in less-developed regions and a glut of funds in developed regions. In China, monetary aggregates are classified into three categories according to liquidity features. The narrowest money is currency in circulation, called M0. The narrow money is M0 plus demand deposits, called M1. And broad money is M1 plus time deposits and savings deposits, called M2. Now the annual rate of change of M2 is the medium-term target of monetary policy in China. The central bank generally targets M2 by 1) predicted annual growth rate of GDP, and 2) predicted annual change rate of consumer prices (CPI as of 2001) and, 3) possible changes in monetary velocity. The implementation of the central bank's monetary policy depends upon the performance of the bank sector and financial market which are subject to the indirect operation of the central bank.

The second is to carry out banking Assets and Liabilities (A&L) ratio management instead of credit ceiling or quota management. A given district, especially a less-developed one where there generally is positive deposit balance, can now autonomously extend its bank lending to clients in line with both the required A&L ratio and lending provisions. It was impossible for it to do so before 1999: its lending business was subject only to the credit quota; funds equivalent to the deposit balance might be transferred into other developed regions by more senior branches or the head office itself of the bank. In contrast, offices in developed regions with positive loan balances cannot now extend its bank lending to clients without constraints as had been the case when most lending expansion at lower branches could and did depend on the borrowing of funds from branch offices or even from the bank's headquarters. This change increases the flexibility of bank lending in less-developed regions. The stimulus comes from different A&L ratios among different banks at the national level and different regional branches at provincial level within a bank. But the authorities require that, variations notwithstanding, banks under supervision maintain A&L ratios averaging 75 per cent, set by the central bank. The differences of A&L ratios among different banks are determined by the central bank; and differences of A&L ratios among different regions within a bank, usually at provincial level, are set by the head office of the bank, which must report to and get permission from the central bank. These differences will be adjusted every couple of years in line with changing conditions.

The third step is to improve the development of the inter-bank market. At the outset of China's exposure to market conditions, participants comprised provincial branches and head offices of SOCBs. This meant that financial institutions located in rural areas and other less-developed regions were unable to borrow funds from other financial institutions and other regions. In 1999, the PBC authorised participation in an inter-bank market for all commercial banks, including SOCBs, JSBs and urban and rural credit co-operatives. The market network covers head offices, provincial branches and prefecture-level sub-branches of national commercial banks and the head offices of city commercial banks and credit co-operatives. Furthermore, the PBC permitted the market entry of securities firms in the first half of 2000.

Box 14.3. **Mechanisms for funds transfer among regions in China*** (*cont.*)

The inter-bank market has three functions. It is responsible for inter-bank transactions of bank fund positions in the short term (less than one year). The transaction depends upon computerised bids and auctions based on spot market information in the network. Every participant in the market has autonomy to conduct business in its own interests. This promotes short-term funds transfer among regions. Another function is to run network services for the open market operations of the central bank (since 1998). The instruments of transactions of the open market operation include repurchase agreements for government bonds, policy bank financial debentures and central bank special bills. Nowadays, refinancing businesses of the central bank to commercial banks is mainly conducted by open market operations instead of credit lending as formerly was the case. Finally, the money market provides network services for handling the computerised bid issuance of book-entry government bonds and policy bank financial debentures.

The fourth step concerns the tentative development of the commercial paper market. Before 1998 there were many restrictions on the development of this market. Some industrial sub-sectors, especially huge SOEs involved in textile, steel, petroleum and coal business areas in developed regions, could take advantage of the policy of guarantees of CP by state bank promise. At that time, it was impossible for SMEs, even those which had good market prospects, to make use of CP to expand their businesses. As of 1999, the PBC loosened the industrial, regional and banking limitations on the CP business and development of bank guarantees for CP has been the initial step. There are no limits on commercial banks', including branches and operating offices of SOCBs, JSBs, city commercial banks and credit co-operatives, supporting enterprises by using CP backed by bank guarantees for their business expansion. The enterprises which are about to take advantage of bank guarantees of commercial paper must be subject to PBC provisions. The requirements are: 1) the CP business must entirely depend on real transactions of goods, proven by signed documents, 2) enterprises should be able to document three consecutive years of profit-making, 3) sound credit records for three consecutive years, 4) enterprises should have favourable market prospects. The bank branch or operating office, which functions as guarantor of the CP, is responsible for due diligence in determining if the required qualifications are met. Eligible enterprises can issue bank-guaranteed CP according to their actual needs. As of 2001, tentative development of this business has emerged in China's coastal regions, and the CP market, including turnover of CP, inter-firm discount and discount by commercial banks, has grown fast. Rediscounting has already become one of the most important PBC monetary policy tools.

Last but no means least, the PBC has launched a series of credit guidance measures to help less-developed regions, especially western regions, to attract more funds from outside.

The *de facto* results achieved are manifest. The annual average growth rate of SOCBs' deposits in western regions was 14.5 per cent between 1995 to 2000, and that for loans was 14.8 per cent. Both rates were higher than the local GDP rate.

---

* This Box was prepared by Dr. Cunzhi Wan, Deputy Director of the Statistics Department of the People's Bank of China, while he was a visiting expert in the OECD Economics Department during June-July 2001.

in other countries do indicate that phased interest liberalisation needs to be carefully co-ordinated in line with market developments in order to prevent distortions. For example, continued control of large bank deposit rates while money market rates are freed can lead to disruptive flows of funds out of banks in periods of rising interest rates. Freeing deposit rates before lending rates are liberalised can unduly squeeze loan margins. Accordingly, authorities may need to be prepared to accelerate the timetable for interest rate liberalisation if circumstances warrant.

Building a sound institutional and supervisory framework for a market-based financial system

The following sections will address key issues related to the supervision of the main financial activities, *i.e.* banking, capital markets and insurance. At the outset, however, one can make some generalisations that apply across the financial sector. In China as in many other countries, the exercise of financial supervision has often been subordinated to other considerations, especially to the support of the government's economic, social and regional objectives. To a large degree this is understandable inasmuch as China operated in a closed state-directed economy where financial institutions essentially validated orders taken elsewhere in the decision making structure. In these circumstances, it would have been pointless to enforce strict prudential rules.

By contrast, as China enters the next phase of its economic development, substantive economic decisions will increasingly be made by the markets, rather than by government directives and the economy will be exposed to international forces to a far greater degree than in the past. Financial deregulation will accelerate, and new financial instruments will be introduced. With the expected rise of funded pension plans, the capital markets will be called upon to shoulder a large share of the responsibility for assuring retirement income. In order to accomplish this expanded mission while minimising the risk of systemic disturbances, market supervisors will have to make significant adaptations. In building market-oriented systems of financial supervision China will be able to make use of the extensive experience that is already available in other markets. In the past few years, market supervisors and other officials from major countries have been working together in various forums to formulate global standards on a number of issues. Bodies such as the Basle Committee on Banking Supervision, the International Organisation of Securities Commissions (IOSCO), the International Association of Insurance Supervisors (IAIS), and the Financial Services Forum (FSF) have participated in the process of setting up recognised standards and best practices. China participates in many of these forums.

Banking

A considerable body of international best practices in Banking Supervision has evolved. Several international groupings, most notably the Basle Committee on Banking Supervision, have formulated a large body of standards that cover aspects of banking supervision.[13] China has been associated with international groups involved in the formulation and implementation of standards.

Official guarantees and deposit insurance

A major underpinning of the legal and regulatory infrastructure for a market-based financial system is a delineation of those activities for which the authorities provide guarantees and those where market participants bear the risk. In many Asian countries it was common not to have formal government guarantees but to allow significant ambiguity about the final responsibility for bank deposits. Market participants were led to believe that the government would not allow financial institutions to fail and that the government would make good on the commitments of banks even in cases of insolvency. This moral hazard arising from expected government support contributed to imprudent risk taking on the part of many banks and investors as well as to unsound investment decisions by non-financial companies. Due to government ownership of banks and industry as well as the continuation of the system of planning, the commitment of the Chinese authorities to support banks is even greater than other Asian countries. The banks are government owned and had little control over their own lending policies. A system of extensive, but informal, guarantees of bank liabilities is clearly a factor encouraging banks to neglect credit analysis and discipline. In order to begin moving toward a regime where financial institutions accept responsibility for their own actions, clearer demarcation of government responsibilities is in order.

One of the main elements in delineating those activities where market participants are expected to bear risk from those the government guarantees is the deposit insurance scheme as is found in most market economies. Under such schemes, the government guarantees that depositors will be compensated for insured deposits even if the institution accepting the deposit becomes insolvent or illiquid.[14] As of now there is no formal system of deposit insurance in China, but it is the presumption of most market participants that all deposits in state banks, at a minimum, are government guaranteed. In other words, market participants act under the assumption that the issue of the creditworthiness of state owned banks can be disregarded, even if these banks would fare badly if normal standards of creditworthiness were applied.

The purposes of deposit insurance schemes are:

- To provide smaller unsophisticated savers with risk free outlets for savings. If no such assurances were provided, smaller unsophisticated savers might hold assets in cash and avoid the formal financial system entirely; and

- To build confidence in the banking system generally by preventing panics and "runs" on banks. Many savers who, lacking adequate information or are unable to assess such information, might be prone to withdraw funds from banks in situations of uncertainty.

When banks can accept guaranteed deposits in unlimited amounts, market competition and pricing is distorted. Banks can take excessive risk without offering adequate risk premiums. Normally, banks' funding costs reflect the markets' perception of the risk of placing funds on deposit with each bank. Indeed, rising funding costs and a loss of markets confidence are often signals of impending difficulty for banks. When the basic principles of mutual surveillance by market participants no longer operates, the banking system can develop incentives to adverse credit selection and excessive risk taking. Excessive access to guaranteed deposits was a major factor in several financial crises, such as the savings and loan crisis in the United States. Therefore, in the current effort to reform financial systems in Asia, efforts are being made to introduce formal deposit insurance schemes, making it clear that any bank liabilities not specifically covered by such insurance are made at the risk of the investor.

Deposit insurance forms one of the justifications for bank supervision. To some degree banks are special institutions that can accept insured deposits and thus gain access to funds at below market rates since no premium for risk is charged. In exchange for this privilege, banks must accept some limitations on their risk taking. Insured deposits are only one privilege accorded banks. Other special privileges of banks are access to central bank credit and to the payments system.

Coverage of deposit insurance is usually limited to a certain amount, with deposits exceeding the amount not covered. Banks are required to disclose those deposits or other products in which the depositors bear the risk and are thus expected to make their own assessment of the risk. For example, money market funds are normally not covered by deposit insurance, even though they have many characteristics in common with bank deposits. If such instruments are introduced in China, they should be clearly labelled as not benefiting from deposit insurance.

Although the government is only obligated to support certain deposits, it may on a case by case basis decide to extend the safety net to a wider set of liabilities. Such expanded guarantees are often extended in times of imminent crises. For example in banking crises in Sweden in the early 1990s or in Japan and the Republic of Korea in the late 1990s, the government decided to extend guarantees rather widely in order to prevent a complete collapse of confidence. In all of these cases, it was decided to phase in partial deposit coverage over a period of years. Thus, partial deposit coverage is scheduled to take effect in 2001 in the Republic of Korea and 2002 in Japan. In some cases, other categories of institutions were included as well as commercial banks. In the specific case of China, where most banks are still contending with basic problems of balance sheet quality and risk management, it would not be practical to introduce a credible system of limited deposit coverage immediately. However, a regime of partial deposit insurance should be an integral part of bank reform. Once a workable programme of bank restructuring is formulated a timetable for a medium term transition to partial deposit insurance can be announced.

In China, the four large SOCBs present a difficult problem. These banks will hold a significant advantage over other banks if a system of limited deposit insurance is introduced, since market participants are likely to decide that they enjoy substantial government support, even if there is no formal guarantee. Thus, international rating agencies regularly assess the degree of government support when assigning ratings to banks. It should be an important policy goal to place these banks on an equal footing with other banks and to encourage the development of prudentially based governance and in-house risk management capacity. Such behaviour is incompatible with unlimited guarantees. It should be the policy that in case of insolvency the government will honour liabilities not explicitly covered by insurance only to the extent that the banking supervisors conclude that it is in the interest of cost-efficient bank rehabilitation to assume such liabilities.

Normally, the deposit insurance system is funded by contributions by banks to an insurance fund. In most cases the deposit insurance system is administered by a specialised official agency, although in a few cases the banks have established a private deposit insurance scheme. All banking institutions, including state-owned institutions that receive insured deposits, should be required to pay insurance premiums. In the long run, the premiums charged by the deposit insurance agency should be proportional to the riskiness of the bank and its activities. Thus, financially sound institutions and those engaging in low risk activities should pay lower premiums than those with weaker balance sheets and/or those engaging in riskier activities. However, Chinese banks are in a period of transition and there is little history of these banks acting as free-standing institutions upon which premiums can be calculated. Thus, it would be unrealistic to impose risk-based variable premiums immediately. The introduction of differentiated premiums should be phased in with limited deposit coverage and progress on bank reform.

The independence and authority of the banking supervisor

In order to be able to fulfil its mission, the bank supervision agency needs sufficient independence from other official bodies and legal and institutional authorities to insist on enforcing high standards, even if this conflicts with other government policy objectives. Two of the most common government policy objectives that potentially conflict with strict prudential supervision are 1) to support objectives such as economic growth, social cohesion or regional development; or 2) to conceal the extent of balance sheet impairment in order to postpone financial and/or industrial restructuring. Examples of the first kind of conflict of objectives include regulatory forbearance accorded banks that finance key economic development projects, that enable firms to maintain employment or make pension payments, or that are active in key regions of the country. Bank supervisors may acquiesce in overstatement of bank balance sheet quality in order to enable the authorities to postpone basic decisions. If bank supervisors were to press hard for remedial action, the banks would have to take action against the borrowers, thereby forcing borrowers to restructure. This may conflict with government priorities.

Banking supervisors are unlikely to insist on high standards when their legal and practical ability to require action is in doubt. When the legal framework in which banks would initiate proceedings against delinquent borrowers is untested, neither the banks nor the supervisors are likely to initiate strong action. Quite frequently, there is also often reluctance to acknowledge the extent of NPL in the banking system since full recognition would reveal the need for large-scale budgetary resources. These considerations, which are highly relevant for China, are visible in most other Asian countries facing the task of bank rehabilitation at this time.

In China, supervisory responsibility is lodged in the People's Bank of China (PBOC) which also acts as the central bank. Many countries maintain responsibility for banking supervision in the central bank but other countries take differing approaches. The question of the optimal institutional setting for financial supervision is considered in the last section of this chapter.

Compliance regulation versus prudential supervision: bank governance and prudential soundness.

Internationally, there is a trend in banking regulation away from an earlier orientation of setting of detailed rules and close monitoring of bank balance sheets for compliance. Instead, the trend is for banks to assume far greater responsibility for their own prudential soundness. In the past, banks in many countries were considered "special" institutions that were expected to serve a wide range of economic and social objectives, such as support of industrial policy, maintenance of employment, development of local communities, and assistance to the government in financing its debts. Banks were subjected to detailed rules about lending policies, often accompanied by strict prohibitions on the range of activities that banks could undertake, tight controls on interest rates and other bank charges, and restrictions on product innovation.

With deregulation, banking has become a highly competitive and innovative industry in which private market participants are constantly challenged to develop new products. Attempts to enforce traditional regulations often lead to excessive rigidity and to banks expending considerable energy on finding means to exploit gaps and inconsistencies in regulations. Instead, banking supervision is based upon an assumption that the primary responsibility for enforcing credit discipline and managing and controlling risk is located in individual banks. Banks are increasingly expected to construct governance systems focused on two overriding concerns: 1) adequate rates of return and 2) prudential soundness. Accordingly, the primary role of the supervisor is not to become involved in the detailed guidance of bank decisions but to be sure that banks have established credible and effective governance structures focused on these two objectives, particularly on meeting prudential standards. A crucial element of those governance structures must be robust internal procedures to manage and control risk.

In the new concept of the roles of the bank and its supervisors, each institution assumes much more control over its own actions, but the supervisor holds the bank strictly accountable for prudential soundness. In order to focus on these objectives those responsible for the governance of the bank, mainly the supervisory board of the bank,[15] are expected to have sufficient autonomy to be accountable for achieving profitability and maintaining or, if necessary improving, the quality of the bank's balance sheet and its exposures in general. It may seem axiomatic to posit these objectives for banks, but it is clear that deviations from this pattern have been common and that such deviations often lie at the origin of banking crises, especially in emerging markets. In China, banks have often been under pressure from governments or allied industrial groups to pursue other aims, and restrictions on bank activity have been such that it was practically impossible for banks to focus on profitability and soundness.

Recent statements by Chinese officials indicate an awareness of possible conflicts among the objectives assigned to banks. One of the stated objectives in listing banks publicly is to strengthen accountability of those responsible for the bank attaining adequate profitability and prudential soundness.[16]

To the extent that bank supervisors believe that institutions have developed adequate governance systems and have been implementing effective risk management and pricing policies, they are normally willing to allow banks more leeway in their decision making and to accept the bank's in-house risk management systems. Chinese banking supervisors report that in keeping with international practice, they have the long term goal of moving away from traditional compliance-oriented supervision toward prudential supervision. Nevertheless, as brought out in the chapter on banking, the incentives now facing Chinese banks remain somewhat diffuse. While banks have been warned to avoid new NPL it is not obvious that they have sufficient autonomy or information to carry out this mandate in a satisfactory manner. Accordingly, while the long term goal of banking supervision should be to move toward prudential supervision, the more immediate objectives of supervisors will have to be 1) to obtain an accurate reading of banks' balance sheets; 2) to require banks to bring their risk management standards to acceptable levels; and 3) to undertake the launching of a regime of prompt corrective action.

Banks' risk management capability

In response to pressures from bank supervisors, rating agencies and shareholders, it is universally accepted that banks should have strong internal credit cultures consisting of a strong in-house capability to analyse credit risk coupled with in-house systems to monitor the granting of credit and the assumption of risk. Credit procedures usually include a commitment of resources to credit analysis capability supported by adequate information systems. Banks typically maintain in-house credit scoring systems and policies that assure that loans are priced in accord with the bank's risk assessment and reviewed by specialised committees that have the authority to act. Bank policies concerning the acceptance and pricing of risk should be written and communicated to the relevant parts of the organisation. In order to enforce adherence within the organisations to credit policies, the credit and risk management functions must have considerable support from senior management and the board. Risk-based pricing tends to raise profitability, an identified weakness of Chinese banks.

479

An adequate credit system provides the management with timely information about the state of bank exposure in various forms to clients by the various parts of the organisation. A bank may have credit exposure to a single company operating through various subsidiaries, while borrowing by various affiliated companies may raise the risk concentration. Similarly, exposure to any given borrower may be increased by guarantees extended by that party. It is an important task of management information to centralise information on exposures inside the bank's credit structure in order to allow the bank's credit review processes to deal with the risk. It is generally observed that management of Chinese banks does not have adequate information about credits granted within their own banks.

To the extent that risk is mitigated by an external guarantee, procedures whereby guarantees are requested and what constitutes an effective guarantee should be specified. To the degree that government guarantees are used to reduce net risk, criteria should be specified whereby these guarantees are specifically accepted and deducted from the bank's total risk to a given borrower. Since many guarantees in China are not formally extended, but given as part of a tacit negotiating process, the exact amount of guarantees that any banks may have and the nature of commitments by various levels of government are unclear. To the extent possible, guarantees should be made explicit and incorporated into banks' credit systems.

An essential part of the credit risk management systems is a reliable loan classification policy. In many advanced countries, the bank's internal credit department is often more rigorous than the banking supervisors in calling attention to problem loans and demanding remedial action. In 1998, the PBOC requested the government-owned banks to set up an experimental system under which loans would be subdivided into five categories: normal, special attention, substandard, doubtful and probable loss. There appears to have been only limited progress in implementing the scheme on a wider basis. Moreover, the definition of NPL as well as rules governing provisions, write-offs and loan disposal are not transparent enough that banks could actually implement such reforms. Beyond this, it is not clear that there would be any benefit for banks to introduce stricter loan classification policies. Rather, banks may have significant incentives to overstate the quality of their loan portfolio. Similarly, there appear to be few incentives to deal with substandard credits either by provisioning adequately or by loan write-offs or asset sales.

Efficient risk management systems also identify the various kinds of risk assumed by banks. Traditional banking has largely been concerned with credit risk, *i.e.* the risk that a given borrower or counterparty would be unable to honour its commitments due to insolvency or illiquidity. As a matter of fact, this is still the major risk facing Chinese banks and will probably be the most serious problem in risk management for Chinese banks for the next few years. However, with liberalisation and innovation, Chinese banks will probably begin to assume other risks, including interest rate risk, market risk (the risk of adverse movements in prices of financial assets), currency risk, liquidity risk and operational risk. Comprehensive risk management systems must measure all these risks and find means to deal with them.

Internal policies concerning risk concentration can result in actions such as refusal of new credits, requests for guarantees, attempts to reduce exposure through sale of credits and greater differentiation in the price of credits. In cases of market risk or interest rate risk, derivatives may be used to hedge risk. As banks develop capability to engage in off-balance-sheet activity, one reaction to a possible rise in credit risk is to engage in a capital market activity in which the risk is transferred to investors.[17] When the credit score of a borrower declines, the bank normally places the borrower on a watch list and begins to implement procedures to monitor closely exposure to the borrower and to communicate concerns. If credits move into low risk classification, decisions must be made about provisioning and/or loan write-offs.

The use of internal capital charges for risks is one of the tools commonly used by banks in internal risk management. In any case, systems must be devised to identify risks, to bring them to the attention of those with designated responsibility for risk management and to decide how to accommodate risk. In the current process of financial restructuring in many Asian countries, banks are undertaking substantial efforts to upgrade internal credit assessment, scoring and decision-making systems.

The preceding paragraphs sketched the outlines of how most banking supervisors expect banks to design their own governance, risk management and credit systems. Realistically, the Chinese banks are not yet ready to operate under a system of flexible prudential supervision, but must be subjected to more direct guidance. However, it should be an important objective of the banking supervisors to encourage banks to build their own systems to the point that they are able to undertake risk management autonomously.

Chinese banks under standard supervisory criteria

As an aid to their own assessment of banks' quality and for use in dialogue with banks under their supervision, supervisors in many countries have evolved systems to evaluate banks' overall financial strength based on a number of factors deemed relevant to prudential soundness. The factors usually registered in these systems include capital adequacy, asset quality, management capability, earnings and liquidity.[18] Supervisors assign scores to institutions based partly upon straightforward numerical ratios and partly upon judgement of the supervisor. Chinese officials are considering incorporating such systems into their own banks' supervisory procedures at this time.

In general, Chinese banks would not be rated highly under most supervisory scoring systems, as can be gleaned from the discussion in Chapter 7 on banking. All SOCBs except one fall below the minimum 8 per cent capital assets ratio generally considered as a minimum by international supervisors. Additionally, the Chinese definition of capital does not accord with international norms. The concept of capital is central to the paradigm in banking in which the governance system is geared to producing adequate returns for shareholders and maintaining prudential soundness. The theoretical owners of the bank have invested their funds in the bank. In order to safeguard the owners' investment and increase their value, the management seeks to take well-measured risk in order to achieve adequate earnings. The situation is somewhat more complicated in the case of SOCBs. With very low or possibly negative capital, there are no external owners of the bank; the management of the bank frequently develops perverse incentives and may engage in excessive risk-taking. Such a situation often leaves the country vulnerable to crisis.

Asset quality of Chinese banks is generally acknowledged to be low, although widespread misclassification of assets makes exact measurement problematic. Recently, banks were permitted to sell NPL to asset management companies. However, it is widely acknowledged that actual NPL may be considerably higher than reported figures. Furthermore, the Chinese system of loan classification gives a very incomplete picture of asset quality. Only loans that are in arrears by three months are categorised as non-performing. But the authorities are experimenting with more forward-looking loan classification schemes, based on international practice, that take into account factors such as the capacity of the borrower's actual and potential cash flows in relation to debt service obligations. Usually systems under which loans are classified according to quality are used in tandem with requirements for provisioning. In well-developed risk management systems banks have in-house loan classifications and provision rules that are used in credit, pricing and provision decisions. Normally, as the quality of a credit declines, an increasingly large percentage of the loan must be set aside in provisions. Current Chinese rules, by contrast, require a uniform 1 per cent provision for all loans.

The Chinese banking supervisors are considering a five-category system modelled on those used in major markets. In addition to outright non-performing loans (*i.e.* those in arrears or rescheduled), this system identifies borrowers warranting varying degrees of special attention. Borrowers in that category include those with doubts about the capacity of earnings to cover interest and principal repayments and/or having other vulnerabilities. Such systems should enable supervisors to have more accurate assessments of bank balance sheets and potential vulnerability in order to gauge more accurately the adequacy of banks' loan provisions and capital. In fact, in China, there are few pressures to identify the quality of bank claims accurately and many incentives to present distorted data. Thus, a banking reform should start by constructing systems to require transparency internally and toward supervisors.

In advanced economies banks are introducing similar credit risk systems into their own credit procedures and in some cases bank supervisors are willing to accept the bank's in-house scoring system as part of supervisory procedures. In the case of China, it appears necessary to begin by relying on official loan classification schemes and gradually offer banks with advanced risk management systems to use their own systems.

Management capacity is one of the factors on which supervisors rate banks. One of the aspects of management is the control of relevant risk. Other important considerations are: the governance structures of the banks, the capability to formulate strategic plans and the content of those plans, the ability to control costs and the coherence of the bank's plan. Generally, bank supervisors should not be called upon to dictate strategic plans to banks but they do have views on whether bank plans are realistic in terms of earnings and balance sheet quality. To date Chinese banks have not been required to formulate autonomous plans but have been required to ratify decisions taken elsewhere. A supervisory regime in which banks are held accountable for their own credit decisions goes hand in hand with gains in real decision-making authority on the part of banks.

Earnings are another yardstick by which banks are commonly measured. Once again, Chinese banks do not measure up well under this standard. Even before adjusting for differing standards for measuring earnings, Chinese banks appear to be distinctly less profitable than their counterparts in other countries. Returns on assets (ROA) among well-managed banks in most countries exceed 100 basis points and a 15 per cent return on equity is considered to be a reasonable target for international banks. (In the United States, Canada, Australia and the United Kingdom, ROAs of the major banks are in the range of 200-300 basis points). As one begins to adjust the data to account for Chinese practices, performance appears even less favourable.

If banks were restructured, there is every reason to believe that Chinese banks could be highly profitable. Chinese banks operate in a rapidly growing market with many dynamic and profitable borrowers present, especially in the private and TVE sectors, but financial resources are in short supply. If banks were free to direct resources to their most promising customers, one would expect margins on lending to be higher than those in more mature banking systems. In other words, if economic signals are allowed to function properly the Chinese banking system should be highly profitable.

The last important measure is liquidity. In general, China would appear to be less vulnerable by this measure than by most other measures.

Corrective action procedures

By most indicators commonly used by banking supervisors, Chinese banks appear to have fundamental problems. Most systems of banking supervision have developed whereby banks that fall short of accepted prudential norms are obliged to take corrective action. Frequently, the legal authority to require such corrective action is incorporated into the law authorising the bank supervisory agency. Usually, as the shortfall from accepted norms increases, the measures are progressively stricter.

As a first step, banks that are in need of adjustment are required to produce plans to address the problems identified by the supervisors in a defined time frame. Usually, targets for improvement are set in quantitative terms with specific deadlines for the accomplishment of tasks. In cases where the shortfall is great, corrective action may include a change in the management, re-capitalisation, merger and/or a resolution of the bank. In China, there is agreement that a serious problem of balance sheet quality, risk management capability, and low profitability exist in the banking system. However, banks have not been required to advance rehabilitation plans, and the supervisory authorities do not have the authority to require corrective action. This problem will have to be addressed by 1) legislative changes to enhance the authority of bank supervisors 2) enhanced institutional capability in the supervisory agency and 3) modifications in the governance regime of banks to increase their responsiveness to prudential issues.

Concerning the capacity of banking supervisors, some encouraging trends can be noted inasmuch as the PBOC has identified critical challenges that must be overcome if Chinese banking supervision is to lift itself up to international norms. At the same time, the PBOC still lacks strong powers to enforce tough rules of prudential supervision and needs considerable institutional strengthening in order to carry out its role as a banking supervisor. At the same time, any reforms in terms of banking supervision are by themselves unlikely to be effective without a simultaneous change in the incentive systems and governance arrangements of the commercial banks.

Capital markets

Future structural changes in capital markets

The capital market, especially the equity market, has undergone impressive growth since its foundations in the early 1990s, but much remains to be done. The initial decision to allow SOEs to issue equity was motivated by two concerns: 1) to assist firms in raising capital and 2) to increase financial oversight over SOEs through discipline by the capital market. The Chinese stock exchanges have attracted large-scale investment from the public but the have not proven effective in imposing financial discipline on SOEs. In practice, SOEs have tended to see public listing as a means to obtain cheap capital with few reciprocal obligations on their part.

In the next phase of its development, the capital market will have to assume a more active role in allocating resources by exposing securities issuers to market scrutiny, thereby placing pressures on issuers to adapt their actions in line with investor expectations. The capital market will be called upon to accept an increased share of the responsibility for the financing of pensions in order to relieve pressures on the overburdened public pension system. SOEs are expected to place more of their equity on the market, thus exposing listed companies to market scrutiny and lessening the capability of insiders and the authorities to influence share prices. Private companies are likely to begin issuance. The domestic retail investors, who dominate the equity market, tend to trade on technical factors and insider information. Institutional investors and foreign investors will probably become major players. Greater professionalism among investors implies making tougher demands regarding disclosure, corporate governance and performance and more emphasis on fundamental analysis. The fixed income market is likely to become more liquid. Portfolios will normally include both debt and equity instruments and investors will compare yields and adjust holdings continuously, with rising use of hedging instruments.

The changing role of market supervisors

With higher market capitalisation, a wider range of investors and more instruments traded, market supervision will evolve. The authorities will on balance have to be less concerned about promoting development of the market and whether investors suffer losses and will need to place greater emphasis on the traditional concerns of securities market supervisors. The goals of market supervisors are usually thus defined: to maintain fair, transparent and efficient markets and to minimise systemic risk. A considerable body of internationally agreed best practices exists in the supervision of capital markets. This collective experience is available to China.[19]

Until recently, Chinese officials have been as concerned with enticing investors into the market as in building a robust regulatory framework. Considerable ambiguity was allowed to develop concerning the commitment of the government to support the market. In the future, however, investors must be allowed to take risks as they see fit, while the authorities' chief concern is to be sure that investors are not deceived about the nature of the risk assumed. Assuming that the market actually becomes more efficient at distinguishing between good and bad issuers, one would expect to see wider dispersions among the prices of equity.

In banking the governance problem tends to be that Chinese banks are insufficiently focused on earnings and prudential soundness. The Chinese investment industry by contrast is well focused on profitability. The main challenge in governance is to devise systems that require intermediaries and investors to observe existing laws and regulations and to act in the interests of investors, rather than in their own interest or those of allied companies. In China, instances of improper dealings (e.g. insider trading, market manipulation and failure to seek best execution) are continually uncovered. In the course, of 2000-2001, the China Securities Regulatory Commission (CSRC) has brought a large number of cases to light. Almost certainly, the heightened publicity given such cases does not mean that the number of offences has risen, but that efforts to expose such malfeasance have been accelerated.

The detection and punishment of wrongdoing is a much more central task for securities market oversight than for banking supervision. The number of transactions requiring oversight is much larger than in banking. At various stages of the investment process the potential exists for fraud, misrepresentation and conflict of interest. The experience of all countries shows that securities markets are highly vulnerable to misuse of market power. This danger is greater yet in emerging markets or in countries where the legal system is weak and untested. Thus, the construction and development of a system of enforcement that provides a fair competitive environment for investment and that earns the confidence of market participants is a critical task going forward.

The sector of the capital market where actions to enforce investor protection are most urgent is the equity market. In a well-functioning capital market investments are made under the presumptions that data released by companies is reasonably accurate and that companies are governed at least partly with the aim of providing investors with a reasonable financial return. When a company fails to perform in line with reasonable market expectations, investors will discount the price of the shares of that company. Poor share performance will make it difficult to raise capital in the future. When the share price falls to low valuations, the company will become vulnerable to take-over. For a variety of reasons the Chinese capital market has not functioned in this manner.

Controlling shareholders, in collaboration with allied securities dealers and some investment funds, have operated in ways that information flows can be controlled and prices can be manipulated. The corporate governance regime of Chinese listed companies has not been attentive to the concerns of minority shareholders. This generalisation needs to be qualified. Even in markets such as China where there are basic doubts about the overall level of respect for the interests of minority shareholders, some companies perform noticeably better than others on this score and this is noted by investors. In those segments of the Chinese market that are open to foreign investors, foreign institutions weigh transparency and attentiveness to the interest of non-controlling investors as part of their investment calculus. As institutional investors, especially foreign institutions, become more significant players in the market, demand for higher standards for disclosure, governance and investor protection are likely to rise.

Apart from ensuring fairness in markets, the minimisation of systemic instability in capital markets is an additional task. Although it is not an area of major concern whether any particular investment project produces returns to investors, the securities regulators have a strong interest in preventing a cycle of speculative prices rises, which as experience shows is often followed by sharp declines in prices. This is especially important in China where equity valuations are very high by international comparison and the market has been driven by manipulative practices and speculation. A number of Asian countries have experienced sharp drops in their equity markets in these conditions.

While the next phase of capital market development will entail more risk of volatility in equity markets, there is no reason to believe that a serious option exists of lessening such risks by slowing liberalisation. Arguably, the experience of the past few years suggests that markets that are transparent with deep institutional investor communities and a wide range of investment instruments are better equipped to avoid asset price bubbles than markets which lack those characteristics. Markets dominated by institutions are more likely to recover quickly after significant price drops. Markets where smaller investors predominate and where the range of investment instruments is narrow are more likely to remain depressed after a bubble bursts.

Building a robust framework for market oversight

As noted above the capital market is highly vulnerable to abuse of agency relationships. The number and complexity of transactions and the potential for abuse are so large that it would not be practical for the supervisor to oversee each operation. Thus, the activities of the securities market supervisor are only part of the overall institutional and regulatory frameworks that seek to assure a fair, efficient and transparent competitive environment. Other important elements include *a*) industry self-regulatory practices and *b*) the internal compliance and audit functions of each institution and *c*) market competition. A successful policy to develop high professional standards will blend all three of these elements in such a way that individual firms will feel the urgency of observing high standards.

In the specific case of China, the need to set standards is made more urgent by the wide ownership and control linkages among government, industry, financial intermediaries and institutional investors as well as a history of using the capital markets to facilitate financing by industry. In economies where private ownership is the prevailing norm, the state, acting as supervisor, can operate as a neutral party to establish rules under which independent issuers and investors interact. In China however, both the issuers and the investors have close links to the state. The main issuers are SOEs. The main intermediaries are securities houses that are owned by the state or SOEs. The securities houses have significant ownership and control relations to the investment management companies.

In most countries, the activities of industry associations and self-regulatory organisations (SROs) complement official regulation. In some cases SROs elaborate standards on issues such as disclosure, the duty to obtain best execution, segregation of client funds, and procedures for listing and trading rules. Some of the useful tools of self-regulation include industry codes best practice, disciplinary committees as well as procedures for investigation and punishment of infractions. Disciplinary procedures and other controls over market conduct constitute important checks on the activities of firms and their employees and can assist the authorities in the process of setting and enforcing rules. SROs have the advantage that they are closer to market practitioners than the supervisors. (On the other hand, SROs may fall under the control of the professionals, especially intermediaries, and promote their interests at the expense of those of the investors.)

The major SROs in China are the two stock exchanges and the *Securities Association of China* (SAC). To date the CSRC has tended to use a highly directive approach, delegating only small amounts of authority to SROs. The stock exchanges in particular have sometimes complained about micro-management by the CSRC. To some degree it is understandable that the CSRC is still involved in more detailed rule setting than its counterparts in other countries, since Chinese intermediaries do not have strong internal control functions and the SROs lack experience. Nevertheless, it is advisable to rely to an expanded degree on greater industry self-regulation. Recent statements by high CSRC officials indicate that more use of SROs will occur in the future.[20]

Within each firm, the compliance and audit function must be to formulate and enforce internal polices that incorporate official regulation and industry standards of practice as well as internal firm policies. It is the responsibility of the internal governance structure of each firm, especially of senior management and the board of directors, to evolve compliance and audit procedures that are adequate to make it possible to survey activities undertaken in various parts of the house, to detect infractions and to punish transgressions.

Finally, market competition is an important element in constructing a sound framework to ensure that market participants act in accord with established standards. In most advanced markets, securities market intermediaries are highly sensitive to the risk that the discovery of irregular practices will lead to a loss of reputation and hence to a loss of business. Firms tend to value their reputation for acting in the client's interest. As professionalism gains, intermediaries find that market competition significantly offsets the information asymmetry that initially favoured the intermediaries. In markets dominated by institutional investors, competition tends to force intermediaries to obtain best execution. Market competition often encourages an intermediary to go beyond what is required in official regulations.

Supervisory capacity

Despite its shortcomings, capacity to enforce prudential standards has been growing over time. After 1997, the CSRC was upgraded to ministerial status, with uncontested mandate to supervise the capital markets. (For more details about the history of securities oversight, see the capital markets chapter). In December 1998, the CSRC's position was consolidated when the Securities Law was enacted. Since 1998, the CSRC has made significant strides toward becoming an independent agency with the institutional capacity to engage in neutral market surveillance. Personnel with improved qualifications have been recruited. The legal powers to investigate and prosecute misdeeds have grown.

In the early months of 2001, the CSRC sent strong signals to the market that it now felt increasingly capable of acting as an independent supervisory body whose main commitment is to market integrity. The CSRC ordered the de-listing of several companies that had not reached minimum profitability requirements. Additionally, cases of insider trading and market manipulation have been prosecuted. The CSRC will seek to enhance its credibility as a market-based supervisor in future years. The fact that the CSRC has been able to step up its campaign to enforce rules of conduct against major firms and securities dealers indicates that institutional capacity to police markets is improving and that the CSRC believes that its campaign enjoys support in official circles. At the same time, the CSRC believes that it is important to obtain additional authorisation in order to be able to require testimony from suspected violators of market regulations and to be able to impose adequate penalties.

Insurance

Before the reform of 1979 the insurance sector played a very marginal role in the economy, with a single supplier, the People's Insurance Company of China (PICC) limited to international trade-related insurance. With reform, insurance was recognised as potentially contributing to economic growth. A 1995 Insurance Law had the joint purpose of imposing more discipline on a growing insurance market as well as promoting its development. In October 1998, the China Insurance Regulatory Commission (CIRC), which reports directly to the State Council, was formed.

The insurance sector is expected to play a more autonomous role in the financial system. As in other financial activities, the capabilities and techniques of the supervisors must be upgraded, while the governance systems of insurance companies, including risk management systems and professional standards, must be raised. Issues concerning the development of the insurance sector have been discussed in detail in Chapter 8.

Institutional investors and the development of capital markets

The most dynamic capital markets in the world are those where institutional investors have a significant presence. Institutional investors have the mission to manage their assets in the interest of their final beneficiaries such as the holders of insurance policies, recipients of pensions or investors in collective investment schemes (CIS). In OECD countries institutional investors tend to be the most sophisticated investors using state of the art investment techniques. Institutional investors also provide a great stimulus to the development of an asset management sector. Thus, the opening of the market will tend to introduce global asset management practices into the Chinese capital market.

The need to develop institutional investors presents an additional challenge to the Chinese authorities. In most OECD countries institutional investors have progressively developed a culture of independence under which they have powerful incentives to act in the interests of their beneficiaries. At the same time, in emerging markets, institutional investors have often been vulnerable to capture by government or by industrial interests, which often see such institutions as a source of easy finance. The establishment of strong governance systems for institutional investors thus is a major priority in the reform of the financial sector.

The responsibility for assuring that institutions act in the interests of their beneficiaries depends upon the nature of the institution. The CSRC is responsible for the oversight of the securities market activities of all institutions and has sole responsibility for CIS. (see Capital Market Chapter). The primary responsibility for oversight of insurance lies with the Insurance Regulatory Commission. As made clear in the preceding section, the insurance supervisors are also seeking to develop the internal governance system for the insurance companies.

Responsibility for oversight of pensions lies elsewhere. In 2001, the government is aiming to introduce the core legislative framework needed to ensure the financial security of occupation pensions and to protect the rights of beneficiaries. Some basic features of this framework have already been identified by the government. The OECD has been taking a leading role in developing governance principles for private pension schemes and China is taking part in OECD efforts to upgrade pension fund governance.

The overall institutional and regulatory structure of the financial sector

The relationship between banking and securities business

One of the current controversies in China is whether it is advisable to restrict the activities of financial institutions to one field of endeavour, such as banking, securities or insurance, or to allow the establishment of financial service organisations that engage in some combination of these activities. In order to address this question it is useful to consider briefly the experience of OECD countries. Some OECD countries, especially the United States, Canada and Japan, traditionally maintained sharp institutional separation between banking and securities activities. Such legal separation reflected an earlier belief that allowing banks to engage in securities operations engendered conflicts of interest. At the other extreme, some countries, notably Germany, had regimes of universal banking. Banking was defined so as to include many capital market operations, and banks were allowed to engage in all such activities. There were many countries that had systems that lay somewhere between these two extremes. It is fair to say that countries with universal banking had bank dominated financial systems where capital markets were less developed than those where securities business was separated from banking. However, the legal separation of banking securities was only one factor that influenced the relative importance of banks and capital markets in financial intermediation. Other relevant factors include the relative size of institutional savings and the ways in which institutional investors were subjected to prudential supervision.

In OECD countries this separation is now much less pronounced than in the past. Those countries that had strict separation of banking and securities have abolished most rules that mandated the separation and those with universal banking have removed many restrictions that previously hampered the development of capital markets. Overall, one can say that considerable convergence in institutional forms is occurring. It can also be added that insurance was frequently separated from other financial activities in the past, but closer linkages between insurance and other forms of finance are now becoming common. The institutional structure that most countries are adopting is of a financial services company in which banking, securities and insurance are undertaken, but separate subsidiaries within the group specialise in each activity.

China currently has a regime of strict institutional separation, but many are questioning whether it would be advisable to change this system. The same reasons that led most countries to abandon institutional separation seem valid for China as well. Therefore, in the long run there is no reason that China should not adopt the institutional model of a unified financial services company. In current circumstances, however, it is also true that the nature of each of these lines of endeavour and the risks assumed in each are significantly different. Given the requirement for institutional strengthening in each of these fields in China at this time, it may be advisable to move only in deliberate steps before ending institutional separation. When the authorities are assured that institutions have mastered each sub-sector of the financial sector and that supervisors have mastered their respective tasks, full integration of financial services expanded powers can be granted.

One way that such a system could be introduced progressively would be to allow only those institutions that have attained the highest possible rating by the supervisors and have maintained those ratings for a number of years to be allowed to form diversified financial groups. As the preceding discussion has made clear, no Chinese institution would currently be allowed to form such companies, but as the overall level of skills rises multi-service licenses could be awarded.

Consolidated or multiple supervisors?

It is a matter of considerable debate inside OECD countries whether all supervisory authority should be concentrated in a single agency or whether it is appropriate to have separate entities to supervise banking, capital markets, insurance and possibly other activities as well. Those favouring unified supervision usually cite the fact that multipurpose financial services are becoming commonplace in major financial markets. Additionally, a certain convergence among products is occurring as banks engage in more off-balance-sheet business and capital market activity and other products are offered that combine elements of several financial products. Some investment products, such as money market funds, are close substitutes for bank deposits and variable annuities combine some elements of investment with elements of insurance. Credit derivatives, which are often purchased by insurance companies, share some characteristics of bank loans. Cross marketing of products is also a major trend.

Equality of regulatory treatment, the need to measure the full range of risks taken inside a financial services company and the need to minimise regulatory arbitrage are cited as factors favouring consolidated regulation. If multiple regulators remain in operation, financial service firms will create products designed to compete with products offered by other institutions, based chiefly on the ability to obtain favourable regulatory treatment. In fact, most OECD countries that have recently undertaken major reviews of their entire systems of financial supervision have tended to opt for a single regulator.

In the last analysis, the issue of single or multiple supervisors should not be a burning one in China at this time. A good case can be made that China should maintain separate regulation, at least for a time. While there is undoubtedly a convergence of market practice occurring globally, a higher priority for China at this stage of its development it to perfect its regulatory skills in each sub-sector of the financial services industry. Since there are distinct features of banking, securities and insurance, China would benefit from a period of development of supervisory skills for each of these specialised fields before considering consolidation. Banking supervision is mostly concerned with the quality of bank balance sheets and banks' credit and risk management capability. Meanwhile, securities supervision tends to focus on setting and enforcing rules to protect investors and prevent misconduct. Finally, insurance supervision is focused on the solvency of institutions that must accept very long-term liabilities.

One related, and much more immediate, question in assessing the overall adequacy of financial supervision is to avoid gaps and inconsistencies. In many Asian countries in particular, intermediaries emerged that did not fit neatly into the traditional categories of banking, securities or insurance. Examples are the finance companies in Thailand or the merchant banks in the Republic of Korea. Partly because they did not fit into the existing categories, they tended to be under supervised and tended to engage in activities that would have aroused suspicion among traditional regulators. Therefore one final word in designing an overall system of financial supervision is that no entity should escape adequate supervision.

Conclusions and recommendations

Financial reforms have been proceeding rapidly since the mid-1990s but the system is still subject to important key weaknesses and remains somewhat behind the real sector in its development. The mismatch between the credit allocated to various business segments and their overall importance to the economy has, if anything, increased in recent years. The financial system does not yet provide adequate incentives and capabilities needed to facilitate the large-scale reallocation of resources and reorganisation of activities and their control that will be needed as trade and investment liberalisation, along with broader economic reforms, proceeds. Remedying these weaknesses will be a critical key to China's success in adjusting to and reaping the maximum benefits from the further international integration of the economy.

The discussion has also suggested certain specific priorities for financial reforms and options for meeting them that can be summarised as follows.

- First, restoring financial soundness through a decisive clean up of financial institution balance sheets is the greatest near-term priority. The government will have to bear the bulk of the burden of the clean up, at least initially, but the cost can be spread out over time. Government support should be accompanied by further tightening of prudential standards that make the institutions strictly accountable for their performances. Permission to undertake new lines of business should be made strictly conditional on specific steps by the institutions to strengthen their governance and management systems, and on adherence to a timetable for raising their capital further over time.

- Second, modern governance structures should be established for SOCB and other financial institutions as soon as possible, as part of broader efforts to improve incentives for profit-oriented behaviour at all state-owned financial institutions. To improve professional standards and accountability, responsibility for appointing and removing senior bank management should be taken from line government agencies and political bodies and vested with the board of directors, subject to the approval of the official financial regulatory authorities.

- Third, the governance systems of financial institutions need to be adapted so that the maintenance of high prudential standards is one of the main objectives of the organisation. Financial intermediaries, such as banks and securities houses, and insurance companies must construct internal credit, risk management and compliance functions that enable the institution to meet prudential requirements. Those responsible for the governance of the institution (usually the supervisory board which then delegates responsibility to the management team) are accountable for the construction of such systems and the ongoing use of these systems to enforce prudential rules. Improved transparency and regular public disclosure of the conditions and operations of financial institutions are also needed to reinforce internal incentives to maintain prudential standards and the focus on commercial objectives.

- Fourth, while the steps now being taken to improve financing for private and other SMEs are important, they will probably need to be broadened if these enterprises are to develop adequately. Among the steps that might be considered are: an acceleration and expansion of the current efforts to provide credit guarantees; and consideration of the development of regional or other "off-board" facilities for the listing and trading of equity in SME. Programmes for SME financing should also be co-ordinated and integrated with broader efforts aimed at SME development. To this end, formulation of a more explicit and comprehensive strategy for development of private and other SMEs to provide a framework and basis for co-ordination of programmes now administered by a range of government agencies would be useful.

- Fifth, supervisors will have to continue to acquire the necessary physical and human capacity to accomplish their tasks. As a starting point, internationally accepted norms and techniques for financial supervision can be adapted to Chinese circumstances. In the past decade and a half, considerable agreement has been reached among international financial supervisors, and basic principles have been enunciated for the supervision of banking, securities and insurance.[21] Additionally, more detailed sets of standards have been elaborated to deal with more precise issues. Capacity building, including training, will be needed in order to enable financial supervisors to assume this broader role.

- Sixth, supervisors will need the authority and independence to exercise surveillance over supervised institutions solely in the interest of prudential soundness and in a way that is not dependent upon other objectives of the government. In cases where shortcomings are found, supervisors will need the power to require action on the part of persons and institutions subject to their supervision or to investigate and prosecute infractions.

489

- Seventh and last, it is an important objective to assure that institutional investors, which are likely to emerge as major players in financial markets, have adequate governance systems. If China succeeds in building institutional savings it will be essential to build mechanisms to assure that the institutions are managed in the interests of final beneficiaries such as investors of COIS insurance policy holders and prospective pensioners. This is an important issue, because these institutions have been vulnerable to capture in emerging markets.

NOTES

1. SOE and other non-financial channels have limited ability to assess creditworthiness. They also have potential adverse incentives, such as the temptation to lend to real estate or other speculative activities, and are not subject to prudential oversight by financial supervisory authorities.

2. The SOCB are potential conduits for such transfers but in practice their operations tend to be regionally segmented. The SOCB are organised as quasi-government departments, with branches and sub-branches at provincial and below provincial levels. At least until recently, these branches were substantially autonomous, and more subject to the influence of local officials than to their head office, as well as constrained in their lending by the amount of funds they were able to collect locally. This pattern has changed in several important respects in recent years, as authority for lending decisions has been moved up to higher offices and as elimination of direct credit quotas has allowed greater scope for intra-bank transfer of funds from surplus to deficit offices. See Box 14.3. for further discussion.

3. Admittedly, bank credit to the private sector is growing rapidly, but this is from a small base and is to a large degree accounted for by increased housing and consumer lending.

4. See Chapter 7 on the banking sector.

5. See the OECD *Economic Surveys* for Republic of Korea for 1998-2000 for discussion of efforts to deal with the banking crisis.

6. See Chapter 7 on the banking sector. At least some of the JSB may be able to restore capital adequacy through listing, but it is much less likely that the SOCB, whose requirements are much larger, will be able to do so. Moreover, listing will require substantial improvement in balance sheets, particularly for JSB.

7. The increase in ownership shown for Japan and some Asian crisis countries reflects acquisitions in the wake of their banking crises. The intention is to return these institutions to private ownership in the future.

8. Largely for this reason, many financial regulatory authorities tend to view public ownership very sceptically, seeing it as increasing moral hazard and other adverse incentives to take excessive risks (see Group of Ten, 1997).

9. This clearly degrades the normal governance paradigm in which boards of directors and managers are held accountable for placing the institution's capital at risk. Nonetheless, it is an important aim of public policy to develop a governance regime for state-owned financial institutions that imposes management accountability as comparably as possible to that of joint-stock or other private institutions

10. For an overview as well as review of individual country policies, see OECD (2000*b*).

11. Guarantee ratios vary considerably. In drawing lessons for China, Lu (2000) argues for a low ratio, noting that in Chinese Taipei it has typically been set around 20 per cent.

12. Spain in the mid-1990s began to introduce participation loans through the government-owned National Innovation Enterprise Association (ENISA). These are subordinated longer-term loans to finance fixed assets, which have "last" status among claims in the event of bankruptcy. See OECD (2000*b*), pp. 175-176.

13. The most comprehensive statement was the "Core Principles for Effective Banking Supervision" issued in 1997. These principles were formulated by the Basle Committee on Banking Supervision, which co-operated with some non-G10 countries, including China, in their formulation. Other issues covered by the Group include risk management, corporate governance of banks, disclosure and co-operation among supervisors.

14. Considerable work has been done through a Working Group of the Financial Stability Forum. This group has issued a number of reports suggesting policy measures that can be taken to strengthen deposit insurance. The most recent comprehensive summary of the work of that group is found in *Report on the Working Group in Deposit Insurance*, Financial Stability Forum, March 2001. See *www.fsforum.org*

15. Chinese corporations have two tier boards. It is assumed that all future Chinese banks will be organised in this manner.

16. *China Daily* 19 April 2001.

17. At the same time it is important not to develop institutions or instruments that merely hide the actual risk that is being assumed. For example in Thailand, banks shifted riskier lending to their allied finance companies. Such activities often occur when supervisory systems leave gaps in coverage. See the final section of this Chapter.

18. Banking supervisors in the United States have developed a CAMEL system that analyses the strength of banks for Capital Asset Management Earnings and Liquidity. Variations on this system are widely used by banking supervisors.

19. The main organisation responsible for the elaboration of such practices is the Intentional Organisation of Securities Commissions (IOSCO) of which China is a member.

20. Statement by CSRC Chairman Zhou, reported in China On Line, 13 April 2001.

21. Basle Core Principles of Banking Supervision, IOSCO Principles of Securities Market Supervision and the IAIS Principles of Insurance Supervision.

BIBLIOGRAPHY

Australia Government Department of Foreign Affairs and Trade (1999),
Asia's Financial Markets, Chapter 12 on China.

Bank for International Settlements (1999a),
"Bank restructuring in practice", BIS *Policy Paper* No. 6, August.

Bank for International Settlements (1999b),
"Strengthening the banking system in China", Proceedings of a conference held in Beijing, BIS *Policy Papers* No. 7, March.

Chien, A. (1999),
"Experience on finance for medium and small enterprises and its credit guarantee system", in Collected Paper from the Symposium on *Micro-Finance and Urban Unemployment in China*, held in Guangzhou, China, 1-3 March, pp. 185-220.

Edey, M. and K. Hviding (1995),
An Assessment of Financial Reform in OECD Countries, Economics Department Working Paper No. 154.

Financial Stability Forum (2001),
Progress Report of the Working Group on Deposit Insurance, March.

Goldstein, Morris and P. Turner (1996),
"Banking crises in emerging market economies: origins and policy options", BIS *Economics Papers*, October.

Group of Ten (1997),
Financial Stability in Emerging Market Economies, Report of the working party on financial stability in emerging market economies.

Han, W. (1999),
"Open up financing service fields and promote the healthy development of small and medium sized enterprises", in Collected Paper from the Symposium on *Micro-Finance and Urban Unemployment in China*, held in Guangzhou, China, 1-3 March, pp. 227-240.

International Finance Corporation (2000),
China private enterprise study, Technical report prepared for the IFC and the State Economic and Trade Commission of the People's Republic of China.

International Organisation of Securities Commissions (IOSCO) (1998),
Objectives and Principles of Securities Regulation, September.

Kumar, A., N. Lardy, W. Albrecht, and T. Chuppe (1997),
"China's non-bank financial institutions: trust and investment companies", *World Bank Discussion* No. 358.

Lardy, N. (1998),
China's Unfinished Revolution, Brookings Institution Press, Washington, DC

Lardy, N. (2000),
When Will China's Financial System Meet China's Needs?, paper for Conference on Policy Reform in China, Center for Research on Economic Development and Policy Reform, Stanford University, Stanford, CA.

Leahy, M., S. Schich, G. Wehinger, F. Pelgrin and T. Thorgeirsson (2001),
"Contributions of financial systems to growth in OECD countries", OECD *Economics Department Working Paper* No. 280, January, Paris.

Lindgren, C-J., G. Garcia and M.I. Saal (1996),
Bank Soundness and Macroeconomic Policy, IMF.

Lu, W. (2000),
"Establishing a credit guarantee system for small and medium sized enterprises in China borrowing helpful experiences", *China Development Review*, Vol. 2, No. 2, April, pp. 75-84.

OECD (2000a),
Reforming China's Enterprises, Paris.

OECD (2000*b*),
  OECD *Small and Medium Enterprise Outlook*, Paris.

OECD (2001*a*),
  Enhancing SME *Competitiveness*, Proceedings of the OECD Ministerial Conference in Bologna.

OECD (2001*b*),
  Venture capital in the present economic cycle, October.

OECD (1996),
  Best Practice Policies for Small and Medium-Sized Enterprises, Paris.

Oppers, E. (1997),
  "Macroeconomic cycles in China", *International Monetary Fund Working Paper* No. 97/135.

Tsuru, K. (2000),
  "Finance and growth: some theoretical considerations and a review of the empirical literature", OECD *Economics Department Working Paper* No. 228, January.

Zhang, J. (1999),
  "Case study on the development of small and medium sized enterprises in Taipei, China" in *Micro-Finance and Urban Unemployment in China*, Proceedings of a World Bank conference held in Guangzhou, China, pp. 145-157.

Chapter 15

PRIORITIES FOR DEVELOPMENT OF CHINA'S CAPITAL MARKETS

TABLE OF CONTENTS

PRIORITIES FOR DEVELOPMENT OF CHINA'S CAPITAL MARKETS[*]

Introduction

This chapter examines the challenges facing the Chinese capital market as it enters its next phase of development, a phase of planned accelerated domestic reform and external liberalisation. The chapter first analyses long-term trends in the capital markets and market supervision, focusing on the current situation and future reform plans. Subsequently, main sub-sectors of the capital market (intermediaries, investors, equity and bond markets) are discussed. Foreign participation in the capital market, including the outlook for liberalisation in coming years, is then addressed. Conclusions and policy recommendations are summarised in the last section of the chapter.

The government's decision in the 1980s to raise funds through the capital markets reflected two goals: 1) to mobilise private savings in order to finance SOEs and 2) to improve SOE performance through public listing. The policy has succeeded beyond the boldest expectations in reaching the first goal. While equity markets were embryonic in 1990, ten years later market capitalisation was equivalent to some 57 per cent of GDP, a figure that compares favourably with those of other Asian countries and many OECD countries (see Figure 15.1). The population has been persuaded to commit a significant part of its savings to the securities market. In addition, the Chinese securities market utilises advanced information and communication technology. Significant progress has been made in building a basic legal and regulatory framework.

Despite its size and technological complexity, the capital market has not been effective in promoting corporate efficiency. Share prices are not well correlated with corporate results. The market, which is dominated by small retail investors who are primarily concerned with short-term trading profits, has frequently been marred by speculation and market manipulation. As mentioned already in

Figure 15.1. **Equity market capitalisation as a share of GDP in selected countries (2000)**

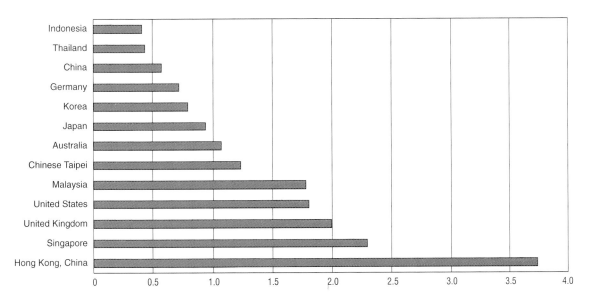

Source: International federation of Stock Exchanges and OECD Secretariat estimates.

---

[*] This chapter was prepared by John Thompson, Counsellor, and Sang-Mok Choi, Project Manager, Directorate for Financial, Fiscal and Enterprise Affairs, OECD.

Chapter 13, standards of disclosure and corporate governance fall short of global norms. Valuations are very high by international comparison even though the listed companies continue to have fundamental problems of profitability. Virtually all funds raised in equity markets have been obtained by SOEs, the sector of the economy where problems of efficiency have been most intractable. The more dynamic non-state sector has been almost completely excluded from the formal capital markets.[1]

In the late 1990s, a decision was made to accelerate reform in order to use the capital market to promote SOE restructuring. In addition, the authorities became convinced that the capital market could assist in providing retirement income for the population through funded pensions, thus easing the large funding problem in the existing pension system.

To enable the capital market to fulfil these ambitious aims, the authorities are taking a number of measures to expedite reforms. The percentage of equity that is publicly traded is programmed to rise considerably as the state places currently non-tradable shares on the market. Meanwhile non-state firms will gain access to the market. The supervisory framework will be strengthened with stricter investor protection rules. Institutional investors, who are expected to become more important players, should bring more professionalism into the market and provide a natural market for a broader range of investment instruments including fixed-income instruments and derivatives. The authorities are also committed to an expanded foreign presence in the capital market. Foreign intermediaries and investors, who generally come from more advanced markets, will inject more competition into the system and encourage upgrading of standards among Chinese market participants.

While substantial reforms are on the horizon, the risk of serious disturbances in the capital market is high at this time. Many characteristics of the market, especially high equity valuations, differences between valuations in restricted and open market sectors, limited risk management capability among major players, the history of manipulation and speculation and the lack of liquidity in many parts of the market give grounds for concern. The decision to allow foreigners into the market while simultaneously deregulating will make it imperative to build a robust institutional and regulatory infrastructure in order to minimise the risk of destabilisation.

Moreover, it is uncertain whether pension reform will be sufficient to generate a pool of institutional savings that will underpin the targeted transformation of the financial system. While this will be a major determinant of the future shape of the capital markets, it lies largely outside the competence of those responsible for capital market supervision.

On a fundamental level, the market has grown in a systemic environment where state ownership of the means of production was the rule and where the legal system did not fully recognise many features of a market-based financial system. It was presumed that state planners would make basic decisions about economic policy and that financial institutions existed to assist planners in monitoring compliance with the plan. The concepts of an independent profit-seeking corporation, owned by and accountable to shareholders, risk-taking by investors and capital markets that monitored corporate performance, were largely absent. Despite the systemic ambiguities that continue to characterise the market up to the present, reforms have been introduced in a pragmatic way and the authorities have been willing to enlarge the number of decisions that are left to market forces and to align their practices with those in major financial markets. It will be necessary to resolve these systemic ambiguities as an increased number of substantive decisions are made by market participants on market-based criteria.

The supervisory framework and the process of reform

Following the adoption of economic reforms in the late 1970s, securities markets developed rapidly. During the 1980s, structural change tended to be driven by spontaneous innovation by market participants or local authorities. Central government officials strained to keep up with market developments and often ratified existing practices. For example, in an atmosphere of frenzied unregulated trading, stock exchanges were formed in Shanghai and Shenzhen in 1990. (For a synopsis of the historical development of the capital markets, see Box 15.1.)

Box 15.1. **Historical overview of capital markets**

While it is somewhat arbitrary to specify stages in the growth of the Chinese capital markets, one can conceive of development proceeding through three stages: 1) a formative period in the late 1970s, 2) the emergence of more formal structures (*e.g.* stock exchanges, corporate laws and regulatory structures) in the early 1990s, and 3) additional reforms after the 1997 Asian crisis.

Informal markets in company stocks first developed with the early stages of reform in the early 1980s. In most cases, initiatives came from enterprises themselves or from local governments without the approval of the central government. Many urban enterprises, usually collective firms, issued debenturesand internal employee shares.[1] At this stage, SOEs, which still had rather easy access to bank credits, only issued on a modest scale. Informal markets in these securities soon developed in cities across the country.

In January 1985, Shanghai Yanzhong Industrial made the first public offering of standardised corporate equity in China. Small over-the-counter markets were established in Shanghai and Shenyang in late 1986, but they did little to restrain speculation or trading. Over-the-counter trading in securities developed in other places in the country, including Shenzhen. The government began issuing bonds in the early 1980s in order to finance its borrowing requirement. Some issues of corporate debt were also launched. Following a set of structural reforms, the government bonds market gained some liquidity after 1992. During this period hectic trading in equities was taking place in Shenzhen while fixed-income trading tended to centre in Shanghai. In response to the proliferation of trading systems and the minimum formal rules in trading, the government attempted to introduce some order.

In the spring of 1990, the establishment of a stock exchange in Shanghai was approved. It was believed that establishing a centralised registration and clearing system for shares was the only way to bring order to otherwise unruly markets. The Shanghai and Shenzhen exchanges both began operation in December 1990. Shenzhen, however, only finally received Beijing's official approval in mid-1991.

In 1992, stock market "fever" broke out in Southeast China. Millions of individuals discovered that fortunes could be made (and lost) through trading of shares. The fever, however, was short-lived. The markets suffered during Beijing's monetary-retrenchment campaigns to restrain inflation during 1993-1995. Excessive issuance of securities, often without central approval had contributed to the inflationary expansion of investment in 1992-1993. The central government tightened the issuance quota for stocks; in 1994-1995, only RMB 1.6 billion (US$194 million) of equity was issued, following RMB 4.3 billion (US$520 million) in 1993.

Efforts to build a formal legal and regulatory framework for the securities sector began with the Trial Measures on Shareholding System in 1992. The legal framework for issuance of equity was made more explicit with the enactment of the Companies Law of 1993, which governs and regulates the establishment, operation, internal management and dissolution of Chinese limited liability companies and joint stock companies. The provisions cover the rights and obligations of shareholders, powers and responsibilities of directors, financial and accounting requirements, termination and liquidation and other areas. The Securities Law was enacted in 1998. A framework for market oversight was begun with the creation of the China Securities Regulatory Commission (CSRC) in 1992.[2]

The central government's attitude to the capital markets evolved significantly during 1996-97. Further reform in the bond market led to the emergence of inter-bank and exchange trading while further reforms strengthened transparency and liquidity in the bond market. After a series of experiments with limited-responsibility contracts, profit retention, and other mechanisms by which the state sought to create better incentives for SOE managers, the government turned to corporatisation as a partial solution to the problem of the resource drain from loss making SOEs.[3] SOE corporatisation entails the creation of enterprises as independent legal persons, a clear delineation and distribution of their assets, and the separation of owners (shareholders, usually the state) and managers. When organised as a limited liability company, Chinese companies are required to appoint supervisory boards, to hold shareholders' meetings and to observe disclosure requirements. In late 1996, the State Council determined that public issuance of SOE equity, and stock markets should be promoted as part of this industrial restructuring programme.

---

1. Firms commonly issued securities like debt, with interest and principal repaid, but with also ownership.
2. Yao pp. 4.5
3. On China's corporatisation experiment, see Hannan, K. *Industrial Change in China: Economic Restructuring and Conflicting Interests*. London: Routledge, 1998. You, J. *China's Enterprise Reform: Changing State/Society Relations after Mao*. London: Routledge, 1998.

From the beginning of the securities markets through the early 1990s, primary regulatory authority was lodged with the People's Bank of China (PBC) which was responsible for all financial regulation. Legislation did not differentiate sharply between the banking and securities business or between commercial banking and central banking. The PBC functioned as central bank and regulatory agency for all financial activities but still retained some features of a commercial bank and investment bank, such as granting credits and launching primary market issues. At the same time local authorities sought to maintain significant control over securities markets. However, securities operations were gaining in size and complexity. With the surge in stock market investment in the late 1980s and early 1990s and with some disturbances related to the stock markets in 1992, awareness grew of the need for more rigorous oversight.

The China Securities Regulatory Commission (CSRC) was formed in 1992, but it did not immediately achieve pre-eminence, even within the field of securities supervision. In subsequent years, jurisdictional uncertainties persisted between the CSRC and the PBC while a prolonged contest ensued between the central and local governments over the right to regulate capital markets.[2]

Until 1997, the CSRC, which was ill equipped and understaffed, was in competition with other agencies, such as the PBC, the State Planning Commission and the provincial and local governments. The two stock exchanges were under the control of their respective municipal governments. The provincial securities offices, which were under the control of the provincial governments, retained significant leeway in setting conditions for listing as well as for the supervision of some activities of securities dealers and markets. There were a number of gaps in regulation. For instance, the government bond (CGB) futures market, established in December 1992, was left mostly unregulated.

In addition to the uncertainties over the exact jurisdiction of the various agencies, these agencies often had somewhat unclear or conflicting mandates. While the enforcement of standards of market integrity was one objective, the facilitation of capital-raising by SOEs, the promotion of the domestic capital market and defence of local interests were other important considerations. True, there was agreement that manipulative practices should not, strictly speaking, be tolerated. Nevertheless, many officials may have been reluctant to act decisively for fear of deflating the mood of buoyancy that was attracting investors into the market. This was especially true since one of the factors enticing investors into equity was the belief that since the issuers were state-owned and the markets state-promoted, the authorities would not permit the market to fall sharply. As the market grew in size and became a significant source for the financing of SOEs, this consideration gained in importance.

In its early years, the CSRC devoted considerable efforts to the preparation of overseas issues particularly H-shares (see section on equities below). While the CSRC had only contested responsibility for the domestic market, it had unquestioned jurisdiction over overseas issues and thus was able to exercise more discipline over companies seeking to list on the Hong Kong Stock Exchange (HKSE) or on foreign exchanges than over companies only listed in Shanghai or Shenzhen. In October 1992, nine SOEs were authorised to list on the HKSE. The CSRC built institutional capacity and a network of contacts related to overseas listings of Chinese companies. Thus, the CSRC sought to promote some convergence with international standards through exposure to world markets. The CSRC also promoted the Hong Kong equities market as a link to the global capital market and as an important stimulus to enterprise reform and capital market development on the mainland.

During the 1990s charges and revelations of irregularities in securities dealings surfaced continually. After 1997, fears that the Asian financial crisis could destabilise the financial sector led to a restructuring of regulation that was announced at the National Financial Work Conference in October 1997. Banks were ordered off the stock exchanges, and their bond trading transferred to a special inter-bank market. It was decided to create a regime mandating strict separation of banking and securities along lines previously enforced in the United States or Japan. As a result of reforms after 1997, the CSRC emerged as the pre-eminent agency responsible for capital markets.[3] The new policy on regulatory structure was recognised in December 1998 by the passage by the National People's Congress (NPC) of the Securities Law, which took effect in July 1999. As part of the reform, the CSRC assumed the functions of all the securities regulatory offices previously controlled by the provincial governments. Moreover, the CSRC, which had previously been isolated in Beijing, established ten regional offices.

With the centralisation of authority in the CSRC, a new phase in capital market development began. The CSRC began to propose a systemic change involving a move from the old system based on a closed market – where Chinese practice deviated significantly from those in other markets – to a progressively open one based on a modernised system of market oversight aligned with international practice. Since 1999, the CSRC has been taking increasingly ambitious measures to modernise the capital markets, upgrade supervision and prepare the country for more competitive conditions. In order to accomplish this, many Chinese citizens with experience in overseas markets – particularly many with experience in Hong Kong, China – were recruited.

Various statements in the past few years indicate that the authorities have reached a consensus that reform must be deepened and that the reform should aim at narrowing the differences between practices in China and those in other markets. For example in October 2000, the Chairman of the CSRC gave a broad view of the expected growth path of the capital markets in the next few years.[4] It was expected that the stock market – whose capitalisation is estimated at about 57 per cent of GDP – would reach twice that ratio in the future. The tradable share of equity would rise even faster as the state released previously non-tradable shares on the market. Private entities as well as SOEs would gain access to the markets. New financial products, including futures and options, would be introduced. Trading over the Internet would become an important feature of China's markets. Institutional investors would become major players. The capital markets will be expected to assume a far larger responsibility for supplying the population with pension income. An internationalisation of activity is expected, with foreign institutions allowed to form joint ventures with intermediaries, such as securities dealers, investment banks and asset management companies. Foreign portfolio investors will gradually be allowed to trade Chinese bonds and equities. Foreign securities will be listed and traded in China.

In the past decade, millions of small investors placed their funds in equities, enabling favoured SOEs to obtain funds while making only minimal concessions to non-controlling investors. Equity valuations remained high, partly because only a relatively small amount of equity was actually traded on the market and also because manipulative practices were not vigorously prosecuted. In its next phase, when the capital market will be expected to exercise discipline over the corporate sector and to contribute to the financing of pensions, it will have to operate under different premises. SOEs will have a larger share of their equity traded on the market and will have to compete for capital with private and foreign issuers, while a market in corporate control is expected to develop. Domestic and international institutional investors will demand higher standards of investor protection and a wider variety of investment instruments.

In late-2000 and 2001 the CSRC has been taking increasingly vigorous action to combat sub-standard practices. Firms that could not meet listing requirements, especially those that did not generate profits for three years or longer have faced de-listing, while enforcement has been stepped up against insider trading and market manipulation. In short, the CSRC is sending very strong signals that its overriding mission is to maintain a fair, efficient, and transparent market, based upon international best practice, regardless of the interests of issuers or intermediaries, while progressively modernising and opening the market.

Many CSRC officials believe that the agency still needs additional powers to investigate wrongdoing and impose sanctions. For example, while it is plain that the CSRC has jurisdiction over institutional investors and securities companies, it has much less power over non-financial companies, which often participate in price manipulation. It is very difficult to obtain the bank accounts of suspected wrongdoers. The sanctions that the CSRC can impose are relatively minor, and usually involve suspension from dealing. To initiate major civil or criminal cases, the CSRC must work through the Ministry of Justice. It will be an important objective to obtain the necessary legal authorisation to grant adequate investigative and punitive powers to the CSRC in the next few years.

Until now the CSRC has been far more proactive than its counterparts in Western countries in promoting market modernisation and regulatory reform. At the same time, individual firms and self-regulatory organisations (SROs) have been marginal in terms of oversight and the initiation of reform. The main SROs in China are 1) the two stock exchanges and 2) the Securities Association of China, the industry body representing the intermediaries.[5] The stock exchanges often complain of excessively detailed setting of listing and trading rules by the CSRC.

Chinese practice in this regard stands in contrast to that of major markets where initiatives to reform and introduce new techniques and products are frequently launched by the private sector, industry associations and SROs, with the securities supervisors only providing broad oversight. Even in cases where the securities regulator initiates action, changes in regulation usually take place only after formalised procedures for consultation with market participants. In OECD countries it has been the norm to shift an increasing share of the burden for observing prudential standards to the individual institutions, industry associations and SROs.

As a temporary expedient, this highly directive stance by the CSRC may be justifiable in view of the relative underdevelopment of the capital market. Continuing revelations of infractions of rules are signs that the industry's capacity to police itself still leaves much to be desired. As a medium-term priority, however, the securities industry will have to assume more responsibility for enforcing standards with the authorities delegating larger responsibilities to firms and SROs.

In 2001, CSRC spokesmen have been insisting that it intends to delegate more supervisory responsibility to SROs in the future, and an important task is to delegate more responsibility to market participants to formulate and enforce standards.[6] In order to move to such a regime, market intermediaries will have to improve their internal risk management and compliance systems while SROs will have to build capacity to investigate alleged infractions and to discipline their own members.

Investors

Retail investors

The Chinese securities market is predominantly one in which individuals invest in shares of SOEs. To this day, retail investors still dominate the equity market, with about 90 per cent of turnover on the stock exchanges originating with retail accounts.[7] It is said that some 60 million household securities accounts have been opened, but this figure must be interpreted with caution. This figure simply represents the number of share accounts opened at the Shanghai and Shenzhen stock exchanges.Many investors trade at both exchanges. Moreover, an unknown number illegally operate multiple accounts.[8] Data from the stock exchanges show that only around 40 per cent of accounts actually hold shares.[9] Some 15 per cent of share accounts trade actively.

Chinese residents have high aggregate savings rates, but retail investors do not have a wide array of choices. Only three categories of financial assets are practically available to such investors: bank accounts, government bonds and equities. In fact, small investors do hold large amounts in bank accounts and government bonds. Other capital market instruments and institutional savings products, which are becoming the predominant form of holding financial assets in OECD countries, are underdeveloped.

Retail equity investors have traditionally not been very concerned with fundamental analyses of corporate performance, and therefore the quality of research supplied by brokers to retail investors is not very high. Similarly, retail investors have not been very demanding in terms of the quality of disclosure or of corporate governance. Retail investors have tended to trade on technical factors, rumours and real or supposed insider information, with the emphasis on short-term trading profits. Chinese investors trade very frequently by comparison to those in other markets. Individual investors commonly hold shares for less than one month.[10] In 2000, the trading turnover ratio was 422 per cent in Shanghai and 372 per cent on the Shenzhen exchange. Comparable ratios in Western markets are typically below 100 per cent.

The prevailing expectations of retail investors clearly represent a problem for reform. These investors have been enticed into the market because the authorities have tacitly accepted a variety of tactics to maintain buoyancy in stock prices. Beyond this, many retail investors undoubtedly believe that the government has an unspoken commitment to support the market. As the stock market enters its new phase, investors will have to be more sensitised to risk and to exercise more careful discrimination among companies.

To the degree that individuals are not capable of performing such analysis they should be encouraged to use institutional forms of investment in order to gain access to professional management. Clearly, it will be a crucial task in the next few years to educate the public about the higher level of judgement that investors will be asked to exercise in the future without provoking a mass exit from equity investment.

Extra-legal investment funds

Although it is true that retail investors dominate the market, there has been a constant pattern of informal investment fund operations on the margins of the recognised financial system. An initial phase of investment fund development took place from 1990-1997. In that period, funds tended to be small and many were not authorised by local bodies or the PBC, rather than the CSRC. The period was characterised by volatility and speculative excesses, with few formal rules governing the formation or operation of funds.[11] Even today there apparently is a significant "grey market" in which "investment consultants", operating outside any recognised legal framework, solicit funds from the public and invest those funds. In many cases the funds are invested through individually-owned accounts. These funds range from small community-based funds, in which funds are invested by informal networks of friends, work colleagues and relatives, to much larger and more professional operations involving large-scale solicitation from the public.

It is difficult to ascertain the actual extent of activity by underground investment funds. According to press reports, a study by analysts at the PBC estimated that funds collected through underground investment funds could be as high as RMB900 billion (about US$108billion), but most analysts believe that this figure is too high. An estimate of total assets of RMB 600 billion is considered more realistic. It is also uncertain to what degree informal funds are being invested in the recognised stock market. These funds may be invested in private companies, property or unlisted securities.[12]

The activities of the underground investment funds have several implications for the capital market. To the degree that these funds are invested in unlisted securities, they may be filling a gap in the range of investment outlets offered to the public, due partly to the policy of restricting access to the formal capital markets to the SOE. These funds may thus be providing capital to dynamic economic sectors, such as private companies. At the same time, to some degree these funds are simply collective investment schemes (CIS) operating outside the formal legal framework. In all likelihood, these schemes do not observe minimal standards regarding disclosure and lack the requisite framework for CIS governance and investor protection. Reportedly, many schemes are promising fixed returns. In many other countries, the informal solicitation of funds by unregulated investment vehicles has been instrumental in generating speculative bubbles and has often led to major losses by large numbers of small investors. It is very important to identify the dimensions of this problem and take measures to bring these schemes within the recognised framework for CIS.

Institutional investors

The Chinese government has been seeking to promote institutional investors, recognising that institutional investors represent a force for improved market quality. These investors tend to be able to engage in more disciplined and professional analysis of issuers thereby encouraging a rise in standards of disclosure and performance. Institutional investors can also reduce volatility.

The Chinese authorities base their hopes for the capability of institutions to transform markets partly on the experience of OECD countries, where an institutionalisation of wealth is transforming financial systems. The assets of institutional investors (pension funds, insurance products or collective investment schemes) are rising as a share of national income and of asset holdings with a proportional decline in holdings of deposits and direct ownership of securities. Investment in institutional savings products enables small investors to obtain portfolio diversification and low cost execution that would otherwise only be available to very large investors. Additionally, rather than relying on their own judgement, investors in institutional savings products can obtain access to professional managers who devote themselves exclusively to analysis of market opportunities using the latest analytic and portfolio management techniques. A diverse investor community spanning a spectrum of investors with varying objectives, (*e.g.* growth, capital protection and income), as well as a variety of time horizons and risk preferences, adds depth to the capital market. Institutional investors measure and manage the risk in such assets while insisting on better disclosure on the part of issuers and credible practices among rating agencies. Moreover, institutional investors are the natural purchasers of asset classes, such as corporate bonds, mortgage bonds, mortgage-backed securities and derivatives.

Institutional investors are crucial to achieving another major Chinese policy goal, the introduction of funded pension schemes. Indeed, one of the forces driving the build-up of institutional savings in OECD countries has been increasing reliance on capital markets to provide retirement income. The assets accumulated for retirement in pension funds, insurance products or collective investment schemes are usually invested in capital market instruments using professional asset management skills.

China is taking some preliminary steps to construct a legal and regulatory framework for retirement savings. Current policies regarding their investments are very cautious. Insurance companies are required to invest most of their assets in government bonds and bank deposits. Recently, authorisation was given to invest small amounts in equities, but only through investment funds. Funded pensions, which are still in a formative stage, were also limited to bank deposits and government bonds but have recently obtained permission to invest in equity. As the legal and regulatory framework for retirement savings matures, regulation should evolve from one of strict prohibition and portfolio allocation guidelines to more flexible governance systems to assure careful analysis and measured risk taking. While insurance companies asset managers and pension funds are major potential capital market players, they can only realise that potential if the necessary legal, institutional and regulatory framework is put in place.

It is worth mentioning that there are close connections among the various forms of retirement-related institutional savings. In particular, CIS (see next section) and insurance products are very frequently eligible for inclusion in pension plans. Many insurance products are designed to allow for a buildup of benefits during an accumulation phase and for a subsequent payment of benefits through an annuity, both of which require adequate investment policies in both phases.

Collective investment schemes (CIS)

The main category of institutional investor that lies in the competence of the securities supervisors is collective investment schemes (CIS). This category includes several forms of open-ended instruments such as investment companies, mutual funds, unit trusts, investment trusts and others. The concept underlying CIS is rather straightforward. While many investment opportunities are available in the capital market, most individuals lack the requisite investment skill and cannot afford sufficiently diversified portfolios or execute large trades. CIS offer individuals a means of pooling their funds and hiring professionals to manage their investments. There are a number of legal and governance structures for CIS, but, whatever its structure, a CIS can be thought of as consisting of three elements: 1) a pooling of resources to attain sufficient size for portfolio diversification and cost-efficient trading; 2) professional portfolio management; and 3) a set of legal and institutional safeguards to assure that the promoters and investment managers of the CIS do not take advantage of the investor.

At this time, there is no firm legal framework for the trust relationship or the collective investment sector in China but a trust law and an investment fund law are under consideration. Pending development of a formal structure, the collective investment sector is operating under temporary rules. Following excesses in the investment fund sector in the early to mid-1990s an attempt to build an orderly framework for CIS began after 14 November 1997, when the State Council Securities Committee issued the *Provisional Measures of the Administration of Securities Investment Funds*, which established a temporary legal basis for the CIS sector under CSRC control. The *Provisional Measures* made some preliminary attempt to spell out the responsibilities of key participants, such as fund managers and depository banks. It was stipulated that all funds must be managed by a separate Fund Management Company (FMC). Only securities companies and investment trust companies were authorised to form FMC, with most actually owned by securities companies.

The *Provisional Measures* further stipulated that:

1. All funds must have CSRC approval;

2. Funds must have paid-up capital of RMB 300 million (US$36 million) and have a minimum term of five years. Any expansion in capital must be approved by the CSRC;

3. 80 per cent of assets must be held in securities (although there appears to be considerable flexibility in the enforcement of this rule). Chinese government bonds must account for no less than 20 per cent of fund assets; and,

4. 90 per cent of the funds' returns have to be distributed to investors as dividends.

Six funds were launched in 1998, each having 2 billion RMB (US$400 million) of assets and a maturity of 15 years. Only closed-end funds were permitted at this time. About half were entirely new funds, but the rest resulted from the restructuring of the old, unstandardised funds to conform to the rules of the *Provisional Measures*. As of June 2000 there were ten FMCs managing 22 funds with assets of RMB50.5 billion. Funds had varying investment styles such as growth, index, mid-caps etc. There are reports that information technology-sector funds will soon be authorised.[13] The funds must be listed on one of the two exchanges. All funds trade at discounts to net asset value (NAV).

The FMCs are emulating techniques of CIS organisation and governance as practised in the major world markets. The funds are organised in contractual form. Each shareholder firm has one board member. The risk control committee includes the General Manager, the Compliance Officer and the Vice General Manager. Funds are required to appoint a custodian bank to hold the assets, supervise the fund managers and calculate NAV. The FMCs are divided into investment management departments, research departments and compliance departments. The investment committee makes large strategic decisions, especially the asset allocation among equities, bonds and money markets. The research department makes specific stock recommendations. The fund managers make the stock picks. Investment and compliance committees provide oversight.

The CIS sector has been one of the fastest growing components of OECD financial systems in the past two decades and one that has gained great credibility with individual investors. This is in large part a reflection of the good performance of OECD bond and equity markets, but it has also resulted from efforts by legislators, regulators and the CIS industry to develop robust internal governance structures and investor protection systems. These systems resolve conflicts of interest and assure that the CIS acts in the interests of final investors. Competition among CIS and improved information flows have also fostered the development of this sector. Because CIS solicit and manage the assets of large numbers of small and often unsophisticated investors, the risk of abuse of agency relationships is present.[14] Trading activity to manipulate markets is one of the more severe abuses of the agency relationship. Other potential problems include excessive trading or use of the CIS to generate revenue for an affiliated financial institution. For example, a CIS could be used to support securities underwritten by an affiliated investment bank or to generate trading revenue for an affiliated broker.

The experience of OECD countries, as well as emerging markets, indicates that the effective oversight of CIS requires a strong legal framework, industry self-regulatory standards, and internal controls based upon strong compliance, information and audit functions. It is the responsibility of the FMC, especially its board, to ensure that such systems are put in place. There is no single legal and governance structure that is agreed to work best in all countries. Instead, there is a considerable range of choice for the structures of CIS. Moreover, a body of best practices in CIS oversight has been developed in international forums especially IOSCO in recent years. These can be used in developing specific rules suited to the Chinese marketplace.

Unlike the structure in China, the great majority of CIS in OECD countries are open-ended. Supervisors and market participants agree that closed-end funds present more problems of governance than open-ended funds. In China, however, concerns have been voiced that since open-ended funds must buy back units if investors were to sell in a market downturn, open-end funds would be forced to liquidate their positions, thus aggravating volatility. Such fears apparently contributed to delays in introducing these funds

The risk of abuse of agency relations, which is always present in a CIS, is still higher in China where the means to safeguard investor interests are not deeply rooted and where many market participants developed bad habits during the two preceding decades when regulatory standards were often unclear and not uniformly enforced. The practices incorporated in the *Provisional Measures* are designed to provide a structure and a tentative set of governance rules to mitigate agency problems.

Despite the attempts to construct adequate internal mechanisms for governance, there have been repeated allegations that recognised Chinese investment funds often collude with SOEs, securities companies and well-placed individuals to push up prices on selected issues. In 2000 and 2001, the CSRC took action to sanction specific cases of stock price manipulation by FMCs.[15] Senior management figures from these companies have been charged with violations of securities laws. It would appear inevitable that the underground funds, which are subject to even less effective scrutiny than the officially recognised funds, are engaging in similar abuses. Instances of continuing improprieties by FMC call attention to the need for institutional safeguards to assure that those in charge of the CIS are operationally separate from related companies and that transactions are reviewed by a competent body. This is turn requires an upgrading of the internal compliance and audit functions of CIS and clear accountability of supervisory boards of FMCs for enforcing adherence to standards.

The legislative framework should be amended to bring all legitimate transactions within the coverage of rules governing CIS. In the end only those CIS that are able to qualify under these laws and regulations should be allowed to continue to solicit funds from the public. An important priority should be to bring the extra legal investment funds with the formal framework.

The CSRC authorised the establishment of new FMC in 2001. Additionally, in June 2001, the CSRC announced that any Chinese company, not merely securities companies or investment trusts, can now apply to open an FMC. This would open the fund management sector to insurance companies, SOEs and banks, and possibly to private companies as well. Financial institutions, such as banks and insurance companies, may try to market funds through their distribution networks. However, banks may face some restriction imposed by banking laws and regulations. The opening of the CIS sector to new participants will broaden distribution channels, but may also raise the risk of new conflicts of interest.

In the past few years, the authorities had been promising to permit the introduction of Western-style open-ended CIS. In November 2000, the CSRC produced its long-awaited guidelines on open-ended funds.[16] These funds will have minimum assets of RMB 5 billion (US$600 million). In September 2001, the first such fund, organised by a domestic fund management company with a foreign partner, was introduced. Despite a soft stock index, the reception among retail investors was very strong. Additional open-ended CIS are expected to be launched in the future.

In the expectation that open-ended CIS will enjoy strong growth in the future, a number of alliances between domestic FMCs and foreign partners are under discussion. Unlike the securities companies which are somewhat ambivalent about the competition from foreign institutions, the FMCs are generally keen to develop skills and want to form strategic alliances or joint ventures with foreign partners. Chinese FMCs hope to gain access to foreign expertise in research, marketing and the operation of open-ended funds.

Intermediaries

Banks

Chinese law mandates the strict separation of banking and securities. These restrictions were imposed in response to abuses that occurred in the 1990s. Several OECD countries, (*e.g.* the United States, Canada and Japan) maintained regimes of strict institutional separation between banking and securities for a number of decades, but all virtually have now been abolished. While China is eventually likely to follow the practice of ending strict institutional separation, there is no particular urgency for it to take such measures. Indeed, there is an argument for allowing each category of institution to perfect skills in its own field of specialisation before expanding into new activities.

The main capital market activity in which banks are active at this time is the government bond market. Banks receive order from retail investors and are active traders in the primary and secondary markets on their behalf, but tend to "buy and hold" investors on their own account. (See section on the bond market later in this chapter.) As noted in the previous section, the CSRC has removed restraints on bank participation in the CIS sector. Certain banks have expressed a desire to enter the CIS market. Banks could form FMCs or use their branch networks to distribute funds. It is not certain whether the PBC will permit banks to engage in such activity.

At the same time, some banks are allegedly participating in equity investments through extra-legal operations. The authorities will have to decide whether they will allow banks to form specialised subsidiaries in order to engage in capital market activities, or to accelerate action enforcement against unauthorised activities by banks in the capital markets activity.

Securities companies

The main capital market intermediaries are the securities companies. At end 2000, there were 102 securities companies. Due to policies of circumscribing the activities of various categories of financial institutions, all securities companies can only engage in a relatively narrow range of operations. Within this already narrow range of operations, securities companies are divided into: *a*) those with "comprehensive" licences, which may engage in the entire range of permitted activities, or *b*) those that are restricted to agency brokerage. Companies with "comprehensive" licences can engage in agency brokerage, underwriting and proprietary trading. They may also form an FMC to manage CIS. As of May 2000, the CSRC had licensed 26 "comprehensive" securities companies. Such authorisation required registered capital of RMB 500 million (US$60 million), net capital of RMB 200 million (US$24 million), three years of profits, some experience of issuance and a clean regulatory record. Prior to the enactment of the Securities Law, there were no legislative constraints on who could underwrite, although the CSRC promulgated administrative regulations in June 1996 that established a qualification system. The limited license requires only registered capital of RMB 50 million.

Chinese securities companies differ considerably from securities companies and investment banks in the major world markets. In the latter markets, investment banks and securities dealers are privately owned and heavily capitalised. A defining feature of their culture is to place the capital of the institution at risk in a range of securities and derivatives operations such as primary market operations, proprietary trading, corporate finance and mergers and acquisitions. Research-based detailed knowledge of the market is a critical part of the skill mix. These institutions have strong in-house risk management systems, utilise sophisticated trading strategies and have strong compliance and risk management systems. The board of directors of the company is accountable to the supervisor for building robust compliance and risk management systems. A high premium is placed on innovation and controlled risk taking.

Chinese intermediaries differ from their foreign counterparts in several critical ways. All of China's securities companies are state-owned, either directly or through SOEs. It is very rare that these companies put large amounts of capital at risk in primary market underwritings or in proprietary trading. Given the lack of depth in the investor community, pressures to produce high quality research have not been strong. Most Chinese companies have limited experience operating in an environment in which strict investor protection rules are enforced. In fact, the securities companies are widely believed to collaborate with investment funds and other market participants to manipulate stock prices. In-house systems for risk management and compliance are not well developed.

Chinese securities companies still depend heavily on commissions from retail customers for revenue. This may well be a source of vulnerability in the future, since the institutionalisation of trading and competition among trading systems are eroding the profitability of agency brokerage in major markets. Although margins have been sustained in retail brokerage until recently, the advent of trading on the Internet has been squeezing margins in this sector as well. There is every reason to expect profitability from agency brokerage activity to diminish in China as it has elsewhere. As a result, there is likely to be consolidation in the Chinese industry as there has been in most countries.[17]

China's securities companies, which are under-financed, are continually seeking to expand their capital and to develop other funding sources in order to engage in a broader range of operations, especially proprietary trading. On several occasions, securities companies have been reprimanded for using customers' funds to finance their own operations. Borrowing from banks was formally prohibited in 1997, but had traditionally been a common practice. Thus, one of the reasons for the development of the repurchase market in government bonds was to enable the securities companies to obtain more liquidity for trading.

Over the past year, the CSRC has enacted a wave of measures designed to enhance liquidity in the secondary market:

1. Securities companies were allowed to buy China government bonds (CGBs) and repurchase agreements (repos) in the inter-bank market.

2. Qualified securities companies were permitted to use share holdings as collateral on bank loans. Loans may not exceed 60 per cent of the market value of the shares only. Comprehensive securities companies can qualify for similar treatment.

3. Listed companies were permitted to trade shares they have held for six months; and

4. Many securities companies have increased their capital base over the past two years under CSRC encouragement.

An additional difference between Chinese and foreign securities companies lies in the area of mergers and acquisitions and corporate finance generally. In most OECD countries, investment banks have diversified skills in this domain as major elements in their corporate strategies. The lack of such capabilities in China is important not only for the securities companies, but also for the economy at large. The corporate sector in OECD countries has made enormous efficiency gains in the past two decades and many analysts agree that the ability to use the capital markets in corporate restructuring has been one of the sources of such gains. Since it is a major policy aim in China to lower debt/equity ratios as part of the broader effort to raise efficiency in the SOE sector, capital market intermediaries must develop the capability to engage in corporate finance as well.

In order to rectify the shortcomings among securities companies, several steps can be taken. One contribution can come from the public listing of securities companies, which will boost capitalisation and provide for enhanced scrutiny of the activities of these companies. Many of the deficiencies in the skill mix can be mitigated through alliances with foreign institutions.

The CSRC has authorised securities companies to increase capital through share issues. Additionally, the CSRC is likely to encourage consolidation in the industry. Consolidation among domestic securities companies is expected over the next few years. This reflects the desire of their owners to gain economies of scale and build nationwide brokerage networks, as well the CSRC's ambition to foster the emergence of a small number of big domestic securities companies that have the potential to develop into investment banks similar to those found in major markets. Within five years, the CSRC is thought to aim at having a core of 8-10 highly capitalised firms with nationwide capability in a broad range of capital market operations. It is likely that the CSRC will grant a select number of companies approval to publicly issue shares. These institutions will have enhanced capability to form alliances with foreign institutions.

Equity markets

Listed companies

As noted previously, the large-scale public flotation of SOE equity has been one of the big successes of the Chinese capital market reform. While equity markets scarcely existed in 1990, more than 1 100 companies were listed in 2000 (see Table 15.1).

Table 15.1. **Development of the equity market 1990-1999**

A. *Number of Chinese listed companies*

	1992	1993	1994	1995	1996	1997	1998	1999
A-shares only	35	140	227	242	431	627	727	822
B-share	0	6.0	4.0	12	16	25	26	26
A and H shares		3.0	6.0	11	14	17	18	19
A and B shares	18	34	54	58	69	76	80	82
Total	53	182	291	324	530	745	851	949
Capital raised from equity issues								
A-share		19.5	5.0	2.3	22.5	65.5	44.3	57.3
H-share		6.1	18.9	3.2	8.4	36.0	3.8	4.7
B-share		3.8	3.8	3.3	4.7	8.1	2.6	0.4
A-share and B-share rights issues		8.2	5.0	6.3	7.0	19.8	33.5	32.1
Total		37.6	32.7	15.1	42.6	129.4	84.2	94.5
Market capitalisation (RMB billion)	105	353	369	347	984	1 753	1 951	2 647
Free float (RMB billion)		86	97	94	287	520	575	821
Market capitalisation/ GDP (%)	4	10	8	6	15	23	25	32
Free float/GDP (%)			2	2	4	7	7	10

B. *Capital raised from equity issuance at home and abroad (RMB billion)*

	1993	1994	1995	1996	1997	1998	1999
A-share	19.5	5	2.3	22.4	65.5	44.3	57.3
H-share	6.1	18.9	3.1	8.4	36	3.8	4.7
B-share	3.8	3.8	3.3	4.7	8.1	2.6	0.4
A-share and b-share rights issues	8.2	5	6.3	7	19.8	33.5	32.1
Total	37.5	32.7	15.0	42.5	129.4	84.2	94.5

Source: China Securities Regulatory Commission.

The vast majority of listed companies are state owned enterprises (SOEs). Public listing of Chinese companies usually begins with a decision by those in control of the SOE, such as a ministry or a local government agency, to transform some of its assets into a joint stock company (corporatisation). While a variety of methods were used in this process in the 1980s, the enactment of the company law in 1994 gave some uniformity to this procedure. This process involves the creation of a balance sheet in conformity with accounting rules for listed companies, approval of articles of incorporation and management structure, the selection of a board of directors and major officers of the company, and an initial shareholder meeting.

Listed companies usually belong to SOE groups that select some of their stronger members for public listing. SOE groups often have a small number of listed companies as well as some unlisted companies.[18] SOE complexes typically have excessive employment, large financial obligations to retired workers and responsibilities for maintaining facilities that are unrelated to their core economic functions. Non-core responsibilities may include operating schools hospitals, housing, and police and fire departments. The process of listing requires firms to take some measures to separate the listed entity from its affiliates.

In practice, the separation between the listed company and its unlisted affiliates is incomplete. At a minimum some unlisted related companies remain important suppliers or customers of the listed company. More seriously, listed companies are embedded in complex groups of listed and unlisted companies that have a web of relationships with various levels of government. The majority of senior managers hold civil service ranks and are selected and remunerated by the SOE group and related

509

government ministries.[19] There is also a parallel structure of the local Communist party that exercises significant influence over the company.[20]

Given that SOEs have been able to obtain large sums on capital markets, while requiring only very limited behavioural changes on the part of listed companies, public listing has been a very attractive proposition. Through the middle of 2001, a listed company typically offered only about 25-35 per cent of its total equity to public investors of all kinds, (*i.e.* employees of the company or retail or institutional investors) (see Figure 15.2). The remaining two-thirds of their equity is held in two forms, the first being state shares representing the state's investment in the company and theoretically owned by the State Council. State shares are not tradable. The second comprises "legal person" shares that are held by SOEs, institutions, authorised social groups or other entities that have been granted "legal person" status. Legal person shares are tradable to a very limited degree, but only among legal persons. In sum, most listed companies continue to be majority-held by the state or organisations closely aligned with the state. As a result of these non-tradable shares, the assertion that equity market capitalisation represents a high share of GDP must be interpreted with some caution.

The government has frequently stated its intention to reduce the non-tradable share of SOE equity significantly over the next few years. The first concrete steps to put that policy into practice occurred on June 14, 2001 when the State Council unveiled its long-awaited regulations on state-share divestment. The Provisional Measures on Management over the Reduction of State Shares to Raise Social Security Funds stipulate that all shareholding companies – including overseas-listed firms – possessing state shares or legal person shares, should sell off their state shares in an amount equal to 10 per cent of their total equity.[21] The sale can take place through IPO or private placement. The resulting revenues will be transferred to the Ministry of Finance (MOF) to offset the deficit of the social security funds. An inter-ministerial group was set up to elaborate the details of the operations. The Group includes the State Planning and Development Committee, the State Economic and Trade Committee, the Ministry of Labour and Social Security, CSRC, the State Social Security Council (SSSC) and State Social Security Funds (SSSF).

While the immediate impact is expected to be modest, the reduction of the non-tradable share of listed companies potentially represents a rise in the ability of non-controlling investors to affect the valuation of companies. In the longer term, wider ownership – along with more institutional ownership and vigorous enforcement of corporate governance rules – should fortify the claims of non-controlling investors for adherence to norms of shareholder value.

Figure 15.2. **Ownership structure of listed companies**

(per cent)

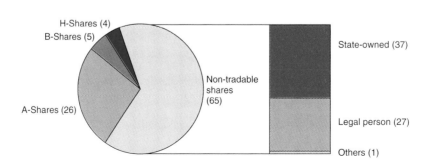

Source: "*This little piggy becomes a market: The challenges of Chinese capital market liberalisation*", Paper prepared for the Organisation for Economic Co-operation and Development (OECD) by Stephen Green, London School of Economics and Royal Institute of International Affairs and David Wall, University of Cambridge and University of London.

Disclosure requirements

Prior to listing, companies must produce the following documents: 1) a prospectus 2) an offering circular and 3) periodic reports as well as special reports on significant matters.[22] The information that must be contained in these documents is specified in CSRC regulations. The supervisory board of the company is responsible for the accuracy of reports, and all accounts must be subjected to an internal audit.

The Ministry of Finance sets accounting standards which may differ among industries. SOEs traditionally used accounting practices based upon the central planning system. In 1993, the Ministry of Finance mandated that SOEs use general principles based on International Accounting Standards (IAS) which have to some degree been incorporated in Chinese accounting principles.[23]

Despite efforts to upgrade standards, repeated examinations of accounts of listed companies show that companies tend to provide false or misleading reports of their actual state of profitability and balance sheet quality. For example, a recent report by the Ministry of Finance estimated that up to 90 per cent of companies distort their published accounts.[24] Accounts can be manipulated by misrepresenting the ways in which funds raised are actually used, concealing related party transactions and hiding or delaying poor earnings results. Inflated earnings reports and/or projections at times of IPO are especially prevalent. Most listed SOE are closely related to larger complexes and to government entities. In some cases, the listed company has not taken sufficient measures to establish a separate identity from its affiliates, such as establishing separate accounts. Earnings from a profitable listed company may be used to fund activities of affiliates. Loan guarantees by listed companies to affiliates are often not reported.

Since 1998, the CSRC has made considerable efforts to crack down on fraudulent IPO applications. Regulations introduced in August 1998 force restructured SOEs to have operated in their final restructured form for at least a year before listing. This is an attempt to prevent hidden debts and falsified profits from coming to light once the firm is listed.[25] Thanks to the toughening of standards following such scandals, the institutional strengthening of the CSRC, and the diminution of local government influence, it appears likely that fewer of the companies now listing have such major problems. Listed firms are required to file financial disclosure reports twice a year. However, the CSRC announced that beginning in the first quarter of 2002 quarterly reports would be required and companies with losses are expected to meet that requirement in the third quarter of 2001.[26] The CSRC requires that listed companies' annual reports be independently audited by certified public accountants. Measures to improve the independence of the auditing profession were begun in 1995, but the validity of these audits is often in question. Independent auditing is still underdeveloped with limited professional accountability.[27]

Better professional standards in undertaking analysis of borrowers are the objective of the Securities Analysts Association of China, which was established in June 2000. Additionally, the CSRC plans to set up an Investors' Institute which will assist investors to seek compensation for investment losses resulting from fraudulent financial reporting or other breaches of law by listed companies.

Domestically listed shares

The categories of shares issued in China are shown in Table 15.2. As of now there are two categories of publicly tradable shares listed on the two Chinese exchanges, A-shares that are only available to Chinese investors and B-shares that until very recently were only available to foreigners.[28] (As explained in the next section, other categories of shares are also reserved for foreigners.) Once a share is issued in a certain category it may not be converted into another share type.

The A shares, which constitute the majority of shares listed in Shanghai and Shenzhen, may only be purchased by Chinese residents. Companies listed exclusively as A-shares tend to be small and unfocused. The size of issues tends to be low. Chinese accounting standards are used and disclosure practices tend to be the weakest for any category of company. Nevertheless, as noted previously, this

Table 15.2. **China's share categories**

Type	Description
A-shares	Domestically listed shares, denominated in local currency. Foreign investors may not own these shares.
B-shares	Domestically listed shares of China-incorporated companies, denominated in US$ in Shanghai and HK$ in Shenzhen. Initially reserved for foreign investors domestic institutions and individuals now make up the majority of trading.
Legal person shares	Roughly a third of every listed firm's equity is transferred to domestic institutions (stock companies, NBFIs, and SOEs with at least one non-state owner) and can not be traded.
State shares	Another third of equity is transferred to the state (central and local government departments, as well as SOEs wholly owned by the state). The ultimate owner is the State Council. Legal person and state shares are not tradable, though they can be transferred with permission from the CSRC. Alongside legal person shares, this practice allows the government to claim that share issuance is not akin to privatisation.
H-shares	Shares of mainland registered companies listed in Hong Kong (China).
Red-chips	Shares of companies registered overseas and listed abroad (principally in Hong Kong, China), having substantial Mainland interests and controlled by affiliates or departments of the Chinese government.

Source: China Securities Regulatory Commission.

market has scored significant success, especially among small Chinese investors, with these stocks trading at very high valuations.

In 1992 a second category of share (B shares) was created. These shares were also listed on the two domestic exchanges, but could only be purchased by foreigners using foreign currency. B-shares listed in Shanghai are denominated in US dollars while those listed in Shenzhen are denominated in Hong Kong dollars. Companies issuing B-shares must present their accounts using international accounting standards.

Unlike the A share market, which made some impressive gains in the 1990s, the B-share markets remained small and illiquid. Of the 108 companies which had issued B-shares by end 1999, only around one fourth had not issued A-shares as well. While the A shares have tended to trade at high multiples, valuations of B shares have been much lower, and closer in fact to those prevailing in major markets. Partly owing to the lack of transparency, most foreign investors have not been large purchasers of B-shares but instead have used other investment instruments. (See next section.) One of the major sources of demand for B-shares has been from Chinese nationals. Although it was not formally permitted for Chinese nationals or firms to buy B shares, there has been considerable leakage, particularly at times when it was thought that the markets would be merged.

In February 2001, the authorities, possibly as a first step in a wider liberalisation, opened the B market to investment by Chinese residents who held foreign currency accounts. In June 2001, it was further decided to open the B-share market to all domestic residents, regardless of whether they had foreign currency accounts. Consequently, the B-share market is now open to both foreigners and Chinese. Following the opening of the B-share market, prices skyrocketed in expectation that the two categories may eventually be merged.

Listing requirements are progressively stricter for each category of share. A firm seeking listing on the A-share market has to produce necessary documents and to meet some essential requirements such as *a*) minimum capital of RMB50 million, *b*) 1000 shareholders with at least 1000 shares each *c*) a minimum of 25 per cent of equity offered for public sale *d*) conformity with rules concerning organisation and governance *e*) a minimum of 3 years of continuous profit.

Overseas issuance

In addition to the purchase of B-shares, foreigners have other possible means of investing in the Chinese equity market. Many Chinese companies have issued equity overseas that is listed on stock exchanges outside the mainland, most frequently on the Hong Kong Stock Exchange (HKSE). These issues, commonly referred to as "H-shares", are reserved for large, strategic and relatively successful SOEs.

Companies seeking listing as H shares must meet yet further requirements beyond those required for A and B share issues. All such companies are obliged to undergo significant restructuring in order to separate themselves from the state and from obligations to the previous constituents of the firm, and to present a corporate structure that has some credibility as a profit-seeking entity. Foreign investment bankers often describe this process as one of "ring fencing" the company. Foreign stock exchanges may impose additional listing requirements.

Since H-shares were the only Chinese stocks that were listed internationally, the CSRC has been able to control listings much more closely than domestic listings and has only approved those that seemed likely to meet the more exacting overseas criteria. In contrast to domestic issues, where the primary market is controlled by Chinese securities houses, major international investment banks are closely involved in advisory work on these issues. The size of issuance tends to be much larger than for those listed domestically. Additionally, standards of quality and transparency are higher since they must first be approved by the CSRC for foreign listing and later approved by the foreign stock exchange on which it will be listed.

By the end of 1999, 49 mainland-incorporated (H-share) companies had listed overseas. While nearly all were listed on the HKSE, several were simultaneously listed on other exchanges, such as New York, London, Tokyo and Singapore. Only two issues were not listed on the HKSE. Total amounts raised came to US$10.6 billion.

An additional means for foreigners to invest in the Chinese market is through the "Red Chips", i.e., companies incorporated in Hong Kong, China but under mainland control. This category of shares was created in 1996 in anticipation of the transfer of sovereignty. Just prior to the transfer of sovereignty in July 1997, this class of share was very popular with foreign investors. The largest and best publicised of these issues was China Telecom. Following a sharp run-up in this market in 1996 and the first half of 1997, a precipitous drop occurred along with the drop in the HKSE in October 1997. There are 64 Red Chips now listed, with total issue amounting to US$23 billion.

International investors seeking exposure to the Chinese equity markets tend to prefer the H-shares to the B-shares. In the first place, the companies that are allowed to list overseas tend to be of higher quality than those with only domestic listings. In addition, the foreign investor obtains some additional protection from the fact that the issuer has met listing and disclosure requirements and is committed to meeting those requirements in the future. The possibilities of obtaining legal redress are also somewhat better on companies that have listed overseas.

Hong Kong, China serves as an important link between the mainland and the international financial market. As noted above, most Chinese companies that list overseas are listed on the HKSE. Mainland enterprises (H shares and Red Chips) are estimated to account for 15 per cent of total listed companies and 27 per cent of the total market capitalisation of the HKSE. Mutual dependence appears to be growing. In 2000, it is estimated that 90 per cent of new listings on the HKSE originated from the mainland while US$14 billion of US$17 billion in Chinese IPO took place through Hong Kong, China.

Primary markets

The requirement of continuous profitability is quite peculiar to China. Most advanced markets have no such requirement. Instead, it is assumed that if a badly performing company is exposed to scrutiny by the market, it will be punished by having its share price driven to low levels, and possibly will become a take-over target. The Chinese authorities apparently believe that their market is not efficient enough to impose such discipline and hence the requirement to maintain profitability is officially enforced. Only one class of common shares may be issued. Companies seeking B-shares are required to supply additional documentation and to present accounts in accord with international accounting principles.

513

Authorisation for issuance

Methods of launching IPO in China differ from those in most other markets. Until 1998, a quota system was used to determine access to listing. Concerning A share issues, an annual quota system was previously used in determining which firms would be allowed to issue equity between the opening of the stock exchanges in 1990 and 1998. Each category has a separate quota with those categories reserved for foreign investors requiring additional approvals. The State Planning Commission (now the State Development and Planning Commission or SDPC) took a leading role in setting allocations. In theory, the quota was linked to the national investment and credit plan. The quota was allocated by province as well as well as by "independent plan municipalities". Within each regional entity, the local authorities granted permission to enterprises to issue equity. Among the criteria used in selecting firms for listing are their performance and their financial importance, including their capability to meet profitability requirements for listing and sectoral priorities. It was widely acknowledged that the quota system gave local governments the capability to list poor-quality companies. Active bargaining among ministries and regions characterised the process of allocating quotas. Although the CSRC technically had to approve issues, no cases of CSRC denial of an application approved by local administrations are known. One stock exchange member is required to act as a sponsor for the listing.

Regulations governing IPO were progressively tightened. In 1995, underwriters were responsible for verifying that issuers fulfil obligations to shareholders for a year following issue. Additionally, an underwriting contract between the underwriter and the issuer must include a one-year guidance period when the underwriter has expanded duties, including assuring disclosure of required information. Regulations defining improper underwriting practices were promulgated in June 1996. While the quote has been abolished in principle, it is unclear whether remnants of the system remain.

Misrepresentation of financial results was widespread. The rules that a firm must have three years of profits before listing were only loosely applied. Restructuring into a corporate form is supposed to be completed before public issuance, but many firms continue to restructure after they have secured a listing. CSRC investigations have revealed that many companies, in co-operation with their underwriters, accountants and lawyers, issued shares on the basis of falsified accounts.

Changes to regulations in July 1998 made it possible to trade legal person shares on a limited basis. No legal person may acquire more than 5 per cent of the company's equity. The regulations divide legal persons into *a)* strategic investors who intend to develop a close relationship with the company and who agree to hold the shares for at least six months and *b)* other legal persons. Ordinary legal persons may trade their shares with other legal persons. At some future time, trading of legal person shares by the general public may be authorised.

The Securities Law that took effect in 1999 introduced more flexibility into the domestic market, but primary issues are still rather tightly controlled in comparison to most advanced markets. Firms must still seek approvals from multiple government departments before applying to the CSRC. The CSRC intervenes in IPO more directly than its counterparts in more advanced markets, which usually operate a registration system under which enterprises wishing to issue shares normally are only required to fulfil a comprehensive set of disclosure requirements. The CSRC, in contrast, does some screening for quality and also verifies that that the firm is in an approved industry and examines the firm's ownership structure.[29] Given the history of fraudulent filings and limited capacity of the market to discriminate between good and bad issuers, some screening by the regulators probably is useful. In the longer run, however, one would expect the market to be able to do more screening and for intermediaries to refuse to underwrite IPO that are likely to fail.

Following screening, the CSRC passes the application materials to its semi-independent Public Offering and Listing Review Committee (POLRC) which makes the final decision on authorisations. The Committee has 80 members, with more than three-fourths of the members independent of the CSRC. Each sub-committee of eight anonymous people meets to consider and vote on the application. The new procedure is considered to be more insulated from political influence than the previous system.

Shares targeted to foreigners, (B-shares and H-shares) are priced using techniques that more closely resemble those used in overseas markets. An initial price is estimated based upon projected earnings and an expected P/E ratio based upon accepted market practice. With this tentative price as a starting point, investment bankers attempt to estimate demand among prospective investors and adjust the final IPO price based on expected demand. Under-pricing is much less prevalent in foreign-targeted issues. Foreign investment banks structure deals in ways that will appeal to foreign institutional investors.

Primary distribution and pricing

As discussed in the preceding paragraph, foreign-targeted issues use techniques comparable to those in most world markets. New domestic issues, which have traditionally been targeted to retail investors, operate under completely different rules. Once issuance is approved, prospective investors must file application forms to purchase the shares and make cash deposits. Issues are heavily oversubscribed, and a lottery determines which investors buy the shares.

Public offers take place mainly through auctions using the electronic trading networks of the stock exchanges. Strategic investors and sponsors take part in IPO on special terms. The lottery system is used to allocate shares in cases of over-subscription. After payments, shares are delivered to investors and secondary trading begins. Due to excess demand at the IPO, trading tended to be feverish in early secondary trading. In addition to the shares traded through public offering a certain amount of an issue can be placed through private placements.

While IPO pricing has evolved significantly over time, there has been a persistent tendency to under-price A-share issues, meaning that the IPO price is usually well below the price at which the stock ultimately trades on the secondary market. One of the main explanations for consistent under-pricing is the traditional technique used in setting IPO prices. The tendency had been to have an offer price that assumes a P/E ratio of 15, *i.e.* a price 15 times the average of the earnings of the three years prior to the IPO. This ratio was roughly comparable to ratios prevailing in many overseas markets in earlier times. However, P/E ratios on domestic Chinese markets were already higher than those in international markets and subsequently tended to rise. In the early years of the stock market, shares tended to trade at seven times their IPO price.

The investment banks that managed primary market issues, usually local firms with connections to the local authorities, tended to approve of this method. Well-connected individuals could trade actively both in the primary market and in early secondary trading with the expectation of short-term trading gains. Since supervision of trading practices was relatively lax at this stage, the possibility for securities houses to engage in "front-running" was also present. The tendency to under-pricing was popular with retail investors since it increases the value of "winning" the IPO lottery. It was also popular with the exchanges since it generates very heavy trading volumes and with underwriters who face limited risks. On the other hand, it means that the issuing company receives less from the IPO than if the offer price were set closer to the expected secondary market price. The CSRC has been allowing underwriters and issuers to experiment with other pricing techniques that give heavier weight to project earnings and that use higher P/E ratios. Some recent IPO have had offer prices that were about 30 times earnings, with demand still very buoyant.

In a sophisticated and competitive market, an unsuccessful IPO would be taken as a sign that the company was of doubtful worth and/or that the underwriter misjudged the market. Consistent under-pricing, on the other hand, would cause an intermediary to lose credibility with issuers. In advanced markets, underwriters compete based partly on their ability to place new issues at prices that are reasonably close to their eventual secondary market prices. The Chinese market has functioned with rationed access limited competition among underwriters and wide price differentials, however.

In 1999, an experiment took place using "book building" techniques for IPO, as are routinely used in major international markets. In this process, the underwriter solicits bids from retail investors while estimating institutional demand through consultation with prospective buyers and determines the final

IPO price. The company chosen for the experimental issue was the Konka Group, a major Chinese manufacturer.[30] The only Chinese investment bank that has foreign equity participation had a key role in managing the offering. The IPO was successful to the extent that all shares were placed. The price in the secondary market tended to decline after the issue, but the decline was in line with a broad decline in the benchmark index. Almost certainly, the funds received by the issuing company were higher than if traditional pricing methods had been used. Nevertheless, trading was less active and the difference between the IPO price and the subsequent secondary market price was significantly less than Chinese investors had come to expect.

In recent IPO, a mix of techniques has been used with book building used for the institutional tranche and the lottery system still used for the larger retail tranches. The exact mix of techniques is agreed between the issuer and the CSRC.

As China moves into its next phase of capital market development, techniques that more closely follow the international primary market practices should be the norm. This would entail: *a*) free access to listing for all companies meeting listing and disclosure requirements, and *b*) market-based pricing of IPO. IPOs is

Although listed companies are mostly SOEs, a few non-state companies have been listed on the Shanghai and Shenzhen boards. To obtain such a listing requires local government backing and the firm must be in a priority industry.[31] Local governments are increasingly championing large non-state firms under their jurisdiction. The tax revenues are beneficial, and a thriving private concern is seen as a symbol of success. There were at least 22 private companies listed at the start of 1999. Most of these companies became listed by acquiring a failed SOE.[32] In the next phase of capital market development, private companies are expected to have access to stock market listings especially through the planned second board. (See below).

Secondary markets

The Shanghai and Shenzhen Exchanges

There are two main stock exchanges, located in Shanghai and Shenzhen, both of which were established in 1990. Both exchanges were created by local governments. However, the central government has gained increasing control over the exchanges, and the CSRC has emerged as the responsible authority under the Regulations on the Securities Exchanges of 1996. Both exchanges operate as non-profit membership organisations. In the 1990s, the two exchanges competed among themselves. The CSRC now oversees the exchanges very closely and appoints the senior staff of each exchange. The CSRC decides on which exchange companies will list, and dual listings are forbidden. In addition to equities (B shares and A shares) both exchanges trade investment fund shares, treasury bonds and corporate bonds.[33] The volume of trading in treasury bonds and related repos is higher in Shanghai.

Only Chinese financial institutions may be members of the stock exchange. Trading in B-shares requires a foreign broker to collect the order and a Chinese broker to execute the order. However, some Chinese brokers have arrangements whereby a foreign broker can use the position of its Chinese counterpart in order to trade directly on the exchange. Trading can take place through a "visible seat" in which a trader located at a station on the trading floor of the exchange manually inputs orders received by telephone. Alternatively, trades can take place though an "invisible seat" in which orders are sent electronically to the exchange's order matching system. B-shares must be traded though a "visible seat". A small amount of direct Internet-based trading also takes place. (Estimates range from 1-5 per cent).

There are no market makers or specialists on the exchanges and no requirement on the part of intermediaries to maintain markets except a general exhortation in the rules to co-operate in maintaining an active market. Both exchanges began with open outcry floor-based trading but are now highly automated, although both exchanges still have trading floors. Trading is now fully automated with a centralised and computerised auction system that matches orders according to a time/price algorithm. The technology supporting the trading platforms is of high quality.

Trading rules are similar in Shanghai and Shenzhen. Both exchanges allow share prices to fluctuate by a maximum of 10 per cent per day, but companies identified by the CSRC as subject to "special treatment" are limited to 5 per cent daily fluctuations. Commissions are fixed but low. All shares are de-materialised and held in book entry form. Each exchange has a central custodian services that holds the securities for shares listed on the exchange and also performs clearing and settlements operations. Each register and clearing company is a wholly owned subsidiary of the exchange. The clearinghouse provides a high degree of security to investors and brokers. Settlement of trades is on a T + 1 basis for A-shares and a T + 3 basis for B-shares (one or three days after the trade, respectively).

While the technology used in equities trading is of high quality, many trading practices leave much to be desired. Many companies that could not meet listing requirements were listed only after filing fraudulent documents and many companies failed to meet requirements for continued listing, especially the requirement of maintaining profitability. CSRC rules provide for de-listing after three years of losses, but until recently corrective action was rather limited. Under-performing companies were re-classified as Special Trading (ST) or Preferential Treatment (PT) meaning that their shares could be traded under restricted conditions, the aim being to encourage related companies to inject assets or restructure their debt in return for equity. As of December 2000, there were 61 ST companies (23 in Shanghai and 38 in Shenzhen) and ten PT companies (seven on the Shanghai Exchange and three in Shenzhen).[34]

Since March 2001, the CSRC has been stepping up its campaign to enforce existing standards and eventually to bring standards closer to those in world markets. Companies failing to improve under these temporary categories will be obliged to undergo full de-listing with their shares ultimately removed from the market and investors compensated.

Since March 2001 the CSRC has been taking strong action against securities companies and FMCs involved in market manipulation. In March the CSRC disciplined 30 senior officials of FMCs involved in price manipulation.[35] In May 2001, four financial consulting firms were fined for fixing the share prices of one company.[36]

It is critical to the detection of market manipulation and insider trading that the markets have audit trails that capture all transactions by price, volume and time of trade. It is unclear whether the Shanghai and Shenzhen exchanges have such capacity, or whether the CSRC has the capability to investigate and prosecute such actions. As a first step toward better enforcement, the CSRC is now studying a set of rules to make sure that securities firms renew all client agreements with clients. Those who do not return their client agreements will be considered suspect accounts and will be cancelled after a grace period.

The planned "second board"

A major overhaul of trader's arrangements has been under discussion for several years. Many market participants believe that the two existing exchanges may be merged into a single exchange based in Shanghai at some future time. A planned "second board" may be located in Shenzhen. The new board would list private companies as well as many innovative and "start-up" companies. CSRC spokesmen cite the experience of other "growth" markets, such as NASDAQ and the Growth and Enterprise Market (GEM) of Hong Kong, China.[37]

The planned second exchange would have more self-regulatory powers than the two existing exchanges. Large SOEs will not be allowed to list. There will be no state and legal person shares for companies listed on this market. In most cases the dominant shareowner will be independent of the state. This second board would have the added advantage in that it would provide a legal channel for firms that have been denied access to the main boards to obtain capital.

517

There will be no requirement of a history of profit on the second board, but disclosure requirements will be stricter and sponsoring securities houses will have responsibility for the security during a period of tutelage. The new board would allow shares to fluctuate 20 or 30 per cent in one day (as opposed to a 10 per cent limit on the main boards at present.)

The reform timetable had initially envisaged that this board would be established in 2001.Contrary to expectations, in late 2001 it appeared that the authorities were relenting in their efforts to open the second board.[38] Officials were particularly concerned about the sharp drops that had occurred on the NASDAQ and other "technology" or "growth" exchanges worldwide. Additionally, the authorities are preoccupied with increasing the tradable shares of already listed companies and with correcting abuses in the recognised market before proceeding with the second board. Thus, despite expectations by market participants, CSRC Chairman Zhou in late 2001 told foreign journalists that the government is not actively considering any proposal to consolidate the two exchanges.

Trends in Equity Prices and Valuations

There have been several cycles in the Chinese market. The mood was euphoric when the market was opened in 1992, as remarks by Deng Xiaoping suggested strong support for the continued development of equity markets. This initial buoyancy received a second impetus in 1993 with the issuance of the first "H" shares. A fairly serious correction occurred in 1994-96 however, as macroeconomic policy became rather restrictive. In 1996-97 issuance accelerated in advance of the transfer of sovereignty in Hong Kong. Additionally, issuance of Red Chips accelerated, with China Telecom most prominent. The pace of issuance slackened after the drop in the HKSE in late 1997 and the Red Chip market fell precipitously. This market has remained at low levels since that time, and these shares trade at very low ratios (see Table 15.3).

The most commonly used measure for equity valuation is the price earnings (P/E) ratio. At the end of 2000, the P/E ratios of the Shanghai and Shenzhen A-shares were 69 and 67, respectively. This ratio was out of all proportion to most other markets. The Chinese market was even expensive in comparison with Japan, traditionally the dearest market in the world. As the market corrected, these ratios declined.

The A-share market has indeed been reasonably strong over time with prices more than doubling between July of 1993 (the launch of the first H-shares) and 2000. Prices more than quadrupled between

Table 15.3. **Valuation of shares in selected markets in December 2001**

	Price/earnings ratios	Dividend yield
Shanghai A	41	0.4
Shanghai B	43	. .
Shenzhen A	42	0.7
Shenzhen B	25	0
Red Chips	11	2.5
H Shares	8	6.6
Hong Kong Stock Exchange (Hang Seng)	15	3.0
Singapore	16	2.3
Korea (KOSPI)	10	1.3
Chinese Taipei	20	1.9
Japan (NIKKEI)	41	0.9
Indonesia	12	2.1
Thailand (SET)	8	1.9
Standard and Poor's	26	1.1
Asia	18	

Source: China Securities Regulatory Commission, BNP Paribas, Bloomberg, UBS Warburg Global Equity, *Financial Times*, Walter and Howie and Secretariat estimates.

the sharp correction of 1995 and 2000. The Chinese domestic market trades at some of the largest valuations in the world. In 2000 and through mid-2001, the Chinese domestic equity market was one of the best performing markets worldwide. In mid-2001, some cooling of the boom became apparent. In the year ending December 2001, both the Shanghai and Shenzhen indexes had lost 20 per cent. Still, the Chinese domestic market trades at some of the highest valuations in the world.

The P/E ratios of categories of shares open to foreigners (H-shares and Red Chips) were much lower and were comparable to those in major markets. More detailed research has shown that shares of the same company trade at very different prices in various markets with the price in the A-share market almost invariably the highest price.[39] The indices which were reserved for foreign investors, (*i.e.* the B-shares, H-shares and Red Chips) were all below their level of July 1993 at the end of 2000. Until mid-2000 prices of B-shares tended to be weak. This category had failed to attract the interest of foreign investors. However, during 2000 and mid-2001 it became widely expected that the market would be opened to Chinese investors and prices began to firm significantly. After Chinese residents were legally authorised to purchase such shares in February 2001, prices shot up, more than doubling between the end of 1999 and mid-2001.

The Red Chip sector boomed in advance of the transfer of power in July 1997, quadrupling in the year before June 1997. However, with the sharp drop of the HKSE after November 1997, this market segment collapsed. While the gyrations in the H-share market have been less severe than in the Red Chips, at the end of 2000 the index of H-shares was also below its level of 1993.

The sharp gyrations in equity indexes in 1991 led to significant shifts in relative valuations. Thus, with the A-share indexes in Shanghai and Shenzhen dropping sharply, the P/E ratio declined considerably, although Chinese markets still were among the most expensive in the world. By contrast, the sharp rise in the B-share indices narrowed the discrepancies between A and B shares.

When considering comparative valuations, it should be remembered that the valuation of the US market, though well below that of the Chinese market, is historically high. This has led many analysts to argue that the US equity market is seriously over-valued. Those who justify the present high valuations argue that American companies have restructured significantly and are now highly focused on producing returns to shareholders. Plainly, Chinese SOEs lack those characteristics. The high valuation of Chinese equities seems even more questionable when it is recalled that the valuations in the US market are calculated using stricter accounting principles than those applied to Chinese companies.

The A-share market is influenced by a different set of factors than the other markets. Thus research concerning the factors influencing the A-share index generally shows a very low correlation with international indices such as the Hang Seng index or the Dow Jones. B-shares have very little correlation with the Dow Jones, but somewhat higher correlation with the Hang Seng index. At the same time, the H-shares and the Red Chips tend to have stronger correlations with foreign indices than with the A-share indices.[40]

No doubt, the relatively low valuation of internationally traded Chinese companies reflect the assessment of international investors who assess the performance of Chinese equities in a global context and compare relative returns categories of assets (bonds, credit spreads, market valuations and so on). Chinese investors, owing to the inconvertibility of the currency and the narrow range of alternative investments, are basically insensitive to these considerations. The exchange, along with market practices in China, has produced valuations that seem to be completely out of line with international norms. Clearly, if the various market segments are merged at some future time, or if capital account liberalisation opens the possibility for greater arbitrage, current valuations of Chinese equities will certainly undergo significant changes.

Chinese equity markets are frequently described as very volatile, but this statement must be carefully qualified. Some researchers have compared the volatility of the NYSE, the HKSE, and the various Chinese markets, and have found that while the NYSE is the least volatile, the Shanghai and Shenzhen A-share indices were less volatile than the Hang Seng index. The larger number of companies, the high volume of trading and lower interest-rate sensitivity were factors explaining the relatively low volatility of the domestic markets.

Bond markets

Although China's bond markets can be traced back as early as the 1950s, the volume of bonds outstanding only began rising substantially after the resumption of issuance in 1981, with the growth of the debt stock accelerating significantly since the mid-1990s. Total debt issues increased from RMB 19.3 billion in 1986 to RMB 601.5 billion in 1999.

The bond market remains dominated by government and quasi-government issues. The issuance of government bonds to finance budget deficits became more significant with the decision to curtail government borrowing from the central bank in 1994. The market has been characterised by a wide variety of instruments such as treasury bonds issued by the central government, financial bonds issued mostly by state-owned policy banks,[41] and bonds issued by SOEs. Government bonds include marketable bonds,[42] and non-marketable bonds (mostly savings bonds targeted to retail investors). In 1998, about one third of government bonds were savings bonds that were sold to individuals. The debt of the state-owned policy banks, which undertake public investment projects, is guaranteed and regarded as quasi-government bonds. Local government bonds and municipal government bonds do not exist because local governments are forbidden from borrowing on their own account (see Figure 15.3).

China's bond market represented about 20 per cent of GDP as of the end of 1999, well below the average for Asia at 40 per cent (see Figure 15.4). The low figure represents *a*) the low (but rapidly growing) stock of government debt and *b*) the absence of sizeable amounts of other categories of debt. This low figure for government debt outstanding may understate the full extent of government liabilities, and in any case the government's expenditures are likely to grow significantly.

Figure 15.3. **Debt Issues in China**

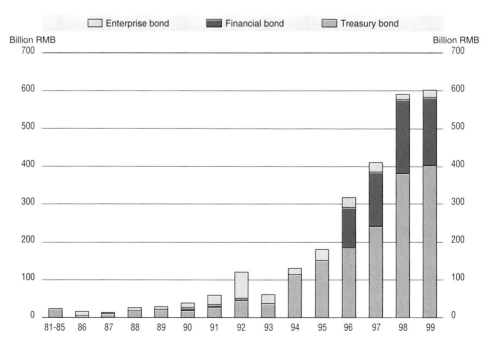

Source: China Securities and Futures Statistical Yearbook.

Figure 15.4. **Comparisons of Asia's bond markets**

(as a per cent of GDP, 1999)

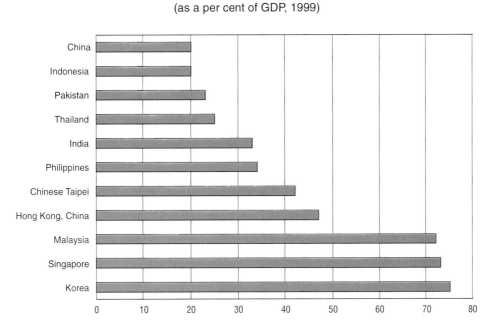

Source: Schroders.

Government bond markets[43]

Market participants

A vibrant government bond market requires active investors and dealers, such as institutional and individual investors[44], and primary dealers.[45] A distinguishing characteristic of most emerging debt markets, including China's, is a lack of institutional investors. In advanced economies, these investors – especially pension funds and insurance companies – have long-term liabilities and thus have a natural demand for longer-term assets. As mentioned in preceding sections, these investors now play a very minor role China at this time, but it is a major policy aim to encourage their growth.

Initially, government bonds were sold mainly to individual investors, and currently, individual investors are still the major holders of government bonds.[46] Banks are the second most important category of holder and their proportion of total government debt has been rising since the mid-1990s. Banks tend to hold bonds in order to earn the spread between their funding cost and the rate of interest on bonds, rather than trading for profit. Since the public holds the predominant share of its assets as bank deposits, the banks have large natural inflow of liabilities and seek acceptable assets. As mentioned in Chapter 7 on banking, banks have been under pressure from the PBC to avoid lending to weak SOEs and thus have sought other assets. As a result, banks have tended to build their portfolios of government bonds which involve zero transaction costs to acquire, give a return over their cost of funds, and carry no credit risk. In normal market circumstances, intense bidding should force bonds yields lower, but current practices have sustained yields at levels that remain attractive to banks.

The authorities in many countries have designated a group of intermediaries (securities firms and/or banks) as primary dealers in the government bond market. These firms obtain privileges in exchange for accepting certain obligations. The privileges may include the right to submit non-competitive bids at auctions, access to inter-dealer broker screens, designation as counterparties for the central banks' open market operations, access to repo financing, and bond borrowing/lending facilities with the central bank. Their obligations typically involve a requirement to place reasonable bids in primary markets, to ensure a fair and orderly secondary market in a range of issues, and to provide the central bank's trading desk with market information.

China's primary dealer system was established in 1993. At the time, 19 securities firms, banks and trust investment companies were selected as primary dealers based on the Regulation on Government Security Primary Dealers. The MOF and the PBC must approve new primary dealers and the number of primary dealers varies, depending on how many qualified institutions are available. Membership status is subject to periodic examination. There were 50 primary dealers as of the end of 1999.

Primary dealers have played an important role in subscribing to government bonds in the primary market. Bidders in primary offerings are mainly primary dealers, although some non-primary dealer financial institutions participate in the bidding process upon the MOF's approval.

In the current global financial environment, international investors are usually part of the investor base of most bond markets. In China, however, domestic debt is, in general, not available to foreign institutions. Since October 1998, designated foreign banks and foreign-owned financial companies have been allowed to participate on a very limited basis in inter-bank trading of government and quasi-government bonds.

Primary market

In China as in other countries, the trend has been to move away from administrative placement of government bonds, in favour of more market-oriented methods.[47] Before 1990, government bonds had been issued only through administrative placement, with banks obliged to accept specified quantities of bonds at government determined rates. After 1991, underwriting syndicates were introduced, and since 1995 auction methods have been used. Despite some progress in introducing market-oriented issue methods, serious obstacles remain. Types of government bonds are complex and segmented.[48] Issuing calendars are not established at regular intervals, with issuance tending to be bunched at certain periods during the year, thus making it difficult for investors to gauge how much new supply will be coming on the market and complicating the management of their own portfolios.

The government tends to utilise all available issuing methods. Additionally, it appears that the government has not fully abandoned its administrative placement methods. The rates on government and quasi-government bonds are expressed as a premium over the equivalent maturity bank deposit rates. Savings bonds are sold through bank underwriters to retail investors while the interest rates are set by the MOF. Book-entry government bonds are auctioned to government underwriters with interest rate guidance. While the auction system permits a more flexible pricing of bonds, the government still sets deposit rates and lending rates. Bidding tends to ensure a comfortable margin for the banking sector and encourages the banks to hold bonds indefinitely rather than to trade.

Maturities include three and six months, and one, two, three, five, seven and ten years, but issuance has been focused on medium-term (2-5 years). Recently, there has been a tendency toward diversification of the maturity profile with a view to smoothing out the payment peak and increase instruments for trading as well as to satisfying better the needs of long-term projects. Therefore, issuance of long-term maturities (more than 5 years) has picked up and an attempt has been made to issue bonds with 30-year maturities. However, bonds with short maturities have been scarce.

By adopting techniques already widely used in major markets, China could add to the liquidity and depth of its bond market. Standardisation of terms of bond issuance, consolidation of issues into a smaller number of categories, and a pre-announced schedule of regular government issuers would encourage a continuous liquid yield curve, which in turn would improve both the efficiency of primary and secondary markets. This will improve liquidity management at the level of the wholesale buyers, and assist the development of benchmark issues. Increased certainty about issue dates and about amounts of government bonds to be issued enables investors to structure the maturity of their investment portfolios in line with the issuing calendar, which lowers the cost of issues. Benchmarks in the major OECD economies establish reference prices or yields for given maturities that are useful for pricing or evaluating yields on other securities with similar maturities. However, gaps in the maturity schedules and uncertainties about forthcoming issues inhibit risk-taking in the bond market.

To develop efficient primary markets for government bonds, fully market-driven primary issuance should be established along with regular issues at the appropriate maturities, pre-announced issue calendars, and a full range of benchmark issues. The price discovery process is enhanced by combining competitive auctions of new issues with issuance through a set of primary dealers who act as underwriters. It is useful to permit foreign firms to become primary dealers on the same basis as domestic firms, which could speed up the adoption of global practices in the local bond market. It is also crucial that the interest rate on government bonds be market-determined, not administratively determined. Benchmarking will be very difficult to establish in China without further deregulation of interest rates. Promoting regular benchmark bond issuance, and rationalising perverse regulations will complete a yield curve for bond pricing and coupon-rate setting.

Building a base for institutional investors and improving access for foreign investors are two key measures for reinforcing domestic bond markets. Focus on institutional investors will permit the offer period to be reduced, and will permit the eventual adoption of an auction system. The government can also more easily issue short-term bills for liquidity management purposes. Developing a mechanism for market access by foreign investors will enhance market breadth, as well as bring in knowledge to the market. As China pursues liberalisation of market entry, its capital market is expected to gradually open up to foreign investors in the next few years.

Secondary market

Secondary markets have been functioning since 1988 when the government allowed the securities held by individuals to be traded over the counter at securities firms or banks. Market trading techniques have advanced with the establishment of the electronic automated quotation system and with the opening of the Shanghai Securities Exchange, the officially recognised market.

One of the distinctive characteristics of the Chinese bond market is that there are two distinct platforms for trading bonds with different participants. Trading takes place on the two stock exchanges (Shanghai and Shenzhen) and in an inter-bank market. The inter-bank platform is mostly used by commercial banks, which tend to be buy-and-hold investors, and has strong demand for new government bond issues. Banks were banned from the exchanges and their bond trading has been transferred to the inter-bank market since late 1997. Currently, stock exchange trading is conducted mainly by securities firms and insurance companies and trading is comparatively active.

The two-tier structure poses inherent difficulties for development of the bond market. The inter-bank market is the largest market for government bonds, as well as for quasi-government bonds. One major problem for the inter-bank market is the lack of a credible inter-bank offer rate-pricing mechanism. Chibor (the China inter-bank offer rate) is not an accurate indicator of the cost of funds because it reflects the average of a small sample of widely differing rates. Large banks, which seek to hold government bonds, set rates that price out the small and local financial institutions.

Liquidity is thin in the secondary market, particularly in the inter-bank bond market. Average daily turnover in the inter-bank bond market is around RMB20 million compared to a total of RMB 1.4 trillion under custody. Transaction turnover in two stock exchanges in 1999 was RMB1828 billion and the ratio of turnover to the outstanding balance was 1.02, a rather low rate by comparison with more dynamic markets.[49]

Trading in government bonds usually involves operations in which a large volume of assets is traded and where margins tend to be very thin. In order to be able to deal profitably, market participants must have adequate risk-management facilities at their disposal. Discontinuities and lack of liquidity at various points on the yield curve raise the risk of trading.

In addition to the primary market practices mentioned above, the lack of liquidity in the secondary market is also due to a lack of capability by all participants, including primary dealers, to fund their dealing positions. Money markets are often cited as a key element in a liquid bond market. Money markets enable non-financial enterprises, banks, brokers, dealers, and institutional investors to manage their cash positions. An efficient mechanism in money markets for financing is repurchase agreements (repos) or, more generally, securities lending and borrowing. Repos enable dealers to take long and short positions in a flexible manner, buying and selling according to customer demand on a relatively small capital base. When there are no repos markets, funding has to be in the form of uncollateralised lines of credit from the banking system.

Until late 1997, commercial banks traded repos on the stock exchanges as well as on the securities trading centres (STC) around the country. They provided a way for securities firms to obtain long-term loans from the banks while formal loans remained prohibited. When the authorities discovered the extent of this illegal practice, banks were banned from the exchanges and their bond trading was transferred to the inter-bank market. In 1999, some securities firms were allowed to participate in the inter-bank market. Within the inter-bank markets in China, repos are mainly conducted in the short-dated maturities.

Liquidity and efficient price discovery in secondary markets are fostered by the development of organised derivatives markets (offering interest-rate futures and options on government securities, for a few benchmark maturities). Dealers and other participants will be more inclined to hold trading portfolios if they can hedge interest-rate risk. In addition, futures markets often have lower transactions costs than underlying cash markets. Such markets now exist in most of the major OECD countries. In China, futures trading on government bonds was halted by the government in 1995 because of a huge treasury bond futures scandal when trading in bond futures soared to very high rates.[50]

Taxation is another factor that affects bond market development. There is currently no business tax on interest income from government bonds and quasi-government bonds. However, trading profit is subject to an 8 per cent business tax and a 33 per cent capital gains tax. This encourages buy-and-hold investment in government bonds rather than active trading.

Other bond markets

The government bond market, which in most countries represents the largest stock of assets, is usually seen as the cornerstone of effective intermediation in the bond market and indeed throughout the entire capital market. A competitive and liquid government bond market provides a benchmark risk-free rate from which other rates on fixed-income assets can be calculated by incorporating spreads to reflect risk and liquidity. Additionally, a liquid government bond market helps investors to establish a theoretical "equity premium" in pricing other assets. Thus, the government bond market is the place to begin building a deep capital market.

Once the government bond market is adequately developed, there are several additional categories of operation that may be well suited to bond finance. State enterprises in the process of restructuring may well be suitable for bond financing, provided that a robust framework for corporate bonds is developed. The financing of privately owned housing will generate possibilities for mortgage bonds or mortgage-backed securities (MBS). Use of such techniques can help banks to cope with maturity mismatches while using their balance sheets more effectively. Infrastructure finance, where China's needs are enormous, is another category of operations that could be well suited to bond finance. China has a large overhang of non-performing assets that have already been removed from the balance sheets of state-owned banks and are currently held by four Asset Management Companies (AMC). The AMC can utilise various capital market techniques to extract value by reselling these assets on secondary markets. Successful asset liquidation through the capital market is also a strong motivation for corporate managers to pursue resolute restructuring policies. This represents an asset class with considerable potential.[51]

Corporate bond markets are not well developed in many countries.[52] Most non-governmental debt is issued by government-guaranteed entities, financial institutions and mortgage institutions. Nevertheless, the corporate debt market is growing in many OECD countries and it is clearly desirable to submit entities to the scrutiny of the credit markets. The corporate bond market in China accounted for less than 5 per cent of the overall bond market. In China, there are a number of formal restrictions on corporate debt issuance. Issuance is still subject to strict quotas and interest rates are subject to administrative control. Corporate bond issuance is subject to approval of the State Economic Planning and Development Commission (SEPDC) and the People's Bank of China (PBC) while coupon rates are set by SPDC. In addition, the quota is infrequently reached and even issues that have received approval are often delayed. As a result, corporate bonds are not priced against a government bond benchmark, as in many other countries. More fundamentally, there are few institutional investors with adequate risk management capability to invest in corporate bonds and to analyse the attendant risks. This uncertainty is aggravated by poor disclosure policies and ambiguities about the responsibilities of government to support SOEs.

It is important to note however, that for non-government bonds, the issue of credit risk becomes significant. Investors will be willing to hold non-government paper in their portfolios, only if they have credible information about the risks that are being assumed. This means that the disclosure and accounting practices, which were identified as issues in the equity market, are also important for the fixed-income market. Similarly, uncertainties about the reliability of payments flows supporting bond payments and about state guarantees must be clarified. For example, most corporate bond issuers in China are SOEs, but the actual degree of state support is unclear.

Assuming that institutional investors become more important players in the bond market, they will increasingly depend upon credit rating agencies that do rigorous analysis of the credit standing of borrowers and analyse the nature of external guarantees. Rating agencies play an important part in nearly all well developed fixed-income markets. While some attempts have been made to begin such agencies in China, it is an important challenge for these institutions to develop institutional capability and independence in order to gain the confidence of investors.

Foreign participation

As noted at several points in this discussion, until now there have been severe limitations on foreign participation of any kind in the Chinese capital markets. The issue of foreign participation deserves some consideration in its own right partly because China is expected to accept substantial commitments to expand the scope of operations permitted to foreign firms and because the policy of limiting foreign presence has an impact throughout the capital market. Chinese practice can be contrasted with the norm among OECD countries, and among many advanced non-OECD countries, which is an integrated capital market in which investors hold international portfolios consisting of debt and equity, compare relative risks and returns throughout the world and allocate capital accordingly. In major markets, foreign presence is significant both in the number of foreign institutions operating in the domestic market and the volume of cross-border business.

China's restrictions on foreign participation are very severe, not only by comparison to OECD countries but to Asian non-OECD countries as well. Historically, many Asian countries had policies of limiting the presence of foreign financial institutions in their domestic capital market. However, it was observed that by segmenting the domestic and international markets, domestic institutions failed to develop the skills that are already present in other financial markets while major parts of the market were neglected. In recognition of the fact that enlarged foreign participation can raise the general level of skills in the capital market, plans are under consideration for a controlled and progressive opening of the market.

In the domestic capital market, foreign institutions are now effectively excluded from virtually all activities involving Chinese domestic investors. Foreign intermediaries cannot deal with Chinese investors in domestic primary offerings, engage in secondary market trading of A-shares, and may not form investment funds or other institutional savings products that are marketed to Chinese residents. Foreign institutions are limited to soliciting orders for B-shares from non-residents, with a Chinese partner required to complete the trade on the exchange. The exclusion of foreigners no doubt perpetuates the tendency to use primary market techniques that differ from those used elsewhere in the world and that cause wide pricing anomalies between Chinese and foreign securities.

Both the Chinese authorities and foreign securities houses see an obvious complementarity between the large pool of savings in China and the skills that foreign institutions can bring to build capacity in areas such as risk management and compliance, proprietary trading and market making, corporate finance, accounting, and portfolio management. It is expected that after liberalisation, foreign firms will be able to form joint ventures with Chinese companies to engage in capital market operations and in portfolio management. The foreign partner will be limited to a 33 per cent stake initially, but foreign ownership will be allowed to rise to 45 per cent after five years.

In all likelihood these joint ventures will specialise in wholesale capital market operations. Foreign joint ventures are likely to concentrate on investment banking to bring more competitive primary marketing techniques to the Chinese market while assisting in the placement of Chinese securities with global investors. This will be particularly important if the distinctions among the various categories of shares are diminished. Corporate restructurings, mergers and acquisitions, derivatives, research and advisory work are also seen as promising. Joint ventures are likely to be used to form FMC.

In the expectation that foreign institutions will eventually be allowed to enter the Chinese domestic market, many foreign securities houses are established in China, most frequently in Shanghai but sometimes in Beijing or other cities. These offices mainly do research on Chinese companies for foreign investors. Foreign firms have been actively seeking Chinese partners, and offering training and advice, most recently in such areas as open-end investment funds and index futures.[53]

Concerning cross-border investment, restrictions are also very tight in comparison to other countries. Foreign investment in the domestic fixed-income market is completely prohibited. The equity market is segmented – if slightly less so than in the past. Additionally, the entry of foreign institutions, which tend to follow more rigorous investment strategies than Chinese investors, will foster the pricing of equity that better reflects the underlying worth of the assets, as well at put pressures on issuers to improve disclosure and governance practices.

All OECD countries have accepted the principle that foreign investors should be allowed to invest without limit in their domestic equity markets, although some countries make exceptions for certain "strategic" industries. Generally, broadening the investor base lowers the cost of capital to issuers. With the great increases in equity issuance that have occurred in the past decade, a growing share of equity in many markets is owned by foreign institutional investors. These investors tend to introduce international expectations concerning disclosure governance and profitability into markets and so encourage listed companies to adhere to global standards. Partly as a result of international investment by institutional investors, shareholder value is becoming an accepted standard by which corporate performance is assessed throughout the world. This is instrumental in the large gains in corporate profitability that have been achieved in North America and Europe in the past decade. Plainly, a larger foreign presence would help the authorities realise their goal of using the capital markets to foster efficiency in the corporate sector (see Chapter 13).

The government is considering measures to enlarge foreign access to Chinese equities. One possible means of implementing the reform would be to merge the A-shares and B-shares. Since arbitrage between foreign and domestic shares would be possible, the logic of having separate H-shares would also be called into question. Instead of fully opening investment to foreigners, the government is repeatedly studying the possible introduction of a system based on the system used in Chinese Taipei of "qualified foreign institutional investors" (QIIs). QIIs would be given direct access to the stock market, but would have to accept some limitations on their capability to withdraw funds from China. (In Chinese Taipei, foreigners must hold the proceeds of asset sales in approved domestic assets for a specified time.) Additionally, ceilings may be imposed on the percentage of total equity that foreigners can own in some or all companies. It should be pointed out that even if planned liberalisation is actually implemented, the Chinese regime would still be fairly restrictive in comparison to other Asian countries.

The authorities have also indicated that they would allow foreign securities to be listed and traded in China. Discussion of this has tended to be less specific than the discussion of the opening of Chinese shares to foreign investment.

Conclusions and recommendations

In the past decade China has succeeded in building a capital market of considerable size, and in attracting a significant volume of savings from the public. This market utilises highly advanced information and communication technology. Significant strides have been made in the organisation, operation and management of intermediaries. A basic legal and regulatory framework has been introduced. Nevertheless, the imbalances that accompanied the growth of capital markets during the past decade are serious enough to necessitate further adjustment.

Reform is particularly urgent at this juncture for two reasons: first, the capital market as it is now structured is not capable of carrying out its expanded mission that includes active project selection, reinforcement of solid corporate governance, and support of a market-based retirement system; second, the system will have to be strengthened in order to withstand the heightened pressure that will accompany modernisation measures, including new financial instruments, increased foreign presence and greater exposure to trends in international financial markets.

Great care must be taken to sequence liberalisation and modernisation measures, for the risk of systemic instability is considerable. Among the factors suggesting a high level of systemic risk are: 1) uneven development of various parts of the financial system, 2) the fragile situation of most banks, 3) the lack of experience of most market participants with risk management systems, 4) excessively high equity valuations and 5) the wide differences in valuations of equity between domestic and international markets.

Policy priorities for the improvement of the capital market

The following paragraphs summarise some of the highest priorities for the next phase of development.[54]

China should continue to build its capacity to exercise supervision over capital market activities and intermediaries in keeping with international best practices. The guiding principle should be that the goal of supervision is to build a fair, transparent, and efficient system to intermediate between issuers and investors in line with best international practice, particularly those embodied in IOSCO principles. Creation of such a robust environment is the best way to assure development of the market. The CSRC should be given adequate investigative and disciplinary powers to carry out its mission. Accounting, disclosure, and audit standards should be aligned with international practices.

In order to reduce moral hazard, accelerated investor education programmes should be undertaken to explain the risk/return characteristics of various investment instruments, including institutional savings products. Those offering investment services should be required to provide full written descriptions of the risks involved in investment products to prospective investors. The investment industry should be actively involved in the investor education programme under the supervision of the CSRC.

Supervision should place increasing responsibility on market participants, emphasising internal compliance, in-house risk management and governance systems and industry standards. Private firms, industry associations and SROs should have greater responsibility for the elaboration of standards. In order to accomplish this, the accountability of private institutions, and particularly of the supervisory boards of such institutions, for compliance with prudential standards should be unambiguous.

The authorities should proceed with their plan to increase the publicly traded share of listed SOEs over the next three years according to a pre-announced timetable. This practice should be implemented in a way that minimises the risk of destabilising the stock market.

All enterprises, whether SOEs, TVEs, or private companies, should have access to the capital markets. Access should be based upon the ability of issuers to meet listing requirements. Practices that lead to consistent underpricing of IPO should be curtailed. Prices at the initial offer should be based upon estimates of supply and demand as agreed between the issuer and the underwriter. All risks in the pricing of primary market issues should be borne by the issuer and the underwriter.

A market in mergers and acquisitions should be developed that should enable companies to transfer control using market mechanisms. These mechanisms should protect the interests of non-controlling shareholders in cases of transfer of control.

Plans to launch the second board should be implemented within one year. Markets in derivatives should be begun within two years.

The differences between the various categories of foreign and domestic shares for companies domiciled on the mainland should be gradually eliminated. As a first step, the differences between A-shares and B-shares should be abolished within two years. This can be achieved regardless of whether China achieves full convertibility on its capital account. This liberalisation measure should be carefully sequenced in order to minimise the risk of destabilising the equity markets where prices of shares available only to domestic residents and to non-residents differ significantly.

Efforts to strengthen shareholder rights and raise standards of corporate governance should be intensified. Companies that do not meet listing requirements, should be subjected to ordinary disciplinary processes.

Action against insider trading and market manipulation should be accelerated. These procedures should be administered by the securities exchanges under the supervision of the CSRC.

All investment funds that solicit funds from the general public should be brought within the formal regulatory framework for collective investment schemes (CIS). A legal and regulatory framework for CIS should be established, based upon one of the models found in major financial markets. CIS should be obliged to observe international standards of valuation and disclosure. An internal governance system for CIS should be developed to adjudicate conflicts of interest and assure the accountability of FMC. The internal compliance and audit functions of CIS should be strengthened. The standards used in the governance of CIS should reflect international standards, especially those elaborated by IOSCO. The CIS industry should be given an active role in the formulation of codes of best practices.

In order to develop institutional savings, the CSRC should co-ordinate with other responsible agencies to assure that comparable reforms are implemented in the insurance and pension fund sectors.

The market for government bonds should be modernised in line with the government's plan. Issue calendars should be regularised and announced in advance. The various categories of government bonds should be consolidated. A market-based system for pricing government debt should be established. A market in futures and options in government debt should be opened. Foreign institutions should be allowed to participate in the government debt market.

The necessary framework for the establishment of markets in mortgage bonds and/or mortgage-backed securities should be created. The necessary legal framework for secondary trading of impaired debt now held by AMC should be established. Credit-rating agencies should be developed, and foreign credit-rating agencies should be allowed to establish in China.

Foreign securities dealers, investment banks and asset managers should be accorded access to the domestic market in keeping with China's commitments to WTO.

NOTES

1. Gregory and Tenev (2001).

2. Lampton (1992).

3. The CSRC has an official rank of a department operating directly under the State Council. Therefore, although its chairman does not sit on the State Council, he is of an equal rank with its members.

4. Speech to OECD/CSRC Round Table on Capital Market Reform in China. Beijing. 24-25 October 2000.

5. The *Securities Association of China* (SAC) formed in 1991 has 145 members including securities firms and trust companies. Like its industry associations elsewhere the SAC:

   1. Acts as an SRO, has several committees, funds management committees, and an IT committee. The SAC formulates codes of conduct;

   2. Serves as a bridge between the CSRC and member firms;

   3. Administers examinations and conducts training programmes;

   4. Provides information to members and publishes information; and

   5. Deals with international counterparts.

6. "CSRC Chairman: Multilayered Regulatory System to be Introduced" *China Online* (*www.chinaonline.com*) 13 April 2001.

7. The Shanghai Stock Exchange had 75 500 institutional investors, compared to 22.6m individual accounts. At end 1999, individual investors on the Shanghai Stock Exchange held RMB 367.3 billion (US$44.4 billion), worth of stocks (89 per cent of market capitalisation), while institutional investors held only RMB 43.9 billion (US$5.3 billion) of stocks (11 per cent).

8. Many such accounts were opened for the purpose of entering the "IPO lottery". Anyone with a registered securities account could enter the competition to buy IPO shares. Since the IPO was commonly priced at a deep discount to secondary market prices, those successful in the lottery were virtually guaranteed large profits in early trading. After April 2000, when the CSRC required a minimum holding of RMB 10 000 (US$1 200) in shares in the secondary market in order to qualify for the IPO lottery, applications dropped drastically.

9. "Institutional investors make up only a small chunk of Shanghai Stock Exchange." *China Online* (*www.chinaonline.com*), 24 May 2000.

10. "Half of China's stock market investors lost money in 1999." *China Online* (*www.chinaonline.com*), 6 January 2000.

11. In the 1990-1993 period, local governments established China's first batch of investment funds. These were all small closed-end funds. The Shenzhen Investment Fund Management Company issued the first such fund, Tianji, in November 1992. It raised RMB 300 million (US$36 million). By 1995, China had 75 such funds, of which only four had received permission to establish from the central PBC. The rest had received authorisation from local administrations, which were keen to maximise investment in local projects. These funds engaged in highly irregular investment practices; many built up losses through real estate, hotel and speculative share investments. They were left largely unregulated. On 19 May 1993, the PBC banned the establishment of new funds. However, given jurisdictional uncertainty between the CSRC and the PBC, policy remained without direction until 1997.

12. "Estimates Grow for Unofficial China Funds", *Financial Times*, 3 July 2001. The Economist Intelligence Unit 9 July 2001 in *China Online* (*www.chinaonline.com*). Also see, *China Online* (*www.chinaonline.com*) 24-25 January 2001.

13. "New guidelines hint at permission for open-end funds." *China Online* (*www.chinaonline.com*), 27 November 2000.

14. For a discussion of agency and governance problems as well as standards and best practices in CIS, see John K. Thompson and Sang Mok Choi "Governance Systems for Collective Investment Schemes in OECD Countries". *Financial Affairs Division. Occasional Paper Number 1*. March 2001.

15. *Finance Asia.Com*. 18 June 2001.

16. EIU, Economist Intelligence Unit. "Off limits." *Business China*, 10 April 2000, 6-7.

17. Everbright Securities and Shenyin Wanguo will merge; Huaxia Securities and Beijing Securities, as well as Guangfa Securities and Guangdong Securities, were reported to be in talks as of late 2000. "Aren't we trendy? Securities companies merging." China Online (*www.chinaonline.com*), 13 July 2000.

    Guangfa, Guoxin, Guotong, Eagle and CITIC Securities are all likely candidates since they have relatively simple share-holding structures and, unlike some of the larger brokers such as Shenyin Wanguo, do not have histories of wrongdoing.

18. For a more detailed discussion of procedures for corporatisation and listing, see Walter and Howie (2001), pp. 38-70.

19. For a discussion of selection and remuneration of managers, see Joe Zhang (2000).

20. MacGregor (2001).

21. *China Online* (*www.chinaonline.com*) 14 June 2001.

22. CSRC, Information Disclosure and Corporate Governance in China.

23. Walter and Howie (2001).

24. See *China Online* (*www.chinaonline.com*) 30 May 2001. In July 2001, the MOF auditors indicated continuing problems with SOE accounts, but noted some improvement. "Review Uncovers US$93 Billion in Irregularities among SOEs" *South China Morning Post* 3 July 2001. Also see Joe Zhang (2000), page 15 ff. According to a survey published in the *Securities Times*, 29 May 2000, 82 per cent of investors believed that reported earnings could not be trusted; also see *The Economist Intelligence Unit* (9 May 2001).

25. Hongguang Industries from Chengdu, Sichuan province is a case in point. Hongguang Industries listed in June 1996 having faked profit records for the previous three years and obtained support from its municipal government in its listing application. It raised RMB 400 million (US$50million). It went on to make losses in 1996 of RMB 100 million (US$12 million), but reported profits of RMB 54 million (US$7 million). In November 1998, the CSRC announced they were investigating Hongguang, and later found evidence of forged documents, bribes and false disclosure.

26. *China Online* (*www.chinaonline.com*) 19 April 2001.

27. This problem was highlighted at a national auditing conference in Beijing in January 2001, at which a State Councillor accused auditors of colluding with their clients to report inflated earnings.

28. Although frequently criticised, even by senior Chinese economists, these categories have endured. Li Yining, one of the Chinese economists responsible for promoting shareholding corporations and stock markets, was involved in drafting the Securities Law. He used this position to argue against the differentiation of share types, and to call for the abolition of state and legal person shares, see Li, Yi Ning (1999).

29. Until 2000, financial institutions and real estate firms were banned from seeking listings, a legacy of the over-investment in such firms in the early 1990s.

30. For details see Walter and Howie (2001), pp. 131-133.

31. The Fuxing Group, a Shanghai-based pharmaceuticals company with genetic research activities, listed in 1998 with Shanghai government backing, raising RMB 348 million (US$42 million). Shaanxi province's Jinhua, a high-tech firm, issued RMB 178 million (US$21 million) worth of shares in 1997.

32. The first known instance of this was in June 1996, when the privately-owned Zunrong Group bought shares in Shenzhen-listed Shenzhonghao.

33. Morgan Stanley Dean Witter (2000). *Shanghai, China Market Summary*. Morgan Stanley Dean Witter. *Shenzhen* 2000, *China Market Summary*. CSRC, 2000, Introduction to China's Securities Markets; Shanghai Stock Exchange 1999 *Fact Book*. Walter and Howie provide interesting historical material on the development of the exchange along with discussion of their operations.

34. Wall and Green (2000), pp. 9-13.

35. *Financial Times*, 25 March 2001.

36. *China Online* (*www.chinaonline.com*) May 1, 2001.

37. Green (2000).

38. For example, see "Shelving plans for a high-tech board" 8 August 2001. Economist Intelligence Unit. *China Online* (*www.chinaonline.com*).

39. For an overview of some related issues, see Fernald and Rogers (1998), "Puzzles in the Chinese Stock Market" Board of Governors of The Federal Reserve System. *Discussion Paper Number* 619 August 1998.

40. A similar discrepancy is visible using the dividend yield as a measure of company valuation. The dividend yield is very low by international comparison, even though dividend yield in many countries are at historic lows. However, Chinese companies do have relatively high payments in the form of bonus shares or rights offerings at favourable prices.

41. There are three policy banks, which are all state-owned banks: China State Development Bank, China Agriculture Development Bank, and China Import and Export Bank.

42. Marketable bonds include book-entry form and bearer form bonds.

43. For a discussion of the main issues and policies in government bond markets, see Blommestein (1999) and Schinasi and Smith (1998).

44. The investors that operate in the wholesale markets are institutional investors (banks, pension funds, insurance companies, mutual funds and hedge funds) and large non-financial corporations with financial surpluses, and those belonging to the retail sector such as small firms, co-operatives and private individuals.

45. Suppliers of bonds include the central government, municipalities, housing finance institutions, infrastructure project financiers and the corporate (mainly industrial) sector. In addition, financial intermediaries exist between suppliers and investors: banks as underwriters and advisers, primary dealers, brokers, etc. They operate alongside other "market builders" such as rating agencies.

46. In China, individual investors hold about 60 per cent of government bonds.

47. In the advanced economies, auctions are now used to issue the bulk of domestic government bonds; in contrast, in markets for corporate bonds, underwriting by syndicates is the norm. It is usually maintained that uniform price auctions (so-called a Dutch auction) outperform discriminatory price auctions by producing a higher average yield at issue.

48. Treasury Bonds include Treasury Bills, Special National Bonds, Construction Bonds, Fiscal Bonds, Inflation-proof Bonds, etc. In addition, they comprise four form bonds such as voucher form, book-entry form, bearer form, and specially allocated bonds, but the main stream is the voucher form and book-entry form bonds. Voucher form bonds and bearer form bonds are targeting individual investors, while book-entry form bonds are only for institutional investors. Specially allocated bonds, which are also called Special Purchaser T-Bonds, were issued only for four state-owned specialised banks to resolve their financial problems.

49. This figure is much lower than those of advanced OECD countries such as the US and Japan, which were 22.0 and 6.9 respectively in 1997.

50. During this incident, treasury bond futures of US$37 billion changed hands during the final eight minutes of trading on 23 February 1995. This scandal was called the "327 Event", named after the contract number. The three-year treasury bonds underlying Contract No. 327 were issued by the Shanghai International Securities Co. Ltd. (SISCO). For more detailed information, see Yao, C., pages 103-109.

51. One relatively successful case of using capital market techniques to extract value from impaired assets is the experience of the Korea Asset Management Company (KAMCO) which has managed to develop a variety of useful techniques. KAMCO is serving as an adviser to Chinese AMC.

52. See Schinasi and Smith (1998).

53. One foreign firm has actually managed to obtain a foothold in the domestic market. Morgan Stanley Dean Witter (MSDW) owns 35 per cent of China International Capital Corporation (CICC) in partnership with China Construction Bank and a Hong Kong-based bank. MSDW is seeking to help the entity adopt best international practices in corporate governance, risk management systems, compliance and research. The joint venture does investment banking for IPO and M&A and has also built capacity in sectors such as investment in non-performing real estate loans. Much revenue has come from advisory work in connection with IPO in order to help the company obtain listings in overseas markers. This may be a model for the kind of joint ventures that could emerge in investment banking and capital market operations.

54. For a similar set of recommendations see Anthony Neoh, "China's Domestic Capital Markets in the New Millennium", Two Parts. 21 and 23 August 2000. *China Online* (*www.chinaonline.com*).

BIBLIOGRAPHY

Anjali Kumar *et al.* (1995),
 China: The Emerging Capital Market (two Volumes.) Washington World Bank.

Anjali Kumar *et al.* (1995)
 China's Non-Bank Financial Institutions: Trust and Investment Companies. Washington World Bank, World Bank Discussion paper No. 358.

Bailey, Warren (1994),
 "Risk and Return on China's New Stock Markets. Some Preliminary Evidence", *Pacific Basin Finance Journal.* 2 243-260.

Blommestein, Hans J., (1999),
 "The Development of Fixed-Income Securities Markets in Emerging Market Economies: Key issues and Policy Actions", *Financial Market Trends* 74, 61-78, OECD, October.

Cheol S. Eun, S. Janakiramanan and Bong-Soo Lee.
 "The Chinese Discount Puzzle." Unpublished Paper. The DuPree College of Management, Georgia Institute of Technology, Atlanta, GA, April 2001.

Chen, G.M., Bong-Soo Lee, and Oliver Rui (1999),
 "Foreign ownership restriction and market segmentation in China's stock markets", *The University of Houston Working Paper.*

Chiu, Andy and Chuck C. Y. Kwok (1998),
 "Auto-Correlation between A Shares and B Shares in the Chinese Stock Markets". *Journal of Financial Research.*

Chui, A.C.W. and Chuck Y. Kwok (1998),
 "Cross-autocorrelation between A- shares and B shares in the Chinese stock market", *Journal of Financial Research* 21, 333-353.

CSRC (2000),
 Information, Disclosure and Corporate Governance in China.

CSRC (2000),
 Introduction to China's Securities Markets, Beijing.

Daborah, Emil (1996),
 The Dual Class System of Stocks in China: Evidence that Location of Ownership Affects Share Prices. Manuscript. Harvard University.

Fernald, John and John H. Rogers (1998),
 "Puzzles in the Chinese Stock Market", Board of Governors of The Federal Reserve System, *Discussion Paper.* 6/9 August.

Gordon, Roger and Wei Li (1998),
 "Government as a discriminating monopoly in the financial market: The case of China", unpublished manuscript.

Green, Stephen (2000),
 "Second Board, Second Chances", *China Online* (*www.chinaonline.com*), 13 October.

Green, Stephen and David Wall (2000),
 "This little piggy becomes a market: The challenges of Chinese capital market liberalisation". Prepared for the Organisation for Economic co-operation and Development (OECD), December.

Gregory, Neil and Stoyan Tenev (2001),
 "The Financing of Private Enterprise in China", *Finance and Development*, March.

Hui, Liu, *Study on the Development of Government Bond Markets in Selected* DMCs: *Country Report People's Republic of China.* Prepared for the Asian Development Bank.

Hu, Xiaoyi (2000),
"The Improvement of Chinese Pension System and Capital Markets", Paper presented at the OECD/CSRC International Round Table on Securities Markets in China, October.

Lampton, D (1992).
"A Plum for a Peach: Bargaining, Interests and Bureaucratic Politics in China", *Bureaucracy, Politics and Decision-Making in Post-Mao China*, edited by K and Lampton Liberthal, D. (1992), 33-58. Berkeley. University of California Press. Lieberthal, K. and Oksenberg, M (1988), *Policy Making in China: Leaders, Structure and Processes*. Princeton: Princeton University Press, Shirk, S. T*he Political Logic of Economic Reform in China*. Berkeley, CA: University of California.

Li, Yi Ning (1999).
Jingji Mantanhu (Economic Discussions), Beijing, Beijing Daxue Chubanshe.

MacGregor, Richard (2001),
"The Little Red Book of Business in China", *Financial Times*, July.

Morgan Stanley Dean Witter (2000),
Shanghai, China Market Summary, October, *Shenzhen, China Market Summary*, October.

Miurin, P. and A. Sommariva (1993),
"The financial reform in Central and Eastern European countries and in China", *Journal of Banking and Finance* 17, 883-911.

Neoh, Anthony (2000),
"China's Domestic Capital Markets in the New Millennium", Two Parts. 21 and 23 August. *China Online (www.chinaonline.com)*.

Procter, Andrew (2000),
"Securities markets and international standards, How can IOSCO objectives and principles of securities regulation be applies to emerging markets?" Paper presented at the OECD/CSRC International Round Table on Securities Markets in China, October.

Publishing House of Law (1999),
The Securities Law of China, Beijing.

Sarkar, Asani., Sugato Chakravarty, and Lifan Wu (1998),
"Information asymmetry, market segmentation, and the pricing of cross-listed shares: Theory and evidence from Chinese A and B shares", *Federal Reserve Bank of New York Working Paper*.

Schinasi, Garry J. and R. Todd Smith,
"Fixed-Income Markets in the United States, Europe, and Japan: Some Lessons for Emerging Markets", IMF *Working Paper* WP/98/173, December 1998.

Shanghai Stock Exchange 1999,
Fact Book.

Su, Dongwei and Belton Fleisher (1997),
"An Empirical Investigation of Underpricing in Chinese IPOs". *Mimeo*, Ohio State.

Sun, Q. and W. H.S. Tong (2000),
"The effect of market segmentation on stock prices: The Chinese syndrome", *Journal of Banking and Finance* 24, 1875-1902.

Tan, Charles X. and others (2000),
"International Trust and Investment Corporations in China", *Moody's Investor Service: Global Credit Research*. New York, July.

Thompson, John K. and Sang Mok Choi (2001),
"Governance Systems for Collective Investment Schemes in OECD Countries". *Financial Affairs Division. Occasional Paper Number*, March.

Walter, Carl E. and Fraser J.T. Howie (2001),
To Get Rich is Glorious: China's Stock Markets in the '80s and '90s, Palgrave.

Yao, Chengxi (1998),
Stock Markets and Futures Markets in the People's Republic of China. Oxford, Oxford University Press.

Yung, Ronald L. and Chen Xingdong (2001),
China Equity Markets: 2001 BNP Paribas Research (2 volumes) Beijing and Hong Kong.

Zhang, Joe (2000),
"China's A-Share Market", UBS Warburg, *Global Equity Research* 30 October.

Zhang, Y.C. and D. Yu (1994),
"China's emerging securities market", *Columbia Journal of World Business* 29, 112-121.

Zhang, Yilei. and W.A. Thomas (1999),
"Operational mechanism and characteristics of China's primary and secondary stock markets", *Journal of Asian Business* 15, 49-64.

Zhou, Xiaochuan (2000),
"Review of Present State and Potential of Chinese Capital Markets" Speech at the OECD/CSRC International Round Table on Securities Markets in China, October 2000.

Chapter 16

LABOUR MARKET AND SOCIAL BENEFIT POLICIES

TABLE OF CONTENTS

LABOUR MARKET AND SOCIAL BENEFIT POLICIES[*]

Introduction

Although trade and investment liberalisation (TIL) is concerned primarily with product and capital markets, its success will depend on the adaptability of the whole economy including the labour market. The obstacles in the latter are considerable. To overcome them, the government must simultaneously tackle the problems that are most urgent in the short term, notably redundancies in state-owned enterprises (SOEs), and pursue a complex agenda of institutional reform that should aim to make the whole labour market more fair and efficient.

China's vast human resources cannot be efficiently employed in the present situation. As in many developing economies the biggest immediate problem is not unemployment, although this exists and is growing, but a prevalence of employment in low-productive forms of agriculture and informal-sector work. More productive jobs are being created at an impressive pace, raising the prospect of much higher incomes in a not-too-distant future. In the meantime, however, major social imbalances persist and in some respects they make a reallocation of human resources more difficult than necessary.

An important measure of labour market efficiency is the extent to which an emerging labour surplus – whether in agriculture or loss-making urban enterprises – can be channelled to the new jobs that are created. This process has been remarkably successful for a long time, especially between about 1980 and the mid-1990s when the labour surplus mainly concerned farmers, of whom (depending on the type of statistics used) well over 100 million seem to have moved to off-farm employment over the period mentioned. This achievement was attributable first of all to the role of township and village enterprises (TVEs), but also to buoyant private business in urban as well as rural areas.[1] But China's agricultural surplus labour can still be counted in hundreds of millions and its long-term decline has shown signs of becoming slower. Following the Asian economic crisis in 1997 and the simultaneous restructuring of many Chinese enterprises, employment in the *urban formal sector* plunged by 12 per cent in two years while TVE employment declined by 2 per cent. In this situation, the urban *informal* economy – about which little is known – appears to represent a principal source of net job creation without which under-employment would have been much more severe.

That so much of the current job creation and labour mobility appears to occur in the informal economy must be regarded as an indication of systemic problems. Although most would agree that informal employment is better than no employment, such jobs are often temporary and sometimes casual in nature, and therefore probably, on average, less likely than formal-sector jobs to foster on-the-job learning and productivity enhancement in the long run. This chapter highlights three systemic factors that seem unnecessarily to discourage or even prevent many job seekers and enterprises from solving their problems within the formal employment systnce, and the manner in which enterprise restructuring and lay-offs are administered.

A key policy objective in the medium-term should be to counteract and eventually eliminate a legacy of labour market segmentation, especially between rural and urban areas. Several policy steps in this direction have been taken during the past two decades, but the combination of *hukou*-related institutional obstacles and tradition continue to restrain and distort rural-urban mobility more than is normal within a national labour market, even taking account of China's size. A complete deregulation would probably, if adopted, raise fears about a possibly large increase of labour supply in urban areas, and these fears are exacerbated in the short term by concern with the plight of redundant SOE workers. Nevertheless, mobility constraints are inefficient because they prevent an optimal use of the country's human resources, and they distort competition between enterprises at different locations. Worse, such

---

[*] This Chapter was written by Anders Reutersward, Principal Administrator, Directorate for Education, Employment, Labour and Social Affairs, OECD. Peter Whiteford, Principal Administrator, and Marie-Ange Maurice, Consultant, also contributed.

constraints can cause long-term damage by reducing incentives for China's rural citizens – the vast majority – to invest in education and training.

Related to the segmented labour market is a considerable income inequality. Estimated household incomes per capita are no less than 2.6 times higher in urban than in rural areas, both nationally and within most provinces. In addition, China's income inequality has a regional dimension with an eastern, mostly coastal area (13 provinces including three big city municipalities[2]) reporting on average 1.6 times higher per-capita income than the average for the rest of the country (see Chapter 21 on Territorial Development). As seen in previous chapters, it is inevitable that coastal provinces benefit the most, at least temporarily, from the present rapid growth for which foreign trade plays a key role. It is then all the more preoccupying that the threat to social consensus this difference can involve is compounded by a rural-urban divide which, however, can and should be gradually reduced.

As an additional cause of inequality in the labour market, public social protection programmes are essentially limited to urban employees, especially in SOEs. The state-sponsored social insurance system – which accounts for the bulk of public social spending – is now being gradually improved and extended to cover all urban workers. But in rural areas, national policy provides only for voluntary and fully self-financed pension insurance of non-agricultural workers, such as those in TVEs. Although a few provinces have introduced additional provisions for the last-mentioned group, it would hardly be possible in the near future – given the income disparities and other factors – to implement social insurance uniformly for all workers in China, nor has this been envisaged by the central government. Nevertheless, when further reforms are introduced within the present urban framework, it will be pertinent to choose solutions that facilitate as far as possible a gradual extension of the social insurance coverage to include additional population groups. Reforms should aim, in particular, to make the insurance affordable and possible to administer under more varying labour market conditions.

The now-emerging urban social protection system, as defined by a series of policy decisions and blueprints at various stages of implementation, has essentially the same main components as in many OECD countries. It features multi-tier pension insurance, health care, sickness, maternity, occupational injury and unemployment insurance as well as a minimum income guarantee of last resort. China can draw potentially useful lessons from international experiences on a number of specific points, as discussed below. But implementing all these programmes in China's nearly 700 cities and 19 000 towns is a daunting task because most of them have little experience of administering social protection which, until now, has been primarily the employers' responsibility. To somewhat reduce the inevitable uncertainty about reform outcomes, China has adopted a practice of experimenting with many detailed programme features as pilot schemes in selected regions before deciding about their possible nationwide introduction.

A major effort of administrative development and staff training will be required. Municipal governments carry the main responsibility for developing front-line office networks that can handle individual cases. Provincial governments have a leadership role to play in order to ensure a correct and equitable administration and to pool financial resources. In addition, provinces will likely be called upon in an increasing number of instances to consider how to address the need for social protection in those rural areas that depend heavily on non-agricultural employment.

Before considering the policy issues in somewhat more detail, the chapter reviews available indicators of social and labour market developments in China and discusses plausible trends in view of trade and investment liberalisation. Three subsequent sections are devoted to possible options for government policy in three main areas: creating a national labour market, reforming social protection, and helping urban workers who lose their jobs.

China's economic restructuring from a social perspective

Previous chapters have shown that agriculture, industry, and service sectors have all greatly improved their performance since economic reforms began in the late 1970s. But most of the growth in the 1990s was recorded in non-agricultural sectors. Monetary incomes from industry and service jobs are now important to rural as well as urban households, reflecting the partly parallel though still quite different development of TVEs, SOEs, and private enterprise.

These positive economic developments have been unevenly distributed. As shown in some detail below, household incomes per capita are particularly high in and around a few big cities, especially Beijing, Shanghai and Tianjin, and in the Pearl River delta in Guangdong province. Average incomes in most other cities are at least one-third lower than in these big-city areas, while in rural areas (except around big cities) they are over two-thirds lower. All these differences encourage labour mobility. In general, however, labour mobility between cities is quantitatively modest in China while the difference between agricultural and non-agricultural incomes emerges as the principal trigger of migration.

Large parts of China still present the image of a predominantly rural country where most of the population is engaged in low-productive forms of farming – at least for part of their working time. However, hardly any region is unaffected by change and in most of them the traditional ways coexist with an expanding modern economy that offers many times higher average incomes. Every year, numerous farmers find it possible to multiply their incomes by a factor of 3 or more by moving to other sectors of activity, or, indeed, by switching from traditional grain production (that is still a duty on farmers, see Chapter I on Agriculture) to more profitable, marketable cash crops in agriculture.[3] Available opportunities for individuals to take such steps successfully are less widespread in inland provinces than in the coastal region; nevertheless, the evidence suggests that a profound transformation of living conditions is underway in most parts of China.

One apparent consequence is that the rural Household Production Responsibility system, which replaced collective farms in 1984, is set to lose some of the economic and social importance it has had until now. As explained above in Chapter I, this system confers to every agricultural household (of which there are about 200 million) a right as well as a duty to cultivate a small land plot, usually around one-half of a hectare.[4] The land entitlement constitutes the principal element of social security in rural areas. As such, it also offers an historical justification of the policy to exclude farmers from public social protection. At the same time, the duty on farmers to produce grain – and the risk of losing the land in case of non-compliance – can have disturbing economic effects because it discourages labour mobility, especially if a job change would require permanent absence from a farm. However, both the rights and the duties involved will become gradually less significant insofar as potential off-farm earnings continue to increase more than the incomes that can be earned from the guaranteed plots.

In urban areas, where much of the recent economic development originates, the spread of market principles along with trade and investment liberalisation has also contributed to new forms of economic insecurity, including a greater sensitivity to cyclical movements in the international economy. A difference here, compared with rural areas, is that the urban groups most negatively affected by economic restructuring are often, or have been until recently, relatively well paid and privileged in terms of housing, social protection and education. By implication, policies to compensate them for job losses can be relatively expensive, and if such compensations are more generous than other workers would receive, it does not necessarily enhance social equity. Nevertheless – as numerous governments have found, for example in transition economies of Central and Eastern Europe – restructuring, privatisation and liquidation of unprofitable enterprises are such crucial economic policy objectives that some extraordinary social policies can be justified to speed up the process. This holds especially when the state owns the problematic enterprises and when it is considered for historical reasons to carry a special commitment towards its employees, as is the case with at least the older SOE workers in China.

The remainder of this section takes a predominantly quantitative approach and reviews the somewhat incomplete statistics that are available for assessing the role of different types of economic activity, looking first at employment data and then at household incomes and wages, followed by some observations about education and labour mobility.

Employment

About half of the employed work on farms...

Total employment, as officially estimated using census-based population statistics, was 706 million in 1999 of which almost 500 million (70 per cent) were in rural areas and 210 million in urban areas (see Figure 16.1 and Table 16.1). But the Urban Labour Force Survey, which gives more detail, suggests that only 155 million persons or 22 per cent were employed in specified types of urban jobs. The even more uncertain statistics available for rural areas indicate that some 127 million or 18 per cent worked in TVEs.[5]

The remainder, accounting for over half of the total employment estimate, is known mainly as a huge residual, making any interpretation quite uncertain. It appears to include, first, around 50 million persons (7 to 8 per cent) in unknown forms of urban activity and somewhat fewer (probably about 20 million or 3 per cent) in unknown forms of rural non-agricultural work. Many of them are probably rural migrants working in and around cities. Secondly, 348 million (49 per cent) are rural working-age inhabitants who, if able-bodied, are assumed by default to work in agriculture. The agricultural employment share rises to 50 per cent if an estimated 6 million urban farmers are included.

Judging from national-level statistics, much of the just-mentioned "unknown" forms of non-agricultural work – both rural and urban areas – belongs to the secondary sector, perhaps especially construction, while a significant part is classified under the tertiary sector (see Tables 16.2 and 16.3) N.B. these "unknown" employment elements are not counted in province-level statistics, which therefore as a rule must be assumed to understate secondary and tertiary-sector employment.

Figure 16.1. **Employment by main type**

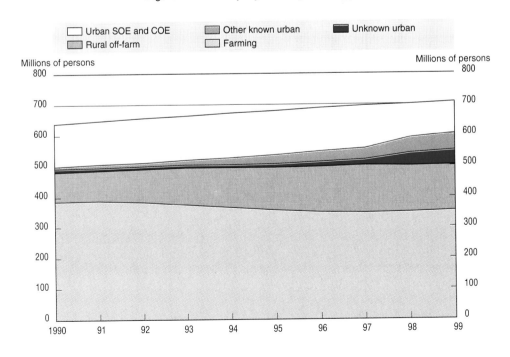

Note: SOE = state-owned enterprises. COE = urban collectively owned enterprises.
Source: See Table 16.1.

Table 16.1. **Urban and rural employment by enterprise type, 1952-1999**
Per cent distribution

	Urban										Rural								Total	
											Farms (primary sector)	Township and village enterprises (TVE)					Unknown (statistical discrepancy)	Rural total		
	SOE	Collective	Share-holding, limited liability etc.*	Other private	Hong Kong (China), Macao or Chinese Taipei funded	Foreign-funded	Self-employed	Farms (primary sector)	Unknown (statistical discrepancy)	Urban total		Collective	Co-operative	Private	Self-employed	TVE total			Per cent	Thou-sands
1952	8	–	–	–	–	–	–	–	4	12	84	–	–	–	–	–	4	88	100	207 290
1962	13	4	–	–	–	–	0.8	–	–	18	82	–	–	–	–	–	–	82	100	259 100
1970	14	4	–	–	–	–	0.3	–	–	18	81	–	–	–	–	–	–	82	100	344 320
1980	19	6	–	–	–	–	0.2	2	–2	25	67	7	–	–	–	7	1	75	100	423 610
1990	16	6	0.2	0.1	–	0.1	1.0	1	2	26	59	7	1.3	6	–	14	1	74	100	639 090
1995	17	5	0.5	0.7	0.4	0.4	2	1	2	28	51	9	1.3	9	–	19	2	72	100	679 470
1996	16	4	0.6	0.9	0.4	0.4	2	1	2	29	50	9	1.4	10	–	20	2	71	100	688 500
1997	16	4	0.7	1.1	0.4	0.4	3	1	3	29	49	8	–	7	4	19	3	71	100	696 000
1998	13	3	1.5	1.4	0.4	0.4	3	1	6	30	49	7	–	7	4	18	4	70	100	699 570
1999	12	2	1.7	1.5	0.4	0.4	3	1	7	30	49	6	–	8	4	18	3	70	100	705 860

* Shareholding companies, jointly owned units, limited liability corporations and limited liability share holding corporations.
Source: *China Statistical Yearbook 2000*, Tables 5-4 (urban areas and total), 5-2 (primary sector); *China Labour Statistical Yearbook 2000*, Table 1-19, and *China TVE Yearbook*, various editions.

Table 16.2. **Employment by economic sector, 1980-1999**
Percent distribution

| | Primary | Secondary | | | | Tertiary | | | | | | | | | Total | |
		Industry	Const-ruction	Unknown (statistical discre-pancy)	Subtotal	Commerce, catering	Transports, communi-cation	Finance, real estate, prospec-ting	Health care, social services	Education, science, culture	Govern-ment, organi-sations	Other	Unknown (statistical discre-pancy)	Subtotal	Per cent	Thousands
1980	69	16	2	–	18	3	2	1	2	3	1	1	–	13	100	423 610
1990	60	15	4	2	21	4	2	1	2	3	2	3	2	19	100	639 100
1995	52	16	5	2	23	6	3	1	2	2	2	7	3	25	100	679 470
1996	50	16	5	3	24	7	3	1	2	2	2	7	3	26	100	688 500
1997	50	15	5	3	24	7	3	1	2	3	2	7	3	26	100	696 000
1998	50	13	5	5	24	7	3	1	2	3	2	7	3	27	100	699 570
1999	50	13	5	5	23	7	3	1	2	2	2	7	3	27	100	705 860

Source: *China Statistical Yearbook 2000*, Tables 5-2 and 5-5.

Table 16.3. **Employment patterns in rural households**

A. *Distribution of active household members by main sector and duration of work*
Millions of economically active persons aged 7 or more

| Household category | Main sector | | | | | | Total |
| | Agriculture | | | Other | | | |
	6 months or more	Under 6 months	Total	6 months or more	Under 6 months*	Total	
Non-agricultural households	–	–	–	43	–	43	43
Agricultural households	353	72	425	94	50	144	519
Total	353	72	425	136	50	186	561

* Persons working off-farm for less than 6 months are not included in the grand total column because they are also counted under agriculture. However, the precise number of persons combining agriculture and other work is unknown. Information about work duration is available only for agricultural households.
Source: *First agricultural census.* See National Bureau of Statistcis, 1998, Table 3-1-3, 3-1-4, 3-1-15.

B. *Rural households members engaged mainly in non-agricultural activity by sector and job location*
Millions of economically active persons aged 7 or more

| Job location | Sector | | | | | |
	Industry	Construction	Transport	Commerce	Other	Total
Rural areas	32	9	6	11	22	79
Urban areas	19	12	3	7	16	57
Total	50	21	9	18	38	136

Source: *First agricultural census.* See National Bureau of Statistics, 1998, Table 3-1-3, 3-1-4, 3-1-15.

The First National Agricultural Census offered somewhat more detail about rural workers in 1997. It found that rural households had 561 million economically active members aged 7 years or more, of whom 57 million worked in urban areas, primarily in industry, construction and commerce (see Table 16.3 and NBS, 1998). Amongst the about 500 million who stayed in rural areas, 353 million were found to work in agriculture for over 6 months per year and a further 72 million worked there for shorter periods. Somewhat surprisingly – considering the just-cited general employment statistics – only about 79 million persons were deemed to have rural non-agricultural jobs as their main activity while 50 million farmers reported non-agricultural work for less than 6 months in the year.

Rural under-employment and *hidden unemployment* are undoubtedly much more widespread than any of these statistics suggest. The average household farm unit of about 0.5 ha is too small to give productive full-time employment to all individuals reported to work there (about two persons per household): many of them must be under-employed unless they have off-farm jobs as a complement. But there is no consensus on how to quantify the problem. "Under-employment" in a narrow sense is sometimes considered as a synonym for "involuntary working-time limitations"; but a more comprehensive concept of "hidden unemployment" can be defined to include *low-productive employment* regardless of working time. Evidently, the numbers concerned by hidden unemployment in this latter definition will depend on what productivity level is regarded as acceptable. If the average GDP contribution per worker in non-agricultural jobs is used as a benchmark, rural hidden unemployment can be estimated to represent a shortfall of over 200 million jobs (see Box 16.1).

Although such calculations are hypothetical, they give an indication of the huge labour reallocations that might occur in China over the next few decades, assuming that general economic conditions remain favourable and that workers and capital are not prevented from moving to where they can gain the highest returns. In other fast-growing economies where industrialisation and urbanisation have been broadly successful, non-agricultural job creation has proved sufficiently buoyant to permit strong declines in agricultural employment without creating very high

---

Box 16.1. Can rural hidden unemployment be measured?

Rural unemployment and under-employment is largely "hidden" behind exaggerated estimates of agricultural employment. Several statistical problems contribute to this result:

- The extent of *part-time work* is unknown in the absence of data about weekly or monthly working time. It is not conceivable, however, that the average household farm in China can give year-round full-time employment to all individuals now reported to work there as a main activity.
- Rural *unemployment* is not measured because it is officially regarded as non-existent.
- Such common features as *mobility* and *multiple-job holding* are not well measured by available statistics because they use different sources and definitions for various parts of the labour market. Some persons working mostly off-farm may be double-counted as employed both in farms and elsewhere, while others are probably counted only under farming, especially if the non-agricultural work is informal.
- The Household Production Responsibility combined with rural tradition can encourage a general tendency to exaggerate the importance of agriculture relative to other activities.

However, quantifying rural unemployment and under-employment in China would have been difficult even if comprehensive statistics were available. Widely-used definitions such as those which the International Labour Organisation (ILO) recommends for labour force surveys were conceived primarily for industrialised and urbanised economies.* Applying them is often problematic under rural conditions, especially in developing countries such as China where much of the potential unemployment and under-employment is hidden as low-productive employment.

A simple calculation shows that 75 million farmers could have produced China's entire agricultural output as reported in 1999, assuming that the GDP contribution per worker employed in farming were equal to the average for non-agricultural work. (The reported GDP contribution per worker was 4.7 times higher in non-agricultural sectors than in agriculture.) The difference between this hypothetical labour requirement of 75 million and the reported farm employment of about 350 million – thus around 275 million – can be considered as a maximum estimate of rural hidden unemployment. If the benchmark GDP contribution per worker in agriculture is set at a modest 50 per cent of the non-agricultural level, the estimate of hidden unemployment declines to 200 million.

---

* The ILO definitions divide the working-age population into three categories: the employed, the unemployed and those not in the labour force. Non-working persons are unemployed if they are able-bodied and seek jobs, otherwise they are not in the labour force. If the surveys include questions about working time, "under-employment" in a narrow sense can be estimated on the basis of the number of part-time workers who say they would like to work more.

---

unemployment. In the Republic of Korea, for example, off-farm employment increased fourfold in absolute terms between 1970 and 1997, permitting the agricultural employment share to decline from over 50 per cent to 11 per cent of the total.[6]

... while off-farm job creation is insufficient in the formal sector

As Figure 16.1 and Table 16.1 show, a steady flow of agricultural labour moving to non-agricultural jobs has been recorded for a long period, with TVEs and urban and rural private business as the principal destinations. But this movement slowed down after the mid-1990s. Considering that the agricultural sector is still burdened by a huge surplus of under-employed workers – most of whom earn very low incomes, see below – it is clear that the slowdown was caused by events on the demand side of the off-farm labour market. In particular, decisions to implement the long-delayed downsizing of urban state-owned and collective enterprises coincided with the negative effects of the Asian economic crisis in 1997, which caused stagnation in a TVE sector that also – partly as a result – entered a period of hurried privatisation and restructuring.

Table 16.4. **Rural household incomes by source**
Net income per capita, per cent

A. All incomes (monetary and in-kind)

	Year				
	1985	1990	1995	1998	1999
Wages	18	20	22	27	29
Farming and related activities**	11	10	4	3	3
Industry and construction	3	6	14	18	20
Services	4	5	5	5	5
Household business income	74	76	71	68	66
Farming and related activities**	64	65	59	54	50
Industry, handicraft and construction	4	5	4	5	6
Services	6	6	8	9	10
Transfers and property income	8	4	6	6	6
Total	100	100	100	100	100
Of which: farming and related activities*	75	74	63	57	53
Income earned in-kind	39	33	37	31	28
Total, 1999 RMB per year	1 311	1 370	1 718	2 132	2 210
Annual real growth rate, per cent*	..	0.9	4.6	7.5	3.7

B. Monetary incomes

	Year				
	1985	1990	1995	1998	1999
Wages	30	30	35	38	40
Household business (farming and other)	58	64	55	54	52
Transfers and property income	12	6	10	8	8
Total	100	100	100	100	100
Total, 1999 RMB per year	799	918	1 091	1 479	1 585
Annual real growth rate, per cent*	..	2.8	3.5	10.7	7.2

*   Average growth rates for the periods between indicated years.
**   Including animal husbandry, forestry, fishing, hunting and gathering.
Source: China Statistical Yearbook 2000, 10-14 and 10-15. The data are derived from official household budget surveys using partly different definitions in urban and rural areas. Wages are assumed to be paid entirely in money. RMB amounts were deflated by the consumer price index (the same as for urban areas).

The slowdown in non-agricultural employment growth after 1997 was partly temporary in nature, related to the international economic crisis. More fundamentally, however, it seems to reflect a process of consolidation in many enterprises whose employment management is being gradually reformed in the face of stronger competition and market discipline. Such institutional changes are mainly driven by domestic factors, but WTO accession and integration in the world economy contribute to making them irreversible.

In this new situation, China will hardly be able to eliminate under-employment unless workers and employers are allowed to act in accordance with market forces. The apparently very strong growth of informal-sector work after 1997 – see especially, the "unknown urban" category in Figure 16.1 – is indicative of systemic problems that seem to prevent much of China's potential for market-driven job creation from occurring within the formal employment system. No systematic information is available about the nature of informal-sector work, but it undoubtedly affects many rural migrants, whose possibilities to work in the urban formal sector are restricted amongst other things by administrative practices related to the household registration system. Laid-off urban workers are also relatively likely to work informally, partly because taking up formal-sector employment would force them to separate permanently from their previous employers (see below).

Coastal provinces are somewhat more urbanised than the inland

As a key indicator of regional disparity, the agricultural shares of total (urban and rural) employment by province show relatively moderate variation. Agriculture represents around 40 per cent of employment in four of the most advanced coastal provinces (Liaoning, Jiangsu, Zhejiang and Guangdong) compared with around 60 per cent in large parts of southwestern and northwestern China and, also, in a few central provinces. For obvious reasons, big cities are outliers in this comparison.[7] But only the southwestern regions of Guizhou, Yunnan and Tibet take extreme positions at the other end with over 70 per cent of employment in agriculture.

Compared with most industrialised countries, even the 40 per cent recorded in coastal China represent a high proportion of agricultural employment. Among OECD countries, only Turkey reports about 40 per cent agricultural employment while the share has fallen to around 20 per cent in such medium-income countries as Mexico and Poland. The employment shares of *industry* in most of coastal China are around 20 per cent, or 25 per cent including construction, which is comparable to many OECD countries, while this proportion is only around 10 per cent in central and western China. Tertiary or *service-sector* employment, finally, represents one of the lowest percentages in the world at less than 30 per cent of total employment. By comparison, services account for 60 to 75 per cent of employment in most OECD countries, and the proportion has recently risen above 50 per cent in numerous middle-income economies, *e.g.* Korea, Mexico and several Central and Eastern European countries. No Chinese province except Beijing reports over 50 per cent service-sector employment.

Given China's peculiar institutions, it is of interest to note that the level of urbanisation appears higher from an economic standpoint than is officially recognised, whether by administrative divisions of the territory or by household registration. Although about half of total employment in 1999 was non-agricultural, only 31 per cent of the population lived in geographic areas administered as urban and as few as 26 per cent belonged to "non-agricultural" households, *i.e.* had non-agricultural *hukou*. Slightly fewer than 10 per cent of the population in rural areas had non-agricultural *hukou*, while probably between one-fourth and one-third of the population in urban areas had agricultural *hukou*.[8]

Above-average percentages of employment in *urban areas* are reported only in big-city municipalities and a few other regions that were urbanised relatively early, especially the northeast. In coastal China except the biggest cities, the administratively recognised "urbanisation" is low despite relatively high proportions of non-agricultural (*i.e.* secondary and tertiary-sector) employment, with the result that over half of the latter is found in officially rural areas (*China Statistical Yearbook* 2000, Tables 5.3 and 5.4). The percentage of rural households having non-agricultural *hukou* is higher in coastal provinces than

Table 16.5.   **Relative wages and real wage growth by type of activity**

Relative wages 1980-1999
Urban average wage = 100

	Type of activity					
	Urban average	SOE	Urban collective enterprises	Private and other urban	TVE	Rural average income*
1980	100	105	82	..	52	57
1985	100	106	84	125	59	60
1990	100	107	79	140	57	53
1995	100	102	71	136	62	45
1997	100	104	70	136	69	50
1998	100	103	71	120	67	45
1999	100	102	69	118	62	41

Note: The urban average wage in 1999 was 8 346 RMB per year.
*   Net income per able-bodied and semi-able-bodied member of rural households.
Source: *China Statistical Yearbook*, 2000; *China TVE Statistical Yearbook*, various editions.

elsewhere – but this percentage is everywhere lower than the proportions of rural workers having non-agricultural employment (NBS, 1998, Tables 2.10, 3.1.4 and 3.1.5). By implication, the rights and duties that the Household Production Responsibility system confers to all agricultural households are legally applicable to a high proportion of the workers with non-agricultural jobs in every province, and especially in the coastal region.

By 1999, non-agricultural employment – whether urban or rural – was found to a large extent in the *private or semi-private sector*, if this notion is understood in a broad sense covering all forms of business not owned by central or local government including the about two-thirds of TVEs that have changed owners in recent years.[9] However, employment in SOEs and collectively-owned firms remained predominant in the biggest cities, perhaps reflecting the special importance there of large enterprises that have been slow to privatise. SOEs and collective enterprises (urban and rural) also continue to prevail in a number of regions on China's periphery to the northeast, west and southwest. The private and semi-private sector often dominates elsewhere – not only along the coast, but also probably in most of the heavily populated inland provinces including Anhui, Jiangxi, Hunan and Henan, and perhaps also in Sichuan.

Incomes and wages

Off-farm employment is important for rural living standards...

Reflecting the relatively slow productivity growth in agriculture, a widening gap in living standards separates households with non-agricultural work incomes from those that depend mainly on agriculture. Thus, it is not only evident that rural per-capita incomes have lagged more and more behind urban ones during the 1990s.[10] In addition, the income distribution across rural areas in different parts of China depends increasingly on the distribution of non-agricultural job opportunities. One result is that the variation in per capita income by province is much greater for rural areas than for urban areas. Western and southwestern regions, having low levels of off-farm employment, stand out not only with the lowest rural incomes but also with the highest ratios, generally surpassing 3, between the urban and rural average incomes in each province.

However uneven the distribution of off-farm job opportunities may be, their growth during the 1990s was sufficiently widespread to ensure that even the rural households, on average, enjoyed significant real-income gains in practically all Chinese provinces. That this positive trend was driven mainly by off-farm employment is clear from rural household budget surveys, which show the share of farm-related incomes declining from 75 per cent in 1990 to 53 per cent in 1999. Because much farm income is received in-kind, the non-agricultural share in monetary incomes must have been well over 50 per cent by 1999. Specifically, 29 per cent of total net rural incomes in 1999 (40 per cent of rural monetary incomes) were wages, mostly from industrial jobs, while another 16 per cent of the total incomes came from non-agricultural household businesses, predominantly in the service sector.[11]

For urban households, by contrast, surveys suggest a more uniform pattern with wages and other employee earnings as the predominant type of income. In this respect, little seems to have changed since 1985 apart from the strong increase in the levels of most incomes. The role of income transfers, especially pensions, has increased to about one-fifth of urban incomes. An analysis by quintile in a distribution of households by per capita income reveals only small variations in the importance of different income types.[12] The relatively well-off urban citizens are more likely to work in SOEs than in collectively-owned enterprises (COEs), and they are often pensioners.

If a food share of over 50 per cent of household consumption expenditure is taken as a sign of economic deprivation, it emerges that only the lowest quintile of urban households are deprived on this definition. Hardly any significant difference between the urban populations in different provinces can be detected here. Again, however, data for rural households show more variation, with average food shares marginally above 50 per cent in most provinces except big cities and the coastal area (*China Statistical Yearbook* 2000, Tables 10.12 and 10.19).

Even in the most advanced coastal provinces, rural per capita incomes in 1999 barely reached one-half of the respective urban levels. Part of the reason is that rural employers in general pay relatively low wages. Statistics for TVEs indicate on average less than two-thirds of urban wages. The difference in labour cost is even greater because urban employers usually contribute at least 20 per cent of the payroll to social insurance (see below). Among TVEs, those that are still under collective (township) ownership tend to pay slightly more than the others.

But the wage differential between TVEs and urban enterprises has become smaller during the 1990s. As Table 16.5 shows, TVE wages did not exceed the average rural income per worker until the late 1980s. By 1998, following a decade of relatively high growth, TVE wages were approximately halfway between the rural and urban averages. This reduction of the wage differential between TVEs and urban enterprises may have resulted from product-market competition. But a trend of integration between urban and rural off-farm labour markets may also be underway, although the speed of convergence is slow.

The special attraction exercised by a few leading big-city labour markets is clearly visible from a comparison of urban wages, which are much higher in Beijing, Shanghai, Tianjin, Zhejiang and Guangdong than the average for any other province.[13] This has also put upward pressure on TVE wages in adjacent rural counties. A further peculiar feature in these regions, apart from Zhejiang, is that urban private and semi-private sector employers pay significantly higher average wages than do SOEs. This may partly have to do with a concentration of foreign investment there. More generally, however, the relatively high wages in big cities are probably a result of both market forces and institutional factors. Government policies to restructure SOEs and privatise some of them, to liberalise the *hukou* system (see below) and to provide more high-quality education outside big-city regions could all serve to temper, if not eliminate, this wage differential.

Apart from the biggest cities, however, urban formal-sector wages show surprisingly little variation between provinces. Indeed, as recorded in 1999, average urban wages were practically the same for most other provinces, usually around 7 000 RMB per year in SOEs and around 5 000 RMB in urban (and rural) collective enterprises. Private-sector wages varied somewhat more. But in most of the densely populated coastal and inland provinces – *i.e.* in the areas where private-sector employment in general is quantitatively most important – urban private and semi-private employers typically pay slightly lower wages than SOEs. Similarly, private and semi-private TVEs pay slightly less than collective TVEs. This pattern, which resembles the situation observed in several countries of Central and Eastern Europe, suggests that private-sector employers are among the most eager to limit their labour costs, presumably as a result of competitive business conditions and hard-budget constraints.[14]

Sample studies conducted in various Chinese regions have pointed to a relatively compressed wage structure within enterprises. Education-related wage premiums appear low by OECD standards, both in rural and urban enterprises, perhaps mainly as a result of mobility constraints that reduce labour-market competition.[15] On the other hand, there is evidence of increasing wage differentials between enterprises depending on economic factors, such as profitability and access to export markets.[16] These wage differentials between enterprises seem to exist regardless of ownership, suggesting that not only privatisation but also management changes in SOEs have rendered their decision-making more responsive to competition and budget limits.

In sum, the current wage distribution seems to reflect the combination of increasing product-market competition and too little labour-market competition. If labour markets become more competitive and less segmented in the future, those wage differences between enterprises that depend on profitability and product-market conditions may well be compressed, while on the other hand the wage differentiation based on individual qualifications can be expected to increase.[17] Considering that a qualification-related wage inequality can be important for the functioning of a competitive labour market, it is all the more desirable to reduce other causes of income inequality that were inherited from the past, including unequal access to education and institutional obstacles to mobility.

Education is often insufficient outside big cities

The prevailing geographic variations in wages also reflect a difference in human capital, as the urban population in general has much better education than the rural population. Again, a few of the biggest cities are particularly advanced, notably with respect to higher education. On the other hand, the educational situation is most often unsatisfactory for rural inhabitants in southwestern and western regions (except Xinjiang) which, as seen above, are the least urbanised.

Illiteracy is twice as common in rural areas as in cities, affecting, respectively, 16 per cent and 8 per cent of the population aged 6 or more. Less than 40 per cent of the rural population in 1999 had attended junior secondary school, compared with two-thirds of the city population. The proportion with senior secondary education was only 5 per cent in rural areas and a modest 31 per cent even in the cities, while almost none in rural areas and 9 per cent in cities had post-secondary education.[18] By comparison, in OECD countries in 1999, on average 62 per cent of the working-age population had completed upper secondary education and 22 per cent had one or more post-secondary degrees (OECD, 2001a).[19]

The situation appears somewhat better for China's young generation, however. In 1999, practically all rural and urban children aged 6-11 (99 per cent) were enrolled in the six-year primary education, while the three-year junior secondary education concerned 57 million pupils or 79 per cent of the 12 to 14 year age group. Senior secondary education was commenced by some 50 per cent of the junior secondary-school graduates, corresponding to 40 per cent of a cohort at the age of 15. But such education, typically located in cities and towns, is frequently of short duration (*e.g.* one year); total enrolment in 1999 was therefore only about 10 million. To this must be added some 5 million pupils in specialised secondary education, often older than 18 years. But institutions for higher education in a more strict sense had only about 4 million students, with about 850 000 graduates annually, corresponding to 4 to 5 per cent of the relevant age cohort. As a measure of geographic concentration, about one-quarter of the post-secondary students were found in the two large areas of Beijing-Tianjin-Hebei and Shanghai-Jiangsu-Zhejiang, and as many were in the northeast, Hubei and Shaanxi. No other provinces showed enrolment rates in excess of the low national average.

In OECD countries around 1999, on average 79 per cent of current youth cohorts attained upper secondary education, with a range of variation from 31 per cent in Mexico to over 90 per cent in Germany, the Netherlands, Japan, the Republic of Korea and the Slovak Republic (OECD, 2001a).[20] The proportion taking one or more post-secondary degrees was 25 per cent on average, ranging from 10 per cent in Turkey and 11 per cent in Mexico to over 30 per cent in Finland, the Netherlands, New Zealand, Norway, Spain, the United Kingdom and the United States.

In sum, the problems of illiteracy and incomplete primary education in China will recede as new generations enter the labour force, but there are still relatively few who attend more than nine or ten years of education. The basic level of education thus attained by most rural and urban youths should facilitate their integration in urbanised labour markets, but it could also raise job expectations that may prove unrealistic in the absence of more specialised skills. Worse, the low proportions of youths attending senior-secondary and higher education – even in urban areas – give reason for concern with their future capacity for lifelong learning, which according to OECD experience is determined to a large extent by the length and quality of education attained in adolescence.[21] There is a risk that employers will not hire persons with less than senior secondary education for the kinds of work that give most opportunity for learning on the job. With a likely gradual shift in labour demand towards more qualified work, a failure to provide youths with sufficient initial education would therefore not only reduce the country's general economic prospects. It could aggravate the problems of labour market segmentation and inequality, putting large numbers at risk of exclusion from the relatively attractive jobs, usually in the formal sector, that offer the highest degrees of stability and the best career opportunities.

For these reasons, a rapid expansion of senior secondary and higher education is highly desirable insofar as it can be afforded. A medium-term policy objective could be to increase the average education attainment towards a level comparable to the situation in OECD countries. This might be achieved by a gradual extension of schooling from the present nine or ten years to about twelve years for most youths and to sixteen or more years for a sizeable minority, perhaps 25 per cent. It falls beyond the scope of this study to determine how soon such an ambitious objective could be reached.[22] But China undoubtedly will need to establish many additional institutions for upper secondary and higher education in the near future, and these should be spread more evenly across the territory than the existing ones.

Indicators of labour mobility

Impediments to labour mobility diminish the chances of a long-term reduction of China's huge rural under-employment. There is a risk that many will not make the best possible use of their skills, nor of their capacity to learn new skills. On the other hand, because some skills are best learnt on the job, it is not necessarily a good sign if some workers change jobs very often.

It is hardly possible to determine any "ideal" level of labour mobility: it may be too high in some labour market groups and too low in others. Studies of labour mobility in OECD countries have also indicated a great deal of variation, with notably different patterns observed in the United States, Japan and Europe. Labour turnover at enterprise level as measured by separations, *i.e.* the proportion of employees who leave jobs per year, has generally been found to vary in the range of 10 to 40 per cent in OECD countries.[23] In Central and Eastern Europe, separation rates as reported by large and medium-sized enterprises generally increased in the early transition years of 1991 to 1994, reaching peak levels mostly in the range of 22 per cent (Slovenia) to 27 per cent (Russia). By 1998, reported separation rates in the same group of countries were between 12 per cent (the Czech Republic) and 25 per cent (Russia).[24] A different mobility measure is the proportion of the population who move house between regions, found to vary between approximately 1 and 4 per cent per year in OECD countries.[25] Both labour turnover and geographic mobility are traditionally higher in the United States than in Europe, while the Japanese labour market seems to combine a considerable geographic mobility with a traditionally low labour turnover, especially in large enterprises. In most countries, the highest mobility is recorded for young people and some unskilled groups.

In China, labour mobility is traditionally low among urban workers and many farmers, while it appears high in a group of rural workers with off-farm employment – perhaps too high in some cases, *e.g.* when workers looking for permanent off-farm employment only find jobs of short duration. In effect, much of the mobility is concentrated in a limited group of workers, the migrants, whose job search is distorted by administrative controls and traditions that tend to confine them to certain segments of the job market.

Gross flows of *urban* workers taking or leaving jobs were markedly small until recently, reflecting the previous norm of lifetime employment. Indeed – contrary to a common perception – urban labour flows in China remained quite moderate by international standards even during the recent wave of lay-offs and enterprise restructuring (see below). A peak was recorded in 1998 with an annual rate of voluntary and involuntary job separations corresponding to 13 per cent of urban formal-sector employment at the beginning of the year. The rate was then 12 per cent in SOEs, 15 per cent in urban collective firms (COEs) and 25 per cent in other formal-sector enterprises (see Table 16.6), the columns to the left of the middle]. The corresponding separation rate in 1999 was lower, on average only 11 per cent, due to fewer lay-offs (counted mostly under "Not on post, etc." in the table).

The reported *hiring* rates – shown to the right of the middle of the table – are extraordinarily low in SOEs and COEs, and much lower than the separation rates. But the "other" group of firms (thus private and semi-private) appear to have normal levels of labour turnover by international standards, with about as many hirings as separations each year. It would seem that the observed downsizing of SOEs and COEs during 1998 and 1999 was achieved as much by low recruitment as it was by lay-offs (or privatisations).[26] Hiring rates in 1999 were under 10 per cent for SOEs and COEs in most provinces except Shanghai. For "other" enterprises, by contrast, hiring rates exceeded 10 per cent in coastal and northeastern provinces, but not in the selected inland provinces. A closer look indicates that the "other" enterprises recruited considerable numbers of workers from the countryside in 1998 and 1999, while SOEs did so only to a small extent. About one-fifth of the hirings in any enterprise type

Table 16.6 **Labour turnover in enterprises in the urban formal sector**
Separations and hirings per year as per cent of employment at the end of the previous year
China in 1998 *and* 1999

Year, enterprise type	Separations						Hirings							*Memorandum:* Employment, end of current year, millions
	Quits (incl. retired)	Dismissed	End of contract	Trans-ferred	Not on post, etc.	Total	From country-side	From cities and towns	From education or army	Transfers within region	Transfers between regions	Other	Total	
1998	**1.9**	**0.8**	**1.9**	**1.7**	**7.0**	**13**	**1.2**	**0.6**	**1.4**	**1.6**	**0.06**	**1.3**	**6**	**127**
SOE	2.0	0.6	1.3	1.8	6.2	12	0.7	0.4	1.5	1.5	0.07	0.8	5	91
COE	1.2	1.0	2.4	1.2	8.8	15	1.2	0.6	0.5	0.8	0.02	0.7	4	20
Other*	2.6	2.8	6.5	2.1	11.3	25	6.1	3.4	2.9	4.8	0.11	7.0	24	17
1999	**1.4**	**0.9**	**2.0**	**1.5**	**4.8**	**11**	**1.3**	**0.7**	**1.5**	**1.4**	**0.04**	**1.4**	**7**	**121**
SOE	1.4	0.6	1.4	1.6	4.2	9	0.7	0.4	1.7	1.5	0.04	1.2	5	86
COE	1.3	1.3	2.7	1.2	6.7	13	1.7	0.7	0.6	0.9	0.02	1.4	5	17
Other*	1.3	1.9	4.6	1.4	5.7	15	4.5	2.5	1.9	1.9	0.07	2.7	14	18

Note: Lay-offs are generally counted as separations under "Not on post, etc.".
* Family-owned businesses are not included.
Source: *China Labour Statistics Yearbook,* 1999 and 2000, Table 4-13, 4-14, 5-7, 5-8, 6-7 and 6-8.

during 1999 were "transfers". But only a very small proportion of these transfers went across provincial borders, possibly also reflecting the limited portability of social insurance (see below).

There appear to be at least 70 to 80 million rural migrants, mostly in urban areas, although available statistics are particularly uncertain on this point. A comparison of citizens' actual residence (where it is known) with the registered one indicates about 70 million migrants.[27] The highest concentrations of migrants are found in the biggest cities and some coastal provinces, particularly in Jiangsu, Guangdong, Shandong and Fujian. But the numbers are significant in practically all provinces, reflecting the fact that many farmers have taken off-farm work not too far from their villages.

The job chances faced by rural job seekers can vary depending on the different recruitment methods used by various groups of employers. A sample study in 1998, conducted in and around some coastal cities, suggested that most SOE workers had been hired as a result of assignment by government bodies and "job inheritance", two methods that still seemed to play a role although they had become less important in recent years.[28] Foreign-owned firms and TVEs (in adjacent rural areas) were found to enjoy more freedom to choose the workers they wanted. One apparent result of the administrative approach to recruitment in SOEs was a greater tendency to discriminate against rural job seekers, and also against women.

Given the rapid pace of change, however, many of the statistics and survey results cited here may already be outdated. Not only does employment in SOEs and COEs become less important compared with other enterprises; firms in these two categories are themselves being gradually reformed, with the result that their management becomes more market-oriented, giving less room for government influence over their business decisions – including recruitment. If the recorded hiring and separation rates in other enterprises are taken as an indicator of the likely direction of change in SOEs and COEs, labour turnover is set to increase substantially. Moreover, urban enterprises will be less and less reticent to hire job seekers of rural origin. This likely development represents a special challenge to public policy, which is the topic of the following section.

Towards a national labour market

Just like product and capital markets, labour markets tend to be less efficient when they are burdened with high transaction costs and other obstacles such as transport problems, scarcity of information, and administrative and cultural barriers. Some obstacles of this nature will always remain, but they can be reduced and China clearly has a potential for much higher efficiency in the allocation of workers to jobs.

Current regulations stipulate that urban enterprises cannot recruit rural labour from another province unless the labour authority finds that local labour cannot meet the demands, quantitatively or in terms of skills.[29] Similar restrictions may also apply to rural labour from the same province and for urban workers from other cities: a city's own workers have the highest priority. Rural *hukou* holders also need residence permits in order to stay in cities. The regulations are applied most strictly in big cities, where typically the migrants are only allowed to take jobs in a small part of the labour market.[30] In practice, recruitment from outside a big city is allowed for two very different job types: high-skill jobs for which there is a shortage of qualified applicants, and low-skilled or otherwise unattractive jobs that urban workers do not want. Evidently, however, enforcement can be difficult and much of the targeted migration is probably not prevented, but diverted to the informal sector.

These regulations have for some time been less restrictive in small cities and towns. Since 1 October 2001, a person with stable work and residence there can normally obtain the local *hukou* registration.[31] But *hukou* policies are still restrictive as a rule in the about 240 larger cities ranked as prefectures or provinces, which typically have around 500 000 inhabitants or more.

The social situation of migrant workers in cities is often precarious because they do not have the same rights as other urban inhabitants with respect to housing, education and social insurance.[32] In principle – as already indicated – agricultural household members can always return to their farms, and many of them probably do so with some regularity. The public authorities of their rural counties of origin are considered to carry some responsibility for them when they are not at home. Not only can they organise job placement, although the main responsibility for this rests on the cities that receive labour; the just-cited regulation instructs authorities at various levels to co-operate in making transport arrangements for migrants, perhaps including an annual return trip for the Spring Festival. Urban employers, for their part, are not allowed to recruit migrants from a rural county without contacting the authorities there, and the migrants must obtain a special card from their home authorities and another certificate from the labour authority of the city to which they move. Undoubtedly, some migrants nevertheless move at their own initiative rather than following official channels, but the numbers are not known.[33]

Hukou and the right to work

The *hukou* household registration system has been the subject of debate for a long time. As far back as 1981 (Feng, 1996),[34] some advocated that the administrative controls it involved be relaxed because they hindered the development of a dynamic labour market. Indeed, in addition to dividing the population by residence – rural or urban – it also divides it according to economic activity: agricultural or non-agricultural. This whole system once had a justification as a basis for food rationing (abolished in the mid-1980s); but, as applied, it also served to hold back mobility.

In spite of the recent liberalisation, rural *hukou* holders are far from having a free choice of jobs. Unless they have certified skills that are in short supply – which is typically not the case – their possibilities of working in large cities are essentially limited to jobs that local residents find unattractive. Many labour movements also remain strictly monitored at the places of departure and arrival, often without any change in *hukou*. The transfer last year of rural workers from Sichuan to the Three Gorges Dam project in Hubei is an example of mobility subject to much official planning, while in other cases it is possible that a majority move on their own initiative or after recommendation by relatives and friends. The largest concentrations of migrants are found in the Pearl River delta (Guangdong) and the Shanghai area, but there are sizeable numbers in all provinces because many do not move far from their places of origin. Though some of the mobility is illegal it often appears to be tolerated by the authorities. Part of it involves the so-called "floating" population that moves from city to city in search of work. This has given rise to a sizeable literature and a multitude of unverifiable estimates of the total number of migrants, ranging from 50 million to 200 million or more.[35]

While most migrants earn higher incomes than is possible in their places of origin, enterprises are probably the main beneficiaries since many of these workers – having a weak bargaining position if they lack urban *hukou* – accept relatively low wages and, often, demand no social insurance. Labour law is difficult to enforce in the informal types of employment, especially for day workers recruited in the streets. Regulations are generally not very firmly applied in labour-intensive manufacturing or in foreign-owned companies, notably in special economic zones and other localities where the authorities have taken special measures to attract investment. Evidently, this is contrary to the principle of "government by law" (*cf.* Zheng, 1999).[36] It must also be noted that China has not ratified all ILO Conventions about core labour standards.[37]

Key policy issues of relevance here are, on the one hand, whether the *hukou* system can be further relaxed or abolished so that more urban jobs become available to rural citizens, and on the other what can be done to increase the chances that labour law can be enforced. Clearly, a policy to phase out *hukou*-related restrictions would contribute to curbing the informal market.

The policy challenge is great in that China's arable land cannot occupy the whole rural population, nor is it likely that accelerated urbanisation around small cities, towns and villages – however important this may be – will solve the rural employment problem entirely. The capacity of enterprises in these areas alone to absorb rural labour is unlikely to be sufficient, even if one assumes that most of the present TVEs will eventually overcome the difficulties they now face in adapting themselves to a changing industrial landscape and to the service economy. Considering that many of the possible new businesses in the future will depend on modern infrastructure, technological investment, and skilled labour, a significant part of the potential job growth for rural workers will undoubtedly be retarded if unnecessary obstacles to labour mobility remain in place.

A continued liberalisation of *hukou* controls is therefore justified.[38] But while this will be advantageous to rural job seekers and to urban enterprises, it poses a special challenge to urban workers, especially in the older generations that previously enjoyed a high level of job security. Because most urban workers have social insurance, it can also place an additional financial burden on the government in the short term. For such reasons it may be pertinent to pursue the continued *hukou* liberalisation gradually over some period of time, moving from smaller to larger cities. Nevertheless, powerful trends in the economy – product-market competition, new principles for enterprise management, and the risk that too much of the necessary job creation will be informal – would seem to motivate a substantial liberalisation in the near future even in the biggest cities.

Reforming social protection[39]

China's social conditions are those of a society that features both modernity and under-development. Although the establishment of market mechanisms has created vast amounts of opportunity, it has also given rise to new inequalities, which the social protection system is ill prepared to deal with. Other inequalities were inherited from the past, and, indeed, the rules of access to social insurance are part of these inequalities as much as a remedy for them.

Of a labour force of over 700 million, only some 20 per cent including civil servants have any form of social insurance, while total spending on social programmes represents about 3 per cent of GDP (see Table 16.7). The expenditure per pensioner is nevertheless high by international standards, resulting in a need for relatively high contribution rates that make it more difficult than necessary to extend the coverage of the population. For workers having access to all available forms of social insurance, the standard contribution rate is about 30 per cent of payroll for employers and 11 per cent of the wage for the workers.[40] But for the vast majority, no social protection is available unless there is a case for using one of China's relatively small relief programmes of last resort, such as disaster relief, support of destitute persons with no family or, in some areas, a guaranteed minimum living standard (see below).

Table 16.7. **Overview of social protection programmes in 1999**

Programme	Expenditure	Contribution revenue	Recipients	Contributors[1]
	Per cent of of GDP		Millions	
Social insurance	2.57	2.70	30	n.a.
Old-age pensions	2.35	2.40	n.a.	95
Occupational injury	0.02	0.03	n.a.	39
Maternity	0.01	0.01	n.a.	29
Health care	0.08	0.11	1	15
Unemployment	0.11	0.15		99
Pensions for civil servants, veterans and related groups	0.44	–	7	–
Other	0.22	–	27	–
Disaster relief	0.04	–	17	–
Social welfare and relief funds	0.06	–	7	–
Pensions for handicapped and bereaved families	0.07	–	4	–
Miscellaneous	0.05	–	–	–
Total	3.23	–	64	–
Memorandum:				
Price-support subsidies (mainly grain)	0.47	–	n.a.	–

n.a. = not available.
1. Persons who pay or for whom employers pay contributions.
Sources: China Statistical Yearbook 2000, China Social Insurance Yearbook 2000, Ministry of Labour and Social Security.

In rural China, the family remains the principal provider of social security for its members, a traditional arrangement that has been codified in the Constitution and other laws. But several factors including low birth rates, dependence on off-farm jobs and migration have combined to exclude many individuals from this safety net. Such concerns may appear premature in a country where the concept of the family is still very broad in scope. But the existence of some 60 million sole children in 1999 obliges one to consider the need for more developed forms of social protection.[41] Judging from experience in OECD countries, the progressive splintering of the family structure will more and more often require the State to substitute itself for the family and provide some income security for individuals.

Social protection policies should also be in harmony with the country's market-driven economic reforms, because sustainable growth is a necessary condition for any lasting improvement in social conditions. Furthermore, these policies must be administered in accordance with the new role of government that is emerging when SOEs are no longer the most important type of enterprise. Social insurance, in particular, is henceforth a public institution and not part of the State's compensation of its own employees. It will be expected to pursue general objectives of public interest such as income security and social equity, which will – in principle and as a long-term objective – be potentially relevant to all rural and urban citizens. However, the very low incomes recorded for part of the rural population makes it impossible to extend social insurance to the whole labour force immediately, and it is important to avoid making promises that cannot be kept.[42] More attention should be paid to the questions of how to continue a gradual extension of the coverage of the population, and which additional population groups should then be given priority.

In practical policy terms, a key principle of the recent and still on-going reforms in urban areas is "de-danweïsation", or phasing out the role of SOEs as "work unit" (*danwei*). This concept encompasses the political, administrative and social order within enterprises that developed in the 1950s and 1960s, including the principle of the "iron rice bowl" (*tiefanwan*: the government's engagement to ensure employment and incomes for urban workers). In the 1980s and most of the 1990s, the "work unit" was the chief vehicle for delivering social benefits, but increasing numbers of enterprises proved unable to pay pensions to their retired workers. Partly for this reason, the policy of "de-danweïsation" of enterprises had been broadly accepted by the end of the 1990s, although it will take some time to implement it everywhere. But the "iron rice bowl" still plays a role as a code-word for the State's historical commitment towards SOE workers. Thus, the government adopted generous transition arrangements for incumbent workers in the context of the recent pension reform (see below), and it has promised that redundant workers will get lay-off benefits and pensions even if their companies are insolvent (the "two guarantees").[43]

In the continued reform activity of the years to come, it will be increasingly important for the government to take a broad approach encompassing the whole economy and labour market. There is a risk that the large number of ministries and government agencies involved in social protection might slow down reform activity. Since 1997, social insurance has been under the responsibility of the former Ministry of Labour, now called the Ministry of Labour and Social Security (MOLSS). But this Ministry has limited contact with rural problems, which largely fall under the Ministry of Agriculture, and it still does not cover the whole social protection system because social assistance is supervised by the Ministry of Civil Affairs (MOCA). Moreover, the choice of methods and pace of reform is often left to provincial and local governments, not to mention the discretion still exercised by company managers in social insurance matters. In this context, the gradual phasing-in of most reforms – typically starting in big cities and coastal regions – has many practical advantages. But a rapid follow-up in the rest of the country is generally desirable, and this requires that the reforms be designed to take account of the persisting regional income disparities.

Different social insurance regimes have been tried in the past

A social insurance programme based on employer contributions was adopted already in 1951 for workers in SOEs and large collective enterprises, but it ceased to be viable during the Cultural Revolution. New regulations were adopted in 1978 and subsequent years, when the first wave of urban unemployment occurred in connection with the return of youths who had been sent to the countryside in the previous years.[44] Since then and until the late 1990s, enterprises alone have carried most of the financial and administrative burden of urban social protection within the *danwei* framework (*cf.* below concerning pension administration).

Following over a decade of preparations and experiments, new principles for social insurance have now been established as far as urban workers are concerned. Employers, employees and the State share the financial responsibility and the funds are to be placed under a common regime at city or prefecture level, once a number of administrative problems have been resolved. Perhaps most important, the coverage of urban formal-sector workers other than in SOEs has been rapidly improved regarding pension and unemployment insurance, though somewhat less for other elements of social insurance.

The remaining two parts of this section are devoted to pensions and social assistance of last resort, while the subsequent section looks at measures for workers who lose their jobs. Other forms of social insurance[45] are not scrutinised in this report, but a few remarks must be made about China's new *health-care insurance*, to which some 50 million workers paid contributions by mid-2001. A range of health-care services that previously were often free of charge for SOE workers have been financed by user fees since 1999, and only the insured can obtain reimbursement. (About 70 per cent of the employer contributions finance hospital treatment and care for serious illness, on condition that it costs over 10 per cent of the annual average wage, up to a ceiling of about four such wages. The employee contributions and 30 per cent of the employer contributions are kept in individual accounts for other expenses.) Provided that – as expected – the number of contributing workers will increase rapidly, this new insurance promises to make the financing of health care more manageable than it was under the previous system, and this should contribute to a long-term development of better health-care provisions. Clearly, however, the high cost of health care compared with the low incomes earned by the large majority of uninsured households, especially in rural areas, raises policy questions of a different order that have not been addressed by this reform.[46]

Pension reform

Extending the coverage of the population...

The social risks associated with a deficient social protection system are perhaps most critical with respect to old-age pensions. The problem is on the one hand that while the population is ageing, too few workers have adequate pension insurance, and on the other that the cost of pension plans where they apply is a heavy burden for enterprises and for society. This cost – representing 84 per cent of total social policy expenses – can distort competition between enterprises that contribute to pension insurance and those that do not. Until now, moreover, pension commitments have been one of the factors making it relatively difficult to restructure SOEs.

By international standards, the proportion of the labour force covered by pension insurance is low in China. Among five large regions in the world, three generally seem to have higher ratios of insured workers to the labour force and lower ratios of pensioners to the old-age population than China (see Table 16.8).[47] Lower ratios than in China between insured workers and the labour force are found mainly in Sub-Saharan Africa – which in other respects is much less advanced than China – and in southern Asia, *e.g.* India, Pakistan, Bangladesh, Indonesia and Vietnam (not detailed in the table).

But the policies pursued during the 1990s have led to a rapid improvement of the pension coverage of China's urban formal-sector employees, for whom the pension insurance in principle is compulsory since 1997. Provincial governments can make it mandatory for the urban self-employed as well. By the end of 2000, the main pension system covered about 104 million active workers, or twice as many as in 1990 (see Table 16.9, Panel A, first column). To this must be added about 30 million civil servants and related groups, who benefit from special pensions paid directly from the state budget.[48] In addition, a voluntary pension system for rural workers – especially in TVEs – was introduced in 1991 and officially has 82 million adherents, but probably only a few of them are effectively covered. This rural programme is based entirely on saving on individual accounts and the accumulated amounts per person are very low.[49] (See Box 16.2 for more details.)

The recent increase in the pension coverage of the urban population can be regarded as a significant policy achievement, in spite of the fact that the coverage of the whole population remains modest by international standards. The urban pension system now covers 90 per cent of all active workers within the groups the government until now has intended to make it compulsory for. However, the significance of this policy achievement was tempered by an increasing number of migrants and informal-sector workers in urban areas, who are not well covered by pension insurance.[50] As a proportion of the estimated total urban employment, the pension system covered constantly about 45 per cent during most of the 1990s before rising to 50 per cent in 2000, or approximately 65 per cent with civil servants (see Table 16.9, Panel A, third column).

The comparatively few urban workers in the formal (or otherwise reported) sector who still lack pension insurance are often self-employed or employees in small private firms, two groups that most countries have found difficult to reach (MOLSS, 2001*a*). Somewhat more disturbing, not least from a perspective of competition policy, is that foreign-owned companies relatively often fail to contribute to public pension insurance – a practice that some local authorities seem to tolerate, perhaps in order to attract foreign direct investment.

Of potentially much greater importance in the long-term, however, is to consider possible ways to ensure acceptable old-age incomes for the rural population. Although this complex issue does not appear to be on the government's immediate policy agenda, there are several reasons to expect that it will become more significant. First, as households find themselves more and more dependent on off-farm incomes, in relative and absolute terms, access to land plots is becoming less satisfactory as a substitute for social insurance. Second, declining birth rates make it more difficult for old people to rely

Table 16.8. **China's pension system compared with selected regions in the world**

A. *Participating active workers, contribution rates and income replacement ratios*

Per cent. China 1995 and 1999 compared with regional averages in the mid-1990s

Region	Participants/ labour force	Contributions/ wage		Average income replacement ratio	Average pension as per cent of GDP per capita
		Pension contributions	All social insurance contributions		
China					
1995	18*	20**	25	69**	78**
1999	18*	25**	30	77**	99**
OECD	90	19	34	38	54
Range	79-98	6-35	14-57	25-49	23-98
Asia and the Pacific	26	14	17	n.a.	n.a.
Range	3-73	3-40	4-46	n.a.	n.a.
Central and Eastern Europe and Former Soviet Union	66	22	31	44	39
Range	32-97	20-45	24-61	24-69	13-92
North Africa and Middle East	41	13	23	55	71
Range	30-82	3-27	13-48	36-78	22-144
Sub-Saharan Africa	6	10	17	n.a.	135
Range	1-18	3-24	6-33	n.a.	40-207
Latin American and Carribean	33	12	21	39	50
Range	11-82	3-29	8-46	13-64	26-64

B. *Dependency ratios and spending*

Per cent. China 1995 and 1999 compared with regional averages in the mid-1990s

Region	Pensioners/active participants	Population 60+/20-59	Pensioners/ population 60+	Pensioners/ Total population	Pension spending as per cent of GDP
China					
1995	26**	17	24*	2*	2*
1999	31**	20	27*	3*	3*
OECD	47	34	102	20	10
Range	27-74	27-42	54-135	8-29	5-15
Asia and the Pacific	20	15	39	3	1
Range	5-56	12-18	1-117	0-6	0-3
Eastern Europe and Former Soviet Union	63	28	136	20	7
Range	47-95	15-39	88-178	11-28	2-14
North Africa and Middle East	30	15	58	4	3
Range	19-50	9-29	5-94	0-10	0-6
Sub-Saharan Africa	7	12	15	1	1
Range	0-37	10-16	0-121	0-10	0-3
Latin American and Carribean	25	17	46	4	3
Range	4-70	12-35	5-152	1-26	0-13

* The regular urban pension system and that for civil servants.
** The regular urban pension system. N.B. employee contribution rates increased every year 1997-2001 (see text).
Source: Calculations based on World Bank data; Palacios and Pallarès-Miralles (2000).

on assistance provided by their children. Third, moreover, the spread of urban value systems can impinge on traditional family responsibilities in many ways.

The great discrepancy between agricultural and non-agricultural incomes makes it difficult, if not impossible, to apply the same pension insurance for the whole population in the foreseeable future. But concerning TVE workers – who earn on average 60 to 70 per cent of urban wages – it should not be

Table 16.9. **The urban old-age pension insurance, 1989-1999**

A. *Workers for whom contributions are paid*

	Millions of workers	Covered workers as per cent of total population	Covered workers as per cent of urban employment	Systemic dependency ratio: contributors per recipient	Revenue as per cent of GDP	Surplus (deficit) as per cent of GDP	Average contribution as per cent of average SOE wage
1990	52	4.6	31	5.4	1.0	0.2	15
1995	87	7.2	46	3.9	1.6	0.2	19
1998	85	6.8	41	3.1	1.9	(0.1)	22
1999	95	7.6	45	3.2	2.4	0.0	24
2000	104	8.2	50	3.3	n.a.	n.a.	n.a.

B. *Pensions*

	Millions of recipients	Recipients as per cent of population	Spending as per cent of GDP	Average pension as per cent of GDP per capita	Average pension as per cent of average SOE wage	Average real pension (1999 RMB per year)
1990	10	0.8	0.8	96	68	3 089
1995	22	1.9	1.5	78	67	4 118
1998	27	2.2	1.9	89	72	5 465
1999	30	2.4	2.4	99	76	6 451
2000	32	2.5	n.a.	n.a.	n.a.	n.a.

Sources: *China Social Insurance Yearbook* 2000, *China Statistical Yearbook* 2000 and information submitted by the Ministry of Labour and Social Security. The figures refer to the main urban pension system which does not concern civil servants.

unrealistic from an economic standpoint to envisage a mandatory pension insurance on approximately the same conditions as for urban workers. Indeed, this may soon be a necessity if the present voluntary pension insurance for rural workers does not generate enough savings to ensure adequate old-age incomes. In view of the likely administrative obstacles, a reform of this nature would have to be implemented gradually, but it should not be unduly delayed. It will justify further reforms of the present urban pension system and its financing in order to make it attractive and possible to implement under more varying conditions.

... requires reforms to make the system affordable

That the inherited pension system in China was designed for a small and often relatively privileged group is evident from information about spending per pensioner (see Table 16.8), Panel A, last column, and Table 16.9, Panel B, fourth column]. The average pension in 1999 was approximately equal to GDP per capita and 76 per cent of the average SOE wage. Internationally, such generous average pensions are rarely found in mandatory programmes designed to cover large parts of the population. As a reflection of the relatively high spending per beneficiary, the rates of employer and employee contributions are also high by most international standards – though lower than in many countries in western and eastern Europe.

The present high spending per pensioner is largely a result of previous policy commitments. For future pensioner generations, reforms adopted in 1997 envisage substantially lower average pensions relative to wages. Significantly, however, these reforms were accompanied by generous transitional arrangements for incumbent workers.[51] Not only was any reduction in spending per pensioner prevented from taking immediate effect, in fact spending increased strongly during the 1990s.

A central component in the reformed urban pension system is still a traditional defined-benefit scheme, but this is now combined with pension saving in state-guaranteed individual accounts, first introduced in 1993. For workers who retire after a normal working life, the reform aims to provide a total pension corresponding to 58 per cent of the average wage, of which the defined-benefit part (the first tier)[52] accounts for 20 percentage points – or 30, if recently planned changes are adopted (see below and Box 16.2)].

Box 16.2. Urban and rural pension systems

A. Urban workers entering the labour market after 1997. (Older workers may benefit from transitional arrangements not described here.)

1. A *pay-as-you-go defined-benefit programme*

Contribution rate: employers usually pay 20 per cent of the payroll, of which at least 17 per cent are used for the defined-benefit programme.

Benefits: 20 per cent of the local average wage after 15 years of work. According to current plans, a further 0.6 per cent will be added for each additional year of work, up to a new benefit ceiling of about 30 per cent of the average wage.

Pension age: 60 for men and professional women, 55 for non-professional women in non-manual jobs, 50 for other women; 55 for men and 45 for women in arduous or unhealthy work.

Disability entitles to early retirement at 50 for men and 45 for women after 10 years of work. In other cases, a disability pension is payable.

Survivor grants if the deceased is an insured worker or pensioner.

2. A *defined-contribution programme (individual accounts)*. This was designed to function as a funded pension system, but most provinces have not saved the contribution revenues: they follow a pay-as-you-go principle. It is then a notional defined-contribution (NDC) programme.

Contribution rate: workers pay 8 per cent. In addition, 3 per cent of the employer contribution of 20 per cent of payroll is transferred to the individual accounts if a worker participates. (The government is considering abolishing this transfer of employer contributions.)

Investment (if any): Handled by local governments, only government bonds allowed. The government guarantees the corresponding rate of interest even if the money is not invested.

Benefits: A monthly amount equal to 1/120 of the savings accumulated before retirement, with interest. – This formula seems to assume ten years' remaining life expectancy. But the pension is payable until the recipient dies, and in any case for ten years during which survivors can become recipients.

Lump sum for workers with less than 15 years of contribution.

Disability, survivor and funeral benefits can also be paid.

Pension age: The same standard pension ages for men and women as under 1 above.

3. *Voluntary pensions schemes provided on market conditions*: Allowed. But employers cannot contribute unless they have fulfilled all obligations under the compulsory pension system.

B. Rural workers

1. A *voluntary defined-contribution programme (individual accounts)*

Contributions: Workers select one of ten contribution rates of which they pay 80 per cent. Their employers pay the rest and benefit from a tax reduction.

Investment: Bank accounts and government bonds.

Benefits: According to the balance on each individual account.

Pension age: 60.

2. *Voluntary pensions schemes provided on market conditions*: Allowed.

The employer contribution, with a standard rate of 20 per cent of the payroll, is currently used to finance all defined-benefit pensions according to previous and current rules. Several provinces with high expenditures according to previous rules, *e.g.* in old industrial areas, have therefore raised the contribution rate above the standard rate, sometimes up to about 30 per cent.[53] Contribution revenues are pooled primarily within cities (for towns: within counties), which is also the level at which average wages are calculated for the purpose of determining individual pensions. If a city's pension fund is in deficit, the provincial government must find enough money to support it so that pensions can be paid.

The national government is not legally obliged to help out, but in 2000 it paid 34 billion RMB to provinces with big imbalances (notably in the northeast), an amount that covered most of the pension subsidies the provinces eventually paid out to cities and counties.

The employees' contribution rate was raised during 2001 to 8 per cent of the wages. This is allocated entirely to the individual accounts – the second tier – where pension entitlements are calculated on the basis of accumulated contributions with some interest (linked with the return to government bonds). In addition to employees' own contributions, 3 per cent of the employer contribution revenues are also assigned to these individual accounts. But according to the governments' most recent plans – currently being tried out in Liaoning province – this transfer of employer contributions to the second tier may soon be abolished, thus reducing the defined-contribution part of future pensions. To compensate, the government would then increase the defined-benefit element of the pension from 20 to about 30 per cent of the average wage in most cases. This would be achieved by paying an additional pension amount related to length of service.

Management of the urban pension system is henceforth entrusted to provincial and local governments and not to enterprises. This "socialisation" process, which should facilitate a restructuring of many SOEs, was more than 90 per cent complete by the end of 2000 (MOLSS, 2001). It involves a considerable administrative effort and it has contributed to a reduction of the previously frequent pension arrears, with reportedly 99 per cent of the pensions paid in time during 2000. (But there are still some accumulated arrears from previous years.) Local governments also collect employer and employee contributions, a task that can be particularly difficult in areas with many insolvent enterprises. However, following several further policy steps to promote enforcement after 1997, compliance on the part of the covered enterprises (not counting the others) was reported to reach 94 per cent in 2000.[54]

The need for continued pension reform

As the above overview shows, recent reforms involve several changes that will make the urban pension system more affordable. Not only will average pensions decline relative to average wages; short-term financial pressures are also tempered by an increasing coverage of the working population and by more effective collection and pooling of contributions. Pensions calculated by the old rules continue to represent a heavy burden, but this does not exclude that the reformed pension system, insofar as the new rules are applied, has been placed on a much sounder financial footing than it would have without the reforms. However, with the huge scope of change currently affecting the Chinese economy and society, it is hardly possible to design a pension system such that it would become immune to the risk of major financial disturbances.

Demographic change is a key factor in the long term. Depending on various assumptions, the so-called dependency ratio between the age group of 15-64 and the age group of 65 and more may decline from nearly 10 at present to about 8 in 2010 and around 3 by 2040. If the dividing line is drawn at age 60, the ratio might decline from about 6 today to 5 in 2010 and just over 2 after 2030.[55] Such *demographic* dependency ratios can be compared with the *systemic* dependency ratio between contributors and beneficiaries in the urban pension system, which declined from over 5 in 1990 to 3.3 in 2000 (see Table 16.9, Panel A, fourth column).

Numerous OECD countries facing similar demographic projections have found it necessary to increase the statutory pension ages.[56] This has not been part of the recent reforms in China, however, in spite of the fact that current pension ages are quite low by international comparison: 60 for men, 50 for most women and 55 for women in non-manual jobs, or less in several cases (see Box 16.2). Some increase in pension ages could therefore be justified in the future, especially perhaps for women, although this may have to be applied with flexibility in order to accommodate the special situations that arise in the context of enterprise restructuring.

Evidently, the future development of the systemic dependency ratio within the urban pension programme will depend not only on demography and on the pension age, but also on the extent to which additional groups of workers are brought into the system. As seen above, the 1990s saw a doubling of the number of contributors – but any positive effect on contribution revenues was offset by a more than threefold increase in the number of pensioners, partly as a result of SOE restructuring. If it is decided in the future to expand the coverage of the present urban pension system, *e.g.* to some areas now under rural administration, the resulting financial effects could depend to a large extent on how these areas are selected. As a rule, however, policies to improve the coverage of the working population will have the greatest chance of success if the ratio between contributions and benefits is attractive to economically sound enterprises and to workers who are not near retirement.

Unfortunately, the high rate of employer contributions in the first tier – required to finance the expensive transitional arrangements for current pensioners and older workers – will make it more difficult than necessary to attract additional contributors in the younger generation. It may also encourage non-compliance in other respects. If the government could finance these transitional arrangements separately, a simple calculation based on the new rules and a systemic dependency ratio of 3.3 – as in 2000 – shows that a contribution rate of 6.1 per cent could finance first-tier pensions equal to 20 per cent of the average wage. If these pensions are raised to 30 per cent of the wage, as planned, a contribution rate of 9.1 per cent would seem adequate. Should the systemic dependency ratio deteriorate to 2, contribution rates of, respectively, 10 or 15 per cent would still suffice under the same assumptions.

Given the government's expensive commitments to the present pensioners and older workers, its policy to impose high contribution rates may still represent the most practical choice: conceivable alternative sources of finance for the transitional arrangements, such as higher income tax or value added tax, would not necessarily be better. However, some differentiation of the contribution rates could be justified, perhaps with lower employer contributions for young workers whose first-tier pensions will also be lower. A possible alternative could be to reduce the contribution rate for low wages, as some other countries with large informal sectors have done (*e.g.* Brazil, Italy, and Ukraine).

Moreover, if the present urban pension system is introduced in some rural areas – where the present older generation receives no pensions – it would seem appropriate to charge substantially lower employer contributions there than in urban areas for a relatively long period. Another possible approach, which would preserve more of the present difference compared with urban areas, could be to introduce only the second pension tier in selected rural areas. Rural enterprises and workers would then be required to contribute only to the individual accounts. Just as in the present urban second tier, the contribution revenues could be either invested or administered according to the notional defined contribution (NDC) model.

Over the next 10 years, spending on pensions can be expected to increase from 2.4 per cent of GDP to between 2.5 and 3 per cent under current rules, not counting civil servants. (This estimate assumes a 15 to 20 per cent deterioration of the dependency ratio and a relatively slow phasing-out of the transitional arrangements for older workers.) Evidently, any increase in the coverage of the population will lead to higher spending – but it will also increase revenues. A key policy challenge is to achieve such an improvement in the ratio between revenues and spending that the contribution rate can be contained, and if possible reduced, in spite of the inevitable ageing of the population.

The role of private pension saving

For the large part of China's population that remains out of the reach of public pension insurance, private saving represents the principal option for old-age financial security – apart from a traditional reliance on families. The population groups without pension insurance typically have below-average incomes, but their earnings are rising and they include a significant number of the relatively well-off, such as employees in foreign-owned urban enterprises and those in TVEs near big cities. In addition, urban workers with social insurance may want to engage in voluntary saving as a complement, an option foreseen as a third tier in the urban pension system (see Box 16.1).

Household saving is already considerable in both urban and rural China, as shown for example by household budget surveys.[57] To the extent that the savings are not invested in family businesses, most of them are probably held in ordinary bank accounts (Asher and Newman, 2001). In this situation, there may be no urgent need for the government to promote private saving in general. But it would be justified, if possible, to facilitate a development of better saving instruments in China's emerging market for financial intermediation, so that the already important savings can be channelled to more profitable investments.

A specific labour-market problem can arise when enterprises' pension plans are not transferable between jobs. (Sometimes, transferability can also be limited in the public pension insurance, *e.g.* when a worker moves to another city or province.) In principle, the government could stipulate in law that all pension contributions and the resulting entitlements must be administered in such a way that individual entitlements can be capitalised and transferred to a different pension administration at any time. However, some employers may legitimately want to offer their employees an incentive to stay on, *e.g.* some additional pension entitlement that would be forfeited in the case of a job quit. In any case, the MOLSS should follow the developments in the labour market and be prepared to propose legislation, if necessary, against pension arrangements that would unduly punish workers who change jobs.

The second tier of the urban pension insurance also involves private saving, albeit controlled by the government, with no individual choice of investment options. Pension authorities can invest the second-tier contributions in government bonds, but in most cases they simply spend them on current (first and second-tier) pensions on a pay-as-you-go basis, crediting the workers' individual saving accounts with notional amounts that represent an implicit government debt to them. With this notional defined contribution (NDC) model there is no need to set up complex fund administrations: pension entitlements are simply calculated as if the money had been invested. This corresponds broadly to the pension reforms recently adopted in several European countries, *e.g.* Italy, Latvia, Poland and Sweden. Although it can seem to conflict with previous Chinese plans for the second tier – which envisaged that it would be funded – NDC probably represents the most practical and pragmatic solution in view of a difficult financing problem in the short term. It must be underlined that there is no difference, from an economic standpoint, between the pay-as-you-go method and "funding" via an accumulation of government bonds: the government will in either case have to finance the same future pension expenditure. (The pay-as-you-go model involves an implicit debt to future pensioners, while bonds – issued by the government to the fund administration – would make this debt explicit.)

A different situation would arise, however, if it were allowed in the future to invest second-tier contributions in other instruments than bonds, for example in the stock market. This would prevent the government from spending the contribution revenues. By implication, it would produce net saving and, if public spending cannot be reduced in the short-term, this would have to be paid for by higher contributions or taxes. Against this economic background, proposals to save and invest the second-tier contributions should have no urgency in the short-term because saving is already considerable in China, and also because – as mentioned – the urban pension contribution rates are high already. Some steps towards a greater use of various investment options could still be worth considering in a long-term perspective, perhaps in connection with other policies designed to make capital markets more efficient and transparent.[58] Much caution would then be required, however, in view of the present weakness of these markets and the lack of transparency in many listed enterprises (Asher and Newman, 2001). In any case, while it is questionable whether China needs to promote any net increase in saving it is clear that the present high rate of pension contributions in the urban formal sector is one of the factors that can distort labour-market competition. A reduction of these contributions should therefore be a top priority in the continued reform efforts, combined with efforts to attract more contribution-paying workers in rural and urban areas.

The last resort: minimum living standard and related programmes

Another recent development is the minimum living standard, a means-tested social assistance programme that is currently being introduced. While such programmes have been envisaged for both rural and urban areas, the greatest policy attention is paid to those in urban areas, where the benefit amounts are higher and where the need for a last-resort income support is seen to increase in the context of rising unemployment and the phasing out of Re-Employment Centres (see below).

The reported number of urban beneficiaries in 2000 was 3.8 million, up from 2.7 million in 1999 (see Table 16.10 and MOLSS, 2001a). The MOLSS estimated that a further 10 million urban workers were eligible but did not receive benefits in 2000. The problem may partly be financial, but another obstacle is the difficulty of assessing the situation of numerous applicant households. The need to develop administrative resources for this task has been recognised as a priority, but it will undoubtedly take some time before it can be done in all cities.[59]

About 80 per cent of the reported beneficiaries in 2000 belonged to specific groups that were known to local authorities, especially the laid-off, retired persons with low pensions and disabled persons. This seems to explain that the use of some previous, partly local programmes in cities declined in 1999 as the minimum living standard was phased in (as seen in the table).

In rural areas, the biggest social programme in terms of beneficiary numbers is one that targets poor farmers and seeks to compensate them for natural disasters, i.e. crop failures. In practice, such support is largely concentrated in regions that are not only poor but characterised by frequent droughts. Another rural programme of some significance is the "five guarantees" (meals, clothes, housing, funeral, and education), which essentially is locally financed. It applies to persons suffering "three withouts": no children, no family, no resources. Most beneficiaries are elderly persons and orphans, and they typically stay in nursing homes or receive grain.

Assuming that the minimum living standard is gradually introduced in the whole country, these traditional programmes are set to lose some of their present significance, although they may still have a role to play for many years. A more important policy problem that could arise in the future, however, concerns the possibility that both urban unemployment and the number of poor rural inhabitants without family relations might increase substantially. In such an event, the minimum living standard could be placed under more severe pressure that would require further consideration of possible ways to improve its targeting and to contain potentially negative effects on work incentives. International experience of various policy options, including the use of small-scale public works for benefit recipients ("workfare), could then be of interest (OECD, 1998 and 1999, and Subbarao, 1993).

Table 16.10. **Recipients of social assistance**

Thousands of persons

	1995	1996	1997	1998	1999
Minimum living standard programme					
Total	–	–	–	1 841	5 317
– Urban	–	–	–	n.a.	2 659
– Rural	–	–	–	n.a.	2 658
Traditional rural relief					
Support of rural poor households (relief funds)	31 528	30 792	26 022	26 917	16 598
Beneficiaries of the Five Guarantees	2 494	2 675	2 791	2 828	3 037
– Periodic and fixed allowances from the government	254	256	218	217	525
– Allowances from rural collectives	2 095	2 130	2 003	2 009	1 954
Older urban programmes					
Support of urban poor households	3 749	2 611	2 683	3 322	1 571
– Allowances from the government	127	200	140	164	232
Support of the laid-off, retired, elderly and disabled former staff and workers	538	535	531	549	515
– 40% of previous wages	239	236	233	249	225
– Periodic and fixed allowances from the government	299	299	298	299	287

Source: China Statistical Yearbook 1999 and 2000, Table 21-51.

Urban lay-offs and unemployment compensation

Lay-off regulations

Under competitive market conditions, employment in a particular enterprise can seldom be guaranteed for a lifetime: there must be some mechanism for permitting separation of workers from an enterprise in cases when the business situation changes for the worse. This was recognised in China from the 1980s, when urban employers began to hire new workers on the basis of individual *contracts*, with employment conditions specified in writing, as an alternative to the implicit or explicit commitments to life-time employment that had prevailed until then. The proportion of contract workers in SOEs increased gradually, surpassing 50 per cent in 1997.[60]

Chinese labour law permits dismissals...

The 1994 Labour Law codified this practice and stipulated that an individual labour contract can be either of indefinite duration ("flexible"), fixed-term or task-related. The two latter types can be used for up to ten years – a very long time by European standards – but after this an indefinite-duration contract is mandatory. Employers can terminate any contract with 30 days' notice in cases of illness or lack of qualification and if "objective conditions ... have greatly changed so that the original labour contract can no longer be carried out", provided, however, that no agreement can be reached by modifying the contract (Article 26). Employment reductions are also allowed if an enterprise has been declared insolvent ("at the brink of bankruptcy") by a court or if it faces major "difficulties in production and management", a concept to be defined by local governments (Article 27).[61] The employer must then inform the trade union and the local labour office. The employer must also pay severance compensation, usually equal to one monthly wage per year of service with a maximum of twelve monthly wages.

These legal regulations resemble those that apply in many OECD countries. They can be regarded as liberal in the sense that employers can select the workers they want to dismiss, albeit in consultation with trade unions and labour offices and subject to some restrictions (*e.g.* concerning disabled persons and pregnant women), and the length of the required notice period is modest. However, the required severance compensations can be relatively expensive to employers. Only a few OECD countries – *e.g.* Italy and Turkey – have laws that require more than a few monthly wages as severance pay in typical cases. (More generous payments can often result from contractual agreements, however.)

... but state-owned enterprises face special obstacles

Although SOE managers are responsible under the Enterprise Law and the Labour Law, they may still have less freedom to act than the latter law suggests. Despite the recent transformation of most SOEs into companies with the State as shareholder, the previously powerful party cells and "mass organisations" are still typically represented in the enterprises, albeit with less formal power over management.[62] Moreover, a significant proportion of SOE employees are not contract workers but older workers who once entered their jobs on the assumption that the State would guarantee lifetime employment. Against this background it is not surprising that SOE managers are under pressure to avoid laying off workers until this has been officially sanctioned and the workers guaranteed special support. In practice, the number of workers an SOE can lay off has therefore become dependent on budgetary decisions by the local government.

SOE employment reached its historical maximum as late as 1995, with over 110 million workers. But by then a vast downsizing effort had been tried in some coastal regions, and it became nation-wide policy from 1995 on. Following regulations in force from 1998, over 20 million workers were laid off in three years as part of the Re-Employment programme (*xiagang*), mainly in SOEs but also in urban collective enterprises (see Table 16.11). By the end of 2000, SOE employment was only about 70 million, while urban collective enterprises had declined even more in relative terms, down to about 15 million. Apart from lay-offs, voluntary job quits and ownership changes (reclassification of enterprises) explained large parts of this decline. The Re-Employment programme appears to account for almost half of the recorded employment decline until now in SOEs, but substantially less in COEs. However, as mentioned already, the total separation rate for SOE workers – including voluntary as well as involuntary terminations of employment – was only 12 per cent in 1998 and 9 per cent in 1999 (see Table 16.6).[63] The fact that SOE employment actually declined much more points to the role of privatisation.

Since 1998, laid-off workers are offered a possibility to enter Re-Employment Centres (REC) within the respective enterprises, where they can stay until they find a job or up to three years. They remain officially employed as long as they are in the REC, but in place of a wage they receive a lower monthly benefit.[64] The government also launched a retraining scheme designed to receive up to 10 million laid-off workers over the period 1998-2000.[65] Only after the three years have elapsed does the employer no longer have any responsibility for them.

Most laid-off workers are reported to find new jobs after some time, but many stay on for at least a year in RECs (see Table 16.11 Panels B and C). Re-employment results appear to have deteriorated in 2000 (MOLSS, 2001a). Among those enrolled in RECs at the end of 1999, slightly over 50 per cent had been there for over a year and the 35-45 year age group was over-represented. The relatively long duration could be taken as evidence that it is difficult to find new jobs. It is possible, however, that many of the laid-off prefer to work in the informal sector for some time while receiving the monthly

Table 16.11. **Laid-off workers and re-employment centres**

A. *Inflows and stocks*

Thousands of workers

Enterprise ownership	Lay-offs per year		Laid-off workers at the end of the year		
	1999	2000	1998	1999	2000
State-owned	6 186	4 480	5 917	6 525	6 570
Urban collective	1 485	n.a.	2 503	2 589	n.a.
Other urban enterprises	144	n.a.	293	257	n.a.
Total	7 815	n.a.	8 713	9 372	9 110

B. *Re-employment and duration of stay in Re-Employment Centres (REC)*

Thousands of workers and per cent distribution

Enterprise ownership	Laid-off workers re-employed via REC during 1999 (1 000 workers)	Laid-off workers at the end of 1999 by duration of stay in REC (% of total)				
		0-1 year	1-2 years	2-3 years	Not in REC	Total
State-owned	4 905	45	43	5	7	100
Urban collective	1 045	14	17	2	68	100
Other urban enterprises	118	16	18	1	65	100
Total	6 067	36	35	4	25	100

C. *Laid off workers in RECs at the end of 1999 by age*

Per cent distribution

Enterprise ownership	Age			
	16-34	35-45	46 or more	Total
State-owned	36	42	22	100
Urban collective	27	49	24	100
Other urban enterprises	36	42	22	100
Total	35	43	22	100

Source: *China Labour Statistics Yearbook 2000,* Ministry of Labour and Social Security (2001).

benefit, something which in general appears to be tolerated. Apart from the benefits, some workers probably delay their search of formal-sector jobs for other reasons; *e.g.* they may want to claim reimbursement of debts that the previous employers owe to them, or they may simply be very attached to these employers.

Notwithstanding these many problems and delays, the evidence until now suggests that the eventual job-finding outcomes are surprisingly good. This general conclusion appears justified even if one takes into account that many seem to receive lower wages in the new jobs, perhaps because they have job-specific skills.[66] The reported re-employment results are probably attributable to several factors. Apart from the support RECs provide, job finding was facilitated by a policy on the part of state-controlled establishments that recruit workers to give priority to laid-off workers, and by the above-mentioned fact that, in spite of the lay-offs, the overall separation rate for SOE workers in China is not particularly high by international standards. Perhaps most important, however, is that urban enterprises of other types have continued to increase their employment (albeit partly in the informal sector). In this broader labour market context, the employment impact of lay-offs in SOEs is not out of line with what would be regarded, if it occurred in the United States or Europe, as a normal rate of labour turnover at enterprise level.

According to current plans, RECs will be phased out in the near future. In a pilot programme in Liaoning, visited by the OECD, no new RECs are to be set up in 2001 and the existing ones have essentially ceased to receive new laid-off workers. Their role will be taken over by unemployment insurance and the above-mentioned minimum living standard.

Unemployment insurance

About 6.5 million workers (3.1 per cent of the urban labour force) were registered as unemployed at the end of 2000 – thus much less than the almost 10 million workers in RECs (who are not counted as unemployed). Registered unemployment is expected to increase over the next few years, both for economic reasons – continued industrial restructuring – and a combination of institutional factors: more laid-off workers leaving RECs and fewer entering them; increasing coverage of the urban labour force by unemployment insurance.

It must be underlined that these administrative unemployment figures are not comparable to the survey-based unemployment statistics used in OECD countries that, as recommended by the ILO, define as unemployed any able-bodied person who does not work but is actively seeking work. While China does not have any data using this definition, it is likely that its officially registered unemployment figures for urban areas understate ILO unemployment in some ways and overstate it in others. Not counted, though potentially ILO-unemployed, are not only the laid-off but perhaps many other job seekers who for various reasons are not registered at the labour offices. On the other hand, in China as elsewhere, official unemployment registers can include many individuals who are not unemployed by the ILO definition, *e.g.* because they have work in the informal sector or are not actively seeking work. In any case, as already observed above, unemployment by any definition can only give a partial picture of the broader problem of under-employment.

Unemployment insurance (UI) has existed in China since the mid-1980s, but its coverage was until recently limited to SOE workers, and not even all of them were covered. After a strong increase during 2000, the number of contributing workers reached 104 million at the end of the year. This still represents a somewhat lower coverage than that of the pension system if civil servants are taken into account. (As seen above, over 130 million urban workers including civil servants have state-managed pension plans.) The programme has been designed to cover all non-agricultural urban workers and its coverage continues to increase. It is financed by employer contributions of 2 per cent of payroll and employee contributions of 1 per cent. (At present, however, almost half of these contribution revenues are transferred to RECs.)

UI benefits are paid for up to two years and replace 60 to 75 per cent of the wage up to a ceiling, determined by provincial governments, which must fall between the minimum living standard (see above) and the minimum wage.[67] At the beginning of 2001, the maximum UI benefits ranged from about

100 to 440 RMB per month, typically corresponding to 120 to 150 per cent of the minimum living standard. As a result, workers with average wages (700 RMB per month in 1999) will probably, in most cases, face an income-replacement ratio of somewhat less than 50 per cent. This ratio corresponds to the situation in many OECD countries, but the two-year benefit duration is relatively long by international comparisons – although the corresponding compensations in several European countries can be more generous in both respects.

To be eligible for UI benefits, a worker must be involuntarily separated from the previous employer and registered as unemployed. Those laid off under the Re-Employment programme will be eligible for UI at the end of the three-year REC period, assuming they do not find work. As in most countries, benefit recipients must regularly visit the local labour office (or the neighbourhood committee), *e.g.* once a month. They must make substantial efforts to seek jobs, and the benefit can be withdrawn if they refuse job offers.

China has begun developing a network of *employment-service* offices for UI administration as well as job information and related measures, and several provinces and cities carry out experiments with computerised labour market information networks. By combining, in the same front-line offices, the legal controls required for UI administration with the more "client-friendly" information and placement services, China has followed a model that has proved appropriate in many OECD countries. In 2000, there were reportedly about 30 000 employment-service offices with 85 000 staff members, of which some 70 per cent belonged to local governments' labour administrations while the rest were managed by other public or private bodies (including trade unions).[68] As a measure of workload, there were on average about 75 registered unemployed persons per staff member, or almost 200 if *xiagang* workers are included. The latter figure appears comparable with reported workloads in the labour offices of many OECD countries.[69]

However, providing counselling and job-search assistance to unemployed persons is a demanding task, and it becomes more difficult when enterprises replace administrative recruitment practices with more market-oriented ones. Urban enterprises reported over 11 million vacant jobs to the employment service in 1999 – a high figure compared with the 8 million hirings in the formal sector – but it cannot be taken for granted that enterprises will accept the candidates proposed by the employment service. To ensure that the services are helpful to employers as well as to job seekers, local authorities will undoubtedly need to develop further their co-operation with the private sector, including many training providers, private employment agencies, newspapers, and Internet-based job search facilities where such exist.

How soon should RECs be phased out?

A topical issue in the present situation is whether RECs can soon be closed, an aim the government declared when it launched its Liaoning pilot programme. A principal argument for such a step is that SOEs and collective enterprises should henceforth be treated in the same way as private enterprises, and, moreover, that some essential parts of a general social protection system are now in place. From a financial point of view, some costs would be moved from enterprises to UI, which, however, already pays part of the costs for RECs. This reform will likely have little net effect on public spending, assuming that job finding can be somewhat accelerated. Nevertheless, in the possible event of a more substantial increase in future unemployment, UI spending is set to rise above the low levels recorded in recent years (0.1 per cent of GDP in 1999).

A possible danger, if RECs are phased out too quickly, is that the introduction of UI may be complicated by an unusually heavy financial burden at the initial stage. In principle, the insurance model may not be the best way to finance all social costs resulting from SOE restructuring, because numerous enterprises began paying insurance contributions only at a time when they were planning to lay off workers or had already done so. This could justify a policy that would permit the government to continue financing these costs by other means than UI, at least in the near future. For such reasons, researchers at the State Council's Development and Research Centre have recommended postponing the introduction of UI in favour of a wider use of the minimum income standard combined with specially financed measures for former SOE workers.[70]

However, the government's current plan to go ahead with UI introduction and to phase out RECs has the advantage that it will remove the programme administration from enterprises, thus permitting them to focus more of their scarce management resources on improving their own business. The recent experience of RECs suggests that a policy to separate the laid-off more quickly from the enterprises may well speed up their job-search activity in many cases.[71] Above all, however, it must be underlined that the necessary downsizing of SOE and COE employment is already well underway, and until now has not led to annual rates of worker separations that can be considered as high by international standards. Against this background, there would seem to be good reason for the government to continue its policy of switching the burden as far as possible from *ad hoc* solutions towards a general social insurance.

Main policy suggestions

A central theme in this chapter concerns the need for China to make better use of its huge human resources. To meet this challenge, the country needs to overcome an inherited pattern of labour market segmentation and establish a national labour market. Mobility obstacles should be reduced, especially between rural and urban jobs and, in urban areas, between informal and formal-sector employment. Institutional features that discourage employers and workers from operating in the formal economy require particular policy attention: a growing informal sector is an indication of malfunctioning in the formal labour market. In policy terms, this notably concerns the *hukou* system and its impact on urban recruitment and wage setting, but also social insurance and other factors, including education.

A continued high pace of non-agricultural job creation will be necessary over a long period in order to eliminate rural poverty and under-employment. This job creation will be most likely to occur if employers and workers are free to decide where they want to invest and work. Much off-farm job growth can and should take place in rural areas, as it has until now, and in the many small cities and towns that have a growth potential. But it must be recognised that the existing well-established urban areas, including big cities, present advantages in terms of infrastructure, access to skilled labour and services that can be difficult to reproduce in the short-term in more newly built-up areas.

The government should therefore continue a policy to phase out *hukou*-related administrative constraints on recruitment in urban enterprises. The effectiveness of these regulations in controlling migration appears *de facto* to have declined over the past two decades, largely as a result of a more competitive economic climate that reduces the possibility for government bodies to influence enterprise decisions. This trend is set to continue because SOEs account for a declining proportion of urban employment, and they are themselves subject to many managerial changes. But unless the government accepts and supports it by appropriate administrative changes, there is a risk that the *hukou*-based regulations – as applied at local level – may both reduce the potential job creation and force a large part of it to occur in the informal sector.

China also needs to improve its *education* system to prepare for a more demanding labour market, especially in rural areas but also in cities. Judging from OECD experience, it may be appropriate as a long-term objective to aim at an increase of the average length of education from the present nine or ten to twelve years for most young people and to sixteen years for, perhaps, about 25 per cent of them. It falls beyond the scope of this study to determine how soon such an objective could possibly be achieved, but China undoubtedly will need to create many additional institutions for secondary and higher education.

On-going reforms of urban *social insurance* have been largely successful until now, but from now on they should take more account of the role of social insurance as a cause of labour market segmentation. High and rising rates of employer and employee contribution are one of the key factors that distort market competition in China, both between urban and rural enterprises and, in urban areas, between enterprises operating in the formal and informal sectors. Compared with this big problem, other much-discussed policy questions such as those concerning a possible funding of second and third-tier pensions have limited importance in the short run, especially since private saving is already substantial. These and other institutional issues will merit careful consideration in the long term in conjunction with the development of more reliable and transparent capital markets.

The transfer of administrative burdens from enterprises to the government and the extension of pension coverage to include most urban formal-sector workers were crucial policy achievements in the past ten years. They will need to be consolidated and reaffirmed in the years to come. Moreover, after recent reforms that will reduce future pensions relative to average wages, along with other changes such as a more effective collection of contributions, the programme has been placed on a much sounder financial footing in the long run. But to preserve financial stability in the face of population ageing, some increase in statutory pension ages will also be desirable in the medium term.

Unfortunately, the reformed urban pension system is burdened by expensive transitional arrangements to protect current pensioners and those who began working before 1997. This burden will probably decline only slowly in the coming ten-year period. Financing the transitional arrangements via the same contributions as the lower pensions stipulated by the new rules may represent a practical solution, but it makes the pension system less attractive than it could be for prospective additional contribution payers. Some differentiation of employer contribution rates, perhaps with lower rates for young workers or for those with relatively low wages, could reduce this problem and, more generally, make it more attractive to work in the formal sector.

For the future, it is also important to consider how to organise social insurance for rural workers, especially those in TVEs. With average wages at 60 to 70 per cent of the urban level, their social and economic conditions are not always as different from the urban situation as the current institutional divisions assume. The existing voluntary pension insurance for rural workers is so little used that it cannot be considered to give adequate old-age income security. A gradual introduction of the present urban pension insurance in rural areas could be a better solution, especially if it can be somewhat adapted to different conditions. As a first step, this could be tried in selected rural areas with high non-agricultural employment, especially around big cities. Because older workers there do not receive pensions and do not benefit from the above-mentioned transitional arrangements, it could be justified to apply an employer contribution rate reduced by half in such areas (10 per cent instead of 20). Another possible strategy, which, however, would preserve a greater difference compared with urban workers, could be to introduce only the second pension tier (saving on individual accounts) as a compulsory element in selected rural areas.

In urban areas, much policy attention is inevitably paid to the restructuring of enterprises and the resulting lay-offs – a relatively new experience in China. Should the government phase out enterprise-managed Re-Employment Centres (REC) and related special arrangements in favour of a wider use of unemployment insurance (UI)? This chapter finds that such a reform – currently tried out as a pilot scheme in Liaoning province – is justified and should be adopted in the whole country. One reason is that the present *"xiagang"* status of the laid-off can have mixed effects, and sometimes probably delays their effective search of formal-sector jobs. Moreover, in spite of the size of restructuring already achieved, available information does not suggest that the lay-off numbers per year as a per cent of SOE and COE employment have been particularly high compared with what most OECD countries would regard as normal labour turnover. Against this background, it appears most rational to deal with the continued restructuring of China's urban enterprises within a general social-insurance framework.

To implement a more widely-used UI, local governments will need to continue their recent development of a modern employment service. Much international experience, analysed by the OECD and other bodies, has potential interest for China in this context. The public employment service will notably need to develop its co-operation with the private sector and experiment with new methods of collecting and disseminating job information. It must also adapt itself to a reduction of its formal powers as a government agency to exercise direct influence on employers' decisions. In China as elsewhere, effective job placement will depend more and more on the quality of the services the employment service can offer to employers and workers.

NOTES

1. Although the term "TVE" (township and village enterprise) has lost some of its previous legal significance, it is still used in statistics and this chapter follows the enterprise classification of the *China Statistical Yearbook* 2000 and the *China TVE Statistical Yearbook* 2000.

2. The term "province" as used here and in the following refers to provinces, autonomous regions and cities administered directly under the national government.

3. According to a recent NBS estimate (quoted in *China Online*, 6 July 2001), 130 million farmers or on average 5.9 million per year switched to non-agricultural work between 1978 and 2000. Switching from grain to cash crops can be difficult, however, due to the limited size of farms, obligations to sell grains to the state and other factors.

4. In 1997, over half of all agricultural households had land holdings in the range of 0.2-0.6 ha. About four-fifths of this land was used to produce grain, with probably about 1.65 crops per year on average, and most households had one to five pigs (NBS, 1998).

5. The NBS' Comprehensive Labour Statistics Reporting System, from which the data in Table 16.1 were compiled, estimated total urban and rural employment in 1999 on the basis of the 1990 census and subsequent sample surveys of population changes. The urban labour force survey is conducted every year, but only covers the specified part of the labour market. Data about TVEs, compiled by the Ministry of Agriculture, are intended to cover all non-agricultural jobs, but a comparison with population-change surveys indicate some under-reporting. The resulting data discrepancies are shown in Table 16.1.

6. In 1970, Republic of Korea's agriculture employed 4.8 million persons or just over half of total employment, but it produced only 23 per cent of GDP. By 1997, farm employment had shrunk to 2.3 million while non-farm employment was almost 19 million. Agriculture then accounted for only 5 per cent of GDP with a GDP contribution per worker less than half of that in other sectors, suggesting that the agricultural employment decline should continue (OECD, 2000c).

7. China's city and town municipalities include both urban and rural areas. Under a city or town government, urban areas are administered by district offices (in large cities) and by street or neighbourhood committees, rural areas by county offices and village committees. Three of the four cities reporting directly to the national government – Beijing, Shanghai and Tianjin – have most of their population under urban administration while the opposite holds in the fourth, Chongqing.

8. A few farms are located in urban areas, but most agricultural *hukou* holders living there are migrants who need a residence permit.

9. *China Statistical Yearbook* 2000, Table 5.4 and *China TVE Yearbook* 2000.

10. See *China Statistical Yearbook*, Tables 10.11 and 10.17. The NBS' household budget surveys are conducted separately for urban and rural areas and generally do not cover rural migrants in urban areas. The comparisons made here concern disposable income per capita for urban households and net income per capita for rural households. In-kind incomes are included for rural households but not for urban ones.

11. See *China Statistical Yearbook*, Tables 10.14 and 10.15. It may also be noted that while 2.8 persons per rural household were considered as members of the labour force in 1999, approximately one of them on average worked off-farm. In urban households on average 1.8 members were employed.

12. *China Statistical Yearbook*, Table 10.4. These household surveys generally do not count rural migrants working in cities. Had they been included, the results would probably have shown more variation.

13. *China Statistical Yearbook* 2000, Table 5.18. For TVE Wages, *cf. China TVE Yearbook*, various editions. Urban employment in Tibet is also relatively well paid, but quantitatively insignificant.

14. *Cf.* for example OECD (2000a), concerning Romania.

15. As noted by Fleischer and Wang (2001), low returns to education are surprising in view of the modest enrolment in post-compulsory education. This contrasts with the situation in Russia, where the large number of such workers can explain a similarly low wage premium for workers with higher education. Fleischer and Wang

attribute China's low returns to education to restrictions on labour mobility and, concerning TVEs, to capital shortage preventing an efficient use of scale economies.

16. Dong and Bowles (2001), in a 1998 survey of enterprises in and around Dalian, Liaoning province, and Xiamen, Fujian province, found that market pressures had forced SOEs to adjust their wages to profitability, leading to higher inter-enterprise differentials. SOEs displayed more wage discrimination between men and women than did foreign-owned firms, a feature the authors interpreted as a heritage from the past. SOEs were also found to discriminate the most against rural workers in general, although foreign-owned firms often seemed to exploit the weak wage-bargaining position of those rural workers whose official documents did not permit them to change jobs without the employers' consent.

17. Qualification-related wage differences seem to have increased during the economic transition in Central and Eastern Europe after 1990 (*e.g.* OECD, 2000a; Vodopivec, 1996). In China, Huang, Caldas and Rebelo (2001) analysed earnings data for SOE workers in Hunan and found that returns to education increased between 1995 and 1998. But they remained modest, especially for secondary education and for women. The highest returns were observed for primary followed by tertiary education.

18. The figures given for cities here do not cover towns, which take intermediate positions in most respects. See *China Population Statistics Yearbook* 2000, Tables 1-15.

19. OECD 2001a, *op. cit.*

20. OECD 2001a, *op. cit.*

21. The International Adult Literacy Survey compared information about continuing education and training (lifelong learning) for working adults with their levels of initial education attainment and literacy. See OECD and Statistics Canada (2000), p. 43.

22. As an approximate historical comparison, the increase in upper-secondary education enrolment (usually age 15-18) to concern a majority of young people occurred in the 1930s in the United States, in the 1950s in Japan, in the 1960s and 1970s in most of Europe and in the 1980s or later in southern Europe.

23. The separation rate used here is the sum of voluntary and involuntary separations, *i.e.* retirements and quits initiated by workers and dismissals or layoffs initiated by employers.

24. Gimpelson and Lippoldt (2000), Table 2.2, and Cazes and Nesporova (2001), Table 3. Most of these estimates were based on enterprise surveys covering large and medium-sized firms. Bulgaria was an extreme case according to Cazes and Nesporova, with recorded separation rates at 36 per cent in 1991, 30 per cent in 1998 and 40 per cent in 1999.

25. (OECD, 1994, Chapter 6.)

26. By comparison, reported hiring rates in Russia remained as high as 19 to 24 per cent throughout the period of 1992 to 1999. In most other Central and Eastern European countries they temporarily declined to between 10 and 15 per cent in the early 1990s, but then recovered to 15 to 20 per cent. Romania, as an extreme case, recorded its lowest hiring rate for industrial enterprises at only 5 per cent in 1992 (Cazes and Nesporova, *ibid.*, and Gimpelson and Lippoldt, *ibid.*).

27. Based on the annual survey of population changes in 1999, this may underestimate the number of migrants. Replies to a more generally phrased question in the survey suggest that about 80 million persons lived in localities other than those where they were registered.

28. Dong and Bowles (*ibid.*) found that 73 per cent of the workers in SOEs and 56 per cent of those in joint ventures had been hired as a result of assignments by government bodies or "job inheritance". The corresponding percentages were 12 per cent in TVEs and 2 per cent in foreign-owned firms.

29. *Interim provisions governing transprovincial and floating employment of rural labour force*, MOLSS Circular 458, 17 November 1994, Article 5.

30. For example, in Dalian only about 10 per cent of the job market was open to job seekers from outside the city.

31. In some localities, *hukou* policies had been liberalised earlier as part of pilot experiments, *e.g.* in Yichun, Jiangxi province, visited by the OECD, and in Jiangsu province (*Zhengquan Shibao*, 29 October 2000).

32. This does not exclude that the presence of numerous migrants has put pressure on urban infrastructures, notably public transport. Housing, education and other facilities are provided to them, but often under conditions that are less attractive than those applicable to urban *hukou* holders.

33. In a township outside Yichun the local labour office arranged placement and transport and possessed detailed information about the migrants from the county, who worked mainly in Guangdong and Shanghai.

34. Feng (1996)

35. For analysis of internal migration and the "floating population" of rural migrants, see Solinger (1997), Cheng Li (1996); Wu (1994); Stembridge (1999).

36. See Zheng (1999) concerning this concept and the development of relevant legislation in the 1990s.

37. China has ratified ILO Convention 100, which bans gender discrimination, and Convention 138 about child labour, which requires countries to adopt a minimum age for work of at least 15 years. But China has not ratified the following conventions: No. 111 concerning discrimination on several grounds in addition to gender; No. 182 requiring action to eliminate the worst forms of labour for children aged up to 18; No. 29 and 105 concerning forced labour; No. 87 and 98 concerning freedom of association.

38. The case for maintaining a restrictive policy towards rural-urban migration would perhaps be stronger if it could not be assumed, as done here, that China's economy will remain sufficiently buoyant to permit most migrants to earn higher incomes than they did as farmers. In the opposite case, one might have considered – as a pessimistic scenario – the risk of migration leading to large concentrations of extreme poverty in cities, as seen in some developing countries with less buoyant economies than China. But while this possibility must not be ignored, the present report's analysis of the Chinese economy and labour market suggests that there is good hope of achieving a better outcome.

39. The term "social protection" as used here covers social insurance and other provisions such as means-tested social assistance.

40. The standard rates of employer contributions are 20 per cent for pension insurance, 2 per cent for unemployment, 6 per cent for health care, up to 1 per cent for maternity and 1 per cent for workplace accidents. Since 2001, employees contribute 8 per cent of their wages for pension insurance, 1 per cent for unemployment and 2 per cent for health care.

41. See Li Shuzhuo, 2001.

42. Russia's experience in the 1990s provides an example of the difficulties faced by a government that had made promises it could not keep. Russia's social insurance in principle covers the whole population, but widespread non-payment and arrears, concerning both contributions and benefits are common. The real value of most benefits, if paid at all, declined dramatically and the system as a whole was largely unable to deal with the new risks encountered by individuals in the market economy (OECD, 2001b).

43. Under special conditions, when SOEs lack funds to pay what they owe to laid-off workers and retirees, the government (MOCA) meets the obligations.

44. The educated young – *zhishi qingnian* – had been sent to the countryside as part of the *xiaxiang* movement during the Cultural Revolution. Their return to the cities in 1979 led to the first sharp increase in unemployment, to 5.8 per cent. This rise was halted by the replacement system – *dingti* – which created jobs for young people by offering their parents early retirement, with pensions paid by companies. See *Feng Lanrui* (1991) and *Li Peilin and Zhang Yi* (2000).

45. The *maternity insurance* pays benefits for 90 days of leave for childbirth, financed via a special fund since 1994. Insurance provisions for *occupational injuries and diseases* have been reformed since 1996. Compensation for workplace accidents depends on the degree of invalidity incurred and can reach 90 per cent of the average local wage, plus a lump sum of 6 to 24 months' wages.

46. A rural co-operative medical system organised at local level (including so-called barefoot doctors) contributed to impressive public-health improvements over a long period until the 1990s, but it has now been essentially dismantled. In recent years, the government has generally preferred to rely on market forces, and rural inhabitants must pay for health care. According to the World Bank (1997), only 10 per cent of the rural population had access to subsidised provisions by the mid-1990s compared to 90 per cent in 1978.

47. These comparisons should be treated with caution because the regional averages are not weighted and the number of countries included depends on data availability.

48. Civil-service pensions replace the whole basic and seniority wage plus, depending on length of service, 40 to 88 per cent of job-related supplements (called position wage and post wage). Former employees of other state institutions receive 50 to 90 per cent of their basic and post wages. Maximum benefits require 35 years of service (MOLSS, 2000).

49. Contributions declined after 1997 due to TVE restructuring. In 2000 they totalled 1.1 billion RBM or under 0.2 per cent of the annual TVE wage bill. Only Shanghai has made participation mandatory in its rural areas, and about half of the contributions nationwide appear to be paid in Shanghai, Shandong, Jiangsu and Zhejiang.

50. Migrants should in principle be included. When they are covered they obtain pension entitlements after 15 years of work; if they leave a city before that they receive a lump sum corresponding to their individual contributions.

51. Only workers who entered the labour force after 1997 are fully covered by new rules. Those who worked and had not retired by 1997 receive benefits as if they had contributed under the new system, plus a transition benefit to protect past entitlements.

52. This section follows the internationally widespread terminology according to which the "first tier" (or "first pillar") refers to defined-benefit pensions, the "second tier' to compulsory defined-contribution and the "third tier" to voluntary defined-contribution schemes. In China, however, the term "second pillar" has been used to

denote a proposed additional defined-benefit element (see below), thus giving the numbers 3 and 4 to the two defined-contribution pillars.

53. Although the "dependency ratio" of contributors to pensioners is 3.3 for the whole country (see Table 16.9), it is only about 1.8 for a number of old industrial cities. Raising the employer contribution rate above the national standard rate requires approval by the Ministry of Finance.

54. MOLSS (2001). Non-payment of contributions is sometimes a result of insolvency, but lack of incentives to pay and poor administration also play a role. To improve efficiency, several provinces have recently moved the responsibility for collecting contributions from labour offices to tax authorities, while a State Council regulation in 1999 underlined the obligation to pay and instructed Labour Inspectors to check compliance. Other government branches are also involved, *e.g.* the Industrial and Commercial offices in charge of enterprise registers.

55. These Secretariat calculations, made for illustrative purposes only, assume constant mortality by age and a constant birth rate. Although broadly corresponding to results obtained by various demographers, *e.g.* Mo Long (2001), they must not be treated as forecasts. Cf. also the projections of the World Bank (1997) and Li Jianmin (2001), all highlighting the threat to social protection posed by population ageing.

56. In addition to reducing the statutory pension ages, it can be important to remove financial incentives to early retirement and disincentives to later retirement. See OECD (1998*b*), which develops principles for pension reform.

57. In 1999, the difference between reported net (disposable) household incomes and consumption expenditures, expressed as a proportion of these incomes, represented 29 per cent in rural households and 21 per cent in urban households.

58. OECD (1998*a*), which developed principles for pension reform, underlined that a development of funded pension systems must go hand in hand with that of financial market infrastructure, including a modern and effective regulatory framework.

59. *The Battle Against Exclusion* (OECD, 1998 and 1999) illustrates and discusses the difficulties faced in administering means-tested social assistance in ten OECD countries.

60. *China Labour Statistics Yearbook*, 1998. Subsequent editions have not shown the proportion of contract workers.

61. Cf. "Provisions on Personnel Reduction due to Economic Reasons in Enterprises", Article 2, in MOLSS (1994b).

62. The 1994 Enterprise Law provided for a gradual transformation of SOEs into companies with the State as shareholder. Such companies are governed by shareholder assemblies, supervisory boards, and management boards.

63. Even in Liaoning and Heilongjang, two provinces with unusually large lay-off numbers under the REC programme, the overall separation rate for SOE workers (as defined above in the text) was a moderate 11 per cent in 1999. This was notably less than in Shanghai, which seems to have a more "normal" labour market by OECD standards with significant rates of both hiring and separations (via REC or not).

64. To finance this benefit, the employer, the State (city or province) and the unemployment insurance fund are expected to pay one-third each. When employers do not pay, the State share is most likely to increase.

65. MOLSS Circular 36 of 1998.

66. Appleton *et al.* (2001) found – based on surveys in six provinces in 2000 – that former laid-off workers in new jobs typically earned less at the time of the survey than they would have done, had they not been laid off. The authors attributed this to the increasing competition for jobs exercised by rural workers. Cf. MOLSS (2001*b*) and Ru and Lu (2001).

67. Each city determines the minimum living standard according to local prices. Provincial governments determine the minimum wages and the maximum UI benefits, usually at varying levels for different cities, suburbs and prefectures. Workers with at least one-year's affiliation to UI can receive benefits for a year, while the maximum duration of 24 months applies to those who contributed for ten years.

68. Depending on local conditions, employment services can be provided by a combination of dedicated labour offices and additional task assignments to offices belonging to the general city administration. Dalian, visited by the OECD, had a central labour office and staff with similar functions in general district and neighbourhood offices.

69. OECD reviews of the public employment service in various countries have generally found that a staffing level corresponding to 100 job seekers per job counsellor is desirable, but the actual staffing in most Member countries is lower, often with 200 or more job seekers per counsellor. N.B. these figures refer only to job counsellors involved in job information and placement, while the figures for China cited in the text include other staff categories. Moreover, the Chinese employment offices cater only for urban areas while those in OECD countries cover all areas.

70. Ge Yanfeng (2000).

573

71. Internationally, there are several examples of cases when keeping redundant workers in the enterprises was found to delay their job-search activity. A Canadian evaluation study covering many enterprise closures, where tripartite bodies (management, trade unions and labour offices) were set up to deal with the lay-offs, found that the activities of these bodies on average had a *negative* impact on the chances that workers would find new jobs. Many workers delayed their job search in the usually vain hope that the tripartite committees would be able to save their jobs (Ekos Research Associates, 1993).

BIBLIOGRAPHY

Appleton,
  Simon, *et al.*, *Towards a Competitive Labour Market? Urban Workers, Rural Migrants, Redundancies and Hardships in China*, International Conference on the Chinese Economy 17-18 May, IDREC, Université d'Auvergne, Clermont Ferrand.

Asher, Mukul, and Newman, David (2001),
  Private Pensions in Asia, OECD, Paris. [DAFFE/AS/PEN/WD(2001)8].

Cazes, Sandrine, and Nesporova, Alena (2001),
  Towards excessive job insecurity in transition economies? Employment Paper No. 23, ILO, Geneva.

Chai Pui Phin,
  The Welfare Policy Implications of China's Ageing Population, Working Paper No.73, Murdoch University, 1992.

Cheng Danfeng, Ed. (2000),
  "China anti-poverty – economical analysis and system planning", Economic sciences edition, 2000, 300 p. (in Chinese).

Dong Xiao-yuan, and BOWLES, Paul (2001),
  Segmentation and Discrimination in China's Emerging Industrial Labour Market, International Conference on the Chinese Economy 17-18 May, IDREC, Université d'Auvergne, Clermont-Ferrand.

Ekos Research Associates (1993),
  Industrial Adjustment Services Program Evaluation, November.

Eyraud, Corinne (1999),
  L'entreprise d'Etat chinoise, de "l'institution sociale totale" vers l'entité économique. Ed. L'Harmattan, Paris, 396 p.

Feng Lanrui (1991),
  "Comparaisons entre les deux grandes vagues de chômage en Chine pendant la dernière décennie". *Revue Internationale des Sciences Sociales*, No. 127.

Feng Lanrui (1996),
  "Chine : 21% de chômeurs à l'horizon 2000". *Perspectives Chinoises* No. 35.

Fleischer, Belton M. and Wang Xiaojun (2001),
  Skill Differentials, Return to Schooling and Market Segmentation in a Transition Economy: The Case of Mainland China, International Conference on the Chinese Economy 17-18 May, IDREC, Université d'Auvergne, Clermont-Ferrand.

Ge Yanfeng (2000),
  "Safeguard the Bottom-line of Social Stability", paper presented by the Development Research Centre at the China Development Forum, 20-21 August, Beijing.

Gimpelson, Vladimir, and Lippoldt, Douglas (2000),
  The Russian Labour Market: Between Transition and Turmoil, Rowman and Littlefield Publishers, Inc., Lanham, Maryland.

Han Liacheng (1998),
  "The Old-Age Insurance System and Fund Management in China", in *Financing Retirement Benefits: The Asia and Pacific Experience*, Social Security Documentation No. 20, International Social Security Association, Geneva.

Huang Xiaoyu, Caldas, José Vaz and Rebelo, Joao (2001),
  Returns to Education during the Reform of State-Owned Enterprises in Hunan, People's Republic of China, International Conference on the Chinese Economy 17-18 May, IDREC, Université d'Auvergne, Clermont Ferrand.

Huchet Jean-François (1996),
  "Quelle retraite pour la Chine? Vers l'établissement d'un système national de protection sociale". *Perspectives Chinoises* No. 36.

James, E. (2001),
  "New Models for Old Age Security – How Can they be Applied in China?", *www.worldbank.org.cn/english/content/466n6200117.shtml*.

Li Jianmin (2001),
"Projections de la population chinoise à l'horizon 2050", version provisoire présentée à la Conférence "La Chine en transition, questions de la population, questions de société", INED, Paris.

Li Peilin and Zhang Yi Eds (2000),
The Analysis of Social Costs of State Enterprises in Transitional China. Beijing, Social Sciences Collection Publishing House, 393 p. (In Chinese.)

Li Shuozhuo (2001),
"Enfants rois et vieillards délaissés : implications socioculturelles de la transition démographique en Chine", version provisoire présentée à la Conférence "La Chine en transition, questions de la population, questions de société", INED, Paris.

Lü Xiaobo and Perry Elizabeth (1997),
Danwei: the Changing Workplace in Historical and Comparative Perspective. Mark Selden Ed; Armonk, ME Sharpe, New York. (Chapter 8).

Maurice, Marie-Ange (1998),
"La protection sociale en R.P. de Chine : traits généraux et réformes majeures. (1949-1998)". Mémoire. Inalco. Paris.

Ru Xin, Lu Xueyi Eds. (2001),
2001: Analyses and Forecasts of China Social Situation. Social Bluebook, Beijing (in chinese).

Mo Long (2001),
"Quel vieillissement démographique pour la Chine?". Article présenté à une Conférence de l'INED "La Chine en transition, questions de transition, questions de population, questions de société", Paris.

Mok Ka-Ho (2000),
Social and Political Development in Post-Reform China, MacMillan Press, London.

Mok Ka-ho and Cai He (1999),
"Beyond Organized Dependence: A study of Workers' Actual and Perceived Living Standards in Guangzhou". *Work, Employment and Society,* Vol. 13, p. 67-82.

MOLSS (Ministry of Labour and Social Protection, formerly Ministry of Labour, 1994a),
Labour Law of the People's Republic of China, Beijing.

MOLSS (1994b),
English-Chinese: Seventeen regulations pertaining to labour law, China Labour Press, Beijing.

MOLSS (2000),
Social Insurance Year Book, Beijing.

MOLSS (2001a),
Issues on Perfecting Social Security System and Re-employment of Laid-off Workers, March 2001, Beijing.

MOLSS (2001b),
"Survey results on laid-off workers and unemployed in ten cities", MOLSS 23/08/2001, *www.molss.gov.cn* (in Chinese).

National Bureau of Statistics (NBS, 2000),
China Price Index and Urban Household Survey Yearbook. China Statistics Press, Beijing.

National Bureau of Statistics (NBS, various editions),
China Statistical Abstract, China Statistics Press, Beijing.

National Bureau of Statistics (NBS, various editions),
China Statistical Yearbook, China Statistics Press, Beijing.

National Bureau of Statistics (NBS, various editions),
China Population Statistics Yearbook, China Statistics Press, Beijing.

National Bureau of Statistics (NBS, 1998),
Abstract of the First National Agricultural Census in China, China Statistics Press, Beijing.

National Bureau of Statistics (NBS, 1998b),
Abstract of the First National Agricultural Census in China: Supplementary tables, China Statistics Press, Beijing.

OECD (1994),
The OECD Jobs Study, Evidence and Explanations, Part II, Paris.

OECD (two volumes in 1998 and one in 1999),
The Battle against Exclusion, Paris.

OECD (1998a),
Maintaining Prosperity in An Ageing Society, Paris.

OECD (2000a),
 Labour Market and Social Policies in Romania, Paris.

OECD (2000b),
 Reforming China's Enterprises, Paris.

OECD (2000c),
 OECD Economic Surveys: Korea 1999-2000, Paris.

OECD and Statistics Canada (2000),
 Literacy in the Information Age, Paris.

OECD (2001a),
 Education at a Glance, Paris.

OECD (2001b),
 The Social Crisis in the Russian Federation, Paris.

Pairault Thierry and Morin Alexandre (1997),
 La Chine au Travail (I): les sources du droit du Travail. CECMC, EHESS, Paris.

Pairault Thierry (1999),
 Les entreprises d'Etat en Chine et la question de leur rentabilité. Historiens et Géographes No. 368.

Palacios, R. and Pallarès-Miralles, M. (2000),
 International Patterns of Pension Provision, *www.worldbank.org/pensions*.

Qian Yingyi (May 2000),
 "The Institutional Foundations of Market Transition in the PR of China". ADB Institute, Tokyo. Working paper No. 9.

Ru Xin, Lu Xueyi Eds. (2000),
 "2000: Analyses and Forecasts of China Social Situation". Beijing, Social Bluebook. (In Chinese)

Ru Xin, Lu Xueyi Eds. (1999),
 "1999: Analyses and Forecasts of China Social Situation". Beijing, Social Bluebook. (In Chinese).

Subbarao, K. *et al.* (1993),
 Safety Net Programs and Poverty Reduction. Lessons from Cross-Country Experience, the World Bank, Washington DC.

Tao Jingzhou, (1999),
 Droit chinois des affaires, Ed. Economica, Paris.

Tian Xiaoyu and WANG Junfang,
 "Apport pour les générations futures – Retour sur un demi-siècle de développement de la protection sociale et du travail en Chine". Beijing, MOLSS, *www.molss.gov.cn/theme/50Years/01.htm* (in Chinese).

United States Social Security Administration (2000),
 Social Security Programs Throughout the World, *www.ssa.gov/policy/pubs/pages/SocialSecurityPrograms.htm*.

Vodopivec, M. (1996),
 "The Slovenian labour market in transition: evidence from micro-data", *Lessons from Labour market Policies in Transition Countries*, OECD, Paris.

Wang, Yan, Xu, Dianqing, Wang, Zhi and Zhai, Fan (2000),
 "Implicit Pension debt, Transition Cost, Options and Impact of China's Pension Reform – A Computable General Equilibrium Analysis", Paper presented at Conference on Globalisation: China's Opportunities and Challenges in the New Century, July, Shanghai.

Wong Chack Kie and Lee Nan Shong (2000),
 "Popular Belief in State Intervention for Social Protection". *Journal of Social Policy* No. 29, 1, 109-116.

Wong Linda and Mac Pherson Stewart Eds. (1995),
 Social Change and Social Policy in contemporary China". Avebury, Hong Kong, Athenaeum Press.

World Bank (1997a),
 Financing Health Care: Issues and Options for China, China 2020, The World Bank, Washington DC.

World Bank (1997b),
 Pension Reform in China :Old age security. The World Bank, Washington DC.

World Bank (1997c),
 Sharing Rising Incomes: Disparities in China, China 2020, The World Bank, Washington DC.

Zheng Yongnian (1999),
 "Du gouvernement par la loi à l'Etat de droit? L'évolution de l'environnement juridique en Chine". *Perspectives Chinoises*, No. 54.

Zhu Zhixin Eds (2000),
 Major definitions of China Statistical System, 2000. China Statistics Press, Beijing.

Chapter 17

ENVIRONMENTAL PRIORITIES
FOR CHINA'S SUSTAINABLE DEVELOPMENT

TABLE OF CONTENTS

Boxes

ENVIRONMENTAL PRIORITIES
FOR CHINA'S SUSTAINABLE DEVELOPMENT[*]

Introduction

China's past two decades of rapid economic growth, urbanisation, and industrialisation have been accompanied by steady deterioration of the environment. For example, the air and water pollution damages, especially the dangers that fine airborne particulates pose to human health, have been estimated to be at least US$54 billion a year – or nearly 8 per cent of GDP in 1995.[1] Water pollution has contaminated over half of monitored urban river sections, which do not even meet the lowest standards necessary for irrigation purposes, putting future access to drinking water under threat. Acid rain in the high-sulfur coal regions of southern and southwestern China threatens to damage 10 per cent of the land area, and may already have reduced crops and forestry productivity by 3 per cent. Soil erosion, deforestation, damage to wetlands and grasslands have resulted in deterioration of China's ecosystems and pose a threat to future agricultural sustainability. Rapid urbanisation has led to additional pressures on water and land resources and the quality of urban air has been deteriorating rapidly. Without reforming economic and environmental policies, restructuring inefficient industries, conserving scarce natural resources and without investing in cleaner material and resource-efficient production, the situation is likely to worsen, affecting potential for further economic growth.

China's environmental situation has become a major factor in determining the country's future economic development. Any analysis of opportunities for, and obstacles to, economic growth linked to trade and investment liberalisation should take environmental issues into account, as trade and investment flows can significantly influence, positively or negatively, the state of the environment.

Several analyses show that liberalised trade and investment regimes can improve resource allocation contributing directly to improvements in protecting the environment, including better use of natural resources. They can also indirectly promote the demand for better quality ambient air, water, and other media. However, in the absence of adequate environmental policies, investment liberalisation may lead to increased production and consumption of polluting goods, or to a non-sustainable use of natural resources, both of which would exacerbate the negative (scale) effects of economic activity for the environment. The analysis of linkages between trade and investment and environmental issues has received growing attention throughout the world, including the OECD region.[2]

This chapter aims to assist the Chinese authorities in identifying areas where analysis is necessary to design and implement policies that would promote the positive impacts of trade and investment liberalisation on the environment and reduce the negative ones. The chapter first presents the main concepts in discussing the relationship between trade and investment and the environment. This is followed by a brief description of key environmental problems in China. A presentation of China's environmental regulatory framework is then provided, together with examples of environmental and sectoral policies and institutions influencing foreign direct investment and trade, as well as examples of negative and positive impacts of different trade and investment patterns in China. The subsequent sections present the main pressures on the environment and the trends in light of changes in trade and investment flows. Finally, the approaches to assessing the effects of trade and investment liberalisation are presented, with examples of the practical application of assessment methodologies in OECD countries and the potential for applying them in China.

---

* This chapter was prepared by Krzysztof Michalak, Peter Borkey, and Christina Tebar-Less, Administrators, and Aki Yamaguchi, Associate Expert from the Environment Directorate, OECD, with the help of consultant Sun Qihong from the Chinese Research Academy of Environmental Sciences and consultant Zhang Shiqiu from the Centre for Environmental Sciences of Beijing University.

General context for relations between trade and investment and the environment

Effects of trade and investment on the environment

As has been shown in other parts of the OECD study, trade and investment promote growth, alter the composition and geographical distribution of economic activities, stimulate competition and facilitate the international diffusion of technologies. Depending on the circumstances, trade and investment can have significant effects, both positive and negative, for the environment. Trade and investment are not the only factors determining these effects, but they both clearly amplify and accelerate them.

Most environmental consequences of trade and investment liberalisation can be characterised by one of five effects (Box 17.1):

- scale – the result of an expansion of world economic output;

- structural – a reallocation of production and consumption worldwide and between sectors;

- technology – the stimulation of technological development and diffusion;

- product – impacts from product trade flows; and

- regulatory – changes in legal instruments.[3]

On the one hand, trade and investment liberalisation – like any policy fostering economic growth – may lead to increased production and consumption of polluting goods or to an expansion in industrial or other polluting activity. This can exert pressures on the environment, such as increased emissions of pollutants and use of resources, rapid urbanisation, or damage to protected areas, and pose problems for pollution control, ecological and public health protection. In OECD countries, scale effects have often tended to outpace efficiency gains in the use of natural resources. In developing countries, including China, these risks are exacerbated due to their often weak environmental policies, as well as weak frameworks for resource tenure and enforcement of ownership rights. Increased economic activity stimulated by trade and investment liberalisation brings into the open or exacerbates distortions and weaknesses of the existing policy framework. This often results in severe environmental degradation. When sources of environmental degradation or under-priced resources (*e.g.* forests, fish, water or air) are not adequately addressed, rapid export growth – while not the root cause – can worsen the problem.

On the other hand, trade and investment liberalisation – when paired with the implementation of strong regulatory frameworks to protect the environment – can have a beneficial impact on the environment by improving resource allocation, promoting economic growth and increasing welfare. For example, trade and foreign direct investment (FDI) can improve structural efficiencies and make new investments in environmental protection possible.

In general, sectoral studies have underscored that trade and investment liberalisation can go hand in hand with environmental improvements. Opportunities to realise economies of scale and the effects of increased competition on efficiency can be expected to lead to welfare gains. For example, liberalisation of environmental goods and services – by opening domestic markets to foreign suppliers by reducing tariffs and other measures – enables advanced know-how and environmental technologies to become more readily available and spurs economic growth and employment. Economic modelling of energy markets has also indicated that trade liberalisation and energy policy reforms would not only increase economic welfare, but also reduce global carbon emissions. Energy subsidies, particularly those encouraging energy consumption by keeping prices below costs, impose a heavy weight on economic efficiency and environmental performance. In this case, reductions in both local and global pollution can accrue from proper pricing.

Trade and investment flows can also assist in abating pollution, or have other positive environmental impacts, through the worldwide dissemination of technologies. With tighter regulations at home, multinational enterprises (MNEs) have a strong incentive to innovate in areas that improve resource efficiency or reduce industrial waste. Once developed, new technologies can be applied on a

---

Box 17.1. Types of trade-related effects

Environmental impacts may stem from the effects of the trade measure or agreement on: 1) the level of trade or of economic activity (*scale effects*); 2) the pattern of economic activity (*structural effects*); 3) technology trade flows (*technology effects*); 4) product trade flows (*product effects*; and 5) legal instruments (*regulatory effects*). These different types of effects can be both positive and negative for the environment.

Scale effects – Scale effects are associated with the overall level of economic activity or the macroeconomic effects resulting from the trade measure or agreement. *Positive scale effects* may result from higher levels of economic growth and financial gain, particularly when appropriate environmental policies are present. *Negative scale effects* may occur when higher levels of economic growth, trade and/or transport bring increased pollution and faster drawdown of resources due to the absence of appropriate environmental policies.

Structural effects – Structural effects are associated with changes in the patterns of economic activity or the microeconomic effects resulting from the trade measure or agreement. *Positive structural effects* may result when trade measures and agreements promote an efficient allocation of resources and efficient patterns of production and consumption. *Negative structural effects* may occur when appropriate environmental policies do not accompany changes in patterns of economic activity, and when environmental costs and benefits are not reflected in the prices of traded goods.

Technology effects – Technology effects are associated with changes in the way products are made depending largely on the technology used. *Positive technology effects* may result when the output of pollution per unit of economic product is reduced. Foreign producers may transfer cleaner technologies abroad when a trade measure or agreement results in a more open market and a business climate more conducive to investment. If there are positive scale effects that generate an increase in income levels, the public may demand a cleaner environment as an expression of their increased national wealth, which in turn will generate demand for cleaner technologies, more stringent pollution standards, and stricter enforcement of existing environmental laws. *Negative technology effects* or the lack of positive effects may occur if neither of the above scenarios eventuates.

Product effects – Product effects are associated with trade in specific products that can enhance or harm the environment. *Positive product effects* may result from increased trade in goods that are environmentally beneficial relative to competing products, such as energy-efficient machinery, low-sulphur coal, or recyclable containers. Positive product effects would also stem from increased trade in environmental goods and technologies themselves, such as equipment for water treatment, waste management, and air quality. *Negative product effects* may result from increased trade in goods which are environmentally sensitive, such as hazardous wastes, dangerous chemicals or endangered species.

Regulatory Effects – Regulatory effects are associated with the legal and policy effects of a trade measure or agreement on environmental regulations, standards and other measures. *Positive regulatory effects* result when trade measures and agreements take care to maintain the ability of governments to pursue appropriate and effective environmental policies. *Negative regulatory effects* may occur when the provisions of the trade measure or agreement undermine the ability of governments to enact and implement appropriate environmental regulations.

Source: *Methodologies for Environmental and Trade Reviews*, OECD, 1994.

---

worldwide basis by the firm in order to benefit from economies of scale. These modern technologies can be licensed directly to foreign producers, imported through abatement equipment or installed directly by MNEs in their foreign affiliates. Foreign direct investment by MNEs can also have positive spillover effects on the technological characteristics of national firms, since local firms may imitate multinationals' technological practices in order to improve their own production practices. However, technology effects need not always be positive. Even if industrial production plants use advanced technologies, foreign direct investment can increase the total environmental burden on a country if before that investment no such plants existed. Also, there have been instances of "technology dumping", where equipment banned in environmentally strict countries (because of its poor environmental performance) is sold to or "dumped" in countries with less demanding environmental standards.

While trade and foreign direct investment are important vehicles for both technological change and diffusion, international capital flows are also an important determinant of the technologies of production. The internationalisation of capital markets, by giving firms access to foreign sources of savings, can ease financial constraints that prevent firms from investing in potentially more efficient and environmentally preferable technologies. In some cases, these financial constraints have arisen from national policies towards foreign capital, such as foreign exchange restrictions, international credit controls, and ownership restrictions.

Whether the simple fact that by contributing to an economy's growth, trade and investment liberalisation contributes to an increased societal demand for a healthier environment remains the subject of debate. While some put forward that wealthier societies are more willing – and able – to pay for protection of the environment, which is supported by evidence illustrating a relationship between per capita income and indicators of environmental quality (the Environmental Kuznets Curve), others contest the causality in this relationship. They maintain that, first, not all measures of environmental quality fit into this pattern, *e.g.* growth contributes monotonically to global emissions of carbon dioxide, levels of waste disposal, and urban congestion. Second, while income growth may well be necessary, it may not be sufficient for environmental improvements.[4]

The pollution haven and halo hypotheses

Long-term environmental impacts of trade and investment will depend in large part on how government environmental policies respond to their pressures and opportunities. For example, the so-called *"pollution haven"* hypothesis implies that competitive forces would move foreign direct investment away from countries with high environmental standards, or attract it towards those with low environmental standards. Closely related to this hypothesis is that of the *"regulatory chill"*, which would reflect resistance to enacting or upgrading home country environmental standards on competitiveness grounds.[5]

It is possible that some countries could be attracted by the idea of relaxing environmental standards or refraining from upgrading low standards in order to attract certain types of investments, and individual firms may be sensitive to the costs of complying with more stringent environmental standards. Foreign direct investment flows to a wide range of industries and companies – some of which are careful environmental stewards, some of which are not. However, empirical research shows that the risk of redeployment of productive resources towards low standard countries is rather small. Environmental costs are only one of a broad number of factors – including quality of infrastructure, access to inputs, wage costs, labour productivity, political risk, the size and growth potential of markets – that investors take into account in location decisions. The costs of adhering to environmental regulations are also typically a small part (on average 2-3 per cent) of total production costs for most firms, although in certain resource-intensive sectors the costs may be higher. Instead, multinational enterprises generally seek *consistent* environmental enforcement, rather than *lax* environmental enforcement. In spite of the strength of empirical findings concerning the relative unimportance of pollution havens, there is some evidence that competitiveness concerns have dampened governments' enthusiasm to raise environmental standards.[6]

The converse notion of *"pollution halos"* suggests that foreign direct investment might promote the establishment of higher environmental standards through technology transfer or via existing management practice within multinational or other firms. For example, a large share of foreign direct investment directed to non-OECD countries is related to privatisation, and privatised firms are typically managed better and more accountably, which tends to reduce waste and pollution. The bulk of international investment is undertaken by large multinational enterprises that typically operate at the highest corporate standard of environmental performance worldwide rather than tailoring their production methods to the level of regulatory enforcement prevailing in host country markets.[7] Close to three-quarters of global foreign direct investment flows originate in, and are directed towards, industrialised countries and are subject to the stringent environmental standards that typically apply in OECD countries. However, it is important that appropriate policies are in place at the national level to ensure that such standards are effectively enforced.

Main features of the state of China's environment

China has experienced a long-term and outstandingly rapid economic growth since its opening-up to the world in 1978. While having significantly improved the quality of life of the large part of the population, economic development has resulted in serious environmental problems, such as widespread water and air pollution, solid waste accumulation, high air pollution, and water scarcity in urban areas. The rural environmental quality has been deteriorating following an expansion of Town and Village Industrial Enterprises (TVIEs) and intensive farming practices. The state of the environment is still worsening and, in several areas, posing obstacles to economic growth.

Water

Economic growth in China has been accompanied by a substantial increase in demand for water. Between 1980 and 1993 urban water consumption increased by 350 per cent and industrial consumption doubled.[8] Demand for water has been increasing at a time when several parts of China experienced water shortages, significant water pollution, and falling groundwater tables as well as flood and drought damage. These factors have aggravated the shortage of water resources, increased costs of water purification, and in cases where appropriate infrastructure has not been in place, threatened the safety of drinking water, thus the health of the population. They also had serious impacts on the safety of industrial and agricultural production and led to losses in the fishing industry. It is estimated that the annual economic loss from water pollution in China reaches between 1.5 to 3 per cent of GDP, having more significant impact than floods and drought.[9] The problems are particularly acute in northern China (*i.e.* north of the Yangze River) and in the catchments of the three rivers: Huai, Hai and Huang (Yellow). These three catchments account for about 35 per cent of total GDP and include the economically and politically important Beijing-Tianjin region.

The main causes of water pollution are industrial wastewater discharge, untreated municipal sewage discharge as well as non-point pollution from agriculture. In recent years, non-point water pollution, which originates from fertiliser and pesticide runoff, and discharges from intensive animal production enterprises, have become serious and can be expected to increase even further.

Quality of surface and coastal water and groundwater

The chemical and biological quality of the surface water is generally low. The main pollutants are organic material from domestic and industrial sources, industrial hydrocarbons, light lubricating oil, plant nutrients and heavy metals. Bacteriological pollution is probably widespread and substantial, though not regularly monitored.

From 1996 to 1998, the water quality in almost all seven main river basins deteriorated (Figure 17.1). Among these river basins, the organic pollution in Liao River, Hai River and Huai River is considered very serious. For instance, in the Hai River the proportion of monitoring sections with water quality classified as Class I to III decreased from 58.9 per cent in 1996 to 28 per cent in 1998, while the share of the sections with Class IV and below jumped from 41.1 per cent in 1996 to 72 per cent in 1998.[10]

It is estimated that 25 per cent of all lakes in China is being adversely affected by eutrophication which is a result of heavy organic pollution and excessive pollution by nutrients (mainly nitrogen and phosphorus) from agricultural production and urbanisation. In 1999, the watershed of Tai Lake (Jiangsu-Zhejiang Provinces) was at medium level of eutrophication while Chao Lake (Anhui Province) and Dianci Lake (Yunnan Province) were hyper-eutrophic. The main consequences of eutrophication are shifts in the biological structure in standing waters, production of toxins potentially poisonous to fish, cattle and humans, and increased costs of water purification.

585

Figure 17.1. **Comparison of surface water quality in seven main rivers in 1996 and 1998**

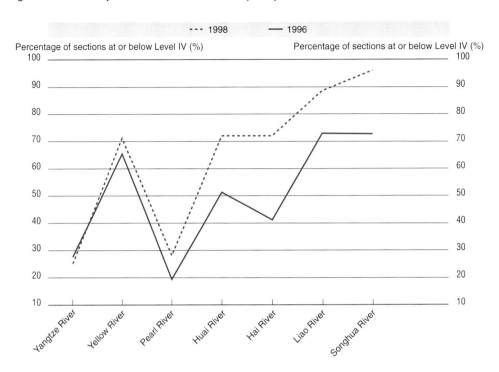

Source: State of the Environment Report, State Administration of Environmental Protection, 1997-1999.

The coastal waters are mainly polluted by increasing industrial and municipal wastewater discharge, solid waste dumping, agricultural run-off and waste from ships. The most serious pollutant is inorganic nitrogen, followed by phosphate and oil. In about one third of the sampling points the coastal waters in China are classified as Class IV[11] or below. An indirect indication of eutrophication in China's coastal areas is the incidence of red tides, which increased significantly during the 1990s.

The quality of groundwater is worsening, particularly in near-surface aquifers and in the vicinity of major cities. The most common pollutants are nitrate, nitrite and ammonia infiltrating groundwater from leaking sewers and overflowing septic tanks. There are no systematic data on contaminants such as pesticides, herbicides, heavy metals or other potentially toxic compounds. In many places over-extraction of groundwater is a serious problem and has not been adequately controlled.

Water availability and use

China has substantial water resources but they are unevenly distributed. On average, per capita water availability in China is 2 343 m³/person/year with the availability being almost four times higher in the southern rivers than the northern rivers.[12] Availability of water in many northern rivers (including the Huai and Huang basins) is lower than 1 000 m³/person/year – which is the internationally accepted definition of water scarcity. In the north, the water resource accounts for only 7.7 per cent while the arable land accounts for 39 per cent and the population for 35 per cent of the total. In the northwestern inland river basins, the land area accounts for 35 per cent while the water resource accounts for only 4.8 per cent. The rainfall is highly seasonal, in most areas 60-80 per cent of precipitation is observed within 4 months of the flood season. Groundwater resources are significant only in the northern river systems, particularly in the lower catchments of the Huai, Hai and Huang Rivers.

The annual water use increased in China from the initial value around 100 billion m^3 in 1949 to 556 billion m^3 in 1997.[13] Water use projections show that 700-800 billion m^3 will be consumed in 2030, approaching the actual water resource availability of 800-900 billion m^3.

Agriculture, industrial and urban residential water use accounts for 75.3 per cent, 20.2 per cent and 4.5 per cent respectively. Contrary to the patterns in most OECD countries, agricultural use is still dominant by far. However, its share in total water use has decreased, along with water consumption for industrial purposes. Conversely, domestic water uses have been increasing rapidly (Figure 17.2). Domestic water consumption in urban areas rose from around 113 litre/capita/day in 1980 to about 230 litre/capita/day in 1997.[14] At the same time, in urban areas in China out of 640 cities more than 300 face water shortages and 100 face severe water scarcities.

The latest national demand projections, prepared in 1999 by the Institute of Water Resources and Hydropower of the Ministry of Water Resources, indicate that the balance between irrigation and other consumptive uses will continue to change in the future. Water use for irrigation purposes is projected to decline from current levels of approximately 75 per cent of total consumption to 50 per cent in 2050. Consumption for urban and industrial purposes will increase significantly. Both of these forms of consumption lead to emissions of polluted water, so it is likely that water pollution pressures will increase substantially.[15]

Inefficient use of water in China is widespread. The average utilisation coefficient of farmland irrigation water is 0.45, while the value in developed countries is 0.7-0.8. The industrial water use per unit of output value was 5-10 times that of the OECD countries. The reuse rate of industrial water was 30-40 per cent while in OECD countries it reaches 75-85 per cent. The loss rate of water use facilities and water supply pipelines in most cities is more than 20 per cent.[16]

Drinking water quality in urban and rural areas

In absolute terms, China has the largest urban population of any country in the world, and urbanisation has been increasing. The official annual growth rate of the urban population through

Figure 17.2. **Changes in water consumption for municipal and industrial purposes, 1990-1999**

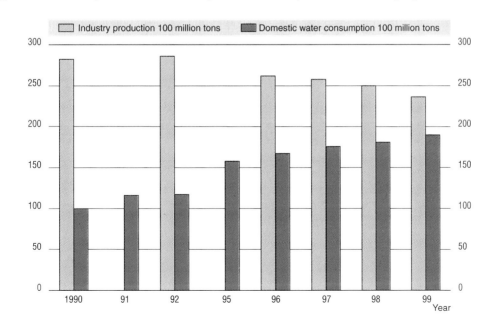

Figure 17.3. **Comparison of discharges wastewater from industry and households, 1991-2000**

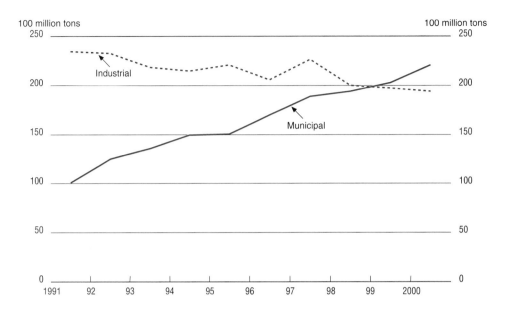

Source: State of the Environment, State Administration of Environmental Protection.

the 1990s was about 3.1 per cent, while the actual rate was probably higher. Urbanisation is expected to accelerate even further over the next 10 to 20 years. The number of officially designated cities increased by about 40 per cent to 668. Total water consumption in designated cities increased at a rate of about 8 per cent per year. Although installed wastewater treatment capacity increased at an even greater rate of about 19 per cent per year, the length of sewers increased at only about half that rate.[17] Although the level of wastewater discharges from industry has decreased, an increased amount of wastewater released from municipal sources will require expansion of municipal wastewater treatment infrastucture (Figure 17.3).

Due to heavy surface water and groundwater pollution and lack of water supply facilities, especially in rural areas, the quality of drinking water in China is low. Even though water supply coverage in the cities was 96.8 per cent in 1998, three-quarters of the drinking water leaving water supply plants did not meet standard requirements.[18] In rural areas, however, the tap water beneficiaries in the late 1990s accounted for only 23.3 per cent of the whole population, half of which is served with drinking water that does not comply with national standards. It should be noted that China's current standards on drinking water quality, introduced in 1986, are much lower than those defined by the World Health Organisation (WHO). For example only 35 quality indicators are measured in China, far less than that of the standards of WHO (49), Japan (59), EU (66) and the US (83). In addition, thresholds for several indicators are lower. For instance, China's standard for turbidity is three to five times lower than that in OECD countries. The standard values in rural areas are even less stringent.

Air pollution

Air pollution is affecting both human health and the environment and it will continue to be one of the major environmental problems in China in the future. Studies carried out by the World Bank have linked the high incidence of premature death in China to serious ambient and indoor pollution. About one third of the territory of China is affected by acid rain, which can retard forest and crop growth and endanger aquatic life. Coal burning is the main contributor to ambient and indoor air pollution in China, but air pollution from motor vehicle emissions is growing fast and is likely to become a major and widespread urban pollution problem over the next 10 years. Re-suspension of surface dust from construction sites and eroded soil are important factors affecting air quality in many northern cities, such as Beijing and Xi'an.

Urban air quality

The main air pollutants are total suspended particulates (TSP) and sulphur dioxide (SO_2). Ambient concentrations of TSP and SO_2 in Chinese cities are among the world's highest. In 1998, seven Chinese cities, with Taiyuan and Beijing ranked the first and third respectively, were among WHO's list of the world's ten most polluted cities in terms of air quality.[19] In 1995, more than one half of 88 cities monitored for SO_2 were above the WHO guidelines (in the cases of cities Taiyuan and Lanzhou by factor 10) and all but two of 87 cities monitored for TSP far exceeded the WHO guidelines.[20]

More recently, rapid expansion of motor vehicle fleets in large cities has heightened ambient pollution by carbon monoxide (CO), nitrogen oxides (NO_x), and related pollutants which contribute to deterioration of the urban air quality by causing serious local photochemical smog pollution (Figure 17.4). The pollution of NO_x in some major cities with a population of more than 1 million (such as Guangzhou, Beijing, Shanghai, Anshan, Wuhan, Zhengzhou, Shenyang, Lanzhou, Dalian, Hangzhou) is growing, exceeding the Class 2 standard[21] by factor 2. Among 60 cities with reported monitoring data, total human exposure to ambient NO_x levels above the Class 2 level increased by almost 60 per cent between 1991 and 1998. Nearly all of the increase occurred in the 32 largest cities. Ambient levels of other pollutants such as carbon monoxide (CO), ozone (O_3) and lead (Pb) are not systematically controlled.

Indoor air pollution is also a serious problem as about 80 per cent of China's people still use solid fuel, such as coal, firewood and crop stalks for cooking and space heating. Burning this fuel in inadequately ventilated households leads to serious indoor air pollution.

Figure 17.4. **Concentrations of NO_x and the trends in motor vehicle numbers in China, 1980-1998**

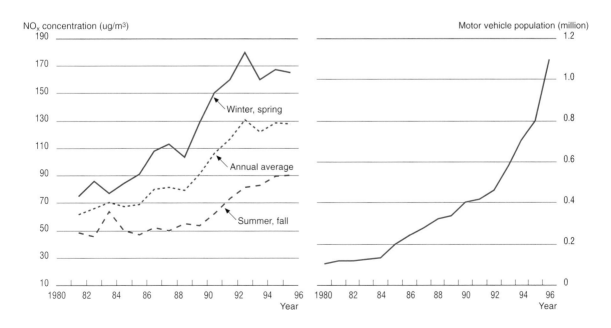

Source: Zhang S., 2001.

Acid rain

Human-induced acid rain deposition in China is mainly associated with SO_2 emissions originating from burning coal with high sulphur content that dominates the fuel mix.

China is among the world's three major acid rain regions, following Europe and North America. After a sharp increase in the areas affected by acid rain pollution in the 1980s, the situation has stabilised in recent years. Serious acid rain pollution, which affects 30 per cent of the country's territory, occurs in some regions of central China, represented by cities such as Chansha, Zhuzhou, Ganzhou and Nanchang.[22]

Impacts of air pollution

Many Chinese cities have concentrations of fine particulates and sulphur dioxide that are the highest in the world. Based on dose-response functions, it was estimated by the World Bank that nearly 178 000 deaths per year or 7 per cent of all deaths in urban areas in China could be prevented if air pollution were reduced to standard levels. Also, 346 000 hospitalisations per year were found associated with the excess levels of air pollution in urban areas. Major consequences of air pollution include respiratory infections, asthma, and chronic bronchitis. The serious health consequences of indoor air pollution due to combustion of coal have been documented in several studies in China.[23]

The decline of forests and crops, damage to buildings and fabrics are examples of acidification. According to a study carried out by the environmental authorities in 1994, the annual economic loss from acid rain in China is about 14 billion RMB, including loss of agriculture and forests products.[24]

Air pollution is also impairing visibility in the cities through light scattering. In Beijing, partly due to high levels of fine particulate and the effect of photochemical smog, low air visibility is frequent in winter. In Guangzhou, visibility decreased from 30 km in the 1960s to 18 km in the 1990s, and the annual sunshine time has also decreased by more than 800 hr over the past 30 years.

Global environmental issues

In terms of air emission, China's two most important global concerns are emissions of carbon dioxide (CO_2) from burning fossil fuel and the production and consumption of ozone-depleting substances (ODS).[25] CO_2 emissions contribute to global warming and ODS to the damage to the ozone layer.

Growth in energy demand, particularly coal, increased rapidly during the first half of the 1990s, which has resulted in a 21 per cent increase of carbon emissions between 1990 and 1998.[26] China's global share of CO_2 emissions increased from 10 per cent to 12 per cent during the 1990s. In the next 20 years, the power sector could become the dominant user of coal, accounting for 50 per cent or more of total coal consumption.

China's consumption of ODS grew by more than 12 per cent per annum from 1986 to 1994. After ODS in developed countries were phased out by 1995, China became the world's largest ODS producer and consumer. Although production and consumption of ODS in China were banned in 1999, a number of cases of ODS import have been recorded.

Waste

Industrial solid waste

Industrial waste, and especially toxic and hazardous waste, can affect the environment and human health, by contaminating the soil and groundwater, by leaching toxic substances such as heavy metals and metalloids, nitrogen compounds, chlorinated compounds and other organics. Industrial solid wastes in China are mostly smelting wastes, coal ash, slag, coal refuses, chemical waste residues, tailings and radioactive wastes. In 1999, 780 million tonnes of industrial solid waste were generated, among which 38.8 million tonnes, including 10.2 million tonnes of hazardous waste, were finally disposed of. The rate of the utilisation and safe disposal of industrial solid waste was only 45.6 per cent and 13.7 per cent respectively.[27]

The discharged industrial wastes have inevitably led to great or potential environmental and health problems. The toxic and hazardous heavy metals and their compounds as well as phenols and radioactive substances can have immediate or potential impact on human health through skin contact, food contamination and respiration. Indirect impacts include the lowering quality of surface water and groundwater, and contamination of soil and ecosystems.

Municipal solid waste

China's annual generation of municipal solid waste (MSW) per capita jumped from 320 kg in the early 1980s to about 540 kg in the 1990s.[28] Due to the rapid growth of cities and urban population, the total amount of solid waste is increasing by 8-10 per cent annually. According to statistics in 668 cities in 1999, over 114 million tonnes of MSW were collected, of which over 72 million tonnes (which account for 63.5 per cent of the total) were treated. The municipal waste composition has changed with the increased share of organic, combustible, recoverable and reusable matters.

Municipal solid waste generation imposes significant environmental pressures, especially when inefficient waste treatment and disposal lead to an accumulative piling of large amounts of solid waste. In 1998, two-thirds of 668 cities were surrounded by solid waste dumping sites, occupying land of about 50 000 ha. Open central landfills are the most applied disposal procedure. In addition, methane – which is generated from the decomposition of organic components in municipal waste disposal sites – may cause explosions. According to recent studies, at least 20 cities experienced such explosion incidents in 1999.[29]

Nature and land

Land degradation

China's growth and development is having a significant impact on its land systems. China is now considered one of the most seriously eroded countries in the world. The Chinese Academy of Sciences (CAS) estimates that in the early 1990s some 375 million hectares, or nearly 40 per cent of the country, were affected by moderate to severe erosion and desertification. The biggest problems are water and wind erosion, followed by salinisation.

Due to over-intensified use of marginal lands, inappropriate use of pesticides and fertilisers, and improper irrigation practices, a number of agricultural ecological problems have occurred. China is experiencing a continuous loss of cultivated area. The Chinese Academy of Sciences has estimated that the net cultivated land area is declining by over 300 000 hectares per year.

Desertification is occurring most visibly in the agro-pastoral zone in northern China. In this area, the most significant contributor to this process over the past 50 years was excessive land reclamation during the 1960s and 1970s, combined with an excessive build-up in livestock numbers in the 1960s. Both were driven by the government's drive for food self-sufficiency. Generally, it appears that the desertification trend throughout the region has progressively worsened through the 1980s and possibly into the 1990s, notwithstanding government control efforts in the late 1980s and 1990s.[30]

Forests

Before 1998, China's forests provided about 40 per cent of the country's rural energy, almost all the panels and lumber for the construction sector, and raw material for the pulp and paper industry. China was the third largest consumer of timber in the world, and was already facing a widening imbalance between supply and demand for wood products. In the early 1990s the forestland area in China was 260 million hectares and the forest area was 130 million ha.[31] The per capita forest area was 0.11 hectares, about 17.2 per cent of the world average figure and ranking the 119th in the world. At the rate of extraction that applied until 1998 (around 300 million m^3/year), the resource had less than 10 years of remaining life.[32]

This situation changed following the devastating floods in the middle reaches of the Yangtze River and in northeast China during the summer of 1998, which many local environmental experts said were caused at least in part by deforestation in the catchments of the rivers in these areas. As a result, the State Council imposed in 1998 a ban on logging in natural forests. The opening of new lands at the expense of forests was prohibited, all construction projects on forestland were frozen for one year; and a new requirement for direct cabinet approval for any occupation of forested land was introduced. In addition, a major new investment programme (Natural Forest Protection Programme – NFPP) was launched to improve natural forest management, covering approximately 95 million hectares of state-owned forests in 17 provinces. Finally, a new land-use law was enacted to promote more efficient use of land and increased afforestation.[33]

Biodiversity

China has one of the greatest ranges of ecological diversity of any country in the world, and probably contains around 10 per cent of all species living on earth. It has an especially high number of plant species (about 30 000), including 3 116 genera, of which 243 are endemic. Vertebrate diversity is also high with 2 340 species, including 499 species of mammals, 1 244 species of birds, 387 species of reptiles, and 274 species of amphibians.[34]

China is also one of the eight original centres of crop diversity in the world. It is the original source of approximately 200 of the world's 1 200 species of cultivated crops. It contains nearly 600 varieties of domesticated animals and poultry. A wide variety of domestic plant and animal species are harvested and used for economic purposes. The Ministry of Agriculture estimates there are more than 3 000 species of wild "economic" plants, including 1 000 species of medicinal plants, 300 species of timber trees, and 500 plants with insecticidal properties. There are also 330 species of "economic" birds, 190 economic mammals, and 60 species of economic fish.

However, biodiversity in China is being threatened due to a large human population, economic development, and excessive utilisation of biological resources and shrinking of natural habitats. It is estimated that 15-20 per cent of the species in China is now endangered. This significantly exceeds the global average that 10-15 per cent of species is considered threatened. Of the 640 species listed in CITES,[35] 156, or nearly 25 per cent, are found in China.

Main pressures on the environment and future trends in light of trade and investment liberalisation

Over the decades unsustainable and inefficient investment, production, and consumption patterns have led to serious deterioration of the environment. These pressures came from rapid industrialisation based on pollution-intensive industries and inefficient technologies, reliance on low-quality coal in the energy sector, and lack of appropriate pollution control technologies. Inefficient practices and the use of low-quality fertilisers and pesticides in agriculture imposed high pressures on human health, water and land resources. Overuse of natural resources, such as water and forests, limited the natural processes of their renewal.

However, recent changes in the structure of the economy, in particular an increasing share of less-polluting industries and the introduction of modern technologies, combined with environmental policies, have led to some significant reduction of environmental pressures. These changes have been, in many cases, stimulated by liberalisation of trade and investment, which created greater competition in the economy, opened up Chinese enterprises' access to modern technologies, and increased the efficiency of operations. Liberalised trade and investment stimulated better use of natural resources and promoted demand for better environment. The gross value of industrial output doubled between 1991 and 1998, while total discharge of major pollutants increased only slightly. Water pollution, especially from small enterprises and TVIEs, decreased significantly, emissions of particulates and other pollutants have been curbed, pressures on water quality from the use of pesticides and fertilisers in agriculture decreased.[36]

In many cases, however, the positive changes have been offset by emerging new problems stemming from the fast growing market economy and continuous population growth. A decrease in the emission of conventional point source pollutants, such as particulates and SO_2, is accompanied by an increased significance of intractable and non-point source pollution. Rapid growth of motor vehicles in urban areas leads to increased CO and NO_x emissions which add to low air quality. Fast urbanisation leads to additional pressures on drinking water resources and increased discharges of untreated wastewater. Urban encroachment has led to the loss of approximately 1 million hectares of cultivated land between 1987 and 1995.

These developments have occurred in the context of weak, or in many cases the lack of adequate, environmental policies. For example, the high speed of urbanisation has not been accompanied by provisions for parallel development of appropriate infrastructure and physical planning policies, and the increased use of motor vehicles has not been accompanied by appropriate exhaust emission standards. It is expected, however, that the continuation of structural changes in the Chinese economy, increased modernisation of the economy through investment and trade liberalisation, along with the parallel application of appropriate policies, will lead to gradual reductions of these pressures in the long-term perspective.

Pressures and trends in the energy sector

China is the world's second energy consumer and the third largest energy producer. It is also the largest producer of coal and the sixth largest producer of crude oil. At the same time, energy consumption, especially generated from coal burning (which currently provides about 76 per cent of China's energy needs), is the main source of anthropogenic air pollution in China. A majority (60 per cent) of the fuel combusted is consumed in the industrial sector, and only 5 per cent in the commercial sector.[37] Sixty five per cent of China's power generating capacity is concentrated in the industrial and heavily polluted east, south central, and southwest regions. China is also the world's second largest emitter of carbon dioxide, accounting for 14 per cent of the world's total emissions, and is projected to become the largest over the next few decades.[38] China's industrial sector is, by far, the largest source of China's carbon emissions, producing 75 per cent of total emissions. Small industrial enterprises (essentially TVIEs) are the main source of particulate emissions, while medium-sized and large industrial enterprises dominate SO_2 emissions, with the main sources being power plants.

Energy efficiency in China is quite low by the standards of industrialised countries. The average thermal efficiency of China's power plants is 25 to 29 per cent compared to rates of 35 and 38 per cent in industrialised countries. In other segments of energy generation the difference is even higher, *e.g.* 52 per cent compared to 72 per cent of industrial boilers, 28 per cent compared to 52 per cent in iron and steel heat generation, and 15 per cent compared to 55 per cent of commercial and household energy use.[39]

Since the early 1990s, China's deficit in energy has sharply increased due to its rapid economic expansion. This gap in China's energy needs and available resources is certain to grow wider in the coming decades. Conscious of its rising dependency on external energy sources and of the need to improve its energy sector efficiency and competitiveness on the world market, China began a radical restructuring and reform of its energy industries and management in 1998, apparently trying to introduce a more market-oriented approach in the energy sector. Chinese power authorities have made improving energy efficiency a priority. It is envisaged to increase the average thermal efficiency of power generation by discouraging the building of small plants, introducing higher efficiency units, and retrofitting or eliminating low-efficiency units. In the power sector, China lacks both the manufacturing capacity to supply the needed generating equipment and the required financial resources. It was estimated that only 80 per cent of the investment needed to meet the year 2000 capacity targets could be generated by domestic resources. Thus, the central government has made attracting foreign direct investment to the power generation sector an explicit goal. Foreign direct investment is not only

Box 17.2. China's challenge to reduce negative environmental impacts

... from mining and the use of coal in the energy sector:

As the world's largest producer and consumer of coal, China faces "special needs" in managing and balancing the environmental consequences of a growing economy fuelled primarily by coal. There are readily identifiable potential areas for environmental improvement throughout the whole of the coal chain. Opportunities exist to improve mining methods to reduce methane emission levels and improve underground mine safety. Management of water and land resources can be improved through the introduction of modern mining practices.

Solid waste disposal is a major problem and can be addressed by increasing the proportion of coal washed. This would have the benefit of improving the quality of coal fed into power stations, thereby improving thermal efficiencies and reducing the costs of boiler maintenance. Significant problems are also caused through the use of high ash coal and the lack of scrubbers in power stations. The pattern of coal use, with so many residential and domestic consumers burning coal directly, is a further significant cause of environmental air pollution.

Many of the environmental problems facing China can be addressed through the transfer of technology in both the mining sector and in the use of coal. However, in China there is strong competition for a limited amount of capital. Whilst the benefits of adopting existing, more efficient technologies may be obvious to the outside world, from China's perspective there must be an economic benefit as well as a social (environmental) benefit for a technology transfer project to rank high in China's overall agenda. This is not a problem peculiar to China; it is common for all developing countries.

In China's case, there is a large potential to significantly improve the country's environmental emission levels through the transfer of existing and proven technology. Much can be done through the exchange and implementation of what is standard practice in the mining and power industries in other parts of the world. Major improvements can be achieved across a wide spectrum of environmental issues with "off-the-shelf" technology transfers. However, in order to take advantage of the available technology, the Chinese authorities must address a number of the legitimate concerns of their foreign partners:

- First, there is a need to fully recognise intellectual property rights and ensure the legal means of protecting these rights.

- Second, China is perceived as a higher risk country which, when coupled with the existing low levels of return, discourages potential investors. Positive encouragement is needed to provide foreign investors with the confidence to invest.

- Third, the implementation of new technology may be slow because of China's desire to develop its own home-grown version. Given the pace of economic development and the escalation in environmental problems resulting from that growth, China may not be able to afford the luxury of waiting for the development of home-grown solutions. China may need to embrace more quickly much of the new technology if it is to achieve acceptable standards of environmental management.

... and by reducing energy subsidies:

Although not primarily prompted by climate change concerns, China has made remarkable progress in reducing energy subsidies since the mid-1980s. This is particularly the case for subsidies to the coal sector. Subsidy rates for coal have fallen from 61 per cent in 1984 to 11 per cent in 1995. At the same time, China removed price controls on coal, and encouraged the development of private coal mines. This subsidy reform has produced multiple benefits. The economic performance of coal mines has improved rapidly, reducing government spending and – along with other policy reforms and technological change – contributing to energy conservation and environmental protection. Energy intensity has fallen by 30 per cent since 1985, leading to energy consumption (in oil equivalents) and CO_2 emissions, respectively, 0.3 billion metric tons and 1.1 billion metric tons less than if the reform had not taken place.

Source: *Coal in the Energy Supply of China*, IEA, 1999.

Figure 17.5. **Domestic supply and net oil import in China**

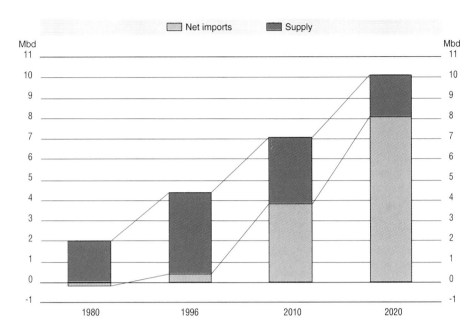

Source: IEA, *World Energy Outlook*, 1998.

attractive as a source of funds, but it also has the potential to enhance energy efficiency by expediting the transfer of advanced and cleaner generating technologies and management techniques. It is estimated that by upgrading technologies in power generation, and in several major industrial energy activities to industrialised-country levels, China could cut 20 per cent of its projected coal consumption. However, there are still some obstacles to the rapid transfer of new technologies to China which relate to establishing an appropriate framework for ensuring intellectual property rights, lowering risks, and reluctance to open the markets to foreign technologies, as well as the proper pricing of energy and electricity (Box 17.2).

Continuing rapid growth will also require diversification of energy sources. The gap between domestic oil and gas production and demand is widening. From 1990 to 1995, China's oil demand grew from 4.3 per cent per year, while oil production increased by only 1.2 per cent. As a result of these trends, China has become a net oil importer and in order to bridge the gap China will need to import more than 8 million barrels a day by 2020 (Figure 17.5). This will make it a major importer in the world oil markets. It is expected that the substitution of high polluting coal by other sources of energy will contribute to reducing environmental pressures and stabilise or lower emissions of "greenhouse gases".

Pressures and trends in industrial development

It is estimated that discharges from industry – including power plants – account for more than 70 per cent of national pollutant emissions. Many polluting industries, dominated by the refining, smelting, metallurgical, chemical, machinery, textiles, leather, timber processing, as well as pulp and paper sectors, are located in densely populated metropolitan areas, exposing urban residents to serious health risks.

In recent years growth has been uneven among various industrial sub-sectors, with some of the most polluting industries experiencing reduction in outputs. This has led to reductions in the overall pollution loads. Many sub-sectors in heavy industry that are important sources of intractable pollution have been growing at rates significantly lower than the all-industrial average. At the same time, less-polluting industries (such as electronics, communications, and household appliances) have been growing at proportionately higher rates. Certainly, not all the "new" industries are without pollution problems, but growth and development favour industries that tend to use fewer raw materials and tend to produce less pollution per unit of output. World Bank estimates show that industrial pollution loads (indexed emission of three major pollutants: COD, sulphur dioxide and soot) increased at much lower rates than industrial output during the 1989-99 period, and that they actually declined after 1995. Some of these effects are the result of an increased regulatory effectiveness, but industrial restructuring also played an important role. The switch to a more competitive, demand-driven industrial sector has also led to an increased earning retention and re-investment. This has increased technological innovation and resource use efficiency, allowing the reduction of industrial pollution intensity per unit of output value.[40]

Industrial restructuring also has narrowed the primary sources of industrial pollution leading to a situation where high quantities of industrial pollution load continued to be emitted by a small sector of industry. As of 1998, just eight industrial sub-sectors were discharging about 85 per cent of all industrial pollution. In several cases, these sub-sectors were making only modest contributions to gross industrial output value (GIOV). For example, the pulp and paper sector generated about 46 per cent of industrial chemical oxygen demand, but only 1.8 per cent of GIOV. The industrial structure is still characterised by relatively polluting upstream manufacturing, but as industrial reform continues, the share of downstream, less polluting, and high value-added manufacturing is expected to increase.[41]

Prior to 1996 TVIEs were a significant source of pollution. Between 1990 and 1995, they increased their combined pollutant emissions by about 120 per cent, while emissions from SOEs actually declined by 9 per cent. Following a major pollution incident in July 1994 in the Huai River, the central government adopted drastic new pollution control measures for TVIEs in 1996, and launched a national campaign to close down some 72 000 highly polluting TVIEs in 15 sub-sectors. About 65 000 were actually shut down, including over 1 000 paper mills. This emergency shutdown programme had a measurable impact on industrial wastewater emissions (although it also had potentially serious adverse social impacts). Some 20 to 30 per cent restarted, either illegally or after bringing their enterprises into compliance with relevant discharge standards.[42]

Further economic restructuring, combined with further liberalisation of trade and investment, will affect various branches of industry as well as their contribution to environmental problems. The industries most adversely affected will be the "smokestack" industries. The reduction in production from this sector will positively influence the environment, as these are usually significant pollution sources and are frequently characterised by their low state of technological development, low product quality, and high consumption of raw materials, including energy and waste. At the same time, it is expected that economic changes will lead to growth in such sectors as electronics, textiles, leather, food processing, and other light manufacturing. Most of these industries are less pollution intensive and their management is more efficient. These factors should help to reduce their contribution to environmental pollution. Some of these industries, such as leather and food processing, can be significant sources of pollution, so it would be important that they are brought into the regulatory network.

The environmental performance of industrial firms depends on the amount of earnings invested in technology improvement, or the installation of new technology. Faced with stronger competition as well as environmental regulations and tougher enforcement, many Chinese enterprises improved the efficiency of resource use. For example, over the past ten years industrial energy intensity declined by 50 per cent. More efficient technology is estimated to account for about one third of this improvement. However, there is still considerably more room for improvement. There is potential for increasing industrial water use efficiency, which has traditionally been very low in China, partly due to low water prices. Some examples include the chemical and paper manufacturing sectors, which are the leading water polluting industries in China. In some areas, particularly north China, increased water scarcity is leading to increased prices and an increased interest on the part of enterprises in water saving technology and other cleaner production strategies.

Since the beginning of the 1990s, the environmental goods and services industry has become a new sector in the Chinese national economy. Although it has developed quickly it accounts now for only 0.85 per cent of GDP. The current structure of this industry is unbalanced with most of the firms (over 90 per cent) operating in coastal provinces and the industry is dominated by small and medium-sized enterprises. The participation of foreign companies is very limited. With the projected increase of investment in protecting the environment and the improvement of the nation's environmental awareness, more environmental pollution control and treatment installations will be needed, and the market demand for these services will significantly increase. It is estimated that the industry will surpass 250 billion RMB of the annual production value and account for over 2 per cent of GDP in the year 2010. The development of this industry, and opening the sector to foreign investors can provide much needed pollution control and treatment equipment and provide additional employment in the Chinese economy.[43]

Pressures and trends in agriculture

The increasing use of fertilisers has been a major factor in the increase in grain and food consumption in China over the last 50 years. Total fertiliser consumption increased by more than 500 per cent between 1980 and 1998, by which time it amounted to about 41 million metric tons a year. Applied fertilisers are the main non-point sources of nutrients that contribute significantly to eutrophication, which occurs in many lakes throughout China and also in near-shore marine areas.

Pesticides played a part in the agricultural sector's growth in output. In the early 1950s, total domestic pesticide production was only about 1 000 tons. By 1999, this increased to about 625 000 tonnes, by which time China had become the second largest producer and consumer in the world. In the early 1980s, China produced high volumes of pesticides with a high proportion of "high-toxicity, high-residue" chemicals. Domestic production of most of these toxic compounds was banned in 1983. As a result, total domestic pesticide production declined by about 60 per cent in 1985. As production recovered through the late 1980s and 1990s, the range of chemicals produced changed, but not very advantageously from an environmental point of view. Two of the top three insecticides produced in 1996 were classified as WHO Class 1 (highest toxicity) chemicals. The ban of high-toxicity chemicals was not completely effective, and there remains a substantial domestic trade, and perhaps also production, of the supposedly banned chemicals. The main environmental effects from the overuse of pesticides are the occurrence of pesticide residues in Chinese food crops and biodiversity impacts. Residues in vegetables, fruit and meat can affect the health of the population in China and other countries through exports.

While per capita grain production has been declining, the consumption of animal products has increased significantly leading to the increase of domestic livestock production. Production of livestock raised in intensive production units can be a significant source of solid and liquid waste, as well as odours. The World Bank estimates that the COD[44] load in untreated piggery wastes was about 2.6 million tonnes in 1996 and will be about 8.2 million tonnes in 2010, representing 28 per cent and 90 per cent respectively of current urban and industrial COD loads. One recent study estimated that, in certain areas within the Huai and Hai River basins, current COD loads from all livestock already amount to between 30 per cent (in Zhangjiakou) and 80 per cent (in Chengde) of industrial COD loads.

In general, it is expected that land-intensive industries, such as forestry products, plantation, and water-intensive grain production and tradition husbandry, would decrease their share in agriculture production. These changes are likely to reduce pressures on land and natural resources, such as water and forests. For example, the grain production sector will experience reductions in the use of chemical fertilisers and pesticides and therefore reduce non-point sources of pollution. It will also reduce the use of water for irrigation purposes.[45]

Pressures and trends in urban development

China's urban population is vast and growing rapidly. The current "official" urban population is estimated at 400 million people, or 30 per cent of the population. Each year during the 1990s, it grew by about 10 million people. It is considered that the actual urban population is much larger, about 455 million, or 36 per cent of the total population. A World Bank model predicts that by the year 2002, 42 per cent of the population, more than 600 million people, will live in urban areas, concentrated in eastern and southeastern provinces.

The Chinese authorities estimate that urbanisation growth rates will be maintained at 0.5-1.0 per cent per annum during the period of the Tenth Five-Year Plan. This implies a substantial increase in urbanisation over the next 10 years. The demand for urban environmental infrastructure, which is already high, will increase accordingly. This will represent another significant environmental challenge for the government. Priority environmental issues in China's urban areas include air pollution, municipal wastewater treatment, solid waste management and urban encroachment in arable land.

Residential and commercial emissions to air, while relatively small compared to industrial emissions, usually cause much more significant pollution effects because of their low emission height and proximity to residential areas. The principal source of this emission is burning fossil fuel. The residential sector accounts for approximately 15 per cent of total use of coal, yet it is estimated that it contributes to more than 30 per cent of urban ground-level air pollution. China has promoted the use of gaseous fuels, especially in large cities. Largely as a result of government investment, about one third of urban residents in China now have access to gas for cooking, and coal-burning households are increasingly turning to the use of cleaner and more efficient briquettes. As a result, SO_2 and TSP pollution have declined significantly.

These reductions, however, have been accompanied by increased pollution from motor vehicles following the sharp increase in the number of cars, especially in the biggest cities. The number of vehicles has tripled between 1986 and 1996, and if the growth rate continues, their number will reach approximately 180 million cars by the year 2020, similar to the number of cars in the US. The main impact of motor vehicles is associated with the poor performance of engines of domestic-made vehicles, which often emit 5-6 times more pollutants (mostly NO_x and CO) than imported cars. Although emissions from individual car engines will decrease, pollution levels may not be affected, as these gains will be offset by the increase in the number of vehicles. It should be noted, however, that a government programme launched in 1997 to phase-out leaded gasoline should help significantly to reduce the health impact of urban transportation. Notwithstanding such initiatives, motor vehicles, and especially passenger cars, will be one of the main sources of urban air pollution in the future, taking account of the current projections of urban transportation growth.

The combination of a rapidly increasing urban population, increasing urban water supply service levels, and increasing per capita urban water consumption, are producing increases in municipal wastewater flows and pollutant loads. According to the SEPA, total wastewater flows and loads from municipal sources now exceed those from industrial sources. Despite double-digit growth of municipal wastewater treatment capacity over the last decade, Chinese cities continue to be under-served by sewers and wastewater treatment plants. It is estimated that only about 2 billion m^3 of non-industrial municipal wastewater received secondary treatment in 1998, representing only about 10 per cent of the total discharge. Given municipal water demand projections, current municipal wastewater treatment capacity will have to be nearly quadrupled over the next 20 years just to maintain the current level of municipal treatment service. If the level of service were to be doubled over the same period, and making no allowance for an increased acceptance of industrial flows, installed capacity would have to increase by six- or seven-fold, which will require massive investments.

There are several main constraints in the effective management of municipal waste in China. First, the current waste management and control system lacks sound regulatory mechanisms. Second, the waste collection and disposal charges are low and they do not cover the costs which are born by the public budgets. Third, unsuitable consumption patterns, including excessive packaging, have led to the increased waste volume. Fourth, the classification and screening system for hazardous waste has not been developed, which leads to contamination of municipal waste by toxic waste, such as batteries and used oil. The recovery and recycling rate of waste is very low, and waste treatment technologies are still at an early stage of development, with lack of facilities or low efficiency.

Substantial policy actions and investment will be required to improve urban environmental quality. Priorities include switching fuel for domestic and residential use; promotion of public transport, as well as increasing the efficiency of motor vehicle engines to reduce air pollution; increased municipal wastewater treatment capacity and extension of sewers to reduce water pollution; and better waste management and treatment. In addition, water and energy conservation as well as waste minimisation programmes should be launched to influence consumer behaviour. These changes, however, have to be underpinned by market-based pricing of environmental services in urban areas to increase incentives to save water and energy, switch to less polluting modes of transport and recover the costs of services.

Development of China's environmental protection policies and regulatory and institutional framework

Early stages of creating the basis for environmental protection in China

China's policy and institutional setting for environmental protection have undergone several transformations over recent decades, reflecting different stages of restructuring and an increasing emphasis placed by the government and society on environmental issues. The preparations for the 1972 United Nations Conference on the Human Environment (UNCHE) in Stockholm gave an important impetus to organising environmental management within the Chinese government. The first countrywide discussion on environmental protection was launched at the first National Conference in 1973. Following on from the conference, further analysis of the environmental consequences of economic development were carried out by a group of experts and officials under the State Council. This work resulted in the publication of a report entitled *Key Points in the Environmental Protection* in 1974. The report stated that China could not afford to adopt the approach of "polluting first and control pollution later" and presented a framework for administrative management of environmental protection at the national level.

As experience with different environmental management approaches accumulated, in 1979 the National People's Congress Standing Committee promulgated a provisional version of China's basic environmental law "The PRC Environmental Protection Law for Trial Implementation". This statute required polluters to comply with pollution and waste discharge standards, directed enterprises to assess environmental impacts of proposed projects, and ensured that new projects satisfied applicable environmental standards. This statute also established national and local environmental agencies. Following this trial period, the formal Environmental Protection Law of the People's Republic of China came into effect in 1989. This legal act now constitutes a basis for China's environmental protection system.[46]

Institutional framework

The first version of China's top environmental agency was the Environmental Protection Office, a unit with a staff of twenty set up in 1974 under the State Council. The office concentrated on planning and had no authority over lower levels of government. In 1982, three years after the promulgation of the trial environmental law, the State Council set up the Ministry of Urban and Rural Construction and Environmental Protection with the Environmental Protection Bureau within its structure. Subsequent reorganisations in 1984 and 1988 elevated the status of the environmental bureau to a separate office. First, the Bureau was renamed the National Environmental Protection Bureau. Its staff doubled in size (from 60 to 120 persons) and it became subordinated to the Ministry of Construction and the State Council's Environmental Protection Commission. The Bureau was then brought out from under the Ministry of Construction and renamed the National Environmental Protection Agency. In making this change, the State Council increased the agency's authority, more than doubled the number of staff (from 120 to 320), and signalled that the State Council attached importance to environmental protection. Like main line ministries, NEPA had direct links to the State Council.

In 1998 China's environmental agency was transformed again, renamed the State Environmental Protection Agency (SEPA) and upgraded to full ministerial rank. The restructuring involved dismantling the Ministry of Forestry and consolidating some of its staff and functions of NEPA. The fact that senior officials from other restructured ministries – Geology and Mineral Resources and the Chemical Industry – were appointed vice-administrators of SEPA, gave this institution even greater weight. With this new structure, the agency was in a better position to influence other government agencies. Notwithstanding this change, SEPA remains far less powerful than some other key ministries or agencies. The 1998 reorganisation unfortunately also dismantled the State Council's Environmental Protection Commission. With membership that included 31 ministries and commissions and several representatives of large enterprises and the media, the Commission had played an active role in policy-making, co-ordinating the environmental efforts of ministries, and assisting in resolving controversies in the proposed laws related to the environment. This change was regarded as a step which weakened the possibilities for proper co-ordination of environmental measures within the State Council.

In general, government organisations involved in environmental protection are organised hierarchically along three lines:

- environmental protection committees of people's congresses, responsible for proposing environmental laws;
- SEPA which formulates environmental policies and programmes, and environmental protection bureaus (EPBs)[47] which implement local and national regulations, and
- environmental protection commissions of people's governments which co-ordinate agency responses to pressing environmental problems.

China's SEPA now plays a key role in designing pollution control policies and programmes, but its role in day-to-day implementation of the regulations is limited. SEPA, which has a staff of a few hundred people, implements rules only for projects undertaken by the sectoral agencies at the national level, or activities that are of national significance. In all other cases, EPBs implement industrial pollution control rules and deal with enterprises on a daily basis.

There are several other administrative units at the national and sub-national level which play a significant role in environmental protection in China. These include sectoral ministries and agencies at the central level, mayor's offices, planning commissions and economic commissions, and industrial, finance and urban construction bureaus at the sub-national level. For example, mayor's offices undertake key decisions on large investment projects involving industrial development and environmental protection. They also settle disputes between the municipal EPBs and enterprises supervised by a municipality's industrial bureaus. Planning commissions at the county level and above are responsible for revising EPBs' environmental protection plans and integrating them into local economic and social development plans. Many industrial bureaus have environmental protection divisions that assist enterprises associated with their bureaus with technical aspects of pollution control.

Current policy and legal framework

In 1996 the National People's Congress approved China's Ninth Five-Year Plan for Social and Economic Development, which for the first time included environmental goals. Several months later, the State Council approved the Ninth Five-Year Plan for Environmental Protection and Long-Term Targets to the Year 2010. Two implementation strategy documents were attached to the latter: one describing a national programme to control total waste discharge (which represented an important shift from concentration-based to mass-based control of pollution emissions), and the second detailing China's "Trans-century Green Projects". The "Trans-century" programme included a list of over 800 pollution abatement projects to be implemented in the context of the Ninth Five-Year Plan.

In the year 2000, China's Tenth Five-Year Plan for Social and Economic Development was elaborated and approved along with the Tenth Five-Year Plan for Environmental Protection. The environmental plan set the new goals for the following five years taking account of progress in implementing the provisions of the previous plan. Its emphasis continued to be placed on further curbing all forms of pollution, including reducing the length of polluted sections in the main rivers, lowering acid deposition across China, and addressing more vigorously pollution from agricultural sources. Other goals included slowing down the trend in destruction of natural habitats and improving environmental quality in major municipalities and regions. Further elaboration of environmental legislation and resource management strategies aimed to strengthen the enforcement of environmental legislation and increase environmental expenditure.

In addition to the basic environmental law of 1989, China has more than twenty special environmental statutes. The State Council, SEPA and other state agencies have issued numerous administrative regulations to implement environmental policies stipulated in the basic and special environmental laws. Many of the priority environmental problems are the subject of national plans and programmes. Several of China's environmental programmes are tied to international agreements, such as the "Country Programme for the Phase-out of Ozone Depleting Substances under the Montreal Protocol".

The current framework of regulations, supplemented by economic, voluntary, and public disclosure instruments, provides a good basis for effective pollution control. The regulatory framework (mainly based on so called "command-and-control" instruments) has been developed in the most comprehensive way (Box 17.3). It includes a number of instruments and programmes, such as environmental discharge and quality standards, Environmental Impact Assessment (EIA) and reporting, a variation of compliance schedules called "pollution control within deadlines", a discharge permit system and pollution control management called "centralised pollution control".

The application of economic instruments for environmental protection has been increasing. This category of instruments includes, *inter alia*, a pollution discharge fee system and non-compliance fees. Under the discharge fee system enterprises must pay fees for releases on air-borne and water-borne pollutants. In addition to paying fees for the release of pollutants beyond standards (non-compliance fee), enterprises violating requirements may have to pay four other kinds of penalty charges, referred to as "four small pieces". These fees serve the purpose of penalising the breaching of environmental requirements, such as long-lasting non-compliance, non-compliance by new enterprises (or failure to comply with administrative orders requiring pollution control by a fixed date), penalty for non- or late fee payment, and finally, the compensation for economic losses or adverse human health effects.[48] A number of other economic instruments have been introduced on an experimental basis, such as sulphur emission fees, emission trading, subsidies for energy saving products, and regulation on refuse credit to high-polluting firms.[49]

In the late 1980s, NEPA proposed an "environmental responsibility system" in which provincial governors, city mayors and county magistrates would be responsible for overall environmental quality in their jurisdictions. Instead of issuing detailed guidelines for implementing an environmental responsibility system, NEPA encouraged local innovation. Some municipalities responded by creating formal contracts between mayors and directors of industrial bureaus, or between mayors and heads of urban districts and rural counties. These contracts spelled out mutually agreed environmental goals and clean-up targets. In some cities, the environmental responsibility system was implemented using informal contracts between EPBs and managers of enterprises. This approach, along with other programmes to promote cleaner production (certification with ISO 14000 standards and environmental labeling) are examples of voluntary instruments (Box 17.4). These instruments have been introduced in environmental management in China only recently, based on the experience of their application in OECD countries. In addition, some information-based instruments and awareness-raising campaigns have also been launched to promote compliance.

Enforcement of, and compliance with, environmental requirements

Despite the complex system of legislative and policy tools in place and the network of environmental officials throughout the country, compliance with environmental regulations remains low, essentially because economic development, and in many cases, social considerations remain

Box 17.3. **Regulatory instruments applied in China's environmental policy**

Emission/discharge and ambient (quality) standards

The 1989 PRC Environmental Protection Law authorised NEPA to establish two types of national standards: ambient (environmental quality) standards and waste discharge/emission standards. Ambient standards are illustrated by restrictions on the minimum allowable concentration of a pollutant in the environment. Discharge/emission standards are exemplified by a limit on the maximum permissible concentration of a pollutant in industrial emissions or discharges, *e.g.* mercury in a factory wastewater release. Local governments may create ambient and discharge standards for pollutants not specified in national standards, and they may also establish more restrictive limiting values for pollutants included in national discharge standards. For a long time China's effluent standards only constrained concentrations and were met by diluting wastewater with uncontaminated water. Pilot schemes have now been launched to introduce mass-based controls on total provincial discharges. In this connection another programme, called "Two Compliance Policy", has been launched. This programme aims to promote compliance with discharge standards and ambient standards at the same time (hence "two compliance") to help the move from concentration-based to mass-based or total pollution load control.

Discharge Permit Systems (DPS)

Under the DPS, environmental protection bureaus issue permits that limit both the quantities and concentrations of pollutants in an enterprise's wastewater and air emissions. DPS rules require enterprises to register with EPBs and apply for a permit. EPBs then allocate allowable pollution loads to enterprises, issue discharge permits, and enforce permit conditions. Unlike other systems and programmes, the DPS has not been affirmed by legislation and is based on administrative edicts.

Pollution control within deadlines

Under the 1989 PRC *Environmental Protection Law* government can require polluting enterprises to control their waste releases by specific dates. Clean-up deadlines for enterprises can only be imposed by national or local people's governments, but local governments sometimes give EPBs the authority to set deadlines. Enterprises that do not abate pollution on time risk being fined or shut down.

Environmental Impact Assessment (EIA) and reporting systems

The EIA requires every project with possibly negative effects on the environment to be reviewed to assess its environmental impacts. Project proposals should contain an analysis of environmental impact and the corresponding preventive measures, and be submitted to the environmental administrative authorities for screening. After the review of the proposal, the applicant needs to engage a qualified firm to prepare an Environmental Impact Report. It is only after the approval by the state or regional environmental authority that the project can be formally launched.

"Three synchronisations" system

The system of "three synchronisations" (called also "Three Simultaneous Steps") requires that the *i*) design, *ii*) construction and *iii*) operation of a new industrial enterprise (or an existing factory expanding or changing its operations) must be synchronised with the design, construction and operation of an appropriate pollution treatment facility. Once the construction of the project is completed, inspection and approval by environmental authorities are required (for large projects, or in case of a dispute at the local level, the approval has to be confirmed by the national level authority). If project operations begin without the approval from the local EPB, the owner of the project can be sanctioned. In many instances, however, the sanctions have not been applied and there are many departures from the above-mentioned procedures, especially by many TVIEs. Overall, however, this programme has played an important role in stimulating investment in pollution abatement facilities at industrial enterprises, especially at new factories.

Centralised pollution control

Until the 1980s, China's pollution reduction efforts focused on treatment by individual enterprises. This strategy has not always been effective, as the costs of individual treatment plants were higher per unit of waste treated than in the case of larger centralised plants. Recognising the possible economic advantages of building large treatment plants, the State Council and the environment agency issued documents requiring governments at all levels to promote centralised control of waste within their jurisdictions.

Source: Environmental Regulations in China: Institutions, Enforcement and Compliance, Ma X., Ortolano L., 2000.

Box 17.4. Voluntary instruments applied in environmental policies in China

Recently adopted requirements to shift to a comprehensive control of technological processes is being encouraged by promotion of the "cleaner production" concept, adoption of ISO 14000 certification[1] procedures, and environmental labeling.

Cleaner production. The Cleaner Production (CP) programme, which started in 1993, encourages enterprises to adopt in-plant waste minimisation technologies as supplements to traditional "end-of-pipe" pollution-control approaches. There is considerable potential in the CP programmes, since many of the older and more polluting enterprises are very inefficient and use outdated production technology. Some successful examples can be found mainly in areas with strong incentives, such as the water-scarce areas of northern China. Nevertheless, the technical capacity to undertake cleaner production audits and feasibility studies has been established such as China National Cleaner Production Centre under the Chinese Research Academy of Environmental Sciences. Institutions like this one have created the foundations for the establishment of an environmental audit service industry and the capacity to respond as the demand for these services develops.

Environmental management standards. The application of ISO 14000 series in China is expected to encourage Chinese companies, directly or indirectly through pressure from purchasers of their products and services, to promote compliance with environmental requirements. Such self-implementation can ease the burden on regulators and foster a corporate culture of compliance, while enhancing the competitiveness of Chinese enterprises in international trade.

The ISO 14000 certification procedures were introduced in 1997, building on a long tradition of standard-setting processes that served to promote business, science and technology. The Standarisation Law of 1988 provides that the state shall encourage the active adoption of international standards. Standarisation under the statute encourages the protection of people's health and safety, the rights of consumers, and the environment; it also promotes resource efficiency as well as economic and technological co-operation with foreign entities and foreign trade.[2]

The introduction of ISO 14000 certification was initiated by SEPA's Office of Environmental Management Systems. Subsequently, a Steering Committee for Environmental Management System Certification was established under the State Council to provide accreditation services for certification bodies and auditors. Several environmental management and consulting centres have been established to conduct ISO 14000 certification, including the Environmental Management Committee of China's Registration Board for Auditors. Initially the adoption rate, as experienced in other countries, was slow. During the first year only 27 enterprises received ISO 14001 certification, but during the subsequent year over 100 enterprises were certified. The majority of the participants are either foreign firms (more than half in the electronics and household appliances industries) or domestic firms engaged in the production of export-oriented goods. Unfortunately, so far the nation's main polluters have not been very active in applying for the environmental certification.

Environmental labeling. In 1994, China began to implement an environmental labeling programme. A number of rules and technical specifications for products eligible for environmental labels have been issued, and over 500 products from 150 enterprises had received such labels by early 1999.

---

1. The ISO 14000 series of environmental management standards have been developed and adopted by the International Organisation for Standardisation (ISO). ISO 14000 series drew heavily on environmental management standards in Great Britain (BS 7750) and the European Union's Eco-Management and Audit Scheme (EMAS). China participated through the process of development and adoption of these standards.
2. PRC *Standarisation Law* (1998)
Source: China: *Environmental Protection, Domestic Policy Trends, Patterns of Participation in Regimes and Compliance with International Norms,* in the China Quarterly, L. Ross, 1998

---

the country's priority at all levels of society. Instances in which, for example, a mayor's office interfered with EPB's decisions on economic grounds are common. A typical case involves a mayor's office that asked an EPB to return fines that an enterprise paid to an EPB. The mayor's office argued that the enterprise had financial problems and that the EPB's fines made the enterprise's position even worse.[50]

Because China's environmental laws are general and often intentionally ambiguous, they allow the State Council, national agencies, and local governments to add details that influence implementation. As most day-to-day implementation of national environmental laws occurs at the local level, local people's congresses and the executive branches of local governments respond to national edicts by producing their own versions of national regulations, notices and other executive orders. Although the laws and regulations issued by these bodies must be consistent with national enactments, they allow for a flexible interpretation of the requirements, which very often leads to compromising environmental objectives. In many cases, the degree of actual compliance and enforcement depends on the region concerned and the personalities involved, as well as the ability of enterprises to comply with the laws. There are cases in which the more strictly environmental policy is applied to richer potential investors, as well as cases in which environmental requirements have been lowered to attract local and foreign investment.

Vagueness of standards in many laws and regulations, combined with the lack of strong enforcement activities and a strong impartial judiciary to interpret the laws and arbitrate legal and regulatory disputes, are other factors allowing widespread non-compliance with environmental requirements. The problems are further magnified by contradictions related to vertical responsibility in environmental administration, and the lack of technical capacity and resources available to SEPA and EPBs to carry out their duties. However, as part of its efforts to strengthen environmental law enforcement, the government revised its criminal code to punish violations against the environment. These steps may provide law enforcement agencies with some powers.

In addition to problems with lax enforcement, the under-pricing of natural resources and environmental services has encouraged their wasteful use, and has not provided appropriate incentive for internalising environmental costs. Despite the fact that China's resources are scarce, prices of energy and water have for a long time been far lower than the actual costs of providing these services. However, great strides are being made to rectify the situation. For example, in recent years the government has raised and partly deregulated coal prices. In most areas, coal prices now cover the costs of production and delivery. In terms of environmental services, many cities and provinces are currently preparing to increase sewage and water charges to consumers and industries. In Taiyuan in Shanxi province, for instance, the price bureaus have announced that water prices would quadruple over the coming years in order to recover supply costs. Shanghai recently increased tap water prices by between 25 and 40 per cent to fund water quality improvement programmes and to make sewage self-financing. Other cities are planning to follow this pattern. In 2001, a proposal was put forward by China's Ministry of Water Resources to increase prices of water in Beijing from 1.6 RMB per cubic meter to 5.0 RMB by 2005 to stimulate water conservation and recover the costs of providing the service.

Environmental regulatory and institutional framework and foreign direct investment and trade

With the introduction of economic reform in 1978, China liberalised foreign trade and investment, which has expedited its integration with the global economy. The reform was vital for generating the inflow of financial resources for investment, and the introduction of modern-technology and know-how. Over the years, however, environmental policies have not been successful in influencing China's decision-making in the area of trade and investment. This occurred in spite of the existence of specific policies and administrative procedures governing, screening, and monitoring trade and investment flows with respect to their impact on the environment. In practice, production costs, market access, and resource availability have been more important considerations in making trade and investment decisions. China has encouraged foreign companies to invest in order to finance its development goals and to assist in opening up its markets, and in many cases environmental requirements have been compromised. As a consequence, trade and investment liberalisation has resulted in several incidents of negative effects on the environment. For example, some foreign firms promoted imports of outdated technologies and polluting or toxic substances, taking advantage of the lower (or more flexible) environmental standards in China. Opening up new trade relations has not always brought about improvements in environmental performance. Some indications at the sector level, as in textile and leather production, show that the quantity of pollution in these sectors has increased as their exports grow.[51]

Over time, however, experience from implementing environmental policies has accumulated, and institutions have become more mature in understanding the environmental impacts of economic activities and the ways to influence them. A number of positive examples have shown that foreign direct investment and trade can result in transferring advanced technologies which improve the performance of polluting industries and reduce energy and resources consumption. At the same time, importing raw materials such as fuels, minerals, petrochemical and rubber products, or paper pulp have reduced negative environmental pressures which could have been exerted by extracting or processing these materials at home. With a growing number of such evidence, the trade and investment liberalisation and environmental interface has recently received greater attention in China. New policies and instruments have been put in place to promote environmentally friendly investment and counteract negative impacts on the environment.

Policy and institutional framework for integrating environmental consideration into trade and investment policies

In general, China does not have separate environmental standards for foreign investment, although some relevant clauses governing foreign investors' environmental behaviour can be found in a number of national laws and regulations. For example, Article 18 of the Constitution contains the principle that all foreign investors must comply with Chinese laws and regulations and meet the host country's environmental standards. Furthermore, Article 30 of the 1998 PRC *Environmental Protection Law* stipulates that imports of environmentally-unfriendly technology and equipment is forbidden. The procedures for regulating the environmental aspects of foreign direct investment are similar to those of domestic firms. The environmental protection programmes and instruments presented earlier (Box 17.3), such as Environmental Impact Assessment and Reporting, the "three synchronisations", registration and licensing systems for discharge of pollutants, and the system of effluent charges are equally applicable to domestic as well as foreign industrial operations.

There are, however, additional specific policies and administrative procedures governing the screening and monitoring of foreign direct investment with respect to their impacts on the environment. According to the "Notice on Reinforcing Environmental Protection Management of Foreign Investment Projects" issued in 1992 foreign investors should prevent environmental pollution and ecological damage, and accept monitoring and supervision by environmental protection authorities. The "Notice" also sets out procedures for screening the environmental implications of investment projects and monitoring the implementation of environmental protection measures. Similar provisions can be found in other regulatory documents, such as "Implementing Regulations on Joint Ventures" or "Regulations of Ocean Oil Exploiting by Foreign Firms". They stipulate that foreign investors are required to comply with relevant environmental laws and that regulations and projects with negative environmental impacts cannot be approved. Some of the regulations in the manufacturing and mining sectors, such as the "Application Form for Establishing Foreign Invested Enterprise in China", require enterprises to present indicators of treatment and control of their pollution releases to the air, land and water (so called "three wastes" indicators). Other examples of such regulations include the 1994 Law of Foreign Trade, the 1995 Law on Contractual Joint Ventures or the 1994 Regulations on the Labour Management in Foreign-Invested Enterprises. All include clauses prohibiting projects with negative impacts on the environment or human health and describe sanctions for breaching environmental regulations.

In 1995, China promulgated "Interim Provisions for Guiding Foreign Investment" and a "Guiding List of Industries for Foreign Investors". Since then the guidelines have been updated regularly reflecting the latest economic developments and policy priorities. In these official documents, foreign direct investment projects are divided in four major categories: *i)* encouraged, *ii)* permitted, *iii)* restricted and *iv)* prohibited. The "encouraged" category includes projects requiring advanced technology to improve products and production processes, increase energy and material efficiency and stimulate effective management of enterprises in general. The "encouraged" projects should also aim to reduce the negative impact on the environment and develop systems to control pollution and increase recycling. The

605|

provisions also encourage investment in the central and western parts of the country which exhibit low pollution levels. Projects that adversely affect human health, pollute the environment, or destroy natural resources fall under category of "prohibited".

These guidelines have enhanced the transparency of the admission and approval process for foreign investors. They also provided guidance for policy implementation agencies in screening foreign direct investment with a view of maximising its benefits to the development process and minimising negative impacts, while protecting the legal rights of investors. On the other hand, government and especially the authorities at the local level, tend to adjust their decisions (often by lowering environmental requirements) in order to improve the local investment climate for foreign investors. One of the arguments used in considering investment flows is that strict environmental regulations would make investment less attractive and discourage foreign investors from locating their operations in the part of the country under consideration. This situation is reinforced by the weak position of the local environmental protection administration, and lack of human capacities to deal with application screening and monitoring mechanisms and procedures. According to one survey, only 97 out of 382 economic development areas in 16 provinces have conducted regional environment assessments. Local officials often ignore the environmental protection laws and regulations, and issue decisions to build polluting projects even in water-source areas or in natural conservation zones. There are cases in which local authorities lowered the environmental standards for foreign investment creating "opposite" double standards.[52]

The problems related to the negative impacts of flexibility of policies and regulations are exacerbated by the lack of appropriate institutional framework for co-ordinating respective policies. The landscape of institutional mechanisms to govern the environmental impacts of international trade and financial flows in China is currently characterised by significant gaps and discontinuities, and important "responsibility vacuums" exist at various levels. The ability of environmental agencies to exert influence over the environmental impacts of foreign trade and investment is constrained by lack of mechanisms to discuss and address conflicts between the goals of economic growth and environmental protection. As already stated, the SEPA's and EPB's influence on sectoral decisions is weak, as the capacity and legitimacy of these agencies are limited. In particular, there is no inter-ministerial body to ensure the integration of environmental consideration into trade and investment policies and decisions. One of the institutions which was helping to co-ordinate cross-sectoral issues was the State Environmental Protection Commission (SEPC) under the State Council, but it was abolished in 1998 as part of the reorganisation of governmental structures.

Examples of environmental impacts of foreign direct investment and trade flows in China

Due to the lack of systematic empirical evidence and a sound analytical framework, it is difficult to provide a comprehensive quantitative analysis of either positive or negative effects of foreign direct investment and trade liberalisation on the environment in China. It is equally difficult to determine whether foreign affiliates' environmental performance is better or worse than that of comparable local firms, as the degree of importance attached to environmental impact of foreign direct investment and trade by local governments and the society varies from one area to another in China. In the coastal areas, which are more economically developed, the desire for environment protection is stronger as a result of the higher level and density of economic development and the existence of higher awareness of environmental pressures resulting from the rapid industrial and urban growth. In such cases it has been easier to act to limit the environmental consequences of industrial development in these areas, and the implementation of environmental policies is more rigorous and effective. In the central and western parts of the country, where development is slower, local governments may have greater interest in attracting foreign direct investment than in protecting the environment. Economic development is often considered of utmost importance and environmental protection is given a low priority. This leads to the situation that environmental measures are frequently remedial rather than preventive.

Over the past two decades, industries such as chemical, petrochemical, leather, printing and dyeing, electroplating, pesticide, pulp and paper, mining and metallurgy, rubber, plastic, construction material, as well as pharmaceutical production, have been among the most attractive for foreign investment in China. They are often referred to as pollution-intensive industries, as they usually rank high in emission intensities of pollutants. A study based on a survey of industrial sectors carried out in 1995 showed that about 30 per cent of foreign direct investment in China was located in pollution-intensive industries, out of which 13 per cent were in highly pollution-intensive industries.[53]

The patterns related to the origins of these investments follow the overall patterns of sources of foreign direct investment. The high share of developing Asian economies investing in pollution-intensive industries is consistent with its overall higher share of their foreign direct investment stock in China. This is possibly due to the rapid change in locational advantage for pollution-intensive industries. An increasing tightening of regulations in the home countries, a lower level of environmental standards and weak monitoring mechanisms in China could be the main reasons for inducing foreign direct investment into those industries.

Very often, an increased focus of foreign direct investment on pollution-intensive industries in China is associated with negative implications for China's environment. The relocation of production into pollution-intensive industries needs, however, to be differentiated from the transfer of pollution itself and large-scale foreign direct investment into these industries has been determined primarily by such factors as labour costs and skills as well as infrastructure and not low environmental standards. In many cases the investments helped to reduce environmental pressures from this highly polluting sector as a number of enterprises with foreign direct investment applied environmentally sound technologies, introduced better management practices and increased pollution control. This has been particularly the case in the pharmaceutical industry, where multinational companies helped that industry to become significantly more environmentally friendly.

As mentioned earlier, China's environmental standards are, in general, lower than those of the OECD countries. Since about 75 per cent of foreign direct investment comes in the form of production equipment, there are cases where foreign investors have transferred to China technological processes that do not meet environmental standards elsewhere. The transfer of production lines that have negative effects on the ozone layer are a case in point. Although there has been strict control over such production lines, around 1 500 foreign-investment firms were established between 1985-1994, most of which produced foaming and rinse products. The majority of the investment in this sector (about 60 per cent) came from Hong Kong and the Republic of Korea. In the face of growing concern regarding these operations, administrative decrees relating to the screening and monitoring of environmental aspects of foreign direct investment came into effect and helped to strengthening control over this type of investment.

Some foreign firms do not pay sufficient attention to pollution prevention, and adequate and effective measures to treat pollution are not applied because enforcement by local environmental authorities is weak or lacking. In July 1997, the NEPA and MOFTEC jointly examined environmental performance of enterprises with foreign capital lower than US$5 million in six provinces (Shandong, Jiangsu, Zhejiang, Fujian, Guangdong, Guangxi). The examination showed that the performance rate of complying with the EIA procedures was 61 per cent on average and compliance with "three simultaneous steps" was 83.5 per cent. These figures for compliance with EIA varied from 28 per cent in Guanxi autonomous region to 96 per cent in Tianjin province.

There are cases of foreign investors setting up enterprises to decompose, renovate and process waste, including metals, electronic appliances, tires, and chemicals. Usually these activities have recycling as the main objective though most of them result in serious environmental pollution. For example, Chinese Taipei used to be an important location for recycling hazardous materials from abroad. In 1993, its environment authorities banned trading in these materials. As a result, a number of Taipei investors relocated their production facilities to the eastern coastal areas in China, such as Shenzhen, Zhuhai and Changzhou. These enterprises continue importing used cells, vehicle plates, computers, adapters and other electrical and electronic components for recycling into China. Most of the incidents happened in the projects financed by medium- and small-scale foreign firms, some with serious environmental consequences (Box 17.5).

On the other hand, there is a growing amount of evidence that foreign direct investment, especially by major multinational companies, has contributed positively to China's environmental protection. Apart from the advantages of technology and management, these investments are usually large

---

Box 17.5. **Examples of negative environmental impacts involving foreign direct investment and trade**

A Hong Kong affiliate invested 16 million dollars in plastic toys production operations in Shenzhen. The firm used a process of adding a large amount of plasticiser, such as dibutyl phthalate (DBP) to polyvinyl chloride (PVC). Substantial amounts of foul and toxic gases, which were produced when the PVC was heated and shaped, were discharged, resulting in severe pollution of the surrounding area. In addition, the noise of its production facilities reached 60 db, far above the national standard. The case was brought to court and the firm was fined HK$20 000 as well as having to pay investigation and lawsuit fees.

Due to an ineffective sewage draining facility, a Sino-Republic of Korean leather manufacturer discharged sewage that surpassed the national standards over 750 times. Many nearby residents complained about severe damage to the surrounding environment. Although the company was amerced three times, it did not take any measures to control the pollution until the case was exposed on a China State TV.

In northeast China, a well-known joint venture was set up in 1992 by a Thai company and a local partner. However, the company began operating without undergoing the appropriate environmental administrative procedures. It was estimated that 30 million tons of highly polluted sewage was discharged through the Yinma river into Songhua river.

A large-scale foreign affiliate located along Shaxi river in Xianyou county launched the production of leather products without paying attention to controlling environmental pollution. Polluted water affected the living and working conditions of tens of thousands of inhabitants in the lower reaches of the river. After discovering these impacts, the factory had to invest a large amount of money to improve its processing facilities. Another foreign leather manufacturer located along Mulan river in Putian city started production without any environment protection measures. The firm discharged a large amount of wastewater directly into Mulan river without proper disposal. This caused strong discontent among residents in nearby areas. Five months later unknown individuals destroyed the factory draining conduit and production had to be terminated.

Import and export patterns may also result in negative environmental impacts. For example, uncontrolled exports of non-ferrous and rare metals, such as wolfram, tin, molybdenum, and antimony, have led to rampant exploitation of such deposits in the Jiangxi Province. Such a development was driven by the rising prices of these minerals on the international market. Some local small-size enterprises and TVIEs have undertaken exploitation without essential mining technologies and supervision. The rate of mineral resources recovery was only 20 per cent, which resulted in the loss of 12 000 tons of wolfram, which was equal to one fourth of the world's wolfram output per year. In addition, a large quantity of hazardous or radioactive substances was discharged from the traditional process of selecting and melting of these minerals, resulting in serious environmental pollution.

The import of old vessels for disassembling scrap steel for sale has been very popular in many Chinese coastal provinces. These old ships were imported mainly from the US, Western Europe, Japan, Hong Kong, and some other economies in the Asian region. Ship disassembling activities in China are dominated by TVIEs. They are usually operated in coastal or bay areas and discharge oily substances, iron, and electric welding directly onto beaches and into the sea. This has not only caused heavy pollution but has also harmed aqua-farming.

Each year, China imports 1.5 to 3 million tonnes of scrap steel, 1 million tons of aluminum, 1.8 million tons of scrap copper and 2 million tons of paper waste. The import of waste as raw materials has some positive aspects in China's economy development providing input for processing and reusing waste materials which are usually labour-intensive activities. However, waste imports can also bring environmental pollution, as in several cases they have been imported for final disposal purposes and not recycling.

Source: The Interface between Foreign Direct Investment and the Environment: The Case of China, Xian G. et al., 1999.

---

compared with domestic firms. They bring significant resources for investment in research and development (R&D), as well as environmental management systems. Some foreign companies have been actively involved in the development of environmental goods and services sector, including waste management and clean-up technologies; others use environmentally friendly technologies in their

---

Box 17.6.   **Examples of positive environmental impacts involving foreign direct investment and trade**

Several local and foreign companies actively participate in adopting international environmental standards. For example, Shanghai Gao Qiao BASF Dispersions Ltd. Co. was the first chemical firm to obtain an ISO14000 certificate in China. BASF has also set up R&D funds for innovation projects in the fields of organic pigment, dyestuff chemistry, and polymer chemistry, as well as new designs for chemical engineering and factory construction. Shanghai Squipp Co., a Sino-American joint venture, was the first pharmaceutical manufacturer in China to obtain an ISO14000 certificate.

Since 1994, when China embarked on environmental labelling certification, 40 out of the 86 firms that obtained such certificates were foreign affiliates.

Liebherr Co. is another example of a foreign company which produce environmentally friendly products. Over the years it has been co-operating with the Chinese manufacturer Haier to produce fluorine-free refrigerators. In the pharmaceutical industry, a large number of major domestic producers have formed joint ventures with foreign companies, and pollution by this industry is now greatly reduced owing to advanced technology and a sound environmental management system.

In the agriculture sector foreign investments helped to increase the production of pesticides that are more effective and less toxic. For example, a joint venture between DuPont and Shanghai Pesticide Factory resulted in the production of a new patented herbicide, which is highly popular for its higher effectiveness and low toxicity.

Some multinational companies operating in China, particularly large ones, have introduced new types of fertilisers which contributed to the improvement of the product structure of fertilisers in China. For example, Aigefu's affiliate in Tianjin produces a highly effective and safer insecticide "deltamethrin". The availability of this product on the market has exerted pressure on domestic firms to apply high environment standards in their production.

Source: *The Interface between Foreign Direct Investment and the Environment: The Case of China, Xian G. et al., 1999.*

---

production. They also generate demonstrative impacts on domestic companies in implementing ISO 14000 standards on other environmental management systems (Box 17.6).

The OECD Guidelines on Multinational Enterprises[54] may provide a useful reference in considering promoting corporate environmental responsibility in order to disseminate best environmental practices introduced by domestic and foreign investors. The Guidelines (originally developed in 1976 as part of the Declaration on International Investment and Multinational Enterprises and revised in 2000) are recommendations addressed by governments to multinational enterprises operating in or from adhering countries (OECD Members as well as Argentina, Brazil and Chile). They provide voluntary principles and standards for responsible business conduct in a variety of areas including employment and industrial relations, human rights, environment, information disclosure, competition, taxation, and science and technology. The environment section now encourages enterprises to raise their environmental performance, through such measures as improved internal environmental management, stronger disclosure of environmental information, and better contingency planning for environmental impacts. Although many business codes of conduct are now publicly available, the Guidelines are the only multilaterally endorsed and comprehensive code that governments are committed to promoting. They aim to promote the positive contributions multinationals can make to economic, environmental and social progress.

Environmental impacts of China's accession to WTO

In general, the main effects of WTO accession should be to continue and probably accelerate changes in the structure of the economy and the patterns and forms of production. Further restructuring

Box 17.7. Possible impacts of WTO accession on the environment

Impacts on water quality

Wastewater discharges from different sectors will vary along with the changes in the structure of the economy that are likely to be encouraged by China's WTO accession. Some preliminary qualitative estimates of overall impacts on water show that total discharge of contaminated water into the environment would slightly decrease following a decrease of pollution from the agriculture sector as pollution from grain production accounts for a fairly large proportion of the total load of contaminated water. For example, Lake Taihu receives wastewater from agriculture production which contains 40 per cent of nitrogen and phosphorus. Some most recent studies suggest that water quality will be affected as follows:

- *The grain production sector* will see reductions in the use of chemical fertilisers and pesticides and therefore a reduction of non-point source pollution (presumably, substantial domestic production of rice, wheat, maize and bean, etc. will be replaced by foreign exports due to price disadvantages);
- *The iron and steel industry* will experience a decrease of wastewater discharges as this sector is likely to reduce outputs;
- *The livestock industry* is likely to increase pollution loads following an increase in livestock production;
- *The textile industry* will see an increase of wastewater discharges;
- *The tertiary industry and residential consumption* is likely to increase its use of water thus increasing discharges of wastewater.

Impacts on air quality

China is likely to increase its imports of cleaner fuels such as oil and natural gas, which would enlarge the proportion of such fuels in energy production and reduce the proportion of coal in China's energy structure. Therefore, environmental pressure resulting from energy consumption on air quality is likely to decline.

However, pressures in the urban air quality will increase. Given the tariff reduction for automobiles, the import of cars will increase following price reductions. Therefore, the rate of motor vehicles in urban areas is likely to increase at an estimated rate of between 5 and 10 per cent per year. Meanwhile, without stricter enforcement related to old cars their emissions will continue to affect air quality. Moreover, there are other major sources affecting urban air quality such as domestic heating and industrial emissions. Without taking adequate measures to enhance pollution control, particularly pollution caused by the increase of automobiles in urban areas, air pollution will increase.

Changes in waste generation trends

Given the probable shrinking of the secondary industry and the growth in the tertiary industry, industrial solid wastes are likely to decrease. This has to be accompanied by appropriate control measures combined with the promotion of cleaner technologies. With urban expansion, however, municipal waste generation will grow. Meanwhile, with the increase in trade volumes and opportunities, there is a possibility of increasing the import of wastes from developed countries if no adequate control procedures are in place. There is also the likelihood that waste would be exported from China to poorer countries.

Impacts on ecosystems

As a WTO member, China could greatly increase its import of timber and timber products to protect its forest resources, and to use both international and domestic markets to maintain food security for its population. With WTO membership, average tariffs for agricultural products will be reduced from 31.5 per cent to 14.5-15 per cent within five years. A tariff-rate quota system will be applied for products such as wheat, rice and cotton, and the import of these products (mainly land-intensive products) will greatly increase as they lose competitive advantages.

From the environmental protection perspective, the increased import of land-intensive agricultural products, such as grain, should lead to reducing land utilisation, lower and more effective application of chemical fertilisers and pesticides. These developments will allow reforestation and afforestation projects to be carried out. This would help China greatly reduce environmental pressure in rural areas and fundamentally halt the trend of ecological degradation. Meanwhile, appropriately guided use of foreign investment could help carry out ecological reconstruction projects, if the Chinese government formulates appropriate incentive policies to encourage the investments.

Source: *Environmental and Trade Implications of China's WTO Accession – A Preliminary Analysis,* Hu T., Wanhua Y., 2000.

of China's economy and its adherence to international trade regimes would lead to the expansion of sectors where China may have comparative advantage, including labour-intensive industries, such as manufacturing, livestock, fruit and vegetables, aqua-culture, non-timber forest products and highly transformed timber products such as furniture and handcraft. Knowledge-based and capital-based industries such as telecommunications, electronics, information technology, community services, banking, insurance, and tourism are also likely to expand.

Very few analyses have been carried out to assess the overall environmental impacts of China's accession to the WTO. One of the most recent (Box 17.7) presents a qualitative analysis of these impacts on the environment. The study predicts that if appropriate policy measures are applied to facilitate rational industrial and agriculture restructuring and effectively address environmental problems, the volume of wastewater discharges to the environment will probably be reduced due to more and better treatment being applied. Although environmental pressure on air quality will also be reduced in general, air quality in urban areas will likely worsen. There is a possibility that the import and export of wastes will grow, and the trend in ecosystem degradation could probably slow down and even be reversed.

Assessing the environmental effects of the liberalisation of trade and investment policies and agreements in OECD countries and in non-members

Over the years several methods of assessing the environmental impacts of national economic development policies and the ways to address them through policy reform have been developed. Environmental impact assessment, valuation of natural and environmental resources, integrated environmental and economic accounting, and the selection, design, and implementation of economic instruments to manage natural resources, are examples of the methods used to assess and address impacts of economic and environmental policies in a number of countries, including China.

With increased trade liberalisation, governments, international organisations, non-governmental organisations and academic institutions have directed their attention to developing methods and conducting various assessments of trade-related policies. These assessments have mainly been concerned with the environmental impact of trade policy, although there has been some investigation of the impacts of environmental policies on trade regimes and also broader social issues. These studies have produced numerous insights into the relationships between trade, the environment and development, as well as highlighting the key factors to consider when examining such relationships.

Similar analyses are being launched in China. They should provide more insights into the relations between trade, investment, and the environment, and an understanding of impacts of the economic and social development on the country's environment. Such analysis can also contribute to the development of the credible and comprehensive approaches to analysing the linkages between trade and the environment, also taking account of development issues.

Environmental reviews of trade policies in OECD countries

Since the early 1990s, the environmental effects of trade liberalisation have figured prominently in OECD work on trade and environment. At its June 1993 meeting at the Ministerial level, the OECD Council recommended that Member governments "examine or review trade and environmental policies and agreements with potentially significant effects on the other policy areas early in their development to assess the implications for the other policy areas and to identify alternative policy options for addressing concerns." It further recommended that governments "follow up as appropriate: to implement policy options, to re-examine policies, agreements and any measures in place and to address any concerns identified in the conclusion of such re-examinations".

That year, the Ministerial Council also endorsed four Procedural Guidelines on trade and environment. The second guideline recommended that OECD governments undertake environmental and trade reviews and follow-up. In the following year the OECD developed a document outlining general methodologies for concluding such reviews. The document, entitled "Methodologies for Environmental and Trade Reviews",[55] presents a menu of options from which countries select when conducting environmental reviews of different types of trade policies and agreements. The choice of which trade policies and agreements should be subject to environmental reviews is left to countries individually or jointly. The nature and scope of these environmental reviews differ according to the country or countries conducting the review and according to the type of trade policy or agreement.

The reviews are intended to focus on a country's domestic trade policies, including their policy approach to international trade agreements. The general purpose of environmental reviews is to inform policy-makers of the environmental consequences of different trade policy measures. The reviews aim to bring broad expertise and perspectives to bear in the interest of further trade-environment policy integration. The reviews are also aimed at assisting in the elaboration of options for addressing the environmental concerns identified, either through the provisions of the trade policy or agreement itself or through complementary mechanisms, including environmental measures and policies.

A number of such reviews have been carried out in OECD countries as well as in other regions. For example, the governments of Canada and the US carried out reviews of NAFTA and the Uruguay Round, the European Commission carried out the review of the EU single market and sponsored a Sustainability Impact Assessment based on EU negotiating proposals for the Millenium Round. In addition some independent studies have been conducted by the World-Wide Fund for Nature (WWF) and the North American Commission for Environmental Cooperation (NACEC). In 1999, the OECD carried out a major stocktaking of several environmental reviews of trade agreements[56] (Box 17.8).

Box 17.8.   **Experience from applying methodologies for environmental assessment of trade liberalisation agreements**

Over the years, significant experience has accumulated from several environmental reviews of trade agreements. The main findings of the stocktaking carried out by the OECD in 1999 were that high political commitment to decide upon and effectively carry out the environmental assessment of trade liberalisation agreements was a necessary condition for a successful assessment. In particular, it was found that an assessment process which was to occur during the negotiation of a trade agreement would need considerable political backing. At the same time, however, it was important to ensure the political independence of the assessment, in order to retain its credibility. Another lesson learned was that the precise purpose of the assessment must be clearly kept in mind when designing and carrying out the assessment. With hindsight, it was apparent that assessments carried out in the past contained two major substantive gaps, by not covering trade in services, especially as regards sub-sectors that have effects on the environment, and investment aspects of trade agreements. At the same time, the need for assessments to examine issues relating to scale, technology, composition and regulatory effects, as noted by the OECD in 1994, was reaffirmed.

The experiences showed that no assessment was a purely technical exercise – there has always been an element of policy assumptions and value judgements. This was considered legitimate, as long as these assumptions and value judgements were transparent. In particular, it was suggested that a set of clear hypotheses be developed that would be tested by the assessment, in order to provide a focus for the exercise. At the same time, it was noted that the assessments would reveal the necessity of trade-offs. It was not considered the task of the assessor to deal with these trade-offs; rather the results of the assessment should be an input into a transparent political process.

Carrying out assessments in developing countries posed special challenges. First, developing countries may not consider it a priority to devote the resources to undertake such analysis. For example, as countries move along the Kuznets curve (whereby environmental conditions get worse before they get better) some may actually "choose to be dirtier". Second, even if that was to be a priority, the possibility was real that the resources and information necessary for the assessment would be lacking. As such, the need for capacity building in this regard in developing countries was emphasised. Third, methodologies that took into account the realities and perspectives of developing countries needed to be improved. Fourth, it was argued that the willingness of developing countries to undertake these assessments would increase, to the extent that the general North-South divide on trade and environment issues was lessened.

Source: *Assessing the Environmental Effects of Trade Liberalisation Agreements: Methodologies*, OECD, 2000.

Assessment of the impacts of trade policies in non-OECD Member countries

Several non-OECD Member countries have started to develop their analytical capabilities to assess the impacts of trade policies, including environmental ones. This is a reflection of an increasing concern over the potential negative impacts of trade liberalisation, particularly on the environmental and natural resources of developing countries and countries in transition where trade has grown most rapidly. These countries have found that economic activities supporting, or supported by, rapidly expanded trade can result in serious environmental degradation when complementary environmental policies are not in place.

Responding to the needs of developing countries to counteract these possible developments, in 1994 the United Nation Environment Programme (UNEP) launched a programme to enhance institutional and human capacities of several governments in developing countries to examine the linkages between trade, environment and development (Box 17.9). The methodology developed by the OECD has been an important reference in that work. In the context of developing countries, the emphasis has been placed on designing innovative approaches to assess and respond to environmental challenges posed by trade policies and relations around the world. In the first cycle, UNEP has worked closely with six countries – Bangladesh, Chile, India, the Philippines, Romania and Uganda – on comprehensive projects to identify the impacts of trade liberalisation on national environmental resources and the use of economic instruments to sustainably manage these impacts.

Through each country project, UNEP sought to build institutional and human resource capacity for analysing alternatives for designing and implementing policies and measures that integrate trade, environment and development. Towards this end, UNEP assisted countries in designing specific mechanisms for managing environmental impacts of macroeconomic reforms, as well as instruments for environmental management in the context of national priorities.

In July 2000, UNEP, together with the Chinese authorities supported by the Agricultural Economics Research Institute (AERI) in Nanjing, launched a study aimed to assess, *ex-ante*, the social, economic and environmental impacts of trade liberalisation in the Chinese cotton production and processing sector

---

Box 17.9. **UNEP work on the development of an integrated assessment of trade-related policies**

In September 1999, UNEP commissioned an International Expert Group on Integrated Assessment to develop the UNEP Reference Manual for the Integrated Assessment of Trade-related Policies. The manual is to be used as a primary reference tool in subsequent country projects supported by UNEP.

The Manual was designed to help conduct integrated assessments of the economic, environmental and social impacts of trade policy and trade liberalisation. This considers the economic, environmental and social effects of trade measures, the linkages between these effects, and aims to build upon this analysis by identifying ways in which the negative consequences can be avoided or mitigated, and ways in which positive effects can be enhanced.

The UNEP manual will also be used as the reference tool in a joint UNEP and UNCTAD's Capacity Building Task Force on Trade, Environment and Development (CBTF). This activity, which was launched in March 2000, provides a framework to help beneficiaries effectively address trade-environment-development issues at the national level and to participate in related deliberations at the international level. The CBTF aims to carry out thematic research and country projects, involving a "learning by doing" process, directly enhancing the capacities of practitioners to assess and manage policy integration challenges in beneficiary countries. Policy dialogue and networking, which are additional elements of the project, aim to allow CBTF beneficiaries to exchange ideas, experiences, and perspectives and to develop partnerships which foster greater co-operation.

Source: *Reference Manual for the Integrated Assessment of Trade-Related Policies*, UNEP (2001).

and to identify policy directions for improved resource allocations and less input-intensive production in the sector. The project, which is currently underway, will provide policy advice for a transition to sustainable development of the cotton sector given China's entry into the WTO, and to strengthen China's negotiation capacity in subsequent rounds of trade talks relating to cotton. Additional studies could concentrate on other priority sectors or products.

Conclusions and recommendations

Since the inception of its "open-door" policy in 1978, China has achieved remarkable progress at a sustained high economic growth rate, rising incomes that have eased poverty, reduced infant mortality, and lengthened life expectancy. However, China entered this period with already heavy pollution loads. Rapid industrialisation and urbanisation have reinforced, and in many cases exacerbated, environmental problems. Serious burdens are imposed on surface and ground waters, air quality in urban areas, as well as land and natural resources, including forestry. Rural environmental quality has been deteriorating as a result of the expansion of TVIEs and intensive farming practices. Evidence suggests that economic growth in China was not environmentally sustainable. As the state of the environment is still worsening the potential for maintaining fast economic growth may be affected.

The most important pressures on the environment came from heavy reliance on low quality coal for energy generation, development of the industrial structure based on pollution-intensive industries which was combined with slow technological progress, agriculture practices imposing high pressure on water and land resources and subsequently on human health. The unsustainable use of natural resources, particularly water and forests, has also been pursued.

Recent changes in the structure of the economy, including in the rural sector, as well as environmental policies applied in the last decade, have led to some significant reduction of environmental impacts. The gross value of industrial output doubled between 1991 and 1998 while total discharge of major pollutants increased only slightly. Water pollution, especially from small enterprises and TVIEs, decreased significantly, emissions of particulates and other pollutants have been curbed, pressures on water quality from the use of pesticides and fertilisers in agriculture have also decreased.

In many cases, however, the positive changes have been offset by emerging new problems stemming from the fast growing market economy and continuous population growth. Rapid growth of motor vehicles is adding to already low air quality in urban areas. Fast urbanisation leads to additional pressures on drinking water resources and increased discharges of untreated wastewater. Urban encroachment has led to the loss of cultivated land. These developments have occurred in the context of weak, or in many cases the lack of, adequate environmental policies. It is expected, however, that the continuation of structural changes of the Chinese economy and increased investment with the parallel application of appropriate policies will lead to gradual reductions of these pressures in the long-term perspective.

Promotion of trade and attraction of foreign investment have been central to the country's efforts to modernise its economy. Many examples from several OECD and non-OECD countries, including China, show that trade and investment liberalisation do promote growth, stimulate competition, and facilitate the international diffusion of technologies. By improving resource allocation, liberalised trade and investment regimes can also directly enhance environmental protection, including better use of natural resources, as well as indirectly promote demand for better quality of ambient air, water and other media. However, in the absence of adequate environmental policies, investment liberalisation may lead to an increased production and consumption of polluting goods, or to a non-sustainable use of natural resources, both of which can exacerbate the negative (scale, structural, technology, product, or regulatory) effects of economic activity on the environment.

China's policies and institutional setting for environmental protection has undergone several transformations over recent decades, reflecting different stages of government restructuring and an increasing emphasis placed by the government on environmental issues. Starting from 1973, protection of the environment has been receiving growing attention. Initial steps to create environmental laws have been modest and spread over time, but they were an important precondition to subsequent development of a comprehensive regulatory and institutional framework for environmental management in China. Experience, which has accumulated over the years, has allowed the effectiveness of environmental regulation and environmental agencies to be improved, and additional instruments to promote better compliance with environmental requirements to be developed. They, in turn, contributed to the reduction of environmental stress in many areas.

Although trade and investment liberalisation can have significant positive and negative environmental impacts, environmental policies in China do not seem to have influenced trade and investment decision-making. In reality production costs, market access, and resource availability have been more important considerations in making trade and investment decisions. China has encouraged investment by foreign companies to finance its development goals and to open up its markets. Environmental requirements have, in many cases, been compromised by local leaders. As a consequence, trade and investment liberalisation has resulted in a number of negative effects on the environment. Some foreign firms, mostly small and medium-sized enterprises, facilitated imports of outdated technologies and polluting or toxic substances, taking advantage of the lower level of environmental standards in China.

Over time, however, as experience from implementing environmental policies has accumulated, environmental institutions have become more mature in understanding the environmental impacts of investments and trade and in designing ways to influence them. A number of positive examples show that foreign direct investment and trade liberalisation can result in transferring advanced technologies which improve the performance of polluting industries and reduced energy and resources consumption. With a growing number of such cases, especially from operations of multinational enterprises, the trade and investment liberalisation-environment interface has recently received greater attention in China. New policies and instruments have been put in place to promote environmentally friendly investment and counteract negative impacts on the environment. For example, China has revised guiding principles for foreign investment, which include a principle to ensure commitments to meet national regulations and international environmental conventions in attracting foreign investment. "Environmentally friendly" production of food is starting to create a basis for sustainable agriculture. China has promoted certification using the ISO 14000 environmental management system and opening up the markets for the development of an environmental goods and services industry. These instruments are, at least in theory, applied to both domestic and foreign investors.

In practice, however, non-compliance with environmental requirements is widespread. Vagueness of standards in many laws and regulations combined with the absence of a strong impartial judiciary to interpret the laws and arbitrate legal and regulatory disputes are important factors. The problems are further magnified by contradictions related to vertical responsibility in environmental administration and the lack of technical capacity and resources available to SEPA and EPBs to carry out their duties.

Furthermore, the institutional mechanisms to assess and manage the environmental impacts of international trade and financial flows in China are currently characterised by significant gaps and discontinuities, and important "responsibility vacuums" exist at various levels. The government's ability to exert influence over the environmental character of foreign trade and investment is often constrained by conflicting goals of economic growth and environmental protection, capacity, and legitimacy effects, particularly with respect to the integration of economic growth and environmental policies, and in adjusting to more stringent "green" requirements in regional and global contexts.

China's recent entry to the WTO will promote further liberalisation of trade and investment and is likely to reinforce the process of restructuring in which the proportion of the tertiary industry will increase and the share of the primary and secondary industries will decrease. As a consequence, overall pollution in China is likely to decrease gradually. In some cases, however, increased trade and investment will lead to situations in which the reduction of pollution per unit of output will be offset by an increase in output volume (*i.e.*, scale effect) or increases of pollution in new sectors, such as transport (*i.e.*, structural effect).

The analyses of linkages between trade, investment and environmental issues have received growing attention throughout the world, including in OECD countries. The studies focused, in particular, on designing the necessary policies to promote positive impacts of trade and investment liberalisation on the environment and reducing the negative ones. Such assessments should be carried out in China using approaches developed in OECD countries, and those applied more recently within the context of the UNEP programme. Such assessments will inform policy-makers in advance of the environmental consequences of different trade policy measures, evaluate trade-related effects on the environment such as product, technology, scale, structural and regulatory effects and suggest the ways for reforming domestic trade and environmental policies, including country policy approaches to international trade and environmental agreements.

As shown above, China's further liberalisation of trade and investment regimes can serve as an opportunity to support processes to strengthen environmental legislation and upgrade environmental standards. At the same time, China faces risks associated with increased trade and investment. In order to minimise negative impacts and promote positive impacts of trade and investment liberalisation the following tasks should be pursued:

- Environmental laws and regulations have to be consistent, transparent, and non-discriminatory so that investors, both domestic and foreign, can make their decisions taking account of what is expected over the medium or long-term perspective. If efforts are not made to ensure the clarity and stability of regulations as well as their consistent enforcement, China may be challenged in the international fora over unfair competition or discriminatory practices which may lead to losing valuable investment. Moreover, environmental regulatory risks may discourage investment. Striking the balance between consistent national environmental requirements and the circumstances that pertain at the local level is a challenge in all large countries and Chinese policy-makers may wish to examine relevant experience from OECD countries.

- Institutional capacity building is essential. This will be required not only to develop, implement and enforce the environmental policy framework at national and local levels, but also to strengthen analytical capacities, including investment analysis, in environmental agencies. More effective and consistent enforcement has to be accompanied by strengthening the capacities and powers of environmental agencies at the national and sub-national level, as well as courts, to interpret environmental laws and to adjudicate disputes between legal and regulatory provisions.

- The assessment of the potential environmental impacts of investment activities has to be consistently applied at various levels. Environmental Impact Assessment procedures at the project level are well understood and should be applied consistently. However, they will not necessarily be adequate to identify and redress potentially harmful scale impacts. Thus, Environmental Impact Assessment procedures should be complemented by applying Strategic Environmental Assessment for priority sectors as well as analysing the potential environmental impacts of foreign direct investment and trade patterns. Various methodologies and models have been developed in OECD countries and elsewhere which could be adapted to the Chinese context. There is also a need to establish co-ordination mechanisms among government agencies to redress the significant gaps and "responsibility vacuums" in integrating environmental, investment and trade policies.

- There is a significant demand in many markets for "environmentally friendly" products. In order to utilise this opportunity, corporate environmental responsibility should be promoted and best practices disseminated, especially among small and medium-sized enterprises. Several steps have already been undertaken in China that can help to respond to such demands, including the introduction of environmental management systems (such as ISO 14000), certification schemes, and environmental labelling. More generally, China may wish to consider other approaches for promoting corporate environmental responsibility in order to disseminate best environmental practices introduced by domestic and foreign investors. The OECD Guidelines on Multinational

Enterprises may provide a useful reference in this regard. Information-based instruments, such as public disclosure or pollutant release registers, could also be used to a greater extent.

- Subsidies and other market-based mechanisms can provide incentives which encourage pollution and inefficient energy use. China should continue its efforts to reduce such distortions and internalise environmental costs in the price system; otherwise trade and investment liberalisation may amplify environmental problems related to such market failures. Similarly, China should continue to move towards full cost-recovery for environmental services. This could provide an opportunity for foreign investors to participate in infrastructure development and operation, for example in the urban water or solid waste disposal sectors. This could release high pressures on the public budgets which have so far had to bear the lion's share of costs of providing those services, as well as introducing more efficient management practices and know-how.

NOTES

1. *China's Environment in the New Century: Clear Water, Blue Skies*, World Bank, 1997.

2. See for example: *Foreign Direct Investment and Environment*, OECD, 1999; *Assessing the Environmental Effects of Trade Liberalisation Agreements: Methodologies*, OECD, 2000; *Sustainable Development: Critical Issues*, OECD, 2001.

3. *Methodologies for Environmental and Trade Reviews*, OECD, 1994.

4. *Foreign Direct Investment and Sustainable Development*, Fortanier F., Maher M., 2000.

5. For further discussion of these concepts see for example: *Foreign Direct Investment and Environment*, OECD, 1999.

6. For example, see *Foreign direct investment and the environment: From pollution havens to sustainable development*, Mabey and McNally, WWF, 1999; *Policy competition for foreign direct investment : A study of competition among governments to attract foreign direct investment*, Oman C., OECD, 1999 and *Trade and Environment*, WTO Special Studies 4, WTO Washington, Nordstrom H. and Vaughan S., 1999.

7. For example, it may be more efficient to run a single set of environmental practices worldwide than to scale back environmental practices at a single overseas location. Also the high visibility of MNEs can make them particularly attractive targets for local enforcement officials, and the ensuing legal difficulties encourage MNEs to be especially conscious of their potential environmental liabilities overseas.

8. *China: Air, Land, and Water: Environmental Priorities for a New Millenium*, World Bank, 2001.

9. *Comprehensive Report on Water Resources Strategy for China's Sustainable Development*, Chinese Academy of Engineering, 2000.

10. China's ambient water quality standards classify water bodies into five categories. The classification scheme is based on types of water uses to be protected and water quality goals. Water designated as Class I have the highest quality I (and can be used for drinking water intakes, fishing and swimming), whereas Class V waters have the poorest quality and can be used only for industrial cooling water and other limited purposes.

11. Class IV is the lowest level stipulated by national seawater quality standard.

12. *China: Air, Land, and Water: Environmental Priorities for a New Millennium*, World Bank, 2001.

13. *Comprehensive Report on Water Resources Strategy for China's Sustainable Development*, Chinese Academy of Engineering, 2000.

14. In OECD countries the individual consumption of water varies between just over 100 litre/capita/day for countries such as the Czech Republic, Portugal or Germany to around 250 litre/capita/day for Australia, Canada and Japan.

15. *China: Air, Land, and Water: Environmental Priorities for a New Millennium*, World Bank, 2001.

16. *Comprehensive Report on Water Resources Strategy for China's Sustainable Development*, Chinese Academy of Engineering, 2000.

17. *China: Air, Land, and Water: Environmental Priorities for a New Millennium*, World Bank, 2001.

18. *State and Characteristics of Urban Water Supply in China*, Cui, Y., Fu T., 2000.

19. *1998-1999 World Resources: A Guide to the Global Environment*, WRI, UNDP, UNEP and World Bank, 1998.

20. *National Environmental Quality Report, 1991-1995*, NEPA, 1996.

21. Class 2 is a national standard for air quality in residential and commercial areas.

22. *State of Environment in China*, SEPA, 20000.

23. See for example: *China's Environment in the New Century: Clear Water, Blue Skies*, World Bank, 1997, *Health and Environment in Sustainable Development: Five years after the Earth Summit*, WHO, 1997 and *World Resources: A Guide to the Global Environment*, WRI, UNDP, UNEP and World Bank, 1998.

24. "More penalties to Curb Acid Rain", in *China Daily*, Zhu Boaxia, 1995.

25. The artificial sources of chlorine and bromine which cause accelerating depletion of the stratospheric ozone layer are chlorofluorocarbons (CFCs of freons) and bromofluorocarbons (halons). CFCs used to be widely applied as propellants in aerosols, coolants in refrigerators and air-conditioning units, foaming agents in the production of insulating and packaging material, and cleaning agents. Halons have been used particularly in fire extinguishers.

26. *China: Air, Land, and Water: Environmental Priorities for a New Millennium*, World Bank, 2001.

27. *State of Environment in China*, SEPA, 2000.

28. "Strategy for Municipal Solid Waste Management in China", Zhu B. (keynote speech presented at ISWA International Symposium on Waste Management in Asia cities, October 2000).

29. "Study on Countermeasures of Municipal Waste in China", Wang Wiping, in *Journal of Natural Resources* Vol. 15, No. 2, 2000.

30. *China: Air, Land, and Water: Environmental Priorities for a New Millennium*, World Bank, 2001.

31. *State of Environment in China*, SEPA, 2000.

32. *China: Air, Land, and Water: Environmental Priorities for a New Millennium*, World Bank, 2001.

33. *Ibid.*

34. *Ibid.*

35. CITES – Convention on International Trade in Endangered Species of Wild Fauna and Flora.

36. *China: Air, Land, and Water: Environmental Priorities for a New Millennium*, World Bank, 2001.

37. *China's Worldwide Quest for Energy Security*, IEA, 2000.

38. While China ranks second in the world behind the US in total energy consumption and carbon emission, its per capita energy consumption and carbon emissions are much lower than the world average. With a growing economy and increasing living standards, however, per capita energy use and carbon emissions are expected to rise.

39. *Foreign Direct Investment in China's Power Sector: Trends, Benefits and Barriers*. Blackman A., Wu X., WRI, 1998.

40. *China: Air, Land, and Water: Environmental Priorities for a New Millennium*, World Bank, 2001.

41. *Ibid.*

42. *Environmental Regulations in China: Institutions, Enforcement and Compliance*, Ma X., Ortolano L., 2000.

43. *Globalisation, Trade, Environment and Sustainable Development: Implications for China and its Entry to the* WTO, Tisdell C., 2000.

44. Because decomposition of organic matter in a river requires oxygen, the level of organic pollution from domestic and industrial sources (mainly sewage) is expressed in chemical oxygen demand (COD).

45. For more detailed discussion of this issue see "Agricultural Prospects and Policies in the Wake of Trade and Investment Liberalisation", CCNM/CHINA(2001)5.

46. *Environmental Regulations in China: Institutions, Enforcement and Compliance*, Ma X., Ortolano L., 2000.

47. EPBs are elements of government at sub-national level, including provincial, municipal, county/district and township levels.

48. *Environmental Regulations in China: Institutions, Enforcement and Compliance*, Ma X., Ortolano L., 2000.

49. *China: Air, Land, and Water: Environmental Priorities for a New Millennium*, World Bank, 2001.

50. *Environmental Regulations in China: Institutions, Enforcement and Compliance*, Ma X., Ortolano L., 2000.

51. *Policy Research on Interactions between China's Foreign Trade and Environmental Protection*, Ye R. et al., 1999.

52. *Policy Research on Interactions between China's Foreign Trade and Environmental Protection*, Ye R. et al., 1999.

53. *The Interface between Foreign Direct Investment and the Environment: The Case of China*, Xian G. et al., 1999.

54. *The OECD Guidelines for Multinational Enterprises. Revision 2000*, OECD, 2000.

55. "Methodologies for Environmental and Trade Reviews" OCDE/GD(94)103.

56. *Assessing the Environmental Effects of Trade Liberalisation Agreements: Methodologies*, OECD, 2000.

BIBLIOGRAPHY

Blackman A., Wu X. (1998),
  "Foreign Direct Investment in China's Power Sector: Trend, Benefits and Barriers", Resources for the Future's Discussion Paper 98-50.

Cao F., Shen X. (2000),
  "Strategies for Trade Liberalisation in Environmental Services in China", paper prepared for the 4th meeting of the 2nd phase of CCICED.

CEA (Chinese Academy of Engineering) (2000),
  Comprehensive Report on Water Resources Strategy for China's Sustainable Development.

Conway T., (1996),
  "ISO 14000 Standards in China; A Trade and Sustainable Development", Perspective paper prepared for the Working Group on Trade and Environment, China Council for International co-operation on Environment and Development (CCICED).

Cui, Y., Fu T. (2000),
  State and Characteristics of Urban Water Supply in China.

Ferris R, *et al.* (2000),
  "Environmental Implications of China's Accession to the WTO: Policy and Law Considerations" in *Sinosphere* Volume 3 Issue 3 Summer 2000.

Fortanier F., Maher M. (2000),
  Foreign Direct Investment and Sustainable Development.

Hu T., Wanghua Y. (2000),
  "Environmental and Trade Implication of China's WTO Accession – A Preliminary Analysis prepared for the Working Group on Trade and Environment", China Council for International co-operation on Environment and Development.

IEA (International Energy Agency) (1998),
  World Economic Outlook.

IEA (International Energy Agency) (1999),
  Coal in the Energy Supply of China.

IEA (International Energy Agency) (2000),
  China's Worldwide Quest for Energy Security.

Ma X., Ortolano L. (2000),
  Environmental Regulations in China: Institutions, Enforcement and Compliance.

Mabey and McNally (1999),
  Foreign direct investment and the environment: From pollution havens to sustainable development, WWF.

NEPA (1996),
  National Environmental Quality Report, 1991-1995.

Nordstrom H. and Vaughan S. (1999),
  Trade and Environment, WTO Special Studies 4, WTO Washington.

OECD (1994),
  Methodologies for Environmental and Trade Reviews OCDE/GD(94)103.

OECD (1999),
  Foreign Direct Investment and Environment.

OECD (1999),
  The Price of Water: Trends in OECD Countries.

OECD (2000),
  Assessing the Environmental Effects of Trade Liberalisation Agreements: Methodologies.

OECD (2000),
   The OECD Guidelines for Multinational Enterprises. Revision 2000.

OECD (2001),
   Sustainable Development: Critical Issues.

Oman C. (1999),
   Policy competition for foreign direct investment: A study of competition among governments to attract foreign direct investment.

PRC Standarisation Law (1998).

Ross L. (1998),
   "China Environmental Protection, Domestic Policy Trends, Patterns of Participation in Regimes and Compliance with International Norms", in The China Quarterly, 1998.

SEPA (2000),
   State of Environment in China.

Stover J. (1999),
   "The Environmental Market in China: Investment Opportunities and Priorities" in Sinosphere Volume 2 Issue 4, Fall 1999.

Sun W., Xia Y. (1999),
   International Investment Rules and Sustainable Development: China's Perspective, CCICED Working Group on Trade and Environment.

Sun Q. (2001),
   "Environmental Situation in China", a background paper for the OECD study.

Tisdell C. at al. (2000),
   Globalisation, Trade, Environmental and Sustainable Development: Implications for China and its Entry to the WTO, draft report on an Economic and Foreign Training Project of AusAID.

UNDP, UNEP, WRI, and WORLD BANK (1998),
   1998-1999 World Resources: A Guide to the Global Environment.

UNEP (1999),
   Trade Liberalisation and the Environment Lessons Learned from Bangladesh, Chile, India, Philippines, Romania and Uganda; A Synthesis Report.

UNEP (2001),
   Reference Manual for the Integrated Assessment of Trade-Related Policies.

USEIA (US Energy Information Administration) (2001),
   China: Environmental Issues (www.eia.doe.gov/emeu/cabs/chinaenv.html).

Wang W. (2000),
   "Study on Countermeasures of Municipal Waste in China", in Journal of Natural Resources Vol. 15, No. 2.

Wheeler D. (2000),
   "Racing to the Bottom? Foreign Investment and Air Quality in Developing Countries", Development Research Group Paper, World Bank.

WHO (World Health Organisation) (1997),
   Health and Environment in Sustainable Development: Five years after the Earth Summit.

WORLD BANK (1997),
   China's Environment in the New Century: Clear Water, Blue Skies.

WORLD BANK (2001),
   China: Air, Land, and Water: Environmental Priorities for a New Millennium.

Wu Ch. (2000),
   "Trade and Sustainability – A China Perspective" in Sinosphere Volume 3 Issue 3 Summer 2000.

Xian G. et al. (1999),
   "The Interface between Foreign Direct Investment and the Environment: The Case of China", Occasional Paper No 3 Report for UNCTAD/DICM Project www.cbs.dk/departments/ikl/cbem.

Xu H. (2000),
   "Environment and China's Entry to the WTO: Urban Sprawl" in Sinosphere Volume 3 Issue 3 Summer 2000.

Ye R. et al. (1999),
   Policy Research on Interactions between China's Foreign Trade and Environmental Protection.

Zhang S., An Sh. (2001),
   "Environmental Implication of Trade and Investment Liberalisation in China", a background paper for the OECD study.

Zhu B. (1995),

"More penalties to Curb Acid Rain", in *China Daily*.

Zhu B. (2000),

"Strategy for Municipal Solid Waste Management in China", (keynote speech presented at ISWA International Symposium on Waste Management in Asian Cities, October 2000).

Chapter 18

THE CURRENT TAX SYSTEM AND PRIORITIES FOR REFORM

TABLE OF CONTENTS

THE CURRENT TAX SYSTEM AND PRIORITIES FOR REFORM[*]

Introduction

Over the past two decades, China has substantially modernised its tax system as social and economic reforms developed towards a socialist market economy and the Chinese market became more and more open to the world. Most of the vestiges of the centrally planned economy disappeared from the tax system after the tax reform in 1994. VAT (Value Added Tax) has been introduced, and all domestic enterprises are subject to a single corporate income tax regardless of ownership. A new income tax has also been introduced to cover both Chinese and non-Chinese individuals.

However, the remaining two-track system for enterprise income tax, one for foreign enterprises and another for domestic enterprises, needs to be merged soon to comply with the national treatment rule of the WTO.

The current tax system excessively relies on revenues from tax turnover (VAT, Business Tax and Consumption Tax). Revenue from income taxation has been seriously eroded by the generous tax incentives provided to foreign and domestic enterprises and by the high threshold in personal income tax. Some of the tax incentives are clearly violating WTO rules and need to be removed. Widening the tax base for income taxation is necessary not only to increase tax revenues but also to use tax more efficiently as a macroeconomic-control policy tool.

Production-type VAT also needs additional reforms. Currently this does not cover all services and is causing distortions in investment decisions through non-creditable input VAT on fixed assets. This also leads to double taxation problems between VAT and the Business Tax. Widening the scope of VAT to include all services, together with reforms in other turnover taxes, is urgently needed.

Partly due to the narrow tax base on incomes and partly due to weaknesses in tax administration, the tax-GDP ratio in China has remained low compared to OECD countries, raising concerns over the sustainability of fiscal balances in the future. Low tax-GDP ratios conceal the existence of very large non-tax revenues from the collection of fees and charges. Non-tax revenues will need to be transformed in tax revenues in order to move towards a more transparent integrated management of fiscal accounts.

Together with further capacity building for tax collection, improving transparency and compliance with tax laws are long-standing agenda items for tax administration in China in the context of trade and investment liberalisation.

Overview of China's taxation

Outline of past tax reforms

Tax is the most important source of fiscal revenue in China. According to statistics provided by the State Tax Administration, tax revenues account for more than 90 per cent of the total fiscal revenue. The share of tax revenue to GDP in China has remained low, however, compared to OECD countries. While the share in China has hovered between 15 and 10 per cent of GDP over the past ten years, for all OECD countries (excluding social security contributions) it has averaged around 27 per cent, showing a slight rise during this period. Nevertheless, as an important policy tool for macroeconomic control, tax has always had an important impact on China's economic and social development.

Tax reforms in the 1980s

In its move towards a socialist market economy in the 1980s, China began to restructure its tax system on a large scale. The major objectives of tax reforms during that decade were: 1) to introduce a

---

[*] This Chapter was prepared by Mrs Zhujian Zhou of the State Administration of Taxation (China), under the supervision of Makoto Nakagawa, Senior Advisor, Centre for Tax Policy and Administration, Directorate for Financial, Fiscal and Enterprise Affairs, OECD.

new tax system to be used as a macroeconomic policy tool, 2) to secure the necessary revenues, 3) to encourage foreign investment, and 4) to adjust the taxation system to allow reforms in state-owned enterprises (SOEs).

The reforms in this area were to bring the Chinese tax system more into line with the new economic policy and to enhance self-management of SOEs. Reforms were introduced in 1983, with steps designated to replace planned profit deductions with taxation. All SOEs were subject to the Individual Income Adjustment Tax that replaced profit deductions. Corporate income taxes were also introduced for both private and collective enterprises.

Reforms were also made in the tax system for foreign-related enterprises. In 1980 and 1981, China allowed the introduction of a corporate income tax law for Chinese-foreign-equity joint ventures and an income tax law concerning foreign enterprises. They were characterised by many tax incentives, light tax burdens and simplified procedures. In 1991, the two laws were incorporated into the current Income Tax Law for Foreign Investment Enterprises and Foreign Enterprises, unifying the tax incentives, tax rates and tax jurisdiction for foreign-funded enterprises. However, differentiated tax treatments for foreign enterprises in corporate income tax were left unchanged.

Within the turnover tax system, the Consolidated Tax on Industries and Commercial Entities introduced in 1958 continued to apply only to non-Chinese enterprises. The Tax on Industry and Commerce, a turnover tax for Chinese enterprises and individuals introduced in the 1970s, was separated into four categories (Product Tax, Value Added Tax, Business Tax, and Salt Tax) in the early 1980s. In the other areas, a new tax on natural resources and a new Personal Income Tax were also introduced.

As a result of these reforms tax revenue substantially increased during the 1980s, with its share of GDP rising from 13 per cent in 1980 to 23 per cent in 1985, when it reached its peak over the past two decades.

Tax reforms in 1994

Although the 1980s tax reforms had radically changed the tax structure in China, more remained to be done. Different income tax systems for domestic enterprises according to categories of ownership were too complicated, causing unfair tax burdens and distortions in competitiveness. There was considerable inequity between tax treatments for foreign-related and domestic enterprises. The turnover tax was complicated by four categories of tax, and coverage of VAT was too narrow. With the rapid development of the market economy and social changes, the tax system was no longer in line with the goals of the Chinese agenda for economic restructuring and growth. This prompted another round of tax reform.

Tax reforms in 1994 were devised 1) to unify tax laws, 2) to equalise tax burdens, 3) to simplify the tax system, 4) to rationalise the decentralised system, 5) to standardise revenue assignment methods between the central and local governments, and 6) to enhance fiscal revenue. It was a comprehensive tax reform and covered almost all taxes in China.

Particularly important was the reform of Value Added Tax. The scope of the tax was expanded to include all industrial production, commercial sales, import of goods, and provision of processing, repairs, and replacement services. Three tax rates were set (standard 17 per cent, 13 per cent for a limited number of goods, and zero per cent for export of goods), considerably simplifying the existing system. The VAT base was expanded to include all entities in China (enterprises and individuals) dealing with taxable goods and services. In this connection, the Consolidated Tax on Industries and Commercial Entities, which had applied only to foreign-related enterprises, was abolished, establishing equal treatment between domestic enterprises and foreign-related enterprises in the field of turnover taxes. An EU-like invoice system was introduced, enabling appropriate tax credit against VAT on inputs on taxable goods and services.

Another important reform was introduced for corporate income taxes for domestic enterprises. The three different corporate income taxes that had applied to different ownership categories of domestic enterprises were unified into one single Enterprise Income Tax. A standard tax rate of 33 per cent now applies to all domestic enterprise regardless of ownership. However, the differentiated treatment between domestic enterprises and foreign-related enterprises was left untouched even after the 1994 reforms.

A new Individual Income Tax, introduced in 1994, abolished the former Individual Income Adjustment Tax and the Urban and Township Individual Industry and Commercial Income Tax (which had been introduced in the 1980s) and the former personal income tax. Under the new system, any individual having resided in China for one or more years has to pay individual income tax on his/her total earnings, including income from abroad. The tax rate for wages, salaries and incomes from individual household production or business operations is progressive (from 5 per cent to 45 per cent for wages and salaries; and from 5 per cent to 35 per cent for other income).

Further new taxes were introduced, such as the Land Appreciation Tax, which applies to any enterprises and individuals who receive income from the transfer of state-owned land use rights. This new tax was introduced following the 1987 reforms on land use in China.

Current tax system for foreign-related taxpayers

After the comprehensive tax reforms in 1994, 25 types of taxes remain. These can be divided into eight categories according to their nature and function (see Table 18.1), of which only 14 types of tax apply to enterprises with foreign investment, foreign enterprises, and foreign individuals. These are: Value Added Tax, Consumption Tax, Business Tax, Income Tax on Enterprises with Foreign Investment and Foreign Enterprises, Individual Income Tax, Resource Tax, Land Appreciation Tax, Urban Real Estate Tax, Vehicle and Vessel Usage Licence Plate Tax, Stamp Tax, Deed Tax, Slaughter Tax, Agriculture Tax, and Customs Duties.

Among the 25 taxes, turnover taxes (Value Added Tax, Consumption Tax and Business Tax) and income taxes have played a dominant role in revenue-raising and income redistribution. The descriptions of their characteristics are outlined in the following sections.

Table 18.1. **China's current tax system**

Category	Type
Turnover taxes	VAT Consumption Tax Business Tax Enterprise Income Tax
Income taxes	Income Taxes on Enterprises with Foreign Investment and Foreign Enterprises Individual Income Tax
Resource taxes	Resource Tax Urban and Township Land Use Tax City Maintenance and Construction Tax Farmland Occupation Tax
Special purpose taxes	Fixed Assets Investment Orientation Regulation Tax (Note: Suspended in January 2000.) Land Appreciation Tax House Property Tax
Property taxes	City Real Estate Tax Inheritance Tax Vehicle and Vessel Usage Tax Vehicle and Vessel Usage Licence Plate Tax Stamp Tax Deed Tax
Agriculture taxes	Agriculture Tax Animal Husbandry Tax
Customs duties	Customs Duties
Behavioural taxes	Slaughter Tax Banquet Tax Security Exchange Tax

Note: Inheritance Tax and Security Exchange Tax have not yet been legislated to date.
Source: State Administration of Taxation (SAT), *Tax system of the People's Republic of China.*

627

Value added tax

VAT is positioned as a central tax. It applies to sales of all goods and imports of goods within the territory of the People's Republic of China but has very limited scope for services. Taxable services under the current VAT are the provision of processing, repairs, and replacement services. VAT only covers services related to industrial activities. Other services are still subject to Business Tax.

A three-tier system applies to VAT. In addition to a standard rate of 17 per cent, a lower rate of 13 per cent is applied to sales and imports of basic subsistence goods such as foodstuffs, water and gas supply, heating, books and magazines, and so on. The lower rate also applies to the agricultural sector, such as sales of fertilisers, agricultural machines, and feed. Export of goods is levied at zero tax rate.

A simplified tax calculation method was adopted for the benefit of small wholesale and retail enterprises. Small businesses dealing with the production of taxable goods and/or services with annual sales of less than RMB 1.0 million are subject to presumptive levy, at 6 per cent of their annual sales turnover. Small businesses dealing with the sale of taxable goods with annual sales of less than RMB 1.8 million are subject to the same rule. The rate has been lowered to 4 per cent since July 1998.

Consumption tax

The consumption tax is an additional excise tax imposed on taxable goods that are considered as luxury goods. They include cigarettes (with 25 to 50 per cent tax rate on an *ad valorem* basis), alcoholic beverages (with 10 to 25 per cent tax rate; for beer, RMB 220 per tonne), jewellery (with five or 10 per cent tax rate on an *ad valorem* basis), gasoline (RMB 0.2 per litre for unleaded fuel), and diesel (RMB 0.1 per litre). Cars are levied at 3 to 8 per cent tax rate, according to the type and cylinder capacity of the vehicle, and motorcycles at 10 per cent. The justification for these excise taxes, as in many countries, is to raise revenue from the consumption of luxury goods and, in the case of tobacco and alcoholic drinks, to penalise smoking and drinking. Starting in 2001, an additional tax burden will be levied at RMB 150 per 50 thousand rolls on cigarettes.

Business tax

The business tax is levied on turnover of taxable services, transfer of intangible assets, or sales of immovable properties in China. For example, financial and insurance business is subject to 8 per cent business tax. Banks will be levied 8 per cent business tax on profits arising from their on-lending business (*i.e.* profits arising from differences between active (lending) and passive (deposits) interest rates). An 8 per cent rate business tax is also levied on profits from securities transactions (capital gains). Insurance companies are also taxed at 8 per cent on profits arising from the difference between original insurance premium and the reinsurance premium paid to the re-insurers.

A business tax rate of 5 per cent applies to services, transfer of intangible assets, and sales of immovable properties and a 3 per cent rate applies to communications and transportation, construction, post and telecommunications, and culture and sports. For entertainment, local governments can levy a business tax rate from 5 to 20 per cent.

The tax rate for financial institutions will be lowered by 1 per cent every year, starting in 2001, to 5 per cent in 2003 (7 per cent in 2001, 6 per cent in 2002 and 5 per cent in 2003). This has been decided in anticipation of the projected impact of WTO on financial institutions in China. The tax rate for entertainment will be unified to 20 per cent by the central government.

Individual income tax

Any individual domiciled in China or with no domicile in China but resident in China for one year or more, shall pay individual income tax on his/her worldwide income. Regardless of domicile or residency status, any individual resident in China for less than one year shall pay Individual Income Tax on his/her income from sources inside China.

Wages and salaries, income from individual household production or business operations and income from contract or lease operations of enterprises or institutions are subject to progressive tax rates. Wages and salaries are taxed with a nine-tiered progressive tax rate varying from 5 per cent to 45 per cent, and other incomes are taxed at a five-tier progressive tax schedule (from 5 per cent to 35 per cent). Remuneration for personal service, author's remuneration, royalties, income from leases of property, income from transfer of property, contingent income and interest, dividends and bonuses are subject to the nominal rate of 20 per cent.

Individual income tax for Chinese individuals is levied on monthly wages and salaries after a lump-sum deduction of RMB 800. Those with no domicile in China but earning wages and salaries from China or domiciled in China and earning wages and salaries from outside China may enjoy additional monthly lump-sum deductions of RMB 3 200.

Enterprise income tax

From 1994, the enterprise income tax applies to all enterprises and organisations in China except foreign investment enterprises (FIEs) and foreign enterprises. The latter are subject to the tax on their worldwide income. Besides the statutory rate of 33 per cent, two lower rates of 18 per cent and 27 per cent are designed for enterprises with lower income. Domestic enterprises with annual taxable income of less than RMB 30 000 are taxed at 18 per cent and those with annual taxable income of more than RMB 30 000 and less than RMB 100 000 are taxed at 27 per cent.

The enterprise income tax is paid to local governments, except for taxes on enterprises serving for central governments and on headquarters of financial institutions, which are paid to the central government.

Foreign enterprises income tax

Income tax on foreign invested enterprises and foreign enterprises (Foreign Enterprises Income Tax, hereinafter referred to as FEIT) applies only to enterprises with foreign investment (Foreign Invested Enterprises; hereinafter referred to as FIEs) and foreign enterprises. As with enterprise income tax, foreign invested enterprises are taxed on their worldwide income, whereas foreign enterprises are taxable only on their Chinese-sourced income.

Foreign invested enterprises and foreign enterprises carrying out business in China on a permanent establishment are taxable on net income at 33 per cent, of which 30 per cent is for central government and 3 per cent for local governments. A tax of 20 per cent of gross income is levied on the Chinese-originated income of foreign enterprises with no permanent establishment in China.

The FEIT is levied on taxable income net of costs, expenses, and losses (with the above exception of foreign enterprises without an establishment in China). Compared with the enterprise income tax for domestic enterprises, the range of before-tax deductions for costs, expenses and losses is wide. The rules for calculating income largely follow internationally accepted accounting principles. Generous tax incentives are contained in the law (which is discussed below).

Tax revenue assignment and legislation

With respect to intergovernmental fiscal relations in China, a tax-sharing system was introduced in 1994. Under the existing system, tax revenue in China is divided into central tax revenue, local tax revenue and the tax revenue shared between the central and local governments. To administer this system, separate national and local tax administrations have been established. The central tax administration is responsible for collecting central taxes and shared taxes. The local tax administration is now part of the finance departments of local governments and collects local taxes. It is financed from local revenues.

The tax system in China is highly centralised. With the exception of a few minor local taxes, local government has no tax legislation authority. Under the current tax laws, the state bodies which have authority on tax laws or tax policy include the National People's Congress and its Standing Committee, the State Council, the Ministry of Finance, and the State Tax Administration. The National People's Congress enacts tax laws. The State Council formulates the administrative regulations and rules concerning taxation. The Ministry of Finance and the State Tax Administration work out the departmental rules (see Chapter 20 on central-local government fiscal relationships).

Tax-GDP *ratio and the tax mix*

There has been a declining trend in the ratio of tax revenue to GDP over the past 20 years (see Table 18.2). The ratio was 22.8 per cent in 1985, when it reached its peak. It then declined to a low of 10.2 per cent in 1996. The decrease halted in 1997 and the ratio started to rise. In 1999, it reached a peak of 13 per cent since the 1994 tax reforms.

Compared with many countries, the tax-GDP ratio in China is still low. The ratio of total tax revenues to GDP in the European Union (EU) was about 42 per cent in 1999. Even excluding social security contributions, the share of total tax revenue to GDP in EU countries was about 30 per cent in 1999. For all OECD countries in 1999, the share of total tax revenue, including social security contributions, was about 37 per cent, and, excluding social security contribution was about 28 per cent.

There are many factors accounting for the decrease of China's tax revenue in proportion to GDP (which will be discussed in detail in the next section).

Tax revenues in China heavily rely on turnover taxes (VAT, Consumption Tax and Business Tax). As shown in Table 18.3, turnover taxes raised 65.1 per cent of total tax revenue in China in 1999, of which 41.3 per cent came from VAT. Due to the differences in definition of tax categories, it is difficult to

Table 18.2. **Total tax revenue in proportion to GDP**

	China	OECD	EU
1985	22.8	33.8 (25.9)	37.9 (27.7)
1990	15.2	35.0 (26.8)	39.2 (28.3)
1995	10.3	36.1	40.0
1999	13.0	37.3 (27.7)	41.6 (30.2)

Note: Figures in parenthesis for all OECD and EU shows total tax revenue excluding social security contribution.
Source: *China Statistical Yearbook, 2000; OECD Revenue Statistics 1965-2000 (2001).*

Table 18.3. **Tax revenue breakdown in percentage**

Type of Tax	Proportion of total tax revenue (%) 1997	Proportion of total tax revenue (%) 1999
Turnover tax	**65.3**	**65.1**
VAT	41.0	41.3
Consumption tax	8.4	7.9
Business tax	15.9	15.9
Tax on incomes	**15.8**	**15.4**
Enterprise Income tax	11.0	9.5
Income tax on enterprises with foreign investment and foreign enterprises	1.7	2.0
Individual Income tax	3.1	3.9
Other taxes	**19.1**	**19.5**
Resource tax	0.7	0.6
City and township land use tax	0.5	0.6
City maintenance and construction tax	3.2	3.0
Fixed assets investment orientation regulation tax	0.9	1.2
House property tax and urban real estate tax	1.5	1.7
Stamp tax	3.1	2.6
Agriculture tax and animal husbandry tax	4.1	4.0
Customs duties	3.8	5.3
Other taxes	1.3	0.5
Total	**100.0**	**100.0**

Source: *Tax Yearbook of China.*

compare precisely the tax mix in China with that of OECD countries. However, the share of taxes on general consumption and on specific goods and services in OECD countries was about 31 to 32 per cent of total tax revenue over the past 25 years (see Table 18.4).

Table 18.4. **Tax structures in OECD countries**

Average percentage share of total tax revenue

	1975	1985	1995	1999
Personal income tax	30	30	27	26
Corporate income tax	8	8	8	9
General consumption tax	13	16	18	19
Specific consumption tax	18	16	13	12
Social security contribution	22	22	25	25
Payroll tax	1	1	1	1
Property tax	6	5	5	5
Other taxes	2	2	3	3
Total	**100**	**100**	**100**	**100**

Source: OECD, *Revenue Statistics, 1965-2000* (2001).

Contrary to most developed countries, revenue from direct taxes is low in China. Tax revenue from Enterprise Income Tax, FEIT, and Individual Income Tax represents only about 15 per cent of total tax revenue, while in OECD countries, the proportion of revenue from personal income tax and corporate income tax to total tax revenue has remained around 35 per cent in recent years (see Tables 18.3 and 18.4).

Implications of trade and investment liberalisation for Chinese taxation

WTO *agreements and the Chinese tax system*

Most of the WTO agreements do not directly require member countries to make policy changes in the area of taxation, the only exception being the rule on the prohibition of export and import subsidies, including tax subsidies. Nevertheless, tax policy is not free from direct and indirect impacts of further liberalisation of trade and investment, given that fundamental policy implications are foreseen in a number of areas in China. The process is likely to prompt another round of tax reforms in China. This section analyses several tax issues that may need to be addressed in the near term.

Tax *policies incompatible with* WTO *principles*

To encourage exports from China or to protect specific domestic goods, the Chinese government has made use of preferential tax treatments. China has also made heavy use of preferential tax treatments to encourage exports. These are likely to be considered as export-promotion or import-substitution subsidies which are prohibited by the WTO agreements.

On the other hand, domestic enterprises enjoy certain tax treatments which are more favourable than those for foreign invested enterprises and foreign enterprises, and which are likely to be regarded as violating the WTO principles of national treatment or non-discrimination.

Tax *subsidies*

Tax subsidies prohibited by WTO principles include the reduction and exemption of direct taxes (typically as in FEIT) directly related to exported goods, and tax refunds and tax exemptions in excess of the payable indirect tax (typically VAT) of similar domestic products. Tax support to import substitution is also prohibited. This includes tax subsidies in the form of reductions of, and exemption

631

from, enterprise income tax, and excessive tax credits against VAT on inputs. Some Chinese tax regulations are likely to violate WTO rules. Examples are as follows:

- Some tax exemptions in FEIT are contingent directly on export performances. For example, export-oriented enterprises with foreign investment may enjoy a further 50 per cent reduction of FEIT if the value of a given year's exported products exceeds 70 per cent of the total value of the products of that year. This will be regarded as a clear violation of WTO rules.

- Some tax measures are used to encourage the use of domestic goods over imported goods. In order to encourage enterprises manufacturing goods for export to use domestically-produced steel, for example, 27 domestic steel companies enjoy VAT exemption on the purchase of steel. These companies include Baoshan, Anshan, and Capital Steel Companies. Moreover, enterprises purchasing steel subject to VAT are entitled to a VAT refund.

- To reduce cotton stocks and encourage enterprises manufacturing goods for export, the government grants tax exemptions, tax credits and refunds for inputs of locally produced cotton. At present, VAT charged by enterprises with foreign investment (FIEs) on their purchase of specified domestically-produced equipment is refunded 100 per cent. Again, these tax treatments appear to be a clear violation of the WTO rules.

Favourable tax treatment for domestic enterprises

While a number of tax incentives are available for foreign-related enterprises, domestic enterprises can also enjoy special tax treatments for which foreign-related enterprises are ineligible. These special tax treatments for domestic enterprises also raise doubts as to their compatibility with WTO principles for national treatment or non-discrimination.

Favourable VAT treatments for domestic enterprises

The current VAT system allows special treatments for domestic enterprises by "imposition first and then refund". For example, state-owned enterprises and domestic group-enterprises dealing with sales of meat, fowl, eggs, fishery products, and vegetables are entitled to immediate refunds of VAT levied on their business. Domestic enterprises engaged in waste goods and materials also enjoy the same treatment. Another example is a VAT treatment for certain domestic self-made products. Computer software developed and sold by domestic taxpayers is initially charged VAT at 17 per cent. However, tax payments exceeding 6 per cent will be refunded afterwards. This treatment is equivalent to a tax subsidy to protect domestically produced goods, which is prohibited by WTO rules.

Favourable enterprise income tax treatment for domestic enterprises

Enterprise income tax, which is applicable only to domestic enterprises, provides some favourable tax treatment that is not available to foreign-related enterprises.

Certain tax holidays are only available to domestic enterprises. For example, service income generated by state-owned science and technology research institutions through technology transfer, the provision of technical consulting, and technical services, or acting as a technology subcontractor, are exempt from income tax.

Domestic enterprises engaging in agricultural production, fisheries, forestry and husbandry are permanently entitled to full income tax exemption. Foreign enterprises in the same industries, however, only receive the standard five-year tax holiday.

Newly established domestic enterprises that engage in services such as trade, tourism and catering may enjoy a one-year income tax exemption or reduction, after approval by the competent tax authorities. Foreign invested enterprises engaging in similar services are ineligible for income tax exemption or reduction, except those in the special economic zones.

Preferential tax treatment for foreign investors

The Chinese government has been using the tax system to achieve its policy goal of attracting foreign direct investment over the past two decades. The number of preferential tax treatments available to foreign invested enterprises and foreign enterprises greatly exceed those available to domestic enterprises and investors. Tax incentives in foreign invested enterprises have played a central role in attracting foreign direct investment. All incentives and concessions are aimed at expanding export potential, improving economic management and development, attaining high levels of technology, and attracting investments in China's favour. The incentives can be classified as follows:

Tax Incentives provided to specified regions

Reduced income tax rates of 15 per cent or 24 per cent, rather than the statutory 30 per cent rate for the central government, apply to foreign invested enterprises and/or foreign enterprises in a number of areas according to the features of their business activities:

- Special economic zones (SEZ) (five zones);
- Open coastal economic zones (OCEZ) (277 zones);
- Economic technological development zones (ETDZ) (32 zones);
- High and new technology zones (52 zones);
- Old urban districts of cities where SEZ and ETDZ are located
- Coastal open cities (14 cities);
- Coastal open areas (260 areas);
- Capital cities of interior provinces (18 cities);
- Open cities along the Yangtze river (six cities);
- National tourism areas (11 zones);
- Bonded areas (13 areas);
- Shanghai Pudong New Area (one area);
- Suzhou Industrial Park (one area)

FIEs located in west China are eligible for a 50 per cent income tax reduction (from the statutory tax rate of 30 per cent to an effective 15 per cent) for an additional three years following the expiry of the normal available tax holiday (see Chapters 10 and 21).

Tax incentives to encourage production type foreign invested enterprises

Foreign invested enterprises engaging in production (for example, machinery, the energy industry, construction, transport) are eligible for two years exemption from income tax starting with the first profit-making year, and a 50 per cent reduction in income tax in the subsequent three years, if their contract period is not less than ten years.

Tax incentives to stimulate specific industries

Chinese-foreign joint ventures engaged in harbour or wharf construction with an operating contract of no less than 15 years may apply for a five-year tax exemption starting with the first profit-making year, and a 50 per cent reduction in the subsequent five years. Foreign invested enterprises classified as technically advanced enterprises may enjoy a three-year extension of the 50 per cent tax reduction. Foreign invested enterprises exporting 70 per cent or more of their output in a given year are eligible for a 50 per cent tax reduction in that year even after the expiry of the normal tax holiday.

Financial institutions with foreign investment exceeding US$10 million and with an operating life of ten years or longer and locating in SEZs or other districts approved by the State Council, qualify for a one-year income tax exemption starting with the first profit-making year, and a 50 per cent tax reduction in the following two years. Foreign invested enterprises located in remote underdeveloped areas with an operating contract of no less than ten years, may apply for 15-30 per cent reductions in their income tax for an additional ten years after the expiry of the two-year exemption and the three-year 50 per cent reduction.

Tax refund on reinvestment

Foreign investors of foreign invested enterprises that reinvest their share of profits in China for a period of no less than five years may obtain a tax refund of 40 per cent of the income tax paid on the amount of reinvestment. If the reinvestment is made in establishing or expanding an export-oriented enterprise or a technologically advanced enterprise in China, the tax refund is 100 per cent. Foreign investors of foreign invested enterprises established in Hainan province (Hainan SEZ) who reinvest their share of profits in Hainan's infrastructure or agricultural development may also obtain a 100 per cent tax refund on the reinvested profit.

These incentives do not apply to domestic enterprises. The Enterprise Income Tax Law contains fewer tax incentives for domestic enterprises or domestic investors. Although its tax rate is 33 per cent, including 3 per cent of local enterprise income tax, many local governments grant foreign invested enterprises local income tax holidays. In fact, the effective tax burden of domestic enterprises is about 24 per cent and the effective tax rate for foreign invested enterprises is around 14.6 per cent.

Rethinking tax incentives

Unlike the tax subsidies discussed above, which are directly contingent on export performance or on use of domestically produced goods over imported goods, and which are clearly in violation of WTO rules, tax incentives more favourable to foreign investors do not directly violate the WTO rules. Those tax incentives have been introduced by the Chinese government to promote foreign investments, to encourage exports and thus to stimulate economic developments in China. However, attention should be drawn to their possible negative effects. These could be summarised as follows:

Distortions in the Chinese market

Foreign investment enterprises and domestic enterprises both operate under the same economic system, confronting the same market. "Super national" tax treatment for foreign enterprises results in unfair competition for domestic enterprises, causing distortions in the Chinese market. It may have discouraged domestic enterprises and domestic investors from accessing the international market.

Intensified regional disparities

One of the important factors determining capital inflows is the expected capital return from investments. Because tax incentives can increase after-tax returns, they play a role in attracting investment, although other factors also play an important role. The coastal regions have far better transportation and communication networks. In 1999, twelve coastal provinces, municipalities and autonomous regions accounted for about 82 per cent, 88 per cent and 87.7 per cent respectively of total foreign investments, contractual foreign funds, and actual use of foreign funds. This high share of foreign investments is probably due to a combination of tax incentives and better transport and communications in the coastal provinces, while central and western regions are penalised on both accounts.

Erosion of tax revenue

Preferential tax treatments contributed to the huge erosion of tax revenues. According to some studies, foreign tax concessions resulted in about RMB 130 billion of erosion in 1996, including customs duty, accounting for 1.5 per cent of GDP. This means that more than 10 per cent of total tax revenue is estimated to be lost every year due to these tax incentives.

Comprehensive review of existing tax incentives is necessary

Although current tax incentives in China for attracting foreign investments are not in clear violation of WTO rules, China's accession to WTO does provide a good opportunity to rethink current schemes. Given the negative effects of tax incentives, China needs to reconsider whether they are still in line with the original policy objectives and whether the latter has been achieved. Since many tax incentives were introduced over the past twenty years in a piecemeal fashion, these complicate the tax system, raising compliance costs for taxpayers and administrative costs for governments. Wide discretionary power attached to the implementation of the schemes may feed corruption.

As explained above, different tax systems for foreign-related enterprises and domestic enterprises are causing problems in China. The current system raises doubts as to whether it is compliant with the WTO rule of national treatment. Unification of the current two-track system for corporate income tax needs urgent consideration by the Chinese government. Reassessing the current tax incentive schemes for attracting foreign investment constitutes an important part of this task.

Problems of the current VAT system

Value Added Tax (VAT) is the most important source of tax revenue. Tax revenue from VAT accounts for about 40 per cent of total tax revenue. There are three types of VAT in the world: production-type VAT, income-type VAT and consumption-type VAT. At present, most countries adopt the consumption-type. VAT also applies to all goods and most services. China has established a production-type VAT, which applies to sales of goods, imports of goods, provision of processing services and industrial repairs and replacement. Under a production-type VAT, the tax levied on purchases of fixed assets necessary for production cannot be credited against VAT charged on sales of products.

The current VAT system in China was designed to suit the particular economic climate in 1993. China was then experiencing double-digit inflation, and cutting capital investments was an important economic policy objective at that time. By adopting production-type VAT, the government did not grant VAT refunds (or deductions) on fixed asset inputs for taxable goods. This played a role in reducing capital investments, cooling off the overheated economy at that time. Since then, however, China has been facing only mild inflation, or even deflation in the past few years. The rationale for production-type VAT, therefore, no longer exists and the side effects of the current VAT system have implications for the development of China's economy.

Current VAT system penalises capital-intensive industries

Because VAT paid on fixed inputs cannot be offset, problems of double taxation arise when VAT is imposed on product sales. It constrains investments, in particular investments for capital-intensive industries like computer and information technology, where intensive capital investments in fixed assets are key to success. The current production-type VAT favours low-tech, labour-intensive industries and penalises high-tech capital-intensive industries.

In this connection, the current VAT system creates imbalances in tax burdens among enterprises with different capital structures. Currently, most energy and raw material extractive industries that require intensive-capital investments are located in the central and western areas of China. Production-type VAT aggravates the tax burden on industries in the region, and may contribute to widening the gap between the regions.

Double taxation problems arising from VAT and business tax

Double taxation problems also arise because of inconsistency between VAT and business tax. Since the current VAT does not cover services of non-industrial business, transportation services are taxed through business tax. For example, an airline company in China has to pay VAT on its purchases of aircraft; however, this VAT on inputs on fixed assets (aircraft) is non refundable from the company's business tax on its provision of transportation services. Neither it is refundable under the current production-type VAT, even if the company's services are subject to VAT. The co-existence of VAT and business tax in the current turnover tax system in China not only complicates the system but also raises serious practical problems for taxpayers.

Moving to consumption-type VAT *is necessary*

It is now urgent that the Chinese government transform the VAT system into the consumption-type and expand the scope of the tax to include all services. VAT on input refunds on the acquisition of fixed assets should be granted under the new system. It is also necessary to reconsider the role of business tax and consumption tax. With the expansion of the scope of VAT, business tax would need to be abolished.

The government might, however, hesitate to proceed with this reform because of the possible negative impact on revenues once the VAT on inputs deduction is granted on fixed assets. Another negative impact could be derived from repealing the right to fully deduct VAT on inputs on exports for foreign-related enterprises, which will be discussed below. Nevertheless, this reform is necessary to expand the VAT tax base to all services and to enhance consistency within the turnover tax system, making Chinese VAT truly compatible with international standards.

Lessons from disputes over VAT refunds for exports

It is an established international practice to exempt VAT on exported goods and services and refund 100 per cent of the VAT on inputs concerned, because the VAT on exports would be borne by the ultimate consumers outside the country of production. The Chinese VAT law follows this international practice. However, due to the unexpectedly large amount of VAT refunds (also due to fraud) at the first stage of the implementation of the current VAT system, in August 1994 the government issued an order to cease refunding VAT on inputs on exports to foreign-related enterprises. Although the government stated in November 1994 that the VAT on inputs to foreign-related enterprises that were established after January 1994 would be refunded, the refund rate was limited to 14 per cent (against the VAT rate of 17 per cent). The refund rate was further lowered to 9 per cent in 1995.

Since then, this issue has been the focus of foreign businesses operating in China, which is of concern to the Chinese government. There are three considerations that need attention.

First, foreign enterprises in China have not yet fully recovered from the placement of VAT on exports, in spite of positive action by the Chinese government. In particular, a government order in 1999 decreed full refunds on exports of major goods like machinery, equipment, electronic devices, transportation equipment and measurement devices. Further actions are expected. The current average rate of recovery is reportedly about 15 per cent – as opposed to the 17 per cent VAT on inputs rate.

Second, the policy change was made in a very discriminatory manner. Domestic enterprises continued to get full refunds on VAT on inputs while foreign-related enterprises were able to recover only part of VAT on inputs on exports. In addition to that, there were differentiated treatments even among the foreign-related enterprises. Those established before the introduction of the new VAT (January 1994) were not entitled to any VAT on inputs refund until very recently (January 2001), while those established after January 1994 were able to recover at least part of their outlays.

Differentiated tax treatments against foreign-related taxpayers with no reasonable grounds have caused concern among foreign investors as to the transparency of tax policies in China (see Chapter 10 on Foreign Direct Investment).

Third, and probably the most serious problem, is the way the tax policy changes were made. Policies written in VAT legislation were overridden by a number of government orders and/or government statements. Some government orders issued from one department contradicted those of other departments. Changes in the refund rate and calculation methods were announced at short intervals, confusing foreign businesses in China.

Changing tax policies without following due legal process raises serious concerns among foreign investors as to China's business environment. Sudden policy changes might be seen as arbitrary.

Business needs predictability. Transparency, stability, and the rule of law are necessary attributes of tax policy and tax administration (see Chapter 11).

Ratio of tax revenue to GDP

There is probably little disagreement over the need to increase the level of taxation in China. As indicated earlier, there has been a declining trend in the ratio of tax revenue to GDP over the past 20 years. Even compared to some developing countries, the ratio in recent years has remained low.

China faces heavy pressure on expenditure in the near term to further develop its social security system, to provide support to unemployed and laid-off workers, and to continue to build infrastructure. It is clear that the current level of tax revenues is insufficient to finance all of these. In 1996, the World Bank estimated China's financing gaps and concluded that additional expenditure needed was equivalent to about 6 per cent of GDP. The major spending gaps are in the areas of health and education (2.3 per cent of GDP) and infrastructure (1 per cent of GDP). Social insurance, pensions and environmental protection are other areas where expenditure gaps now exist or are likely to occur. There are many factors explaining the decrease of tax revenue as a percentage of GDP. The main factors are as follows:

Decline in tax revenues due to changes in the ownership system

China's ownership structure has undergone a fundamental change over the past two decades, from very heavy reliance on state-owned enterprises to a mixed economy where non-state-owned enterprises play a very important role. GDP of non-state-owned enterprises was RMB 4 348 billion accounting for 58 per cent of total GDP in 1997. It was 44 per cent in 1978. With regard to industry, state-owned enterprises account for 34 per cent of the industrial added value, and non-state-owned enterprises 66 per cent. By 1998, the domestic private sector had grown to about 27 per cent of GDP, but tax contribution by the non-state-owned sector was not proportionate to its increased role in the whole economy. This is an important factor in explaining the low tax-GDP ratio. In 1997, the turnover tax burden of state-owned industrial and commercial enterprises was over 6 per cent and that of non-state-owned industrial and commercial enterprises was 4 per cent. The income tax burden of state-owned industrial and commercial enterprises was 28 per cent and that of non-state-owned industrial and commercial enterprises was 20 per cent.

Tax incentives for foreign-related enterprises may account for the relatively low income tax burden of non-state-owned industrial and commercial enterprises. But it should be mentioned that the tax revenue from foreign investment enterprises and foreign enterprises accounts for 16 per cent of the total tax revenue, ranking first among the non-state-owned sector. In 1999, the revenue of state-owned enterprises accounted for 50 per cent; collectively-owned enterprises accounted for 12 per cent, holding companies 11 per cent, individual industrial and commercial households 6 per cent, privatised enterprises 2.6 per cent, co-operative holding companies 1.6 per cent, joint ventures 1.2 per cent and other enterprises about 1 per cent. When the same tax system is applied, difference in treatments from the tax administration is likely to be another important factor explaining different tax burdens among enterprises depending on their category of ownership.

Decline in tax revenues due to change in the structure of production

Because different sectors make different contributions to tax revenue, changes to the production structure will affect the volume of tax revenue. The proportion of the primary and tertiary sectors to GDP decreased gradually between 1993 and 1996 while that of industry slightly increased. China has been applying a light tax burden to the primary sector. The tax burden of the primary sector rose gradually while that of secondary and tertiary sectors continued to fall. Since the main source of tax revenue are the secondary and tertiary sectors, the change of tax burdens for the two kinds of activity negatively affect the growth of the tax-GDP ratio.

Sharp rise in non-tax revenue

China's ratio of tax revenue to GDP has been low. Between 1990 and 1996, the highest tax ratio to GDP was 13.6 per cent in 1990 and the lowest was 10.2 per cent in 1996. Notably these were even lower than some developing countries' standards. The low tax revenue has partly been made up for by a relatively high level of "extra-budgetary' revenues, most of which are collected by, and accrued to local governments (see Chapter 20 on central-local government fiscal relations). Officially authorised extra-budgetary revenues have averaged about 4 per cent of GDP since 1997, or nearly one-third of tax revenues. While their exact amount is not publicly known, discretionary fees and charges collected by local governments are reported to have grown rapidly during the 1990s and may now substantially exceed authorised extra-budgetary revenues. Some sources report that total extra-budgetary revenues, including those reported in official sources, plus other fees and charges collected by local governments but which are either discretionary or not reported in official sources, amount to at least 8 to 10 per cent of GDP, and possibly to as much as 15 per cent of GDP. If the higher figure is correct, extra-budgetary revenues exceed the amount of tax revenues. However, again, due to a lack of official statistics, it is difficult to verify those figures.

At sub-national levels, the unduly high ratio of non-tax revenue to GDP is prominent. In some areas, charges and fees exceed local tax revenue, and even exceed the budget revenue. The following are some examples. According to (incomplete) statistics, in Hebei province, the total charges and fees were RMB 14.6 billion, 1.7 times the level of tax revenue in 1996. According to a 1997 survey of 91 individual households and private enterprises in Yueyanglou district, Yueyang city, Hunan province, they paid RMB 4.44 million in fees and charges, and RMB 2.05 million in taxes. For the Yueyanglou district, the total amount of fees and charges was RMB 33.7 million, of which RMB 2.0 million is budgetary revenue governed by the financial department, accounting for only 5.9 per cent of the total.

In October 1999, the Office for Reduction of Enterprise Burdens of the State Council announced that central government departments had cancelled 39 items of unreasonable fees and charges, amounting to RMB 6.9 billion, after a government resolution aimed at curbing arbitrary levy was approved in 1997. In addition, provincial governments eliminated 4 288 items, incorporated 76 items and lowered the criteria of 89 items, reducing RMB 32.7 billion of fees and other charges. Sub-province governments also reduced 21 410 items, amounting to RMB 13.9 billion.

Because fees and charges are accrued to local governments and specified departments, they tend to put more effort into collecting fees and charges than taxes. For example, electricity departments can cut off electricity if charges are not paid. Therefore, the collection of fees and charges increases more rapidly than tax revenue. This results in the erosion of tax revenue. While the tax-GDP ratio is relatively low, the actual financial burden to enterprises is high. This system creates disincentives to businesses and hampers the development of the economy.

The random collection of fees and charges also has other negative effects. It squeezes out tax revenue, hampers effective fiscal management and budgetary control and leads to misallocation of funds. It also distorts businesses' long-term decisions and hinders the attraction of foreign investment.

Moreover, the random application of fees and charges that are collected and spent at the discretion of government departments affects the transparency of China's governmental policies. In accordance with WTO principles, the implementation of a member's laws and regulations should be standardised and transparent.

There are many reasons for the random collection of charges and fees such as swelling administrative structures, and multiple tiers of administration. While the hands of local governments are tied in terms of tax legislation, there is no strict limitation on them not to collect fees and funds. When their tax revenues cannot meet their need to maintain operation, collection of fees and charges is a way out (see Chapter 20 on central-local government fiscal relations).

Agriculture tax and actual peasant burdens

China has a rural population of about 0.9 billion. Although the agricultural tax only accounts for a small amount of the total tax revenue, its impact on incomes should not be underestimated. As a labour-intensive industry, agriculture, which is under comparatively high protection, will be greatly affected by trade and investment liberalisation. The government should consider easing the negative impact on peasant income.

Agriculture tax

Agriculture tax is the most ancient tax in China, traceable back to the Shang Dynasty. The current tax provisions are fixed by the Agricultural Tax Law of the People's Republic China of 1958. It still features the ancient field-tax (Tianfu) system. Taxpayers of the agriculture tax include co-operative economic entities, enterprises, other entities, peasants and other individuals who are engaged in agricultural production and receive agricultural income. The agriculture tax adopts regionally differentiated flat rates. Although the national average rate is 15.5 per cent of the yield in a normal year, the currently implemented average rate is 8.8 per cent and the actual burden is only about 2.5 per cent. In most cases, the agricultural tax is paid in kind, *i.e.* in grain, and the final settlement is made in currency. The tax on specific agricultural products is computed on an *ad valorem* basis ranging between five per cent and 25 per cent.

Actual peasant burden

The so-called "peasant burden" problem became increasingly serious during the 1990s, raising nationwide concern (see also Chapter 1). Reforming the agriculture taxation and fees system and reducing the peasant burden are regarded as very important for rural stability. According to current laws and regulations, this burden could be classified into the following four categories:

- Taxes. These include the agriculture tax and tax on agricultural specific products that are paid by farmers engaged in agricultural production.

- The "three village levies and five-unified township fees" (three *tiliu* and five *tongchou*) and compulsory rural labour. The levies are the contributions by farmers to the public accumulation fund, the public welfare fund, and administrative fees. The fees are the five items of 1) township and village education, 2) family planning, 3) township and village transport construction, 4) militia exercises, and 5) social expenses. According to the regulations by the State Council in 1991, the "three village levies and five-unified township fees" should not exceed five per cent of farmer's previous annual average net income per capita.

- Miscellaneous fees stemming from *ad hoc* regulations.

- The fulfilment produce order to farms set by the state.

Problems concerning the "peasant burden"

Heavy non-tax burden

According to a "peasant burden" survey of 5 000 farm households conducted by the State Administration of Taxation in 1997, the tax burden of peasants was only RMB 46 per household, accounting for 24 per cent of the total household peasant burden of RMB 195. The non-tax burden, which was RMB 49, accounting for 76 per cent of the total, was much higher. In the non-tax burden, the "three village levies and five-unified township fees" accounted for 34 per cent, rural compulsory labour (converted into RMB) 31 per cent, and apportionment for raising funds 13 per cent of the total peasant burden.

Heavier tax burden in the less developed regions

Due to the low-income level in the less developed regions, although in absolute terms the average peasant burden in these areas is comparatively smaller, its proportion to total peasant income is high. According to a survey of the 125 townships (see Table 18.5), in rural regions where the agricultural GDP per farmer is less than RMB 3000, the average burden is RMB 115.2, accounting for 6.6 per cent, while in the regions where the agricultural GDP per farmer is over RMB 11000, the average burden is RMB 212.8 accounting for 0.8 per cent.

Table 18.5. **Average peasant tax burden in regions with different income levels, 1997**
Monetary unit: RMB

Groups by annual income per farmer (RMB)	Average burden per farmer (RMB)	Average burden in proportion to average agriculture GDP (%)
Less than 3 000	115.2	6.6
3 000-5 000	165.1	4.3
5 000-7 000	128.4	2.1
7 000-9 000	216.8	2.6
9 000-11 000	166.0	1.7
More than 11 000	212.8	0.8

Source: Secretariat calculations based on Chinese data.

Problems with the agriculture tax

High nominal tax rate and low effective tax burden

Securing a stable tax burden has been an important policy in implementing the agriculture tax. The existing tax targets were fixed in 1961. Due to the difference between the actual output and taxable output, the actual tax burden is decreasing. In 1996, the actual agricultural output was 544.6 kilograms of grains per household and the taxable output was only 142.4 kilograms, accounting for 26 per cent of the actual output. The effective tax burden was 9.3 per cent in 1961, 4.4 per cent in 1978, and 2.3 per cent in 1996, while the nominal rate of the agriculture tax is 15.5 per cent. The big difference between nominal tax rate and effective tax burden is that it makes the tax base and tax rate meaningless, and the agriculture tax revenue decreases.

Gap between the current land area and taxable land area

With economic development and rapid population increase, taxable lands are decreasing every year. During 1978-1996, the population rose by 21.7 per cent to reach 1.2 billion. Meanwhile, cultivated land fell by 4.5 per cent from 9 939 km^2 to 9 491 km^2. It decreased by 22.6 per cent per capita. In some areas, the newly cultivated land after the expiry of the exemption period is not included in the taxable land. In some areas, losses caused by the reduction of taxable lands are compensated with higher tax on the existing taxable area so as to fulfil the assessed task, resulting in an unequal tax burden.

Shift from agriculture tax revenue to fees at local government level

The agriculture tax system was introduced under the centrally planned economy. It has not been reformed despite the rapid development of agriculture, resulting in the decrease in agriculture tax revenue. After the implementation of the revenue-sharing system, the agriculture tax revenue becomes the major financial source of county and township level governments. Because limited tax revenues could not meet the increasing needs of government expenditures, local governments financed the required spending programmes through arbitrary collection of fees and charges.

Efforts at reforming agriculture tax

In recent years, the Chinese government has initiated trial reforms of the agriculture tax in some regions so as to lighten the peasants' burden and normalise revenue distribution. These could be summarised into three main points: 1) Changing fees into taxes, namely, incorporating "three village levies and five-unified township fees" into taxes; 2) Reassessing the tax base; and 3) Cancelling unreasonable fees.

The programme aims to raise the rate of agriculture tax to 8.4 per cent. The "three village levies and five-unified township fees", and the random collection of fees and charges will be cancelled. It will be up to the central government to take measures to fill the possibly large gap between revenue and public expenditures.

Conclusion and reflections on future tax reforms

Directions for tax reforms in China

As China has progressively opened up its market over the last twenty years, the tax system has developed in pace with economic and social developments. Further opening up of China's trade and investments is expected to have significant effects on the Chinese economy in the short term, as well as in the medium and long term. These should provide impetus for another round of tax reforms in China and for improving tax administration.

The Chinese State Administration of Taxation (SAT) officials have indicated the directions of tax reforms in the near future as follows:

1. Tax policies incompatible with WTO principles should be modified.
2. Tax measures compatible with WTO principles should be formulated to foster the adjustment of industrial and capital structures and improve the competitiveness of national industries in the international market.
3. Income taxes for domestic enterprises and foreign investment enterprises will be gradually unified to maintain the tax equity principle and implement "national treatment". Tax incentives will be revised to promote China's economic policy and developments in certain industries.
4. The ratio of tax revenue to GDP will be raised.
5. Production-type VAT will be changed into consumption-type tax.
6. Tax should replace fees, including in agriculture. Some new taxes will be introduced, such as inheritance, gift tax, and petroleum tax.
7. Elements of the consumption and business tax will be adjusted.
8. The coverage of individual income tax will be enlarged, with a view of income redistribution in favour of the poor.
9. The country will also step up the reform of local taxes, including merging, and amending vehicle and vessel usage tax, vehicle and vessel-usage license-plate tax, real estate tax, urban real estate tax and urban and township land-use tax.

As already discussed in this paper, these reforms are relevant and need to be carried out without delay. Nevertheless, other considerations in adjusting tax policy to the needs of trade and investment liberalisation should also be taken into account.

Cautious approach to tax incentives

Although most of the current tax incentives for attracting foreign investments are not necessarily against WTO rules, they need to be rationalised and be more focused. This concerns the reform to merge the double-tracked corporate income tax system. Given the huge budgetary cost attached to the current tax incentives (nearly 10 per cent of total tax revenues), it is necessary to streamline the current system. Starting with the abolishment of the tax incentives directly linked to export-promotion/import-substitution, China should carefully review each of the existing tax incentives, whether the expected policy goals have been achieved, and whether benefits exceed costs. For example, tax benefits to production-type foreign invested enterprises should be abolished, or at least carefully prioritised.

China should be cautious in introducing new tax incentives. A shift to a wider use of accelerated depreciation rather than outright tax exemption and tax deduction should be considered. In the long run, China should consider replacing incentives by expenditure programmes, where policy goals could be more focused and the government could have more control.

New tax system for the new economic structure

In contemplating changes to the tax system, the government should carefully take into account social and economic developments likely to be fostered from the further opening up of China's market. Service business in trade, distribution, transportation, telecommunications and financial services will grow faster as private, domestic or foreign investments flow into the service sector. All of this will have effects on individual income distribution.

Tax reforms to further expand the tax base on consumption and on incomes should be sought. Expansion of the scope of VAT to include all services with adjustments in business tax is urgently needed. At the same time, the refund of VAT on inputs on fixed assets should be introduced to avoid distortions in investment decisions. The currently high thresholds for personal income tax should be reassessed. Reforming the current structure of personal income tax – where various kinds of incomes are taxed separately – and introducing a more integrated tax system for personal incomes, could also be considered. Other reforms to increase the tax revenue share from income taxation should be sought. This would not only contribute to increasing tax revenues but also provide the government with macroeconomic policy tools.

Replacing fees with taxes

How to deal with the issue of non-tax revenues will probably be one of the most difficult challenges for the government. Collecting fees and charges undermines transparency, leads to wider discretion by local governments, goes against an integrated management of fiscal accounts and leads to a reduced tax base. Given these negative aspects, it would be ideal to turn all collected fees and charges into taxes and to collect them as on-budget revenues. This will provide greater transparency to the public accounts and allow governments much wider flexibility and control of fiscal policy.

However, solving this issue is not as straightforward in practice. Given the huge size of non-tax revenue in China (almost equal to tax revenue), tax sharing between the central and the local governments would first need to be addressed. The central and the local governments would need to agree on expenditure programmes and their respective responsibilities under the programmes, maybe even including the size of the government. This is far from easy.

On balance, the current approach taken by the Chinese government looks practical. Unjustifiable random collection of fees should be halted by the central government, while replacing fees by taxes should be implemented on a case-by-case basis. Reforms in the agriculture tax are in the right direction. A petrol tax to raise revenue for building roads, now under consideration, also represents the correct approach to tax reforms.

Nevertheless, more efforts should be made to enhance transparency and to improve public accounts. It is unjustifiable that nearly half of fiscal revenues are collected and spent off budget. It is important to identify whether they are earmarked revenues, user charges, or general finance. At the same time, and more fundamentally, continuous efforts should be made to improve fiscal relations between the central and the local government.

Towards more transparent tax administration

Tax policy and tax administration are two sides of the same coin. Tax policy written in tax legislation would mean nothing unless it is implemented in practice through tax administration. New challenges for tax policy from further trade and investment liberalisation are also new challenges for the tax administration.

Probably the biggest challenge is to improve transparency in tax administration in China. Transparency in policy/administration is a requirement in the WTO rules. As seen in the episode of the treatment of VAT on inputs refund on exports, international business has been from time to time disconcerted by sudden changes in tax policies and/or by discretionary tax administration. These were often made without any legal grounding and government injunctions were often more important than laws. Complaints from international businesses in China that tax treatments are often different from region to region or from city to city are not rare, pointing to inconsistent tax administration. All these practices raise concerns as to the extent of transparency and rule of law in China's tax administration, which is part of the business environment. Improved compliance with international practice is strongly expected.

Another area of concern is capacity building. The fact that the SAT's human resources were halved in recent years raises a serious concern. Prospects of increased business operations in China by non-Chinese enterprises and individuals will put stronger pressure on the tax administration, particularly on international tax issues, involving tax treaties and/or transfer pricing issues. Capacity building in international tax administration is urgent.

The agenda for tax administration is not a light one. Moving to improved tax administration will surely be a lengthy process, but should not be postponed. In the long run, this reform could be among the most profound and important bearings of trade and investment liberalisation under WTO.

BIBLIOGRAPHY

Bahl, Roy. 1999,
  Fiscal Policy in China, Taxation and Intergovernmental Fiscal Relations, The 1990 Institute, p. 9.

Clark, Steven 2000,
  "Corporate Tax Incentives for Foreign Direct Investment – A Guide for Economies in Transition", in OECD, Unpublished Paper.

International co-operation and Exchange Department of State Administration of Taxation, the People's Republic of China. 1996,
  Tax Legislation of the People's Republic of China, China Tax Publishing House.

Li, Jinyan. 2000,
  "WTO and China's Tax Policy", *Tax Notes International*, Volume 20, Number 22, pp. 2451-2459.

Ni, Hongri 2000,
  Entry into the WTO should Adjust the Different tax Incentives toward Domestic Enterprises and Foreign Investment Enterprises, Tax Study, 10, pp. 13-18.

State Administration of Taxation,
  Tax System of the People's Republic of China.

State Administration of Taxation. 2000,
  The problems with Peasant burden and the Reform of Agriculture tax system, Tax study, 4,5.

Wang Chengyao. 2000,
  The Tax Requirements of WTO Principle and the Adjustment of tax policy, Finance Study, 7, pp. 2-22.

Wong, Cassie and Jim Chung. 2001,
  "WTO Accession Propels Chinese Tax Reform", *Tax Notes International*, Volume 22, Number 6, pp. 667-672.

Zuo, Liu. 1999,
  "Changing fees into Tax should Become the Main Task for the Next Step of Tax System Reform", A paper for the 1999 National tax theory Seminar, China Tax Publishing House, pp. 343-352.

Chapter 19

PUBLIC SECTOR BUDGET MANAGEMENT ISSUES

TABLE OF CONTENTS

PUBLIC SECTOR BUDGET MANAGEMENT ISSUES*

Introduction

During the past two decades, China has embarked on a series of profound economic reforms aimed at transforming a centrally planned economy into a market-based economy. The modernisation of budget institutions and processes has, however, lagged behind in the overall economic reforms in China. The current system reflects more the systems traditionally in place in planned economies.

The budget does not have the same stature as it does in OECD Member countries, where the budget is generally the single most important government policy document and is the primary vehicle for reconciling policy objectives and implementing them in concrete terms. The current status of the budget in China is a legacy of the planned economy whereby it was primarily a financing and accounting device, and all major policy decisions were made in the Plan. The importance of the budget is, however, increasing significantly and rapidly as China moves away from the planned economy.

The Chinese authorities recognise that the budget system needs to be reformed and have embarked on significant steps towards that end. Many of these reforms are in the initial phases but despite the great challenges ahead, the great progress that has been achieved in a very short period of time should not be overlooked. A fully reformed budgeting structure will foster coherence, transparency and accountability in all areas of government policy-making and implementation. This is a fundamental governance aspect, supporting further trade and investment liberalisation.

This chapter seeks to highlight the current situation in China and reforms that have been announced or implemented, and compare this with current practice in OECD Member countries.

The chapter is divided into three sections. The first one deals with the budget formulation process and the overall scope of the budget. The second discusses the role of parliament in the budget process. The third section comments on budget implementation issues.

Budget formulation process

Until very recently, it was very difficult to even talk of a budget formulation process as existing in China. The budget consisted of several separate parts with very broad categories. The official budget documentation amounted to but a few pages. In practice, there was practically no difference between budget formulation and budget implementation. The two activities went together hand-in-hand throughout the year, and consisted of negotiations between spending ministries and the Ministry of Finance. In fact, it was not uncommon for the budgets of ministries and agencies to be known only at the end of the year. The budget was in effect an *ex post*, rather than an *ex ante* document. Efforts have begun to reform this situation, bringing the budget formulation process more in line with that of OECD Member countries (see Box 19.1).

Comprehensive budget

Unlike the case in OECD Member countries, the Chinese budget does not encompass all revenues and expenditures.

There are numerous fees and charges, legal and otherwise, collected outside of the budget. This is primarily a problem at the provincial and local levels (see Chapter 20), but they also exist at the central level (see Chapter 18 on the current tax system). Despite the fact that the Chinese authorities have been moving against the practice of extra-budgetary funds for quite a long time, they are still very common.[1]

* This Chapter was prepared by Jón Blöndal, Principal Administrator, Budgeting and Management, Public Management Service, OECD.

Box 19.1.   **Key features of the budget formulation process in OECD Member countries**

- The budget is comprehensive, encompassing all revenues and expenditures.
- Realistic forecasts of revenues and expenditures are made for each category.
- The budget is classified in terms of appropriations for ministries and agencies.
- The annual budget process takes place in the context of multi-year expenditure frameworks.
- The annual budget process operates according to a highly disciplined timetable with clear divisions of roles between the finance ministry and other ministries.
- The budget is increasingly presented in terms of results to be achieved for appropriations, either as outcomes or outputs.

Various social expenditures, such as surplus labour (hidden unemployment), pensions, health care, housing, and education are undertaken by state-owned enterprises on behalf of their employees rather than by the government, or the individuals themselves. Separating these social functions is a key task of state-owned enterprise reform in China. These social functions are also a major contributing factor to the amount of non-performing loans in the banking system. This obscures the role and scope of the budget in China as very large amounts of public expenditures are financed outside of the budget in this manner.

The budget is divided into a separate operating budget and a separate capital budget. The capital budget is not decided by the Ministry of Finance, but rather by the State Development Planning Commission (SDPC) which passes approved projects on to the Ministry of Finance as a "fait accompli". The Ministry of Finance establishes the overall level of funding for projects in aggregate, but the SDPC selects and approves individual projects without regard for their subsequent operating costs. For example, it could decide to build a new National Library that would call for huge additional operating costs each year. The Ministry of Finance would have no opportunity to challenge the implications of that decision. This highlights the problems of separate decision-making procedures for operations and capital.

Decisions on the number of staff and their remuneration are not made in the budget, but by the State Commission Office for Public Service and the Ministry of Personnel. The budget simply finances the consequences of their decisions that are taken with no effective collaboration between them. In recent years, the focus has been on downsizing government so the number of staff has not been an issue. However, remuneration has been, as significant increases have been awarded. The fact that remuneration is set centrally, without regard to budget, is a problem.[2]

Ensuring the comprehensiveness of the budget is a prerequisite for the budget – assuming its role as the key policy document of the government as in OECD Member countries. Although the above problems are all recognised in China, progress in remedying them has been very slow with no substantial advances having in fact been made in recent years.

Realistic forecasts of revenues and expenditures

The Chinese budget process, even to the extent that revenues and expenditures are included in the budget in the first place, has been based on unrealistic projections of revenues and expenditures. Both projections are significantly, and systematically, lower than can be expected to materialise under any realistic scenario. This goes well beyond what could be termed "prudence" in formulating the budget. It is in fact a means to circumvent the formal budget process. The official budget proposal may be set in accordance with official priorities when introduced to parliament, but then in-year adjustments are made on an *ad hoc* basis and undermine the priority setting exercise. For example, education and agriculture, which are government priorities in the original budget, are generally disregarded in any in-year adjustments. The in-year proceeds of fiscal stimulus packages are also appropriated without regard to the government's original priority areas. The net result is that the final budget bears little resemblance to the priorities announced by the government when the original budget was introduced. This undermines the very purpose of the budget as applied in OECD Member countries.

The government is making efforts at reforms in this area, which should be seen also in the context of the new classification of the budget as described below.

New budget classification

The Chinese budget used to be divided into 29 broad functional categories. This did not coincide with the ministries and agencies responsible for the expenditures. For example, there was a broad category for education expenditure in the budget. This category was meant to finance education-related expenditures in all ministries; it was not meant to finance only the operations of the Ministry of Education. As a result, budget negotiations continued well into the fiscal year, as there was no official budget for each ministry and agency.

Under pressure from the National People's Congress (see next section), the Government has embarked on reforms in this area with the introduction of "departmental budgets". These were introduced on a pilot basis in the 2000 budget process for four ministries and agencies. Currently, this has been expanded to 24 ministries and agencies. When complete, a total of 170 departmental budgets will be produced. In terms of detail, the new budgets represent the opposite extreme of the previous ones. The budgets are about 100-200 pages each, with expenditures disaggregated by items of expenditure at a great level of detail. Experience in OECD Member countries shows that disaggregation at such a level is unrealistic in practice. With time, a more balanced approach will have to be arrived at. Significantly, the organisational budgets are not publicly available.

The fundamental nature of this reform cannot be overestimated. It is a basic principle of budgeting in OECD Member countries that there is a specific organisation accountable for the expenditure. For the first time this is now the case in China, with the budget as enacted by parliament. This reform is in its infancy, and may have been overdone as to the level of detail of the budgets, but the success of this reform will spur on the other reforms outlined in this section.

Multi-year expenditure frameworks

All OECD Member countries employ multi-year expenditure frameworks as an essential tool for budgeting. Each year's budget does not start with a "blank sheet of paper", but rather with deviations from a previously established framework. It is common for multi-year expenditure frameworks to extend 2-5 years beyond the next budget in Member countries. They are made on a rolling basis with a new year added at the end of the horizon with each new budget. There are no such multi-year expenditure frameworks in China. It would appear that the Chinese authorities view this as a "second-generation" reform.

Disciplined timetable and clear division of roles

The budget formulation process adheres to a very disciplined timetable in OECD Member countries with relatively long lead times and a clear division of roles between the different actors. Box 19.2 depicts a typical budget formulation timetable in Member countries, using the example of Sweden:

The Chinese budget formulation process deviates from this in virtually all aspects:

- As noted above there is no multi-year budget frameworks in China.
- Member countries generally apply a top-down budgeting system, which fosters a more strategic, policy-oriented direction to budget formulation. This entails Cabinet agreeing on the total

---

Box 19.2.   **Budget formulation timetable – Sweden**

January-March	Minister of Finance updates the Multi-year budget framework based on budget submission from spending ministries.
Mid-March	Minister of Finance presents to Cabinet his budget recommendations for the coming year and the following two years.
End March	Cabinet Budget Meeting takes place where the total level of expenditure for the coming year and the following two years is approved as well as indicative funding levels for each of 27 Expenditure Areas.
April-May	Spending ministries finalise allocations among individual appropriations within their respective Expenditure Areas.
June-August	Budget documentation prepared.
Early September	Cabinet agrees on the final budget proposal to be presented to parliament.
20 September	Budget bill is presented to Parliament.
1 January	Fiscal Year begins.

---

amount to be spent and how this is divided in aggregate by different policy areas. Then, each spending ministry is responsible for allocating funds among its various programmes within the aggregate level set. By contrast, in China the budget formulation process is a bottom-up exercise with the Ministry of Finance reacting to each proposal from spending ministries. This is a time-consuming exercise, focused on game playing between spending ministries and the Ministry of Finance. Furthermore, it serves to obscure government-wide policy priorities.

- The budget formulation process in China begins very late in the year. The decisions made in March in the timetable in Box 19.2 are not made until October or November in China, although efforts are being undertaken to start this process earlier. This reflects the fact that the budget formulation process and the budget implementation process in China have essentially worked hand-in-hand in the past.

- The budget is not submitted to parliament prior to the start of the fiscal year. This is discussed in detail in the next section.

- The internal organisational structure of the Ministry of Finance has until very recently been very different from that found in OECD Member countries. In China, spending ministries did not submit their budget requests to the budget office. Rather, different parts of each ministry's budget proposal were handled by different parts of the Ministry of Finance. For example, administrative expenditures were handled by one unit, requests for education/training funding by another, and so on. Co-ordination of these activities was very weak. In 2000, a fundamental re-organisation of the Ministry of Finance took place replacing functional lines with organisational units. There is, for example, a division in the Ministry of Finance that overviews the whole budget of the Ministry of Education. This is in line with practice in OECD Member countries and is a direct follow-on of the introduction of departmental budgets. It should be noted that this reform appears to have proceeded remarkably smoothly.

Focus on results

The Chinese budget is very input-oriented, focusing on the breakdown of expenditures in each organisation rather than on outcomes. This is in itself a major advance in China, as the previous functional budgets did not even offer this basic input information. OECD Member countries are now increasingly budgeting on the basis of outcomes and outputs, *i.e.* the results expected from each organisation. This involves costing government services, which in turn involves the adoption of accrual accounting and budgeting practices. The Chinese authorities have shown great interest in studying these developments and view this as the next step for budget reform in China.

Role of parliament

The National People's Congress (NPC) is China's parliament. Constitutionally, it is the highest organ of state power. However, it has been argued that it is inferior in power to the State Council and to several intra-Communist Party organs. This is not to say that the NPC can be characterised as a "rubber stamp" institution. In recent years, it has begun to increasingly assert its power. Observers attribute this to several factors. First, it is in line with the general opening of the Chinese economy and society since 1978. Second, the NPC is composed of representatives of the provinces and there are significant strains in national-provincial relations in China, especially in the field of budgeting. Other factors may also be at play.

The NPC is composed of 2 979 delegates selected (mostly) on a provincial basis for 5-year terms. The NPC meets in plenary session for two weeks each year, usually in March. This plenary session can be portrayed as a ceremonial occasion as most of the "real" power of the NPC is vested in the Standing Committee of the National People's Congress. It is composed of 155 NPC members and meets regularly throughout the year. There are also nine specialised committees and two commissions. The committees are formally sub-committees of the NPC as such, although all of their members come from the Standing Committee. The commissions are formally sub-committees of the Standing Committee of the NPC. In practice, this means that commissions report to the committees which, in turn, report to the NPC in plenary session.

Role of the committees

Up until 1999, the budget was examined by the Economic and Finance Committee of the NPC. In 1998, it was decided to establish a special Budget Commission of the Standing Committee of the NPC, which became operational in 1999. The chairman of the Budget Commission is the vice-chairman of the Economic and Finance Committee. The Budget Commission can be seen as a sub-committee of the Economic and Finance Committee. The Economic and Finance Committee has 27 members at present whereas the Budget Commission has ten members. The Budget Commission consists of members of the NPC and commission staff. For example, the Staff Director of the Commission is also a member of the Commission. The Commission has a professional staff of nine at present, which has been approved to increase to nineteen.

The formal duties assigned to the Budget Commission are three-fold. First, to assist in reviewing and approving the government's budget proposal. Second, to monitor the implementation of the budget and to undertake any related special studies. Third, to draft laws relating to the formulation and implementation of the budget. All of these functions are carried out on behalf of the Economic and Finance Committee.

The NPC ascribes under-performance in the budget to three factors that inhibit them in fulfilling their duties. First, the lack of resources relative to the finance ministry. The establishment of the Budget Commission is supposed to be a key step in rectifying this. Second, the lack of effective working methods. Third, the need to systematise and formalise the budget process to a much greater degree. The implementation of organisational budgets is a major advance in this area. The preponderance of informal (non-transparent) mechanisms for budget decision-making is, however, a continuing problem.

Parliamentary budget process

The fiscal year is the calendar year. However, as the NPC only meets in plenary session in March, the budget is not enacted until well into the fiscal year. This is an entrenched structural problem, as changing the fiscal year, or moving the meeting time of the NPC, are not authorised. As noted above, the significant work of the NPC takes place in the Standing Committee, and it has been suggested that the Standing Committee grant "interim approval" to the budget proposal prior to the start of the fiscal year.

The NPC in plenary session would then give its final approval in March once the fiscal year underway. It is striking that the parliamentary budget process at present *begins* after the start of the fiscal year.

The government formally presents its budget proposal to the NPC at the beginning of the plenary session in March. The NPC in plenary session has therefore only 2 weeks to deliberate. The parliamentary budget process, however, starts in January – about 6-8 weeks prior to the submission of the budget proposal to the NPC in plenary session. During this "preliminary stage", the Budget Commission and the Ministry of Finance (MOF) hold discussions on the content of the budget proposal. These discussions are characterised as "formal" in nature. The venue for the discussions alternates between the NPC and the MOF. In essence, the Ministry of Finance presents a draft budget for their comments. The introduction of organisational budgets is a prerequisite for the NPC being able to assume a more powerful role in the budgeting process.

All of the NPC's efforts to influence the direction of budget policy take place during this preliminary stage. Once the budget is introduced, the NPC can only approve (or reject) the budget in total but cannot amend it. There are, however, no rules against members of the NPC in plenary session proposing changes. If thirty or more People's Representatives jointly make a motion, this must be considered by the NPC. There are, however, no formal procedures for how to deal with such a motion. Reportedly, several years ago a group of People's Representatives submitted a motion calling for the government to take stronger measures to eliminate the budget deficit, with no further specifics. This was considered a "political" matter and forwarded to the State Council "for resolution".

At the conclusion of this preliminary stage, the Budget Commission submits a formal report to the Economic and Finance Committee which, in turn, would "recommend" changes to the Ministry of Finance. The Ministry of Finance has *never* rejected any proposal made by the Committee. The increased role of the NPC in the budget process comes primarily from making bolder recommendations to the Ministry of Finance. For example, organisational budgets were introduced following NPC's recommendation. Formalising this stage of the budget process would appear to be an important reform objective in coming years to make it more transparent.

In the course of the fiscal year, representatives of the Ministry of Finance appear quarterly before the Economic and Finance Committee to report on the implementation of the budget. The presentation by the Ministry of Finance focuses on the budget aggregates and on any specific issue that the Committee decides. For example, education spending has recently been a major focus. Notwithstanding this, in-year adjustments to the budget have generally been made with no consultations or approval by the NPC.

This also serves to highlight the particular nature of legislation passed by the NPC. "Laws" approved by the NPC are not binding laws. Two examples highlight this. First, various legislations in China call for spending on a specific activity to grow by a certain percentage annually, or to grow "faster" than overall spending. These calls are universally ignored in practice. Second, the creation of organisational budgets was first mandated in the new organic budget law of 1994. It was not until 2001, however, following strong pressures by the NPC, that the organisational budget was actually presented. Whether the NPC will be able to gain a more assertive role in the budget remains open to conjecture.

Budget implementation

The key reform being implemented in this area is the introduction of a treasury management system. Treasury management can be defined as the manner in which the government implements the budget, *i.e.* how it manages its cash receipts and cash payments. At present, China can best be described as having *no* effective central treasury management system in place.

Treasury management is a fundamental aspect of budget implementation in OECD Member countries. It has three primary objectives. First, to reduce the government's interest expenditure by investing any idle funds. Second, to prevent abuse from taking place by putting in place effective controls for the receipts and disbursement of funds. Third, to provide *immediate* information on the government's financial position. The government's treasury management system also provides information on the economy. For example, the government's tax revenue is one of the indicators of economic activity in Member countries. Therefore, the treasury management system can alert the government to any actions it may need to take to stimulate or dampen demand in the economy.

Current state of affairs

There are over 13 000 government organisations at all levels of government in China, which operate a plethora of separate bank accounts in commercial banks. Each one of these accounts will have idle and often significant balances that the Ministry of Finance has no ability to manage.

Government revenue collection organisations first deposit revenue in their own accounts. The money often stays there for a long period of time before being turned over to the Ministry of Finance, as the revenue collection organisations benefit from the interest earned their accounts. There are also abuses, as significant amounts of revenue are never turned over to the Ministry of Finance.

Government organisations receive lump sums for their operations from the Ministry of Finance at regular intervals. The Ministry of Finance deposits these funds in accounts held by central government organisations in commercial banks. These organisations in turn deposit the money in the accounts of various subsidiary organisations. This cascading process often involves six layers before reaching the final end user. Delays in making the money available are common, as each organisation on the ladder benefits from higher interest income the longer it keeps hold of the funds.

This system is also open to abuse, as there are no effective controls on what the money is actually spent on. All organisations are to report to the Ministry of Finance on their use of funds, but this takes place long after the actual utilisation, is highly aggregated, and incomplete.

The legal framework for treasury management is incomplete. It is also unclear, given the existence of many extra-budgetary funds, what specifically constitutes government revenue for treasury management purposes. Furthermore, the exact role of the Ministry of Finance in supervising the treasury management system is not unequivocal at present.

Proposed reforms

The State Council has approved reforms to the treasury management system in China that will bring it into line with those of OECD Member countries. The reforms will be implemented in a step-by-step process, following an initial pilot project. This project, which includes six central government and ten provincial government ministries, was initiated on 1 July 2001. More ministries and sub-national government will be progressively included in the new treasury management system. No deadline has been set, however, for the completion of this reform, *i.e.* when *all* government organisations will be included in the new system. There is reportedly strong resistance to the reforms by many government organisations.

The Ministry of Finance will establish a Treasury Single Account at the People's Bank of China. All revenue will enter this account and all expenditures will be paid from this account.

Separate bank accounts will be created for each government organisation at commercial banks. Each government organisation will pay its obligations to third parties from these accounts. The accounts will, however, be very different from the accounts that government organisations presently have in commercial banks: *First*, the Ministry of Finance will have to approve each of the accounts. *Second*, each transaction from these accounts will be via the Ministry of Finance Payment Centre (see below), rather than directly by each organisation. *Third*, the accounts will be "swept" overnight, *i.e.* the balance of the accounts at the close of each business day will be zero as any remaining balance will be transferred to the Treasury Single Account at the People's Bank. As a result, the government will be able to centralise treasury management.

Government organisations will also be permitted to open special accounts for extra-budgetary funds and special purpose funds. These funds can be seen as the equivalent of trust funds and specialised social insurance funds in OECD Member countries. As part of this reform, the number of such funds will be substantially reduced in China. The balances of these accounts will be swept overnight and form part of the central treasury management system.

The Ministry of Finance will also permit government organisations to open accounts for small amounts, which will have overnight balances. These are essentially "petty cash" accounts in order for government organisations to pay minor day-to-day expenses.

Comparison with OECD experiences

Role of Ministry of Finance and scope of treasury management

The Ministry of Finance is always and inherently in charge of the treasury management function in OECD Member countries; without a central organisation in charge, effective treasury management is not feasible. For the same reason, all revenues go into the central treasury management system and all expenditures are paid from the central treasury management system in OECD Member countries, *i.e.* no transaction takes place outside the central treasury management system. User charges and other "proprietary" revenue are all deposited into the treasury management system. In cases where separate "off-budget" accounts are held for social insurance programmes, these balances are managed as part of the central treasury management system.

These features are enshrined in the organic budget laws of OECD Member countries. As noted above, the situation in China currently diverges from this in important respects. The proposed reforms, however, address all of these issues.

Role of the central bank

The role of the central bank in treasury management varies in OECD Member countries. Regardless of these differences, the monetary policy function of the central bank is clearly separated from that of fiscal agent of the government.

China's reforms have opted for a very limited role of the central bank in the treasury management system. Several reasons are given for this: First, the central bank does not have the capacity to act as the government's payment agent. The cost of the treasury management system operating through commercial banks is much lower. Second, it is believed that the central bank should be primarily concerned with monetary policy. Third, the central bank should be monitoring the commercial banks in their function of the government's payment agents. It could not do so if it was the government's payment agent.

This rationale for a limited role for the central bank is familiar in OECD Member countries. It should be noted that the role of the central bank depends on local circumstances; there is no "right" or "wrong" role.

Role of commercial bank accounts

In cases where government organisations in OECD Member countries have their own bank accounts in commercial banks, these balances are "swept" overnight into the Treasury Single Account in the central bank where it would be managed effectively. In that sense, there is no difference from a treasury management point of view in whether government organisations have accounts in commercial banks or if they have sub-accounts/ledger accounts in the central bank. The existence of accounts in commercial banks does in no way imply that those government organisations have freedom to collect or spend money at will. The existence of such bank accounts does however imply a banking relationship and the Ministry of Finance will need to devote resources to negotiating expected performance levels and monitoring the actual performance of the commercial bank against those expectations.

In OECD Member countries where organisations have accounts in commercial banks, they are normally accompanied by a series of incentives (allowing interest to be earned and paid) in order to decentralise cash management procedures. These practices are considered "leading edge" in OECD Member countries and rely on a very sophisticated banking system.

Reporting

Extensive reporting is made, based on the information in the treasury management system. These include reports on the government's cash balance at the end of each day and monthly reports on the government's revenue and expenditures by categories of organisations and expenditure. Such reports are publicly available in OECD Member countries.

Fiscal reporting of this kind is not practiced in China at present and the proposed reforms do not envisage those reports being made publicly available.

Cash forecasting

It is striking that the proposed reforms in China do not include cash forecasting. This is a fundamental and inherent part of the treasury management function in OECD Member countries. Cash forecasting is made on the basis of historical patterns for revenue collection and payment disbursement and adjusted for any known special payment. Such forecasts are made for each day and are made public; financial markets follow any differences between forecasts and actual outcome very carefully and if gaps emerge, financial markets "punish" governments by increasing the premium in interest rates.

Conclusion

The planned establishment of the Treasury Single Account is of fundamental importance for making the implementation of the budget effective and efficient. It has the potential to do for budget execution what departmental budgets will do for budget formulation, *i.e.* put the basic infrastructure in place that will then allow more sophisticated reforms to take place. Resistance to this reform comes from many vested interests. The implementation of this reform is also very complex from a technical point of view, and its success is by no means a foregone conclusion. Three factors, however, augur well for its successful implementation. First, the reforms enjoy strong political support from the very highest leaders of the country. Second, a great amount of preparation has gone into the development of China's treasury management system and tailor-making it for local circumstances. Finally, the new system has been pilot tested in a number of areas with very successful results. It is important, however, to recognise that the full implementation of this system will take several years.

NOTES

1. It is important to note that these extra-budgetary funds should not automatically be equated with corruption. Assignment of expenditures to levels of government often operates on a cascading system in China with each level of government pushing down responsibility for certain functions to the next level below. This is generally not accompanied by commensurate revenue sources to cover the expenditures. The fact that this cascading system generally ends at the lowest level, where the use of extra-budgetary funds is also the most prevalent, is not a coincidence. Local governments are not allowed to officially levy taxes, so they resort to these means of financing.

2. Remuneration for public employees is set uniformly throughout the country, despite the fact that the capacity to pay wages varies significantly from one region to another. In fact it is common for remuneration to be made on the basis of the capacity of the cities on the eastern coast. This leads to substantial arrears in salary payments in other areas which simply cannot afford them.

Chapter 20

ISSUES CONCERNING CENTRAL-LOCAL GOVERNMENT FISCAL RELATIONS

TABLE OF CONTENTS

ISSUES CONCERNING CENTRAL-LOCAL GOVERNMENT FISCAL RELATIONS[*]

Introduction

Improving the relations between central and local government has been an important focus of China's fiscal reform since the beginning of economic reforms in 1979. While preserving the unity of the system as a whole, central-local government fiscal relations have undergone four major reforms during the past twenty years. These reforms have established a form of "fiscal federalism" in which local governments have clearly defined responsibilities and incentives to collect revenue and carry out expenditures in accordance with nationally determined norms. The ultimate objectives of these reforms have been to stimulate the development of the Chinese economy, improve the allocation of income and resources, and to bolster macroeconomic performance. Continued fiscal reforms to improve inter-governmental fiscal relations are necessary to sustain the growth of the Chinese economy in the new century as well as to facilitate adjustment to trade and investment liberalisation and complete the transformation to a market economy.

In this context, this chapter focuses on the current situation and problems of local finance in China. In order to analyse and identify the characteristics and problems of local finance, the first section discusses developments in fiscal reforms since 1979 and lays out the current framework of central-local government fiscal relations. The next section discusses the main features and problems of local finance from the viewpoint of central and local relations. This is followed by a discussion of the increasing regional disparity in fiscal revenues and the effects of the current system of central-local government relations on this. It will then be possible to draw conclusions and stress the necessary areas of reform for China.

Overall, the analysis will suggest two conclusions concerning the fiscal relationship between central and local governments.

- First, there would seem to be a serious problem of imbalance between the budget revenue and expenditure responsibilities of local government. Due to mismatches in the division of responsibility and functions among different levels of government, local government expenditure has increased steadily and is heavily dependent upon central transfers and extra-budgetary revenues. This problem affects not only the normal operation of local government, but also the ability to promote economic development and pursue economic reform.

- Second, the most serious problem of central-local government relations is the great disparity between regions, which reflects the large differences in tax bases and growth rates among provinces. The current transfer system has been completely inadequate to deal with these differences because most of the transfer allocations are based upon local revenue growth, and the role of the general transfer aimed at decreasing regional differences has been strictly limited.

General framework of the Chinese fiscal system

China's governmental hierarchy has five levels, with a total of some 50 000 entities. The fiscal system has a structure corresponding to that of the government, consisting of the central government and four lower levels referred to as local government. The local government comprises 1) thirty-one provincial-level localities, including twenty-two provinces, four municipalities with significant independent power directly under the central government, and five autonomous regions; 2) over three hundred and thirty-five prefectures and cities at the prefecture level; 3) over two thousand, one hundred and forty-two counties, autonomous counties and cities at the county level; and 4) about forty-

---

[*] This Chapter was prepared by Ms Wei Wang, Research Fellow, Development Research Centre of the State Council, China under the supervision of Charles Pigott, Senior Economist, Non-Member Economies Division, Economics Department, OECD.

Figure 20.1. **Framework of the fiscal system in China**

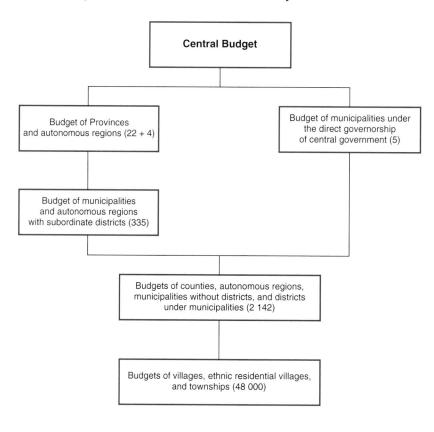

Source: Ministry of Finance of China: The Fiscal System in China, *www.mof.gov.cn.*

eight thousand townships, towns and city districts. The last three levels are known as the sub-provincial levels of government and operate under the authority of the provincial level (see Figure 20.1).

The present system of central-local government fiscal relations represents the culmination of four major past reforms of fiscal administration (see Box 20.1). The first of these reforms was undertaken in 1980 and the last, which is the basis for the current system, was enacted in 1994. Each of these reforms has fundamentally reshaped financial relations among various levels of government. The overall thrust of the reforms has been decentralisation in the implementation of budget policies based on increasingly explicit rules governing the allocation of revenues and the assignment of responsibilities for expenditures.

Structure of the current system

The current system of central-local government fiscal relations was defined by the 1994 reform that was undertaken to support the goal of establishing a Socialist Market Economy System. The core of the reform is a nationwide Tax Sharing System (TSS), which establishes a multilevel network of mechanisms for revenue collection and distribution. However, the division of responsibilities and various related expenditures between the central and local governments was not revised.

Box 20.1. Evolution of China's central-local government fiscal arrangements

From 1980 to 1993, according to the principle of "simplifying administration and decentralisation" and the principle of "offering incentives to both the local government and the central government", intergovernmental fiscal relations were restructured towards a system of "getting the food from one's own kitchen" in three phases.

Firstly, in 1980 a fiscal revenue-sharing system known as "dividing revenue and spending between different level of governments, permitting each level to be responsible for its own financing" began to be implemented. Under this system, central-provincial fiscal sharing rules were established by the central government, whereas provincial-municipal relations were governed by the province, and this principle extended to lower levels. According to the revenue sharing rule, all revenue no longer automatically accrued to the central government. The central government designated revenues from each tax as being "central fixed revenue" (accruing to the central government), "local fixed revenue" or "shared revenue". Shared revenue was divided between the central government and local government according to negotiated but flexible contracts.

Secondly, in 1985 a system called "dividing the taxes by kinds, checking and ratifying revenue and spending, letting each level of government be responsible for itself " was brought into effect.

Finally, from 1988, the fiscal contracting system or the fiscal responsibility system (caizheng baogan zhi) was widely practised. Under this system, provincial governments each negotiated a fixed tax quota with the central government, with collections in excess of that level being retained at the local level. This new system created strong incentives for the local government to conceal information about local revenue from the centre, since otherwise they would face a "ratchet effect", as this information was valuable at the time that fiscal contracts were renegotiated. Furthermore, since profits of many of the new enterprises in the rapidly expanding township and village enterprises accrued to the benefit of "local shareholders", there was a continued incentive to shift deficits to the centre and hide profits from taxation. Thus, the system heightened an asymmetry, in that local government absorbed excess revenues, while the deficits were covered by the central government.

Going through the reform above, the system of letting each level of government be responsible for its own finance led to a steady decline in the fiscal resources of the central government (see Figure 20.1). This situation led to a radical reform of the fiscal system that was initiated in 1994.

The key specific elements of the assignment of responsibilities under the current system are as follows.

- Revenues are divided between central and local governments based on the principle of "matching responsibility with financial capacity". Taxes deemed necessary for the protection of national interests and to carry out macroeconomic adjustment are designated as "central taxes" accruing entirely to the central government (see Table 20.1). Taxes directly related to economic development are classified as "shared taxes" and are divided between central and local governments, while taxes suitable for collection by local governments are classified as "local taxes". State tax agencies are responsible for collecting central government and shared taxes, while local taxes are collected by local government agencies which are subject to local governments.

- The central government is responsible for expenditures on national defence, the conduct of foreign relations, administration of central government agencies, as well as spending on economic restructuring and adjustments related to macroeconomic policies. Local governments are assigned responsibility for local government administration and for supporting economic and social development within their jurisdictions. In effect, this devolves most responsibility for education, health, and other social benefits to the local level.

Table 20.1. **Tax revenue assignments (2000)**

Category	Tax	Central share %
Central taxes	Domestic excise taxes	100
	Customs duties	100
	VAT and excise taxes on imports	100
	Income on deposit interest	100
Local taxes	Personal income tax	0
	City and township land use tax	0
	Farmland occupation tax	0
	Fixed assets investment orientation tax	0
	Land appreciation tax	0
	House property tax	0
	Urban real estate tax	0
	Vehicle and vessel use tax	0
	Deed tax	0
	Slaughter tax	0
	Banquet tax	0
	Agricultural and animal husbandry taxes	0
Shared taxes	Domestic VAT	75
	Business tax	
	– railroads, headquarters of bank or insurance companies	100
	– all others	0
	Enterprise income tax	
	– Railroads, headquarters of financial institutions and insurance companies belonging to the central government	100
	– all others	0
	Income tax on foreign and foreign funded banks	100
	Income tax on foreign and foreign funded nonbanks	0
	Resource tax	
	– if paid by offshore oil companies	100
	– all others	0
	City maintenance and construction tax	
	– if paid by railroads, headquarters of banks or insurance companies	100
	– all others	0
	Securities tax	
	– if collected on stock transactions	88
	– all other transactions	0

Source: State Administration of Taxation, *Tax System of the People's Republic of China.*

- Gaps between expenditure responsibilities and revenues are addressed by an inter-governmental (central-local) transfer payment system, details of which are discussed further below.

- Decisions about the content of all budgets are highly centralised. In particular, 1) all taxes and rates are set by the central government, while local governments have only limited rights to set rates for few local taxes; 2) local governments do not have the right to grant exemptions or reductions from provisions of the relevant tax laws; and 3) local governments have no right to issue debt or to borrow from the People's Bank of China (PBC). Shortfalls in financing for local government expenditures are supposed to be covered by transfer payments or subsidies from central government – or, to the extent these do not suffice, by spending cutbacks.

- Budgets are nationally co-ordinated but managed separately at the central government and at the four lower government levels. The national budget is composed of the central government budget and provincial and local government budgets. As stipulated by the Budget Law of the

People's Republic of China, the draft annual budgets and final accounts for the national and central government must be reviewed and approved by the National People's Congress (NPC). The draft budgets for local government are reviewed by the corresponding level of the NPC, even though the local NPC has only a limited role in budget supervision and management. The central and local budget adjustment plans and final accounts must be reviewed and approved by the standing committees of the NPC and local congresses (see Chapter 19 on public sector budget management issues).

The inter-governmental transfer system is composed of five elements whose relative importance is changing:

- A base factor related to the revenue collected in 1993, the year before the last reform, and whose importance in determining the overall transfer is declining.

- Revenue returned equal to an additional 30 per cent of the increase in the VAT and other excise tax revenues (on top of the 25 per cent specified in the tax sharing arrangement) above the previous year.

- Special purpose subsidies and grants in hundreds of earmarked categories, such as grain procurement, price subsidies, and transfers to cover shortfalls in local pension funds.

- General transfers, called transfer payments in the transition period, similar to those widely used in OECD countries.

- Miscellaneous transfers.

Overall the transfer system represents a hybrid between the earlier approach to revenue distribution and the current system. In particular, the second element in the above list is similar to the pre-1993 "matching" system in which relatively rapidly growing provinces received proportionately larger rebates than slower growing provinces. The third and fourth elements reflect the more recent move toward basing transfers on local needs. However, in practice, the special purpose subsidies and grants (the third element) tend to be distributed according to a variety of economic, social, administrative, and political considerations that often bear little relation to fundamental needs. The general transfers are still a relatively small part of the total transfers, although their importance is growing.

The 1994 reform has been followed by important shifts in the trend of revenues and spending for both central and local governments. For most of the reform period, although revenues and expenditures grew quite rapidly, they fell behind the pace of overall GDP growth. As a result, the ratio of government budget revenue and expenditure to GDP declined steadily between 1980 and 1994, with tax revenues reaching a low of just above 10 per cent of GDP in 1994. This decline, as well as the relatively low overall level of government tax revenues, is unusual by international standards. For example in OECD countries, the ratio of government revenue to GDP increased from 26.9 per cent of GDP in 1965 to 36.5 per cent in 2000. The decline in the revenue ratio in China is mainly attributable to three factors:

- The shift in the weighting of national income distribution away from government towards individuals and enterprises.[1]

- The declining economic share and profitability of state owned enterprises SOEs, which have been the main tax base, due to increased competition and, more recently, their structural problems.

- Inefficiencies in tax collection and incomplete compliance that have led to substantial underpayment of certain taxes.

The decline in revenue has complicated the government's ability to promote economic development and pursue economic reforms. It has also had important effects on the fiscal relations between local and central governments. The share of central government revenue fell with the total revenue ratio during 1980-1994, reaching an exceptionally low level of 22 per cent in 1993 (Figure 20.2). A major objective of the 1994 reform was to redress this imbalance. The central government share of total budget revenue rose to above 55.7 per cent in the immediate aftermath of the 1994 reform and has

Figure 20.2. **Central/local shares of government budget revenue**

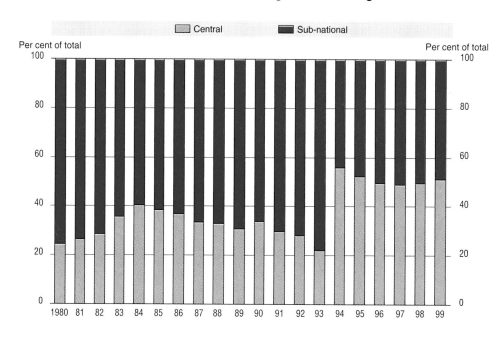

Source: China Statistical Yearbook, 2000.

since stabilised at about 50 per cent in 1998-1999 after falling slightly in 1995-1997. In parallel, aggregate tax revenues have recovered significantly, rising by more than twice the rate of nominal GDP since 1994, and reaching nearly 13.3 per cent of GDP in 2000. The rapid increase in tax revenue partly reflects strong efforts to improve collection of taxes due from non-state enterprises and other segments where collection has been relatively weak.

Implications for the characteristics of local government finances

The 1994 reforms are largely responsible for several important characteristic features of local government finances and their relation to the central government.

First, fiscal decentralisation is relatively high in China. The two most commonly employed measures of fiscal decentralisation are the share of the local budget in the consolidated state budget and the degree to which local budgets are financed from revenues raised from local sources as opposed to transfers from the central government. From 1994 to 1999, the share of local budget revenue to the total raised by all government levels in China ranged between 44.3 and 49.4 per cent, which is close to the ratios found in a number of developed federal states, such as the United States and Germany.[2] The share of local expenditure to the total is nearly 70 per cent (Figure 20.3), which is comparatively high in relation to other transition countries and some developed countries.[3] The share of the transfer from the central government in aggregate local revenue has remained at 40 per cent since 1994, and such a level is also somewhat high by international standards. Since the local government budget accounts for a heavy portion of the total budget resources of China, the fiscal problems that exist in local government have had an important influence on the effectiveness and efficiency of China's overall fiscal system and policy.

Second, local governments have been taking on an increasing share of total government spending but their share of revenue has fluctuated. The budget expenditure ratio of local government to the total has increased rapidly, from 45.7 per cent in 1980 and 67.4 per cent in 1990, to 68.5 per cent in 1999

Figure 20.3. **Central/local shares of government expenditure**

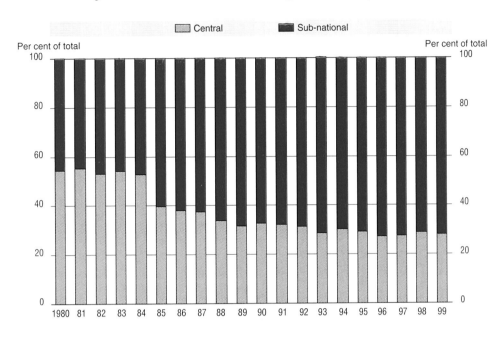

Source: *China Statistical Yearbook*, 2000.

(see Figure 20.3). The increasing and high level of expenditure of local government indicates that local governments have taken on more responsibilities over the past two decades. The reason behind the increasing expenditure of local government will be discussed below. In contrast, the distribution of budget revenue between central and local government has fluctuated over the four rounds of fiscal reform. In the last reform, the ratio of local government revenue to the total fell from about one-third before 1994 to about half that level between 1994 and 1999, as the fiscal position of the central government was strengthened.

Third, local governments rely heavily upon transfers from the central government and upon extra-budgetary funds. At the local government level in China, there are three kinds of fiscal resources that can be used to match the increasing spending requirement derived from assigned responsibilities and ambitious development plans. As Table 20.2 indicates, budget revenue has been the largest revenue category and its ratio to the total local government revenue has increased steadily from 36.8 per cent in 1994 to 44.1 per cent in 1998. Transfer payments from the central government have been another important fiscal revenue source for local government, even though their portion in total local revenue has declined from 38 per cent in 1994 to 29.4 per cent in 1998. Taking into consideration their share of central government expenditure and their ratio to GDP (Table 20.3), transfers from the central government have become the most important means for redistribution of fiscal resources. On the other hand, local government has been nearly as heavily dependent on extra-budgetary funds. Although the government considers extra-budgetary funds to be fiscal resources, they are managed separately from the budget. In China, extra-budgetary funds, which consist of surtaxes, levies and charges accruing to government and administrative units, have grown rapidly, from 2.6 per cent of GDP in 1978 to 4 per cent of GDP in 1998.[4] Among these extra-budgetary funds, local government has taken the main share for the past 20 years. In 1998, the total extra-budgetary revenue was around RMB 308.2 billion, and almost 95 per cent of it belonged to local governments. From 1994 to 1998, local extra-budgetary funds contributed about a quarter of the total local government revenue. Such a tendency reflected the fact that local governments have been heavily reliant on extra-budgetary resources.

Table 20.2. **Revenue structure of local government since 1994**

RMB 100 million

	Total revenue (1)=(2)+(4)+(5)	Budget revenue (2)	Of which: tax revenue (3)	Transfers (4)	Extra-budget revenue (5)	Ratio (%) (3)/(2)	Ratio (%) (2)/(1)	Ratio (%) (4)/(1)	Ratio (%) (5)/(1)
1994	6 280.0	2 311.6	2 294.9	2 389.2	1 579.2	99.3	36.8	38.0	25.2
1995	7 608.7	2 985.6	2 832.8	2 534.2	2 088.9	94.9	39.2	33.3	27.5
1996	9 415.1	3 746.9	3 449.0	2 722.5	2 945.7	92.0	39.8	28.9	31.3
1997	9 961.8	4 424.2	4 002.0	2 856.7	2 680.9	90.5	44.4	28.7	26.9
1998	11 286.6	4 984.0	4 438.5	3 321.5	2 981.1	89.1	44.1	29.4	26.5
1999	n.a.	5 594.9	4 959.9	n.a.	n.a.	88.7	n.a.	n.a.	n.a.

n.a.: not available.

Notes: Total Revenue is the total of local budget revenue, transfers from the central government and extra-budget revenue.

Budget revenue for local government consists of tax revenue, less subsidies to cover SOE losses plus some official special fees and charges.

Source: *China Statistical Yearbook* (2000); *Finance Yearbook of China* (1999).

Table 20.3. **Scale of the inter-government transfer**

Transfer	1996	1997	1998	1999
Total transfer (billion RMB)	271.6	285.4	332.3	409.5
Ratio to GDP (%)	4.0	3.8	4.2	5.0
Share of central expenditure (%)	49.9	45.7	41.4	41.7
Share of local revenue (%)	42.1	39.2	40.1	42.3

Source: New China Fifty Years' Government Finance Statistics; *Statistics Yearbook*, 2000.

Fourth, local taxes have not been the main source of the overall tax revenues accruing to local government. Tax revenue has been the main source of government on-budget revenue since 1985. For the general government and for the central government, the ratio of tax revenue to total on-budget revenue was about 93.3 per cent and 97.8 per cent, respectively, in 1999. However, for local government, the ratio of tax revenue to on-budget revenue has decreased from 99.3 in 1994 to 88.7 in 1999.

VAT and business tax are the main taxes for China's general government, and accounted for 36.3 and 15.9 per cent of total taxes, respectively, in 1999 (see Table 20.4). For central government, the main tax revenue is generated from VAT, which accounted for 50.3 per cent in 1999. The three major taxes accruing entirely to the central government account for an additional one-third of its total tax revenues. Local government tax revenues are somewhat less concentrated than those of the central government. Nearly half of local government tax revenues come from VAT and business taxes. The remainder of local government tax revenue is generated from the eleven local taxes and the local portion of shared taxes other than VAT and business tax. The three most important local taxes are the individual income tax, the tax on the use of urban land, and agriculture taxes, which together accounted for 27.6 per cent of the total local tax revenue.

Finally, local government expenditure is focused upon operating expenses for education, health care, culture, and other social needs, on capital construction and expenses for local government administration. As Table 20.5 shows, economic construction expenditure has the largest share in the budget outlays for all levels of the government as a whole, although the share has fallen from 58.2 per cent in 1980 to 38.7 per cent in 1998. In OECD countries, the ratio of such expenditures to total government outlays ranges between 5 and 19 per cent. The much higher ratio for China reflects the understandably greater priority given in government fiscal policy to promoting economic development.

Table 20.4. **Tax revenue structure for central and local governments in 1999**
Per cent share of total revenue collected

Taxes	Total	Central Government	Local Government
Total tax revenue	100	100	100
Value-added Tax (VAT) |S|	36.3	50.3	20.2
Business Tax |S|	15.9	4.2	29.5
Consumption Tax (CT) |C|	7.7	13.9	0
Tariffs |C|	5.3	9.8	0
CT & VAT on Import goods |C|	5.2	9.7	0
Enterprise Income Tax |S|	11.5	7.8	15.7
Agriculture taxes |L|	4.0	0	7.3
Security Exchange Stamp Duty |S|	2.6	3.8	1.4
Individual Income Tax |L|	3.9	0	8.4
Tax on Using Urban Land |L|	5.5	0	11.9
Other	2.1	0.5	5.6

Notes: |S| = Shared Tax |C| = Central Tax |L| = Local Tax.
Agricultural Taxes include the agricultural tax, animal husbandry tax, tax on cultivated land, tax on special agricultural products and the contract tax.
Source: *Tax Yearbook of China*, 2000; *China Statistical Yearbook*, 2000.

Table 20.5. **Expenditure structure of local government (%)**

Item	Ratio to the total		
	1991	1994	1998
1. Expenditure for Capital Construction	8.4	7.3	10.1
2. Innovation and New Product Promotion Funds	5.1	7.3	6.4
3. Expenditure for Price Subsidies	14.8	5.5	4.5
4. Expenditure for Local Government Administration	13.6	16.6	16.1
5. Operating Expenses for Culture, Education, Science and Health Care	27.2	28.2	24.9
6. Operating Expenses for Industrial, Commercial and Communication Department	0.1	1.6	1.0
7. Expenditure for Social Welfare	2.9	2.3	2.1
8. Agriculture Aids and Development	9.6	8.8	7.2
9. Others	18.3	22.4	26.8
Total	100	100	100

Note: Expenditure for government administration includes public security, prosecutorial work and the court of justice.
Source: *Finance Yearbook of China*, 1999.

At a local government level, about two-thirds of the budget expenditure was spent on supporting economic development and on local government administration. The average growth of total local government expenditure was 16.3 per cent in the period of 1991-1999. The expenditure for capital construction, innovation, and new product promotion, as well as operating expenses for local government administration, increased even more rapidly and their share of total expenditure rose by 1.5, 0.9, and 2.5 percentage points respectively in the same period. However, local government expenditure on culture, education, science, and health care, which had been the largest expenditure responsibility for the local government in the early 1990s, has grown less rapidly than total spending (by an average of 1.1 percentage points between 1991 and 1998), and its share of total spending has fallen.

The main problems of central-local government fiscal relations

In order to meet the requirement of the market-oriented economy, the Chinese government announced in 2000 the establishment of a new nationwide government fiscal system within three to five

667

years. Given that China's local government accounted for more than 70 per cent of budgetary expenditure and about half of the budgetary revenue, it will be critical to further reform to identify problems and entry points for reform at a local level. Establishing an effective local fiscal management system and a healthy relationship between central and local governments will be fundamental for the new fiscal system.

Unclear responsibility and expenditure assignment for local government

The assignment of expenditure responsibility in the 1994 fiscal system reform is still at the level of principles without clarification of details and institutional guarantees. As a result, local government expenditure has been expanding and is now larger than its tax revenue. Given that it accounts for more than 70 per cent of the budgetary expenditure of the government as a whole, local government seems to have taken on much more responsibility than the central government.

In general, it is necessary to allocate government expenditure among the different government levels according to their responsibility for guaranteeing the supply of public services, and to avoid shifting the burden of responsibility between different levels of government. The reasons behind this are as follows:

- First, *the division of responsibility has been quite general* since the beginning of the 1994 reform. The result has been confusion and overlaps in expenditure assignment. On paper, the division of expenditure responsibilities between central and local government is in line with public finance theory and international best practices. In practice, however, there are a lot of similarities in the activities and corresponding expenditure outlays among different levels of government (see Table 20.6). Except for a few items identified as mainly local or central government responsibilities, most expenditure items have been shared between central and local government, although the degree of sharing is quite different depending on the item. Some sharing of responsibilities is inevitable, especially in economic development areas such as capital investment, and research and development (R&D) activities. However, some responsibilities that should be borne by the central government, for example the redistribution of national revenue and national defence, are also shared by local governments.

Table 20.6. **Share of central and local governments in major expenditure items**

Per cent share of total spending in each category

Expenditure item	Central Government Ratio	Local Government Ratio
1. Expenditure for Capital Construction	43.9	56.1
2. Circulation Fund for SOE	50.7	49.3
3. Innovation and New Product Promotion Funds	23.1	76.9
4. Geological Prospecting Expenditure	98.8	1.2
5. Expenditure for Government Administration	6.9	93.1
6. Operating Expense for Industrial, Commercial and Communication Department	38.2	61.8
7. Operating Expenses for Culture, Education, Science and Health Care	11.2	88.8
8. Expenditure for National Defence	99.3	0.7
9. Expenditure for Armed Police Troops		
10. Expenditure for Social Security and Welfare	3.7	96.3
11. Agriculture Aids	10.9	89.1
12. Price Subsidies	51.1	48.9
13. Expenditure for Urban Maintenance and Construction	0	100
14. Aid Funds for less developed regions	0	100
15. Others	26.3	73.6
Total	28.9	71.1

Note: All data is for 1998.
Source: Finance Yearbook of China, 1999.

- Second, *local governments still engage in activities that are not normally carried out by governments in other countries.* Some of these activities derive from the pre-reform and early reform periods when local government was still involved in providing products and services that should have been provided by the private sector. For example, in 1998, subsidies to loss-making SOEs and other payments to SOEs amounted to RMB 27.9 billion, and outlays for price subsidies reached RMB 34.8 billion. Together, these two items accounted for 8.4 per cent of local government expenditure.

- Third, *local government expenditures are not allocated efficiently* and as a result they are unable to adequately fund important areas for which they are primarily responsible. The structure of local government budgetary expenditure provides such evidence. For example, in 1998 the shares of local government spending in China going to education, social security, and healthcare were lower than the 30.5, 20, and 10.1 per cent levels in transition countries such as Hungary. China's lower share of spending on these areas is partly attributable to the relatively high share of spending going to local government administration.

- Fourth, *local government expenditure has often been affected by the reform and planning policies of central government.* The mandates on local governments from these policies have usually been imposed without providing any financial resources to carry them out. For example, in 1998 the central government decided to bring all state owned enterprises in coal mining, geology and some universities under the control of local governments, while petrochemical enterprises were placed under the control of the central government. Under this policy, eighteen coal mining enterprises, together with 141 953 employees and retired workers, were transferred to the Hunan provincial government. Despite central government subsidies, the government of the province is still heavily burdened by social security and other social welfare expenditures for those employees and retired workers, particularly because the inefficient operations of the eighteen coal mining companies are not able to provide sufficient revenues for this purpose. Another example is the policy regarding grain pricing and procurement. Local government is required to contribute to the grain price support funds at the ratio of 1.1 to 1 with the central government. In addition, local government is also required to pay for losses incurred in the procurement at official guaranteed prices by the state-owned grain trading enterprises.

For these reasons, it is necessary for China to clarify and rationalise expenditure responsibility, not only for local government but for the central government as well. Establishment of more appropriate expenditure assignments and responsibilities, along with more efficient allocation of fiscal resources, will help local governments to shed unnecessary burdens and improve their ability to provide public goods and service to society.

Lack of effectiveness and ability to guarantee the sustainable growth of regional budget revenue

Even though the 1994 tax-sharing reforms improved the division of revenue between central and local government, local governments have not been authorised to adjust local taxes according to their needs. As a result of the new pattern of revenue assignments introduced in the 1994 reform, the central government's revenue situation has improved in terms of the ratio of its revenue to the total. However, the failure to revise expenditure assignments has left local governments with a large fiscal gap in some places, especially at the county and township level. However, the central government has strengthened its transfer payments to local government since the 1994 reform. In 1999, the total amount of transfers from central government was approximately RMB 4 100 million, which accounted for almost 70 per cent of central government revenue of the same year and 42 per cent of the total local government revenue. A fiscal gap existed for the local government, suggesting that they had not been provided with sufficient institutional arrangements to finance themselves and to reach an equilibrium between expenditure responsibilities and revenue capacity.

The new tax-sharing system (TSS) weakened local revenue strength, and potential fiscal risk has been growing rapidly. Under the fiscal contract system, local government had benefited greatly from the turnover taxes generated from township and village enterprises (TVEs). Under the TSS, however, local governments have smaller claim to VAT. The lower the level of government, the smaller the gain from VAT because the major share belongs to central government and each succeeding sub-provincial level successively extracts a portion for its own use. As a result, the tax revenue increase at levels of government was lower than the collective increase for the province as a whole. Another important issue concerning local government finances is the potential for increasing fiscal risk. For example, in 1998, eighteen counties in Hubei province reported a fiscal deficit, whose cumulative total was RMB 273.5 million. Among these counties, four had deficits which were over 50 per cent of their revenue, and, in the county with the highest deficit, the fiscal gap was 123 per cent of the county's revenue.

Local governments were given limited tax-setting abilities under the 1994 reform. They can only modify the rates and bases for a few minor taxes, and all other revenue decisions need to be taken by the central government. This factor has given rise to continuing incentives for local government to raise revenue outside the formal budget system, in the form of fees and charges that accrue to locally managed extra-budgetary funds. Indeed, although the share of central government extra-budget revenue to the total had fallen from an average of 50.4 per cent during 1989-93 to 7.9 per cent during 1994-1999, this was not the case at the local government level. There the ratio has remained around 40 per cent over the period from 1989 to 1998.

In a sense, rising extra-budget funds have contributed much to support the operation and development plans of local government. However, they have brought more serious negative effects to local governments, as well as to the central government. Such negative effects are: 1) to squeeze the normal tax base, which is one of the main reasons for China's fiscal contracting; 2) to destroy fiscal discipline and encourage behaviour without cost constraints; and, 3) to lead to corruption and to undermine confidence in the government. Fortunately, the central government has already taken some policy measures with the aim of curtailing the extra-budget funds. The State Council Document No.29 of 1997 is one of the important measures that aim to clarify and limit the authority for setting fees and levies. Another important reform policy is the recent measure on "Rural Tax and Fees", which seeks to encourage the wider emulation of the reform experience in Anhui province. However, until now, the central government has not produced a comprehensive reform plan to deal with the extra-budget funds.

In addition, local governments have no right to borrow in order to meet their increasing expenditure requirements. In fact it is common for local government to use more indirect methods to borrow. The typical practice is for the local government to borrow from a local ("window") enterprise, while providing a loan guarantee to allow the enterprise to obtain the funds. For example, Yichang, a prefecture city in Hubei province, borrowed up to RMB 1.08 billion in 1998 through local financial institutions in this manner.

Lack of consistency in intergovernmental relations from the upper to the bottom level

The purpose of the reform introduced after 1994 was to establish a multi-level fiscal system framework based on a tax-sharing system. After six years of practise, such a fiscal framework has not been implemented thoroughly in terms of tax sharing. The reform package of 1994 had specified only the assignment of taxes between the central and provincial governments, and left each province to determine how to share the province's part among its lower levels. The tax-sharing relationship has been established in principle, even though the fiscal contract still exists somewhere between the central and provincial government. However, intergovernmental relations within provinces present different characteristics.

The absence of guidelines on the division of the twelve local taxes, and on the apportionment of local shared tax between different levels of government below the provincial level, has led to diverse sharing patterns across the nation. Some provinces have simply applied the formula for sharing through to lower levels, while some provinces and prefecture units have added their own layers to the system. For example, the provincial government of Guizhou province takes 10 per cent of the locally retained 25 per cent of VAT, and 50 per cent of the incremental portion of the four local taxes – land occupation tax, land appreciation tax, revenue from land leases and the resource tax.

Another important issue affecting local government finances is revenue growth targets. Such targets were introduced by the Ministry of Finance (MOF) for 1994, with the aim of preventing provincial governments from inflating their collections in 1993 (the central government having decided to take 1993 as the base year for the TSS reform and to guarantee that local governments received at least the 1993 level after reform), and to ensure adequate revenue growth in 1994 and thereafter. Even though the MOF did not issue revenue growth targets after 1994, the practice seems to have continued at sub-national levels and has been the most important incentive for sub-provincial tax collection. For example, Puding county, a nationally designated poor country in Guizhou, received a revenue growth target of 20 per cent for 1997 from its provincial government. To meet this target, the county finance bureau had to set contracts targeting revenue growth of 15 per cent to 25 per cent per year for its eleven subordinated townships and towns. Collective and township officials who met the targets were rewarded, while those who failed to meet the targets were penalised with a fine.

Based upon the above analysis, it is possible to conclude that the fiscal contract relation within provinces has been an important source of the problems in the overall central-local government fiscal relationship. The current system for allocating taxes among the provincial government levels is not a genuine tax-sharing mechanism and further reforms to improve the system need to be implemented.

Regional fiscal disparities and the effects of the current fiscal system

While the local governments' overall fiscal resources have been strengthened over the years, the distribution of those resources among different regions has not been balanced. Regional fiscal disparities can be seen through the following indicators:

- **Budget revenue in relation to economic output.** Among the thirty-one provinces, there is a big gap in the ratio of budgetary revenue to GDP by region. For example, in 1998 the difference between the highest and lowest ratio was about 16.9 per cent (see Table 20.7). Table 20.7 indicates that eastern or coastal regions have a higher ratio of budget revenue to GDP than central or western regions (except for Yunnan province, due to its large tobacco industry).

- **Per capita budget revenues and spending.** Table 20.8 indicates that the per capita budget revenue and expenditure in the eastern region is much higher than in the middle and west regions. For example, per capita budget revenue and expenditure in Shanghai, which are the highest China, are about 14.6 and 8.8 times higher than that in Guizhou province, where the ratios are the lowest.

- **Differences in the growth rate of budgetary revenue.** From 1994 to 1998, local government budget revenue increased at an average annual rate of 16.2 per cent. Growth in most eastern provinces, notably Shanghai and Guangdong, was above the national average, while growth was generally below the average in central provinces and roughly equal to the national average in western provinces.

Table 20.7. **Differences in ratio of budget revenue to GDP by region**

Per cent

	1994		1998	
Top three provinces	Yunnan	26.6	Yunnan	22.9
	Shanghai	17.5	Shanghai	18.0
	Tianjin	13.7	Beijing	17.9
Bottom three provinces	Tibet	3.4	Tibet	6.0
	Anhui	6.8	Sichuan	6.8
	Xinjiang	7.0	Jiangxi	7.97

Source: New China Fifty Years' Government Finance Statistics; China Statistical Yearbook, 2000.

Table 20.8. **Budget disparities among selected regions (1998)**

Regions	Per capita budget revenue (RMB)	Per capita budget expenditure (RMB)	Budget revenue increase rate (annual average 1994-1998) (%)
East			
Shanghai	2 606.4	3 218.4	17.5
Guangdong	902.9	1 163.3	16.5
Tianjin	1 061.8	1 444.3	15.8
Central			
Sichuan	233.4	379.3	7.9
Hunan	241.8	422.1	10.9
Anhui	258.6	393.2	24.1
West			
Shaanxi	260.5	463.8	17.3
Gansu	215.6	500.1	13.2
Guizhou	179.9	366.4	15.9

Source: New China Fifty Years' Government Finance Statistics; China Statistical Yearbook, 2000.

Effects of the tax-sharing system on regional fiscal disparities

Increasing regional disparity in economic development has been one of the prominent problems in China for a long time. There are many theories about the various influences and factors behind the disparity, including differences in resources allocation, industry structure, and economic policies. However, there is no doubt that the weak current fiscal system has done little to ameliorate regional fiscal disparities.

As discussed above, local budget tax revenue comes mainly from the shared VAT and business taxes under the current fiscal system. In general, the tax base of VAT and business tax covers the secondary (manufacturing) and tertiary (service) industries. This helps to explain why coastal provinces, where the share of GDP of secondary and tertiary industries is relatively high, also have a comparatively high ratio of local tax revenue to GDP (Table 20.9). In contrast, the GDP of central and western provinces is relatively more concentrated in primary industries, in particular agriculture, which tend to be more lightly taxed than other industries. For local taxes, such as the personal income tax, a similar pattern can be seen. Coastal regions have higher average household income and therefore a proportionately larger yield from personal income taxes than central or interior regions.

In theory, equalising the distribution of revenue and expenditures is one of the important functions of inter-regional transfer payments in the fiscal system. However, the current Chinese transfer system established by the 1994 reform has done little to reduce regional fiscal disparities, especially the unequal distribution of gaps between revenue and expenditure needs.

In the pre-1994 system, the central transfer to provinces consisted of three components: quota subsidies, earmarked grants, and other subsidies. Since the 1994 reform, two new kinds of transfer payments, "returned revenue" and a "transition transfer", have been introduced, while the above three components were retained.

Among the five transfer components, the fixed subsidies under the old system aimed to guarantee local government the same level of revenue as in 1993. As revenue increased over time, such subsidies gradually declined in importance. From 1996 to 1998, the ratio of fixed subsidies under the old system to the total transfer decreased by 0.7 per cent, to 3.4 per cent. Thus, the fixed subsidies inherited from the earlier system do not have any capacity to equalise revenue distribution.

Table 20.9. **Analysis of budget revenue and transfers in selected provinces**

Region	Ratio to GDP (%)			Budget revenue rank	Transfer from Central Government (RMB 100 millions)
	Primary industry	Secondary industry	Tertiary industry		
Coast					
Beijing	4.0	38.9	57.1	5	106.7
Shanghai	1.9	48.4	49.6	2	216.8
Guangdong	12.1	50.4	37.5	1	196.4
Jiangsu	13.2	50.7	36.1	4	192.6
Central					
Anhui	25.9	43.6	30.5	13	98.8
Hubei	16.9	49.0	34.1	12	136.5
Henan	24.5	45.6	29.8	8	136.1
Sichuan	25.6	41.8	32.7	10	124.2
West					
Shanxi	18.0	42.7	39.2	20	63.3
Gansu	21.0	44.1	34.9	27	71.6
Guizhou	29.7	39.7	30.5	24	70.9

Note: Average income is average per capita annual income of urban households.
Source: *China Statistical Yearbook*, 2000.

Returned revenue has become the main component of the central transfer to provinces. In 1998, returned revenue accounted for 62.7 per cent of the total central transfer (see Table 20.10). The amount of returned revenue is based on increases in tax revenues collected by a province. Accordingly, those provinces which are growing most rapidly, and which can thus more easily increase their revenue collections, benefit most under this transfer arrangement. In effect, the returned revenue acts mostly as an incentive to local governments to collect revenues accruing to the central government.

Special purpose subsidies or earmarked grants are another important transfer component, which accounted for 26.4 per cent of the total transfer in 1998. In China, earmarked grants are used as a policy instrument for central government to regulate local governments' behaviour and to direct local expenditure to central government policy priorities. Almost all areas of local government expenditures are financed in part by earmarked grants. In practice, there are no normative rules or regulations on the distribution of the earmarked grants. The distribution usually depends both upon negotiations between the local and central government and its agencies, and on the local government's other fiscal resources, because local governments are always required to match the grants together with a certain amount of local funds. This system again benefits wealthier regions compared to poorer regions.

Table 20.10. **Share of different types of transfer in total transfers**
%

Items	1996	1997	1998
Total transfer	100.0	100.0	100.0
Returned revenue	71.7	70.5	62.4
Fixed subsidies under old system	4.1	4.1	3.4
Earmarked grants	18.0	18.1	26.4
Transition period transfer	1.3	1.3	1.8
All other transfers	4.9	5.8	5.7

Source: *New China Fifty Years' Government Finance Statistics*.

The transition transfer is the only component of the central-local transfer mechanism that is designed to equalise fiscal resources. Unfortunately, the transition transfer is the smallest component in the mechanism and only accounted for 1.8 per cent of the total transfer in 1999. It is obvious that the equalisation effects of the transition transfer are very limited and overwhelmed by the other components of the inter-governmental transfer system.

This is indicated by the fact that the distribution of the central transfer payment among provinces is similar to that of budget revenue (see the last column in Table 20.9). The wealthier a province, the higher its proportionate share of the central government transfer. This demonstrates further that the current fiscal system favours regions with a high development level and does not provide a mechanism to equalise fiscal resources among different regions.

Conclusion

The fiscal features and problems of local government as discussed above show that the objectives of the multilevel tax-sharing fiscal system established in 1994 have not been fully achieved, and that there is a need for further reform. The main priorities for reform are as follows.

- **To clarify and define the responsibilities and relevant expenditures for different levels of government.** To define government responsibilities according to their functions in the market economy is a keystone for China to establish an efficient multilevel tax-sharing system, and therefore a precondition to optimising and rationalising the expenditure structure for all levels of government.

- **To improve local taxes and to implement the TSS within the provincial level government.** A lack of main categories and sharing principles of local tax within provincial government has been an important obstacle for the implementation of TSS reform. It is necessary and urgent to bolster local revenue by rationalising local tax categories and granting provincial governments some flexibility to set local taxes and their rates.

- **To reform the intergovernmental transfer** mechanism in order to achieve a more equal distribution of fiscal resources among regions. On the one hand, this means simplifying and consolidating the current five transfers into two categories of equalisation and earmarked grants. On the other hand, it implies basing the transfer formula on local economic needs and resources, rather than on existing tax bases.

- **To redesign the budget law to provide institutional guarantees for the central-local fiscal relationship.** A sound institutional arrangement for intergovernmental fiscal relations based on explicit law would not only establish confidence in the central government. More importantly, it would limit the fiscal resource allocation authority of different levels and departments of the government and improve their management so as to achieve greater cost-effectiveness.

NOTES

1. According to the data of the China National Account of NBS, the ratio of government in GNDI (Gross National Disposable Income) decreased from 33.9 per cent in 1978 to 17.5 per cent in 1998, while the ratio for enterprises and individuals, increased by 16.4 per cent in the same period.

2. In Germany and the US, the share of local government revenue to the total was about 52 per cent and 51 per cent respectively in 1998.

3. According to OECD statistics, the share of local budget expenditure to the total of Germany and Switzerland were higher than 70 per cent, and most of the countries were between 50-60 per cent; developing countries like Brazil, Russia and India were around 50 per cent, or even lower.

4. See the *China Statistics Yearbook* for 2000 and the *Finance Yearbook of China* for 1999.

BIBLIOGRAPHY

References in English

Bernstein, Thomas P. and Lu Xiaobo (2000).
"Taxation without representation: peasants, the central government and local States in the reform China". *The China Quarterly*, 2000.

Blanchard, Olivier and Andrei Shliefer (2000),
"Federalism with and without Political Centralisation: China versus Russia". Working Paper 7616, National Bureau of Economic Research, USA.

Chung, Jae Ho (2000),
"Regional disparities, policy choices and state capacity in China", *China Perspectives*, No. 31 September-October 2000.

Ehtisam Ahmad, Keping Li and Thomas Richardson (2000),
"Decentralisation in China?" Conference on fiscal decentralisation.

A. Lavrov, J. Litwack, D. Sutherland (2001),
Fiscal federalist relations in Russia: A case for subnational autonomy.

Richardson, Thomas,
"Recent developments in China's intergovermental finance system".

OECD (2001),
Managing public expenditure: Some emerging policy issues and a framework for analysis. Economics Department Working Paper (ECO/WKP (2001)11), OECD.

OECD (2001),
Contributions of financial systems to growth in the OECD countries. Economics Department. Working Paper No. 280 (ECO/WKP (2001) 6.

Wong, Christine P.W. (2000),
"Central-Local Relations Revisited – The 1994 tax-sharing reform and public expenditure management in China". *China Perspective*, No. 31 September-October 2000.

World Bank (2000),
"China: managing public expenditures for better results – Country Economic memorandum". Report No. 20342-CHA of the World Bank.

References in Chinese

Chinese Academy of Science,
Regions Development Report of China.

CHENG Jianguo,
"Prospect of the Tax Sharing System Reform in China". *China Economic Times*, Jan. 19, 2001.

Development Research Centre of the State Council, China (1998),
Fiscal Policy Issues in the Economic Restructuring Process. Research on the Strategic Restructuring of the State Owned Economy.

Ministry of Finance of the PRC,
The Fiscal System in China. www.mof.gov.cn

Ministry of Finance of the PRC,
Finance Yearbook of China (1999).

NI Hongri and Chen Dong,
"Policy and Reform of Fiscal and Taxation: Retrospect of the Ninth Five-year Periods and Prospect of the Tenth Five-year Period". *Cai Zheng Yan Jiu* No. 9, 2000.

National Tax Bureau of the PRC,
Tax Yearbook of China (2000).

Research on Local Fiscal Risk,
Cai Zheng Yan Jiu No. 4, 2000.

Yang Canming,
"Fiscal Policy Alternatives for the Tenth Five-Year Planning". Magazine of *Cai Zheng* and *Taxation* No. 5, 2000.

Zhang Juliang,
"Some Thinking on Improving the Current Governmental Transfer Payment System". *Magazine of Cai Zheng and Taxation* No. 12, 2000.

Zhang Hongli, Lin Guifeng and XIA Xiande,
"Ear-marked Grants of Central Government to Local Government". *Cai Zheng Yan Jiu* No. 5, 2000.

Zhu Qiuxia,
"Purpose and Alternatives of the Fiscal System Reform in China – Analysis on the Fiscal Relations between Central and Local Government Since Tax Reform in 1994". Magazine of *Cai Zheng and Taxation* No. 4, 1998.

Zhou Ye An,
"International Comparison on Local Fiscal Revenue and Expenditure". Magazine of *Cai Zheng and Taxation* No. 7, 2000.

Chapter 21

CHINA'S REGIONAL DEVELOPMENT: PROSPECTS AND POLICIES

TABLE OF CONTENTS

Tables

CHINA'S REGIONAL DEVELOPMENT: PROSPECTS AND POLICIES[*]

Introduction

The purpose of this chapter is to assess the extent to which the widening of regional disparities that has been observed in China since 1990 is likely to be increased by further trade and investment liberalisation and to identify appropriate policy responses in light of OECD experience. Indeed, while China's accession to the WTO should on the whole have a positive effect on the level of growth, it may have considerable individual and sectoral, but also territorial, redistributive effects. In particular, there could be a widening of the territorial divide between coastal areas and the interior, and between town and country, and the creation of new rifts between north and south and within major metropolitan areas. The need for political and social stability demands that these disparities be limited, which entails the adoption of a balanced and sustainable development strategy.

That strategy must include actions to break the isolation of certain territories (by installing transport and communications infrastructure), to allow greater mobility of persons, goods and capital, and thus to develop an internal market, ensure macroeconomic stability, establish an institutional framework that can reconcile transition and development, and to provide territories with sufficient resources to meet the responsibilities that have been devolved to them.

This chapter is divided into four parts. The first reviews the nature and extent of territorial disparities in China. The second analyses the policies that the Chinese authorities have implemented to reduce them over the past twenty years, drawing on the experience of certain OECD countries. The third assesses the potential impact of trade and investment liberalisation on those disparities. The fourth presents the main lessons that can be drawn from the experience of OECD countries as regards regional development policy. Finally, the conclusion proposes a set of recommendations for making this liberalisation an opportunity for territorial development in China.

Long-standing and sharp disparities

Disparities in territorial development have existed in China for a long time. Today these disparities are highly disturbing: the absolute differential (as measured by per capita GNP) between the poorest province (Guizhou) and the richest one (Shanghai) is 14 to 1(Démurger, 2000). Following the launch of reforms in 1978, the differential between provincial per capita incomes narrowed initially, and then began to widen once again in the 1990s.

China's geo-economic divides

The inequalities of development in China vary, depending on which geographic scale and which indicator are chosen to measure them. Lin *et al.* (1999) propose several decompositions of the main sources of disparities in China, by using a decomposable Theil index, which makes it possible to assess the relative contributions of the various geographic divides to the overall level of territorial inequalities.

When decomposing the overall regional income disparity into internal disparities of per capita income in the rural and urban areas and urban-rural income disparity, they find that the urban/rural contrast explains more than 50 per cent of the territorial inequalities in China over the entire reform period. This contrast, which is already a sharp one when measured by macroeconomic indicators, becomes even sharper if social indicators are used. The differential ranges from 2.5 to 11 for all macroeconomic indicators – GDP, income, consumption, per capita savings (see Table 21.1).

---

[*] This chapter was prepared by Sylvie Démurger, Chercheur, Centre d'Études et de Recherches sur la Chine, Clermont-Ferrand (France) and Gilles Lelong under the supervision of Bernard Hugonnier, Director, Territorial Development Service, OECD. It incorporates material from consultant report written by Ms Shantong Li, Director General, Department of Development Strategy, Development Research Centre of the State Council, China.

Table 21.1. **The urban/rural development gap**

Indicator (per capita)	Real income (1995)	Savings deposits (1995)	Consumption (1995)
Ratio town : country	2.79	11.4	3.41

Source: Xu (1997) and Li (1999, Table 3).

The use of social indicators amplifies this urban/rural divide. With an indicator of income in the broad sense – *i.e.* encompassing social transfers (health care and education benefits, unemployment benefits, housing subsidies and old-age pensions) – the gap between urban and rural areas is 4 to 1. In rural areas, 17.6 per cent of the population is poor, versus only 0.4 per cent in urban areas (Gustafsson and Li, 1998). A rural resident spends 62.40 renmimbi per year on personal health care versus 179.68 for urban residents. Seventy-four per cent of urban households are equipped with plumbing facilities, versus only 7 per cent of rural households. Lastly, for refrigerators, the figures are 78 per cent of urban households and only 11 per cent of those in rural areas. Where health services are concerned, however, the gap is much less deep as a result of policies set in place during the pre-reform period.

The urban/rural dichotomy and the divide between coastal and inland provinces often overlap, since the western and central regions are essentially rural. In the five most successful coastal provinces (Guangdong, Fujian, Zhejiang, Jiangsu and Shandong), per capita income growth between 1980 and 1996 averaged between 6.4 and 9.2 per cent per annum in rural areas and between 5.5 and 7.9 per cent in urban areas. The corresponding figures for 11 other provinces[1] were 3.9 to 7.3 per cent in rural areas and 3.6 to 6.5 per cent in urban areas (Gang *et al.*, 1997). Per capita income in the wealthiest provinces, in purchasing power parities, is now double to triple that of the poorest provinces.

Disparities between provinces reveal not only the contrast between coastal China and inland China, but also, more subtly, China's division into economic macro-regions. China can be divided into four economic macro-regions (Naughton, 1999; Giroir, 1999 and Gipouloux, 1998).

The city-provinces (Beijing, Shanghai and Tianjin) are prosperous and outward-reaching commercial, industrial and administrative centres which have 85 per cent of their workforce employed in secondary and tertiary industries, and their per capita GDP is nearly double that of the coastal provinces. The presence there of the most prosperous State-owned enterprises provides subcontracting opportunities for the rural firms that are springing up on the periphery.

The three northeastern provinces (Heilongjiang, Jilin and Liaoning) have made up the industrial heart of China. It is an area undergoing major restructuring in response to challenges similar to those of the transitional economies of Central and Eastern Europe. The structure of production is that of the Soviet model, dominated by heavy industry. Discriminatory measures against private businesses persist. Transport infrastructure is colonial-style, geared towards the extraction and export of raw materials and dominated by the Harbin-Dalian railway.

The seven coastal provinces (Shandong, Fujian, Guangdong, Zhejiang, Jiangsu, Hainan and Hebei) enjoy income above the national average and owe their recent vitality to the policy of reform and openness in effect since 1978. Their success is attributable to the remarkable growth of rural enterprises since the early 1980s and the crucial role of foreign direct investment.

Lastly, the six central agricultural provinces (Anhui, Hubei, Hunan, Henan, Jiangxi and Shanxi) and the twelve western provinces (Shaanxi, Inner Mongolia, Xinjiang, Tibet, Qinghai, Ningxia, Gansu, Sichuan, Yunnan, Guizhou, Chongqing and Guangxi) have per capita income and GDP levels that are below the national averages. Ownership is largely in State hands, and the secondary and tertiary sectors employ between 30 and 40 per cent of the labour force in those areas. Some of these provinces (*e.g.* Shaanxi) hold substantial mineral and (sometimes) other natural resources. These regions do, however, enjoy a major tourism potential, which has yet to be adequately exploited. The western provinces, which *inter alia* were traversed by the famous silk route, boast a wealth of architectural and cultural treasures.

Finally, intra-provincial disparities can also be accounted for by using county-level data (Lin *et al.*, 1999). The results indicate that in 1992 per capita income disparities in most provinces were smaller than per capita income disparities for China as a whole. The only exceptions are Guangdong, Yunnan, Gansu and Sichuan. Moreover, within the large metropolitan areas there is a trend towards socio-spatial segregation between prosperous central and near outlying areas, on the one hand, and "hamlets" peopled by immigrant workers clustered by provincial origin (*e.g.* the Xinjiang and Henan hamlets of Beijing) (He, 2000) and located further out from the centre, on the other.

Diversity that is more economic than social

The territorial divide between the coast and the interior differs, depending on the indicator used to measure it (Pairault, 1999). Macroeconomic indicators accentuate geo-economic divides. Regional per capita GDP differentials expressed in PPP show gaps of 1 to 9 (UNDP, 1999). Shanghai has a per capita GDP level, expressed in PPP, equivalent to that of Republic of Korea or Argentina. Fujian has a GDP equivalent to that of South Africa or Thailand. Lastly, Tibet's GDP is equivalent to that of Cameroon, and Gansu's to that of Mozambique.

The best infrastructure, a majority of township and village enterprises, and the bulk of foreign direct investment are concentrated in the most dynamic coastal provinces: over 85 per cent of China's foreign direct investment and foreign trade is concentrated in the coastal provinces. In contrast, more than half of the poorest 80 million Chinese live in western provinces (Sichuan, Gansu, Guizhou, Yunnan, Qinghai, Shaanxi, Ningxia, Tibet and Xinjiang). This part of the country attracts less than 5 per cent of aggregate foreign investment in China (see Table 21.2).

Table 21.2. **Disparities between provinces: economic indicators, 1999**

Provinces	GDP (RMB million)	Per capita GDP (RMB)	Average yearly wage (RMB)	FDI (US$ million)	Rural enterprises[1]
Beijing	217 446	19 846	14 054	1 975	96
Tianjin	145 006	15 976	11 056	1 764	114
Hebei	456 919	6 932	7 022	1 042	788
Shanxi	150 678	4 727	6 065	391	317
In. Mongolia	126 820	5 350	6 347	65	385
Liaoning	417 169	10 086	7 895	1 062	439
Jilin	166 956	6 341	7 158	301	249
Heilongjiang	289 741	7 660	7 094	318	149
Shanghai	403 496	30 805	16 641	2 837	150
Jiangsu	769 782	10 665	9 171	6 078	821
Zhejiang	536 489	12 037	11 201	1 233	814
Anhui	290 859	4 707	6 516	261	496
Fujian	355 024	10 797	9 490	4 024	530
Jiangxi	196 298	4 661	6 749	321	307
Shandong	766 210	8 673	7 656	2 259	1 281
Henan	457 610	4 894	6 194	521	858
Hubei	385 799	6 514	6 991	915	657
Hunan	332 675	5 105	7 269	654	922
Guangdong	846 431	11 728	12 245	11 658	1 178
Guangxi	195 326	4 148	6 776	635	344
Hainan	47 123	6 383	6 865	484	27
Chongqing	147 971	4 826	7 182	239	144
Sichuan	371 161	4 452	7 249	341	586
Guizhou	91 186	2 475	6 595	41	128
Yunnan	185 574	4 452	8 276	154	235
Tibet	10 561	4 262	12 962		2
Shaanxi	148 761	4 101	6 931	242	391
Gansu	93 198	3 668	7 427	41	149
Qinghai	23 839	4 662	9 081	5	23
Ningxia	24 149	4 473	7 392	51	49
Xinjiang	116 855	6 470	7 611	24	75

1. Number of workers per 10 000 in the labour force.
Source: *China Statistical Yearbook* (2000).

The ranking remains the same if it is based on the Human Development Index (HDI) (see Table 21.3), although there are some differentials–negative for Shanxi, Inner Mongolia, Liaoning, Hunan, Sichuan, Shaanxi and Guizhou; and positive for Fujian, Jiangxi, Qinghai and Ningxia. These differentials would suggest a lesser degree of social diversity.

The apparently lesser social uniformity in fact conceals sharp disparities, which emerge fairly clearly when more specific indicators are used. For life expectancy and school enrolment rates, the results are as concentrated as those for GDP. For both of these indicators, there is a strong correlation with per capita GDP ($R = 0.78$ for life expectancy and $R = 0.70$ for the school enrolment rate). The provinces of Gansu, Yunnan, Qinghai, Guizhou and Ningxia, which are all remote inland provinces, have the greatest deficit in education.

In contrast, with regard to training and literacy levels, the correlation with the growth rate is slight, the correlation coefficient being relatively low ($R = 0.38$ in 1997) (Pairault, 1999). For the sake of strategic priorities and the imperative of industrialisation, northern and western provinces were favoured under pre-reform education policies. In contrast, the southeastern provinces, which today are the most dynamic, were long left behind, and their performance in terms of literacy rates is very mediocre.

Table 21.3. **Disparities between provinces: social indicators and digital divide**

Provinces	HDI rank[1] 1995	Health care services[2] 1999	Illiteracy (%) 1999	Computers per 100 population 1997
Beijing	2	477	6.45	12.20
Tianjin	3	310	8.03	5.00
Hebei	12	303	11.42	1.57
Shanxi	14	268	9.14	1.35
In. Mongolia	22	319	16.44	1.13
Liaoning	7	288	7.18	1.45
Jilin	13	251	6.81	0.84
Heilongjiang	10	200	9.77	0.86
Shanghai	1	364	8.68	8.60
Jiangsu	6	190	16.79	2.22
Zhejiang	5	373	15.70	3.08
Anhui	19	109	20.28	1.05
Fujian	8	306	18.46	2.24
Jiangxi	23	190	13.15	1.78
Shandong	9	164	20.15	1.77
Henan	16	124	16.31	1.09
Hubei	17	190	14.98	1.36
Hunan	20	273	11.13	2.68
Guangdong	4	174	9.23	9.05
Guangxi	18	283	12.35	1.58
Hainan	11	323	14.58	1.60
Chongqing		313	14.75	4.00
Sichuan	21	382	16.77	1.80
Guizhou	29	262	24.46	1.20
Yunnan	26	283	24.34	1.58
Tibet	30	490	66.18	n.a.
Shaanxi	25	292	18.29	0.91
Gansu	27	353	25.64	2.20
Qinghai	28	472	30.52	1.78
Ningxia	24	265	23.32	1.06
Xinjiang	15	372	9.77	0.99

n.a: not available.
1.   HDI: Human Development Index.
2.   Number of hospitals, clinics, maternity facilities and dispensaries per million population.
Source: UNDP (1995) and *China Statistical Yearbook* (2000).

A *convergence process active in the* 1980s, *interrupted in the* 1990s

The launching of reforms in 1978 led over the ensuing decade to a gradual reduction in the dispersion of per capita income. But in the first half of the 1990s, the overall level of disparities began to rise anew, in particular because of the aggravation of the territorial divide between coastal provinces and those in the interior.

The relative convergence of the 1980s

Whichever indicators of inequality are used (Gini index, Theil index, coefficient of variation or log variance), the trend in the dispersion of per capita GDP between Chinese provinces testifies to the existence of a certain degree of convergence during the 1980s (See in particular, Lin *et al.*, 1999; Démurger, 2000 and Zhang, 2001).[2]

Thus, using the variance of the logarithm indicator, Figure 21.1 shows a slight tendency towards a reduction in cross-province dispersion of per capita GDP until 1990, which can be explained by a variety of phenomena: a greater role played by market mechanisms, a rise of agricultural prices relative to prices of manufactures, the remarkable vitality of rural enterprises, which raised the growth rate in rural provinces and, at least until the mid-1980s, a reduction in the urban/rural divide.

As shown by Figure 21.1, the reduction of inequalities within the three large regional areas (coast, centre and west), measured by their respective intra-regional variance, more than offset the widening of disparities between those areas (inter-regional variance) up to the end of the 1980s. This stems from the fact that while the three municipalities (Beijing, Tianjin and Shanghai) had relatively low growth rates over the decade, the southern coastal provinces, which had started out with an income level lower than the national average, experienced very rapid growth. Positive discrimination policies on their behalf encouraged the development of a dynamic industry through foreign direct investment and rural enterprises, which resulted in an unprecedented shake-up of the regional economic hierarchy (Naughton, 1999). The remarkable take-off of provinces such as Guangdong and Fujian illustrates this shake-up.

Figure 21.1. **Dispersion trends measured by the log variance of per capita GDP, 1978-1998**

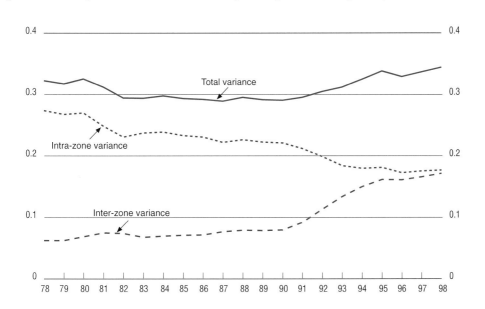

Source: Démurger (2000). Data updated by the author.

The trend since the 1990s

As Figure 21.1 shows, at the beginning of the 1990s, while convergence continued to improve within the three large areas, a reversal of the trend took place, both for China as a whole and between the regions. This stemmed in particular from the growing difficulties of township and village enterprises and from a policy to promote urban development, implying a growing urban-rural gap.

This relatively generous policy of urban income subsidies was financed by a double tapping of rural incomes: an increase in local taxes on farm households, plus an inflationary rise in the tax on rural income because of an unusually accommodating monetary policy. This policy had channels of transmission that were especially sensitive in rural areas because of both productivity differentials and the rise in the prices of non-tradable goods. This triggered a loss of purchasing power in certain provinces.

The persistence of price distortions also contributed to a renewal of regional protectionism from the end of the 1980s, mostly at the initiative of interior provinces (Lee, 1998). Customs barriers, whether tariff-based or not, impeded inter-regional trade and thereby reduced the least advanced regions' chances for development. Thus, as noted by Lee (1998), local protectionism has not subsided in the 1990s but according to the evidence, it seems that regional barriers mainly remain on capital market, and not much on product market (except for a few products, such as autos and beer). Besides, barriers to cross-provincial business investment and mergers/acquisitions seem to be a lot greater.

Finally, the divergence process between coastal provinces and municipalities on the one hand and interior provinces on the other hand has had a self-sustaining dynamic with a true hysteresis effect on regional comparative advantage, as concerns attracting foreign direct investment in particular. The correlation between regional growth and foreign direct investment is very strong. Institutional factors (*e.g.* guarantees of individual and family property rights), transport infrastructure and human capital in the broad sense (encompassing public health and education), which play a considerable role in regional growth (Démurger, 2001), are also important in attracting foreign direct investment (World Bank, 1997 and Oman, 1999).

Underlying factors behind the difference in economic performance among regions

The role of regional policy

Although regional co-operation and co-ordinated regional development have been emphasised in nearly all planning documents from the Sixth Five-Year Plan to the Tenth, the Special Economic Zone policies emphasised in the Seventh Five-Year Plan and the opening of Shanghai-Pudong plus the extension of the opening measures listed in the Ninth Five-Year Plan have had a larger impact on the pattern of regional development. The distribution of the various opening zones among the three regions (west, central and coastal) has had a high impact on the inflow of foreign direct investment. It can be seen from Table 21.4 that the eastern region has the highest number of open cities and zones. The openness also has a tremendous impact on differences of economic performance among regions due to liberalisation of trade and investment and other forms of international co-operation.

The underdeveloped western region still manifests urban-rural disparities due to market forces. There is also a shift of investment in fixed assets among these three regions. There are no detailed data available for savings in different regions, but the data of investment on fixed assets point to mobility of investment and capital from the relatively underdeveloped western region into the eastern region simulated by a search for higher returns on capital. This shift of investment is also affected by the credit allocation of the banking system from the plan. Table 21.5 shows this shift of investment in fixed assets among the three regions in different planning periods. It can be seen from this table that for investment in fixed assets there is an increase in the share of the eastern region from 26.9 per cent (in "Third Five", the lowest of all periods) to 54.2 per cent (in the "Eighth Five", the highest of all periods), while there is a decreasing share of investment in fixed assets in the western region from 34.0 per cent (in the "Third Five", the highest of all periods) down to 14.7 per cent (in "Eighth Five", the lowest of all periods).

Table 21.4. **Spatial distribution of various preferential zones for foreign investors (1979-1994)**

Type of zone	Eastern region	Central region	Western region	Total for the country
Free trade zone	13			13
Special economic zone	5			5
Economic technological development zone	26	4	2	32
Pudong, new area	1			1
Coastal opening cities	14			14
Coastal economic development zone (municipality, county) (CEDZ)	260			260
Open cities along rivers (mainly Yangtze River)		6	3	9
Open cities along borders (municipality, county, town)	2	5	6	13
Border economic co-operative zone	3	4	6	13
Other open cities (capital of province or autonomous region)	2	8	8	18

Source: *Retrospect and Perspective of China's Economic Development* 1979-2020 (Chinese), Chief Editor: Wang Mengkui, Deputy Editor: Wang Huijiong and Li Shantong.

Table 21.5. **Share of investment of capital construction in three regions in different planning periods**

Region	1953-1957 "First five"	1958-1962 "Second five"	1963-1965 "Adjustment period"	1966-1970 "Third five"	1971-1975 "Fourth five"
Eastern	36.9	38.4	34.9	26.9	35.5
Central	28.8	34.0	32.7	29.8	29.9
Western	18.8	22.0	25.6	34.0	24.5

Region	1976-1980 "Fifth five"	1981-1985 "Sixth five"	1986-1990 "Seventh five"	1991-1995 "Eighth five"	1996-1998. Previous three years of "ninth five"
Eastern	42.2	47.7	51.7	54.2	52.5
Central	30.1	29.3	24.4	23.5	23.2
Western	19.9	17.2	15.8	14.7	15.6

Source: *China's Investment on Fixed Assets, Annual Statistics* (1950-1995).

The role of other factors

Different performance of SOEs in different regions

The level of performance by State-owned industrial enterprises is not, in general, satisfactory. This is especially so in the western region. It is reported that the performance by SOEs in 2000 is better, but the data are not available yet. Table 21.6 presents major indicators of performance by major industrial SOEs in different regions in 1999. It can be seen from Table 21.6 that SOEs in the Eastern region perform better than those in the Western region, *i.e.* they generally have lower asset to liability ratios and higher ratios of profit to industrial costs than the national average.

Development of non-State enterprises of different regions

China has encouraged the development of different ownership enterprise systems through a gradualist approach. The 1980s witnessed rapid growth of town and village enterprises. Revision of the constitution in 1999 accorded equal legal status to enterprises under different ownership systems. The revised constitution states that "the non-public economy in the form of individual economy or private economy within the scope framed in the law are essential components of the socialist market economy". As discussed in Chapters 2 and 5, non-State enterprises of the Eastern region have a much higher value added in production than the Central or Western regions.

687

Table 21.6. **Profits and debt of industrial firms in the state sector by Province, 1999**

	Profits/production costs	Assets/debt (%)	Share of the State sector in industrial production (%)[1]
National average	2.89	61.98	48.6
Beijing	3.63	60.16	73.0
Tianjin	−1.60	65.92	31.8
Hebei	3.20	59.92	55.0
Shanxi	0.59	65.54	67.0
Inner Mongolia	−0.65	61.54	84.0
Liaoning	0.76	59.96	66.0
Jilin	1.55	66.78	84.0
Heilongjiang	15.43	64.88	83.0
Shanghai	5.57	50.95	51.0
Jiangsu	2.61	60.30	31.0
Zhejiang	5.25	52.24	21.0
Anhui	0.83	61.31	64.0
Fujian	6.36	60.62	33.0
Jiangxi	−1.09	70.34	81.0
Shandong	3.24	62.87	40.0
Henan	1.12	65.56	51.0
Hubei	1.94	65.03	60.0
Hunan	0.12	70.21	66.0
Guangdong	5.80	57.22	28.0
Guangxi	−0.02	69.81	69.0
Hainan	−0.63	73.73	72.0
Chongqing	−2.36	67.50	71.0
Sichuan	0.57	63.66	66.0
Guizhou	0.36	69.02	81.0
Yunnan	8.80	52.81	81.0
Tibet	14.42	35.60	78.0
Shaanxi	−0.95	69.77	77.0
Gansu	−1.85	69.83	78.0
Qinghai	−0.75	66.48	87.0
Ningxia	−0.90	67.78	78.0
Xinjiang	−0.16	63.35	88.0

1. Only firms with independent accounting systems are included in the figures (this excludes firms with business receipts of less than 5 million RMB.
Source: Zhongguo tongji nianjian (2000), *China Statistical Yearbook*, p. 433.

Fiscal revenue income and expenditure of different regions

The Chinese fiscal system has been undergoing reform since the late 1970s. China's budget system served China well under central planning but it increasingly falls short of the demands that China's emerging socialist market economy imposes. The structure of the taxation system and budgetary practices of China lag behind the economic decentralisation from the reform period. Further improvements for complete development of the taxation system, such as broadening the tax base, adjustment of tax rates and tax items, clarification of the rights and responsibilities of central and local governments are required. As a rule the central government receives a higher share of revenue income than the sum of revenues of provincial governments, while the total expenditure of local governments is higher than that of the central government. For the country as a whole, the ratio of expenditure of local government to central government is 2.18. Jilin, Inner Mongolia, Guizhou, Yunnan, Tibet, Gansu, Qinghai, Ningxia and Xinjiang have a ratio of fiscal expenditure/fiscal revenue higher than the national total. These, with the exception of Jilin province, are designated as poor jurisdictions in the Western region. See Chapter 20 for more detailed discussion of this issue.

Difference in development of infrastructure and urbanisation

Differences in the development of infrastructure and rates of urbanisation have been manifest throughout past years. Table 21.7 compares infrastructure and rate of urbanisation in 1998.

Table 21.7. **Comparison of infrastructure and rate of urbanisation (1998)**

	Railway (km/10^4 km^2)	Highway (km/10^4 km^2)	Length of postal routes (km/10^4 km^2)	Length of long distance optical cable line (km/10^4 km^2)	Telephone set (set/100 persons)	Rate of urbanisation
National total	82.2	1 331.7	2 972.8	202.19	10.5	28.3
Eastern	220.2	3 853.0	11 392.9	490.94	17.1	33.8
Central	184.3	2 267.8	3 835.3	366.76	7.7	26.6
Western	35.9	712.6	1 456.1	117.31	5.4	20.7

Source: Based upon Special Issue of Statistical Information – Guide for Western Regional Development, *China Social Science Publisher* 2000.

Difference in development of human resources

Although the Chinese government has paid attention to the development of human resources in the western region, where the growth rate of indices of human resources is generally higher than that of the national average, the large disparity of human resource development before the establishment of PRC, and the other social economic factors before and after the launch of economic reform, mean, however, that there are still large differences in the human resource development of the western region compared to the whole nation. For instance, the population of the western region represents 27 per cent of the national total, but it comprises around 54 per cent of the illiterate citizens in the nation as a whole. This becomes a crucial factor of constraint in the socio-economic development of the western region.

The western region is also underdeveloped in scientific and technological capabilities. The development of education, along with capabilities in S&T, promote human resource development. Improvements in the quality of the labour force are essential components for the development of the western region. A World Bank Report on Gansu province pointed out that "Increased labour mobility and rapid change in the structure of employment in Gansu will depend greatly on improvements in basic education... Most important of all, however, is the need to improve the qualification of teachers..."[3] This comment is valid not only for Gansu province, but is applicable to other provinces and autonomous regions of the western region as well.

Policy strategies and territorial development

Two major strategies have been deployed by the Chinese authorities over the past fifty years: the central planning of the pre-reform period, and the "creative market decentralisation" of the reform period. Since the beginning of the reforms, the Chinese authorities have not been much aware of the need for balanced regional development, and it is only recently that they have chosen a new course, perhaps out of fear of centrifugal tendencies and the expression of a certain irredentism by national minorities.

Strategies of the past: central planning and creative market decentralisation

Central planning: 1950-80

In none of the three forms it took – the industrialisation-oriented deconcentration of the "Great Leap Forward", the emphasis on regional self-reliance in the aftermath of the Great Leap Forward, or the redistributive centralisation of the "Third Front" – did pre-reform development strategy have much impact on reducing territorial disparities (Yang, 1997).

Box 21.1. The regional dimension of China's planning system

China's central planning before the 1980s was rather different from the former Soviet Model of Planning, which was very much centralised, whereas the planning system of China had undergone several cycles of centralisation and decentralisation since 1956. This explains why regional authorities had acquired a certain level of experience in planning based upon the former Soviet Model.

During the First Five-Year Planning period (1953-57), China implemented a regional co-operative administrative level intermediate between the central and provincial levels. There were six intermediate administrative regions: North-eastern region (Liaoning, Jilin, Heilongjiang), Northern region (Beijing, Tianjin, Hebei, Shanxi, Inner Mongolia), Eastern (Shanghai, Jiangsu, Zhejiang, Anhui, Fujian, Jiangxi, Shandong), Central Southern (Henan, Hubei, Hunan, Guangdong, Guangxi), Southwestern (Sichuan, Guizhou, Yunnan, Tibet) and Northwestern (Shaanxi, Gansu, Qinghai, Ningxia, Xingjiang). During this period there were 156 key projects. The distribution of those projects was heavily biased in favour of interior regions (for instance Northeastern region: 56 projects; Southwestern region: 33 projects). The eastern region was allocated only 5 projects. The Second Five-Year Planning period (1958-62), was also the period of the "Great Leap Forward".* Regional policy was to achieve a balanced distribution of industry and an independent and self-sufficient economic system within each administrative region and province. Projects (large, medium and small) under construction reached more than 210 000 and a strategy of adjustment was implemented from 1963-65. In the "Third Five" (1963-67) and "Fourth Five" (1968-72), the major planning focus was defence-oriented. "Third Line" construction was stressed, and locations of projects were in large part in Yunnan, Guizhou, Sichuan, Shannxi, Gansu and the western part of Henan, Hubei, Hunan. Until the period of the Fifth Five-Year Plan (1976-80), there was a shift of location and investment to the eastern part. There were nine projects located in the eastern part, and six in the western part among the 22 large projects tied to imported equipment. The excessive scale of capital construction in this period precipitated further adjustments.

Since the launch of economic reform and opening to the outside world in the late 1970s, China has embarked on the gradual reform of its planning system. There are explicit regional policies listed in the planning document since the Sixth Five-Year Plan (1981-85) up to the recently announced Tenth Five-Year Plan (2001-05). There are several broad preconceptions of regional policies and there is also the evolution of regional concepts and policies in this period. The major aspects are as follows:

- There have been various concepts for classification of regions. One concept is the classification into coastal region, hinterland, minority region and so on. This concept is derived from traditional notions within the former planning system (and is maintained in the Sixth Five-Year Plan). The other concept is that of classifying the regions into eastern, central and western region according to geographical location. In addition, minority, poorer regions are added. The rural-urban relationship is introduced as a subject of study and the concept is initiated in the Seventh Five-Year Plan (1986-90).

- Although China had prepared five Five-Year Plans before its reform and opening to the outside world, there were no explicit regional policies and benefits from such policies would accrue only in some regions. Targeting sectoral policy was very much emphasised. With heavy industry as the foundation, the iron and steel sector, machinery sector *inter alia* were targeted, but this sectoral targeting was not incorporated into regional development. The so-called "Third Line Construction" was defence-oriented rather than explicit regional policy. Fiscal allocation (or transfer payment) was the major macroeconomic policy prior to the 1980s. Since the launch of economic reform and opening, there have been steps towards classification of the regions, and before the Tenth Five-Year Plan there were statements of regional policy. A change is emerging away from sectoral to regional targeting. But there is no consistent statement on the regions in the planning documents of Sixth Five-Year Plan to Ninth Five-Year Plan. There is also no integration of macroeconomic, social environmental and industrial policy. In China's Tenth Five-Year Plan, development of the western region was declared to be a major strategy; there is also some integration of sectoral policies *vis-à-vis* the eastern, central and western regions. There is a need to study China's regional development within the framework of co-ordinated macroeconomic policy (fiscal, monetary, trade), social policy (poverty alleviation, income distribution), environmental policy (sustainable development) and industrial policy.

---

* The name given to the development policy launched in China at the end of 1957, which was intended to speed up the development process by a 20 to 30 per cent industrial growth rate. The success of this venture has been very difficult to assess because of other events which were occurring simultaneously. (Abstracted from *The* MIT *Dictionary of Modern Economics*, Third Edition, edited by Pearce, D.W., The MIT Press, 1989).

The strategy of the Great Leap Forward (1958-60) was to encourage the accumulation of capital and urban development. It entailed tapping peasant income through a redistributive system of farm and industrial pricing and administrative limitations on the mobility of rural workers. The outcome of the concentration of capital in urban areas, and of the *Hukou* system, was to reduce the stock of available capital per rural worker and to create a redundancy of farm labour. These two effects led to a reduction in apparent labour productivity in rural areas and widened the divide between urban and rural areas (Cook, 1999).

Following the collapse of the Great Leap Forward and the ensuing famine period in 1960-62, the Chinese authorities encouraged regional economic self-sufficiency. This self-reliance policy was anchored on both ideals of egalitarianism and considerations of national security. Its principle was that each province should build up relatively independent industrial systems and be self-sufficient in industrial as well as food production.

The "Third Front" strategy was implemented in the mid-1960s, out of security and strategic defence considerations. It implied a massive move, as well as in-site construction, of industrial enterprises to inland provinces, through the centralisation of investment decisions, which made it possible to redistribute productive resources amongst the provinces. But the policy's impact on territorial disparities was limited because of the economic inaccuracy of most projects planned in the Third Front policy, which led to a wasteful use of funds and gave poor economic results (Yang, 1997). In the 1960s, the Third Front policy laid waste to more than two-thirds of China's gross fixed capital formation and had only a marginal effect on growth rates in the central and northern provinces (Naughton, 1999).

Creative market decentralisation: 1980-90

With the 1982 Constitution a new era began, since the Constitution devolved substantial powers to the provinces, which became the driving force in China's economic and political transition (Montinolla, Qian and Weingast, 1995). The provinces are now free to set price levels, within the framework of a system of local public markets; the regional minimum wage; and regional investment and customs tariffs, as part of their new trade-related powers. In the course of the reforms, provinces (and/or cities) were given more and more authority to approve foreign direct investment in certain industrial sectors without the central government's prior consent. In the early 1990s, they embarked upon a vast programme of restructuring and privatisation of the local public sector. Competition law is also being formulated at the regional level.

Local governance was unquestionably improved as well. The Party's central apparatus was scaled back, and while appointments of local leaders still require the centre's prior consent, those leaders act ever more independently of Beijing (Li and Lian, 1999). The first direct election of municipal authorities took place in 1998. At that time, the Carter Foundation of Atlanta contributed to the installation of pilot computer systems to tally votes in the villages in which elections were held.

While the role of guilds and other interest groups (such as the famous "Nanking Transporters' Guild" between the two world wars) was a characteristic of coastal provinces only, the spectacular expansion of the local press and of village associations testifies to the growing role played by civil society in rural and inland provinces. While the number of traditional peasant tax rebellions increases, judicial settlement of disputes between elite groups and local populations is now implemented, with a particularly steep rise in tax disputes (Bianco, 2000).

Decentralisation also involved a strategy of positive discrimination in favour of the southern coastal provinces. *Inter alia*, this was the goal of the so-called "opening-up" policy deployed in the 1980s with the creation of "Special Economic Zones". While this was accompanied by a propagation effect within the coastal provinces (Démurger, 2000), the dominant outcome of this policy of positive discrimination was nonetheless to widen the territorial divide between the coast and the interior.

The fiscal distribution that resulted from the reform period among provinces is severely unbalanced. As a rule, the richest (coastal) provinces can raise higher amounts of revenue from local taxes (levied on their dynamic secondary and tertiary industries) and they can spend more on

691

Box 21.2. Special Economic Zones and Economic Development Zones

These economic zones can be defined as geographic areas within a given territory in which selected economic activities are fostered through preferential tax policies and regulations. While creation of special economic zones (SEZs) is a prerogative of the central government, development zones are set up by the provinces.

In the 1980s, five special economic zones – Shenzhen, Zhuhai and Shantou in Guangdong province, Xiamen in Fujian province, and then Hainan Island – were created at the initiative of the State Council. These areas were chosen *inter alia* because of their coastal locations and, especially, their proximity to Hong Kong, China, Macao and Chinese Taipei.

These zones, enjoying preferential tax treatment and provided in the 1980s and 1990s with quality infrastructure, were to serve as laboratories for China's reforms. They were also to be the starting point for an inward drive to the inland provinces, thanks to FDI-related technology transfers. foreign direct investment flows in these zones increased 30-fold between 1980 and 1995. As is the case for similar areas set up in the OECD countries, their attractiveness to foreign direct investment is attributable less to the start-up benefits they offer than to their geographic location, the quality of their labour force and infrastructure, and their relative judicial security. Taking advantage of rising costs in Hong Kong, China and Chinese Taipei, these SEZs were able to set up local capital markets, including venture capital markets. Stock exchanges were set up in Shenzhen and Shanghai (Pudong). The Dalian economic development zone, which was set up by Liaoning province in the 1990s, has new business incubators that have spawned start-ups in the forefront of technological progress.

The economic performance of these zones is remarkable. The vitality of foreign trade and FDI-related technology transfers have generated a considerable rise in productivity, inducing a growth rate far in excess of the (already very high) national average. Shenzhen, for example, experienced real growth of 35.5 per cent per annum between 1985 and 1995, while the growth rate for China as a whole was 10 per cent. The extent to which this growth is propagated to neighbouring provinces (through technology transfers and learning by doing), although perceptible, remains limited (Ge, 1999).

developing an attractive business environment, by building quality infrastructure, training a skilled labour force, etc. On the contrary, the poorest (non-coastal) provinces are trapped into a vicious circle of a low level of both revenue and expenditure and an inadequate equalisation mechanism (see Chapter 20 on Issues concerning central-local government fiscal relations).

The current route: seeking balanced development

Reducing disparities between coastal and inland provinces is now a core priority of the Chinese authorities. They are determined to put a halt to the widening territorial divide by helping the inland provinces to better exploit their comparative advantages, and especially the abundance of raw materials. This objective is set forth clearly in the introductions to the Eighth, Ninth and Tenth Five-Year Plans.

More recently, a general programme for developing the west was formulated in connection with the Tenth Five-Year Plan (see Box 21.3). To achieve this objective, the authorities have two types of instruments at their disposal: infrastructure policy and tax policy.

Infrastructure policy

The Chinese government has embarked upon a vast infrastructure programme to bring the inland provinces out of their isolation. During the 1990s, spending on infrastructure as a proportion of GDP rose from 1.26 per cent to 4.5 per cent. Under the Tenth Five-Year Plan, RMB 800 billion is to be expended to finance infrastructure and attract foreign investors. This policy of heavy and light infrastructure was introduced at two levels–that of the central State and that of the provinces.

Box 21.3. **The western development strategy**

Launched by the Chinese government in 1999, the Western Development Strategy was officialised in March 2000 by the creation of a specific agency to oversee its implementation (*Office of the Leading Group for Western Region Development*). This office comes directly under the State Council and is directed by the chairman of the State Planning and Development Commission. The aim of this strategy is to narrow the disparities in income and development between the coastal provinces and the western provinces by creating an environment conducive to the development of the twelve western provinces concerned, namely Inner Mongolia, Shaanxi, Gansu, Qinghai, Ningxia, Xinjiang, Tibet, Sichuan, the municipality of Chongqing, Guizhou, Yunnan and Guangxi.

The aims of the strategy are to:

- Promote infrastructure development, chiefly by central government funding.
- Attract investment by putting in place preferential policies, in particular preferential tax regimes.
- Promote environmental protection, especially in areas subject to erosion.
- Foster an environment conducive to the development of science and technology-related activities, and to attracting skilled labour.
- Encourage the involvement of the coastal provinces in their neighbours' development.

Some measures have already been announced and implemented since 1 January 2001 for a 10-year period. They include *inter alia* additional public expenditure, increased support and lower tax rates. Nearly 100 billion RMB per year are due to be spent by the central government in the western region, financed by bond issues, bank loans and other investment. Corporate profit tax will be cut from 33 per cent to 15 per cent for local and foreign enterprises. Private enterprises will be given more freedom, which should put them on an equal footing with State enterprises. Lastly, various incentives are scheduled to be introduced to attract investment in capital-intensive industries such as energy, transport and telecommunications.

Beijing has managed to give priority to major infrastructure without neglecting the development of minor infrastructure. Projects recently approved by the State Planning Board for the Tenth Five-Year Plan include the construction of 150 000 km of new motorways in the western provinces and the laying of 955 km of railroad track linking Xian (Shaanxi) and Hefei (Anhui).[4] Other infrastructure projects include telecommunications networks and dams in western China. To be able to deliver on this promise, Beijing would like to float a US$12 billion bond issue to finance natural gas pipelines and electric power plants (official figure from the State Planning Board). A 4 200 km gas pipeline is also being built between the Tarim basin in Xinjiang and Shanghai. Lastly, Beijing is trying to foster co-operation between TVEs in the interior and those in coastal provinces, and to set up "technological project zones" to spur dissemination of innovations from the most dynamic coastal provinces to interior provinces.

For their part, the central and western provinces have put the emphasis on transport and communications infrastructure so they can exploit their abundant natural resources: non-ferrous metals in Gansu; potash mines in Quinghai; oil in Xinjiang; coal and natural gas in Shanxi, Shaanxi and Inner Mongolia; hydro-electric resources in Sichuan and Guizhou; and phosphorus in Yunnan, Guizhou and Hubei.

The combination of these policies renewed the momentum for development in certain western and central regions, while rising factor costs in the coastal provinces tended to drive investments towards the inland provinces, prompting new industries, including some Western firms, to establish a presence in western China.

Tax measures

The central authorities have made massive use of tax measures. The privileges heretofore accorded to SEZs have now been extended to large interior metropolitan areas like Chongqing and Wuhan. As a rule, such positive tax discrimination, which also generates major distortions, can hardly

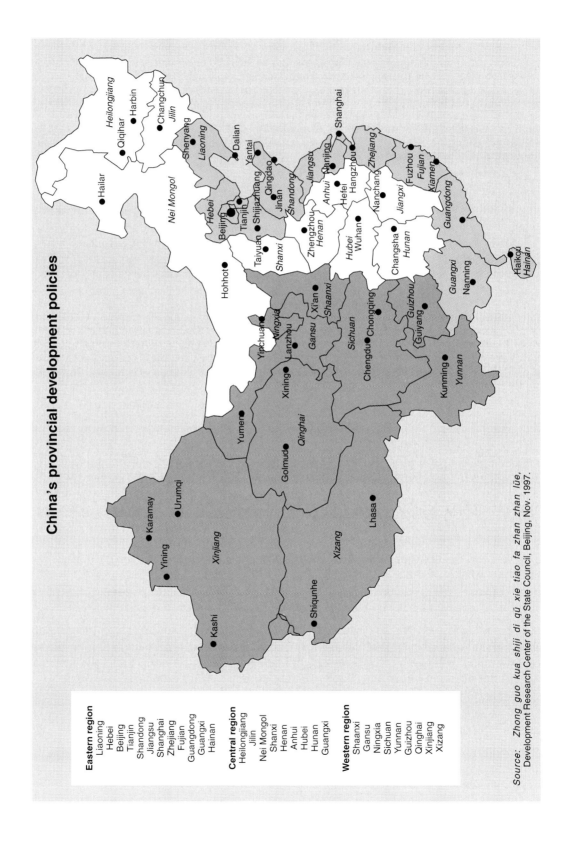

China's provincial development policies

Eastern region
Liaoning
Hebei
Beijing
Tianjin
Shandong
Jiangsu
Shanghai
Zhejiang
Fujian
Guangdong
Guangxi
Hainan

Central region
Heilongjiang
Jilin
Nei Mongol
Shanxi
Henan
Anhui
Hubei
Hunan
Guangxi

Western region
Shaanxi
Gansu
Ningxia
Sichuan
Yunnan
Guizhou
Qinghai
Xinjiang
Xizang

Source: Zhong guo kua shiji di qū xie tiao fa zhan zhan lüe,
Development Research Center of the State Council, Beijing, Nov. 1997.

offset the comparative disadvantage of geographic isolation. Inadequate and low quality infrastructure combined with relatively less opportunities in remote provinces make these tax measures much less attractive for entrepreneurs than was the case in coastal provinces.

The fiscal reform of 1994, and the one begun in 1999, attempted to make up for the problems generated by decentralisation by increasing the budgetary preponderance of the State (see Chapter 20). Local budgets' share of aggregate general government budgets fell from 70 per cent to 50 per cent in the latter half of the 1990s (Zhang, 1999). A new system of horizontal equalisation was also set up in 1995, based on budget transfers from provinces having per capita GDP at least 25 per cent above the national average to those where it is at least 25 per cent below.

Despite these provisions, the resources of the poorest provinces have remained quite limited. The actual latitude available to local authorities is still quite important, since their revenue also include extra-budget revenue. With regard to regional disparities, this extra-budget financing adds to the overall inequality since provinces' capacity to raise funds mainly depends on local industrial activity and income. The tax reforms therefore seem inadequate to offset decentralisation, which would appear to penalise rural provinces. This certainly explains why in March 2001 Chinese Prime Minister Zhu Rongji announced a reform plan to unify the system of taxation for farmers with a flat 7 per cent tax on all their income. This will entail a reorganisation of local governments and the institution of subsidies from Beijing.

On the expenditure side, the outcome is quite similar since the decentralisation process has been accompanied by a decentralisation of certain expenditure responsibilities to local governments. This is the case for education whose funding mainly falls within the competence of local governments. As poor provinces cannot raise as many funds as rich provinces, the decentralisation of expenditures also entails further inequalities.

Preferential policies for foreign direct investment are also supplemented (see Table 21.8).

Table 21.8. **Preferential policies for FDI in the central and the west regions**

1. FDI which can play the advantages of human and natural resources of the central and the west regions and is consistent with national industrial development policy can be classified as encouraged category, and therefore, enjoy the preferential treatment of tariff free and value added tax exemption for imported equipment and technology.

2. Approval conditions and degree of market openness for FDI projects under the restricted category or subject to foreign ownership control can be more open in the central and the west regions than in the east region.

3. Central government will take the priority to set up a group of key projects in the central and west regions, including agriculture, water conservancy, transport, energy, raw materials and environment protection, to attract FDI, and will provide full support for complementary funds and other related measures.

4. Large and medium sized state-owned enterprises and military enterprises transferring to civilian purpose in the central and west regions are encouraged to attract FDI to participate in technology innovation.

5. FIEs in the east region are encouraged to invest in the central and the west regions. The invested enterprises can enjoy corresponding preferential treatment if the share of foreign investors' investment exceeds 25 per cent.

6. The experiment permitted by the central government to open new sectors and industries to FDI can be carried out in the east region and in the central and the west regions simultaneously. The provincial capital cities of the central and the west regions can carry out experiments to open commerce, foreign trade and tourist agency to FDI. FDI in the provincial capital cities, border cities, cities along the Changjiang River, economic and technological development zones, and new technological development zones and Shaanxi Yangling agricultural development zone of the central and the west regions will be granted the same preferential policies. Provincial authorities in the central and the west regions will be empowered to authorise FDI worth up to US$30 million.

7. Starting from January 1, 2000, FIEs classified as encouraged category located in the central and the west regions can enjoy 15 per cent enterprise income tax rate for three years after the expiry of the current preferential taxation policies. For enterprises which are at the same time regarded as technology advanced enterprises or export-oriented enterprises and whose export value of the year reaches more than 70 per cent of the total output value, enterprise income tax can be collected at a tax rate reduced by half, but the reduced tax rate should not be lower than 10 per cent.

8. Foreign banks are encouraged to set up representative offices or set up bank branches in the central and the west regions.

9. The central government has issued the "Catalogue of Advantageous Sectors for Foreign Direct Investment in the Central and the West Regions".

Source: Office of the West Development Leading Group of the State Council (2000), *Guojia Zhichi Xibu Dakaifa de Youguan Zhengce Cuoshi* [State's Relevant Policies and Measures on Supporting the Development of West Areas].

WTO accession: the consequences for regional development in China

To explore the likely consequences of China's upcoming accession to the WTO, we shall take three approaches. The first is to examine the results from a two-region CGE model built by China's Development Research Centre of the State Council; the second is to analyse input on the impact by industry from the various research and analysis that has been conducted to date; the third is to classify China's 31 provinces into six major categories, on the basis of economic specialisation, in order to get a clearer idea of the consequences of liberalisation on each one.

A *two-region* CGE *model*

To investigate the regional impact of China's WTO accession in a comprehensive and consistent framework, a two-region Chinese Computed General Equilibrium (CGE) model is utilised in this analysis. The consistent modelling framework brings together a broad range of elements involved, and permits exploration of impacts from different perspectives. The model seeks to quantify the impact of China's accession to the WTO, and provide empirical evidence to understand the challenge and opportunities it brings to relevant parties.

Based on the China-US agreement on market accession, the following four aspects of WTO membership are simulated: 1) tariff reduction on industrial products; 2) elimination of quotas on industrial products by 2005; 3) agricultural trade liberalisation, *i.e.* tariff reduction for agricultural products, introduction of tariff rate quota system for agricultural goods; 4) the phase-out of Multi-Fibre Arrangement (MFA) quota on textiles and clothing under the WTO Agreement on Textiles and Clothing

---

Box 21.4. The two-region Chinese CGE model

The Chinese CGE model used here is closely related to the applied general equilibrium model already used extensively over the past two decades to analyse the impact of trade policy reform (see Derivis, de Melo and Robinson, 1982; de Melo, 1988; Shoven and Whalley, 1992; de Melo and Tarr, 1992; Hertel, 1997). But the regional disaggregation in the model, which specifies Guangdong and the rest of China as endogenous agents and allows for inter-regional and national-regional feedback, makes it possible to discern the impact on coastal and inland areas of trade or other policy reforms.

An important feature of the CGE model is the explicit treatment of two separate foreign trading regimes. As pointed out by Naughton (1996), China had established two separate trading regimes by 1986-87. One is the export processing or export promotion regime, which is extremely open, with most foreign-invested firms and parts of domestic firm participating in it. The other is the traditional, but increasingly reformed, ordinary trade regime. Since the 1990s export processing has grown rapidly, accounting for more than half of all exports. Obviously, to analyse the external trade behaviour and the impact of alternative changes of trade policy in such an economy, it is very important to have an explicit treatment of its dualistic foreign trading regimes in the model.

In the extension from single region Chinese CGE model to multi-region setting, two regions – Guangdong province and rest of China – are specified, each with a demand and production structure, and inter-regional trade in commodities and services. The interregional factor mobility and intergovernmental transfer are also introduced in the model. Guangdong province is located in southern China, neighbouring Hong Kong, China and Macao. As the largest economy in China, it accounts for nearly 40 per cent of national foreign trade. The development of Guangdong since 1978 and its economic structure could serve as a representation of China's coastal area.

The model assumes imperfect inter-regional factor mobility to reflect the policy and institutional factors that limit regional factor movement, as well as the location preference of residents. The movement of capital is driven by the relative rental rates across regions and the constant elasticity of transformation, while movement of labour is determined by the relative real income across regions plus the constant elasticity of transformation. The real income of labour is defined as the wage plus *per capita* net intergovernmental transfer income.

(ATC). The analysis therefore at best captures only one part of the issue. Given the availability of data and limitations of modelling technology, it does not take into account other major aspects of WTO membership, such as the reduction of barriers in service trade and foreign investment, the protection of intellectual property rights, securing market access, enforcement of commitment, and co-operation in dispute settlement.

A base case projection for the next ten years is established first, which determines a reference growth trajectory, in absence of trade or other reforms. It assumes that China will continue its grain self-sufficient policy, and that import quotas on agricultural goods will grow at 3 per cent annually from 2001-10.

National impact

Annex 2 reports the main efficiency and other macroeconomic indicators under the scenario of China's WTO accession as described by this model.

Regional effects

The benefits of trade liberalisation will also be spread unevenly across regions. The greater the share of a given provincial industrial output of a kind relatively favoured by accession, the greater will be the benefits for the province. Conversely, the greater the share of any given provincial output from industries which are relatively disadvantaged by China's WTO accession, the smaller will be the benefits for the province. Moreover, the more dependent the provinces are on foreign trade, the more those provinces will gain from accession, especially those provinces whose foreign trade mostly operated under the ordinary trade regime.

The uneven distribution of benefits from China's WTO accession is confirmed in Table 21.9. The simulation results show that the real GDP of Guangdong will increase by 5.7 per cent in 2010 relative to base case, while real GDP in the rest of China will only increase by 0.56 per cent. The increase of GDP in Guangdong is around 122 billion RMBs, accounting for 55 per cent of national GDP gain.

The model shows that with WTO accession the growth of investment in Guangdong rises higher than private consumption, while in the rest of China the increase of investment due to accession is almost zero. The different pattern of investment growth between Guangdong and the rest of China results from changes in domestic capital flows, which are driven by relative rental rates of capital among regions. The more rapid economic growth and expansion of export sectors in Guangdong will raise the local return of production factors, attracting inflows of capital. In contrast, the rest of China will

Table 21.9. **Major macroeconomic effects on Guangdong and rest of China, 2010**
Percentage change relative to base case

	Guangdong	Rest of China
EV (% of GDP)	5.09	0.36
GDP	5.71	0.56
Consumption	4.81	0.68
Investment	7.95	0.01
Exports	15.66	18.06
Imports	13.03	18.57
Inter-regional exports	–4.13	2.46
Inter-regional imports	2.46	–4.13
Trade surplus	–18.90	14.31
GDP deflator	–0.28	–0.07
Per capita households income		
Urban	1.14	1.28
Rural	2.20	0.56
Labour force	2.32	–0.16

Note: EV = Hicksian equivalent variation of the welfare gain.
Source: simulation results.

experience greater capital net outflow. As a result of increased capital outflow, the trade surplus of the rest of China in 2010 will increase by 14.3 per cent but its investment ratio to GDP will decline.

Expansion of foreign trade is significant for both economies. The increase of exports and imports in Guangdong is smaller than elsewhere China. Two factors account for this. Firstly, the share of agricultural imports in Guangdong is much smaller than the national average. Agricultural trade liberalisation under the WTO accession framework will not result in dramatic increases in agricultural imports for Guangdong. Secondly, the export dependency of Guangdong is higher than the rest of China. Even a small expansion of exports could induce a large increase of factor prices in Guangdong. Due to the imperfect factor mobility across regions, the relatively rapid growth of factor costs would weaken the competitiveness of Guangdong's products, resulting in relatively less expansion of its exports.

The changes in inter-regional trade and trade surplus are driven by inter-regional capital flows. The increased capital inflow to Guangdong will reduce the exports of Guangdong to the rest of China, and increase its imports from the rest of China. The trade surplus of Guangdong will decline by 19 per cent. Because of the high share of processing exports in total exports, the dependence of exports on intermediate inputs from inter-regional imports is small. As suggested by the simulation results, it is likely that expansion of foreign trade will bring about a large increase of inter-regional trade.

More rapid economic growth increases the demands of the labour force. The rising wages in Guangdong will divert the labour force from the rest of China to Guangdong. The labour force and overall population of Guangdong will increase by 2.3 per cent in 2010, boosted by migration from elsewhere in China. The labour force in the rest of China will decline by 0.16 per cent.

These simulation results suggest that at regional level, the coastal area will gain more from trade expansion and increased exports of labour-intensive goods, but the inland provinces, especially provinces specialising in agricultural production, may experience losses.

Insights from the literature by industry

On the basis of the studies reviewed in Annex 2, it emerges that it is labour-intensive sectors that will benefit from liberalisation. This finding, which is consistent with the theory of comparative advantage, leads to projections of increased production, employment and exports in light industries and non-grain farm output. Conversely, industries that are land – and capital – intensive should see their production decline and replaced by imports. In particular, this may be the case with regard to grain and automobiles.

More specifically, as regards agriculture, relatively labour-intensive activities (*e.g.* production of fruit, vegetables and aquacultural produce) may benefit from liberalisation. In contrast, Chinese grain production would be hit by foreign competition, especially from large world producers like the United States and Australia. In this context, trade liberalisation is likely to be seen as a further cause of deterioration in farmers' living conditions, which, coupled with the fact that rural incomes have been virtually flat since 1997, could widen the gap between rural and urban areas.

As regards industry, it is light industry that should reap the main benefits from liberalisation; in particular, the textile and clothing industries would appear to be the main beneficiaries, irrespective of the simulations considered. The unskilled, labour-intensive clothing sector already accounts for a large share of China's exports (15 per cent in 1999) thanks to remarkable growth in the 1990s.[5] The leading world exporter of clothing since 1994, China accounted for 16.7 per cent of world clothing exports in 1998. The most optimistic of the simulations done on China project a further substantial increase in its share of world textile exports due to the phasing-out of the Multi-Fibre Agreement by 2005, but according to some estimates the short-term gain may be smaller because numerous safeguard clauses will still be imposed after 2005.

In contrast, for capital and/or technology intensive sectors, the impact is projected to be negative due to the higher cost of capital. This would be the case for heavy industry in particular but also for sectors that at present are very protected, like the automobile sector.[6] Lastly, services, which figure only slightly in the simulations, should benefit to a small extent from trade liberalisation by around 2010.

Beyond the outcome of CGE models, however, more descriptive analyses would suggest that there will be short-term adjustment costs, potentially substantial in some sectors. While the expected long-term effects are clearly positive thanks to the efficiency gains resulting from heightened foreign competition, it is this same competition that may in the short term trigger a crisis in those sectors, which at present are very heavily protected. Moreover, losses are expected to be recorded in public services (education, transport and health care) due to the expected drop in government revenue linked to tariff barriers.

The typological approach

Sectoral analysis of the gains and losses from trade liberalisation naturally entails differentiating between the impacts on rural areas and urban areas. As China is still a very rural country, with on average 75 per cent of the employed population located in rural areas in 1999, it is important to distinguish between these effects. When one examines the breakdown by province, one sees that even in the northeast provinces, the traditional industrial basins of pre-reform China, rural employment represents over half of total employment (see Table 21.10). This markedly rural distribution of the employed population means that, regardless of the regions considered, it is of crucial importance to gauge the impact of liberalisation on rural areas. As regards rural populations, the main question posed by the sectoral studies is whether the projected negative effect on grain production and farm incomes could be offset by the positive effect on the textile industry, which is widely developed in rural areas in

Table 21.10. **Typology of Chinese provinces**

Zone	Municipalities	Coast	Northeast	Centre	Southwest	Northwest	National
Population distribution in % (1999)	3.0	31.0	8.6	28.6	19.5	9.3	
Area in %	0.4	9.2	8.2	10.7	14.2	57.3	
GDP composition (1999)							
Primary sector	3.1	14.5	15.1	21.6	24.8	21.9	167
Secondary sector	45.8	49.3	48.8	44.4	40.7	41.6	46.5
of which: Industry	39.8	43.0	42.9	38.5	33.6	31.6	40.0
Tertiary sector	51.1	36.1	36.1	34.0	34.5	36.4	36.8
Structure of employment (1999)							
Share of rural employment in total employment	34.4	75.6	53.7	78.6	84.5	69.5	75.0
Share of TVEs in rural employment	60.7	35.9	34.0	25.2	13.2	29.2	27.1
Share of SOEs in urban employment	55.5	49.0	55.3	55.6	60.8	63.4	55.0
Share of primary sector in total employment	14.6	46.3	44.4	58.0	65.7	57.7	53.6
Distribution of main crop production (1999)							
Cereals	1.3	30.1	13.8	29.,5	16.4	8.9	
Cotton	0.3	22.2	0.1	38.4	2.1	37.0	
Fibres	0	6.5	31.5	42.0	14.4	5.6	
Industrial structure							
Share of light industry in industrial production (1999)	36.1	50.3	21.7	36.2	42.5	25.0	42.0
Share of mining in the industry of each region (1995)	2.2	8.1	31.9	13.5	9.9	25.6	12.4
Share of chemical industry in the manufacturing industry of each region (1995)	6.3	7.9	9.0	7.1	8.3	8.7	7.7
Share of textile industry in the manufacturing industry of each region (1995)	9.4	17.8	3.6	9.1	3.6	8.9	11.8
Textile industry[*]							
Distribution of the added value of the textile industry (1995)	11.5	64.7	2.8	14.4	3.1	3.5	
Distribution of the added value of the textile industry generated by TVEs (1998)	8.8	76.8	2.9	9.7	1.0	0.9	

Note: The "textile" industry comprises the textile, clothing and leather sectors.
Source: China Statistical Yearbook (2000), China TVE Yearbook (1999) and 1995 industrial census.

the form of TVEs. This would require that rural industrial activities absorb the surplus labour in the agricultural sector as discussed in Chapters 2 and 3. Thus, it is in non-agricultural employment that provincial disparities appear to be the most marked. While provinces like Guangdong or Fujian are ostensibly more rural (above average), nearly half of rural jobs are provided by TVEs, *i.e.* substantially more than the national average of 25 per cent in 1999. Conversely, it is in the remotest provinces like the southwest that rural industry is the least developed. This being so, if potentially surplus labour is located in rural areas a long way from labour markets (those of the textile industry for example), the matter of labour mobility and migration is likely to become particularly acute.

The provinces can be divided into six major regional groups, which take account not only of the official tripartite classification (coastal, centre and western) but also of the economic characteristics shared by certain provinces. The six groups, as shown in Table 21.10, are as follows:

- *Municipalities* (Beijing, Tianjin and Shanghai).
- *Coast* (Hebei, Jiangsu, Zhejiang, Fujian, Shandong, Guangdong and Hainan).
- *Northeast* (Liaoning, Jilin and Heilongjiang).
- *Centre* (Shanxi, Anhui, Jiangxi, Henan, Hubei and Hunan).
- *Northwest* (Inner Mongolia, Shaanxi, Gansu, Qinghai, Ningxia, Xinjiang and Tibet).
- *Southwest* (Sichuan, Chongqing, Guizhou, Yunnan and Guangxi).

The last two groups (northwest and southwest) comprise the twelve provinces considered to be western provinces in the Western Development Strategy.

As Table 21.11 suggests, the degree of integration of the Chinese provinces into the world economy, as measured by foreign trade and foreign direct investment flows, varies widely from one province to another. Export ratios are 3 to 4 times higher along the coast than in the central or western provinces. They also indicate the much greater integration of the coastal provinces into international trade, and their dependence on exports, mainly of manufactured goods. If we compare the ratio of exports to total supply,[7] as measured by the sum of GDP and imports, the gap between the degree of openness of the coast and the interior is smaller, mainly due to the municipalities, which are big exporters, but it also reveals, symmetrically, the low import content of supply in the inland provinces. Virtually all China's foreign trade in 1999 thus came from the coastal provinces and municipalities despite a slight regional diversification of inward direct investment (80 per cent of which, however, is still concentrated in these two zones). While the weight of the coastal regions in China's foreign trade as well as in foreign direct investment fell slightly in the 1990s, it is still well in excess of their weight in China's economic structure, and in employment of course.

Table 21.11. **Degree of integration of Chinese regional economies into the world economy**[1]

Share of each group in :	Exports			Imports		Openness[2]		Inward direct investment
	Total	Manufacturing	Enterprises with foreign capital	Total	Enterprises with foreign capital	In % of GDP	In % of the total supply	
Municipalities	18.0	13.3	18.4	30.5	24.9	37.9	24.5	16.5
Coast	69.1	70.7	73.8	58.5	65.9	29.5	24.3	67.1
Northeast	5.2	5.2	5.6	4.8	5.5	9.6	9.0	4.2
Centre	3.8	5.9	1.3	2.6	2.4	3.4	3.3	7.7
Southwest	2.2	3.1	0.6	2.0	1.0	3.6	3.5	3.5
Northwest	1.8	1.7	0.4	1.6	0.4	5.2	5.0	1.1
Total	**100**	**100**	**100**	**100**	**100**			**100**

1. 1999 figures except for manufacturing exports (1997 data).
2. The degree of openness measures the ratio of exports to GDP, and to the sum of GDP and imports, respectively.
Source: *China Statistical Yearbook* (2000); *Almanac of China's Foreign Economic Relations and Trade* (1998).

The limited presence of the central and western provinces in foreign markets is ascribable not only to policies that are less market-friendly, but also to the fact that the economies of these regions are less dynamic. The question thus arises as to whether liberalisation represents an opportunity for these provinces in terms of growth and integration into the world economy. To answer this question, it is necessary to look at the economic structure of these regions more closely in order to identify their potential strengths and weaknesses and to evaluate the cost-benefits of China's accession to the WTO for these specific regions.

Table 21.10 provides a statistical overview of the economic structure by main zone and highlights the very different characteristics of each zone. Bearing in mind the sectoral results of the simulations of the expected impact of WTO accession on the one hand, and the structure of the different regional economies on another, it is natural to find that there are "winners" and "losers" in the regional breakdown, which reflect sectoral gains and losses. On the one hand, the municipalities and coastal provinces, whose weight in the primary sector and extractive industries is relatively small, but large in the TVEs and light industry, especially the textile industry, should be able to benefit from trade liberalisation, by exploiting their comparative advantage in light industry, which can absorb surplus labour from the countryside.[8] On the other hand, the ability of the provinces in the northeast, centre, and west to benefit from trade liberalisation is likely to be more limited on account of certain structural and natural handicaps.

The northwest, which contains 10 per cent of China's population on 57 per cent of its territory, is characterised by the predominance of heavy and state industry, especially mining, on account of the region's abundant mineral resources. Conversely, the rugged terrain and arid natural conditions are not conducive to the development of large-scale agricultural production apart from cotton-growing, with the region providing over a third of national production of that crop. These characteristics give the northwest a comparative advantage in natural resources, but excessive specialisation in this area can have (and has had) adverse effects. The region's industrial base is still weak, with very little light industry, well below the national average. Given the unfavourable natural conditions and the fact that the region is cut off from the rest of the country, it is unlikely that the development of light industry – where the prospects for growth lie – will be easy or spontaneous. Transport and market access are also big problems for these provinces.

The geographical situation of **the southwestern provinces** is not conducive to economic development. Cut off from the rest of the country, handicapped by undulating or mountainous terrain, they have experienced little industrial development, either during the period of central planning or since the introduction of reforms. Enjoying a tropical climate that lends itself to agriculture and allows several harvests a year, they have remained essentially agricultural. In 1999, nearly 85 per cent of jobs were still agricultural. As Table 21.10 shows, industrial rural employment (in TVEs) is very underdeveloped.

The question of the geographical isolation of the northwest and southwest regions is very important from the standpoint of the implementation of the Western Region Development Programme and the economic liberalisation that WTO accession will bring. Given the difficult natural conditions, with the problems they pose to entrepreneurs in terms of transport costs and returns on investment, preferential policies by themselves will not suffice to generate flows of investment to these provinces and hasten their industrial development. Their geographical isolation also means that the projected negative impact of WTO accession on rural incomes is liable to be all the greater in the western regions, since they are not only highly dependent on agriculture, but there is no simple alternative available, one of the prerequisites for the reallocation of farm labour to industry being the existence of an environment conducive to industrial development.

The economic situation of the **northeast provinces** is very different from those in the west, since as the former industrial base of pre-reform China, the share of the rural population is well below the national average. With agriculture representing only a relatively small part of the economy, these provinces should be less affected by the negative effects of liberalisation on the agricultural sector. In contrast, their industrial structure is geared essentially to heavy industry, which accounted for nearly 80 per cent of their industrial output in 1999, and especially to mining, which alone accounted for almost a third of industrial value added in 1995. To this should be added a large number of State enterprises, which still employ more than half the urban labour force, in those same industries. The problems that the northeastern provinces are going to encounter are thus very different from those of the western provinces, since they will have to cope with industrial restructuring in urban areas, the pace of which is likely to be speeded up by accession to the WTO. The challenge facing these provinces, whose income level is relatively high owing to the preferential policy during the pre-reform period, is to develop new industries on an industrial base that already exists but which is inefficient and, by and large, obsolete, and to absorb *urban* labour that is very much in over-supply.

Lastly, densely populated and rather rural, **the central provinces** conform to the national average, as shown by the statistics in Table 21.10. Thus, while they should experience the negative impact of trade liberalisation on the agricultural sector, they should also be able to develop existing light industry, chiefly by increasing their share of national textile production.

In conclusion, it emerges from the analysis that three regional groups may potentially suffer from liberalisation (the northwest, the southwest and the northeast), and two groups stand to benefit from it (the municipalities and the coast). In terms of the trend of disparities, this would mean a potential widening of the divide if no back-up policies were introduced to attenuate the negative effects of liberalisation. The proposed typology highlights the importance of differentiating economic policy goals and instruments according to regions. In the case of the western provinces, the main objectives should be to end their isolation and to develop an industrial structure, which at present does not exist. As for the northeastern provinces, the priority should be the restructuring of the industrial sector.

Regional development and increasing economic interdependence: the experience of OECD countries

Unemployment in OECD countries is highly concentrated in certain regions and locations. Some types of regions are apparently more adaptable or resilient than others. Statistics show that unemployment rates remain, on average, higher in rural than in predominantly urban areas in many OECD countries because of structural impediments related to low population density, lack of critical mass, and geographical isolation in a number of countryside areas. The unemployed in rural regions make up over 30 per cent of the total unemployed in a majority of OECD countries. Some rural regions are nevertheless increasingly diverse and a number have performed well recently, creating jobs and wealth sometimes at a more sustained rate than in metropolitan areas.

In a context of increasing economic interdependence and the globalisation processes, not all regions are responding alike. For example, globalisation of company strategies is now reinforcing agglomeration processes in urban or intermediate areas that offer various resources and externalities needed for modernisation of economic structures or innovation. Although world trade continues to be an important driving force for growth in most Member countries (it has for several years been expanding twice as fast as economic activity – except in 1998), it is mainly the most advanced regions (those with economic activities with a high skills and capital content) that reap the benefit of doing business on international markets. Thus most major countries still have limited geographical diversification of trade (only 20 American states earn more than 10 per cent of their GDP from exports; in France, 5 out of 22 regions are responsible for over half of the country's sales abroad). Winning regions are those with a solid export base and notably with a sectoral distribution of activities emphasising mostly globalised industries such as pharmaceuticals, electrical and non-electrical machinery, basic chemicals, scientific instruments, textiles, electronics, and services to firms.

Growth in foreign direct investment (FDI) is another phenomenon associated with globalisation. Strengthened by economic recovery, foreign direct investment represents very large amounts (for instance, since 1980 it has grown three times faster than domestic investment in the EU). A number of factors determine the attractiveness of regions for investors: proximity to markets, quality and availability of labour, appropriate infrastructure (transport and telecommunications), quality of life, cultural similarities, and presence of other companies (clusters). In this case the polarisation effect promotes agglomeration. However, there are no hard and fast rules. Recognition as a dynamic region is not necessarily permanent. Experience shows that long-term success can be ensured by means of well-designed policies.

During the past 20 years, most of the governments of OECD Member countries have developed comprehensive regional policies, to which they continue to allocate significant funds. Many countries consider that reducing imbalances and economic gaps between regions is the principal way to attain given fundamental social objectives – such as social cohesion and mutual support. Mechanisms for restoring balance between regions are currently being used to reach these goals in both federal and unitary states. They are a recurrent subject of discussion in debates about construction within the European Community (*e.g.* the structural funds policy). Sometimes balanced regional development is a right enshrined in constitutions or the law (*e.g.*, Spain, Germany and France), and sometimes, as in the Nordic countries, making living standards equal, although not laid down in the law, remains a major goal of central government.

Although these strategic objectives are not being called into question, it is clear that the instruments and methods of intervention adopted almost everywhere to attain them are increasingly subject to debate. Thus, there is now agreement that policies based on redistribution mechanisms involving direct assistance to enterprises, technocratic approach to heavy infrastructure, or support to declining economic activities do little to stimulate growth and employment in the regions concerned and may even be costly blind alleys.

The setbacks or partial setbacks countries have experienced can teach useful lessons about government failures (OECD, 2001). For example:

- *The inadequacy of pouring massive amounts of assistance through bureaucratic channels into lagging regions.* Italy provides a good example of a considerable effort to channel funds to its southern region (the Mezzogiorno) by means of a government agency provided with ample funds.[9] Behind the particularly poor results obtained (increased disparities[10] between 1980 and 1995) lies a simplistic view of the reasons for lagging development and industrial conversion. First, the small wage differential between south and north (wages are negotiated at central level) held back any flow of investment to the south. Second, weakness of social capital in the Mezzogiorno (where the sense of individual initiative is limited and inclination to undertake collective action low) has favoured a culture of dependence on assistance and multiplied obstacles to development.

- *Artificial interventions.* Reindustrialisation efforts in many countries have been focused on a small number of sites in order to pin down industrial development, benefit from the effects of scale, and absorb labour made available by a stagnant primary sector or from restructuring sectors in decline. Even in the long view, such so-called poles of growth strategies have been relatively unsuccessful. They have often been costly, combining large-scale infrastructure projects, enterprise zones, and expensive tax incentives. The investments made have generally paid little attention to local and regional industrial cultures and have at best turned sites into exporting islands. Many examples can be given (Lorraine and southern France, Pouilles and Basilicate in Italy, the Walloon Region in Belgium).

- *Launch of major infrastructure projects without taking regional demand into account.* Motorways, airports, ports and bridges are examples of projects that have improved the accessibility of non-metropolitan regions, sometimes beyond their capacity to fully utilise them.

- *Maintenance of direct assistance to declining sectors in order to protect local economic activities.* Such practices were employed on a large scale in the 1980s in most European countries and in traditional sectors generally did little more than delay adjustment. The approach, which has been almost universally abandoned, appears to persist in the new European OECD Member countries (such as Poland or the Czech Republic) – and particularly in the Republic of Korea – by means of banking subsidies or by keeping enterprises within the public sector.

- *Short termism.* A conflict usually exists between infrastructural long-term development needs that tend to concern weaker regions, and immediate imperatives to alleviate bottlenecks that concern stronger areas where growth is leading to the emergence of excess demand capacity. In the case of financial constraints, there is a bias towards meeting short-term needs and often allocating funds to wealthier regions.

Generally speaking, these diagnoses are no longer in dispute and a change of direction has taken place almost everywhere in recent years. Although the new policies vary from country to country in response to factors associated with historical events, economic conditions or political institutions, such updating of regional policies displays some common features. Greater weight is given to a new approach including regional activities in policies to encourage competitiveness by taking all regions into account, by adjusting procedures to the specific requirements of each, and often by granting them wider responsibilities over economic development. In other words, the task of regional policies is no longer to redistribute growth between regions. Its top priority is to maximise the potential of each region and its contribution to national growth.

As territories have fragmented, the goals, targets, and prospects of regional policies are also changing. National authorities are much less concerned with systematically reducing gaps in wealth and employment between regions. Their efforts are instead directed increasingly to assisting each region to identify and achieve its own development potential. It is now recognised that no single model of development exists but that there is instead a wide variety of paths to growth.

As a result, policies are increasingly framed as policy mixes adapted to the needs and opportunities offered by territories. This is, however, no easy task. Not only must appropriate locally-conceived development strategies be introduced (promoting SMEs, business enterprise, infrastructure, and resource management) together with policies for attracting foreign investment, but major contingent factors also have to be taken into account such as *i)* the knowledge-based society, *ii)* the expansion of the "new economy", *iii)* the need for enhanced quality of life, and *iv)* the development of local and institutional co-operation, notably between urban and adjacent rural areas.

Conclusion: priorities for China in light of OECD experiences

The main challenge facing China at present concerns the development of rural areas. Drawing on the experiences of OECD countries, emphasis should be placed on:

- Policies to improve the accessibility of rural regions and their attractiveness through the development and maintenance of appropriate infrastructures (transport, communications, health, education, etc.).

- Policies to diversify the economic base through niche market production and labelling, in order to link niche products with the historical/cultural image of the local area.

- Policies to facilitate the creation of SMEs through the development of business incubators, and to increase their competitiveness by supporting the development of clusters of enterprises.

- Policies to enhance the economic potential of small and medium-sized towns, to encourage them to specialise and to foster the creation of networks within the framework of a spatial-functional division of labour, information, services and infrastructures.

- Rural amenity policies which develop local consensus, establish conditions for a more significant contribution to rural economic development by public amenity goods, and provide incentives which stimulate amenity provision through market mechanisms.

- Policies to induce the development of partnerships between cities and counties to foster the development of joint projects with sufficient financing.

However, amongst the many remaining main factors which handicap at present the development of rural regions, three main ones would need to be urgently addressed: local public finance; local education systems and internal economic integration. A certain number of major reforms should thus be undertaken to ensure the feasibility of the development of these regions so that China's economy can reap the full benefits of trade and investment liberalisation.

Reforming local public finance

Comparisons with international experiences suggest that the Chinese budgetary regime is extraordinarily decentralised. The process of decentralisation tends to exacerbate regional disparities. Moreover, the extent of decentralisation is in fact much greater than the trends indicated in the budgetary data because of the increasing reliance on off-budget funds. Several reforms in public finance are needed to both enhance the predictability and transparency of local public finance and promote a fair redistribution system among provinces (see Chapters 19 and 20).

These reforms include the definition of a clear and detailed division of responsibilities for spending and revenue allocation, the abolition of arbitrary off-budget fees and levies, and the simplification of the structure of provincial taxation (27 taxes at the sole discretion of Chinese regions!). Central government currently accounts for only about 10 per cent of total expenditures on "culture, education and health" – the category that encompasses 80-90 per cent of social expenditures in the Chinese budget (Wong, 1995). Such functions should be returned from the local level (townships, districts and municipalities) to higher tiers of government (provinces or the central State).

A formal programme of earmarked/conditional transfers should also be established, targeted to achieve a number of well-defined policy goals such as poverty alleviation and achieving minimum standards in basic services (education, health, and social security). These grants aimed at promoting local public services should be paid on the basis of the cost and quality of the services rendered. The central government should set up monitoring mechanisms for this type of vertical grants.

Lastly, the current scheme should be replaced by a system of horizontal equalisation whereby rich local governments provide more support for poor ones (as do the German *Länder*). The new equalisation system should only take into account disparities in tax-raising capacities. Grants for fiscal equalisation should be entirely unconditional. The equalisation system should provide all local governments with adequate financial resources without, however, loosening local budget constraints. The effectiveness of the system also requires increasing the size of the central budget.

Reforming the system of local education and training

Balanced economic development in China requires an active education policy capable of giving the population the training that is needed to fill the country's increasing requirements for skilled labour. This will entail continued emphasis on making basic education universal, and on developing vocational and technical training throughout China. Given the widening disparities between provinces and between rural areas and urban ones, and in the delivery and quality of education services, it is necessary to reconsider how the education system is funded, in respect of disadvantaged areas in particular.

The decentralisation process that accompanied the reforms undertaken by China over the past 20 years has profoundly altered the way in which the Chinese education system is financed. Since responsibility for primary and secondary education has now been devolved to local (below the county level) governments, funding is far more heavily dependent on these governments' capacity to raise the necessary funds from local populations, leading to *de facto* inequality depending on the basis of wealth levels.

Clearly a redistribution system exists to benefit poor regions, but this system remains highly marginal in relation to needs. The system is based on priority allocation to disadvantaged areas of categorical grants by higher levels of government (the provinces or the State), in respect of specific educational objectives (*e.g.* repairing school buildings, teacher training, technical education, etc.).

Despite substantial efforts to diversify revenue sources in recent years, the Chinese education system suffers from a funding shortfall. With education spending representing a mere 2.5 per cent of GNP, China trails behind other countries with a comparable level of development. Given the substantial resource constraints in rural areas and the at times high tuition fees, the State's commitment to basic education remains more necessary than ever to ensure that the education system achieves a minimum level of performance throughout the entire country. *Inter alia*, this will require Beijing to earmark substantially increased resources for basic education, and that disadvantaged areas be given priority in the allocation of these resources (see above). Moreover, the redistribution of central and provincial government financing to lower echelons of local government, and to villages in particular, should be made systematic in order to ease the budget squeeze on the poorest regions.

While the 1986 law imposing nine years of compulsory education (primary and the first half of secondary school) boosted schooling rates and lowered illiteracy in the youngest age cohorts, sharp disparities persist, depending on place of residence and sex. For example, people living in western provinces, as well as women, are over-represented in the illiterate population, which, while less than 15 per cent for the country as a whole, rises to nearly 40 per cent for the women of Qinghai province. In this context, it is important to set priority goals that are differentiated by region, and to put the emphasis, through awareness-building campaigns and welfare payments, on the most highly disadvantaged families, on the education of girls, too many of whom in rural areas still drop out after primary school, *inter alia* because of the high cost of education.

Lastly, special attention needs to be paid to improving schooling conditions in disadvantaged areas. Teacher training in rural areas is often still rudimentary, and the variety of languages and dialects spoken in certain remote areas (due to the presence of numerous minorities) confronts education with an additional difficulty.

Creation of a genuine single domestic market

Given its geographic expanse and the size of its population, but also that of its 31 constituent provinces, China cannot be compared to any other country. It would seem more appropriate to make comparisons with either the European Union (EU) or the North American Free Trade Agreement (NAFTA). The primary objective of both of these undertakings is integration – integration that is of course limited to trade and investment in the case of NAFTA, but which for the EU extends well beyond these aspects to a host of other areas.

The EU's case involves 15 countries – soon to be around 30 – seeking, through a comprehensive process of convergence, to create a genuine single European market. Agricultural policy and regional policy are already under the responsibility of Brussels, which expends nearly 1 per cent of Europe's GNP on these areas each year. Trade and competition policies are also centralised, whereas monetary and currency policies are the sole responsibility of the European Central Bank. For the future, other areas of policy convergence are currently under study, involving taxation, the environment, education, social affairs and so on.

In addition, everything has been undertaken in Europe to facilitate the free movement of goods, services, capital and persons, and the establishment of businesses that enjoy relatively similar – and ultimately even more similar – operating conditions regardless of where they are located, while convergence is also taking place in the realms of competition law, taxation and social cover.

At the opposite end of the spectrum, with the extensive decentralisation that it has been undertaking for years, China seems to be moving the other way, *i.e.* towards a fragmentation of its market, giving the various provinces increasing autonomy over economic, tax and social affairs. Internal mobility is still limited for goods, capital, persons and businesses alike; taxation differs widely from one province to another, due in particular to off-budget revenue; in some provinces, public services, such as education, may be privatised; there are several different bodies of competition law; the rules and conditions for establishing a business differ by province, as do customs regimes; lastly, Beijing has scant budgetary capacity to harness a nationwide infrastructure development policy for genuine land-use planning. For all these reasons, China would appear to be headed not towards a single domestic market, but towards a juxtaposition of provinces without any great level of coherence or cohesion. Moreover, aid for the poorest regions is quite meagre in comparison with the EU's structural funds, and a similar remark could be made in respect of agriculture, which by European standards seems to receive little aid.

This policy, which would seem antithetical to the integration policies of Europe or North America, poses major problems: the difficulty for businesses to attain nationwide size and thus to become more competitive thanks to economies of scale; a lack of flexibility of domestic markets, including the labour market, with mobility of production factors being an essential condition of market efficiency; the difficulty of introducing structural reforms, and especially regulatory reforms, given the large (and rising) volume of provincial regulations; widening disparities between coastal regions and the interior, and between rural areas and urban ones, which could ultimately trigger a certain social instability and adversely affect the rise in China's overall level of prosperity. Major reforms are therefore crucial for the construction of the single domestic market that China lacks.

In addition, creating a single market in China cannot be dissociated from providing equal access to infrastructure and public services all over the country as well as developing partnerships between local communities to favour a better cohesion of local policies. In these two aspects, several policies implemented in OECD countries could prove to be instructive. In Canada, equal access to public services is being supported by an equalisation programme for provinces that cannot generate revenue otherwise at a reasonable level of taxation (OECD, 2001). Special funds are made available to allow these provinces to provide public services according to their own priorities at levels comparable to what is found elsewhere. The development of local partnerships has been at the core of several OECD countries' recent experience to exploit potential synergies and ensure co-operation between the Central State and the regions. This has been notably the case in the United States where the National Rural Development Partnership (NRDP) promotes *"partnerships between agencies and their departments and with the private sector in order to facilitate grassroots approaches to development in conjunction with financial support and expertise from government bodies"* (OECD, 2001, p. 189).

NOTES

1. Liaoning, Jilin, Heilongjiang, Anhui, Henan, Hubei, Hunan, Sichuan, Shaanxi, Gansu and Ningxia.

2. Trends in the dispersion of per capita income in the Chinese provinces are well documented in recent literature.

3. China (1988), "Growth and development in Gansu province", *World Bank Country Study*.

4. The cost of these projects is estimated at US$2.8 billion.

5. China's clothing exports have more than doubled since 1992, totalling US$30 billion in 1999.

6. Moreover, this sector is all the more likely to be hit by competition in that, on the whole, it is inefficient, since the firms that compose it are small. This prevents it from benefiting from the economies of scale that usually characterise the sector.

7. By calculating this ratio, it is possible to correct partially the degree of openness as measured solely by exports/GDP, since by taking account of the import content of exports, it makes exports (which represent turnover and not value added) and GDP more comparable.

8. One could, however, draw attention to the risks associated with early restructuring of the financial sector, for the municipalities in particular.

9. This kind of unprecedented regional intervention was abandoned in 1995 and the relevant (European) funds are now disbursed by various ministries following "usual" procedures.

10. Per capita income declined relative to the Centre and North. Production is also down and unemployment at the end of the period was almost five times the figure for the northern part of the country.

BIBLIOGRAPHY

Anderson, K. (1997),
"On the Complexities of China's WTO Accession", *World Economy*, Vol. 20, September, pp. 749-772.

Aubert, C. (1999),
"Agriculture chinoise, des grains et des hommes", in Larivière, J.P. (dir. pub.): *La Chine et les Chinois de la diaspora*, CNED-SEDES.

Barro, R.J. and X. Sala-I-Martin (1992),
"Convergence", *Journal of Political Economy*, Vol. 100, No. 2, pp. 223-251.

Bhattacharyya, A. and E. Parker (1999),
"Labor productivity and migration in Chinese agriculture: a stochastic frontier approach", *China Economic Review*, Vol. 10, No. 1, pp. 59-74.

Bianco, L. (2000),
"La recrudescence de l'agitation rurale", in Fabre, G. (dir. pub.): *Chine : le piège des inégalités*, La Documentation française, février, pp. 64-68.

Carter, C. (2000),
"China's trade integration and impacts on factor markets", in *China's Agriculture in the International Trading System*, proceedings from the OECD Workshop, Paris, 16-17 November.

Cheng, J.Y.S. and M. ZHANG (1998),
"An Analysis of Regional Differences in China and the Delayed Development of the Central and Western Regions ", *Issues and Studies*, Vol. 34, No. 2, February, pp. 35-68.

COOK, S. (1999),
"Surplus Labour and Productivity in Chinese Agriculture: Evidence from Household Survey Data", in *Journal of Development Studies*, Vol. 35, No. 3, February, pp. 16-44.

Démurger, S. (2001),
"Infrastructure Development and Economic Growth: An Explanation for Regional Disparities in China?", *Journal of Comparative Economics*, Vol. 29, No. 1, March, pp. 95-117.

Démurger, S. (2000),
Economic Opening and Growth in China, OECD Development Centre Studies, Paris.

Gang, F., D.H Perkins and L. Sabin (1997),
"People's Republic of China: Economic Performance and Prospects", *Asian Development Review*, Vol. 15, No. 2, pp. 43-85.

Ge W. (1999),
"Special Economic Zones and the Opening of the Chinese Economy: Some lessons for Economic Liberalization", *World Development*, Vol. 27, No. 7, July 1999, pp. 1267-1285.

Gipouloux, F. (1998),
"Intégration ou désintégration", *Perspectives chinoises*.

Giroir, G. (1999),
"La crise des industries d'Etat et re-développement dans le Nord-Est chinois", in Fur, A., P. Gentelle and T. Pairault (dir. pub.): *Economie et régions de la Chine*, collection cursus.

Gustafsson, B. and S. Li. (1998),
"The Structure of Chinese Poverty, 1988", *The Developing Economies*, Vol. 36, No. 4, December, pp. 387-406.

He, Q. (2000),
"Migration paysanne et délinquance urbaine", in Fabre, G. (dir. pub.): *Chine : le piège des inégalités*, La Documentation française, February, pp. 70-73.

Ianchovichina, E., W. Martin and E. Fukase (2000),
Assessing the Implications of Merchandise Trade Liberalization in China's Accession to the WTO, World Bank, July.

Fan, M. and Y. Zheng (2000),
"The Impact of China's Trade Liberalization for WTO – A Computable General Equilibrium Analysis", CASS, *mimeo*, (Conference on Global Economic Analysis, Melbourne).

Lee, P.K. (1998),
"Local Economic Protectionism in China's Economic Reform", *Development Policy Review*, Vol. 16, No. 3, September, pp. 281-303.

Li, S. (1999),
"L'évolution des inégalités de revenu individuel dans la Chine en transition", *Revue d'Economie du Développement*, No. 1-2, June, pp. 159-182.

Li, S. and P. Lian (1999),
"Decentralisation and coordination: China's credible commitment to preserve the market under authoritarianism", *China Economic Review*, Vol. 10, No. 2, pp. 161-190.

Li, S. and F. Zhai (1999),
"China's WTO Accession and Implications for National and Provincial Economies", Development Research Centre, *mimeo*.

Li, X. and A. Lejour (2000),
"The Sectoral Impact of China's Access to WTO – A Dynamic CGE Analysis", CASS and Netherlands Bureau for Economic Policy Analysis, *mimeo*, June.

Lin, J.Y., F. Cai and Z. Li (1999),
"Conséquences des réformes économiques sur les disparités régionales en Chine", *Revue d'Economie du Développement*, No. 1-2, June, pp. 7-32.

Maddison, A. (1998),
Chinese Economic Performance in the Long Run, OECD Development Centre Studies, Paris.

Montinolla, G., Y. Qian and B. Weingast (1995),
"Federalism Chinese Style, The Political Basis for Economic Success in China", *World Politics*, No. 48, October, pp. 50-81.

Morrison, W.M. (2001),
"A Review of Major Studies that Examine the Economic Effects of China's Accession to the World Trade Organisation", *mimeo*, February.

Naughton, B. (1999),
"Causes et conséquences des disparités dans la croissance économique des provinces chinoises", *Revue d'Economie du Développement*, No. 1-2, June, pp. 33-70.

O'Connor, D. (2000),
"Rural industrial development in Vietnam and China: a study in contrasts", *Technical Papers*, OECD Development Centre, April.

OECD (2001),
OECD *Territorial Outlook* 2001, Paris.

Pairault, T. (1999),
"Développement et dynamiques provinciales", in Fur, A., P. Gentelle and T. Pairault (dir. pub.): *Economie et régions de la Chine*, collection cursus.

Park, A. (2001),
"Trade integration and the prospects for rural enterprise development in China", *China's Agriculture in the International Trading System*, proceedings from the OECD Workshop, Paris, 16-17 November 2000. OECD, 2001

PNUD (1999),
The China Human Development Report, Oxford University Press.

Qian, Y. and B. Weingast (1995),
"China's Transition to Markets: Market-Preserving Federalism, Chinese Style", *Essays in Public Policy*, Hoover Institution.

Qian, Y. and B. Weingast (1998),
"From federalism Chinese style to privatisation, Chinese style", Centre For Economic Policy Research.

Wang, Z. (1999),
"The Impact of China's WTO Entry on the World Labor-intensive Export Market. A Recursive Dynamic CGE Analysis", *World Economy*, Vol. 22, May, pp. 379-405.

Xu, L. (2000),
"L'évolution des différences de revenus", in Fabre, G. (dir. pub.): *Chine : le piège des inégalités*, La Documentation française, February, pp. 42-43.

Yang, D. (1997),
> *Beyond Beijing – Liberalization and the regions in China, Routledge Studies in China in Transition*, Routledge, London and New York.

Yang, Y. (1996),
> "China's WTO membership: What's at Stake?", *World Economy*, Vol. 19, November, pp. 661-682.

Zhang, L., (1999),
> "Chinese Central-provincial Fiscal relationships, Budgetary decline and the Impact of the 1994 Fiscal reform: An Evaluation", *China Quarterly*, No. 157, March, pp. 115-141.

Zhang, W. (2001),
> "Rethinking Regional Disparity in China", *Economics of Planning*.

Internet references on the western development strategy

www.westchina.gov.cn/english/index.htm
> (Official site of the "Office of the Leading Group for Western Region Development of the State Council").

www.chinadaily.net/highlights/west/index.html
> (Site of the *China Daily* devoted to the programme for the development of the western provinces).

http://english.peopledaily.com.cn/zhuanti/Zhuanti_13.html
> (Site of the *China Daily* devoted to the programme for the development of the western provinces).

Chapter 22

MACROECONOMIC POLICY PRIORITIES TO REALISE THE BENEFITS OF TRADE AND INVESTMENT LIBERALISATION

TABLE OF CONTENTS

MACROECONOMIC POLICY PRIORITIES TO REALISE THE BENEFITS OF TRADE AND INVESTMENT LIBERALISATION[*]

The extensive changes the Chinese economy will undergo during this decade pose important challenges to macroeconomic performance and policy. Sound macroeconomic performance – namely adequate real growth with low inflation and sustainable external and budget accounts – will provide an important support to economic reforms and greatly facilitate adjustments to trade and investment liberalisation. However, unstable macroeconomic conditions are likely to make these changes much more difficult. At the same time, trade and investment liberalisation together with other economic reforms will pose important challenges to macroeconomic policies. These include large-scale turnover in labour markets as employment is reallocated, potential deflationary pressures arising from displacement of labour and falling profits in declining sectors, rising demands on public finances, and increasing needs by businesses for access to international financial markets. These challenges would arise even if there were less trade and investment liberalisation than is now in prospect. However, as in other areas, trade and investment liberalisation affects some of the priorities for macroeconomic policy.

This chapter considers three aspects of China's macroeconomic policies over the coming decade. These concern macroeconomic policies to maintain internal balance between potential output and aggregate demand and external equilibrium in the balance of payments, public finances, and exchange rate and capital control policies.

The discussion highlights three key specific macroeconomic challenges. The first is to sustain real growth at a level that is adequate to improve the utilisation of China's labour force. The second is to establish a sustainable fiscal position while allowing spending to rise to support China's economic development needs. And the third is to gradually increase the flexibility of the exchange rate and capital account regimes. Each of these challenges is closely intertwined with the structural developments and reforms discussed in other chapters of this study. Maintaining adequate real growth requires not only an appropriate stance of macroeconomic policies but also progress on financial reforms, improvement in enterprise financial positions, and other policies to address conditions that now impair the transmission of macroeconomic policies. Sustaining fiscal policy that is both sound and meets China's development needs will require not only better collection of taxes but also efforts to reduce wasteful spending and to address distortions in central-local government fiscal relations. And while liberalisation of the exchange rate and capital control regime is ultimately necessary, its pace is contingent on reforms to improve incentives for prudent financial behaviour and on development of domestic financial markets.

Sustaining real growth while improving resource utilisation

This section reviews the forces underlying China's recent macroeconomic performance and then considers the main challenges for macroeconomic performance that are likely to be encountered over the next five to ten years. While performance both domestically and externally over the past five years appears quite favourable compared to many other emerging market economies, it has also masked some problems.

Forces underlying recent macroeconomic performance

China has sustained an enviable growth performance for most of the reform period. Real GDP growth as measured by official figures averaged 9.2 per cent during the 1980s and more than 10 per cent during 1990-98. Admittedly, official figures probably overstate actual growth,[1] but even so, China's performance appears broadly comparable with that of other countries that have grown exceptionally rapidly

---

[*] This chapter was written by Charles Pigott, Principal Economist, Economics Department, OECD and Jian-Guang Shen, Bank of Finland and consultant to the OECD Economics Department during 2001.

during the post-war period, notably Japan and the Republic of Korea, and, more recently, several other "Asian tigers".[2] Exports and imports have grown even more rapidly than GDP since the mid-1980s . As a result, China's economy is now substantially more open to trade than it was at the beginning of the reform period, and more open than a number of other major developing countries such as India and Brazil (Table 21.11). China's relative openness compared to other countries at a comparable stage of development is even greater in terms of foreign direct investment (FDI). China's inflation performance has been more mixed, as there have been several episodes of overheating since the beginning of reforms during which, in the worst cases, CPI inflation rose to the low twenties (see Oppers, 1997). China, however, has not undergone the prolonged periods of very high inflation suffered by some other developing countries at various times over the past three decades.

Since the early 1990s, however, China's growth has fallen steadily, reaching a trough of 7.1 per cent in 1999 and then recovering modestly to 8 per cent in 2000 and 7.3 per cent in 2001. Part of this slowdown reflects the cooling of the cyclical boom during 1992-94. However, real GDP growth since 1996 has averaged 8.25 per cent, well below the pace of the prior fifteen years. All segments of industry have been affected, but the change has been particularly pronounced for collective enterprises, which were formerly the largest contributors to China's aggregate real growth. The slowdown in Chinese growth is all the more notable given that China was relatively unaffected by the Asian crisis and by the fact that export growth has remained generally quite robust. Inflation has essentially disappeared during this period, indeed giving way to deflation in aggregate consumer prices until recently. These conditions suggest that there has been a significant shift in China's macroeconomic performance that is more than purely cyclical in character.

Trends in employment (Figure 21.1) strengthen this impression.[3] During the latter half of the 1980s, the Chinese economy added nearly 13.6 million net jobs annually, but the increase dropped to less than two-thirds of this amount (8.1 million) in the first half of the 1990s. The fall in employment growth during this period occurred largely in rural areas as labour exited from agricultural activities, and happened despite continued strong growth in employment by township and village enterprises (TVEs). Employment growth in TVE declined in the latter 1990s, and the impact on aggregate employment was accentuated by labour shedding of state owned enterprises (SOEs) and other urban enterprises beginning around 1997. Since 1995, aggregate employment increases have averaged 6.7 million per year, less than half the pace of the latter 1980s, and barely sufficient to keep up with the natural increase in the overall labour force.[4] The overall result of these trends has been a marked increase in slack in both rural and urban labour markets. Estimates cited in Chapter 16 suggest that more than 200 million rural workers are either unemployed in the rural sector, or substantially under-employed. As much as half of these are thought to have taken up work in the informal sector in cities, but many of these workers are probably under-employed as well. The unemployment rate among urban workers in the formal sector has also risen sharply, and is now probably more than 10 per cent.[5]

Table 22.1. **Openess to international trade**

1999

	Exports + imports as share of GDP (%)
China	37.8
United States	18.9
Euro Area	25.7
Germany	48.1
Japan	16.8
Brazil	20.1
India	18.2
Indonesia	51.1
Russia	70.0
Mexico	59.4
Korea	64.9

Source: *International Financial Statistics,* International Monetary Fund.

Figure 22.1. **Employment growth**

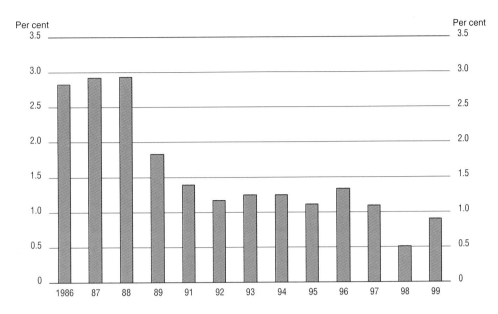

Source: *China Statistical Yearbook*, 2000.

One possible explanation for the growth slowdown, suggested by the earlier experiences of Japan and the Republic of Korea, is that China is undergoing a natural decline in potential growth due to diminished opportunities to raise factor productivity. Potential growth in Japan and the Republic of Korea declined as the productivity gains from transferring labour from agriculture to higher productivity jobs in industry and from absorbing readily available technology and other know-how from abroad became exhausted. However these conditions do not seem to apply to China's current situation since the share of labour in agriculture is still quite high and there is much under-employed labour.[6]

A more plausible explanation for the slowdown in growth lies in several related structural conditions that became increasingly acute during the 1990s. The first is the over-capacity and excess inventories accumulated during the investment bubble during (roughly) 1992-94. These excesses have led to falling prices for key industrial goods over much of the latter half of the 1990s. The shift in agricultural support policies beginning in 1995 contributed to the development of substantial agricultural surpluses and decline in market prices, although the effect on farmers was partly mitigated by price supports. Rural income growth has been further set back in recent years by the slowdown in employment absorption by TVE. The second condition is the rising debt loads and falling profits experienced by SOEs as well as TVEs during the 1990s. This deterioration in performances was partly due to the first condition and was (particularly for TVE) further aggravated by the downturn in export demand in the wake of the 1997 Asian crisis. However, the poor financial condition of these enterprises is more fundamentally the heritage of their "policy burdens" – such as the requirement to sustain excess labour and provide social benefits – together with substantial operating inefficiencies due to insufficient scale of production, obsolete equipment, outmoded technology, and poor organisation of operations.[7]

A third factor has been the virtual "credit crunch" in lending to much of the enterprise sector precipitated by the tightening of bank lending standards starting in 1996 (see Chapter 14 on the financial system). This tightening was a response to growing non-performing loans (NPLs) of the business sector. To a substantial degree, the accumulation of these loans reflects the use of bank lending to provide effective subsidies to businesses and so postpone the adverse impact on aggregate demand of the growing structural problems of enterprises. This use of bank lending has added to the adverse impacts by contributing to the current extreme conservatism in bank lending.

The net result of the three factors has been a substantial slowdown in income growth in rural areas and severely constrained cash flow of enterprises. The former has depressed growth in rural consumption – which accounts for about half of total consumption – since the mid-1990s. The deterioration of corporate financial positions has led to a marked decline in capital spending by both SOE and non-state enterprises, although this has been partially masked by increases in government infrastructure spending. Capital spending by non-state enterprises has been especially weak, due in part to their difficulty in obtaining bank credit.[8]

Some of the conditions depressing growth appear to be improving. In particular, enterprise profits rose mildly in 1999, from a very low base, more than doubled in 2000, and increased further in 2001 (see Chapter 4, Figure 4.4). The recent figures probably do not yet fully reflect the substantial reduction in SOE workforces since 1997, in part because enterprises bear much of the cost of the re-employment centres to which laid-off SOE workers are initially transferred. The re-employment of workers now in these centres (or transfer to general unemployment rolls if they are not able to find employment) should reduce SOE costs and provide some further boost to profits over the next several years. Consistent with the rising profits, the business survey taken by the People's Bank of China points to a significant improvement in business sentiment during 2000 and 2001, particularly in prospects for capital spending and assessments of inventory levels (See the discussion in Chapter 4 on industry prospects). There appears to be less improvement in assessments of capacity utilisation and access to bank lending. Moreover, there is little sign yet of improvement in rural income growth, or of an appreciable recovery in capital spending by non-state enterprises.

Authorities have sought to counter the deflationary forces from structural problems with expansionary macroeconomic policies. There have been six interest rate reductions since 1996, bringing the benchmark one-year loan rate down from just about 12 per cent to 5.85 per cent at present; bank demand deposit rates are now just below 1 per cent. The effect of these reductions on aggregate demand has been severely blunted, however, by the extreme caution banks are now exercising in their lending. The burden of macroeconomic policy support for demand has largely been borne by fiscal policy. Bond financed infrastructure spending by the government directly contributed more than 1 percentage point to annual GDP growth over 1998-2000, and as much as half of total capital spending. Its importance was probably even greater to the extent that it helped prevent a vicious circle of mutually reinforcing declines in demand and enterprise financial conditions. However, as discussed further in the next section, the scope for future fiscal stimulus to support growth may be narrowing.

Maintaining adequate growth as trade and investment liberalisation proceed

Maintaining adequate growth is arguably the central challenge for China's macroeconomic policy in the coming decade. To meet this challenge, macroeconomic policies will need to sustain growth in line with China's potential while containing inflation and maintaining an adequate balance in China's external accounts.

The current five-year plan envisages average GDP growth of 7 per cent during 2001-05. Based on recent trends, this is probably close to the minimum growth that will be needed simply to maintain the existing level of slack in the labour force. However, the level of growth that is adequate in terms of China's longer-term development goals depends on two conditions that are becoming increasingly important. The first is the need to improve utilisation of China's human resources by progressively reabsorbing into productive employment the unemployed and under-employed labour that has been built up over the past decade. The second is the need to achieve more balanced growth among China's regions as part of a broader process of containing and ultimately reducing income inequalities between provinces, and between rural and urban areas within provinces. The Western Economic Development initiative represents an official recognition of the importance of this need. These goals are important both to the quality of China's macroeconomic performance and to the objective of achieving "growth with equity".

In order to improve utilisation of the labour force, China's real GDP will at some point have to grow significantly above its potential for a number of years. The required rate of growth will probably have to be significantly above the pace recorded since 1996.[9] Moreover, urban areas are likely to have to create a larger fraction of aggregate job increases than they have in the past. Even with restructuring, the impetus provided from WTO, and their future development in interior provinces, rural industries seem unlikely to be able to regain the pace of job creation they achieved during the high watermark in the early 1990s (see Chapter 2 on rural enterprises and Chapter 16 on labour market and social policies). However it will be difficult to achieve sufficient growth to improve resource utilisation until current structural problems are substantially reduced. Attempting to do so now, through more macroeconomic stimulus, would likely lead to severe bottlenecks and risk igniting inflationary pressures.

By itself, trade and investment liberalisation is unlikely to appreciably improve labour utilisation. The studies reviewed in Annex 2 suggest that entry into WTO on terms comparable to those of China's accession could raise real GDP by a cumulative amount of between 1 and 5 per cent within five to ten years after accession. This works out to an increase in average real growth over the decade of 0.1 to 0.5 percentage points annually. Estimates in the lower end of this range typically are based on "static" gains, such as the direct changes in demand and reallocation of resources among activities to accommodate them engendered by liberalisation of trade flows. The estimates in the higher end take into account potential "dynamic" gains, such as increased productivity growth, as well as the liberalisation of non-tariff barriers. The associated impacts on employment are modest, even though the overall effect of trade and investment liberalisation is to boost growth of relatively labour-intensive industries. These relatively modest effects reflect the fact that China's economy is already substantially open to international trade as a result of the trade liberalisation since the mid-1980s. Largely as a result, there should be little risk that China will undergo the extensive disruptions throughout industry experienced by Russia during its transition.[10]

Trade and investment liberalisation could have important indirect impacts on real growth, but these will depend upon other economic reforms. Liberalisation is likely to have mixed effects on the deflationary forces engendered by existing structural problems and their aggregate impact may differ depending on the time horizon. Employment and profits are likely to improve in labour intensive industries, where profit rates have been below the average for industry as a whole. However much of the positive effects are unlikely to be manifest until the Multi-Fibre Agreement (MFA) lapses in 2005. Trade and investment liberalisation will reduce employment and profits in automobile and other heavy industries relative to the levels they would otherwise be expected to attain, and the effects are likely to be manifest somewhat earlier.[11] These industries are now generally more profitable than the prospective gainers from trade and investment liberalisation and also tend to be more intensive users of external credit.

The net impact of trade and investment liberalisation on aggregate spending industry profits in the medium-term should be modest and increasingly positive in the longer-term – under two conditions. The first is that progress is made in reforms to facilitate business sector restructuring, and the second is that real GDP growth does not fall substantially further from the pace of recent years. Under these conditions, aggregate industry profits should continue to recover as enterprises reap the benefits of their labour shedding and other efforts to improve efficiency.[12]

Nevertheless, if these two conditions are not met, particularly if business sector restructuring becomes stalled, there is a risk that the negative impact on aggregate spending from adversely impacted industries could outweigh the positive impact from industries that benefit in the medium-term. Reforms to address current structural weaknesses are crucial to contain this risk. For example, an onset of new non-performing loans from declining industries is more likely to impair the ability of the banking system to supply credit needed to sustain aggregate growth if banks continue to suffer from inadequate capital and low profits. As indicated in Chapters 4 and 5, extensive reorganisation and restructuring will be needed in labour-intensive sectors to realise the potential benefits from TIL while sectors that are adversely affected initially also need to undergo extensive restructuring before they can resume growing. Other chapters document the serious obstacles to these adjustments that now exist, such as the administrative constraints on mergers and acquisitions and weaknesses in property rights regimes that discourage technology transfers.

The "dynamic" impacts on macroeconomic performance from trade and investment liberalisation are potentially large but difficult to estimate. Increased competition and access to foreign know-how created by greater scope for foreign enterprises in the domestic economy has the potential to engender "virtuous circles" of improving management skills, technology, and operating efficiency for domestic firms. If sufficiently pervasive, these could significantly raise aggregate productivity. The extent to which these dynamic gains are realised again depends critically upon the success of broader reforms. In particular, improvements in enterprise governance, intellectual property right protection, the efficiency of credit allocation, and competition will be necessary if domestic firms are to have the internal capabilities and incentives to exploit opportunities offered by the opening to international markets.

Greater balance in regional development is important both to the goal of improving labour utilisation and to realising China's aggregate growth potential. Coastal cities cannot be expected to absorb all of the underemployed rural workers without incurring undue pollution or congestion. Migration of capital, through increased physical investment, will ultimately be needed in interior provinces to achieve full employment of the labour force. Greater balance in regional development could raise China's overall growth potential by better exploiting productivity gains from regional specialisation and achieving a more efficient geographic allocation of labour and capital. The potential impact on labour costs of the substantial wage differences between interior regions and the coast (and between rural and urban areas) are at least partly offset by lack of physical infrastructure and relatively low human capital in the interior.[13] Capital mobility is also restricted by excessively costly government regulations and red tape imposed by local governments, unclear property rights, lack of transparency in laws and regulations, and local government resistance to acquisition of local firms by businesses from other provinces. Elimination of such barriers would make it easier to exploit the lower wages in interior provinces, thereby raising the return to capital and boosting aggregate labour productivity.[14]

As documented in earlier chapters, the direct effects of trade and investment liberalisation will accentuate rather than reduce existing gaps in regional growth, at least in the medium-term. Most of the increase in foreign direct investment from trade and investment liberalisation is expected to go to coastal provinces. There may be some expansion of foreign direct investment to a few well-situated urban areas in the central region, but this is likely to be limited in both overall quantity and geographic scope.[15] As indicated by the simulations reported in Chapter 21 on regional prospects and policies, coastal regions are also likely to benefit disproportionately from the increased exports arising from trade and investment liberalisation, since labour intensive industries are now concentrated in these regions. The present system for allocating revenues and expenditures between the central and local governments, which effectively tends to channel government resources toward the most rapidly growing areas (see Chapter 20 on central-local government fiscal relations), is likely to further aggravate regional disparities. The analysis in Chapters 2-3 on the rural economy imply that these forces may also accentuate the income gap between urban workers and those workers dependent on agriculture or rural industries for their income.

Finally, while structural reforms are essential, macroeconomic demand management will continue to be important to improving labour utilisation and achieving more balanced growth among regions. Over the longer-term, the supply-side improvements from successful adjustment to trade and investment liberalisation and implementation of broader reforms will help to support demand by increasing growth in factor inputs and in raising productivity growth. Nevertheless, unevenness in the adjustment processes may produce fluctuations in demand that macroeconomic policies will need to address. At least in the first several years of trade and investment liberalisation implementation, macroeconomic policy is likely to have to continue to support demand growth to counter deflationary forces from enterprise and rural sector structural problems.

Moreover, while sustaining real growth, macroeconomic policy also needs to continue to be vigilant in containing inflation pressures. China's past experiences with macroeconomic overheating underscore the risks of excessive credit creation and inflation that can arise during cyclical upturns. While inflation risks now seem quite low in the current environment of excess supply in many product markets and restricted credit supplies, they could well rise with trade and investment liberalisation. In particular, the expected influx in foreign investment, stimulus to spending by domestic enterprises, and increase in exports arising from trade and investment liberalisation – particularly given the likelihood they will be concentrated in coastal provinces – have the potential to fuel an investment boom that could lead to excessive growth in aggregate demand if not adequately restrained by policy.

While fiscal policy has taken most of the burden of demand management in recent years, monetary policy will likely have to play a more important role in the future. The People's Bank of China (PBC) has been developing its "indirect" instruments, notably the central bank discount rate and reserve management, as a basis for more flexible, market-oriented, monetary policy management in the future. These steps, together with prudential and other financial reforms taken since the mid-1990s, have been aimed in part at ensuring that the loss of credit control that occurred in the early 1990s does not recur. However, the transmission mechanisms through which monetary policy influences market signals that shape demand have been blunted by the conservatism in bank leading noted earlier, and are further impaired by the limited flexibility of interest rates and underdeveloped state of financial markets. Under these circumstances, it becomes difficult for monetary policy to stimulate demand without undermining bank prudential standards or slipping into excessive stimulus. In this context, improvement in the effectiveness of monetary policy will depend importantly on restoration of financial soundness to banks and improvement of their accountability as commercial entities (so that they resume lending to creditworthy customers while maintaining prudent lending standards). Greater flexibility for interest rates to vary with market forces will also be required.

Implications for external balance

China's balance of payments has remained quite healthy over the past ten years. The current account has been in surplus since 1993 and reached a peak of 4 per cent of GDP in 1997, although it has since fallen back to 1.9 per cent in 2000 (Figure 22.2). The current account surpluses together with strong foreign direct investment inflows have sustained a balance of payments surplus for much of this period. As a result, China's international reserves have increased by nearly seven-fold since 1993, and are now more than 100 per cent of external debt and nearly 12 months of total imports. These ratios are relatively favourable by international and historical standards, as is the external debt ratio to GDP (now about 10 per cent).

The ultimate effects of trade and investment liberalisation on China's trade and current account balances are difficult to assess. Macroeconomic performances in the aftermath of trade liberalisation have been mixed. In some countries current account balances have deteriorated while in others they have improved (Figure 22.3). This underscores the fact that the evolution of the external balances depends on the policies and other circumstances that accompany trade and investment liberalisation. Empirical studies of the impact of China's WTO entry suggest that it will significantly increase the growth of both imports and exports but by comparable amounts, so that the net effect on the trade balance will probably be moderate but of uncertain sign (see Annex 2).

Trade and investment liberalisation could lead to further deterioration in China's trade and current account balances in the medium-term, however. OECD projections (OECD, 2001) imply that China's current account surplus will largely disappear by 2003, even though exports are likely to continue to grow faster than their external market.[16] The rapid projected growth in imports is attributable partly to the reduction of tariffs and other trade barriers starting in 2002, along with continued strong growth in purchases of foreign capital equipment as Chinese enterprises seek to upgrade their production capabilities. The trade balance may fall further through 2005 and, together with continuation of the decline in the services balance that has been underway since the mid-1990s, could push the current account into deficit by the middle of this decade[17]. While a change from the pattern prevalent during the 1990s, the deficit is likely to be modest by comparison with those often incurred by developing countries, and, by itself, should not present any serious risk to the sustainability of the external accounts. Moreover, the boost to exports provided by the termination of the MFA should help to stabilise the current account balance, and could well lead to an improvement after 2005.

Trade and investment liberalisation has potentially favourable implications for key components of China's capital accounts. Studies suggest that foreign direct investment inflows could double from their current level in the medium-term with China's WTO accession (see Chapter 10 on foreign direct

Figure 22.2. **Current account and trade balances**

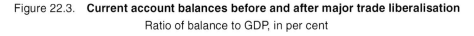

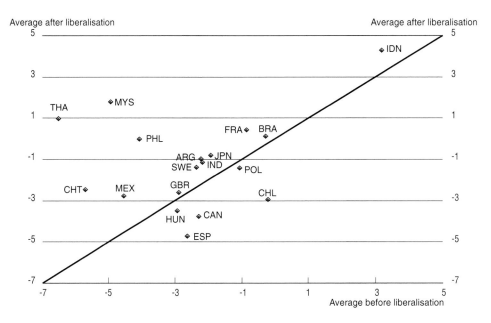

Source: IMF, *International Financial Statistics*.

Figure 22.3. **Current account balances before and after major trade liberalisation**
Ratio of balance to GDP, in per cent

Note: Before liberalisation is the average of the five years prior to the liberalisation ; after liberalisation is the average of the year of the liberalisation
and four years after. Trade balances for: Chile, Chinese Taipei, France, Indonesia, Japan, Spain, Sweden and United Kingdom.
Source: IMF, *International Financial Statistics, Statistical Data Book of Chinese Taipei.*

Figure 22.4. **Growth in China's exports and their market**

Annual per cent change

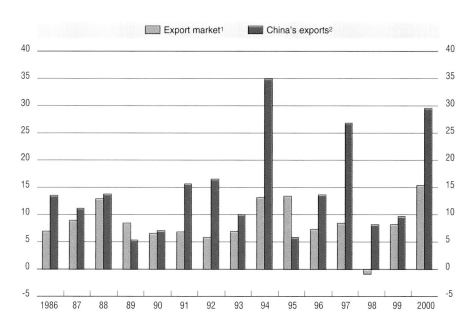

Note: Average gap (China's exports growth – Export market growth):

      1990-2000   7.9
      1995-2000   7.0

1. Export market growth: average growth in China's trading partners, weighted by their share in china's total exports.
2. Export growth in the annual growth in real merchandise exports. Figures are based on OECD Secretariat estimates of the price deflator for exports.
Source: OECD.

investment prospects and policies). Portfolio inflows are also likely to increase as the stock market and other capital markets develop, although the amount will depend on the extent to which foreign access to these markets is increased.

Overall, therefore, trade and investment liberalisation by itself does not seem to present obvious risks to China's external accounts. The key to maintaining sustainability in these accounts will lie with the success of domestic macroeconomic and financial policies in maintaining aggregate demand in line with potential non-inflationary growth, and in containing financial excesses. There are, however, some uncertainties surrounding the effects of trade and investment liberalisation, particularly if these conditions are not met. There is a possibility that trade and investment liberalisation, together with other changes in the domestic and international economy, will lead to a change in the equilibrium (real) exchange rate. Theoretical literature and existing evidence are again ambiguous on this point: depending on accompanying circumstances, a country's terms of trade may either improve or deteriorate with trade liberalisation. The impact on the nominal exchange rate also depends on the domestic rate of inflation versus that of trading partners. Thus, the direction, magnitude, or timing of a change in the exchange rate parity – if it is needed – cannot be predicted with any confidence. However these considerations do suggest that China will need increased flexibility in its exchange rate arrangements in the future.

Even greater uncertainties attend the evolution of China's capital accounts. Portfolio and short-term capital flows are not directly affected by China's WTO commitments and their evolution will be shaped substantially by the capital control regime. As argued in the last section of this chapter, China is likely to need to partially relax capital controls over the medium-term, but to retain some controls until financial markets are better developed and enterprise governance and external market disciplines are strengthened. China is not, however, likely to continue to have the insulation from external financial shocks it had during the 1997 Asian crisis for much longer. And the importance of internal macroeconomic and financial stability to sustainable external accounts is likely to increase.

Challenges to fiscal policy

As illustrated by many chapters in this study, China's public finances will face substantial new demands over the coming decade. These demands arise most immediately from the need to restore solvency to financial institutions, and from spending to facilitate adjustments to trade and investment liberalisation and other economic reforms. Additional demands will arise from increased spending on education, research and development, and other programmes important to economic development but which have been under-funded, and, over the longer term, from pension, medical, and other benefits of future workers and retirees. Dealing with these demands will require extensive restructuring of revenues and expenditures and greater capacity for debt management.

This section focuses on three issues concerning prospects for China's public finances over the next five to ten years. The first is the extent to which there are constraints on China's ability to afford the costs associated with economic reforms and the adjustments to trade and investment liberalisation. The second concerns the requirements needed to manage the cost of reforms in a way that does not prejudice fiscal sustainability over the longer term. The third is the ability, given these requirements, for fiscal policy to continue to provide stimulus to support aggregate demand.

The current status of public finances

From a purely macroeconomic perspective, China's public finances appear rather favourable. Under official definitions, the government deficit was about 2.8 per cent of GDP[18] in 2000. Domestic public debt was 21 per cent of GDP and official foreign debt about 10 per cent (Table 22.2). Although noticeably higher than in the mid-1990s, these figures are moderate by the standards of OECD countries as well as other emerging market economies.

A deeper look at the figures underlying the macro aggregates reveals a less favourable picture in three respects. First, the level of revenues that the government can effectively deploy to alternative uses is relatively limited. General government revenues are only slightly greater than 20 per cent of GDP,

Table 22.2. **Government finances**

Per cent of GDP

	1994	1997	1999	2000[1]
General government revenue[2]	16.8	17.4	20.4	20.9
On-budget	11.2	11.6	13.9	14.6
Extra-budget	4.0	3.8	3.9	3.8
Social insurance funds	1.6	2.0	2.6	2.5
General Government spending[2]	17.5	17.7	22.3	23.6
On-budget	12.4	12.3	16.1	17.4
Extra-budget	3.7	3.6	3.7	3.7
Social insurance funds	1.4	1.8	2.5	2.5
Budget deficit	−0.7	−0.3	−1.9	−2.7
On-budget	−1.2	−0.7	−2.2	−2.8
Memoranda:				
Government debt (domestic)				21.0
Interest on government debt				
Share of GDP				0.8
Share of on-budget revenue				5.5

1. Figures for 2000 are estimates based on partial data.
2. Figures exclude intra-government budget funds and fees amounting to about 1.3 per cent of GDP in 1999. Unsanctioned *ad-hoc* fees and charges imposed by local governments, and whose amount is not known, are also excluded.
Source: China Statistical Yearbook, 2000; Secretariat estimates.

compared to the higher levels found in OECD countries as well as many emerging market economies (Table 22.3). Moreover, nearly one-third of these revenues come from social insurance and "extra-budget" funds (mainly) raised by local governments to finance specific projects. Explicit ("on-budget") tax revenues – which are the most fungible of government resources – fell relative to GDP for much of the reform period and, despite a recovery after the tax reform in 1994, are still only 14.6 per cent of GDP. This ratio is also relatively low by international standards. The relatively low level of taxes is partly a reflection of the heavy reliance on indirect business taxes as opposed to personal income and other direct taxes, and of the proportionately lower (explicit) taxes paid by non-state enterprises as opposed to SOEs.

Local governments and other agencies in China also collect a substantial amount of funds in the form of *ad hoc* charges on farmers, local businesses, and other entities that are not recorded in official statistics or sanctioned by existing tax laws or codes. As discussed in Chapter 18 on tax policies and Chapter 20 on central-local government fiscal relations, these fees have grown rapidly in recent years and are now quite substantial.[19] If the fees are added to the explicit revenues, it is less clear that China's governments collect less than their counterparts in other countries. However these *ad hoc* revenues are even less fungible than the extra-budget funds and social insurance funds. Moreover, while probably used to some degree to meet social needs that are under-funded in the explicit government budgets, a substantial portion seem to be appropriated for personal use by officials or otherwise wasted from a social point of view. Key sectors, notably rural enterprises and farmers, which seem to have relatively light burdens in terms of explicit taxation, apparently have much greater burdens once the *ad hoc* fees are accounted for. The apparent contradiction between the scarcity of government revenues to meet development needs and the heavy effective tax burdens borne by most segments of the economy is a key indication of the overall inefficiency of the tax system.

Second, China's current government expenditures are deceptively moderate because key areas are under-funded. In particular, expenditures on education (World Bank, 1997) and on research and development (see Chapter 6 on technology challenges) are relatively low. These limits are at least partly responsible for China's lower level of educational attainment compared to OECD countries[20] and for the outmoded technology in much of industry. Spending on infrastructure (at least until recently) and on the environment has also not kept pace sufficiently with the development of the overall economy. Additional revenues are likely to be required by the Western Economic Development programme and government support needed to facilitate adjustments to trade and investment

Table 22.3. **Government on-budget revenues as share of GDP**
1999

	Share
China[1]	20.4
OECD average	37.8
United States	31.0
European Union	45.0
France	50.5
Germany	44.5
Italy	44.9
United Kingdom	40.5
Japan	37.6
Other emerging market economies	
Brazil	31.7
India	18.8
Indonesia	17.3
Russia[2]	29.8

1. China data are Secretariat estimates [see notes to previous table on Government finances].
2. Data are for 1998.
Note: Data include payments to social insurance funds.
Source: International Monetary Fund; OECD Secretariat compilations and estimates.

liberalisation. As a result, the ratio of revenues is likely to have to continue to rise if China is to adequately support its economic development and social needs.

Third, China's official public debt seriously understates the government's true obligations because burdens the government will almost certainly have to assume have not yet been explicitly recognised. As discussed further in Chapter 14, restoring capital adequacy to the major state banks (SOCBs) alone is likely to entail a cost equivalent to around 20 per cent of GDP. The more thorough clean up of financial institution balance sheets recommended in this study could cost between 30 and 60 per cent of GDP, depending on how serious the non-performing loans turn out to be and other circumstances. (See Chapter 14 on developing the financial system and financial regulatory policies).

These considerations suggest that the effective constraints on China's fiscal policy are greater than suggested by official figures on its current debt and government deficit. In effect, China's government at present has insufficient fiscal resources at its deposal to adequately support its development or to meet social needs. The large prospective burdens on public finances have raised doubts about whether China can afford the full cost of its reforms, or whether a fiscal crisis can be avoided.[21] However, as argued below, the situation is not this dire and there remains scope to put public finances on a sustainable foundation. The real constraints on China's fiscal policy depend less on the burdens that will need to be assumed in the near-term than on the evolution of the government's capacity to meet essential demands, and to constrain other demands, in the future.

The potential for increased revenue

China's tax revenues grew considerably faster than GDP between 1994 and 1999, by 15.8 per cent compared to 11.9 per cent for nominal GDP (Table 22.4). Business taxes on services, which grew by 20 per cent annually during that period, were the largest contributor to the overall increase, followed by personal income taxes and profit taxes paid by foreign enterprises. This increase has been reinforced by a more than doubling of tariff revenues since 1999 resulting from the government's crackdown on smuggling. The result is that tax revenues as a share of GDP were 2 percentage points higher in 1999 than in 1995, and nearly 3 percentage points above the trough in 1996.[22]

Much of the growth of taxes relative to GDP is attributable to improvement in tax yields from services, personal income, and other areas where collection and compliance have been particularly weak. Business taxes have been further boosted by the more rapid growth in services than in GDP as a whole, and by the increase in the turnover tax on financial services from 5 per cent to 8 per cent beginning in 1997.

There remains significant scope to further increase revenues relative to GDP, for at least two reasons. First, collective and other non-state enterprises, although subject legally to the same tax rates

Table 22.4. **Annual growth in tax revenue, 1994-1999**

	Annual average growth (%)
Total	15.8
Value-added taxes	11.0
Business taxes	20.0
Consumption taxes	11.0
Tariff revenue	15.5
Corporate profits taxes- total	6.3
SOE	0.9
Collective enterprises	11.7
Foreign-funded enterprises	35.3
Personal income taxes	41.5

Note: Value-added taxes are levied primarily on industry while business taxes are levied on revenue of service and some other tertiary activities.
Source: *China Statistical Yearbook*, 2000.

Figure 22.5. **Tax revenue scenarios**
Per cent of GDP

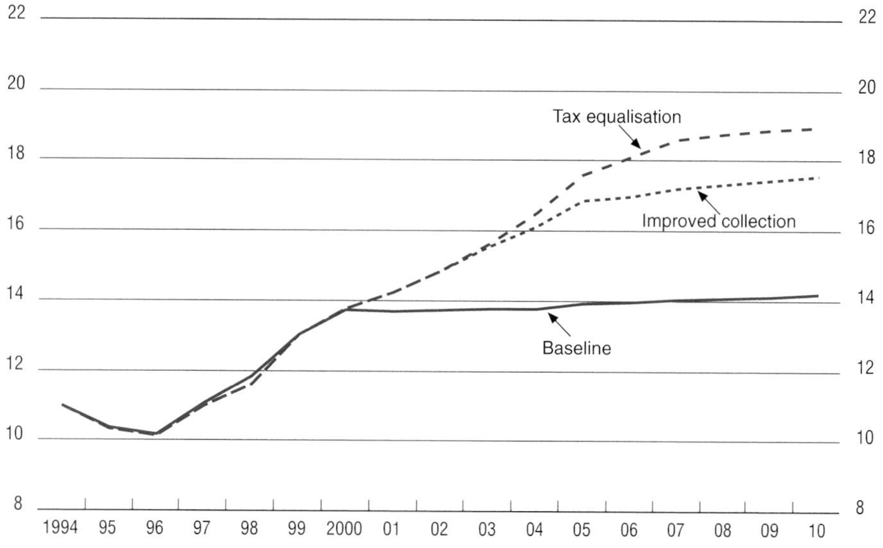

Note: All scenarios are based on real GDP growth of 7 per cent from 2003-2005 and 8 per cent from 2005-2010, and inflation of 2 per cent from 2002 onward. Projected tariff revenues are based on Secretariat estimates of import growth after WTO and the WTO mandated fall in the average tariff rate. Income from services and urban incomes are assumed to grow faster than GDP in line with the experience of the latter half of the 1990s. The "baseline scenario" assumes no further improvement in tax collection, no changes in current tax provisions, and limited further improvement in enterprise profits. The "improved collection" scenario assumes VAT, business tax, and income taxes paid by collectives rise to 90-95 per cent of the amount owed by 2010; the ratio of personal income taxes paid by urban households rises from 4 per cent in 1999 to 8 per cent in 2010 through improved collection and compliance and elimination of some exemptions; and enterprise profits rise further relative to GDP compared to the baseline. The "tax equalisation" scenario assumes that preferences on the VAT, business income, and import duties for FIE are eliminated by 2006 and that the personal income rises further to 10 per cent of urban household incomes through elimination of additional exemptions.
Source: OECD Secretariat calculations.

as SOEs in practice pay considerably less.[23] Rough estimates suggest that the value-added tax collected in 1999 was on the order of 75 per cent of the total theoretical liability of enterprises.[24] Collectives also pay proportionately less in income taxes than SOEs. There is also significant under-collection of the business tax (applied to revenue in service sectors) and in personal income taxes. Second, revenue from SOEs and domestic non-state enterprises has been depressed by the decline in corporate profits to very low levels during the 1990s. As indicated earlier, profits have been recovering since 1998 and are likely to improve further as (and provided) capacity utilisation improves and the gains from labour shedding, debt reduction, and other reforms are manifest.

Figure 22.5 provides a rough illustration of the potential for increasing government tax revenues as a share of GDP under various assumptions about growth in the tax bases, how much collection can be improved and other factors. These scenarios are intended as simply illustrative of the possibilities rather than as predictions. Nor should the increases in individual tax revenues underlying the hypothetical scenarios be taken literally: as indicated below, there are a number of possible ways in which total taxes could be increased by a given amount.

The first (baseline) scenario assumes that there are no changes in tax policies other than those already enacted or required by trade and investment liberalisation,[25] no significant further improvement in compliance or collection rates, and only modest further recovery in enterprise profits relative to GDP after 2001. Value-added taxes and most other taxes grow in line with their tax base in the baseline, at the rate of nominal GDP (see note to Figure 22.5). Non-state enterprises continue to pay proportionately less tax than SOEs, and new foreign enterprise entrants receive the same tax preferences as those now

727|

accorded to existing foreign invested enterprises (FIEs).[26] The ratio of government revenues rises slightly due to the assumed further improvement in profits of SOEs and to the more rapid growth of services than of GDP. However growth in taxes is substantially slower during 2000-10 than during the previous five years. Tax revenue is still only slightly above 14 per cent of GDP in 2010 and only about 1 percentage point higher than in 1999. This scenario should be regarded as pessimistic in that the recent trend toward improved collection and compliance stops and enterprise profits do not fully recover.

In the second "improved collection" scenario, the trend toward improved tax collection and compliance of recent years continues and enterprise profits rise further relative to GDP after 2001. The personal income tax yield is doubled relative to its base as a result of better collection and elimination of some exemptions.[27] Taken together, these assumptions imply a substantial increase in tax, as well as total government revenues: taxes rise by slightly more than 3 percentage points between 1999 and 2005, and by a modest amount further by the end of the ten year horizon. Most of this increase reflects higher VAT and business income tax payments relative to GDP. The growth in tax revenues is still somewhat slower than that actually recorded during 1994-99.

Further increases in tax revenues could be obtained by changes to current tax laws that authorities have endorsed in principle or indicated that they are considering. One possible step that could raise substantial revenue would be to equalise tax treatment between foreign enterprises and domestic enterprises by eliminating preferential exemptions now enjoyed by the former.[28] This, together with the elimination of additional exemptions on the personal income tax, could bolster revenues by another 1 to 1.5 percentage points of GDP by the end of the decade. (The third "tax equalisation" scenario in Figure 22.5 assumes this equalisation begins to occur in 2005.)

While only roughly indicative, the scenarios suggest that there is significant scope to raise government revenues through more effective application of existing tax laws and equalisation of tax treatment among enterprises. While more fundamental changes in tax structure may be desirable on other grounds, they do not appear to be essential to achieve a significant increase in government revenues relative to GDP. However, to ensure that the overall burden of government resource extraction on the economy does not increase further, steps to increase government revenues will need to be accompanied by other reforms to improve the efficiency of the tax system and curtail the resort to unauthorised and distorting levies by local governments.

Prospects for expenditures

China's expenditure has been growing even faster than revenue in recent years. Official budget expenditures reached 17.4 per cent of GDP in 2000, nearly 50 per cent above the ratio in 1995, while spending including off-budget outlays was around 21 per cent of GDP. Infrastructure spending, which has been carried out partly to support aggregate demand growth, has grown most rapidly and accounts for nearly one-third of the overall increase in on-budget outlays. However, virtually all other major categories of spending (except explicit government subsidies to enterprises, which are quite low) have also grown more rapidly than GDP. In addition, there has been a marked rise in interest payments on the government debt, although these are still fairly modest – about 5.5 per cent of total (on-budget) revenues and less than 1 per cent of GDP.

These increases have made up much of the gap between the level of expenditures earlier studies have suggested are needed to bring China's social programmes to a level comparable with other countries with similar *per capita* income, and to adequately exploit its development potential. In particular, the World Bank (1997) report suggested that total on-budget and extra-budget revenues be raised to 20.2 per cent of GDP, or 4.5 percentage points higher than the level in 1994 but only 1 percentage point greater than in 2000. The growth in infrastructure spending that has occurred over the past five years has largely achieved the increase called for in the World Bank recommendations.

Other important components of spending have not risen as fast as infrastructure outlays, however. In particular, spending on education and related activities important to human capital development and technology capabilities have risen by only about one-third of the amount (3.6 per cent of GDP) recommended in the World Bank report. These earlier studies do not fully take into account new demands on spending that have arisen in recent years, in particular the prospective increase in national defence outlays or additional needs for infrastructure and other spending to support the Western Economic Development initiative. Nor do they include government funding to facilitate adjustments to trade and investment liberalisation, for example for support and retraining of displaced workers.

Although the uncertainties are large, these considerations suggest that further increases in government spending relative to GDP are both likely and desirable. A plausible but probably conservative estimate is that budget plus extra-budget expenditures need to rise by at least 2 to 3 percentage points of GDP over the next five to ten years. In addition, social insurance outlays are likely to rise further, perhaps by around 0.5 to 1 percentage points of GDP (see Chapter 16 on labour market and social policies). Such increases would raise general government spending to nearly 25 per cent of GDP (excluding interest payments on the government debt), but would entail noticeably slower growth in expenditure during 2000-10 than over the past five years.[29] The increase in government spending could be greater if worker displacements and other adjustments entailed by trade and investment liberalisation and ongoing reforms are larger, or other spending needs to be increased more rapidly, than expected at present.

Is *fiscal policy sustainable?*

The trends in revenues and spending provide a basis for some rough scenarios for China's fiscal position over this decade. As with the tax revenue scenarios, these budget scenarios should be viewed as hypothetical illustrations of the range of possibilities and key forces determining the evolution of the deficit and debt rather than as predictions. The basic assumptions underlying the scenarios are summarised in Table 22.5. Each of these scenarios assumes that the government cleans up the balance sheets of the banks and rural credit co-operatives. In order to gauge potential fiscal strains, the scenarios are based on a relatively pessimistic estimate that the clean-up will entail a cost equal to about 50 per cent of 2000 GDP (which is in the upper portion of the range developed in Chapter 14) that is taken on over 2001-2003.[30] A further critical assumption is that financial institutions are able to contain future NPL so that the government does not have to pay for another financial system clean up.[31]

The first scenario assumes that revenues grow in line with the baseline case described earlier, in which current tax provisions and collection rates are largely unchanged. General government revenues are unchanged in relation to GDP but expenditures grow more rapidly as authorities finance key development needs described in the last sub-section. This and the other scenarios also incorporate the costs and revenues involved in the "pay-as-you-go" first pillar described in the section of Chapter 16 on social benefits, in which coverage is gradually extended while benefit rates are reduced so that the funds remain in balance.

This scenario mainly serves to underscore a point already apparent, namely that China is unlikely to be able to sustain adequate government spending to meet its development needs without a significant further increase in revenues relative to GDP. The primary budget deficit remains in substantial deficit throughout the horizon and government debt continues to rise. Debt is not yet at a clearly untenable level even by 2010, but is still rising and could reach an untenable level in the next decade if the gap between (non-interest) expenditures and revenues were to remain. Moreover the scenario is probably too optimistic, since the growth in debt is moderated by the fact that the assumed real interest rate on government debt, while higher than the rate now being paid, is still below the growth of the economy.[32] Under a more realistic scenario, the real interest rate on government debt would very probably rise to higher levels, as investors became increasingly concerned over the viability of public finances.

The second scenario incorporates the revenue path of the second case discussed earlier, in which taxes and general government revenue rise significantly in relation to GDP. Other assumptions, about the debt needed to restore financial soundness and to fund pensions, are the same as in the first scenario. In this scenario, the primary government deficit first rises but then tapers off and reaches a small surplus by the end of the decade. Domestic government debt peaks at just above 60 per cent of GDP (over 70 per cent including foreign debt), but then declines by nearly 10 percentage points over the remainder of the decade. Government interest payments on domestic public debt rise to 3.7 per cent of GDP (about 21 per cent of on-budget government revenue) in the middle of the decade but

729

Table 22.5. **Scenarios for government finances**
Per cent of GDP

	2000	2005	2010
Scenario I (unchanged tax ratio)			
Government debt	21.7	69.5	74.5
General government budget deficit	−2.5	−7.2	−8.1
Primary deficit	−1.7	−3.2	−3.5
General government expenditure	23.6	28.5	29.6
Interest payments on government debt	0.8	4.1	4.6
General government revenue	21.1	21.2	21.5
Scenario II (improved collection and compliance)			
Government debt	21.7	60.7	50.1
General government budget deficit	−2.5	−3.8	−3.0
Primary deficit	−1.7	0.0	0.3
General government expenditure	23.6	28.1	28.3
Interest payments on government debt	0.8	3.7	3.3
General government revenue	21.1	24.4	25.3
Scenario III (continued fiscal stimulus through 2004)			
Government debt	21.7	71.2	63.5
General government budget deficit	−2.5	−6.5	−4.2
Primary deficit	−1.7	−2.2	−0.2
General government expenditure	23.6	30.6	29.1
Interest payments on government debt	0.8	4.2	4.1
General government revenue	21.1	24.2	24.8
Memorandum:			
Scenario II with higher real interest rates			
Government debt	21.8	66.3	65.7
General government budget deficit	−2.5	−5.8	−6.2
Primary deficit	−1.7	−0.3	−0.2
General government expenditure	23.6	30.1	31.2
Interest payments on government debt	0.8	5.5	6.0
General government revenue	21.1	24.3	25.0

Note: Scenario I: tax revenue/GDP ratio is roughly flat after 2000, on-budget revenues rise by 3.4 percentage points of GDP between 1999 and 2010, debt from the financial system clean up of about 50 per cent of 2000 GDP is assumed, and real interest rates on government debt average about 4.5 per cent compared to average real GDP growth of 7.5 per cent.
Scenario II: same as Scenario I except that tax revenues rise further relative to GDP;
Scenario III: same as Scenario II but with spending rising by 1 per cent of GDP further in each of 2003-05, and then falling back to the Scenario II spending by 2010.
Memorandum scenario; same as scenario II except that the real interest rate equals real GDP growth from 2003 on.
Source: OECD Secretariat calculations.

then fall back. Overall this scenario is relatively benign, particularly given the large amount of debt taken on from the financial system.[33] As in the first scenario, the growth in debt and debt service is moderated by the positive gap between the economy's real growth and the interest rate paid on government debt. However the outcome would not be drastically altered, although it would be less favourable, if the real interest rate were to equal the real growth rate of GDP (see Table 22.5). Such a real rate is both high compared to China's historical experience and implies a nominal interest rate on government debt substantially above the present rate on government bonds.

It is important to emphasise that this second scenario is not a prediction. Rather it indicates that it should be possible to accommodate necessary or desirable additions to spending with revenue increases that appear feasible in view of recent trends and plausible assumptions about improvements in collection. The outcome is hardly assured and is likely to be valid only if there is reasonable progress on reforms discussed in other chapters. Two conditions are essential. First, future NPL, of financial institutions must be contained: further periodic bail-outs would very likely drive government debt to untenable levels or require the imposition of heavy tax burdens that could impair the development of the real economy.[34] Second, pension and other social benefit costs need to be carefully managed and benefit rates reduced over time as coverage is extended.

In addition, continued progress on improving the financial and competitive performance of enterprises is also important to ensure that the key tax bases expand at least as rapidly as GDP. As noted earlier, *ad hoc* fees and taxes now being imposed by local authorities need to be substantially reduced, if not curtailed, if the increase in tax revenues assumed in the scenario is not to lead to excessive burdens on enterprises and individuals. Moreover, efforts to reduce waste, duplication, and misallocation of spending are likely to be necessary if the increases in spending are to be sufficient to meet development needs.[35] If these conditions are not met, authorities are likely to continue to face painful tradeoffs between the funding needed to support economic reforms and development and fiscal soundness. Indeed these tradeoffs could become more acute. On the other hand, success in carrying out these reforms has the potential to create a "win-win" situation in which public finances are established on a sustainable basis, government revenues to support China's development are increased, while the overall burden of government resource extraction on the economy is reduced.

Box 22.1. **Conditions for a sound and sustainable fiscal position**

- Government tax revenues rise sufficiently relative to GDP to meet additional spending needs.
- The financial system maintains sound credit standards so that future NPLs are contained.
- Pension reforms succeed in establishing sustainable benefit levels.
- Waste in current spending is reduced and incentives for local governments to impose *ad hoc* taxes are contained.
- Enterprise performances continue to improve.

Finally, the second scenario also helps illuminate the potential constraints on fiscal stimulus to support real growth. These constraints are shaped by the need to limit the primary budget deficit so that government debt does not rise continuously. This means that any near-term increase in the primary deficit caused by fiscal stimulus has to be offset at some point by fiscal contraction of a comparable magnitude. The net benefits of fiscal stimulus to support growth for a time depend upon whether aggregate demand growth has been sufficiently restored to withstand the negative shock when the fiscal contraction has to begin.

In the second scenario discussed earlier, the net contribution of the budget to growth (which can be roughly measured by the change in the general government balance in relation to GDP) is considerably smaller during 2001-05 than it has been during 1998-2000.[36] Fiscal stimulus largely abates by 2001 and gives way to moderate contraction from 2004 onward. The third scenario provides an indication of the effect of continuing fiscal stimulus at a rate comparable to that during 1998-2000. This scenario is based on the revenue and spending paths in the second scenario but assumes that fiscal stimulus equivalent to 1 per cent of GDP per year is added in 2001-03 in order to support demand growth during the period when adjustments to trade and investment liberalisation are likely to be particularly intense. The stimulus is then withdrawn over the next five years as expenditure returns to its level in the main scenario. In this alternative, debt peaks at over 70 per cent of GDP and is still nearly two-thirds of GDP at the end of the horizon.

This alternative suggests that while it would be possible to continue fiscal stimulus somewhat further, the scope is probably moderate in terms of both magnitude and duration. Given the uncertainties about how rapidly revenues can be increased, other debts that may have to be assumed by the government, and interest rates, the scope for continued stimulus is probably more likely to be less than greater than the scenario implies.

China's exchange rate and capital control regimes

China's exchange rate system is officially registered as a floating exchange rate regime with current account convertibility but without capital account convertibility. In 1994, the authorities abolished the dual exchange rate and implemented significant reforms in the foreign exchange system. This comprises a compulsory foreign exchange settlement system, in which all foreign exchange earnings by domestic enterprises must be sold to authorised foreign exchange banks, while enterprises are entitled to purchase foreign exchange upon proof of a commercial contract requiring foreign exchange payment (Box 22.2). The system was revised in 1996 to allow foreign funded enterprises to retain their foreign exchange earnings. After a series of further measures to ease restrictions on foreign exchange trading, China officially achieved current account convertibility for the renminbi (RMB) at the end of 1996.

Box 22.2.   **China's foreign exchange market**

Since the beginning of 1994, China's exchange rate has been determined in an inter-bank foreign exchange market, the China Foreign Exchange Trading Centre (CFETC). In addition to the main task of providing a platform for foreign exchange trading, the CFETC also provides settlement services. The main players in the market are the central bank (PBC), the designated foreign exchange banks and non-bank financial institutions. There are a total of 300 participants, including the foreign banks. Each designated foreign exchange bank is assigned a foreign exchange margin in the foreign exchange settlement system. The designated foreign exchange banks have to enter the market whenever their margin exceeds the limit.

Table 23.   **Share of foreign exchange market during 1999**

	Buy	Sell
Chinese banks	60.0%	81.1%*
Foreign banks	11.6%	18.5%
Central banks	28.4%	..

*   Over 50% are from Bank of China alone.
Source: China Financial Development Report, 2000.

China's current foreign exchange market is still hampered by some problems. The Bank of China, and to a lesser extent the other three wholly state-owned banks, dominate trading. Due to the compulsory foreign exchange settlement system and other controls on transactions, market conditions do not adequately reflect the underlying supply and demand for foreign exchange of market participants or the economy as a whole. The physical market in various centres dominates trading and is characterised by public quotations and centralised deal-making organised by the CFETC. However, the physical market has high costs and more restrictions, *e.g.* in limited official hours for trading and in the geographic locations where trading can take place. The products of the foreign exchange trading centre are very simple. Only foreign currencies are traded in the centre – the US dollar, the HK dollar and the yen. Foreign exchange products are very basic and there are no currency futures or options trading.

The market is currently overly dominated by the central bank, while other market participants are heavily constrained by the foreign exchange controls. With trade and investment liberalisation, the need for more flexible access to foreign exchange and other international financial markets is likely to intensify. In order to improve the efficiency of the foreign exchange market, the present compulsory foreign exchange settlement system needs to be phased out. It should be replaced, in a step-by-step fashion, by a voluntary system that more accurately reflects the needs of market participants, and which allows the exchange rate to be more responsive to market conditions.

As stated in Box 22.2, China's exchange rate is administered in the China Foreign Exchange Trading Centre (CFETC). The advent of this system was marked by fluctuations and gradual appreciation of the exchange rate from its initial level of RMB 8.7 per U.S. dollar during 1994 and part of 1995. However, after 1995, including during and after the Asian crisis, China's exchange rate has been effectively maintained by central bank intervention at around RMB 8.3 per US dollar.

China's effectively fixed exchange-rate parity is supported by an elaborate system of capital account controls maintained through administrative measures. China has encouraged inflows of foreign direct investment, but has severely restricted foreign portfolio investment inflows and foreign borrowing by enterprises and financial institutions, especially short-term foreign borrowing. As a result, medium and long-term borrowings dominate China's foreign debt, most of which is sovereign debt.

China now faces the challenge of adapting its exchange rate and capital control regimes to support its integration into international markets. As argued below, the choice of end-point is the easiest aspect of this task. The more difficult challenge is to manage the transition to the end-points in a way that contains risks to economic stability while balancing the need for greater exchange rate flexibility, autonomy in domestic monetary policy, the needs of domestic businesses to access international financial markets, and the development of domestic financial markets.

The choice of exchange rate regime

There are roughly eight different arrangements for the exchange rate system. These range from the "hard pegs" involved in a common currency (where the country lacks its own separate legal tender) and currency board, to a pegged rate within a band ("soft peg"), a crawling peg, a crawling band, managed floating with no pre-announced exchange rate path and free floating. As Frankel (1999) states, no single exchange rate system is optimal for all countries for all time. The choice of the exchange rate systems depends on the capital control regime and the extent of development of the domestic financial markets – conditions that also have important implications for the financial stability of the economy.

Box 22.3 summarises the benefits and disadvantages of four exchange rate regimes that are most relevant to China: fixed and floating exchange rate regimes, as well as two intermediate arrangements.

Box 22.3. **Benefits and disadvantages of different exchange rate regimes (under free mobility of capital)**

	Benefits	Disadvantages
Fixed exchange rate regimes	Stable currency in (at least) nominal terms. Potentially high credibility	No monetary autonomy when capital is mobile; adjustment to external real shocks falls entirely on the domestic economy
Crawling pegs	Relatively stable real exchange rate.	Low monetary autonomy and limited ability to offset external real shocks. Difficult to design rules for "crawling"
Floating within a band (target zone)	Restricts currency swings. Provides some limited monetary policy autonomy and limited flexibility to offset external shocks.	Vulnerable to speculative currency attacks. Design of the band is difficult.
Floating exchange rate regimes	Allows a domestic-oriented monetary policy. The exchange rate adjusts to external shocks, insulating the domestic economy in some cases.	Currency risks to domestic financial institutions and non-financial enterprises. Risk of exchange rate fluctuations that impose disruptions to the domestic economy.

733

Fixed exchange rate regime: stability but limited flexibility

A fixed exchange rate regime has the benefit of preventing wide fluctuations in both the real and nominal value of the economy. Wide swings in the exchange rate in China's present circumstances, when other macroeconomic instruments are constrained and structural distortions are widespread, could lead to undesirable disruptions in the domestic economy. In addition, a fixed exchange rate can be used as a nominal anchor to contain inflation, since a central bank in a developing country is sometimes short of credibility and insufficiently independent to fight inflation effectively. Pegging the currency to one or a group of countries with a more stable inflation environment allows authorities to "import" credibility to deal with inflation (Herrendorf, 1997).

However, the fixed exchange rate system poses potential problems for China, even without the liberalisation of capital account controls. As the currency is pegged against the US dollar, it is not flexible to respond to various internal and external shocks, nor to changes in the value of the US dollar against other major currencies, notably the yen and the euro. Chinese enterprises and banks need to hedge against currency risks related to movements among these major currencies, particularly when, as before the 1997 Asian crises, the fluctuations have been large.

During the Asian crisis, China's authorities maintained the fixed exchange rate parity, in part because devaluation probably would have prompted further declines in other Asian currencies. But when Chinese exports suffered, the government had to resort to other measures, such as an increase in the (value-added) tax rebate to stimulate exports.[37] Thus stability in the exchange rate effectively imposed a cost in terms of lower fiscal revenues. In recent years, China's current account surplus and strong foreign direct investment inflows have put upward pressure on the RMB at certain times. To counter this pressure, the central bank has had to intervene to maintain the fixed parity. However such intervention either has to be sterilised – not an easy task given the limits of domestic financial markets – or allowed to raise the monetary base, with the risk to the PBC's control of domestic credit.

With trade and investment liberalisation accelerating in the coming years, China will face more shocks, some nominal, others real. The primary drawback of the fixed exchange rate policy is that it deprives authorities of a relatively flexible means for adjusting to real shocks and maintaining external balance. With a fixed exchange rate, domestic prices and wages will have to adjust to external real disturbances. The costs, particularly when the shock requires deflation of domestic prices and wages, can be quite painful. Maintenance of a fixed exchange rate parity since the Asian crisis may have aggravated the domestic deflation in China of recent years.

Furthermore, it is not possible to have a fixed exchange rate, free capital mobility, and an independent, domestic-oriented monetary policy at the same time. (This has been called the "impossible trinity" of monetary policy). Recent experience shows that the commitment to a fixed current peg under free capital mobility needs to become progressively "harder" as the capital account is liberalised. Ultimately this means joining a currency union or the adoption of a currency board, neither of which seems likely or appropriate given the size of China's economy. Moreover, once the capital account is liberalised, a fixed exchange rate system will require the central bank to relinquish autonomous monetary policy. However, as argued below, a domestic-oriented monetary policy is likely to be necessary to adequately manage domestic demand and financial conditions in the near to medium-term. Thus a more flexible exchange rate policy is likely to be required as capital controls are eased.

Floating exchange rate regime: greater flexibility under the right financial conditions

A floating exchange rate regime can remedy many of the drawbacks of a fixed exchange rate system. A floating exchange rate allows a country to adjust to both external and internal shocks. The currency is free to vary to offset divergences between domestic and foreign inflation, and so maintain the economy's competitiveness on international markets. Movement in the exchange rate acts like a safety valve, adjusting to reflect the balance of various factors, such as cross-border capital flows and differentials between international and domestic interest rates. In principle, a country can maintain stability in the real exchange rate in the face of these shocks through adjustment of the nominal exchange rate. With a fixed exchange rate, it is domestic prices and wages that have to adjust.

After the liberalisation of the capital account, in theory, monetary policy will face a trade off between exchange rate and interest rate policy. A floating exchange rate regime will allow the central bank to retain some degree of autonomy for monetary policy to set domestic interest rates on the basis of the requirements of the domestic economy.

However, the requirements for a successful floating system are also rather demanding. In particular, capital controls need to be substantially liberalised if the foreign exchange market is to be efficient enough to accurately price the exchange rate. For China, reforms to develop money and capital markets, restructure and recapitalise the banking sector, and to improve corporate governance are likely to be necessary if a floating exchange rate is to adequately reflect underlying economic fundamentals and not lead to serious disruptions in the domestic economy. The hardening of budget constraints of state-owned banks and enterprises is essential in this regard to avoid incentives to take on excessive foreign exchange risks. The need to contain prudential risks when financial discipline in the domestic economy is weak is one reason why the PBC has sought to limit open foreign exchange positions of enterprises and financial institutions.

For a floating exchange rate regime to be beneficial to the domestic economy, interest rates need to be free to vary with market conditions rather than fixed by regulation. Otherwise, the interest rate differential with abroad may give distorted signals for international capital flows, causing the exchange rate to deviate from the rate justified by underlying economic fundamentals. Under-developed domestic financial markets can create similar distortions. Under-developed domestic markets also limit the ability of monetary authorities to insulate the economy from speculative capital inflows ("hot money") or other unwanted pressures on the exchange rate, since, as noted earlier, they make it difficult to conduct sterilised intervention in the foreign exchange market.

These considerations suggest that, as with the United States, the European Union, and Japan, a floating exchange rate will ultimately be most appropriate to China's circumstances. However such a system is not feasible at present, and is unlikely to be desirable until capital control liberalisation and other conditions necessary for its achievement are in place.

Intermediate arrangements: floating within a band and a crawling peg

As noted earlier, China's current exchange rate parity may well have to change before the conditions for a free float are established. Adoption of a crawling peg, in which the exchange rate varies with the ratio of domestic prices relative to those of foreign competitors, or a float within a band, has the potential attraction of combining some of the benefits of a fixed parity with those of a floating rate system. In theory, a crawling peg can ensure a relatively stable real exchange rate and avoid unwarranted gains or loss of competitiveness when domestic or foreign inflation changes. In theory also, a float within a moderately wide band ("soft peg") provides greater flexibility for monetary policy to deal with external shocks, while avoiding excessive fluctuations in the currency's value beyond those warranted by economic fundamentals.

However, the practical difficulties of these intermediate arrangements are significant. Particularly in highly open economies, a crawling peg runs the risk of validating domestic inflation shocks and undermining the credibility of authorities' commitment to price stability. Choosing the correct basket of currencies against which to peg and the measure of inflation with which to index the exchange rate also involves difficult technical issues. The benefits of a crawling peg tend to be greatest when domestic inflation rates differ substantially from those of trading partners. The benefits for China, where inflation domestically as well as internationally is now quite low, would seem to be limited.

Currency crises during the 1990s indicate that soft pegs can be quite vulnerable to "speculative attacks" when the exchange rate approaches the limit of the band.[38] Wider bands may (but not necessarily) reduce this risk but also increase vulnerability to unwarranted exchange rate fluctuations.

The lesson of the European crises is that maintenance of soft pegs for extended periods is quite difficult when there is free capital mobility.

Nevertheless, a limited widening of the band within which the exchange rate is allowed to vary may be appropriate for China during the transition to a regime of liberalised capital controls and free floating. Authorities have undertaken some limited experiments with band widening in recent years. Such a widening, provided it was accompanied by some broadening of access to the foreign exchange market and relaxation of restrictions on trading, could help to promote the development of the foreign exchange market. A wider band would allow more flexibility to deal with external shocks, while avoiding the problems from attempting to maintain a floating exchange rate before the capital account was liberalised and domestic financial markets are sufficiently developed. A wider band might make it easier to change the central parity when conditions warrant – although this is by no means assured. As Eichengreen *et al.* (1998) have argued, exit from a fixed peg under capital controls is best undertaken before confidence in the peg has begun to decline, and when the country enjoys a favourable net capital flow situation. While these conditions now apply to China, there is no guarantee that they will continue to do so.

The need for phased liberalisation of China's capital control regime

The Chinese authorities have endorsed capital account convertibility as a desirable ultimate goal. Indeed, the authorities raised the possibility just before the 1997 Asian crisis that this might be achieved early in the following decade. That crisis has led to a reconsideration of those plans, however, and capital account convertibility is now regarded as a longer-term objective.

Controls are necessary in the present environment

China's current capital controls can be regarded as a "second best" policy in which under-developed markets, extensive financial weakness, lack of market discipline, and asymmetric information create incentives for excessive risk taking and other imprudent financial behaviour. In China, the main agents in the markets often do not have adequate internal mechanisms to maintain prudential norms and to control risk: in particular; SOEs and SOCBs are still characterised by weak governance structures and are faced with soft budget constraints in many cases. The weaknesses in these mechanisms and the potential problems they can cause are underscored by the substantial number of financial irregularities, such as the excessive risk-taking by many trust and investment companies (TIC), which have come to light in recent years. These problems also illustrate the need, despite much progress in recent years, for further strengthening of the capabilities of financial supervisory authorities.

Capital controls in China have substantially insulated the domestic financial markets from changes in conditions in international financial markets, and are an important reason why China was able to escape the 1997 Asian financial crises. These crises illustrate the risk of extensive liberalisation of capital controls before the necessary domestic foundations of adequate market discipline, reasonably developed financial markets, and strong supervisory capabilities are developed. A number of currency and financial crises over the past decade are attributable in part to premature capital account liberalisation before domestic financial distortions were removed. These include the crises in Finland and Sweden in 1991-92, Mexico in 1994, and Indonesia, Thailand and the Republic of Korea in 1997 (see Furman and Stiglitz, 1998; Ariz *et al*, 2000).

The timing of China's capital control liberalisation also depends on the degree to which independent monetary policy will be needed to meet the needs of the domestic economy. As noted earlier, macroeconomic policy will need to be able to support the higher real GDP growth required to improve labour utilisation, once structural reforms make this possible without engendering inflation. Monetary policy may have to supply much of the support, given the limits on fiscal stimulus consistent with sound public finances. Less than perfect capital mobility gives authorities somewhat greater flexibility to maintain interest rates below those prevailing internationally while still limiting exchange rate fluctuations that could be disruptive to the domestic economy.

Progressive liberalisation will be needed over time

Despite the need to maintain controls in the current environment, capital account liberalisation is likely to become increasingly necessary as trade and investment liberalisation proceeds. Strains on China's capital account controls have become increasingly evident in several ways.

- Existing controls impose excessive costs on the commercial banks that are authorised to deal in foreign exchange. Only the head offices are authorised to enter the market itself and their permitted transactions are based on the consolidated foreign exchange position of the bank as a whole. When branches of the banks receive orders for foreign exchange they cannot meet out of their own reserves, they must first apply to the head office, which, if its consolidated position is insufficient, must then go into the market. Branches sometimes have difficulty executing customer orders on time because of this cumbersome procedure and tend to maintain higher foreign exchange reserves than would otherwise be necessary.

- Limits on positions and trading by other participants mean that the PBC effectively dominates market trading. Its share has averaged nearly 25 per cent of total trading in the market, and has sometimes risen to over 50 per cent.

- Controls also create difficulties for domestic enterprises. Under the present compulsory foreign exchange settlement system, domestic enterprises needing to trade foreign exchange are not always able to sufficiently adjust their foreign exchange holdings to deal with repetitive but small needs, as well as urgent needs in some cases. In addition, the documentation requirements for individual foreign exchange transactions can be a tedious process that can expose enterprises to unwarranted exchange rate risks.

Moreover, evasion of the controls is widespread. Incentives to evade the controls are often strong and the ability of foreign exchange banks and supervisory authorities to enforce the controls is limited. This has led to widespread abuses, including: over-invoicing of declared imports and evasion through the use of links to Hong Kong, China. The limited control is reflected in the large errors and omissions in China's balance of payments accounts: in recent years, the current account surplus plus net recorded capital inflows has greatly exceeded the increase in foreign exchange reserves, indicating substantial unrecorded capital outflows. Numerous examples further underscore the porous nature of the controls. For example, the international trust and investment companies (ITICs) borrowed extensively from abroad in the beginning and middle of the 1990s. Many of these foreign loans were neither approved nor registered with the State Administration for Foreign Exchange (SAFE). (The Fujian and Guangdong cases each involved amounts over US$6 billion.) As with such regulations generally, the stringency of the controls and the high transaction costs of adhering to them encourage evasion and complicate the task of accurately measuring the underlying trends in the balance of payments.

More fundamentally, continued capital controls are ultimately inconsistent with the broader goal of promoting China's integration into the world economy. In the medium-term, foreign investors in China as well as domestic businesses with significant international activities are likely to need more flexible access to international financial markets. The increased presence of foreign banks in China's market and the growing participation of large Chinese enterprises and banks in world markets is likely to increasingly blur the distinction between domestic and international financial markets and add to strains on the current system of capital controls (Xie, 2001). On the other hand, greater freedom for international capital flows could help significantly to improve breadth, efficiency, and competition in domestic financial markets. China's domestic stock markets and its listed companies can benefit from foreign investment, particularly as only a limited number of firms are likely to be able to list in foreign markets. The development of the government and other bond markets could also benefit by allowing more access for foreign investment.

Considerations shaping the transition

Liberalisation of capital controls to establish capital account convertibility is thus the second end point toward which China's exchange rate and capital control regimes will need to move toward in coming years. The more difficult questions concern the way in which this transition, and that toward a more flexible exchange rate, is to be made. International experience does not provide specific blueprints for accomplishing this transition but it does suggest that there are significant risks both in excessive speed and in undue delay in capital account liberalisation. The risks of premature liberalisation of capital controls are now especially great for China because of the poor financial conditions of enterprises and financial institutions, weak corporate governance, and the incomplete development of financial regulatory and supervisory capabilities. However, delay in liberalising the capital account also involves potentially high costs, since it limits the pace at which the exchange rate regime can be made more flexible as well as the benefits of liberalised capital flows to the development of domestic financial markets and to the overall economy.

China's circumstances suggest that the following specific considerations are likely to be important in shaping the transition in the medium-term.

- The substantial amount of unrecorded capital outflows suggests that the rigidity of the current regime may be encouraging evasion. Partial liberalisation of controls to allow domestic enterprises and banks more flexible access to foreign exchange, while at the same time improving procedures for reporting and enforcement, could help to improve compliance.

- Partial liberalisation is also likely to be needed to develop a more efficient foreign exchange market.

- Until the current distortions in the domestic financial system are substantially reduced, the capabilities of financial regulators to detect and limit imprudent financial behaviour will be critical to the pace of capital account liberalisation.

- Liberalisation, within the next several years, of portfolio inflows into the stock market through merger of the now separate markets for foreign and domestic investors and the government bond market would help to develop those markets. The risks should be limited, although merger of the stock markets may lead initially to declines in domestic equity prices, which appear overvalued by international standards (See Chapter 15 on capital markets).

These considerations suggest that a phased liberalisation of the exchange rate and capital control regime should begin in the near term and proceed in a co-ordinated manner in line with the development of domestic financial markets and financial regulatory/supervisory capabilities. The main near-term goals are: to develop a broader and more efficient foreign exchange market in which leading banks take on a greater role as market makers; to reduce evasion and improve reporting of capital outflows; and to begin to liberalise foreign access to domestic capital markets. Several specific steps would help to achieve these objectives. The first is to allow domestic foreign exchange banks greater flexibility in their foreign exchange operations, perhaps by allowing major branches to enter the market directly, while the head office is held accountable for their activities. The second is to give domestic enterprises greater flexibility to retain foreign exchange earnings and to purchase foreign exchange when needed. And a third would be to implement official plans to merge the foreign and domestic segments of the stock markets, while preparing to allow foreign entry into the government bond market within the next several years.

Conclusions and policy implications

Macroeconomic performance will be very important to sustaining economic reforms while making a satisfactory adjustment to trade and investment liberalisation. A stable macroeconomic environment – robust real growth, low inflation, and sustainable external accounts – are essential to facilitate the redeployment of labour, restructuring of enterprises, financial system recovery, and other structural adjustments that need to occur over the coming decade. As experiences of other countries have repeatedly shown, an unstable macroeconomic environment at least makes such adjustments much more difficult and protracted, and often prevents or reverses them. In China, macroeconomic policy needs not only to avoid instability, but also to improve in certain respects on recent macroeconomic performance in order to provide a more supportive environment for structural adjustment. The key challenges in this regard are to ensure adequate real growth in the sense described earlier while maintaining balance in China's external accounts; to increase government financial resources sufficiently to support China's development needs; and to ensure adequate flexibility in the exchange rate and capital account regimes.

These challenges are made all the more difficult by the strong dependence of macroeconomic performance on structural developments in the economy. The deflationary forces now being engendered by structural problems of enterprises and the rural sector are not likely to disappear for some time and in some areas may be accentuated by adjustments to trade and investment liberalisation and other reforms. Adjustments to trade and investment liberalisation will create uneven demand pressures across business segments and regions. The limited geographic integration of the economy and restricted factor mobility may further aggravate differences in the balance of supply and demand across sectors. As OECD experiences, notably those of many European countries, have shown, such structural unevenness seriously complicates aggregate demand management by making it more difficult to achieve full utilisation of resources without generating unacceptable inflationary pressures. Limited integration, the imbalances in central-local government fiscal relations, and differing regulatory treatment of state-owned, collective, private, and foreign enterprises have complicated the task of mobilising adequate government revenue. The pace of capital account and exchange rate liberalisation is necessarily constrained so long as inadequate corporate governance and financial discipline create incentives for imprudent financial activities.

In these circumstances, effective macroeconomic policies together with progress on structural reforms are likely to be needed to sustain adequate macroeconomic performance. To carry out their role, macroeconomic policy instruments will need to become more effective and flexible than they are now. The need for macroeconomic policies to support aggregate demand is likely to remain in the near term, but policy may well have to deal with potential economic overheating in the future once banks' financial conditions improve and the simulative portion of the effects of trade and investment liberalisation accumulate. The scope for using fiscal policy in demand management is likely to narrow as debt rises with the recapitalisation of the financial system and other demands. China should be able to avoid fiscal crisis provided it can raise government revenues to a more adequate level of GDP, contain future NPL, implement programmes to contain future pension burdens and allocate fiscal expenditures more efficiently. Monetary policy will have to assume a greater role in demand management, but its effectiveness will depend on the success of financial reforms in reducing the present weaknesses in credit allocation, and on greater interest rate flexibility. China's increasing integration with the international economy and the parallel changes in the domestic economies are likely to increase the need for access to international financial markets and will have significant, but difficult to predict, effects on relative prices and other forces shaping the external accounts. Dealing with these changes will require progressively greater flexibility in the exchange rate regime and in international capital controls, but liberalisation in these areas will be dependent on progress on domestic financial reforms.

To achieve these goals, the discussion in this chapter has highlighted several recommendations concerning the priorities for macroeconomic policies.

- *Achievement of aggregate real growth sufficient to progressively reduce the surplus of workers in the economy over time should be an explicit goal of economic policy.*

  Achievement of full employment is likely to take longer than the current decade to fulfil, but real growth will have to exceed potential for a number of years if significant progress is to be made. The required growth is likely to be above the pace achieved in the past several years. At least in the near term, this goal is unlikely to be achievable by macroeconomic policies alone and will require substantial progress on labour market, enterprise, and other structural reforms.

- *Increasing government tax revenues relative to GDP along with measures to improve the efficiency with which revenues are used should be a central priority of macroeconomic policy.*

  Higher government revenues that can be effectively deployed where most needed are essential to fund the increased expenditures that will be needed to provide adequate support to economic development and expand social benefit programmes. Given the demands that the public sector is likely to have to meet, higher revenues are likely to be necessary to contain risks to fiscal soundness. Efforts to increase tax revenues need to be accompanied by complementary reforms to increase the efficiency of the overall tax system, curtail unauthorised levies, and improve the allocation of revenues that are discussed in other chapters of this study.

- *Interest rate deregulation should be achieved in the near term and extend at least to bank loan rates and interest rates on large deposits.*

  This step, which was also recommended in Chapter 14 on financial system development, is essential to improving the effectiveness of monetary policy in the near term, and to liberalisation of the exchange rate and capital account regimes.

- *Further development of the money and government bond markets should be given high priority in the medium term.*

  Development of a broader and more flexible money market along the lines suggested in Chapter 14 on financial system development is essential to improvement of the monetary policy transmission mechanism. The prospective rise in government debt will require a broader and more flexible government bond market, particularly the secondary market.

- *The flexibility of the exchange rate regime needs to be increased progressively, with the longer-term goal of establishing a floating exchange rate regime in step with liberalisation of the capital account and development of domestic financial markets.*

  The stability afforded by the current regime will continue to be important for the next several years. Over a longer period, greater flexibility, especially in the real exchange rate, is likely to be needed to adjust to the changes in the domestic and international economy that will come with trade and investment liberalisation and other developments. A more flexible mechanism for varying the nominal exchange rate will be needed if China is to maintain external balance while avoiding the speculative pressures that have too often accompanied adjustable exchange rate parity regimes in other countries. In the longer term, China, as with other major economies, is likely to find a floating exchange rate regime most desirable from this standpoint.

- *The capital control regime should be progressively liberalised, with near-term measures to improve the efficiency of the foreign exchange market and proceeding thereafter in line with the development of domestic financial markets; the strengthening of financial supervision and improvement in corporate governance and financial discipline.*

- Existing capital controls should be partially relaxed over the next several years to allow enterprises more flexible access to foreign exchange and to create a broader and more efficient foreign exchange market. Relaxation of controls on portfolio flows would help spur the development of domestic equity and bond markets, but supervisory mechanisms to control abuses may need to be strengthened first. While capital account liberalisation needs to be "sequenced" with domestic financial system reforms, undue delay is likely to slow the development of domestic financial markets and constrain progress toward a more flexible exchange rate regime.

NOTES

1. Various studies suggest that official figures may overstate China's average real growth during the reform period by about 2 to 3 percentage points. Improvements in statistical methods during the 1990s and other factors probably have reduced the overstatement on average, but the bias probably varies with economic circumstances. Alternative estimates developed by Rawski (2000) suggest that real growth in 1998 may have been less than half the official figure of 8 per cent.

2. China's performance also appears quite respectable but not exceptional in terms of the modest contribution to growth from productivity improvements rather than increases in material inputs (see Young, 2000). However "extensive growth" with little or no generalised productivity growth has been typical in centrally planned economies and there is evidence that growth in other Asian developing countries has followed this pattern (*e.g.* Krugman, 1994). Subsequent studies have challenged this conclusion (see Chen, 1997), however, and underscore the difficulties of adequately measuring productivity growth.

3. For further details on the employment trends summarised here, see the discussion in Chapter 16 on labour markets and policies; and the overview of adjustments in industry in Chapter 4.

4. Employment growth has very likely fallen below the growth in the labour force in recent years. Average employment growth during 1995-99 was about 1.0 per cent. Figures reported by the World Bank (*World Bank Development Indicators*, 2000) project that the labour force will grow by 0.8 per cent annually between 1998 and 2010, but the rate has probably been somewhat higher over the past several years, given that labour force growth over 1980-98 averaged 1.8 per cent annually.

5. Because of the presently limited coverage of the unemployment insurance system, the official unemployment rate is well below the true rate.

6. The slowdown in potential growth in Japan and the Republic of Korea also occurred at a substantially more advanced stage of development, as indicated by per capita income, than where China is now.

7. See Chapters 4 and 5 on industry prospects and industry reorganisation, respectively.

8. Chinese statistics do not clearly separate capital spending by state owned enterprises from infrastructure and other fixed investment by government agencies. Coverage of investment of non-state enterprises is incomplete and so official figures need to be taken with some caution. Except for fixed investment by state entities, data are available only on an annual basis, which makes it difficult to assess recent trends in investment by non-state enterprises.

9. Employment growth is likely to have to return to something like the pace of the early 1990s for a number of years to achieve something like full employment. To the extent productivity growth rises with trade and investment liberalisation, the aggregate real GDP growth needed to create jobs at this pace will be even higher than that recorded during the early 1990s.

10. Extensive declines in sales and production and drop in real growth followed Russia's trade opening in the early 1990s. This negative shock reflects the fact that a large portion of Russian industry was not competitive on world markets at the prevailing exchange rate. In contrast, there is little evidence that China's currency is seriously overvalued.

11. The loss of market share likely to be incurred by domestic automobile producers – the biggest prospective losers from WTO – is likely to be at least partially mitigated by strong growth in domestic demand for autos. (Indeed, studies predict that the output of the domestic auto industry will continue to grow, although less rapidly than it would in the absence of WTO). See Chapter 4.

12. See OECD (2000), especially Chapter 3.

13. A variety of studies have argued that returns to capital are at least offset by barriers of this sort that are either not subject to change, or likely to change only very slowly. See, for example, Chapter 21. The consequence is illustrated by the simulations of Zhai and Li (2000) reported in that chapter: trade liberalisation leads to a flow of capital from low wage interior regions to the coast, and to an increase in the growth differential between the coast and interior, due to the assumption that total factor productivity is substantially lower in the interior. The result would be different if total factor productivity differences were allowed to converge over time (say as regional barriers to capital mobility were reduced), with capital likely to flow from high wage to low wage areas

while the gap in growth rates among the regions narrows. Aggregate real growth would also be higher in this scenario due to the improvement in capital productivity.

14. Indeed this is already occurring in some cases; for example, Shanghai textile firms, with the encouragement of local authorities, have been moving operations requiring lower skilled workers to interior locations where wages are significantly lower than those in Shanghai.

15. Foreign firms have significant presence in several interior cities, such as Wuhan in Hubei province and Chongqing in Sichuan that may be further encouraged by the development of the Yangtze River valley region and, in the case of Chongqing, by the economic spillovers from the Three Gorges Dam. The prospects for other major interior cities are less clear, however. In any case, most observers expect that coastal cities such as Shanghai and Guangzhou will continue to be by far the largest recipients of foreign direct investment flows in the aftermath of trade and investment liberalisation.

16. These projections assume that nearly all the direct trade impacts of trade and investment liberalisation occur after 2002.

17. From a macroeconomic perspective, the decline in the current account can be viewed as the result of a revival in domestic investment as enterprise profits and cash flow improve. Similarly, the surplus that developed during the mid-1990s was the counterpart of the decline in domestic consumption and investment spending.

18. OECD Secretariat estimates. See OECD (2001a).

19. Indeed, as indicated in Chapter 18, unsanctioned fees that do not appear in official statistics may amount to at least 5 per cent of GDP, and possibly significantly more.

20. Education attainment in rural areas is particularly low, whereas that in cities compares more favourably to that of OECD and other emerging economies. For further discussion, see Chapter 16 on labour market and social policies.

21. See, for example, Lardy (2000).

22. Tax revenues are being boosted further by the policy, beginning in 2000, of converting some extra-budget fees and revenues into taxes. This conversion does not, however, contribute to the growth of overall revenue.

23. As an indication of the underpayment, the legal value-added tax rate is 17 per cent for all enterprises, but total value-added taxes collected are only 11 per cent of industry value-added in 1999, roughly the same as the average for 1994-95. This somewhat understates the compliance rate because smaller firms pay a lower rate and because foreign invested firms are exempt from the VAT for the first several years of their operation in China. For more detailed analysis of the difference in tax burdens of SOEs and non-state enterprises, see OECD (2000), Chapter 2 and the Appendix.

24. This estimate is based on comparing the VAT tax ratio of 17 per cent applied to all but smaller enterprises against the actual value-added tax they paid. The figure is in line with an earlier estimate by the World Bank (World Bank, 1996) for the mid-1990s. The actual ratio of VAT paid to industry value-added has risen only slightly since the mid-1990s.

25. As indicated in the survey of WTO impacts, the effective tariff rate is slated to drop by nearly one-half, from around 4 per cent at present. This is largely offset by the projected acceleration in import growth due to trade and investment liberalisation.

26. Tax preferences for existing foreign enterprises expire over time, and while often extended, are unlikely to be fully replaced; partly for this reason, income taxes paid by FIE rise faster than nominal GDP growth in the baseline. The government's commitment to move toward national treatment suggests that new foreign direct investment will receive somewhat less favourable treatment (although that will also depend on the sector distribution of FDI).

27. The 1997 World Bank study estimated that the personal income tax could be doubled as a share of GDP by eliminating certain exemptions, although the ratio of the tax to total wages was lower than it is now.

28. These include exemption from the VAT and corporate income tax for several years after establishment (and which in practice is often extended) and the right to duty-free imports of capital goods not accorded to domestic enterprises.

29. Growth in total on-budget expenditures at the average pace over 1995-99 (nearly 18 per cent) through 2005 would raise their ratio to GDP by nearly 7 percentage points over the 2000 level (this assumes nominal GDP growth of 10 per cent annually). If off budget spending were to remain constant as a share of GDP, total government spending would reach nearly 29 per cent of GDP by 2005. An increase of this magnitude seems unlikely, both in view of projected spending needs and the constraints likely to be imposed by available revenues.

30. In present value terms, the assumed cost is 45 per cent of 2000 GDP.

31. The scenarios here are consistent with those outlined in Lardy (2000). The outcomes there are much less favourable because it is assumed that 20 per cent of new lending by banks through 2008 becomes non-

performing and that the government has to bear the resulting cost. The more optimistic outcomes here should be viewed as conditional on banks' ability to contain NPL, not as a prediction that they necessarily will do so. This depends on the success of other financial reforms discussed in Chapters 7 and 14.

32. With the real interest rate on government debt below the real growth rate, a modest primary government deficit is consistent with a stable government debt to GDP ratio.

33. This scenario corresponds most closely to the most optimistic case described in Lardy (2000), in which it is assumed, as here, that banks are able to contain NPL.

34. As illustrated by Lardy (2000), failure to contain NPL is the most likely circumstance under which a fiscal crisis could develop in China. To illustrate, an incidence of 10 per cent on new SOCB lending in coming years (which is well below the average incidence in the past), could, under reasonable assumptions, amount to an amortised charge on public finances of several percentage points of GDP annually. If financed by additional government borrowing, public debt would continue to rise toward untenable levels in relation to GDP. Financing the charge through higher taxes or cuts in other government spending would very likely be detrimental to the development of the real economy.

35. See in particular Chapter 20 on central-local government fiscal relations.

36. Although China does not formulate official multi-year budgets, this pattern is consistent with the budget for 2001, which implies modest drop in the budget deficit. See the projections for China in the OECD (2001a).

37. Under accepted international trade practice, China is permitted to rebate value-added tax paid on domestically produced products that are exported. In practice, authorities have typically refunded only part of the tax paid but have progressively increased the rebate rate since 1997.

38. For analyses of currency crises in the European Union, see Eichengreen and Wyplosz (1993) and Funke (1996).

BIBLIOGRAPHY

Ariyoshi, A., K. Habermeier, B. Laurens, I. Ötker-Robe, J. Canales-Kriljenko, A. Kirilenko (2000),
Capital Controls: Country Experiences with Their Use and Liberalization, International Monetary Fund Occasional Paper, No. 190.

Aziz, J., F. Caramazza, R. Salgado (2000),
Currency Crises: In Search of Common Elements. International Monetary Fund Working Paper 00/67.

Chen, E.K.Y. (1997),
"The total factor productivity debate: determinants of growth in East Asia", *Asian Pacific Economic Literature*, 11:1, May.

China Financial Development Report 2000,
Shanghai University of Economics and Finance Publishing House.

Eichengreen, B., P. Masson, H. Bredenkamp, B. Johnston, J. Hamann, E. Jadresic, I. Ötker (1998),
Exit strategies; Policy options for countries seeking greater exchange rate flexibility. International Monetary Fund Occasional Paper, 168.

Eichengreen, B., C. Wyplosz (1993),
"The Unstable EMS", *Brookings Papers on Economic Activity*, 1/1993, pp. 51-143.

Frankel, J. (1999),
No Single Currency Regime Is Right for All Countries or at all times. National Bureau of Economic Research Working Paper No. 7338.

Funke, N. (1996),
"The Vulnerability of Fixed Exchange Rate Regimes: The Role of Economic Fundamentals", *OECD-Economic-Studies*; 0(26), pages 1578-76.

Furman, J., J. Stiglitz (1998),
"Economic Crises: Evidence and Insights From East Asia", *Brookings Papers on Economic Activity*, No. 2, 1-135.

Herrendorf, B. (1997),
"Importing Credibility through Exchange Rate Pegging", *The Economic Journal* 107, pp. 687-694, (May).

International Bank for Reconstruction and Development (1997),
China 2020.

International Bank for Reconstruction and Development (2000),
World development indicators, 2000

International Monetary Fund (2000),
India: recent economic developments, (December).

Krugman, P. (1994),
"The Myth of Asia's Miracle", *Foreign Affairs*, November.

Lardy, N. (2000),
"Fiscal Sustainability: between a rock and a hard place", *China Economic Quarterly*.

National Bureau of Statistics of China (2000),
China Statistical Yearbook.

OECD (2000),
Reforming China's enterprises.

OECD (2001a),
OECD *Economic Outlook*, 70 (December).

OECD (2001b),
OECD *Economic Surveys: Brazil* (July).

Oppers, S.E. (1997),
Macroeconomic cycles in China, International Monetary Fund Working Paper No. 97/135

People's Bank of China (2000),
China Financial Outlook 2000.

People's Bank of China (1998-2000),
Fiscal and Finance Issues, various issues.

Rawski, T. (2000),
China by the numbers: how reform affected Chinese economic statistics, available on the author's web site: *www.pitt.edu/~tgrawsk*, (December).

Xie, Ping (2001),
"Optimal sequence of China's financial sector reform and opening-up to the rest of the world: an institutional perspective". In Kyung T. Lee, Justin Yifu Lin, and Si Joong Kim (editors), *China's integration with the world economy: repercussions of China's accession to the* WTO, Korea Institute for International Economic Policy.

Young, A. (2000),
Gold into base metals: productivity growth in the People's Republic of China during the reform period, National Economic Bureau of Economic Research Working Paper, No. 7856, August.

Zhai, F. and S. Li (2000),
"Quantitative analysis and evaluation of the impact of entry to WTO on China's economy", *China Development Review*, Development Research Centre of the State Council of the People's Republic of China

Annex I

SUMMARY OF CHINA'S COMMITMENTS UNDER WTO

TABLE OF CONTENTS

SUMMARY OF CHINA'S COMMITMENTS UNDER WTO

China's commitments under WTO represent the consolidation of the 37 bilateral agreements with the United States, the European Union, and other WTO members. This consolidation is based on the principle of most favoured nation, under which the most favourable concession made to any one country in a given area is automatically extended to all other members. The commitments also incorporate several multilateral agreements with the WTO working party concerning modalities by which China will carry out its obligations and responsibilities. The first section of this annex provides an overview of the main elements of China's WTO accession commitments, while the second section summarises the key commitments contained in the Protocol and Working Party report.

Main elements of market access commitments

China's market access commitments include the elimination or reduction of tariff rates and relaxation of various non-tariff restrictions, including removal of barriers to imports of agricultural products, and reduction in quotas on trade in services. In overall terms, these commitments are substantially broader than those made by other developing countries that have joined the WTO.

Tariffs

Since the early 1990s, China's average tariff rate has fallen significantly from over 40 per cent to around 15 per cent, but it is still relatively high compared to the average 6 per cent tariff rate of WTO members. During the accession process, China agreed to bind all tariffs for imported goods and make substantial reductions in duties of many products.[1] After implementing all the commitments made, China's average tariff level for agricultural goods will decrease from an average of 18.9 per cent to an average of 15 per cent. The range on individual products is from 0 to 65 per cent, with the higher rates applied to cereals. For industrial goods, the average tariff will go down from an average of 14.8 per cent to 8.9 per cent with a range from 0 to 47 per cent, with the highest rates applied to photographic film and automobiles and related products. Some tariffs were eliminated upon accession, with most other reductions completed by the end of 2004, and in no case later than 2010.

Since its accession, China also participates in the Information Technology Agreement (ITA), eliminating tariffs on products such as computers, telecommunications equipment and semiconductors. Tariffs on these information technology products will be cut from an average level of 13.3 per cent to zero by 2005. China also agreed to a large reduction in tariffs for autos and auto parts that have been highly protected from import competition by high duties and various non-tariff restrictions. Tariffs on autos will fall from 80-100 per cent to 25 per cent and tariffs on auto parts reduced to an average rate of 10 per cent by 2006 (see Table A.1.1).

Non-tariff measures

Besides the reduction of tariffs, China also made commitments to phase out quotas, licenses, tendering requirements, and other quantitative restrictions that restrict trade in industrial goods – some upon accession, many others within the two following years, and the rest within five years. For example, all quotas on civil aircraft, medical equipment, and IT products were eliminated upon accession. For automobiles and key parts, quotas will rise by 15 per cent annually (initial quota value of 6 billion US$) until all licenses and quotas are eliminated by 1 January 2005.

China also committed to progressively liberalise the availability and scope of trading rights so that, within three years after accession, all enterprises in China – foreign owned and domestic – will have the right to directly sell goods throughout the customs territory of China.[2]

Table A.1.1. **Tariff reduction after China's accession to the WTO**

Sector or selected sub-sector	Level in 2001 (%)	Tariff level after WTO accession (%)	Difference between 2001 applied and agreed rates (%)
Agriculture: average	18.9	15 (1.1. 2005)	3.9
Industrial products: average	14.8	8.9 (1.1. 2005)	5.9
IT products[1]	13.3	0 (1.1. 2005)	13.3
Automobiles	80-100	25 (1.7. 2006)	55-75
Textiles and apparel	25.4	11.7 (1.1. 2005)	13.7
Steel	10.6	8.1 (1.1. 2004)	2.5

1. IT refers to information technology.
Source: OECD Secretariat estimates based on Protocol on the Accession of the People's Republic of China, Annex 8: Schedule CLII.

China's formal inclusion, as a result of its WTO membership, in the International Agreement on Textiles and Clothing (commonly known as the Multi-Fibre Agreement, or MFA) represents its primary direct gain in terms of improved access for its exports to foreign markets. As for all WTO members, the existing bilateral quotas on China's textile and clothing exports imposed under the MFA are due to be phased out by 31 December 2004. However a provision of China's bilateral agreement with the US, and which is incorporated in its accession agreement, provides for a "safeguard" mechanism lasting through 2008, under which textile-importing countries may restrict imports if they are deemed to have led to disruption of the domestic market.

Agriculture

In addition to the reduction in agricultural tariffs, China has made commitments in other areas concerning quantitative import restrictions and trade-distorting domestic subsidies.

Tariff rate quotas

Previous quantitative import restrictions on various agricultural bulk commodities such as wheat, corn, rice, sugar, and cotton will be eliminated and replaced by a tariff-rate-quota (TRQ) system under which a specified quantity will be allowed to enter at a low tariff (not to exceed 10 per cent), with imports above the limit being assessed at a higher duty (Table A.1.2). The quota limits are due to be raised annually through 2004, with the quotas for soybeans and palm oil eliminated in 2006 and replaced with a flat tariff of 9 per cent.

TRQs on a number of other products will be replaced by a single tariff rate applying regardless of the amount imported. These products include barley, soybeans, rape-seed (canola), peanut oil, sunflower seed oil, corn oil, and cottonseed oil.

Trading rights

For many goods, the right to import will be expanded beyond government agents to include non-government entities. China has agreed to phase in these expanded trading rights over three years. Trade in some goods, including wheat, corn, rice, cotton and soybean oil, will continue to be channelled through state trading enterprises (STEs). But commitments have been made to phase out STE monopolies by allocating minimum amounts of the import quotas to non-state trading enterprises, as seen in Table A.1.2. State trading will, however, continue for a range of agricultural and other key commodities, although WTO rules impose significant disciplines on the protection that state trading enterprises can provide.

Table A.1.2. **Schedule of tariff-rate quotas for agricultural products**

Product	Year[1]	Quota quantity (million metric tons)	Within-quota tariff rate (%)	Share reserved to state-trading enterprises (%)
Wheat	2001	7.88	1-10	90
	2004	9.64	1-10	90
Corn	2001	5.18	1-10	71
	2004	7.20	1-10	60
Rice	2001	3.32	1, 9	50
	2004	5.32	1, 9	50
Soybean oil[2]	2001	2.12	9	42
	2005	3.59	9	10
Palm oil[2]	2001	2.10	9	42
	2005	3.17	9	10
Rape-seed oil	2001	0.74	9	42
	2005	1.24	9	10
Sugar	2001	1.68	20	70
	2004	1.95	15	70
Wool	2001	0.25	1	
	2004	0.29	1	
Cotton	2001	0.78	1	33
	2004	0.89	1	33

1. The figures in the first row indicate volumes or rates for calendar year 2001; the year in the second row indicates the date (referring to 1 January of the year indicated) when the final quota quantity is achieved.
2. Tariff quotas to be eliminated on 1 January 2006.
Source: Protocol on the Accession of the People's Republic of China, Annex 8: Schedule CLII, Part I, Section I-B Tariff Quotas.

Export subsidies and other domestic support policies

China has committed not to use export subsidies for agricultural products. China has also committed to cap and reduce trade-distorting domestic subsidies for agricultural production.[3] It has agreed to limit its farm subsidies to 8.5 per cent of the value of farm output, as measured by the WTO's Aggregate Measurement of Support (AMS), both for general support and for each specific product.[4]

Services

China has made a broad range of commitments to open up its services sector to foreign investment and participation gradually after its entry into the WTO. Table A.1.3 summarises the main points of the agreements.

The financial services sector, previously severely restricted to foreign participation, will be opened up considerably, especially in banking and insurance. China's commitments in these, and other, sectors, concern restrictions that have applied specifically to foreign businesses, and do not directly affect regulatory and other provisions that apply to domestic as well as foreign firms.

- In banking, upon accession, foreign financial institutions were permitted to provide foreign currency services to all enterprises. Foreign financial institutions will be permitted to provide local currency services – including deposit-taking, loans, and other services – to Chinese enterprises by two years after accession. Within five years of accession, foreign financial institutions will be permitted to provide local currency services to Chinese individuals as well. Non-bank financing institutions were permitted to provide auto financing upon accession.

- In securities, foreign financial institutions' firms will be allowed to have up to a 49 per cent equity interest in domestic fund management businesses three years after accession. Foreign underwriters will be allowed to establish joint ventures, with foreign minority ownership not exceeding 33 per cent.

Table A.1.3.   **China's market access commitments in selected services sectors**

Selected sector or sub-sector	China's commitments
Financial	
Banking and other financial services	*Geographic coverage* • Foreign currency business: there are no geographic restrictions since accession. • Local currency business: geographic restrictions will be phased out as follows. Upon accession, Shanghai, Shenzhen, Tianjin and Dalian; within one year after accession, Guangzhou, Zhuhai, Qingdao, Nangjing and Wuhan; within two years after accession, Jinan, Fuzhou, Chengdu and Chongqing; within three years after accession, Kunming, Beijing and Xiamen; and within four years after accession, Shantou, Ningbo, Shenyang and Xi'an. Within five years after accession, all geographic restrictions will be removed. *Clients* • For foreign currency business, foreign financial institutions were permitted to provide services in China without restriction upon accession. • For local currency business, within two years after accession, foreign financial institutions will be permitted to provide services to Chinese enterprises. Within five years after accession, foreign financial institutions will be permitted to provide services to Chinese individuals as well. Foreign financial institutions licensed for local currency business in one region of China may service clients in any other region that has been opened for such business. *Licensing* • Foreign financial institutions with total assets of more than US$10 billion (at the end of the year prior to filing the application) are eligible to establish a subsidiary of a foreign bank or a foreign financial company in China. Such institutions are also eligible to establish a Chinese-foreign joint venture bank or finance company. Foreign financial institutions with total assets of more than US$20 billion (at the end of the year prior to filing the application) are eligible to establish a branch of a foreign bank in China. • Qualifications for foreign financial institutions to engage in local currency business are as follows: three years business operation in China and a record of positive profits for two consecutive years prior to the application. *Auto financing* • Foreign non-bank financial institutions were permitted to provide auto financing upon accession.
Securities	• Foreign securities institutions may engage directly (without Chinese intermediary) in B- share business. • Upon accession, foreign investors were permitted to establish joint ventures to conduct domestic securities investment fund management business. The maximum permitted foreign equity stake was 33 per cent upon accession, and will rise to 49 per cent within three years after accession. Within three years after accession, foreign securities institutions will be permitted to establish joint ventures, with a maximum equity stake of one third, to engage (without Chinese intermediary) in underwriting all types of shares as well as government and corporate bonds, to engage in trading of B and H-shares and bonds, and to participate in the launching of investment funds.
Insurance	*Form of establishment* • Foreign non-life insurers are permitted to establish as branches, or as joint ventures with 51 per cent ownership. • Within two years after accession, foreign non-life insurers will be permitted to establish wholly-owned subsidiaries. • Upon accession, foreign life insurers were permitted 50 per cent ownership in a joint venture with the partner of their choice. *Geographic coverage* • Upon accession, foreign life and non-life insurers, and insurance brokers were permitted to provide services in Shanghai, Guangzhou, Dalian, Shenzhen and Foshan; within two years after accession, they will be permitted to provide services in: Beijing, Chengdu, Chongqing, Fuzhou, Suzhou, Xiamen, Ningbo, Shenyang, Wuhan and Tianjin. • Within three years after accession, there will be no geographic restrictions. *Business scope* • Upon accession, foreign non-life insurers were permitted to provide "master policy" insurance/insurance of large-scale commercial risks, with no geographic restrictions. • Within 2 years after accession, foreign non-life insurers were permitted to provide the full range of non-life insurance services to both foreign and domestic clients. • Foreign insurers were permitted to provide individual (not group) insurance to foreigners and Chinese citizens upon accession. Within three years after accession, foreign insurers will be permitted to provide health insurance, group insurance and pension/annuities insurance to foreigners and Chinese citizens.

Table A.1.3. **China's market access commitments in selected services sectors** (*cont.*)

Selected sector or sub-sector	China's commitments
	Licenses • Upon accession, licenses can now be issued with no economic needs test or quantitative limits on licenses. • Qualifications for establishing a foreign owned or invested insurance institution are as follows: – The investor shall be a foreign insurance company with more than 30 years of establishment experience in a WTO member; – It shall have had a representative office for two consecutive years in China; – It shall have total assets of more than US$5 billion at the end of the year prior to application, except for insurance brokers. Minimum total assets required for establishing a foreign insurance brokerage are: US$500 million upon accession; US$400 million within one year after accession; US$300 million within two years after accession; and US$200 million within four years after accession. *Reinsurance* • The current requirement that domestic and foreign insurers must cede 20 per cent of the gross premium that they receive locally to the state-owned China Reinsurance Company will be phased out within four years after accession.

Distribution

Wholesale trade and commission agents	• Within one year after accession, foreign service suppliers may establish joint ventures to engage in the commission agents' business and wholesale business of all imported and domestically produced products, except for certain excluded items. Of these items, foreigner invested wholesale firms will be permitted to engage in distribution of books, newspapers and magazines, pharmaceutical products, pesticides, and mulching films by three years after accession, and to distribute chemical, and crude and processed oil after five years. • Within two years after accession, foreign majority ownership in distribution services will be permitted and no geographic or quantitative restrictions will apply.
Retailing (excluding tobacco)	• Upon accession, Zhengzhou and Wuhan were immediately open to joint venture retailing enterprises. Within two years after accession, foreign majority control will be permitted in joint venture retailing enterprises, which will be allowed to operate in all other provincial capitals, as well as Chongqing and Ningbo. • Foreign service providers will be permitted to engage in the retailing of all products, except for books, newspapers and magazines within one year after accession; pharmaceutical products, pesticides, mulching films and processed oil within three years after accession; chemical fertilisers within five years after accession.
Franchising and other	• Market access three years after accession.

Business

Legal	• Geographic and quantitative limitations will be eliminated within one year after accession. • All representatives shall be resident in China no less than six months each year. The representative office shall not employ Chinese lawyers registered outside of China.
Accounting, auditing and bookkeeping	• Partners or professional accountants employed by incorporated accounting firms are limited to Certified Public Accountants (CPAs) licensed by the Chinese authorities. • Foreign accounting firms are permitted to affiliate with Chinese firms. • Upon accession, issuance of licenses to those foreigners who have passed the Chinese national CPA examination are accorded national treatment.
Taxation	• Foreign firms providing tax services will be permitted to establish wholly owned subsidiaries within six years after accession.
Medical and dental	• Foreign service suppliers are permitted to establish joint venture hospitals or clinics with Chinese partners, subject to quantitative limitations in line with China's needs. Foreign majority ownership permitted. • The majority of doctors and medical personnel of joint venture hospitals and clinics shall be of Chinese nationality.
Computer and related	• Certified engineers, or personnel with bachelor's degree (or above) and three years of experience in these fields are allowed to provide services. • For software and data processing services, only joint ventures are allowed, with foreign majority ownership permitted.

Table A.1.3. **China's market access commitments in selected services sectors** (*cont.*)

Selected sector or sub-sector	China's commitments
Communication	
Courier services	• Within four years after accession, foreign service suppliers will be permitted to establish wholly-owned subsidiaries.
Tele-communications	• Upon accession, foreign service suppliers were permitted to establish joint venture value-added telecommunication enterprises, and provide services in the cities of Shanghai, Guangzhou and Beijing. Foreign investment in joint ventures shall not exceed 30 per cent.
	• Within two years after accession, geographic restrictions will be abolished and the maximum foreign equity share raised to 50 per cent.
Audio-visual	*Videos and sound recording distribution*
	• Foreign suppliers are permitted to establish contractual joint ventures with Chinese partners to engage in the distribution of audio-visual products, excluding motion pictures.
	• China allows the importation of motion pictures for theatrical release on a revenue-sharing basis, subject to an annual ceiling of 20.
	Cinema theatre
	• Foreign services providers are permitted to construct and/or renovate cinema theatres in conjunction with domestic providers, with foreign share not exceeding 49 per cent.
Tourism and travel related	
Hotels and restaurants	• Within four years after accession, wholly foreign-owned subsidiaries will be permitted.
Travel agency and tour operator	• Foreign services suppliers who meet certain conditions are permitted to provide services in the form of joint-venture travel agencies and tour operators in the holiday resorts designated by the Chinese government in the cities of Beijing, Shanghai, Guangzhou and Xi'an upon accession.
	• Within six years after accession, wholly foreign-owned subsidiaries will be permitted and geographic restrictions will be removed.

Source: Protocol on the Accession of the People's Republic of China, Annex 9: Schedule of Specific Commitments on Services.

• In the insurance sector, geographic restrictions on foreign firms will be removed altogether within three years and the scope of permitted business activities for foreign insurers will be significantly expanded. Foreign non-life insurers will be permitted to operate as wholly-owned subsidiaries within two years after accession. Foreign life insurers will be required to operate on a joint venture basis, with a maximum equity share of 50 per cent. Current restrictions on reinsurance activities by foreign as well as domestic firms will also be phased out in four years.

China has also committed to open up the distribution sector, including wholesale trade, retailing and franchising. All restrictions on distribution activities by foreign firms will be phased out for most products over three years. In telecommunications, foreign service suppliers will be permitted to invest up to 50 per cent in joint ventures within two years after accession, and geographic restrictions on their activities will be removed by that time. Business services, including legal, auditing, accounting, computer, and rental and leasing services, will also be gradually opened up to foreign participation over the next six years.

Protocol and working party report commitments

China's WTO membership negotiations also took place in the multilateral framework of the WTO Working Party, whose focus was to ensure that China would conform its trade regime to all the rules, practices, and obligations required by WTO agreements. The results of these multilateral negotiations were finalised in an accession protocol and working party report that outline the terms of China's membership.

Trade framework

Administration of the trade regime: China has committed to ensure uniform and transparent administration of its trade regime subject to judicial review. The provisions of WTO Agreement and the Protocol apply uniformly to the entire customs territory of China, including border trade regions and minority autonomous areas, Special Economic Zones, open coastal cities, economic and technical development zones and other areas where special regimes for tariffs, taxes and regulations are established (collectively referred to as "special economic areas"). China's local regulations, rules and other measures of local governments at the sub-national level will conform to the obligations undertaken in the WTO Agreement and the Protocol.

Special economic areas: Imports by the special economic areas will receive the same treatment as other imports. China will notify the WTO within 60 days of any changes in trade measures pertaining to special economic areas.

Special trade arrangements: Upon accession, China had to eliminate or bring into conformity with the WTO Agreement all special trade arrangements, including barter trade arrangements, with third countries and separate customs territories that are not in conformity with the WTO Agreement.

Right to trade: China is committed to progressively liberalise the right to trade, so that all enterprises in China will have the right to import and export goods throughout the customs territory of China, subject to exceptions for some designated goods where state trading enterprises are given preference. The government is also obligated to ensure that import purchasing procedures of state trading enterprises are finally transparent and in compliance with the WTO Agreement.

Economic policies

Non-discrimination: Foreign individuals and enterprises and foreign-funded enterprises are accorded treatment no less favourable than that accorded to other individuals and enterprises with respect to: a) the procurement of inputs and goods and services necessary for production and the conditions under which goods are produced, marketed or sold in the domestic market and for export; and b) the prices and availability of goods and services supplied by national and sub-national authorities and public or state enterprises, in areas including transportation, energy, basic telecommunications, other utilities and factors of production.

Subsidies: China has committed to implement the Agreement on Subsidies and Countervailing Measures (SCM). It had to eliminate, upon accession, all export subsidies as well as all subsidies contingent upon the use of domestic rather than imported goods, except for those exceptions specified in the Agreement.[5] Value-added tax rebates will be applied only to exported products and not to domestically consumed products.

State-owned and state-invested enterprises: China will seek to ensure that all state-owned and state-invested enterprises make purchases and sales based solely on commercial considerations, *e.g.* price, quality, marketability and availability. In addition, the government will not influence, directly or indirectly, commercial decisions by state-owned or state-invested enterprises, including those pertaining to the quantity, value or country of origin of any goods purchased or sold, except in a manner consistent with the WTO Agreement.

Price controls: China has committed to allow prices for traded goods and services in every sector to be determined by market forces, subject to certain exceptions specified in the accession agreement, and to eliminate multi-tier pricing practices for such goods and services. It will publish in an official journal list of goods and services subject to state pricing and changes thereto.

Foreign exchange and payments: China will carry out its obligations with respect to foreign exchange (forex) transactions in accordance with the provisions of the WTO Agreement and other related declarations and decisions of the WTO. China agrees to current account convertibility under the terms of Article VIII of the IMF's Articles of Agreement, which provides that "no member shall, without the approval of the Fund, impose restrictions on the making of payments and transfers for current international transactions".

Trade-related investment measures: China agreed to fully comply with the Trade-Related Investment Measures (TRIMs) Agreement upon accession, which required the elimination of trade-restrictive and distorting investment measures, *i.e.* those that required local content or trade balancing or those that restricted a firm's access to foreign exchange or level of exports. China has committed to ensure that the distribution of import licences, quotas, tariff-rate quotas, or any forms of import approval applied by national or sub-national authorities, are not subject to conditions such as the existence of competing domestic suppliers, or performance requirements of any kind, such as local content, offsets, technology transfer, export performance or the conduct of research and development in China.

Trade-related intellectual property regime

China agreed to implement the WTO's Agreement on Trade-Related Intellectual Property Rights (TRIPs) in full from the date of accession. This agreement defines both the scope and enforcement procedures of intellectual property rights in various areas including copyrights, trademarks, patents, geographic indications, industrial designs, layout designs of integrated circuits, protection of undisclosed information, and control of anti-competitive practices in contracts.

The government also had to make amendments to its Patent Law, Copyright Law and the Trademark Law, as well as relevant implementing rules covering different areas of the TRIPs Agreement, upon accession. China has also committed to modify relevant laws, regulations and other measures in compliance with the TRIPs agreement so as to ensure national and most-favoured nation for intellectual property rights for foreigner holders.

Standards and regulatory measures

Import and export licensing: China has agreed to implement the WTO Agreement and provisions of the Agreement on Import Licensing Procedures. Procedures used for licensing will be made transparent and formulated and applied so that they do not restrict trade unduly. Foreign individuals and foreign-owned or funded enterprises will be accorded treatment no less favourable than that accorded to other individuals and enterprises in the distribution of import and export licenses and quotas.

Technical barriers to trade: China will, upon accession, bring into compliance with the Technical Barriers to Trade (TBT) Agreement all technical regulations, standards and conformity assessment procedures. Upon accession, China is committed to ensure that the same technical regulations, standards and conformity assessment procedures are applied to both imported and domestic products.

The government was also obligated to notify the WTO within 30 days after accession about all laws, regulations and other measures relating to its *sanitary and phytosanitary standards*, including product coverage and relevant international standards, guidelines and recommendations.

Compliance and safeguard mechanisms

Price comparability in determining subsidies and dumping: China has agreed to allow WTO members to use either Chinese prices or an alternative methodology in determining dumping, subsidies and countervailing measures. In anti-dumping cases, this provision will expire 15 years after accession.

Transitional safeguard mechanism: China has agreed to allow WTO members to avail themselves of a product-specific safeguard process to regulate import levels of specific products in the event of market disruptions from surges of Chinese imports for a duration of 12 years following China's accession. In textiles and clothing, the safeguard mechanism will be available until the end of 2008.

Transitional review mechanism: Within one year after accession, the relevant subsidiary bodies of the WTO will review the implementation by China of the WTO Agreement and of the related provisions of the Protocol. China can also raise issues relating to the reservations or any other specific commitments made by other Members in the Protocol in those subsidiary bodies.

NOTES

1. China's specific market accession commitments are detailed in the Schedule of Concessions and Commitments on Goods annexed to the Protocol on its WTO accession.

2. Annex 2A of the Protocol lists those goods which continue to be subject to state trading in accordance with the Protocol. According to the Annex, China will maintain import state trading for wheat, corn, rice, vegetable oils, sugar, tobacco, crude and processed oils, chemical fertiliser, and cotton. In addition, China will maintain export state trading for tea, rice, corn, soy bean, coal, crude and processed oils, silk and unbleached silk, a variety of cotton products, and several kinds of tungsten and ammonium products.

3. In the WTO Agreement on Agriculture, domestic support measures that have, at most, a minimal impact on trade ("green box" policies) are excluded from reduction commitments. Such policies include general government services, for example in the areas of research, disease control, infrastructure and food security. It also includes direct payments to producers, for example certain forms of income support, structural adjustment assistance, direct payments under environmental programmes and under regional assistance programmes.

4. The WTO Agreement on Agriculture limits the total AMS to 5 per cent in the case of developed countries and 10 per cent in the case of developing countries. In addition to the green box policies, other policies might not be included in the AMS, including: direct payments under production-limiting programmes; certain government assistance measures to encourage agricultural and rural development in developing countries; and other support which makes up only a low proportion of the value of production of individual products or the value of total agricultural production.

5. The SCM Agreement recognises "non-actionable" subsidies, which include subsidies involving assistance to industrial research and pre-competitive development activity, assistance to disadvantaged regions, or certain type of assistance for adapting existing facilities to new environmental requirements imposed by law and/or regulations.

Annex II

SUMMARY OF STUDIES OF THE IMPACT OF WTO ON CHINA

TABLE OF CONTENTS

SUMMARY OF STUDIES OF THE IMPACT OF WTO ON CHINA[1]

Abstract

This annex provides an overview and comparison of major studies written between 1996 and 2000 that use some type of computable general equilibrium (CGE) model to estimate the effects on China's economy from its accession to the World Trade Organisation (WTO). Many of the studies listed use the Global Trade Analysis Project (GTAP), a project conducted at Purdue University that provides a model for world trade and production.

A study that estimates the welfare costs of China's protectionist trade polices on 25 product sectors is also reviewed. While it does not specifically address China's WTO accession, it may provide some additional insight into the possible effects of trade liberalisation in China. Also reviewed are studies that attempt to measure services trade barriers in China, although they do not specifically address China's WTO offers on services. Finally, various articles that assess certain economic aspects of China's WTO accession are listed, although the details of their analysis are generally not available.

The major findings of the studies differ markedly, but the majority of them indicate major gains to China's economy from its WTO accession, especially through efficiency gains. However, trade liberalisation will likely create both winners and losers. Most of the studies project that China's textile and apparel sectors would benefit greatly from China's WTO accession, due to the phase-out and removal of quotas on China's textile and apparel exports that would occur with China's accession. On the other hand, some heavy industry sectors, such as autos, and certain land-intensive agricultural sectors, such as wheat and corn, may contract as a result of China's WTO entry.

Most of the studies limit their analysis to the effects of China's tariff cut offers and the removal of textile and apparel quotas on Chinese exports; they generally do not address the full range of trade liberalisation measures (such as the removal of non-tariff barriers and reducing restrictions on foreign investment) that China has committed to in bilateral and multilateral trade negotiations for WTO membership. In addition, of the 36 bilateral agreements China has concluded with WTO members, only the November 1999 US-China WTO agreement has been made available. *Thus it is likely that most of the studies reviewed significantly understate the likely effects of China's WTO accession.*

This annex is divided into three sections. The first section provides a summary of China's current trade regime and describes issues that were addressed in negotiations for its WTO accession. The second section provides an overview and comparison of the major findings of the various studies in regard to projected effects on the economy as a whole as well as on various sectors. The concluding remarks in the third section include an evaluation of the models used to analyse the effects of China's WTO accession.

China's trade regime

China has been negotiating to become a member of the General Agreement on Tariffs and Trade (GATT), and its successor organisation, the WTO, since 1986. In preparation for membership, China has, over time, slashed tariffs and removed a number of non-tariff barriers. The simple average Chinese tariff rate has been reduced from 42.9 per cent in 1992 to 23.6 per cent in 1996 to 17.5 per cent in 1999 (weighted averages tend to be slightly higher). The Chinese government stated that average tariffs fell to 16.5 per cent in 1999 and to 15.3 per cent at the beginning of 2001.

Despite recent reductions in trade barriers, China remains a difficult market to penetrate for many foreign firms due largely to Chinese government policies that attempt to protect and promote domestic industries. Chinese trade policies generally attempt to encourage imports of products which are deemed beneficial to China's economic development and growth (and which generally are not produced in China), such as high technology, as well as machinery and raw materials used in the manufacture of products for export. In many cases, preferential trade policies are used to encourage these priority imports. Goods and services not considered to be high priority, or which compete directly with domestic Chinese firms, often face an extensive array of tariff and non-tariff barriers. Such policies make it difficult to export products directly to China. As a result, many foreign firms have established production facilities in China to gain access to its market, although they face a wide variety of barriers as well. Major Chinese barriers **before WTO** included:

- *High tariffs on selected products.* While average tariffs have fallen, they remained high for selected items, such as autos and various agricultural products, which can rise to over 100 per cent.

- *Restrictions on agriculture.* China utilised a number of non-tariff barriers, including quotas and tariff rate quotas, (*i.e.*, application of a higher tariff rate to imported goods after a specified quantity of the item has entered the country at a lower prevailing rate), trading rights limits (*i.e.*, exclusive right to import given to selected firms or agencies), license requirements, and restrictive sanitary and phytosanitary (SPS) standards, to limit agricultural imports in order to protect domestic producers.

- *Restrictive non-tariff measures* (NTMs) *on industrial goods.* China used NTMs (such as quotas, tendering requirements, import licenses, import substitution policies, and registration and certification requirements) to control the level of certain manufactured imports into China. While China removed over 1,000 quotas and licenses on selected products under a 1992 market access agreement with the United States, as of late 1997, it officially maintained NTMs on 385 tariff-line items.

- *Restrictions on services.* China's services sectors (such as banking, insurance, telecommunications, and various professional services) are heavily regulated by the government and were largely closed to foreign service providers, except for a few firms that are allowed to operate in certain cities on an experimental basis.

- *Non-transparent trade rules and regulations.* Despite efforts by the government to improve transparency, several problems remain. China's trade laws and regulations were often secretly formulated, unpublished, unevenly enforced, and variable across provinces, making it difficult for exporters to determine what rules and regulations apply to their products. In addition, foreign firms found it difficult to gain access to government trade rule-making agencies to appeal new trade rules and regulations.

- *Trading rights.* China restricted the number and types of entities in China that are allowed to import products into China, which limits the ability of both Chinese and foreign firms in China to obtain imported products. Foreign companies were not permitted to directly engage in trade in China.

- *Distribution rights.* Most foreign companies were prohibited from selling their products directly to Chinese consumers.

- *Investment restrictions.* Foreign investors had to agree to contract provisions, which stipulate technology transfers, exporting a certain share of production, and commitments on local content. Other problems faced by foreign firms in China included the denial of national treatment (*i.e.*, foreign firms are treated less favourably than domestic firms), foreign exchange controls, distribution and marketing restrictions, and the lack of rule of law.

- *Lack of national treatment and other discriminatory policies.* In addition to the tariff and non-tariff barriers cited above, China conditions, or imposes restrictions, on participation in the Chinese economy based upon the nationality of the entity concerned.

Comparison of major findings from studies that examine the economic effects of China's WTO accession

Macroeconomic effects

Table A.2.1 provides a summary of projections from ten of the major studies surveyed on changes to China's GDP and economic welfare resulting from its accession to the WTO. Table A.2.2 lists projected

Table A.2.1. **Projections of changes to China's GDP and economic welfare from Its WTO accession**

	GDP		Economic Welfare	
	Static	Static + growth	Static	Static + growth
Yang (1996) 3 scenarios: 1) Developing, 2) Developed, 3) All tariffs cut to 10% (change from 1992 tariffs) Change over baseline: 2005 ($1992)	1) 4.0% 2) 4.4% 3) 7.7%		1) $18 billion 2) $19 billion 3) $27 billion	
Anderson (1997)1995 weighted average tariffs are cut from 30% in 1995 to 16% by 2005. Change over baseline: 2005 ($1992)			$27 billion (3.0%)	
Bach *et al.* (1997) Ave. weighted tariff cut from 30.4% in 1992 to 16.1% in 2005. Change over baseline: 2005 ($1992)			$17-31 billion, depending on how tariff exemptions are modeled	
Wang (1997)1996 tariff rates cut by 35%. Baseline year: 1992 ($1992)			$10 billion	$20 billion
USITC (1999), China's April 1999 offer (tariffs only)* Baseline year: 1998 ($1998)	0.9%	4.1%	–$2.9 billion	$20 billion
Li and Lejour (1999) (Tariffs only) All tariffs eliminated in 2010 Baseline year : 2020 ($1992)	–0.7		$30 billion	
World Bank I (2000) Nov. 1999 US-China Agreement (Cuts from 1997 tariff levels) Baseline year: 2005 ($1995)			$28.6 billion	
Fan and Zheng (2000)Nov. 1999 US-China Agreement (tariffs only) Baseline year: 1998	0.06%	0.6%		
Zhai and Li (2000) 1997 tariff levels cut 40% from 1998-2000, removal of certain non-tariff barriers, and replace all agric. quotas with a flat 10% tariff Baseline year: 2005	1.5%		1.2%	
Lejour (2000)1995 tariffs are cut 50% and certain non-tariff barriers removed. 3 tariff models: 1) statutory rates, 2) average applied rate 3) estimated applied exemptions for intermediate and investment goods. Baseline year: 2020 ($1995)	1) 2.1% 2) 1.4% 3) 1.7%		() $53 billion 2) $10 billion 3) $8 billion	

*   The USITC study separately examined the effects of eliminating textile and apparel export quotas on China's economy, projecting the phase-out in 2010 would raise GDP by $9.2 billion and economic welfare by $8.4 billion.

changes to exports and imports from WTO accession from six of the studies. Most of these studies predict that China's WTO accession would boost its GDP, economic welfare, and trade. However, the magnitude of these results vary widely across studies due to a number of factors, such as the different model specification, the different assumptions to project a baseline, and differences in time periods utilised. Other major factors that appear to affect the results of these studies include:

- *Whether (or not) the phase-out of quotas on China's textile and apparel exports that would occur with China's WTO accession is factored into the analysis.* Studies that factor in the elimination of the China's textile and apparel export quotas in their simulations generally found significantly higher gains to GDP and trade than those studies that excluded consideration of the quota phase-out.[2] For example Li and Lejour (1999) exclude consideration of the elimination of quotas in their analysis, focusing only on China's tariff reductions (which they simulated to be reduced to zero by 2010). Their analysis estimated that, while this scenario would result in consumer welfare gains of $30 billion by 2010, it would lead to a 0.7 per cent reduction in GNP. Fan and Zheng (2000) also excluded consideration of the export quota phase-out in their analysis of the November 1999 US-China WTO agreement, estimating that WTO accession would raise real GDP by only 0.06 per cent. On the other hand, the USITC (1999) separately examined the economic effects of eliminating the export quotas, estimating that in 2010, China's GDP and economic welfare would rise by $9.2 billion and

Table A.2.2. **Projections of changes to China's exports and imports from its WTO accession**

	Export Volume		Import Volume	
	Static	Static + growth	Static	Static + growth
Yang (1996) 3 scenarios: 1) Developing, 2) Developed, and 3) All tariffs cut to 10% Change over baseline: 2005 ($1992)	1) 30% 2) 35% 3) 81%		1) 36% 2) 46% 3) 119%	
Anderson (1997) 1995 weighted average tariffs are cut from 30% in 1995 to 16% by 2005 Change over baseline: 2005 ($1992)	$61 billion		$47 billion	
Wang (1997) 1996 tariff rates cut by 35%. Baseline year: 1992 ($1992)	$62 billion	$66 billion	$44 billion	$48 billion
USITC (1999), China's April 1999 offer (tariffs only)* Baseline year: 1998	10.1%	12.2%	11.9%	14.%
Fan and Zheng (2000) Nov. 1999 US-China Agreement (tariffs only) Baseline year: 1998	5.7%	5.4%	7.3%	9.1%
Lejour (2000) 1995 tariffs are reduced by 50% and certain non-tariff barriers removed. Three tariff models: 1) statutory rates, 2) average applied rate 3) estimated applied exemptions for intermediate and investment goods. Baseline year: 2020	26.9%		25.8%	

* The USITC study separately examined the effects on China's economy from eliminating quotas on China's textile and apparel exports, projecting the phase-out would increase exports by $16.3 billion and imports by $10.9 billion.

$8.4 billion respectively, and trade volume would increase by $27.2 billion. This would seem to indicate that the phase-out of the quotas on China's textile and apparel exports would have a major effect on the Chinese economy.[3]

- *Differences in assumptions on the magnitude of tariff cuts as well as how these are factored in across sectors.* Assumptions on tariff cuts range from 26 per cent to 100 per cent, and studies differ according to which year's tariff schedule was used to compare with the estimated amount of tariff cuts.[4] A survey of the studies shows a strong correlation between the level of assumed liberalisation used to analyse China's WTO accession and the degree to which economic welfare is projected to rise as a result of liberalisation.[5] In addition, several studies simply apply an across-the board tariff cut to all sectors, while others (primarily those that use details of the November 1999 US-China WTO agreement) apply different tariff cuts to different sectors. These factors may also affect various estimates of the effects of China's trade liberalisation.

- *Whether or not China's use of tariff exemptions on certain imports is factored into the analysis.* Several studies, including those done by Bach *et al.* (1999), The World Bank II (2000), and Lejour (2000), indicate that China maintains a unique trade regime *vis-à-vis* the rest of the world. A large share of imported products used by export-oriented firms and foreign-invested firms in China receive preferential tariff treatment. Many of these imports enter the country duty-free or are subject to reduced duties. The World Bank estimates that in 1998 only around 25 per cent of all imports entered as ordinary trade, subject to normal customs. Thus, China's effective tariff rates appear to be far below statutory tariff rates. Several studies estimate that failure to account for these tariff exemptions could significantly overstate (or in some cases understate) the economic impact of China's tariff reductions.[6] Some studies try to factor in China's tariff exemptions in their simulations. Different approaches are used. One approach applies the overall effective tariff rate (*i.e.*, the value of all tariffs collected divided by the value of imports) to all imports in the simulations. A second method attempts to factor in the tariff exemptions applied to certain products, while applying the statutory rates to imports not covered by preferential policies.[7]

- *The use of static, versus dynamic, measurements of the effects of trade liberalisation.* Most of the studies estimate the static gains from trade liberalisation, that is, the economic benefits caused by efficiency gains through a more efficient use of resources. Other studies, including Wang (1997), USITC (1999), and Fan and Zheng (2000) estimate the static, as well as the dynamic growth effects of trade liberalisation; the latter includes the additional growth that may occur when static growth produces additional income and savings, which increases capital stock and hence promotes greater economic growth. The estimates for dynamic plus growth gains from trade liberalisation are generally much larger than the data on the static effects. For example, USITC (1999) estimated the static gains to China's GDP from the tariff provisions of its April 1999 offer at 0.9 per cent; this figure rises to 4.1 per cent when dynamic effects are introduced. The same result occurs with economic welfare: under a static model, China's economic welfare declines by nearly $3 billion (due to a decline in China's terms of trade), but under the dynamic model, economic welfare increases by $20 billion, due to long term rises in incomes. Wang (1997) found that the dynamic growth estimates of gains to China's economic welfare was double that of the static estimate ($20 billion versus $10 billion). The USITC (1999), in its analysis of the effects of the MFA quota phase-out, estimated that China would increase imports of capital-intensive equipment, which would produce greater gains in total factor productivity for the economy as a whole. Thus, it appears that studies that only measure static gains may understate the long-term gains for China from its WTO accession.

Studies that predict large gains to GDP from WTO accession state that reforms enhance efficiency of resource allocation through increased specialisation according to comparative advantage. In addition, the removal of high protective rates would be equivalent to a real depreciation, enhancing international competitiveness of China's industries, while eliminating the export quotas on China's textile and apparel products would further increase the competitiveness of those sectors, boosting their exports.

Some studies predict some short-term disruption in China's economy, due to increased competition and the reallocation of resources away from protected and/or less competitive sectors to sectors where China has more of a comparative advantage. For example, analysis by Zhai and Li (2000) predict that (under their assumptions of trade liberalisation) WTO membership would displace 9.6 million rural agricultural workers, but that millions of jobs would be created in light industry (especially textiles and apparel) and service sectors. The same study predicted that trade liberalisation would increase income disparity between rural and urban areas. This indicates that trade liberalisation, while beneficial in the long-run, could be somewhat painful for some sectors in the short run, and may require government action to help smooth out this transition.

As noted, most of the studies that examined China's WTO accession failed to consider in their analysis the full range of trade barriers (*i.e.*, tariff and non-tariff barriers) that China erects against imports, and the potential effects that would result from their removal. However, an Institute for International Economics (IIE) study examined the combined costs of tariff and non-tariff barriers on 25 major industries in China in 1994 and concluded that the static benefits to consumers from full liberalisation of these sectors would amount to $35 billion, about 6.2 per cent of GNP. The study further estimated that if the entire Chinese economy was liberalised, static welfare benefits could reach $79 billion, or 14 per cent of GNP. While somewhat outdated (since China has removed several non-tariff barriers since 1994), this study indicates that China's non-tariff barriers are substantial and that their removal would likely have a significant impact on China's economy.

Effects on industry

Most of the studies rely on models that reflect classic economic theory to project possible effects of China's WTO accession on its industrial sectors. For example, most studies indicate that China has a comparative advantage in labour-intensive production *vis-à-vis* the rest of the world, but has less of an advantage in land and capital. Hence, it is argued that China's economy would gain significantly if it focused more of its resources on labour-intensive industries, and trade for those products where it does not have a comparative advantage (*i.e.*, land-intensive and capital-intensive products). Various studies document how China uses a variety of trade barriers in order to promote the development of industries it deems necessary for China's economic development, but state that such barriers distort the most efficient use of resources throughout the economy.

While the removal of trade barriers is expected to provide overall gains to the economy, such reforms would likely produce both "winners" and "losers"; that is, some industries will expand, while other will contract.[8] However, as previously noted, most of the studies limit their analysis to the effects of cuts in tariff barriers and the elimination of quotas on China's textile and apparel exports, but do not measure the effects of the reduction of non-tariff barriers.[9] Thus, such studies fail to capture the full extent of the effects of China's WTO accession on its industries.[10]

The projected effects on China's industrial sectors from its WTO accession differ across studies, due in part to different assumptions used on the degree of liberalisation that would take place from China's accession. Fan and Zheng (1999) state that the effects of WTO entry on various sectors depend largely on whether an industry is domestic-oriented or export-oriented. If an industry is export-oriented, it would likely benefit from China's trade liberalisation. If the industry is domestic-oriented, then trade liberalisation could negatively affect that sector. The majority of studies project the textile and apparel sectors to be the biggest "winners" in terms of increased output, while heavy industry sectors, such as the auto/transportation sector, are projected to be the biggest "losers" from trade liberalisation.[11] The remaining part of this section examines the projected effects of WTO accession on China's textile, apparel, and road vehicle sectors. Additional information and data on the effects on other sectors can be found in Box A.2.1.

Textiles and apparel

Nearly all of the studies indicate that China's textile and apparel sectors would gain substantially from China's WTO accession, mainly because China's exports of such products are currently sharply limited by quotas imposed by developed countries.[12] Under the Uruguay Round's Agreement on Textile and Clothing (ATC), WTO members agreed to phase out and eliminate, over a 10-year period (1995-2005), quota arrangements with other WTO members that were originally authorised under the Multi-Fibre Agreement (MFA).[13]

Limitations on Chinese exports under the MFA are believed to have had a significant effect on the size and growth of China's textile and apparel industries (since this sector is very export-oriented). In addition, since China only recently became a member of the WTO, it has not benefited from the expansion of quotas that have taken place under the ATC since 1995, while current members of the WTO have been able to expand their exports of such products.[14]

China's accession to the WTO will enable it to enjoy the phase-out of the MFA quotas. Many of the studies indicate that, because production of textiles and clothing is labour-intensive (where China enjoys a comparative advantage), the lowering of trade barriers would lead to significant increases in China's output and exports of such products.[15] However, the November 1999 US-China agreement also includes provisions that would enable the United States (and presumably all WTO members once all negotiations are completed), to employ safeguard provisions (for 12 years) to limit textile and apparel imports from China if an increase of such imports caused or threatened to cause market disruption to domestic industries. The use of such safeguards against Chinese imports could limit (or delay) the potential gains from increased output and exports of textile and apparel productions that would otherwise result from China's WTO accession.[16]

Table A.2.3 summarises the major findings of the studies that include the phase-out of MFA quotas in their simulations on the effects of China's WTO accession.[17] They show that WTO accession would have a significant effect on China's textile and apparel sectors, although the extent of such effects varies from study to study (especially for textiles) due in part to different assumptions used. Nearly all of the studies that factored in the effects of removing the MFA quotas predicted that textile and apparel would be by far the biggest overall winners from China's WTO accession in terms of increased production, exports, and employment. Yang (1996) determined that textiles and clothing would be the only expanding industries under WTO accession; nearly all other industrial sectors would decline. Wang (1997) estimated that China's exports of textiles and apparel would increase by nearly $62 billion (in 1992 dollars) with WTO accession, constituting 95 per cent of the total increased exports that would result from trade liberalisation, and that China would more than double its share of world exports of these products (from 14 per cent to 30 per cent). Zhai and Li (2000) project that WTO accession will raise employment in the apparel and textile sectors by 3.6 million and 2.8 million, respectively in 2005. Output and exports of apparel/clothing increases sharply under all of the studies in Table A.2.3.[18]

Output of textiles (when this sector is separated out from apparel) increases in a majority of the simulations in Table A.2.3 with the exception of the first model in Lejour (2000) when nominal tariffs are cut in half. This would cause textile output to decline by 16 per cent in 2020 relative to the baseline. However, if tariff exemptions granted to intermediate imports intermediates are factored in, textile output is predicted to increase by between 1 and 6 per cent. Textile imports increase significantly in each simulation due largely to the expansion of the apparel/clothing sector.

Table A.2.3. **Projected effects of WTO entry on Chinese textile and apparel sectors**

Study	Output	Employment	Exports	Imports	Comments
Yang (1996) 3 scenarios: 1) Developing 2) Developed 3) All tariffs cut to 10% Change over baseline: 2005	Clothing: 1) 246% 2) 253% 3) 335% Textiles: 1) 35% 2) 37% 3) 4%				These are the only two sectors that expand under WTO accession.
Wang (1997) Change over baseline: 1992 Static plus growth measurement			Combined textiles and apparel: $62 billion (accounts for 95% of total increase in exports form WTO entry)	$18 billion (accounts for 38% of total increase in exports form WTO entry)	Share of world exports more than doubles (from 14% to 30%).
Wang (1999) % change over baseline: 2010	Clothing: 44% Textiles: 12%	Clothing: 39% Textiles: 6%	Clothing: 67% Textiles: 18%	Clothing: 37% Textiles: 112%	
World Bank I (2000) 1995-2005 % growth rate without WTO entry and with WTO entry.	Apparel No WTO: 7% WTO:264% Textiles No WTO: 2% WTO: 88%		Apparel No WTO: 5% WTO: 375% Textiles: No WTO: 45% WTO: 107%	Apparel: No WTO: 58% WTO: 818% Textiles: No WTO: 87% WTO: 272%	
Zhai and Li (2000) change over baseline: 2005 ($1995)	Apparel: $63 billion (74%) Textiles: $47 billion (26%)	Apparel: 3.6 mil. Textiles: 2.8 mil.	Apparel: $59 billion (214%) Textiles: $22 billion (64%)	Apparel: $1 billion (124%) Textiles: $19. billion (86%)	
Lejour (2000)50% tariff cut using 3 models: 1) full tariffs, 2) reduced tariffs, 3) exempted % change over baseline: 2020	Apparel: 1) 60% 2) 55% 3) 55% Textiles: 1) −16% 2) 1% 3) 6%				The effect of trade liberalisation on textiles is strongly affected by how tariff exemptions are modelled.

Road vehicles

Several of the studies indicate that China's output of road vehicles will be significantly affected by China's WTO accession, mainly because of the sharp cut in tariffs on imports in this sector that are expected to occur after accession, and because the sector is relatively capital intensive (rather than labour intensive where China has more of a comparative advantage). Table A.2.4 provides simulation results from five studies on the effects of WTO accession on China's road vehicles sector. Output decreases sharply in nearly all of the simulations. The World Bank I (2000) projects that without WTO accession, output of automobiles would increase by 190 per cent from 1995-2005, but with accession, output would decline by 4 per cent. Wang (1999) and Zhai and Li (2000) project that motor vehicle output would decline by 21 per cent and 15 per cent respectively, compared to their baseline estimates. Yang (1996) projects output of transport equipment would fall under two scenarios (when tariffs are cut by 26 per cent and 36 per cent) from its baseline projection in 2005, but under scenario 3, when all tariffs are reduced to 10 per cent, output increases by 27 per cent. The increase in output under scenario 3 results from big cuts in the costs of intermediate inputs used by the industry.[19] Lejour (2000) estimates that a 50 per cent cut in nominal tariffs would cause China's output of motor vehicles to fall by 62 per cent. However, if tariff exemptions that are given to intermediate goods are factored in (to reflect estimates that applied tariffs are lower than statutory tariffs), then output falls by half as much (around 30 per cent).

Wang (1999) estimated that employment in the motor vehicles sector would fall by 24 per cent, while Zhai and Li projected employment would drop by 15 per cent (or 500,000 workers). The same studies project that sector imports would rise sharply from WTO accession: 136 per cent in Wang (1999) and 105 per cent ($5 billion) in Zhai and Li (2000).[20] Wang (1999) and the World Bank I (2000) estimated that, despite decreases in output to motor vehicles, exports of such products would rise, due to improvements

Table A.2.4. **Projected effects of WTO entry on China's road vehicle sector***

Study	Output	Employment	Exports	Imports	Comments
Yang (1996) (transport equipment) 3 scenarios: 1) Developing 2) Developed 3) All tariffs cut to 10%. % Change over baseline: 1992	1) −21% 2) −15% 3) 27%				Output of transport equipment increases under 3) due to big cut in costs of intermediate inputs to the industry.
Wang 1999 (motor vehicles) % change over baseline: 2010	−21%	−24%	45%	136%	
World Bank I (2005) (autos) 1995-2005 % growth rate without WTO Entry and With WTO Entry.	No WTO: 190% WTO: −4%		No WTO: 648% WTO: 2,523%	No WTO: 25% WTO: 556%	
Zhai and Li (2000) change over baseline: 2005 ($1995)	−$9.8 billion (−15%)	−0.5 billion (−15%)	-$0.1 billion (−8%)	$5 billion (105%)	
Lejour (2000) (motor vehicles) 50% tariff cut using 3 models: 1) full tariffs, 2) reduced tariffs, 3) exempted imports % change over baseline in 2020	(1) −62% (2) −31% (3) −30%				Modeling for tariff exemptions under 2) and 3) sharply reduces the level of projected losses in 1)

* Studies listed used different classifications for road vehicles, and hence, comparative data should be interpreted with caution.

in efficiency from trade liberalisation. However, Zhai and Li (2000) project exports would decline by 15 per cent ($0.5 billion) with trade liberalisation.

Effects on agriculture

The effects on China's agricultural sectors from its WTO accession appear to be somewhat more difficult to measure than the effects on industrial sectors due largely to the complex nature of China's protectionist policies on agriculture. In addition to high tariffs on many agricultural products, agriculture also relies on subsidies and a wide variety of non-tariff barriers to protect domestic production. In general, China's non-tariff barriers and use of subsidies appear to be significantly more effective in restricting agricultural imports than tariff barriers.

Several economic models, such as the GTAP, do not contain data on the effects of China's non-tariff barriers. The studies that focused only on the effects of tariff barriers on agricultural products generally found that WTO accession would have a relatively minor effect on China's agricultural sectors, while those studies that included the effects of subsidies and tariff and non-tariff barriers estimated their removal or reduction would have a significant effects on production and trade of certain commodities.

Many of the studies state that China's agricultural policies have caused Chinese farmers to concentrate on the production of land-intensive crops (such as wheat, corn, and oilseeds), where it does not hold a comparative advantage, and away from the production of labour-intensive crops (such as fruit and vegetables) where it does have a comparative advantage. It appears that such policies are mainly geared towards keeping China relatively self-sufficient in grain production. However, these policies are costly to the Chinese economy because domestic prices for agricultural products (such as corn and wheat) are above world prices.[21] Such policies also prevent resources from going to more productive sectors of the economy.

Most of the studies project that the importance of agricultural production (and export) to China's economy (output and export) will decline in the future (under their baseline projection) and that China's accession to the WTO will accelerate this trend (although they differ on the extent of changes). For example, Anderson (1997) notes that agriculture's output as a share of total output has declined sharply since the 1970s. He projects that agriculture's share of China's total output would decline by 42 per cent between 1992 and 2005 (from 22 per cent to 13 per cent) without WTO entry. With WTO accession, the decline in agriculture's output share would slightly accelerate to 46 per cent.[22]

Several studies found a strong correlation between the elimination of MFA quotas on Chinese textile and apparel exports and changes to China's agricultural production and trade. For example, Wang (1999) estimates that the elimination of MFA quotas on China's exports would lead to a substantial boost in Chinese production, employment, and exports of textile and apparel products. He states that the expansion of the labour-intensive manufacturing sector would bid productive resources away from farming, boost domestic demand for food products, and increase agricultural imports (while decreasing exports). Wang (1999) estimated that production and employment in wheat, other grains, and plant fibres (such as cotton) would fall and imports of these products would rise substantially.[23]

Non-tariff barriers

Some of the studies attempt to factor in the effects of cutting non-tariff barriers to agricultural trade. Huang *et al.* (1999) examined the effects of fully liberalising China's trade regime for agriculture by eliminating tariffs, non-tariff barriers, and subsidies for seven grain products (rice, wheat, maize, soybean, sweet potato, potato, and other grains) and seven animal products (pork, beef, mutton, poultry, egg, milk, and fish) between 2000 and 2005. The authors determined that under present conditions and policies China would be able to meet most of its agricultural needs domestically, although prices for many commodities would remain above world prices. Under the free trade scenario, domestic prices for most grains (except rice) would fall, leading to a drop in farm incomes and a sharp increase in grain imports, especially maize and corn. Domestic consumption would rise by 29.2 million tons in 2005 (due to lower prices), much of it met by increased imports, which would increase by 23.4 million tons over the baseline.

On the other hand, production of most animal products (except milk) would increase – especially pork, egg, and poultry, which would benefit from lower feed prices. Huang *et al.* predict that China would boost net exports of animal products by 7.8 million tons in 2005.

Zhai and Li (2000) develop a simulation that includes partial liberalisation of China's agricultural trade regime. On top of a 40 per cent tariff cut of 1997 tariff rates across all sectors, elimination of MFA quotas, and a phase-out of nine industrial non-tariff barriers, the authors assume a scenario in which agricultural imports are allowed to grow from 3 per cent of total Chinese production to 5 per cent (all of which is phased in from 1998-2005). After 2005, all agricultural import quotas are replaced with a flat 10 per cent tariff. The authors estimate that the elimination of agricultural quotas would have a dramatic impact on highly protected agricultural sectors. It would lead to lower domestic prices for many products, which in many cases would lead to lower production and employment in several sectors, and cause a large increase in imports. For example, domestic output of wheat, cotton, and rice would fall by 9.0 per cent, 22.6 per cent, and 1.4 per cent, respectively. Combined employment in these three sectors would fall by 12.8 million workers. On the other hand, production and employment would increase for livestock and processed food. Overall, agricultural imports would increase by 220 per cent over the baseline in 2005.[24] As a result of the full terms of the WTO accession scenario, incomes of rural workers would decline, while those of urban workers would rise, leading to greater income disparity between the rural and urban areas of China. Zhai and Li (2000) project that WTO accession will raise GDP by 1.5 per cent in 2005, with nearly two-thirds of these gains coming from agricultural liberalisation.

Studies that analyse the agriculture provisions of the November 1999 US-China trade agreement

Two of the major studies surveyed here examine the agriculture trade provisions in the November 1999 US-China trade agreement, including the World Bank I (2000) and the OECD (2000).[25] The World Bank study estimates that no liberalisation is required by China in agriculture from the November US-China 1999 agreement (except for those products subject mainly to high tariff barriers) because the bindings for products subject to TRQs are estimated to be above the previous rates of protection.[26] As a result, the World Bank found that agricultural liberalisation would have a relatively minor overall effect on Chinese agricultural output and trade, although the full package of liberalisation would boost output of meat and livestock and dairy products. It would also lead to greater imports of such products as meat and livestock, oilseeds, and other agriculture. The reduction of tariffs on beverages and tobacco is projected to have a significant impact on this sector. Output falls by 66.9 per cent, and imports rise by 6 570.1 per cent.

The OECD agriculture study examines the effects of the US-China WTO agreement and the May 2000 EU-China agreement on China's production and trade in grains, oilseeds, and certain livestock. It estimated that imports of grains and oilseeds would increase by 2.0 million and 2.5 million tons in 2005 over the baseline (non-WTO accession). Lower feed costs would modestly boost production of various animal products, such as pork.[27]

Other factors

Several of the studies that examine the effects of China's WTO offers on agriculture describe a number of factors that may influence the extent trade liberalisation will affect its agricultural production and trade. For example, both Huang and Chen (2000) and Zhai and Li (2000) discuss the effects their simulations would have on the Chinese government's goal of maintaining at least a 95 per cent self-sufficiency rate in grains. Zhai and Li (2000) estimated China's grain self-sufficiency rate would still be very high under their simulation–92.3 per cent in 2005. Huang *et al.*'s (2000) total trade liberalisation simulation is estimated to cause this rate to fall to 88 per cent in 2005. Huang *et al.* (2000) estimate that this rate could be raised to 97 per cent if the government raised expenditures for agricultural research by a certain level. Thus, steps by the Chinese government to boost agricultural productivity could affect the level of future imports following WTO accession.

The OECD (2000) study estimated that the increases in Chinese imports of grains and oilseeds resulting from China's implementation of the trade liberalisation measures in the US-China and EU-China WTO trade agreements would be substantially enhanced if China also eliminated its trade-distorting agricultural subsidies. For example, with the bilateral WTO agreement provisions, China's imports of coarse grains are estimated to rise by 0.7 million tons in 2005. This level would rise to 7.0 million tons if domestic subsidies were also eliminated. The study further noted that the increase of processed agricultural imports would depend in part on the ability of domestic industries to improve their efficiency, which might be accomplished through the use of government subsidies. The extent to which China will be able to use agricultural subsides will thus likely have a significant effect on China's agricultural production and trade after it joins the WTO.[28]

Services[29]

Services are an important and growing component of the Chinese economy, contributing 33 per cent to China's GDP in 1998 compared with 21 per cent in 1980.[30] None of the studies surveyed address the provisions on services China has agreed to in its bilateral and multilateral WTO negotiations, and hence there are no data that estimate their possible impact.[31] However, since China's services industries (such as banking, insurance, telecommunications, etc.) are currently largely closed to foreign companies, it is reasonable to believe that China's WTO offers on services would likely have a significant effect on many of its domestic services industries, as well as on the economy as a whole (*i.e.*, efficiency gains, etc.).[32] In addition, liberalisation of trade in services would also significantly improve the ability of foreign firms to market and distribute their products in China, a factor that is not reflected in the studies that mainly examine the effects of China's tariff offers.

A number of CGE studies have been undertaken that include preliminary estimates of the economic costs of services barriers for various countries, including China.[33] Measurements of service barriers are incorporated into CGE models by converting them to 1) revenue-generating tariff equivalents, 2) cost-raising measures, or 3) rent-creating measures. Nonetheless these studies generally include very rough estimates of the effects of reducing certain services barriers by a certain percentage or eliminating them altogether.[34] Such studies may help shed light as to the extent of services barriers in China as well as the possible effects on economic welfare that might occur from reductions in such barriers. It is also clear that such estimates must also be interpreted with great caution since the methodologies used to measure the economic costs of services barriers are very imprecise.[35] The studies can be divided between those that do not explicitly model the different modes of services supply and those that model foreign direct investment (FDI) in service sectors. Three studies that do not explicitly model the different modes of services supply include:

- **The Australia Department of Foreign Affairs and Trade**, using the GTAP model (version 4, 1995 base year) and utilising estimates of tariff equivalents of services trade barriers,[36] projects that a 50 per cent reduction in China's barriers on services would boost economic welfare by $9.8 billion annually.[37]

- **Robinson *et al.***, uses the GTAP database (version 4) and estimates of tariff equivalents of services trade barriers.[38] The model also contains a function linking trade performance and total factor productivity (*i.e.*, increased imports raises the level of technology). The study estimated that a 50 per cent cut in barriers to services would raise China's economic welfare as a percentage of GDP by 0.34 per cent annually; this figure rises to 1.55 per cent when gains from technology transfers are factored in.

- **Chada *et al.*** uses the GTAP database (version 4), and extrapolates data to 2005 to incorporate the implementation of the Uruguay Round agreements.[39] The study estimated that a 33 per cent reduction in tariff equivalents by China on services would raise economic welfare by $11.8 billion.

Studies that explicitly model the different modes of services supply include:

- **Verikios and Zhang** use a modified version of the GTAP (version 4) database (the FTAP Model) which incorporates a bilateral treatment of FDI.[40] The FTAP model also incorporates assumptions of imperfect capital mobility, increasing returns to scale, and large-group monopolistic competition in all sectors. FTAP also distinguishes barriers to commercial presence from those that affect other modes of supply, and non-discriminatory barriers to market access from discriminatory restrictions on national treatment. Services barriers are modelled as tax equivalents that generate rents. The effects of eliminating services barriers in communications services and banking services in a post-Uruguay Round environment (*i.e.*, after 2005) is examined. The authors estimate that China's economic welfare would rise by $4.5 billion if trade barriers on communications services were eliminated, and $2.0 billion if trade barriers in financial services (finance, insurance, and business services) were eliminated.[41]

- **Dee and Hanslow** use the same FTAP model utilised by Verikios and Zhang.[42] The authors assume the estimates of barriers to communications and financial services (similar to those used above) to be typical of most other services (including services related to trade, transport, finance, business, and recreational services). They estimate that the removal by China of all of its services trade barriers would raise economic welfare by $90.9 billion in 2005.[43]

Other studies

This section briefly discusses four other major articles that examine China's WTO accession. They are listed because they make assessments that may add to the understanding of the possible economic effects of China's WTO accession. In three out of four cases, however, the methodology used in the analysis is not available.

- The US Department of Agriculture (USDA), using its Country Linked System of models (CLS), estimates that China's WTO accession (based on the November 1999 US-China WTO agreement) would raise its combined net imports of corn, wheat, rice, cotton, and soybeans and their products by an average annual level of $1.5 billion between 2000 and 2009 over its baseline projection (which assumes no Chinese WTO accession). This growth is mainly caused by trade liberalising measures that will require China to convert quotas into tariff-rate quotas (and to expand them over time), allow a limited level of non-state trade in agricultural commodities, and remove restrictive sanitary and phyto-sanitary (SPS) standards.[44]

- The United Nations Conference on Trade and Development (UNCTAD) estimated that in the short term, China's WTO accession would have only a small effect on foreign direct investment (FDI) flows into China, as investors take a wait and see attitude while reforms are being implemented. However, in the medium-term, UNCTAD predicts FDI flows into China could reach $60 billion (from current levels of about $40 billion) and possibly $100 billion annually if cross-border mergers and acquisitions were to be allowed.[45]

- The International Monetary Fund (IMF) estimated that WTO accession would cause China's real GDP to fall by 0.3 per cent in 2001 (which at that time was the first year of expected WTO membership for China), but then to rise by 0.1 per cent in 2002, 0.6 per cent in 2003, 0.6 per cent in 2004, and 0.8 per cent in 2005. Tariff reductions would increase imports and lead to deterioration in China's current account balance; that balance declines by 10.5 billion in 2005. WTO accession puts competitive pressures on a number of sectors, including agriculture, automobiles, certain capital-intensive sectors (including telecommunications), and the banking system. China's textile industry benefits greatly from the removal of quotas by 2005. In the long run, increased competition produces efficiency gains and improvements to total factor productivity.[46]

- An article by Goldman Sachs' examined China's reported April 1999 offer to the United States and projected that China's WTO accession would significantly boost China's economic growth, foreign investment, and trade. According to the article, trade liberalisation and greater openness would boost productivity, expanding GDP growth by an additional 0.5 per cent per year by 2005. China's total trade (exports plus imports) and FDI flows would nearly double by 2005.[47] Tariff cuts would generate $65 billion in additional Chinese imports by 2005, elimination of non-tariff barriers would raise imports by $20-$30 billion, while increased foreign investment would generate another

$20 billion in new imports (equipment, raw materials, etc.). In total, imports would rise $230-$260 billion by 2005. The elimination of MFA quotas would double China's textile and clothing products to $70 billion annually.[48]

Concluding remarks

Nearly all of the studies surveyed in this report conclude that China's economy will benefit from its WTO accession, although the estimated level of economic gains differs across studies. In addition, such studies differ widely as to which Chinese industries would benefit or be harmed by WTO entry. It is difficult to evaluate which of the studies surveyed provides the most accurate and comprehensive assessment of the impact of China's WTO entry on its economy, largely because none of them reflect all of the offers China has made in all of its bilateral and multilateral negotiations. A second major problem in assessing the usefulness of the studies surveyed is that most attempt to measure only the economic effects of China's tariff cut offers and the elimination of textile and apparel quotas on Chinese exports, but fail to reflect China's significant offers on non-tariff barriers (such as trading rights, distribution rights, quotas, import licensing, SPS restrictions, etc.) and services, which, many analysts argue, could have a bigger impact on China's economy than its tariff reductions. Part of the problem here is a lack of data, not only on China's WTO offers on non-tariff barriers and services, but also the tariff equivalent effects of these restrictions. Thus, it seems highly likely that the studies surveyed significantly understate the actual effects China's WTO accession will have on its economy and sectors. Finally, there are several aspects of China's economy that differ sharply from various assumptions used by standard CGE economic models and thus it is unclear to what extent such models can accurately reflect changes to China's economy from trade liberalisation.

Several studies use the November 1999 US-China WTO trade agreement or descriptions of a preliminary agreement that reportedly was reached in April 1999 (and closely resembled the agreement that was finalised in November 1999) in their simulations. Of the 36 bilateral WTO trade agreements China has reached, the US agreement is the only accord that has been released in its entirety (March 2000). Prior to its release, the US government made available detailed descriptions of most aspects of the agreement. The EU and other countries have released only general descriptions of their agreements with China. The US agreement with China is significant due to the extensive tariff reductions China offered on industrial goods (average tariffs lowered from 24.6 per cent to 9.4 per cent) and the tariffication of most of China's non-tariff barriers on agriculture (as well as sharp cuts in tariffs on certain agricultural products). The CGE studies that use either the preliminary April 1999 agreement or the November 1999 agreement include those done by: the USITC (1999), the World Bank I (2000), Fan and Zheng (2000), and the OECD (2000). However, these studies do not consider the costs of non-tariff barriers. Zhai and Li (2000) and Lejour (2000) include estimates of non-tariff trade barriers on selected industrial sectors, but exclude estimates of non-tariff barriers on agriculture, and neither specifically examine the November 1999 China-US WTO agreement.

Several of the studies attempt to factor in the tariff cuts China has made in recent years into the baseline used; many use China's 1997 average tariff rates, for example. On the one hand, this approach produces estimates of the economic effects further tariff cuts would have on the Chinese economy once it becomes a WTO member. However, since China has made such tariff cuts in preparation for WTO membership, not factoring these reductions into the simulation may underestimate the full effects of China's WTO membership.

Analysis by Bach *et al.* (1997), the World Bank (2000, study II), and Lejour (2000) indicate that applied tariff rates in China are significantly below statutory rates due to preferential tariff policies applied to imported investment and intermediate inputs used in the production of goods for export. Their analysis indicates that failure to model for tariff exemptions in simulations may overstate (or in some cases understate) the effects of China's WTO accession (in terms of tariff cuts) on economic welfare and change in output of various sectors.

Most of the studies that analyse the economic effects of China's accession to the WTO use either a custom-built single country model of the Chinese economy or a multi-regional model of the world economy. The main advantage of using a single-country model is the ability to include more sectoral detail and to examine unique aspects of a single economy. For example, Zhai and Li (2000) introduce two separate trade regimes in their model: ordinary trade and processing trade.

Limitations of the GTAP model for analysing China's WTO accession

One of the most commonly used multi-regional models is Global Trade Analysis Project (GTAP). The standard GTAP can be used to estimate the macroeconomic and sectoral effects of a policy change, such as a tariff cut, to a particular economy (such as China) as well as to other regions and economies in the model. Despite its usefulness in analysing the possible economic effects of China's WTO accession, the GTAP (as well as most multi-regional models) has certain limitations, especially as it applies to China:

- The GTAP model contains data on China's tariffs, but not on estimates of the tariff-equivalents of China's non-tariff barriers (although it has such estimates for certain other countries). As noted earlier, Chinese non-tariff barriers constitute a major barrier to trade for many products, especially agriculture. Failure to consider these barriers will underestimate the likely macroeconomic and sectoral effects of China's WTO entry.

- The GTAP model assumes perfect competition. While China has implemented a wide number of market reforms over the past several years, the government is still heavily involved in regulating the economy. Nearly one quarter of industrial production comes from state-owned enterprises which receive preferential treatment from the government, such as preferential access to bank loans and exclusive rights in trade, services, and production in certain sectors. Thus, the Chinese market is far from being perfectly competitive.

- The GTAP model assumes constant returns to scale. However, various studies indicate that trade liberalisation enables countries to import more capital, which improves productivity, and hence increases growth. As a result, such models may understate the gains from liberalisation.

- The GTAP model assumes that labour is mobile across sectors. In China, however, labour mobility is restricted by a number of policies and economic factors. Thus, a re-allocation of resources from one sector of the economy to another sector, due to trade liberalisation, is likely to cause a certain level of employment disruption in China in the short term, which may not be reflected in the standard GTAP model. Failure to account for this factor may overstate welfare gains from trade liberalisation.

- The standard GTAP model is not a dynamic model with endogenous growth built in. Hence the growth effects that would likely result from increased foreign investment in China after its WTO accession may not be reflected in the simulation.

Box A.2.1. **Summary of major findings of China WTO studies**

Study	Model used	Assumption on China's WTO entry	Changes from baseline and major findings
Yang (1996) ($1992)	GTAP Base case is projection of world economy: 1992-2005 (with UR agreements).	Three scenarios for China's WTO entry: 1) developing 2) developed 3) developing plus all tariffs reduced to a maximum of 10 per cent (tariff cut and levelling).	The effect of trade liberalisation is much more beneficial when all tariffs are reduced to a maximum of 10 per cent, GDP change for 1) 4.0 per cent, 2) 4.4 per cent, and 3) 7.7 per cent. Welfare change for 1) $18.0 billion, 2) $19.1 billion, and 3) $27.4 billion. Export volumes up for 1) 29.8 per cent, 2) 35.4 per cent, and 3) 81.2 per cent Import volumes up for 1) 35.9 per cent, 2) 45.5 per cent, and 3) 119 per cent. Largest winners under scenario 3) are clothing, other manufactures, and transport equipment Largest losers are beverages and tobacco, fisheries, and machinery and equipment. Effects on agricultural output are minimal.
Anderson (1997) ($1992)	GTAP Base Projections of the world economy for 1992-2005. Simulations estimate effects of UR with and without China and Chinese Taipei	China's 1995 WTO offer (weighted average of tariffs falls from 30 per cent in 1992 to 16 per cent by 2005).	In 2005: Real exports increase by $61 billion; Real imports increase by $47 billion; Welfare increases by $26.6 billion (3.0 per cent) Change in trade balances: 1992-2005 ($ billions): agriculture (−13.3), other primary (−10.9), light manufactures (58.6), heavy manufactures (−32.9) WTO accession has only a minor effect on China's agriculture.
Bach, Martin, and Stevens (1997) ($1992)	GTAP (the baseline scenario is the world economy (1992-2005) without the effect of the UR agreements. Looks at the effects on China's economic welfare from its 1994 WTO tariff offer; factors in tariff exemptions on certain imports	China's September 1994 offer (average weighted tariff declines from 30.4 per cent in 1992 to 16.1 per cent in 2005)	Using standard measures of tariff restrictiveness, the estimated welfare gains to China from its tariff offer are $22 billion. Two different methods for measuring China's tariff exemptions yields welfare gains of $17 billion and $31 billion.
Wang (1997) ($1992)	GTAP (1992). Effects of UR with and without Chinese Taipei in the WTO	China's 1996 tariff cuts factored in. In addition, tariffs are reduced by an additional 35 per cent	Affects of China's accession in 1992: Static gains to welfare = $10 billion (2.6 per cent of GNP) Static + growth gains to welfare = $20.3 billion (5.5 per cent of GNP). Export volume increases $65.7 billion Import volume increases by $47.2 billion China substantially increases labour-intensive exports (especially textiles and apparel) and increases imports of manufactured intermediates and machinery and equipment. China's world share of output of textiles and apparel would more than double. Net agricultural imports increase by $8.4 billion.
McKibbin and Wilcoxen (1998)	A dynamic inter-temporal general equilibrium model (DIGEM): G-Cubed (1991-2020), which. Incorporates financial flows.	1) 1997 statutory tariff rates are gradually reduced to zero by 2010. 2) China implements financial reforms that increase the returns from investing in China by 1 per cent in 1998, 2 per cent in 1999, and 3 per cent from 2000 onwards.	1) In 1998, GDP growth slows as industries adjust, but after 1998 economy grows more quickly, and by 2010, GDP growth is 0.85 per cent higher. Real exports initially fall, then rise in the long run; real imports increase sharply (3 per cent in 2010). 2) Financial flows into China increase very quickly and boost GDP growth. Real exports decrease, real imports increase.

775

Box A.2.1. **Summary of major findings of China WTO studies** (*cont.*)

Study	Model used	Assumption on China's WTO entry	Changes from baseline and major findings
Wang (1999)	GTAP with a focus on the impact of the elimination of MFA quotas on China's exports. Baseline period is 1995-2010.	On top of tariff cuts made in Oct. 1997, China cuts tariff rates on industrial products by an additional 40 per cent (by 2010), and quotas on agricultural products are replaced with a 15 per cent tariff by 2005.	By 2010: Overall production increases by 1.8 per cent. Exports rise by 14.4 per cent. Imports rise by 20.2 per cent. Clothing sector is big winner. Auto sector is big loser.
USITC (1999) ($1998)	GTAP, version 4 (1998 baseline year)	Separately examines China's April 1999 offer to the U.S., and phase-out of MFA quotas.	Effects of April 1999 tariff offer (1998) Static effects: real GDP increases 0.9 per cent; Static + growth effects on real GDP, 4.1 per cent; Static effects on welfare, −0.3 per cent; Static + growth effects on welfare, 2.1 per cent Static effects on total exports, 10.1 per cent Static effects on total imports, 11.9 Static + growth effects on exports, 12.2 per cent; Static + growth effects on imports, 14.3 per cent Output of wearing apparel, footwear, and light manufactures increases substantially, output of oilseeds declines. Effects of MFA quota phase-out in 2010 ($1998): GDP increases by $9.2 billion Welfare increases by $8.4 billion Exports increase by $16.3 billion Imports increase by $10.9 billion.
Li and Lejour (1999) ($1992)	Chinese CGE model (1992-2020). Factors in tariff exemptions on imports, but does not consider the phase-out of MFA quotas	Tariffs are cut 40 per cent during 1992-2000 (to reflect actual cuts that have been made); from 2000-2010; tariffs cut 10 per cent each year until they are eliminated in 2010 and kept at zero through 2020.	Large welfare gain ($30 billion annually), but slight decline in GDP (−0.7 per cent). Electrical machinery and equipment and textiles and apparel benefit from WTO accession, but most other sectors lose slightly.
Huang *et al.* (2000) (Only examines agriculture)	CCAP Agriculture Policy Simulation and Projection Model (CAPSiM). A country model. Base period begins in 1995 with projections through 2000. Model examines WTO effects for 2000-2005.	Gradual liberalisation of 14 major agricultural commodities (7 grain products and 7 animal products) after 2000 and completely phase out all trade barriers by 2005.	From 2000-2005: Without WTO entry, China meets most of its agricultural needs domestically, although prices for many commodities remain higher than world prices. With WTO entry, domestic prices for most grain products (except rice) fall, leading to drop in domestic prices, and an increase in imports from foreign sources; prices for meat products increase. Trade liberalisation could challenge China's policy of maintaining a 95 per cent grain self-sufficiency rate; it may drop from 98 per cent in the mid-1990s to 88 per cent in 2005. China would be able to obtain a 97 per cent grain self-sufficiency rate by 2020 by increasing agricultural research expenditures.
Ianchovichina *et al.* (2000) (World Bank I)	GTAP (1995-2000)	The US-China November 1999 agreement compared to 1997 tariff rates.	Consumer welfare rises by $28.6 billion Output of textiles and wearing apparel increase sharply; output of autos and beverages and tobacco fall. Exports of textiles, wearing apparel, and autos rise sharply; exports of beverages and tobacco and various agricultural produces decline sharply. Imports of beverages and tobacco, textiles, wearing apparel, and autos rise sharply. Wages of unskilled workers will grow twice as fast as the wages of skilled workers

Box A.2.1. **Summary of major findings of China WTO studies** (*cont.*)

Study	Model used	Assumption on China's WTO entry	Changes from baseline and major findings
World Bank II (2000) ($1995)	GTAP-DE (modified to include tariff exemptions): 1995-2000	China's August 1998 offer to WTO Working Party to reduce tariffs on manufactured. products by 20 per cent (over 1997 tariffs)	Under GTAP, welfare increases by $35.6 billion. Under GTAP-DE, welfare increases by $24.4 billion. Failure to account for duty exemptions on imports may significantly overstate gains from trade liberalisation, especially on sectors. Under GTAP-DE, China's share of world exports rise by 1.8 per cent and imports 1.4 per cent in 2005 than the baseline projection. Welfare gains in 2005 = $28.6.1 billion. Substantial increase in China's world output share of apparel. Large increase in China's export share of autos and a number of high tech sectors. Protection of agriculture remains largely unchanged, but imports of certain agricultural products rise.
Fan and Zheng (2000)	CGE model, PRCGEM 1997 used to project effects in 1998	November 1999 US-China WTO agreement (changes from 1999 statutory tariff rates). Examines tariff cuts but not elimination of MFA quotas.	Tariff cuts have minor, but positive, effects In 1998: Static gains to GDP = .06 per cent Static + growth gains to GDP =0.6 per cent Static gains to exports = 5.7 per cent Static + growth gains to exports = 5.4 per cent Static gains to imports 7.3 per cent Static + growth gains to imports = 9.1 per cent Largest sector winner in terms of per cent change in output would be meters (4.7 per cent); biggest loser would be metal ore (–2.1 per cent). Biggest per cent increase in exports: electronic equipment (10.7 per cent). Biggest per cent increase in imports: wood (18.7 per cent).
Zhai and Li (2000)	CGE model built for the Trade and Environment Programme at OECD factors in tariff exemptions on imports (1995-2010).	1) Implementation of actual 1997 tariff and NTB reduction + 2) UR implementation + 3) gradual 40 per cent cut in 1997 tariff rates from 1998-2005 and removal of non-tariff barriers in nine industrial sectors + 4) agricultural trade liberalisation (1998-2004), import quotas eliminated by 2005 and replaced with a 10 per cent import tariff + 5) phase out of MFA by 2005.	In 2005: GDP increases by 1.5 per cent Welfare increases by 1.2 per cent Exports increase by 26.9 per cent Imports increase by 25.8 per cent Overall gains to the economy unevenly distributed: Urban household welfare increases, while rural welfare declines. Output of highly protected agricultural and some capital-intensive industrial sectors (autos, instruments, cotton, wheat, etc.) would contract significantly, while various labour intensive industries, especially textile and clothing would benefit significantly. Around 9.6 million agricultural workers will be transformed to other sectors.
Lejour (2000)	GTAP and WorldScan Two separate types of tariff exemptions examined (1995-2020	Tariffs are reduced by 50 per cent. Three tariff models 1) statutory rates, 2) all tariffs reduced by two-thirds to mimic actual 1995 collection rates, 3) tariffs reduced only for imports used as intermediate goods and investment goods.	In 2020: GDP growth for 1) 2.1 per cent, 2) 1.4 per cent, 3) 1.7 per cent; Welfare growth ($ billion) for 1) 52.9, 2) 9.5, 3) 8.2; Under 1), 2) and 3) volume of production for wearing apparel increases the most, while that of motor vehicles decreases the most. The magnitude of sectoral effects depends whether tariff exemptions are introduced and in which way they are modelled.

777

Box A.2.1.   **Summary of major findings of China WTO studies** (*cont.*)

Study	Model used	Assumption on China's WTO entry	Changes from baseline and major findings
Walmsley and Hertel (2000) ($2000)	Dynamic GTAP Baseline is 2000-2020.	1) China's WTO offer as of August 1998; WTO; tariff cuts and textile quotas phased out by 2005. 2) Delay in phase-out of MFA quotas.	Cumulative increase in real GDP = 8.6 per cent. Cumulative increase in welfare = $27.1 billion. Cumulative increase in exports = 35.2 per cent. Cumulative increase in imports = 39.4 per cent Delay in phase-out in MFA quotas slightly slows GDP growth.
OECD 2000	OECD Aglink model	November 1999 US-China agreement and oilseed provisions of the May 2000 EU-China agreement. Examines grains, oilseeds, and certain livestock products	Grain imports increase by 2 million tons, oilseeds by 2.5 million tons. Domestic demand for pork and chicken increase due to lower tariffs. Chicken imports increase but pork demand met by domestic producers, due to the benefit of lower costs for feed. As urban incomes rise, a rise in demand for milk products Grain imports would be substantially higher after WTO accession if distortionary subsidies were eliminated.
Other studies			
Zhang, Zhang, and Wan (1998)	Computable partial equilibrium model	Estimates of tariff and tariff equivalent of non-tariff barriers (NTBs) of 25 "protected industries." NTBs estimated through price surveys of China's trading companies	For 1994, China's consumer surplus loss from trade protection for the 25 products totalled $35 billion (6.2 per cent of GNP), suggesting large gains from liberalisation. Trade liberalisation would lower index of landed prices of these products from 1.00 to 0.68, and the CIF value of imports would increase by 37.6 per cent. The price index for comparable domestic goods would fall from 1.00 to 0.90. Large short-term adjustments. Output of protected firms would drop by $40 billion (or 32 per cent), and lost jobs could total 11.2 million.
Goldman Sachs (1999)	n.a.	China's April 1999 offer	GDP grows by an additional 0.5 per cent Total trade and investment nearly double by 2005.
USDA (2000).	Country Linked System of models (CLS) developed by USDA (2000-2009)	November 1999 US-China trade agreement. Focuses largely on the effects of expanding TRQs. Examines the effects on corn, wheat, rice, cotton, and soybeans and their products.	Between 2000 and 2009, China's average annual net imports of selected agricultural products increases by $1.5 billion over baseline.
UNCTAD (2000)	n.a.	n.a.	In the medium-term, FDI in China could reach $60 billion, and possibly $100 billion annually if cross-border mergers and acquisitions are allowed.
IMF (2000)	NA	November 1999 US-China Agreement. Assumes China's accession in 2001. Estimates of differences between China WTO and non-WTO scenarios.	GDP falls by 0.3 per cent in 2001, then rises by 0.1 per cent in 2002, 0.6 per cent in 2003, 0.6 per cent in 2004, and 0.8 per cent in 2005. Current account balance deteriorates after 2001, falling by $10.5 billion in 2005 (as tariff cuts boost demand). But this trend will reverse, as quotas on textiles and apparel are eliminated and foreign investment in China increases. In near term, increased competitive pressure on agriculture, automobiles, certain capital-intensive sectors, and the banking system. But increased competition will increase productivity. Short-term employment disruptions and increase in income disparities, but employment growth should pick up over time.

NOTES

1. This annex was prepared by Wayne Morrison, Specialist in International Trade and Finance, Congressional Research Service, Library of Congress, Washington, DC under supervision from George Holliday, Principal Administrator, Trade Directorate, OECD.

2. Some studies excluded consideration of the effects of the quota elimination, focusing instead on the unilateral trade liberalisation measures China had to make to join the WTO.

3. This conclusion is influenced by the fact that the economic costs of the quotas on China's textiles and apparel have been estimated and included in several of the models used.

4. As noted, China has significantly liberalised its trade regime over the past few years. Some of the WTO studies factor in these tariff reductions, while others do not. Differences in assumptions of the magnitude of tariff reductions between the WTO and non-WTO scenarios could lead to different results among studies.

5. For example, Yang (1996), who examines three scenarios of Chinese trade liberalisation, found that both China's GDP and economic welfare rose higher when more extensive levels of trade liberalisation were assumed.

6. The World Bank II (2000) study estimated that failure to account for the duty exemptions on imports for production of exports would overstate estimates of the increase in China's welfare from WTO accession by about 50 per cent. However, analysis by Bach *et al.* (1997) uses a "trade restrictiveness index" to measure the welfare effects of tariffs with high variance; they estimated gains to economic welfare would be nearly 50 per cent higher compared to simulations that estimated the effects of statutory tariff rate reductions.

7. However, the authors who use these models admit that detailed Chinese data on tariff exemptions are limited, making it difficult to make precise estimates of tariff exemptions by sector.

8. Some of the losers of trade liberalisation may be so in the short term, but not necessarily in the long run, since exposing protected (and presumably inefficient) Chinese firms to greater competition could improve their efficiency and make them more competitive in world markets. Thus, some studies found that, while the output of certain protected Chinese industries would decline after WTO accession, their exports would increase due to gains in efficiency.

9. Most of the studies measure the quotas on textiles and apparel as export taxes.

10. For example, under the US-China trade agreement of November 1999, China agreed to significantly cut tariffs on autos, from the current rate of 80-100 per cent, to 25 per cent by 2006. However, China also agreed to eliminate a wide variety of non-tariff barriers (which would likely have a significant impact on China's auto industry as well) including quotas, restrictions on trading and distribution rights, and requirements on foreign auto investors regarding local content and technology transfer.

11. It is difficult to make direct comparisons of WTO effects of sectors across studies due to differences in commodity descriptions and groupings that are used. In addition, many studies list the percentage change in output, employment, and trade over the baseline, but don't provide data on the actual increase or decrease in value terms or number of workers, making it difficult to judge the magnitude that trade liberalisation will have on the sector as a whole. For example, if imports of autos were currently very low, doubling imports would not likely have much of an effect on China's domestic auto industry.

12. Despite these limitations, China is the world's largest exporter of textile and apparel.

13. The MFA originally came into effect in 1974 and was extended six times. It authorised members of the GATT (the predecessor to the WTO) prior to 1995, to negotiate bilateral trade agreements on textile and clothing quotas with other countries. The MFA was a departure from GATT free trade rules on other products. While China was not a GATT member, it was pressured to agree to quota limits by other GATT members. The ATC replaced the MFA beginning in 1995. However, countries that are not WTO members do not benefit from the phase-out of textile and apparel quotas and hence are subject to the same conditions that existed under the MFA. Thus, textile and apparel quotas imposed on Chinese exports are generally referred to in most studies as MFA quotas.

14. For example, under the current US-China textile agreement, Chinese export quotas are only allowed to expand by only 1 per cent annually.

15. According to the USITC, a significant share of China's apparel production comes from foreign-invested firms in China, while China's textile industry is dominated by rather inefficient Chinese state-owned enterprises.

16. Anderson (1997) estimated that freezing China's MFA quotas at 1992 levels would reduce China's exports and imports by $6.0 billion and $3.9 billion ($1992) respectively in 2005. Walmsley and Hertel estimated that delaying the elimination of MFA quotas until 2010 would slightly lower China's GDP (over the years 2000-2020), and shift a greater share of production to other sectors, such as electronics, in the short-run than would otherwise occur if the MFA quotas were eliminated in 2005.

17. In some cases, textiles and apparel are combined into one category, while in other cases they are reported separately. Some studies use the term "clothing" instead of "apparel."

18. Clothing imports rise as well in percentage terms, but it is likely that this is measured from a small base.

19. Yang notes, however, that these estimates were made using the average tariff level (37.5 per cent) for all transport equipment imports, which does not reveal the high tariff on motor vehicles. Yang states that had the industry been disaggregated, motor vehicle production would probably decline, while the production of other products would increase even more.

20. The World Bank I (2000) projects that without accession, automobile imports would rise by 25 per cent from 1992-2005, but with accession imports would surge by 556 per cent.

21. Many of the studies surveyed indicated that rice prices in China are below world prices, and hence estimate minor changes in China's rice imports resulting from WTO membership.

22. Anderson (1997) uses the GTAP model and thus does not consider the costs of non-tariff barriers and subsidies.

23. In Wang (1999), production of wheat falls by 15.7 per cent, other grains by 8.8 per cent and plant fibres by 11.6 per cent. Employment in these sectors falls by 16.1 per cent, 9.2 per cent, and 12.9 per cent respectively. Imports in these sectors rise by 108.3 per cent, 130.3 per cent, and 150.0 per cent respectively.

24. In particular, imports of cotton rise significantly due in part to the expansion of China's textile and apparel sectors.

25. Also worth noting is a 2000 US Department of Agriculture study. It focuses mainly on the effects of the TRQ provisions in the US-China WTO agreement on corn, wheat, rice, cotton, and soybeans and their products. It estimated that China's WTO accession would boost the combined level of imports of these products by nearly $2 billion over its baseline projection (non-WTO accession) in 2005, with the largest increases coming from corn, wheat, and cotton.

26. The World Bank notes difficulties involved in assessing the degree of agricultural reform that would be brought about by WTO accession, such as over how to measure the levels of protection that would prevail in the absence of WTO accession, especially since non-tariff barriers constitute the most significant restrictions on agricultural imports and there are no conclusive data on the costs of these barriers. In addition, the level of protection for certain agricultural products has varied from year to year, based on administrative decisions by the government on the quantity of imports (especially for wheat). In some years, China's imports of wheat and corn have exceeded the TRQ levels agreed to in the November 1999 WTO agreement.

27. The study notes that production of pork would rise by 800,000 tons over the baseline (a 2 per cent increase). The author explains that a large share of pork production currently comes from small family farm units, but projects that WTO reforms will lead to an expansion of specialised household farms and commercial pig operations.

28. At the time of writing, this issue was still being negotiated in the WTO Working Party.

29. This section draws largely on a study done by the OECD entitled: *Quantification of Costs to National Welfare From Barriers to Services Trade: A Literature Review*, August 2000, Report number TD/TC/WP (2000)24.

30. This level is quite low compared to that of developed countries and even that of many developing countries, indicating that China's service economy is very underdeveloped. *Source*: The World Bank, *World Development Indicators*, 2000, p. 186.

31. The lack of analysis of the effects on China's service offers is a reflection of the limited amount of analysis that has been performed on the effects of services trade liberalisation in general. This arises from problems in attempting to measure the economic effects of non-tariff barriers (such as quantitative restrictions and government regulations on foreign investment in such sectors) imposed against foreign services providers. In addition, data on trade in services across countries (especially for developing countries such as China) are limited and incomplete compared to data on merchandise trade. Because these studies do not specifically address China's WTO accession, only a general description of them is provided (*i.e.*, they are not discussed in the section of this report that individually examines in detail studies on WTO accession).

32. For example, the US Trade Representative's 1998 report on "Foreign Trade Barriers" stated that "China's market for services today remains essentially closed." The 1999 Foreign Trade Barriers report noted that "restrictive investment laws, lack of transparency in administrative procedures and arbitrary application of regulations and laws severely limit US service exports and investment in China, especially in the financial services, telecommunications, audio-visual, distribution, professional services and travel and tourism sectors."

33. This section draws largely on a study done by the OECD entitled: *Quantification of Costs to National Welfare From Barriers to Services Trade: A Literature Review*, August 2000, Report number TD/TC/WP(2000)24.

34. Some of these studies focus only on services, while others look at the effects of percentage cuts in barriers on both goods and services.

35. Because these studies do not specifically examine China's WTO offer on services, they are not described in great detail.

36. These estimates are taken from a study by Bernard Hoekman entitled: *Tentative First Steps, an Assessment of the Uruguay Round Agreement on Services*, the World Bank, Policy Research Working Paper 1455, (1995). Hoekman derived these estimates from the General Agreement on Trade in Services (GATS) scheduled commitments of WTO members using a three-category weighting method to measure the degree of restrictiveness. However, Hoekman's calculations do not include all barriers to services. In addition, the weighing method fails to distinguish between barriers in terms of their effects on the economy.

37. Australian Department of Foreign Affairs and Trade. *Global Trade Reform: Maintaining Momentum*, 1999.

38. Robinson, S., Z. Wang and W. Martin, *Capturing the Implications of Services Trade Liberalisation*, Invited Paper at the Second Annual Conference on Global Economic Analysis, Ebberuk, Denmark, 1999.

39. Chadha, R., D. Brown, and R. Stern, *Computational Analysis of the Impact on India of the Uruguay Round and the Forthcoming WTO Trade Negotiations*, University of Michigan, Discussion Paper No. 459, Marcy 2000.

40. Verikos, G. and X. Zhang. *Sectoral Impact of Liberalising Trade in Service*, paper presented to the Third Conference on Global Economic Analysis, Melbourne, June 2000.

41. These projections were based on estimates of barriers to communications and financial services taken from other studies.

42. Dee P. and K. Hanslow. *Multilateral Liberalisation of Services Trade*, Productivity Commission Staff Research Paper, March 2000.

43. It is worth noting that the study determined that 68 per cent of the projected welfare gains from a global elimination of all services would accrue to China, an indication that China's services sector is highly protected.

44. USDA, Economic Research Service. *China's WTO Accession Would Boost US Agricultural Exports and Farm Income*, Agricultural Outlook, March 2000, p. 11.16.

45. UNCTAD. *World Investment Report 2000: Cross-border Merges and Acquisitions and Development*, 2000, p. 55.

46. IMF. *World Economic Outlook*, October 2000, Box 1.3, p. 63-65.

47. Total trade would rise to $600 billion by 2005.

48. Goldman Sachs, *Global Economics*, by Fred Hu, Paper No. 14, April 26, 1999, p. 1.

BIBLIOGRAPHY

Anderson, Kym,
  On the Complexities of China's WTO Accession, World Economy, Vol. 20, September 1997, p. 749-772.

Australian Department of Foreign Affairs and Trade,
  Global Trade Reform: Maintaining Momentum, 1999.

Bach, Christian F., Will Martin, and Jennifer A Stevens,
  China and the WTO: Tariff Offers, Exemptions, and Welfare Implications, April 17, 1997.

Chadha, R., D. Brown, and R. Stern,
  Computational Analysis of the Impact on India of the Uruguay Round and the Forthcoming WTO Trade Negotiations, University of Michigan, Discussion Paper No. 459, Marcy 2000.

Dee P. and K. Hanslow,
  Multilateral Liberalisation o f Services Trade, Productivity Commission Staff Research Paper, March 2000.

Fan, Mingtai and Yuxin Zheng,
  The Impact of China's Trade Liberalisation for WTO Accession – A Computable General Analysis, Chinese Academy of Social Sciences, 2000.

Goldman Sachs,
  Global Economics, by Fred Hu, Paper No. 14, April 26, 1999, p. 1.

Huang, Jikun and Chen Chunlai (Centre For Chinese Agricultural Policy, Chinese Academy of Agricultural Sciences), Scott Rozelle (University of California, Davis), and Francis Tuan (ERS, USDA),
  Trade Liberalisation and China's Food Economy in the 21st Century: Implications to China's National Food Security, 1999.

IMF,
  World Economic Outlook, October 2000, Box 1.3, p. 63-65.

Ianchovichina, Elena, Will Martin, and Emiko Fukase,
  Assessing the Implications of Merchandise Trade Liberalisation in China's Accession to the WTO, the World Bank, July 26, 2000.

Ianchovichina, Elena, Will Martin, and Emiko Fukase,
  Introducing Export Processing Schemes into GTAP, the World Bank, November 2000.

Lejour, Arjan,
  China and the WTO: the Impact on China and the World Economy, CPB, the Netherlands Bureau for Economic Policy Analysis, March 2000.

Li, Xuesong and Arjan Lejour,
  Impact of China Access to WTO – A Dynamic CGE Analysis, Chinese Academy o f Social Sciences; and CPB, Netherlands Bureau for Economic Analysis, October 1999.

McKibbin, Warwick and Peter Wilcoxen,
  The Global Impacts of Trade and Financial Reform in China, Asia Pacific School of Economics and Management, Working Paper 98-3, 1998.

OECD,
  Changes in China's Agricultural Trade Policy Regime: Impacts on Agricultural Production, Consumption, Prices, and Trade (prepared by Josef Schmidhuber), November 2000, Report CCNM/CHINA/CA(2000)22.

OECD,
  Quantification of Costs to National Welfare From Barriers to Services Trade: A Literature Review, August 2000, Report number TD/TC/WP(2000)24.

Robinson, S., Z. Wang and W. Martin,
  Capturing the Implications of Services Trade Liberalisation, Invited Paper at the Second Annual Conference on Global Economic Analysis, Ebberuk, Denmark, 1999.

UNCTAD,
  World Investment Report 2000: Cross-border Merges and Acquisitions and Development, 2000, p. 55.

USDA,
> Economic Research Service. *China's WTO Accession Would Boost* US *Ag Exports and Farm Income*, Agricultural Outlook, March 200, p. 11.16.

US International Trade Commission (USITC),
> *Assessment of the Economic Effects on the United States of China's Accession to the* WTO, Publication 3229, September 1999.

Verikos, G. and X. Zhang,
> *Sectoral Impact of Liberalising Trade in Service*, paper presented to the Third Conference on Global Economic Analysis, Melbourne, June 2000.

Walmsley, Terrie L. and Thomas W. Hertel,
> *China's Accession to the* WTO: *Timing is Everything*. Centre for Global Trade Analysis, Purdue University, September 2000.

Wang, Zhi,
> *The Impact of China and Taiwan Joining the World Trade Organisation on* US *and World Agricultural Trade*, A Computable General Equilibrium Analysis, Economic Research Services, US Department of Agriculture, 1997.

Wang, Zhi,
> *The Impact of China's* WTO *Entry on the World Labour-intensive Export Market. A Recursive Dynamic* CGE *Analysis*, World Economy, Vol. 22, May 1999, p. 379-405.

Yang, Yongzhen,
> *China's* WTO *Membership: What's at Stake?* World Economy, Vol. 19, November 1996, p. 661-682.

Zhai, Fan, and Shantong Li,
> *The Implications of China's Accession to the* WTO *on China's Economy, Development Research Centre*, the State Council, May 2000.

Zhang, Shuguang, Yansheng Zhang, and Zhogix Wan,
> *Measuring the Costs of Protection in China, Institute for International Economics*, November 1998.

Annex III

MANAGING RAPID EXPANSION OF TERTIARY EDUCATION PROVISION

TABLE OF CONTENTS

MANAGING RAPID EXPANSION OF TERTIARY EDUCATION PROVISION[1]

Introduction

In 1998 the OECD published a comparative report on the first years of tertiary education.[2] This thematic study, which looked at developments in 12 OECD countries, provides a comprehensive, forward-looking comparative analysis of how systems, institutions and individual learners are responding – and will need to continue to respond – to changing conditions, including how to accommodate large volume participation (now the norm in OECD countries); how to ensure that tertiary-level learning options appropriately and effectively meet the needs and interests of learners as well as the demands of the economy and society; and how to address the competing demands and constraints on public and private budgets in meeting the costs.

In this context the terms "tertiary education" and the "first years" used in the OECD report require explanation. "Tertiary" refers to a stage or level of programmes and learning beyond secondary education that is provided through universities and other types of institutions and arrangements, is undertaken full- or part-time, in residence or at a distance, and is pursued by young and older adults. The "first years" are those leading to an initial qualification recognised to be of value in the labour market. Universities and other tertiary education institutions account for most of the volume and diversity of students in the first years of tertiary education, but now increasingly complemented by new arrangements for tertiary-level learning outside of the sector.

China, too, is in the midst of a major economic reform process in which education, and in particular at the higher levels, has a pivotal role in helping to sustain the growth potential of the country. Grasping the opportunities presented by the knowledge society and the growing impact of technology and the Internet will depend on equipping people, young and old, with the intellectual, technical and inter-personal skills of the 21st century. The Chinese authorities and the OECD agreed it would be valuable to embark on a study of the very extensive developments in tertiary education in China, against the background of the comparative framework established for the OECD study, so that the experience gained both in OECD countries and in China might provide the basis for informing policy reform more generally. The co-operation that already exists between the OECD and China through the World Education Indicators programme and the OECD Programme for International Student Assessment has provided an excellent starting point for this new co-operative venture.

The study team brought together a range of national and international experience in tertiary education, in the same way as the teams that had conducted visits in the other countries participating in the larger OECD comparative activity. The team was very conscious that a visit of less than two weeks to China permitted only a fleeting glimpse of a country of immense size and population, with an unsurpassed richness of history, culture and educational tradition. The team was equally conscious of the risks of generalising conclusions from visits that took them only to Beijing and to Shaanxi Province. However, the extensive briefings provided by the Ministry of Education (MoE), the many Central and Provincial Government officials, as well as the professors and leaders of the institutions themselves and those in the private sector, allowed insights into current developments that have guided the study team in the preparation of this report. The team wishes to recognise the openness and frankness of the discussions and readiness of their interlocutors to answer the unending series of questions posed, which helped with understanding what are very complex and difficult reforms being put in place and provided the necessary confidence to frame this report and the ideas put forward in it.

The team particularly wishes to express its appreciation to Mr. Zheng Fuzhi, Deputy-Director General, Department of Development Planning, in the Ministry of Education, Mr. Fan Wenyao, Deputy Director General, National Center for Education Development Research, Professor Wang Xiaohui, Director of the Centre's Comparative Education Division, and their colleagues. In meetings and conversations with them over the course of the visit, the team was able to explore a wide range of options for tertiary education.

On this, the team also had the benefit of Professor Wang, Beijing Normal University, who accompanied the team on its study visit.

It is not claimed here that there is one single blueprint for successful national education policies – there is not. As described in the Country Notes prepared by OECD study teams for each of the 12 countries that already have participated in this comparative exercise, the distinctiveness of national characteristics is evident from the OECD countries themselves. But this should not stand in the way of greater international exposure of tertiary education systems and reinforced co-operation, especially in the exchange of students and faculty as well as research. It is hoped that the views offered in this document based on the comparative experience of other countries will provide some input into the consideration of future developments in China.

The context

The importance attached to the place of learning and education in the current reforms in China was evident from the many conversations which took place during the study visit. The fact that a Working Group on Science and Education has been established under the chairmanship of the Premier is clear evidence of the support for the reform effort in education at the highest political level. As China embraces the knowledge-based economy of the 21st century, the emphasis on the development of the human capital that will ensure China's transition to a middle-income country by 2020 was uppermost in the minds of those met by the team.

China's open-door policy over the past twenty years has been remarkably successful in achieving high and sustained rates of economic growth. During the period since 1978, GDP growth has averaged 9.8% annually. The proportion of the population in absolute poverty has fallen from more than half in 1978 to 8% (under national definitions) in 1997. By 1997, China had become the world's fifth largest trader and second largest recipient of foreign direct investment. These aggregate trends, of course, conceal complex patterns of diversity across the Provinces, with the coastal regions continuing to achieve the more dynamic development.

Moving into the learning society poses real challenges for Chinese education, as it does for the education systems of all countries. Learning is no longer the preserve of the young. Education and learning systems must now provide for a spectrum of needs that are not bound by age. Compulsory education, on which there is a particular emphasis in China, has the responsibility to set the foundation for lifelong learning, by creating in each individual the ability and the motivation to continue the process of learning throughout life. As a very perceptive paper prepared by China for the 2000 APEC Education Ministers Meeting in Singapore put it, "the survival and development of each member of human society will increasingly depend on lifelong learning and creative activities".[3] This is a challenge familiar to policy makers across the world. In the OECD countries it has been recognised that building learning systems that address the needs of the lifelong learner can only be achieved through a strategic and global approach that embraces in the reform process all programmes and institutions.

An initial impression that inevitably strikes an outside observer of Chinese education is of a very fragmented system. Responsibility for managing and funding its various aspects has long been invested in a range of Ministries, and other Central, Provincial and Municipal authorities. Adult tertiary education seems to reside in a separate system, somehow apart from the "main" tasks of tertiary education institutions. This segmentation has not permitted the development of a comprehensive and holistic approach to the reform of the whole system.

The current ambitious reforms in China are aimed not only at addressing these shortcomings but also at introducing, in the words of the APEC discussion paper, "comprehensive innovation in education in order to meet the constantly changing social life and new patterns of economic growth". This report explores how the reforms seem to be framed and are developing, as seen from the perspective of OECD countries and recent experience in the OECD area.

The concerns that motivated the OECD's Redefining Tertiary Education are very similar to those that the team was told were driving reform in China. They include:

- extensive and expanding student participation;
- greater diversity in those seeking access to tertiary education;
- changing needs and expectations of students, families, employers and the community;
- growing concerns over quality and purpose;
- emerging scenarios for lifelong learning;
- competing demands for scarce public resources;
- challenges and opportunities offered by information and communication technologies.

Although the reform and restructuring of the universities and other tertiary education institutions in China began some years ago, the process has considerably accelerated especially over the past two years.

Expansion and access

In 1999 long-term aims were set by China for the development of all types of education towards the year 2010. The goal for tertiary education was to achieve an enrolment ratio of 15% of the 18-22 age group. There are fairly clear indications that that target will be achieved ahead of time. The team had the impression from its discussions that there are extensive developments, internal and external to the education system, that will have considerable bearing on how that goal can and indeed should be achieved before 2010.

First there are the pressures of the knowledge society and the prevalence of technology driving radical changes in the labour market, the nature of employment and the new and different skills and qualifications that are now needed. Economic development over the past twenty years has enabled China to become the world's fifth largest trading partner and the process towards membership of the WTO will offer opportunities and challenges, especially to those sectors of the Chinese economy that will be exposed to greater international competition. All of this, together with the declared intention that China will become a middle-income country by 2020, will call out for more highly skilled people. Add to that the burgeoning social demand for education and the pressures for rapid expansion seem overwhelming.

Second, within the education system itself, although the reform and restructuring of the Universities and other tertiary institutions began some years ago, the process has considerably accelerated especially over the past two years. In 1999 the gross enrolment rate for tertiary education[4] was 10.5% and 11% in 2000, with 11 million students receiving all types of tertiary education – twice as many as in 1990. This represents a 17% increase over 1999 and illustrates the flexibility and the increased capacity that the restructuring has introduced into the system. According to analyses carried out by the National Center for Education Development Research, the 15% goal could be achieved around 2005-2006 just at the moment when the youth demographic curve reaches its peak.

But entering university is only one part of the story. Successful completion is the other. Typically 20-25% of university entrants in OECD countries do not complete their studies on schedule. University survival rates differ among countries, in ways that are not fully explained by participation rates. For example, the United States has a high access and a high dropout rate, while Finland, New Zealand and the United Kingdom have high participation rates and low dropout rates.[5] Other factors are at work, including in some countries a reinforcement of policies and practices that can work to foster success and completion.

Expansion implies a transition from an elite to a mass system. That transition also implies that tertiary education shifts from being a "public" good to a "semi-public" good. The explosion in participation is a direct response to combined social and economic demand. As economic conditions improve and the

789

Chinese people enjoy more prosperous lifestyles, the demands and expectations of parents for the education of their children grow, especially for university education. It is no longer simply a question of aspiring to attend a university, but, rather, of going to a good one. While in the past families built up savings in order to pass the wealth on to their children, they are now more interested in using these savings (estimated at 60 trillion RMB) to invest in their children's education. This is a distinctive Chinese cultural feature, which is not found in countries that opt for high levels of public spending. The evolution towards a large-volume system in China may well follow a different path from that taken in some European countries.

Though the numbers of students involved are far smaller, many OECD countries have witnessed very significant increases of the order of 50% and more in tertiary education enrolments between 1990 and 1997. Enrolments more than doubled in Portugal, Poland, Hungary; increased by nearly 90 percent in Turkey and the United Kingdom; grew by around 50 per cent in the Czech Republic, Ireland, Korea, New Zealand and Sweden.[6] The experiences in implementing these increases and in otherwise managing the changing world of tertiary education contain lessons that might be useful to China as she undertakes these ambitious policies.

For example, typical Chinese assumptions about undergraduate education seem to include:

a) eligible students are very recently graduated from secondary schools;

b) students live in residence, on-campus, at the colleges and universities;

c) students attend full-time courses;

d) students graduate in 3 or 4 years depending on the programme; and

e) students learn in settings where there is one full-time faculty person for every 15 or so students.

In fact, every one of these assumptions is being challenged in many OECD countries. The typical student in the United States is 27 years old, lives off-campus, goes to school part-time and is going to a two-year community college. Those who go to four-year colleges average 24 years of age, take 6 years to graduate, live off-campus and work part-time. And the ratio of students to faculty varies greatly across America. To a greater or lesser extent, many of these patterns can be seen in such other OECD countries as Sweden, Australia, the Netherlands, Germany and the United Kingdom; partly as a consequence of growth itself, tendencies in these directions now are evident in nearly all OECD countries.

When the typical assumptions under gird a national policy for expansion of tertiary education, the result is the expansion of existing facilities or the development of new facilities that are expensive, take time to build and that are often at a great distance from the population of students that lack access. One of the interesting characteristics of many OECD national systems of tertiary education is that over 50% of students go to a school located within 25 miles of their home. This is true even within the large nations.

Moreover a rapid expansion of this sort will usually require either a substantial increase in the workload of existing faculty and/or the training and hiring of a large number of new faculty in a very limited time. Although the Ministry of Education plan calls for a dramatic expansion of graduate students, most of these highly talented people will end up in the professions or private industry rather than as members of the professoriate. Therefore, should such massive growth in demand be met in more or less conventional ways, one result could be a substantial reduction in quality due to the extra workload for existing staff and/or the recruitment of untrained staff.

Finally, two other considerations are important. The first concerns the supply and equality of access, as the number of regular tertiary education students expands in a dramatic fashion over the next decade. Although there are a substantial number of talented students in China who apply and do not now obtain admission as undergraduates, just as many more have not had the opportunity to take the kinds of courses of study that would prepare them to go on to University. These students exist in the provinces of the East as well as the West. Many are in secondary schools that do not have the necessary expertise on the faculty to enable their students to effectively prepare for examinations. By way of comparison, average completion rates at the upper secondary level in China are 48% – though in urban centres such as Beijing rates can reach 92% – against average OECD completion rates of 80% but with some countries exceeding 90%. As access is expanded these students, too, need to be given the opportunity to compete for places.

The second consideration has to do with adult students, particular those who did not pass examinations. In many OECD countries, there are opportunities for these students to try again for entry to all types of tertiary education including university studies. Often the criterion for their admission is a combination of success in life and in courses in tertiary institutions such as community colleges in the United States rather than success on a single university entrance examination (access systems which have often been found to have less than perfect reliability). In countries where the flows between tertiary education institutions are more limited, such as Norway or Denmark, rely on other options to draw in such students. The Mjoes Commission in Norway has proposed open access for any adult who has completed secondary education or its equivalent, a policy of long standing in New Zealand. Sweden's 25 plus 5 scheme sets aside places for adults who are 25 years old and have five years of relevant work experience.

These policies have had the effect of opening up for adults all forms of tertiary education. Substantial numbers of these students, particularly those who were under-prepared for, or opted out of the initial university examination, go on to graduate and move into important places in society. Further, there are also those students in areas where economic performance is good and jobs available who go into employment directly from school. A second or even a third chance to go to university or other forms of tertiary education is a growing characteristic of learning societies. No country can afford to lose talent.

The solution to the problems posed in the preceding paragraphs, as many countries have discovered, is an approach to expansion that focuses on quality and access together, is nimble and open to innovation, attendant to local needs and resources and varied in strategy. China has a variety of resources and policies already in place that will facilitate expansion. These include Project 211, an aggressive effort to expand and improve the system so that at the beginning of the 21st Century China will have 100 universities and a group of key disciplinary areas of first class quality; decentralisation, leaving to the Provinces responsibility for about 900 tertiary education institutions which should make them more attuned to local needs; a private sector (profit and not-for-profit) that is eagerly looking to expand; and an emerging and enlightened set of projects and policies to expand the use of technology, particularly in the area of distance education.

Perhaps the most critical component will be how the MoE steers rather than controls, and works to ensure the access of the poor and underserved. Each of the efforts already underway needs attention. Project 211 could serve only a narrow proportion of the society, or it could support and help improve universities and other forms of tertiary education across the nation; decentralisation of authority over former national universities to the Provinces will succeed in improving their quality and reach only if they have the necessary resources, including resources to support the retirement and health care systems that they have inherited; the private sector will only expand with quality and speed if MoE regulations support thoughtful accreditation and oversight, reflecting their distinctive profiles and roles, and enable the growth and continuation of the institutions over time; distance education and related technology initiatives will succeed if the MoE can strike the proper balance between oversight and stimulation and can support a serious programme in applied research and knowledge dissemination.

A *vision for the future*

Confronted with similar concerns about how to respond to continuing growth and large-volume participation, the OECD comparative study found that an important first step was to establish a coherent and inclusive vision for any future educational reform. As the Secretariat report on the most recent developments in OECD countries observes, authorities have set out and continue to stress a broad vision of education at the tertiary level, encompassing a range of providers including universities and giving particular attention to linkages to the labour market and society more widely. The team considers that developing such a holistic and inclusive vision is a prerequisite for successful educational reform as China builds the human capital needed to move towards becoming a middle-income country by the year 2020. Such a vision would be very much in line with the conclusions of the plenum of the Central Committee on 10 October 2000 that " … a major strategic task for the future is to train, attract and give full play to talented personnel and that efforts should be made to vigorously develop human resources, step up the development of education and build up a huge contingent of quality talents".

A number of important elements of such a vision are now falling into place. The discussion paper prepared for the recent APEC Education Ministerial meeting laid out clear objectives to guide "a new round of educational reforms and innovations". The team was also informed that the 10th Five-Year Plan now in preparation would be different from its predecessors in that it would be drafted "according to the market" and would remain at the macro-level, providing directions rather than prescribing detailed implementation of educational programmes. However, one aspect that underpins the approach of most countries is the acceptance that learning should be a lifelong process. This implies that the learning system should be seen as an interlocking whole, offering opportunities to all ages. This does not seem to be the case in China. The team was left with the impression that at present adult education is somehow set apart. Integrating adult learning into the overall approach will be essential if China is to seize the opportunities of the knowledge society.

It should be possible to build upon these and other elements, which will be explored in this report to develop an approach that will allow the education system to be steered at the strategic level by the Ministry of Education, with implementation taking place at local level. The question of steering will be returned to later in this report.

The team agrees with the Ministry of Education vision for the future that combines the idea of a lifelong learning network with the goal of increasing access to tertiary education. There is a lot to learn from the experiences of OECD and non-OECD countries about how these goals can be jointly achieved. From the meeting with officials in Xi' an and Beijing it was clear that two issues in particular will be critical.

Who will be the providers? From discussions with the Ministry, university officials and local and provincial officials, the impression received is that responsibility for tertiary education would be distributed among a variety of providers. The team would like to underline here the importance of the providers being open to the needs of all age groups. The traditional providers (public and private universities) will continue to be the intellectual leaders and will provide most of the instruction, at least for the short run. For the West and other rural areas, there may be a need for new institutions established locally or regionally that would be closely aligned and responsive to local community and Provincial needs and that would not be residential. Public or private, these institutions might also serve as stepping stones to university and may, or may not, have collaborative relationships with existing universities. Both types of relationships are to be found in OECD countries. In either case, traditional and new institutions would provide on site and distance education. For the entire nation there would be an aggressive and nimble but thoughtfully regulated private sector that would range from providing content and hardware to other providers to providing content to consumers.

How will quality be assured, including in the distance education programs? During discussions, the following approach seemed to evolve as a candidate: the MoE and the Provinces would agree on a guidance and oversight system that would have four parts:

a) regulations and accreditation requirements for private providers that reinforce quality without overly restricting the market or narrowly defining content, context and method of teaching and learning;

b) a strategy for continuously assessing the quality of all (distance and on-site) new providers, consisting of independent expert evaluations of content and pedagogy, continuous and public feedback from users (students), and, when appropriate, exit examinations approved by the state for graduation or certification;

c) high quality research and development sponsored by the MoE that would provide direction and information to providers about how best to implement distance education; and

d) a system to provide all consumers with good information about their choices for tertiary education.

Restructuring

Changes in tertiary education provision are already evident, driven by the shifts in oversight of tertiary education institutions from line Ministries to the MoE and for all but a select group of leading research universities from the Central Government to the Provinces. A key motive for those shifts is to permit a concentration, consolidation and targeting of resources on leading universities in an effort to harness and capitalise on the expertise for teaching and research at the highest level. The team was privileged to visit such universities in Beijing and Xi'an, and to discuss important links with the institutes and programmes of the Academy of Sciences and with the economic sector. The importance of their current and potential contributions is appreciated.

As has been noted, the expansion now anticipated and desired will be responding to demands for tertiary education that are more diverse in terms of student backgrounds and interests and of needs in the labour market. The Ministry implicitly recognises this aspect of demand. In the expanded system, students will be participating in a variety of ways: part-time as well as full-time; at a distance as well as informal, on-site studies; and particularly through IT-based delivery of programmes offered by universities. Further, the Provincial oversight of some 900 institutions along with substantial provision through private providers is expected to bring study programmes more in line with local demands and needs. And, study options for adults remain available through a range of providers.

These elements of diversity in tertiary-level provision – existing, new and in view – are welcome. The OECD team carrying out the study visit of Portugal put such diversity in its wider context: "The country needs a diversity of talent, and a diversified approach to the educating and skilling of that talent."

As participation increases, it is expected that demand will create further pressures on existing structures and arrangements for provision. First, the experience in OECD countries suggests that growing demand leads to even greater departures from formerly limited and narrow options and isolated, closed study programmes, *i.e.* growing diversity whether in the form of expanded options for study in programmes other than regular university degree programmes or diversity within university programmes. Second, diversity appears to lead to a breaching of rigid boundaries. Put another way, categories of students can no longer be so easily distinguished according to programme enrolment: full- and part-time students are less easy to identify clearly, with respect to their backgrounds as well as current activities (concurrent work, for example) and programmes of study; young and mature age, working and "inactive", fee-paying and publicly supported students now are more likely to sit alongside each other in classrooms, laboratories, libraries and computing centres. This point has been made earlier with respect to adults; such a blurring has potential implications for the structure and functioning of the tertiary education system as a whole. Finally, growing and diverse demands combine with constraints on public and family budgets to call for even more creative, innovative thinking about ways to foster diversity in provision. These are matters that continue to occupy policy attention in most OECD countries.

Among the areas for further development in the course of expansion, the following might be noted:

• Further development of tertiary-level institutions and programmes outside of universities. In some OECD countries, these institutions have developed with a strongly vocational orientation from vocational secondary schools (*e.g.* Denmark and France); in others, as distinct new forms of tertiary education [*e.g.*, IUTs (Institut Universitaire de Technologie), also in France; technological universities in Mexico]. There are also the models of United States and Canadian community colleges and of further education in Australia and the United Kingdom. While each of these institutional sectors reflects their national contexts, they share two key features: a unique blending of vocationally-oriented and general studies and a spread of provision into under-served localities.

• Mergers of institutions, in ways that enable economies of scale and also new profiles, *e.g.* blending academic with more applied study orientations. The team heard of such aims in the universities visited, and note parallel developments strongly driven by policy in such countries as Belgium (Flemish Community) and Australia.

- Partnerships between institutions, particularly crossing Provincial boundaries to co-operate with institutions in the Western Provinces. Again, the team was told about such arrangements.

- Expanding private higher and tertiary education, including arrangements for overseas providers. OECD countries differ in the extent of private tertiary education provision, but the Portuguese case merits attention as a country that rapidly expanded enrolment through new private tertiary education institutions.

- New forms of co-operation in teaching and learning, with research institutes and with enterprises. In various discussions, these forms were described as already in place.

The variety of options and arrangements imply a diversity of institutions and providers in a framework which allows for a certain flexibility and responsiveness. The policy challenge is how to realise such a restructuring of tertiary education. The most promising policy orientation seems to be one that combines strong measures (*e.g.* a distinctive and strengthened tertiary education sector, new distance education arrangements) and weak measures (allowing private and overseas providers). Whatever the balance and mix, the Central Government has a key role to play in setting out a broad framework and putting in place incentives and conditions under which these options can grow in response to demand. This is the approach followed, in different ways, in OECD countries.

Specific policies can encourage, rather than impede, such restructuring. First, quality assurance needs to be adapted in ways that allow for a more diverse set of learning options. Instead of a single "standard", the challenge will be to arrive at a set of standards that correspond to the distinctive objectives of study programmes available, through universities, public or private, or a range of other providers. This challenge remains on the policy agenda in the OECD area. Second, means are needed to permit and ease movement into and across programmes, institutions, segments and systems. Access routes for adults into regular university and other tertiary education programmes have already been mentioned. Ireland's new Qualifications Authority has as one of its responsibilities to promote recognition of learning within and between institutions as well as internationally. Third, public funds – whether from the Central Government or Provincial Government – should be provided on the basis of criteria that allow for institutional initiative and encourage varied forms of co-operation. With regard to the national universities, for example, public funds can be earmarked partly in support of new networking arrangements much as the French contracting policy is used to bring together enterprises and universities in a region.

Distance education and other technology initiatives

Most of the OECD countries and many other nations are entering into uncharted territory as they attempt to fulfil the promise of information technology (IT) to create educational quality and opportunity for millions of students around the world. China, along with a number of other large nations, has the chance to carry out an experiment of incredible magnitude and importance as it figures out how to harness this resource.

The goal set out by the MoE is to establish a comprehensive lifelong learning system with IT as its backbone by 2010. In the meantime, to succeed in reaching its interim goals for expansion of undergraduate and adult education, China will need steady step-by-step progress as it crosses this challenging river. The stepping-stones are there to be placed or discovered and used. The team is aware of some and the following is but an illustration of the sort of developments that are taking place:

- As early as 1995 the MoE, with the help of China's key universities established the China Education and Research Computer Network (Cernet) which by the beginning of 2000 connected up some 550 universities, middle and primary schools, reaching 2 million users in 80 cities.

- Simultaneously, the nation's plans include stretching fibre-optic wiring across huge expanses with information carried the "last mile" via wireless technology. Already satellite supported wireless technology provides significant coverage of rural areas. These will eventually be broadband technologies.

- As part of the Cernet the MoE has been working with primary and middle schools to support students and teachers to be competent in using the computer and the Internet. The MoE has also established teaching networks in the Central and Western Provinces to combat illiteracy and foster the training of teachers.

- In August 2000 "thirty-one Chinese universities were approved to run pilot projects for distance learning".[7] Twenty-six of the universities will be allowed to enrol students who participated in the national higher-education entrance exams and adult higher-education entrance exam. They can also offer their own entrance exams. The other five will only be able to offer courses to students who take the adult higher-education exam.

- A number of universities are aggressively moving into the delivery of courses on-line. The Hong Kong Open University makes 85 programmes leading to Bachelors and Graduate degrees and 155 courses available to a current enrolment of 25 000 throughout Hong Kong.[8] A number of the universities in the 31 recently approved as pilot projects for distance learning have been developing their capacity and relationships for a few years.[9] Chinaonline.com recently posted a web site summarising some of these activities.[10]

- Finally, the private sector is moving into the distance learning space. According to a report of 4 October 2000, online, long-distance education in China is set to receive a major boost. Citicorp Capital Asia (Taiwan) Ltd. and the Internet Data Group, along with other investors, recently invested a total of USD 5 million in the PRCEDU Co., a Web site providing long-distance education. PRCEDU will use this investment to continue developing its educational software. The company is located in Beijing, has 160 employees, and seeks to become the largest online educational platform service provider in China.[11] The platforms will make it easy for universities and companies to develop and deliver distance education courses. This is a critical software infrastructure development.

This is an excellent start but there are many steps to go to reach the goal of a lifelong learning system based on IT. The remoteness of the Western Provinces, the need to assure quality along with access and equity, the lack of experience with aggressive private and international sectors, the challenge of putting broadband access throughout the nation, the need to design and evaluate courses and programmes that are appropriate for many ages and levels of experience – all of these are challenges for the next decade.

The prize, though, could be extraordinary. The team believes that China is poised to become a significant leader in the new economy. To succeed in that goal the full development of the nation's human capital is critical. This cannot be accomplished in the near future, in the timeframe of the new economic revolution, unless dramatic steps are taken to modernise the delivery of education. China has the opportunity to carry out in just a few years what it has taken many Western countries decades to accomplish – to leapfrog generations in the development of access for all qualified to a quality experience in tertiary education.

A number of mechanisms are already, or could be, in place to support efforts in this area. The 211 project participants (100 well-established universities) might collaborate with new institutions in the West or other rural areas to provide on-site and distance learning. The 31-school distance learning demonstration project could be a garden for an aggressive research effort to study strategies for the effective and efficient delivery of distance learning, adding to the knowledge accumulating from similar advanced-level distance education programmes, such as Open Universities in the UK, Germany, the Netherlands and Japan and Stanford University's Masters' Degree programme in Engineering (see Box). Private dot-com companies that supply, twenty-four hours a day and seven days a week, tutoring, professional development for teachers and professors, data gathering and organisation strategies, and exemplary courses from around the world, will all spring up and want access to the education market.

Box A.3.1. **Delivering degrees at a distance. Stanford's Master's degree in engineering**

Stanford University has been providing a master's degree in engineering through distance learning for over a decade. The basic model is that a private sector firm contracts with the university to provide the course materials (videos or CDs of lectures, reading lists, assignments and so on) for a small group of students. The course materials are on the web and available to the students. The students at the firm are expected to do the same work as students on campus and take the same exams, which are typically graded at the university. The way that the students experience the course and the learning environment are different from the way they would have learned at the university.

"... The twist, though, is that once the engineers received the video they'd replay it in their own small study group, but in a special way. Every three minutes or so they'd stop the tape and talk about what they'd just seen, ask each other if there were any questions or ambiguities, and resolve them on the spot. Forward they would go, a few minutes at a time, with lots of talk and double-checking, until they were through the tape and everybody understood the whole lesson. What they were doing, in terms we used earlier, was socially constructing their own meaning of the material... The results were that students taking the course this way outperformed the ones actually taking the classes live. Today, the approach has been tried ... with college students, even with California prison inmates; most of the students who've tried it got half a grade point better grades than the regular students. This account is not meant as a commentary on regular Stanford classes! Rather it is used to describe an elegantly simple idea, low-tech and low-cost, ..."

John Seeley Brown (2000), "Growing up digital", *Change* (March/April 2000), p. 17.

Financing

Shortage of resources, both human and financial, is the common currency of all education systems. China is no different in that respect. The team was consistently told of the problems caused by the financial implications of the reforms. China devotes less than 3% of GDP to all levels of education combined. This compares with 4.8% in Brazil, a country at a more or less comparable stage of development. The average expenditure, from all sources, across the OECD countries is 6.1% of GDP, ranging from 7.4% in Korea to 4.2% in Luxembourg. In almost all OECD countries, between 1990 and 1996 expenditure of education grew faster than, or kept pace with, national wealth. It is the MoE's intention to increase the level of spending to 4% of GDP. This will still leave spending in China behind that of many other countries. The importance attached to education by the Chinese authorities has resulted in the input into education being increased by 1% of the total Government budget each year. The team was informed that the education sector is benefiting more in terms of financing than other public sectors. The Central authorities have asked the Provincial authorities to match their commitment.

Funding of public programmes is limited by the generalised problem of the low level of government revenues in China. Tax revenues amount to about 12% of GDP, around half that of other countries at a similar stage, *e.g.* India, Brazil. Broadening the tax base is a general objective but success could boost the resources available to education among other public programmes.

The pattern of education expenditure differs from that of OECD countries (Table 1). The bulk of expenditure in China, 67.8%, is devoted to compulsory education (primary and lower secondary) which accounts for 77.1% of enrolments. Upper secondary accounts for 8.4% of overall public expenditure on education, and 10.3% of enrolments. Tertiary education receives 21.8% of public expenditure on education, while accounting for 2.4% of total enrolments. In the OECD by contrast the proportions of

Table A.3.1. **Percentage distribution of enrolment and expenditure by level of education**
(full- and part-time)

	China (1997)		OECD (1998)	
	Enrolment	Expenditure	Enrolment	Expenditure
Pre-primary	9.7%	1.9%	11.5	6.7
Primary and lower secondary	77.1	67.8	52.5	43.1
Upper secondary	10.3	8.4	20.4	22.4
Post-secondary, non-tertiary			1.5	1.7
All tertiary	2.4	21.8	14.0	22.4

Note: OECD data are country averages. Expenditure data for OECD countries are for 1997.
Source: OECD (1999), *Investing in Education: Analysis of the 1999 World Education Indicators*, Paris; OECD (2000), *Education at a Glance: OECD Indicators*, Paris.

educational spending are, on average, 43.1% for primary and lower secondary; 22.4% for upper secondary; and 22.4% for all tertiary.

Funding at the institutional level in China comes from a number of sources. While the most successful universities benefit from revenues from the commercialisation of their research efforts, others especially at the Provincial level depend heavily on Central and Provincial Government funding. For leading institutions, such as Quinghua and Peking Universities, approximately one-third of operating costs are financed through funds from the MoE. Tuition fees account for 7-8% of financing at these institutions, although the team was told that at Peking University, for example, student financial support exceeds the amount of fees received. The remainder of expenditures are financed from sales of technology (through university enterprises or science parks), research contracts and donations.

The situation at the Provincial level is particularly precarious, especially after the transfer of some national universities to provincial control and the recent increase in enrolments. The transfers, although welcomed as a means of decentralising the system and strengthening the linkages between these institutions and the local economy and its education system, has brought in its wake funding difficulties. In Shaanxi Province, 17 universities have been transferred to the Provincial Government, making a total of 32 provincial institutions and reducing the number of national universities to 7. Central Government funding to all institutions, however, has been maintained at the same amount as before the expansion in enrolments and this is expected to continue under current policy. The patterns of financing tertiary education in the Province have evolved, as shown in Table 2.

The combination of flat rate contribution from Central Government, which will, over time, represent a declining share of funding, and the outstanding question of how the transfer of pension, health and other liabilities to the Provincial Government will be handled, will inevitably restrict Shaanxi Province's ability to reach the 15% enrolment target by 2005, let alone their self-declared aim of 20% by 2010, notwithstanding the Provincial authorities intention to invest in tertiary education 20% of the increase in local government income. French experience here is instructive. The policy for deconcentration, with an aim to provide for a wider distribution of tertiary education institutions and enrolment outside of Paris,

Table A.3.2. **Patterns of financing tertiary education (Shaanxi province)**

	1996	1999
Tuition fees	5%	15%
National contribution	85	60-70
Revenues from technology transfer, etc.	3-4	8-10
Donations	7	7

has been successful in achieving a rapid expansion of provision across the country and a certain sharing of costs between regional and national levels. The geographic balance of institutions and programmes proved less easy to realise, as did the control of recurrent costs.

As part of the national policy to serve the West, Shaanxi Province has been host to many national universities. As a result of the concentration of institutions, the Province is rated fourth of all the Chinese Provinces in the provision of tertiary education. Paradoxically, however, in terms of economic development, it ranks twentieth out of the 30 provinces. As a result of this status of provider of education, the Province attracts 40-50% of its students from other provinces, but does not benefit from any financial contribution from the "sending" provinces. No one spoken to questioned this role, but this inherited situation is one that will be difficult to sustain. While the team applauds the aim of extending provision in this way to students from less well-served areas, if quality is to be maintained, careful consideration will have to be given to both expanding provision in the other provinces, including in new and different ways (perhaps, along the lines described in the preceding section). Further, to ensure better cost sharing, by drawing on the resources and experience of the institutions in the Eastern urban areas (*e.g.* through co-operative ventures, assistance programmes and mentoring) as well as by establishing a system of funding that allows financing to follow the student (a policy practised in many OECD countries).

Sweden, Norway and New Zealand provide three different approaches to such arrangements. In Sweden, university colleges are located within a unified system and, although distinct institutions, draw and benefit from expertise provided by universities. Some college staff hold posts as professors at an associated university. Network Norway has a similar aim: to bring resources and expertise available throughout the country so that individual colleges and universities will collaborate and complement each other. Single institutions are expected to function as "nodes" within the network, with quality assured and programmes strengthened through collaboration with the single institution benefiting from the experience and specialities of other institutions. Research institutions and foundations can participate, and communication links are extended also to private colleges, business and industry and central and regional authorities. In Sweden and Norway, the strategy seeks to support and extend the work of the colleges while allowing and encouraging them to respond to local needs. Following a very different approach, universities in New Zealand have established linkages with polytechnics in other localities. Massey University, a leader in distance education, also moved to establish a branch campus outside its traditional "catchment" area.

Cost-effectiveness remains a major preoccupation. Some 40% of the institutions have less than 3 000 students and the case for reorganisation and restructuring seems strong. Outsourcing the provision of student and faculty accommodation and dining facilities is already taking place to reduce the direct burden on the institutions' financial and administrative resources. The Ministry of Finance in Beijing stated its intention to set up a system to evaluate the cost-effectiveness of funding.

Tuition fees are an accepted part of education in China. Fees are normally charged in all post-compulsory institutions. In some cases, private and key schools command substantial fees: USD 4 000 per annum was not considered unusual at leading primary schools. Fees vary according to the institution, the course and the economic status of the student.

OECD countries have a range of approaches to financing via tuition fees. While some have a policy of charging fees for tuition, others maintain their attachment to a publicly funded system. But, even in such "no-fees" countries, the principle of public funding has limits. Denmark expects institutions offering Open Education courses, on a part-time basis and to adults in the evenings, to charge up to 20% of the costs. In Finland and Sweden, students and their families shoulder part of the costs of maintenance. But what is common is the recognition that because of the pressure on public expenditure of all sorts, greater innovation and creativity has to be deployed in funding education and other public programmes. To make expansion possible and effective the resources of the whole community need to be mobilised. Since the benefits of higher levels of education accrue to both society and individuals, both public and private investment is generally recognised to be justified. Equally, it is recognised that tuition fees should not in themselves create barriers to participation and that there should be arrangements in place to ensure that able students from low-income backgrounds are not excluded from pursuing higher levels of learning.

Various possibilities already exist for students to gain support for their studies – including grants; loans of up to 8 000 RMB (approx. USD 966) per annum, with, for the poorest, half the interest rate subsidised by the MoE; fees forgone; scholarships (including from companies); and self-help in the shape of part-time work by the student themselves.

Private universities

Out of a total of 100 private universities that have been established only 37 have been recognised to offer degree courses. Since there is, as yet, no law on the establishment of private universities (now being discussed), the existing institutions operate under the 1998 Law on Higher Education, which stipulates that all institutions should operate on a not-for-profit basis. This lack of clarity raises some uncertainties about the status of these institutions in terms of ownership of the assets.

Some public funding is provided amounting to about 8% of total costs. The remainder of expenditure is covered by fees which vary according to the category of student:

- Ordinary students   7 000 to 8 000 RMB (approx. USD 845-966) per annum.
- Adult students   2 000 RMB (approx. USD 241) per annum.
- Self-taught adult students   4 000 RMB (approx. USD 483) per annum.
  (preparing for graduation examinations)

The content of courses is decidedly market-oriented and students are enrolled with no guarantees given on getting a job after graduation. The private university visited by the team had a very good record: with 98.3% of graduates finding employment, its placement rate approaches the essentially universal employment experience of graduates from the most prestigious universities such as Quinghua. As participation increases and restructuring of the economy gathers pace, market-responsiveness will be key to the success of the private institutions.

Private universities that respond rapidly and nimbly to the changing demands of the labour market of the new economy could provide some of the diversity and flexibility that the Chinese education system will require. The early enactment of a law on private universities would provide a more solid legal basis and more certainty for the operation of these institutions in future.

Labour market linkages

As the Chinese economy has diversified, so, too, has the structure of the labour market. During the past ten years, non-State enterprises have been the main source of new jobs. With employment in the State Owned Enterprises (SOEs) and the urban collectives on the decline, the private enterprise sector now accounts for almost all the net growth in employment in the urban economy. In rural areas, where 80% of the population lives, the Township and Village Enterprises (TVEs), together with the private enterprises, are the main sources of employment growth.[12] (See also Table 3.)

The share of the labour force in agriculture, which stood at 70% in 1978, is now down to 45%. It is the tertiary sector that has witnessed strongest growth in employment share over this same period, up from 12% to 29% of the labour force. That share is expected to grow to 36 per cent by 2010. The industrial sector, too, has seen its share of employment increase to 26 percent, from 17 per cent in 1978 (Table 4).

The team learned in Xi'an that the downsizing of the SOEs has had a significant impact on the local labour market. It was only in 2000, after three lean years, that the demand for graduates showned any upturn. Of the 70 000 graduates – 30 000 from the universities and 40 000 from the vocational schools – some 80% are reported to find their jobs through what is described as "mutual choice" employment. The remaining 20% were assigned jobs by the Government. However, students tend to avoid seeking employment in those areas where economic development is low. They prefer the attraction of the

Table A.3.3. **Number of enterprises and employment by type, 1990 and 1998**

	1990	1998	1990	1998
	Number (000s)	Number (000s)	Employees (000s)	Employees (000s)
State-owned	1 152	1 836	104	91
Private	98	1 201	2	17
TVE	18 504	20 039	93	125
Foreign	25	228	1	6
Collective	3 382	3 736	35	19

Note: "Private" include individual-owned, shareholding, limited liability corporations and others; "foreign" also include investment from Hong Kong, Macao and Taiwan. TVE are not based on ownership, but geographical locations of sponsors. They are founded by towns, villages or individuals in rural areas, and are mostly collective or private.

Source: World Bank (2000), *China's development strategy: The knowledge and innovation perspective*, Washington, D.C.

burgeoning labour markets of the Eastern urban centres. In order to encourage graduates to go to the less developed areas, incentives are on offer. For example, for Government jobs in these regions the probationary period is waived, salaries can be increased by one or two steps, subsidies are available, and after an initial contract of 5-8 years the individual has the right to move elsewhere. Some 28% of graduates in 1999-2000 found employment in the private sector, and efforts are being made to establish favourable working conditions that would encourage graduates to seek employment on the private and TVE sectors in the rural areas.

The placement of tertiary education institutions may provide another incentive to retain or attract graduates to less developed regions. Norway has advanced such a view, seeing programmes offered in its tertiary education institutions in the less densely populated northern area as part of a strategy to keep students – and graduates – in those regions. Programme offerings have been expanded through arrangements with co-operating universities and colleges in other regions, an approach to which attention has already been drawn.

Job assignment is no longer practised but for those graduates who wish to protect their "cadre status", *i.e.* the right to public employment, all employment contracts are subject to specific durations. Contracts in the townships of 6 years (in low development areas) of 5-8 years and fixed term contracts in the private sector negotiated by the employers and the individual, will guarantee continued cadre status. These arrangements, which undoubtedly provide an element of security for some in a period of transition, carry with them a clear risk of hindering labour market flexibility and deterring employees and employers from coming to the sort of arrangements that would suit each of them. The team was pleased to learn later in Beijing that the concept of "cadre status" is to be abandoned and that everyone will be considered as an employee. The "right" that cadre status has implied will disappear. This will be important in allowing everyone to make the most appropriate employment choices in response to the information available on labour market opportunities.

It has been noted in other countries faced with rapid economic transformation that improving efficiency and longer-term competitivity depends on a virtuous circle of mutually reinforcing progress on

Table A.3.4. **Employment share by sector, 1978 and 2000**

	1978	2000
Agriculture	70.5%	45.0%
Industry	17.4	26.0
Tertiary	12.1	29.0

Source: World Bank (2000), *China's development strategy: The knowledge and innovation perspective*, Washington, DC.

a wide range of reforms and on the growth of the economy as a whole. An effective labour market will contribute to the overall economy as well as benefiting from economic growth. If labour markets are to function effectively, information about vacancies, skill demands, training opportunities, salaries etc. must be readily available, to all – students, employed and unemployed – and in as user-friendly and transparent way as possible. As the private share of jobs expands, so, too, will it be necessary to ensure the availability of information and guidance to potential job seekers.

Labour market developments have already had an impact upon the educational institutions, their courses and the way in which they operate. With the abandonment of the job assignment system in 1996, students now secure their employment through the labour market. As a result, the whole of the tertiary education sector is being restructured to respond to the needs of what is a rapidly evolving market. This entails recasting the curriculum to ensure a broader knowledge base and eliminate the over-specialisation that existed previously. Students in the words of one leading educationalist "are to become flexible and adaptable to rapidly changing needs". "Creativity" is now the watchword. These changes are also affecting the design of school curriculum and examinations. It is widely accepted that the new economy will demand new skills, rounder individuals with interpersonal skills.

The team has heard of major reorganisation of courses with many areas of study, where employment prospects are declining or even disappearing, being dropped with the aim of establishing more broadly-based majors focusing on the "new" areas such as technology and telecommunications (computer science, bio-technology etc.). The prospect of WTO membership loomed large in the thoughts of many of those with whom discussions were had, as did the need to concentrate on improvements in those areas where the Chinese economy does not come up to international standards.

Conclusion: steering and the expansion of tertiary education

So far in this report have been reviewed the sorts of issues that appeared to be the main elements of a possible vision for the development of a greatly expanded tertiary education system in China. This concluding section turns to the question of steering that system. One of the first questions facing all partners is where should leadership rest? Responding to that requires answers to related questions. What should be the scope of leadership? What instruments should be used to transmit or mediate that leadership? Which responsibilities should be bundled together to maximise effective leadership? Which responsibilities should be separated to enhance efficiency and reduce friction, ambiguity and duplication?

The OECD countries have answered these questions differently. The federal nations have answered them differently from the nation states, which, in turn, have answered them in differing ways. Those few nations with robust private university sectors have different approaches to questions of regulation and student financing than those who regard university education as essentially a public good. The younger nations have addressed quality assurance issues differently from the nations laying claim to the oldest universities.

Context notwithstanding, a set of key assumptions shapes approaches to governance:

- Tertiary education is a "semi-public" good. By this it has been argued tertiary education contributes to the nation as a whole, to the economy, to the community and to the body of knowledge shared by all. Of course, it also contributes to the capacities and wealth of individuals – giving them a private benefit. This mixture of public and private benefit characterises the current and likely future tertiary system in China, as it does in OECD countries.

- National ministries should be small in size and strategic in focus. The recent reductions in the size of the Ministry of Education and other national agencies in China align with this view. By way of corollary, with a slimmer national government, greater authority is vested in the provinces, municipalities and institutions. The same aims and tendencies are to be found in the OECD area.

- Greater emphasis on individual choice: of institutions, of course of study, of pathways and of occupation. In China, the move away from the assignment system whereby graduates are allocated to a particular employer to one of "mutual choice" with assignment occurring only when no agreement can be reached is an example of increased choice.

This constellation of assumptions and the appreciation of different governance models around the world led the team to frame these questions in terms of steering. In English this is distinct from notions of "controlling", " governing" and "managing"; all of these words imply a degree of singular authority and system responsiveness. Steering can be imagined as the act of driving a car: sitting behind the engine, the source of power, with a destination in mind and a limited number of gauges and external signposts to guide and inform decisions. You have the capacity to speed up, slow down, turn and reverse.

With this metaphor and the three assumptions in mind the team offers the following comments as the basis for a broader discussion about the appropriate mix of steering mechanisms for China's tertiary education system in the next twenty years, as it moves towards large-volume participation with greater equality of access and higher quality.

Strategic instruments for steering

The experience of OECD countries and transition economies shows that essential functions for governing a growing, large-volume tertiary education system providing a range of learning options to a diverse student population may be identified as follows:

- formulating and setting goals for the tertiary education system within the national education system as a whole, which reflect the desired economic and social development of the country;
- elaborating and enforcing a legal framework for the effective operation of public and private institutions of tertiary education;
- designing, financing and implementing national programmes to foster the achievement of national goals;
- promoting equality of access to tertiary education – urban and rural, young and older adult;
- providing accurate and timely information about the supply, demand and value of particular skills and qualifications;
- fostering, financing and evaluating the research and innovation dimensions of the tertiary education sector;
- assuring high quality teaching, learning and research in the interests of the nation and individuals; and
- reporting on a regular basis about the efficiency, effectiveness and quality of the tertiary education system.

These eight functions are to a large degree interdependent: more weight on one function might reduce the need for another or reduce the intensity with which it is carried out.

Drawing upon the issues explored earlier, the team comments in greater detail on each of the eight functions and raises questions about the appropriate locus of responsibility.

Formulating goals

In setting goals for tertiary education, OECD countries have increasingly recognised that this level of education is one, albeit important, part of a national education system. Ensuring appropriate linkages and relationships between levels of education is seen as essential, if the system as a whole is to be effective. All levels of the tertiary system should be involved in goal setting and formulation. In China, at the national level, goal setting can be done through the five-year plan. The Ministry of Education's current thinking – to see the five-year plan as a set of strategies and guidelines rather than a platform of finely specified targets and mandated actions – seems to be just right. This approach allows Provinces and institutions to build on their particular strengths and to take into account local circumstances even as important national objectives are being pursued. This more strategic approach to goal setting should also be adopted by Provincial education authorities in working with tertiary institutions, and particularly the universities. This approach would enhance institutional autonomy (a matter which is returned to below).

National goal formulation depends on good, relevant and reliable data. The example of a target for expansion is instructive. Differences were noted in how various levels and different types of tertiary education institution were responding (or planning to respond) to growth. Some premier universities seemed reluctant to increase capacity, because of physical constraints and because of a concern that quality would be undermined at a time when there was also a national goal of creating world-class universities. Other types of tertiary education institution were keen to expand so they could respond to changes in demand from individuals and employers. In many cases, the expansion of provision in these types of institution appeared to be constrained by the lengthy approval process for national funds for the necessary capital works. In this respect, holding the funds for expansion in Beijing seems to be an unnecessary degree of central control.

Taken together, these two observations help to illustrate the importance of expressing goals in a way that takes into account linkages and trade-offs. While concrete and simple targets such as the proportion of an age cohort enrolled in tertiary education have powerful symbolic and signalling effects, they can also impede the pursuit of other goals such as quality and market responsiveness and neglect the kinds of complementarities and linkages needed to realise the goals.

As China's socialist market economy continues to evolve and develop there will be marked and quite rapid changes in the levels and types of skills and qualifications required. While these cannot be "planned" they can be anticipated in a very broad sense (drawing from experiences in other transition economies and by modelling likely changes in the occupational structure). Indeed the team was struck by the consistency in changes of demand that were identified at the national, Provincial and institutional levels. Students already are choosing to move towards fields like computing sciences, informatics, telecommunications and applied sciences and to move away from – if not seeking to complement and balance – theoretical studies and narrow specialisations.

A *legal framework*

Most OECD countries have explicit laws that set out the roles and responsibilities of institutions offering tertiary education. These laws usually define the accountability and reporting requirements of tertiary education institutions (particularly those receiving public funds or awarding nationally-recognised qualifications). In some countries, the relevant legislation also specifies the criteria for the establishment and regulation of private institutions. It is through such legislation and the related regulatory framework that most OECD countries are trying to address emerging issues of programmes and studies offered by cross-border, ICT-based or private providers.

The experience of other countries is that supporting legislation and regulatory frameworks are highly desirable. Particularly with regard to private tertiary education providers, the legislation and regulations resolve questions about the ownership of institutional property and assets. In so doing, they provide for the certainty in operations and clarity in legal status needed to attract private source funding.

Programmes *addressing national goals*

In the OECD area, setting goals, writing laws and advocating change has not been sufficient to encourage and enable change in programmes, teaching and learning. Most countries now design, finance and evaluate programmes and projects that aim to influence providers to undertake change. The team heard about and saw examples of such efforts during in China. To take one example, the 211 project already appeared to be having a significant impact on the universities involved.

The development and design of such initiatives have proved to be more effective when they are informed both by the empirical assessment of earlier interventions and by the active participation of experts and officials from institutions that are expected to implement the desired changes. Relevance, feasibility and practicability are enhanced when this involvement is built in to the early stages of design.

This formal involvement acknowledges the autonomy of tertiary education institutions; it also supports the development in each institution of the capacity to effectively exercise that autonomy.

Equality of access

China has a long-standing commitment to equality of access to tertiary education. An elaborate infrastructure for self-study students and the education of peasants, workers and minorities has been in place for some time. However, as is true in OECD countries, minorities and women tend to be under-represented in the highest demand programmes, and participation by otherwise capable young people from poor families or geographically remote areas are deterred by the direct and indirect costs.

Student loans, both mortgage-type and income-contingent, and grants for tertiary study are common equity strategies in many OECD countries.[13] The different experiences and models warrant study by the Ministry of Education, in order to better evaluate the successes and failures of the pilot loan schemes currently underway at the institutional, municipal and Provincial levels.

There is a strong case for the use of public funds to finance tertiary education. But this should not obviate individuals from bearing some of the costs of participation in tertiary education. As well as contributing to the public good, individuals receive a private benefit through higher incomes as a result of participation and completion of studies at this level. In a number of OECD countries, this is now seen as justification for some individual contribution toward tuition or maintenance. The burden of such contributions is eased not only through access to loan financing (with extended repayment arrangements) but also by contributed service, such as service in remote areas for a limited period of time. Both options exist in China.

The use of public funds for these purposes should not crowd out private sector funding. Indeed, in most OECD countries where private source funding accounts for a growing share of expenditure on tertiary education, public expenditure also has increased. Further, in transition economies, a student loan scheme offers an important opportunity to diversify the financial sector and to create credit opportunities.

While costs play a role in the decisions of young people and adults to participate in tertiary education, relatively lower rates of participation from lower income groups, ethnic and linguistic minorities and (in some countries) women reflect partly the failure of schooling to retain and adequately prepare students from these groups. This remains a policy priority in OECD countries as much as in China, where the quality, relevance and accessibility of primary and secondary education require attention and investment. As far as the team could tell, the issue is most pressing in the poorer Western Provinces where significant numbers of children fail to enrol in or complete primary education.

Supply and demand information

Reliable and timely information about the demand for and value of particular skills and qualifications plays a key role in a more market-oriented, demand-driven tertiary education system. Information of this type helps students make choices about programs of study and possible futures. It also helps institutions anticipate changes in demand.

In support of "mutual choice" employment in China, Provincial and local authorities are producing handbooks on the number of graduates by field of study and the number of employers interested in recruiting from these fields. While useful, this information appears to be incomplete because it does not provide reliable information on the "value" of particular qualifications (especially in the private sector). Information on such matters is transmitted more often by word of mouth or the popular media. Some Provincial and municipal authorities seek to build information bridges between tertiary education institutions and employers, but it was the impression of the team that these constructive endeavours were partial in scope and coverage. They often failed to pick up information on changing demands for skills and qualifications, generally and within particular occupations; the emerging market-oriented economy and the rapidly developing private sector are poorly covered. Specialist institutions and private providers seemed to be more aware of changes in supply and demand of those with specific tertiary-level qualifications; many had responded by changing course combinations, offering new courses and making significant investments in information technology (both to support teaching computer sciences and other digitally-based programmes and to improve the quality of teaching and learning).

Research and innovation

In China, the position of research and innovation in tertiary education seems to be uncertain. Research historically was publicly financed through a system of national institutes. Although this is now changing, research, teaching and learning and industrial application remain separated. In a market-oriented economy, the separation of these functions makes knowledge diffusion, increased productivity and innovation more difficult. The challenge of how to foster greater complementarity across these functions is familiar to OECD countries, and no less difficult there than in China.

The team noted, in particular, that university-based research findings are being transformed into productive enterprises, either owned and operated by the university itself or through a private sector incubator or holding company. The revenues generated through such activities make an important contribution to the overall level of resources available to universities. But, this too is a matter of some concern, if the volume of such arrangements unduly divert leadership in the universities from other key areas of teaching, fundamental research and wider networking in support of improved schooling and other types of tertiary education. Experience in OECD countries suggests that the transfer of research findings and enterprise links do not have to compete with key missions of the university. However, efforts need to be made to maintain balance and to foster the complementarities afforded by such arrangements.

Teaching and learning

In all countries – China no less than those in the OECD area – there is a pressing need to lift the quality of teaching and learning. Although there was limited opportunity to observe teaching in the course of the visit, the team was impressed by the opportunities for practical learning – building on a solid grounding in theoretical work – provided in a private university. Policies to improve teaching and learning centre on recruitment of new faculty, opportunities for faculty to gain higher degrees (domestically and internationally) and "twinning" with leading universities. These are reasonable approaches, with counterparts in OECD countries, where there also are efforts to evaluate, support and improve teaching particularly in the first years of tertiary education.

Reporting

Reporting should occur routinely, systematically, in a timely manner and in an accessible form; reporting should come from all levels of the tertiary education system and all institutions. Reports should focus on the use of funds and on the quality and results of learning, teaching and knowledge creation.

Such reports emerge as essential elements in systems that allow more institutional autonomy and flexibility. It was put this way by the UNESCO and World Bank Task Force on Higher Education: "Accountability does not imply uncontrolled interference, but it does impose a requirement to periodically explain actions and have successes and failures examined in a transparent fashion".[14] Accountability is the natural counterpart of autonomy.

Sharing responsibility for these functions

It remains to identify the levels at which responsibility for each of these functions is lodged. China's tertiary education system is very heterogeneous with many different forms of institutions serving different populations and offering different qualifications. It is similar, in this respect, to most OECD countries, a number of which have taken steps to increase further diversity in provision and to extend participation in all forms of tertiary education to adults. In the face of this diversity, it is possible only to offer general principles that should figure in the consideration of responsibilities of different levels of governance, institutions and partners in steering tertiary education.

- *Setting explicit goals and reporting on progress towards those goals.* All levels and sectors of the system share these responsibilities. The goals should align with a clear national vision for all education and learning. The Central Government has the responsibility to lead goal setting and reporting processes, but those processes will be most effective when carried out in close co-operation with ministries with economic and social functions and in consultation with private enterprise, civil society, Provincial Governments and educational institutions at secondary as well as tertiary levels.

- *Promoting equality of access.* This responsibility is shared across governance levels and with institutions. The Ministry of Education has a particular responsibility to ensure that schools prepare *all* young people – regardless of family income, geographic region or locality, ethnicity or gender – for participation in tertiary education and to encourage and enable participation of adults in a wider range of tertiary-level learning opportunities.

- *Establishing a legal framework and designing and financing of programmes to support national goals.* A national agency responsible for the strategic direction of tertiary education should assume responsibility for these matters. OECD countries vest the responsibility for these tasks in the Ministry of Education or a designated tertiary education commission. In either case, the agency should either be responsible directly for all or none of the tertiary education institutions. The team notes that many countries have taken steps to separate responsibility for the legal framework from the direct responsibility for provision. Such a separation allows for a more flexible and pro-active response to cross-border or private provision as well as for a balanced handling of competing demands from the full range of public tertiary education institutions (some of which have had a preferential relationship with a regulatory or financing agency).

- *Improving teaching and learning.* This is primarily the responsibility of each tertiary education institution. Given the growing importance the globalisation of knowledge and the long-standing value of cross-border co-operation in scholarship and research, a system-wide investment in tertiary education faculty exchange, co-operative research and upgrading of academic qualifications should be made by Central Government. The Central Government responsibility extends to support for quality improvement initiatives and co-operative arrangements to establish standards.

- *Gathering and disseminating reliable market information.* At present, responsibility in this area is highly diffused and should, in the view of the team, remain so. In OECD countries, the Ministry of Labour, statistics or census bureaus, trade unions, employers and professional associations often collect and provide such information. In some countries, the data are collected and made available on a commercial basis by newspapers and publishers. The Ministry of Education should take on as its responsibility the encouragement of these and other groups to develop and disseminate such information widely – to potential students, employers and tertiary education institutions. The team's view is that a diversity of sources of such information is to be welcomed. The benefits to more informed and improved choices and planning outweigh redundancy, duplication and uneven coverage by some information providers.

The approach to reform in China is one of gradualism – "following the stepping stones across the river". Nonetheless, the pace and depth of tertiary education reform have increased markedly in the past two years. Successful tertiary education reform will not be achieved in isolation, as both quality and success in primary and secondary education and increased adult participation in further education and training (including at the tertiary level) represent important complementary elements to reform from a lifelong learning perspective. Nor will the hoped-for contributions of tertiary education to economic development and overall well-being be realised by the universities alone; all forms of tertiary-level studies – degree- and certificate-awarding, academic and vocationally-oriented, full- and part-time, resident and at a distance, ICT-based – need to be reinforced and extended, and supported through linkages with the leading universities. Changes in these areas may require thinking about the "unthinkable", where further reflection on new ways to improve access to learning across the country and across the life cycle will lead to consideration of other departures from existing arrangements and provision. Indeed, the reforms in train already reveal some attention to these aspects, too.

There will be much to learn – in China, but also in OECD countries – from the efforts underway. If the results of these efforts are monitored with the vision and goals in view and policies are adapted in the light of what is learned, tertiary education will figure prominently as the entire education system is harnessed in support of achieving the goal of middle-income status by 2020.

NOTES

1. This report was prepared by Alan Wagner and Tom Alexander of the OECD Directorate for Education, Labour and social affairs, based on the results of a field study. Members of the study team were: Thomas J. Alexander (Former Director for Education, Employment, Labour and Social Affairs, OECD; Senior Research Fellow, Department of Educational Studies, University of Oxford, United Kingdom), Agneta Bladh (State Secretary, Ministry of Education and Science; Member, OECD Education Committee, Sweden), Alan Ruby (Sector Manager for Human Development, East Asia and Pacific Region, The World Bank; Former Deputy Secretary, Department of Employment, Education and Training, Australia; Former Member and Chair, OECD Education Committee Australia), Marshall S. Smith (Professor School of Education, Stanford University; Former Deputy Secretary of Education, United States Department of Education; Former Member, OECD Education Committee, United States, and Alan Wagner (OECD Secretariat). The PRC team was headed by Ms. Yu Wei, Vice Minister of Education; Mr. Zhang Li, Director of the National Centre for Education Development Research; Mr. Zheng Fuzhi, Deputy Dirctor General, Department of Development Planning; Mr. Fan Wenyao, Deputy Director of the National Centre for Education Development Research; and Ms. Yang Xiuwen, research specialist of the National Centre for Education Development Research.

2. OECD (1998), *Redefining Tertiary Education*, Paris.

3. The People's Republic of China (2000), "Innovation in Education for the 21st Century" Discussion paper presented at the 2nd APEC Education Ministerial Meeting, 2000.

4. TEIs (tertiary education institutions) consists of universities, 4- and 2-year colleges, 3-year colleges (polytechnics), advanced vocational education institutions (community colleges) and branch schools. Adult TEIs consists of radio/TV universities, workers'/peasants' colleges, institutes of administration, educational colleges (in-service training course), independent correspondence colleges, evening schools, short-cycle courses. The enrollment data refer to individuals enrolled in these establishments, at tertiary level. Tertiary level, in this case, means that the programmes are aimed at those who have completed the full cycle of secondary schooling.

5. OECD (2000), *Education at a Glance*; OECD Indicators 2000, Paris.

6. OECD (2000), *Education at a Glance*: OECD Indicators 2000, Paris.

7. See *www.chinaonline.com/topstories/000814/c400081112.asp*

8. *www.oli.hk/about.html*

9. For example, "besides planning and implementing distance learning in Shanghai, the Shanghai Jiao Tong University centre is also in charge of developing distance learning technology – a key task of the 9th 5-year plan. Meanwhile the centre is holding several domestic collaboration exercises on distance learning technology such as the one with Shanghai Jiaotong University, Fudan University, Shanghai medical University, Shanghai University, Shanghai Broadcast and T.V. University. In addition to the domestic projects mentioned above, the centre has also gone international by receiving such aids as the Intel Research Fund, AT&T Research Fund and Yuanzhi Engineering University Research Fund from Taiwan. Presently, the centre has already set up extensive co-operative research relations with numerous universities in Taiwan, Japan, USA and German etc." *www.dlc.sjtu.edu.cn/English/lab_Eng.htm* Both Quinghua and Peking Universities in Beijing have similar efforts underway.

10. *www.chinaonline.com/refer/edu_servi ces/currentnews/secure/B200080305.asp*

11. *www.chinaonline.com/issues/econ_new s/currentnews/secure/c00092602.asp*

12. OECD (2000), *Reforming China's Enterprises*, Paris.

13. OECD (1998), "Paying for tertiary education: The learner perspective," *Education Policy Analysis* 1998, Paris; OECD (1999), "Tertiary education: Extending the benefits of growth to new groups", *Education Policy Analysis* 1999, Paris.

14. The Task Force on Higher Education (2000), *Higher Education in Developing Countries: Peril and Promise*, The World Bank and UNESCO.

Annex IV

MAIN ECONOMIC INDICATORS FOR CHINA

The statistics presented in this annex were first published in the March 2002 edition of *Main Economic Indicators*.

CHINA

		1998	1999	2000	2001	1999 Q4	2000 Q1	Q2	Q3	Q4	2001 Q1	Q2	Q3	Q4
NATIONAL ACCOUNTS														
Current prices														
Final consumption	CNY bln	4640.6	5005.5											
Households	CNY bln	3692.1	3943.2											
Government[1]	CNY bln	948.5	1062.3											
Gross capital formation	CNY bln	3039.6	3141.7											
Gross fixed capital formation	CNY bln	2818.1	2964.6											
Change in stocks	CNY bln	221.5	177.0											
Gross domestic product[2]	CNY bln	7834.5	8205.4	8940.4		8205.4	1817.3	3949.1	6212.4	8940.4	1989.5	4294.2	6722.7	
GDP per capita	CNY	6277	6517	6902										
PRODUCTION														
Indices of production														
Industry excluding construction[3]	SPPY=100													
Commodity output[4]														
Coal	tonnes '000		80199	70775	80040	86468	61331	73317	70284	78169	71307	80329	77808	90715
Crude steel	tonnes '000	9511	10304	10526	11879	10993	9954	10446	10548	11157	10918	11393	11906	13297
Cement	tonnes '000	44667	44982	48617	52136	50105	37855	54141	50897	51574	40188	55510	54317	58530
Crude petroleum	tonnes '000	13417	13365	13519	13736	13448	13512	13514	13530	13521	13540	13745	13796	13864
Electricity	Gwh mln	97	101	109	118	103	102	108	115	113	109	116	126	123
BUSINESS AND CONSUMER OPINIONS														
Business tendency surveys														
Business climate	% balance					1	0	4	7	8	5	9		
Sales: level	% balance					-3	-5	3	2	2	0	3		
Order books: level[5]	% balance					-18	-17	13	-12	-12	-11	-9		
Finished goods stocks: level	% balance					8	9	3	5	3	4	5		
Judgement on capacity utilisation	% balance					-32	-35	-31	-29	-28	-28	-26		
Consumer surveys														
Consumer confidence indicator	normal=100													
DOMESTIC DEMAND														
Retail sales														
Value	CNY bln	2934.3	3113.4	3415.3	3759.5	898.6	839.5	785.4	808.8	981.7	925.6	865.9	887.8	1080.2
sa	CNY bln					808.4	828.0	840.5	860.7	883.0	911.1	927.5	945.6	971.4
LABOUR														
Employment														
Total - labour force survey	Millions	699.6	705.9	711.5	730.3									
Unemployment[6]														
Level - registered	Millions	5.7	5.8	5.8			5.6	5.6	5.8	5.9	6.1			
Rate - registered	%	3.1	3.1	3.1			3.0	3.0	3.1	3.1	3.2			
Labour compensation														
Monthly earnings[7]	CNY	7479	8319	9333		8319	2096	4164	6309	9333	2343	4694	7197	
PRICES														
Producer prices														
Industry	SPPY=100	95.9	97.6	102.8										
Consumer prices														
All items	SPPY=100	99.2	98.6	100.4										
Food	SPPY=100	96.8	95.8	97.4										
Fuel and electricity	SPPY=100													
Services	SPPY=100	110.1	110.6	114.1										

More detailed methodological information at http//www.oecd.org/std/mei. Footnotes appear at the end of the table.

		2001 Feb	Mar	Apr	May	Jun	Jul	Aug	Sep	Oct	Nov	Dec	2002 Jan	Var sur 12 mois
COMPTES NATIONAUX														
Prix courants														
Consommation finale	CNY mld													7.9
Ménages	CNY mld													6.8
Administrations publiques[1]	CNY mld													12.0
Formation brute de capital	CNY mld													3.4
Formation brute de capital fixe	CNY mld													5.2
Variations des stocks	CNY mld													
Produit intérieur brut[2]	CNY mld													9.0
PIB par habitant	CNY													5.9
PRODUCTION														
Indices de production														
Industrie non compris la construction[3]	SPPY=100	119.0	112.1	111.5	110.2	110.1	108.1	108.1	109.5	108.8	107.9	108.7		
Quantités produites[4]														
Charbon	tonnes '000	67974	82494	79422	80626	80938	74142	78100	81181	83893	88065	100187		15.4
Acier brut	tonnes '000	10276	11376	11040	11454	11687	11934	11887	11896	12668	12872	14351	14500	30.6
Ciment	tonnes '000	34794	52231	54875	56702	54952	51573	54165	57213	56356	56386	62848	46952	40.0
Pétrole brut	tonnes '000	12765	14336	13569	14057	13610	13852	14025	13510	14070	13627	13895		1.1
Électricité	Gwh mln	106	117	112	118	119	131	127	119	118	120	131	132	27.0
OPINIONS DES INDUSTRIELS ET DES MÉNAGES														
Enquêtes de conjoncture (entreprises)														
Climat des affaires	solde en %													
Niveau des ventes	solde en %													
Carnets de commande: niveau[5]	solde en %													
Stocks de produits finis: niveau	solde en %													
Jugement sur l'util. Des capacités	solde en %													
Enquêtes auprès des ménages														
Confiance des consommateurs	normal=100	97	97	98	97	97	98							
DEMANDE INTÉRIEURE														
Ventes au détail														
Valeur	CNY mld	304.7	287.6	282.1	293.0	290.9	285.1	288.9	313.7	334.7	342.2	403.3		9.6
cvs	CNY mld	300.1	302.5	304.5	313.1	309.9	312.2	314.7	318.7	323.9	323.3	324.1		9.7
MAIN-D'OEUVRE														
Emploi														
Total - enquête sur la population active	Millions													2.6
Chômage[6]														
Niveau - inscrits	Millions													0.2
Taux - inscrits	%													
Rémunération du travail														
Gains mensuels[7]	CNY													
PRIX														
Prix à la production														
Industrie	SPPY=100	100.9	100.2	99.9	99.8	99.4	98.7	98.0	97.1	96.9	96.3			
Prix à la consommation														
Total	SPPY=100	100.0	100.8	101.6	101.7	101.4	101.5	101.0	99.9	100.2	99.7	99.7	99.0	
Alimentation	SPPY=100	96.7	99.0	101.3	101.7	101.0	101.5	100.2	100.3	100.8	99.2	99.2	98.1	
Combustibles et électricité	SPPY=100													
Services	SPPY=100	109.3	109.5	109.6	109.4	109.1	108.9	108.8	101.9	102.1	102.0	101.6		

Des informations méthodologiques plus détaillées sur http//www.oecd.org/std/mei. Les notes se trouvent en fin de tableau

CHINA *(continued)*

		1998	1999	2000	2001	1999 Q4	2000 Q1	2000 Q2	2000 Q3	2000 Q4	2001 Q1	2001 Q2	2001 Q3	2001 Q4
FINANCE														
Monetary aggregates[8]														
Monetary aggregate (M1)	CNY bln	3895	4584	5315	5987	4584	4516	4802	5062	5315	5303	5519	5682	5987
Monetary aggregate (M2)	CNY bln	10450	11990	13461	15830	11990	12258	12661	13047	13461	13874	14781	15182	15830
Share prices														
Shangai composite index	1995=100	206.5	248.8	341.7	349.5	258.5	303.1	339.7	357.5	366.5	368.4	393.3	331.3	305.1
Exchange rates[4]														
USD: spot	Cents/CNY	12.08	12.08	12.08	12.08	12.08	12.08	12.08	12.08	12.08	12.08	12.08	12.08	12.08
External finance[8]														
Official reserves excluding gold	USD bln	145.0	154.7	165.6	212.2	154.7	156.8	158.6	160.1	165.6	175.8	180.8	195.8	212.2
External debt: total	USD bln	146.0	151.8	145.7										
INTERNATIONAL TRADE[4]														
Imports c.i.f.	USD bln	11.69	13.81	18.76	20.30	16.04	15.50	18.54	20.33	20.65	18.18	20.64	21.66	20.71
sa	USD bln					14.17	18.32	18.60	20.17	18.50	21.30	20.73	21.43	18.54
Exports f.o.b.	USD bln	15.31	16.24	20.77	22.22	19.32	17.24	20.93	22.59	22.32	19.76	21.89	23.47	23.76
sa	USD bln					17.34	20.55	21.27	21.44	20.19	23.43	22.32	22.24	21.45
Net trade (f.o.b.-c.i.f.)	USD bln	3.62	2.43	2.01	1.92	3.27	1.74	2.39	2.26	1.66	1.57	1.25	1.82	3.05
sa	USD bln					3.17	2.23	2.67	1.27	1.68	2.14	1.59	0.81	2.91
Exports / imports	%	131	118	111	109	120	111	113	111	108	109	106	108	115
sa	%					123	112	114	106	109	110	108	104	116
Imports c.i.f. from EU15	USD bln	1.73	2.12	2.57	2.99	2.34	2.14	2.51	2.70	2.93	2.69	3.00	3.00	3.26
Exports f.o.b. to EU15	USD bln	2.35	2.53	3.18	3.40	2.97	2.80	3.23	3.44	3.26	3.27	3.35	3.32	3.66
Net trade (f.o.b.-c.i.f.) with EU15	USD bln	0.62	0.40	0.61	0.41	0.63	0.66	0.72	0.74	0.33	0.58	0.34	0.32	0.40
BALANCE OF PAYMENTS[9]														
Current balance	USD mln	29324	15667	20519								5099		
Balance on goods	USD mln	46614	36206	34474								13443		
Balance on services	USD mln	-4925	-7509	-5600								-3211		
Balance on income	USD mln	-16644	-17973	-14666								-8609		
Balance on current transfers	USD mln	4278	4943	6311								3476		
Capital and financial balance	USD mln	-12747	-863	-8626								3403		
Change in reserve assets	USD mln	-6426	-8505	-10548								-15572		
Net errors and omissions	USD mln	-16576	-14804	-11893								-8502		

(1) Covers both individual and collective consumption.
(2) Quarterly data are cumulative. The estimate for the year 1998 is a revised figure and there is a small discrepancy with the figure of the 4th quarter of 1998.
(3) Index of industrial value added.
(4) Monthly averages.
(5) Domestic order level only.
(6) Urban unemployment figures.
(7) Average annual nominal wage.
(8) End of period.
(9) Semestrial data.

| 2001 | | | | | | | | | | | 2002 | 12 month change | | | |
Feb	Mar	Apr	May	Jun	Jul	Aug	Sep	Oct	Nov	Dec	Jan	Var sur 12 mois			
														FINANCE	
														Agrégats monétaires[8]	
5200	5303	5326	5342	5519	5350	5581	5682	5611	5658	5987		*12.7*		Agrégat monétaire (M1)	*CNY mld*
13621	13874	13995	13902	14781	14923	14994	15182	15150	15409	15830		*17.6*		Agrégat monétaire (M2)	*CNY mld*
														Cours des actions	
352.8	380.5	381.6	398.8	399.4	345.8	330.3	317.8	304.2	314.8	296.4		*-20.6*		Bourse de Shangai: Indice synthétique	*1995=100*
														Taux de change[4]	
12.08	12.08	12.08	12.08	12.08	12.08	12.08	12.08	12.08	12.08	12.07	12.08	*0.0*		USD: comptant	*Cents/CNY*
														Finances extérieures[8]	
174.8	175.8	177.2	179.0	180.8	184.5	190.1	195.8	203.0	208.3	212.2	217.4	*28.9*		Réserves officielles or exclu	*USD mld*
														Dette extérieure: total	*USD mld*
														COMMERCE INTERNATIONAL[4]	
18.23	20.77	21.86	18.81	21.25	20.96	22.16	21.85	18.90	20.85	22.39	18.97	*22.0*		Importations c.a.f.	*USD mld*
22.88	20.78	21.45	20.57	20.16	20.86	22.24	21.19	20.11	19.53	15.97	24.63	*21.7*	*cvs*		*USD mld*
19.20	23.14	22.79	20.81	22.08	22.89	23.54	23.99	22.79	24.00	24.50	21.70	*28.2*		Exportations f.a.b.	*USD mld*
25.20	23.16	23.01	22.02	21.91	22.19	21.89	22.63	22.12	23.27	18.97	28.15	*28.3*	*cvs*		*USD mld*
0.97	2.37	0.93	2.00	0.83	1.93	1.38	2.14	3.89	3.16	2.11	2.73			Solde commercial (f.a.b.-c.a.f.)	*USD mld*
2.32	2.38	1.56	1.45	1.75	1.33	-0.34	1.44	2.00	3.74	3.00	3.52		*cvs*		*USD mld*
105	111	104	111	104	109	106	110	121	115	109	114			Exportations / importations	*%*
110	111	107	107	109	106	98	107	110	119	119	114		*cvs*		*%*
2.70	3.05	3.22	2.79	3.00	3.00	3.33	2.67	2.96	3.26	3.57		*9.9*		Importations c.a.f. de EU15	*USD mld*
3.22	3.52	3.55	3.15	3.34	3.40	3.54	3.01	3.17	3.72	4.09		*19.2*		Exportations f.a.b. vers EU15	*USD mld*
0.52	0.47	0.33	0.36	0.34	0.40	0.21	0.34	0.21	0.46	0.52				Solde commercial (f.a.b.-c.a.f.) avec EU15	*USD mld*
														BALANCE DES PAIEMENTS[9]	
														Balance des transactions courantes	*USD mln*
														Balance des biens	*USD mln*
														Balance des services	*USD mln*
														Balance des revenus	*USD mln*
														Balance des transferts courants	*USD mln*
														Balance financière et de capital	*USD mln*
														Variation des avoirs de réserves	*USD mln*
														Erreurs et omissions nettes	*USD mln*

(1) Couvre la consommation collective et la consommation individuelle des administrations publiques.
(2) Les données trimestrielles sont cumulatives. Le chiffre pour l'année 1998 est un chiffre révisé, et il existe une légère différence avec le chiffre du 4ème trimestre de 1998.
(3) Indice de la valeur ajoutée dans l'industrie.
(4) Moyennes mensuelles.
(5) Niveau des commandes intérieures uniquement.
(6) Données du chômage dans les villes.
(7) Salaire nominal annuel moyen.
(8) Fin de période.
(9) Données semestrielles.

OECD PUBLICATIONS, 2, rue André-Pascal, 75775 PARIS CEDEX 16
PRINTED IN FRANCE
(14 2002 04 1 P) ISBN 92-64-19707-9 – No. 52351 2002